THE CAMBRIDGE HISTORY OF
# RUSSIA

The third volume of the Cambridge History of Russia provides an authoritative political, intellectual, social and cultural history of the trials and triumphs of Russia and the Soviet Union during the twentieth century. It encompasses not only the ethnically Russian part of the country but also the non-Russian peoples of the tsarist and Soviet multinational states and of the post-Soviet republics. Beginning with the revolutions of the early twentieth century, chapters move through the 1920s to the Stalinist 1930s, the Second World War, the post-Stalin years and the decline and collapse of the USSR. The contributors attempt to go beyond the divisions that marred the historiography of the USSR during the Cold War to look for new syntheses and understandings. The volume is also the first major undertaking by historians and political scientists to use the new primary and archival sources that have become available since the break-up of the USSR.

RONALD GRIGOR SUNY is Charles Tilly Collegiate Professor of Social and Political History at the University of Michigan, and Emeritus Professor of Political Science and History at the University of Chicago. His many publications on Russian history include *Looking Toward Ararat: Armenian Modern History* (1993), and *The Soviet Experiment: Russia, the USSR, and the Successor States* (1998).

THE CAMBRIDGE HISTORY OF
# RUSSIA

This is a definitive new history of Russia from early Rus' to the successor states that emerged after the collapse of the Soviet Union. Volume I encompasses developments before the reign of Peter I; volume II covers the 'imperial era', from Peter's time to the fall of the monarchy in March 1917; and volume III continues the story through to the end of the twentieth century. At the core of all three volumes are the Russians, the lands which they have inhabited and the polities that ruled them while other peoples and territories have also been given generous coverage for the periods when they came under Riurikid, Romanov and Soviet rule. The distinct voices of individual contributors provide a multitude of perspectives on Russia's diverse and controversial millennial history.

Volumes in the series

Volume I
*From Early Rus' to 1689*
Edited by Maureen Perrie

Volume II
*Imperial Russia, 1689–1917*
Edited by Dominic Lieven

Volume III
*The Twentieth Century*
Edited by Ronald Grigor Suny

# THE CAMBRIDGE
# HISTORY OF
# RUSSIA

★

## VOLUME III
## The Twentieth Century

★

*Edited by*
RONALD GRIGOR SUNY

*University of Michigan* and *University of Chicago*

CAMBRIDGE
UNIVERSITY PRESS

University Printing House, Cambridge CB2 8BS, United Kingdom

Cambridge University Press is part of the University of Cambridge.

It furthers the University's mission by disseminating knowledge in the pursuit of education, learning and research at the highest international levels of excellence.

www.cambridge.org
Information on this title: www.cambridge.org/9781107660991

© Cambridge University Press 2006

First published 2006
Reprinted 2010
First paperback edition 2015

*A catalogue record for this publication is available from the British Library*

ISBN 978-0-521-81144-6 Hardback
ISBN 978-1-107-66099-1 Paperback

# Contents

*List of illustrations*   viii
*List of maps*   x
*Notes on contributors*   xi
*Acknowledgements*   xiv
*Note on transliteration and dates*   xv
*Chronology*   xvi
*List of abbreviations*   xxii

Introduction   *1*

1 · Reading Russia and the Soviet Union in the twentieth century: how the 'West'
wrote its history of the USSR   *5*
RONALD GRIGOR SUNY

PART I
RUSSIA AND THE SOVIET UNION: THE STORY
THROUGH TIME

2 · Russia's *fin de siècle*, 1900–1914   *67*
MARK D. STEINBERG

3 · The First World War, 1914–1918   *94*
MARK VON HAGEN

4 · The revolutions of 1917–1918   *114*
S. A. SMITH

5 · The Russian civil war, 1917–1922   *140*
DONALD J. RALEIGH

Contents

6 · Building a new state and society: NEP, 1921–1928    168
ALAN BALL

7 · Stalinism, 1928–1940    192
DAVID R. SHEARER

8 · Patriotic war, 1941–1945    217
JOHN BARBER AND MARK HARRISON

9 · Stalin and his circle    243
YORAM GORLIZKI AND OLEG KHLEVNIUK

10 · The Khrushchev period, 1953–1964    268
WILLIAM TAUBMAN

11 · The Brezhnev era    292
STEPHEN E. HANSON

12 · The Gorbachev era    316
ARCHIE BROWN

13 · The Russian Federation    352
MICHAEL McFAUL

PART II
RUSSIA AND THE SOVIET UNION: THEMES
AND TRENDS

14 · Economic and demographic change: Russia's age of
economic extremes    383
PETER GATRELL

15 · Transforming peasants in the twentieth century: dilemmas of Russian, Soviet
and post-Soviet development    411
ESTHER KINGSTON-MANN

16 · Workers and industrialisation    440
LEWIS H. SIEGELBAUM

Contents

17 · Women and the state    468
BARBARA ALPERN ENGEL

18 · Non-Russians in the Soviet Union and after    495
JEREMY SMITH

19 · The western republics: Ukraine, Belarus, Moldova and the Baltics    522
SERHY YEKELCHYK

20 · Science, technology and modernity    549
DAVID HOLLOWAY

21 · Culture, 1900–1945    579
JAMES VON GELDERN

22 · The politics of culture, 1945–2000    605
JOSEPHINE WOLL

23 · Comintern and Soviet foreign policy, 1919–1941    636
JONATHAN HASLAM

24 · Moscow's foreign policy, 1945–2000: identities, institutions
and interests    662
TED HOPF

25 · The Soviet Union and the road to communism    706
LARS T. LIH

*Bibliography    732*
*Index    793*

# Illustrations

The plates will be found between pages 344–345

1 The last emperor of Russia, Nicholas II. Slavic and Baltic Division, New York Public Library, Astor, Lenox and Tilden Foundations
2 Poster *Le Spectre de la Rose*, 1911. The New York Public Library
3 Metropolitan Sergei. Credit Novosti (London)
4 Demonstration of soldiers' wives, 1917. New York Public Library
5 Trotsky, Lenin, Kamenev, May 1920. Slavic and Baltic Division, New York Public Library, Astor, Lenox and Tilden Foundations
6 Baroness Ol'ga Wrangel's visit to the Emperor Nicholas Military School in Gallipoli, c.1921. Gallipoli album. Militaria (uncatalogued), André Savine Collection, Wilson Library, University of North Carolina at Chapel Hill
7 May Day demonstration, Leningrad, 1924
8 Soviet poster by I. Nivinskii: 'Women join the co-operatives!', Rare Books Division, New York Public Library, Astor, Lenox and Tilden Foundations
9 Anti-religious poster 'Religion is poison. Safeguard the children' (1930). From the Hoover Institution Archives, Poster Collection, RU/SU650
10 Soviet poster 'Every collective farm peasant . . . has the opportunity to live like a human being' (1934)
11 P. Filonov, *Portrait of Stalin*. Reproduced by permission of the State Russian Museum, St Petersburg
12 Aleksei Stakhanov with car (1936). From: Leah Bendavid-Val (ed.), *Propaganda & Dreams: Photographing the 1930s in the USSR and the US* (Zurich and New York: Stemmle Publishers GmbH, 1999)
13 Two posters celebrating the multinational character of the Soviet Union
14 Muscovites listen as Prime Minister Viacheslav Molotov announces the outbreak of the war, 22 June 1941
15 Red Army soldiers in Stalingrad, winter 1942–February 1943. Credit Novosti (London)
16 Soviet poster 'Who receives the national income?' (1950)
17 Nikita Khrushchev and Fidel Castro. © AP/EMPICS
18 Soviet space capsule *Vostok* © Bettmann/CORBIS
19 Russian tanks in the streets of Prague, Czechoslovakia, 1968. Credit Novosti (London)

20 Parade float of the factory named 'Comintern', 1968. © Daniel C. Waugh

21 Brezhnev and Ford, 1974. Courtesy Gerald R. Ford Library

22 Still from *Ballad of a Soldier* (1959). © BFI stills, posters and designs

23 Soviet poster from the early years of *Perestroika* (1986) showing General
Secretary Mikhail Gorbachev meeting with energy workers in Tiumen'.
From the Hoover Institution Archive, Poster Collection, RU/SU 2318

24 Groznyi in ruins, 1996. Credit Novosti (London)

25 Yeltsin and Putin, Moscow, 2001. Credit Novosti (London)

# Maps

5.1 European Russia during the civil war, 1918–21. From *Soviet Experiment: Russia, the U.S.S.R., and the Successor States* by Ronald Grigor Suny, copyright © 1997 by Ronald Suny. Used by permission of Oxford University Press, Inc. *page* 141

8.1 The USSR and Europe at the end of the Second World War. From *Soviet Experiment: Russia, the U.S.S.R., and the Successor States* by Ronald Grigor Suny, copyright © 1997 by Ronald Suny. Used by permission of Oxford University Press, Inc. 218

12.1 Commonwealth of Independent States 350

13.1 Ethnic republics in 1994 353

# Notes on contributors

ALAN BALL is Professor of History at Marquette University and the author of *Russia's Last Capitalists: The Nepmen, 1921–1929* (1987) and *And Now My Soul is Hardened: Abandoned Children in Soviet Russia, 1918–1930* (1994).

JOHN BARBER is Senior Lecturer in History at King's College, Cambridge University and the author of *Soviet Historians in Crisis, 1928–32* (1981), and, with Mark Harrison, *The Soviet Home Front, 1941–1945: A Social and Economic History of the USSR in World War II* (1991).

ARCHIE BROWN is Professor of Politics at St Antony's, Oxford, and the author of *The Gorbachev Factor* (1996) and the editor of *Contemporary Russian Politics: A Reader* (2001).

BARBARA ALPERN ENGEL is Professor of History at the University of Colorado and the author of *Between Fields and the City: Women, Work, and Family in Russia, 1861–1914* (1995) and *A History of Russia's Women: 1700–2000* (2003).

PETER GATRELL is Professor of History at the University of Manchester and the author of *The Tsarist Economy, 1850–1917* (1986) and *A Whole Empire Walking: Refugees in Russia during the First World War* (1999).

YORAM GORLIZKI is Senior Lecturer in Government at the University of Manchester and the author, with Oleg Khlevniuk, of *Cold Peace: Stalin and the Soviet Ruling Circle, 1945–1953* (2004).

STEPHEN E. HANSON is Associate Professor of Political Science at the University of Washington and the author of *Time and Revolution: Marxism and the Design of Soviet Institutions* (1997) and co-author, with Richard Anderson, Jr., M. Steven Fish and Philip Roeder, of *Postcommunism and the Theory of Democracy* (2001).

MARK HARRISON is Professor of Economics at the University of Warwick and the author of *Soviet Planning in Peace and War 1938–1945* (1985) and *Accounting for War: Soviet Production, Employment, and the Defence Burden, 1940–1945* (1996).

JONATHAN HASLAM is Professor of the History of International Relations, Cambridge University, and the author of *The Soviet Union and the Struggle for Collective Security in Europe, 1933–39* (1984) and *The Vices of Integrity: E. H. Carr, 1892–1982* (2000).

DAVID HOLLOWAY is Raymond A. Spruance Professor of International History and Professor of Political Science at Stanford University and the author of *The Soviet Union and the Arms Race* (1983) and *Stalin and the Bomb: The Soviet Union and Atomic Energy, 1939–1956* (1994).

TED HOPF is Professor of Political Science at Ohio State University and the author of *Peripheral Visions: Deterrence Theory and American Foreign Policy in the Third World, 1965–1990* (1994) and *Social Construction of International Politics: Identities and Foreign Policies, Moscow 1955 and 1999* (2002).

OLEG KHLEVNIUK is a Senior Research Fellow in the Russian State Archives and the author of *In Stalin's Shadow: The Career of 'Sergo' Ordzhonikidze* (1995) and, with Yoram Gorlizki, *Cold Peace: Stalin and the Soviet Ruling Circle, 1945–1953* (2004).

ESTHER KINGSTON-MANN is Professor of History at the University of Massachusetts, Boston, and the author of *Lenin and the Problem of Marxist Peasant Revolution* (1983) and *In Search of the True West: Culture, Economics and Problems of Russian Development* (1999).

LARS T. LIH is an independent researcher based in Montreal and the author of *Bread and Authority in Russia, 1914–1921* (1990) and co-editor, with Oleg V. Naumov, Oleg Khlevniuk and Catherine Fitzpatrick, of *Stalin's Letters to Molotov, 1925–1936: Revelations from the Russian Archives* (1995).

MICHAEL McFAUL is Peter and Helen Bing Senior Fellow at the Hoover Institution and Associate Professor of Political Science, Stanford University, and the author of *Russia's Unfinished Revolution: Political Change from Gorbachev to Putin* (2001) and, with James Goldgeier, *Power and Purpose: American Policy toward Russia after the Cold War* (2003).

DONALD J. RALEIGH is the Jay Richard Judson Distinguished Professor of History at the University of North Carolina, Chapel Hill, and the author of *Revolution on the Volga: 1917 in Saratov* (1986) and *Experiencing Russia's Civil War: Politics, Society, and Revolutionary Culture in Saratov, 1917–1922* (2002).

DAVID R. SHEARER is Associate Professor of History at the University of Delaware and the author of *Industry, State, and Society in Stalin's Russia, 1926–1934* (1996).

LEWIS H. SIEGELBAUM is Professor of History at Michigan State University and the author of *Stakhanovism and the Politics of Productivity in the USSR 1935–1941* (1988) and *Soviet State and Society Between Revolutions, 1918–1929* (1992).

JEREMY R. SMITH is Lecturer in Twentieth Century Russian History at the University of Birmingham and the author of *The Bolsheviks and the National Question, 1917–1923* (1999) and editor of *Beyond the Limits: The Concept of Space in Russian History and Culture* (1999).

S. A. SMITH is Professor of History at the University of Essex and the author of *Red Petrograd: Revolution in the Factories, 1917–18* (1983) and *Like Cattle and Horses: Nationalism and Labor in Shanghai, 1895–1927* (2002)

MARK D. STEINBERG is Professor of History at the University of Illinois, Urbana-Champaign, and the author of *Moral Communities: The Culture of Class Relations in the Russian Printing Industry, 1867–1907* (1992) and *Proletarian Imagination: Self, Modernity, and the Sacred in Russia, 1910–1925* (2002).

RONALD GRIGOR SUNY is Charles Tilly Collegiate Professor of Social and Political History at the University of Michigan, and Emeritus Professor of Political Science and History at the University of Chicago and the author of *The Revenge of the Past: Nationalism, Revolution, and the Collapse of the Soviet Union* (1993) and *The Soviet Experiment: Russia, the USSR, and the Successor States* (1998).

WILLIAM TAUBMAN is the Bertrand Snell Professor of Political Science at Amherst College and the author of *Stalin's American Policy: From Entente to Détente to Cold War* (1982) and *Khrushchev: The Man and his Era* (2003).

JAMES VON GELDERN is Professor of German and Russian Studies at Macalester College and the author of *Bolshevik Festivals, 1917–1920* (1993) and the co-editor, with Richard Stites, of *Mass Culture in Soviet Russia: Tales, Poems, Songs, Movies, Plays, and Folklore, 1917–1953* (1995).

MARK VON HAGEN is Professor of Russian, Ukrainian and Eurasian History at Columbia University and the author of *Soldiers in the Proletarian Dictatorship: The Red Army and the Soviet Socialist State, 1917–1930* (1990) and co-editor, with Karen Barkey, of *After Empire: Multiethnic Societies and Nation-Building: The Soviet Union and the Russian, Ottoman and Habsburg Empires* (1997).

JOSEPHINE WOLL is Professor of German and Russian at Howard University and author of *Invented Truth: Soviet Reality and the Literary Imagination of Iurii Trifonov* (1991) and *Real Images: Soviet Cinema and the Thaw* (2000).

SERHY YEKELCHYK is Assistant Professor of History at the University of Victoria and the author of *The Awakening of a Nation: Toward a Theory of the Ukrainian National Movement in the Second Half of the Nineteenth Century* (1994) and *Stalin's Empire of Memory: Russian-Ukrainian Relations in Soviet Historical Imagination* (2004).

# Acknowledgements

Every effort has been made to secure necessary permissions to reproduce copyright material in this work, though in some cases it has proved impossible to trace copyright holders. If any omissions are brought to our notice, we will be happy to include appropriate acknowledgements on reprinting.

# Note on transliteration and dates

The system of transliteration from Cyrillic used in this volume is that of the Library of Congress, without diacritics. The soft sign is denoted by an apostrophe but is omitted from the most common place names, which are given in their English forms (such as Moscow, St Petersburg, Archangel). For those countries that changed their official names with the collapse of the Soviet Union – Belorussia/Belarus, Kirgizia/Kyrgyzstan, Moldavia/Moldova, Turkmenia/Turkmenistan – we have used the first form up to August 1991 and the second form afterwards. Anglicised name-forms are used for the most well-known political, literary and artistic figures (e.g. Leon Trotsky, Boris Yeltsin, Maxim Gorky), even though this may lead to inconsistency at times. Translations within the text are those of the individual contributors to this volume unless otherwise specified in the footnotes. Dates pre-1918 are given according to the 'new-style' Gregorian calendar, although in the Chronology the 'old-style' Julian calendar dates are also given in brackets.

# Chronology

1894    Tsar Nicholas II came to the throne

1902    Vladimir Lenin published *What Is To Be Done?*

1903    Second Congress of the Russian Social Democratic Workers' Party split into the Bolsheviks and Mensheviks

1904    Outbreak of the Russo-Japanese war

1905    9 January: Bloody Sunday

        30 October: Nicholas II issued the October manifesto

1911    Assassination of Prime Minister Petr Stolypin.

1914    1 August: Germany declared war on Russia; outbreak of First World War

1917    8–13 March (23–8 February ) – the 'February Revolution'

        15 (2) March: Nicholas II abdicated

        17 April: Lenin announced his 'April Theses' calling for all power to the soviets

        14 (1) May: After the 'April Crisis', the coalition government was formed

        1 July (18 June): 'Kerensky Offensive' began

        16–18 (3–5) July: the 'July Days' led to a reaction against the Bolsheviks

        6–13 September (24–31 August): the 'mutiny' of General Lavr Kornilov

        7 November (25 October): The 'October Revolution' established 'Soviet power'

        15 (2) December: Soviet Russia signed an armistice with Germany

1918    18 (5) January: First (and last) session of the Constituent Assembly

        3 March: Soviet government signed Treaty of Brest-Litovsk with Central Powers

        19 March: the Left SRs resigned from the Sovnarkom

        May: revolt of the Czechoslovak legions, which seized the Trans-Siberian Railway

        26–8 May: Georgia, Armenia and Azerbaijan declared independence from Russia

        16–17 July: murder by local Bolsheviks of Nicholas II and his family in Ekaterinburg

        31 July: fall of the Baku Commune

        July: First Constitution of the Russian Soviet Federated Socialist Republic adopted

        2 September: systematic terror launched by the government against their enemies

1919    March: Eighth Congress of the RKP (b) decided to form a Political Bureau
        (Politburo), an Organisational Bureau (Orgburo) and a Secretariat with a
        principal responsible secretary
        2–6 March: First Congress of the Third International (Comintern)
1920    25 April: Pilsudski's Poland invaded Ukraine, beginning the Russo-Polish war
        1–7 September: First Congress of the Peoples of the East was held in Baku
1921    28 February–18 March: revolt of the sailors at Kronstadt
        8–16 March: Tenth Congress of the RKP (b); defeat of the Workers'
        Opposition and the passing of the resolution against organised factions within
        the party; introduction of the New Economic Policy (NEP)
1922    16 April: Treaty of Rapallo signed with Germany
        May: Soviet government arrested Patriarch Tikhon, head of the Russian
        Orthodox Church
        June: trial of the Right SRs
        8 June: Glavlit, the censorship authority, established
        August: Soviet government decided to deport over 160 intellectuals
        4 August: Red cavalry killed Enver Pasha and put down the Basmachi rebellion
        30 December: the USSR was formally inaugurated
1923    9 March: a stroke incapacitated Lenin, removing him from politics.
        Triumvirate of Stalin, Zinoviev and Kamenev
1924    21 January: death of Lenin
        31 January: Constitution of the USSR was ratified
        April–May: Stalin's lectures on *Foundations of Leninism*
        December: Stalin promoted idea of 'Socialism in One Country', along with
        Bukharin
1925    January: Trotsky replaced as Commissar of War by Mikhail Frunze
        18–31 December: the Stalin–Bukharin 'centrist' position triumphed over the
        Opposition at the Fourteenth Congress of the RKP (b)
1926    April: united opposition formed by Trotsky and Zinoviev
        November: the Code on Marriage, Family, and Guardianship was adopted
1927    May: Great Britain broke off relations with the Soviet Union and set off a 'war
        scare'
        Autumn: peasants began reducing grain sales to the state authorities
        Eisenstein's film *October (Ten Days that Shook the World)* released
        12–19 December: Fifteenth Congress of the VKP (b) called for a Five-Year Plan
        of economic development and voluntary collectivisation
1928    18 May–5 July: Shakhty trial
        17 July–1 September: Sixth Congress of the Comintern adopted the 'social
        fascist' line
        30 September: Bukharin's 'Notes of an Economist' published in *Pravda*
1929    9–10 February: the Politburo condemned Bukharin, Rykov and Tomskii
        21 December: Stalin's fiftieth birthday, the beginning of the 'Stalin Cult'
1930    2 March: Stalin's article 'Dizzy with Success' reversed the collectivisation drive
        14 April: Suicide of Mayakovsky
        July: Litvinov replaced Chicherin as People's Commissar of Foreign Affairs

|      | November: Molotov replaced Rykov as chairman of Sovnarkom; Ordzhonikidze became the head of the industrialisation drive |
|------|---|

November: Molotov replaced Rykov as chairman of Sovnarkom;
Ordzhonikidze became the head of the industrialisation drive
November–December: trial of the 'Industrial Party'

1931 21 June: Stalin spoke against equalisation of wages and attacks on 'specialists'; end of the 'Cultural Revolution'; beginning of the 'Great Retreat'
October: Stalin published his letter to *Proletarian Revolution* on writing party history

1932 November: Stalin's wife, Nadezhda Allilueva, committed suicide
December: introduction of the internal passport system for urban population
Famine in Ukraine (1932–3)

1933 May: suicide of Mykola Skrypnyk as a result of attacks on Ukrainian 'nationalists'
16 November: United States and Soviet Union established diplomatic relations

1934 26 January–10 February: Seventeenth Congress of the VKP (b), the 'Congress of the Victors'
August: First Congress of Soviet Writers adopted 'Socialist Realism' as official style
18 September: USSR entered the League of Nations
1 December: the assassination of Kirov
Vasil'ev brothers' film, *Chapaev*, released

1935 2 May: Franco-Soviet Treaty of Mutual Assistance
July–August: Seventh Congress of the Comintern adopted 'Popular Front' line
30 August: beginning of the Stakhanovite campaign

1936 27 June: New laws on prohibiting abortion and tightening the structure of the family
19–24 August: Moscow 'show trial' of Zinoviev and Kamenev, who were convicted and shot
5 December: Constitution of the USSR adopted

1937 28 January: attack on Shostakovich's opera, *Lady Macbeth of Mtsensk*
23–30 January: Moscow 'show trial' of Radek, Piatakov, Sokol'nikov and Serebriakov
18 February: Ordzhonikidze committed suicide
May–June: purge of army officers; secret trial and execution of Tukhachevskii and other top military commanders. Height of the Great Purges, the 'Ezhovshchina'

1938 Eisenstein's film *Aleksandr Nevskii* released; Meyerhold's theatre closed
2–13 March: Moscow 'show trial' of Bukharin and Radek
13 March: Russian language was made compulsory in all Soviet schools
September: the *Short Course of the History of the Communist Party* published
December: Beria replaced Ezhov as head of the NKVD

1939 23 August: Molotov–Ribbentrop Pact of Non-Aggression between the USSR and Germany
17 September: Soviet forces invaded Poland
30 November–12 March 1940 – Russo-Finnish war
14 December: USSR expelled from the League of Nations

| | |
|---|---|
| 1940 | 8–11 April: Soviet secret police murder thousands of Polish officers at Katyn |
| | 3–6 August: Lithuania, Latvia and Estonia joined the Soviet Union |
| | 20 August: the assassination of Trotsky in Coyoacan, Mexico |
| 1941 | 22 June: Germany invaded the Soviet Union |
| | 8 September: Leningrad surrounded; beginning of the 900-day 'Siege of Leningrad' |
| | 30 September–spring 1942: the Battle of Moscow |
| 1942 | 17 July–2 February 1943: Battle of Stalingrad |
| 1943 | 23 May: dissolution of the Comintern |
| | 5 July–23 August: Battle of Kursk |
| | 28 November–1 December: the Tehran Conference |
| | November–December: deportation of the Karachais and Kalmyks; later (February–March 1944) the Chechens, Ingushi and Balkars; and (May) the Crimean Tatars |
| 1944 | 1 January: a new Soviet anthem replaced the 'Internationale' |
| | October: Stalin and Churchill concluded the 'percentages agreement' |
| 1945 | 4–11 February: Yalta Conference |
| | 8–9 May: the war in Europe ended |
| | 17 July–2 August: Potsdam Conference |
| | 8 August: USSR declared war on Japan |
| | 24 October: founding of the United Nations |
| 1946 | 9 February: Stalin's 'Pre-election Speech' |
| | 14 August: attack on Zoshchenko and Akhmatova; beginning of the *Zhdanovshchina* |
| 1947 | September: founding of the Cominform |
| 1948 | 13 January: murder of the Jewish actor Solomon Mikhoels |
| | 27 March: rupture of relations between Stalin and Tito's Yugoslavia |
| | 24 June–5 May 1949: Berlin Blockade |
| | 13 July–7 August: Academy of Agricultural Sciences forced to adopt Lysenkoism |
| 1949 | The 'Leningrad Affair' |
| | 29 August: USSR exploded its first atomic bomb |
| | 1 October: founding of the People's Republic of China |
| 1950 | 26 June: North Korea invaded the south and began the Korean war |
| 1952 | 5–14 October: Nineteenth Congress of the VKP (b) |
| | October: Stalin published *Economic Problems of Socialism in the USSR* |
| 1953 | 13 January: announcement of the 'Doctors' Plot' |
| | 5 March: death of Stalin. Malenkov became chairman of Council of Ministers |
| | June: workers' uprising in East Germany |
| | 26 June: arrest of Beria |
| | September: Khrushchev became First Secretary of the Communist Party |
| 1955 | 8 February: Bulganin replaced Malenkov as chairman of the Council of Ministers |
| | 14 May: formation of the Warsaw Pact |
| | July: Geneva Summit Conference |

| | |
|---|---|
| 1956 | 14–25 February: Twentieth Congress of the CPSU; Khrushchev's 'Secret Speech' |
| | April: dissolution of the Cominform |
| | 23 October–4 November: Soviet army put down revolution in Hungary |
| 1957 | 17–29 June: 'Anti-party Group' (Malenkov, Molotov and Kaganovich) acted against Khrushchev |
| | 4 October: Soviet Union launched *Sputnik*, the first artificial satellite of the Earth |
| 1958 | 27 March: Khrushchev replaced Bulganin as chairman of the Council of Ministers |
| | October–November: campaign against Nobel Prize winner, Boris Pasternak |
| | 27 November: Khrushchev initiated the Berlin Crisis |
| 1959 | September: Khrushchev visited the United States; 'Spirit of Camp David' |
| 1960 | 1 May: American U-2 spy plane shot down over the Soviet Union |
| 1961 | 12 April: Yuri Gagarin became the first man in space |
| | June: Khrushchev and Kennedy met in Vienna |
| | August: the Berlin Wall was built |
| | 17–31 October: Twenty-Second Congress of the CPSU. Stalin's body removed from the Lenin Mausoleum |
| 1962 | 2 June: riots in Novocherkassk |
| | 22–8 October: Cuban Missile Crisis |
| 1963 | 5 August: Nuclear Test Ban Treaty signed |
| 1964 | 14 October: Khrushchev removed as first secretary by the Central Committee and replaced by Brezhnev |
| 1965 | Kosygin attempted to introduce economic reforms |
| | 24 April: Armenians marched in Erevan to mark fiftieth anniversary of genocide |
| 1966 | 10–14 February: Trial of Siniavskii and Daniel' |
| 1968 | 20–1 August: Soviet army invaded and occupied Czechoslovakia |
| 1969 | October: Solzhenitsyn won the Nobel Prize for Literature |
| 1971 | 3 September: Four-Power agreement signed on status of Berlin |
| 1972 | 22–30 May: Brezhnev and Nixon signed SALT I in Moscow. Period of détente |
| 1975 | 1 August: Helsinki Accords signed |
| | December: Sakharov won the Nobel Prize for Peace |
| 1977 | 7 October: adoption of new Constitution of the USSR |
| 1979 | 24–6 December: Soviet troops moved into Afghanistan to back Marxist government |
| 1982 | 10 November: Brezhnev died and was succeeded by Andropov |
| 1983 | 1 September: Soviet jet shot down Korean airliner 007 |
| 1984 | 9 February: Andropov died and was succeeded by Chernenko |
| 1985 | 10 March: Chernenko died and was succeeded by Gorbachev |
| 1986 | 26 April: Chernobyl', nuclear accident |
| | October: Gorbachev and Reagan met in Reykjavik, Iceland |
| | December: Gorbachev invited Sakharov to return to Moscow from exile |

|      | December: Kazakhs demonstrated in protest against appointment of a Russian party chief |
|------|---|
| 1987 | October–November: Yeltsin demoted after he criticised the party leadership |
| 1988 | February: crisis over Nagorno-Karabakh erupted |
|      | 28 June: Nineteenth Conference of the CPSU opened |
| 1989 | 9 April: violent suppression of demonstrators in Tbilisi, Georgia |
|      | 25 May: Congress of People's Deputies convened |
|      | 9 November: the Berlin Wall was torn down |
| 1990 | January: Soviet troops moved into Azerbaijan to quell riots and restore order |
|      | 6 March: Article Six of the Soviet Constitution removed |
|      | 15 October: Gorbachev won the Nobel Peace Prize |
| 1991 | 17 March: referendum on the future structure of the USSR |
|      | 12 June: Yeltsin elected president of the Russian Federation |
|      | 18–21 August: attempted coup against Gorbachev failed |
|      | 25 December: Gorbachev resigned as president of the Soviet Union |
|      | 31 December: end of the Union of Soviet Socialist Republics |
| 1992 | 2 January: Gaidar launched 'shock therapy' economic policy |
|      | March: Shevardnadze returned to power in Georgia |
|      | 14 December: Gaidar was replaced by Chernomyrdin as prime minister |
| 1993 | 25 April: referendum supported Yeltsin's reform policies |
|      | June: Aliev returned to power in Azerbaijan, overthrowing the Popular Front |
|      | 21 September: Yeltsin dissolved the Russian parliament and called elections to a State Duma |
|      | 3–4 October: clashes between forces backing the parliament and those backing the president |
|      | 12 December: elections to the State Duma rejected the radical reformers and supported nationalists and former Communists; ratification of the new Constitution |
| 1994 | May: Armenia, Azerbaijan, Karabakh and Russia agreed to a ceasefire in the Karabakh war |
|      | 11 December: Russian troops invaded Chechnya |
| 1996 | June–July: Yeltsin won re-election as president of the Russian Federation |
|      | 31 August: peace agreement signed between Moscow and Chechnya |
| 1999 | 31 December: Yeltsin resigned, and Putin became acting president |
| 2000 | 26 March: Vladimir Putin elected president of the Russian Federation |
| 2004 | 14 March: Putin re-elected president of the Russian Federation |

# Abbreviations

| | |
|---|---|
| APRF | *Arkhiv prezidenta Rossiiskoi Federatsii* (Archive of the President of the Russian Federation) |
| ASR | *Avtonomnaia sovetskaia respublika* (Autonomous Soviet Republic) |
| Basmachestvo | Pan-Turkic movement in Central Asia, 1918–28 |
| BPF | Belorussian Popular Front |
| Cheka | *Chrezvychainaia komissiia* (Extraordinary Commission to Combat Counter-revolution and Sabotage) |
| CIS | Commonwealth of Independent States |
| COMECON | Council for Mutual Economic Assistance |
| Comintern | *Kommunisticheskii internatsional* (an organisation based in Moscow that devised strategies for Communist Parties around the world) |
| CP(b)U | Communist Party (Bolshevik) of Ukraine |
| CPRF | Communist Party of the Russian Federation |
| CPSU | Communist Party of the Soviet Union |
| Dashnaks | members of the Armenian Revolutionary Federation (*Dashnaktsutiun*) |
| DCs | Democratic Centralists |
| GASO | *Gosudarstvennyi arkhiv Saratovskoi oblasti* (State Archive of Saratov Region) |
| GIAgM | *Gosudarstvennyi istoricheskii arkhiv goroda Moskvy* (State Historical Archive of the City of Moscow) |
| GKO (alternatively GOKO) | *Gosudarstvennyi komitet oborony* – the Soviet war cabinet (1941–5) |
| *glasnost'* | 'Openness;' policies ending censorship under Mikhail Gorbachev, 1985–91 |
| *glavki* | chief industrial branch administrations |
| Gosplan | *Gosudarstvennaia planovaia komissiia* (State Planning Commission) |
| Gulag | *Gosudarstvennoe upravlenie lagerei* (State Administration of Camps) |
| Hummet | 'Energy'; early Muslim socialist party in Transcaucasia |
| ILWCH | *International Labor and Working-Class History* |

| | |
|---|---|
| IMEMO | Institute of World Economics and International Relations |
| Ittifak | 'Independence'; a post-Soviet Tatar political movement |
| JAC | Jewish Anti-Fascist Committee |
| Kadets | Constitutional Democratic Party |
| KGB | *Komitet gosudarstvennoi bezopastnosti* (Committee for State Security), the Soviet political police in the late Soviet period, successor to Cheka, GPU, OGPU, NKVD and other organisations |
| khozraschet | *khoziaistvennyi raschet* (cost-accounting basis) |
| kombedy | committees of poor peasants |
| Komsomol | *Kommunisticheskii soiuz molodezhi* (Communist Youth League) |
| Komuch | Committee to Save the Constituent Assembly |
| Korenizatsiia | 'Rooting' or 'indigenisation'; Soviet nationality policies, 1920s |
| Narkomnats | Commissariat of Nationalities |
| Narkomprod | Food Supply Commissariat |
| Narkompros | Commissariat of Enlightenment |
| NATO | North Atlantic Treaty Organisation |
| NEP | *Novaia ekonomicheskaia politika* (New Economic Policy) |
| NKVD | *Narodnyi komissariat vnutrennykh del* (People's Commissarist of Internal Affairs) |
| NOT | *Nauchnaia organizatsiia truda* (Scientific Organisation of Labour) |
| NTR | *Nauchno-tekhnologicheskaia revoliutsiia* (Scientific-Technological Revolution) |
| OGPU | United Main Political Administration (political police, successor to the ChEKA and GPU, predecessor of the NKVD) |
| OUN | *Orhanizatsiia ukrainskykh natsionalistiv* (Organisation of Ukrainian Nationalists) |
| perestroika | 'restructuring'; the reformist policies of Mikhail Gorbachev, 1985–91 |
| Politburo | Political Bureau of the Central Committee of the CPSU |
| politruk | *politicheskii rukovoditel'* (political adviser to military officers in the Red Army) |
| Proletkul't | proletarian cultural-educational organisations |
| PSS | *Polnoe sobranie sochinenii* (Complete Works) |
| Rabfak | Worker faculties |
| Rabkrin | Workers'–Peasants' Inspectorate |
| RAPM | Russian Association of Proletarian Musicians |
| RAPP | Russian Association of Proletarian Writers |
| RCs | Revolutionary Communists |
| RGANI | *Rossiiskii gosudarstvennyi arkhiv noveishei istorii* (Russian State Archive of Contemporary History) |
| RGASPI | *Rossiiskii gosudartvennyi arkhiv sotsial'noi-politicheskoi istorii* (Russian State Archive of Social and Political History), |

|  |  |
|---|---|
|  | the former archive of the Communist Party of the Soviet Union, TsPA |
| RSDRP | *Rossiiskaia sotsial-demokraticheskaia rabochaia partiia* (Russian Social Democratic Workers' Party) |
| RSFSR | *Rossiiskaia Sovetskaia Federativnaia Sotsialisticheskaia Respublika* (Russian Soviet Federative Socialist Republic) |
| *samizdat* | 'self-published;' the underground dissident publications in the Soviet Union |
| Sovnarkhoz | Supreme Economic Council |
| Sovnarkom | Council of People's Commissars |
| SR | Socialist Revolutionary |
| SSR | *Sovetskaia Sotsialisticheskaia Respublika* (Soviet Socialist Republic) |
| STKs | *Sovety trudovykh kollektivov* (Councils of Labour Collectives) |
| Transcaucasian Sejm | Representative assembly in Transcaucasia, April 1918 |
| TsDNISO | *Tsentr dokumentatsii noveishei istorii Saratovskoi oblasti* (Centre for the Documentation of the Recent History of the Saratov Region) |
| Ukrainian Central Rada | Ukrainian national government, formed 1917 |
| USA | United States of America |
| USSR | Union of Soviet Socialist Republics |
| VTsIK | Central Executive Committee of the Soviets |
| VTsIOM | All-Soviet (later All-Russian) Institute for Public Opinion |

# Introduction

RONALD GRIGOR SUNY

The history of Russia in the twentieth century (and particularly the Soviet period) has undergone several important historiographical shifts in emphasis, style, methodology and interpretation. From a story largely centred on the state, its leaders and the intellectual elite, Russian history became a tale of social structures, class formation and struggles and fascination with revolution and radical social transformation. Political and intellectual history was followed by the wave of social history, and a whole generation of scholars spent their productive years investigating workers, peasants, bureaucrats, industry and agriculture. From the revolution attention moved to the 1920s, on to the Stalinist 1930s, and at the turn of the new century has crossed the barrier of the Second World War (largely neglecting the war itself) into the late Stalin period (1945–53) and beyond. In the last decade and a half the 'cultural' or 'linguistic turn' in historical studies belatedly influenced a new concentration on cultural topics among Russianists – celebrations and rituals, representations and myths, as well as memory and subjectivity. One revisionism followed another, often with unpleasant displays of hostility between schools and generations. The totalitarian model, undermined by social historians in the 1970s, proved to have several more lives to live and reappeared in a 'neo-totalitarian' version that owed much of its vision to a darker reading of the effects of the Enlightenment and modernity.

The historiography of the USSR was divided by the Cold War chasm between East and West and by political passions in the West that kept Left and Right in rival camps. On the methodological front deductions from abstract models, perhaps necessitated by the difficulty of doing archival work in the Soviet Union, gave way by the 1960s to work in Soviet libraries and archives. The access to primary sources expanded exponentially with the collapse of the USSR, and the end of the Cold War allowed scholars in Russia and the West to work more closely together than in the past, even though polemics about the Soviet experience continued to disturb the academy. While the end of the

I

great divide between Soviet East and capitalist West portended the possibility of a neutral, balanced history of Russia in the twentieth century, old disputes proved to be tenacious.

Still, Russian historiography has benefited enormously from the newly available source base that made possible readings that earlier could only be imagined. One can even say that the dynamic political conflicts among scholars in the past have actually enriched the field in the variety of approaches taken by historians. At the moment there are people practising political, economic, social and cultural history and dealing with topics that earlier had been on the margins – sexuality, violence, the inner workings of the top Soviet leadership, non-Russian peoples and the textures of everyday life in the USSR.

It is easy enough to begin with the observation that Russia, while part of Europe (at least in the opinion of some), has had distinguishing features and experiences that made its evolution from autocratic monarchy to democracy far more difficult, far more protracted, than it was for a few privileged Western countries. Not only was tsarist Russia a relatively poor and over-extended member of the great states of the continent, but the new Soviet state was born in the midst of the most ferocious and wasteful war that humankind had fought up to that time. A new level of acceptable violence marked Europe in the years of the First World War. Having seized power in the capital city, the new socialist rulers of Russia fought fiercely for over three years to win a civil war against monarchist generals, increasingly conservative liberal politicians, peasant armies, foreign interventionists, nationalists and more moderate socialist parties. By the end of the war the new state had acquired habits and practices of authoritarian rule. The revolutionary utopia of emancipation, equality and popular power competed with a counter-utopia of efficiency, production and social control from above. The Soviets eliminated rival political parties, clamped down on factions within their own party and pretentiously identified their dictatorship as a new form of democracy, superior to the Western variety. The Communists progressively narrowed the scope of those who could participate in real politics until, first, there was only one faction in the party making decisions and eventually only one man – Joseph Stalin.

Once Stalin had achieved pre-eminence by the end of the 1920s, he launched a second 'revolution', this one from above, initiated by the party/state itself. The ruling apparatus of Stalin loyalists nationalised totally what was left of the autonomous economy and expanded police terror to unprecedented dimensions. The new Stalinist system that metastasised out of Leninism resurrected the leather-jacket Bolshevism of the civil war and violently imposed collectivised agriculture on the peasant majority, pell-mell industrialisation on workers and a cultural straitjacket on the intelligentsia. Far more repressive than Lenin had been, Stalinist state domination of every aspect of social life transformed the Soviet continent from a backward peasant country into a poorly industrialised and urban one. The Stalinist years were marked by deep contradictions: visible progress in industry accompanied by devastation and stagnation in agriculture; a police regime that saw enemies everywhere at a time when millions energetically and enthusiastically worked to build their idea of socialism; cultural revival and massive expansion of literacy and education coinciding with a cloud of censorship that darkened the field of expression; and the adoption of the 'most democratic constitution in the world' while real freedoms and political participation evaporated into memories.

However brutal and costly the excesses of Stalinism, however tragic and heroic the Soviet struggle against Fascism during the Second World War, and however devastated by the practice of mass terror, Soviet society slowly evolved into a modern, articulated urban society with many features shared with other developed countries. After Stalin's death in 1953, many in the West recognised that the USSR had become a somewhat more benign society and tolerable enemy than had been proposed by the Cold Warriors. The 1960s and 1970s were a particularly fruitful moment for Western scholarship on the Soviet Union, as the possibility to visit the country and work in archives allowed a more empirical investigation of earlier mysteries. With the development in the late 1960s of social history, historians in the West began exploring the origins of the Soviet regime, most particularly in the revolutionary year 1917, and they radically revised the view of the October Revolution as a Bolshevik conspiracy with little popular support. Other 'revisionists' went on to challenge the degree of state control over society during the Stalin years and emphasised the procedures by which workers and others maintained small degrees of autonomy from the all-pervasive state. Gradually the totalitarian model that dominated in the 1940s and 1950s lost its potency and was largely rejected by the generation of social historians.

From its origins Soviet studies was closely involved with real-world politics, and during the years of détente the Soviet Union was seen through the prism of the 'developmental' or 'modernisation' model. Implicit in this interpretation was a sense that the social evolution of the Soviet system could eventually lead to a more open, even pluralistic regime. The potential for democratic evolution of the system seemed to be confirmed by the efforts of Gorbachev in the late 1980s to restrain the power of the Communist Party, awaken public opinion and political participation through *glasnost'*, and allow greater freedom to the non-Russian peoples of the Soviet borderlands. Yet with the failure of the

Gorbachev revolution this reading of Soviet history was bitterly attacked by the more conservative who harked back to more fatalistic interpretations – that the USSR was condemned by Russian political culture or its utopian drive for an anti-capitalist alternative to a dismal collapse.

This volume of the *Cambridge History of Russia* deals with the twentieth century in the Russian world chronologically and thematically in order to provide readers with clear narratives as well as a variety of interpretations so that they may sort through the various controversies of the Soviet past. The volume is not simply a history of the ethnically Russian part of the country but rather of the two great multinational states – tsarist and Soviet – as well as the post-Soviet republics. Although inevitably the bulk of the narrative will deal with Russians, the conviction of the editor is that the history of Russia would be incomplete without the accompanying and contributing histories of the non-Russian peoples of the empire. Among the unifying themes of the volume are: the tensions between nations and empire in the evolution of the Russian and Soviet states; the oscillation between reform and revolution, usually from above but at times from below as well; state building and state collapse; and modernisation and modernity. For the historians and political scientists who have contributed to this work, understanding the present and future of Russia, the Soviet Union and the non-Russian peoples can only come by exploring the experiences through which they have become what they are.

# Reading Russia and the Soviet Union in the twentieth century: how the 'West' wrote its history of the USSR

RONALD GRIGOR SUNY

From its very beginnings the historiography of Russia in the twentieth century has been much more than an object of coolly detached scholarly contemplation. Many observers saw the USSR as the major enemy of Western civilisation, the principal threat to the stability of nations and empires, a scourge that sought to undermine the fundamental values of decent human societies. For others the Soviet Union promised an alternative to the degradations of capitalism and the fraudulent claims of bourgeois democracy, represented the bulwark of Enlightenment values against the menace of Fascism, and preserved the last best hope of colonised peoples. In the Western academy the Soviet Union was most often imagined to be an aberration in the normal course of modern history, an unfortunate detour from the rise of liberalism that bred its own evil opposite, travelling its very own *Sonderweg* that led eventually (or inevitably) to collapse and ruin. The very endeavour of writing a balanced narrative required a commitment to standards of scholarship suspect to those either militantly opposed to or supportive of the Soviet enterprise. At times, as in the years just after the revolution or during the Cold War, scholarship too often served masters other than itself. While much worthy analysis came

My gratitude is extended to Robert V. Daniels, Georgi Derluguian, David C. Engerman, Peter Holquist, Valerie Kivelson, Terry Martin, Norman Naimark, Lewis Siegelbaum, Josephine Woll and members of the Russian Studies Workshop at the University of Chicago for critical readings of earlier versions of this chapter. This essay discusses primarily the attitudes and understandings of Western observers, more precisely the scholarship and ideational framings of professional historians and social scientists, about the Soviet Union as a state, a society and a political project. More attention is paid to Anglo-American work, and particularly to American views, since arguably they set the tone and parameters of the field through much of the century. This account should be supplemented by reviews of other language literatures, e.g. Laurent Jalabert, *Le Grand Débat: les universitaires français – historiens et géographes – et les pays communists de 1945 à 1991* (Toulouse: Groupe de Recherche en Histoire Immédiate, Maison de la Recherche, Université de Toulouse Le Mirail, 2001).

from people deeply committed to or critical of the Soviet project, a studied neutrality was difficult (though possible) in an environment in which one's work was always subject to political judgement.

With the opening of the Soviet Union and its archives to researchers from abroad, beginning in the Gorbachev years, professional historians and social scientists produced empirically grounded and theoretically informed works that avoided the worst polemical excesses of earlier years. Yet, even those who claimed to be unaffected by the battles of former generations were themselves the product of what went before. The educator still had to be educated. While the end of the Cold War and the collapse of the Soviet Union permitted a greater degree of detachment than had been possible before, the Soviet story – itself so important an ingredient in the self-construction of the modern 'West' – remains one of deep contestation.

## The prehistory of Soviet history

'At the beginning of [the twentieth century]', wrote Christopher Lasch in his study of American liberals and the Russian Revolution,

> people in the West took it as a matter of course that they lived in a civilization surpassing any which history had been able to record. They assumed that their own particular customs, institutions and ideas had universal validity; that having showered their blessings upon the countries of western Europe and North America, those institutions were destined to be carried to the furthest reaches of the earth, and bring light to those living in darkness.[1]

Those sentences retain their relevance at the beginning of the twenty-first century. Western, particularly American, attitudes and understandings of Russia and the Soviet Union unfolded in the last hundred years within a broad discourse of optimism about human progress that relied on the comforting thought that capitalist democracy represented the best possible solution to human society, if not the 'end of history'. Within that universe of ideas Russians were constructed as people fundamentally different from Westerners, with deep, largely immutable national characteristics. Ideas of a 'Russian soul' or an essentially spiritual or collectivist nature guided the interpretations and policy prescriptions of foreign observers. This tradition dated back to the very first travellers to Muscovy. In his *Notes Upon Russia (1517–1549)*

---

1 Christopher Lasch, *The American Liberals and the Russian Revolution* (New York and London: Columbia University Press, 1962; paperback edn: McGraw Hill, 1972), p. 1. All references in this chapter are from the latest edition listed, unless otherwise noted.

Sigismund von Herberstein wrote, 'The people enjoy slavery more than free-dom', observations echoed by Adam Olearius in the seventeenth century, who saw Russians as 'comfortable in slavery' who require 'cudgels and whips' to be forced to work. Montesquieu and others believed that national character was determined by climate and geography, and the harsh environment in which Russians lived had produced a barbarous and uncivilised people, ungovernable, lacking discipline, lazy, superstitious, subject to despotism, yet collective, pas-sionate, poetical and musical. The adjectives differed from writer to writer, yet they clustered around the instinctual and emotional pole of human behaviour rather than the cognitive and rational. Race and blood, more than culture and choice, decided what Russians were able to do. In order to make them civilised and modern, it was often asserted, force and rule from above was unavoid-able. Ironically, the spokesmen of civilisation justified the use of violence and terror on the backward and passive people of Russia as the necessary means to modernity.

The most influential works on Russia in the early twentieth century were the great classics of nineteenth-century travellers and scholars, like the Marquis de Custine, Baron August von Haxthausen, Donald Mackenzie Wallace, Alfred Rambaud, Anatole Leroy-Beaulieu and George Kennan, the best-selling author of *Siberia and the Exile System*.[2] France offered the most professional academic study of Russia, and the influential Leroy-Beaulieu's eloquent descriptions of the patience, submissiveness, lack of individuality and fatalism of the Russians contributed to the ubiquitous sense of a Slavic character that contrasted with the Gallic, Anglo-Saxon or Teutonic. Ameri-can writers, such as Kennan and Eugene Schuyler, subscribed equally to such ideas of nationality, but rather than climate or geography as causative, they emphasised the role of institutions, such as tsarism, in generating a national character that in some ways was mutable.[3] Kennan first went to Russia in 1865, became an amateur ethnographer, and grew to admire the courageous

2 Marquis de Custine, *Journey for Our Time: The Journals of Marquis de Custine*, ed. and trans. Phyllis Penn Kohler (1843; New York: Pellegrini and Cudahy, 1951); Baron August von Haxthausen, *The Russian Empire: Its People, Institutions and Resources*, 2 vols., trans. Robert Farie (1847; London: Chapman and Hall, 1856); Sir Donald Mackenzie Wallace, *Russia on the Eve of War and Revolution*, ed. and intro. Cyril E. Black (1877; New York: Random House, 1961); Alfred Rambaud, *The History of Russia from the Earliest Times to 1877*, trans. Leonora B. Lang, 2 vols. (1878; New York: Hovendon Company, 1886); Anatole Leroy-Beaulieu, *The Empire of the Tsars and the Russians*, 3 vols., trans. Zénaïde A. Ragozin (New York: Knickerbocker Press, 1902); George F. Kennan, *Siberia and the Exile System*, 2 vols. (New York: Century, 1891).
3 David C. Engerman, *Modernization from the Other Shore: American Intellectuals and the Romance of Russian Development* (Cambridge, Mass.: Harvard University Press, 2003), pp. 28–53.

revolutionaries ('educated, reasonable self-controlled gentlemen, not different in any essential respect from one's self') that he encountered in Siberian exile.[4] For his sympathies the tsarist government banned him from Russia, placing him in a long line of interpreters whose exposures of Russian life and politics would be so punished.

Russia as an autocracy remained the political 'other' of Western democracy and republicanism, and it was with great joy and relief that liberals, including President Woodrow Wilson, greeted the February Revolution of 1917 as 'the impossible dream' realised. Now the new Russian government could be enlisted in the Great War to make 'the world safe for democracy'.[5] But the Bolshevik seizure of power in Petrograd turned the liberal world upside down. For Wilson's secretary of state, Robert Lansing, Bolshevism was 'the worst form of anarchism', 'the madness of famished men'.[6] In the years immediately following the October Revolution the first accounts of the new regime reaching the West were by journalists and diplomats. The radical freelance journalist John Reed, his wife and fellow radical Louise Bryant, Bessie Beatty of the *San Francisco Bulletin*, the British journalist Arthur Ransome and Congregational minister Albert Rhys Williams all witnessed events in 1917 and conveyed the immediacy and excitement of the revolutionary days to an eager public back home.[7] After several trips to Russia, the progressive writer Lincoln Steffens told his friends, 'I have seen the future and it works.' Enthusiasm for the revolution propelled liberals and socialists further to the Left, and small Communist parties emerged from the radical wing of Social Democracy. From the Right came sensationalist accounts of atrocities, debauchery and tyranny, leavened with the repeated assurance that the days of the Bolsheviks were numbered. *L'Echo*

---

4 Ibid., p. 37.
5 On American views of Russia and the revolution, see Lasch, *The American Liberals and the Russian Revolution*; and N. Gordon Levin, Jr., *Woodrow Wilson and World Politics: America's Response to War and Revolution* (Oxford: Oxford University Press, 1968); Peter G. Filene, *Americans and the Soviet Experiment, 1917–1933* (Cambridge, Mass.: Harvard University Press, 1967); Peter G. Filene (ed.), *American Views of Soviet Russia, 1917–1965* (Homewood, Ill.: Dorsey Press, 1968).
6 Arno J. Mayer, *Politics and Diplomacy of Peacemaking: Containment and Counterrevolution at Versailles, 1918–1919* (New York: Alfred P. Knopf, 1967), p. 260. See also his *Political Origins of the New Diplomacy, 1917–1918* (New Haven: Yale University Press, 1959).
7 John Reed, *Ten Days that Shook the World* (New York: Boni and Liveright, 1919); Louise Bryant, *Six Months in Russia: An Observer's Account of Russia before and during the Proletarian Dictatorship* (New York: George H. Doran, 1918); Bessie Beatty, *The Red Heart of Russia* (New York: Century, 1918); Arthur Ransome, *Russia in 1919* (New York: B. W. Huebsch, 1919); *The Crisis in Russia* (London: Allen and Unwin, 1921); Albert Rhys Williams, *Through the Russian Revolution* (New York: Boni and Liveright, 1921). See also the accounts in Filene, *Americans and the Soviet Experiment*; Filene, *American Views of Soviet Russia*; Lasch, *The American Liberals and the Russian Revolution*.

*de Paris* and the London *Morning Post*, as well as papers throughout Western Europe and the United States, wrote that the Bolsheviks were 'servants of Germany' or 'Russian Jews of German extraction'.[8] The *New York Times* so frequently predicted the fall of the Communists that two young journalists, Walter Lippmann and Charles Merz, exposed their misreadings in a long piece in *The New Republic*.[9]

The Western reaction to the Bolsheviks approached panic. Officials and advisers to the Wilson administration spoke of Russia as drunk, the country as mad, taken over by a mob, the people victims of an 'outburst of elemental forces', 'sheep without a shepherd', a terrible fate for a country in which 'there were simply too few brains per square mile'.[10] Slightly more generously, American ambassador David Francis told the State Department that the Bolsheviks might be just what Russia needed: strong men for a people that do not value human life and 'will obey strength . . . and nothing else'.[11] To allay fears of domestic revolution the American government deported over two hundred political radicals in December 1919 to the land of the Soviets on the *Buford*, an old ship dubbed 'the Red Ark'. The virus of Bolshevism seemed pervasive, and powerful voices raised fears of international subversion. The arsenal of the Right included the familiar weapon of anti-Semitism. In early 1920 Winston Churchill told demonstrators that the Bolsheviks 'believe in the international Soviet of the Russian and Polish Jews'.[12] Baron N. Wrangel opened his account of the Bolshevik revolution with the words 'The sons of Israel had carried out their mission; and Germany's agents, having become the representatives of Russia, signed peace with their patron at Brest-Litovsk'.[13]

8 Walter Laqueur, *The Fate of the Revolution: Interpretations of Soviet History from 1917 to the Present* (London: Macmillan, 1967; revised edn New York and London: Collier Books, 1987), p. 8.
9 'Thirty different times the power of the Soviets was definitely described as being on the wane. Twenty times there was news of a serious counter-revolutionary menace. Five times was the explicit statement made that the regime was certain to collapse. And fourteen times that collapse was said to be in progress. Four times Lenin and Trotzky were planning flight. Three times they had already fled. Five times the Soviets were "tottering." Three times their fall was "imminent" . . . Twice Lenin had planned retirement; once he had been killed; and three times he was thrown in prison' (Walter Lippmann and Charles Merz, 'A Test of the News', *The New Republic* (Supplement), 4 Aug. 1920; cited in Engerman, *Modernization from the Other Shore*, pp. 198–9).
10 Quotations from Engerman, *Modernization from the Other Shore*, pp. 94, 95.
11 Ibid., p. 98.
12 *Times* (London), 5 Jan. 1920; cited in E. Malcolm Carroll, *Soviet Communism and Western Opinion, 1919–1921*, ed. Frederic B. M. Hollyday (Chapel Hill: University of North Carolina Press, 1965), p. 13.
13 *From Serfdom to Bolshevism: The Memoirs of Baron N. Wrangel, 1847–1920*, trans. Brian and Beatrix Lunn (Philadelphia: J. B. Lippincott, 1927), p. 291.

Western reading publics, hungry for news and analyses of the enigmatic social experiment under way in Soviet Russia, turned to journalists and scholars for information. The philosopher Bertrand Russell, who had accompanied a delegation of the British Labour Party to Russia in 1919, rejected Bolshevism for two reasons: 'the price mankind must pay to achieve communism by Bolshevik methods is too terrible; and secondly, . . . even after paying the price I do not believe the result would be what the Bolsheviks profess to desire.'[14] Other radical dissenters included the anarchist Emma Goldman, who spent nearly two years in Bolshevik Russia only to break decisively with the Soviets after the repression of the Kronstadt mutiny in March 1921.[15]

The historian Bernard Pares had begun visiting Russia regularly from 1898 and reported on the beginnings of parliamentarianism in Russia after 1905. As British military observer to the Russian army he remained in the country from the outbreak of the First World War until the early days of the Soviet government. After service as British commissioner to Admiral Kolchak's anti-Bolshevik White government, Pares taught Russian history at the University of London, where he founded *The Slavonic Review* in 1922 and directed the new School of Slavonic Studies. A friend of the liberal leader Pavel Miliukov and supporter of constitutional monarchy in Russia, by the 1930s Pares had become more sympathetic to the Soviets and an advocate of Anglo-Russian rapprochement. Like most of his contemporaries, Pares believed that climate and environment shaped the Russians. 'The happy instinctive character of clever children,' he wrote, 'so open, so kindly and so attractive, still remains; but the interludes of depression or idleness are longer than is normal.'[16] In part because of his reliance on the concept of 'national character', widely accepted among scholars, journalists and diplomats, Pares's influence remained strong, particularly during the years of the Anglo-American–Soviet alliance. But with the coming of the Cold War, he, like others 'soft on communism', was denounced as an apologist for Stalin.[17]

In the United States the most important of the few scholars studying Russia were Archibald Cary Coolidge at Harvard and Samuel Northrup Harper of the University of Chicago. For Coolidge, the variety of 'head types' found

14 Bertrand Russell, *The Practice and Theory of Bolshevism* (London, 1920; New York: Simon and Schuster, 1964), p. 101.
15 Emma Goldman, *My Disillusionment in Russia* (New York: Doubleday, Page and Co., 1923; London: C. W. Daniel, 1925).
16 Sir Bernard Pares, *Russia between Reform and Revolution: Fundamentals of Russian History and Character*, ed. and intro. Francis B. Randall (New York: Schocken Books, 1962), p. 3. The book was first published in 1907.
17 On Pares, see Laqueur, *The Fate of the Revolution*, pp. 173–5.

among Slavs was evidence that they were a mixture of many different races, and while autocracy might be repugnant to the 'Anglo-Saxon', it appeared to be appropriate for Russians.[18] After working with Herbert Hoover's American Relief Administration (ARA) during the famine of 1921–2, he concluded that the famine was largely the result of the peasants' passivity, lethargy and oriental fatalism, not to mention the 'stupidity, ignorance, inefficiency and above all meddlesomeness' of Russians more generally.[19] The principal mentor of American experts on the Soviet Union in the inter-war period, Coolidge trained the first generation of professional scholars and diplomats. One of his students, Frank Golder, also worked for Hoover's ARA and was an early advocate of Russia's reconstruction, a prerequisite, he felt, for ridding the country of the 'Bolos'. Golder went on to work at the Hoover Institution of War, Peace and Revolution at Stanford University, collecting important collections of documents that make up the major archive for Soviet history in the West.[20]

Samuel Harper, the son of William Rainey Harper, the president of the University of Chicago, shared the dominant notions of Russian national character, which for him included deep emotions, irregular work habits, apathy, lethargy, pessimism and lack of 'backbone'.[21] Harper was a witness to Bloody Sunday in 1905 and, like his friend Pares, a fervent defender of Russian liberals who eventually succumbed to the romance of communism. Russians may have been governed more by emotion and passion than reason, he argued, but they possessed an instinct for democracy. In 1926 he accepted an assignment from his colleague, chairman of the political science department at Chicago, Charles E. Merriam, arguably the most influential figure in American political science between the wars, to study methods of indoctrinating children with the love of the state. Russia, along with Fascist Italy, was to be the principal laboratory for this research. Merriam was fascinated with the successes of civic education in Mussolini's Italy, while other political scientists saw virtues in Hitler's Germany.[22] For Merriam creating patriotic loyalty to the state was a technical problem, not a matter of culture, and the Soviet Union, which had rejected nationalism and the traditional ties to old Russia, was a 'striking experiment' to create 'de novo a type of political loyalty to, and interest in a new order of things'.[23] In *The Making of Citizens* (1931), he concluded that the

18 Engerman, *Modernization from the Other Shore*, pp. 60–1.    19 Ibid., p. 110.
20 Terrence Emmons and Bertrand M. Patenaude (eds.), *War, Revolution, and Peace in Russia: The Passages of Frank Golder, 1914–1927* (Stanford, Calif.: Hoover Institution Press, 1988).
21 Ibid., p. 65.
22 Ido Oren, *Our Enemies and US: America's Rivalries and the Making of Political Science* (Ithaca, N.Y.: Cornell University Press, 2003), pp. 47–90.
23 Ibid., pp. 59–60.

revolution had employed the emotions generated by festivals, the Red Flag, the Internationale and mass meetings and demonstrations effectively to establish 'a form of democratic nationalism'.[24]

To study what they called 'civic education', something akin to what later would be known as 'nation-building', Harper and Merriam travelled to Russia together in 1926. Guided by Maurice Hindus, an influential journalist sympathetic to the Soviet experiment, Harper visited villages where he became enthusiastic about the Bolshevik educational programme. Impressed by Soviet efforts to modernise the peasantry, he supported their industrialisation drive.[25] This led eventually to estrangement from the State Department specialists on Russia with whom Harper had worked for over a decade. In the mid-1930s he wrote positively about constitutional developments in the USSR, and his 1937 book, *The Government of the Soviet Union*, made the case for democratic, participatory institutions in the Soviet system. He rationalised the Moscow trials and never publicly criticised Stalin. When Harper defended the Nazi–Soviet Pact of 1939 as a shrewd manoeuvre, students abandoned his classes and faculty colleagues shunned him. Only after the Soviets became allies of the United States in 1941 did he enjoy a few twilight years of public recognition, even appearing with Charlie Chaplin and Carl Sandburg at a mass 'Salute to our Russian Ally'.[26]

## Seeing the future work

Through the inter-war years the Soviet Union offered many intellectuals a vision of a preferred future outside and beyond capitalism, but contained within the hope and faith in the USSR and communism were the seeds of disillusionment and despair. Writers made ritualistic visits to Moscow and formed friendships with other political pilgrims. In November 1927 novelist Theodore Dreiser accepted an invitation to tour the USSR, and his secretary remembered an evening at the Grand Hotel with Dorothy Thomas, Sinclair Lewis, Scott Nearing and Louis Fischer, followed by a visit to New York Times correspondent Walter Duranty.[27] By the early 1930s, many 'Russianists' had moved decisively to the Left. The sociologist Jerome Davis, who taught at Dartmouth

24 Ibid., p. 61; Charles E. Merriam, *The Making of Citizens: A Comparative Study of Methods of Civic Training* (Chicago: University of Chicago Press, 1931), p. 222.
25 Samuel N. Harper, *The Russia I Believe in: The Memoirs of Samuel N. Harper, 1902–1941*, ed. Paul V. Harper (Chicago: University of Chicago Press, 1945).
26 Oren, *Our Enemies and US*, pp. 111–16.
27 Ruth Epperson Kennell, *Theodore Dreiser and the Soviet Union, 1927–1945* (New York: International Publishers, 1969), pp. 25–6.

and Yale, advocated recognition of the USSR and was ultimately fired from Yale for condemning capitalism.[28] Paul Douglas, a distinguished University of Chicago labour economist, enthusiastically but mistakenly predicted that Soviet trade unions would soon overtake the Communist Party as the most powerful institution in the country.[29] Robert Kerner, a Russian historian at the University of Missouri, gave up what he had called 'racial metaphysics' (he said he had studied the Slavs as the 'largest white group in the world') to investigate environmental and historical factors, work that culminated in his *The Urge to the Sea* (1942). The epitome of professional Russian history in the inter-war period, Geroid Tanquary Robinson of Columbia University, was attracted to radical thought early in his life and dedicated his scholarship to a re-evaluation of the much-maligned Russian peasantry. His magnum opus, *Rural Russia under the Old Regime* (1932), the first substantial historical work by an American scholar that was based on extensive work in the Soviet archives, challenged the prevalent notion of peasant lethargy and passivity. Influenced by the 'New Historians' who turned to the study of everyday life and borrowed insights from the other social sciences, he worked to distinguish professional historical writing, which looked to the past to explain the present (or other pasts), from journalism or punditry, which used the past and present to project into and predict the future.

'Collectively', writes David C. Engerman, these new professional experts on Russia – Harper, Kerner, Davis, Douglas, Robinson, Vera Micheles Dean and Leo Pasvolsky – 'offered more reasons to support Soviet rule than to challenge it'.[30] They played down ideology as they elevated national, geographic or even racial characteristics. Russia, they believed, had affected communism much more than communism Russia. The small cohort of American diplomats (George Kennan, Charles 'Chip' Bohlen, Loy Henderson and the first ambassador to the USSR, William Bullitt) who manned the new US embassy in Moscow after recognition of the Soviet Union in 1933 shared similar attitudes. Kennan reported that in order to understand Russia he 'had to weigh the effects of climate on character, the results of century-long conflict with the Asiatic hordes, the influence of medieval Byzantium, the national origins of the people, and the geographic characteristics of the country'.[31] Influenced by the German sociologist Klaus Mehnert's study of Soviet youth, Kennan noted how young people were carried away by the 'romance of economic development' to the point that they were relieved 'to a large extent of the curses

---

28  Engerman, *Modernization from the Other Shore*, pp. 132–6.
29  Ibid., p. 136. He later turned to politics and was elected Democratic senator from Illinois.
30  Ibid., p. 152.    31  Ibid., p. 258.

of egotism, romanticism, daydreaming, introspection, and perplexity which befall the young of bourgeois countries'.[32] To demonstrate the continuity and consistency of Russian character of life, Kennan sent home an 1850 diplomatic dispatch, passing it off as if it were current![33]

In the years of the First Five-Year Plan, Western writing reached a crescendo of praise for the Soviets' energy and sacrifice, their idealism and attendant suffering endured in the drive for modernisation. The post-First World War cultural critique of unbridled capitalism developed by American thinkers like John Dewey and Thorstein Veblen encouraged many intellectuals to consider the lessons that capitalist democracies might learn from the Soviets. Western Leftists and liberals hoped that engineers, planners and technocrats would be inspired by Soviet planning to discipline the anarchy of capitalism. In 'An Appeal to Progressives', contrasting the economic breakdown in the West with the successes of Soviet planned development, the critic Edmund Wilson proclaimed that American radicals and progressives 'must take Communism away from the Communists . . . asserting emphatically that their ultimate goal is the ownership of the means of production by the government and an industrial rather than a regional representation'.[34] The educator George Counts waxed rhapsodic about the brave experiment in the USSR and its challenge to America, though within a few years he turned into a leading anti-communist. As economist Stuart Chase put it in 1932, 'Why should the Russians have all the fun of remaking the world?'[35] John Dewey expressed the mood of many when he wrote that the Soviet Union was 'the most interesting [experiment] going on upon our globe – though I am quite frank to say that for selfish reasons I prefer seeing it tried out in Russia rather than in my own country'.[36]

Even the evident negative aspects of a huge country in turmoil did not dampen the enthusiasm for Stalin's revolution from above. Popular historian Will Durant travelled to Russia in 1932, witnessed starvation, but was still able to write, 'The challenge of the Five-Year Plan is moral as well as economic. It is a direct challenge to the smugness and complacency which characterize American thinking on our own chaotic system.' Future historians, he predicted, would look upon 'planned social control as the most significant single achievement of our day'.[37] That same year the Black writer Langston Hughes,

32 Ibid., p. 255; Klaus Mehnert, *Die Jugend in Sowjetrussland* (Berlin: S. Fischer, 1932), pp. 34–9.
33 Engerman, *Modernization from the Other Shore*, p. 260.
34 Edmund Wilson, 'An Appeal to Progressives', *The New Republic* 45 (14 Jan. 1931): 234–8; Filene, *American Views*, pp. 76–7.
35 Engerman, *Modernization from the Other Shore*, p. 165.     36 Ibid., p. 184.
37 Will Durant, *The Tragedy of Russia: Impressions from a Brief Visit* (New York: Simon and Schuster, 1933, p. 21; Filene, *American Views*, p. 89.

already interested in socialism, visited the USSR with other writers to produce a documentary. Inspired by what he saw – a land of poverty and hope, struggle but no racism or economic stratification – he wrote a poem, 'One More "S" in the U. S. A.', for his comrades. Decades later the anti-communist Senator Joseph McCarthy brought him before his committee to discuss publicly his political involvement with Communists.[38]

Journalism occupied the ideological front line. With the introduction of by-lines and a new emphasis on conceptualisation and interpretation instead of simple reportage, newspapermen (and they were almost all men) evaluated and made judgements. Reporters became familiar figures in popular culture, and, as celebrities back home, those posted in Russia gradually became identified with one political position or another. Of the handful of American correspondents in Moscow, Maurice Hindus stood out as a sympathetic native of the country about which he wrote. Unlike those who relied on Soviet ideological pronouncements or a reading of the Marxist classics as a guide to understanding what was going on in Russia, Hindus chose to 'be in the country, wander around, observe and listen, ask questions and digest answers to obtain some comprehension of the sweep and meaning of these events'.[39] He befriended men and women of letters, like John Dewey and George Bernard Shaw (whom he guided through the USSR on a celebrated trip), and once was prevailed upon by F. Scott Fitzgerald's psychiatrist to allay the novelist's fears of a coming communist revolution in America. To his critics, Hindus was naive, apologetic and even duplicitous. One of his fellow correspondents, the disillusioned Eugene Lyons, considered Hindus to be one of the most industrious of Stalin's apologists.[40] Whatever his faults or insights, Hindus developed and popularised a particular form of reporting on the Soviet Union – one emulated later with enormous success by Alexander Werth, Hedrick Smith, Robert Kaiser, David Shipler, Andrea Lee, Martin Walker, David Remnik and others – that combined personal observations, telling anecdotes and revealing detail to provide a textured picture of the USSR that supplemented and undercut more partisan portraits.

The *Christian Science Monitor*'s William Henry Chamberlin came as a socialist in 1922 and left as an opponent of Soviet Communism in 1934. In those twelve years he researched and wrote a classic two-volume history of the

38 Langston Hughes, *I Wonder as I Wander: An Autobiographical Journey* (New York: Rinehart, 1956).
39 Maurice Hindus, *A Traveler in Two Worlds*, intro. Milton Hindus (Garden City, N.Y.: Doubleday, 1971), p. 311.
40 Eugene Lyons, *Assignment in Utopia* (New York: Harcourt Brace, 1937).

Russian Revolution that, along with Trotsky's account, remained for nearly a quarter of a century the principal narrative of 1917 and the civil war.[41] *The Nation's* Louis Fischer was an early Zionist, who became disillusioned when he served in the Jewish Legion in Palestine and came to Russia in 1922 to find 'a brighter future' in the 'kingdom of the underdog'. His two-volume study of Soviet foreign policy, *The Soviets in World Affairs* (1930), was a careful rebuttal to the polemics about Soviet international ambitions. Lyons was very friendly to the Soviets when he arrived in Moscow at the end of 1927 and wrote positively about Stalin in a 1931 interview before he turned bitterly against them with his *Assignment in Utopia* (1937). Duranty, the acknowledged dean of the Moscow press corps, stayed for a decade and a half, won a Pulitzer Prize in 1932, refused to recognise the great famine in Ukraine of that year and often justified what he observed with the phrase, 'You can't make an omelet without breaking eggs'.[42]

Several European journalists were more critical earlier than the Americans: Malcolm Muggeridge of the *Manchester Guardian* reported on the famine months before his American counterparts; and Paul Scheffer of the *Berliner Tageblatt* was refused re-entry after he wrote about the violence of mass collectivisation. One of the most dramatic defections was by Max Eastman, a Leftist celebrity, formerly the bohemian editor of the radical journal *Masses*, who had enjoyed notoriety as the representative of the Left Opposition in America and promoted Trotsky's line in *Since Lenin Died* (1925) and *Leon Trotsky: Portrait of a Youth* (1926). The translator of Trotsky's extraordinary *History of the Russian Revolution* (1932), he attacked Stalin's cultural policies in *Artists in Uniform* (1934). By the mid-1930s his doubts about Marxism led him to conclude that Stalinism was the logical outcome of Leninism, a position that Trotsky rejected.[43] In time Eastman became a leading anti-communist, even defending the necessity of 'exposing' Communists during the McCarthy years.[44]

41 William Henry Chamberlin, *The Russian Revolution, 1917–1921* (New York: Macmillan, 1935; New York: Grosset and Dunlap, 1965).
42 Engerman, *Modernization from the Other Shore*, pp. 199–243; S. J. Taylor, *Stalin's Apologist: Walter Duranty: The New York Times's Man in Moscow* (New York and Oxford: Oxford University Press, 1990). See also the recent controversy over rescinding Duranty's Pulitzer Prize: Jacques Steinberg, 'Times Should Lose Pulitzer from 30's, Consultant Says', *New York Times*, 23 Oct. 2003; 'Word for Word/The Soft Touch: From Our Man in Moscow, In Praise of Stalinism's Future', *New York Times*, 26 Oct. 2003.
43 Alan M. Wald, *The New York Intellectuals: The Rise and Decline of the Anti-Stalinist Left from the 1930s to the 1980s* (Chapel Hill: University of North Carolina Press, 1987), pp. 112–18, 154–6.
44 Ibid., p. 273. Eastman himself denied that he was ever a 'follower' of Trotsky, though he was closely associated with the opposition to Stalin and Stalinism. (See his 'Biographical

The great ideological and political struggles that pitted liberals against conservatives, socialists against communists, the Left and Centre against Fascists intensified with the coming of the Great Depression. Like a litmus test of one's political loyalties, one's attitude towards the Soviet Union separated people who otherwise might have been allies. Communists by the 1930s were unquestioning supporters of Stalinism and the General Line. Their democratic critics included liberals and Europe's Social Democrats, among whom the exiled Mensheviks used their contacts within the country to contribute knowledgeable analyses in their journals and newspapers, most importantly *Sotsialisticheskii vestnik* (Socialist Herald). To their left were varieties of Trotskyists, most agreeing with Trotsky that the Soviet Union had suffered a Thermidorian reaction and become a deformed workers' state.[45] For Trotsky the USSR was ruled, not by a dictatorship of the proletariat, but by 'a hitherto unheard of apparatus of compulsion', an uncontrolled bureaucracy dominating the masses.[46] Stalin's personal triumph was that of the bureaucracy, which perfectly reflected his own 'petty bourgeois outlook', and his state had 'acquired a totalitarian-bureaucratic character'.[47] Impeccably Marxist, Trotsky provided an impressive structuralist alternative to the more common accounts based on national character or rationalisation of the Soviet system as an effective model of statist developmentalism.

In the second half of the 1930s the threat posed by Fascism intensified the personal, political and psychological struggles of the politically minded and politically active. While some embraced Stalinism, even as it devoured millions of its own people, as the best defence against the radical Right, others denounced the great experiment as a grand deception. The show trials of 1936–8 swept away loyal Bolsheviks, many of whom had been close comrades of Lenin, for their alleged links to an 'anti-Soviet Trotskyite' conspiracy. John Dewey, novelist James T. Farrell and other intellectuals formed the American Committee for the Defense of Leon Trotsky, and the 'Dewey Commission' travelled to Coyoacan, Mexico, to interrogate Trotsky. It concluded that none of the charges levelled against Trotsky and his son was true.[48] But equally

Introduction' to Max Eastman, *Reflections on the Failure of Socialism* (New York: Grosset and Dunlap, 1955), pp. 7–20.)

45 Leon Trotsky, *The Revolution Betrayed: What is the Soviet Union and Where is it Going?*, trans. Max Eastman (1937; New York: Pathfinder Press, 1972), pp. 19, 47, 61.

46 Ibid., p. 52.    47 Ibid., pp. 93, 97, 108.

48 *The Case of Leon Trotsky: Report of Hearings on the Charges Made against Him in the Moscow Trials by the Preliminary Commission of Inquiry* (New York: Merit Publishers, 1937); *Not Guilty: Report of the Commission of Inquiry into the Charges Made against Leon Trotsky in the Moscow Trials* (New York: Harper and Brothers, 1938). See also, Alan Wald, 'Memories of the John Dewey Commission: Forty Years Later', *Antioch Review* (1977): pp. 438–51.

eminent intellectuals – among them Dreiser, Fischer, playwright Lillian Hellman, artist Rockwell Kent, author Nathaniel West and journalist Heywood Broun – denounced the Commission's findings and urged American liberals not to support enemies of the USSR, 'a country recognised as engaged in improving conditions for all its people' that should 'be permitted to decide for itself what measures of protection are necessary against treasonable plots to assassinate and overthrow its leadership and involve it in war with foreign powers'.[49] Confusion and self-delusion about the USSR affected even the American ambassador to Moscow, the political appointee Joseph E. Davies, who attended the Bukharin trial and later wrote that he was astonished that such crimes could have been committed by Old Bolsheviks.[50]

Despite forced collectivisation, the consequent famine and the Great Purges, many on the Left retained their passion for Soviet socialism until Stalin himself delivered a body blow to their faith with the August 1939 non-aggression pact with Nazi Germany. Fellow-travellers found it hard to travel down this road, and Communist parties around the world haemorrhaged members. *The New Republic*, which had supported the Soviet Union for decades, reversed itself when Stalin attacked Finland. Many who had resisted the concept of 'totalitarianism', which collapsed Stalinism and Nazism into a single analytical category, suddenly saw merit in this formulation. In 1940 Edmund Wilson published *To the Finland Station*, an excursion through the prehistory and history of Marxism in thought and in power.[51] Once a Communist, later an admirer of Trotsky, Wilson questioned the sureties of his earlier faith and ended up with praise for Marxism's moral and social vision while rejecting the authoritarianism and statism of the Soviet model.[52] Arthur Koestler, the son of Hungarian Jews, explored his loss of faith in the Communist movement in his novel *Darkness at Noon* (1940). Basing his hero on Bukharin, Koestler told the story of an idealistic Soviet leader, Rubashov, who agrees to confess to imaginary crimes as his last contribution to the revolutionary cause. Along with George Orwell's distopian novels, Koestler's exploration into the mind of a Bolshevik would become one of the defining literary portraits in the anti-communist arsenal in the post-war years.

With the Nazi invasion of the USSR in June 1941, attitudes shifted once again, spawning an outpouring of writing on Russia and the Soviet Union.

---

49 'An Open Letter to American Liberals', *Soviet Russia Today* 6 (Mar. 1937): 14–15; Filene, *American Views*, p. 119.

50 Joseph E. Davies, *Mission to Moscow* (New York: Simon and Schuster, 1941), pp. 269–72.

51 Edmund Wilson, *To the Finland Station: A Study in the Writing and Acting of History* (Garden City, N.Y.: Doubleday, 1940; Anchor Books, 1953).

52 Wald, *The New York Intellectuals*, pp. 157–63.

Some two hundred books were published in the United States in 1943–5 alone. Ambassador Davies's memoir, *Mission to Moscow* (December 1941), sold 700,000 copies and was memorialised in a splashy Hollywood film that lauded Soviet achievements, 'convicted' those charged at the Moscow trials, justified the Soviet attack on Finland and portrayed Stalin as a benign avuncular patriarch. A grotesque piece of war propaganda, playing fast and loose with historical fact, the film was widely panned in the press, and leading 'progressive' intellectuals, including Dewey, Dwight MacDonald, Wilson, Eastman, Sidney Hook, Farrell and socialist Norman Thomas, signed public protests against it. Four years after the film's opening in 1943, Warner Brothers reacted to the onset of the Cold War by ordering all release prints destroyed.[53]

One of the most important and influential scholarly works of the period was by the Russian-born émigré sociologist Nicholas S. Timasheff, whose *The Great Retreat* showed in detail how the Soviet state had abandoned its original revolutionary programme and internationalist agenda in the mid-1930s and turned into a traditional Great Power.[54] Instead of the radical levelling of social classes of the early 1930s, Stalinism re-established new hierarchies based on wage differentials, education, party affiliation and loyalty to the state. The Great Retreat represented the triumph of the 'national structure', Russian history and the needs and desires of the people over 'an anonymous body of international workers'.[55] Rather than betraying the revolution, the Retreat signalled its nationalisation and domestication, the victory of reality and 'objective facts' over utopianism and radical experimentation. The book appeared in 1946 just after the high-point of Soviet–American co-operation, clearly a reflection of the Yalta spirit of the immediate pre-Cold War years. Timasheff predicted that the revolutionary years were over; faith in the Marxist doctrine had faded and a future development towards democracy was possible. Here he echoed his collaborator, fellow Russian-born sociologist Pitirim Sorokin of Harvard, who in his *Russia and the United States* (1944) proposed that Russia and the United

53 Clayton R. Koppes and Gregory D. Black, *Hollywood Goes to War: How Politics, Profits and Propaganda Shaped World War II Movies* (New York: Free Press, 1987; Berkeley and Los Angeles: University of California Press, 1990), pp. 185–221. Other pro-Soviet films of the war years included: *North Star*, written by Lillian Hellman; *Song of Russia*; *Days of Glory*; *Counter-Attack*; *Three Russian Girls*; and *Boy from Stalingrad*.
54 Nicholas S. Timasheff, *The Great Retreat: The Growth and Decline of Communism in Russia* (New York: E. P. Dutton, 1946). An earlier reference to 'the Great Retreat' can be found in C. L. R. James, *World Revolution, 1917–1936: The Rise and Fall of the Communist International* (New York: Pioneer Publishers, 1937). Born in Trinidad, James emigrated to Britain where he became a leading Trotskyist. Best known for his study of the Haitian revolution, *The Black Jacobins* (1938), he was also the translator of Souvarine's biography of Stalin into English.
55 Timasheff, *The Great Retreat*, pp. 361–2.

States were meant to be allies, not enemies, and that the two societies were indeed converging along the lines of all other highly industrialised societies. This 'convergence thesis' would eventually become standard in the modernisation literature of the 1950s, and both in its introduction and its elaboration it was part of a general political recommendation for understanding, tolerance, patience and entente between the Soviet Union and the Western powers.

## The Cold War and professional sovietology

In late 1945 American public opinion was generally positive about the Soviet Union. A *Fortune* poll in September showed that only a quarter of the population believed that the USSR would attempt to spread communism into Eastern Europe. By July 1946 more than half of those polled felt that Moscow aimed to dominate as much of the world as possible.[56] Within government and in the public sphere opposing formulations of the Soviet Union contended with one another. Vice-President and later Secretary of Commerce Henry A. Wallace used Russian character to explain why a 'get tough with Russia' policy would only result in tougher Russians. Others like Walter Lippmann warned that not recognising Soviet interests in Eastern Europe would lead to a 'cold war'. But far more influential, and eventually hegemonic, were the views of a number of State Department specialists, most importantly George Kennan, who did not trust the Soviet leadership.

In 1946 Kennan sent his famous 'Long Telegram' from Moscow, reiterating that Russian behaviour was best explained by national characteristics. The inherent, intractable, immutable characteristics of the Russians as 'Asiatics' required the use of countervailing force to contain the Soviets' aggressive tendencies. When he published his views in *Foreign Affairs*, famously signing the article 'X', Kennan abruptly shifted his position from considering Marxism largely irrelevant to emphasising the importance of Marxist doctrine. 'The political personality of Soviet power as we know it today', he wrote, 'is the product of ideology and circumstances: ideology inherited by the present Soviet leaders from the movement in which they had their political origin, and circumstances of the power which they now have exercised for nearly three decades in Russia.'[57] Soviet ideology included the idea of the innate antagonism between capitalism and socialism and the infallibility of the Kremlin as the

56 John Lewis Gaddis, *The United States and the Origins of the Cold War, 1941–1947* (New York and London: Columbia University Press, 1972), p. 321.
57 'X' [George F. Kennan], 'The Sources of Soviet Conduct', *Foreign Affairs* 25 (July 1947): 566.

sole repository of truth. Though his explanation had changed from national character to ideology, Kennan's prescription for US foreign policy remained the same: the USSR was a rival, not a partner, and the United States had no other course but containment of Russian expansive tendencies.[58]

Under the imperatives of the American government's apprehension about Soviet expansionism, a profession of 'sovietologists' began to form, primarily in the United States. In 1946 the first American centre of Russian studies, the Russian Institute, was founded at Columbia University, soon to be followed by the Russian Research Center at Harvard (1948). The first 'area studies' centres in the United States became prototypes for a new direction in social science research, bringing together various disciplines to look intensively at a particular society and culture. A generation of scholars, many of whom had had wartime experience in the military or intelligence work, worked closely with governmental agencies and on official projects sponsored by the CIA or the military. Most importantly the air force funded the Harvard Interview Project, questioning thousands of Soviet émigrés and producing valuable information on daily life and thought in the USSR, as well as guides for target selection and psychological warfare. In 1950 the Institute for the Study of the USSR was founded in Munich. Secretly funded by the CIA until it was closed in 1971, the Institute produced numerous volumes and journals by émigré writers that confirmed the worst expectations of Western readers. More interesting to scholars was the American government-sponsored journal *Problems of Communism*, edited from 1952 to 1970 by a sceptical scion of the Polish Jewish Bund, Abraham Brumberg, which managed to condemn the Soviet Union as a totalitarian tyranny while avoiding the worst excesses of anti-communist hysteria.

American scholars, particularly political scientists and sociologists, were caught in a schizophrenic tension between their disciplinary identity as detached scientists and their political commitment to (and often financial dependency on) the American state. Challenged by McCarthyism, historians and political scientists sought shelter behind their claims to objectivity, even as they joined in the general anti-communist patriotism of the day. Across the social sciences 'Marx was replaced by Freud; the word "capitalism" dropped out of social theory; and class became stratification'.[59] A group of social scientists

---

58 The point about the shift from national character to ideology is made convincingly by Engerman, *Modernization from the Other Shore*, pp. 264–71.

59 Thomas Bender, 'Politics, Intellect, and the American University, 1945–1995', in Thomas Bender and Carl E. Schorske (eds.), *American Academic Culture in Transformation: Fifty Years, Four Disciplines* (Princeton: Princeton University Press, 1997), p. 29.

at the University of Chicago deliberately chose the term 'behavioural sciences' to describe their endeavour, trying to appear neutral and not scare off congressional funders who 'might confound social science with socialism'.[60] The benefits of working in tandem with the interests of the state were enormous; the dangers of non-conformity were omnipresent. Two of the founders of Columbia's Russian Institute, Soviet legal expert John N. Hazard and Soviet literature specialist Ernest J. Simmons, were named by Senator McCarthy in 1953 as members of the 'Communist conspiracy'.[61] The intellectual historian H. Stuart Hughes was dismissed as associate director of Harvard's Russian Research Center when a trustee of the Carnegie Corporation, a major funder of the Center, complained that Hughes supported the 1948 Henry Wallace presidential campaign.[62] In Britain the most prominent historian of Russia, E. H. Carr, reported in 1950 that 'It had become very difficult . . . to speak dispassionately about Russia except in a "very woolly Christian kind of way" without endangering, if not your bread and butter, then your legitimate hopes of advancement', and the Marxist historian Eric J. Hobsbawm affirmed that 'there is no question that the principle of freedom of expression did not apply to communist and Marxist views, at least in the official media'.[63]

## The totalitarian model

With the collapse of the Grand Alliance, the more sympathetic renderings of Stalin's USSR popular during the war gave way to the powerful image of 'Red Fascism' that melded the practices of Nazi Germany with the Soviet Union. In order to conceptualise these terror-based one-party ideological regimes, political scientists elaborated the concept of 'totalitarianism'. Carl Friedrich and Zbigniew Brzezinski formulated the classic definition of totalitarianism with its six systemic characteristics: a ruling ideology, a single party typically led by one man, a terroristic police, a communications monopoly, a weapons monopoly and a centrally directed economy.[64] Such states, with their mass

60 John G. Gunnell, *The Descent of Political Theory: The Genealogy of an American Vocation* (Chicago: University of Chicago Press, 1993), p. 218.
61 Stephen F. Cohen, *Rethinking the Soviet Experience: Politics and History Since 1917* (New York and Oxford: Oxford University Press, 1985), p. 17.
62 Charles Thomas O'Connell, 'Social Structure and Science: Soviet Studies at Harvard', Ph.D. diss, UCLA, 1990; Martin Oppenheimer, 'Social Scientists and War Criminals', *New Politics* 6, 3 (NS) (Summer 1997): 77–87.
63 Both citations are from Eric Hobsbawm, *Interesting Times: A Twentieth-Century Life* (London: Allen Lane, 2002), p. 183.
64 Carl J. Friedrich and Zbigniew K. Brzezinski, *Totalitarian Dictatorship and Autocracy* (Cambridge, Mass.: Harvard University Press, 1956; revised edn, New York: Frederick A.

manipulation, suppression of voluntary associations, violence and expansionism, were contrasted with liberal democratic, pluralistic societies. Because such systems were able to suppress effectively internal dissension, many theorists concluded, they would never change unless overthrown from outside.

The T-model dominated scholarship, particularly in political science, through the 1950s well into the 1960s, a time when the academy was intimately involved in the global struggle that pitted the West against the Soviet Union, its 'satellite' states and anti-colonial nationalism. The model of a gargantuan prison state, 'a huge reformatory in which the primary difference between the forced labour camps and the rest of the Soviet Union is that inside the camps the regimen is much more brutal and humiliating', was compelling both because high Stalinism matched much of the image of a degenerated autocracy and because Soviet restrictions and censorship eliminated most other sources, like travellers, journalists and scholars with in-country experience.[65] The image of an imperialist totalitarianism, spreading its red grip over the globe, was at one and the same time the product of Western anxieties and the producer of inflated fears. George Orwell, already well known for his satire on Soviet politics, *Animal Farm* (1945), produced the most effective literary vision of totalitarianism in his popular novel *Nineteen Eighty-four* (1949). Its hero, Winston Smith, tries futilely to revolt against the totally administered society presided over by Big Brother, but by novel's end he has been ground into submission and spouts the doublespeak slogans of the regime. The political philosopher Hannah Arendt, a refugee from Nazism, provided the most sophisticated and subtle interpretation of *The Origins of Totalitarianism* which she connected to anti-Semitism, nationalism, imperialism and the replacement of class politics by mass politics.[66]

Scholars explained the origins and spread of totalitarianism in various ways. Arendt linked totalitarianism with the coming of mass democracy; Waldemar Gurian saw the source in the utopian ambitions of Leftist politicians; Stefan Possony tied it to the personality of Lenin, Robert C. Tucker to the personality of Stalin; and Nathan Leites employed psychoanalytic concepts to write about the psychopathology of the Bolshevik elite, distinguished primarily by paranoia. The anthropologists Geoffrey Gorer and Margaret Mead reverted to

Praeger, 1966), p. 22. See also Carl J. Friedrich (ed.), *Totalitarianism* (Cambridge, Mass.: Harvard University Press, 1954; New York: Grosset and Dunlap, 1964).

65 Merle Fainsod, *How Russia is Ruled* (Cambridge, Mass.: Harvard University Press, 1953), p. 482.

66 Hannah Arendt, *The Origins of Totalitarianism* (New York: Harcourt, Brace, 1951). For a history of the concept of totalitarianism, see Abbott Gleason, *Totalitarianism: The Inner History of the Cold War* (New York and Oxford: Oxford University Press, 1995).

the ever-handy notion of national character, in this case patterns of inbred sub-missiveness to authority caused by the peasant practice of swaddling Russian infants.[67] Russians were not quite like other human beings. 'They endure physical suffering with great stoicism and are indifferent about the physical sufferings of others . . . [Therefore] No techniques are yet available for eradi-cating the all-pervasive suspicion which Great Russians, leaders and led alike, feel towards the rest of the world. This suspicion springs from unconscious and therefore irrational sources and will not be calmed, more than momentarily, by rational actions.'[68] The positive vision of 'civic education' put forth in the 1920s gave way to the image of 'brain-washing'. In 1949 George Counts, who eighteen years earlier had written *The Soviet Challenge to America* (1931), now co-authored with Nucia Lodge *The Country of the Blind: The Soviet System of Mind Control* (1949).

The totalitarian approach turned an apt if not wholly accurate description into a model, complete with predictions of future trajectories. The concept exaggerated similarities and underestimated differences between quite dis-tinct regimes, ignoring the contrast between an egalitarian, internationalist doctrine (Marxism) that the Soviet regime failed to realise and the inegali-tarian, racist and imperialist ideology (Fascism) that the Nazis implemented only too well. Little was said about the different dynamics in a state capi-talist system with private ownership of property (Nazi Germany) and those operating in a completely state-dominated economy with almost no produc-tion for the market (Stalin's USSR), or how an advanced industrial economy geared essentially to war and territorial expansion (Nazi Germany) differed from a programme for modernising a backward, peasant society and trans-forming it into an industrial, urban one (Stalinist Soviet Union). The T-model led many political scientists and historians to deal almost exclusively with the state, the centre and the top of the political pyramid, and make deductions from a supposedly fixed ideology, while largely ignoring social dynamics and the shifts and improvisations that characterised both Soviet and Nazi policies.

---

67 This catalogue of causes is indebted to Alfred Meyer, 'Coming to Terms with the Past', *Russian Review*, 45, 4 (Oct. 1986): 403; Waldemar Gurian, *Bolshevism: An Introduction to Soviet Communism* (Notre Dame, Ind.: University of Notre Dame Press, 1956); Stefan Possony, *Lenin: The Compulsive Revolutionary* (Chicago: Henry Regnery, 1964); Robert C. Tucker, *Stalin As Revolutionary, 1879–1929* (New York: Norton, 1973); Margaret Mead, *Soviet Attitudes toward Authority: An Interdisciplinary Approach to Problems of Soviet Character* (New York: McGraw-Hill, 1951); Nathan Leites, *The Operational Code of the Politburo* (New York: McGraw-Hill, 1951); *A Study of Bolshevism* (Glencoe, Ill.: Free Press, 1953); Geoffrey Gorer and John Rickman, *The People of Great Russia: A Psychological Study* (New York: Chanticleer Press, 1950).
68 Gorer and Rickman, *The People of Great Russia*, pp. 189, 191–2.

Even more pernicious were the predictive parallels: since Nazi Germany had acted in an expansionist, aggressive way, it could be expected that another totalitarian regime would also be aggressive and expansionist. Indeed, during the Cold War Western media and governments fostered the notion that the USSR was poised and ready to invade Western Europe. Any concessions to Soviet Communism were labelled 'appeasement', a direct analogy to Western negotiations with the Nazis in the 1930s.

Ironically, not only changing reality, but the findings of specific studies, belied the model. The most influential text, Merle Fainsod's *How Russia is Ruled*, the key text in the field for over a decade, appeared within months of Stalin's death and saw little evidence that the Soviet system would change. Yet later when Fainsod used an extraordinary cache of Soviet archives captured by the German invaders to write a ground-breaking study, *Smolensk under Soviet Rule* (1958), he exposed a level of complexity that made 'generalizing processes' like 'urbanization, industrialization, collectivization, secularization, bureaucratization, and totalitarianization . . . seem rather pallid and abstract'.[69] His younger colleague, Barrington Moore, Jr., asked the important question, what was the relationship between Leninist ideology and the actual policies and products of the Soviet regime under Stalin, and concluded that the Bolshevik ideology of ends – greater equality, empowerment of working people, internationalism – had been trumped by the Bolshevik ideology of means – 'the need for authority and discipline'. The 'means have swallowed up and distorted the original ends'. Instead of 'humane anarchism', the very elasticity of communist doctrine allowed for the entry of nationalism, pragmatism and inequalities that ultimately used anti-authoritarian ideas to justify and support an authoritarian regime.[70] In a second book Moore shifted from a language of authority to the then current vocabulary of totalitarianism and elaborated a range of possible scenarios for the USSR, ranging from a rationalist technocracy to a traditionalist despotism. The Soviet state would continue to require terror, however, if it meant to remain a dynamic regime.[71]

69 Merle Fainsod, *Smolensk under Soviet Rule* (Cambridge, Mass.: Harvard University Press, 1958; Rand Corporation, 1958; Vintage Books, 1963), p. 446. For a Russian look at the effect of the Smolensk archive on American sovietology, see Evgenii Kodin, *Smolenskii arkhiv i amerikanskaia sovetologiia* (Smolensk: SGPU, 1998).

70 Barrington Moore, Jr., *Soviet Politics – The Dilemma of Power: The Role of Ideas in Social Change* (Cambridge, Mass.: Harvard University Press, 1950; New York: Harper Torchbook, 1965), pp. 1–12, 402–5, 430. See also his *Terror and Progress: Some Sources of Change and Stability in the Soviet Dictatorship* (Cambridge, Mass.: Harvard University Press, 1954; New York: Harper Torchbook, 1966).

71 Barrington Moore, *Terror and Progress*, pp. xiii–xiv, 173–4, 179–231.

As the Cold War consensus of the 1950s gave way to a growing discomfort with American policy, especially when containment of the Soviet threat turned into the military intervention in Vietnam, the Soviet Union itself was evolving away from Stalinism. Nikita Khrushchev ended the indiscriminate mass terror, loosened the state's hold on the population, and opened small windows to the West. Increasingly, the regime attempted to govern through material satisfaction of popular needs and encouraged popular initiative. The monolithic Stalinist empire in Eastern Europe showed signs of what was called 'polycentrism', a variety of 'roads to socialism', with somewhat increased autonomy, if not real independence, from the Kremlin. And after nearly two decades of T-model dominance, the first serious critiques of totalitarianism appeared, first from political scientists, and later from historians.

In 1965 Princeton political scientist and former diplomat Robert C. Tucker attempted to refine the concept of totalitarianism by analysing the personalities of the dictators and concluded that the system of totalitarianism was not the cause of the massive violence of the late 1930s; rather, terror was in large part an expression of the needs of the dictatorial personality of Stalin.[72] In a more radical vein Herbert J. Spiro and Benjamin R. Barber claimed that the concept of totalitarianism was the foundation of 'American Counter-Ideology' in the Cold War years. Totalitarianism theory had played an important role in the reorientation of American foreign policy by helping 'to explain away German and Japanese behavior under the wartime regimes and thereby to justify the radical reversal of alliances after the war'. A purported 'logic of totalitarianism' provided an all-encompassing explanation of Communist behaviour, which led to suspicion of liberation movements in the Third World, a sense that international law and organisations were insufficiently strong to thwart totalitarian movements and a justification of 'the consequent necessity of considering the use of force – even thermonuclear force – in the settlement of world issues'.[73] Totalitarian theory was a deployed ideological construction of the world that

---

72 Robert C. Tucker, 'The Dictator and Totalitarianism', *World Politics* 17, 4 (July 1965): 555–83.
73 Herbert J. Spiro and Benjamin R. Barber presented a paper on totalitarianism at the 1967 meeting of the American Political Science Association. The quotations here are from the published version, 'Counter-Ideological Uses of "Totalitarianism"', in *Politics and Society* 1, 1 (Nov. 1970) (pp. 3–21): 9; see also, Herbert J. Spiro, 'Totalitarianism', in *International Encyclopedia of the Social Sciences* (New York: Macmillan and Free Press, 1968–76), vol. xvi, pp. 106b–112b. At the invitation of Professor William G. Rosenberg of the University of Michigan I presented a paper on the panel, 'Uses of the Soviet Past – A Critical Review', at the 1970 meeting of the American Association for the Advancement of Slavic Studies. The response from many in the audience to the paper, 'The Abuses of the Soviet Past', which primarily criticised the totalitarian model, was hostile, even accusatory. I decided not to pursue this line of inquiry in print until many years later.

denied its own ideological nature at a time when leading American thinkers proclaimed 'the end of ideology'.[74]

Scholars had to shift their views or jigger with the model. For Merle Fainsod in 1953, terror had been the 'linchpin of modern totalitarianism', but ten years after Stalin's death he revised that sentence to read: 'Every totalitarian regime makes some place for terror in its system of controls.' In 1956 Brzezinski wrote that terror is 'the most universal characteristic of totalitarianism'.[75] But in 1962 he reconsidered: terror is no longer essential; the USSR is now a 'voluntarist totalitarian system' in which 'persuasion, indoctrination, and social control can work more effectively'.[76] Yet in that same year Harvard political scientist Adam B. Ulam insisted that 'the essence of the Soviet political system' is not 'transient aberrations arising out of willful and illegal acts of individuals', but is, rather, 'imposed by the logic of totalitarianism'. Given the immutable laws that follow from that logic, 'in a totalitarian state terror can never be abolished entirely'.[77] When the evidence of the waning of terror appeared to undermine that argument, Ulam spoke of a 'sane pattern of totalitarianism, in contrast to the extreme of Stalin's despotism' and claimed that terror was 'interfering with the objectives of totalitarianism itself'.[78] But since Stalinism itself had earlier been seen as the archetype itself of totalitarianism and terror its essence, Ulam inadvertently laid bare the fundamental confusion and contradictions of the concept.

From the mid-1960s a younger generation of historians, many of them excited by the possibilities of a 'social history' that looked beyond the state to examine society, were travelling to the Soviet Union through expanded academic exchange programmes. The luckiest among them were privileged to work in heavily restricted archives, but all of them saw at first hand the intricacies, complexities and contradictions of everyday Soviet life that fitted poorly with the totalitarian image of ubiquitous fear and rigid conformity.

74 On the end of ideology discussion, see Daniel Bell, *The End of Ideology: On the Exhaustion of Political Ideas in the Fifties* (Glencoe, Ill.: Free Press, 1960; Cambridge, Mass.: Harvard University Press, 2000); and Nils Gilman, *Mandarins of the Future: Modernization Theory in Cold War America* (Baltimore: Johns Hopkins University Press, 2003), pp. 56–62, 109–10.

75 Zbigniew K. Brzezinski, *The Permanent Purge – Politics in Soviet Totalitarianism* (Cambridge, Mass.: Harvard University Press, 1956), p. 27.

76 Zbigniew K. Brzezinski, *Ideology and Power in Soviet Politics* (New York: Praeger, 1962), pp. 80, 88–9.

77 Adam B. Ulam, 'The Russian Political System', in Samuel H. Beer and Adam B. Ulam (eds.), *Patters of Government: The Major Political Systems of Europe*, 2nd edn revised (New York: Random House, 1962), pp. 670, 656, 646; cited in Spiro and Barber, 'Counter-Ideological Uses', pp. 13–14.

78 Ulam, 'The Russian Political System', p. 646; Spiro and Barber, 'Counter-Ideological Uses', p. 19.

Excited by the idea of a 'history from the bottom up', social historians pointed out that by concentrating on the political elite and the repressive apparatus, the totalitarian approach neglected to note that in the actual experience of these societies the regime was unable to achieve the full expectation of the totalitarian model, that is, the absolute and total control over the whole of society and the atomisation of the population. What was truly totalitarian in Stalinism or Nazism were the intentions and aspirations of rulers like Hitler or Stalin, who may have had ambitions to create a society in which the party and people were one and in which interests of all were harmonised and all dissent destroyed. But the control of so-called totalitarian states was never so total as to turn the people into 'little screws' (Stalin's words) to do the bidding of the state. Despite all the limitations of the model, scholars writing in this tradition illuminated anomalous aspects of the Stalinist and post-Stalinist regimes that contradicted the fundaments of totalitarianism. At the same time, though less widely regarded, critics of liberalism and market society, from the Marxists of the Frankfurt School to post-modernist cultural theorists, took note of the 'totalitarian' effects of modernity more generally – of technology, industrialism, commercialism and capitalism – which were excluded from the original model.[79]

## The modernisation paradigm

The Cold War American academy celebrated the achievements of American society and politics, which had reached an unprecedented level of stability and prosperity. Historians of the 'consensus school' held that Americans were united by their shared fundamental values; political scientists compared the pluralistic, democratic norm of the United States to other societies, usually unfavourably. America was 'the good society itself in operation', 'with the most developed set of political and class relations', 'the image of the European future', a model for the rest of the globe.[80] Western social science worked from an assumed Western master narrative brought to bear on non-Western

79 Key texts for the Marxists are: Max Horkheimer and Theodor W. Adorno, *Dialectic of Enlightenment* (New York: Seabury Press, 1972), originally published as *Dialektik der Aufklärung* (New York: Social Studies Association, 1944); Herbert Marcuse, *Soviet Marxism: A Critical Analysis* (New York: Columbia University Press, 1958); *One-Dimensional Man* (Boston: Beacon Press, 1964); and *Negations* (Boston: Beacon Press, 1968). For post-modernist critics, see Zygmunt Bauman, *Modernity and the Holocaust* (Ithaca, N.Y.: Cornell University Press, 1989); and his *Intimations of Postmodernity* (London and New York: Routledge, 1992).
80 From Seymour Martin Lipset, *Political Man: The Social Bases of Politics* (Garden City, N.Y.: Doubleday, 1960), as cited in Oren, *Our Enemies and US*, p. 126.

societies: they too were expected to evolve as had Western Europe from theocratic to secular values, from status to contract, from more restricted to freer capitalist economies, from *Gemeinschaft* to *Gesellschaft*, in a word, from tradition to modernity.

Elaborating ideas from the classical social theorists Emile Durkheim and Max Weber, modernisation theory proposed that societies would progressively assume greater control over nature and human suffering through developments in science, technology, mass education, economic growth and urbanisation. While Marxism may also be understood as a theory of modernisation, complete with its own theory of history that reached beyond capitalism to socialism, what might be called 'liberal modernisation theory' was elaborated in opposition to Marxism and claimed that the best road to modernity lay through capitalism (though not necessarily through democracy as well), with no necessary transcendence to a post-capitalist socialism.[81] Since the modern was usually construed to be American liberal capitalist democracy, this powerful, evolving discourse of development and democracy legitimised a new post-colonial role for the developed world vis-à-vis the underdeveloped. The West would lead the less fortunate into prosperity and modernity, stability and progress, and the South (and later the East) would follow.

Modernisationists were divided between optimists, who held that all people had the capacity to reach Western norms if they had the will or managed the transition properly, and pessimists, who believed that not all non-Western cultures were able to modernise and reach democracy. For an optimist like Gabriel Almond, one of the most prominent comparative politics scholars of his generation, human history was generally seen to be progressive, leading upward, inevitably, to something that looked like the developed West.[82] Classic works such as Seymour Martin Lipset's *Political Man: The Social Bases of Politics* (1960) and Almond and Sidney Verba's *The Civic Culture* (1963) considered a democratic political culture with civic values of trust and tolerance, crucial prerequisites for democracy that would somehow have to be instilled in modernising societies. Democracy, development and anti-communism were values which went together. As in the years following the First World War, so during

---

81 The classic statement on the priority of order over democracy in the process of development can be found in Samuel P. Huntington, *Political Order in Changing Societies* (New Haven: Yale University Press, 1968). Huntington saw the USSR and other Soviet-style states as examples of a high level of development and social stability. On modernisation theory, see Gilman, *Mandarins of the Future*.

82 Gabriel Almond, *Political Development: Essays in Heuristic Theory* (Boston: Little, Brown, 1970), p. 232.

the Cold War, poverty was not only undesirable but a positive danger precisely because it inflamed minds and could potentially lead to communism.

The Soviet Union presented the modernisationists with an anomalous example of a perverse road to modernity that looked very seductive to anti-imperialist revolutionaries. With American scholarship intimately linked to the global struggle against Soviet Communism, the modernisation paradigm both provided an argument for the universal developmental pattern from traditional society to modern, a path that the Third World was fated to follow, and touted the superiority and more complete modernity of capitalist democracy American-style. A team of researchers and writers at MIT's Center for International Studies (CENIS), worked in the modernisation mode, developing analyses of the deviant Soviet road. CENIS, a conduit between the university community and the national government, had been established with CIA funding and directed by Max Millikan, former assistant director of the intelligence agency. No specialist on the Soviet Union, the MIT economic historian Walt Whitman Rostow published *The Dynamics of Soviet Society* (1952), in which he and his team argued that Soviet politics and society were driven by the 'priority of power'. Where ideology came into conflict with the pursuit of power, ideology lost out.[83] After being turned over to the CIA and the State Department and vetted by Philip Mosely of Columbia's Russian Institute and others before it was declassified and published, Rostow's study was released to the public as a work of independent scholarship.[84]

In his later and much more influential book, *The Stages of Economic Growth: A Non-Communist Manifesto* (1960), Rostow proposed that peoples moved from traditional society through the preconditions for take-off, to take-off, on to the drive to maturity and finally to the age of high mass-consumption. He trumpeted that Russia, 'as a great nation, well endowed by nature and history to create a modern economy and a modern society', was in fact developing

83 W. W. Rostow and Alfred Levin, *The Dynamics of Soviet Society* (New York: W. W. Norton, 1952; Mentor Books, 1954), p. 89.
84 Allan A. Needell, 'Project Troy and the Cold War Annexation of the Social Sciences', in Christopher Simpson (ed.), *Universities and Empire: Money and Politics in the Social Sciences During the Cold War* (New York: New Press, 1998), p. 23; Bruce Cumings, 'Boundary Displacement: Area Studies and International Studies During and After the Cold War,' ibid., pp. 167–8. Then at Harvard, historian Robert V. Daniels worked on the project at MIT because Harvard had a rule against classified research and farmed such work out to other institutions. Daniels disagreed with Rostow's single factor analysis – that the pursuit of power was a complete explanation – and eventually broke with Rostow over authorial credit before the commercial publication of the book. (Personal communication with the author, 19 March 2004.)

parallel to the West.[85] But traditional society gave way slowly in Russia, and its take-off came only in the mid-1980s, thirty years after the United States, and its drive to maturity in the First Five-Year Plans. Its growth was remarkable, but there was no need for alarm in the West, for its growth was built on under-consumption. Communism, which for Rostow was 'a disease of the transition', 'is likely to wither in the age of high mass-consumption'.[86]

Most sovietologists shared the general assumptions of modernisation theory, and the most fervent adherents of the totalitarian concept made valiant attempts to preserve the T-model in the face of the challenge from the more dynamic modernisation paradigm or to reconcile the two. In a 1961 discussion, Brzezinski distinguished between the 'totalitarian breakthrough' of Stalinism that destroyed the old order and created the framework for the new and the post-terror totalitarianism of the Khrushchev period.[87] The latter looked much more like the corporate system described by John Armstrong in his study of Ukrainian bureaucrats, managed by the 'Red Executives' analysed by David Granick and Joseph Berliner.[88] Brzezinski pointed out that Soviet ideology was no longer about revolution but the link that legitimised the rule of the party by tying it to the project of technical and economic modernisation. Whereas Brzezinski argued that 'indoctrination has replaced terror as the most distinctive feature of the system', Alfred G. Meyer went further: 'acceptance and internalization of the central principles of the ideology have replaced both terror and frenetic indoctrination.' In what he called 'spontaneous totalitarianism', Meyer noted that 'Soviet citizens have become more satisfied, loyal, and co-operative'.[89] The USSR was simply a giant 'company town' in which all of life was organised by the company.

85 W. W. Rostow, *The Stages of Economic Growth: A Non-Communist Manifesto* (Cambridge: Cambridge University Press, 1960), p. 104.
86 Ibid., pp. 163, 133. Rostow later became a key adviser to President Lyndon Baines Johnson and an architect of the American intervention in Vietnam.
87 Zbigniew Brzezinski, 'The Nature of the Soviet System', *Slavic Review* 20, 3 (Oct. 1961): 351–68.
88 David Granick, *The Red Executive: A Study of the Organization Man in Russian Industry* (Garden City, N.Y.: Doubleday, 1960); Joseph S. Berliner, *Factory and Manager in the USSR* (Cambridge, Mass.: Harvard University Press, 1957).
89 Brzezinski, 'The Nature of the Soviet System'; Alfred G. Meyer, 'USSR, Incorporated', *Slavic Review* 20, 3 (Oct. 1961): 369–76. Among the most influential authorities on modernisation theory as applied to the Soviet Union was Princeton's Cyril E. Black, who edited *The Transformation of Russian Society: Aspects of Social Change Since 1861* (Cambridge, Mass.: Harvard University Press, 1960), and later organised the team that published Cyril E. Black, Marius B. Jansen, Herbert S. Levine, Marion J. Levy, Jr., Henry Rosovsky, Gilbert Rozman, Henry D. Smith, II, S. Frederick Starr, *The Modernization of Japan and Russia: A Comparative Study* (New York: Free Press, 1975).

The two models, however, differed fundamentally. The T-model was based on sharp differences between communist and liberal societies, while the modernisation paradigm proposed a universal and shared development. For many writing in the modernisation mode, the Soviet Union appeared as less aberrant than in the earlier model, a somewhat rougher alternative programme of social and economic development. While some writers expected that the outcome of modernisation would be democratic, more conservative authors were willing to settle for stability and order rather than representation of the popular will. For Samuel P. Huntington, a critic of liberal modernisation theory, communists were not only good at overthrowing governments but at making them. 'They may not provide liberty, but they do provide authority; they do create governments that can govern.'[90]

By the 1960s it was evident to observers from the Right and Left that the Soviet Union had recovered from the practice of mass terror, was unlikely to return to it, and was slowly evolving into a modern, articulated urban society with many features shared with other developed countries. In the years when modernisation theory, and its kissing cousin, convergence theory, held sway, the overall impression was that the Soviet Union could become a much more benign society and tolerable enemy than had been proposed by the totalitarian theorists.[91] Later conservative critics would read this rejection of exceptionalism as a failure to emphasise adequately the stark differences between the West and the Soviet Bloc and to suggest a 'moral equivalence' between them. Deploying the anodyne language of social science, modernisation theory seemed to some to apologise for the worst excesses of Soviet socialism and excuse the violence and forceful use of state power as a necessary externality of development. Social disorder, violence, even genocide could be explained as part of the modernisation process. If Kemal Atatürk was acceptable as a moderniser, why not Lenin or Stalin?[92]

90 Huntington, *Political Order in Changing Societies*, p. 8; Gilman, *Mandarins of the Future*, pp. 228–34.
91 Among works in the 'modernisation school' that continued to subscribe to the language of totalitarianism, one might include Raymond A. Bauer, Alex Inkeles and Clyde Kluckhohn, *How the Soviet System Works: Cultural, Psychological and Social Themes* (Cambridge, Mass.: Harvard University Press, 1956; New York: Vintage Books, 1961); Alex Inkeles and Raymond A. Bauer, *The Soviet Citizen: Daily Life in a Totalitarian Society* (Cambridge, Mass.: Harvard University Press, 1961). Moshe Lewin, *Political Undercurrents of Soviet Economic Debates: From Bukharin to the Modern Reformers* (Princeton: Princeton University Press, 1974), uses a modified modernisation framework but without the liberal telos. For an account that rejects the convergence thesis, see Zbigniew Brzezinski and Samuel Huntington, *Political Power: USA/USSR* (New York: Viking Press, 1964).
92 In a famous essay in the journal *Encounter*, economic historian Alec Nove asked, 'Was Stalin Really Necessary?' (Apr. 1962). And he concluded that the 'whole-hog Stalin ... was

## Alternatives

Even though government and many scholars were deeply entrenched in an unmodulated condemnation of all Soviet policies and practices from the late 1940s through much of the 1960s, no single discourse ever dominated Russian/Soviet studies. A number of influential scholars – E. H. Carr, Isaac Deutscher, Theodore von Laue, Alec Nove, Moshe Lewin, Alexander Dallin and Robert C. Tucker – offered alternative pictures of the varieties of Bolshevism and possible trajectories. Edward Hallett Carr was a British diplomat, a journalist, a distinguished realist theorist of international relations, an advocate of appeasement in the 1930s, a philosopher of history and the prolific author of a multi-volume history of the Soviet Union, 1917–29.[93] Even in the 1930s when Carr had been sympathetic to the Soviet project, what he called 'the Religion of the Kilowatt and the Machine', he was critical of Western Communists and 'fellow-travellers', like the British Marxist economist Maurice Dobb and the Fabian socialists Beatrice and Sidney Webb, who ignored the 'darker sides of the Soviet régime' and defended them 'by transparent sophistry'.[94] During the Second World War, at the moment when the Soviet army and popular endurance halted the Nazi advance, Carr 'revived [his] initial faith in the Russian revolution as a great achievement and a historical turning-point'. 'Looking back on the 1930s,' he later wrote, 'I came to feel that my preoccupation with the purges and brutalities of Stalinism had distorted my perspective. The black spots were real enough, but looking exclusively at them destroyed one's vision of what was really happening.'[95] For more than thirty years, Carr worked on his Soviet history as a story of a desperate and valiant attempt to go beyond bourgeois capitalism in a country where capitalism was weak, democracy absent and the standard of living abysmally low. Politically Carr was committed to democratic socialism, to greater equality than was found

---

not "necessary", but the possibility of a Stalin was a necessary consequence of the effort of a minority group to keep power and to carry out a vast social-economic revolution in a very short time. And *some* elements were, in those circumstances, scarcely avoidable.' (*Was Stalin Really Necessary? Some Problems of Soviet Political Economy* (London: Allen and Unwin, 1964) (pp. 17–39), p. 32.) See also, James Millar and Alec Nove, 'A Debate on Collectivization: Was Stalin Really Necessary?' *Problems of Communism* 25 (July–Aug. 1976): 49–66.

93 Jonathan Haslam, *The Vices of Integrity: E. H. Carr, 1892–1982* (London and New York: Verso, 1999); E. H. Carr, *A History of Soviet Russia*, 14 vols. (London and Basingstoke: Macmillan, 1950–78).

94 R. W. Davies, 'Introduction', to Edward Hallett Carr, *The Russian Revolution, From Lenin to Stalin (1917–1929)* (London: Palgrave, 2003), pp. xvi–xvii; Maurice Dobb, *Soviet Economic Development since 1917* (London: Routledge, 1948); Beatrice and Sidney Webb, *Soviet Communism: A New Civilisation?*, 2 vols. (London: Longman, Green, 1935).

95 Davies, 'Introduction', p. xvii.

in most capitalist societies, and believed in public control and planning of the economic process and a stronger state exercising remedial and constructive functions.[96] Shortly before his death, he glumly remarked to his collaborator Tamara Deutscher, 'The left is foolish and the right is vicious.'[97]

His volume on the Bolshevik revolution appeared in 1950 and challenged the dominant émigré historiography on the October Revolution as a sinister *coup d'état*. Carr stood between the Mensheviks, who thought that bourgeois democracy could have been built in Russia, and the Bolsheviks, who took the risk of seizing power in a country ill-prepared for 'a direct transition from the most backward to the most advanced forms of political and economic organisation . . . without the long experience and training which bourgeois democracy, with all its faults had afforded in the west'.[98] Turning later to the 1920s, Carr eschewed a struggle-for-power tale for a narrative that placed the feuding Bolsheviks within the larger economic and social setting. He tied Stalin's victories over Trotsky, Zinoviev and Bukharin to his ability to sense and manipulate opportunities that arose from the play of social forces. Still later Carr argued that collectivisation was unavoidable, given Russia's limited resources for industrialisation, and on this issue he differed from his collaborator, R. W. Davies, who had become convinced that industrialisation at a modest pace had been possible within the framework of the New Economic Policy.[99] Carr's work was criticised for its sense of inevitability that tended to justify what happened as necessary and to avoid alternative possibilities.[100] Yet in its extraordinary breadth and depth (a study of twelve momentous years in fourteen volumes), Carr's history combined a sensitivity to political contingency, as in his analysis of Stalin's rise, and an attention to personality and character, as in his different assessments of Lenin and Stalin, with attention to structural determinations, like the ever-present constraints of Russian backwardness.

96 Ibid., p. xviii.
97 Tamara Deutscher, 'E. H. Carr – A Personal Memoir', *New Left Review* 137 (Jan.–Feb. 1983): 85.
98 E. H. Carr, *A History of Soviet Russia: The Bolshevik Revolution, 1917–1923* (London: Macmillan, 1950; Pelican Books, 1966), vol. I, p. III.
99 Davies, 'Introduction', p. xxxiv.
100 Carr's critics were often impressed by his industriousness and command of the material but wary of his stances towards the Soviet Union. Historian James Billington wrote, 'The work is scrupulously honest and thorough in detail, but the perspective of the whole remains that of a restrained but admiring recording angel of the Leninist Central Committee' (*World Politics* (Apr. 1966): 463). And even his good friend Isaac Deutscher thought Carr too much the political instead of social historian, who 'is inclined to view the State as the maker of society rather than society the maker of the State' (*Soviet Studies* 6 (1954–5): 340; Isaac Deutscher, *Heretics and Renegades and Other Essays* (Indianapolis and New York: Bobbs-Merrill, 1969), p. 95; cited in Davies, 'Introduction', p. xxx).

Carr's friend Isaac Deutscher was a lifelong rebel: a Jew who broke with religious orthodoxy and wrote poetry in Polish; a bourgeois who joined the outlawed Communist Party of Poland; a Communist who in 1932 was expelled from the party for his anti-Stalinist opposition; a Trotskyist who remained independent and critical of the movement; and finally a historian who produced some of the most important works on Soviet history in his day but was shunned by academia.[101] In exile in England, both from his native Poland and the communist milieu in which he had matured, Deutscher turned first to journalism and then to a biography of Stalin, which appeared in 1949.[102] A 'study [of] the politics rather than the private affairs of Stalin', this monumental work by 'an unrepentant Marxist' challenged the liberal and conservative orthodoxies of the Cold War years and sought to rescue socialism from its popular conflation into Stalinism.[103] Deutscher laid out a law of revolution in which 'each great revolution begins with a phenomenal outburst of popular energy, impatience, anger, and hope. Each ends in the weariness, exhaustion, and disillusionment of the revolutionary people . . . The leaders are unable to keep their early promises . . . [The revolutionary government] now forfeits at least one of its honourable attributes – it ceases to be government by the people.'[104] As in Trotsky's treatment so in Deutscher's, Stalin had been hooked by history. He became 'both the leader and the exploiter of a tragic, self-contradictory but creative revolution'.[105]

A year later Deutscher reviewed a powerful collection of memoirs by six prominent former Communists, the widely read *The God that Failed*, edited by the British socialist Richard Crossman. At that time a parade of former Communists – among them André Malraux, Ruth Fischer, Whittaker Chambers – had become public eyewitnesses of the nature of the movement and the USSR, all the more credible and authentic in the eyes of the public by virtue of their experience within and break with the party. Within a few years those who stayed loyal to Communist parties would be regarded by much of the public,

101 Tamara Deutscher, 'On the Bibliography of Isaac Deutscher's Writings', *Canadian Slavic Studies* 3, 3 (Fall 1969): 473–89. See also the reminiscences in David Horowitz (ed.), *Isaac Deutscher: The Man and his Work* (London: MacDonald, 1971).

102 Isaac Deutscher, *Stalin: A Political Biography* (Oxford: Oxford University Press, 1949; Vintage paperback edn: New York, 1960; 2nd edn: Oxford and New York, 1966). Page references to Deutscher are from the 2nd edn.

103 Ibid., p. xv. 'Unrepentant Marxist' comes from one of Deutscher's most severe critics, Leopold Labedz. See his two-part article, 'Deutscher as Historian and Prophet', *Survey* 41 (Apr. 1962): 120–44; 'Deutscher as Historian and Prophet, II', 3, 104: 146–64. For a more balanced critique of Deutscher's work, see J. I. Gleisner, 'Isaac Deutscher and Soviet Russia', Centre for Russian and East European Studies, University of Birmingham, Discussion Papers, Series RC/C, no. 5, Mar. 1971.

104 Deutscher, *Stalin*, pp. 173–5.     105 Ibid., p. 569.

particularly in the United States, as spies for the Soviet Union. Deutscher was pained, not so much by the apostasies of the ex-Communists, as by their embrace of capitalism. While he saw the ex-Communist as an 'inverted Stalinist', who 'ceases to oppose capitalism' but 'continues to see the world in black and white, [though] now the colours are differently distributed', Deutscher believed that the god was not bound to fail.[106] Himself a passionate opponent of Stalinism, Deutscher sought to distance what the Soviet Union had become from what the Bolsheviks had originally intended and from the possibility of a different socialism. His idealism and utopian aspiration distinguished him from Carr's pragmatism and realism. His three-volume biography of Trotsky at once celebrated the intellectual and revolutionary and soberly revealed his faults and frailties.[107] Summing up his interpretation of the failure of socialism in the Soviet Union, he wrote: 'In the whole experience of modern man there had been nothing as sublime and as repulsive as the first Workers' State and the first essay in "building socialism".'[108] 'There can be no greater tragedy than that of a great revolution's succumbing to the mailed fist that was to defend it from its enemies. There can be no spectacle as disgusting as that of a post-revolutionary tyranny dressed up in the banners of liberty.'[109]

In the small world of British sovietology, Carr, the Deutschers, R. W. Davies and Rudolf Schlesinger, the Marxist founder of Glasgow's Institute of Soviet and East European Studies and the journal *Soviet Studies*, stood on one side. On the other were the Oxford philosopher Isaiah Berlin, London School of Economics historian Leonard Schapiro, Hugh Seton Watson, David Footman and much of the academic establishment. Carr was extremely critical of Schapiro's *Origins of the Communist Autocracy* (1955) and fought with Berlin over its publication.[110] Carr never received the appointment he desired at Oxford and ended up back at his own alma mater, Trinity College, Cambridge, at the age of sixty-three. His collaborator, Davies, became a leading figure at the Centre for Russian and East European Studies of the University of Birmingham, established in 1963, and it was to Birmingham that Moshe Lewin came to teach Soviet history in 1968.

A socialist Zionist from his youth, Lewin escaped from his native Vilno ahead of the advancing Germans thanks to peasant Red Army soldiers who disobeyed their officer and winked him aboard their retreating truck. In wartime USSR

106 Deutscher, *Heretics and Renegades*, p. 15.
107 Isaac Deutscher, *The Prophet Armed: Trotsky 1879–1921; The Prophet Unarmed: Trotsky 1921–1929; The Prophet Outcast: Trotsky 1929–1940* (New York and London: Oxford University Press, 1954, 1959, 1963).
108 Ibid., vol. III, p. 510.    109 Deutscher, *Heretics and Renegades*, p. 12.
110 Haslam, *The Vices of Integrity*, pp. 157–65.

he worked on collective farms, in a mine and a factory before entering a Soviet officer's school. He then returned to Poland and later emigrated to Israel. Upset with the direction that the Israeli state took during the 1950s, he began studying history, moving on to Paris where he worked with Roger Portal and was deeply influenced by the social historical *Annales* school and by his friend, the sociologist Basile Kerblay. After teaching in Paris and Birmingham, he moved to the University of Pennsylvania in 1978 where he and Alfred Rieber organised a series of seminars that brought a generation of younger historians from the study of Imperial Russia to the post-1917 period.

Lewin considered himself a 'historian of society', rather than simply of a regime. 'It is not a state that has a society but a society that has a state'.[111] His *Russian Peasants and Soviet Power* (1966) was the first empirical study of collectivisation in the West, and it was followed by his influential study, *Lenin's Last Struggle* (1967).[112] In sprawling essays on Stalinism he enveloped great social processes in succinct and pungent phrases: 'quicksand society', a 'ruling class without tenure'.[113] Lewin resurrected a Lenin who learned from his errors and tried at the end of his life to make serious readjustments in nationality policy and the nature of the bureaucratic state. Although he failed in his last struggle, Lenin's testament remained a demonstration that there were alternatives to Stalinism within Bolshevism. Lewin's reading of Leninism challenged the view of Bolshevism as a single consistent ideology that supplied ready formulae for the future. For Lewin, Bukharin offered another path to economic development, but once Stalin embarked on a war against the peasantry the massive machinery of repression opened the way to a particularly ferocious, despotic autocracy and mass terror.[114]

## From political science to social history

By the time Lewin arrived in the United States, the privileges of material resources, state support and perceived national interest had made the American

---

111 Personal communication with the author, 13 Mar. 2004.

112 Moshe Lewin, *La Paysannerie et le pouvoir soviétique, 1928–1930* (La Haye: Mouton, 1966); *Russian Peasants and Soviet Power: A Study of Collectivization*, trans. Irene Nove (Evanston, Ill.: Northwestern University Press, 1968); *Le Dernier Combat de Lénine* (Paris: Minuit, 1967); *Lenin's Last Struggle* (New York: Random House, 1968).

113 Moshe Lewin, *The Making of the Soviet System: Essays in the Social History of Interwar Russia* (New York: Pantheon Books, 1985); *Russia – USSR – Russia: The Drive and Drift of a Superstate* (New York: New Press, 1995).

114 Lewin, *Political Undercurrents in Soviet Economic Debates; Le Siècle soviétique* (Paris: Fayard / Le Monde diplomatique, 2003); originally in English and published as *Russia's Twentieth Century: The Collapse of the Soviet System* (London: Verso, 2005).

sovietological establishment the most prolific and influential purveyor of information on the Soviet Union and its allies outside the USSR. A veritable army of government employees, journalists, scholars and private consultants were hard at work analysing and pronouncing on the Soviet Union. In a real sense the view of the other side forged in America not only shaped the policy of one great superpower, but determined the limits of the dialogue between 'West' and 'East'. While the interpretations produced by American journalists and professional sovietologists were by no means uniform, the usual language used to describe the other great superpower was consistently negative – aggressive, expansionistic, paranoid, corrupt, brutal, monolithic, stagnant. Exchange students going to the USSR for a year of study routinely spoke of 'going into' and 'out of' the Soviet Union, as into and out of a prison, instead of the conventional 'to' and 'from' used for travel to other countries. Language itself reproduced the sense of Russia's alien nature, its inaccessibility and opaqueness.

Few professional historians in American universities studied Russia before the 1960s; fewer still ventured past the years of revolution until the 1980s. The doyen of Russian imperial history at Harvard, Michael Karpovich, stopped at the fall of tsarism in February 1917, 'announcing that with that event Russian history had come to an end'.[115] He and his colleague, the economic historian Alexander Gerschenkron, celebrated the cultural and economic progress that the late tsarist regime had made but which had been derailed with the wrong turn taken by the Bolsheviks. Marc Raeff at Columbia, the eloquent author of original studies of Russian intellectuals and officials, was equally suspicious of the ability seriously to study history after the divide of 1917. George Vernadsky at Yale focused primarily on early and medieval Russia that emphasised Russia's unique Eurasian character. Given that most archives in the Soviet Union were either closed or highly restricted to the few exchange students who ventured to Moscow or Leningrad beginning in the late 1950s, what history of the post-revolutionary period was written before the 1970s was left almost entirely to political scientists, rather than historians. Robert Vincent Daniels's study of Communist oppositions in Soviet Russia in the 1920s, an exemplary case of historically informed political science, presented the full array of socialist alternatives imagined by the early revolutionaries and argued that the origins of Stalinist totalitarianism lay in the victory of the Leninist current within Bolshevism over the Leftist opposition, 'the triumph of reality over program'. Stalin typified 'practical power and the accommodation to circumstances'

---

115 Meyer, 'Coming to Terms with the Past', p. 403.

that won out over 'the original revolutionary objectives' which proved 'to be chimerical'.[116]

Russian studies in the United States ranged from more liberal, or what might be called 'détentist', views of the USSR to fervently anti-Communist interpretations that criticised mainstream sovietology from the Right. With Karpovich's retirement from the Harvard chair, the leading candidates were two of his students, Martin Malia and Richard Pipes, who in the next generation would become, along with Robert Conquest of the Hoover Institution, the leading representatives of conservative views in the profession. Harvard gave the nod to Pipes, whose first major work was an encyclopedic study of the non-Russian peoples during the revolution and civil war that portrayed the Bolshevik revolution and the Soviet state as a fundamentally imperial arrangement, a colonial relationship between Russia and the borderlands.[117] Using the activities and proclamations of nationalist leaders or writers as indicators of the attitudes of whole peoples, he played down the widespread support for socialist programmes, particularly in the early years of the revolution and civil war, and touted the authenticity and legitimacy of the nationalists' formulations to the artificiality of the Communists' claims.

Robert Conquest, born in the year of the revolution, was a poet, novelist, political scientist and historian. Educated at Oxford, he joined the British Communist Party in 1937 but soon moved to the right. While serving in the Information and Research Department (IRD) of the Foreign Office (1948–56), a department known to the Soviets but kept secret from the Western public, he promoted and produced 'research precisely into the areas of fact then denied, or lied about by Sovietophiles'.[118] Even George Orwell supplied the IRD with 'a list of people he knew whose attitudes to Stalinism he distrusted'.[119] In the late 1960s Conquest edited seven volumes of material from IRD on Soviet politics,

116 Robert Vincent Daniels, *The Conscience of the Revolution: Communist Opposition in Soviet Russia* (Cambridge, Mass.: Harvard University Press, 1960), pp. 4–5.
117 Richard Pipes, *The Formation of the Soviet Union: Communism and Nationalism, 1917–1923* (Cambridge, Mass: Harvard University Press, 1954; revised edn, 1997). Similar views of Russian/Soviet imperialism were expressed in other works of the time: Walter Kolarz, *Russia and her Colonies* (New York: Frederick A. Praeger, 1952); Olaf Caroe, *Soviet Empire: The Turks of Central Asia and Stalinism* (New York, 1953); Robert Conquest, *The Soviet Deportation of Nationalities* (London: Macmillan, 1960), reprinted and expanded as *The Nation Killers: The Soviet Deportation of Nationalities* (London: Macmillan, 1970); Hugh Seton-Watson, *The New Imperialism* (Chester Springs, Pa.: 1962); and outside scholarship: US Congress, Senate Committee on the Judiciary, *The Soviet Empire* (Washington, 1958; revised edn, 1965).
118 Robert Conquest, 'In Celia's Office', *Hoover Digest* (1999), no. 2; www-hoover.stanford. edu/publications/digest/992/conquest.html, p. 3.
119 Ibid.

without acknowledgement that the books' source was a secret government agency or that the publisher, Frederick A. Praeger, was subsidised by the CIA. His first major book (of scholarship; he was already known for his poetry and science fiction) was a carefully detailed study of the political power struggle from the late Stalin years to Khrushchev's triumph.[120] But far more influential was his mammoth study of the Stalin Terror in 1968, which, like Aleksandr Solzhenitsyn's *Gulag Archipelago* some years later, stunned its readers with the gruesome details of the mass killings, torture, imprisonment and exiling of millions of innocent victims.[121] No elaborate theories for the purges were advanced, only the simple argument that 'Stalin's personal drives were the motive force of the Purge'.

For Conquest Stalinism was the apogee of Soviet communism, and the secret police and the terror its underlying essence. In another widely read book he argued that the Ukrainian famine of 1931–33 was a deliberate, state-initiated genocide against the Ukrainian peasantry.[122] Most scholars rejected this claim, seeing the famine as following from a badly conceived and miscalculated policy of excessive requisitioning of grain, but not as directed specifically against ethnic Ukrainians. Disputes about his exaggerated claims of the numbers of victims of Stalin's crimes went on until the Soviet archives forced the field to lower its estimates.[123] Yet for all the controversy stirred by his writing, Conquest was revered by conservatives, enjoyed a full-time research position at the Hoover Institution from 1981, and was 'on cheek-kissing terms' with Margaret Thatcher and Condoleezza Rice.[124]

Interest in the Soviet Union exploded in the United States with the Soviet launching of the first artificial earth satellite, *Sputnik*, in October 1957. A near hysteria about the USA falling behind the USSR in technology, science and

120 Robert Conquest, *Power and Policy in the USSR: The Struggle for Stalin's Succession, 1945–1960* (London: Macmillan, 1961).
121 Robert Conquest, *The Great Terror: Stalin's Purge of the Thirties* (London: Macmillan, 1968); *The Great Terror: A Reassessment* (New York: Oxford University Press, 1990).
122 Robert Conquest, *Harvest of Sorrow: Soviet Collectivization and the Terror-Famine* (New York and Oxford: Oxford University Press, 1986).
123 This subject remains highly controversial. For example, Conquest estimated 15 million deaths in the collectivisation and famine, while a study based on archival records by R. W. Davies and S. G. Wheatcroft lowers that figure to 5,700,000. The total number of lives destroyed by the Stalinist regime in the 1930s is closer to 10–11 million than the 20–30 million estimated earlier. From 1930 to 1953, over 3,778,000 people were sentenced for counter-revolutionary activity or crimes against the state; of those, 786,000 were executed; at the time of Stalin's death, there were 2,526,000 prisoners in the USSR and another 3,815,000 in special settlements or exile. (Ronald Grigor Suny, *The Soviet Experiment: Russia, the USSR, and the Successor States* (New York and Oxford: Oxford University Press, 1998), p. 266.)
124 Conquest, 'In Celia's Office', p. 2.

education led to a pouring of funding into Soviet and East European studies. Yet the focus of attention remained on regime studies and foreign policy. In the 1960s political scientists focused on the distribution of power within the Soviet elite and the processes of decision-making. Well within the larger paradigm of totalitarianism, Kremlinology looked intently for elite conflict, even peering at the line-up on the Lenin Mausoleum to detect who was on top. Slow to revise their models of the USSR, scholars underestimated the significance of Khrushchev's de-Stalinisation reforms, emphasising instead the dysfunctional and brutal aspects of a regime seen as largely static and unchanging. Moscow's resort to force in the Soviet Bloc – suppressing the revolution in Hungary in 1956 and the 'Prague Spring' in Czechoslovakia in 1968 – only confirmed the images of a redeployed and only slightly modified Stalinism. But increasingly the evident differences, and even rivalries, between Communist regimes, as well as the growing variation and contention within Eastern Bloc countries led some observers to question the idea of Communism as monolithic, unchanging and driven simply by ideology or a single source of power.

Sovietology stood somewhat distant from mainstream political science, which employed an empiricism and observation that was impossible for students of the USSR. The 'behaviouralist revolution' in political science in the 1960s was palely reflected in Soviet studies and was soon replaced by policy analysis, comparative case studies and the deployment of concepts borrowed from Western studies such as corporatism, pluralism, interest groups and civil society. Turning to the study of the Soviet Union as a 'political system', a 'process of interaction between certain environmental influences and the consciously directed actions of a small elite group of individuals working through a highly centralised institutional structure', scholars now emphasised the environmental, cultural and historically determined constraints on the Soviet leaders, rather than their revolutionary project to transform society or their total control over the population.[125] They investigated how decisions were made; which interest groups influenced policy choices and were to have their demands satisfied; how popular compliance and the legitimacy of the regime was sustained in the absence of Stalinist terror; and whether the system could adapt to the changing international environment. By looking at institutions and how they functioned, many sovietologists noted the structural similarities and practices the Soviet system shared with other political systems.[126]

---

125 Richard Cornell (ed.), *The Soviet Political System: A Book of Readings* (Englewood Cliffs, N.J.: Prentice Hall, 1970), p. 3.
126 For Alfred G. Meyer, a bureaucratic model of the USSR was needed to supplement the outdated totalitarian model. (See his 'The Comparative Study of Communist Political

A particularly influential methodology in Soviet studies – and in which sovietology made an impact on mainstream political science – was the political culture approach. The concept possessed a long pedigree, going back at least to René Fülöp-Miller's *The Mind and Face of Bolshevism* (1927) and Harper's work on civic training, if not to earlier work on national character.[127] In part a reaction against the psychocultural studies of the 1940s that had attributed political attitudes of a national population to child-rearing and family practices (e.g. the swaddling thesis), political culture studies held that political systems were affected by political attitudes and behaviours that made up a separate cultural sphere available for analysis.[128] Beliefs, values and symbols provided a subjective orientation to politics that defined the universe in which political action took place.[129] Associated with Frederick Barghoorn, Robert C. Tucker and the British political scientists Stephen White and Archie Brown, political culture focused on consistencies in political behaviour and attitudes over the *longue durée*.[130] Tucker's 'continuity thesis', for example, connected Stalin's autocracy to tsarism, the Communist Party to the pre-revolutionary nobility, and collectivisation to peasant serfdom. Harvard medievalist Edward Keenan carried this path-dependent version of political culture even further in a determinist direction when he explored the influence of what he called 'Muscovite political folkways' on the Soviet Union. As impressive as such megahistorical connections appear, the political culture approach faltered when it tried to explain change over time or the precise

Systems', *Slavic Review* 26, 1 (Mar. 1967): 3–12.) For Meyer an important difference was 'that Communist systems are sovereign bureaucracies, whereas other bureaucracies exist and operate within larger societal frameworks'.

127 René Fülöp-Miller (1891–1963), *Geist und Gesicht des Bolschewismus : Darstellung und Kritik des kulturellen Lebens in Sowjet-Russland* (Zurich: Amalthea-Verlag, 1926); *The Mind and Face of Bolshevism: An Examination of Cultural Life in Soviet Russia* (London and New York: G. P. Putnam's Sons, 1927); Samuel Northrup Harper, *Civic Training: Making Bolsheviks* (Chicago: University of Chicago Press, 1931).

128 Ruth Benedict, *The Chrysanthemum and the Sword: Patterns of Japanese Culture* (Boston: Houghton Mifflin, 1946); Margaret Mead, *Soviet Attitudes toward Authority: An Interdisciplinary Approach to Problems of Soviet Character* (New York: McGraw-Hill, 1951); Nathan Leites, *The Operational Code of the Politburo* (New York: The Rand Corporation 1951); *A Study of Bolshevism* (New York: Free Press, 1953); Gorer and Rickman, *The People of Great Russia*.

129 Lucian Pye and Sidney Verba (eds.), *Political Culture and Political Development* (Princeton: Princeton University Press, 1965), p. 513; Robert C. Tucker, *Political Culture and Leadership in Soviet Russia: From Lenin to Gorbachev* (New York: W. W. Norton, 1987), p. 3.

130 Frederick C. Barghoorn, *Politics in the USSR* (Boston: Little, Brown, 1966, 1972); Stephen White, *Political Culture in Soviet Politics* (London: Macmillan, 1979); Archie Brown, *Political Culture and Communist Studies* (Armonk, N.Y.: M. E. Sharpe, 1985).

mechanisms that carried the culture from generation to generation over centuries.[131]

Tucker supplemented political culture with studies of the dictator and turned to psycho-history as a way to understand Stalin. As a young American diplomat stationed in Moscow in the last years of Stalin's rule, Tucker became enthralled by Karen Horney's *Neurosis and Human Growth*, particularly her concept of the 'neurotic character structure'. Adverse emotional experiences in early life, wrote Horney, may lead to formation of an idealised image of oneself, which may then be adopted as an *idealised self*, which has to be realised in action, in a search for glory. Walking down Gorky Street sometime in 1951, Tucker began to wonder if the grandiose images of the Stalin cult were not an idealised self, Stalin's own 'monstrously inflated vision of himself'.[132] Stalin's rise to power and his autocracy were to be understood as the outcome of four major influences – Stalin's personality, the nature of Bolshevism, the Soviet regime's historical situation in the 1920s and the historical political culture of Russia ('a tradition of autocracy and popular acceptance of it'). Despite Tucker's attempt to explain history through personality, psycho-history had little resonance in the profession. Most historians were unimpressed by an approach that underplayed ideas and circumstances and treated historical figures as neurotic or psychopathic.[133] Rather than Freud, it was Marx and Weber who influenced the next generation of historians, as they turned from a focus on personality and politics to the study of society, ordinary people, large structures and impersonal forces.

## The first revisionism: 1917

The political and social turmoil of the 1960s – civil rights struggles, opposition to the Vietnam War, student challenges to the university and resistance to imperial dominance, whether Western colonialist or Communist – had a profound effect on the academy in general, historical writing in particular and sovietology even more specifically. Young scholars in the late 1960s

---

131 For an alternative look at early Russian political culture, see Valerie A. Kivelson, *Autocracy in the Provinces: The Muscovite Gentry and Political Culture in the Seventeenth Century* (Stanford, Calif.: Stanford University Press, 1996).

132 Robert C. Tucker, 'A Stalin Biographer's Memoir', in Samuel Baron and Carl Pletsch (eds.), *Introspection in Biography* (Hillsdale, N.J.: Analytic Press, 1985), pp. 251–2; Tucker, 'Memoir of a Stalin Biographer', *University: A Princeton Magazine* (Winter 1983): 2.

133 Psycho-historical methodologies are more prevalent in pre-Soviet than Soviet historiography.

questioned not only the Cold War orthodoxies about the Manichean division of free world from slave, but also the usually unquestioned liberal assumptions about valueless social science. While detachment and neutrality were valued as methodology, the concern for a history with relevance to the politics of one's own time and place gave rise to a deep scepticism about the histories that had been written to date. 'Social history', 'radical history' and 'history from below' were in their earliest formations challenges to the political narratives and state-centred histories of earlier years. They were self-consciously 'revisionist'.

The Cold War convictions that Soviet expansionism had forced a reluctant United States to turn from isolationism to a global containment policy, that the Cold War was almost entirely the fault of Stalin's territorial and political ambitions and that if left unchecked by Western power Communism would conquer the world were seriously challenged in the 1960s by a revisionist scholarship on the origins of the Cold War. Moderate revisionists allotted blame for the division of the world to both superpowers, while more radical revisionists proposed that the United States, in its dedication to 'making the world safe for free market capitalism', was the principal culprit. The historians who wrote the new Cold War histories were almost exclusively historians of American foreign policy who had only limited knowledge of Soviet history and no access to Soviet archives. No parallel history from the Soviet side would be available until the end of the Cold War. Yet the revisionist undermining of the orthodox liberal consensus profoundly affected many young scholars who were then able to interrogate hitherto axiomatic foundational notions about the Soviet Union and the nature of communism.

Beginning in the late 1960s, younger historians of Russia, primarily in the United States, began to dismantle the dominant political interpretation of the 1917 Revolution, with its emphasis on the power of ideology, personality and political intrigue, and to reconceptualise the conflict as a struggle between social classes. The older interpretation, largely synthesised by anti-Bolshevik veterans of the revolution, had argued that the Russian Revolution was an unfortunate intervention that ended a potentially liberalising political evolution of tsarism from autocracy through constitutional reforms to a Western-style parliamentary system. The democratic institutions created in February 1917 failed to withstand the dual onslaught from the Germans and the Leninists and collapsed in a conspiratorial coup organised by a party that was neither genuinely popular nor able to maintain itself in power except through repression and terror. Informed by participants' memoirs, a visceral anti-Leninism and a steady focus on political manoeuvring and personalities, this paradigm depicted Bolsheviks as rootless conspirators representing no authentic interests of those who foolishly followed them.

The social historians writing on 1917 in the 1970s and 1980s proposed a more structuralist appreciation of the movements of social groups and a displacement of the former emphasis on leaders and high politics. By looking below the political surface at the actions and aspirations of workers and soldiers, they revealed a deep and deepening social polarisation between the top and bottom of Russian society that undermined the Provisional Government by preventing the consolidation of a political consensus – Menshevik leader Iraklii Tsereteli's concept of an all-national unity of the 'vital forces' of the country – so desired by moderate socialists and liberals. Rather than being dupes of radical intellectuals, workers articulated their own concept of autonomy and lawfulness at the factory level, while peasant soldiers developed a keen sense of what kind of war (and for what regime) they were willing to fight. More convincingly than any of their political opponents, the Bolsheviks pushed for a government of the lower classes institutionalised in the soviets, advocated workers' control over industry and an end to the war. By the early autumn of 1917, a coincidence of lower-class aspirations and the Bolshevik programme resulted in elected Leninist majorities in the soviets of both Petrograd and Moscow and the strategic support of soldiers on the northern and western fronts. But, after a relatively easy accession to power, the Bolsheviks, never a majority movement in peasant Russia, were faced by dissolution of political authority, complete collapse of the economy and disintegration of the country along ethnic lines. As Russia slid into civil war, the Bolsheviks embarked on a programme of regenerating state power that involved economic centralisation and the use of violence and terror against their opponents.

The political/personality approach of the orthodox school, revived later in Pipes's multi-volume treatment, usually noted the social radicalisation but offered no explanation of the growing gap between the propertied classes and the *demokratiia* (as the socialists styled their constituents), except the disgust of the workers, soldiers and sailors with the vacillations of the moderate socialists and the effectiveness of Bolshevik propaganda.[134] Historians of Russian labour described the growing desperation of workers after the inflationary erosion of their wage gains of the early months of the revolution and the lockouts and closures of factories. The parallel radicalisation of soldiers turned the ranks against officers as the government and the moderate leadership of the

---

134 Richard Pipes, *The Russian Revolution* (New York: Alfred A. Knopf, 1990); *Russia under the Bolshevik Regime* (New York: Alfred A. Knopf, 1993); *Three Whys of the Russian Revolution* (London: Pimlico, 1998).

soviets failed to end the war. As the revolutionary year progressed, *tsentsovoe obshchestvo* (propertied society) and the liberal intelligentsia grew increasingly hostile towards the lower classes and the plethora of committees and councils, which they believed undermined legitimately constituted authority. Taken together these works demonstrated that the Bolsheviks came to power in 1917 with considerable popular support in the largest cities of the empire. What remained a matter of dispute was the degree, consistency, durability and meaning of that support.

Recognising that revolutions, by their very nature, are illegitimate, extra-legal actions overthrowing constituted political regimes, social historians did not explicitly pose the question of their 'legitimacy' as if Soviet power required the sanction of academic historians. On the other hand, the 'political conspiratorial' interpretation, dominant in the West for the first fifty years of Soviet power, implied the illegitimacy of the Communist government and contained within it a powerful argument for political opposition to the Soviet regime. Conservative historians, such as Malia and Pipes, rejected the notion that the revolution 'had gone wrong' in the years after Lenin or been 'betrayed' by Stalin, and argued instead that 'Stalin was Lenin writ large, and there cannot be a democratic source to return to'.[135] In the late 1980s and 1990s Soviet intellectuals, disillusioned by the economic and moral failures of the Soviet system, found these views, as well as the concept of totalitarianism, consonant with their own evolving alienation from Marxism. When Gorbachev proposed a rereading of Soviet history but tried to limit the critique to Stalinism, daring intellectuals opened (after 1987) a more fundamental attack on the legacy of the revolution. The interpretation of the October seizure of power as either a *coup d'état* without popular support or as the result of a fortuitous series of accidents in the midst of the 'galloping chaos' of the revolution re-emerged, first among Soviet activists and politicians, journalists and publicists and later in the West in the discussion around the publication of Pipes's own study of the Revolutions of 1917.[136] Yet most Western specialists writing on the revolution considered the thesis that the revolution was popular, both in the sense

135 Martin Malia, 'The Hunt for the True October', *Commentary* 92, 4 (Oct. 1991): 21–2. Pipes makes a similar argument: 'The elite that rules Soviet Russia lacks a legitimate claim to authority . . . Lenin, Trotsky, and their associates seized power by force, overthrowing an ineffective but democratic government. The government they founded, in other words, derives from a violent act carried out by a tiny minority' (Richard Pipes, 'Why Russians Act Like Russians', *Air Force Magazine* (June 1970): 51–5; cited in Louis Menasche, 'Demystifying the Russian Revolution', *Radical History Review* 18 (Fall 1978): 153).
136 An earlier version of the accidental nature of the October Revolution can be found in Robert V. Daniels, *Red October: The Bolshevik Revolution of 1917* (New York: Charles Scribner's Sons, 1967); Pipes, *The Russian Revolution*.

of involving masses of people and broad support for Soviet power (if not the Bolshevik party itself), 'incontrovertible'.[137]

By the 1980s, despite the resistance of Pipes and a few others, the revisionist position had swept the field of 1917 studies, and the term 'revisionism' migrated to characterise a group of social historians investigating the vicissitudes of the working class and the upheavals of the Stalin years.

## The fate of labour history: from social to cultural

Social history was never a unified practice, either in its methodologies or its interests, but rather a range of approaches, from social 'scientific' quantification to cultural anthropologies, concerned with the expansion of the field of historical enquiry. The major effect of the turn to the social was the broadening of the very conception of the political in two important ways. First, borrowing from the insights of feminism and the legacy of the New Left that the 'personal is political', politics was now seen as deeply embedded in the social realm, in aspects of everyday life far beyond the state and political institutions.[138] The turn towards social history reduced the concern with labour politics, but 'politics in the broader sense – the power relations of various social groups and interests – intruded in the lives of Russian workers too directly and persistently to be ignored'.[139] Second, the realm of politics was recontextualised within society, so that the state and political actors were seen as constrained by social possibilities and influenced by actors and processes outside political institutions.[140] Not surprisingly, this rethinking of power relations would eventually involve consideration of cultural and discursive hegemony and exploration of 'the images of power and authority, the popular mentalities of subordination'.[141]

The great wave of interest in the Russian working class crested in the last decades of the Soviet experience, only to crash on the rocks of state socialism's demise. Some labour historians in Britain and the United States challenged Soviet narratives of growing class cohesion and radical consciousness in the years up to the revolution with counter-stories of decomposition,

137 Terence Emmons, 'Unsacred History', *The New Republic*, 5 Nov. 1990: 36.
138 Geoff Eley, 'Edward Thompson, Social History and Political Culture: The Making of a Working-Class Public, 1780–1850', in Harvey J. Kaye and Keith McClelland (eds.), *E. P. Thompson: Critical Perspectives* (Philadelphia: Temple University Press, 1990), p. 13.
139 Ziva Galili, 'Workers, Strikes, and Revolution in Late Imperial Russia', *International Labor and Working-Class History* 38 (Fall, 1990): 69.
140 Here the work of Moshe Lewin has been particularly influential, integrating political history with his own brand of historical sociology.
141 The phrase is E. P. Thompson's, quoted in Eley, 'Edward Thompson, Social History and Political Culture', p. 16.

fragmentation and accommodation, while others elaborated a grand march of labour not far removed from the Soviet account. From peasant to peasant worker to hereditary proletarian, the Russian worker moved from the world of the village to the factory, encountering along the way more 'conscious' worker activists and Social Democratic intellectuals, who enlightened the worker to his true interests and revolutionary political role. Workers' experience involved the unfolding of an immanent sense of class, the 'discovery' of class and the eventuality, even inevitability, of revolutionary consciousness (under the right circumstances or with the strategic intervention of radical intellectuals). Categories, as well as narrative devices, were drawn either from sources themselves saturated with Marxist understandings or directly from Soviet works.

The classic picture of Soviet labour in the 1930s had been provided by the former Menshevik Solomon Schwarz, who wrote in 1951 about the draconian labour laws that had essentially tied workers to factories and eliminated their ability to resist.[142] By the 1980s the focus had shifted from an emphasis on state intervention and repression to the nature of the work process and the informal organisation of the shop floor. Several accounts, eventually dubbed 'revisionist', related the enthusiasm of workers for the exertions of rapid industrialisation of the early 1930s. Young skilled workers joined the 'offensives' against 'bourgeois' specialists, moderate union leaders and others dubbed 'enemy'. This group of workers in particular, standing between their older, skilled co-workers disoriented by the industrialisation drive and peasant migrants to the factories, were committed to the notion of building socialism.[143] Tens of thousands of radicalised workers left for the countryside to 'convince' the peasants to join the collective farms.[144] Rather than successfully 'atomising' the working class, the state, powerful as it appeared, was limited in its ability to coerce workers. With working hands scarce, workers found areas of autonomy in which they could 'bargain' with the state, and factory bosses had to compete with one another for skilled labour. Even as they lost the ability to act in an organised fashion, in thousands of small ways workers were able to affect the system.[145] Shop-floor studies and micro-histories

---

142 Solomon Schwarz, *Labor in the Soviet Union* (New York: Praeger, 1951).

143 Sheila Fitzpatrick, *Education and Social Mobility in the Soviet Union, 1921–1934* (Cambridge: Cambridge University Press, 1979); Hiroaki Kuromiya, *Stalin's Industrial Revolution: Politics and Workers, 1928–1932* (Cambridge: Cambridge University Press, 1988).

144 Lynne Viola, *The Best Sons of the Fatherland: Workers in the Vanguard of Soviet Collectivization* (Oxford: Oxford University Press, 1987).

145 Lewis Siegelbaum, *Stakhanovism and the Politics of Productivity in the USSR, 1935–1941* (Cambridge: Cambridge University Press, 1988); Donald Filtzer, *Soviet Workers and Stalinist Industrialization: The Formation of Modern Soviet Production Relations, 1928–1941* (Armonk, N.Y.: M. E. Sharpe, 1986).

undermined the overly simple political interpretation of Stalinist society and, more particularly, the totalitarian model, in which an all-powerful state rendered an atomised population completely impotent.

Social history was often uncomfortable with its pedigree in Marxism and a base-substructure model of explanation ('it's the economy, stupid!'). Following the pioneering work in other historiographies by E. P. Thompson, William H. Sewell, Jr., Gareth Stedman Jones, Joan Wallach Scott and others, Russian historians began to pay more attention to language, culture and the available repertoire of ideas.[146] Investigating class formation in the post-Thompsonian period involved not only exploring the structures of the capitalist mode of production or the behaviour of workers during protests and strikes, but also the discourses in which workers expressed their sense of self, defined their 'interests', and articulated their sense of power or, more likely, powerlessness. Whatever the experience of workers might have been, the availability of an intense conversation about class among the intellectuals closest to them provided images and language with which to articulate and reconceive their position. While structures and social positions, or even 'experience', influence, shape and limit social actors, they do not lead to action or create meaning in and of themselves. The discourses, cultures and universes of available meanings through which actors mediate their life experience all have to be added into the mix.[147]

## The study of Stalinism: the next revisionism

The term 'Stalinism' has its own genealogy, beginning in the mid-1920s even before the system that would bear its name yet existed. Trotsky applied the word to the moderate 'centrist' tendencies within the party stemming from the 'ebbing of revolution' and identified with his opponent, Stalin.[148]

146 E. P. Thompson, *The Making of the English Working Class* (London: Victor Gollancz, 1963); Gareth Stedman Jones, *Languages of Class: Studies in English Working Class History, 1832–1982* (Cambridge: Cambridge University Press, 1983); William H. Sewell, Jr., *Work and Revolution in France: The Language of Labor from the Old Regime to 1848* (Cambridge: Cambridge University Press, 1980); Joan Wallach Scott, *Gender and the Politics of History* (New York: Columbia University Press, 1988).

147 For work that reflects the interest in language, discourse and representation, see Orlando Figes and Boris Kolonitskii, *Interpreting the Russian Revolution: The Language and Symbols of 1917* (New Haven: Yale University Press, 1999); and Mark D. Steinberg, *Voices of Revolution, 1917* (New Haven and London: Yale University Press, 2001); and his *Proletarian Imagination: Self, Modernity, and the Sacred in Russia, 1910–1925* (Ithaca, N.Y.: Cornell University Press, 2002).

148 Robert H. McNeal, 'Trotskyist Interpretations of Stalinism', in Robert C. Tucker (ed.), *Stalinism: Essays in Historical Interpretation* (New York: Norton, 1977), p. 31.

By 1935 Trotsky's use of Stalinism gravitated closer to the Marxist meaning of 'Bonapartism' or 'Thermidor', 'the crudest form of opportunism and social patriotism'.[149] Even before Trotsky's murder in August 1940, Stalinism had become a way of characterising the particular form of social and political organisation in the Soviet Union, distinct from capitalism but for Trotskyists and other non-Communist radicals not quite socialist. Not until the falling away of the totalitarian model, however, did scholars bring the term Stalinism into social science discussion as a socio-political formation to be analysed in its own right. For Tucker Stalinism 'represented, among other things, a far-reaching Russification of the already somewhat Russified earlier (Leninist) Soviet political culture'.[150] For his younger colleague at Princeton, Stephen F. Cohen, 'Stalinism was not simply nationalism, bureaucratization, absence of democracy, censorship, police repression, and the rest in any precedented sense . . . Instead Stalinism was excess, extraordinary extremism, in each.'[151] Taking a more social historical perspective, Lewin saw Stalinism as a deeply contradictory phenomenon:

> The Stalinist development brought about a different outcome: as the country was surging ahead in economic and military terms, it was moving backwards, compared to the later period in tsarism and even the NEP, in terms of social and political freedoms. This was not only a specific and blatant case of development without emancipation; it was, in fact, a retreat into a tighter-than-ever harnessing of society to the state bureaucracy, which became the main social vehicle of the state's policies and ethos.[152]

Stalinism was now a way of describing a stage of development of non-capitalist statist regimes in developing countries dominated by a Leninist party, as well as an indictment of undemocratic, failed socialist societies.

A key question dividing Soviet studies was the issue of continuity (or rupture) between the regimes of Lenin and Stalin. Was Stalinism implicit in original Marxism or the Leninist version, or had there been alternatives open to the Bolsheviks? Along with Tucker and Lewin, Cohen was one of the major opponents of the view that saw Stalin as the logical or even inevitable outcome of Leninism. While it had its roots in earlier experiences, Stalinism was qualitatively different from anything that went before or came after.[153] Original

149 Ibid., p. 34.
150 Tucker, 'Introduction: Stalinism and Comparative Communism', in Tucker, *Stalinism*, p. xviii.
151 Cohen, 'Bolshevism and Stalinism', in Tucker, *Stalinism*, p. 12.
152 Lewin, 'The Social Background of Stalinism', in Tucker, *Stalinism*, p. 126.
153 Stephen F. Cohen, *Rethinking the Soviet Experience: Politics and History Since 1917* (New York and Oxford: Oxford University Press, 1985), p. 48.

Bolshevism had been a diverse political movement in which Leninism was but one, albeit the dominant, strain. In the years of the New Economic Policy (1921–8) Bolsheviks, far from united in their plans for the future socialist society, presided over a far more tolerant and pluralistic social order than would follow after Stalin's revolution from above. Stalin's policies of 1929–33 rejected the gradualist Bukharinist programme of slower but steady growth within the framework of NEP and in its place built a new state that 'was less a product of Bolshevik programs or planning than of desperate attempts to cope with the social pandemonium and crises created by the Stalinist leadership itself in 1929–33'.[154]

The cohort of social historians of Stalinism that emerged in the 1980s was not particularly interested in broad synthetic interpretations of Stalinism or Marxist-inspired typologies. Their challenge was directed against the top-down, state-intervention-into-society approach and proposed looking primarily at society, while at the same time disaggregating what was meant by society. They looked for initiative from below, popular resistance to the regime's agenda, as well as sources of support for radical transformation.[155] Some stressed the improvisation of state policies, the chaos of the state machinery, the lack of control in the countryside. Others attempted to diminish the role of Stalin. As they painted a picture quite different from the totalitarian vision of effective dominance from above and atomisation below, these revisionists came under withering attack from more traditional scholars, who saw them as self-deluded apologists for Stalin at best and incompetent, venal falsifiers at worst.[156]

For Sheila Fitzpatrick, the standard Trotskyist formulation of the bureaucracy standing over and dominating society was far too simplistic, for the lower echelons of the bureaucracy were as much dominated as dominating.[157] Fascinated by the upward social mobility into the elite that characterised early Soviet society, she introduced Western audiences to the *vydvizhentsy* (those thrust upward from the working class).[158] In contrast to those Western scholars who argued that the erosion of the working class was key to the

154 Ibid., p. 64. See his *Bukharin and the Bolshevik Revolution: A Political Biography, 1888–1938* (New York: Alfred A. Knopf, 1973).
155 For a bold attempt to find initiative for state policies from below, see Sheila Fitzpatrick (ed.), *Cultural Revolution in Russia, 1928–1931* (Bloomington and London: Indiana University Press, 1978).
156 See e. g. Richard Pipes, *Vixi, Memoirs of a Non-Belonger* (New Haven and London: Yale University Press, 2003), pp. 126, 221–3, 242.
157 Sheila Fitzpatrick, 'New Perspectives on Stalinism', *Russian Review* 45, 4 (Oct. 1986): 361–2.
158 Fitzpatrick, *Education and Social Mobility*.

eventual evolution of the Bolshevik regime from a dictatorship of the proletariat to a dictatorship of the bureaucracy, Fitzpatrick contended that the
real meaning of the revolution was the coming to power of former workers who occupied the key party and state positions in significant numbers.
'The Bolsheviks', according to Fitzpatrick, 'had made an absurd, undeliverable
promise to the working class when they talked of a "dictatorship of the proletariat". The oxymoron of a "ruling proletariat", appealing though it might be
to dialectical thinkers, was not realizable in the real world.'[159] Workers, in her
view, had become 'masters' of Russian society by moving into the old masters'
jobs. The *longue durée* of the revolution became a tale of upward social mobility
that encompassed modernisation (escape from backwardness), class (the fate
of the workers) and revolutionary violence (how the regime dealt with its
enemies).[160]

Along with the collectivisation of peasant agriculture and the vicious de-
kulakisation campaigns, the principal subject of enquiry for revisionist historians in the 1980s was the Great Terror of the late 1930s. Earlier, political scientists,
like Brzezinski, had proposed that purging was a permanent and necessary
component of totalitarianism in lieu of elections.[161] Solzhenitsyn, whose fiction
and quasi-historical writing on the *Gulag Archipelago* had enormous effect in the
West, saw the purges as simply the most extreme manifestation of the amoral-
ity of the Marxist vision, and the *Ezhovshchina* as an inherent and inevitable
part of the Soviet system.[162] Tucker and Conquest saw the Great Purges as an
effort 'to achieve an unrestricted personal dictatorship with a totality of power
that [Stalin] did not yet possess in 1934'.[163] Initiation of the purges came from
Stalin, who guided and prodded the arrests, show trials and executions forward,
aided by the closest members of his entourage. Similarly Lewin argued that
the purges were the excessive repression that Stalin required to turn a naturally
oligarchic bureaucratic system into his personal autocracy. Here personality
and politics merged. Stalin could not 'let the sprawling administration settle

159 Sheila Fitzpatrick, 'The Bolshevik Dilemma: Class, Culture and Politics in the Early
Soviet Years', *Slavic Review* 47, 4 (Winter 1988): 599–613.
160 Sheila Fitzpatrick, *The Russian Revolution 1917–1932* (Oxford and New York: Oxford
University Press, 1984), p. 8; 2nd edn (1994), pp. 9–13. Fitzpatrick's interpretation of
the revolution took a darker tone in the 2nd edn, published after the collapse of the
Soviet Union. Revolution here is about illusions and disillusions, euphoria, madness
and unrealised expectations (pp. 8–9).
161 Brzezinski, *The Permanent Purge*.
162 Alexander Solzhenitsyn, *The Gulag Archipelago, 1918–1956: An Experiment in Literary
Investigation* (various editions, 1973–8).
163 Tucker, 'Introduction: Stalin, Bukharin, and History as Conspiracy', in Tucker and
Cohen (eds.), *The Great Purge Trial* (New York: Grosset and Dunlap, 1965), p. xxix;
Conquest, *The Great Terror*, p. 62.

and get encrusted in their chairs and habits', which 'could also encourage them to try and curtail the power of the very top and the personalized ruling style of the chief of the state – and this was probably a real prospect the paranoid leader did not relish'.[164]

Revisionists explained the purges as a more extreme form of political infighting. High-level personal rivalries, disputes over the direction of the modernisation programme, and conflicts between centre and periphery were at the base of the killing. J. Arch Getty argued that 'the Ezhovshchina was rather a radical, even hysterical, *reaction* to bureaucracy. The entrenched officeholders were destroyed from above and below in a chaotic wave of voluntarism and revolutionary Puritanism.'[165] Dissatisfaction with Stalin's rule and with the harsh material conditions was palpable in the mid-1930s, wrote Gabor T. Rittersporn, and the purges were fed by popular discontent with corruption, inefficiency and the arbitrariness of those in power.[166] Several writers focused on the effects of the purges rather than their causes, implying that intentions may be read into the results. A. L. Unger, Kendall E. Bailes and Fitzpatrick showed how a new 'leading stratum' of Soviet-educated 'specialists' replaced the Old Bolsheviks and 'bourgeois specialists'.[167] The largest numbers of beneficiaries were promoted workers and party rank-and-file, young technicians, who would make up the Soviet elite through the post-Stalin period until Gorbachev took power. Stalin, wrote Fitzpatrick, saw the old party bosses less as revolutionaries than 'as Soviet boyars (feudal lords) and himself as a latter-day Ivan the Terrible, who had to destroy the boyars to build a modern nation state and a new service nobility'.[168]

Soviet power, however, could never rule by terror alone. In Weberian terms, the regime needed to base itself on more than raw power; it needed to create legitimated authority with a degree of acquiescence or even consent from the people. Social historians were able to record both displays of enthusiasm and active, bloody resistance. Lynne Viola recorded over 13,700 peasant disturbances and more than 1,000 assassinations of officials in 1930 alone, while

---

164 Lewin, *The Making of the Soviet System*, p. 309.

165 J. Arch Getty, *Origins of the Great Purges: The Soviet Communist Party Reconsidered, 1933–1938* (Cambridge: Cambridge University Press, 1985), p. 206.

166 Gabor T. Rittersporn, *Stalinist Simplifications and Soviet Complications: Social Tensions and Political Conflicts in the USSR 1933–1953* (Chur, Switzerland: Harwood, 1991).

167 A. L. Unger, 'Stalin's Renewal of the Leading Stratum: A Note on the Great Purge', *Soviet Studies* 20, 3 (Jan. 1969): 321–30; Kendall E. Bailes, *Technology and Society under Lenin and Stalin: Origins of the Soviet Technical Intelligentsia, 1917–1941* (Princeton: Princeton University Press, 1978), pp. 268, 413; Sheila Fitzpatrick, 'Stalin and the Making of a New Elite', *Slavic Review* 38, 3 (Sept. 1979): 377–402.

168 Fitzpatrick, *The Russian Revolution*, p. 159.

Jeffrey Rossman uncovered significant worker resistance in the textile industry under Stalin, protests accompanied by the rhetoric of class struggle and
commitment to the revolution.[169] Sarah Davies read through police reports
(*svodki*) to discover that popular opinion in Stalin's Russia was contradictory
and multivalent, borrowing the themes set down by the regime and sometimes
turning them in new directions.[170] Workers, for example, favoured the affirmation action measures during the First Five-Year Plan that gave them and their
families privileged access to education but were dismayed at the conservative
'Great Retreat' of the mid-1930s. Davies's Russians do not fit the stereotype
of a downtrodden people fatally bound by an authoritarian political culture.
Given half a chance, as during the elections of 1937, Soviet citizens brought
their more democratic ideas to the political process. Along with grumbling
about the lack of bread and alienation from those with privileges, ordinary
Soviets retained a faith in the revolution and socialism and preserved a sense
that the egalitarian promise of 1917 had been violated. Class resentments and
suspicion of those in power marched along with patriotism and a sense of social
entitlement.

## From above to below, from centre to periphery

Revisionism's assault on older interpretations of Communism during the
years of détente (roughly 1965–75) gained such wide acceptance within the
academy in the late 1970s and early 1980s that conservatives felt beleaguered
and marginalised in the profession. Yet representatives of earlier conceptuali-
sations still had the greater resonance outside the circles of specialists, within
the public sphere, and in government. Zbigniew Brzezinski served as National
Security Adviser to President Jimmy Carter (1977–81), while Richard Pipes
spent two years on the National Security Council as resident expert on the
USSR early in the administration of Ronald Reagan (1981–3). Brzezinski was
instrumental in the turn towards a harder line towards the Soviet Union,
which after the Soviet intervention in Afghanistan in December 1979 escalated
into a covert war aiding Muslim militants against the Kabul government and
the Soviets. Pipes proudly took credit for toughening the anti-Soviet line of

169 Lynne Viola, *Peasant Rebels under Stalin: Collectivization and the Culture of Peasant Resistance*
(New York: Oxford University Press, 1996), pp. 105, 136, *passim*; Jeffrey Rossman, 'The
Teikovo Cotton Workers' Strike of April 1932: Class, Gender, and Identity Politics in
Stalin's Russia', *Russian Review* 56, 1 (Jan. 1997): 44–69.
170 Sarah Davies, *Popular Opinion in Stalin's Russia: Terror, Propaganda and Dissent, 1934–1941*
(Cambridge: Cambridge University Press, 1997).

President Reagan, already a dedicated anti-Communist but prone at times to sentimentality.[171] As a historian primarily of tsarist Russia, he brought back to Washington views based on ideas of national character and culture that had long been abandoned by professional historians.[172]

Political history had often meant little more than the story of great men, monarchs and warriors, while social history was by its nature inclusive, bringing in workers, women and ethnic minorities. As more women entered the field, gender studies gained a deserved respectability. Gail Lapidus's pioneering study was followed by monographs on women workers, the women's liberation movement, Soviet policies towards women and the baleful effects of a liberation that kept them subordinate and subject to the 'double burden' of work outside and inside the home. Just as it had once been acceptable for historians to treat all humankind as if it were male, so the study of Imperial Russia and the Soviet Union was long treated unapologetically as if these empires were homogeneously Russian. For the first several decades, émigrés with strong emotional and political affiliations with nationalist movements and personal experiences of the brutalities of Stalinism were the principal writers on non-Russians. Their studies, so often pungently partisan and viscerally anti-Communist, were relegated to a peripheral, second-rank ghetto within Soviet studies and associated with the right-wing politics of the 'captive nations'. Nationalities were homogenised; distinctions between them and within them were underplayed; and political repression and economic development, with little attention to ethnocultural mediation, appeared adequate to explain the fate of non-Russian peoples within the Soviet system. Since studying many nationalities was prohibitively costly and linguistically unfeasible, one nationality (in the case of the Harvard Project on the Soviet Social System, the Ukrainians) was chosen to stand in for the rest.

Though in Friedrich and Brzezinski's *locus classicus* of the totalitarian model nationalities were not mentioned as potential 'islands of separateness', along with family, Church, universities, writers and artists, in time scholars began to think of the non-Russian nationalities as possible 'sources of cleavage' in the Soviet system and, therefore, of significance. Inkeles and Bauer noted

---

171 Pipes, *Vixi*, pp. 163–8.
172 Of Russians he wrote: 'Centuries of life under a harsh and capricious climate and an equally harsh and capricious government had taught them to submit to fate. At the first sign of trouble they withdraw like turtles into their shells and wait for the danger to pass. Their great strength lies in their ability to survive even under the most adverse conditions; their great weakness is their unwillingness to rebel against adversity. They simply take misfortune in stride; they are much better down than up. If they no longer can take it, they drink themselves into a stupor' (Ibid., pp. 239–240; see also, pp. 62–3).

that 'national and ethnic membership constitutes a basis for loyalties and identifications which cut across the lines of class, political affiliation, and generation'.[173] In the wake of the dismantling of the totalitarian model, more empirical and historical studies focused on non-Russians. Zvi Gitelman, like Gregory J. Massell, told a story of Communist failure 'to combine modernization and ethnic maintenance', largely because of the poor fit between the developmental plans of the party and the reservoir of traditions and interests of the ethnic population. Secularised Jewish Communists set out to destroy the old order among the Jews, Bolshevise Jewish workers and reconstruct Jewish life on a 'socialist' basis, but as successful as they were in eliminating Zionism and Hebrew culture and encouraging Yiddish culture, they failed to 'eradicate religion, so firmly rooted in Jewish life'.[174] In Central Asia the failure to mobilise women as a 'surrogate proletariat' with which to overturn the patriarchal social regime led to a curious accommodation with traditional society.[175]

Much sovietological work on nationalities and nationalism accepted uncritically a commonsensical view of nationality as a relatively observable, objective phenomenon based on a community of language, culture, shared myths of origin or kinship, perhaps territory. Nationalism was seen as the release of denied desires and authentic, perhaps primordial, aspirations. This 'Sleeping Beauty' view of nationality and nationalism contrasted with a more historicised view that gravitated towards a post-modernist understanding of nationality as a constructed category, an 'imagined community'. A 'Bride of Frankenstein' view of nationality and nationalism asserted that, far from being a natural component of human relations, something like kinship or family, nationality and the nation are created (or invented) in a complex political process in which intellectuals and activists play a formative role. Rather than the nation giving rise to nationalism, it is nationalism that gives rise to the nation. Rather than primordial, the nation is a modern socio-political construct. By the 1990s this 'modernist' view of the construction of nations within the Soviet empire began to appear in a number of studies in the Soviet field.[176]

173 Inkeles and Bauer, *The Soviet Citizen*, p. 339.
174 Zvi Gitelman, *Jewish Nationality and Soviet Politics: The Jewish Sections of the CPSU, 1917–1930* (Princeton: Princeton University Press, 1972), pp. 3–4, 6–7, 491–2.
175 Gregory J. Massell, *The Surrogate Proletariat: Moslem Women and Revolutionary Strategies in Soviet Central Asia, 1919–1929* (Princeton: Princeton University Press, 1974).
176 Ronald Grigor Suny, *The Revenge of the Past: Nationalism, Revolution, and the Collapse of the Soviet Union* (Stanford, Calif.: Stanford University Press, 1993); Yuri Slezkine, 'The Soviet Union as a Communal Apartment, or How a Socialist State Promoted Ethnic Particularism', *Slavic Review* 53, 2 (Summer 1994): 414–52; *Arctic Mirrors: Russia and the*

## Soviet studies in the post-Soviet world

By the 1990s the former Soviet Union had become a historical object, an imperial relic to be studied in the archives, rather than an actual enemy standing defi-
antly against the West. At the same time the dominance of social history gave
way to greater acceptance of new cultural approaches. Instead of British Marxists or the Italian Communist Antonio Gramsci, the principal influences now
came from French social and cultural theorists, such as Michel Foucault and
Pierre Bourdieu; the German political theorist Jürgen Habermas; the American
cultural anthropologist Clifford Geertz; and the Russian literary theorist
Mikhail Bakhtin. Scholars gravitated to investigating cultural phenomena, like
rituals and festivals, popular and ethnic culture and the daily life of ordinary
people, topics that increasingly became possible to investigate with the opening of Soviet archives at the end of the 1980s. Fitzpatrick's own work turned in
an ethnographic direction, as she scoured the archives to reconstruct the lost
lives of ordinary workers and peasants.[177] Historians moved on from the 1930s
to 'late' Stalinism and into the post-Stalin period. The 'cultural turn' led to an
interest in the mentalities and subjectivities of ordinary Soviet citizens.

As a popular consensus developed that nothing less than history itself has
decisively proven the Soviet experience a dismal failure, historians of Communist *anciens regimes* turned to summing up the history of the recent past.[178]
Among the more inspired post-mortems was Martin Malia's *The Soviet Tragedy*,
which turned the positive progress of modernisation into a darker view of
modernity. Launching a sustained, ferocious attack on Western sovietology,
which, in his view, contributed to a fundamental misconception and misunderstanding of the Soviet system by consistently elevating the centrality of society
and reducing ideology and politics to reflections of the socio-economic base,
Malia put ideology back at the centre of causation with the claim that the

*Small Peoples of the North* (Ithaca, N.Y.: Cornell University Press, 1994); Terry Martin, *The Affirmative Action Empire: Nations and Nationalism in the Soviet Union, 1923–1939* (Ithaca, N.Y., and London: Cornell University Press, 2001).

177 Sheila Fitzpatrick, *Stalin's Peasants: Resistance and Survival in the Russian Village after Collectivization* (New York and Oxford: Oxford University Press, 1994); *Everyday Stalinism: Ordinary Life in Extraordinary Times: Soviet Russia in the 1930s* (New York and Oxford: Oxford University Press, 1999).

178 Martin Malia, *The Soviet Tragedy: A History of Socialism in Russia, 1917–1991* (New York: Free Press, 1994); François Furet. *The Passing of an Illusion: The Idea of Communism in the Twentieth Century*, trans. Deborah Furet (Chicago: University of Chicago Press, 1999); Stéphane Courtois, Nicolas Werth, Jean-Louis Panné, Andrzej Paczkowski, Karel Bartošek, Jean-Louis Margolin, *The Black Book of Communism: Crimes, Terror, Repression*, trans. Jonathan Murphy and Mark Kramer (Cambridge, Mass.: Harvard University Press, 1999); John Earl Haynes and Harvey Klehr, *In Denial: Historians, Communism, and Espionage* (San Francisco: Encounter Books, 2003).

Soviet leadership worked consistently to implement integral socialism, that is, full non-capitalism. In one of his most redolent phrases, he concluded, 'In sum, there is no such thing as socialism, and the Soviet Union built it.'[179] Because the moral idea of socialism is utopian and unrealisable, the only way it could be 'realised' on the ground was through the terroristic means that Lenin and Stalin used. The collapse of the Soviet system was inevitable; the regime was illegitimate and doomed from the beginning; its end was inscribed in its 'genetic code'.

Malia placed the Soviet project in the larger problematic of modernity from the Enlightenment on. Socialism, the logical extension of the idea of democracy, was the highest form of this modernist illusion. In a similar vein Stephen Kotkin offered a seminal study of the building of the industrial monument, Magnitogorsk, in which he borrowed insights from Foucault to show how Stalin's subjects learned to 'speak Bolshevik' as they built 'a new civilisation'.[180] Kotkin dismissed the idea of 'the Russian Revolution as the embodiment of a lost social democracy, or, conversely, as a legitimation of Western society through negative example'. Instead, he likened 'the Russian Revolution to a mirror in which various elements of the modernity found outside the USSR are displayed in alternately undeveloped, exaggerated, and familiar forms'.[181] Like Malia, Kotkin saw ideology as having 'a structure derived from the bedrock proposition that, whatever socialism might be, it could not be capitalism. The use of capitalism as an anti-world helps explain why, despite the near total improvisation, the socialism built under Stalin coalesced into a "system" that could be readily explained within the framework of October.'[182] Positioning himself apart from both Fitzpatrick, who argued that Stalinism was the conservative triumph of a new post-revolutionary elite, and Lewin, who saw that triumph as a betrayal of the initial promise of the revolution (preserved by Lenin) and a backward form of modernisation, Kotkin argued that what Stalin built was socialism, the only real fully non-capitalist socialism the world has ever seen.[183]

If a political dedication to socialism was rendered 'academic' for most Western scholars after 1991, particularly in the United States, interest in the internal workings of the Soviet system, the USSR as a distinct culture, the construction of subjects and subjectivity and the officially ascribed and self-generated identifications of Soviet citizens remained high. Neither the notion of atomised,

---

179 Ibid., p. 496.
180 Stephen Kotkin, *Magnetic Mountain: Stalinism as a Civilization* (Berkeley and Los Angeles: University of California Press, 1995).
181 Ibid., p. 387.     182 Ibid., p. 400.     183 Ibid., pp. 5, 379 n. 21.

cowed 'little screws' or crypto-liberals acting as if they were believers adequately captured the full, complex range of Soviet subjectivity. Different people, and sometimes the same individual, could both resist and genuinely conform, support the regime performatively or with real enthusiasm. Even dissent was most often articulated within 'the larger frame of the Soviet Revolution', appropriating the language of the regime itself.[184] That frame was extraordinarily powerful, as are hegemonic discursive formations in any society, but it also was never without contradictions, anomalies or imprecise meanings that allowed for different readings and spaces for action. Soviet power, Foucault would have told us, had its creative side as well as its repressive aspects and constituted a landscape of categories and identifications that may have precluded 'any broad, organised resistance challenging the Soviet state', but also permitted much small-scale subversion of the system, from evasion of duties, slowdowns at the workplace and evasion of orders from above.[185] As historians as different as Lewin, Fitzpatrick and Malia have contended, ordinary citizens agreed with the regime that together they were building socialism, even as they incessantly complained about the failure of the authorities 'to deliver the goods'.

While post-Soviet scholars rejected the concept of modernisation, with its optimism about the universality and beneficence of that process, a darker, more critical view of modernity became the talisman for a distinct group of younger historians who wished to contest the idea of Soviet exceptionalism.[186] An unusually protean term, modernity was used to explain everything from human rights to the Holocaust. Following the lead of theorists like Zygmunt Bauman and James Scott, the 'modernity school' noted how Bolsheviks, like other modernisers, attempted to create a modern world by scientific study of society, careful enumeration and categorisation of the population and the

---

184 Jochen Hellbeck, 'Speaking Out: Languages of Affirmation and Dissent in Stalinist Russia', *Kritika* 1, 1 (Winter 2000): 74.
185 Ibid., p. 80.
186 See e. g. David L. Hoffman and Yanni Kotsonis (eds.), *Russian Modernity: Politics, Knowledge, Practices* (New York: St Martin's Press, 2000); Amir Weiner, *Making Sense of War: The Second World War and the Fate of the Bolshevik Revolution* (Princeton: Princeton University Press, 2001); Peter Holquist, '"Information is the Alpha and Omega of Our Work": Bolshevik Surveillance in its Pan-European Context', *Journal of Modern History* 69, 3 (Sept. 1997): 415–50. While eclectic and inclusive in its selection of articles, the journal *Kritika: Explorations in Russian and Eurasian History*, which began publication in the winter of 2000, has established itself as the mouthpiece of what its editors conceive of as 'post-revisionist' scholarship, attempting to move beyond the debates of the Cold War years. (See, particularly, the editorial introduction, 'Really-existing Revisionism?' in *Kritika* 2, 4 (Fall 2001): 707–11.)

application of planning and administration.[187] For Russianists the frame of 'modernity' presented an all-encompassing comparative syndrome in which the Soviet experiment appeared to be a particularly misguided effort that led to unprecedented violence and state-initiated bloodshed.

In reaction to the 'modernity school' some historians and political scientists, attentive to the insights of Max Weber, considered the neo-traditionalist aspects of the Soviet experience that denied or contradicted the move to a generalised modernity.[188] Simply put, the modernity school emphasised what was similar between the West and the Soviet Union, and the neo-traditionalists were fascinated by what made the USSR distinct. Modernity was concerned with the discursive universe in which ideas of progress and subjugation of nature led to state policies that promoted the internalisation and naturalisation of Enlightenment values. Neo-traditionalism was more interested in social practices, down to the everyday behaviours of ordinary people. Whereas modernity talked about the 'disenchantment of the world', in Weber's characterisation of secularisation, neo-traditionalists were impressed by the persistence of religion, superstition and traditional beliefs, habits and customs. Their attention was turned to status and rank consciousness, personalities and personal ties (in Russia phenomena such as *blat* (pull, personal connections), family circles, *tolkachy* (facilitators)), patron–client networks, petitioning and deference patterns. Kenneth Jowitt saw neo-traditionalism as a corruption of the modernist ideals of the revolutionary project, while sociologist Andrew Walder, in an influential study of Chinese Neo-traditionalism (1986), argued that the more the regime tried to implement its core principles, the more neo-traditional elements came forth.[189] Abolishing the market and attempting to plan production and distribution led to soft budgeting, shortages, distribution systems based on rationing or privileged access. Petitioning was an effective substitute for recourse to the law or the possibility of public action. The end of a free press

187 Bauman wrote, 'In my view, the communist system was the extremely spectacular dramatization of the Enlightenment message . . . I think that people who celebrate the collapse of communism, as I do, celebrate more than that without always knowing it. They celebrate the end of modernity actually, because what collapsed was the most decisive attempt to make modernity work; and it failed. It failed as blatantly as the attempt was blatant' (*Intimations of Postmodernity*, pp. 221–2).

188 Terry Martin, 'Modernization or Neo-Traditionalism? Ascribed Nationality and Soviet Primordialism', in Sheila Fitzpatrick (ed.), *Stalinism, New Directions* (New York and London: Routledge, 2000), pp. 348–67; Kenneth Jowitt, 'Neo-Traditionalism' (1983), reprinted in his *New World Disorder: The Leninist Extinction* (Berkeley: University of California Press, 1992), pp. 121–58; Victor Zaslavsky, *The Neo-Stalinist State: Class, Ethnicity, and Consensus in Soviet Society* (Armonk, N.Y.: M. E. Sharpe, 1982).

189 Andrew G. Walder, *Neo-traditionalism: Work and Authority in Chinese Industry* (Berkeley: University of California Press, 1986).

elevated the importance of gossip and rumour, and the efforts of a modernising state to construct nationality eventually led to embedding peoples in a story of primordialist ethnogenesis. The reintroduction of ascribed identities, resurrecting the idea if not the actual categories of *soslovnost'* (legally ascribed categories), was characteristic of the inter-war period, in the way the Soviets dealt with both class and nationality.[190]

After 1991 sovietological political scientists had lost their subject and turned to a cluster of new questions: how did a great state self-destruct; why did the Cold War end; will the 'transition' from command to market economy, from dictatorship to democracy, be successful; are post-Soviet transitions comparable to democratisation in capitalist states?[191] Several explained the Gorbachev 'revolution' as largely emanating from the very top of the Soviet political structure and emphasised the agency of the General Secretary, his chief opponent, Boris Yeltsin, and other actors over structural factors. Others focused on institutions, the actual 'Soviet constitution' of power and the loss of confidence and eventual defection of Soviet *apparatchiki* to the side of the marketeers and self-styled democrats. Still others argued that Leninist nationality policies had created a structure of national polities within the USSR that fostered potent nationalist constituencies and proved to be a 'time bomb' that with the weakening of central power tore the union apart. Rather than nationalism as the chief catalyst of state collapse, they found that state weakness and disintegration precipitated nationalist movements.[192]

'Transitologists' who had studied the fall of Latin American and Iberian dictatorships had developed a model of democratisation that largely eschewed the cultural, social and economic prerequisites for successful democratisation that modernisation theorists had proposed. Instead, they argued that getting the process right – namely negotiating a 'pact' between the old rulers and the emerging opposition – was the best guarantee for effective democratic transition.[193] Post-sovietologists disputed the universal applicability of

190 Sheila Fitzpatrick, 'Ascribing Class: The Construction of Social Identity in Soviet Russia', in Fitzpatrick (ed.), *Stalinism, New Directions*, pp. 20–46; Martin, *The Affirmative Action Empire*.
191 For an analytical and critical review of post-sovietology, see David D. Laitin, 'Post-Soviet Politics', *Annual Review of Political Science*, 2000, 3: 117–48.
192 Suny, *The Revenge of the Past*; Rogers Brubaker, *Nationalism Reframed* (Cambridge, Mass.: Cambridge University Press, 1996).
193 Guillermo O'Donnell and Philippe C. Schmitter, *Transitions from Authoritarian Rule: Tentative Conclusions about Uncertain Democracies* (Baltimore: Johns Hopkins University Press, 1986); Adam Przeworski, *Democracy and the Market: Political and Economic Reforms in Eastern Europe and Latin America* (Cambridge: Cambridge University Press, 1991); and Adam Przeworksi et al., *Sustainable Democracy* (Cambridge: Cambridge University Press, 1995).

the transitological model by specifying the differences between non-market economies and capitalist societies and authoritarian dictatorships in the West and 'totalitarian' states in the East.[194] Michael McFaul showed how the transition in Russia was revolutionary, occurred without pacting, and involved mass participation – all of which were excluded from the original model.[195] But as the new century began and Vladimir Putin solidified his power in the Kremlin, the jury remained out on how consolidated, liberal or effectively representative Russian (or, for that matter, Ukrainian, Armenian or any other) democracy was.

Even as it claimed to break with the old sovietology, Western scholarship reproduced many of its older concerns a decade and a half after the dissolution of the Soviet Union and remained true to fundamental assumptions deriving from Western liberalism. The T-model had counterposed the indoctrinated, believing 'Soviet Man' against an imagined, free, liberal individual in the West, a person self-directed and capable of independent thought.[196] Cold War scholars were dismayed by the destruction of the individual in Sovietised societies and the inability of citizens to resist the regime effectively. They found it hard to believe in the authentic commitment of people to such an illiberal project as Stalinism or to accept the legitimacy of such political deviance from a Whig trajectory. Images of Koestler's Rubashov confessing to crimes he had not committed or Orwell's Winston Smith capitulating to Big Brother powerfully conveyed Soviet socialism's threat to liberal individuality. Yet, as social historians had demonstrated, Soviet subjects were neither atomised nor completely terrorised and propagandised victims of the system; they managed to adapt to and even shape the contours imposed from above.

When post-Soviet scholars or journalists looked back at the seventy-four years of the Soviet experience, they most often turned to the Stalinist horrors as the emblem of Leninist hubris. In 1999 a team of scholars produced a massive

194 Valerie Bunce, *Subversive Institutions: The Design and the Destruction of Socialism and the State* (Cambridge: Cambridge University Press, 1999); Michael McFaul, *Russia's Unfinished Revolution: Political Change from Gorbachev to Putin* (Ithaca, N.Y.: Cornell University Press, 2001); Philippe C. Schmitter with Terry Lynn Karl, 'The Conceptual Travels of Transitologists and Consolidologists: How Far to the East Should They Attempt to Go?' *Slavic Review* 53, 1 (Spring 1994): 173–85; Valerie Bunce, 'Should Transitologists Be Grounded?' *Slavic Review* 54, 1 (Spring 1995): 111–27; Terry Lynn Karl and Philippe C. Schmitter, 'From an Iron Curtain to a Paper Curtain: Grounding Transitologists or Students of Postcommunism?' *Slavic Review* 54, 4 (Winter 1995): 965–978; and Valerie Bunce, 'Paper Curtains and Paper Tigers', ibid., pp. 979–87.
195 McFaul, *Russia's Unfinished Revolution.*
196 For development of this theme, to which this paragraph is indebted, see the insightful discussion in Anna Krylova, 'The Tenacious Liberal Subject in Soviet Studies', *Kritika* 1, 1 (Winter 2000): 119–46.

catalogue of crimes, terror and repression by Soviet-style communisms. *The Black Book of Communism* contended that 'Communist regimes did not just commit criminal acts (all states do so on occasion); they were criminal enterprises in their very essence: on principle, so to speak, they all ruled lawlessly, by violence and without regard for human life.'[197] Given this foundational claim, it followed that 'there never was a benign, initial phase of communism before some mythical "wrong turn" threw it off track'.[198] Its violence was a deliberative, not a reactive, policy of the revolutionary regimes and was based in Marxist 'science' that elevated the class struggle to the central driving force of history. The aim of *The Black Book* was not only to show that the very essence of communism was terror as a form of rule, but even more ambitiously to demonstrate that communism was not just comparable to fascism but was actually worse than Nazism. *The Black Book* lay the burden of guilt on intellectuals, those who thought up, spread and justified the idea that liberation and secular salvation ought to be purchased at any price.

Yet in its attempt to judge Soviet killing by the standard of Nazi crimes, *The Black Book* actually de-historicised Soviet violence. Context and causation were less important than the equation with the colossal, seemingly inexplicable evil that led to the Holocaust. These claims led to an intense international debate around *The Black Book* that recapitulated arguments that had divided historians of the Soviet Union for decades: is explanation to be sought in the social or the ideological? Is there an essential connection between all communist movements that stems from communism's roots in Leninism that produces the violence that has accompanied them in all parts of the world? Or are these movements, while related, more particularly the products of their own social, political and cultural environments?

For all the claims that the old controversies of the Cold War had ended with the end of the Soviet Union, the problematical meaning of the Soviet Union remains an open question among scholars and in the public sphere. While some continue to look for some deep essence that determined the nature of the USSR, others search for the contradictions and anomalies that disrupt any easy model. Neutrality remains a worthy if elusive stance, complete objectivity an unattainable ideal. While conservative scholars celebrate what they see as the victory of their views over 'left-wing' sovietology, and the pursuit of modernity appears dubious to many scholars, Russian and Soviet studies, ironically, hold firm to the broad liberal values that marked Western attitudes towards the East a century ago. Without a 'socialist' alternative with which to contend,

---

197 Courtois et al., *The Black Book of Communism*, p. xvii.    198 Ibid., p. xviii.

pundits proclaim that the expectations of the modernisationists have been realised – a single world gravitating towards capitalist democracy. The West continues to regard itself as superior in what is now called the globalising world, and its most zealous advocates are prepared to export its political and economic forms, even if it requires military force, against the resistance of those who reject Western modernity and its liberal values. The states of the former Soviet Union exist in a twilight of a failed socialism but without the full light of the anticipated democratic capitalist dawn. As those who had insisted that capitalist economics and democratic politics would wipe away the East's deviant past confront the persistence of Soviet institutions, practices and attitudes long after the collapse, they must humbly reconsider the power of that past. Whether one thinks of this as the 'Leninist legacy' or Soviet path dependency or the continuities of a relatively fixed Russian (or Georgian or Uzbek) political culture, looking backwards in order to understand the present and future has become ever more imperative for social science.

# PART ONE

# RUSSIA AND THE SOVIET UNION: THE STORY THROUGH TIME

2

# Russia's *fin de siècle*, 1900–1914

## MARK D. STEINBERG

The critical years from the turn of the century to the eve of the First World War were a time of uncertainty and crisis for Russia's old political, social and cultural order, but also a time of possibility, imagination and daring. A chronological narrative of events is one way to retell this contradictory story. Still useful too is rehearsing the old debate about whether Russia was heading towards revolution in these pre-war years (the 'pessimistic' interpretation as it has been named in the historiography and in much classroom pedagogy) or was on a path, had it not been for the burdens and stresses of war, towards resolving tensions and creating a viable civil society and an adequately reformed political order (the 'optimistic' narrative). The conventional narrative of successive events and likely outcomes, however, suggests more coherence, pattern and telos than the times warrant. To understand these years as both an end time and a beginning, and especially to understand the perceptions, values and expectations with which Russians lived these years and entered the war, the revolution and the new Soviet era, we must focus on the more complexly textured flux of everyday life and how people perceived these experiences and imagined change.

## History as event

The years 1900–14 are full of events marking these times as extraordinary years of change and consequence. In 1903, as part of the government's ongoing efforts to strengthen the state by stimulating the expansion of a modern industrial economy, the great Trans-Siberian Railway was completed, symbolising both the growth of the railroad as an engine of industrial development (the driving idea of the minister of finance, Sergei Witte) and the imperial reach of the state.[1] In the same year, in direct opposition to this growing power of the state,

[1] T. H. Von Laue, *Sergei Witte and the Industrialization of Russia* (New York: Atheneum, 1969).

members of the Marxist Russian Social Democratic Workers' Party, meeting at its second congress in Brussels and then London (the stillborn founding congress was in 1898), created an organisation designed to incite and lead democratic and social revolution in Russia, though it also split into two factions, the Bolsheviks and the Mensheviks, over questions of how disciplined and closed such a party should be.[2]

The year 1904 saw the start of the Russo-Japanese war, a disastrous conflict sparked by Russia's expansion into China and Korea in the face of Japan's own regional desires, further fuelled by Russian overconfidence and racist contempt for the Japanese. The assassination by revolutionaries in the summer of 1904 of the notoriously conservative minister of internal affairs, Viacheslav Plehve, and his replacement by Prince Dmitrii Sviatopolk-Mirskii, who openly spoke as few tsarist officials had before of finding ways for the voice of 'society' to be heard, initiated what many expectantly called a political 'spring' in relations between state and society. A 'banquet campaign', inspired by the French example of 1847–8, was staged by increasingly well-organised liberals, who gathered over dinner and drinks to make fervent speeches and pass resolutions calling for democratising political change.[3] And then came the 'Revolution' of 1905, an unprecedented empire-wide upheaval, set in motion by the violent suppression on 9 January ('Bloody Sunday') in St Petersburg of a mass procession of workers with a petition for the tsar. The revolution had many faces: workers' and students' strikes, demonstrations (both dignified and rowdy) stretching through city streets, spates of vandalism and other periodic violence, assassinations of government officials, naval mutinies, nationalist movements in the imperial borderlands, anti-Jewish pogroms and other reactionary protest and violence, and, by the end of the year, a series of armed uprisings, violently suppressed.[4] These revolutionary upheavals extracted a remarkable concession from the government: Nicholas II's 'October manifesto', which for the first time in Russian history guaranteed a measure of civil liberties and a parliament (the State Duma) with legislative powers.

The years following the 1905 Revolution were marked by a succession of contradictory events. New fundamental laws in 1906 established the legislative Duma but also restricted its authority in many ways – not least of which was the complete lack of parliamentary control over the appointment or dismissal of

2 Leopold Haimson, *The Russian Marxists and the Origins of Bolshevism* (Cambridge, Mass.: Harvard University Press, 1955).
3 Abraham Ascher, *The Revolution of 1905: Russia in Disarray* (Stanford, Calif.: Stanford University Press, 1988), pp. 53–6, 66–70.
4 Ibid.

cabinet ministers. Trade unions and strikes were legalised, but police retained extensive authority to monitor union activities and to close unions for engaging in illegal political activities or even allowing political speeches at meetings. Greater press freedom was guaranteed, but in practice was subject to constant harassment, punitive fines and closure for overstepping the bounds of tolerated free speech. In the early summer of 1907, the new prime minister, Petr Stolypin, seeking to defuse persistent criticism of the government by liberals and the Left in the first and second State Dumas (the first Duma closed after seventy-three days, the second lasted three months), revised the electoral law, reducing representation by peasants, workers and non-Russian nationalities, and increasing that of the gentry, hoping to ensure that the new Duma would be more compliant. Stolypin's 'coup', as it was dubbed, proved effective, in the short term, in quietening the Duma. Stolypin was similarly effective, again at least in the short term, in 'pacifying', as it was then called, continuing political and social unrest in the country. During 1906–7, disagreeable publications were shut down by the hundreds and summary courts martial tried and sentenced hundreds of individuals accused of sedition. In the first few months, more than a thousand people were executed, inspiring grim ironic talk of 'Stolypin's necktie' – the noose. These repressions were not without reason: assassinations or attempts on the lives of tsarist officials were frequent during 1906. Characteristically, Stolypin paired his political authoritarianism with a commitment to modernising social reform in Russia, visible above all in laws he was able to pass designed to break up the traditional peasant commune in the hope of leading rural society away from dangerous communalism and out of what many saw as its destabilising backwardness.[5]

The relative stability of the years between 1907 and the start of war in 1914 – a time when many who dreamed of change spoke of Russia as mired in political darkness, stifling repression, of bleak hopelessness – were marred (or brightened, depending on one's point of view) by unsettling events. Terrorist assassinations continued, in defiance of Stolypin's harsh repressions; indeed in 1911, Stolypin himself was fatally shot, in the presence of the tsar, while at a theatre in Kiev. The year before, the writer Lev Tolstoy's death inspired widespread public acts of mourning for a man who had been excommunicated by the Orthodox Church in 1901 for his influential denial of much of Church

---

5 Abraham Ascher, *The Revolution of 1905: Authority Restored* (Stanford, Calif.: Stanford University Press, 1992); Ascher, *P. A. Stolypin: The Search for Stability in Late Imperial Russia* (Stanford, Calif.: Stanford University Press, 2001); Victoria Bonnell, *Roots of Rebellion: Workers' Politics and Organizations in St. Petersburg and Moscow, 1900–1914* (Berkeley: University of California Press, 1983).

dogma and ritual in favour of an ethical religion of inward purity and virtuous practice; adding to his sins and popularity, Tolstoy had made use of his status as a moral prophet to openly criticise the brutality of the government of Stolypin and Nicholas II. A new wave of strikes broke out beginning in 1910, though especially in the wake of news of the violent death of over a hundred striking workers attacked by government troops in 1912 in the Lena goldfields in Siberia. But perhaps the most ominous events of these years, which filled the daily press, took place abroad. Russians closely followed the Balkan wars of 1912 and 1913. For many, these were struggles for independence by Slavic Orthodox nations, necessarily and justly backed by Russia. But many also saw in these distant conflicts threatening signs of a much greater European war.

## The political ideology of autocracy

As we look beneath the surfaces of these events, it is useful to begin with ideas about the nature of state power in Russia, which were more complex than is allowed by the simple definition of Russia's political order as an 'autocracy'. The Fundamental Laws continued to insist that the Russian emperor (as the tsar was also called since Peter the Great) was a monarch with 'autocratic and unlimited' power, a redundancy meant to suggest both the lack of formal bounds to his authority and the personal nature of his sacred authority and will. In the wake of the manifesto of 17 October 1905, the stipulation that the tsar's authority was 'unlimited' was reluctantly dropped: the new Fundamental Laws of 1906 defined the monarch as holding 'Supreme Autocratic Power', impressive but not 'unlimited', for the law also recognised the new authority of the legislative State Duma.[6]

In practice, even before the 1905 Revolution, the tsar's power was not boundless in its reach nor could it all emanate directly from his own person. Although all servants of the state were in theory accountable to the tsar, Russia's legions of officials and bureaucrats necessarily exercised considerable practical power. It is impossible to speak, for example, of the policies of the imperial regime in its final decades without recognising the influence of ministers such as Konstantin Pobedonostsev, Sergei Witte or Petr Stolypin. Their influence, however, was contradictory. On the one hand, Pobedonostsev, a tutor to Nicholas II as well as to his father and the lay official (Chief Procurator) in charge of the Orthodox Church from 1880 to 1905, fought vigorously and, for many years, effectively

---

6 *Svod zakonov Rossiiskoi imperii* (St Petersburg: Obshchestvennaia pol'za, 1897), vol. 1, p. 2; *Svod zakonov Rossiiskoi imperii* (St Petersburg: Zakonovedenie, 1913), vol. 1, p. 2; Ascher, *The Revolution of 1905: Authority Restored*, pp. 63–71.

against any concessions to civil liberties and constitutionalist reform, which he viewed as a dangerous course inspired by the fundamental philosophical error, derived from the Enlightenment, of belief in the perfectibility of man and society.[7] By contrast, Witte and Stolypin, leading government ministers, each eventually holding the post of prime minister (Witte 1903–6 and Stolypin 1906–11) and both loyal to the principle that Russia required and that God had willed a strong state, recognised the need for political and social reform to restore stability to Russia after 1905. Witte's advice, to which Nicholas turned in desperation amidst the upheavals of 1905, was crucial to the decision to issue the October manifesto. And without Stolypin's 'drive and persistence' and 'commanding presence', a recent historian has written, the state's policy of intertwined reform and repression in the years 1906–11 is 'inconceivable'.[8]

Still, the tsar retained, even after 1905, substantial power. He alone appointed and dismissed ministers and he, not the Duma, controlled the bureaucracy, foreign policy, the military and the Church. He retained, by law, veto power over all legislation, the right to dissolve the Duma and hold new elections, and the right to declare martial law. He felt growing regret in his final years for the concessions he made in 1905–6 under duress and did much to undo them. Indeed, it has been argued persuasively that Nicholas II (supported and encouraged by prominent conservative figures) was ultimately a force for instability in the emerging political order of late Imperial Russia. While ministers like Witte and Stolypin and the legislators of the Duma worked to construct a stable polity around the ideal of a modernised autocracy ruling according to law and over a society of citizens, Nicholas II was at the forefront of those embracing a political vision that sought to resituate legitimate state power in the person of the emperor. To put this in more political-philosophical terms, 'rather than accommodating the monarchy to the demands for a civic nation', Nicholas II and his allies 'redefined the concept of nation to make it a mythical attribute of the monarch'.[9]

As a symbolic and performative accompaniment to these ideas, and to quite tangible policies of authoritarian control, the last tsar engaged in an elaborate effort to demonstrate publicly that the legitimacy and even efficacy of his immense authority was grounded not in constitutional relationships with various constituencies of the nation or the empire but in his own personal

7 Konstantin Pobedonostsev, *Moskovskii sbornik* (Moscow, 1896), trans. as *Reflections of a Russian Statesman* (Ann Arbor: University of Michigan Press, 1965); Robert Byrnes, *Pobedonostsev: His Life and Thought* (Bloomington: Indiana University Press, 1968).

8 Ascher, *P. A. Stolypin*, p. 392; Ascher, *The Revolution of 1905: Authority Restored*, p. 263.

9 Richard S. Wortman, *Scenarios of Power: Myth and Ceremony in Russian Monarchy*, vol. II (Princeton: Princeton University Press, 2000), p. 12.

virtue (devotion to duty, orderliness in private and public life, familial devotion and love, religious piety) and in the mystical bond of mutual devotion and love uniting tsar and 'people' (by which was meant mainly those whom Nicholas called the 'true Russian people'). Public rituals of national 'communion' and 'love', often gesturing to an idealised pre-modern past, proliferated, such as Easter celebrations in the pre-Petrine capital of Moscow signalling the tsar's communion with the nation and tradition, or journeys of remembrance and dynastic nationalism into the Russian heartland during the 1913 tercentenary of Romanov rule, or the ceremony on Palace Square at the outbreak of war in 1914 when Nicholas, with tears in his eyes, exchanged ritual bows with his people.[10] Nicholas II was not alone, of course, in imagining Russia's salvation to lie in an ideal of the paternal state standing above society – free and independent of government bureaucracy, fractious political parties, selfish social groups and individuals and even law itself – to defend the common good, care for the poor and downtrodden and advance principle over vested interest. Ultimately, the official embrace of this vision of the Russian political nation would contribute to the rejection of monarchy in 1917. But its echoes would also play a part in how state and party were envisioned later in the twentieth century.

## Intellectuals and ideologies of dissent

Russia's growing class of educated men and women offered a wealth of alternative visions of power and society to those of the monarch, the state and their conservative supporters. In spirit, many educated liberals and radicals in the early twentieth century felt themselves to be heirs to the traditions of the nineteenth-century 'intelligentsia', a group distinguished not by education alone, nor even by a shared interest in ideas, but by a cultural and political identity constituted in opposition to a repressive order and in the pursuit of the common good and universal values. Like these forebears, they often suffered as individuals for daring to criticise and act against the established order. Still, they managed to meet together, to form clandestine 'circles' (*kruzhki*), and to organise a series of oppositional parties, ranging from liberals to Social Democrats and neo-populists to militant communists and anarchists.

10 Ibid., vol. II, chs. 9–14; Andrew Verner, *The Crisis of the Russian Autocracy: Nicholas II and the 1905 Revolution* (Princeton: Princeton University Press, 1990); Dominic Lieven, *Nicholas II: Emperor of All the Russias* (New York: St Martin's Press, 1994); Mark Steinberg, 'Introduction', in Steinberg and Vladimir M. Khrustalëv, *The Fall of the Romanovs: Political Dreams and Personal Struggles in a Time of Revolution* (New Haven: Yale University Press, 1995).

On the moderate Left, liberals were divided over strategy and tactics – reflected especially in the post-1905 split between the Left-liberal Constitutional Democratic Party (Kadets) and the relatively pro-government Union of 17 October (Octobrists). But they shared a common set of goals for transforming Russia into a strong and modern polity: the rule of law replacing the arbitrary will of autocrat, bureaucrats and police; basic civil rights (freedom of conscience, religion, speech, assembly) for all citizens of the empire; a democratic parliament (Kadets viewed the system established after 1905 as incomplete); strong local self-government (many liberals were involved in the *zemstvo* councils of rural self-government or in city councils); and social reforms to ensure social stability and justice, such as extension of public education, moderate land reform to make more land available to peasants and protective labour legislation. They also believed strongly in the need for personal moral transformation, making individuals into modern selves inspired by values of individual initiative, self-reliance, self-improvement, discipline and rationality. In many respects, like the monarchy itself, liberals viewed themselves as acting for the national good rather than the interests of any particular class. This was especially true of the Kadets, who vehemently insisted that they were 'above class' and even 'above party'. The good they sought to promote was, of course, the good of the individual – a liberal touchstone – but also the development of a national community founded on free association and patriotic solidarity.[11]

Socialists shared the democratic goals of the liberals as well as the philosophical logic underpinning liberal democracy: that political and social change ought to promote the freedom and dignity of the human person by removing the social, cultural and political constraints that hindered the full development of the individual. But socialists approached this ideal with the radical insistence that only a transformation root and branch of all social and political relationships, and of the values informing these, could set Russia on the path to true emancipation. Indeed, dissatisfied with the anomic logic of liberal individualism (though many Russian liberals also worried about the dangers of excessive individualism), socialists favoured linking self-realisation with communal notions of solidarity and interdependent interests.

11 Shmuel Galai, *The Liberation Movement in Russia, 1900–1905* (Cambridge: Cambridge University Press, 1973); William Rosenberg, *Liberals in the Russian Revolution: The Constitutional Democratic Party, 1917–1921* (Princeton: Princeton University Press, 1974), pt. 1; Richard Pipes, *Struve*, 2 vols. (Cambridge, Mass.: Harvard University Press, 1970 and 1980).

Various underground socialist organisations emerged in the early years of the century. Populist socialists were organised after 1901 around the Socialist Revolutionary Party (the SRs) and partly represented after 1906 by the Trudovik (Labourist) faction in the State Duma. Ideologically, they viewed the whole labouring *narod*, the common people, as their constituency, and socialism as a future society embodying, above all, the ethical values of community and liberty. Marxists, who were increasingly numerous and influential and organised around the Russian Social Democratic Workers' Party, believed they possessed a more 'scientific' and rationalistic understanding of society and history. Socialism, for Marxists, was the historically certain, and more rational and progressive, successor to capitalism, and the industrial proletariat alone, not some idealised 'people', was the social class whose interests and efforts would bring this new order into being. This simple divide between populists and Marxists inadequately suggests the intricate divisions among socialists, though. Populists differed among themselves over issues such as the use of terror, the actual vitality and theoretical importance of peasant communalism and whether and on what terms to ally with liberals. Marxists differed among themselves – often with considerable rancour – over questions of organisation (how centralised and authoritarian the party should be), tactics (such as whether workers should ally with other classes), strategy (whether Russia was ready for socialism) and philosophy (e.g. the relative importance of ethics and revolutionary faith versus scientific reason).[12]

The intellectual differences between two leading Marxists, Vladimir Ul'ianov (known by his party pseudonym Lenin) and Iulii Tsederbaum (Martov), illustrate some of the diversity and complexity that lay behind party programmes. In many ways, Martov fitted well into the long history of the Russian intelligentsia, especially in his passionate preoccupation with the idea of justice. When he discovered Marxism, he found compelling not only Marxist arguments about the natural progress of history and the centrality of the working class but the moral idealism embedded in this rationalist ideology: an end to inequality and suffering, injustice and coercion and Russia's humiliating backwardness as a nation.[13] Lenin also approached politics with passion, but his was

12 Haimson, *The Russian Marxists*; Oliver Radkey, *The Agrarian Foes of Bolshevism* (New York: Columbia University Press, 1958); Abraham Ascher, *Pavel Axelrod and the Development of Menshevism* (Cambridge, Mass.: Harvard University Press, 1972); Manfred Hildermeier, *The Russian Socialist Revolutionary Party before the First World War* (New York: St Martin's Press, 2000).

13 Israel Getzler, *Martov: A Political Biography of a Russian Social Democrat* (Cambridge: Cambridge University Press, 1967); Haimson, *The Russian Marxists*.

a passion more of reason than of moral sensibility, focused more on the goal of liberation than on the uplifting process of struggle. Indeed, Lenin repeatedly made it clear that he despised the political moralising so common to Russian socialism. For Lenin, the revolution was a matter of rationality and discipline not the romantic heroism of the struggle for justice, goodness and right.[14]

These different sensibilities were reflected in different approaches to key political notions. Everyone, it seemed, from liberals to radical socialists, embraced democracy. Martov – and perhaps most Russian Marxists in the pre-war years – was attracted to Marxism precisely for its democratic promise. They believed that political representation and civil freedoms were goods in themselves, though necessarily needing to be supplemented by the democracy of social rights. Lenin, by contrast, was among those who embraced social and political democracy as a goal, but not for its own sake. Rather, Lenin argued, Bolsheviks viewed political democracy as having mainly instrumental value, as enabling workers more effectively to fight for socialism. Along similar lines, while Martov was among those who believed strongly in what might be called the consciousness-raising benefits of the experience of struggle (hence his opposition in 1903 to Lenin's advocacy of a vanguard party limited to disciplined professional revolutionaries), Lenin emphasised the centrality in raising consciousness of imposed rationality and leadership. As he famously argued in *What Is To Be Done* (1902), left to themselves workers were unable to see beyond the economic struggle and understand that their interests lay in overthrowing the existing social system.[15] If socialists were to do more than 'gaze with awe ... upon the "posterior" of the Russian proletariat',[16] Lenin wrote in his characteristically biting style, it was necessary to create a party (and later critics would suggest that this was the kernel of Lenin's approach to the Soviet state) of full-time revolutionaries to direct the mass movement, who embodied the full consciousness that the masses lacked and were obedient to party discipline. In practice, these differences were not absolute. By the eve of the war, both parties were to be found playing large and similar roles among workers: helping to establish and lead workers' organisations and spreading socialist ideas among workers, students and others through underground publications and everyday agitational talk. And the results were

---

14 V. I. Lenin, 'Who Are the "Friends of the People" ' (1894), *PSS*, vol. 1, pp. 325–31, 460; Robert Service, *Lenin: A Political Life*, vol. 1 (Bloomington: Indiana University Press, 1985); Haimson, *The Russian Marxists*.

15 V. I. Lenin, *What Is To Be Done?* (1902), in Robert Tucker (ed.), *The Lenin Anthology* (New York: Norton, 1975), pp. 12–114.

16 Lenin, *What Is To Be Done?*, p. 65.

impressive. Though these parties had relatively few members, and large numbers of workers could not understand what they saw as the pointless and harmful squabbling between Mensheviks and Bolsheviks, the influence of socialist ideas among workers, students and others was considerable. But as the popularity of socialism grew, so did the variety of motivating logics and approaches.

Across the political spectrum, from liberals to socialists, the 'woman question' was an essential, if frequently unsettling, issue in debates about democratic change in Russia. If, as most agreed, democratic change meant creating a society in which the dignity and rights of the individual were respected and individuals were able to participate actively in the public sphere, the situation of women was clearly in dire need of change. Women were widely viewed as morally and intellectually different and weak and women's civic roles and personal autonomy were circumscribed. Since the mid-1800s, however, such patriarchalism had been persistently challenged by activist men and increasingly by publicly active women. Often paired with programmes for the emancipation of all people, activists targeted the particular humiliations women endured: sexual harassment, domestic violence, prostitution, lack of education, lack of training for employment, lower wages, undeveloped social supports for maternity and childcare, lack of legal protections and civil rights.

The movement for women's emancipation gained particular force and urgency during and after the 1905 Revolution, as women, though not given the vote, were often heard at meetings appealing for respect as human beings and for equal rights as citizens, and as a series of women's organisations and publications emerged to promote the cause. As a movement, the struggle to improve the situation of women was as divided as the larger political world; and it divided that world. On the one hand, many activists fought directly to overcome women's inferior status, and spoke of the particular sufferings of women in public and private life. On the other hand, many women, especially socialists, argued that feminism, which focused on women's particular needs, risked fragmenting the common cause, which must be to free all people from the restrictions of the old order. Only as part of this 'larger' cause, it was said, could women be emancipated.[17]

17 Richard Stites, *The Women's Liberation Movement in Russia* (Princeton: Princeton University Press, 1978); Linda Edmondson, *Feminism in Russia, 1900–17* (Stanford, Calif.: Stanford University Press, 1984); Barbara Clements, Barbara Engel and Christine Worobec (eds.), *Russia's Women: Accommodation, Resistance, Transformation* (Berkeley: University of California Press, 1991).

## In the public sphere

For women and men, the expansion of the public sphere in the late 1800s and early 1900s was one of the most consequential developments in Russian life. The growth of this critically important civic space – the domain of social life in which organised associations mediate between the individual and the state, citizens communicate with one another on matters of general interest, public opinion takes form and the state is restrained in its influence and compulsion – dramatically altered the Russian social and cultural terrain, indeed the very texture of individuals' lives, but also had enormous implications for politics. Arguably, it provided the essential foundation for the possibility of democratic civil society. The 1905 Revolution unleashed civic opinion and organisation, enabled further by the partial civil rights promised by the reform legislation that followed, but the history of civic organisations and public opinion was older. Especially since the late 1800s, voluntary associations had proliferated, including learned societies, literacy and temperance societies, business and professional associations, philanthropic and service organisations, workers' mutual assistance funds and varied cultural associations and circles. Already before the de facto press freedoms of 1905 and the freeing of the press from preliminary censorship in 1906, the printed word, including mass-circulation daily newspapers and a burgeoning book market, had become a powerful medium for disseminating and exchanging information and ideas. In addition, universities, public schools, law courts, organisations of local rural and urban self-government and even the Church stood on the uncertain boundaries of being at once state and civil institutions, though offering an important space for individuals to engage with the emerging public life.[18]

This public sphere could not have emerged with such intensity had it not been for the ongoing economic and social modernisation of the country. Material and social life were changing: the industrial sphere expanded, evidenced by rising numbers of factories and other businesses and innovations in technology; the size and populations of urban areas grew; a commercial

---

18 On civil society, see esp. Edith Clowes, Samuel Kassow and James West (eds.), *Between Tsar and People: Educated Society and the Quest for Public Identity in Late Imperial Russia* (Princeton: Princeton University Press, 1991); and Joseph Bradley, 'Subjects into Citizens: Societies, Civil Society, and Autocracy in Tsarist Russia', *American Historical Review* 107, 4 (Oct. 2002): 1094–123. On the press, literacy and reading, see Jeffrey Brooks, *When Russia Learned to Read: Literacy and Popular Literature, 1861–1917* (Princeton: Princeton University Press, 1985); and Louise McReynolds, *The News under Russia's Old Regime* (Princeton: Princeton University Press, 1991).

sphere expanded, marked by increasing numbers of consumer goods and new forms of commerce such as department stores and arcades, which tangibly transformed everyday material life; growing also was a middle class of urban professionals, business owners, salaried employees and others; literacy spread, as did the regularity of reading, creating a growing market for the expanding press; and social and geographic mobility made Russia in many ways a country on the move as peasants, workers and the educated journeyed between city and country, between various places and types of work and between occupations and even class levels.

The daily press was a chronicle of the unsettling and inspiring uncertainties of modern life in Russia. Its images of everyday public life were often positive and confident: stories of scientific knowledge and technical know-how; entrepreneurial success and opportunities for upward mobility; the increasing role of institutions of culture (museums, schools, libraries, exhibitions, theatres); the growth of civic organisation (scientific, technical, philanthropic); and the civilising effects of the constructed beauty and ordered space of city streets and buildings. But the daily press was also filled with a sense of the disquieting forms and rhythms of the modern: a widespread tendency to esteem material values over spiritual values; the egoistic and predatory practices of the growing class of 'capitalists'; frightening attacks on respectable citizens and civic order by 'hooligans'; the pervasive dangers and depredations of con-artists, thieves and burglars; sexual licentiousness and debauchery; prostitution, rape and murder; an epidemic of suicides; widespread public drunkenness; neglected and abandoned children (who often turned to street crime and vice); and spreading morbidity – especially diseases such as syphilis that were seen as resulting from loose morals, or tuberculosis or cholera that were seen as nurtured by urban congestion.[19]

Sex, consumption and popular entertainment were widely and publicly discussed as touchstones for interpreting the meaning of modern public life and the nature of the modern self. Civic discussion of sex often propounded liberal ideals about the individual: personal autonomy, rights to privacy and

19 This summary of images of the modern city in the daily press is drawn primarily from the St Petersburg mass-circulation dailies *Gazeta-Kopeika* and *Peterburgskii listok* from 1908 to 1914. See also Joseph Bradley, *Muzhik and Muscovite: Urbanization in Late Imperial Russia* (Berkeley: University of California Press, 1985); Daniel Brower, *The Russian City between Tradition and Modernity, 1850–1900* (Berkeley: University of California Press, 1990); Joan Neuberger, *Hooliganism: Crime, Culture, and Power in St. Petersburg, 1900–1914* (Berkeley: University of California Press, 1993); Catriona Kelly and David Shepherd (eds.), *Constructing Culture in the Age of Revolution: 1881–1940* (Oxford: Oxford University Press, 1998), p.2; Mark Steinberg, *Proletarian Imagination: Self, Modernity, and the Sacred in Russia, 1910–1925* (Ithaca, N. Y.: Cornell University Press, 2002), pp. 5–9, 147–81.

happiness and the rule of law. But these accounts also dwelled on the need for sexual order, rationality and control, reflecting anxieties about unleashed individualities.[20] The emergence of a consumer culture similarly impressed many observers as both desirable and disconcerting. Department stores and glass-covered arcades (*passazhi*) displayed goods and objects of visual pleasure and desire which stimulated notions of being fashionable and respectable – that is, modern materialist and consumerist identities – but also confused identities and raised the spectre of threatening self-creation.[21] Urban mass entertainments particularly disturbed the 'culturalist' intelligentsia as the consumption of crass and debasing pleasures rather than the acquisition of uplifting knowledge or the improvement of taste. City spaces filled with opportunities for unenlightened public pleasure: music halls, nightclubs, *cafés chantants*, 'pleasure gardens', cheap theatres and cinemas. These entertainments were especially aimed at the growing urban middling and working classes. Reading tastes often seemed hardly less uplifting. Newspapers 'pandered to crude instincts' with stories of 'scandal' and sensation, while 'boulevard' fiction, often serialised in the press and made available in cheap pamphlets, eroded traditional popular and national values in favour of preoccupations with adventure, individual daring (and suffering), exotic locales and behaviours, material success (or loss) and a pervading moral cynicism.[22]

The unsettling and contradictory character of modern life was also visible in art and literature. One can speak of a pervading 'decadence' in Russian expressive culture, a characteristic sense of disintegration and displacement, even a foreboding, though also an imaginative anticipation, of an approaching 'end' that might also be a beginning. Some embraced a melancholy mood. Some turned to an escapist aestheticism: the old world was dying, but at least it should be a beautiful death. Some nurtured a cosmopolitan 'nostalgia for world culture' or turned back to Russia's 'pure' national traditions. Some dwelled on the self as both a new source of meaning and a dark source of danger. And some, especially the 'Futurists', engaged in iconoclastic rebellion in the name of the new and the modern, evoking in their works the noise of factories and of the marketplace and the textures of iron and glass, and challenging 'philistine' tastes and perceptions with bizarre public

20 Laura Engelstein, *The Keys to Happiness: Sex and the Search for Modernity in Fin-de-Siècle Russia* (Ithaca, N. Y.: Cornell University Press, 1992).
21 Kelly and Shepherd (eds.), *Constructing Culture*, pp. 107–13.
22 Ibid., 113–41; Richard Stites, *Russian Popular Culture* (Cambridge: Cambridge University Press, 1992), ch. 1; Louise McReynolds, *Russia at Play: Leisure Activities at the End of the Tsarist Era* (Ithaca, N. Y.: Cornell University Press, 2002).

behaviour and 'trans-rational' words and images meant to herald the new and transcendent.[23]

## Sacred stories

The final decades of the imperial order in Russia were also marked by spiritual searching and crisis – a complex upheaval often reduced historiographically to the simple image of a 'religious renaissance'. These were years during which many educated Russians sought to return to the Church and revitalise their faith. But even more evident were non-conformist paths of spiritual searching known as God-Seeking. Writers, artists and intellectuals in large numbers were drawn to private prayer, mysticism, spiritualism, theosophy, Eastern religions and other idealisations of imagination, feeling and mystical connections between all things. A fascination with elemental feeling, with the unconscious and the mythic, proliferated along with visions of coming catastrophe and redemption. The visible forms of God-Seeking were extensive. A series of 'Religious-Philosophical Meetings' was held in St Petersburg in 1901–3, bringing together prominent intellectuals and clergy to explore together ways to reconcile the Church with the growing if undogmatic desire among the educated for spiritual meaning in life. Especially after 1905, various religious societies arose, though much of this religious upheaval was informal: circles and salons, séances, private prayer. Some clergy also sought to revitalise Orthodox faith, most famously the charismatic Father John of Kronstadt, who, until his death in 1908 (though his followers remained active long after), emphasised Christian living and sought to restore fervency and the presence of the miraculous in liturgical celebration.[24]

One sees a similarly renewed vigour and variety in religious life and spirituality among the lower classes, especially after the upheavals of 1905. Among

23 S. A. Vengerov (ed.), *Russkaia literatura XX veka* (Moscow, 1914), vol. 1, pp. 1–26; Camilla Gray, *The Russian Experiment in Art, 1863–1922* (London: Thames and Hudson, 1962). Vladimir Markov, *Russian Futurism: A History* (Berkeley: University of California Press, 1968); Katerina Clark, *Petersburg, Crucible of Cultural Revolution* (Cambridge, Mass.: Harvard University Press, 1995).
24 A. S. Pankratov, *Ishchushchie boga* (Moscow, 1911); George L. Kline, *Religious and Anti-Religious Thought in Russia* (Chicago: University of Chicago Press, 1968); Maria Carlson, *'No Religion Higher Than Truth': A History of the Theosophical Movement in Russia, 1875–1922* (Princeton: Princeton University Press, 1993); Catherine Evtuhov, *The Cross and the Sickle: Sergei Bulgakov and the Fate of Russian Religious Philosophy, 1890–1920* (Ithaca, N. Y.: Cornell University Press, 1997); Nadieszda Kizenko, *A Prodigal Saint: Father John of Kronstadt and the Russian People* (University Park, Pa.: Pennsylvania State University Press, 2000); Vera Shevzov, *Russian Orthodoxy on the Eve of Revolution* (Oxford: Oxford University Press, 2004).

the peasantry we see widespread interest in spiritual-ethical literature and non-conformist moral-spiritual movements; an upsurge in pilgrimage and other devotions to sacred spaces and objects (especially icons); persistent beliefs in the presence and power of the supernatural (apparitions, possession, walking-dead, demons, spirits, miracles and magic); the renewed vitality of local 'ecclesial communities' actively shaping their own ritual and spiritual lives, sometimes in the absence of clergy, and defining their own sacred places and forms of piety; and the proliferation of what the Orthodox establishment branded as 'sectarianism', including both non-Orthodox Christian denominations, notably Baptists, and various forms of deviant popular Orthodoxy and mysticism.[25] Among urban workers, the often-described decline in Orthodox belief and practice was complicated by a rise of alternative forms of religious faith and enthusiasm. This popular urban religious revival included workers' gatherings in taverns to talk about religion; followers of individual mystics and healers; adulation of Lev Tolstoy as well as popular Tolstoyan movements; the charismatic movement known as the 'Brethren' (*brattsy*), which attracted thousands of workers to an ideal of moral living, to the promise of salvation in this life and to impassioned preaching; and growing congregations of religious dissenters and sectarians. The Orthodox Church hierarchy frequently branded these and other movements as sectarian, and the Church actively tried to restore its influence among the urban population by challenging 'sectarians' to debates, attacking them in a flurry of pamphlets and on occasion (as against the Brethren) anathematising and excommunicating the most visible leaders.[26]

While these organisational forms reveal the shape and extent of Russia's religious upheaval, its significance as a sign of these unsettled times and of the widespread search for answers and meanings is most evident in the words and images individuals created to speak of what troubled them spiritually about the world and of what they desired and imagined. The strong desire in these years to reinterpret the world was joined by a desire to re-enchant it as well. In 1902, Aleksandr Benua (Benois), the leader of the World of Art movement, noted the widespread feeling that the reigning 'materialism' of

25 In addition to previous references, also Gregory Freeze, 'Subversive Piety: Religion and the Political Crisis in Late Imperial Russia', *Journal of Modern History* 68 (June 1996): 308–50; Laura Engelstein, *Castration and the Heavenly Kingdom* (Ithaca, N.Y.: Cornell University Press, 1999); Christine Worobec, *Possessed: Women, Witches, and Demons in Imperial Russia* (DeKalb: Northern Illinois University Press, 2001); Steinberg, *Proletarian Imagination*, ch. 6.
26 A. S. Prugavin, '*Brattsy*' *i trezvenniki* (Moscow, 1912); A. I. Klibanov, *Istoriia religioznogo sektantstva v Rossii* (Moscow, 1965); Engelstein, *Castration and the Heavenly Kingdom*.

the age was too 'astonishingly simple' to answer essential questions about the meaning of the world, too shallow in its answers to satisfy what people needed, and was therefore being replaced, in all the arts, by the 'mystical spirit of poetry'.[27] Symbolist writers like Andrei Belyi sought to penetrate appearances to discover the spiritual essences of things (and of the human self), by exalting imagination, elemental feeling and intuition. Many visual artists, especially after 1905, were similarly drawn towards a spiritual understanding of the power and function of images.[28] In intellectual circles, a sensation-creating volume of essays appeared in 1909 under the title *Vekhi* (Landmarks or Signposts), authored by a group of leading left-wing intellectuals, mostly former Marxists, who bluntly repudiated the materialism and atheism that had dominated the thought of the intelligentsia for generations as leading inevitably to failure and moral disaster. At the same time, some writers were drawn to a new Messianism, an apocalyptic (if often dark) faith in a coming catastrophe out of which a great redemption would come. The discontent with materialism and the allure of religious and mystical perceptions and imagination reached into unexpected places in these years. Among Marxists, a group associated with the Bolshevik Party (including the future leader of the Proletkul't, Aleksandr Bogdanov, the future commissar of enlightenment, Anatolii Lunacharskii, and the popular writer Maxim Gorky) elaborated in 1908–9 a re-enchanted Marxism known as God-Building. Feeling the cold rationalism, materialism and determinism of traditional Marxism inadequate to inspire a revolutionary mass movement, they insisted on the need to appeal to the subconscious and the emotional, to recapture for the revolution, in Lunacharskii's words, the power of 'myth', in order to create a new faith that placed humanity where God had been but retained a religious spirit of passion, moral certainty and the promise of deliverance from evil and death.[29]

## Proletarians

Marxists tended to take an essentialist view of the proletariat: this was the class destined by the logic of history to emancipate humanity from injustice and oppression. No Marxists, least of all the Bolsheviks, believed this would

27 Aleksandr Benua, *Istoriia russkoi zhivopisi v XIX veke* (Moscow: Respublika, 1998), pp. 343–4.
28 Gray, *Russian Experiment in Art*.
29 A. V. Lunacharskii, *Religiia i sotsializm*, 2 vols. (St Petersburg, 1908 and 1911). See also Kline, *Religious and Anti-Religious Thought in Russia*, ch. 4; Jutta Scherrer, 'L'intelligentsia russe: sa quête da la "vérité religieuse du socialisme"', *Le temps de la réflexion*, 1981, no. 2: 134–51. See also Steinberg, *Proletarian Imagination*, ch. 6.

happen until workers were brought to 'consciousness' (*soznatel'nost'*) of their historical situation and mission. But the content of consciousness was not in doubt: a conscious 'proletarian' understood the dehumanising essence of capitalism, felt a sense of collective identity with his class, and recognised the destiny of workers to overthrow capitalism through revolution in order to create, for all humanity, a socialist order. This imagined proletariat was not entirely a fantasy. But the real history of workers in the early twentieth century was considerably more complex. Ultimately, both this ideological construct and the actual conditions and visions of workers would play a critical part in the history of the revolution and the Soviet experiment.

The most visible (and, for many, troubling) sign of Russia's industrialisation and urban development since the late 1800s was the great visibility of large numbers of industrial workers (42–3 per cent of the populations of St Petersburg and Moscow in 1910–12, and 49 per cent in Baku, for example), uprooted from the countryside and left to fend for themselves in the harsh world of the city.[30] Working conditions had been eased in the late 1800s by labour legislation, which established a factory inspectorate, regulated female and child labour and limited the working day. But conditions remained difficult: overcrowded housing with often deplorable sanitary conditions, an exhausting work-day (on the eve of the war a ten-hour work-day six days a week was the average), widespread disease (notably tuberculosis) and high rates of premature mortality (made worse by pervasive alcoholism), constant risk of injury from poor safety conditions, harsh discipline (rules and fines, at best, but sometimes foremen's fists) and inadequate wages. The characteristic benefits of urban industrial life could be just as dangerous from the point of view of social and political stability. Acquiring new skills, even simply learning to cope with city life, often gave workers a sense of self-respect and confidence, raising desires and expectations. The elaborate commercial culture of early twentieth-century Russian cities nurtured desire and hope as well as envy and anger. And urban workers were likely to be or become literate, exposing them to a range of new experiences and ideas. Indeed, the very act of reading and becoming more 'cultured' encouraged many commoners to feel a sense of self-esteem that made the ordinary deprivations, hardships and humiliations of lower-class life more difficult to endure.[31]

---

30 A. G. Rashin, *Naselenie Rossii za 100 let (1811–1913 gg): statisticheskie ocherki* (Moscow: Gosudarstvennoe statisticheskoe izdatel'stvo, 1956), pp. 320–47.
31 See esp. Leopold Haimson, 'The Problem of Social Stability in Urban Russia, 1905–1917' (pt. 1), *Slavic Review* 23, 4 (Dec. 1964): 619–42; Reginald Zelnik, 'Russian Bebels', *Russian Review* 35, 3 and 4 (July 1976 and Oct. 1976); Bonnell, *Roots of Rebellion*.

The most visible sign of worker discontent was strikes and, beginning in 1905, the growth of trade unions. The upheavals of 1905, in which economic and political demands were constantly interconnected, were unprecedented in vehemence and scale, though foreshadowed by widespread strikes in 1896–7, 1901 and 1903. During 1905, strikes broke out in almost every industry and every part of the country, and workers began forming illegal trade unions, which, along with strikes, were legalised in the wake of the October manifesto (strikes in December 1905, unions in March 1906). The government clearly hoped (and radicals feared) that legalising strikes and unions and allowing workers to vote for representatives to the new State Duma would give workers effective channels for redressing their grievances, thus leading the labour movement onto a more peaceful path. Initially, this appeared to be precisely what happened. Thousands of workers joined the legal unions and concentrated on attaining better economic conditions. The leaders of these unions, and many members, became increasingly cautious, so as not to give the government an excuse to close the unions down. And, among the socialist parties, workers tended to choose as their leaders Mensheviks, who emphasised, for the short term, legal struggle for realisable and mainly liberal-democratic gains. This moderation of the labour movement might have continued had not the tsarist government acted in ways that aggravated workers' political attitudes. Although trade unions were legal, they were under the close surveillance and control of the police, who regularly closed meetings, arrested leaders and shut down union papers. Meanwhile, employers endeavoured, often with success, to take back economic gains workers had made in 1905, and to form their own strong organisations. When the strike movement revived in 1910–14, workers' frustrations were sharply visible, not only in the stubborn persistence of strikers and the revival of political demands but also in the growing popularity of the more radical Bolsheviks. In the autumn of 1912, Bolsheviks won a majority of workers' votes to the Duma in almost all industrial electoral districts. Many unions elected Bolshevik majorities to their governing boards.[32]

It bears remembering that social and political discontent is a social and cultural construction as much as a natural response to material conditions, tangible relationships or political restrictions. Workers had to see their conditions not as the inevitable lot of the poor but as correctable wrongs. They needed a language of justice and right and a belief that alternatives existed. Workers constructed such a vocabulary partly out of traditional sources of moral judgement: religious ethics and communitarian values, for example.

32 Bonnell, *Roots of Rebellion*; Haimson, 'The Problem of Social Stability'.

But fresher sources abounded. Magazines, newspapers, pamphlets and books widely disseminated ideas about universal rights, the natural equality of all human beings and the mutability of every political order. Whatever the sources, notions of justice, entitlement and progress were becoming unsettlingly widespread among Russia's urban poor. These arguments were evident, for example, in demands presented during strikes. Beside appeals for economic or political change (higher wages, shorter hours, civil rights), many demands focused on what have been termed 'moral issues' (or 'dignity issues'). The most obvious of these was the demand for 'polite address'. But even ordinary economic demands for higher wages, shorter hours and cleaner lavatories, were interpreted as necessary so that workers might 'live like human beings'. In the trade union press, we often hear workers speaking of their identity as 'human beings' not 'machines' (or 'slaves' or 'cattle') and their consequent human 'rights'. Popular discontent, of course, was not simply about justice, democracy and rights. It also contained a great deal of anger and resentment. Once aroused to open protest, workers could express a desire to punish and humiliate, even to dehumanise, those who stood above them and whom they blamed for their sufferings. In this spirit, workers put foremen or employers in wheelbarrows, dumped trash on their heads and rolled them out of the shop and into the streets, or, less ceremoniously, beat them, occasionally to death. Plebeian lives encouraged the poor to dream of revenge and reversal as well as of justice.[33]

Evidence of worker 'consciousness' and protest hardly exhausts the story of working-class mentalities in the pre-war years. As any 'conscious' worker would readily admit (and often complained) too many workers were lost in a dire state of 'unenlightened melancholy, impenetrable scepticism, and stagnant inertia'.[34] In practice, according to frequent accounts by dismayed working-class activists, this meant (and the talk here was mainly about men) too much alcohol, workers lying to their wives about wages squandered on drink (along with contempt for, and violence against, women), vulgar swearing, sexual licentiousness and crass tastes in boulevard fiction, the music hall and trashy popular cinema. Working-class women were viewed as victims in all this and as lost in 'backwardness' and 'passivity'. In a way, the cultural behaviour of ordinary workers could be seen as a type of defiance against elite moral norms and, by extension, a form of protest against class domination. But, activists constantly worried, such rebellion did not point to any alternative. On the

---

33 See Bonnell, *Roots of Rebellion*.
34 A. Zorin [Aleksei Gastev], 'Sredi tramvaishchikov (nabrosok)', *Edinstvo* 12 (21 Dec. 1909): 11.

contrary, it seemed a mark of disillusionment and 'impenetrable scepticism', of escapism and ephemeral pleasure at best.

## In the countryside

The vast majority of Russians were peasants – at 85 per cent, Russia had the highest proportion of rural dwellers in Europe on the eve of the First World War.[35] A great deal of everyday peasant life had changed little since the abolition of serfdom in 1861 and even from earlier times. Work, community, family and religion remained the hallmarks of everyday life in the village. Subsistence family farming and handicraft manufacture were still central to the texture of everyday life, little changed by technological innovation. Village life was largely controlled by the commune (*obshchina* or *mir*), acting most often through its assembly of male heads of household. The commune held collective title to local peasant lands and made the major decisions about land use (what work should be done in each field, when to do it and by which methods) and periodically, according to tradition, redistributed the holdings, which were divided into scattered strips, among peasant families on the basis of a calculus of hands to work and mouths to feed. The commune also carried out a range of fiscal, administrative and community functions: tax collection, military recruitment, granting or refusing permission to individuals to work away from the village, investigating and punishing petty crimes and misdemeanours, maintaining roads and bridges and the local church or chapel, dealing with outsiders and caring for needy members of the community. The village community was not simply a structural fact of life, but also a cultural value, as can be seen vividly in the collective enforcement of community values and order – through rituals of charivari (*vozhdenie*), which publicly humiliated offenders against community interests and norms, and occasional collective violence, some of it startlingly brutal, against deviants and criminals. Community solidarity was a moral value as well as a way to survive in a harsh world. The family household remained the foundational unit of everyday peasant social and economic life. Within the family, the male head of household exercised enormous power: controlling, sometimes brutally, behaviour in his household, representing the family at assemblies of the village commune, and holding village administrative, police and judicial posts. In this patriarchal world, women were relegated to domestic and some farming work and to ceremonial life.

35 *Rossiia 1913 god: Statistiko-dokumental'nyi spravochnik* (St Petersburg: Blits, 1995), pp. 23, 219.

Religious life, in which women had the largest role to play, was an Orthodoxy (though Old Belief was strong in many areas of the country and sectarianism common) that complexly blended folk, magical and Church traditions. The timing and form of rituals and celebrations, belief in the pervasiveness of powerful unseen spirits and forces (God, saints, Satan, devils, sprites), reliance on holy men and women (from priests to folk healers), belief in the porous boundary between the worlds of the living and the dead and belief in the power of material objects to embody the sacred (relics, holy water, ritual gestures, icons, incantations, potions and herbs), all partook of both Orthodox traditions and what the Church and educated Russians sometimes called 'pagan' residues to create a lived folk Christianity (a vital, syncretic mix poorly captured by the notion of a 'dual-faith', or *dvoeverie*, in which an essential paganism was only superficially masked by a 'veneer' of Christian faith) that helped make the world meaningful to peasants and give them some measure of control.[36]

Evidence of profound changes in the experiences and expectations of peasants in these years is no less impressive. Most visibly, peasants were becoming increasingly engaged politically, especially in the wake of the 1905 Revolution. The abolition of serfdom had left peasants with only part of the land they believed by right belonged to them (it was a sacred verity that land must belong to those who work it), requiring peasants to pay rent or work for wages on the land of others. Noble landownership declined precipitously in these years, with peasant communes purchasing or leasing much of this land, and there is evidence that overall peasant poverty gradually diminished. Still, 'land hunger', as it was widely called, and the old dream of 'black repartition', the redistribution of all the land into the hands of the peasantry, remained stubbornly compelling, nurtured by both the relative poverty peasants felt and their notions of moral right. 'Disturbances' and everyday forms of resistance continued. In the midst of the national crisis of 1905–7, when the possibilities for change seemed high, peasants voiced their discontent and desires openly in petitions to the government and through new political organisations such as the All-Russian Peasant Union. They also took direct action, seizing land,

---

36 Ben Eklof and Stephen Frank (eds.), *The World of the Russian Peasant: Post-Emancipation Culture and Society* (Boston: Unwin Hyman, 1990); Christine Worobec, *Peasant Russia: Family and Community in the Post-Emancipation Period* (Princeton: Princeton University Press, 1991); Barbara Engel, *Between Fields and the City: Women, Work and Family in Russia, 1861–1914* (Cambridge: Cambridge University Press, 1995), ch. 1; Stephen Frank, *Crime, Cultural Conflict, and Justice in Rural Russia, 1856–1914* (Berkeley: University of California Press, 1999).

taking and redistributing grain, pillaging landlords' property and burning manor houses.[37]

No less important, peasants were less and less a 'world apart', as they have sometimes been characterised, and more and more entwined in Russia's modern transformation. External changes facilitated this, though what most decisively altered peasants' everyday lives were their own actions and choices. After the turn of the century, the government moved towards removing some of the disabilities that marked peasants as a distinct and legally inferior social estate: collective responsibility for tax payment was ended in 1903, corporal punishment was abolished in 1904 and, in 1906, Prime Minister Petr Stolypin promulgated a reform that allowed individual peasants to withdraw from the commune and establish independent farmsteads, though relatively few did. Outsiders (educated reformers, teachers, clergy and others) were increasing in evidence in the villages, organising co-operatives, mutual assistance organisations, lectures and readings, theatres and temperance organisations. The rapid expansion of schooling and literacy and the massive rise in newspapers and literature directed at common people (the illiterate could hear these read and discussed in village taverns and tearooms) exposed peasants in unprecedented ways to knowledge of the larger world. Changing economic opportunities were especially important. Migration to industrial and urban work touched the lives of millions of peasants – the migrants themselves but also their kin and fellow villagers when these individuals returned to the countryside after seasonal or temporary industrial or commercial work, or at least on holidays, or after becoming sick or aged.

As peasants responded to these new experiences and to their own desires, everyday peasant life visibly changed. Many peasants, especially younger men and women who had been to the city, demonstrated new social mores (for example, in personal and sexual relations); began wearing urban-style dress, either bought in urban shops or hand-sewn on the model of pictures in magazines; and purchased, or at least desired, commodities such as clocks, urban furniture, stylish boots and hats, porcelain dishes and cosmetics. Especially for peasants able to experience life beyond the village (through work but also reading), this new knowledge stimulated new desires and expectations. What was said of peasant women who had worked in the city can be

37 Maureen Perrie, 'The Russian Peasant Movement in 1905–7', in Eklof and Frank, *The World of the Russian Peasant*, pp. 193–218; Barbara Engel, 'Women, Men, and Languages of Peasant Resistance, 1870–1907', in Stephen Frank and Mark Steinberg (eds.), *Cultures in Flux: Lower-Class Values, Practices, and Resistance in Late Imperial Russia* (Princeton: Princeton University Press, 1994), pp. 34–53.

said of many individual peasants in these years whose lives were no longer confined by traditional spaces and knowledges: they were 'distinguished by livelier speech, greater independence, and a more obstinate character'. These changes brought pleasure, but also potential frustration and danger.[38]

## Nation and empire

The fundamental question of Russian nationhood was also in flux, and under siege, in these years. As a political entity, of course, Russia was not a single ethnic nation but an empire that included large numbers of Ukrainians, Poles, Belorussians, Turkic peoples, Jews, Roma (gypsies), Germans, Finns, Lithuanians, Latvians, Estonians, Georgians, Armenians and many others, some of whom could claim histories of once having their own states and others who were discovering and inventing themselves as nations. Non-Russian 'minorities', based on native language, were already a slight majority in the empire at the time of the 1897 census.[39] The empire's national complexity was no less visible in the strong presence, despite many restrictive laws, of ethnic and religious minorities in urban centres, especially in business and the professions. But how was this imperial society understood? Historians have debated the utility of categories such as empire, imperialism, colonialism, orientalism, frontier and borderlands. At the level of state policy, certainly, it would be foolhardy to apply any single model: the treatment of Jews, Catholic Poles, Orthodox Ukrainians, Muslim Tatars or Uzbeks and 'pagan' Evenks, for example, was not uniform. Also, local policies, driven by imperial administrators and educators who often better understood local needs and possibilities, could differ from the policy directives coming from St Petersburg. And individuals were treated differently depending on their professions and their degree of assimilation. Most of all, as recent scholars have shown, state policy towards

38 Engel, *Between Fields and the City*, quotation p. 82; Frank, *Crime, Cultural Conflict, and Justice in Rural Russia*; Frank and Steinberg, *Cultures in Flux*, ch. 5; Brooks, *When Russia Learned to Read*; Ben Eklof, *Russian Peasant Schools: Officialdom, Village Culture, and Popular Pedagogy, 1861–1914* (Berkeley: University of California Press, 1986); Jeffrey Burds, *Peasant Dreams and Market Politics: Labor Migration and the Russian Village, 1861–1905* (Pittsburgh: University of Pittsburgh Press, 1998); Boris Mironov (with Ben Eklof), *The Social History of Imperial Russia, 1700–1917* (Boulder, Colo.: Westview Press, 2000).
39 Of the entire population of the empire, excluding Finland, only 44.9 per cent spoke Russian (not including Belorussian and Ukrainian, though the census viewed these as sub-categories of Russian) as their native language. N. A. Troinitskii (ed.), *Pervaia vseobshchaia perepis' naseleniia Rossiiskoi Imperii, 1897 g.*, vyp. 7 (St Petersburg, n.p., 1905), pp. 1–9.

the empire's peoples, even in any single case, was 'enormously ambiguous, variable, uncertain, and contested'.[40]

On the one hand, the government of Nicholas II, and the tsar personally, actively promoted a renewed Russian nationalism that often had dire conse-quences for those defined as outside the national fold. Official images of the tsar's loving communion with his 'people' pointedly excluded non-Russian nationalities. Conversely, he blamed non-Russians (especially Jews) for the dis-turbances of 1905. For Nicholas II and his nationalist allies, it was time again to establish state and society on 'unique Russian principles', which meant 'that unity between Tsar and all *Rus'* . . . as there was of old'. To speak of Russia as *Rus'*, of course, was to offer up an idealised national past, a pure national Russia before imperial expansion or Westernisation, in place of the complex realities of *Rossiia* the empire.[41] In practice, the state had since the late 1800s been promoting an aggressive 'Russification' of non-Russian nationalities: insisting on Russian as the language of education and administration, promoting the settlement of ethnic Russians in the borderlands, supporting active Orthodox missionary work and building Orthodox churches throughout the empire, increasing quotas on Jews and some other groups in higher education, tolerat-ing and perhaps even instigating anti-Jewish violence ('pogroms'), reducing the representation of non-Russian national parties in the Duma and suppressing radical nationalist parties and demonstrations.

The government's approach to empire and nation was not a simple matter of Russian nationalist revivalism and the repression of the 'Other', however. Indeed, 'Russification' could also be a policy of trying to assimilate various ethnic groups (or at least individuals) into a common imperial polity, and could mean in practice limited respect for local customs, education in native languages and an active if circumscribed role in administration or education for non-Russians themselves, all in the pursuit of a deeper integration. Imperial diversity was sometimes visibly celebrated in rituals such as the tsar's corona-tion or the arrival in the borderlands of imperial dignitaries.[42] But apparent celebration of the empire's many peoples was often entwined with a compli-cating ideology of national hierarchy and mission. Russian national identity,

40 Robert Geraci, *Window on the East: National and Imperial Identities in Late Tsarist Russia* (Ithaca, N.Y.: Cornell University Press, 2001), p. 344.
41 Wortman, *Scenarios of Power*, vol. II, p. 397 (quote), 495, 497. Major-General A. Elchaninov, *The Tsar and his People* (London: Hodder and Stoughton, 1913); Steinberg and Khrustalëv, *Fall of the Romanovs*, 'Introduction'.
42 Wortman, *Scenarios of Power*, vol. II, p. 351; Dov Yaroshevskii, 'Empire and Citizenship', in Daniel Brower and Edward Lazzerini (eds.), *Russia's Orient: Imperial Borderlands and Peoples, 1700–1917* (Bloomington: Indiana University Press, 1997), pp. 58–9.

for many leaders of state and society, was constructed upon notions of Russia as a 'civilised' nation bringing 'order' and 'culture' to 'backward' peoples. Even the reforms of 1905–6, which stipulated religious tolerance and greater possibilities for native leaders to play active roles in civic life, were conceived as part of the effort to integrate the various peoples of the empire into a coherent whole, marked by ideals of citizenship, of a non-parochial common good, and even of the universalism of empire.[43] Such talk clashed with other official discourses that relegated Russia's diversity to the shadows and focused on the mythic recovery of the purified national spirit of old *Rus'*. Still, the dominant official vision remained that of integration and uniformity. This was sometimes elaborated in generous and inclusive ways; but most often, especially in the final years of the empire, the model (however contradictory and unstable) was a polity that was simultaneously national-Russian and imperial.[44]

The perspectives and actions of non-Russians themselves greatly complicated efforts to strengthen the empire. The late 1800s and early 1900s were a time of widespread cultural awakening and nationalist activism. Many groups – Poles, Ukrainians, Finns, Balts, Jews, Georgians, Armenians, Muslims and others – defined themselves as 'nations' and organised movements seeking cultural autonomy and perhaps an independent nation-state, though many activists (especially socialists) saw national revival and emancipation best served in common cause with Russians to fight for civil rights and democracy for all within the empire. Changes in the lives and expectations of non-Russians, however, were not limited to the history of political and nationalist movements. For many non-Russian communities, these were also years of social and cultural change and exploring of new possibilities and new identities – probably more than we know, as historians are still only beginning to recover and retell these 'other' Russian histories.

Among Jews, for example, we see the rise around the turn of the century and after of schools promoting Hebrew or Yiddish (each with quite different national agendas) along with growing numbers of Russian-educated Jews; the emergence of a new Jewish literature, written in both Hebrew and Yiddish, and of a Jewish periodical press; increasing secular studies in the yeshivas; the rise of both mysticism and secularising trends within religious life; organised political movements of both Jewish socialism, which sought a transformed Russian Empire, and Zionism, which sought salvation in a new land; and large numbers of Jews living and working outside the Pale of Settlement, often

---

43 Brower and Lazzerini (eds.), *Russia's Orient*, chs. 3 and 7.
44 Theodore Weeks, *Nation and State in Late Imperial Russia* (DeKalb: Northern Illinois University Press, 1996).

negotiating complex new identities as 'Russian Jews'. Boundaries (not just of settlement but of culture) were far from stable or absolute in Jewish life in these years: we know, for example, that religious Jews were attracted to secular ideologies and that secular radicals might be attracted to prayer and even mysticism. What is certain is that it was no longer possible to speak of Jewish life in Russia, even in the Pale and least of all among the Jewish populations of cities like Kiev, Odessa and St Petersburg, as ghettoised and tradition-bound. Indeed, widespread anti-Jewish prejudice and hatred seemed less a timeless response to Jewish 'otherness' than a reaction to Russia's intensifying crisis and the increasing visibility of Jews in public life.[45]

We see a similar movement of cultural revival and reform, and of civic visibility and engagement, especially after 1905, among Russia's Muslims. Organisations proliferated – including libraries, charities, credit unions, national congresses and political unions and parties – expressing ideologies ranging from liberalism and socialism to Pan-Islamism and Pan-Turkism. The drive for cultural reform was especially strong. The Jadid (new-method) movement in Islamic education – which grew into a widespread movement of cultural and social reform, echoing trends throughout the Muslim world – sought to create a new modern Muslim steeped both in a revitalised and 'purified' Islam and in modern cosmopolitan knowledge. A major sign and catalyst of change was the growth of native-language publishing, including influential magazines such as the satirical *Mulla Nasreddin* from Tiflis, which elaborated a new hybrid discourse that blended the world-view of Western modernity (thus, for example, satirising Muslim 'backwardness' and advocating women's rights) with Muslim identities and values (though these too were to be debated and renewed).[46]

Many non-Russian communities and individuals sought to articulate the meaning of their own 'national' selves and their relationships to others. As an ideal, many sought to be hybrids at once reconnected to their national and religious traditions, free to practise this culture and faith how they wished and imbued with a modern knowledge and identity. Others, just as fervently, resisted challenges to tradition and viewed reformers and those with hybrid ethnic and religious identities with hostility. The sense of crisis and opportunity

45 Zvi Gitelman, *A Century of Ambivalence: The Jews of Russia and the Soviet Union, 1881 to the Present* (Bloomington: Indiana University Press, 2001); Benjamin Nathans, *Beyond the Pale: The Jewish Encounter with Late Imperial Russia* (Berkeley: University of California Press, 2002).
46 Geraci, *Window on the East*; Brower and Lazzerini, *Russia's Orient*; Adeeb Khalid, *The Politics of Muslim Cultural Reform: Jadidism in Central Asia* (Berkeley: University of California Press, 1998).

that marked so much of the Russian *fin de siècle* was evident in the experience of being a non-Russian subject of the empire, as well as in state policy towards the nationalities 'problem'.

## Fin de siècle

The contemporary sense that Russian life in the early years of the twentieth century had become deeply unstable and contradictory highlights the characteristic modernity of Russia's historical moment. Modern displacement – of people, traditions, the order of public spaces, identities and values – was everywhere. So was the modern ambiguity of pervading progress and collapse, possibility and crisis. Historians have long debated whether pre-war Russia was heading towards inevitable crisis and revolution or towards creating a viable civil society and a reformed political order. This chapter has pointed to evidence for the visibility and plausibility of both narratives. But the focus has been beneath these surfaces to a still deeper contradictoriness. A working-class author, looking back on these years through the wake of the war, revolution and civil war that followed, described the experience of this age as ambiguously marked by 'unexpected pains and joys' and by 'tragedies of immense weight appearing at every step', as a time when 'people sicken, go mad from exhaustion, but really live'.[47] As this writer understood, as late as 1914, the greatest tragedies and joys were still to come.

47 N. Liashko, 'O byte i literature perekhodnogo vremeni', *Kuznitsa* 8 (Apr.–Sept. 1921): 29–30, 34.

# 3

# The First World War, 1914–1918

MARK VON HAGEN

The Russian Empire entered what became known as the First World War in the summer of 1914 as a Great Power on the Eurasian continent; four years later, the Russian Empire was no more. In its place was a Bolshevik rump state surrounded by a ring of hostile powers who shared some loyalty to the values of the Old Regime, or a conservative version of the Provisional Government. The notable exception to this was Menshevik-dominated Georgia in Transcaucasia, which pursued a moderate but socialist transformation of its society. Although all the Central European dynastic empires (Austria-Hungary, the Ottomans, Germany and Russia) failed to survive the suicidal war, what succeeded the Russian Empire, namely, the Soviet socialist state, was unlike any other successor regime. Many of the origins of that Soviet state, and the civil war that did so much to shape it, can be traced to the preceding world war: new political techniques and practices, the polarisation of mass politics, the militarisation of society and a social revolution that brought to power a new set of elites determined to transform society even further while in the midst of mobilising for its own war of self-defence against domestic and foreign enemies. The war demanded unprecedented mobilisation of society and economy against formidable enemies to the west and south. The industrial mobilisation alone triggered 'a crisis in growth – a modernisation crisis in thin disguise'.[1] But the economic crisis, with its attendant dislocations and disruptions, unfolded against the backdrop of an impressive societal recruitment; the involvement of millions of subjects in the war effort raised demands for political reform and exacerbated the crisis of the Old Regime.

## The outbreak of war

The outbreak of war followed from the absence of any effective international mechanisms for resolving interstate conflicts on the European continent

---

1 Norman Stone, *The Eastern Front, 1914–1917* (New York: Penguin, 1998), p. 14.

after the decline of the system of 'balance of power'. The previous diplomatic arrangements were predicated on no single power gaining overwhelming influence over the affairs of Europe. That balance was disrupted by the rise of a powerful German Reich in Central Europe that was committed to a position of world power under its aggressive emperor, Wilhelm II. Faced with new threats on its western borders, Russia abandoned its traditional nineteenth-century royalist alliance with Germany and Austria-Hungary for a new set of relationships, the Triple Entente, with the constitutional monarchy of Great Britain and republican France, in the 1890s. The immediate *casus belli* was an Austrian ultimatum to Serbia after the assassination of the Habsburg heir, Archduke Francis Ferdinand, and his wife in Sarajevo on 28 June 1914; Russia and Austria-Hungary were divided over other issues of growing contention as well, particularly the fate of Austrian eastern Galicia (today's western Ukraine), where pre-war tensions involved several sensational espionage trials and fears of annexation. Influential German elites, for their part, developed plans to detach the western borderlands of the Russian Empire and reduce their eastern rival to a medium-sized and non-threatening power.

It was these western borderlands (today's Poland, Ukraine, Belarus, Lithuania, Latvia and Estonia) which witnessed the war's most devastating violence and whose social structures were unintentionally and dramatically transformed even before the revolutions of 1917 proper. This set of battle-grounds became known as the eastern front of the First World War and remains much less well known in English-language literature than the western front that pitted Germany against France and Britain. Transcaucasia (today's Georgia, Armenia and Azerbaijan) also became another important front in the war after the Ottoman Empire joined the Central Powers in late October 1914. Here, too, the war strained local resources, destroyed moderate, nascent civil societies and pitted ethnic and social groups against one another in violent struggles for survival.

Although most elites in Russia (as was true for the other belligerent powers) dreaded the outcome of a major continental war, the proclamation of war in July 1914 was greeted in educated society with a wave of patriotism and some willingness to suspend the opposition to the obstreperous regime of Emperor Nicholas II. Russian elites naively shared the certainty of their counterparts across the continent that the war would be over by Christmas. The call-up of soldiers to military service was less of a patriotic manifestation, with draft riots and other violence providing the first foretaste of the war's challenge to social cohesion.[2] The standing army of the tsar, 1,423,000, was augmented by 5 million new troops by the end of the year. From 1914 to 1916, the last year soldiers were conscripted for the imperial army, 14.4 million men were called to service; by 1917, 37 per cent of the male population of working age was serving in the army. (The Central Powers' numbers, including the armies of Germany, Austria-Hungary, Turkey and Bulgaria, reached 25,100,000, but were fighting on the two major fronts.) Despite the numerical advantages the Russian army enjoyed, its troops faced several disadvantages against the German forces; these included technical matters, such as relatively inadequate railroad lines to transport troops around the fronts, organisational problems caused by political conflicts at the top of the army (particularly between the supreme commander Grand Prince Nikolai Nikolaevich and the minister of war, General Sukhomlinov), and the general inefficiency and corruption of much of the Russian state apparatus. Still, the Germans' Schlieffen Plan called for initially concentrating the major military efforts on the western front, affording some small measure of respite to the Russians in the east.

## Military campaigns: 1914–16

During the first months of the war, the eastern front formed north–south from the East Prussian marshes to the Carpathian Mountains. The Russian (First and Second) armies first confronted the Germans in East Prussia and defeated them at Gumbinnen. They were not allowed to savour their victory long before the Germans turned the tables on them at the Battle of Tannenberg, which ended in disaster for the Russians, who lost 90,000 prisoners and 122,000 casualties. The first battles revealed the scandalous shortage of rifles in the Russian army (one for every three soldiers). In a subsequent defeat, the First Battle of the Masurian Lakes, the Russians lost another 45,000 prisoners and 100,000 men killed and wounded. The pain of these defeats was partly allayed when the Russians defeated their Austrian counterparts in Galicia and occupied Lemberg (Lwow/L'viv/L'vov) and other important fortress cities for nearly eight months. Austria lost 300,000 men, including 100,000 prisoners, in a blow from which it never quite recovered. The Germans provided the new momentum on the side of the Central Powers with a successful push towards Russian Poland in October.

---

2 In the opinion of Vladimir Gurko, 'the war excited neither patriotism nor indignation among the peasants and factory workers'. *Features and Figures of the Past: Government and Opinion in the Reign of Nicholas II* (New York, 1958), p. 528.

With a stalemate quickly developing on the western front, the German leadership was persuaded to make the eastern front a higher priority in 1915, a policy which bore fruit in the first major Russian retreat of the war. (It was also during the campaign against Warsaw that the Germans first used poison gas in the war.) The Second Battle of the Masurian Lakes in February ended in the Russians' retreat from East Prussia. After the fall of the fortress of Przemysl, the Russians lost 126,000 prisoners. Lemberg fell in June, Warsaw and Brest-Litovsk in August and the German advance was halted only in November. In the meantime, Emperor Nicholas II, against the advice of most of his counsellors, dismissed his great-uncle in August and insisted on taking personal command of his armies. The army's admission that 500,000 soldiers had deserted during the first year of war, most of them into German and Austrian prisoner-of-war camps, effectively surrendering to the enemy, raised alarm among the military and political elite.

A new army Chief of Staff, General Mikhail Alekseev, was able to rebuild much of the shattered Russian forces and 1916 brought short-lived victory to the Russian side with the successful June–July offensive of General Aleksei Brusilov, one of the best generals in the Russian camp. Another set of devastating Austrian defeats nearly took the Habsburg monarchy out of the war, but the Germans came to the rescue and Brusilov's advances had outrun his supply lines. Once again, casualties were staggering on both sides (1,412,000 Russian casualties, including 212,000 POWs; 750,000 Austro-Hungarian casualties, 380,000 of them POWs) and contributed to broad demoralisation among both military and civilian populations. Though the war would drag on for another two murderous years, the Russian army, after the defeat of the Brusilov offensive, never again threatened the Germans' domination of Eastern Europe. It was the Germans' own defeat in 1918, combined with revolution at home and international pressure, that forced them to abandon the borderlands between Russia and the Reich, and even then they stayed on in various arrangements until Allied High Commissions could organise a transfer of power, for example, in the Baltic states.

## The martial law regime and its consequences

On 16 July 1914, wide swaths of the Russian Empire were placed under martial law; this included not only the front-line regions and a broad band of territory behind the lines. It also included the two capitals, Moscow and Petrograd (recently renamed to reflect a more patriotic Slavic identity against the German enemy and its culture). Military authorities had virtually unlimited authority to overturn the decisions of local civilian governments; Russia's tenuous achievements in establishing some autonomy for civilian self-rule in the empire were effectively reversed in a matter of months.[3] The army set up a 'Chancellery for Civilian Administration' to co-ordinate its rule over the population, and the expansion of the power and authority of the army proceeded with little effective resistance. The Duma, which had already had its powers trimmed in Nicholas's determination to roll back the concessions he had made under pressure in 1905, suffered further limitations with the war and had virtually no power to influence the course of the war. Several wartime finance measures, especially the imposition of taxes, were passed by special enactments of the government, without consulting the Duma. Duma deputies at best could use the parliament as a tribune to voice their opposition criticism of the regime, but they had no power over the military budget, war aims or the conduct of the war. Interior Minister Nikolai Maklakov led the government's assault on the Duma; the government declared its intention to extend use of the Clause 87 of the Fundamental Laws, banned press coverage of meetings of the Council of Ministers and effectively abandoned the principle of parliamentary immunity. After a largely ceremonial session on 26 July the government refused to reconvene the parliament until it needed a state budget passed. The Fourth Duma met for three days (27–9 January 1915) and was dismissed again until November. And, thanks to the Stolypin *coup d'état* of June 1907, the electoral franchise shaped a conservative, Russian nationalist majority in the Fourth Duma (which convened from 1912 to 1917) with virtually no representation from the non-Russian populations or the non-propertied classes. The war, far from saving the Duma as it was hoped by the moderate parties who declared the *union sacrée*, instead offered the government an opportunity to reduce the Fourth Duma from a legislative to a consultative assembly.[4]

The military managed to free itself, however, even from the Petrograd bureaucracies, the Council of Ministers, and wilfully disregarded decisions passed by the State Council, the conservative upper house of the relatively new Russian parliament. For example, in 1915 Chief of Staff Nikolai Ianushkevich, in the name of national security or military strategic interests and evoking the war against Napoleon in 1812, ordered a scorched-earth policy to deny the Germans and Austrians any advantage from the reoccupied territories

3 For a description of the martial law regime, see Daniel Graf, 'The Reign of the Generals: Military Government in Western Russia, 1914–1915', Ph. D. diss., University of Nebraska, 1972.
4 See Raymond Pearson, *The Russian Moderates and the Crisis of Tsarism, 1914–1917* (New York: Barnes and Noble, 1977).

in Poland and Galicia, over the clear objections of the State Council. The scorched-earth policy made conditions much less tolerable for any future Russian reoccupation, but short-term considerations appeared to win out over longer-term rationale. That policy was also one more illustration of the increasing brutalisation of the war and its devastating impact on the civilian population that fell in its wake.

Occupation policy in the first months of the war was another site for the exercise of the military's new powers. Lemberg's military governor-general, Georgii Bobrinskii, oversaw the expulsion of enemy aliens (German and Austrian citizens) and the arrest and deportation of thousands of Polish, Jewish and Ukrainian community leaders whose loyalty was suspect to the interior of the empire, thereby giving rise to radical émigré circles in nearly every major European Russian city. Martial law authorities confiscated personal and communal property, particularly that of religious, educational and cultural institutions, and transferred them to new owners in violation of any due process or judicial norms. To staff the occupation administration, the Russian military authorities deployed hundreds of local bureaucrats and notables from the south-west provinces, a stronghold of Russian nationalist parties and movements shaped by a largely anti-Polish and anti-Jewish politics of Old Regime elite self-defence. And, under the cover of the Russian occupation, several politically engaged hierarchs of the Orthodox Church, notably Archbishop Evlogii, launched a new campaign for the reconversion of the Galician population to its 'traditional' Orthodox faith from its Greek-Catholic apostasy.

Most Russian subjects in the interior provinces were provisionally spared these massive new intrusions into local social life, but when the retreat of 1915 threw the front lines and the martial law regime far to the east, they too got their first taste of the redrawn borders between civilian and military authority. Moreover, the retreat of the Russian army also brought into the imperial heartland millions of refugees (2.7 million in 1915, which grew to 3.3 million by May 1916) for whom little or no provision had been made by the imperial government. These refugees, not surprisingly, quickly overwhelmed local resources and their alien presence provoked pogroms.

Finally, the military authorities began experimenting with modern techniques of political control over the populations under their expanding authority, particularly in the area of surveillance. A 'Temporary Statute on Military Censorship' introduced a regime of press and postal controls after the outbreak of war. For the first time, the army began monitoring its soldiers' correspondence for signs of discontent or disloyalty to the dynasty and empire; the expansion of surveillance marked both a quantitative and qualitative change over any previous efforts of the tsarist bureaucracy. And after the Great Retreat of 1915 and the re-emergence of a vocal opposition in the Duma, the Ministry of Internal Affairs extended the surveillance practices to civilian society. The army also began to invest the first substantial resources in wartime propaganda to persuade the largely conscript army of the righteousness of the Russian cause. Russian conscripts were sent to the front with a vague message of pan-Slavic liberation of their suffering brothers under Habsburg rule overlaid with an insistence on Teutonic barbarism, illustrated, for example, by the atrocities committed by the retreating Hungarian (*sic*) forces in 1914. The war was cast as a fight for survival between German militarism and Slavic, Orthodox civilisation. The rhetoric of titanic struggle contributed to the totalisation of the war and the sense that no sacrifice was too great for the cause.

## The nationalisation of the empire

The wartime propaganda was one factor in the polarisation of large parts of the imperial population along ethnic or national lines. As in other multinational empires, ethnic and class identities frequently reinforced one another; ethnic groups occupied particular socio-economic niches in the imperial political economy. The relative ethnic peace of the pre-war period was shattered by the war and its policies of ethnic discrimination and militarisation, beginning in the borderlands and moving quickly to the centre.[5] Above all, any Russian subject with German ancestry became a potential target of 'patriotic self-defence' groups, which were vigilante groups who destroyed property and injured or killed individuals. This was true even in the capitals where maximum security measures were ostensibly in place. In one particularly violent outburst, Moscow mobs destroyed 800 'German' businesses in May 1915. During the first months of the war, the Volynian German population, which had resided in the area as peaceable agriculturists for decades, was brutally uprooted and resettled inland by military order. This was not, by the way, a trend encouraged by the court, who rather feared its consequences, given the German ancestry of the Empress Alexandra and even more distant members of the Romanov family. The number of Baltic and other German nobles who served in the officer corps and throughout the imperial bureaucracy fed a steady stream of rumours about the court's signing a separate peace with the enemy or, more ominously, working for Russia's defeat by the Germans.

---

5 See Eric Lohr, *Nationalizing the Russian Empire: The Campaign against Enemy Aliens during World War I* (Cambridge, Mass.: Harvard University Press, 2003).

The favourite scapegoat of the Russian nationalist Right, of course, had been the Jews, whose often German-sounding names presented the political anti-Semites with all the evidence they needed of the Jews' divided or non-existent loyalty for the Romanov throne and the Russian Empire. The military command, too, was rife with vicious anti-Semites, beginning with Chief of Staff Ianushkevich, who banned Jewish employees in the public organisations that worked behind the front lines in support of the army. Anti-Jewish measures in occupied Galicia spread back into the rear as local military authorities, seemingly on their own initiative, refused to receive Jewish conscripts into their camps and fortresses. Despite the presence of hundreds of thousands of Jewish conscripts in the army, the tone set from above held that Jews were unsuitable soldierly material and incapable of genuine Russian patriotism. These already firmly held prejudices were not only given new life in the conditions of the martial law regime, but the 1915 retreat marked a historic break in imperial policy towards the Jews when the Pale of Settlement was informally ended. Hundreds of thousands of Jews from the western borderlands now sought shelter and new lives in interior provinces that had never seen any or such large numbers of non-Christian aliens. The military made the least provision for accommodating the Jewish refugees from the war zone and often put obstacles in their way.

As was true for nearly all the refugees who fled from the war zone to the relative security of the interior during the war, so, too, Jewish community leaders in the empire began to organise refugee relief for their co-religionists and co-ethnics.[6] These sorts of non-governmental organisations emerged to fill the gap left by the inadequate response of the imperial officials. (The Tatyana Society, symbolically headed by one of the emperor's daughters, made little dent in the massive social crisis provoked by the refugee problem.) But because most of these organisations defined themselves along ethnic lines, they had the unintended consequence of further reinforcing not just ethnic or national identities, but increasingly exclusivist ones. An applicant for aid had to demonstrate that she was a full-blooded member of the Jewish, Latvian, Polish or other nation. However much good these organisations were able to do for the refugee population, the presence of millions of uprooted human beings left them vulnerable to the often radical appeals of oppositionist parties. The politics of desperation – survival in conditions of economic disorganisation and loss of local control – found fertile ground among the displaced populations

---

6 See Peter Gatrell, *A Whole Empire Walking* (Bloomington: Indiana University Press, 1999).

who had to leave behind their institutions of communal control and self-support.

The Poles were another popular target of the nationalist right, but the Russian government found itself in the curious position of competing with the Germans for Polish loyalties by promising ever-increasing measures of autonomy and unification for a post-war Poland. The Germans started the rivalry by promising to restore a united Poland after the Central Powers' victory; the Russians followed quickly with their own promise to return Poland to the map of Europe under Russian protection, of course. The Germans, in support of their war aims of detaching the 'borderlands' from the Russian Empire, supported oppositionist parties and movements in the League of Foreign Peoples of Russia that embraced Poles, Finns, Ukrainians, Georgians and many others. It was not only the Poles who took heart from this international rivalry for their loyalties; other nations of the empire, particularly the Ukrainians and Finns, began to point to the Polish example as appropriate for their aspirations too. When Nicholas II promised Armenians 'a shining future' on a visit to the Caucasus, they, too, expected dramatic changes in the post-war world. Still, many high-ranking military authorities, and their provisional allies in the public organisations, continued to hold Poles in considerable suspicion and resented the promises made to this periodically rebellious (and ungrateful) subject people. For those Russian nationalists who battled the Ukrainian (and, to a lesser degree, the Belorussian) national movement of the early twentieth century, it was the Poles who were primarily the instigators of any sense of distinct Ukrainian nationality that had emerged over the centuries. To 'win back' the Ukrainians from their Polonised culture and their Greek-Catholic faith, it was also necessary to battle the Roman Catholic and Polish influence in the western borderlands.

In support of the Polish 'project' of the Russian government, the army authorised the creation of separate Polish military formations early in the war. Elsewhere, exile communities in the Russian Empire, from Serbs to Czechs, were also offered the opportunity to organise their own national units to take part in the liberation of their people from the Germanic enemies. Before long, the Russian authorities were recruiting such national military units from among the numerous prisoners of war in Russian camps. Armenians similarly were permitted to organise volunteer military units after the entry of the Turks into the war, also in the name of national liberation. In retrospect, the arming of national liberation movements might have seemed a suicidal policy departure for the multinational Russian Empire, but it was following the practice of most of the belligerents. The Germans outfitted anti-Russian Finnish, Polish and eventually Ukrainian units; for the army of Austria-Hungary armed units manned by ethnic groups who had their counterparts across the border were not much of a departure, but a long-standing principle of military organisation, though much criticised. One of the consequences, nonetheless, of the Russian experiments along these lines was the rise of the politics of the nationalisation of the imperial army, which would split not only the army high command, but soldiers' organisations across the empire and civilian organisations and parties as well. During 1917, nearly every major non-Russian national movement began making claims for their own armed forces.

Although all the ethnic and confessional communities of the empire pro-claimed their solidarity with the emperor's war (even those many groups who had no formal representative in the Duma), the wartime climate of suspi-cion, espionage and treason spread from the western borderlands, where the fighting was most intense, into the rest of the empire. After the entry of the Ottoman Empire into the war on the side of the Central Powers, the Turkic and Muslim populations of the empire came under increasing scrutiny, despite generally low levels of flight or oppositionist sentiment. The campaigns on the Caucasian front also soon resulted in a large influx of Armenian refugees from the Turkish forced march and massacre of 1915; most of them ended up in the first major city across the border, Baku, which was also home to Azeri Turks and others. Despite the efforts of the enthusiastically pro-Armenian Viceroy Vorontsov-Dashkov in Tiflis, the Armenians suffered new pogroms after their escape from the Ottoman Turks on the part of local Turks who were, similar to their counterparts in European Russia, largely overwhelmed by the influx of new populations without income, housing and community resources.

The most violent ethnic conflict of the war came in the Steppe region and Turkestan (today's Central Asia) in 1916. The army, haemorrhaging from the devastating losses during the first two years of fighting, insisted on a labour mobilisation of ethnic groups previously exempt from military service in June 1916. Throughout July and August the Turkic natives, largely Kazakhs and Kirgiz, rose up against the Russian and Ukrainian peasants who had only recently been resettled in the area as part of Stolypin's solution to the agrarian problem. Conflict over land use and other resources provided the broader context for the bloodletting, but the immediate excuse was the call-up to labour service. As many as 1,000,000 Kazakhs and Kirgiz lost their lives in the widespread pogroms or fled to Chinese Turkestan across the eastern border. Only in mid-January 1917 did Russian officials regain control over the region. In the meantime, 9,000 Slavic homesteads had been destroyed and 3,500 settlers killed in what looked very much like a conventional colonial war.

In short, the wartime policies and the economic hardships that were their mostly unintended consequences shaped a hardening of ethnic and national identities that quickly filled the ideological space after the abdication of Nicholas II and the discrediting of the monarchical principle. This dynamic is key to understanding the dismantling of the Russian Empire in 1917 and beyond.

## The politics of war

The war shaped a dramatic transformation of political life in the Russian Empire. At one level, that of the autocrat, it was as if little had changed. Nicholas II seemed as determined as ever to undermine his own government in the name of defence of his autocratic prerogatives. But the poor performance of the Russian army in the first year of the war, and especially the 'Great Retreat' and munitions crisis of 1915, emboldened the opposition to challenge the court for new political reforms. The Progressive Bloc, a coalition of parties from progressive nationalists to Kadets, demanded among other things a government of confidence, amnesty for those convicted or deported without trial on religious and political grounds, the repeal of discriminatory measures against Poles, Jews, Ukrainians and religious minorities, concessions to Finland and the extension of local self-government – in other words, respect for the constitution. The emperor angrily prorogued the Duma and decided to leave for the front to replace his great-uncle as commander-in-chief. That decision was certain to introduce yet more confusion and lack of co-ordination in the government, as court intrigues and constant personnel replacements came to replace policy-making; the possibility of any co-operation with 'society', even in the Duma, seemed more and more remote.

Still, the moderate opposition was able and willing to cloak itself in the cause of patriotism in its conflict with the autocracy to a far greater degree than it had during the Russo-Japanese war. Oppositionist patriotism, in the form of a defence of Russia's Great Power status and the integrity of the empire, united the Right and Centre parties of the political spectrum. The Bolsheviks had cast the lone votes against war credits for the government in the Duma and were promptly arrested on charges of treason, and they were joined by the Mensheviks in a resolution condemning the war and the political and social order that had brought it about. The two largest socialist parties, the Mensheviks and Socialist Revolutionaries, quickly faced splits in their leadership over rival programmes of internationalism and the pursuit of immediate peace or more patriotic justifications for war in the name of combating German militarism. Here was born the ideology of defencism (and later, revolutionary defencism), a type of left-wing patriotism that would play a large role during 1917 and after.[7] The revolutionary parties, or at least a large part of their mass membership, thereby began to express an ideological justification for the further pursuit of war and the mobilisation of society in that cause. Against a European-wide tradition of anti-militarism and international peace, this development portended a new era of revolutionary politics. Still, by 1917 society was poised to reorganise itself along lines of war and peace, even if those lines were frequently shifting.

Perhaps an even more important development of the early war years than the relative impotence of the legal political parties and the tacit dissolution of the Duma was the, in part, compensatory rise of what has been recently described as 'the parastatal complex',[8] semi-public, semi-state structures that were summoned into being by the tragically evident shortcomings of the government in outfitting its own war effort and by the political class of educated society demanding a role in this war effort. The largest and most influential of these organisations were: the union of *zemstvos*, the union of towns and the war industries committees. The *zemstvos*, organs of local self-government, were the first to propose an expanded role for society when they founded the All-Russian Union for the Relief of Sick and Wounded Soldiers. The Moscow provincial *zemstvo* convened an emergency session on 7 August 1914, and succeeded in enlisting thirty-five provincial *zemstvos* in its relief initiative. The tsar reluctantly acknowledged their offer, and ungraciously warned that their existence would be limited to the duration of the war. A loose agreement divided up the empire between the Red Cross and the War Ministry, on the one hand, and the union on the other, with the Red Cross serving the immediate front-line area. In fact, the unions' legal status remained unsettled throughout their existence because the Duma was unable to pass legislation regulating their activities; this extra-legal, or illegal, status, was characteristic of several of the agencies that emerged during the war years. This seeming disability notwithstanding, the expansion of *zemstvo* activities significantly transformed local government and

7 See Ziva Galili y Garcia, 'Origins of Revolutionary Defensism: I. G. Tsereteli and the "Siberian Zimmerwaldists"', *Slavic Review* 41 (Sept. 1982): 454–76; George Katkov, *Russia 1917: The February Revolution* (New York: Harper and Row, 1967), pp. 23–37.
8 See Peter Holquist, *Making War, Forging Revolution* (Cambridge, Mass.: Harvard University Press, 2002), pp. 4, 21, 26–7, 28, 30, 38. Holquist adapts this term from historian of Germany Michael Geyer, 'The Stigma of Violence, Nationalism and War in Twentieth Century Germany', *German Studies Review*, special issue (1992): 75–110.

forced open the franchise of the local bodies to include large numbers of the technical and professional intelligentsia. As an indicator of their semi-public, semi-state status, *zemstvo* doctors were exempt from the draft.[9] From their initial charge to aid in the evacuation of wounded soldiers from the front, the unions moved into army supply of food and clothing, civilian public health and food supply, refugee relief and other spheres.

As the war situation deteriorated, the parastatal complex expanded its activities to help mobilise industry more effectively, in effect becoming an integral part of the military supply administration. In response to the munitions crisis of the first year of the war, patriotic business circles created the war industries committees in mid-1915 and brought together representatives of the government, business, public organisations and eventually labour, in a revolutionary departure from Russia's traditional administrative practices, but here, too, in the name of mobilising the economy more effectively for the war effort.[10] The issue of working-class participation forced the socialist parties to face squarely the dilemmas of defencism in late 1915 and they split over their tactics towards collaborating with the 'bourgeois' government. Initially, Menshevik Internationalists and Bolsheviks were in a minority in advocating boycott on the grounds that workers must not support a bourgeois government engaged in an imperialistic war. The leaders of the war industries committees themselves, the industrialists of Moscow and the provinces, largely supported what they called 'healthy militarism' in the name of 'Great Russia'. Though they contributed significantly to the mobilisation of industry for the war, their efforts were frustrated by continuing governmental intransigence, their own disunity and growing social conflicts articulated by the workers' groups that formed throughout the country under their aegis. The imperial government even embarked on a brief experiment to integrate the war effort with the creation of a Special Council for Defence in August 1915.

Later initiatives of the parastatal complex extended to the food supply and the efforts to overcome the failings of the market in getting food to where it needed to be delivered. If we add to this the previously mentioned organisations that arose to tend to the needs of refugees, we have a picture of tremendous, unprecedented self-mobilisation of society in the cause of war. This was as much a 'societalisation' of the military as it was a militarisation of society,[11]

---

9 See William Ewing Gleason, 'The All-Russian Union of Towns and the All-Russian Union of Zemstvos in World War I: 1914–1917', Ph. D. diss., Indiana University, 1972.
10 See Lewis Siegelbaum, *The Politics of Industrial Mobilization, 1914–1917: A Study of the War-Industries Committees* (New York: St Martin's Press, 1983).
11 Holquist, *Making War*, pp. 211–12.

in which relations between the civilian and military elites were remarkably intimate. Characteristically, the chairman of the unions, Prince L'vov, was fond of extolling the 'unity of the army and the people', and the conflation of civilian and military spheres of the Russian state was proceeding at an alarming pace. The model for many in the public organisations was the wartime economy of Germany, but with less reliance on a far less-developed Russian market economy and an even larger role for the state than in Germany itself. As Nicholas II persistently undermined the legitimacy and functioning of the official state institutions, the military and the parastatal complex took over more and more of the state's actual functioning. In so doing, they also came to see themselves as a rival state and increasingly challenged the autocracy on its right to rule on the basis of that experience. Indeed, by 1916, the chairman of the Council of Ministers, B. V. Shtiurmer, warned that Russia would soon have two governments; and in April 1916 the government banned all public congresses and conferences, but had to back down in the face of public pressure. Other government officials and members of the court also feared the ambitions of the war industries committees and saw in them a source of sedition, 'a second government' or even 'revolutionary organ'. That the centre of both the unions' activities and the war industries committees' most energetic opposition was in Moscow underlined the emerging split within the Russian ruling elite.

## Revolution and the transformation of war

It was probably only the delegation from army headquarters that could have persuaded Nicholas II to abdicate 'for the sake of saving Russia and for the victorious ending of the war' in March 1917. And so the war that Nicholas had reluctantly embarked upon and almost wilfully mismanaged brought him down together with the dynasty itself. The Provisional Government that took power in Petrograd was nothing less than the new elite of the parastatal complex that had grown up in the interstices of government inefficiency during the wartime years. The new prime minister, Prince L'vov, was chairman of the All-Russian Union of *Zemstvos*; Russia's first-ever civilian war minister, Aleksandr Guchkov, was chairman of the Moscow War Industries Committee. Other ministers in the new cabinet (Tereshchenko, Manuilov) shared similar wartime experiences in the public organisations. The new government proceeded to dismiss local officials and replace them with 'their people', often introducing a great deal of confusion into local administration. At the same time, they appealed to 'society' to join with them in the new politics and to help consolidate the 'revolution'.

These appeals were heeded not only by educated society, but by organisations that quickly mobilised to speak for labour, peasants, soldiers, Cossacks
and any number of other groups that had felt excluded or marginalised in the
imperial political order: urban and rural soviets, trade unions, factory committees, workers' militias, food and land committees and others. They took
advantage of the new freedoms to call organisational congresses and make
their own claims to the revolution's agenda of transformation. The organisations took on themselves very practical functions largely out of self-defence
when the traditional forces of law and order lost control over the country, but
they also articulated various ideologies of self-rule and self-government (and
freedom from external authorities) in their local affairs. This was a new type
of parastatal complex emerging in response to the perceived elite politics of
educated society and its organisations.[12]

In particular, workers and peasants, parallel to and often overlapping with
various national groups, began arming themselves against marauders in Red
Guards, factory militias and partisan detachments in a further stage of the inter-
penetration of society and army and in a militarisation of the class divisions
of imperial society. At the same time, the new political class, both the Provisional Government representatives of educated society and the self-proclaimed
spokesmen of democracy (the soldiers, workers and peasants) in the Petrograd
Soviet coalition of moderate socialist parties, appealed to the soldiers to support the revolution and the new state. This change in attitude towards the
army was remarkable and was the result of the wartime evolution of attitudes towards patriotism and the war itself on the part of nearly all the major
political parties. Now that the autocracy was no more and the 'Revolution'
was in power, society was expected to understand the need for continued
mobilisation and sacrifice for the war against the German enemy. Revolutionary defencism permitted a good part of the socialist Left to join with the
liberals of the Provisional Government in patriotic unity. The opposition to
the war did not go away, however, and splits deepened among the socialists
and anarchists between revolutionary defencists, internationalists who sought
an honourable, democratic peace and a small but growing minority movement, led by Lenin and the Bolsheviks, who called for Russia's defeat and the
radicalisation of the revolution.

12 On these organisations, see John L. H. Keep, *The Russian Revolution: A Study in Mass
Mobilization* (New York: Norton, 1976), though Keep's focus is not on the extension of
the parastatal complex to the previously disfranchised layers of the population, but their
co-optation by the Bolsheviks during 1917 and 1918.

The extension of political citizenship to the soldiers in Orders No. 1 and 2 in March 1917 marked a new stage in the conflation of political and military power in Russia. Soldiers made use of their new freedoms to demand democratic reforms of the army, including the election of soldiers' committees to run day-to-day affairs in units. Although intended only for the Petrograd garrison, this new military order spread throughout the disintegrating imperial army as soldiers entered political life as defenders of revolutionary Russia. There were alarming signs of the coming civil war in the army as well, as officers deemed insufficiently sympathetic to the revolution were executed by self-appointed revolutionary committees.

The return of émigrés and exiles from years abroad or in Siberia contributed to a general radicalisation of politics towards the left. This included the rise of an important set of non-Russian national proto-elites who began to seize part of the local political resources that were available in the growing vacuum of central control. In Ukraine, Georgia, Latvia, Finland and elsewhere, the new elites began challenging the parastatal complex that had come to power in Petrograd over the terms of rule and governance. The Provisional Government preferred to postpone any restructuring of the former empire until the convocation of the Constituent Assembly, but the continued deterioration of the centre's authority brought forth the response of escalating demands for autonomy for local decision makers. Here, too, soldiers played important, if sometimes conflicting, roles. The army, too, was not only not spared the general economic deterioration of the country, but probably suffered more and was asked a greater sacrifice. Deteriorating morale in the army led Aleksandr Kerensky, the prime minister of the third coalition Provisional Government, to conclude that a new offensive was the only solution to the further Bolshevisation of the soldiers. That disastrous June offensive against the Central Powers marked the end of the imperial army as an institution and its transformation into a variety of successor militaries. Kerensky, incidentally, in a new stage of the conflation of military and civilian spheres, added to his responsibilities as prime minister those of war minister.

The failed offensive also weakened the resistance of the army high command to another proposed solution to the Bolshevisation of the soldiers, namely, the nationalisation of the imperial army. The largest such movement was among the Ukrainians, who argued that allowing soldiers to fight alongside their co-nationals would enable the military to mobilise their fighting spirit and better defend their native land. This movement spread to other non-Russian groups and frequently provoked counter-mobilisations on the part of self-identified 'Russian' soldiers. The conflicts of the early years of the war, especially in the prisoner-of-war camps, were now infiltrating the army itself. And the constant rhythm of army and national congresses and conferences and the reassignments and reorganisations that were agreed to in the name of these nationalisations led to further disorganisation in the military and the collapse of its fighting capacity. The deterioration of the generals' place in politics was captured by the failure of the coup by General Lavr Kornilov in August, which was itself intended as a move largely to reverse the decline in order and security.

The Bolsheviks who seized power in October 1917 proclaimed peace to all the belligerent powers and hoped that they would have a peaceful breathing spell to consolidate their new regime. The Germans, though they had supported just such a revolutionary outcome in Russia from the beginning of the war (and had sent the Bolshevik leader Vladimir Lenin back from his exile in Zurich across German-occupied Central Europe), saw an opportunity to break the stalemate of the previous year and advanced on the fledgling revolutionary dictatorship. The splits that had transformed the politics of moderate socialists now were replicated in the republic of soviets. Revolutionary defencism moved yet further to the left and allowed the mobilisation of war to be harnessed to a programme of socialist transformation of the nation. The hard-headed Lenin, however, had little initial faith in the demoralised soldiers to defend the latest version of the revolution; he fought hard for peace with the Germans. After they had occupied most of Ukraine, Belorussia and the Baltic coast, and only after he threatened to resign his party and state posts, did Lenin get his way. He bought peace with the surrender of the western borderlands to the enemy and was not forgiven for many years by patriotic Bolsheviks who wanted to carry the international revolutionary war to Europe and beyond. (Other Russian nationalist forces also considered the Brest Treaty a betrayal of 'Russia's' national interests.)

Still, even the initial experience with the steamrollering German army during the winter of 1917–18 forced another epochal change on the Bolshevik Party, which had not only opposed the war but had also been opposed to a standing, professional army. In the spring of 1918, the party leadership began to jettison its objections to an effective, bureaucratic fighting force and its previous attachment to a democratic, militia force that would unite a democratic citizenry in self-defence. Though the Bolsheviks' real baptism by fire would come in the civil war fought against the Whites and other rivals, the German invasion of winter 1917–18 was their wake-up call and had been prepared by the ongoing realignment of socialism and war mobilisation that was captured by the slogan of revolutionary defencism and the general trend of conflating military and civilian spheres.

Moreover, the Bolsheviks carried further the innovations in political-military organisation that the Provisional Government had introduced in 1917 under Kerensky. Not trusting in the spontaneous politics of the soldiers but acknowledging their potential as cultural and organisational forces in the country, the Provisional Government created a 'Bureau for Socio-Political Enlightenment' and eventually an entire Political Directorate of the War Ministry to channel the considerable political energies of the soldiers in support of the regime. The Bolsheviks waited only until April 1918 before it replicated this experiment with its own Political Directorate of the Workers' and Peasants' Red Army. The conflation of civilian and military spheres that Kerensky attempted to push forward from the summer of 1917 was finally accomplished by the Bolsheviks in their creation of the Council of Defence. The new form of parastatal complex that had emerged over the course of 1917, the soviet network of local organs of self-administration, was attached to the new war mobilisation effort as the revolution spread across a war-weary population.

## 1918, the final year of war: occupation and intervention

After the winter assault of the Central Powers, the eastern front became the occupation regime of Germany and Austria-Hungary over the lands they acquired under the harsh and exploitative terms of the Treaty of Brest-Litovsk.[13] The war had taken its toll on the Central Powers, too, and the Russian Revolutions of 1917 had created new senses of possibility for oppositionist politicians there too. Not surprisingly, new revolutionary governments supplanted the dynastic monarchies very shortly after the capitulation of Germany and Austria-Hungary in November 1918. In the intervening year, the two armies served to shield a series of recently proclaimed sovereign states along the western and southern borders of Bolshevik Russia. From Finland to Georgia the Central Powers appeared to have accomplished one of their most important wartime goals, the detaching of the borderland peoples (*Randvölker*) from the Russian heartland. Only now that a genuinely revolutionary regime was in place in Petrograd (soon to relocate to Moscow), Germany and Austria-Hungary (and the other major belligerent powers as well) began to fear the

13 See John W. Wheeler-Bennett, *Brest-Litovsk: The Forgotten Peace, March 1918* (London: Macmillan, 1938).

'contagion' would spread to their own war-weary and weakened populations. Early in the war Lenin had called for the transformation of the international war into a global civil war. That threat came much closer to realisation due to the continued involvement of the major belligerent powers in the conflicts on the territory of the now former Russian Empire.

The war also continued by proxy when the Entente Powers recognised the Bolsheviks' leading rivals, the volunteer army of South Russia, as the legitimate successor government of Russia, especially after the Bolsheviks signed the peace treaty with the Central Powers and thereby threatened to give the Germans one more respite on the eastern front. In order to keep Russia in the war, mainly the British, French and American (soon joined by the Japanese) governments sent advisers, some arms and military equipment to the anti-Bolshevik forces who became known as the Whites. The core of the White movement was former imperial military men, but they were joined by representatives of the former civilian political elites of the Provisional Government, who had recently been Centrist-Left in their politics but who mostly moved rapidly to the right over the course of 1917. Among other platforms, they persisted in their patriotic defence of the integrity of the Russian Empire as they had earlier in the war. Because these anti-Bolshevik proto-states (the most important in the south of Denikin and Wrangel, Siberia under Admiral Kolchak and the north-east under General Yudenich) were forced to operate on the peripheries of the former empire, however, in borderland regions of ethnically very mixed populations (and certainly not necessarily dominated by Russian nationals), this politics undermined their cause, especially when the Bolsheviks (and even Woodrow Wilson) were promising varying degrees of national self-determination. Not surprisingly, the Whites made scant progress in uniting the anti-Bolshevik forces across the empire, notably the Cossacks, Ukrainians, Finns and Turko-Muslim peoples. In fact, they were barely able to sustain a united front among themselves over such fundamental issues as the conduct of the anti-Bolshevik war or how much of the recently overturned political and socio-economic orders to restore.

Even had the White military and political leadership been able to forge a more unified front, the Entente allies, too, quarrelled among themselves over the post-war order; both their leaders and their local representatives had little understanding of the local conditions or national political forces where they chose to intervene, and they also faced war-weary populations back home and in their overseas colonies. The relatively insignificant material contributions of the foreign supporters of intervention in Russian affairs nonetheless helped to prolong the violence and fighting of the civil war for at least three years after the formal end of the world war itself in November 1918. And it provided the Bolshevik state with one of its most powerful founding myths, that of 'capitalist encirclement'. The Russian Soviet Republic declared itself an armed camp and began to build its own form of socialist state under the pressures of wartime mobilisation of economy and society. This was to be only one of many lasting legacies of this brutal, modern, total world war.

# 4

# The Revolutions of 1917–1918

S. A. SMITH

On 23 February 1917 thousands of female textile workers and housewives took to the streets of Petrograd to protest against the bread shortage and to mark International Women's Day.[1] Their protest occurred against a background of industrial unrest – only the day before, workers at the giant Putilov plant had been locked out – and their demonstration quickly drew in workers, especially in the militant Vyborg district. By the following day, more than 200,000 workers were on strike. The leaders of the revolutionary parties were taken by surprise at the speed with which the protests gathered momentum, but experienced activists, who included Bolsheviks, anti-war Socialist Revolutionaries (SRs) and non-aligned Social Democrats, gave direction to the movement in the working-class districts.[2] By 25 February students and members of the middle classes had joined the crowds in the city centre, singing the Marseillaise, waving red flags and bearing banners proclaiming 'Down with the War' and 'Down with the Tsarist Government'. Soldiers from the garrison proved reluctant to clear the demonstrators from the streets. On Sunday, 26 February, however, they were ordered to fire on the crowds and by the end of the day hundreds had been killed or wounded. The next day proved to be a turning-point. On the morning of 27 February, the Volynskii regiment mutinied and by evening 66,700 soldiers had followed their lead. Demonstrators freed prisoners from the Kresty jail,

---

1 The following is based on: Tsuyoshi Hasegawa, *The February Revolution: Petrograd, 1917* (Seattle: University of Washington Press, 1981); Orlando Figes, *A People's Tragedy: The Russian Revolution, 1891–1924* (London: Jonathan Cape, 1996), ch. 8; Marc Ferro, *The Russian Revolution of February 1917* (London: Routledge and Kegan Paul, 1972); George Katkov, *Russia 1917: The February Revolution* (London: Longman, 1967); E. N. Burdzhalov, *Russia's Second Revolution: The February 1917 Uprising in Petrograd*, trans. Donald J. Raleigh (Bloomington: Indiana University Press, 1987); E. N. Burdzhalov, *Vtoraia russkaia revoliutsiia: Moskva, front, periferiia* (Moscow: Nauka, 1971).

2 Michael Melancon, *The Socialist Revolutionaries and the Russian Anti-War Movement, 1914–1917* (Columbus: Ohio State University Press, 1990); D. A. Longley, 'The Mezhraionka, International Women's Day: In Response to Michael Melancon', *Soviet Studies* 4, 41 (1989): 625–45; James D. White, 'The February Revolution and the Bolshevik District Committee', *Soviet Studies* 4, 41 (1989): 603–24.

set fire to police stations, 'blinded' portraits of the tsar and 'roasted', that is, set alight, the crowned two-headed eagle, symbol of the Romanov dynasty.[3] Despite orders from Tsar Nicholas II – with apparent support from the high command – to crush the uprising, the military authorities were unable to summon sufficient loyal troops to do so.

On 27 February pro-war Mensheviks associated with the Workers' Group of the War Industries Committee moved to assert their authority by calling on all factories and military units to elect delegates to a soviet, or council, designed as a temporary organ to direct the revolutionary movement. Within a week 1,200 deputies had been elected to the Petrograd Soviet.[4] On the night of 27 February, the tsar's cabinet resigned, after proposing that the tsar establish a military dictatorship. The liberal politicians in the Duma, who had hitherto reacted to the insurgency with indecision, now formed a temporary committee to restore order and realise their long-standing aspiration of a constitutional monarchy. They endeavoured to persuade the military high command that only the abdication of Nicholas in favour of his son could ensure the successful prolongation of the war. The generals did not need much persuading. Only two corps commanders would offer their services to the tsar, and only a couple would later resign rather than swear loyalty to the Provisional Government. Among the tens of thousands of officers promoted during the war, there was general sympathy for the revolution. Faced with the loss of confidence of his generals, Nicholas abdicated in favour of his brother, Grand Duke Mikhail. It did not take much to persuade Mikhail that the masses would not accept this outcome and, as a result, on 3 March the 300-year-old Romanov dynasty came to an end.[5] Few bemoaned the passing of tsarism. The Bloody Sunday massacre of 1905 had shattered popular faith in a benevolent tsar, and residual loyalty to Nicholas had been swept away during the war by rumours of sexual shenanigans and pro-German sympathies at court.

The two forces that brought down the monarchy – the movement of workers and soldiers and the middle-class parliamentary opposition – became institutionalised in the post-revolutionary political order, which soon became known as 'dual power'. The Duma committee, which had formed on 27 February, was acutely aware that it had no authority among the masses. Only on 2 March, after political infighting, did it draw up a list of members of a Provisional

3 Orlando Figes and Boris Kolonitskii, *Interpreting the Russian Revolution: The Language and Symbols of 1917* (New Haven: Yale University Press, 1999), p. 48.
4 Iu. S. Tokarev, *Petrogradskii sovet rabochikh i soldatskikh deputatov v marte i aprele 1917 g.* (Leningrad: Nauka, 1976), p. 120.
5 Mark D. Steinberg and Vladimir M. Khrustalëv, *The Fall of the Romanovs* (New Haven: Yale University Press, 1995 ), pp. 61–5.

Government. Headed by Prince G. E. L'vov, a landowner with a record of service to the zemstvos, it was broadly representative of professional and business interests and liberal, even mildly populist in its politics. The only organised political force within the new government were the Kadets, a liberal party increasingly defined by its intransigent defence of the imperial-national state. In its manifesto of 2 March, the Provisional Government committed itself to a far-reaching programme of civil and political rights, promising to convoke a Constituent Assembly to determine the shape of the future polity. It said nothing, however, about the burning issues of war and land. This was in keeping with the Kadet view that the February events constituted a political but not a social revolution.

In a bid to widen their base of support, the Duma politicians pressed the Petrograd Soviet to join the new government. Only Aleksandr Kerensky, a radical lawyer, agreed to do so, proclaiming that he would be hostage of the 'democracy' within the bourgeois government. The rest of the left-wing Mensheviks and SRs on the Executive Committee (EC) of the Soviet rejected the invitation to join the government since they believed Russia was undergoing a 'bourgeois' revolution and was destined to undergo a long period of capitalist development and parliamentary democracy before it would be ripe for socialism. At the same time, they rejected calls, such as that which came from the Vyborg district committee of the Bolshevik Party, to make the Soviet the provisional government, since they feared that this might provoke conservative elements in the army to crush the revolution.[6] On 2 March, therefore, the Soviet agreed that it would support the Provisional Government in so far as it carried out a programme of democratic reform but would not be bound by its domestic or foreign policies.[7] Thus was born 'dual power', wherein the Provisional Government enjoyed formal authority but the Soviet EC enjoyed real power, by virtue of its influence over the garrison and workers in transport and communications and general support among the populace. Some have cast doubt on the adequacy of the 'dual power' formulation, correctly pointing out that even at this stage real power lay with the workers and soldiers rather than the EC.[8] Nevertheless, it has the merit of reminding us that from the outset the new revolutionary order expressed the deep social division between the 'democracy' and propertied society.

6 David A. Longley, 'Divisions in the Bolshevik Party in March 1917', Soviet Studies 24, 1 (1972–3): 61–76.
7 Petrogradskii Sovet rabochikh i soldatskikh deputatov v 1917 godu, vol. 1 (Leningrad: Nauka, 1991), p. 59.
8 T. Hasegawa, 'The Problem of Power in the February Revolution', Canadian Slavonic Papers 14 (1972): 611–32.

Outside Petrograd dual power was less in evidence. In most places a broad alliance of social groups formed committees of public organisations that ejected police and tsarist officials, maintained order and food supply and later oversaw the democratisation of the municipal dumas and rural *zemstvos*. In March, 79 such committees were set up at provincial level, 651 at county (*uezd*) level and over 9,000 at township (*volost'*) level.[9] The committee in faraway Irkutsk was typical in defining its task as 'carrying the revolution to its conclusion and strengthening the foundations of freedom and popular power'.[10] Unlike the soviets, whose rising popularity would soon undermine them, the committees were not defined by political partisanship. In the township-level committees in Saratov province, for example, no fewer than three-quarters of members were non-party.[11] In seeking to establish its authority in the localities, the Provisional Government chose to bypass these committees and to appoint provincial and county commissars, many of whom were chairs of county *zemstvos* who hailed from landed or middle-class backgrounds and who did not command popular favour. Grass-roots pressure to democratise *zemstvos* and municipal dumas soon built up: by mid-October, dumas had been re-elected in 650 out of 798 towns.[12] The democratisation of the *zemstvos* and the rise of the soviets spelt the end of the public committees. The Provisional Government never established effective authority in the localities and, as the social and political crisis deepened in summer 1917, power became ever more fragmented. In a crucial sphere such as food supply, for example, the government supply organs, working in tandem with the co-operatives, competed with the respective food-supply commissions of the soviet, the local garrison, trade unions and factory committees.

In the countryside the revolution swept away land captains, township elders and village constables and replaced them with township committees elected by the peasants.[13] By July these were ubiquitous – there being over 15,000

9 G. A. Gerasimenko, 'Transformatsiia vlasti v Rossii v 1917 g.', *Otechestvennaia istoriia*, 1997, no. 1: 63.
10 G. A. Gerasimenko, *Pervyi akt narodovlastiia v Rossii: obshchestvennye ispolnitel'nye komitety 1917 g.* (Moscow: NIKA, 1992), p. 132.
11 Ibid., p. 106.
12 Kh. M. Astrakhan, *Bol'sheviki i ikh politicheskie protivniki v 1917 godu* (Leningrad: Lenizdat, 1973), p. 365.
13 The discussion of the peasants here and below is based on: J. L. H. Keep, *The Russian Revolution: A Study in Mass Mobilization* (New York: Norton, 1976), p. 3; Graeme J. Gill, *Peasants and Government in the Russian Revolution* (London: Macmillan, 1979); John Channon, 'The Peasantry in the Revolutions of 1917', in E. R. Frankel et al. (eds.), *Revolution in Russia: Reassessments of 1917* (Cambridge: Cambridge University Press, 1992), pp. 105–30; Orlando Figes, *Peasant Russia, Civil War: The Volga Countryside in Revolution (1917–21)* (Oxford: Clarendon Press, 1989), ch. 2; Maureen Perrie, 'The Peasants', in Robert Service

townships across the country – and later some adopted the appellation 'soviet'. The government attempted to strengthen its authority by setting up land and food committees at township level, but these were soon taken over by the peasants. Meanwhile the authority of the village gathering was strengthened, as younger sons, landless labourers, village intelligentsia (scribes, teachers, vets and doctors) and even some women began to participate in its deliberations. The revolution thus substantially reduced the degree of interference in village life by external authority and after October the peasants came to associate this unprecedented degree of self-government with soviet power.

In the course of spring 1917, some 700 soviets were formed, involving around 200,000 deputies.[14] By October, 1,429 soviets functioned in Russia, 706 of which consisted of workers' and soldiers' deputies, 235 of workers', soldiers' and peasants' deputies, 455 of peasants' deputies, and 33 of soldiers' deputies.[15] They represented about one-third of the population. Soviets saw themselves as representing the 'revolutionary democracy', a bloc of social groups comprising workers, soldiers and peasants, and often stretching to include white-collar employees and professionals, such as teachers, journalists, lawyers or doctors, and in some cases representatives of ethnic minorities. The Omsk soviet described itself as the 'sole representative of the local proletariat and of the general labouring masses of the local population and army'.[16] The basic principles of soviet democracy were that deputies were elected directly by and were subject to immediate recall by those they represented. The Mensheviks and SRs, who were the leading force in the soviets until autumn, saw their function as being to exercise 'control' over local government in the interests of revolutionary democracy. Soviets generally did not see themselves as rivals to elected organs of local government and championed the democratisation of dumas and the speedy election of a Constituent Assembly. In practice, they soon took on tasks of practical administration, concerning themselves with everything from fuel supply, to education, to policing.[17] In a small number of cases, soviets declared themselves the sole authority in a particular locality: in Kronstadt the soviet, which consisted of 96 Bolsheviks, 96 non-party deputies,

(ed.), *Society and Politics in the Russian Revolution* (London: Macmillan, 1992), pp. 12–34; Christopher Read, *From Tsar to Soviets* (London: UCL Press, 1996), ch. 5.
14 Gerasimenko, 'Transformatsiia', p. 64.
15 N. N. Smirnov, 'The Soviets', in Edward Acton et al. (eds.), *Critical Companion to the Russian Revolution, 1914–1921* (London: Arnold, 1997), p. 432.
16 Gosarkhiv Omskoi oblasti, f. R-662, op.1, d.8, l.1.
17 Israel Getzler, 'The Soviets as Agents of Democratisation', in Frankel et al., *Revolution in Russia*, pp. 17–33.

73 Left SRs, 13 Mensheviks and 7 anarchists, caused a furore when it refused to recognise the government in May.[18]

## The aspirations of the masses

Liberty and democracy were the watchwords of the February Revolution. New symbols of liberty, of republic and of justice, drawn mainly from the French Revolution and the European socialist and labour movements, made their appearance. 'Free Russia' was personified as a beautiful woman in national costume or as a heroine breaking the chains of tsarism, wearing a laurel wreath, or bearing a shield.[19] These symbols were embraced by all who identified the February Revolution with liberation from autocracy.[20] Red, once a colour to cause the propertied classes to tremble, became an emblem of the revolution.[21] All agreed that, in order to realise freedom, they must organise collectively. 'Organise!' screamed placards and orators on the streets, and as people organised, interest in politics grew exponentially. John Reed, the American journalist who later came to witness the revolution, observed: 'For months in Petrograd, and all over Russia, every street-corner was a public tribune. In railway-trains, street-cars, always the spurting up of impromptu debate, everywhere.'[22]

Yet from the first, the scope of the democratic revolution was in dispute. For the privileged classes, the overthrow of autocracy had been an act of self-preservation necessitated by the need to bring victory in war and engender a renaissance of the Russian people. For the lower classes, liberty and democracy signalled nothing short of a social revolution that would entail the comprehensive destruction of the old order and the construction of a new way of life in accordance with justice and freedom. Even peasants proclaimed themselves free citizens and showed a rudimentary familiarity with notions of a constitution, a democratic republic, civil and political rights. Yet for them, as for the lower classes in general, democracy was principally about solving their

18 Israel Getzler, *Kronstadt, 1917–1921: The Fate of a Soviet Democracy* (Cambridge: Cambridge University Press, 1983), p. 66.
19 P. K. Kornakov, 'Simvolika i rituály revoliutsii 1917 g.', in *Anatomiia revoliutsii: 1917 god v revoliutsii – massy, partii, vlast'* (St Petersburg: Glagol', 1994), pp. 356–65; Richard Stites, 'The Role of Ritual and Symbols', in Acton et al., *Critical Companion*, pp. 565–71.
20 Figes and Kolonitskii, *Interpreting*, p. 69.
21 B. I. Kolonitskii, *Simvoly vlasti i bor'ba za vlast'* (St Petersburg: Dmitrii Bulanin, 2001), pp. 250–84.
22 John Reed, *Ten Days that Shook the World* (Harmondsworth: Penguin, 1970), p. 40.

pressing socio-economic problems and only secondarily about questions of law and political representation.[23]

There were around nine million men in uniform in 1917 and soldiers were to become a force of huge importance in promoting the social revolution.[24] Though they lacked the high level of organisation of workers, they were crucial in weakening the Provisional Government, in politicising the peasantry and, after October, in establishing soviet power. Soldiers and sailors greeted the downfall of the tsar with joy, seeing in it a signal to overthrow the oppressive command structure of the tsarist army. Tyrannical officers were removed and sometimes killed – lynchings being worst in the Baltic Fleet, with Kronstadt sailors killing about fifty officers. Soldiers celebrated the fact that they were now citizens of free Russia, and demanded an end to degrading treatment, the right to meet and petition, and improvements in condition and pay. Crucially, they formed committees at each level of the army hierarchy. This drive to democratise relations between officers and men was authorised on 1 March by Order No. 1 of the Petrograd Soviet, which proved to be its most radical undertaking. General M. V. Alekseev pronounced the Order 'the means by which the army I command will be destroyed'.[25] In practice, the soldiers' committees were dominated by more educated elements, including non-commissioned officers, medical and clerical staff, who had little desire to sabotage the operational effectiveness of the army. Most soldiers wanted a speedy peace, but did not wish to expose free revolutionary Russia to Austro-German attack. At the same time, if democratisation did not mean – at least in the spring and early summer – the disintegration of the army as a fighting force, it was clear that it could no longer be relied upon to perform its customary function of suppressing domestic disorder.

Industrial workers were the most politicised, organised and strategically positioned of all social groups in 1917.[26] Something like two-thirds were recent

23 Mark D. Steinberg, *Voices of Revolution, 1917. Documents*, trans. Marian Schwartz (New Haven: Yale University Press, 2001), pp. 10, 13.
24 The following is based on A. K. Wildman, *The End of the Russian Imperial Army: The Old Army and the Soldiers' Revolt (March–April 1917)* (Princeton: Princeton University Press, 1980); Evan Mawdsley, *The Russian Baltic Fleet: War and Politics, February 1917–April 1918* (London: Macmillan, 1978); Evan Mawdsley, 'Soldiers and Sailors', in Service (ed.), *Society and Politics*, pp. 103–19; Norman Stone, *The Eastern Front, 1914–1917* (London: Hodder and Stoughton, 1975); Howard White, '1917 in the Rear Garrison', in Linda Edmondson and Peter Waldron (eds.), *Economy and Society in Russia and the Soviet Union, 1860–1930* (London: Macmillan, 1992), pp. 152–68.
25 R. P. Browder and A. F. Kerensky (eds.), *The Russian Provisional Government, 1917*, vol. II (Stanford, Calif.: Stanford University Press, 1961), p. 851.
26 The following is based on Tim McDaniel, *Autocracy, Capitalism, and Revolution in Russia* (Berkeley: University of California Press, 1988); D. H. Kaiser (ed.), *The Workers' Revolution*

recruits to industry, either peasant migrants or women who had taken up jobs in the war industries. Yet this was a working class defined by an unusual degree of class consciousness. From the end of the nineteenth century, a layer of so-called 'conscious' workers, drawn mainly from the ranks of skilled, literate young men, had emerged, partly under the tutelage of revolutionary intellectuals, who provided leadership in moments of conflict, and, crucially, served as the conduit through which class politics touched a wider lower-class constituency. During the revolution workers determined that the overthrow of tsarism be followed by the overthrow of 'autocracy' on the shop floor. Hated foremen and administrators were driven out, the old rule books were torn up and factory committees were set up, especially among metalworkers, to represent workers' interests to management. Russian industrialists were not as well organised as their employees, mainly because they were divided by region and branch of industry. Moscow textile manufacturers favoured a more liberal industrial relations policy than the metalworking and engineering manufacturers of Petrograd, who had been far more supportive of tsarism, because of their dependence on state orders.[27] For a brief period following February, sections of employers came out in favour of a liberal policy that entailed a formal eight-hour day (perhaps the most pressing demand of labour), improved wages and conditions, arbitration of industrial disputes, and co-responsibility of factory committees in regulating workplace relations.[28] The factory committees took on a wide range of tasks, including overseeing hiring and firing, guarding the factory, labour discipline and organising food supplies. They were the most influential of the plethora of labour organisations that emerged. Significantly, they were the first to register the shift in lower-class support away from the moderate socialists to the Bolsheviks. In late May the first conference of Petrograd factory committees overwhelmingly passed a Bolshevik resolution on control of the economy.[29]

*in Russia, 1917* (Cambridge: Cambridge University Press, 1987); Diane Koenker, *Moscow Workers and the 1917 Revolution* (Princeton: Princeton University Press, 1981); R. A. Wade, *Red Guards and Workers' Militias in the Russian Revolution* (Stanford, Calif.: Stanford University Press, 1984).

27 Ziva Galili, 'Commercial-Industrial Circles in Revolution: The Failure of "Industrial Progressivism" ', in Frankel et al., *Revolution in Russia*, pp. 188–216; P. V. Volobuev, *Proletariat i burzhuaziia v 1917 godu* (Moscow: Mysl', 1964).

28 V. I. Cherniaev, 'Rabochii kontrol' i al'ternativy ego razvitiia v 1917 g.', in *Rabochie i rossiiskoe obshchestvo: vtoraia polovina XIX-nachalo XX veka* (St Petersburg: Glagol', 1994), pp. 164–77; D. O. Churakov, *Russkaia revoliutsiia i rabochee samoupravlenie 1917* (Moscow: AIRO-XX, 1998), pp. 35–41.

29 S. A. Smith, *Red Petrograd: Revolution in the Factories, 1917–18* (Cambridge: Cambridge University Press, 1983), chs. 3–4.

In 1917 gender was not a category of political mobilisation in the same way as class, youth or nationality. Despite their role in triggering the events that led to the February Revolution, women soon found themselves on the margins of revolutionary politics.[30] In March middle-class feminists mobilised to ensure that women received the vote; but as soon as this was granted, their movement lost influence. Most of its leaders were nationalistically inclined and some went on to form the women's 'death battalions', the only instance of women playing a combat role in the First World War. Many educated women threw themselves into work in educational and cultural organisations, the co-operatives and political parties. The one partial exception to the rule of women not organising as women were food riots in which mainly lower-class housewives, especially soldiers' wives, clashed with traders and shopkeepers over the price and availability of goods and with local governments over the miserable allowances paid to combatants' families.[31] Women workers, who comprised a third of the workforce, participated in strikes and trade unions, but were not prominent in the labour movement, partly because of their responsibilities as wives and mothers, partly because of their lower levels of literacy and partly because they were perceived as 'backward' by labour organisers, who unwittingly forged an organisational culture which marginalised them. Despite the fact that the Bolsheviks would not countenance separate organisations for working women, they did most to group them into class organisations, thanks to the initiative of a few leading women, such as Aleksandra Kollontai.[32] In the Constituent Assembly elections, interestingly, turn-out was higher among rural women than among rural men (77 per cent against 70 per cent).[33]

## The politics of war, March to July 1917

Despite the talk of 'unity of all the vital forces of the nation', the issue of war divided the Soviet leaders and the Provisional Government. The minister of

---

30 The following is based on: Linda H. Edmondson, *Feminism in Russia, 1900–1917* (London: Heinemann, 1984); Richard Stites, *The Women's Liberation Movement in Russia* (Princeton: Princeton University Press, 1978); Richard Abraham, 'Mariia L. Bochkareva and the Russian Amazons of 1917', in Linda Edmondson (ed.), *Women and Society in Russia and the Soviet Union* (Cambridge: Cambridge University Press, 1992), pp. 124–44.

31 Barbara Alpern Engel, 'Not by Bread Alone: Subsistence Riots in Russia during World War One', *Journal of Modern History* 69 (1997): 696–721.

32 Moira Donald, 'Bolshevik Activity among Working Women of Petrograd in 1917', *International Review of Social History* 27 (1982): 129–60; Beatrice Farnsworth, *Aleksandra Kollontai: Socialism, Feminism, and the Bolshevik Revolution* (Stanford, Calif.: Stanford University Press, 1980).

33 L. G. Protasov, *Vserossiiskoe uchreditel'noe sobranie: istoriia rozhdeniia i gibeli* (Moscow: Rosspen, 1997), p. 233.

foreign affairs, Pavel Miliukov, typified government thinking in believing that the revolution would unleash a surge of patriotic feeling that would carry Russia to victory in the war. By contrast, the Soviet leaders wished to see a 'democratic' peace entailing the renunciation of annexations and indemnities, although pending that, they were anxious not to leave Russia vulnerable to Austro-German attack. It was the Georgian Menshevik, I. G. Tsereteli, who crafted a compromise, known as 'revolutionary defencism', designed to uphold national defence while pressing the Provisional Government to work for a comprehensive peace settlement.[34] However, on 18 April Miliukov sent a note to the Allies that spoke of prosecution of war to 'decisive victory' and gave a heavy hint that Russia would stand by the terms of the secret treaties, which included annexations and indemnities. Soldiers and workers came out onto the streets of the capital to demand Miliukov's resignation, and Bolsheviks bore banners declaring 'Down with the Provisional Government'. With Miliukov's resignation on 2 May, Prince L'vov pressed members of the Soviet EC to join a coalition government. Tsereteli managed to overcome the reluctance of Mensheviks to participate in a 'bourgeois' government, convincing them that this would strengthen the chances for peace. Socialists accepted six places in the new government, alongside eight 'bourgeois' representatives. It proved to be a ruinous decision, since in the eyes of the masses it identified the moderate socialists with government policy.

The Mensheviks and SRs dominated the popular movement in spring and summer 1917. In late May 537 SR delegates confronted a mere fourteen Bolsheviks at the First Congress of Peasant Soviets. At the beginning of June, 285 SRs, 248 Mensheviks and only 105 Bolsheviks attended the First All-Russian Congress of Soviets.[35] The First World War had caused Mensheviks and SRs to split between internationalists, who refused to support either side in the war, and defencists, who believed that an Allied victory would represent a triumph of democracy over Austro-German militarism. Tsereteli's policy of 'revolutionary defencism' did something to heal the rift in the Menshevik Party, but the decision to join the coalition opened up new divisions. From summer L. Martov, leader of the internationalist wing, advocated the creation of a purely socialist government and the imposition of direct state controls on industry. But the centre-right insisted that there was no alternative to a coalition with

---

34 Rex A. Wade, *The Russian Revolution, 1917* (Cambridge: Cambridge University Press, 2000), ch. 3; Ziva Galili, A. P. Nenarokov et al. (eds.), *Men'sheviki v 1917 godu*, vol. I: *Ot fevralia do iul'skikh sobytii* (Moscow: Progress-Akademiia, 1994), pp. 55–70.

35 Oskar Anweiler, *The Soviets: The Russian Workers', Peasants' and Soldiers' Councils, 1905–21* (New York: Pantheon, 1974), pp. 121–3.

the 'bourgeoisie' given that socialism was not yet feasible in Russia. It is difficult to estimate the number of Mensheviks, since many provincial organisations of the Russian Social Democratic Workers' Party had declined to split into Menshevik and Bolshevik factions.[36] By May there may have been as many as 100,000, half of them in Georgia, the faction's stronghold; this probably rose to nearly 200,000 by autumn, only to fall to 150,000 by December. Intellectuals dominated the leadership of the Mensheviks, but its members were overwhelmingly workers.[37]

The SRs were the largest political party in 1917. In spring they had about half a million members, which rose to 700,000 by autumn (including Left SRs).[38] They were seen as the party of the peasantry, since they had invested much energy into organising the villages in 1905–7, but they also had a strong base in the factories and armed forces.[39] The February Revolution exacerbated divisions within the party. Viktor Chernov, leader of the centrist majority, approved the policy of coalition on the grounds that it would increase the influence of the 'democracy' within government. He took up the post of minister of agriculture and was active in preparing land redistribution, but his support for legality and 'state-mindedness' alienated him from the party's peasant base. The Left SRs, who were hostile to the 'imperialist' war, began to crystallise as a distinct faction in May; they supported the peasants' seizure of landowners' estates and favoured a homogeneous socialist government rather than a coalition with the 'bourgeoisie'. Their influence grew, and by autumn a majority of party organisations in the provinces had come out in favour of soviet power.

On 3 April, V. I. Lenin returned to Russia from Switzerland. Apart from a six-month stay in 1905–6, he had been away from his native land for almost seventeen years and his record as a revolutionary was largely one of failure.[40] Yet his hatred of liberalism and parliamentarism, his implacable opposition to

36 Ziva Galili, *The Menshevik Leaders in the Russian Revolution: Social Realities and Political Strategies* (Princeton: Princeton University Press, 1989).
37 Z. Galili et al. (eds.), *Men'sheviki v 1917 godu*, vol. II: *Ot Iul'skikh sobytii do kornilovskogo miatezha* (Moscow: Progress-Akademiia, 1995), pp. 48–9; V. I. Miller, 'K voprosu o sravnitel'noi chislennosti partii bol'shevikov i men'shevikov v 1917 g.', *Voprosy istorii KPSS* 12 (1988): 118 (109–118).
38 Astrakhan, *Bol'sheviki*, p. 233.
39 The following is based on O. H. Radkey, *The Agrarian Foes of Bolshevism* (New York: Columbia University Press, 1958); Melancon, *Socialist Revolutionaries*; Sarah Badcock, '"We're for the Muzhiks' Party!"': Peasant Support for the Socialist Revolutionary Party During 1917', *Europe–Asia Studies* 53, 1 (2001): 133–49.
40 The following is based on Robert Service, *Lenin: A Political Life*, vol. II: *Worlds in Collision* (London: Macmillan, 1991); James D. White, *Lenin: The Practice and Theory of Revolution* (London: Palgrave, 2001); Beryl Williams, *Lenin* (Harlow: Longman, 2000).

the 'imperialist' war and his appreciation of the mass appeal of soviets oriented him well to the new conditions in Russia. Prior to his return, the Bolshevik Party was also divided, the return of L. B. Kamenev and Joseph Stalin from Siberian exile having committed it to qualified support for the Provisional Government, a revolutionary defencist position on the war and to negotiations with the Mensheviks to reunify the RSDRP. In his April Theses Lenin fulminated against these policies, insisting that there could be no support for the government of 'capitalists and landlords', that the character of the war had not changed, and that the Bolsheviks should campaign for power to be transferred to a state-wide system of soviets. The war had convinced Lenin that capitalism was bankrupt and that socialism was now on the agenda internationally. L. D. Trotsky welcomed his conversion to a view that the revolution in Russia could trigger international socialist revolution. Though more unified politically than the other socialist parties, the Bolsheviks nevertheless remained rather diverse; the more moderate views of Kamenev or G. E. Zinoviev continued to command support, so that key committees like those in Moscow and Kiev would oppose the plan to seize power in October.[41] Owing to wartime repression, the number of Bolsheviks may have fallen as low as 10,000, but in the course of 1917 tens of thousands of workers, soldiers and sailors flooded into the party, knowing little Marx but seeing in the Bolsheviks the most committed defenders of their class interests. By October party membership had risen to at least 350,000.[42]

Six Mensheviks and SRs entered the government on 5 May, believing that their action would hasten the advent of peace. Almost immediately, they became involved in Kerensky's preparations for a new military offensive. This was motivated by his desire to see Russia honour her treaty obligations to the Allies and be guaranteed a place in the comity of democratic states. Kerensky toured the fronts, frenetically whipping up support for an offensive. On 18–19 July only forty-eight battalions refused to go into battle, but most had rallied for the last time. The offensive was a fiasco and led to about 150,000 losses and a larger number of deserters.[43] In its wake the Russian army unravelled as soldiers despaired of seeing an end to the bloodshed, grew angry at the unequal burden of sacrifice and determined to lay hands on gentry estates.

41 Robert Service, *The Bolshevik Party in Revolution: A Study in Organizational Change, 1917–1923* (London: Macmillan, 1979), p. 56.
42 Miller, 'K voprosu', p. 118.
43 Figes, *People's Tragedy*, p. 408; *Velikaia oktiabr'skaia sotsialisticheskaia revoliutsiia: entsiklopediia* (Moscow: Sovetskaia entsiklopediia, 1987), p. 208.

Left SRs and Bolsheviks – whose support was now growing – found their denunciation of the war falling on receptive ears.[44]

On 3 July the Kadet ministers resigned from the government, ostensibly over concessions made to Ukrainian nationalism.[45] By 2 a.m., 60,000 to 70,000 armed soldiers and workers had surrounded the Tauride Palace in Petrograd to demand that the Central Executive Committee of the Soviets (VTsIK) take power. The latter condemned the demonstration as 'counter-revolutionary' and denounced the Bolsheviks for attempting to 'dictate with bayonets' the policy of the Soviets. Although lower-level Bolshevik organisations were involved in the demonstration, party leaders considered this attempted uprising premature. As more and more soldiers and workers came onto the streets, however, they decided to lead the movement. By the next day, a semi-insurrection was under way. That night the government brought in troops to protect the Soviet, and news that a powerful force was on its way from the northern front, together with the increasingly ugly character of the demonstrations (estimates of total dead and wounded in two days of rioting ran to 400), caused regiments that had been raring for action to lose heart. Kerensky vowed 'severe retribution' on the insurgents and issued orders for the arrest of leading Bolsheviks and for the closure of their newspapers. On 7 July, he formed a 'government of salvation of the revolution' and on 21 July, after threatening to resign, persuaded the Kadets to join a second coalition government. It looked as though the Bolshevik goose had been truly cooked.

## The peasant revolution

The political awareness of the peasantry was low, but historians often exaggerate the cultural and political isolation of the village. In the last decades of tsarism, the expanding market for agricultural goods, large-scale migration, the impact of urban consumer culture, rising rates of literacy, mass conscription, and the arrival of refugees, had brought new ideas and values to the village.[46] In 1917 soldiers returning from the front played a vital role in bringing politics into the village, as did agitators sent by urban soviets and labour organisations. The Petrograd Soviet of Peasant Deputies, for example, sent

44 A. K. Wildman, *The End of the Russian Imperial Army: The Road to Soviet Power and Peace* (Princeton: Princeton University Press, 1987); Read, *From Tsar*, ch. 6

45 The following is based on: Alexander Rabinowitch, *Prelude to Revolution: The Petrograd Bolsheviks and the July 1917 Uprising* (Bloomington: Indiana University Press, 1968); O. N. Znamenskii, *Iul'skii krizis 1917 goda* (Leningrad: Nauka, 1964).

46 Stephen Frank and Mark Steinberg (eds.), *Cultures in Flux: Lower-Class Values, Practices and Resistance in Late Imperial Russia* (Princeton: Princeton University Press, 1994).

about 3,000 agitators into the countryside, armed with agitational literature produced at a cost of 65,000 roubles.[47] Educated folk were full of tales about the political ignorance of the peasantry, but peasants latched on to elements in the discourse of revolution – such as those of self-government, citizenship and socialism – reinterpreting them according to their lights.[48] Dissatisfaction over the state grain monopoly and the slow progress on land reform caused peasants gradually to become disillusioned with the Provisional Government. This, together with a desperate desire to see peace, a growing attraction to soviet power and an idealised vision of socialism, strengthened peasant support in autumn 1917 for the Left SRs and, to a lesser extent, the Bolsheviks.

The first issue that brought peasants into conflict with the government was that of the state grain monopoly. The war had seen a small decline in the amount of grain grown but, more worryingly, a more substantial fall in the amount of grain marketed, from one quarter of the harvest in 1913 to one sixth in 1917. Peasants had little incentive to sell grain given galloping inflation and the shortage of consumer goods. The Provisional Government's efforts to force peasants to sell grain at fixed prices provoked them into concealing grain or turning it into alcohol.[49] The second issue that brought peasants into conflict with the government was that of land redistribution. Peasants believed that the revolution would redress the historic wrong done to them at the time of the emancipation of the serfs by transferring gentry, Church and state lands into the hands of those who worked them. The new government, however, had no stomach for carrying out a massive land reform at a time of war. Moreover, it was split between Kadets, who insisted that landlords be fully compensated for land taken from them, and Chernov, who wished to see the orderly transfer of land via the land committees to those who worked it. With a view to allowing the Constituent Assembly to decide the question, the government set up a somewhat bureaucratic structure of land committees to prepare a detailed land settlement, region by region. This only served to heighten peasant expectations.

From late spring, a struggle began between peasants and landlords. Initially, peasants were cautious, testing the capacity of local authorities to curb their

---

47  Michael Hickey, 'Urban *Zemliachestva* and Rural Revolution: Petrograd and the Smolensk Countryside in 1917', *Soviet and Post-Soviet Review* 23, 2 (1996): 143–60; Michael Melancon, 'Soldiers, Peasant-Soldiers, and Peasant-Workers and their Organisations in Petrograd: Ground-Level Revolution during the Early Months of 1917', *Soviet and Post-Soviet Review* 23, 2 (1996): 183 (161–90).
48  Figes and Kolonitskii, *Interpreting*, ch. 5.
49  L. T. Lih, *Bread and Authority in Russia, 1914–21* (Berkeley: University of California Press, 1990), ch. 3.

encroachments on landlord property. They unilaterally reduced or failed to pay rent, grazed cattle illegally on the landowners' estates, stole wood from their forests and took over uncultivated tracts of gentry land on the pretext that it would otherwise remain unsown. In the non-Black Earth zone, where dairy and livestock farming were critical, they tried to get their hands on mead-ows and pasture. Seeing the inability of local commissars to respond, illegal acts multiplied, levelling off during harvest from mid-July to mid-August, but climbing sharply from September. Generally, the village gathering authorised these actions, returning soldiers often spurring it on. By autumn the agrarian movement was in full swing, with peasants increasingly seizing gentry land, equipment and livestock and distributing them outright. The movement was fiercest in the overcrowded central Black Earth and middle Volga provinces and in Ukraine. The government introduced martial law in Tambov, Orel, Tula, Riazan', Penza and Saratov provinces, but soldiers in rear garrisons could not be relied upon to put down peasant rebels. The Union of Landowners and Farmers castigated the government for failing to defend the rights of private property.[50]

## Political polarisation

By summer the economy was buckling under the strain of war.[51] In the first half of 1917 production of fuel and raw materials fell by over a third and gross factory output over the year fell by 36 per cent compared with 1916. As a result, enterprises closed and by October nearly half a million workers had been laid off. The crisis was aggravated by mounting chaos in the transport system, which meant that grain and industrial supplies failed to get through to the towns. The government debt rose to an astronomical 49 billion roubles, of which 11.2 billion was owed on foreign loans, and the government reacted by printing money, further fuelling inflation. Between July and October prices rose fourfold and in Moscow and Petrograd the real value of wages halved in the second half of the year.

As the economic crisis deepened, class conflict intensified. Between February and October, 2.5 million workers went on strike, stoppages increas-ing in scale as the year wore on, but becoming ever harder to win.[52] The trade

50 John Channon, 'The Landowners', in Service, *Society and Politics*, pp. 120–46.
51 The following is based on Paul Flenley, 'Industrial Relations and the Economic Cri-sis of 1917', *Revolutionary Russia* 4, 2 (1991): 184–209; *Velikaia oktiabr'skaia entsiklopediia*, pp. 593–4.
52 D. P. Koenker and W. G. Rosenberg, *Strikes and Revolution in Russia, 1917* (Princeton: Princeton University Press, 1989).

unions, which by October had over two million members, were organised mainly along industry-wide lines. They endeavoured to negotiate collective wage agreements with employers' organisations, but negotiations were protracted and served to exacerbate class antagonism.[53] For their part, the factory committees implemented workers' control of production to prevent what they believed to be widespread 'sabotage' by employers. Workers' control signified the close monitoring of the activities of management, rather than its displacement, but it was fed by deep-seated aspirations for workplace democracy. The idea of workers' control, though not emanating from any political party, was taken up by Bolsheviks, anarchists and some Left SRs; it proved to be a key reason why worker support shifted in their favour. By contrast, the insistence of the moderate socialists that only state regulation could restore order to the economy – and that 'control' by individual factory committees only exacerbated the crisis – was another cause of their undoing.[54] Industrialists, resenting any infringement of their right to manage, resorted to ever more extreme measures, including lockouts and the closure of mines and factories in the Urals and Donbass.[55] Having failed to form a single national organisation to represent their interests, they, too, became alienated from the 'socialist' government.

By summer a discourse of class was in the ascendant, symbolised in the substitution of the word 'comrade' for 'citizen' as the favoured form of address.[56] Given the underdevelopment of class relations in Russia, and the key role played in the revolution by non-class groups such as soldiers and nationalist movements, this was a remarkable development. After all, the language of class, at least in its Marxist guise, had entered politics only since 1905. Yet it proved easily assimilable since it played on a binary opposition that ran deep in popular culture between 'them', the *verkhi*, that is those at the top, and 'us', the *nizy*, that is those at the bottom. People's identities, of course, were multiple – one was not only a worker, but a Russian, a woman, a young person – yet 'class' came to reconfigure identities of nation, gender and youth in its own terms. 'We' could signify the working class, 'proletarian youth', 'working women', the 'toiling people' (i.e. peasants as well as workers) or 'revolutionary democracy'. 'They' could signify capitalists, landlords, army generals or, at its most visceral, the *burzhui*, anyone with an overbearing manner, an education,

53 D. P. Koenker, 'The Trade Unions', in Acton et al., *Critical Companion*, p. 450 (pp. 446–56).
54 Smith, *Red Petrograd*, ch. 7.
55 T. H. Friedgut, *Iuzovka and Revolution*, vol. II: *Politics and Revolution in Russia's Donbass, 1869–1924* (Princeton: Princeton University Press, 1994), ch. 8.
56 Kolonitskii, *Simvoly vlasti*, pp. 303–14.

soft hands or spectacles.[57] Faced by what they perceived to be an elemental
conflict tearing the heart out of the Russian nation, the Kadets struggled to
uphold a conception of 'state-mindedness', appealing to Russians to set aside
all class and sectional strife.[58] In 1918 the liberal P. V. Struve characterised the
Russian Revolution as 'the first case in world history of the triumph of internationalism and the class idea over nationalism and the national idea'.[59] But
this was only partly true. For if exponents of class politics rejected the Kadet
vision of the nation under siege – as well as the moderate socialist vision of
'unity of all the vital forces of the nation' – the exponents of class politics never
entirely rejected the appeal to the nation: rather they engaged in a struggle to
redefine the 'nation' in terms of its toiling people, playing on the ambivalence
that inheres in the Russian word *narod*, which can mean both 'nation' and
'common people'.[60]

If Russian nationalism was in crisis by summer 1917, nationalism among the
non-Russian people was in the ascendant.[61] From the late nineteenth century,
the tsarist state had been destabilised by rising nationalisms, although these
played no direct part in its demise. At the time of the February Revolution
nationalism was developed extremely unevenly across the empire – strong in
the Baltic and the Caucasus, weak in Central Asia – and movements to form
independent nation-states proved irresistible only in Poland and Finland. Initially, nationalists demanded rights of cultural self-expression, such as schooling
or religious services in native languages, the formation of military units along
ethnic lines, and a measure of political autonomy within the framework of a
federal Russian state. The typical aspiration was encapsulated in the slogan
of the liberal and moderate socialist Ukrainian National Council, known as

57 L. H. Haimson, 'The Problem of Social Identities in Early Twentieth Century Russia',
   *Slavic Review* 47, 1 (1988): 1–20; B. I. Kolonitskii, 'Antibourgeois Propaganda and Anti-
   *Burzhui* Consciousness in 1917', *Russian Review* 53, 2 (1994): 183–96; Michael C. Hickey, 'The
   Rise and Fall of Smolensk's Moderate Socialists: The Politics of Class and the Rhetoric of
   Crisis in 1917', in Donald J. Raleigh (ed.), *Provincial Landscapes: Local Dimensions of Soviet
   Power, 1917–53* (Pittsburgh: University of Pittsburgh Press, 2001), pp. 14–35.
58 W. G. Rosenberg, *Liberals in the Russian Revolution: The Constitutional Democratic Party,
   1917–21* (Princeton: Princeton University Press, 1974), pp. 134–70.
59 P. V. Struve, 'Istoricheskii smysl' russkoi revoliutsii i nasional'nye zadachi', in *Iz glubiny:
   sbornik statei o russkoi revoliutsii* (1918; Moscow: Moskovskii universitet, 1990), p. 235.
60 *Revoliutsionnoe dvizhenie v Rossii v avguste v 1917 g. Razgrom kornilovskogo miatezha*
   (Moscow: Akademiia Nauk, 1959), pp. 103, 407; V. F. Shishkin, *Velikii Oktiabr' i prole-
   tarskii moral'* (Moscow: Mysl', 1976), pp. 41–2, 49.
61 The following is based on Mark von Hagen, 'The Great War and the Mobilization of
   Ethnicity in the Russian Empire', in Barnett R. Rubin and Jack Snyder (eds.), *Post-Soviet
   Political Order: Conflict and State-Building* (New York: Routledge, 1998), pp. 34–57; Ronald
   G. Suny, 'Nationalism and Class in the Russian Revolution', in Frankel et al., *Revolution
   in Russia*, pp. 219–46; Stephen Jones, 'The Non-Russian Nationalities', in Service, *Society
   and Politics*, pp. 35–63.

the Rada: 'Long Live Autonomous Ukraine in a Federated Russia'. The Provisional Government assumed that by abrogating discriminatory legislation against national minorities it would 'solve' the national question. Its reluctance to concede more substantial autonomy was motivated by fear that nationalist movements were being used by Germany – a not unreasonable supposition if one looks to their later record in the Baltic – and by an emotional commitment to a unified Russian state, especially strong among the Kadets. As a result of this reluctance, nationalist politicians stepped up demands for autonomy, at the same time as they tacked to the left in order to keep in step with the growing radicalism of peasants and workers, whose support they needed if they were to create viable nation-states.[62] When in September Kerensky finally endorsed the principle of self-determination 'but only on such principles as the Constituent Assembly shall determine', it was too little and too late.[63] Nevertheless if nationalism became one more force undermining the viability of the state, the strength of nationalist sentiment should not be exaggerated. In most non-Russian areas, demands for radical social and economic policies eclipsed purely nationalist demands. Workers, for example, generally inclined to class politics rather than nationalist politics; and though peasants liked parties that spoke to them in their own language and defended local interests, they proved unreliable supporters of 'their' nation-states when called upon to fight in their defence. In general, but not invariably, nationalism proved successful where it was reinforced by class divisions, as in Latvia, Estonia or Georgia.

In autumn 1917 a psychological break occurred in the public mood, with the euphoria of the spring giving way to anxiety, even to a sense of impending doom. This was most evident in many elements that made up Russia's heterogeneous middle classes. The intelligentsia, which had long been losing coherence as an ethically and ideologically defined group, lost confidence in the common people whose interests it had always claimed to champion. By autumn many felt that the existence of civilisation was menaced by the 'dark masses'; so fearful were they that sections of the press referred to them as the 'i.i.', which stood for 'terrified intellectuals'.[64] Students, in the van of the struggle against autocracy between 1899 and 1905, had ceased in the intervening years automatically to identify with the Left. When 272 delegates arrived for the All-Russian Congress of Students on 15 May they proved unable to

---

62 V. P. Buldakov, 'Imperstvo i rossiiskaia revoliutsionnost', pt. 2, *Otechestvennaia istoriia*, 1997, no. 2: 24–7 (20–47).

63 Wade, *Russian Revolution*, p. 148.

64 O. N. Znamenskii, *Intelligentsiia nakanune velikogo oktiabria (fevral'–oktiabr' 1917 g.)* (Leningrad: Nauka, 1988), p. 299. For a more positive depiction, see Christopher Read, 'The Cultural Intelligentsia', in Service, *Society and Politics*, pp. 86–102.

forge a common programme, declaring themselves 'necessary to no one, and our resolutions binding on no one'.[65] Professional groups, such as lawyers, doctors, teachers or engineers, showed rather more confidence. One of the paradoxes of the revolution was that as the power of the state weakened, its reach – via the regulatory economic organs and democratised local administrations – expanded, and opportunities for professionals, managerial and technical staff increased accordingly.[66] The liberal and technical professions, however, showed little political coherence, with lower-status groups, such as primary-school teachers or medical assistants, orienting towards 'revolutionary democracy', and higher-status groups, such as doctors or secondary-school teachers, orienting towards the Kadets.[67] Beneath professionals were salaried employees (*sluzhashchie*), a diverse group comprising white-collar workers in public institutions, industry and commerce, and numbering close to 2 million. Their tendency was to align politically with the 'proletariat' by forming trade unions, although hostility towards them on the part of blue-collar workers was by no means uncommon.[68] Salaried employees, along with the lower ranks of professionals, were part of the heterogeneous lower-middle strata, whose ranks also included artisans, traders and rentiers, and who numbered about 14 million by 1915.[69] Many of the latter turned against socialist 'chatterers' in the soviets, demanding a 'strong power' to defend property and security.[70]

Following the July Days, Kerensky, now prime minister, cultivated an image as a 'man of destiny' summoned to 'save Russia'.[71] On 12 July he restored the death penalty at the front, and a week later military censorship. On 19 July he

---

65 Znamenskii, *Intelligentsiia*, pp. 301, 275; A. P. Kupaigorodskaia, 'Petrogradskoe studench-estvo i oktiabr'', in *Oktiabr'skoe vooruzhennoe vosstanie v Petrograde* (Moscow: Nauka, 1980), pp. 241–8.

66 Daniel Orlovsky, 'The Lower Middle Strata in 1917', in Acton et al. (eds.), *Critical Companion*, pp. 529–33; W. G. Rosenberg, 'Social Mediations and State Constructions in Revolutionary Russia', *Social History* 19, 2 (1994): 169–88.

67 Howard White, 'The Urban Middle Classes', in Service, *Society and Politics*, pp. 72–5 (64–85).

68 Ibid., pp. 79–80; Smith, *Red Petrograd*, pp. 134–8; 233–4.

69 N. I. Vostrikov, *Bor'ba za massy: gorodskie srednie sloi nakanune oktiabria* (Moscow: Mysl', 1970), p. 15.

70 N. P. Druzhinin, *Meshchanskoe dvizhenie 1906–17 gg.* (Iaroslavl', 1917).

71 The account of the Kornilov rebellion is based on: J. L. Munck, *The Kornilov Revolt: A Critical Examination of Sources* (Aarhus: Aarhus University Press, 1987); G. Ioffe, *Semnadtsatyi god: Lenin, Kerenskii, Kornilov* (Moscow: Nauka, 1995), p. 132; J. D. White 'The Kornilov Affair – A Study in Counter-Revolution', *Soviet Studies* 20, 2 (1968–9): 187–205; Allan Wildman, 'Officers of the General Staff and the Kornilov Movement', in Frankel et al. (eds.), *Revolution in Russia*, pp. 76–101; A. F. Kerensky, *The Prelude to Bolshevism: The Kornilov Rebellion* (New York: Haskell, 1972). For the view that Kornilov was betrayed at the last minute by Kerensky, see George Katkov, *Russia 1917: The Kornilov Affair* (London: Longman, 1980).

appointed General L. G. Kornilov supreme commander-in-chief of the army. Kerensky hoped to use the reactionary general to bolster his image as a strong man and to restore frayed relations with the Kadets, many of whom talked openly about the need for military dictatorship to save Russia from anarchy. Kornilov and Kerensky entered into negotiations on the need to establish 'firm government', which both understood to mean crushing not only the Bolsheviks but also the soviets. Kerensky, however, demurred at demands to restore the death penalty in the rear and to militarise defence factories and the railways. On 26 August Kerensky received what he took to be an ultimatum from Kornilov demanding that all military and civil authority be placed in the hands of a dictator. Accusing him of conspiring to overthrow the government, he sent a telegram on 27 August relieving Kornilov of his duties. The latter ignored it, ordering his troops to advance on Petrograd. Kerensky had no option but to turn to the Soviet to prevent Kornilov's troops from reaching the capital.

Henceforth politics was a theatre of shadows with the real battles for power going on in society. Kerensky formed a five-person 'directory', a personal dictatorship in all but name, in which he had virtually complete responsibility for military as well as civil affairs. But now even Mensheviks and SRs would not countenance a government containing Kadets, since they had been blatantly implicated in the Kornilov rebellion.[72] The depth of the crisis among the moderate socialists was revealed at the Democratic Conference (14–19 September), called to rally 'democratic' organisations behind the government.[73] This proved unable to resolve the question of whether or not the government should involve 'bourgeois' forces. On 25 September Kerensky went ahead and formed a third coalition, but failed to win ratification from the Petrograd Soviet.

## The Bolshevik seizure of power

The Kornilov rebellion dramatised the danger of counter-revolution and starkly underlined the feebleness of the Kerensky regime. Crucially, it triggered a spectacular recovery by the Bolsheviks after the setback they had suffered following the July Days. The party's consistent opposition to the government of 'capitalists and landowners', its rejection of the 'imperialist' war, its calls for land to the peasants, for power to the soviets and for workers'

72 Geoffrey Swain, *The Origins of the Russian Civil War* (London: Longman, 1996), pp. 23–38.
73 Z. Galili et al. (eds.), *Men'sheviki v 1917 godu*, vol. III, p. 1 (Moscow: Rosspen, 1996), pp. 13–34.

control now seemed to hundreds of thousands of workers and soldiers to provide a way forward.[74] In the first half of September, eighty soviets in large and
medium towns backed the call for a transfer of power to the soviets. No one
was entirely sure what the slogan 'All Power to the Soviets', which belonged
as much to anarchists, Left SRs and some Mensheviks as to the Bolsheviks,
actually meant. While hiding in Finland, Lenin had written his most utopian
work, *State and Revolution*, which outlined his vision of a 'commune state' in
which the three pillars of the bourgeois state – the police, standing army and
the bureaucracy – would be smashed and in which parliamentary democracy
would be replaced by direct democracy based on the soviets.[75] But it is unlikely
that many – even in the Bolshevik Party – understood the slogan in that way.
For most it meant severing the alliance with the 'bourgeoisie' and forming a
socialist government consisting of all parties in VTsIK pending the convening
of a Constituent Assembly.[76]

Seeing the surge in popular support for the Bolsheviks, Lenin became convinced that nationally as well as internationally the time was ripe for the
Bolsheviks to seize power in the name of the soviets.[77] He blitzed the Central
Committee with demands that it prepare an insurrection, even threatening to
resign on 29 September. 'History will not forgive us if we do not assume power
now.'[78] The majority of the leadership was unenthusiastic, believing that it
would be better to allow power to pass democratically to the soviets by waiting
for the Second Congress of Soviets, scheduled to open on 20 October. Having
returned in secret to Petrograd, Lenin on 10 October persuaded the Central
Committee to commit itself to the overthrow of the Provisional Government.
Significantly, no timetable was set (see Plate 5). Zinoviev and Kamenev were
bitterly opposed to the decision, believing that the conditions for socialist revolution did not yet exist and that an insurrection was likely to be crushed.
As late as 16 October, the mood in the party was against an insurrection and
the decision of Zinoviev and Kamenev to make public their opposition drove

74 David Mandel, *The Petrograd Workers and the Soviet Seizure of Power: From the July Days
1917 to July 1918* (London: Macmillan, 1984); D. P. Koenker, 'The Evolution of Party
Consciousness in 1917: The Case of Moscow Workers', *Soviet Studies* 30, 1 (1978): 38–62.
75 Neil Harding, 'Lenin, Socialism and the State', in Frankel et al. (eds.), *Revolution in Russia*,
pp. 287–303; Service, *Lenin: A Political Life*, vol. II, pp. 216–28.
76 Mandel, *Petrograd Workers*, pp. 232–43; Wade, *Russian Revolution*, p. 213; Read, *From Tsar*,
pp. 160, 176–7.
77 The following is based on Alexander Rabinowitch, *The Bolsheviks Come to Power: The
Revolution of 1917 in Petrograd* (New York: Norton, 1976); Marc Ferro, *October 1917: A
Social History of the October Revolution* (London: Routledge and Kegan Paul, 1980), ch. 8.
78 V. I. Lenin, 'The Bolsheviks Must Assume Power', in V. I. Lenin, *Between the Two
Revolutions: Articles and Speeches of 1917* (Moscow: Progress, 1971), p. 392; in Lenin, *Collected
Works* (Moscow: Progress, 1972), vol. XXVI, pp. 19–21.

Lenin to a paroxysm of fury. It fell to Trotsky, now chair of the Petrograd Soviet, to make practical preparations, which he did, not by following Lenin's suggestion of an attack on the capital by sailors and soldiers of the northern front, but by associating an insurrection with the defence of the Petrograd garrison.[79]

On 6 October the government had announced that half the garrison was to be moved out of the capital to defend it against the onward advance of the German army. The Soviet interpreted this as an attempt to rid Petrograd of its most revolutionary elements, and on 9 October created an embryonic Military-Revolutionary Committee (MRC) to resist the transfer. This was the organisation that Trotsky used to unseat the government. On 20 October the government ordered the transfer of troops to begin, but the MRC ordered them not to move without its permission. On the night of 23–4 October, Kerensky ordered the Bolshevik printing press to be shut down, as a prelude to moving against the MRC, thus giving Trotsky another pretext to take 'defensive' action. On 24 October military units, backed by armed bands of workers, known as Red Guards, took control of bridges, railway stations and other strategic points. Kerensky fled, unable to muster troops to resist the insurgents. By the morning of 25 October only the Winter Palace remained to be taken. That afternoon Lenin appeared for the first time in public since July, proclaiming to the Petrograd Soviet that the Provisional Government was overthrown. 'In Russia we must now set about building a proletarian socialist state.' At 10.40 p.m. the Second Congress of Soviets finally opened, the artillery bombardment of the Winter Palace audible in the distance. The Mensheviks and SRs denounced the insurrection as a provocation to civil war and walked out, Trotsky's taunt echoing in their ears: 'You are miserable bankrupts; your role is played out. Go where you ought to be: into the dustbin of history.'[80]

## The establishment of Bolshevik dictatorship

The Bolsheviks determined to break with the vacillation of the Provisional Government by issuing decrees on the urgent questions of peace, land and workers' control of industry.[81] On 26 October they issued a peace decree

---

79 James D. White, *The Russian Revolution, 1917–21: A Short History* (London: Arnold, 1994), pp. 160–7.
80 Isaac Deutscher, *The Prophet Armed: Trotsky, 1879–1921* (Oxford: Oxford University Press, 1954), p. 314.
81 The following is based on Roy Medvedev, *The October Revolution*, trans. George Saunders (New York: Columbia Press, 1979), p. 3; Keep, *Russian Revolution*, p. 4; J. L. H. Keep (ed.),

calling on all the belligerent powers to begin peace talks on the basis of no annexations or indemnities and self-determination for national minorities. The rejection by the Entente of this proposal led to the Bolsheviks suing for a separate peace with Germany. German terms proved to be tough and Lenin's insistence that they be accepted caused what was arguably the deepest schism ever experienced by the Bolshevik Party.[82] On 18 February the German high command lost patience with Trotsky's stalling tactics and sent 700,000 troops into Russia where they met virtually no resistance. On 23 February it proffered terms even more draconian. At the crucial meeting of the Central Committee that evening, opponents of peace gained four votes against seven in favour of acceptance, while four supporters of Trotsky's formula of 'No war, no peace' abstained. The peace treaty, signed at Brest-Litovsk on 3 March, was massively punitive: the Baltic provinces, a large part of Belorussia and the whole of the Ukraine were excised from the former empire.

On 26 October the Bolshevik government also issued a Land Decree that legitimised the spontaneous land seizures by formally confiscating all gentry, Church and crown lands and transferring them to peasant use.[83] Significantly, it did not embody the Bolshevik policy of 'nationalising' land – that is, of taking it directly into state ownership – but the SR policy of 'socialisation', whereby land 'passes into the use of the entire toiling people'. This left individual communes free to decide how much land should be distributed and whether it should be apportioned on the basis of the number of 'eaters' or able-bodied members in each household. The idea of socialising land proved hugely popular. The decree precipitated a wave of land confiscation: in the central provinces three-quarters of landowners' land was confiscated between November and January 1918.[84] How much better off peasants were as a result of the land redistribution is hard to say, since there was no uniformity in the amount of land they received, even within a single township. Slightly more than half of communes received no additional land, usually because there was no adjacent estate that could be confiscated. And since two-thirds of confiscated land was already rented to peasants, the amount of new land that became available represented just

The Debate on Soviet Power: Minutes of the All-Russian Central Executive Committee of Soviets, October 1917–January 1918 (Oxford: Clarendon Press, 1979).
82  Ronald I. Kowalski, The Bolshevik Party in Conflict: The Left Communist Opposition of 1918 (London: Macmillan, 1991).
83  The following is based on: John Channon, 'The Bolsheviks and the Peasantry: The Land Question during the First Eight Months of Soviet Power', Slavonic and East European Studies 66, 4 (1988): 593–624; Keep, Russian Revolution, p. 5; Figes, Peasant Russia, ch. 3.
84  I. A. Trifonov, Likvidatsiia ekspluatatorskikh klassov v SSSR (Moscow: Politizdat, 1975), p. 90

over a fifth of the entire cultivated area. Following redistribution, about three-quarters of households had allotments of up to 4 *desiatiny* (4.4 hectares), plus a horse and one or two cows. This was sufficient for a basic level of subsistence, but no more.

If the slogan 'All Power to the Soviets' was widely understood to mean the transfer of power to a coalition consisting of *all* socialist parties, the Bolsheviks nevertheless went ahead on 26 October and formed a Council of People's Commissars (Sovnarkom) exclusively from members of their own party. Talks with the Mensheviks and SRs to form a coalition government got under way, but were scuttled by the intransigence of hard-liners on all sides. Five Bolsheviks resigned from the Sovnarkom when ordered to withdraw from the talks, saying 'we consider a purely Bolshevik government has no choice but to maintain itself by political terror'. In due course, seven Left SRs did join the new government, having been assured that the Sovnarkom would be accountable to the VTsIK – something that never happened – and they engineered the fusion of VTsIK with the All-Russian Soviet of Peasant Deputies, whose SR-dominated executive had backed military resistance to the Bolsheviks.

Soviet power was established with surprising ease, a reflection of the popularity of the idea of devolving power to the toilers.[85] In towns and regions with a relatively homogeneous working class, such as the Central Industrial Region or the mining settlements of the Urals, Bolsheviks and their Left SR and anarchist allies asserted 'soviet power' quickly with little opposition. In big commercial and industrial cities with a more diverse social structure, such as Moscow, Smolensk or the Volga cities of Kazan', Samara, Saratov, Tsaritsyn, the Bolsheviks enjoyed a plurality of votes in the soviets but faced a strong challenge from the moderate socialist bloc. Here 'soviet power' was often established by the local military-revolutionary committee – of which there were 350 nationwide – or by the garrison. Finally, there were the less industrially developed towns, towns of more medium size, or the capitals of overwhelmingly agricultural provinces, such as those in the central Black Earth provinces, where the SRs and Mensheviks were heavily ensconced in the soviets. Here moderate socialists put up staunch resistance to soviet power, as did Cossacks and nationalist movements such as the Ukrainian Rada.

The Constituent Assembly symbolised the people's power at the heart of the revolution and the Bolsheviks made much political capital out of the Provisional Government's decision to postpone elections to it. Yet once in government, Lenin insisted that there could be no going back to a parliamentary

85 The following is based on: Keep, *Russian Revolution*, chs. 26 and 27.

regime now that soviet power, a superior form of democracy in his view, had been established. The Bolsheviks nevertheless decided to allow elections to go ahead. In all, 48.4 million valid votes were cast, of which the SRs gained 19.1m. (39.5 per cent), the Bolsheviks 10.9m. (22.5 per cent), the Kadets 2.2m. (4.5 per cent) and the Mensheviks 1.5m. (3.2 per cent). Over 7 million voted for non-Russian socialist parties, including two-thirds of Ukrainians. The SRs were thus the clear winners, their vote concentrated in the countryside. The main voters for the Bolsheviks were workers and 42 per cent of the 5.5m. soldiers.[86] This represented the peak of popular support for the Bolsheviks: hereinafter they would lose support as soldiers returned to their villages and as worker disaffection grew. On 5 January the Assembly opened in dispiriting circumstances. The delegates elected Chernov chair and voted to discuss the SR agenda. In the small hours of the morning, the sailor's leader, A. G. Zhelezniakov, announced that 'the guard is getting tired' and put an end to its proceedings for ever.

The Bolshevik seizure of power is often presented as a conspiratorial coup against a democratic government. It had all the elements of a coup – albeit one advertised in advance – except for the fact that a coup implies the seizure of a functioning state machine. Arguably, Russia had not had this since February. The reasons for the failure of the Provisional Government are not hard to pinpoint. Lacking legitimacy from the first, it relied on the moderate socialists in the Soviet to make its writ run. From summer, it was engulfed by a concatenation of crises – at the front, in the countryside, in the economy and in the non-Russian periphery. Few governments could have coped with such a situation, and certainly not without an army to rely on. Many argue that democratic government was a non-starter in Russia in 1917. This may underestimate the extent of enthusiasm for 'democracy' in 1917. It is true, however, that from the first a heavily 'socialised' conception of democracy vied with a liberal conception tied to the defence of private property. Perhaps if the Petrograd Soviet had taken power in March when it had the chance, perhaps if it had hastened to summon the Constituent Assembly and to tackle the land question, the SRs and Mensheviks might have been able to consolidate a parliamentary regime. In the wake of the Kornilov rebellion, a majority of moderate socialists came round to the view that the coalition with the 'bourgeoisie' must end, but that, of course, was not their view in spring. More crucially, on the vital matter of the war there were many in the SR Party whose instincts were little different from those of Kerensky. Therein lay the rub. For the fate of democracy in 1917 was ultimately sealed by the decision of liberals

---

86 Protasov, *Vserossisskoe*, pp. 164, 168.

and moderate socialists to continue the war. It was the war that focused the otherwise disparate grievances of the people. It was the war that exacerbated the deep polarisation in society to a murderous extent. It was the war, in the last analysis, that made the Bolshevik seizure of power irresistible.

The Bolsheviks satisfied the demands of tens of millions on the burning issues of peace and land, but their promise to transfer power to the soviets proved to be very short-lived and severely incomplete. Historians debate the extent to which the speedy rise of one-party dictatorship was due to Bolshevik authoritarianism or to circumstances. There can be little doubt that the Bolsheviks' course of action was powerfully dictated by circumstances such as an imploding economy, a collapsing army, spiralling lawlessness, a disintegrating empire, the fragmentation of state authority and, not least, by extensive opposition to their rule. At the same time, they were never blind instruments of fate. The lesson that Lenin and Trotsky drew from the experience of 1917 was that breadth of representation in government spelt weakness; and in their determination to re-establish strong government – something that millions craved – they did not scruple to use dictatorial methods. By closing the Constituent Assembly they signalled that they were ready to wage war in defence of their regime not only against the exploiting classes, but against the socialist camp. The dissolution of the assembly doomed the chances of democracy in Russia for seventy years and for that the Bolsheviks bear the largest share of blame. Yet the prospects for a democratic socialist regime had by this stage become extremely tenuous. True, some 70 per cent of peasants voted in the assembly elections, but they did so less out of enthusiasm for parliamentary politics than out of a desire to see the assembly legalise their title to the land. Once it became clear that they had no reason to fear on that score, they acquiesced in the assembly's dissolution. The grim fact is that by 1918 the real choice facing the Russian people was one between anarchy or some form of dictatorship.[87]

87 This argument is worked out in S. A. Smith, *The Russian Revolution: A Very Short Introduction* (Oxford: Oxford University Press, 2002).

# 5

# The Russian civil war, 1917–1922

DONALD J. RALEIGH

While the story of the Russian Revolution has often been retold, the historiography of the event's most decisive chapter, the civil war, remains remarkably underdeveloped. A generation ago, the nature of available sources as well as dominant paradigms in the historical profession led Western historians of the civil war to focus on military operations, Allied intervention and politics at the top. This scholarship pinned the blame for the resulting Communist dictatorship on Marxist-Leninist ideology and/or Russia's backwardness and authoritarian political culture. In the 1980s, interest in social history and Bolshevik cultural experimentation stimulated publication of new academic and popular overviews of the civil war,[1] and also of a landmark collaborative volume that shifted the explanation for the Communist dictatorship from conscious political will and ideology to the circumstances of the ordeal.[2] The first full-scale investigations of the civil war in Petrograd and Moscow appeared as well.[3] Some studies issued at this time cast the period as a 'formative' one, emphasising that the Bolshevik behaviour, language, policies and appearance that emerged during 1917–21 served as models for policies later implemented under Joseph Stalin.[4]

Although Soviet historians writing on 1917 often produced results that were not entirely invalidated by ideological content, this is less the case in regard to the civil war, whose history they patently falsified, undoubtedly owing to

1 The best of these is Evan Mawdsley, *The Russian Civil War* (Boston: Allen and Unwin, 1987).
2 Diane P. Koenker, William G. Rosenberg and Ronald G. Suny (eds.), *Party, State, and Society in the Russian Civil War: Explorations in Social History* (Bloomington: Indiana University Press, 1989).
3 Mary McAuley, *Bread and Justice: State and Society in Petrograd, 1917–1922* (Oxford: Oxford University Press, 1991); and Richard Sakwa, *Soviet Communists in Power: A Study of Moscow during the Civil War, 1918–21* (Basingstoke: Macmillan, 1988).
4 Sheila Fitzpatrick, 'The Civil War as a Formative Experience', in Abbott Gleason, Peter Kenez and Richard Stites (eds.), *Bolshevik Culture: Experiment and Order in the Russian Revolution* (Bloomington: Indiana University Press, 1985), pp. 57–9, 71.

Map 5.1. European Russia during the civil war, 1918–21

mass discontent with Bolshevik practices after 1918. Focusing on the political and military aspects of the civil war, Soviet historians published a 'canonical' five-volume survey of the subject between 1935 and 1960.[5] World war and the partial discrediting of Stalinist scholarship following the Soviet leader's death in 1953 help to explain the delay in issuing the last volumes in the series. Like their Western counterparts, Soviet historians by the 1980s had begun to devote more attention to the 1918–21 phase of the Russian Revolution, resulting in the

5 M. Gor'kii et al., *Istoriia grazhdanskoi voiny v SSSR* (Moscow: 'Istoriia grazhdanskoi voiny', 1935, 1942, 1957, 1959, 1960).

release of a two-volume authoritative survey to replace the one begun during the Stalin years.[6] They debated periodisation of the civil war, acknowledged opposition parties and regional differences, examined party and state institutions and re-evaluated War Communism. However, they failed to engage deeper interpretive issues or to address the degree of popular opposition to Bolshevik policies.

The opening of the archives has allowed historians to revisit old questions and also to conceptualise the civil war in fresh ways. Lenin became the object of this first trajectory. Underscoring his disregard for human life, new writing on the founder of the Soviet state draws on long-sealed documents to confirm his willingness to resort to terror and repression. Such literature breathed new life into the long-standing argument that Stalinism represented the inevitable consequence of Leninism.[7] An attempt to expose the 'revisionist' historians' intellectual dead end and to convict the Bolsheviks of crimes similar to those perpetrated under Stalin mars an otherwise valuable study of the civil war published in 1994.[8] More importantly, unprecedented archival access and changing intellectual paradigms encouraged historians to carry out local case studies informed by cultural approaches and by an interest in daily life. These works show how the experiential aspects of the civil war constrained and enabled later Soviet history, pointing out that many features of the Soviet system that we associate with the Stalin era were not only practised, but also *embedded* during the 1914–22 period.[9] Shifting focus away from Lenin and Bolshevik ideology, these investigations interpret this outcome as the consequence of a complex dynamic shaped, among other things, by Russia's political tradition and culture, Bolshevik ideology and the dire political, economic and military crises starting with the First World War and strongly reinforced by the mythologised experience of surviving the civil war. Some of these studies conclude that the 1920s contained few real alternatives to a Stalinist-like system. Herein lies the civil war's significance.

---

6  N. N. Azovtsev (ed.), *Grazhdanskaia voina v SSSR* (Moscow: Voennoe izdatel'stvo Ministerstva oborony SSSR, 1980, 1986).

7  Dmitrii Volkogonov, *Lenin: Life and Legacy*, trans. Harold Shukman (London: Harper-Collins, 1994); Richard Pipes (ed.), *The Unknown Lenin: From the Secret Archive* (New Haven: Yale University Press, 1996); and Robert Service, *Lenin: A Biography* (Cambridge, Mass.: Harvard University Press, 2000).

8  Vladimir N. Brovkin, *Behind the Front Lines of the Civil War: Political Parties and Social Movements in Russia, 1918–1922* (Princeton: Princeton University Press, 1994).

9  Igor' Narskii, *Zhizn' v katastrofe: Budni naseleniia Urala v 1917–1922 gg.* (Moscow: Rosspen, 2001); Donald J. Raleigh, *Experiencing Russia's Civil War: Politics, Society, and Revolutionary Culture in Saratov, 1917–1922* (Princeton: Princeton University Press, 2002); and Peter Holquist, *Making War, Forging Revolution: Russia's Continuum of Crisis, 1914–1921* (Cambridge, Mass.: Harvard University Press, 2002).

## Overview

The origins of the Russian civil war can be found in the desacralisation of the tsarist autocracy that took place in the years before the First World War; in the social polarisations that shaped politics before and during 1917; and in the Bolshevik leadership's belief in the efficacy of civil war, the imminence of world revolution and the value of applying coercion in setting up a dictatorship of the proletariat. When did the civil war begin? Historians have made compelling cases for a variety of starting points, yet dating the event to October 1917 makes the most sense, because that is how contemporaries saw things. Armed opposition to the new Council of People's Commissars (Sovnarkom) arose immediately after the Second Congress of Soviets ratified the Bolshevik decree on land and declaration of peace, when officers of the imperial army formed the first counter-force known as the volunteer army, based in southern Russia. Ironically, the widespread belief among the population that Bolshevik power would soon crumble accompanied what Lenin, and subsequent generations of Soviet historians, called the 'triumphal march' of Soviet power as the Bolsheviks consolidated their hold in cities across central Russia.

During the civil war the Bolsheviks or Reds, renamed Communists in 1918, waged war against the Whites, a term used to refer to all factions that took up arms against the Bolsheviks. The Whites were a more diverse group than the Bolshevik label of 'counter-revolution' suggests. Those who represented the country's business and landowning elite often expressed monarchist sentiments. Historically guarding the empire's borders, Cossack military units enjoyed self-government and other privileges that likewise made them a conservative force. But many White officers had opposed the autocracy and some even harboured reformist beliefs. Much more complicated were the Bolsheviks' relations with Russia's moderate socialists, the Mensheviks and Socialist Revolutionaries (SRs) and both parties' numerous offshoots, who wished to establish a government that would include all socialist parties. Frequently subsumed within the wider conflict between Reds and Whites, the internecine struggle within the socialist camp over rival views of the meaning of revolution prevailed during much of 1918, persisted throughout the civil war, and flared up once again after the Bolsheviks routed the Whites in 1920.[10]

Fearing a White victory, the moderate socialist parties threw their support behind the Reds at critical junctures, thereby complicating this scenario. Moreover, left-wing factions within these parties forged alliances with the

10 See Geoffrey Swain, *The Origins of the Russian Civil War* (London and New York: Longman, 1996).

Bolsheviks. For instance, until mid-1918 the Bolsheviks stayed afloat in part owing to the support of the Left SRs, who broke from their parent party following October 1917. Accepting commissariats in the new government, the Left SRs believed they could influence Bolshevik policies towards Russia's peasant majority. In some locales the Bolshevik–Left SR coalition even weathered the controversy over the Brest-Litovsk Peace in March 1918, which ceded eastern Poland, the Baltic states, Finland and Ukraine to Germany, as well as Transcaucasia to Turkey, in return for an end to hostilities. Ratifying the treaty sundered the alliance with the Left SRs, who withdrew from the Lenin government in protest, and also sparked heated controversy within the Communist Party, especially among the so-called Left Communists led by Nikolai Bukharin, who backed a revolutionary war against Germany. Renegade Left SRs later formed a new party called the Revolutionary Communists (RCs), who participated in a ruling coalition with the Bolsheviks in many Volga provinces and the Urals. Committed to Soviet power, the RCs perceived otherwise questionable Bolshevik practices as the consequence of temporary circumstances brought about by civil war. The Bolshevik attitude towards the RCs and other groups that supported the Reds reflected the overall strength of Soviet power at any given time. Exercising power through a dynamic of co-optation amid repression, they manipulated their populist allies before orchestrating their merger with the Communists in 1920.[11]

Because political opposition to the Bolsheviks became more resolved after they closed down the Constituent Assembly in January 1918, the Lenin government established the Red Army under Leon Trotsky. He promptly recruited ex-tsarist officers to command the Reds, appointing political commissars to all units to monitor such officers and the ideological education of recruits. This early phase of the civil war ended with a spate of armed conflicts in Russian towns along the Volga in May and June 1918 between Bolshevik-run soviets and Czechoslovak legionnaires. Prisoners of war from the Austro-Hungarian armies, they were slated to be transported back to the western front in order to join the Allies in the fight to defeat the Central Powers. Their clash with the Soviet government emboldened the SR opposition to set up an anti-Bolshevik government, the Committee to Save the Constituent Assembly, *Komuch*, in the Volga city of Samara in June 1918. Many delegates elected to the Constituent Assembly congregated there before the city fell to the Bolsheviks that November. Meanwhile, the Bolsheviks expelled Mensheviks and SRs from local

11 Donald J. Raleigh, 'Co-optation amid Repression: The Revolutionary Communists in Saratov Province, 1918–1920', *Cahiers du Monde russe* 40, 4 (1999): 625–56.

soviets, while the Kadets met in the Siberian city of Omsk in June to establish a Provisional Siberian Government. The rivalry between Samara and Omsk resulted in a state conference that met in Ufa in September, the last attempt to form from below a national force to oppose Bolshevism. Drawing representatives from disparate bodies, the Ufa Conference set up a compromise five-member Directory. But in November the military removed the socialists from it and installed Admiral Kolchak in power. He kept his headquarters in Siberia, remaining official leader of the White movement until defeat forced him to resign in early 1920.

Although its role is often exaggerated, international intervention bolstered the White cause and fuelled Bolshevik paranoia, providing 'evidence' for the party's depictions of the Whites as traitorous agents of imperialist foreign powers. Maintaining an apprehensive attitude towards the Whites whom many in the West viewed as reactionaries, the Allies dispatched troops to Russia to secure military supplies needed in the war against Germany. Their involvement deepened as they came to see the Bolsheviks as a hostile force that promoted world revolution, renounced the tsarist government's debts and concluded a separate peace with Germany. Allied intervention on behalf of the Whites became more active with the end of the First World War in November 1918, when the British, French, Japanese, Americans and a dozen other powers sent troops to Russian ports and rail junctures. Revolutionary stirrings in Germany, the founding of the Third Communist International in Moscow in March 1919 and the temporary establishment of Béla Kun's Hungarian Soviet Republic at roughly the same time heightened the Allies' fears of a Red menace. Yet the Allied governments could not justify intervention in Russia to their own war-weary people. Lacking a common purpose and resolve, and often suspicious of one another, the Allies extended only half-hearted support to the Whites, whom they left in the lurch by withdrawing from Russia in 1919 and 1920 – except for the Japanese who kept troops in Siberia.

Both Reds and Whites turned to terror in the second half of 1918 as a substitute for popular support. Calls to overthrow Soviet power, followed by the assassination of German Ambassador Count Mirbach in July, which the Bolsheviks depicted as the start of a Left SR uprising designed to undercut the Brest-Litovsk Peace, provided the Bolsheviks with an excuse to repress their one-time radical populist allies and to undermine the Left SRs' hold over the villages. Moreover, with Lenin's approval, local Bolsheviks in Ekaterinburg executed Tsar Nicholas II and his family on 16 July 1918. Following an attempt on Lenin's life on 30 August, the Bolsheviks unleashed the Red Terror aimed at eliminating political opponents within the civilian population.

The Extraordinary Commission to Combat Counter-revolution and Sabotage (Cheka), set up in December 1917 under Feliks Dzerzhinsky, carried out the terror.

Seeking to reverse social revolution, the Whites savagely waged their own ideological war that justified the use of terror to avenge those who had been wronged by the revolution. Although the Whites never applied terror as systematically as the Bolsheviks, White Terror was equally horrifying and arbitrary. Putting to death Communists and their sympathisers, and massacring Jews in Ukraine and elsewhere,[12] the Whites posed a more serious threat to the Reds after the Allies backed the Whites' cause. Until their defeat in 1920, White forces controlled much of Siberia and southern Russia, while the Reds, who moved their capital to Moscow in March 1918, clung desperately to the Russian heartland.

The Whites' unsuccessful three-pronged attack against Moscow in March 1919 decided the military outcome of their war against the Reds. Despite their initial success, the Whites went down in defeat that November, after which their routed forces replaced General Anton Denikin with Petr Wrangel, the most competent of all the White officers. Coinciding with an invasion of Russia by forces of the newly resurrected Polish state, the Whites opened their final offensive in the spring of 1920. When Red forces overcame Wrangel's army in November, he and his troops retreated back to Crimea from which they then withdrew from Russia. In the meantime, the Bolsheviks' conflict with the Poles ended in stalemate; the belligerent parties signed an armistice in October 1920, followed by the Treaty of Riga in 1921, which transferred parts of Ukraine and Belorussia to Poland.

Although at civil war's end the difference between victory and defeat seemed a small one, it is hard to imagine how the Whites might have prevailed in the ordeal: the Constituent Assembly elections made clear that over 80 per cent of the population had voted for socialist parties. The Whites simply lacked mass appeal in a war in which most people were reluctant to get involved. Concentrated on the periphery, the Whites relied on Allied bullets and ordnance to fight the Reds. True, a more determined Allied intervention might have tipped the scales in the Whites' favour in the military conflict, but their failure was as much political as it was military. Recent scholarship reaffirms the ineptitude and corruption of the White forces, emphasising that their virtual government misunderstood the relationship between social policy and military

---

12 Orlando Figes, *A People's Tragedy: The Russian Revolution, 1891–1924* (London: Jonathan Cape, 1996), pp. 563–4, 656–9, 665, 676–9, 717.

success.[13] Moreover, the alliance with the moderate socialists, made frail by lack of a common ideology to unite them, contributed to the Whites' political failures, as did the hollow appeal of their slogan, 'One, Great, and Indivisible Russia'.[14]

Apart from their military encounters with the Whites, the Bolsheviks also had to contend with a front behind their own lines because of the appeal of rival socialist parties and because Bolshevik economic policies alienated much of the working class and drove the peasantry to rise up against the requisitioning of grain and related measures. Viewing October 1917 as a stage in the bourgeois-democratic revolution, the Menshevik Party refused to take part in an armed struggle against the Bolsheviks, but found their neutrality difficult to sustain when the White threat intensified. The party's political and ideological concessions to the Bolsheviks, however, damaged its identity, even its ideals, thus jeopardising its support among workers. Adopting hard-line policies towards Right Menshevik critics opposed to accommodating the Bolsheviks, the Menshevik Central Committee disbanded certain local party organisations, and expelled members from others.[15] True, some Right SRs experienced a short-lived period of co-operation with the Bolsheviks during the White offensive of 1919, but for the most part they threatened the Soviet government with the possibility of forming a third front comprising all other socialist groups. Given the far-reaching opposition to Bolshevik rule by 1920, Mensheviks and SRs believed the Leninists would be forced to co-opt the Menshevik/SR programme or face defeat. This encouraged them, as well as anarchist groups, to step up their agitation against the Bolsheviks at the end of the year.

The activities of the rival socialist parties provided the frame for popular revolt. Recent studies underscore the vast scale of the crisis of early 1921, documenting workers' strikes and armed peasant rebellions in many locales.[16] Peasant discontent, which the Communists called the Green movement, and mass worker unrest convinced the party to replace its unpopular economic policies known, in retrospect, as War Communism – characterised by

13 Jonathan Smele, *Civil War in Siberia: The Anti-Bolshevik Government of Admiral Kolchak, 1918–1920* (New York: Cambridge University Press, 1996); and Norman G. O. Pereira, *White Siberia: The Politics of Civil War* (Montreal and Kingston: McGill-Queen's University Press, 1996).
14 Susan Z. Rupp, 'Conflict and Crippled Compromise: Civil-War Politics in the East and the Ufa State Conference', *Russian Review* 56 (1997): 249–64.
15 Brovkin, *Behind*, pp. 244–6.
16 Raleigh, *Experiencing*, ch.12; and Jonathan Aves, *Workers against Lenin: Labour Protest and the Bolshevik Dictatorship* (London: Tauris Academic Studies, 1996).

economic centralisation, nationalisation of industry and land and compulsory requisitioning of grain – with the New Economic Policy (NEP), which
swapped the hated grain requisitioning with a tax in kind and restored some
legal private economic activity. The necessity of this shift in policy was made
clear when, in early March 1921, sailors of the Kronstadt naval fortress rose
up against the Bolsheviks whom they had helped bring to power. Demanding
the restoration of Soviet democracy without Communists, the sailors met
with brutal repression. Although most historians view the Kronstadt uprising,
worker disturbances, the Green movement and the introduction of the NEP
as the last acts of the civil war, after which the party mopped up remaining
pockets of opposition in the borderlands, the famine of 1921 marks the real
conclusion to the conflict, for it helped to keep the Bolsheviks in power by rob-
bing the population of initiative. Holding broad swaths of the country tightly
in its grip until late 1923, the famine and related epidemic diseases took an
estimated 5 million lives; countless more would have perished had it not been
for foreign relief.

Moreover, the Bolshevik Party took advantage of mass starvation to end its
stalemate with the Orthodox Church. Turning many believers against the new
order, the Bolsheviks had forced through a separation of Church and state in
1917 and removed schools from Church supervision. Once famine hit hard, the
party leadership promoted the cause of Orthodox clergy loyal to Soviet power,
so-called red priests, or renovationists. They supported the party's determination to use Church valuables to finance famine relief, hoping thereby to
strengthen their own position. Popular opposition to what soon amounted
to a government confiscation of Church valuables, however, triggered violent confrontations. Viewing these as evidence of a growing conspiracy, party
leaders allied with the renovationists. But this move was one of expedience,
for 'the Politburo planned to discard them in the final stage of destroying the
church'.[17]

The defeat of the Whites, the end of the war with Poland and famine made
it possible for the Lenin government to focus on regaining breakaway territories in Central Asia, Transcaucasia, Siberia and elsewhere, where issues of
nationalism, ethnicity, religion, class, foreign intervention and differing levels of
economic development and ways of life complicated local civil wars. Russians
had comprised approximately 50 per cent of the tsarist empire's multinational
population. At times tolerant, but increasingly contradictory and even repressive, tsarist nationality policies had given rise to numerous grievances among

17 Edward E. Roslof, *Red Priests: Renovationism, Russian Orthodoxy, and Revolution, 1905–1946*
(Bloomington: Indiana University Press, 2002), pp. 39–73, quote on p. 72.

the non-Russian population. Yet only a minority of intellectuals in the outlying areas before 1914 championed the emergence of independent states. The situation in Poland and perhaps Finland was the exception to this generalisation. The Revolution of 1917, however, gave impetus to national movements in Ukraine and elsewhere.

As Marxists engaged in an international struggle on behalf of the interests of the proletariat, the Bolsheviks backed self-determination of nations. This policy contributed to the destabilisation of the Provisional Government, and also created problems for the Bolsheviks once they took power. In January 1918 Sovnarkom's Commissariat of Nationalities (Narkomnats) headed by Stalin confirmed the Soviet government's support for self-determination of the country's minorities, characterising the new state as a federation of Soviet republics. The first Soviet constitution of July 1918 reiterated these claims, without specifying the nature of federalism. The cost of survival, however, made it necessary to be pragmatic and flexible: Lenin made clear already in early 1918 that the interests of socialism were more important than the right of self-determination. The sober reality of ruling, disappointment over the failure of world revolution, fear of hostile border states that could serve as bases for new intervention and the Soviet state's inability to prevent the emergence of an independent Poland, Finland, Latvia, Lithuania and Estonia, shaped emerging Soviet nationality politics.

Fostered by intellectuals and politicians, local nationalisms tended to develop into political movements with popular support in territories most affected by industrial development, whereas national consciousness arose more slowly where local nationalities had little presence in towns. Often, however, class and ethnic conflicts became entangled as these territories turned into major battlefields of the civil war and arenas of foreign intervention. The situation in regard to Ukraine illustrates these points. The Ukrainian authorities had demanded autonomy from the Provisional Government, and the Bolsheviks recognised Ukraine's independence at the end of 1917. But Ukraine's support of General Kaledin and the consequences of the short-lived Brest-Litovsk Peace with Germany dramatised the dangers of an unfriendly border state. Soon the activities of peasant rebel Nestor Makhno obscured the intertwining hostilities among Reds, Whites, Ukrainian nationalists, Germans and Poles, as Ukraine changed hands frequently. Under the black flag of anarchism, Makhno first formed a loose alliance with the Communists, but then battled against Red and White alike until Red forces crushed his army in 1920. With its rich farmland, developed industry and complex ethnic and social situation that included a sizeable Russian population in the cities, Ukraine was too important to the emerging Soviet state to be allowed to go its separate way. In Belorussia, nationalists had declared their independence under German protection in 1918, but this effort at statehood failed with Germany's withdrawal from the war. Nevertheless, the signing of the Treaty of Riga forced the Bolsheviks to give up parts of both Western Ukraine and Belorussia.

The Bolsheviks also had to accept other circumstances not to their liking. Recognising the non-socialist government set up in Finland in 1918, they backed an unsuccessful Red Army uprising in the former tsarist territory, after which they had to bow to political realities. With Germany's patronage, the Baltic states of Latvia, Estonia and Lithuania achieved their independence in a similar manner. Declaring their independence in 1918, the states floundered after Germany's defeat since coherent nationalist movements had not set them up. Yet with the assistance of the British navy and of units from the German army, they managed to prevail against the Red Army and local socialists.

In the Caucasus, Georgian Mensheviks, Armenian Dashnaks and Azeri Musavat established independent regimes in 1918. Because these states had developed so unevenly in the preceding decades, their nationalist movements remained distinct. Thus, when they attempted a short-lived experiment at federalism, irreconcilable differences and the territorial claims they had on each other forced them to turn to foreign protectors for self-defence. The Germans, followed by the British, came to the aid of the popular Georgian socialist republic set up by Mensheviks. Meanwhile, the Turks assisted their co-Muslim Azeris, while the Allies expressed support for the Armenians. The defeat of the Germans and the Turks, and the withdrawal of the British made it possible for ethnic strife to break out between Azeris and Armenians in Baku, especially since the Soviet government that held power briefly in the city in 1918 failed to rally the ethnically diverse region around the platform of Soviet power. The Red Army invaded Armenia and Azerbaijan in 1920, and Georgia the following year. Meeting with stiff resistance from religious leaders and guerrilla forces in mountain regions of the northern Caucasus, Soviet forces eventually overcame opposition there, too.

The situation in the Islamic regions of Russia proved to be particularly difficult to handle, since Islam, like Marxism, also espoused internationalist sentiments and there was always the fear that these feelings would find expression in support for the idea of a pan-Turkic state. By the late nineteenth century, elements within Russia's Muslim elite felt at home within a broader community of the world's Muslims. Some of Russia's Muslim intellectuals, the Jadids, advocated a complete reform of culture and society to meet the modern world's challenges. Embracing modernity and searching for what it meant to be Muslim, they encountered resistance from Muslim society's leaders, ever the more so because some would-be reformers had become socialists. To be sure, notions of statehood remained inchoate, but Jadids among the Crimean Tatar population did criticise tsarist policies, while war and revolution added impetus to anti-Russian feelings. Violent anti-European uprisings flared up in Central Asia in 1916, leaving embittered feelings on both sides. Moreover, the revolution emboldened the All-Russian Muslim Congress to press claims against the Provisional Government. Disintegration of state power further pitted reformers against traditional elites and Muslims against Russian settlers. For instance, angry clashes between Russian-controlled soviets and natives in Tashkent and Kazan' prompted some Muslims to side with the Whites. But this marriage of convenience was short-lived, since the Whites failed to dispel fears that they were little more than Russian oppressors.

Appreciating the need to win support within the Muslim world, the Bolsheviks granted autonomy to the Bashkirs in 1919 and to the Tatars in 1920. However, the party faced a diverse partisan movement deep in Central Asia that drew support from all classes but whose separate parts often fought for different reasons. Recapturing the khanates of Bukhara and Khiva in 1920, the Bolsheviks continued to face stubborn opposition elsewhere from armed bands of Islamic guerrillas, whom the Bolsheviks labelled brigands, or *basmachi*. They resisted the Red Army takeover until 1923. Given political realities, some Jadids joined the Communists in order to fulfil their vision of transforming Muslim society.

The Bolsheviks' victory in the civil war led to the founding of the Union of Soviet Socialist Republics (USSR) in December 1922. Under the supervision of Narkomnats, the Soviet government set up a federation, granting statehood within the framework of the Soviet Russian state to those territories it had recaptured. Seeing the nationalist threat as a serious one – including that among Russians, which had the potential to provoke defensive nationalism among others – Lenin and Stalin supported the development of non-Russian territories and downplayed Russian institutions, hoping to create a centralised, multi-ethnic, anti-imperial, socialist state, an 'affirmative action empire'.[18]

## The Bolshevik party-state

War, geopolitics and the prolonged crisis beginning in 1914 shaped the emerging Bolshevik party-state, which differed radically from the utopian views of

18 Terry Martin, *The Affirmative Action Empire: Nations and Nationalism in the Soviet Union, 1923–1939* (Ithaca, N. Y.: Cornell University Press, 2001).

the commune state that Lenin had formulated in 1917 in his *State and Revolution*. True, political power devolved to the locales for much of the civil war, but this was not by design. In many localities, revolutionary leaders headed up their own councils of people's commissars (*sovnarkomy*), which frequently declared themselves independent republics or communes. Localism emerged because each local unit of administration had to rely on its own resources to establish state power. In these dire circumstances, the revolutionary soviets became transformed into pillars of the state bureaucracy as their plenums lost influence and their executive committees and presidiums came to govern Russia. These small bands of revolutionaries justified their actions by insisting that opposition to Soviet power had made them necessary.

From the Sovnarkom's perspective, localism made it difficult to prosecute the war effort. To combat separatist tendencies, the Commissariat of Internal Affairs purged soviet executive committees of those opposed to centralism and turned party organisations into overseers of local soviets. The gradual implementation of the Soviet constitution helped to transform the country's network of soviets into pillars of state power by more narrowly defining their functions, making them financially dependent upon the Centre, and obliging local soviets to execute the decrees of higher organs of power. As a result, some soviets no longer held elections. In others, the party ended secret balloting and organised Communist election victories or had to settle for majorities of 'unaffiliated' deputies forced to conceal their real party preferences.

The government's attempts to centralise the political system gained momentum at the Eighth Party Congress in March 1919, as a result of which a principle of dual subordination was introduced: all administrative departments formed by soviet executive committees became subordinate to them but also to the corresponding Moscow commissariats. The debate over how centralised the new state should be, however, was fuelled by the Democratic Centralists (DCs), who believed that the decline in elective offices and collective decision-making had caused a malaise within the party. The DCs supported the integrity of the soviets vis-à-vis local party organisations and the Centre, opposing Moscow's periodic redistribution of cadres. The DCs debated these issues before the 1919 party congress and later led a full-scale attack against 'bureaucratic centralism'. But true reform 'remained a dead letter'[19] because open debate threatened the party's tenuous hold on power.

---

19 Leonard Schapiro, *The Origin of the Communist Autocracy: Political Opposition in the Soviet State. First Phase, 1917–1922*, 2nd edn (Cambridge, Mass.: Harvard University Press, 1977), p. 223.

To be sure, the cultural frame that defined the parameters of Bolshevik civil-war practices was rooted in centuries of autocracy characterised by Russia's frail representative institutions; low levels of popular participation in political life; centralisation; a bureaucratic, authoritarian government with broad powers; and highly personalised political attachments.[20] Yet political culture does absorb new influences from historical experience. The conditions of the 1914–21 period endowed civic practices with exaggerated, even grotesque features. Some historians ground the party elite's maximalism in the circumstances of the First World War, which created a new political type prone to apply military methods to civilian life. The attitudes and skills the new leaders acquired during a period of destruction, violence, social unrest, hunger and shortages of all kinds made them enemies of compromise who believed that anything that served the proletariat was moral. Such beliefs fed corruption, abuses of power and arbitrary behaviour, as well as a system of privileges that kept the party afloat often in a sea of indifference and hostility from the people whose support they lost.[21] Moreover, in promoting the use of violence in public life, the civil war affected the political attitudes not only of Bolsheviks: a synchronous birth of 'strong power' forms of government emerged among both Reds and Whites, producing *chrezvychaishchina*, or forms of government based on mass terror, which left a deep mark on the country's political culture.[22] Although Russia's vulnerable democratic traditions continued to coexist with Soviet power, the civil-war experience reduced the likelihood that the democratic strains in Russian public life would supplant the authoritarian ones.

The civil war widened access to the political elite for members of all revolutionary parties, young adults, women, national minorities and the poorly educated, creating not a workers' party, but a plebeian one, run mainly by intellectuals. Throughout the conflict, workers made up roughly 40 per cent of the party's membership and the peasantry 20 per cent. Officials and members of the intelligentsia accounted for the rest, and perhaps for this reason the party remained better educated than the population at large. Approximately

---

20 Stephen White, 'The USSR: Patterns of Autocracy and Industrialization', in Archie Brown and Jack Gray (eds.), *Political Culture and Political Change in Communist States*, 2nd edn (New York: Holmes and Meier, 1979), p. 25.
21 E. G. Gimpel'son, 'Sovetskie upravlentsy: Politicheskii i nravstvennyi oblik (1917–1920 gg.)', *Otechestvennaia istoriia*, 1997, no. 5: 45–52; and Fitzpatrick, 'The Civil War', pp. 57–76.
22 See Gennadij Bordjugov, 'Chrezvychainye mery i "Chrezvychaishchina" v Sovetskoi respublike i drugikh gosudarstvennykh obrazovaniiakh na territorii Rossii v 1918–1920 gg.', *Cahiers du Monde russe* 38, 1–2 (1997): 29–44; and V. P. Buldakov, *Krasnaia smuta: Priroda i posledstviia revoliutsionnogo nasiliia* (Moscow: Rosspen, 1997).

1.5 million people enrolled in the party between 1917 and 1920, but fewer than half a million members were left by 1922.[23] Moreover, at this time the over-whelming majority of party members had joined it in 1919–20.[24] Civil-war circumstances had propelled recent converts into positions of prominence, but Old Bolsheviks monopolised the political leadership, which also con-tained a larger percentage of minority nationalities than among the rank and file.

Dramatising their differences from non-Communists, the Bolsheviks cast themselves as disciplined, hard, selfless, dedicated, committed, honest and sober. The gulf existing between Bolshevik self-representation and individual party members' personal attributes was so large, however, that party diehards mistrusted the rank and file. Party leader L. B. Krasin, for instance, opined that 90 per cent of the party's members were 'unscrupulous time-servers'.[25] Appreciating the powerful role of cultural constraints, the party enrolled thou-sands of young recruits on probation, maintaining a revolving-door policy and expelling members who compromised it. The most serious attempts to flush the party of undesirable elements took place in the spring of 1919, when 46.8 per cent of the party's total membership was excluded. During the purge of 1920, 28.6 per cent of the party's members were expelled, and in 1921, 24.8 per cent.[26]

One of the most widespread problems that purging the party sought to remedy was corruption. Blaming it for the Whites' success, the party made corruption a class issue by depicting it as a 'dirty' form of class relationships inherited from old Russia, as bourgeois specialists and former tsarist bureau-crats obtained administrative positions – and rations – 'simply by applying for party membership the day before applying for the job itself'.[27] Indeed, in 1918, necessity forced the Bolsheviks to co-opt into the emerging state appa-ratus individuals whose political views were often inimical to Bolshevism: the Bolsheviks needed their class enemy not only to run the machinery of state but also to blame when its (mal)functioning provoked mass discontent. The process of 'othering' the bourgeoisie likewise had practical limitations because the vicissitudes of class war could be turned on and off during this time of terrible shortages with a bribe or valuable personal contact.

23 Jonathan R. Adelman, 'The Development of the Soviet Party Apparat in the Civil War: Center, Localities, and Nationality Areas', *Russian History* 9, pt. 1 (1982): 91–2.
24 T. H. Rigby, 'The Soviet Political Elite', *British Journal of Political Science* 1 (1971): 418–19, 422, 436.
25 Cited in Gimpel'son, 'Sovetskie upravlentsy', 44.
26 Adelman, 'Development', p. 97. See also Narskii, *Zhizn'*, pp. 452–61.
27 Robert Service, *The Bolshevik Party in Revolution, 1917–1923: A Study in Organizational Change* (New York: Barnes and Noble, 1979), p. 90.

The consequences of the Bolsheviks' arbitrary policies proved difficult to eradicate. When the party in April 1919 broadened the activities of the State Control Commission to do something about the problem of corruption, the commission found malfeasance, theft, speculation and other forms of corruption in virtually all Soviet institutions. As part of a national campaign to curb abuses of power, restore discipline, cut down on red tape, revive industry and overcome growing worker alienation from the party by involving workers in participatory practices, the party replaced the State Control Commission in 1920 with the Workers'–Peasants' Inspectorate (*Rabkrin*). But it too failed to remedy the problem because of the billiard-ball interaction of circumstances, ideologically fuelled initiatives, rivalries, misunderstandings, deep cultural patterns and the unbelievably awful functioning of essentially all institutions and organisations.

## Revolution and culture

Bolshevik cultural policies underscore the complex interaction between the empowering environment of revolution, utopian stirrings of Communists and intellectuals alike, Russian cultural practices and the larger contemporary arena of Western and even American culture.[28] Bent on retaining power and the symbols of legitimacy, the Bolsheviks disagreed over how best to implement new cultural practices, which they saw as essential to the success of their revolution. Like the French Revolutionaries, they sought to create a new national will through revolutionary ideology. Although some party members opposed the complete destruction of the cultural past and instead sought to 'proletarianise' it by making it more accessible, others promoted efforts to sweep away old cultural forms.

The institution most identified with cultural revolution was Proletkul't, organised in October 1918. An acronym for proletarian cultural-educational organisations, Proletkul't aimed to awaken independent creative activity among the proletariat. Without a common vision of what 'proletarian culture' was or ought to be, cultural activists showed that their struggle 'was just as contestuous as the efforts to change the political and economic foundations of Soviet society'.[29] Their efforts reveal that an intelligentsia divided among itself,

---

28 Katerina Clark, *Petersburg: Crucible of Cultural Revolution* (Cambridge, Mass.: Harvard University Press, 1995).
29 Lynn Mally, *Culture of the Future: The Proletkult Movement in Revolutionary Russia* (Berkeley and Los Angeles: University of California Press, 1990), p. xviii.

but mostly ill-disposed toward a marketplace in culture, played the leading role in promoting proletarian culture, and for this reason had limited success.[30]

In its hurried drive to reconstitute society, the Soviet government abolished titles, private property and ranks. It fashioned a new language, social hierarchies (and divisions), rituals and festivals, myths, revolutionary morality and revolutionary justice. It emancipated women by promulgating a radical family code in 1918. It separated Church and state. It modernised the alphabet, introduced calendar reform, and sought to make revolution itself a tradition. Revolutionary songs, party newspapers, slogans, pamphlets, brochures, elections and festivals acquired new meaning. For instance, Bolshevik festivals left little room for spontaneity and popular initiative. Revolutionaries also sought to obscure the past by making it difficult to observe traditional holidays, especially religious ones.

The Communists likewise fashioned a new public ideological language that, in erasing the difference between ideas and reality, liberated them from the need to provide any logical proof for their claims.[31] Communism's public language emphasised distrust of the class other; a hierarchy of class, soviets, privileges, even of countries; coercion as the necessary means that justified the hoped-for ends; and a national ideology as opposed to a parochial one. The specifics of the ever-changing narrative are less important than how it underscored the battle of the new world against the old, the need to sacrifice, and the despicable nature of the opposition. By the time the civil war drew to a close, the Bolsheviks were proclaiming that the Communist victory and survival of the Soviet state were inevitable, that capitalism was doomed, and that it would trigger a new war and world revolution. This conveyed the message that resistance was not only improper, but also futile. In promising a glorious future, the Bolsheviks thus inscribed historically delayed gratification into their narrative of revolution, which they presented to the population through newspapers, propaganda efforts, visual arts and other forms.[32] During periods of vulnerability the party took additional measures to propagate its views; however, these frenzied efforts only underscored how little cultural capital the Communists had at this point. Indeed, to make their ideology the ruling one, the Bolsheviks took over the state educational system, giving literacy and the spread of 'enlightenment' a top priority

30 James R. Von Geldern, *Bolshevik Festivals, 1917–1920* (Berkeley and Los Angeles: University of California Press, 1993), p. 72.
31 Mikhail N. Epstein, *After the Future: The Paradoxes of Postmodernism* (Amherst: University of Massachusetts Press, 1995), pp. 102–3, 118, 154–5, 161.
32 Raleigh, *Experiencing*, ch. 7.

in order to facilitate the reception of their propaganda, but met with stiff opposition.

As party leaders and intellectuals quarrelled among themselves over how best to effect cultural change, practices immersed in everyday life continued to direct people's perceptions along more familiar, less revolutionary pathways, preventing a complete destruction of past culture. Ultimately, the Bolsheviks sacralised a new world that privileged workers and at times peasants not only through class-based policies but also through the construction of a heroic narrative of the revolution that reflected new social hierarchies. While this narrative of integration – and exclusion – made it possible for later generations of Soviet leaders to co-opt and mobilise individuals and groups, the ready employment of the despotic power of the state to effect cultural change helped obscure the fact that the party had failed to establish cultural domination, while its ideology continued to invite argument.

## War Communism and Russia's peasant majority

The economic formation that prevailed between 1918 and March 1921 has subsequently come to be known as War Communism. A term lacking analytical precision, it was originally popularised by L. Kritsman, its leading spokesperson, and used by Lenin to discredit the opposition. In elucidating the term, the partisan and scholarly literatures either emphasise the role of ideology in implementing 'communist' economic principles during civil-war conditions, or downplay it, underscoring instead the emergency nature of the measures enacted.[33] Yet the lessons learned are less about the new economic order itself than about the significance of *how* the Bolsheviks attempted to put it into practice.

Civil war in industry started immediately after October 1917, when the Bolsheviks limited private property and the market, encouraging workers' control and nationalising banks.[34] Economic localism soon clashed with centralising impulses against a background of various ideological legacies. These included the tsarist wartime economic model in place since 1915 in which state intervention and control played a major role, and utopian Marxist visions of a socialist economy, which presumed an inherent hostility in class relations and

---

33 See Silvana Malle, *The Economic Organization of War Communism, 1918–1921* (Cambridge: Cambridge University Press, 1985), pp. 1–28; and S. A. Pavliuchenkov, *Voennyi kommunizm v Rossii: Vlast' i massy* (Moscow: RKT-Istoriia, 1997), pp. 16–44.
34 Pavliuchenkov, *Voennyi kommunizm*, 23–4; and E. G. Gimpel'son, *Formirovanie Sovetskoi politicheskoi sistemy, 1917–1923 gg.* (Moscow: Nauka, 1995), p. 96.

the superiority of socialist principles.[35] Although previous state policies shaped economic practices during the civil war, Bolshevik ideology transformed practices of state intervention by justifying coercion. This point is manifested in the implementation of the food dictatorship and nationalisation of industry in 1918; in the obligatory grain quota assessment or *razverstka* and co-optation of the consumer co-operatives in 1919; and in the militarisation of labour and greater use of violence in the countryside in 1920.

The Soviet government created an organ responsible for economic life, the Supreme Economic Council (Sovnarkhoz), and urged local soviets to establish provincial councils. Industrial breakdown in 1918 posed the most pressing problem for local economic councils, which likewise navigated the rocky transition from workers' control to centralisation, and resolved which industries to nationalise and how to improve transportation, becoming embroiled in inter-agency squabbles in the process, particularly with the Food Supply Commissariat (Narkomprod). But pragmatism as well as conflict coloured the relationship between local councils and Moscow, especially since industries managed by the Centre had a greater chance of securing fuel to keep operating. The military threat also defined local councils' activities as some of their departments worked exclusively for the Red Army and eventually all of them did so to some degree. Their main problem, however, remained lack of clearly defined jurisdiction between the councils and local agencies of Moscow's chief industrial branch administrations (*glavki*).

Growing food shortages accompanied the collapse of industrial production. The problem had begun already during the war and gained momentum in 1917, when local agencies proved reluctant to release resources, fearing the destabilising consequences of the scarcity of food. As civil war unfolded, provincial agencies struggled to satisfy both local and larger demands on food supplies. To cope with the crisis, the Soviet government set up the Food Supply Commissariat on 27 May 1918. Local agencies soon registered the population in order to issue rations cards according to a class principle that privileged workers and discriminated against the bourgeoisie. The class principle of doling out food proved to be largely symbolic, however, owing to a constant reclassification of professions and to the fact that members of the bourgeoisie often took jobs in the bureaucracy to obtain rations.[36] The Bolsheviks' co-opting of the consumer co-operatives, responsible for distributing food and other items, further exacerbated the distribution of food and other essentials. Oppositional socialists

35 Jacques Sapir, 'La Guerre civile et l'économie de guerre: Origines du système soviétique', *Cahiers du Monde russe* 38, 1–2 (1997): 9–28.
36 McAuley, *Bread and Justice*, pp. 286–94.

fought to retain the co-operatives' independence, adding to the difficulty the Bolsheviks had in taking them over.

Centring on procurement, Bolshevik economic practices alienated the peasantry and contributed to the famine of 1921–3. The party launched its first annual grain procurement programme in August 1918; however, the breakdown of the state infrastructure made procurement highly problematic. Shortages of employees in the procurement bodies, the parallelism of government organisations, destruction caused by the Whites, transportation difficulties and sundry decrees issued by local executive committees undermined campaigns. Moreover, the peasants' reluctance to hand over grain convinced the Bolsheviks to foment class war in the countryside by introducing committees of the village poor (*kombedy*). In the summer and autumn of 1918 brigades of Narkomprod's Food Army (*prodarmiia*), comprising workers from the capitals and other industrial cities, participated in the government's procurement programme. Most of them ended up speculating in grain, thereby sabotaging the Soviet government's system of fixed prices.

The exchange of manufactured goods for agricultural products (*tovaroobmen*) served as the linchpin of procurement. Established by a decree of 2 April 1918, *tovaroobmen* became mandatory for thirteen 'grain producing' provinces.[37] This involved setting up a food monopoly, abolishing private trade and establishing fixed prices, creating central supply organs and combating 'speculation'. Despite unfavourable sowing conditions in the spring of 1919 and the disruption of civil war, the government's assessment in 1919 represented a significant increase over the previous year. Acknowledging that a black market in just about everything undermined state procurement efforts, the party justified the use of force to carry out requisitioning. Although repression sparked disturbances throughout the countryside, the Bolsheviks needed to rely on the measures to hold onto power while they tried to effect the changes that they believed would make coercion unnecessary in the long run. To be sure, the peasantry designed their own strategies to ward off domination. The result was famine. The introduction of NEP was made possible only after a massive social and political rejection of War Communism on the part not only of the peasantry, but also of workers and elements in the party and state apparatus.

But it did not have to be that way. Until mid-1918 village autonomy flourished as the peasants finished the social revolution in the villages, liquidating gentry

37 See M. I. Davydov, 'Gosudarstvennyi tovaroobmen mezhdu gorodom i derevnei v 1918–1921 gg.', *Istoricheskie zapiski* 108 (1982): 33–59.

landholding and promoting a levelling process. In fact, the Right SRs' bid for power failed in part because the peasantry, satisfied with the land settlement, remained neutral before that summer. However, the Communist Party's decision on 11 June 1918 to establish *kombedy* to promote social revolution in the villages, facilitate grain collection and curb free trade marked a tragic turn in the party's course in the countryside. Combined with the introduction of the grain monopoly and food dictatorship in May and the first mobilisations into the Red Army, the party's resolve to manufacture class war in the villages represented the beginning of the end of the fleeting period of peasant self-rule.[38] These measures also exacerbated the rift between town and country, strained relations between the Bolsheviks and Left SRs, and eventually forced the Bolsheviks to reject their own policies.

Although the Red Army served as an institution of socialisation, mandatory service also turned the countryside against the Communists, as is evinced in the colossal rate of desertion. Soldiers deserted because they wanted to be left alone, because they were concerned about the fate of their loved ones, because of the terrible conditions in the ranks and because of their opposition to specific policies such as requisitioning and the imposition of an extraordinary tax. The failure of rural soviets to work the fields of Red Army men contributed to the problem, as did the vile conditions in military hospitals. The party applied carrot and stick measures to deserters, including execution, the taking of hostages and amnesties, yet between 1918 and 1920 probably over half of all of those drafted deserted.[39]

Ultimately, the ideology of Bolshevism, as well as a strain in Russian intellectual life that viewed the countryside in a negative light, drove the Bolsheviks to force unfavourable rates of exchange on the peasants. In fact, the language the party used in describing the peasantry – ' disorganised', 'poor and ignorant know-nothings', who lacked 'consciousness' because they were 'politically illiterate' and had a 'low cultural level' – bears some striking similarities to the language of colonialism.[40] Communists blamed the 'darkness' of the village for the peasants' antipathy towards Soviet power, susceptibility to rumours and failure to understand the imminence of world revolution. They understood

38 Orlando Figes, *Peasant Russia, Civil War: The Volga Countryside in Revolution (1917–1921)* (Oxford: Oxford University Press, 1989), p. 71.
39 Raleigh, *Experiencing*, pp. 332–7; and Mark Von Hagen, *Soldiers in the Proletarian Dictatorship: The Red Army and the Soviet Socialist State, 1917–1930* (Ithaca, N.Y.: Cornell University Press, 1990), pp. 69–79.
40 Alvin W. Gouldner, 'Stalinism: A Study of Internal Colonialism', in *Political Power and Social Theory: A Research Annual* (Greenwich, Conn., 1978): 209–59; 212, 216, 238; S. V. Leonov, *Rozhdenie Sovetskoi imperii: Gosudarstvo i ideologiia, 1917–1922 gg.* (Moscow: Dialog MGU, 1997), p. 183.

that the peasantry demonstrated little interest in Communism, seeking solace in the argument that economic ruin caused the peasantry's lack of enthusiasm. That is, if Communism had worked, the peasantry would have been all for it.

In 1919 forced requisitioning replaced the hitherto haphazard approach to obtaining grain deliveries. Discontent stemming from unfair quotas and from confiscations surfaced immediately, as a result of which punitive measures proved necessary to realise the state's objectives. One illustrative episode from Saratov province involved an armed unit under the command of N. A. Cheremukhin in the summer of 1919, which violently struck out against desertion and the brewing of illicit spirits. Known in party circles for his 'tact, experience . . . and devotion to the interests of the Revolution', Cheremukhin torched 283 households in the village of Malinovka. Applying 'revolutionary justice', he confiscated 'kulak property', levied contributions on entire villages that participated in anti-Soviet uprisings and shot 'active opponents of Soviet power, deserters, kulaks, and chronic brewers of moonshine'. Between July and September his forces executed 139 people in an attempt to break the spirit of those opposed to Soviet decrees. Party members, non-Communists and Red Army units protested against Cheremukhin's repression.[41] But local party boss V. A. Radus-Zen'kovich insisted that Cheremukhin's detachment 'did not use force at all'.[42] Such episodes made it certain that peasants would later welcome armed peasant bands bent on overthrowing Bolshevik power.

Beginning in mid-1918, peasant rebellions against Communist policies represented attempts to restore an earlier, partially mythical, time before Soviet power, which had done plenty to drive the peasantry into the opposition. Soviet power mobilised peasant youth. It brought in hungry urban workers from the outside to wrench grain from the countryside. It created havoc when it set up the *kombedy*. It levied an extraordinary tax. It attacked religion. It threatened traditional power and gender relations. It subjected the peasantry to abuses of power that exceeded anything rural inhabitants had experienced before. As a result, peasant bands known as Greens composed of deserters and others surfaced in 1918 and again in 1919 during the White offensive. Triggering uprisings in Tambov, the Volga and Urals regions, Ukraine and Siberia, the peasant revolt reached a crescendo in 1920 and 1921, when Lenin remarked

---

41 Gosudarstvennyi arkhiv Saratovskoi oblasti (GASO), f. 521, op. 1, d. 445, ll. 4–6, 19–21, 59, 76, 85, 102; f. 521, op. 1, d. 445, ll. 60–61 ob, 63–63 ob, 67; and Tsentr Dokumentatsii Noveishei Istorii Saratovskoi Oblasti (TsDNISO), f. 151/95, op. 2, d. 8, l. 17.

42 See Pavliuchenkov, *Voennyi kommunizm*, pp. 208–11; and V. A. Radus-Zen'kovich, *Stranitsy geroicheskogo proshlogo. Vospominaniia i stat'i* (Moscow: Gosudarstvennoe izdatel'stvo politicheskoi literatury, 1960), p. 39.

that this 'counter-revolution is without doubt more dangerous than Denikin, Yudenich, and Kolchak taken together'.[43]

Although the SR Party might not have orchestrated the peasant revolt, SR values – including violence – provided the political frame for the peasant rebels' programme.[44] Despite some differences in the demands of particular groups, the Greens did not oppose Soviet power, but rather the specific policies of War Communism and the arbitrary lording over them of 'vampire-Communists, Jews and commissar-usurpers'. Seeking to put an end to 'Bolshevik tyranny', the Greens advocated restoration of the Constituent Assembly. The relative isolation of local communities and the subaltern nature of the peasant world made it unlikely that a peasant revolt triggered by one-time Red Army men would succeed without outside leadership and organisation, but the Bolsheviks feared that the spate of uprisings could have tipped the scales against the party because of the potent ferment in the cities. Interrupting grain requisitioning and agricultural production, the Greens killed Communists whenever they encountered them, destroyed collective farms, disbanded Soviet agencies and seized seed, agricultural products and livestock, thereby exacerbating food shortages in the cities.

The party's decision to employ force in the villages also contributed to the famine of 1921–3, which provided the Bolsheviks with an opportunity they exploited to fortify their position. Although climatic conditions played a role in the famine's origins, the major cause was Bolshevik agricultural policies.[45] Moscow did not knowingly allow the famine to develop, but it ignored local reports until late spring 1921, when mass discontent and chilling news on the magnitude of the potential human suffering put an end to any doubts about the gravity of the crisis.

If the civil war was a process whereby a fractious society renegotiated its values, then the government's rapacious policies in the villages, the rupture of market relations and the increase in savagery strengthened the internal mechanisms of cohesion in the countryside and the appeal of landownership at the expense of whatever collectivist principles might have existed. Largely alienated from power, the peasant withdrew into the local economy and everyday

43 V. I. Lenin, *Polnoe sobranie sochinenii*, vol. XLIII (Moscow: Gosudarstvennœ izdatel'stvo politicheskoi literatury, 1970), p. 24.
44 Seth Singleton, 'The Tambov Revolt (1920–1921)', *Slavic Review* 25, 3 (1966): 502. See also Oliver Radkey, *The Unknown Civil War in Soviet Russia: A Study of the Green Movement in the Tambov Region, 1920–1921* (Stanford, Calif.: Hoover Institution Press, 1976).
45 James W. Long, 'The Volga Germans and the Famine of 1921', *Russian Review* 51, 4 (1992): 510; Markus Wehner, 'Golod 1921–1922 gg. v Samarskoi gubernii i reaktsiia Sovetskogo pravitel'stva', *Cahiers du Monde russe* 38, 1–2 (1997): 223–42.

life. In order to survive, the peasant had to become more self-sufficient by the winter of 1918–19. The famine furthered this trend. Ironically, by the end of the civil war many peasants rejected communal land tenure even though during the revolution they had clamoured for egalitarian distribution.[46]

## Workers against Bolsheviks

Although the Bolsheviks understood and depicted the events of October 1917 as a workers' revolution, many workers became alienated from the new party-state. Their world-view shaped by ideology, Bolsheviks interpreted workers' estrangement as the consequence of de-urbanisation during the civil war, and not as a change in workers' attitudes, maintaining that the number of 'real' proletarians (in effect, a metaphysical concept tautologically defined as a worker who supported the party) simply had declined. The social turmoil at this time did reduce the size of Russia's working class and reconfigure its gender and age composition. Many workers perished; most who enrolled in the Communist Party left their factory benches to serve in the burgeoning state bureaucracy. Others entered the Red Army, returned to the villages or joined the ranks of the unemployed. Yet a substantial core of urban workers remained in the factories, and their attitudes towards the Bolsheviks were indeed transformed. Working-class consciousness did not disappear during the civil war, but found expression in resistance to and circumvention of Bolshevik practices, both in the implicit language of symbolic activity such as labour absenteeism and foot-dragging, and in more antagonistic ways. A consciousness based on their experience of dealing with the Bolsheviks gave some workers their own collective identities outside those the Bolsheviks created for them. While economic hardship certainly galvanised workers during the civil war, they also blamed the Bolsheviks for the rift within the democracy, political repression and the betrayal of the promises of 1917.

Debate over issues of labour policy already rocked the party in the weeks following October 1917, when the Bolsheviks reconsidered the role factory committees and trade unions would play under the new regime. As factory committees began to run rather than supervise factory administrations, the Bolsheviks realised that spontaneous industrial democracy could become a political handicap. As a result, they reorganised unions by industry, thereby undermining the factory committees, and then made the unions extensions of party organs. This transformation proved to be highly contested, especially

46 Figes, *Peasant Russia*, p. 59.

since Mensheviks backed independent trade unions. Workers, in the meantime, enrolled in them to obtain larger rations. The union leadership's support in 1920 of centralisation, discipline and labour conscription further alienated them from workers. Tensions within the Communist Party over labour conscription and other controversial policies resulted in angry debate over what role unions should play in the post-war environment, involving the so-called Workers' Opposition associated with A. G. Shliapnikov, the Democratic Centralists, as well as Lenin and Trotsky. Strictly a party affair, the debate did not appeal to workers.[47]

The further deterioration of the economy – as well as discontent over broken political promises – drove many workers into the opposition. The collapse of the economy resulted in factory closures and unemployment. Wages did not keep up with prices, despite a chaotic system of bonus pay. To survive, workers were forced to rely on the black market and on other survival strategies such as pilfering, absenteeism and shirking responsibilities. The economic experience of civil war thus left an indelible imprint on their individual and mass consciousness by shaping a culture of mutual dependence in conditions of utmost want. Growing indifference towards work and a drop in labour discipline had manifested themselves already in 1918. The situation deteriorated in 1919, when fuel shortages shut down factories.

Needing working-class support in order to justify and rationalise the dictatorship of the proletariat they claimed to have established, the Bolsheviks endowed workers with a symbolic capital that the party manipulated through its control over the language used to give meaning to the term 'worker'. Invoking class as a weapon of exclusion and inclusion in their efforts to reconfigure Russian culture, the Bolsheviks reconstructed a working-class identity. Given the claims the party made about the working class, the new identity the party formulated for workers became something one attained through correct behaviour. Class had become a social-psychological and political projection in which any act of opposition brought symbolic expulsion from the ranks of the true proletariat and confinement to the ranks of an inferior class 'other'. As one Communist put it, 'given his class position a worker can be nothing but a Communist'.[48]

The party viewed workers hierarchically, casting highly skilled members of the industrial proletariat as the conscious revolutionary vanguard that

---

47 See Larry E. Holmes, 'For the Revolution Redeemed: The Workers Opposition in the Bolshevik Party 1919–1921', *Carl Beck Papers in Russian and East European Studies*, no. 802 (Pittsburgh: Center for Russian and East European Studies, 1990): 6–9.
48 TsDNISO, f. 136, op. 1, d. 9, l. 7.

supported Soviet power. But it was precisely these workers who challenged the Bolsheviks the most.[49] Denying workers agency, the party depicted dissatisfaction among skilled workers as temporary wavering caused by the deceptive propaganda practices of rival socialist parties, and opposition among unskilled and female workers as the result of their lack of consciousness. As the civil war deepened, the Bolsheviks blamed the physical disappearance of the working class for labour conflicts, representing opposition as the work of counter-revolutionaries, saboteurs and misguided peasant workers.

Although economic issues provided the venue for voicing dissatisfaction, workers' actions indicate that they understood economic life as contested political ground. Workers expressed their consciousness in routine acts of resistance and circumvention: voting against Communist candidates and resolutions, abstaining from voting when elections lacked real choices, foot-dragging, inertia, absenteeism, pilfering, dissimulation, co-opting Soviet public language and practices and using them to their advantage, spreading rumours and so on. They opposed one-party rule, the silencing of the opposition press, attempts to co-opt labour organs and other repressive measures. Such opposition often amounted to demands for secret ballots during elections to factory committees and soviets. For their part, the Bolsheviks alternated between repression and solicitousness, depending upon how vulnerable they felt, but remained determined to control, manipulate and repress the workers' movement so as not to encourage the opposition.[50]

After thrashing the White armies in 1920, the Bolsheviks devoted all of their energies to 'peaceful construction', to attempts to address industrial collapse, transportation breakdown, shrinking rations and dying cities. The party declared war on economic ruin, filth, disease and hunger, addressing the need to restore industry, raise productivity and mobilise labour armies at the rear. It extended labour bonuses and introduced a labour ration based on the type of work one did. It stepped up its campaign to involve citizens in unpopular volunteer workdays (*subbotniki*). It set up labour disciplinary courts to deal with absenteeism, instituted one-person management and restructured unions to raise productivity. These measures, as well as use of bourgeois specialists, piece-rate wages and labour books to control movement, provoked waves of unrest in Russia, uniting workers who otherwise had little in common and once again showing how they created themselves as workers. In turn, labour disturbances ended a period of relaxation in the party's tolerance of rival socialist parties, just as it gave rise to opposition groups within the Communist Party.

49 Aves, *Workers against Lenin*, passim.
50 Raleigh, *Experiencing*, pp. 367–77; and Narskii, *Zhizn'*, pp. 461–8.

While workers' strikes in Petrograd at this time are well known and usually viewed as a prelude to the soldiers' revolt at Kronstadt in March 1921, recent research documents similar ferment in Moscow and perhaps most provincial capitals. In fact, the party announced the end of grain requisitioning and approved the NEP not only in response to rural unrest, but also in response to the powerful wave of industrial strikes – which the party represented as a work slowdown or *volynka* – in key urban centres.[51] In Saratov, for instance, an 'all but general strike' broke out, which the party brutally repressed by sentencing 219 workers to death and others to various prison terms, and by expanding its network of informants throughout the province.[52]

## Conclusion

In accounting for the Bolshevik victory in the civil war, historians have emphasised the self-sacrifice, relative discipline and centralised nature of the Bolshevik Party; its control over the Russian heartland and its resources; the military and political weaknesses of the Whites, particularly their failure to promote popular social policies; the subaltern nature of the Green opposition; the inability of the Bolsheviks' opponents to overcome their differences; the tentative nature of Allied intervention; the effectiveness of Bolshevik propaganda and terror; and, during the initial stage of the conflict, the support of many workers and peasants. In defeating the Whites the Bolsheviks had survived the civil war, but the crisis of March 1921 suggests that mass discontent could have continued to fuel the conflict. It did not, owing to the concessions ushered in by the NEP, which gave the impression that the Leninists had fallen under the influence of their rivals' programmes, and which took the edge off the opposition, since so many longed to have order restored. The famine also helped to keep the Bolsheviks in power by preventing popular discontent from flaring up again.

The Russian civil war caused wide-scale devastation, economic ruin, loss of life through military operations and disease and the emigration of an estimated 1–2 million middle- and upper-class Russians. Most estimates of human losses during the ordeal range from 7 million to 8 million, of which more than 5 million were civilian casualties of fighting, repression and disease. These figures do not include the estimated 5 million who died from the famine of 1921–3. Moreover, the civil war produced a steep decline in the standard of living, causing the destruction of much of the country's infrastructure.

---

51 Aves, *Workers against Lenin*, 111–57; and Raleigh, *Experiencing*, ch. 12.
52 Raleigh, *Experiencing*, pp. 387–91.

Industrial production fell to less than 30 per cent of the pre-1914 level and the amount of land under cultivation decreased sharply.[53] Soviet policies resulted in a large measure of de-urbanization, created a transient problem of enormous proportions, militarised civilian life, ruined infrastructures, turned towns into breeding grounds for diseases, increased the death rate and victimised children.

Furthermore, War Communism strengthened the authoritarian streak in Russian political culture by creating an economic order characterised by centralisation, state ownership, compulsion, the extraction of surpluses, forced allocation of labour and a distribution system that rhetorically privileged the toiling classes. Six years of hostilities, of wartime production that exhausted supplies, machinery and labour, and of ideologically inspired and circumstantially applied economic policies had shattered the state's infrastructure, depleted its resources, brutalised its people and brought them to the brink of physical exhaustion and emotional despair. In political terms, the party's economic policies contributed to the consolidation of a one-party state and the repression of civil society as the population turned its attention to honing basic survival strategies. In practical terms, the price of survival was the temporary naturalisation of economic life, famine and the entrenchment of a black market and a system of privileges for party members.

The sheer enormity of the convulsion shattered traditional social relations. Although it has been argued that a 'primitivisation' of the whole social system occurred,[54] it was not simply a matter of regression, but also of *new* structuring, which focused on the necessities of physical survival. People had little time for political involvement, resulting in 'estrangement from the state',[55] and contributing to the Bolsheviks' winning the civil war. Everyday practices mediated or modified in these extreme circumstances of political chaos and economic collapse became part of the social fabric, as the desire to survive and withdraw from public life created problems that proved difficult to solve and undermined subsequent state efforts to reconfigure society. In this regard, the civil war was not a formative experience, but a *defining* one, for it ordained how the Bolsheviks would, in subsequent years, realise their plan for social engineering: many of the practices we associate with the Stalinist era became an integral part of the new order already during the civil war, as did the population's strategies of accommodation and resistance.

---

53 Mawdsley, *The Russian Civil War*, p. 287.
54 Moshe Lewin, 'The Civil War: Dynamics and Legacy', in Koenker et al., *Party, State, and Society*, p. 416.
55 Robert Argenbright, 'Bolsheviks, Baggers and Railroaders: Political Power and Social Space, 1917–1921', *Russian Review* 52, 4 (1993): 509.

6

# Building a new state and society: NEP, 1921–1928

ALAN BALL

As 1921 dawned, the Bolsheviks could proclaim themselves victors in the civil war and celebrate an accomplishment that would stand as one of the great triumphs in official lore for the rest of the Soviet era. At the same time they presided over a nation whose borders were uncertain and whose peasantry protested ever more aggressively against grain requisitioning and other measures of the civil war that continued beyond the conflict itself. In fact, growing opposition to these exactions was the principal development that convinced Lenin to change course in the direction of what soon became known as the New Economic Policy. By February, in Tambov province alone, tens of thousands of peasant fighters faced Bolshevik commanders who could not be certain of the loyalty of their own troops. Similar peasant violence gripped many other regions, and some areas, notably the lower Volga provinces and Siberia, were not pacified until the summer of 1922. In Moscow, Petrograd and other principal cities, diminishing food rations in the winter of 1920–1 sparked strikes among workers who had backed the Bolsheviks during the civil war. Mutiny at the Kronstadt naval base in March 1921 may have delivered the severest shock, given that the sailors' support for the Bolsheviks reached back to 1917. But the inflamed countryside had already convinced Lenin that a new approach was required, and he made this clear in March to delegates at the Tenth Party Congress who approved what turned out to be the first major plank of the New Economic Policy. To be sure, none of this signalled a wavering of the Bolsheviks' political monopoly, for they continued to arrest leaders of other parties active beside them in the revolutionary ferment of previous years. Only the Bolshevik (Communist) Party remained to guide the nation to socialism, and even this vanguard faced tighter discipline during the 1920s. On Lenin's initiative, the same Tenth Party Congress that authorised dramatic economic concessions also ordered an end to factions in the party itself.[1]

---

1 Vladimir Brovkin, *Behind the Front Lines of the Civil War: Political Parties and Social Movements in Russia, 1918–1922* (Princeton: Princeton University Press, 1994); Robert Service, *Lenin: A Political Life*, vol. III: *The Iron Ring* (London: Macmillan, 1995).

The New Economic Policy (NEP) emerged neither as a single decree nor a planned progression but as a label pinned eventually on a series of measures that appeared over the course of several months beginning in the spring of 1921. NEP was 'new' – that is, a departure from the practices of the civil-war era – in a number of ways. Most important initially, grain requisitions were replaced by a fixed tax, lower than the grain requisition targets. Soon peasants were also allowed to sell at free-market prices any produce left after their taxes had been paid. Not long thereafter, most of the rest of the population received the right to engage in small-scale trade and manufacturing, with the result that cities and towns followed the countryside in acquiring a legal private economic sector that coexisted with state-run factories and stores.[2]

Large-scale industry, retained by the state, also found itself placed on a new footing. No longer could enterprises expect to receive raw materials and other resources from Moscow, and they could not rely on the state to absorb their output regardless of cost or demand for the products. Wartime privation and turmoil had undermined such support in any case, but NEP did so officially. Efforts to administer industry from Moscow had grown so unwieldy during the civil war that the state now sought to place thousands of its factories on a cost-accounting basis (*khozraschet*). Individual enterprises were grouped into trusts, organised most often according to activity – the State Association of Metal Factories, for instance, or the Moscow Machine Building Trust. Whether subordinated directly to the Supreme Economic Council in Moscow or to local economic councils, a trust's factories were now instructed to cut expenses and produce goods that could be marketed successfully to other state customers or, in some instances, to private entrepreneurs. They could not anticipate automatic assistance from Moscow, where officials were busy cutting the central budget sharply in an effort to gain control over spending that had borne little relation to actual government resources during the civil war.

This aspect of NEP did not mean that the Bolshevik leadership had abandoned dreams of a centrally planned system of state industry, just as the legalisation of private trade did not replace the long-term goal of socialism. In fact, NEP's initial year witnessed not only the announcement of *khozraschet* and the concessions to private enterprise, but also the formation of the state planning agency (Gosplan). However, the time seemed propitious for theory rather than practice, as Gosplan's employees occupied themselves more with the study of

---

2 Alan Ball, *Russia's Last Capitalists: The Nepmen, 1921–1929* (Berkeley: University of California Press, 1987).

planning than its implementation. Vital factories might receive orders and subsidies from the centre, and provincial party secretaries intervened on occasion in the operation of local industry. But economists in Moscow had no means of obtaining comprehensive data about the nation's trusts and individual enterprises that would have been necessary to establish a planned economy – little suspecting that such a campaign was less than a decade away.[3]

Ambitious social and economic projects appeared far beyond reach in 1921 amid the accumulated death and destruction inherited from the First World War and the civil war. Millions of city residents had perished, emigrated or returned to the villages of peasant relatives, leaving Russia even less an urban society than it had been at the end of the nineteenth century. Metropolises tended to experience the largest proportional declines, with Moscow and Petrograd losing more than half of a combined population that had reached 4 million by 1917. The nation's industrial workforce shrank even more rapidly than the general urban population during the civil war, gutting the class on whom the Bolsheviks depended most for support. By 1922 only 1.6 million people were counted as workers, less than two-thirds the number shortly before the First World War.[4]

This proved to be the low point, however, as cities recovered in the comparative calm of NEP and again attracted millions of peasants seeking permanent or seasonal work. Demobilisation reduced the Red Army's ranks from 4.1 million to 1.6 million in 1921, worsening overpopulation in the hungry countryside and boosting migration to cities. Roughly a million peasants settled permanently in towns during the decade's middle years, and a few million more arrived for temporary employment – accounting together for over 75 per cent of urban population growth at this time. While not all sought industrial occupations, enough did to help swell the proletariat to the neighbourhood of 5.6 million and ease fears that the regime's pillar of social support was eroding.

At last the Soviet state emerged from nearly a decade of crises that had plagued the people of the region and their successive governments. The death rate declined steadily, and in 1925 the nation's population passed the level it had reached before the First World War. Meanwhile, currency reform eliminated

3 David Shearer, *Industry, State, and Society in Stalin's Russia, 1926–1934* (Ithaca, N.Y.: Cornell University Press, 1996); Alec Nove, *An Economic History of the USSR*, 2nd edn (London: Penguin Books, 1989).
4 Diane Koenker, William Rosenberg and Ronald Suny (eds.), *Party, State, and Society in the Russian Civil War: Explorations in Social History* (Bloomington: Indiana University Press, 1989); Lewis Siegelbaum, *Soviet State and Society Between Revolutions, 1918–1929* (Cambridge: Cambridge University Press, 1992); Sheila Fitzpatrick, *The Russian Revolution*, 2nd edn (Oxford: Oxford University Press, 1994).

the inflation that had rendered the rouble nearly worthless over the period 1921–3, and by fiscal year 1923/4 the government had managed to produce a balanced budget, with a surplus following in 1924/5. Industrial production, both heavy and light, as well as foreign trade improved far above the abysmal levels of the civil war and the beginning of NEP. Rail transport recovered so impressively that in 1926 it surpassed the level of traffic in 1913, to say nothing of 1921. As the number of workers increased, the improvement in their standard of living seemed all the more striking when measured against their plight just a few years before.[5]

Encouraging as these signs were for those promoting the construction of socialism's foundation, NEP also encompassed a variety of developments difficult to reconcile with Bolshevik visions. More galling than private trade itself was an atmosphere of extravagant consumption among newly wealthy entrepreneurs and others in the largest cities. In contrast to the privation and egalitarian dreams of War Communism, the Soviet Union's principal urban centres seemed to have joined the Roaring Twenties. 'Moscow made merry', observed the Menshevik Fedor Dan in the winter of 1921–2, 'treating itself with pastries, fine candies, fruits, and delicacies. Theatres and concerts were packed, women were again flaunting luxurious apparel, furs, and diamonds.' Casinos and nightclubs opened, American jazz bands arrived and Hollywood's movies reached Soviet screens by the hundreds, exceeding the number of Soviet films released from 1924 until the end of NEP.[6]

The raucous nightlife seemed particularly unpalatable to Bolsheviks because it flourished alongside extensive social misfortune, especially during the decade's early years. In the second half of 1921, a famine withered countless villages in the Volga basin, all the way from the Chuvash Autonomous Region and the Tatar Republic through Simbirsk, Samara, Saratov and Tsaritsyn provinces down to Astrakhan' on the Caspian Sea. Beyond the Volga region, starvation extended as far north as Viatka province, as far east as Cheliabinsk and the Bashkir and Kirghiz republics and west as far as southern Ukraine. Severe drought that year, combined with the legacy of protracted warfare, had given rise to a catastrophe destined to claim at least 5 million lives. Not until the end of 1922 did a better harvest and a relief campaign mounted by

---

5 Roger Pethybridge, *One Step Backwards, Two Steps Forward: Soviet Society and Politics in the New Economic Policy* (Oxford: Oxford University Press, 1990); Nove, *Economic History*; Siegelbaum, *Soviet State and Society*.

6 F. I. Dan, *Dva goda skitanii* (Berlin: Sklad izd. Russische Bucherzentrale Obrazowanje, 1922), p. 253; Denise Youngblood, *Movies for the Masses: Popular Cinema and Soviet Society in the 1920s* (Cambridge: Cambridge University Press, 1992).

foreign organisations (notably, Herbert Hoover's American Relief Administration) provide reason for hope. Alarm over the nation's food supply faded
through the following year, but other evidence of human trauma persisted.

Millions of juveniles had already found themselves abandoned or otherwise
homeless in the seven years before 1921, as families disintegrated through
violence, starvation or disease brought by the First World War and the civil
war. The subsequent Volga famine played an even greater role in severing
youths from their parents, and destitute juveniles flooded numerous Soviet
cities at the beginning of NEP. Street children gained recruits not only through
the deaths of mothers and fathers but also when parents abandoned dependants
they could no longer feed. Principal municipalities in the Volga epicentre of the
famine accumulated hundreds of new waifs each day by the spring of 1922,
and cities at major rail junctions in the region contained tens of thousands.

In the early 1920s, estimates of the nation's contingent of street children
settled at around 7 million, including tens of thousands drawn to Moscow itself.
Whether in the capital or provincial towns, they laboured to sustain themselves
through begging, petty street trade, theft and prostitution. Almost at once
they overwhelmed orphanages into which they were crammed. Revolutionary
visions of collective childcare – to emancipate women from household chores
and instil socialist principles in a new generation – dissolved in the reality of
institutions that could offer little more than a piece of bread and a spot on the
floor, and from which children often departed as fugitives or corpses. Not until
the middle of the decade did the number of street children decline steadily,
providing reason at last for optimism that a blight the Bolsheviks associated
with capitalist society could be removed from their own.[7]

For that to happen, however, the circumstances of families and especially
single mothers would have to improve considerably, and here NEP generated mixed results. Industry, for example, revived briskly, but women seeking
employment encountered new obstacles at the factory gate and inside. They
had poured into the proletariat during the First World War and represented
close to half of the industrial labour force that remained at the beginning of
1921, many of them working in branches of production where they could not
have expected employment in 1913. As labour patterns reverted during NEP
to gender divisions more common before 1914, women were concentrated in
textiles and other light industries and in lower-paying, lower-skilled occupations – if they were able to escape the 'last hired, first fired' retrenchment at

---

7 Alan Ball, *And Now My Soul is Hardened: Abandoned Children in Soviet Russia, 1918–1930*
(Berkeley: University of California Press, 1994).

enterprises placed on *khozraschet*. A variety of other factors appear to have played a part in augmenting the ranks of unemployed women, including a belief among employers that men, on average, possessed a higher level of industrial skills and could cope more readily with heavy physical labour. Party organisations also instructed state labour exchanges to assign priority to placing demobilised soldiers in jobs, while labour laws barred women from certain industrial occupations and stipulated that they receive substantial time off for maternity and the care of sick children. All of this hindered women in competing for jobs against male candidates who arrived on the scene in large numbers beginning in 1921. By 1923, women and juveniles (also protected under labour laws that restricted their use by factory directors) accounted for over half of all unemployed workers.[8]

Thus, labour laws formulated to benefit women with such rights as generous maternity leave yielded results in practice that were difficult to celebrate. Much the same could be said of broader Bolshevik legislation on women and the family. Less than a year after the revolution, a Code on Marriage, the Family and Guardianship had proclaimed equal standing for men and women regarding divorce and alimony, while removing legal stigmas attached to 'illegitimate' children and their mothers. In 1926 a new Family Code recognised de facto marriage, effectively eliminating the legal distinction between common-law and officially registered unions. Modified alimony and child-support provisions from the first code were joined by a declaration that property acquired during marriage belonged jointly to husband and wife. When a relationship turned sour, divorce could be obtained as easily as sending a postcard of notification to one's partner.

These measures, intended as a stride towards emancipation and equality, met with a chilly reception from most Soviet women during NEP. Three out of four were peasants, and patriarchal views on family relations proved tenacious in the countryside. Even in the cities, reformers found women more cautious than exultant over the new freedom of divorce and the legal acceptance of unregistered relationships. They suspected, correctly, that alimony would be difficult to collect, and that men, more than women, would avail themselves of the new opportunity to secure divorce on demand at a time when NEP had opened a forbidding landscape before single mothers. The same budget-cutting imperatives that had prompted the state to place factories on *khozraschet* also led to reductions in government spending on childcare

8 Wendy Goldman, *Women at the Gates: Gender and Industry in Stalin's Russia* (Cambridge: Cambridge University Press, 2002).

facilities and other social services sorely needed by women left to support children on their own. For the jurists who drafted these codes, talk of liberation clashed with reality throughout the period and found little support even from the intended beneficiaries.[9]

Nowhere was this more glaring than in Soviet Central Asia, once activists embarked on a drive to emancipate Muslim women from a variety of customs deeply rooted in the region. During the mid- to later years of the decade, a series of laws banned such practices as polygamy and the abduction of a fiancée, while strengthening women's property rights in marriage. Mutual consent paved the way for divorce, and courts favoured women more often than not in cases where spouses failed to reach agreement. Taken together, the laws invited women to enjoy public rights equal to men – an endeavour described by Bolsheviks as vital to modernise a region they viewed as backward. The Women's Section of the party and the Communist Youth League (Komsomol) often led the charge by staging public events at which women removed their long veils or renounced other traditions. These efforts assumed the form of an all-out campaign by 1927, but most Central Asian women (let alone men) saw little to tempt them. The few who did unveil, adopt Russian clothing or join the Komsomol risked ostracism and, in scattered instances, murder. Eventually, at the end of the decade, Moscow reined in the endeavour. The hostility it caused had come to seem counter-productive and a distraction from goals more important to the new Stalinist leadership bent on industrialising the nation.[10]

* * * * *

The frustrating venture in Central Asia underscored one of the challenges faced by the Bolsheviks from the moment of their revolutionary triumph. They presided over scores of non-Slavic regions whose inhabitants had not always relished their experience as part of the tsarist empire and now contemplated warily a union of soviet republics. In 1921 the fragmented remains of the tsarist empire included six republics bearing the name Soviet – the Russian Soviet Federative Socialist Republic (by far the largest) and counterparts in Ukraine, Belorussia, Georgia, Armenia and Azerbaijan – along with more nebulous 'republics' in Central Asia and the Far East. Bilateral treaties signed

9 Wendy Goldman, *Women, the State, and Revolution: Soviet Family Policy and Social Life, 1917–1936* (Cambridge: Cambridge University Press, 1993).
10 Hélène Carrère d'Encausse, *The Great Challenge: Nationalities and the Bolshevik State, 1917–1930* (New York: Holmes and Meier, 1992); Douglas Northrop, 'Nationalising Backwardness: Gender, Empire, and Uzbek Identity', in Ronald Suny and Terry Martin (eds.), *A State of Nations: Empire and Nation-Making in the Age of Lenin and Stalin* (Oxford: Oxford University Press, 2001).

between the Russian Republic (RSFSR) and the other five created a confusing impression that suggested both an understanding between independent nations and an administrative reform of a single state, depending on the portion of the document consulted. As Bolshevik leaders prevailed in the civil war, they gained the opportunity to exert their will in outlying regions and thereby address this unstable equilibrium. From 1920 to 1922, taking advantage of the leading role played by the Russian Communist Party in all six republics, Moscow transferred an ever-larger share of authority to itself. Even the Commissariats for Foreign Affairs, symbolic bastions of independence in the other five republics, yielded to the Kremlin and allowed Russia to speak for all six at the Genoa Conference early in 1922. This vexed Ukrainian officials in particular, but dismay over evaporating sovereignty rang out most loudly in a smaller republic further south.

Not long after the Red Army conquered Georgia in February 1921, friction developed between Georgian Bolsheviks leading the new Georgian Soviet Republic and plenipotentiaries sent from Moscow to supervise government in the Caucasus. Regarding the formation of a union of soviet republics, for instance, the Georgians desired to preserve their republic's individual identity and enter on the same terms as, say, the Ukrainians rather than as part of a single Transcaucasian Republic that would also include Armenia and Azerbaijan. Moscow's representatives, led by Sergo Ordzhonikidze and backed by Stalin, insisted that all three join the Soviet Union together as one republic. The dispute grew bitter – Ordzhonikidze pinning the label of selfish nationalism on the Georgians who responded with charges of Great Russian chauvinism – and by 1922 it had alarmed Lenin. He had no particular objection to bringing Georgia into the Soviet Union as part of a Transcaucasian Republic, but he, more than Stalin or Ordzhonikidze, was troubled by cries of Great Russian chauvinism, which he described as much more reprehensible than local nationalism rising in defence of a small region menaced by large powers. Lenin also showed concern about propaganda consequences that might ensue in other soviet republics and abroad from heavy-handed treatment of the Georgian comrades. Nevertheless, his misgivings over the process under way in Georgia were not fundamental, and as his health deteriorated he watched Georgia pressed into a Transcaucasian Republic that signed a treaty with the RSFSR, Ukraine and Belorussia, joining them all in a new Soviet Union on 30 December 1922.

In this larger venture, too, Lenin did not see eye to eye with Stalin, though here again the difference was more a matter of methods and appearances than ultimate goals. Lenin argued that each republic should participate in the Soviet Union as, ostensibly, an equal, independent member, while Stalin showed less patience for such language and favoured a more streamlined structure that left no doubt over the dominance of central authority. Lenin, in other words, demonstrated a lighter touch regarding the diverse national units of the Soviet Union, but he, like Stalin, intended to maintain control through the Communist Party, whose centralised apparatus extended through all of the republics and ethnic 'autonomous regions' that made up the state. As the process worked itself out – a constitution for the Soviet Union was drafted in the summer of 1923 and approved by the All-Union Congress of Soviets on 31 January 1924 – Stalin made more verbal concessions than Lenin. But in the Soviet state that emerged there could be no doubt that authority resided in Moscow rather than the constituent republics.[11]

That said, for the remainder of NEP party leaders indicated that they would not rely solely on military pacification and Politburo commands. The Soviet Union took shape as an assemblage of national or ethnic units, and the Kremlin advanced the line that national identity was an inevitable feature of incipient socialism as well as capitalism. Following Lenin, the party even stipulated that past Russian oppression had indeed given rise to valid complaints among numerous ethnic groups now inhabiting the Soviet Union. The proper policy, then, was to accept national sentiment and steer it in healthy directions, away from those who might fan such passions in opposition to socialism and the Soviet state. As long as national loyalties did not threaten Soviet unity, they might be permitted as a means of rendering Soviet rule more palatable. If power could be made to seem local rather than Russian, in other words, the leadership would take great strides in holding the Soviet Union together and gaining support for its policies. Such was the party's strategy during NEP, and it unfolded along two lines. The state declared its intent to support (or even help create) national languages and cultures, while also seeking local people to fill positions in the administrative organisations of their regions. If this could be done, the face of authority would appear less alien and incomprehensible.

The party's approach, known eventually as indigenisation (korenizatsiia), soon produced striking changes. Local candidates were heavily recruited for party membership in their republics and smaller regions, transforming party ranks filled mainly by Russians just a few years before. By 1927, for example, over half the members and candidate members of the Communist Party in a

11 Jeremy Smith, The Bolsheviks and the National Question, 1917–23 (New York: St Martin's Press, 1999); Carrère d'Encausse, Great Challenge; Terry Martin, 'An Affirmative Action Empire: The Soviet Union as the Highest Form of Imperialism', in Suny and Martin, State of Nations.

number of republics (Ukraine, Belorussia, Armenia and Georgia) belonged to the republic's titular nationality, while in Central Asia over 40 per cent of the party's cadre in Uzbekistan and Tajikistan came from the local, non-Russian population. As for administrative bodies, notably the executive committees of regional soviets, non-Russians accounted for two-thirds to four-fifths of the membership in Ukraine, Belorussia, Azerbaijan, Armenia, Turkmenistan and Uzbekistan.

At the same time the party encouraged the use of indigenous languages and art forms as tools for promoting socialist practices. With this approach, 'national in form, socialist in content' as Stalin put it, the Kremlin's proprietors hoped not only to pacify but to guide their multi-ethnic domain to a new society where, eventually, a universal socialism would supplant the scores of national cultures whose narrower outlook the community had finally outgrown. It was a tolerant strategy, characteristic of NEP's concessions in other areas, but this also made it another of NEP's gambles. Just as no one could be certain about the consequences of permitting private trade on the road to socialism, it remained to be seen if national forms might eclipse or disfigure socialist content.[12]

In the meantime, though, NEP's largest gamble lay elsewhere, for whatever the nature of Moscow's policy towards the nation's far-flung ethnic groups, most Soviet citizens were Slavic peasants. This enduring aspect of Russian life the revolution could not change, at least during NEP, and peasant villages with their traditional communes continued to dominate the landscape as they had for centuries. But if the events initiated in 1917 left Soviet Russia a peasant society, they nevertheless transformed the countryside. Gone were the nobles' estates and even many of the most substantial peasant holdings. Over 100 million peasants had seized these properties and parcelled them out among themselves, yielding a rural panorama that consisted almost entirely of small plots. Roughly 85 per cent of the Russian Republic's peasant households worked fields of less than 11 acres in 1922 and did so with fewer than two draught animals per family. Although a more modern plough had largely replaced the archaic wooden scratch-plough by the end of the decade, most work was still performed manually by humans and horses. As late as 1928, hand labour accounted for three-quarters of the spring sowing, and it took place in fields where less than 1 per cent of the ploughing had been done by tractors.

12 George Liber, *Soviet Nationality Policy, Urban Growth, and Identity Change in the Ukrainian SSR, 1923–1934* (Cambridge: Cambridge University Press, 1992); Martin, 'Affirmative Action Empire'; Smith, *Bolsheviks and National Question*.

Here were the people the Kremlin hoped to mollify in 1921 by abandoning grain requisitions and permitting free trade of surplus produce. The new grain tax for 1921/2 was set at 57 per cent of the requisition target for the previous year, and only a fraction of this was actually collected. Even in the best of conditions the Bolsheviks' fledgling government was not capable of fanning out through the boundless countryside to gather the tax, and 1921 was far from the best of years. The famine that had begun to strangle several grain-producing provinces in the Volga basin, combined with the disruption of agriculture left by the civil war, yielded a grain harvest of less than half the average garnered before the First World War. So severe was the famine that stricken regions found the grain tax waived altogether as fields dried up and life drained from villages. Only by late 1922 had the worst passed. The nation's peasants improved their harvest almost 40 per cent that year, and the following one was better still. After 1922 the rural population grew rapidly until the end of the decade and as early as 1926 approached 120 million (over 80 per cent of the nation's total). That same year, the grain harvest exceeded the best return of the tsarist era, while the number of cows, pigs, sheep and goats had already recovered to totals above pre-war levels. At last the peasantry closed a decade of calamities that had begun in 1914 and extinguished as many as 15–20 million lives.[13]

The Bolsheviks, of course, sought not a return to life as it had been before these storms, but a new, socialist countryside. Although NEP signalled no wavering in this desire, it did announce that the transition would be made peacefully. Whatever Lenin had said about the peasants previously, he felt by 1921 that a union or bond between workers and peasants – called the *smychka* and symbolised by the hammer-and-sickle emblem – was not only essential for the survival of his government but also represented the key for building socialism in Russia. As the country industrialised, the proletariat would supply the peasants with manufactured household goods and agricultural equipment (especially tractors) through such channels as rural co-operatives, while peasants would deliver food to the co-operatives for shipment to their urban comrades. Such an exchange, it was hoped, would breathe life into the *smychka* and serve to persuade peasants to join (or form) co-operatives. They would not be forced. Lenin and other Bolshevik defenders of NEP believed that co-operatives possessed such striking advantages over conventional

13 Viktor Danilov, *Rural Russia under the New Regime*, trans. Orlando Figes (London: Hutchinson, 1988); Moshe Lewin, *Russian Peasants and Soviet Power: A Study of Collectivization* (Evanston, Ill.: Northwestern University Press, 1968); Nove, *Economic History*.

village ways that peasants could be enticed to join, once model co-operatives were established for them to observe.

To be sure, it would require some time to launch such a network throughout the country and revive industry to the point where it could saturate the co-operatives with attractive goods. But the passing of the civil war gave the Bolsheviks time, and by the end of 1922 it finally seemed to be on their side in the villages. Co-operatives marked the beginning, and once they were securely rooted, peasants would be prepared to recognise the virtues of pooling their strips of land in collective farms. The advantages of mechanisation and other modern techniques demonstrated on model collective farms would convince peasants to drop their attachment to the unproductive practices of bygone generations. Then, as collective farms gained members at an accelerating pace without coercion reminiscent of the civil war's grain requisitioning, Bolsheviks would witness the triumph of socialism in the countryside. So ran official hopes during NEP.

One thing that did carry over from the civil war was the Bolsheviks' view of a stratified rural society. Out in the villages, they affirmed, lived three distinct groups. Poor peasants (roughly one-third of the total) possessed little or no land and often worked as hired labourers. Their 'proletarian' condition was thought to render them natural allies for the party's rural policies. A much larger group, the 'middle peasants', were described as those with enough land and livestock to support a meagre existence. Winning them over to co-operatives and ultimately socialism would demand considerable exertion, party officials believed, and it became the Kremlin's most ambitious goal in the countryside during NEP. Whenever these efforts proved frustrating, Bolsheviks commonly pointed in blame at a third rural category, the kulaks. In Soviet ideology these villagers loomed as a rapacious elite, perhaps 3–5 per cent of the peasant community. More prosperous in terms of land, livestock and equipment, they were said to fill the role of rural capitalists exploiting the hired labour of other peasants in a manner suggested by their label *kulak* – a fist. Together with the Nepmen (as private traders were dubbed), they appeared to Bolsheviks as the 'new bourgeoisie', and like the Nepmen they experienced discrimination in such forms as higher taxes and deprivation of the right to vote.[14]

All in all, though, peasants identified as kulaks were tolerated during NEP and experienced less badgering than did urban private traders who operated more directly under the gaze of the authorities. Compared to the years preceding and following NEP, the countryside appeared tranquil. Departing nobles

14 Siegelbaum, *Soviet State and Society.*

and other owners of large estates abandoned fields, forests and meadows to the peasants, whose tax obligations to the Soviet regime were not backbreaking. Indeed, the new government left the peasants largely to their own devices, with rural agitators only occasional visitors to most villages. If some peasants responded warmly to Bolshevik forays – campaigns to spread literacy, for example, or to introduce modern agricultural or medical techniques – they did not set the tone in most villages. Here, life went on in harmony with traditions that the peasantry had found congenial for generations. When harvests began setting post-revolutionary records by the middle of the decade, it seemed that Russian history had rarely smiled as brightly on the villages. No doubt few peasants cared or even realised that the recovery did little to promote NEP's strategy for transforming their lives. But the scant progress towards socialism did not escape notice among Bolsheviks, and it became a matter of greater urgency as the years passed.

In many respects, then, NEP embraced practices that revolutionaries viewed with misgiving but felt compelled to tolerate temporarily. This delay on the journey to socialism might be attributed to the failure of revolution to erupt in Western countries, or to the destruction left by the civil war, or to stubborn habits rooted in the population. Whatever the explanation, though, much of NEP from the activist's vantage point amounted to concessions that must yield as soon as possible to superior arrangements appropriate in a socialist community. This was obvious regarding the Nepmen and peasant society, which did not fit visions of a planned economy supplying necessities to one and all. In the juridical realm, too, partisans described the family codes as temporary rather than socialist. The drafters conceded, for instance, that child-rearing would have to remain centred in traditional family units for a time, until the state acquired the means to provide a more enlightened upbringing in collective settings. Nor were myriad differences among nationalities expected to figure in the community desired by Bolshevik prophets. *Korenizatsiia* took shape as an attempt to help unify the country and commence the process of socialist development necessary to produce a future generation no longer concerned with the disparate cultural norms of a fractious past. Analogous concessions appeared in other endeavours, and taken together they produced a landscape in which socialism remained on the horizon.

* * * * *

Thus, while most peasants and other Soviet citizens doubtless welcomed NEP as a distinct improvement over the policies and misery of War Communism, many Bolsheviks viewed the legalisation of private business activity with consternation. It seemed naive to speak of a brief, orderly retreat when the doors were opening again to the 'bourgeoisie', the class said to have been overthrown in the 'Great October Socialist Revolution' of 1917. Such concerns surfaced regularly at party meetings, forcing Lenin to argue time and again that a hostile peasantry would doom the revolution in a country still overwhelmingly rural. NEP has been called a peasant Brest-Litovsk, and so it began – with concessions unpalatable to Bolsheviks but indispensable, Lenin insisted, for them to retain power.

Pacification of the countryside was not the only reason for tolerating private economic activity, as Lenin explained on the basis of assumptions widely shared among Bolsheviks. All could agree, for instance, that socialism presupposed a thoroughly industrialised country because industrialisation provided both a large proletariat and sufficient productive capacity to fulfil the material requirements of the entire population. In addition, it seemed clear to most party members that they would not industrialise the nation without amassing a grain surplus. Grain could be exported to obtain foreign currency for purchasing Western technical expertise, and it would be essential for feeding the growing proletariat. Yet the state could not gather this surplus through coercion, having adopted the 'peasant Brest-Litovsk'. The heart of NEP lay in a hope that peasants would produce a surplus through incentives rather than compulsion, and Lenin defended the legalisation of private trade as an important means for inducing the peasantry to boost production. Private entrepreneurs (and not the state) possessed the numbers, experience and initiative to offer the peasants desirable products and thereby encourage them to raise more grain for the market. Anyone who increased the flow of goods between cities and countryside helped build socialism, Lenin wrote in 1921, and this included private traders. 'It may seem a paradox: private capitalism in the role of socialism's accomplice? It is in no way a paradox, but rather a completely incontestable economic fact.'[15]

Still, as private traders gained control of most retail trade in 1921–2 and ran circles around inexperienced state enterprises, only an optimistic Bolshevik could accept the spectacle calmly and regard Nepmen as 'socialism's accomplices'. Facing considerable unease in the party on this score, Lenin returned often to the argument during the last years of his life. 'The idea of building communism with communist hands is childish, completely childish', he lectured the Eleventh Party Congress in March 1922. 'Communists are only a

15 V. I. Lenin, *Polnoe sobranie sochinenii*, 5th edn, 55 vols. (Moscow: Gosizdpolit, 1958–65) (hereafter cited as Lenin, *PSS*), vol. XLIII, p. 233.

drop in the sea, a drop in the sea of people . . . We can direct the economy if communists can build it with bourgeois hands, while learning from this bourgeoisie and directing it down the road we want it to follow.'[16]

How long this would take, Lenin was less certain. NEP had been adopted 'seriously and for a long time', he emphasised at party meetings, while also acknowledging that he could not specify how many years the Bolsheviks would require to operate the economy efficiently and render the private sector obsolete. Uncertainty over NEP's duration might not have proved so divisive for the Bolsheviks had Lenin continued to steer the party as he had in the contentious transition from War Communism to NEP. But his death in 1924, three months before his fifty-fourth birthday, left the party with neither a clear sense of how long to abide by NEP, nor a consensus on how to end it whenever the appropriate time seemed at hand. As a result, when debate over NEP's future tore the party after Lenin's death, both those who desired to end NEP in short order and those who wanted to prolong it could claim to be following a Leninist path.

In the meantime, NEP had sanctioned a struggle between the private sector and the state for the preference of the peasantry and the remainder of the population. Could the state provide satisfactory merchandise and service to entice citizens from private shops and marketplaces? For Lenin this was a vital question, as he emphasised in one of his last works, written for the Twelfth Party Congress in January 1923: 'In the final analysis the fate of our republic will depend on whether the peasantry sides with the working class, preserving this alliance, or allows the "Nepmen", i.e. the new bourgeoisie, to separate it from the workers, to split off from them.'[17] Not only were the stakes high, but Lenin could even betray concern on occasion that the party appeared to be losing the contest – a misgiving soon recalled by those determined to end NEP without delay.

\* \* \* \* \*

At the beginning of the 1920s Lenin was clearly the most formidable of the Bolshevik leaders. He did not always get his way in party disputes, but his prestige and influence stood unrivalled. No one else could have taken the party on such an abrupt – and, for many Bolsheviks, unpopular – change of course as the implementation of the New Economic Policy. Among Lenin's colleagues in the Politburo, Trotsky seemed the most prestigious in 1922 because of his prominent role in the October Revolution and his moulding of the Red Army that saved the revolution during the civil war. If the question of party leadership

16 Lenin, *PSS*, vol. XLV, p. 98.    17 Ibid., pp. 387–8.

*after* Lenin were to arise, Trotsky's name would occur first to most Bolsheviks, whether they viewed his possible ascension with enthusiasm or alarm.[18]

The latter emotion proved more common among other members of the Politburo, including Stalin. His service to the party had not been as spectacular as Trotsky's during the revolution or civil war, and now, at the beginning of the new decade, he devoted himself to offices in the party bureaucracy that did not signal his leadership ambitions to associates in the Politburo. Neither the Central Committee's Organisational Bureau, where Stalin had served since its inception in 1919, nor its Secretariat, which he joined in 1922 as General Secretary, was regarded originally as a locus of power. But their responsibilities – including the promotion or transfer of provincial cadres and the appointment of party personnel to carry out decisions of the leadership – provided a stream of opportunities for an ambitious figure to expand his own influence. This Stalin did, advancing local officials who showed potential as allies, while obstructing the careers of those seemingly beholden to Trotsky and other rivals. If Stalin's offices appeared benignly administrative at NEP's birth, some in the party, including Lenin, formed a different impression before long.

In May 1922 Lenin suffered a stroke that removed him from political and governmental activities for several months. He had not recovered fully when he returned to work in October, and by December more strokes left him partially paralysed. Aware that the rivalry between Trotsky and Stalin had not ended along with the civil war, and spurred by his physical deterioration to set down words of guidance for the party, he dictated a series of notes to his secretary that became known as his Testament. Over a period of nearly two weeks at the end of 1922 and the beginning of the new year, Lenin gave voice to assessments and recommendations that he hoped would be presented to the next party congress. Some of his attention focused on suggestions for reorganising the party – expanding the Central Committee, for instance, in the hope that this would yield a body less susceptible to factional paralysis or schism. But he seemed most troubled by the tension between Trotsky and Stalin. The early notes did not clearly favour either man, but Lenin's final dictation abandoned a dispassionate listing of various party leaders' strengths and shortcomings to

18 The following pages on the party debates and power struggle during NEP are informed by discussions in numerous works, including: Stephen Cohen, *Bukharin and the Bolshevik Revolution: A Political Biography, 1888–1938* (Oxford: Oxford University Press, 1980); Robert Tucker, *Stalin as Revolutionary, 1879–1929: A Study in History and Personality* (New York: Norton, 1973); Isaac Deutscher, *The Prophet Unarmed: Trotsky, 1921–1929* (London: Oxford University Press, 1959); Michal Reiman, *The Birth of Stalinism: The USSR on the Eve of the 'Second Revolution'*, trans. George Saunders (Bloomington: Indiana University Press, 1987); and Alexander Erlich, *The Soviet Industrialization Debate, 1924–1928* (Cambridge, Mass.: Harvard University Press, 1960).

direct a scorching attack on the General Secretary alone. 'Stalin is too rude', Lenin declared, 'and this shortcoming, though quite tolerable in our midst and in relations among us communists, becomes intolerable in the position of General Secretary.'[19] He urged the party to find a way to remove Stalin from this position.

It is not entirely clear what prompted Lenin to change his assessment of Stalin so dramatically in less than two weeks. Perhaps he was reacting to an abusive phone call made by Stalin to Lenin's wife, who had taken down a note that Lenin asked her to convey to Trotsky (hindering the doctors' efforts to care for Lenin, claimed Stalin). Also, Lenin had probably learned enough by this time to develop vexation over Stalin's bare-knuckled approach to curtailing Georgian autonomy. In any case, through January and February 1923 Lenin grew increasingly concerned with Stalin's treatment of the Georgians. At the beginning of March he contacted Trotsky on the subject of taking up the Georgian case and broached an even more dramatic move to deprive Stalin of his political power. That same day, however, Lenin's health deteriorated sharply. Almost at once another stroke paralysed much of his body and eliminated his power of speech, thereby ending his political career well before he died in January 1924.

The final collapse of Lenin's health in the spring of 1923 triggered the decisive phase of the struggle between Trotsky and Stalin, with Stalin gaining the upper hand through his alliance with Politburo colleagues Grigorii Zinoviev and Lev Kamenev. To Stalin's partners in this triumvirate, Trotsky appeared the obvious menace – a high-voltage personality inclined to thrust himself into the position vacated by Lenin. Trotsky mounted an ineffectual effort to challenge the triumvirate and could not dislodge them from their pre-eminent position in the Politburo. Lenin's Testament lay in the shadows until May 1924, when it was disclosed to the Central Committee in what must have been a tense session. After the reading, Zinoviev rose to defuse Lenin's alarm over Stalin. The leadership's harmonious work over the past few months demonstrated that Lenin need not have harboured any anxiety over the party's General Secretary, Zinoviev explained, while Trotsky and Stalin remained silent. The party would not publish Lenin's Testament in Stalin's lifetime.

A few months later, in the autumn of 1924, Trotsky published a long essay titled *The Lessons of October* in which he discussed mistakes that revolutionaries might make when the moment for action arrived. Here he singled out Zinoviev and Kamenev for their opposition to Lenin's determination to seize

---

19 Lenin, *PSS*, vol. XLV, p. 346.

power in the October Revolution. They responded in kind by reviewing Trotsky's numerous, often bitter, disputes with Lenin prior to Trotsky's belated entry into the Bolsheviks' ranks. Stalin furthered the campaign to contrast Trotsky and Lenin, notably in a speech titled 'Trotskyism or Leninism?', but he also hounded Trotsky on a broader theoretical plane, dismissing the latter's 'pessimistic' notion of 'permanent revolution'. How could one have so little confidence in the Soviet proletariat and Communist Party to imagine that revolution must spread to the West before the Soviet Union could build socialism, he asked. Surely the nation's progressive forces could build 'socialism in one country' without having to wait for assistance from the West that might be expected following the international triumph of the revolution. The ultimate victory of communism presumed the spread of revolution to the West, of course, but in the meantime, contended Stalin, the Soviet Union could set out to construct socialism on its own.

By the beginning of 1925, Trotsky's position had deteriorated sufficiently for the Central Committee to remove him as commissar of war. The victory, however, did not belong to Zinoviev and Kamenev, for as Trotsky's star dimmed, Stalin began to distance himself from them in order to form a new alliance with another set of Politburo members: Nikolai Bukharin, Aleksei Rykov and Mikhail Tomskii. All three accepted the general assumptions behind the notion of constructing 'socialism in one country', and they believed that the New Economic Policy represented the most prudent course to follow towards this end.

Zinoviev and Kamenev, joined in 1926 by their former adversary Trotsky, were more inclined to view NEP as a retreat from socialism, a dangerous concession to the nation's 'new bourgeoisie', and an inadequate policy for extracting enough grain from the countryside to support a rate of industrial growth that they deemed essential. This 'Left Opposition' became the principal political challenge to Stalin and his new allies in 1926–7, which meant that Stalin emerged as a gradualist and defender of NEP. Whether he was genuinely comfortable in this guise or whether it merely served the temporary requirements of factional struggle, he left most of the public defence of NEP to Bukharin and the others, while he toiled to derail the careers of officials linked to the opposition.

In this respect, the Stalin–Bukharin faction succeeded with such efficiency that the Left Opposition was thoroughly routed by 1927. During the previous year, Trotsky, Zinoviev and Kamenev all lost their Politburo seats, and in 1927 the Central Committee dismissed them as well. In November, after authorities thwarted demonstrations planned by the Left Opposition to marshal popular support on the tenth anniversary of the revolution, Trotsky and Zinoviev were expelled from the party altogether. Two months later, Trotsky and numerous followers found themselves exiled to distant parts of the land, in Trotsky's case the Central Asian city of Alma-Ata. No longer did the party contain a Left Opposition of any potency, and, to some observers, NEP had never appeared more secure.

But just as Stalin had parted company in 1925 with Zinoviev and Kamenev, he now abandoned Bukharin, Rykov and Tomskii to join forces with more recent arrivals at the party's summit, men whose ascent owed much to Stalin's patronage. Among these new supporters – including Viacheslav Molotov, Kliment Voroshilov, Sergei Kirov, Anastas Mikoyan and Lazar Kaganovich – Stalin proceeded to embrace policies in 1928 that matched or exceeded the militancy demanded by the Left Opposition just a year or two earlier. Thus began the climactic stage of debate, a struggle in the party over the two policy options recognised by the Bolsheviks throughout the 1920s. While the champions of each approach rose and fell (or switched sides) over the years, as did the emphases placed on specific issues, the principal dispute remained recognisable and reached the point of starkest contrast between the contending options in 1928–9. The outcome would put an end to NEP.

By this time, Bukharin's pronouncements had marked him as the most prominent advocate of maintaining NEP for an indefinite period, certain to be measured in years. He could accept such modifications as slightly higher taxes on the peasantry, but nothing that would threaten NEP's original foundation – including a peasant's option to dispose of surplus produce at free-market prices and the opportunity for others to engage in private trade beyond the countryside. In general, Bukharin and colleagues of similar mind believed that NEP should continue until the party succeeded in a number of vital tasks. First, the state had to convince (not force) peasants to join co-operatives or other forms of collective life. As noted previously, this might be accomplished by establishing model co-operatives, supplying them generously with consumer goods and equipment, and letting the peasants see for themselves that the new organisations yielded a more bountiful life. Then it would not be difficult to persuade them to join co-operatives and collective farms, thereby enabling the countryside to make the turn to socialism. Bukharin was confident about the eventual triumph of large-scale, socialist practices, but this outcome would beckon only after the state had learned to manage its own sector of the economy productively enough to supply and distribute a substantial volume of goods to the countryside. Until then, NEP's acceptance of traditional peasant agriculture would have to continue.

So, too, with the toleration of private vendors in cities. The advantages of 'socialist' trade would prove decisive, Bukharin maintained, as state stores and co-operatives supplied merchandise at the lowest possible prices – a public service distinct from the inclination of Nepmen to charge as much as the market could bear. Consumers would flock to the 'socialist sector', and private shops would wither for lack of customers. Bukharin did not relish the Nepmen, and he could support taxing them more heavily than co-operatives. But he rejected the adoption of 'administrative measures' (such as confiscatory taxation, seizure of goods and arrest) to eliminate private economic activity. Were the state to liquidate private traders before it could replace them itself, the result would not be socialism but 'trade deserts', a term used to describe locales where few goods were available.

All of this meant that those inclined to accept NEP indefinitely were also prepared to accept a modest rate of industrial growth. In the Bolshevik mind, rapid industrialisation required (1) a large grain surplus (to feed a mushrooming proletariat and export in exchange for foreign technology) and (2) investment decisions that favoured heavy industry as much as possible. Steel mills, coal mines, hydroelectric projects and machine shops turned out products that could be used to produce still more factories, while light (consumer goods) industry did not. Neither of these things – a massive grain surplus and over-whelming investment in heavy industry – seemed compatible with the New Economic Policy. NEP anticipated the production of a large quantity of con-sumer goods, enough to turn state stores into successful competitors with urban private entrepreneurs and to stock rural co-operatives sufficiently to win the favour of the peasantry. Not only that, NEP took funds from the state budget (which might otherwise have been devoted to heavy industrial projects) in the form of payments to obtain peasants' surplus grain. Both of these aspects of NEP left the budget with less in the short run for heavy industry, while failing over the years to accumulate a substantial grain reserve for the state. To Bukharin and prominent allies like Rykov and Tomskii, none of this seemed cause for anything more than modifying NEP. The state might raise taxes on the kulaks, they could agree, but it should also offer peasants higher prices for the grain they marketed. Such incentives continued to figure in the strategies of NEP's defenders, for they understood that the primacy of coercion would signal the end of the path taken in 1921.

There were others in the party, however, who favoured a decisive change, and without further delay. For some with this outlook, NEP seemed to threaten cultural contamination from diverse sources, including nightclubs, casinos, jazz and Hollywood films common in the nation's largest cities. Here, capitalist decadence rather than socialist fervour seemed in the offing, and a campaign would soon erupt to generate a proletarian culture suitable for the new society said to be close at hand. But the main thrust of NEP's most formidable Bolshevik opponents took place along the 'industrial front', where critics dismissed Bukharin's course as incompatible with industrialisation at a pace necessary to construct socialism and defend the nation.

Stalin's voice could be heard most clearly in this chorus, revealing that he had lost patience with NEP as a means to provide the state with grain to export in substantial volume. By 1928, developments 'on the grain front' indicated that he was parting company with Bukharin and other former allies. The preceding year's harvest had not been poor, but during the last quarter of 1927 the state acquired little more than half the grain it had received during the corresponding period in 1926. Peasants were withholding supplies from the market, apparently for a variety of reasons that included the insufficient price offered by the state and the scarcity of manufactured consumer goods. They preferred to sell other crops and animal products for which prices were more favourable, while retaining grain to build up herds of livestock or in anticipation of better prices to come. At any rate, the party faced a problem that Stalin seized to promote stern measures more reminiscent of War Communism than NEP. Local officials received instructions to force peasants to 'sell' grain to the state at low prices, and Stalin himself toured Siberia in January–February 1928, ordering administrators to crack down on peasants hoarding grain. Keeping a surplus off the market was legal under NEP, but Stalin described it as a crime ('speculation'), permitting authorities to confiscate the produce in question. Like-minded Bolshevik leaders toured other grain-producing regions, and their efforts helped net the state two-thirds more grain during the first quarter of 1928 than in the same three months of the previous year.

Bolsheviks more devoted to the continuation of NEP were appalled by the coercive nature of the 'extraordinary measures' and by Stalin's remarks in Siberia about pushing forward with sweeping collectivisation. Their criticism prompted Stalin to beat a brief verbal retreat. He rejected talk of NEP's demise and condemned 'excesses' of over-zealous procurement officials here and there. At the same time, he continued to defend his approach to collecting grain, and when shortages reappeared later in the year, he again supported the extraction of 'surpluses' through forced delivery and confiscation. With every month in 1928 it grew more fanciful to suppose that anyone could quickly regain the peasants' trust in NEP, which encouraged party members to presume that increased pressure remained the only alternative. This was probably Stalin's intent all along, but the effect of the 'extraordinary measures' in any case tended to steer Bolsheviks towards a conclusion that some form of collectivisation represented the solution to their seemingly chronic difficulty in amassing enough grain for the army, the proletariat and the export market.

Stalin and his new allies dismissed suggestions from Politburo colleagues to obtain more grain by offering the peasants higher prices and additional consumer goods. These options, consistent with NEP, would have drained funds from heavy industry and other portions of the budget. At a Central Committee plenum in July 1928, Stalin bluntly defended the maintenance of prices unfavourable to peasants in order to extract 'tribute' to support industrialisation. The government's recent difficulties in collecting grain stemmed not from misguided prices, he explained, but from class struggle spearheaded by the kulaks, whose opposition had to be vanquished. Nor was the Stalinist faction prepared to 'coddle' the Nepmen much longer. Private entrepreneurs had no place in socialism, and if socialism was now proclaimed to be close at hand, the Nepmen must leave the scene in short order. For this to happen in harmony with NEP, the party would have to invest far more in the production of consumer goods and a network of state stores (again, at the expense of heavy industry). With such a course unacceptable to Stalin and his supporters, it soon became clear that 'administrative measures' rather than economic competition would be the road taken to liquidate the 'new bourgeoisie'.

Other groups, never popular with the Bolsheviks but regarded during NEP as vital for economic recovery, now joined the Nepmen and kulaks as targets of unsettling rhetoric. The term 'bourgeois specialist' – referring to non-party engineers, economists and other technical experts employed by the state – surfaced ominously in the press as a label for people allegedly responsible for shortages and other economic difficulties that grew more common with the onset of rapid industrialisation at the end of the decade. As early as 1928 the Kremlin staged a trial of fifty-three engineers from the coal industry, accusing them of sabotaging the mining facilities in which they worked. These proceedings, the well-publicised Shakhty trial, alarmed Bukharin and Rykov among others, but they could not shield bourgeois specialists from what became a series of such prosecutions continuing into the 1930s. Once the nation accelerated its drive to socialism, Stalin declared, bourgeois counter-revolutionary elements would, in desperation, intensify their opposition. Let there be no doubt, he added, that true Bolsheviks possessed the resolve to crush this sedition.

As struggle in the party ran its course through 1928–9, Stalin's faction triumphed in part because of his superior command of the party's apparatus. As noted above, Stalin's position and temperament allowed him to advance the careers of supporters and undermine opponents far more effectively than did any of his chief rivals – Trotsky first, then Zinoviev, Kamenev and Trotsky together, and finally Bukharin, Rykov and Tomskii. By the end of the decade, most of Stalin's new confederates in the party leadership owed their rise largely to him. He understood the power of patronage and exploited it tirelessly throughout the decade.

However, Stalin's defeat of Bukharin, Rykov and Tomskii did not stem solely from administrative manoeuvring. He offered the party an alternative that enjoyed considerable appeal among Bolsheviks – a bold end to the retreat and concessions of NEP. The government really was failing to boost grain exports during NEP, and, in fact, by 1927/8 they had dwindled to a meagre level not only several times lower than in mid-NEP but a tiny fraction of the grain exported before the First World War. While industrial production had increased during the first five years of NEP, it had done so largely through the revitalisation of existing enterprises previously damaged or otherwise dormant for lack of resources. Thereafter, the same rate of industrial growth, to say nothing of an increase, would require substantially greater investment than the Soviet regime had managed so far. The government's experience during the 1920s offered no guarantee that this could be accomplished through reforms within the framework of the New Economic Policy. If Western scholars have approached unanimity in deeming a continuation of NEP preferable to the carnage of the 1930s, Bolsheviks in 1928 had a different perspective, unburdened by knowledge of their fate under Stalin. For many of them, NEP had failed to hasten economic modernisation and the arrival of socialism. How long would Lenin himself have been prepared to accept modest industrial growth, if that were the best that NEP could offer into the 1930s?

Stalin for one had seen enough, and he readily found party members in agreement. They invoked the 'revolutionary-heroic' tradition of the party, recalling the Lenin of the October Revolution rather than the Lenin of 1921. The time for patient, gradual measures was over, they proclaimed. True Bolsheviks must now complete the revolution, finishing the work begun by the party in 1917 and defended heroically by the Red Army during the civil war. 'There are no fortresses Bolsheviks cannot storm', ran a slogan that captured the tone favoured by the new leadership. While it is impossible to establish what percentage of party members approved the path urged by Stalin – by no means all local officials jumped to employ the severe grain-collection methods of 1928, for example – there was certainly room for profitable campaigning against NEP inside a party devoted to socialism.

As 1928 gave way to 1929, Stalin's grip tightened. In April, Bukharin lost his positions as editor of *Pravda*, the party's flagship daily, and as head of the Comintern, an organisation based in Moscow that devised strategies for Communist Parties around the world. By the end of the year he had been expelled from the Politburo, while new leaders embarked on a series of policies that were completely incompatible with the party line of 1925. NEP was dead, though no decree materialised to announce the fact, just as none had appeared in 1921 to proclaim its birth. On occasion, Soviet authors even alleged that a modified NEP continued well into the 1930s. More often it was simply ignored, having been shoved into an unmarked grave by an offensive that featured massive collectivisation of agriculture and breathtaking industrialisation according to five-year plans. Not until the nation lay on its own deathbed half a century later, with some reformers already casting furtive glances to the capitalist West for alternatives, would NEP be recalled in the Soviet Union as a worthy path to socialism. In the meantime, new Stalinist policies became the centrepiece of a different Soviet model that would be recommended to socialist aspirants far and wide for decades to come.

7

# Stalinism, 1928–1940

DAVID R. SHEARER

In the late 1920s, the ruling Communist Party of the Soviet Union, under the leadership of its General Secretary, Joseph Stalin, launched a series of 'socialist offensives', a revolution that transformed the country. Within a few short years, the USSR bore little resemblance to the country it had been. In the 1920s, the Soviet Union was a minor industrial power, a poor but resource-rich country, based on a large but primitive agrarian network of small-hold peasant farms. By the late 1930s, very few individual farms remained. The country's agricultural production had been forcibly reorganised on a massive and mechanised scale. Most of the rural population lived on huge state-managed agrifarm complexes. Through state planning and forced investment, industrial production had doubled, then tripled and quadrupled. By the beginning of the Second World War, the Soviet Union had become an industrial military power on the scale of the most advanced countries. The Great Patriotic War, as the Second World War was called, accelerated these modernising processes, and brought about other major changes. The country, which had been nearly 80 per cent rural in the late 1920s, was, by the early 1950s, becoming increasingly urbanised, mobile and educated. Literacy rates had soared as the result of intensive state spending on education. Roads, rail lines, radio and air travel connected the previously isolated parts of the country. Cultures that had had no language boasted their own schools, organised national institutions, written literary traditions and legal status as nations within the Soviet state. From an ethnically dominant Russian Empire, the Soviet Union was transformed into a state of constitutionally organised nations. By the time of Stalin's death in March 1953, the USSR had become an industrial, military and nuclear giant. It was one of only two global 'superpowers'. The Soviet Union's power was rivalled and checked only by the power of the United States.

This modernising revolution from above was one of the most remarkable achievements of the twentieth century, and one of the costliest in human lives. Stalin's revolution was full of brutal and shocking contradictions, even in such a brutally shocking century as the twentieth. The belief that they were building socialism motivated party and state leaders with a sincere concern to construct towns, build roads and schools, to introduce scientific methods of farming, to modernise industries and to uplift culture. This same belief allowed leaders to destroy churches, synagogues and mosques, move populations wholesale, impoverish and work the population to the point of starvation and to imprison and shoot massive numbers of people. Soviet leaders claimed that they were building socialism and human dignity; what they created was an industrial-military state built, in large part, on the back of a slave labour system unprecedented in modern history. Stalinist officials, with few exceptions, saw no contradiction in their motives or actions. All were part of a grand historical mission to construct a new, specifically socialist, kind of modernity. This chapter describes the state and society that developed out of Stalin's revolution from above.

## Industrialisation, collectivisation and class war

To Stalinist leaders, building socialism in one country meant, first and foremost, modernising and expanding the country's basic industrial sectors: iron and steel production, mining, metallurgy and machine building, energy generation and timber extraction, and, of course, agriculture. During the 1930s, but especially in the years of the First Five-Year Plan, 1928–32, the Soviet state poured funds into the construction of heavy industrial projects, a 'bacchanalian' orgy of planning, spending and construction, as one economist put it.[1] The results were dramatic, truly heroic on a historical scale, even while enormously wasteful and costly in both human and financial terms. These years of the Soviet industrial revolution have been made famous by the names of some of the world's largest construction projects. This was the era of Magnitogorsk, a metal city of 100,000 workers and families that was raised within the span of half a decade from the plains of central Siberia. No less dramatic was the raising of Kuznetsstroi, another metallurgical and machine-building giant. The hydroelectric dam at Dneprostroi, started in 1928, generated its first power in 1934. The Volga River–White Sea canal system was built almost entirely by the killing machine of forced labour, yet it also stands as a major engineering feat. Tractor and locomotive manufacturing plants rose or were renovated and modernised. Military weapons, tanks, ships and aeroplane production also increased as secret military factories were constructed.

1 Naum Jasny, *Soviet Industrialization, 1928–1952* (Chicago: Chicago University Press, 1961).

The litany of statistics chronicling Soviet industrial achievements under Stalin was and still is impressive. In the Russian Republic, alone, construction of new energy sources jumped the number of kilowatt hours of energy generated from 3.2 billion in 1928 to 31 billion in 1940. Coal production increased from 10 to 73 million tons per year, iron ore from 1 to $5\frac{1}{2}$ million tons, steel from 2 to 9 million tons. The Soviet Union went from an importer to an exporter of natural gas, producing 560 million metric tons by 1932.[2]

The drive for socialist industrialisation was impressive, but it was only one aspect of Stalin's revolution, one front of the socialist offensive. The second major front of the socialist offensive was played out in the countryside in the campaigns to collectivise agriculture. State control of the countryside was crucial, according to Stalinist leaders, if the effort to construct Soviet socialism was to succeed. It was through the international sale of agricultural surplus that industrialisation had to be financed and that the socialist cities were to be fed, yet throughout the 1920s, the countryside had been purportedly in the hands of a petty-bourgeois, anti-Soviet, private farm class. These 'rich' peasants, or kulaks in Bolshevik parlance, held the revolution hostage to the whims of the market and threatened the socialist sector by withholding grain from the state. The grain crises of 1927 and 1928 seemed to prove this point. Although the harvests in those years had been reasonably good, state agencies experienced serious difficulties meeting their procurement quotas. Peasant producers preferred to sell to private buyers at higher prices than those offered by state buyers, or they withheld their grain altogether from the urban markets. In any case, the procurement crises of the late 1920s brought to a head the constraints on state-sponsored modernisation that faced the regime. Moderates within the party hierarchy such as Nikolai Bukharin and Mikhail Tomskii argued for tax and pricing mechanisms to coax grain from the countryside. They warned against any forced or repressive measures that would strain social and economic relations with private producers at a time when the government could ill afford such problems. They repeated Lenin's maxim that there be no third revolution to threaten the NEP truce between workers and peasants, town and countryside.

Stalin and those around him took a different and increasingly militant view. They argued that to placate the kulak class would only place the government and its plans in greater jeopardy. Stalin argued for outright requisitioning of grain at state prices, and he instituted such methods during personal visits

2 Iu. A. Poliakov et al., *Naselenie Rossii v XX veke. Istoricheskie ocherki*, vol. 1: *1900–1939* (Moscow, 2000), p. 220.

to the Urals and Siberia in early 1928. Moderate party leaders opposed these policies. They were taken aback by Stalin's 'feudal-military' exploitation of peasants, and they accused Stalin of taking unilateral action against the party's policies of conciliation. This charge was true, but Stalin by then had won over the majority of the members of the party's top political bureau, the Politburo. In February 1929, the General Secretary forced a humiliating showdown with the moderates in the Politburo and the party's Central Committee.

Citing claims of popular support from workers and poor peasants, and with the backing of the party elite, Stalin launched the infamous collectivisation drive of the First Five-Year Plan period. Mass propaganda campaigns created an aura of legitimacy, even as Stalinist leaders mobilised local party committees, political police, internal security forces and even military units and volunteer gangs from urban factories. These were the shock troops that enforced the order to collectivise. In the course of the ensuing several years, using persuasion and propaganda, but often outright force, the regime methodically destroyed the system of private land tenure in the country and organised agricultural production into large, state-administered farming administrations. Peasants and villages were organised either into collective farms, the *kolkhozy*, or into state farm administrations called *sovkhozy*. *Kolkhozy* were supposedly voluntary co-operative farm organisations, whereas *sovkhozy* were farms owned outright by the state, which paid peasant farmers as hired labour, a rural proletariat.

The campaign to collectivise agriculture was harsh, often brutal, and evoked strong peasant resistance. Official versions did not deny the fact of resistance but depicted it as part of the class struggle of rich, exploiting kulaks against socialism. Official versions claimed that the vast majority of poor peasants supported the regime and collectivisation. The judgement of most scholars, however, is that resistance was widespread, that there existed a broad peasant solidarity against the regime, and that collectivisation amounted to a general war against the countryside, not just a targeted class war against the kulak class enemy.[3] However one describes the collectivisation drive, it was horrific in its costs. Anyone who resisted collectivisation could be, and usually was, branded a kulak. Police and party officials confiscated the property and livestock of these individuals, arrested them and their families and exiled them to penal

3 V. P. Danilov et al. (eds.), *Tragediia sovetskoi derevni. Kollektivizatsiia i raskulachivanie. Doku-mentry i materialy v 5 tomakh, 1927–1939* (Moscow, 2000–3); R. W. Davies, *The Socialist Offensive: The Collectivization of Soviet Agriculture, 1929–1930* (Cambridge, Mass.: Harvard University Press, 1980); Andrea Graziosi, 'Collectivization, Peasant Revolts, and Government Policies through the Reports of the Ukranian GPU', *Cahiers du Monde russe et soviétique* 35, 3 (1994): 437–631; Lynne Viola, *Peasant Rebels under Stalin: Collectivization and the Culture of Peasant Resistance* (New York: Oxford University Press, 1996).

colonies, or even executed them as class enemies. In 1930 and 1931, the two most intense years of forced collectivisation and 'de-kulakisation', authorities deported 1.8 million peasants (about 400,000 households) as class enemies who had resisted collectivisation. The great majority of these peasants were deported to penal farms or settlements in remote areas of the country in Siberia, northern Russia and Central Asia. Many others were dispossessed and resettled into special farms in their home districts. By conservative estimates, well over 2 million rural inhabitants were deported by the end of 1933, when the regime ended the policy of forced mass collectivisation, and this does not include the unknown but surely large number of peasants who were executed, killed in outright fighting, or who died of harsh conditions even before they reached their places of exile.

By 1933, the regime had driven nearly 60 per cent of peasant households to join collective farms, although, remarkably, some 40 per cent or so of peasant families had managed to hold out against the wave of collectivisation. Individual peasant farms – *edinolichniki* – continued to exist legally, despite harsh tax and procurement policies and severe pressure to join collective farms. In 1930 and 1931, in fact, when the regime briefly relaxed coercive measures of collectivisation, peasants streamed out of collectives, reducing the overall proportion to a low of 21 per cent.[4] Only by offering lucrative tax and other incentives could the regime begin to reverse the decline in collectivisation, and only by allowing peasants the right to own livestock and to farm their own plots was the regime able, finally, to persuade peasants to return to collectives in large numbers. By 1935, collectives encompassed about 83 per cent of peasant households, although by the end of the decade this number had declined to 63 per cent. In the most significant grain-growing areas, in Ukraine and western Siberia, the regime ensured that collectivisation reached nearly 100 per cent.

Agricultural production was severely disrupted as a consequence of the social war in the countryside, and the cost in livestock was also devastating. By 1934, the number of cattle, sheep, horses and pigs in the USSR was approximately half of what it had been in 1929, due in no small part to the peasant slaughter of livestock in protest against state policies. The cost in human lives of collectivisation was appalling, even above and beyond the wrenching costs of the de-kulakisation campaigns. In 1932, a combination of factors – poor harvests, agricultural disruption caused by collectivisation and high state grain procurement quotas – precipitated famine in areas of Ukraine, the North Caucasus and central Russia, which left over 5 million people dead by the time

---

4 Viola, *Peasant Rebels*, p. 28,

the situation eased in late 1933 and 1934. Although the famine hit Ukraine hard, it was not, as some historians argue, a purposefully genocidal policy against Ukrainians.[5] Stalinist leaders certainly used the famine to break peasant resistance to collectivisation, and very likely to punish the Ukrainian countryside for having long resisted Soviet power. Still, no evidence has surfaced to suggest that the famine was planned, and it affected broad segments of the Russian and other non-Ukrainian populations both in Ukraine and in Russia.

Despite the excesses and costs, the Stalinists achieved their goal – a state-controlled agrarian sector. Beginning in 1930, state grain procurements increased dramatically, almost doubling yearly, despite the decline in harvests during the hard years of 1932 and 1933. In fact, the Soviet government continued to export grain even during the famine, and the regime trumpeted collectivisation as a triumph of socialist modernisation. At first glance, it was. Collectivisation seemed to satisfy the regime's insatiable appetite for grain, and the state's agencies poured out statistics to prove that collectivisation had resulted in a large net transfer of economic and labour resources from agriculture to industry. For all the propaganda, however, the results of collectivisation were mixed. Many economic historians, and other students of Soviet history, argue that the costs of collectivisation, even in economic terms, far exceeded the benefits to the regime. The regime gained control over grain, but was forced to invest far greater amounts of money and supplies in agriculture than it got out of that sector.[6] The administrative costs alone were enormous and remained uncalculated, as did the massive investment needed to maintain police and party surveillance over the rural population. Productivity remained relatively low throughout much of the 1930s, despite the regime's goal to 'tractorise' the countryside, and many collective farms amounted to no more than paper fronts for traditional household and village farm economies.[7] Still, in all, collectivisation altered the rural life of the country. The regime's harsh measures brought Soviet power, finally, to the countryside, and it did so with a vengeance. Party and police presence became pervasive in rural areas, as did the institutions of Soviet authority. Moreover, along with collectivisation came severe restrictions on peasants' freedom of movement. Rural inhabitants were forbidden to travel without the written permission of local authorities,

5 Robert Conquest, *The Harvest of Sorrow: Soviet Collectivization and the Terror-Famine* (New York and Oxford: Oxford University Press, 1986).
6 R. W. Davies, *The Soviet Economy in Turmoil, 1929–1930* (Cambridge, Mass.: Harvard University Press, 1989), p. ix.
7 Sheila Fitzpatrick, *Stalin's Peasants: Resistance and Survival in the Russian Village after Collectivization* (New York: Oxford University Press, 1994); V. B. Zhiromskaia, *Demograficheskaia istoriia Rossii v 1930-e gody* (Moscow, 2001), p. 167.

and collective farm workers were, by and large, excluded from receiving the internal passports necessary to travel and to move from one location or place of work to another. Collectivisation bound peasants once again to the land in a way that many regarded as a second serfdom.

Peasants were not the only segment of the population affected by Stalin's socialist offensive against capitalist revivals. Destruction of the private farm economy went hand in glove with a general assault on private trade and other market remnants of NEP. The regime drove out the private trade networks, at first through increasingly heavy taxation, and then through decrees outlawing any private sale of goods. Police began arresting traders and middlemen – the officially reviled NEPmen of the 1920s. Authorities closed commission resale stores, they even banned local farm markets, and for a time even forbade the resale of personal property between individuals. All trading and any exchange of goods was to be done through state-approved stores, co-operatives, or through state-controlled rationing systems.

Stalinist leaders attempted to replace market mechanisms with the elements of a planned, socialist economy. The state's planning agency, Gosplan, took on the expanding burden not only of industrial investment, but of planning for all aspects of the Soviet economy. Through its series of five-year plans, the agency and its burgeoning number of commissions set priorities for the country's different economic sectors based on political priorities decided by the party leaders. Gosplan established prices and determined production and distribution quotas.

As with other aspects of the socialist offensive, the sudden thrust of the state into the private economy came at a high cost. State agencies were woefully unprepared for the task of supplanting private markets. Shortages racked the economy in all basic commodities. Goods disappeared even from state stores and were costly when they did appear. Hidden inflation from shortages and deficit industrial investment devastated the value of the currency, dropping it by more than half by the end of 1930. Rationing, which had begun as early as 1928 for bread, broadened to include almost all staple goods. Many areas of the country moved to barter of the few goods that existed, and families began to use any items of metal value on the black markets that sprang up outside the official price and rationing systems. Assessing the effects of this informal economy, one official commented ironically that it amounted to a social redistribution of wealth in unanticipated ways.

Such unanticipated consequences affected urban workers as well as rural inhabitants. The value of wages plummeted and, during the early 1930s, many state enterprises were so strapped for cash that they failed routinely to meet wage payments. This was due, of course, not only to money shortages, but also to widespread corruption and graft within the rapidly expanding state economic system. During the early 1930s, workers relied increasingly for food and other basic necessities on the growing rationing system in their workplaces and through trade union organisations. In order to keep a steady workforce, factory administrations suddenly found themselves in the business of providing housing, food and clothing shops, cafeterias, remedial education and other services that were not part of their production tasks for the state. In effect, they were forced to fill the vacuum left by the collapsing service and trade economy. This kind of corporatist economy was not what state planners had had in mind by a socialist revolution, but neither was it a capitalist economy.[8]

## The domestic and international contexts

Stalin's industrial and agrarian revolution marked a radical break with the state capitalism of the 1920s, the gradualist policies of economic development and the social armistice that had underpinned NEP. Some of the most prominent leaders in the party opposed Stalin's plunge into social war and socialist modernisation, yet the Stalinists, supported by significant numbers within the party, believed that radical measures were necessary, and the grain crisis of the late 1920s was only one of several events that convinced Stalin that the revolution itself was in jeopardy. Domestically, the grain crisis was a signal to Stalin and those around him of the gathering strength of anti-Bolshevik social forces. In the mid-1920s, voting for local soviets had showed a small but disturbing trend towards support of former Menshevik and SR candidates.[9] Bolshevik leaders were convinced that this vote reflected strong pressure from kulaks and local private employers on poor peasants to vote anti-Bolshevik or not to vote at all. Moreover, finance commissariat studies claimed to show an alarming growth of private capital in the country, as opposed to only moderate rates of growth of the state's revenues.

These trends were disturbing enough, but they seemed to herald a growing capitalist backlash inside the Soviet Union at a time when the country found itself increasingly isolated internationally. The virulent destruction of the communist movement in China in 1927 and the triumph of the nationalists

8 Stephen Kotkin, *Magnetic Mountain: Stalinism as a Civilization* (Berkeley: University of California Press, 1995); David R. Shearer, *Industry, State, and Society in Stalin's Russia, 1926–1934* (Ithaca, N.Y.: Cornell University Press, 1996).
9 Michel Reiman, *The Birth of Stalinism: The USSR on the Eve of the 'Second Revolution'*, trans. George Saunders (Bloomington: Indiana University Press, 1987), p. 44; Markus Wehner, *Bauernpolitik im proletarischen Staat* (Cologne: Boehlau Verlag, 1998), p. 257.

suddenly presented Soviet leaders with a major threat along their weak and long southern borders. Moreover, the Chinese disaster occurred at the same time that the British government broke off relations and threatened war against the Soviet Union. The Soviet budget was already over-extended and foreign governments, led by the British example, expressed reluctance to offer the investment credits the Soviets needed for increased industrial development. By the late 1920s, the Soviet Union was weak, isolated and seemed to face a growing domestic as well as international threat. Such was the perception of the Soviet leaders, and not only Soviet leaders. In 1927, the German ambassador in Moscow cabled his superiors in Berlin to prepare a German response in the event that the Bolshevik government should collapse.[10]

In these conditions, Stalin turned inward. He became convinced that building socialism in one country was the only alternative left to the Soviet Union, and he believed that the country needed to modernise quickly. In 1929, Stalin delivered the famous speech in which he declared the need to make up one hundred years of backwardness in ten, lest the country and the revolution be crushed. He called on the party and the working class once again to renew the revolution – to destroy the kulak class, once and for all, and to industrialise the country for its own defence. Stalin's revolution had begun.

## Social dynamics and population movements

Policies of rapid industrialisation and forced collectivisation produced dramatic population and demographic shifts during the 1930s and altered both the regional and urban–rural balance in the country. In some areas, these policies – combined with the effects of widespread famine – precipitated death and migration on a nearly biblical scale. The forced relocation of populations, policies of mass repression and the reconstruction of different nationalities added to the momentous and often calamitous changes experienced by the Soviet population under Stalin's rule. Industrialisation alone accounted for a significant growth in the number of urban centres and urban populations. In the years between the 1926 and 1937 all-union censuses, the overall population of the Soviet Union increased from 147 million to 162 million – about a 9 per cent increase – but the urban population in the country doubled during the same period, from about 26 million to 52 million. Only 18 per cent of that increase came from natural growth rates of the urban population, while about two-thirds (63 per cent) resulted from in-migration to existing cities and

10 Reiman, *The Birth of Stalinism*, p. 48.

towns. Almost 20 per cent of the growth in urban populations resulted from the industrial transformation of rural population centres into cities and towns. In the Russian Republic alone, the number of population centres classified as cities increased from 461 to 571. The number of cities with populations over 50,000 increased from 57 to 110. In the country as a whole, the number of population centres classified as urban centres increased in the years between 1926 and 1937 from 1,240 to 2,364.

Rural areas emptied as cities filled up. In 1926, the urban population made up 18 per cent of the overall population of the USSR, but by the late 1930s, urban areas accounted for 30 per cent of the population. The most significant population shifts occurred, of course, during the early 1930s, the years of rapid industrialisation and collectivisation, and while all areas of the country were affected, the growth in industrial urbanisation affected some areas more than others. The greater Moscow and Leningrad urban areas experienced significant growth, their populations doubling during the late 1920s and 1930s. Areas such as eastern and western Siberia, the Urals and the Volga coal and industrial basin underwent rapid, almost unchecked, growth in their overall populations, and especially in their urban populations. These were the areas of the country that the regime targeted for intensive industrial development and mineral and other natural resource extraction. During the 1930s, the population of the Far Eastern administrative district soared 376 per cent. The population of eastern Siberia expanded by 331 per cent, western Siberia by 294 per cent, and the Urals by 263 per cent. The mining and industrial city of Kemerovo, in western Siberia, saw a sixfold increase in its population; Cheliabinsk, not far away, experienced a fourfold population increase, as did the rail, river and manufacturing centre of Barnaul, south of Novosibirsk. Cities such as Novosibirsk, Sverdlovsk (the once and future Ekaterinburg), Vladivostok and Khabarovsk (the administrative centre of the eastern Siberian district) saw their populations triple during the late 1920s and 1930s.

These population shifts resulted from industrialisation, but also from the regime's systematic policies of repression, particularly against peasants, socially marginalised groups and certain national minorities. Major population shifts also came about as the result of a dramatic increase in forced labour populations, and from mass migration due to famine. During the early 1930s, de-kulakisation depleted rural areas, especially in the western parts of the USSR, of supposed class enemies.[11] Famine took its toll, either by killing large

---

11 On kulak deportations, see esp. V. N. Zemskov, *Spetspereselentsy v SSSR, 1930–1960* (Moscow, 2003).

numbers of people or by forcing others to flee stricken areas. After 1932, mass deportations of peasants tapered off as the regime turned its attention to 'cleansing' major urban and industrial areas of socially marginalised and economically unproductive populations. Using newly enacted residence laws, police conducted mass sweeps of cities, industrial areas and border regions to rid them of what were described as 'anti-Soviet' and 'socially danger-ous' elements – criminals, wanderers, the indigent and the dispossessed, even orphans – the social detritus of Stalin's modernisation policies.[12] At the same time, the regime began large-scale deportations of certain nationalities. In the western borderlands, police singled out Poles and Germans for removal as early as 1932 and 1933. Deportations of Finnish-related populations began in Karelia and around Leningrad in earnest in the middle 1930s and continued up through the Finnish war in 1940. Fearful of 'Asian' solidarity with the Japanese expansion in China, Soviet authorities deported 172,000 Soviet citizens of Korean descent from Far Eastern border areas in 1937 and 1938. During the Second World War, Stalin ordered the removal of a number of populations supposedly sympathetic to German occupation forces and desirous of achieving national independence. The most infamous of these deportations resulted in the removal of the entire Chechen people and the Crimean Tatar population, shipped en masse to Central Asia.[13]

Most deported populations, some several million over the course of the 1930s, were resettled either in penal labour colonies or in the infamous forced labour camps in the eastern interior areas of the USSR. Large sections of the Urals, Siberia and Central Asia became the favoured dumping ground for unwanted or supposedly dangerous populations, as did the northern districts of European Russia. The turnover of camp populations varied dramatically from year to year due to death, escape and release of prisoners, but overall the camp populations grew steadily from about 179,000 in 1930 to half a million by 1934. The huge influx of prisoners during the Great Purges in 1937 and 1938 swelled camp populations to 1.5 million by 1940. Similarly, the populations of police-run prisons and colonies jumped during the 1930s, reaching 254,354 in 1935, according to official figures, and 887,635 by 1938. Slightly more than 250,000 of those held in prisons and labour colonies in 1938 were located in

12 On the campaigns for 'social defence,' see especially Paul Hagenloh, ' "Socially Harmful Elements" ' and the Great Terror', in Sheila Fitzpatrick (ed.), *Stalinism: New Directions* (London: Routledge, 2000), pp. 286–308; and David R. Shearer, 'Social Disorder, Mass Repression, and the NKVD during the 1930s' *Cahiers du Monde Russe et Soviétique* 42, nos. 2,3,4 (Apr.– Dec. 2001): 505–34.
13 Pavel Polian, *Ne po svoei vole . . . Istoriia i geografiia prinuditel'nykh migratsii v SSSR* (Moscow: O. G. I. - Memorial, 2001).

the Urals, Central Asia and Siberia. If the number of prisoners held in labour camps grew rapidly throughout the 1930s, the numbers of those deported as kulaks peaked in the early 1930s and then declined steadily. As noted above, however, most of the peasant deportations were also to the newly opened colonial areas in the eastern part of the country. In 1932, for example, nearly 1.1 million of the 1.3 million 'special settlers' – the kulak *spetspereselentsy* – lived in the Urals, Kazakhstan or in the agricultural regions of western Siberia.[14]

The Soviet regime exploited these populations ruthlessly as a source of extractive labour, and the Gulag and settlement colonies became, in time, an integral part of the Soviet state's economic planning system. This was especially true for the colonial development of raw materials industries such as logging and precious metal mining, but also for agriculture. As a result of these policies, the eastern regions of the country experienced a remarkable increase in overall population during the 1930s. So much so, that the head of the state's statistical agency, I. A. Kraval', recommended to the Politburo that the 1937 census undercount the population of Siberia so as to hide the extent of the demographic shift to that part of the country.

Along with massive migration, both forced and unforced, Stalinist policies also created social dislocation on a massive scale, and authorities were hard pressed to cope with the resulting social disorder. In the first half of the 1930s, especially, waves of migrants, both legal and illegal, overwhelmed local communities and even large cities. The population of abandoned, runaway or orphaned children rose rapidly from approximately 129,000 in 1929 to well over half a million by 1934, and these figures counted only numbers that were officially registered in the woefully inadequate and understaffed children's homes. Abandoned or orphaned mostly as the result of policies of de-kulakisation and conditions of famine, hundreds of thousands of children made their way to cities. Having no home and no work, socially alienated because of their background and the violence that made them homeless, the population of abandoned, runaway or orphaned children contributed to the growing and serious waves of petty criminality that marked city streets, marketplaces, train stations and other public areas. Millions of other people – rough peasants and dispossessed populations – also poured into the cities, factories and industrial construction sites. People were fleeing collectivisation and famine, running from penal colonies or just seeking a better life. Shanty towns, slums and raw campsites mushroomed on the outskirts of cities. Sometimes, whole villages

14 For the most comprehensive figures on camp populations and distribution, see *GULAG (Glavnoe Upravlenie Lagerei) 1918–1960* (Moscow, 2000), esp. pp. 410–35. For kulak colony figures, see Zemskov, *Spetspereselentsy v SSSR*.

appeared at the gates of shops, negotiating directly with foremen for work, food and shelter.

The sudden influx of migrants into cities and industrial sites strained public services and scarce housing and food supplies, and focused all that was modern and brutally primitive about Soviet socialism during the inter-war decade. Novosibirsk, for example, the administrative centre of western Siberia, shone with the gleam of Soviet modernity. The district executive committee building, designed by the famous architect A. D. Kriachkov, and completed in 1933, won honourable mention at the Paris architectural fair in 1938. The city lavished funds on construction of the largest opera house east of Moscow in 1934, another architectural marvel and a palace of culture for the people. In contrast, the city of Barnaul, an industrial pit five hours by train south of Novosibirsk, could boast only two city buses in 1935. These served an impoverished population of 92,000. The city could not generate enough electricity to illuminate street lights. Thousands of people suffered, while others died, of intestinal infections and malaria due to a lack of clean drinking water. Much of the city's population lived in the squalour of makeshift shanty huts and bathed in the industrially fouled waters of the Ob' River. Police rarely ventured into the burgeoning shanty towns, and public welfare programmes failed to cope. The city had no paved sidewalks and few paved roadways.[15]

The regime faced problems of control and legitimacy in rural as well as urban areas. Despite the regime's attempt to extend Soviet power, Soviet authority outside major cities and towns remained weak throughout much of the 1930s. The experience of Soviet power at local levels differed considerably from that wielded by the powerful centralised political institutions of the party. As often as not, local officials felt like they were holding a besieged outpost rather than wielding power as a ruling class. Reports by local political police officers and party heads reflected their sense of isolation. Many local officials sought transfers from 'backward' rural regions to urban or more centrally located postings, and the strains of isolation drove more than a few rural authorities to suicide. Political officials worried about the small number of Communist 'actives' in their areas. They also worried about the growing number of peasant households withdrawing from collective farms and the hostile moods of *kolkhozniki*. Pointed disrespect for officials, both symbolic and real,

15 On 'ruralisation' of cities, see Moshe Lewin, *The Making of the Soviet System: Essays in the Social History of Interwar Russia* (New York: Pantheon Books, 1985). See also David Hoffmann, *Peasant Metropolis: Social Identities in Moscow, 1929–1941* (Ithaca, N.Y.: Cornell University Press, 1994). On Siberia, see David Shearer, 'Modernity and Backwardness on the Soviet Frontier', in Donald Raleigh (ed.), *Provincial Landscapes: Local Dimensions of Soviet Power, 1917–1953* (Pittsburgh: University of Pittsburgh Press, 2001), pp. 194–216.

resulted in violence and even murder. At times, local officials expressed open fear of confrontation with collective-farm peasants, and officials took threats against their lives as a serious possibility. Vandalism and theft of state property, including and especially rustling of animals, continued on a widespread scale. Armed and mounted bandits roamed large parts of the countryside requiring, in some instances, small-scale military campaigns to suppress them. In mixed ethnic areas, non-Russian populations frequently protected bandits and other outlaws from authorities. And, as rumours about a new constitution gathered force in 1935 and 1936, local leaders also worried about the revival of religious activity. Believing that they would be protected under new laws, lay priests and sectarians of all denominations began to proselytise again. Itinerant preachers spoke, at times to large gatherings of rural inhabitants, alternately promising to establish Christian collective farms or to bring God's judgement on the collective-farm system.

## Consolidating Stalin's revolution: the victory of socialism and the retreat to conservatism

The cataclysmic social upheaval created by Stalin's modernising revolution left lasting effects, but the country experienced a relative period of stabilisation after mid-decade, and this was due largely to moderating policies implemented by Stalinist leaders. Stalin signalled this turn and gave the hint of a social truce in his famous victory speech at the Seventeenth Party Congress in 1934. In this major speech, Stalin proclaimed that the victory of socialism had been won in the USSR. He declared that organised class opposition had been broken and that the country had set the foundation for a socialist economy and society. He warned of the continued threat of enemies within and without, and of the difficult historical tasks that still lay ahead. He cautioned that because of continuing dangers, the party, the police and the state needed to remain strong and vigilant against the enemies who would try to undermine the Soviet achievement. Yet the vision of the near future that Stalin then laid before the congress was one of consolidation and amelioration, even a retreat, in some respects, from the extreme policies of the First Five-Year Plan period. Leaders did, in fact, shift investment priorities in the Second Five-Year Plan in order to ease food and other shortages and to compensate for the catastrophic decline in living standards. In rural areas of the country, the regime legalised small-scale market exchange again, and a new Stalinist 'charter' allowed *kolkhozniki* to own some livestock and to cultivate small private plots of land for their own use. The effect of these changes was immediate and beneficial. Food became available, if not plentiful, on a regular basis. While collective and state farms continued to under-produce, the small private plots of peasants saved the country from further starvation. Private farm plots made up only about 10–12 per cent of the arable land, but accounted for nearly two-thirds of the produce sold in the country during these years. *Edinolichniki*, although distrusted by the regime, provided an invaluable economic niche of support for the collective-farm system and became the core of a revived artisan culture in the countryside. These private economic activities, grudgingly permitted by the regime, quickly formed the basis of a new, second economy, which became indispensable for the maintenance of the state's huge and increasingly unwieldy official economy.

## Culture and morality in the service of socialism

Stalinist leaders continued to pour money into military and heavy industrial development, but the regime also turned its attention during the mid- and late 1930s to the social, cultural and moral tasks of socialist construction. Cultural history is often given second place in discussions of the 1930s, even though cultural construction was an important aspect of Stalinism. The regime made significant efforts to extend basic education and health care to the population. The Stalinist regime tried hard to control what the public read and saw, but it wanted and needed a public that was literate and educated. As a result, the plans for economic development of any region (indeed, of the whole country) always included estimates for the construction of schools, numbers of clinics, teachers, doctors, nurses and even movie houses. In Novosibirsk, the gleaming centre of the new Siberia, the huge central opera house was completed in 1934, before the new central executive building and long before expansion of party headquarters. Every factory and workers' barracks had its newspaper boards, Red Reading Corners and literacy classes, and trade union organisations as well as local soviets provided free technical and basic education for citizens of all ages.

Stalinist educational achievements were impressive. Although the regime had promoted literacy and basic education throughout the 1920s, school attendance for all children became mandatory at the beginning of the 1930s. Many adults were also encouraged to take basic literacy classes. By the end of the decade, nearly 75 per cent of the adult population could read, a remarkable achievement compared to a literacy rate of 41 per cent, according to the 1926 census. Among children aged twelve to nineteen, literacy rates, according to the 1937 census, had reached 90 per cent. Some of the most significant advances occurred in rural and non-Russian areas and among women. Soviet authorities regarded education as a primary weapon in the struggle against what they considered backwardness, especially against traditional influences of religion and indigenous ethnic culture. The regime targeted women, especially, as a traditionally oppressed social group, but also because they were considered essential to the socialist education of children. As a result, the regime put significant effort into spreading educational opportunities in rural and non-Russian areas and among women. By the late 1930s literacy rates among all women in Russia reached over 80 per cent.[16]

The Stalinist regime lavished large amounts of money on art, literary production, film and other forms of entertainment. Art became, under Stalin, a form of social mobilisation, a means to bind the populace to the regime, and as Stalin extended state power into what had been private sectors of the economy, so too the Stalinist regime extended state control into the sphere of art and culture and into all aspects of public and private life. Indeed, in Stalin's socialist revolution, there was to be no distinction between public and private. 'The private life is dead', insisted Pasternak's character Strelnikov, in the novel *Doctor Zhivago*, and this phrase epitomised how life was to be lived in the new socialist motherland. Under Stalin, all art, culture and morality was to be put in the service of building socialism. Artists were to act as 'engineers of the soul', in Stalin's famous phrase. Their job was to construct the socialist individual, just as structural engineers were responsible for constructing buildings, roads, hydroelectric dams and steel mills.

Socialist realism became the criterion by which all art and culture was to be measured. The doctrine of socialist realism came, in fact, from Stalin, refined by the writer Maxim Gorky, as a way to describe life in direct, understandable ways, but in ways that would uplift the subject towards the goals of fulfilling socialism. Socialist realism was a dogma of art that was unapologetically didactic. It was not necessarily a recipe for saccharine sweet or escapist depictions of socialist plenty and happiness, even though much of socialist realist art degenerated to that level. The doctrine, as applied by censors, and even by Stalin himself, allowed for, and even demanded, the portrayal of conflict and sacrifice, even tragedy, but always with a moral message. That message was that the cause of building socialism was greater than the individual, that the individual found self-realisation only by denying selfish interests, by dissolving individual will into the will of the collective, and by giving the self completely to the cause of socialism and in the striving for socialism.

16 Zhiromskaia, *Demograficheskaia istoriia Rossii*, pp. 179–84.

In practice, socialist realism found expression in representational and clearly programmatic forms, whether in literature, music, painting, film or other artistic genres. And while the dogma dictated the form in general, it did not entirely stifle creativity or breed simplicity. Socialist realist art did not always take the form of 'boy meets tractor'. In music, for example, the composers Dmitrii Shostakovich and Sergei Prokofiev abandoned the high formalist experimentation of their earlier careers after serious political censure and public humiliation. Both composers turned back to classical melodic and symphonic forms, but they continued to produce great works of music. The writer Valentin Katayev's novel *Time Forward!* (*Vremia vpered*) – about the heroic struggles by a young couple to overcome adversity and even sabotage on an industrial construction site – became a much and often poorly copied model of socialist realism in action. The movie *Chapaev* (1934) provided film history as well as Soviet audiences with grand action and heroes on a larger-than-life scale. Sergei Eisenstein's film epics *Aleksandr Nevskii* and *Ivan Groznyi* (Ivan the Terrible) are regarded as movie classics, just as Shostakovich's music score for *Aleksandr Nevskii* ranks as a musical and choral classic.

If socialist realism did not entirely stifle creativity, neither did it preclude truly popular forms of entertainment. American jazz music found an enthusiastic audience in the USSR during the 1930s, as did Charlie Chaplin movies. The country had no lack of its own schmaltzy radio ballroom crooners. P. Mikhailov was one of the best known, though by no means the only, of the radio singers of the late 1930s. His song 'The Setting Sun' was one of the most popular of the period – a syrupy ballad about palm trees and moonlight on an exotic Black Sea shore. Escapist musicals, Hollywood style, were also popular, but with a revolutionary Soviet twist. The film *A Wealthy Bride* (*Bogataia nevesta*) (1937) portrayed the life of joy and plenty on a collective farm. It showed often on the wide screen, replete with copious amounts of food and drink, boisterous pranks, light romance and big choral numbers involving happy singing peasants in fecund marketplaces and in fields redolent of grain.

The Stalinist regime enforced aesthetic norms by extending monopoly control over the organisation of all cultural production. Intrusion of the state into the country's cultural life went hand in glove with the extension of state power into the economy. Culture became a front, in the militarised language of the day, just as did the economy, in the campaign to mobilise the country to build socialism. Thus, any artist or writer who worked professionally had to belong to a corresponding union, which was closely regulated by the party and subject to state censorship review. Decisions about what constituted acceptable socialist realist art could be arbitrary and depended greatly on the political and even personal politics of the union organisations, censorship boards and the artists themselves. Shostakovich, for example, regularly introduced modernist elements into his music. He covered himself and his music with a politically acceptable title or dedication, but while the lack of exactitude in aesthetic definitions allowed some leeway in artistic endeavour, that vagueness could also be dangerous. Shostakovich found himself more than once fearing for his life as well as his artistic career under the scrutiny of Stalin's personal displeasure. Many artists wrote or composed 'for the desk drawer', realising that their work would very likely not pass censors, or deciding simply not to take the risk of being public cultural figures. Others abandoned creative production and retreated into safer but related activities. The writer Boris Pasternak spent much of the 1930s and 1940s producing his now famous series of translations of Shakespeare into Russian.

The middle 1930s witnessed a conservative turn in Stalin's social as well as cultural policies. The new Soviet morality rebuffed the liberalising trends of the 1920s and the cultural revolution of the early 1930s and heralded a return to traditionally gendered roles. 'Communist virtue' for men extolled patriarchal values of manliness and patriotism, duty and discipline, and family. The heroine welder in Ostrovskii's *How the Steel was Tempered* (*Kak zakalialas' stal'*) – who could smoke, curse and shimmy down ropes from high altitudes just as well as any man – no longer provided a role model for women. Soviet advertising in the relative abundance of the mid- and late 1930s appealed to women as domestic and feminine consumers, not as revolutionary equals with men.[17] In the new morality, women were encouraged to provide the moral and emotional support for their worker husbands in the building of socialism. Official propaganda stressed child-bearing as the highest duty for women under socialism. Family and education were touted as the foundation of socialist society.[18]

Stringent laws reinforced these values. The series of family laws passed in 1936 were the most comprehensive of these and reversed many of the progressive statutes of the 1926 set of family laws. The new laws affirmed the nuclear family and made divorce more difficult to obtain. Abortion became a criminal offence once again, with severe jail penalties for both women and abortionists, although women continued to have abortions, and doctors continued to give them in large numbers. Child-support laws were strengthened, as were

---

17 Amy Randall, 'The Campaign for Soviet Trade: Creating Socialist Retail Trade in the 1930s', Ph. D. diss., Princeton University, 2000.
18 David Hoffmann, *Socialist Values: The Cultural Norms of Soviet Modernity, 1917–1941* (Ithaca, N.Y.: Cornell University Press, 2003).

criminal statutes for men, primarily, failing to provide court-ordered family support. For a brief period, police even considered the idea of placing a special stamp in the internal passports of men who owed child support so that they could be traced.

## Nationality under Stalin

Stalinist leaders sought to reconstruct Soviet nationalities on the same broad scale that they did society, culture and moral values. The peoples of the Soviet Union were to be mapped, schematised and rationalised – engineered, in a word – just as was the land, the economy and the human soul. Constructing nationality was not unique to Stalinism or to the Soviet Union. Most European states engaged in some form of nation-building, based on criteria of inclusion and exclusion, but the Soviet experiment differed fundamentally from the nation-building projects of other states. The Soviet state was not a nation-state, such as France or Germany, but a state of nations, a conglomeration of national political governments under a central controlling state system. The only other state resembling this model had been the Austro-Hungarian Empire, which had been torn asunder by the strains of the Great War. Stalin understood – or at least he thought he understood – the explosive potential of national identity and, while he did not openly repudiate the conciliatory policies of the 1920s, he gave nationality issues a new politicised importance that they had not had.

During the 1930s, Soviet officials continued to encourage the development of national cultures and institutions under the rubric 'national in form, socialist in content'. This policy, begun in the 1920s, included the rooting (*korenizat-siia*) of different ethnic groups in their own republics, autonomous regions and oblasts. In contrast to the relatively laissez-faire policies of the 1920s, however, nationality policies of the 1930s reflected the same highly structured, top-down character of other Stalinist state-building projects. Rather than allowing different ethnic groups to develop their own cultural traditions, Soviet officials in the 1930s aggressively organised officially sanctioned forms of nationality. Ethnographic studies burgeoned as scholars worked closely with officials to create over fifty written languages for peoples who had had no written forms of culture. Small nationalities were created and consolidated out of various nomadic cultures, and the state assigned to them their own territories. Alphabets were reformed and folk traditions were officially celebrated, all within the encompassing context of the brotherhood of Soviet peoples.

Stalinist nationality policies had a sharp political edge to them, and not all nationalities were encouraged equally, as had been the policy in the 1920s. Stalin elevated Russian national culture, in particular, to pride of place and it was celebrated as the predominant culture among all the Soviet cultures. The ascendancy of Russian culture and Russian forms of patriotism was reinforced during the war, and several attempts were promoted, although rejected by Stalin, to create a specifically Russian Communist Party along the lines of other republic party organisations. Stalin rejected this trend, fearing that a Russian party could potentially form a rival centre of power. While he rejected an openly assimilationist nationality policy, Stalin nonetheless permitted Russians a dominant role in party affairs. Russian migration was encouraged into non-Russian areas, and Russian national culture went with the new immigrants. Russian language was instituted as the universal language of education and state affairs. Leaders took care to foster indigenous national elites, especially within the party structure, but most of the leading party and state positions at the republic and oblast levels were held by ethnic Russians, usually outsiders appointed from Moscow. Non-Russian institutions, organisations and journals inside the Russian republic were closed or scaled back as the Russian republic was Russified, and nationalities were territorialised in the 1930s in a way that had not been the case earlier. Institutions promoting ethnic consciousness and culture were confined, generally, to the territories designated for particular national groups.[19]

As the discussion above implies, national identity gained a new prominence in Soviet society, even as categories of social class began to wane in importance as a means to determine one's identity and relation to state authority. In the early 1930s, when the state first issued internal passports, citizens were required to identify their national identity as well as their social-class status, yet class still counted as the primary defining criterion of inclusion and exclusion. The mass repressions associated with collectivisation and de-kulakisation were based on class and, initially, residence and rationing privileges associated with the new passport system were also based on social criteria of class and occupation. Then came the so-called victory of socialism in 1934, the officially announced defeat of organised class opposition in the country. The announcement of this victory did not end political repression, nor did it signal the end of class struggle, according to Stalin. Indeed, Stalin anticipated that the struggle against the

19 Terry Martin, *The Affirmative Action Empire: Nations and Nationalism in the Soviet Union, 1923–1939* (Ithaca, N.Y.: Cornell University Press, 2001); R. G. Suny and Terry Martin (eds.), *A State of Nations: Empire and Nation-Making in the Age of Lenin and Stalin* (Oxford: Oxford University Press, 2001).

enemies of Soviet socialism would intensify as the socialist state grew stronger and anti-Soviet 'elements' grew more desperate, but Stalin also anticipated that the character of the state's struggle against its enemies would change as the nature of resistance also changed. What, exactly, Stalin anticipated is impossible to know, but the nature of repression and the criteria of inclusion and exclusion underwent a marked change during the 1930s. As early as 1933, deportations of so-called anti-Soviet elements from western border regions targeted specific national groups of Poles, Belorussians and Ukrainians. Stalin was especially suspicious of Ukrainian separatism, since resistance to collectivisation had been particularly strong in that republic and in the western border areas of the country. As the 1930s wore on, Stalin also came to mistrust certain other ethnic groups, which he suspected of having potential loyalties outside the USSR. By 1936, most campaigns of mass repression were being carried out against groups defined by national or ethnic rather than social criteria, and while the great mass purges of 1937–8 started against so-called kulak and other marginalised social categories, these were quickly superseded by the great campaigns against Germans, Poles, Finns and Asian populations in the Soviet Far East. During the war, mass deportations continued, especially of ethnic groups from the Caucasus regions, which Stalin suspected of separatist and collaborationist tendencies, and in the years after the war, Soviet police and military units fought against strong Ukrainian separatist movements. By the early 1950s, nationality had almost all but replaced class as the most important criterion of Soviet identity, at least within the pre-Second World War borders of the USSR.

## Mass repression, police and the militarised state

In late July 1937, N. I. Ezhov, the head of the political police and the Commissariat of the Interior, issued the now infamous operational order no. 447. That order began one of the most bizarre, tragic and inexplicable episodes of Soviet history – the mass operations of repression of 1937 and 1938. By decree of the Politburo, the political police were charged to begin mass shooting or imprisonment of several categories of what regime leaders considered socially harmful elements. Leaders regarded former kulaks, bandits and recidivist criminals among the most dangerous of these groups, alongside members of anti-Soviet parties, White Guardists, returned émigrés, churchmen and sectarians and gendarmes and former officials of the tsarist government. By the end of November 1938, when leaders stopped the operations, nearly 766,000 individuals had been caught up in the police sweeps. Nearly 385,000 of those individuals had been arrested as category I enemies. Those who fell into this category were scheduled to be shot, while the remaining arrestees, in category II, were to receive labour camp sentences from five to ten years.

There exists almost nothing in open archives and other sources to explain fully the motivation behind these massive social purges, but we can at least understand the dynamics of the purges and something of the motivation behind them. We can compare the great social purges of the late 1930s to the campaigns of repression that preceded and followed them, and in this way place them within the context of a larger discussion of mass repression under Stalin. As in the early 1930s, and after several years of relative stability, the regime turned again on peasants during the *Ezhovshchina*. Collective and state farmers, as well as individual farmers (*kolkhozniki*, *sovkhozniki*, and *edinolichniki*), were arrested in the tens of thousands. Yet, the mass repressions of the late 1930s were more than a second de-kulakisation. Criminal elements, former convicts, sectarians and a host of other marginalised populations, along with farm workers, local Soviet officials and freeholder peasants, became targets of the state's campaigns of mass repression. As noted above, the repressions of 1937 and 1938 also encompassed significant numbers of national minorities, arrested under analogous operational orders. If the campaigns of mass repression began as a purge of socially suspect groups, they turned into a campaign of ethnic cleansing against 'enemy' nations.[20]

Here, then, were the elements that gave the Great Purges their particular characteristics and virulence. The de-kulakisation, social order and national deportation campaigns of the preceding years formed the background for the mass repressions of the late 1930s. The mechanisms employed during the repressions of 1937 and 1938 were similar to those used earlier to contain or dispose of undesirable populations and, in 1937 and 1938, the police targeted many of the same groups. Yet it was not just the threat of class war or social disorder that generated the mass repressions of the late 1930s. The threat of war introduced a xenophobic element into Soviet policies of repression and gave to those policies a sense of political urgency. By 1937, leaders were convinced that oppositionists, working with foreign agents, were actively organising socially disaffected populations into a fifth-column force. Authorities worried that invasion, which seemed increasingly likely in the late 1930s, would be the signal for armed uprisings by these groups, as well as by potentially hostile national populations. Each of these concerns – over social disorder, political opposition and national contamination – had generated separate political responses and

---

20 Terry Martin, 'The Origins of Soviet Ethnic Cleansing', *Journal of Modern History* 70 (1998): 813–61.

operational policies of repression throughout the previous years. These political fears and operational initiatives coalesced in 1937 and 1938. The various fears of Soviet leaders combined in a deadly way within the context of imminent war and invasion and generated the vicious purges of those years. Ezhov, on orders from Stalin, launched the massive purge of Soviet society in 1937–8 in order to destroy what Stalinist leaders believed was the social base for armed overthrow of the Soviet government.[21]

Stalinist leaders employed the full coercive power of the state to achieve their objectives of socialist construction. Indeed, Stalin's use of mass repression as a normal instrument of policy defined one of the distinguishing characteristics of his regime. Lenin used mass repression brutally and without hesitation during the emergency of the civil war, yet he always regarded mass repression as an extraordinary means of revolutionary struggle. Repression was not to be employed against party members or as a normal means of governance. Hence the original name of the Cheka, the *chrezvychainaia kommissia*, the 'Extraordinary' Commission. During collectivisation and de-kulakisation, Stalin engaged in mass forms of repression still in this manner – as part of a revolutionary class war to establish Soviet power and the dictatorship of the party. Ironically, however, the 'victory' of socialism in 1933 and 1934 not only marked the end of class war; it also ended any pretence to class-specific forms of repression. Police used administrative forms of mass repression against an ever-widening range of social and then ethnic groups. During the mid-1930s, especially, mass repression became the primary way authorities dealt with social disorder, engaging in large-scale police round-ups and passport sweeps to cleanse cities of marginalised and other supposedly anti-Soviet social groups. By 1935, for example, police had even taken over the country's massive orphan problem, with near sole jurisdiction to sweep orphan and unsupervised children into police-run rehabilitation camps. Leaders used mass forms of expulsion and deportation to redistribute the Soviet population, to construct politically acceptable national identities, to protect the country's borders, to colonise land and exploit resources, and to impose public order and economic discipline on Soviet society. Stalin, in other words, turned the extraordinary use of repression against political enemies into an ordinary instrument of state governance. Stalin's use of mass repression set his regime apart from its Leninist predecessor and from the selective use of repression employed by successive Soviet regimes.

21 For this particular argument, see Shearer, 'Social Disorder, Mass Repression, and the NKVD'.

The political police operated as the main instrument of repression, and one of several coercive organs centralised under the NKVD, the Commissariat of the Interior. The NKVD also included the infamous Gulag, or labour camp administration, the border guard forces, the NKVD's interior troops and the regular or civil police, the *militsiia*. During the 1930s, reforms took away local Soviet authority over the *militsiia* and subordinated the civil police to the state's centralised political police administration. This was a key part of Stalin's statist revolution and it had important consequences. Placing the civil police under control of the political police led inevitably during the decade to the merging of the two institutions and their respective functions – maintaining social order and protecting state security. As a result, the civil police were drawn increasingly into the business of mass repression, and the political police became drawn more and more into the coercive repression of day-to-day crimes and the resolution, through administrative forms of repression, of the country's major social problems.

The conflation of civil and political police functions was unintentional and it politicised the social sphere in a way uncharacteristic of the pre- and post-Stalin eras. It was the police, primarily through the constant campaigns of mass repression, social categorisation and deportation, which, unwittingly, became the primary institution within the Soviet state to define and reconstruct the social-geographic and national-ethnic landscape of the country. Police usurped and politicised many functions of the civil government. Still, it is inaccurate to describe the Soviet state under Stalin simply as a police state. The political police never attempted to gain control over the government or the party. Except for a brief period during the Great Purges in the late 1930s, party officials maintained control over the police. Stalin always had final control over the NKVD. Moreover, Stalinist officials always regarded the use of special police powers as a temporary response to conditions of national crisis, even though the methods of mass police repression became, in effect, a normal means of governance under Stalin. The word in Russian that best describes the process that occurred during the 1930s is *voennizatsiia*, or militarisation of the state's institutions of social and civil order. *Voennizatsiia* was a word consciously used at the time and later by Soviet leaders to describe the martial-law or emergency-law state that Stalin built. And even though police were given sweeping emergency powers, the civil state was never entirely abrogated. Its institutions were, at least formally, strengthened by the 1936 constitution. Authorities of civil state institutions – in the procuracy, the judiciary and in local Soviet governments – continued with more or less success to assert their authority. In fact, Ezhov began to disentangle civil and political police structures even before the mass purges of the late 1930s. This process continued unevenly under Ezhov's successor, Lavrentii Beria, until the two institutions were finally and completely separated in the early 1950s. For as much as Stalinist leaders constructed the apparatus of a militarised state socialism, they also set the constitutional groundwork for a Soviet civil socialism. This was a dual heritage, which they passed on to their successors.

## Conclusion

Stalin's revolution drove the USSR headlong into the twentieth century and it brought into being a peculiarly despotic and militarised form of state socialism. Ideology and political habits, as well as personality, shaped the actions of Stalin and those around him. Elements of continuity carried over from earlier periods of Soviet and even Russian history, especially from the Leninist legacy of the War Communism period. Yet the actions of Stalinist leaders cannot be explained simply by reference to some essential ideology or political practice.[22] The mechanisms of power, the policies of repression and policing and the bureaucratic apparatus of dictatorship that we know as Stalinism were unanticipated by Marxist-Leninist ideology or practice. Stalinism grew out of a unique combination of circumstances – a weak governing state, an increasingly hostile international context and a series of unforeseen crises, both domestic and external. The international context was especially important in shaping Stalin's brand of socialism. Stalin's personality gave to his dictatorship its despotic and uniquely vicious character, but the militarised aspects of Stalinism may be attributed as well to the growing fears of war and enemy encirclement. Stalin's successors struggled with the legacy left by his dictatorship, but as the circumstances passed that created Stalinism so did Stalinism. After the dictator's death in 1953, the character of the Soviet regime and Soviet society evolved in other directions.

22 Zbigniew Brzezinski, *The Grand Failure: The Birth and Death of Communism in the Twentieth Century* (New York: Scribner, 1989); Walter Laqueur, *The Dream that Failed: Reflections on the Soviet Union* (New York: Oxford University Press, 1994); Martin Malia, *The Soviet Tragedy: A History of Socialism in Russia, 1917–1991* (New York: Free Press, 1994); Richard Pipes, *Communism, the Vanished Specter* (New York: Oxford University Press, 1994).

8

# Patriotic War, 1941–1945

JOHN BARBER AND MARK HARRISON

Standing squarely in the middle of the Soviet Union's timeline is the Great Patriotic War, the Russian name for the eastern front of the Second World War. In recent years historians have tended to give this war less importance than it deserves. One reason may be that we are particularly interested in Stalin and Stalinism. This has led us to pay more attention to the changes following the death of one man, Stalin, in March 1953, than to those that flowed from an event involving the deaths of 25 million. The war was more than just an interlude between the 'pre-war' and 'post-war' periods.[1] It changed the lives of hundreds of millions of individuals. For the survivors, it also changed the world in which they lived.

This chapter asks: Why did the Soviet Union find itself at war with Germany in 1941? What, briefly, happened in the war? Why did the Soviet war effort not collapse within a few weeks as many observers reasonably expected, most importantly those in Berlin? How was the Red Army rebuilt out of the ashes of early defeats? What were the consequences of defeat and victory for the Soviet state, society and economy? All this does not convey much of the personal experience of war, for which the reader must turn to narrative history and memoir.[2]

## The road to war

Why, on Sunday, 22 June 1941, did the Soviet Union find itself suddenly at war (see Plate 14)? The reasons are to be found in gambles and miscalculations by

The authors thank R.W. Davies, Simon Ertz and Jon Petrie for valuable comments and advice.

1 Amir Weiner, *Making Sense of War: The Second World War and the Fate of the Bolshevik Revolution* (Princeton: Princeton University Press, 2001).
2 Forty years on there is still no more evocative work in the English language than Alexander Werth's *Russia at War, 1941–1945* (London: Barrie and Rockliffe, 1964).

Territory gained by the USSR,
1939–41 and in 1945

White
Sea

SWEDEN

FINLAND

NORWAY

Vyborg

Helsinki

Leningrad

Tallinn

Baltic
Sea

ESTONIA

DENMARK

Riga

Moscow

LATVIA

LITHUANIA

Kaliningrad

Vilnius

Minsk

NETHERLANDS

Berlin

BELORUSSIA

BELGIUM

GDR
(EAST GERMANY)

Warsaw

POLAND

Kiev

FRG
(WEST GERMANY)

Prague

L'vov

UKRAINE

CZECHOSLOVAKIA

TRANSCARPATHIA

FRANCE

Vienna

BESSARABIA
(MOLDAVIA)

AUSTRIA

Budapest

HUNGARY

ROMANIA

ITALY

Bucharest

Belgrade

Black Sea

YUGOSLAVIA

BULGARIA

Sofia

ALBANIA

GREECE

TURKEY

Map 8.1. The USSR and Europe at the end of the Second World War

all the Great Powers over the preceding forty years. During the nineteenth century international trade, lending and migration developed without much restriction. Great empires arose but did not much impede the movement of goods or people. By the twentieth century, however, several newly industrialising countries were turning to economic stabilisation by controlling and diverting trade to secure economic self-sufficiency within colonial boundaries. German leaders wanted to insulate Germany from the world by creating a closed trading bloc based on a new empire. To get an empire they launched a naval arms race that ended in Germany's military and diplomatic encirclement by Britain, France and Russia. To break out of containment they attacked France and Russia and this led to the First World War; the war brought death and destruction on a previously unimagined scale and defeat and revolution for Russia, their allies and themselves.

The First World War further undermined the international economic order. World markets were weakened by Britain's post-war economic difficulties and by Allied policies that isolated and punished Germany for the aggression of 1914 and Russia for treachery in 1917. France and America competed with Britain for gold. The slump of 1929 sent deflationary shock waves rippling around the world. In the 1930s the Great Powers struggled for national shares in a shrunken world market. The international economy disintegrated into a few relatively closed trading blocs.

The British, French and Dutch reorganised their trade on protected colonial lines, but Germany and Italy did not have colonies to exploit. Hitler led Germany back to the dream of an empire in Central and Eastern Europe; this threatened war with other interested regional powers. Germany's attacks on Czechoslovakia, Poland (which drew in France and Britain) and the Soviet Union aimed to create 'living space' for ethnic Germans through genocide and resettlement. Italy and the states of the former Austro-Hungarian Empire formed more exclusive trading links. Mussolini wanted the Mediterranean and a share of Africa for Italy, and eventually joined the war on France and Britain to get them. The Americans and Japanese competed in East Asia and the Pacific. The Japanese campaign in the Far East was both a grab at the British, French and Dutch colonies and a counter-measure against American commercial warfare. All these actions were gambles and most turned out disastrously for everyone including the gamblers themselves.

In the inter-war years the Soviet Union, largely shut out of Western markets, but blessed by a large population and an immense territory, developed within closed frontiers. The Soviet strategy of building 'socialism in a single country' showed both similarities and differences in comparison with national economic developments in Germany, Italy and Japan. Among the differences were its inclusive if paternalistic multinational ethic of the Soviet family of nations with the Russians as 'elder brother', and the modernising goals that Stalin imposed by decree upon the Soviet economic space. Unlike the Nazis, the Communists did not preach racial hatred and extermination, although they did preach class hatred.

There were also some similarities. One was the control of foreign trade; the Bolsheviks were happy to trade with Western Europe and the United States, but only if the trade was under their direct control and did not pose a competitive threat to Soviet industry. After 1931, conditions at home and abroad became so unfavourable that controlled trade gave way to almost no trade at all; apart from a handful of 'strategic' commodities the Soviet economy became virtually closed. Another parallel lay in the fact that during the 1930s the Soviet Union pursued economic security within the closed space of a 'single country' that was actually organised on colonial lines inherited from the old Russian Empire; this is something that Germany, Italy and Japan still had to achieve through empire-building and war.

The Soviet Union was an active partner in the process that led to the opening of the 'eastern front' on 22 June 1941. Soviet war preparations began in the 1920s, long before Hitler's accession to power, at a time when France and Poland were seen as more likely antagonists.

The decisions to rearm the country and to industrialise it went hand in hand.[3] The context for these decisions was the Soviet leadership's perception of internal and external threats and their knowledge of history. They feared internal threats because they saw the economy and their own regime as fragile: implementing the early plans for ambitious public-sector investment led to growing consumer shortages and urban discontent. As a result they feared each minor disturbance of the international order all the more. The 'war scare' of 1927 reminded them that the government of an economically and militarily backward country could be undermined by events abroad at any moment: external difficulties would immediately accentuate internal tensions with the peasantry who supplied food and military recruits and with the urban workers who would have to tighten their belts. They could not forget the

3 N. S. Simonov, '"Strengthen the Defence of the Land of the Soviets"': The 1927 "War Alarm" and its Consequences', *Europe–Asia Studies* 48, 8 (1996); R.W. Davies and Mark Harrison, 'The Soviet Military-Economic Effort under the Second Five-Year Plan (1933–1937)', *Europe–Asia Studies* 49, 3 (1997); Lennart Samuelson, *Plans for Stalin's War Machine: Tukhachevskii and Military-Economic Planning, 1925–41* (London and Basingstoke: Macmillan, 2000); Andrei K. Sokolov, 'Before Stalinism: The Defense Industry of Soviet Russia in the 1920s', *Comparative Economic Studies* 47, 2 (June 2005): 437–55.

Russian experience of the First World War, when the industrial mobilisation of a poorly integrated agrarian economy for modern warfare had ended in economic collapse and the overthrow of the government. The possibility of a repetition could only be eliminated by countering internal and external threats simultaneously, in other words by executing forced industrialisation for sustained rearmament while bringing society, and especially the peasantry, under greater control. Thus, although the 1927 war scare was just a scare, with no real threat of immediate war, it served to trigger change. The results included Stalin's dictatorship, collective farming and a centralised command economy.

In the mid-1930s the abstract threat of war gave way to real threats from Germany and Japan. Soviet war preparations took the form of accelerated war production and ambitious mobilisation planning. The true extent of militarisation is still debated, and some historians have raised the question of whether Soviet war plans were ultimately designed to counter aggression or to wage aggressive war against the enemy.[4] It is now clear from the archives that Stalin's generals sometimes entertained the idea of a pre-emptive strike, and attack as the best means of defence was the official military doctrine of the time; Stalin himself, however, was trying to head off Hitler's colonial ambitions and had no plans to conquer Europe.

Stalinist dictatorship and terror left bloody fingerprints on war preparations, most notably in the devastating purge of the Red Army command staff in 1937/8. They also undermined Soviet efforts to build collective security against Hitler with Poland, France and Britain, since few foreign leaders wished to ally themselves with a regime that seemed to be either rotten with traitors or intent on devouring itself. As a result, following desultory negotiations with Britain and France in the summer of 1939, Stalin accepted an offer of friendship from Hitler; in August their foreign ministers Molotov and Ribbentrop signed a treaty of trade and non-aggression that secretly divided Poland between them and plunged France and Britain into war with Germany.[5] In this way Stalin

4  The Russian protagonist of the latter view was Viktor Suvorov (Rezun), *Ice-Breaker: Who Started the Second World War?* (London: Hamish Hamilton, 1990). On similar lines see also Richard C. Raack, *Stalin's Drive to the West, 1938–1941: The Origins of the Cold War* (Stanford, Calif.: Stanford University Press, 1995); Albert L. Weeks, *Stalin's Other War: Soviet Grand Strategy, 1939–1941* (Lanham, Md.: Rowman and Littlefield, 2002). The ample grounds for scepticism have been ably mapped by Teddy J. Ulricks, 'The Icebreaker Controversy: Did Stalin Plan to Attack Hitler?' *Slavic Review* 58, 3 (1999), and, at greater length, by Gabriel Gorodetsky, *Grand Delusion: Stalin and the German Invasion of Russia* (New Haven: Yale University Press, 1999); Evan Mawdsley, 'Crossing the Rubicon: Soviet Plans for Offensive War in 1940–1941', *International History Review* 25, 4 (2003), adduces further evidence and interpretation.

5  On Soviet foreign policy in the 1930s see Jonathan Haslam's two volumes, *The Soviet Union and the Struggle for Collective Security in Europe, 1933–39* (London: Macmillan, 1984),

bought two more years of peace, although this was peace only in a relative sense and was mainly used for further war preparations. While selling war materials to Germany Stalin assimilated eastern Poland, annexed the Baltic states and the northern part of Romania, attacked Finland and continued to expand war production and military enrolment.

In the summer of 1940 Hitler decided to end the 'peace'. Having conquered France, he found that Britain would not come to terms; the reason, he thought, was that the British were counting on an undefeated Soviet Union in Germany's rear. He decided to remove the Soviet Union from the equation as quickly as possible; he could then conclude the war in the West and win a German empire in the East at a single stroke. A year later he launched the greatest land invasion force in history against the Soviet Union.

The Soviet Union remained at peace with Japan until August 1945, a result of the Red Army's success in resisting a probing Japanese border incursion in the Far East in the spring and summer of 1939. As war elsewhere became more likely, each side became more anxious to avoid renewed conflict, and the result was the Soviet–Japanese non-aggression pact of April 1941. Both sides honoured this treaty until the last weeks of the Pacific war, when the Soviet Union declared war on Japan and routed the Japanese army in north China.

## The eastern front

In June 1941 Hitler ordered his generals to destroy the Red Army and secure most of the Soviet territory in Europe. German forces swept into the Baltic region, Belorussia, Ukraine, which now incorporated eastern Poland, and Russia itself. Stalin and his armies were taken by surprise. Hundreds of thousands of Soviet troops fell into encirclement. By the end of September, having advanced more than a thousand kilometres on a front more than a thousand kilometres wide, the Germans had captured Kiev, put a stranglehold on Leningrad and were approaching Moscow.[6]

and *The Soviet Union and the Threat from the East, 1933–41: Moscow, Tokyo and the Prelude to the Pacific War* (London: Macmillan, 1992); Geoffrey Roberts, *The Soviet Union and the Origins of the Second World War: Russo-German Relations and the Road to War, 1933–1941* (Basingstoke: Macmillan, 1995); and Derek Watson, 'Molotov, the Making of the Grand Alliance and the Second Front, 1939–1942', *Europe–Asia Studies* 54, 1 (2002): 51–85.

6 Among many excellent works that describe the Soviet side of the eastern front see Werth, *Russia at War*; Seweryn Bialer, *Stalin and his Generals: Soviet Military Memoirs of World War II* (New York: Pegasus, 1969); Harrison Salisbury, *The 900 Days: The Siege of Leningrad* (London: Pan, 1969); books and articles by John Erickson including *The Soviet High Command: A Military-Political History, 1918–1941* (London: Macmillan, 1962), followed by *Stalin's War with Germany*, vol. I: *The Road to Stalingrad*, and vol. II: *The Road*

The German advance was rapid and the resistance was chaotic and disorganised at first. But the invaders suffered unexpectedly heavy losses. Moreover, they were met by scorched earth: the retreating defenders removed or wrecked the industries and essential services of the abandoned territories before the occupiers arrived. German supply lines were stretched to the limit and beyond.

In the autumn of 1941 Stalin rallied his people using nationalist appeals and harsh discipline. Desperate resistance denied Hitler his quick victory. Leningrad starved but did not surrender and Moscow was saved. This was Hitler's first setback in continental Europe. In the next year there were inconclusive moves and counter-moves on each side, but the German successes were more striking. During 1942 German forces advanced hundreds of kilometres in the south towards Stalingrad and the Caucasian oilfields. These forces were then destroyed by the Red Army's defence of Stalingrad and its winter counter-offensive (see Plate 15).

Their position now untenable, the German forces in the south began a long retreat. In the summer of 1943 Hitler staged his last eastern offensive near Kursk; the German offensive failed and was answered by a more devastating Soviet counter-offensive. The German army could no longer hope for a stalemate and its eventual expulsion from Russia became inevitable. Even so, the German army did not collapse in defeat. The Red Army's journey from Kursk to Berlin took nearly two years of bloody fighting.

The eastern front was one aspect of a global process. In the month after the invasion the British and Soviet governments signed a mutual assistance pact, and in August the Americans extended Lend-Lease to the Soviet Union. The Japanese attack on Pearl Harbor in December 1941, followed by a German declaration of war, brought America into the conflict and the wartime

to Berlin (London: Weidenfeld and Nicolson, 1975 and 1983); his 'Red Army Battlefield Performance, 1941–1945: The System and the Soldier', in Paul Addison and Angus Calder (eds.), Time to Kill: The Soldier's Experience of War in the West, 1939–1945 (London: Pimlico 1997); John Erickson and David Dilks (eds.), Barbarossa: The Axis and the Allies (Edinburgh: Edinburgh University Press, 1994); three volumes by David M. Glantz, From the Don to the Dnepr: Soviet Offensive Operations, December 1942–August 1943 (London: Cass, 1991), When Titans Clashed: How the Red Army Stopped Hitler with Jonathan House (Lawrence: University Press of Kansas, 1995), and Stumbling Colossus: The Red Army on the Eve of World War (Lawrence: University Press of Kansas, 1998); Richard Overy, Russia's War (London: Allen Lane, 1997); Bernd Wegner (ed.), From Peace to War: Germany, Soviet Russia, and the World, 1939–1941 (Providence, R.I.: Berghahn, 1997); Antony Beevor, Stalingrad (London: Viking, 1998), and Berlin: The Downfall, 1945 (London: Viking 2002); Geoffrey Roberts, Victory at Stalingrad: The Battle that Changed History (London: Longman, 2000). For a wider perspective see Gerhard L. Weinberg, A World at Arms: A Global History of World War II (Cambridge: Cambridge University Press, 1995).

alliance of the United Nations was born. After this there were two theatres of operations, in Europe and the Pacific, and in Europe there were two fronts, in the West and the East. Everywhere the war followed a common pattern: until the end of 1942 the Allies faced unremitting defeat; the turning points came simultaneously at Alamein in the West, Stalingrad in the East and Guadalcanal in the Pacific; after that the Allies were winning more or less continuously until the end in 1945.

The Soviet experience of warfare was very different from that of the British and American allies. The Soviet Union was the poorest and most populous of the three; its share in their pre-war population was one half but its share in their pre-war output was only one quarter.[7] Moreover it was on Soviet territory that Hitler had marked out his empire, and the Soviet Union suffered deep territorial losses in the first eighteen months of the war. Because of this and the great wartime expansion in the US economy, the Soviet share in total Allied output in the decisive years 1942–4 fell to only 15 per cent. Despite this, the Soviet Union contributed half of total Allied military manpower in the same period. More surprisingly Soviet industry also contributed one in four Allied combat aircraft, one in three artillery pieces and machine guns, two-fifths of armoured vehicles and infantry rifles, half the machine pistols and two-thirds of the mortars in the Allied armies. On the other hand, the Soviet contribution to Allied naval power was negligible; without navies Britain and America could not have invaded Europe or attacked Japan, and America could not have aided Britain or the Soviet Union.

The particular Soviet contribution to the Allied war effort was to engage the enemy on land from the first to the last day of the war. In Churchill's words, the Red Army 'tore the guts' out of the German military machine. For three years it faced approximately 90 per cent of the German army's fighting strength. After the Allied D-Day landings in Normandy in June 1944 two-thirds of the Wehrmacht remained on the eastern front. The scale of fighting on the eastern front exceeded that in the West by an order of magnitude. At Alamein in Egypt in the autumn of 1942 the Germans lost 50,000 men,

---

7 On the Soviet economy in wartime see Susan J. Linz (ed.), *The Impact of World War II on the Soviet Union* (Totowa, N.J.: Rowman and Allanheld, 1985); Mark Harrison, *Soviet Planning in Peace and War, 1938–1945* (Cambridge: Cambridge University Press, 1985); Mark Harrison, *Accounting for War: Soviet Production, Employment, and the Defence Burden, 1940–1945* (Cambridge: Cambridge University Press, 1996); Jacques Sapir, 'The Economics of War in the Soviet Union during World War II', in Ian Kershaw and Moshe Lewin (eds.), *Stalinism and Nazism: Dictatorships in Comparison* (Cambridge: Cambridge University Press, 1997); and for a comparative view Mark Harrison (ed.), *The Economics of World War II: Six Great Powers in International Comparison* (Cambridge: Cambridge University Press, 1998).

1,700 guns and 500 tanks; at Stalingrad they lost 800,000 men, 10,000 guns and 2,000 tanks.[8]

Unlike its campaign in the West, Germany's war in the East was one of annexation and extermination. Hitler planned to depopulate the Ukraine and European Russia to make room for German settlement and a food surplus for the German army. The urban population would have to migrate or starve. Soviet prisoners of war would be allowed to die; former Communist officials would be killed. Mass shootings behind the front line would clear the territory of Jews; this policy was eventually replaced by systematic deportations to mechanised death camps.

Our picture of Soviet war losses remains incomplete. We know that the Soviet Union suffered the vast majority of Allied war deaths, roughly 25 million. This figure could be too high or too low by one million; most Soviet war fatalities went unreported, so the total must be estimated statistically from the number of deaths that exceeded normal peacetime mortality.[9] In comparison, the United States suffered 400,000 war deaths and Britain 350,000.

Causes of death were many. A first distinction is between war deaths among soldiers and civilians.[10] Red Army records indicate 8.7 million known military deaths. Roughly 6.9 million died on the battlefield or behind the front line; this figure, spread over four years, suggests that Red Army losses on an *average* day ran at about twice the Allied losses on D-Day. In addition, 4.6 million soldiers were reported captured or missing, or killed and missing in units that were cut off and failed to report losses. Of these, 2.8 million were later repatriated or re-enlisted, suggesting a net total of 1.8 million deaths in captivity and 8.7 million Red Army deaths in all.

The figure of 8.7 million is actually a lower limit. The official figures leave out at least half a million deaths of men who went missing during mobilisation because they were caught up in the invasion before being registered in their units. But the true number may be higher. German records show a total of 5.8 million Soviet prisoners, of whom not 1.8 but 3.3 million had died by May 1944. If Germans were counting more thoroughly than Russians, as seems likely up

---

8 I. C. B. Dear (ed.), *The Oxford Companion to the Second World War* (Oxford: Oxford University Press, 1994), p. 326.

9 Michael Ellman and Sergei Maksudov, 'Soviet Deaths in the Great Patriotic War', *Europe–Asia Studies* 46, 4 (1994); Mark Harrison, 'Counting Soviet Deaths in the Great Patriotic War: Comment', *Europe–Asia Studies* 55, 6 (2003), provides the basis for our figure of 25 ± 1 million.

10 The detailed breakdown in this and the following paragraph is from G. F. Krivosheev, V. M. Andronikov, P. D. Burikov, V. V. Gurkin, A. I. Kruglov, E. I. Rodionov and M. V. Filimoshin, *Rossiia i SSSR v voinakh XX veka. Statisticheskoe issledovanie* (Moscow: OLMA-PRESS, 2003), esp. pp. 229, 233, 237 and 457.

to this point in the war, then a large gap remains in the Soviet records.Finally, the Red Army figures omit deaths among armed partisans, included in civilian deaths under German occupation.

Soviet civilian war deaths fall into two groups: some died under German occupation and the rest in the Soviet-controlled interior. Premature deaths under occupation have been estimated at 13.7 million, including 7.4 million killed in hot or cold blood, another 2.2 million taken to Germany and worked to death, and the remaining 4.1 million died of overwork, hunger or disease. Among the 7.4 million killed were more than two million Jews who vanished into the Holocaust; the rest died in partisan fighting, reprisals and so forth.[11]

How many were the war deaths in the Soviet interior? If we combine 8.7 million, the lower limit on military deaths, with 13.7 premature civilian deaths under German occupation, and subtract both from 25 million war deaths in the population as a whole, we find a 2.6 million residual. The scope for error in this number is very wide. It could be too high by a million or more extra prisoner-of-war deaths in the German records. It could be too high or too low by another million, being the margin of error around overall war deaths. But in fact war deaths in the Soviet interior cannot have been less than 2 million. Heightened mortality in Soviet labour camps killed three-quarters of a million inmates. Another quarter of a million died during the deportation of entire ethnic groups such as the Volga Germans and later the Chechens who, Stalin believed, had harboured collaborators with the German occupiers. The Leningrad district saw 800,000 hunger deaths during the terrible siege of 1941–4. These three categories alone make 1.8 million deaths. In addition, there were air raids and mass evacuations, the conditions of work, nutrition and public health declined, and recorded death rates rose.[12]

Were these all truly 'war' deaths? Was Hitler to blame, or Stalin? It is true that forced labour and deportations were part of the normal apparatus of Stalinist

11 Jewish deaths were up to one million from the Soviet Union within its 1939 frontiers, one million from eastern Poland, and two to three hundred thousand from the Baltic and other territories annexed in 1940. Israel Gutman and Robert Rozett, 'Estimated Jewish Losses in the Holocaust', in Israel Gutman (ed.), *Encyclopedia of the Holocaust*, vol. IV (New York: Macmillan, 1990).

12 Peacetime deaths in the camps and colonies of the Gulag were 2.6 per cent per year from figures for 1936–40 and 1946–50 given by A. I. Kokurin and N. V. Petrov (eds.), *GULAG (Glavnoe Upravlenie Lagerei). 1918–1960* (Moscow: Materik, 2002), pp. 441–2. Applied to the Gulag population between 1941 and 1945, this figure yields a wartime excess of about 750,000 deaths. On deaths arising from deportations see Overy, *Russia's War*, p. 233. On deaths in Leningrad, John Barber and Andrei Dreniskevich (eds.), *Zhizn' i smert' v blokadnom Leningrade. Istoriko-meditsinskii aspekt* (St Petersburg: Dmitrii Bulanin, 2001). On death rates across the country and in Siberia, John Barber and Mark Harrison, *The Soviet Home Front: A Social and Economic History of the USSR in World War II* (London: Longman, 1991), p. 88.

repression. For example, Stalin sent millions of people to labour camps where overwork and poor conditions raised mortality in peacetime well above the norm in the rest of society. Because of the war, however, food availability fell to a point where more people were sure to die. Hitler caused this situation, and in this sense he chose *how many died*. Stalin chose *who died*; he sent some of them to the Gulag and allowed the conditions there to worsen further. If Hitler had not decided on war, Stalin would not have had to select the victims. Thus, they were both responsible but in different ways.

In short, the general picture of Soviet war losses suggests a jigsaw puzzle. The general outline is clear: people died in colossal numbers in many different miserable or terrible circumstances. But the individual pieces of the puzzle still do not fit well; some overlap and others are yet to be found.

In 1945 Stalin declared that the country had passed the 'test' of war. If the war was a test, however, few citizens had passed unscathed. Of those alive when war broke out, almost one in five was dead. Of those still living, millions were scarred by physical and emotional trauma, by lost families and lost treasured possessions, and by the horrors they had been caught up in. Moreover, the everyday life of most people remained grindingly hard, as they laboured in the following years to cover the costs of demobilising the army and industry and rebuilding shattered communities and workplaces.[13]

The Soviet economy had lost a fifth of its human assets and a quarter to a third of its physical wealth.[14] The simultaneous destruction of physical and human assets normally brings transient losses but not lasting impoverishment. The transient losses arise because the people and assets that remain must be adapted to each other before being recombined, and this takes time. Losses of productivity and incomes only persist when the allocation system cannot cope or suffers lasting damage. In the Soviet case the allocation system was undamaged. Economic demobilisation and the reconversion of industry to peacetime production, although unexpectedly difficult, restored civilian output to pre-war levels within a single five-year plan. A more demanding yardstick for recovery would be the return of output to its extrapolated pre-war trend. In this sense recovery was more prolonged; during each post-war decade only half the remaining gap was closed, so that productivity and living standards were still somewhat depressed by the war in the 1970s.[15]

---

13 Don Filtzer, *Soviet Workers and Late Stalinism: Labour and the Restoration of the Stalinist System after World War II* (Cambridge: Cambridge University Press, 2002).

14 Harrison, *Accounting for War*, 162.

15 Mark Harrison, 'Trends in Soviet Labour Productivity, 1928–1985: War, Postwar Recovery, and Slowdown', *European Review of Economic History* 2, 2 (1998).

## On the edge of collapse

John Keegan has pointed out that most battles are won not when the enemy is destroyed physically, but when her will to resist is destroyed.[16] For Germany, the problem was that the Soviet will to resist did not collapse. Instead, Soviet resistance proved unexpectedly resilient. At the same time, from the summer of 1941 to the victory at Stalingrad in the winter of 1942/3 a Soviet collapse was not far off for much of the time.

Even before June 1941 the Wehrmacht had won an aura of invincibility. It had conquered Czechoslovakia, Poland, Netherlands, Belgium, Luxembourg, France, Norway, Denmark, Greece and Yugoslavia. Its reputation was enhanced by the ease with which it occupied the Baltic region and Western Ukraine and the warmth of its initial reception.

In contrast, Red Army morale was low. The rank and file, mostly of peasant origin, had harsh memories of the forced collectivisation of agriculture and the famine of 1932/3. The officer corps was inexperienced and traumatised by the purges of 1937/8.[17] In the campaigns of 1939 and 1940, and particularly the 'winter war' against Finland, successes were mixed and casualties were heavy. Rather than fight, many deserted or assaulted their commanders. In the first months of the war with Germany millions of Red Army soldiers rejected orders that prohibited retreat or surrender. In captivity, with starvation the alternative, thousands chose to put on a German uniform; as a result, while civilians collaborated with the occupiers in all theatres, the Red Army was the only combat organisation in this war to find its own men fighting on the other side under the captured Red Army General Vlasov.[18] The Germans also succeeded in recruiting national 'legions' from ethnic groups in the occupied areas.

As the Germans advanced, the cities of western and central Russia became choked with refugees bearing news of catastrophic setbacks and armies falling back along a thousand-kilometre front.[19] Some Soviet citizens planned for defeat: in the countryside, anticipating the arrival of German troops, peasants secretly planned to share out state grain stocks and collective livestock and fields. Some trains evacuating the Soviet defence factories of the war zones to the safety of the interior were plundered as they moved eastward in late

---

16 John Keegan, *The Face of Battle* (Harmondsworth: Penguin, 1978).
17 On the Red Army before and during the war see, in addition to the military histories already cited, Roger R. Reese, *The Soviet Military Experience* (London: Routledge, 2000).
18 Catherine Andreyev, *Vlasov and the Russian Liberation Movement: Soviet Reality and Emigré Theories* (Cambridge: Cambridge University Press, 1987).
19 On wartime conditions see Barber and Harrison, *Soviet Home Front*.

1941. In the Moscow 'panic' of October 1941, with the enemy close to the city, crowds rioted and looted public property.

In the urban economy widespread labour indiscipline was reflected in persistent lateness, absenteeism and illegal quitting.[20] Food crimes became endemic: people stole food from the state and from each other. Military and civilian food administrators stole rations for their own consumption and for sideline trade. Civilians forged and traded ration cards.[21] Red Army units helped themselves to civilian stocks. In besieged Leningrad's terrible winter of 1941 food crimes reached the extreme of cannibalism.[22]

In the white heat of the German advance the core of the dictatorship threatened to melt down. Stalin experienced the outbreak of war as a severe psychological blow and momentarily left the bridge; because they could not replace him, or were not brave enough to do so or believed that he was secretly testing their loyalty, his subordinates helped him to regain control by forming a war cabinet, the State Defence Committee or GKO, around him as leader.[23] At many lower levels the normal processes of the Soviet state stopped or, if they tried to carry on business as usual, became irrelevant. Economic planners, for example, went on setting quotas and allocating supplies, although the supplies had been captured by the enemy while the quotas were too modest to replace the losses, let alone accumulate the means to fight back.

## Unexpected resilience

The Soviet collapse that German plans relied on never came. Instead, Stalin declared a 'great patriotic war' against the invader, deliberately echoing Russia's previous 'patriotic war' against Napoleon in 1812.

---

20 Filtzer, *Soviet Workers and Late Stalinism*.
21 William Moskoff, *The Bread of Affliction: The Food Supply in the USSR during World War II* (Cambridge: Cambridge University Press, 1990).
22 Barber, *Zhizn' i smert'*.
23 Dmitrii Volkogonov, *Triumf i tragediia: politicheskii portret I. V. Stalina*, vol. II, pt. I (Moscow: Novosti, 1989). Other views of Stalin and Soviet wartime politics are provided by G. A. Kumanev, *Riadom so Stalinym. Otkrovennye svidetel'stva. Vstrechi, besedy, interv'iu, dokumenty* (Moscow: Bylina, 1999); A. N. Mertsalov and L. A. Mertsalov, *Stalinizm i voina* (Moscow: Terra-Knizhnyi klub, 1998); A. I. Mikoian, *Tak bylo. Razmyshleniia o minuvshem* (Moscow: Vagrius, 1999); Konstantin Simonov, *Glazami cheloveka moego pokoleniia. Razmyshleniia o I.V. Staline* (Moscow: Novosti, 1989); and V. A. Torchinov and A. M. Leontiuk, *Vokrug Stalina. Istoriko-biograficheskii spravochnik* (St Petersburg: Filologicheskii fakul'tet Sankt-Peterburgskogo gosudarstvennogo universiteta, 2000). Many such recent and intimate revelations are compiled and summarised in English by Simon Sebag Montefiore, *Stalin: The Court of the Red Tsar* (London: Weidenfeld and Nicolson, 2003). For traditional views of Stalin in wartime see also Bialer, *Stalin and his Generals*.

How was Soviet resistance maintained? The main features of the Soviet system of government on the outbreak of war were Stalin's personal dictatorship, a centralised bureaucracy with overlapping party and state apparatuses, and a secret police with extensive powers to intervene in political, economic and military affairs. This regime organised the Soviet war effort and mobilised its human and material resources. There were some adjustments to the system but continuity was more evident than change.

In the short term, however, this regimented society and its planned economy were mobilised not on lines laid down in carefully co-ordinated plans and approved procedures but by improvised emergency measures. From the Kremlin to the front line and the remote interior, individual political and military leaders on the spot took the initiatives that enabled survival and resistance.

The resilience was not just military; the war efforts on the home front and the fighting front are a single story. Patriotic feeling is part of this story, but Soviet resistance cannot be explained by patriotic feeling alone, no matter how widespread. This is because war requires collective action, but nations and armies consist of individuals. War presents each person with a choice: on the battlefield each must choose to fight or flee and, on the home front, to work or shirk. If others do their duty, then each individual's small contribution can make little difference; if others abandon their posts, one person's resistance is futile. Regardless of personal interest in the common struggle, each must be tempted to flee or shirk. The moment that this logic takes hold on one side is the turning point.

The main task of each side on the eastern front was not to kill and be killed. Rather, it was to organise their own forces of the front and rear in such a way that each person could feel the value of their own contribution, and feel confident in the collective efforts of their comrades, while closing off the opportunities for each to desert the struggle; and at the same time to disorganise the enemy by persuading its forces individually to abandon resistance and to defect.

A feature of the eastern front, which contributed to the astonishingly high levels of killing on both sides, was that both the Soviet Union and Germany proved adept at solving their own problems of organisation and morale as they arose; but each was unable to disrupt the other's efforts, for example by making surrender attractive to enemy soldiers. One factor was the German forces' dreadful treatment of Soviet civilians and prisoners of war: this soon made clear that no one on the Soviet side could expect to gain from surrender. Less obviously, it also ensured that no German soldier could expect much better if Germany lost. Thus it committed both sides to war to the death.

In short, three factors held the Soviet war effort together and sustained resistance. First, for each citizen who expected or hoped for German victory there were several others who wanted patriotic resistance to succeed. These were the ones who tightened their belts and shouldered new burdens without complaint. In farms, factories and offices they worked overtime, ploughed and harvested by hand, rationalised production, saved metal and power and boosted output. At the front they dug in and fought although injured, leaderless and cut off. To the Nazi ideologues they were ignorant Slavs who carried on killing pointlessly because they were too stupid to know when they were beaten. To their own people they were heroes.

Second, the authorities supported this patriotic feeling by promoting resistance and punishing defeatism. They suppressed information about Red Army setbacks and casualties. They executed many for spreading 'defeatism' by telling the truth about events on the front line. In the autumn of 1941 Moscow and Leningrad were closed to refugees from the occupied areas to prevent the spread of information about Soviet defeats. The evacuation of civilians from both Leningrad and Stalingrad was delayed to hide the real military situation.

Stalin imposed severe penalties on defeatism in the army. His Order no. 270 of 16 August 1941 stigmatised the behaviour of Soviet soldiers who allowed themselves to be taken prisoner as 'betrayal of the Motherland' and imposed social and financial penalties on prisoners' families. Following a military panic at Rostov-on-Don, his Order no. 227 of 28 July 1942 ('Not a Step Back') ordered the deployment of 'blocking detachments' behind the lines to shoot men retreating without orders and officers who allowed their units to disintegrate; the order was rescinded, however, four months later. The barbarity of these orders should be measured against the desperation of the situation. Although their burden was severe and unjust, it was still in the interest of each individual soldier to maintain the discipline of all.

The authorities doggedly pursued 'deserters' from war work on the industrial front and sentenced hundreds of thousands to terms in prisons and labour camps while the war continued. They punished food crimes harshly, not infrequently by shooting. The secret police remained a powerful and ubiquitous instrument for repressing discontent. This role was heightened by the severe hardships and military setbacks and the questioning of authority that resulted. Civilians and soldiers suspected of disloyalty risked summary arrest and punishment.

Third, although German intentions were not advertised, the realities of German occupation and captivity soon destroyed the illusion of an alternative to resistance.[24] For civilians under occupation, the gains from collaboration were pitiful; Hitler did not offer the one thing that many Russian and Ukrainian peasants hoped for, the dissolution of the collective farms. This was because he wanted to use the collective farms to get more grain for Germany and eventually to pass them on to German settlers, not back to indigenous peasants. On the other hand, the occupation authorities did permit some de-collectivisation in the North Caucasus and this was effective in stimulating local collaboration.

People living in the Russian and Ukrainian zones of German conquest were treated brutally, with results that we have already mentioned. Systematic brutality resulted from German war aims, one of which was to loot food and materials so that famine spread through the zone of occupation. Another aim was to exterminate the Jews, so that the German advance was followed immediately by mass killings. The occupation authorities answered resistance with hostage-taking and merciless reprisals. Later in the war the growing pressure led to a labour shortage in Germany, and many Soviet civilians were deported to Germany as slave labourers. In this setting, random brutality towards civilians was also commonplace: German policy permitted soldiers and officials to kill, rape, burn and loot for private ends. Finally, Soviet soldiers taken prisoner fared no better; many were starved or worked to death. Of the survivors, many were shipped to Germany as slave labourers. Red Army political officers faced summary execution at the front.

It may be asked why Hitler did not try to win over the Russians and Ukrainians and to make surrender more inviting for Soviet soldiers. He wanted to uphold racial distinctions and expected to win the war quickly without having to induce a Soviet surrender. While this was not the case, his policy delivered one unexpected benefit. When Germany began to lose the war, it stiffened military morale that German troops understood they could expect no better treatment from the other side. Thus Hitler's policy was counter-productive while the German army was on the offensive, but it paid off in retreat by diminishing the value to German soldiers of the option to surrender.

As a result, the outcome of the war was decided not by morale but by military mass. Since both sides proved equally determined to make a fight of it, and neither could be persuaded to surrender, it became a matter of kill-and-be-killed after all, so victory went to the army that was bigger, better equipped

---

24 Alexander Dallin's *German Rule in Russia, 1941–1945* (New York: St Martin's Press, 1957; revised edn Boulder, Colo.: Westview Press, 1981) remains the classic account.

and more able to kill and stand being killed. Although the Red Army suffered much higher casualties than the Wehrmacht, it proved able to return from such losses, regain the initiative and eventually acquire a decisive quantitative superiority.

Underlying military mass was the economy. In wartime the Soviet Union was more thoroughly mobilised economically than Germany and supplied the front with a greater volume of resources. This is something that could hardly have been predicted. Anyone reviewing the experience of the poorer countries in the First World War, including Russia, would have forecast a speedy Soviet economic collapse hastened by the attempt to mobilise resources from a shrinking territory.

On the eve of war the Soviet and German economies were of roughly equal size; taking into account the territorial gains of 1939/40, the real national product of the Soviet economy in 1940 may have exceeded Germany's by a small margin. Between 1940 and 1942 the German economy expanded somewhat, while the level of Soviet output was slashed by invasion; as a result, in 1942 Soviet output was only two-thirds the German level. Despite this, in 1942 the Soviet Union not only fielded armed forces more numerous than Germany's, which is not surprising given the Soviet demographic advantage, but also armed and equipped them at substantially higher levels. The railway evacuation of factories and equipment from the war zones shifted the geographical centre of the war economy hundreds of kilometres to the east. By 1943 three-fifths of Soviet output was devoted to the war effort, the highest proportion observed at the time in any economy that did not subsequently collapse under the strain.[25]

There was little detailed planning behind this; the important decisions were made in a chaotic, unco-ordinated sequence. The civilian economy was neglected and declined rapidly; by 1942 the production of food, fuels and metals had fallen by half or more. Living standards fell on average by two-fifths, while millions were severely overworked and undernourished; however, the state procurement of food from collective farms ensured that industrial workers and soldiers were less likely to starve than peasants. Despite this, the economy might have collapsed without victory at Stalingrad at the start of 1943. Foreign aid, mostly American, also relieved the pressure; it added about 5 per cent to Soviet resources available in 1942 and 10 per cent in each of 1943 and 1944. In 1943 economic controls became more centralised and some resources were restored to civilian uses.[26]

25 Mark Harrison, 'The Economics of World War II: An Overview', in Harrison (ed.), *Economics of World War II*, p. 21.

26 Harrison, *Soviet Planning in Peace and War*, chs. 2 and 4, and *Accounting for War*, chs. 6 and 7.

How did an economy made smaller than Germany's by invasion still out-produce Germany in weapons and equipment? Surprising though this may seem, the Soviet economy did not have a superior ability to repress consumption. By 1942 both countries were supplying more than three-fifths of their national output to the war effort, so this was not the source of Soviet advantage. Stalin's command system may have had an advantage in repressing consumption more rapidly; the Soviet economy approached this level of mobilisation in a far shorter period of time.

The main advantage on the Soviet side was that the resources available for mobilisation were used with far greater efficiency.[27] This resulted from mass production. In the inter-war period artisan methods still dominated the production of most weapons in most countries, other than small arms and ammunition. In wartime craft technologies still offered advantages of quality and ease of adaptation, but these were overwhelmed by the gains of volume and unit cost that mass production offered. The German, Japanese and Italian war industries were unable to realise these gains, or realised them too late, because of corporate structures based on the craft system, political commitments to the social status of the artisan and strategic preferences for quality over quantity of weaponry. In the American market economy these had never counted for much, and in the Soviet command system they had already been substantially overcome before the war.

The quantitative superiority in weaponry of the Allies generally, and specifically of the Soviet Union over Germany, came from supplying standardised products in a limited assortment, interchangeable parts, specialised factories and industrial equipment, an inexorable conveyor-belt system of serial manufacture, and deskilled workers who lacked the qualifications and discretion to play at design or modify specifications. Huge factories turned out proven designs in long production runs that poured rising quantities of destructive power onto the battlefield.

## The Red Army in defeat and victory

A contest over the nature of revolutionary military organisation began in March 1917, when the Petrograd Soviet decreed that soldiers could challenge their officers' commands. While the army of Imperial Russia disintegrated, the Red Guard emerged as a voluntary organisation of revolutionaries chosen for

27 Mark Harrison, 'Wartime Mobilisation: A German Comparison', in John Barber and Mark Harrison (eds.), *The Soviet Defence Industry Complex from Stalin to Khrushchev* (London and Basingstoke: Macmillan, 2000).

working-class origin and political consciousness. But when revolution turned into civil war these founding principles had to face the realities of modern military combat. Trotsky, then commissar for war, responded by instituting conscription from the peasantry and the restoration of an officer corps recruited from imperial army commanders willing to serve the new regime.

The Workers' and Peasants' Red Army that Trotsky created reflected a sweeping compromise of political principles with military imperatives: professional elements combined with a territorial militia, military training of the rank and file side by side with political education and party guidance, and dual command with military officers' orders subject to verification by political 'commissars'; the latter term, used widely in English and German, approximates only loosely to the Russian *politruk* (short for *politicheskii rukovoditel'*: political guide or leader). After the civil war Trotsky's successor, Frunze, introduced military reforms that created a General Staff and unified military discipline. Over the next quarter-century the Red Army evolved from its radical origins to a modern military organisation.

A feature of the revolutionary tradition in the Red Army was its emphasis on offensive operations, and specifically in the counter-offensive as the best means of defence. Underlying this was the belief that, in a world polarised between capitalism and communism, no country could attack the Soviet Union without risking mutiny at the front and revolution in its rear. Therefore, the moment when it was attacked was the best moment for the Red Army to launch a counter-attack. When this proved to be an illusion, Red Army doctrines shifted to a more defensive stance based on a war of attrition and falling back on reserves. Then, when forced industrialisation created the prospect of a motorised mass army with armoured and air forces capable of striking deep into the enemy's flanks and rear, Tukhachevskii's concept of 'deep battle' again radicalised Red Army thinking.[28]

The size of the armed forces followed a U-shaped curve in the inter-war years. It stood at 5 million at the end of the civil war in 1921 and 5 million again at the German invasion of 1941. In the 1920s wholesale demobilisation and cost-cutting took the Red Army and Navy down to little more than half a million. In the 1930s modernisation and recruitment reversed the decline. The Red Army of 1941, with its thousands of tanks and aircraft, bore little visible comparison with the ragged-trousered regiments who had won the civil war.

Beneath the surface, the new army was nearer in spirit to the old one than might appear. It was difficult to break the mould of the civil war. One

28 Samuelson, *Plans for Stalin's War Machine.*

problem was that, as numbers expanded, the quality of personnel deteriorated amongst both rank and file and officers. It was impossible to recruit officers in sufficient numbers, give them a professional training and pay them enough to command with integrity and competence. Another was the cost of re-equipping the rapidly growing numbers with motorised armour and aviation at a time of exceptional change in tank and aircraft technologies. The industry of a low-income, capital-scarce country could not produce new weapons in sufficient numbers to equip the army uniformly in the current state of the arts; instead, the army had to deploy new and obsolete weapons side by side.

Then in 1937/8, in the middle of rapid expansion, Stalin forced the Red Army through a major backward step in the bloody purge that he inflicted on its leadership. Most commanding officers down to the level of corps commanders were executed; altogether, more than twenty thousand officers were discharged after arrest or expulsion from the party. Stalin carried out the purge because he feared the potential for a fifth column to develop in the armed forces, as in other structures of Soviet society, that would emerge in wartime to collaborate with an adversary and hand over the key to the gates.[29] He determined to destroy this possibility in advance by savage repression. He believed that this would leave the army and society better prepared for war.

Stalin succeeded in that the purge turned the army's command staff, terrorised and morally broken, into his absolutely obedient instrument. At the same time, while continuing to grow rapidly in numbers, it declined further in quality. Officer recruitment and training had to fill thousands of new posts and at the same time replace thousands of empty ones. The mass promotions that resulted had a strongly accidental character; they placed many competent but poorly qualified soldiers in commanding positions and many incompetent ones beside them. Bad leadership brought falling morale amongst the rank and file. The army paid heavily for incompetent military leadership at war with Finland in 1939/40, and more heavily still in the June 1941 invasion.

The backward step that the Red Army took in 1937 was expressed in its organisation and thinking. Organisationally, Stalin sought to compensate for officers' collapsing prestige and competence by returning to the model of dual command: in 1937 military commanders again lost their undivided authority to issue orders, which had to be countersigned by the corresponding *politruk* (political commissar). Unified command was restored in 1940; then, in the military chaos of 1941 following the German invasion, Stalin once more returned to

29 Oleg Khlevniuk, 'The Objectives of the Great Terror, 1937–1938', in Julian Cooper, Maureen Perrie and E. A. Rees (eds.), *Soviet History, 1917–53: Essays in Honour of R. W. Davies* (London and Basingstoke: St Martin's Press, 1995).

the *politruk* system, finally restoring unified command in the military reforms of 1942.

In military thinking the Red Army also took a step back, marked by a return to the cult of the offensive. The main reason was Stalin's fear of defeatist tendencies in the armed forces; since retreat was the first stage of defeat, his logic ran, the easiest way to identify defeatism was to connect it with plans for Tukhachevskii's 'deep battle', which envisaged meeting the enemy's invasion by stepping back and regrouping before launching a counter-offensive. Thus, the advocates of operations in depth were accused of conspiring with Nazi leaders to hand over territory. As a result, when war broke out many officers found it easier to surrender to the Wehrmacht than to retreat against Stalin's orders.

Soviet military plans for an enemy attack became dominated by crude notions of frontier defence involving an immediate counter-offensive that would take the battle to the enemy's territory. Stalin now hoped to deter German aggression by massing Soviet forces on the frontier, apparently ready to attack. This was a dangerous bluff; it calmed fears and stimulated complacency in Moscow, while observers in Berlin were not taken in. The revived cult of the offensive also had consequences for the economy. The planned war mobilisation of industry was based on a short offensive campaign and a quick victory. Threats of air attack and territorial loss could not be discussed while such fears were equated with treason. As a result, air defence and the dispersal of industry from vulnerable frontier regions were neglected.

Stalin was surprised and shocked when Hitler launched his invasion. Having convinced himself that Hitler would not invade, he had rejected several warnings received through diplomatic and intelligence channels, believing them to be disinformation. When the invasion came, he was slow to react and slow to adapt. Better anticipation might not have prevented considerable territorial losses but could have saved millions of soldiers from the encirclements that resulted in captivity and death. After the war there was tension between Stalin and his generals over how they should share the credit for final victory and blame for early defeats. In 1941 Stalin covered his own responsibility for misjudging Hitler's plans by shooting several generals. The army had its revenge in 1956 when Khrushchev caricatured Stalin planning wartime military operations on a globe.

The war completed the Red Army's transition to a modern fighting force, but the process was complicated and there were more backward steps before progress was resumed. As commander-in-chief, Stalin improvised a high command, the Stavka, and took detailed control of military operations. He demanded ceaseless counter-attacks, regardless of circumstances, and indeed, in the circumstances of the time, when field communications were inoperative and strategic co-ordination did not exist, there was often no alternative to unthinking resistance on the lines of 'death before surrender'. This gave rise to episodes of both legendary heroism and despicable brutality. Over time Stalin ceded more and more operational command to his generals while keeping control of grand strategy.

For a time the army threatened to become de-professionalised again. Reservists were called up en masse and sent to the front with minimal training. More than 30 million men and women were mobilised in total. The concepts of a territorial militia and voluntary motivation were promoted by recruiting 'home guard' detachments in the towns threatened by enemy occupation. These were pitched into defensive battle, lightly armed and with a few hours' training, and most were killed. The few survivors were eventually integrated into the Red Army. At the same time, partisan armies grew on the occupied territories behind German lines, sometimes based on the remnants of Red Army units cut off in the retreat; these, too, were gradually brought under the control of the General Staff. Once the tide had turned and the Red Army began to recover occupied territory, it refilled its ranks by scooping up able-bodied men remaining in the towns and villages on the way. Offsetting these were high levels of desertion that persisted in 1943 and 1944, even after the war's outcome was certain.

The annihilating losses of 1941 and 1942 instituted a vicious cycle of rapid replacement with ever-younger and less-experienced personnel who suffered casualties and loss of equipment at dreadful rates. This affected the whole army, including the officer corps. At the end of the war most commanding officers still lacked a proper military education, and most units were still commanded by officers whose level of responsibility exceeded their substantive rank.

In the end, three things saved the Red Army. First, at each level enough of its units included a core of survivors who, after the baptism of fire, had acquired enough battlefield experience to hold the unit together and teach new recruits to live longer. Second, in 1941 and the summer of 1942, when the army's morale was cracking, Stalin shored it up with merciless discipline. In October 1942 he followed this with reforms that finally abolished dual command by the political commissars and restored a number of traditional gradations of rank and merit. Third, the economy did not collapse; Soviet industry was mobilised and poured out weapons at a higher rate than Germany. As a result, despite atrocious losses and wastage of equipment, the Soviet soldier of 1942 was already better equipped than the soldier he faced in armament, though not yet in rations, kit or transport. In 1943 and 1944 this advantage rose steadily.

By the end of the war the Red Army was no longer an army of riflemen supported by a few tanks and aircraft but a modern combined armed force. But successful modernisation did not bar soldiers from traditional pursuits such as looting and sexual violence, respectively encouraged and permitted by the Red Army on a wide scale in occupied Germany in the spring of 1945.

## Government and politics

The war ended in triumph for Soviet power. Whether or not the Soviet Union has left anything else of lasting value, it did at least put a stop to Hitler's imperial dreams and murderous designs. This may have been the Soviet Union's most positive contribution to the balance sheet of the twentieth century.

Millions of ordinary people were intoxicated with joy at the announcement of the victory and celebrated it wildly in city squares and village streets. But some of the aspirations with which they greeted the post-war period were not met. Many hoped that the enemy's defeat could be followed by political relaxation and greater cultural openness. They felt the war had shown the people deserved to be trusted more by its leaders. But this was not a lesson that the leaders drew. The Soviet state became more secretive, Soviet society became more cut off and Stalin prepared new purges.[30] Ten years would pass before Khrushchev opened up social and historical discourse in a way that was radical and shocking compared with the stuffy conformity of Stalinism, but pathetically limited by the standards of the wider world.

As for the social divisions that the war had opened up, Stalin preferred vengeance to reconciliation. While the Germans retreated he selected entire national minorities suspected of collaboration for mass deportation to Siberia. The Vlasov officers were executed and the men imprisoned without forgiveness. No one returned from forced labour in Germany or from prisoner-of-war camp without being 'filtered' by the NKVD. Party members who had survived German occupation had to account for their wartime conduct and show that they had resisted actively.[31]

There were other consequences. The Soviet victory projected the Red Army into the heart of Europe. It transformed the Soviet Union from a regional

---

30 Yoram Gorlizki, 'Ordinary Stalinism: The Council of Ministers and the Soviet Neo-Patrimonial State, 1946–1953', *Journal of Modern History* 74, 4 (2002): 699–736.

31 Weiner, *Making Sense of War*.

power to a global superpower; Stalin became a world leader. It strengthened his dictatorship and the role of the secret police.

Nothing illustrates Stalin's personal predominance better than the lack of challenge to his leadership at the most critical moments of the war. As head of GKO and Sovnarkom, defence commissar, supreme commander-in-chief and General Secretary of the Communist Party, Stalin's authority over Soviet political, economic and military affairs was absolute. From the moment when his colleagues asked him to lead the war cabinet Stalin exercised greater influence over his country's war effort than any other national leader in the Second World War. Washing away his mistakes and miscalculations in 1941 and 1942, the victory of 1945 further strengthened his already unassailable position.

The establishment of the five-man GKO was a first step to a comprehensive system of wartime administration that institutionalised pre-war trends. GKO functioned with marked informality. Meetings were convened at short notice, without written agendas or minutes, with a wide and varying cast of supernumeraries. It had only a small staff; responsibility for executing decisions was delegated to plenipotentiaries and to local defence committees with sweeping powers. But it was vested, in Stalin's words, with 'all the power and authority of the State'. Its decisions bound every Soviet organisation and citizen. No Soviet political institution before or after possessed such powers. Another pre-war trend that continued in wartime was the growth in influence of the government apparatus through which most GKO decisions were implemented. Its heightened importance was reflected in Stalin's becoming chairman of Sovnarkom on the eve of war and thus head of government.

The role of central party bodies declined correspondingly. The purges of 1937/8 had already diminished the role of the Politburo. Before the war it met with declining frequency; all important decisions were taken by Stalin with a few of its members, and issued in its name. During the war the Politburo met infrequently and the Central Committee only once; there were no party congresses or conferences. It was at the local level that the party played an important role in mobilising the population and organising propaganda. It did this despite the departure of many members for the front; in many areas party cells ceased to exist.

The NKVD played several key roles. While repressing discontent and defeatism, it reported on mass opinion to Stalin. In military affairs it organised partisans and the 'penal battalions' recruited from labour camps. In the economy it supplied forced labour to logging, mining and construction, and to high-security branches of industry. These roles gave it a central place in wartime government. Beria, its head, was a member of GKO throughout the war and deputy chairman from 1944, as well as deputy chairman of Sovnarkom. Not accidentally, reports from him and other security chiefs constituted the largest part of Stalin's wartime correspondence.

In economic life the overall results of the war were conservative and further entrenched the command system. The war gave a halo of legitimacy to centralised planning, mass production and standardisation. It showed that the Soviet economy's mobilisation capacities, tried out before the war in the campaigns to 'build socialism' by collectivising peasant farming and industrialising the country, could be used just as effectively for military purposes: the Soviet economy had devoted the same high proportion of national resources to the war as much wealthier market economies without collapsing.[32]

Had the war changed anything? At one level Hitler had made his point. Germany had fought two world wars to divert Europe from the class struggle and polarise it on national lines. The Second World War largely put an end to class warfare in the Soviet Union. By the end of the war nationality and ethnicity had replaced class origin in Soviet society as a basis of selection for promotion and repression.[33]

Other influences made the post-war economy and society more militarised than before. The country had paid a heavy price in 1941 for lack of preparedness. In the post-war years a higher level of economic preparedness was sustained so as to avoid a lengthy conversion period in the opening phase of the next war. This implied larger peacetime allocations to maintain combat-ready stocks of weapons and reserve production facilities to be mobilised quickly at need.

After an initial post-war demobilisation, the Soviet defence industry began to grow again in the context of the US nuclear threat and the Korean war. Before the Second World War, defence plants were heavily concentrated in the western and southern regions of the European USSR, often relying on far-flung suppliers. The Second World War shifted the centre of gravity of the Soviet defence industry hundreds of kilometres eastward to the Urals and Western Siberia. There, huge evacuated factories were grafted onto remote rural localities. A by-product was that the defence industry was increasingly concentrated on Russian Federation territory.

After the war, despite some westward reverse evacuation, the new war economy of the Urals and Siberia was kept in existence. The weapon factories of the remote interior were developed into giant, vertically integrated production complexes based on closed, self-sufficient 'company towns'. Their existence was a closely guarded secret: they were literally taken off the map.

32 Harrison, *Accounting for War*.  33 Weiner, *Making Sense of War*.

The post-war Soviet economy carried a defence burden that was heavier in proportion to GNP than the burdens carried by the main NATO powers. Whether or how this contributed to slow Soviet post-war economic growth or the eventual breakdown of the economy are questions on which economists find it hard to agree; there was certainly a substantial loss to Soviet consumers that accumulated over many years.

Finally, the war established a new generation that would succeed Stalin. At the close of the war in Europe GKO members comprised Stalin (65), Molotov (55), Kaganovich (51), Bulganin (50), Mikoyan (49), Beria (46), Malenkov (43) and Voznesenskii (41); Voroshilov (64) had been made to resign in November 1944. Members of the Politburo included Khrushchev (51) and Zhdanov (49). Stalin's successors would be drawn from among those in their forties and early fifties.[34] These were selected in several stages. First, the purges of 1937/8 cleared their way for recruitment into the political elite. Then they were tested by the war and by Stalin's last years. Those who outlived Stalin became the great survivors of the post-war Soviet political system. Once they were young and innovative. Having fought their way to the top in their youth, they became unwilling to contemplate new upheavals in old age. The war had taught them the wrong lessons. Unable to adapt to new times, they made an important contribution to the Soviet Union's long-term decay.

34 John Crowfoot and Mark Harrison, 'The USSR Council of Ministers under Late Stalinism, 1945–54: Its Production Branch Composition and the Requirements of National Economy and Policy', *Soviet Studies* 42, 1 (1990): 41–60.

# 9

# Stalin and his circle

YORAM GORLIZKI AND OLEG KHLEVNIUK

Research in recent years has highlighted the limits of the Stalinist state. Aside from the numerous forms of resistance, both physical and symbolic, which they faced, Soviet bureaucracies under Stalin often lacked the resources or co-ordination to provide a consistent and effective system of administration. In between campaigns, as one commentator has noted of the countryside in the late 1930s, 'neglect by Soviet power was as characteristic as coercion, and perhaps sometimes even as much resented'.[1] Despite these limitations, the Stalinist state did have the capacity to mobilise its officials and to transform the lives of its citizens. The most powerful state-sponsored campaigns overturned traditional modes of existence and effected reorganisations against which the combined forces of armed rebellion and popular resistance would prove to be no match.[2] Although some enjoyed the support of activists on the ground, the most important campaigns of this kind were driven from above, usually from the very summit of the political system. Some of the key turning points of this period, such as forced collectivisation, the Great Purges, and the onset of the Cold War, were the consequence of decisions taken by a small leadership group around Stalin. Although Stalin attracted the support of a variety of constituencies within Soviet society, he was never a mere cipher for these groups, but was rather a powerful and independent force in a social order that would come to bear his name.

Stalin's personality left a giant imprint on the Soviet system. The leader's approach to solving problems was, first, overwhelmingly coercive. While this was not entirely exceptional, given the Bolshevik state's origins in revolution and civil war, Stalin ratcheted up the combination of pressure and violence to new levels. This devotion to force was an important factor in converting an

---

1 Sheila Fitzpatrick, *Stalin's Peasants: Resistance and Survival in the Russian Village after Collectivization* (New York: Oxford University Press, 1994), p. 174.
2 See e.g. Lynne Viola, *Peasant Rebels under Stalin: Collectivization and the Culture of Peasant Resistance* (New York: Oxford University Press, 1996), pp. 238–9.

already brutal regime into a terrorist dictatorship, the excesses of which were gratuitous and unnecessary by any standards.[3] On matters of policy Stalin was also extremely stubborn. Ideological concessions and policy retreats were, on the whole, only wrung out of him under considerable duress, normally when the country was teetering on the edge of crisis. Augmented by a personality cult, which tended to present it as a mark of the leader's 'infallibility', this obduracy would, as towards the end of his life, when Stalin steadfastly blocked much-needed reforms in key sectors, cost his country dear.

For all its brutality and bloody-mindedness, this position of 'firmness' did, from Stalin's perspective, serve a particular purpose: to secure his own position as the leader of a separate, powerful and respected socialist state. Many of Stalin's actions were guided by quite rational calculations towards the attainment of this goal.[4] While this pragmatism has most often been observed in Stalin's behaviour on the international stage, it was also evident in domestic affairs. Perhaps nowhere was this more apparent than in Stalin's relations with his immediate colleagues. Despite a reputation for arbitrary brutality, Stalin systematically promoted younger functionaries and treated with great care those high-level leaders whose qualities, either as workers or as symbols of the revolution, he valued; after the Great Purges in particular, this was a group towards which the leader exhibited a surprising degree of self-restraint and moderation.[5]

The attention Stalin paid his colleagues was fully merited, for these deputies played an indispensable role in running the Soviet state. Well known in their own right, most members of the Politburo managed important portfolios and headed powerful personal networks. In two periods – during the war and in the early 1950s – Stalin was forced to hand over complete control of certain jurisdictions to this leadership substratum. Rather than being an inherently stable or inert form of rule, Stalin's one-man dictatorship was repeatedly in tension with powerful oligarchic tendencies.[6] Maintaining the upper hand

---

3 See Alec Nove, *Was Stalin Really Necessary? Some Problems of Soviet Political Economy* (London: George Allen and Unwin, 1964), pp. 27–32.
4 For an alternative view, which lends greater weight to the irrational aspects of Stalin's behaviour, see Roy Medvedev, *Let History Judge: The Origins and Consequences of Stalinism*, revised edn (New York: Oxford University Press, 1989).
5 An early version of this argument may be found in T. H. Rigby, 'Was Stalin a Disloyal Patron?' *Soviet Studies* 38, 3 (1986): 311–24.
6 Oligarchy is classically viewed as inherently unstable and displaying a propensity to dissolve either into a pattern of individual dominance or into a more diffuse distribution of power. Under Stalin, however, one detects repeated shifts in the opposite direction, from one-man dictatorship towards oligarchical forms of decision-making. Cf. T. H. Rigby, 'The Soviet Leadership: Towards a Self-Stabilizing Oligarchy?' *Soviet Studies* 22, 2 (1970): 167–8.

would prove to be a taxing business, one which would keep the ageing leader on his toes.

Stalin's relations with his deputies were not fixed or constant over time. In this chapter their evolution is divided into four phases. We begin by assessing the rise of the Stalinist faction in the 1920s. The consolidation of dictatorship from the 1920s to the late 1930s and the operation of the Stalinist dictatorship at its peak, following the Great Purges, is the subject of the second section. The chapter then goes on to examine Stalin and his entourage during the war years, a period of marked decentralisation. The chapter concludes by looking at Stalin's last years, as the decision-making structures of the post-Stalin era began to take shape.

## Rise of the Stalinist faction

With victory in the civil war, the locus of political struggle in the early 1920s shifted to the upper reaches of the Bolshevik Party. In the lead-up to Lenin's death, the broad collegial leadership which had existed under him dissolved into factions, usually consisting of short-term tactical alliances. The consolidation of a 'Stalinist faction' out of these groupings was the result of an extremely convoluted process and an outcome which few would have predicted.

The first stage took place from the end of 1923 to 1924, when a solid majority formed within the Politburo against Leon Trotsky, whose impetuous behaviour and poor political judgement stoked up widespread unease within the leadership.[7] To co-ordinate their stand, in August 1924 a 'septet' was created, consisting of six members of the Politburo (that is, all of the Politburo, apart from Trotsky) and the chair of the Central Control Commission, Valerian Kuibyshev. It was this 'septet' which took the key decisions, bringing to official sessions of the Politburo (attended by Trotsky) resolutions which it had agreed beforehand. Once Trotsky had been sidelined, however, the septet's coherence quickly evaporated, and it soon broke off into two wings, with the minority group, consisting of Kamenev and Zinoviev, eventually drifting off towards Trotsky. Following a bitter dispute, all three leaders of the Zinoviev–Trotsky bloc were expelled from the Politburo in autumn 1927.

---

7 Recent research suggests that Stalin was able to provide leadership in the Politburo's struggle with Trotsky precisely because, in the words of one commentator, 'he had a good case'. See Lars Lih, 'Introduction', in Lars T. Lih, Oleg V. Naumov and Oleg V. Khlevniuk, *Stalin's Letters to Molotov* (New Haven: Yale University Press, 1995), pp. 19–24, esp. p. 23.

With a clear majority ending up in Stalin's inner circle of the 1930s, it is tempting to think of the Politburo of late 1927 as staunchly 'Stalinist'. At this stage, however, rank-and-file members of the Politburo still enjoyed a considerable degree of latitude. Their autonomy was bolstered by the still-prevailing norm of 'collective leadership' which rested on a comparatively clear-cut division of labour within the cabinet. Apart from Stalin himself, who led the party apparatus, Aleksei Rykov chaired the Council of People's Commissars (Sovnarkom, which managed the economy), and Nikolai Bukharin acted as chief ideologist to the party. So long as no one leader fully dominated the summit of the political system, other members of the Politburo remained more or less free to pursue their own course. The same applied to the middle layers of the power pyramid, the members of the Central Committee, on whose votes much would depend in the coming power struggle.

Relatively free of constraints, members of the Politburo were allowed to migrate from one ad hoc alignment to another, depending on the issue at hand. The looseness of the 'Stalinist faction' was evident, for example, in the summer of 1927 when the break in diplomatic relations with Britain, the murder of the Soviet ambassador in Poland and the clampdown against the Communists in China, placed it under enormous strain. Stalin, on vacation in the south, received regular dispatches from Molotov on Politburo debates. Molotov reported that one group, including those who were ostensibly Stalin's followers, such as Ordzhonikidze, Voroshilov and Rudzutak, had criticised the policies being implemented in China, with Voroshilov, who would later emerge as one of Stalin's most fanatical supporters, going so far as to ' "roundly condemn" [your] leadership over the last two years'.[8] Another issue on which opinions were divided was whether Trotsky and Zinoviev should be immediately expelled from the Central Committee. Some of Stalin's allies, such as Kalinin, Ordzhonikidze and Voroshilov, argued that the matter should be deferred until the party congress. Stalin, still in the south, fumed at this, though to little avail. It was only after Stalin insisted that his vote be counted in absentia, and when, at the last moment, one Politburo member, Kalinin, switched sides that, on 20 June 1927, the Politburo decided, by the slimmest of margins, to have the two expelled.[9]

The one exception to this pattern of fluid alignments was the stand taken by Viacheslav Molotov. From his appointment as secretary of the Central Committee in 1921, Molotov had pledged his unswerving loyalty to Stalin,

8 RGASPI f. 558, op. 11, d. 767, ll. 35–9, 45–8, 56–60.
9 RGASPI f. 558, op. 11, d. 767, ll. 35–9, 45–8; 71, op. 11, ll. 13–14.

and for much of the 1920s he remained his only unconditional supporter on the Politburo. This absolute allegiance would prove to be one of Stalin's most important assets in the struggle which unfolded in 1928, once the united opposition of Trotsky and Zinoviev had finally been crushed, and the Politburo 'majority' had lost the common enemy against which it had closed ranks in earlier years.

One fact that would play a major role in bringing the Stalinist faction into line was a debate that emerged in 1928. Having encountered serious economic difficulties, above all in the countryside, the Politburo adopted a series of 'emergency measures', which included the forced expropriation of grain from the peasantry and the suppression of private trade. At first there were no significant disagreements over the use of this 'extraordinary approach'. It was only when it became apparent that this ostensibly temporary strategy was to be frozen into a permanent mode of government that two groups began to form in the Politburo. The first, led by Stalin, insisted on a continuation of the measures. The second, represented by Rykov, Bukharin and Tomskii, called for a retreat, even if this meant granting concessions.

One of the principal reasons why the Stalin group triumphed was that their message was more closely attuned to the sentiments of rank-and-file members of the party. Stalin's definition of the situation in terms of class war, and his use of slogans such as 'assault on the Kulak', appealed to the mores of War Communism which continued to carry great resonance for many Bolsheviks.[10] Stalin also possessed key organisational resources, not the least of which was his control, as General Secretary of the Central Committee, of personnel assignments within the party apparatus.[11]

This did not mean, however, that Stalin's victory was in any way predetermined. Among second-level officials on the Central Committee, as well as among Politburo members themselves, there remained a strong willingness to resolve the conflict amicably. Many Central Committee members feared a large-scale conflict which might destroy the balance of power within the Politburo and thereby their own 'parliamentary' role as the Politburo's final court of appeal. Even more seriously, Central Committee and Politburo members

---

10 See e.g. Robert C. Tucker, 'Stalinism as Revolution from Above', in Tucker (ed.), *Stalinism: Essays in Historical Interpretation* (New York: Norton, 1977), p. 93; Hiroaki Kuromiya, *Stalin's Industrial Revolution 1928–1932* (Cambridge: Cambridge University Press, 1988), 109–112.

11 The classical case for what would become known as the 'circular flow of power' can be found in Robert V. Daniels, *The Conscience of the Revolution* (Cambridge, Mass.: Harvard University Press, 1960).

recognised that a split in the cabinet would force them to take sides, and to risk their own career in the case of defeat. Reflecting this mood, Ordzhonikidze wrote to Rykov in November 1928: 'I am frankly imploring you to bring about a reconciliation between Bukharin and Stalin . . . It is laughable, of course, to speak of your "replacement" or of Bukharin's, or of Tomskii's. That really would be madness. It is true that relations between Stalin and Bukharin have taken a turn for the worse, but we must do all we can to reconcile them. And this can be done . . . In general, Aleksei, we must approach with inordinate care any issues which might plunge us into a "fight". We need the greatest self-control not to let all this come to blows.'[12]

The impetus to break this delicate equilibrium came from Stalin, who seemed determined to force a choice on his Politburo colleagues. To this end, he did his utmost to open up a rift within the Politburo. 'Andreev is fully behind the Central Committee position,' he wrote to Molotov. 'Tomskii, it turns out, tried (at the plenum) to "wear him down" . . . but was unable to "lure" him'; 'under no circumstances', Stalin noted on another occasion, 'should we let Tomskii (let alone anyone else) "sway" Kuibyshev or Mikoyan'.[13] It is likely that Stalin also used blackmail to firm up his alliance. In December 1928 and March 1929 the Central Control Commission received materials from the archives of the tsarist police which showed that two current members of the Politburo, Mikhail Kalinin and Ian Rudzutak, had years earlier betrayed other revolutionaries. The fact that these documents, which were sufficient to have the two expelled, or even arrested, had surfaced at the same time as the struggle with the 'Rightists' was coming to a head is unlikely to have been a matter of chance.[14]

An important consequence of the victory over the 'Rightists' was the formation within the Politburo not simply of a majority faction, but of one relatively unified group under Stalin. Although still a collective body, this group was no longer an alliance of equals. It was now headed by a single leader, who had disposed of the original cast of would-be successors to Lenin. No longer able to manoeuvre between leadership contenders, the position of rank-and-file members of the Politburo and of the Central Committee had been seriously weakened. Thus, following the tumultuous policy clashes of late 1928 and early 1929, the rough balance of power at the apex of the political order, which had persisted throughout the 1920s, was finally broken.

12 A.V. Kvashonkin et al., *Sovetskoe rukovodstvo. Perepiska. 1928–1941* (Moscow: Rosspen, 1999), pp. 58–9.
13 RGASPI f. 82, op. 2, d. 1420, ll. 200, 220.
14 RGASPI f. 85 new acquisitions, d. 2, ll. 1–11, 28–30.

## From oligarchy to dictatorship

With the defeat of the 'Rightists', Stalin's position was strengthened. Lazar Kaganovich, Sergei Kirov and Stanislav Kosior were now repaid for their loyalty to Stalin with full membership of the Politburo, while a number of others who had supported Stalin – Andrei Andreev, Anastas Mikoyan, Grigorii Petrovskii, Sergei Syrtsov and Vlas Chubar – had made it onto the Politburo as candidate members. After a brief pause, Stalin continued his purge of the cabinet. In December 1930 a former loyalist, Syrtsov, was removed from the Politburo for vocal dissent and for his ties to another critic, the first secretary of the Transcaucasian Regional Committee, Vissarion Lominadze, while the last 'Rightist', Aleksei Rykov was also expelled, and his place on the Politburo taken by Sergo Ordzhonikidze.

Although an important staging post on the road to dictatorship, the leadership system of the early 1930s is best viewed as a phase of unconsolidated oligarchic rule. In this system, Politburo members still retained considerable political influence. In leading a key department of government, every member of the Politburo not only took operational decisions and controlled considerable resources, but formed around himself an extensive network of personally devoted functionaries. While intrusions into the personal domain of a Politburo member were possible they were, as a rule, accompanied by unholy scandals. The significance of these Politburo 'patrimonies' was such that Stalin himself would have to take them seriously.

This pattern of relationships became most fully apparent in 1931, when the Politburo had to face up to the effects of its radical policies, which included food shortages, housing crises, labour disturbances, deportations and rebellion. The sense of deepening crisis led to very real showdowns on the Politburo. In what would become a common refrain, Stalin blamed many of the country's woes on the shoddy work and departmental egoism of his colleagues. Politburo members in turn resisted Stalin's onslaught with whatever means they had, including the threat of resignation. One of the fiercest clashes arose in connection with orders for imported goods. Despite a steep rise in foreign debts, the economic commissariats insisted on an increase in deliveries from abroad. Although Stalin accused his colleagues of wrecking the state budget, his demands that new orders be rescinded went unheeded. In September 1931, he finally issued an ultimatum, declaring that he would cut short his vacation and return to Moscow for a special sitting of the Politburo.[15] Stalin's

15 R. W. Davies et al. (eds.), *The Stalin–Kaganovich Correspondence, 1931–1936* (New Haven: Yale University Press, 2003), pp. 46–7.

manoeuvre, which resembled his tactics over the expulsion of Trotsky and Zinoviev in 1927, was a response to the still powerful oligarchic forces which continued to constrain him. Yet while the earlier dispute had centred on an essentially political question, the new one – and others like it – revolved around the economic issue of resource allocation. Battles over economic and organisational questions of this kind were a typical feature of leadership debates in the early 1930s.

The existence of such conflicts should not be confused with the view that Stalin was surrounded by 'radicals' and 'moderates', between whose stands the leader continuously vacillated. Certainly, recent research does not lend much support to this position, nor to the view that there were 'factions' as such in the Politburo at all in this period.[16] In fact, virtually all conflicts in the Politburo appear to have been driven by bureaucratic interests, rather than by questions of principle or ideology. Hence, the same member of the Politburo could at any one time adopt a 'moderate' position and at others 'radical' ones, depending on the particular needs and requirements of the department which he headed.[17]

In fact, most members of the Politburo were 'moderates' in the sense that they had an interest in maintaining unconsolidated oligarchical rule and, through that, preserving overall stability within the system. The personal rights and jurisdictions of Politburo members remained the final barrier preventing the establishment of a full-blown personal dictatorship at the centre. Attempts by Politburo members to preserve these oligarchic privileges added up to a defence of a more 'moderate' line, marked by certain checks and balances. We may observe this phenomenon most clearly in the conflicts which flared up between Stalin and his long-term friend and Politburo colleague, Sergo Ordzhonikidze.

One of the best-known leaders of the 1930s, Ordzhonikidze headed the Commissariat of Heavy Industry, a powerful portfolio which became the institutional symbol of Soviet industrialisation. As he learned to defend the interests of his own department and to attract qualified, enterprising managers to work

16 This view of a stand-off between 'moderate' members of the higher leadership (Kirov, Kuibyshev, Ordzhonikidze) and 'radicals', who advocated an intensification of repression (Molotov, Kaganovich, Ezhov) has, among other things, been used to account for one of the most important political events of the 1930s – the murder on 1 December 1934 of the head of the Leningrad party organisation Sergei Kirov. As a supposed 'moderate', Kirov was ostensibly murdered on the orders of Stalin, who saw in Kirov a potential competitor. While this version of events is based on indirect evidence and on memoirs, no specific evidence of Stalin's participation in the murder has ever surfaced.

17 See Sheila Fitzpatrick, 'Ordzhonikidze's Takeover of Vesenkha: A Case Study in Soviet Bureaucratic Politics', *Soviet Studies* 37, 2 (1985).

under him, Ordzhonikidze turned into a proponent of moderation within the leadership. The slightest attempt to encroach on his department was warded off, and Ordzhonikidze guarded his traditional right to 'punish or pardon' his own people with great fervour. It was on these grounds that Ordzhonikidze had regular run-ins with other leaders, most notably Stalin.[18] Their differences reached a head in 1936, as Stalin began a sweeping purge of Soviet official-dom which included sanctioning the arrest of Ordzhonikidze's elder brother. Although Ordzhonikidze put up a stout defence of his own particular patri-mony, the scope of resistance was limited. Rather than engaging in principled opposition, Ordzhonikidze's main goal appears to have been to convince Stalin to end attacks on Ordzhonikidze's 'own' people. Ordzhonikidze's eventual sui-cide on 18 February 1937, on the eve of the Central Committee plenum which pronounced a policy of widening repression, amounted to a last desperate act of defiance against Stalin's onslaught on Politburo prerogatives.

Faced with the choice of fighting for the last vestiges of collective rule or succumbing to the shrill demands from Stalin on carrying out a mass purge, most members of the Politburo and of the Central Committee capitulated.[19] The mass terror which followed numbered among its victims hundreds of thousands of ordinary citizens, as well as party-state officials at all levels.[20] The epidemic of arrests and confessions opened up leads implicating those around Stalin. For the first time in Soviet history members and candidates of the Politburo – Kosior, Chubar, Eikhe, Rudzutak and Postyshev – were arrested and executed. By the end of the purges, two members of the Politburo had been executed, one, Ordzhonikidze, had committed suicide and three candidate members had been shot. Close aides and relations of other Politburo leaders were also defenceless against the purge. The wife of the head of state, Mikhail Kalinin, was sent to the camps, while the case of Molotov's wife, Polina Zhemchuzhina, came up several times at Politburo meetings. Although she narrowly escaped prosecution, Zhemchuzhina was dismissed as commissar of fish industries, thereby sending a further pointed message to her husband and his cabinet colleagues. In asserting his power to have anyone he wished fired, prosecuted or killed, Stalin had attained the truest hallmark of a tyrant.[21]

18 Oleg Khlevniuk, *In Stalin's Shadow. The Career of 'Sergo' Ordzhonikidze* (Armonk, N.Y.: M. E. Sharpe, 1995).
19 For a useful collection of documents on the purge of the party, see J. Arch Getty and Oleg V. Naumov (eds.), *The Road to Terror: Stalin and the Self-Destruction of the Bolsheviks, 1932–1939* (New Haven: Yale University Press, 1999).
20 This is discussed at greater length in Chapter 7.
21 For this view of Stalin as 'tyrant', see T. H. Rigby 'Stalinism and the Mono-organisational Society', in Tucker, *Stalinism*, pp. 53–76.

The late 1930s may be regarded as the high water mark of Stalin's dictator-ship, a fact underscored by two key developments. First, Stalin now promoted a new cohort of junior figures who had played no role during the revolution and owed their rise entirely to the dictator. In March 1939, following the Eighteenth Party Congress two young Stalinists, Zhdanov and Khrushchev, were elected as full members of the Politburo, while the new commissar of internal affairs, Lavrentii Beria, was made a candidate member. They were joined in Febru-ary 1941 by three other up-and-coming career administrators, Nikolai Voz-nesenskii, Georgii Malenkov and Aleksandr Shcherbakov, who also became candidate members. Each of these figures performed clearly designated roles. The thirty-nine-year-old Beria had been summoned from Georgia to work in Moscow in August 1938, when Stalin decided to appoint him, in place of Ezhov, as commissar of internal affairs. Stalin had already formed a favourable impression of Beria in the early 1930s. Nominating him as first secretary of the Transcaucasian regional committee, Stalin, in a letter of 12 August 1932, had observed: 'Beria makes a good impression. He is a fine organiser, is business-like, and is an able worker.'[22] In 1937, a second member of the new cohort, Georgii Malenkov, was only thirty-five. By this time he had already served in a number of party posts including, as of 1934, as head of the department of leading party agencies at the Central Committee. Set up to assert control over regional leaders, the department assumed a critical role during the purges, affording Malenkov direct and regular access to Stalin. Following the Eighteenth Party Congress, at which Malenkov delivered one of the major speeches, he became a Central Committee secretary. In March 1941, a third member of this new cohort, the thirty-seven-year-old chair of Gosplan, Nikolai Voznesenskii, was chosen by Stalin as first deputy chair of Sovnarkom. Prior to his promotion to Moscow, Voznesenskii had worked in Leningrad under Zhdanov, and it is quite possible that Zhdanov had recommended Voznesenskii to Stalin. At the same time it is clear that Stalin rated Voznesenskii highly as a specialist and as a person who was fully committed to the Stalinist cause. In becom-ing first deputy prime minister, Voznesenskii had, like Beria and Malenkov, leapfrogged over a number of more senior and experienced Politburo members.

The second measure of Stalin's supremacy was the ease with which he manipulated decision-making structures to suit his own needs. The years 1937–8 had witnessed the end of the 'old' Politburo as a collective decision-making body. On 14 April 1937 two Politburo commissions were established

22 RGASPI f. 81, op. 3, d. 99, ll. 154–5.

for the consideration of high-level secret issues. These were then superseded by a smaller 'ruling group' of the Politburo, the so-called 'quintet' which, apart from Stalin, consisted of Molotov, Mikoyan, Voroshilov and Kaganovich. While this group convened regularly in Stalin's office, the formal Politburo, as a collective body with well-defined procedures, ceased to function. On 17 January 1941 Stalin explained the principles behind the new arrangement: 'We at the Central Committee have not convened a meeting of the Politburo for four to five months now. All questions are prepared directly by Zhdanov, Malenkov, and others at meetings with specialist colleagues and, far from losing out, the leadership system as a whole has actually improved.'[23]

A further indicator of Stalin's new status was his own appointment as chair of Sovnarkom in May 1941, a move which finally confirmed Stalin as absolute leader of the country (and not simply of the party) and as successor to Lenin (who had himself served as head of Sovnarkom). The appointment appears to have been carefully orchestrated by Stalin. Following a succession of attacks on the then head of Sovnarkom, Molotov, on 28 April 1941 Stalin sent members of the higher leadership a note: 'I think it is no longer possible to carry on "running things" like this. I suggest we raise the matter at the Politburo.'[24] On 4 May 1941 a Politburo resolution drew up a new pecking order. In addition to having been sacked as chair of Sovnarkom, Molotov, now a regular deputy chair, had been overtaken by Voznesenskii, who had been made first deputy chair in March. At the same time, in a break with existing party conventions, Zhdanov was officially designated as Stalin's 'deputy' in the party, with responsibility for directing the work of the party apparatus.[25]

With these reorganisations a new dictatorial order was consolidated. Stalin now held the two supreme offices of the party-state and had appointed as his first deputies not old colleagues, but new figures, Zhdanov and Voznesenskii. The dictator was in turn supported by an informally constituted 'ruling group' (now expanded from the original 'quintet' to include recently promoted figures such as Voznesenskii, Zhdanov, Malenkov and Beria) which met at his discretion and drew up decisions, depending on Stalin's wishes, either in the name of the Politburo or of Sovnarkom.

At the first session of the new bureau of Sovnarkom on 9 May 1941, Stalin once again reminded his companions of their dependence on his good will. Molotov, who had presented a paper on bonuses for engineers and who, as we

23 V. A. Malyshev, 'Dnevnik narkoma', Istochnik, 1997, no. 5: 114.
24 RGASPI f. 558, op. 11, d. 769, ll. 176–176 ob.
25 O.V. Khlevniuk et al. (eds.), Stalinskoe Politbiuro v 30-e gody (Moscow: AIRO–XX, 1995), pp. 34–5; APRF f. 3, op. 52, d. 251, ll. 58–60.

have seen, had been Stalin's most faithful follower, bore the brunt of Stalin's attack. Iakov Chadaev, who took the minutes of the meeting, recalls:

> Stalin did not conceal his disapproval of Molotov. He very impatiently listened to Molotov's rather prolix responses to comments from members of the bureau . . . It seemed as if Stalin was attacking Molotov as an adversary and that he was doing so from a position of strength . . . Molotov's breathing began to quicken, and at times he would let out a deep sigh. He fidgeted on his stool and murmured something to himself. By the end he could take it no longer:
> 'Easier said than done,' Molotov pronounced in a low but cutting voice. Stalin picked up [Molotov's] words.
> 'It has long been well known,' said Stalin, 'that the person who is afraid of criticism is a coward.'
> Molotov winced, but kept quiet – the other members of the Politburo sat silently, burying their noses in the papers . . . At this meeting I was again convinced of the power and greatness of Stalin. Stalin's companions feared him like the devil. They would agree with him on practically anything.[26]

On the eve of war Stalin had become a fully fledged dictator. Without concerning himself with notions of 'collegiality', he settled some of the most important issues of the day single-handedly. Accordingly there is not even a perfunctory reference in the Politburo records to the most historic decisions of the day, such as the signing of the Nazi–Soviet pact of August 1939. At the same time, it would be wrong to think that, even at this stage, all the elements of 'oligarchic' leadership had vanished. Even at the height of dictatorship there continued to exist, albeit in a weakened and attenuated form, in-built forces pushing towards oligarchic or collegial rule. These found expression in the relative autonomy of Politburo leaders in dealing with everyday operational issues and in the emergence of powerful networks of patron–client relations tying Politburo leaders to circles of dependants beneath them. This tension between personal dictatorship and oligarchical rule would carry on into the war period and beyond.

## War years

The months leading to the war revealed the downside of Stalin's obstinate nature and of the highly concentrated system of decision-making he had created. In addition to blocking much-needed reorganisations of the General Staff, Stalin dismissed a series of detailed intelligence reports on the German

26 Chadaev, personal archive.

build-up for war as 'provocations'.[27] Stalin's state of denial reached a head on the first day of the German attack. 'I only saw Stalin confused once,' Zhukov later recalled, 'and that was at daybreak on 22 June 1941.'[28] For most of the first morning, Stalin still clung to the hope that this was an act of provocation instigated by the German generals without Hitler's knowledge or consent. Such hope evaporated, however, with the official declaration of war by the German ambassador, Schulenburg, later on in the morning. 'During that first day [Stalin] was unable to pull himself together and take hold of events,' recounted Zhukov.[29]

In the first months of the war Stalin committed a succession of blunders. By mid-October, as the Germans approached Moscow, the leader's confidence had reached a low ebb. In a break with precedent, Stalin let the commander of the Moscow front, Georgii Zhukov, have a free hand in organising the city's defence. Observers recall Zhukov treating Stalin brusquely and even rejecting his advice:

> [Stalin's] eyes had lost their old steadiness; his voice lacked assurance. But I was even more surprised by Zhukov's behaviour. He spoke in a sharp commanding tone. It looked as if Zhukov was really the superior officer here. And Stalin accepted this as proper. At times a kind of bafflement even crossed his face.[30]

The summer and autumn of 1941 saw Stalin weaker than possibly at any time since coming to power. Yet the vulnerability of the Soviet system in these months meant that the ruling circle now needed Stalin more than ever. On 30 June four leaders, Molotov, Malenkov, Beria and Voroshilov, gathered in Molotov's office and decided to create a State Defence Committee (GKO) to take overall command of the war effort. When the four visited Stalin at his dacha, to which he had retreated in despair two days earlier, following the fall of Minsk, it was to beseech him to head the new committee. Despite the leader's temporary fall from grace, this approach by Stalin's deputies was not at all surprising. After over a decade of ceaseless propaganda, the cult of Stalin had assumed significant proportions as a popular motivator. The aura around Stalin also served to integrate the country's decision-making bodies and to co-ordinate the higher ranks of leaders and decision makers. Among top officials,

27 Iurii Gor'kov, *Gosudarstvennyi Komitet Oborony postanovliaet. 1941–1945. Tsifry i dokumenty* (Moscow: Olma Press, 2002), pp. 16–17, 51, 483–9, 554.
28 Georgii Zhukov, *Vospominaniia i razmyshlenniia*, 10th edn (Moscow: APN, 1990), vol. II, p. 106.
29 Ibid.
30 Colonel General P. A. Belov, cited in Seweryn Bialer (ed.), *Stalin and his Generals: Soviet Military Memoirs of World War II* (London: Souvenir Press, 1970), p. 296.

Stalin's word carried more weight than did that of any general or ordinary Politburo member. When the high command (Stavka) was established on the second day of the war, and the commissar of defence, General Timoshenko, was appointed its head, none of the nine Politburo members who served on it 'showed any intention of taking orders from the commissar'.[31] It was only later, on 19 July, when Stalin himself became commissar of defence, and then on 8 August, when he became supreme commander-in-chief of the Soviet armed forces, that the Stavka gained genuine authority.

Despite a profusion of new bodies, such as the GKO and the Stavka, there were important continuities with pre-war structures. While the GKO was given overall command of the war effort, and it was directly modelled on the Council of Workers' and Peasants' Defence from the civil war, it was a pre-eminently civilian body. With all its members from the Politburo, the GKO was, in key respects, the direct successor to the Politburo's 'ruling circle', whose membership and operating norms Stalin had shaped in the preceding years. Setting up the GKO gave formal cover for Stalin's civilian ruling circle to exercise unlimited powers as a 'war cabinet'. These included the authority to reorganise the armed forces, to take charge of military production, to undertake personnel changes, and to control the agencies of repression.

At the same time, the GKO epitomised the versatility of the Soviet system in adjusting to conditions of crisis. Under the GKO the mode of governance over subordinate bodies shifted with remarkable speed to an emergency regime.[32] Under this system procedures were simplified in the extreme. 'Meetings of the GKO in the usual sense of the term – that is, with definite agendas, secretaries and protocols – did not take place. Procedures for reaching agreement with [other agencies] were reduced to a minimum,' recalled General Khrulev.[33] Given the overlap in membership between the GKO, the Politburo and Sovnarkom, it was not always apparent in what capacity a meeting had been convened, nor on whose authority a resolution had been passed.

In addition to heading the Politburo and Sovnarkom, Stalin chaired meetings of the GKO and the Stavka, acted as commissar of defence and, as of

---

31 N. G. Kuznetsov, cited in A. A. Pechenkin, 'Gosudarstvennyi komitet oborony v 1941 godu', *Otechestvennaia istoriia* 4–5 (1994): 134–5.

32 See Sanford R. Lieberman, 'Crisis Management in the USSR: Wartime System of Administration and Control', in Susan Linz (ed.), *The Impact of World War II on the Soviet Union* (Totowa, N.J.: Rowman and Allanhead, 1985). The term 'emergency regime' comes from John Barber and Mark Harrison, *The Soviet Home Front 1941–1945: A Social and Economic History of the USSR in World War II* (London: Longman, 1991), pp. 197–200.

33 A. V. Khrulev. 'Stanovlenie strategicheskogo tyla v Velikoi Otechestvennoi voine', *Voenno-istoricheskii zhurnal* 6 (1961): 66; cited in Lieberman, 'Crisis Management', p. 61.

14 September 1942, led a new key GKO Transport Committee. The extraordinary burdens on Stalin left him with no choice but to completely let go of certain leadership functions on which he had earlier kept half an eye. The main beneficiaries of this process of delegation were Stalin's companions on the GKO, who were now given full and unqualified charge of whole sectors of the war effort. Thus members of the GKO were entrusted with the authority to convene meetings and to arrive at decisions of importance under their own steam, without reference to the overburdened leader.

The emergency regime, consisting of plenipotentiaries, ad hoc committees and very high levels of autonomy for GKO members, was particularly well suited to the early phase of the war. Yet while well adapted to a situation of crisis, this system of decision-making was far from effective over the long term. In many areas, the conversion of the economy to munitions production was carried too far, as a result of which by 1942 it was the dwindling stocks of coal, oil, iron and steel, rather than limited munitions capacity, which had become the key factor constraining the Soviet war effort.[34] Greater co-ordination was required to rectify these imbalances. A big step in this direction was achieved on 8 December 1942 with the formation of a GKO Operations bureau, and with the reconstitution, also on that day, of the Sovnarkom bureau which took up responsibility for considering economic plans and the state budget, as well as for overseeing the work of economic commissariats not under the jurisdiction of the GKO bureau. As the war progressed, the authority and status of both bureaux grew.[35]

It is significant that Stalin played no part on either bureau. As the war unfolded, the delegation of powers to GKO members and the emergence of a more balanced and co-ordinated system of economic decision-making was matched by a narrowing of Stalin's commitments, which focused increasingly on military issues and foreign affairs. Further, as Stalin's grasp of military matters improved, the obstinacy he had displayed in the early stages of the war gave way to a certain pragmatism. From the spring of 1942 Stalin removed incompetent cronies such as Voroshilov and Budennyi as well as political appointees such as Kulik and Mekhlis on whom he had relied earlier. In October 1942 Stalin also abolished political commissars – political appointees who shadowed military leaders at the front – and he became more willing to defer matters of strategic leadership to a group of senior military figures on the Stavka. Further,

34  Barber and Harrison, *The Soviet Home Front*, pp. 132, 136.
35  Thus on 16 May 1944 Beria, the head of the GKO bureau, was made deputy chair of GKO and three days later, on 19 May 1944 the bureau's jurisdiction was widened from 14 to 21 commissariats and its responsibilities enhanced.

whereas in the first months of the war virtually every bungled operation had resulted in executions, Stalin was now willing to heed the advice of top military aides in sparing the lives of commanders in the field.[36]

The war had caught Stalin off guard and highlighted the flaws of the one-sided form of government he had fashioned in the preceding years. At the same time, the war also showed how mutually interdependent Stalin's leadership was with the social and administrative system which had formed in the 1930s. In the early days of the conflict, Stalin's deputies saw that they needed Stalin and the cult which surrounded him to boost morale and to co-ordinate the higher ranks of Soviet officialdom. For his part, in the guise of the State Defence Committee, Stalin was able to keep his ruling circle and informal modes of decision-making similar to those he had installed before the war. The one major difference was that, with the advent of an 'emergency regime', Stalin was compelled to hand over total responsibility for certain spheres to his deputies. Originally constituted on an informal basis, this delegation of powers was formalised with the establishment of the GKO and Sovnarkom bureaux in December 1942. It was this relatively decentralised system of wartime governance which lasted until the effective end of hostilities in May 1945.

## Post-war dictatorship

During the war Stalin had delegated large swaths of authority to his deputies and set aside ideological differences with his coalition partners. Soon, however, a souring of relations with the West would bring a swift end to the relaxation of the war years. In a programmatic speech to voters of 9 February 1946, Stalin once again highlighted the need to strengthen the sinews of national power, most notably heavy industry. The laying out of long-term plan priorities was accompanied by a newly belligerent rhetoric in which Stalin sought, to quote one commentator, to transform the post-war period 'into a *new prewar period*' in which a 'postulated external danger [was] the primary fact of national life and the internal policies of the government [were] a compulsive response to it'.[37] This return to the ideological matrix of the pre-war years was matched by a much harsher and less accommodating approach to his Politburo companions. Here too, the leader clawed back the discretion he had ceded during the war and, in a series of attacks, resurrected the relations of strict subservience and control which had predominated in the late 1930s.

36  See Gor'kov, *Gosudarstvennyi Komitet*, pp. 81–4.
37  Robert C. Tucker, *The Soviet Political Mind* (New York: Norton, 1971), pp. 91, 89 (italics in the original).

On 4 September 1945 the GKO was dissolved and a month later Stalin left Moscow for his first major break from the capital in almost a decade, leaving affairs of state in the hands of a 'quartet' consisting of Molotov, Malenkov, Beria and Mikoyan. While in Sochi the leader closely followed events in Moscow, receiving between twenty and thirty documents a day, and became increasingly dismayed by what he regarded as the 'independent' political line being pursued by Molotov in relations with the Western powers. Matters reached a head at the beginning of December, when Stalin launched a vicious assault on Molotov: 'None of us has the right to change the course of our policies unilaterally,' Stalin argued. 'But Molotov has accorded himself this right. Why, and on what grounds?' 'I can no longer regard this comrade as my first deputy,' Stalin concluded. Stalin sent the message to the other members of the quartet – but not to Molotov – and asked that they read it out to him. On 7 December the triumvirate reported: 'We summoned Molotov and read out your telegram in full. After some hesitation Molotov admitted that he had made many mistakes but he regarded the lack of trust in him as unjust, and shed some tears.' On the same day Molotov sent his own reply to Stalin. 'Your ciphered message is filled with deep distrust towards me, both as a Bolshevik and as a person, which I take as a most serious party warning for all my further work. I shall try through deeds to regain your trust, in which every honest Bolshevik sees not only personal trust, but also the trust of the party, which is dearer to me than my own life.'[38]

To resurrect the relations of strict subordination of the immediate pre-war years, Stalin visited attacks of similar severity on each member of his quartet.[39] Mikoyan's apology, which Stalin extracted from him in the autumn of 1946, would prove to be quite typical: 'Of course neither I nor others', Mikoyan conceded, 'can frame questions quite like you. I shall devote all my energy so that I may learn from you how to work correctly. I shall do all I can to draw the lessons from your stern criticism, so that it is turned to good use in my further work under your fatherly guidance.'[40]

At the same time, given their qualities either as revolutionary symbols or as hard-working administrators – it was for these reasons that they were in the ruling circle to begin with – Stalin was reluctant to dispense with the services of any member of the quartet altogether. Instead, he sought to curb

38 RGASPI f. 558, op. 11, d. 99, ll. 95, 120.
39 See Yoram Gorlizki and Oleg Khlevniuk, *Cold Peace: Stalin and the Soviet Ruling Circle, 1945–1953* (New York: Oxford University Press, 2004), pp. 19–29.
40 RGASPI f. 558, op. 11, d. 765, ll. 113–14.

the independence they had gained during the war and to bring about a return to the status quo ante of the first post-purge years.

The personal subjugation of Stalin's close circle was accompanied by a reorganisation of the country's top decision-making bodies. Within the Politburo itself, Stalin soon re-established the intrinsically fluid and patrimonial arrangements of the late 1930s. Convening the Politburo as an informally constituted 'ruling group' offered Stalin several advantages. Apart from arranging its meetings as and when he wished, Stalin could bypass the tedious procedure for having members formally elected by the Central Committee. It was, for example, nearly five months before Voznesenskii's election as a full member of the Politburo, that Stalin dictated a Politburo resolution that the 'sextet [i.e. the ruling group] add to its roster the chair of Gosplan [the State Planning Commission], comrade Voznesenskii, so that it now be known as the septet'.[41] Often, admission to the ruling group was not accompanied by any formal resolutions as such. Without any official decision to go by, it is only indirectly that we may infer that Kaganovich was admitted to it on his return to Moscow from Kiev in December 1947, so that the 'septet' became an 'octet', and that Bulganin joined in February 1948, swelling the group into a 'novenary'.

As much as it suited Stalin to have relatively informal arrangements at the very highest levels, he and his colleagues did not lose sight of the need for effective administration lower down. Thus the relatively rule-less activity of a Politburo dominated by him went hand in hand with greater institutionalisation elsewhere, most notably at the Council of Ministers (Sovmin), the successor to Sovnarkom. Particularly important in this respect was a resolution of 8 February 1947 'On the Organisation of the Council of Ministers', which laid out a clear division of labour between the Politburo and Sovmin in which the former, led by Stalin, was accorded the right to consider all matters of a 'political' nature, such as governmental appointments, issues relating to defence, foreign policy and internal security, while Sovmin, without Stalin, was expected to deal with all mainstream economic issues and matters of everyday governmental administration. The February resolution also marked the consolidation of a new supra-ministerial order at Sovmin, consisting of a hierarchy of sectoral committees attended by specialists which met at regular intervals and complied with clearly established procedures.[42]

41 O.V. Khlevniuk et al. (eds.), *Politburo TsK VKP(b) i Sovet Ministrov SSSR 1945–1953* (Moscow: Rosspen, 2002), p. 38.
42 See Yoram Gorlizki, 'Ordinary Stalinism: The Council of Ministers and the Soviet Neo-patrimonial State, 1945–1953', *Journal of Modern History* 74, 4 (Dec. 2002): 705–15.

In the post-war period Stalin thus operated through two committees: the Politburo, over which he almost always presided, and the main bureau of the Council of Ministers, which nearly always convened without him. The combination of Stalin's highly personalised leadership, as represented by the Politburo, and the technocratic features of Sovmin, allowed Stalin to marry personal-autocratic features of rule with modern committee-based decision-making.

The consolidation of two key features of the early post-war period – the tightening of Stalin's grip over his deputies and the establishment of a split system of leadership committees – was not an entirely smooth or continuous affair. One flashpoint which would disfigure the leadership system was a purge, orchestrated by Stalin, which would come to be known as the Leningrad Affair.[43] Its immediate trigger was a scandal surrounding a seemingly innocuous all-Russian wholesale fair held in Leningrad from 10 to 20 January 1949. When it emerged that proper authorisation for the fair had not been granted, the three leaders who had organised the fair, M. I. Rodionov, P. S. Popkov and the Central Committee secretary, A. A. Kuznetsov, all of whom had long-running ties to the city, were taken to task. To stave off allegations of his own links with this group, the Politburo member Voznesenskii, himself from Leningrad, admitted to Stalin that the previous year Popkov had approached Voznesenskii with a request that the latter act as a 'patron' of Leningrad. This revelation was to have disastrous consequences, for the idea that any leader other than Stalin could exercise 'patronage' over a territory was entirely anathema to the dictator. On 15 February Kuznetsov, along with Popkov and Rodionov, were dismissed, and Vosnesenskii was given a stern warning.

One factor which may have fuelled the Leningrad Affair was the existence of two loose groupings within the leadership, one consisting of natives of the city associated with the deceased former Leningrad first secretary, Andrei Zhdanov, and the other headed by two thrusting young Politburo leaders, Malenkov and Beria.[44] There is little evidence, however, that any member of either group aimed to have their adversaries killed. Ever conscious of Stalin's volatile state of mind, both groups knew that a fresh round of bloodletting at the very highest levels could easily swerve out of control and claim other

43 See Robert Conquest, *Power and Policy in the USSR* (London: Macmillan, 1961), ch.5; and Gorlizki and Khlevniuk, *Cold Peace*, pp. 79–89.
44 For a different interpretation which emphasises the ideological and policy differences between these groups, see Werner G. Hahn, *Postwar Soviet Politics: The Fall of Zhdanov and the Defeat of Moderation, 1946–53* (Ithaca, N.Y.: Cornell University Press, 1982).

victims, not least themselves. The key role in taking this affair over the edge and turning it into a mini blood-purge would belong to Stalin.

Although Voznesenskii had earned a reprieve in February, his dismissal would follow shortly afterwards. As a member of the younger generation of Politburo leaders, Voznesenskii, who had seen no revolutionary service and whose symbolic worth was limited, had been promoted and retained by Stalin solely on the basis of his organisational talents and reliability. As the head of Gosplan, Vosnesenskii's main assignment was to provide the political leadership under Stalin with accurate information on the economy. When Stalin discovered, towards the end of February, that Voznesenskii had deliberately massaged economic statistics, his retribution was swift. On 5 March Vosnesenskii was dismissed as chair of Gosplan and two days later he was forced out of the Politburo.

For some time, Stalin vacillated over what to do with Vosnesenskii. After several months the latter's fate was sealed when he was charged with losing secret documents. In a last-ditch attempt to earn Stalin's forgiveness Voznesenskii pleaded in a letter: 'I appeal to the Central Committee and to you, comrade Stalin, and beg you to pardon me . . . and to believe that you are dealing with a man who has learned his lesson . . .'[45] Waving aside this appeal, on 11 September 1949 the Politburo confirmed a recommendation of the Commission of Party Control to have Voznesenskii expelled from the Central Committee and to hand him over for trial.[46] On 27 October 1949 Voznesenskii was arrested and joined Kuznetsov and the others, who had been detained earlier that summer. Following a year of confinement and interrogations Voznesenskii and the other 'Leningraders' were convicted at a secret trial in September 1950 and executed on 1 October.

In selecting his victim and moment of retribution Stalin was often quite unpredictable, and, accordingly, he could turn virtually any untoward circumstance into a pretext for punishment. We cannot be certain about what tipped the balance in this instance. It is clear, however, that a number of established Stalinist norms had been violated. The strict hierarchy of decision-making had been flouted and there appeared to be evidence that a Moscow-based network of senior leaders had exercised patronage over regional clients in Leningrad. For his part, Voznesenskii had violated his assignment, which involved providing accurate statistics to the Politburo. At the same time, despite the potential, frequently realised in the 1930s, for ever-expanding networks to be

45 APRF f. 3, op. 54, d. 26, ll. 78–91.    46 RGASPI f. 17, op. 163, d. 1530, l. 154.

implicated in such a purge, the scope of the Leningrad Affair would prove to be surprisingly narrow.

## Last years

After the drama of 1949, the next two years were a period of relative calm and moderation within the leadership, as the ageing dictator spent an increasing amount of time in the south. On this basis the higher leadership began to consolidate and to lay the foundations of collective rule. While Stalin was out of the capital, issues within the Politburo's brief were discussed at meetings of a Stalin-less ruling group, known as the 'septet', which operated as a collective decision-making body. At its sessions questions appear to have been properly debated and authentic fact-finding commissions were set up for supplementary investigation of contentious issues. Indeed, the septet's work methods when Stalin was away began to approximate the pattern of Politburo decision-making which had prevailed prior to the establishment of a full-blown dictatorship.

Arguably of greater significance were the regular meetings of the supreme governmental agency in this period, the Bureau of the Presidium of the Council of Ministers. At the time of its foundation on 7 April 1950 the bureau consisted of five members, Bulganin, Beria, Kaganovich, Mikoyan and Molotov, who were joined by a sixth member, Malenkov, in mid-April, and by a seventh, Nikita Khrushchev, who began attending its meetings on 2 September 1950. While the bureau consisted entirely of members of the Politburo's ruling group, unlike the Politburo it *never* met with Stalin, not even when Stalin was in Moscow. At the same time, the bureau convened very regularly, normally once a week. Thus the ruling group of the Politburo had regular opportunities to meet without Stalin and outside the very framework of the Politburo in order to discuss issues of national importance within a committee structure with a clear membership, well-defined procedures and set agendas. These meetings afforded an embryonic collective leadership the opportunity to meet regularly and to forge a set of mutual understandings.

There are indications that in his last year Stalin settled on what might be termed an anti-oligarchic strategy aimed at undercutting the relatively stable and independent system of collective leadership which had taken hold over the previous two years, especially at the Council of Ministers. Stalin's strategy consisted of three elements. First, in December 1951 Stalin finally called a party congress, which convened the following October. The congress afforded Stalin a convenient pretext for loosening the ties of senior Politburo members to the

Council of Ministers and for focusing attention instead on a new Central Committee Presidium Bureau, which would meet under him. The second prong of Stalin's anti-oligarchic strategy was an onslaught on two Politburo veterans, Molotov and Mikoyan, who were left out of the Central Committee Bureau. As on earlier occasions, for example in 1941 and 1945, Stalin reserved his most stinging attack for Molotov. At the post-congress plenum, making explicit reference to the events of autumn 1945 described earlier, Stalin openly accused Molotov of cowardice, capitulationism and, critically, of personal betrayal. These accusations were all the more astounding for the fact that they ran against the widely held perception of Molotov as Stalin's most devoted follower.

The third and boldest element of Stalin's anti-oligarchic strategy was the fabrication of a notional 'conspiracy' by a group of mostly Jewish doctors to murder members of the Soviet leadership. 'Jewish nationalists', Stalin told a session of the Presidium on 1 December 1952, 'believe that their nation has been saved by the United States (there they can become rich, bourgeois and so on). They believe they are obliged to the Americans. Among the doctors there are many Jewish nationalists.'[47] On 13 January 1953 the national daily, *Pravda*, published a TASS bulletin, originally dictated by Stalin, and a lead editorial, commissioned and heavily edited by him, on the activities of a group of 'doctor-wreckers' most of whom, it claimed, were the tools of an 'international Jewish Zionist organisation'.[48] The publication ushered in a frenzied nationwide campaign with heavy anti-Semitic overtones and led to yet more arrests.

Concocting the Doctors' Plot served a dual purpose. First, it demonstrated Stalin's undiminished control of the secret police, a factor which continued to underpin his control of Politburo colleagues. The plot, secondly, was designed to prevent Stalin's fellow leaders from lapsing into a 'spirit of geopolitical complacency'.[49] Paradoxically the USSR's achievements over the previous decade, which included its defeat of Nazi Germany, the acquisition of a ring of buffer states in Eastern Europe and the testing of the atom bomb in 1949, had presented Stalin with a problem, namely the view, seemingly widely held by other members of the leadership, that the country's new-found strength and security could enable it to relax and to focus on domestic issues. The Doctors' Plot was, to quote Robert Tucker, 'Stalin's desperate attempt to dramatise the postulated persistence of the capitalist encirclement'.[50]

47 Malyshev, 'Dnevnik narkoma', pp. 140–1.     48 RGASPI f. 558, op. 11, d. 157, ll. 29–33.
49 The phrase is from Tucker, *Soviet Political Mind*, p. 95.
50 Ibid., pp. 95–6. Also see Khlevniuk et al., *Politburo TsK VKP(b) i Sovet Ministrov SSSR 1945–1953*, p. 393.

It was a measure of Stalin's unimpeachable authority that there were no open challenges to his rule over these last months. At the same time, Stalin was unable to take any of the thrusts of his anti-oligarchic strategy as far as he may have wished. Thus, for example, the organisation of the Central Committee Presidium Bureau, the equivalent of which Stalin had dominated for over twenty years, was made part of Khrushchev's brief, and, in a further break with tradition, it was resolved that, in Stalin's absence, the cabinet could be chaired by Malenkov, Khrushchev or Bulganin.[51] Stalin also appears to have dispensed with the services of his long-standing aide and the head of the special sector, Aleksandr Poskrebyshev, a month or so before his death.[52] The second prong of Stalin's strategy, the excommunication of Molotov and Mikoyan, also appears to have had limited success. Stalin's displeasure towards Mikoyan and Molotov had virtually no bearing on the attitudes of other top leaders towards the two, who were covertly told of leadership meetings and quickly reassumed their positions once Stalin died.[53] Third, despite the frenzied and bigoted atmosphere it created, the purge implications of the Doctors' Plot should not be overstated. Unlike the Great Terror in the 1930s, which had been supported in public by all top Politburo leaders, this campaign was waged by secondary functionaries, mostly from the Central Committee apparatus, and did not receive a public endorsement from any of Stalin's inner circle.[54] Equally, claims that the regime planned to hold public show trials, or to deport Jews to special camps in the east, much as other ethnic minorities had been 'cleansed' and relocated during the war, now appear to be misplaced.[55]

It appears that in Stalin's last months his poor health and declining energy had begun to take their toll. Certainly, whatever plans Stalin had in store for his colleagues and for the country's Jews were cut short by a sudden deterioration in his health. On 1 March 1953 Stalin, unusually, did not call on his staff. When, late that evening, the assistant warden of the dacha brought in the post, he found Stalin lying on the floor. On their arrival the following morning Stalin's physicians diagnosed a brain haemorrhage, and the next day they informed the

51 APRF f. 3, op. 22, d. 12, l. 3.
52 RGANI f. 2, op. 1, d. 65, ll. 26, 28–9; RGASPI f. 83, op. 1, d. 7, ll. 75–6 cf. 73; N. S. Khrushchev, Vospominaniia (Moscow: Moskovskie novosti, 1999), vol. II, pp. 109–10.
53 Anastas Mikoyan, Tak bylo (Moscow: Vagrius, 1999), pp. 557–8. Also see G. V. Kostyrchenko, Tainaia politika Stalina (Moscow: Mezhdunarodnye otnosheniia, 2001), pp. 683–85.
54 This was a point made by Adam Ulam, Stalin: The Man and his Era (New York, Viking, 1974), p. 738.
55 See Samson Madieveski, '1953: La Déportation des Juifs Soviétiques était-elle programmée', Cahiers du Monde russe et soviétique, 41, 4 (2000): 563–67; and Kostyrchenko, Tainaia politika, pp. 676–7.

ruling group that the leader had no hope of recovery. By 8.00 p.m. on 5 March, while Stalin was technically still alive (he died at 9.50 p.m.), the ruling group had convened a joint session of the Presidium and of the Central Committee.[56] Notwithstanding the turmoil of Stalin's last months, the leadership would rely on the collegial decision-making structures and mutual understandings forged in the proceding years, to see itself through the uncertainties of the early post-Stalin transition.

## Conclusion

The entrenchment of Stalin's dictatorship was a multi-stage process in which oligarchic tendencies were persistently represented. By the end of the 1920s a fully-fledged Stalinist faction had been formed, yet there were still strong elements of collective rule. At this stage Stalin still had to accommodate the cut and thrust of high-level bureaucratic politics and to win colleagues onto his side. Any semblance of resistance was only crushed with the purges of the late 1930s which left the Politburo and Central Committee, newly infused with a young cohort of Stalin appointees, as institutionally malleable bodies subject to the dictator's whims. For Stalin the leadership system of the late 1930s represented the high-water mark of dictatorship, an ideal to which the leader would strive to return in later years.

At the height of his powers, in March 1939 Stalin declared to the Eighteenth Party Congress that 'there is no doubt that we will not use again the method of the mass purge'. Although we are unlikely ever to know whether Stalin seriously intended to keep his pledge, there are indications from the post-war years that Stalin recognised the benefits of relative equilibrium within the political system. Despite the devastating personal consequences for those involved, the Leningrad Affair of 1949 was the only occasion after the 1930s in which high-ranking politicians lost their lives, and the purges of the personal networks which accompanied it were relatively confined in scope. Equally, when, in the early 1950s, oligarchic tendencies began to set in and to constrain Stalin's leadership, as they had in the early 1930s, the anti-oligarchic strategy pursued by Stalin was far less bloody or robust than it had been when Stalin had broken the back of the 1930s collective leadership, fifteen years before.

The latter phase of Stalin's life has sometimes been depicted as a time of Stalin's mental decline and of the system's institutional disarray.[57] In fact from

---

56 Khlevniuk et al., *Politburo TsK VKP(b) i Sovet Ministrov SSSR 1945–1953*, pp. 101–4.
57 See e.g. Ulam, *Stalin*, pp. 652, 665–70, 686.

the second phase of the war on, we find evidence of institutional consolidation. As for Stalin himself, we see a rationalisation of his own commitments, as the leader shed a variety of secondary duties and focused on a narrow range of core activities. As Stalin grew older and his powers waned, he was forced to relinquish even more of these. It is in the Doctors' Plot that we find, distilled to their essence, the two irreducible functions that Stalin could never let go of. In this final, desperate, lunge he turned to repression and ideology in order to counter oligarchical forces which, despite his own supreme dictatorial powers, would never quite go away.

# 10

# The Khrushchev period, 1953–1964

## WILLIAM TAUBMAN

The Twentieth Congress of the Soviet Communist Party convened on 14 February 1956 in the Great Kremlin Palace. On 25 February, the day the congress was slated to end, Soviet delegates attended an unscheduled secret session at which their leader, Nikita Khrushchev, talked for nearly four hours with one intermission. His speech was a devastating attack on Joseph Stalin. Stalin was guilty of 'a grave abuse of power'. During his reign 'mass arrests and deportation of thousands and thousands of people, and execution without trial or normal investigation, created insecurity, fear, and even desperation'. Stalinist charges of counter-revolutionary crimes had been 'absurd, wild and contrary to common sense'. Innocent people had confessed to such crimes 'because of physical methods of pressure, torture, reducing them to unconsciousness, depriving them of judgement, taking away their human dignity'. Stalin himself had been personally responsible for all this: he 'personally called in the interrogator, gave him instructions, and told him which methods to use, methods that were simple – to beat, beat and once again, beat'. 'Honest and innocent Communists' had been tortured and killed. Khrushchev assailed Stalin for incompetent wartime leadership, for 'monstrous' deportations of whole Caucasian peoples, for a 'mania of greatness', and 'nauseatingly false' adulation and self-adulation.[1]

Khrushchev's indictment was neither complete nor unalloyed. The Stalin he portrayed had been a paragon until the mid-1930s. Although oppositionists had not deserved 'physical annihilation', they had been 'ideological and political enemies'. Khrushchev not only spared Lenin and the Soviet regime itself, he glorified them, but his speech stunned his audience. Many in the hall

---

This chapter draws extensively on my book, *Khrushchev: The Man and his Era* (New York: Norton, 2003).

1 'O kul'te lichnosti i ego posledstviiakh: doklad pervogo sekretaria TsK KPSS tov. Khrushcheva N. S. XX s"ezdu Kommunisticheskoi partii Sovetskogo Soiuza', in *Izvestiia TsK KPSS* 3 (1989): 131, 133, 144–5, 149, 154–5.

were unreconstructed Stalinists. Others, who had secretly feared and hated Stalin, could not believe his successor secretly shared their view. The speech was met with 'a deathly silence', Vladimir Semichastnyi, who would later become Khrushchev's KGB chief, recalled. 'We didn't look at each other as we came down from the balcony,' remembered Aleksandr Yakovlev, then a minor Central Committee functionary, and later Mikhail Gorbachev's collaborator in *perestroika*, 'whether from shame or shock or from the simple unexpectedness of it.'[2]

Khrushchev's speech was supposed to be kept secret. However, the ruling Presidium approved distributing it to local party committees; local authorities read the text to millions of party members and others around the country; and Polish Communist leaders allowed thousands of copies to circulate, one of which reached the US Central Intelligence Agency. The US State Department eventually released the text to the *New York Times*, which published it on 4 June 1956.

'I very much doubt Father wanted to keep it secret', recalled Khrushchev's son Sergei. 'He wanted to bring the report to the people. The secrecy of the session was only a formal concession on his part...'[3] Yet, at numerous meetings at which the speech was read and discussed, criticism of Stalin exploded way beyond Khrushchev's. Why had it taken so long to admit Stalin's crimes? Had not current leaders been his accomplices? Why had Khrushchev himself kept silent for so long? Was not the Soviet system itself the real culprit? Some meetings tried to call for rights and freedoms, and for multi-party elections to guarantee them.[4] In April 1956, the KGB reported that portraits and busts of Stalin had been defaced or torn down, that Communists at one party meeting had declared him 'an enemy of the people', and at another had demanded his body be removed from the Lenin–Stalin mausoleum. On the other hand, those who defended Stalin included not only unreconstructed party officials but ordinary citizens, some of whom hailed Stalin for 'punishing' the party and police officials who had oppressed them.[5] In Stalin's native Georgia, some 60,000 people carried flowers to his monument, and when some of them

---

2 Semichastnyi's recollection in 'Taina zakrytogo doklada', *Sovershenno sekretno* 1 (1996): 4. Yakovlev quoted in Iurii V. Aksiutin, 'Novye dokumenty byvshego arkhiva TsK', in *XX s"ezd: materialy konferentsii k 40 – letiu SS s"ezda KPSS* (Moscow: Aprel'-85, 1996), p. 127.

3 Sergei N. Khrushchev, *Nikita Khrushchev and the Creation of a Superpower* (University Park, Pa.: Pennsylvania State University Press, 2000), p. 99.

4 See Iurii Aksiutin, 'Popular Responses to Khrushchev', in William Taubman, Sergei Khrushchev and Abbott Gleason (eds.), *Nikita Khrushchev* (New Haven: Yale University Press, 2000), pp. 182–92.

5 See Mikhail S. Gorbachev, *Memoirs* (New York: Doubleday, 1995), pp. 61–3.

marched on the radio station, at least twenty demonstrators were killed in the clashes with troops.[6]

Not long after his 'secret' speech, 'Khrushchev sensed the blow had been too powerful, and . . . increasingly he sought to limit the boundaries of critical analysis, lest it end up polarising society . . .'[7] His retreat climaxed in a Central Committee resolution of 30 June which blamed Stalin at most for 'serious errors'.[8] However, the retreat came too late to prevent turmoil in Poland and a revolution in Hungary, which Soviet troops crushed at a cost of some 20,000 Hungarian and 1,500 Soviet casualties.

## Personality and history

The year 1956 was pivotal in the Khrushchev period. De-Stalinisation was at the heart of his effort to reform Soviet Communism. But in the years that followed, virtually all his reforms were marked by the kind of alternating advance and retreat that occurred in 1956. What triggered the burst of change that was central to the Khrushchev years? What limited it? Why did the reforms of the Khrushchev period go as far as they did, but no further? Answers to these questions can be found at the intersection of personality and history, of Khrushchev and his character, on the one hand, and, on the other, impersonal forces such as Stalin's legacy, the nature of the Soviet system, the influence of the world outside the USSR, even the nature of nuclear weapons.

Three conditions justify singling out a political leader and his or her personality as decisive influences on events. Obviously, such a leader must have the sheer political power to affect those events. Second, a leader who acts idiosyncratically, rather than doing what others would do in his position, is not simply reacting to the dictates of a situation, or reflecting values that he and his colleagues share. Thirdly, actions that are particularly costly and self-destructive are likely to be products of internal drives and compulsions rather than of external circumstances.[9]

---

6 V. A. Kozlov, *Massovye besporiadki v SSSR pri Khrushcheve i Brezhneve (1953–nachalo 1980)* (Novosibirsk: Sibirskii khronograf, 1999), p. 160.

7 Aleksei Adzhubei, *Krushenie illiuzii* (Moscow: Interbuk, 1991), p. 145.

8 Resolution translated in *The Anti-Stalin Campaign and International Communism*, ed. Russian Institute of Columbia University (New York: Columbia University Press, 1956), pp. 282, 291, 293.

9 See Sidney Hook, *The Hero in History: A Study in Limitation and Possibility* (New York: John Day, 1943), pp. 151–83; Fred I. Greenstein, *Personality and Politics: Problems of Evidence, Inference and Conceptualization* (Chicago: Markham, 1969), pp. 33–68; Faye Crosby, 'Evaluating Psychohistorical Explanations', *Psychohistory Review* 2 (1979): pp. 6–16.

Khrushchev fits all three criteria. Stalin's successor may have wielded less power than his former master, but more than enough to allow him to initiate reforms and then throttle them back. Perhaps his most important decisions (to unmask Stalin in 1956, to dispatch nuclear missiles to Cuba in 1962 and then suddenly to remove those missiles) were moves which, in all probability, no other Soviet leader of his time would have made. In a sense, Khrushchev's life is a stunning success story (if one does not count the corpses over which he clambered on his way to the top), but no sooner had he survived and succeeded Stalin, and assumed full power himself, than he began making devastating miscalculations, which ended in his unceremonious removal in October 1964.

Yet, Khrushchev also acted in a historical context that shaped and limited him. Having come to political maturity under Stalin and served for years in the dictator's inner circle, Khrushchev himself was a Stalinist before he became a 'de-Stalinist'. In addition, Stalin's legacy – a dysfunctional economy, a super-centralised polity and a self-isolating foreign policy – was nearly insurmountable. Martin Malia goes so far as to contend that the Soviet system which Khrushchev tried to reform was essentially unreformable.[10] Kremlinologists like Myron Rush, Carl Linden and Michel Tatu have portrayed Kremlin power struggles that determined Khrushchev's policies.[11] Stephen F. Cohen pointed to the 'larger political forces in Soviet officialdom and society', particularly the 'friends and foes of change', which influenced the pace and pattern of de-Stalinisation.[12] Not to mention the effect of Russian inertia, explicated, for example, by Tim McDaniel in *The Agony of the Russian Idea*,[13] but characterised more crudely by Khrushchev in a 1963 conversation with Fidel Castro: 'You'd think I, as first secretary, could change anything in this country. Like hell I can! No matter what changes I propose and carry out, everything stays the same. Russia's like a tub full of dough, you put your hand in it, down to the bottom, and you think you're master of the situation. When you first pull out your hand, a little hole remains, but then, before your very eyes, the dough expands into a spongy, puffy mass. That's what Russia is like!'[14]

10 Martin Malia, *The Soviet Tragedy: A History of Socialism in Russia, 1917–1991* (New York: Free Press, 1994).
11 Michel Tatu, *Power in the Kremlin: From Khrushchev to Kosygin*, trans. Helen Katel (New York: Viking, 1969); Carl Linden, *Khrushchev and the Soviet Leadership: 1957–1964* (Baltimore: Johns Hopkins University Press, 1966).
12 Stephen F. Cohen, *Rethinking the Soviet Experience: Politics and History Since 1917* (New York: Oxford University Press, 1985), pp. 93–157.
13 Tim McDaniel, *The Agony of the Russian Idea* (Princeton: Princeton University Press, 1996).
14 N. C. Leonov, *Likholet'e* (Moscow: Terra, 1997), p. 73.

The outside world posed both mortal threats and irresistible opportunities to a superpower on the make like the USSR. Pursuing 'expansion and
coexistence'[15] simultaneously was difficult for any Soviet leader. As Alexander
Yanov has argued, the United States 'consistently [tried] to undermine a Soviet
reformist leader, thus practically shutting one of the rare Russian windows into
political modernity and inviting a ferocious arms race'.[16] But Khrushchev himself was also at fault: the awesome power of nuclear weapons reinforced his
conviction that war with the United States would be an unmitigated catastrophe, but it also tempted him to engage in nuclear bluff and blackmail that
ended up endangering Soviet security as well as his own.

## Biography

Khrushchev was born on 15 April 1894 in the poor southern Russian village
of Kalinovka, and his childhood there profoundly shaped his character. His
parents dreamed of owning land and a horse but did not obtain either. His
father, who later worked in the mines of Iuzovka in the Donbass, was a failure
in the eyes of Khrushchev's mother, a strong-willed woman who invested her
hopes in her son. That made it all the more important for Khrushchev to outdo
his father, yet the very success he craved risked evoking guilt at succeeding
where his father had not. The fact that Khrushchev had no more than two
to four years of elementary education not only equipped him ill to cope with
governing a vast transcontinental state, it also explains the insecurity he felt,
especially when jousting with the intelligentsia, and the super-sensitivity to
slight which made him vindictive towards those he thought had demeaned or
betrayed him. His parents' religiosity helps to account for his sense of rectitude
and for the conscience that endured even after he violated his own moral code
by becoming Stalin's accomplice in terror.

From 1908 until the late 1920s, Khrushchev lived and worked mostly in the
Donbass. Until the revolution, he laboured as a metalworker whose ambition
was to become an engineer. The revolution and civil war 'distracted' him into
Bolshevik politics (he joined the party in 1918), witness the fact that he twice
returned to an educational path that seemed designed to lead to an industrial

15 Adam B. Ulam, *Expansion and Coexistence: Soviet Foreign Policy, 1917–1973* (New York:
Holt, Rinehart and Winston, 1974).

16 Alexander Yanov, 'In the Grip of the Adversarial Paradigm: The Case of Nikita Sergeevich
Khrushchev in Retrospect', in Robert O. Crummey (ed.), *Reform in Russia and the USSR:
Past and Prospects* (Urbana: University of Illinois Press, 1989), p. 169.

career. Strange as it may sound, Khrushchev might have made a better manager than a political leader whose native gifts sustained him during his rise to the top, but failed him when he reached the summit of power. Both in 1925 and 1930, he chose careers in the Communist Party apparatus, first in Ukraine, then in Moscow, where he quickly became Moscow party boss. Returning to Ukraine as party leader in 1938, he remained there (except for the war years) until Stalin summoned him back to Moscow in 1949.

During the 1930s and 1940s, Khrushchev played a central role in Stalinism. His positive contributions included supervising construction of the Moscow metro, energising Ukrainian agriculture and industry after the Great Purges, and attempting to ameliorate the post-war famine which Stalin's draconian policies caused. On the other hand, as he himself later admitted, his arms were 'up to the elbows in blood' of those who perished in the purges. 'That', he continued shortly before he died, 'is the most terrible thing that lies in my soul'.[17] Khrushchev believed in socialism and took great pride in his role in 'building' it. But he also felt a deep guilt about his complicity in Stalinism, guilt that helps to explain both his anti-Stalin campaign and why he retreated from it lest his own complicity be fully revealed.

The 'secret speech' was a sign of Khrushchev's repentance. As early as 1940 he confided his sense of anger about Stalin's terror to a childhood friend in the Donbass: 'Don't blame me for all that. I'm not involved in that. When I can, I'll settle with that "Mudakshvili" [Khrushchev altered Stalin's real name, Dzhugashvili, by playing on the Russian word for 'prick', *mudak*] in full. I don't forgive him any of them – not Kirov, not Iakir, not Tukhachevskii, not the simplest worker or peasant.'[18]

Stalin was Khrushchev's mentor and tormentor, the man who raised him to the heights, but mocked him for his limitations as he did so. Khrushchev managed to survive and succeed Stalin by playing the simple peasant slogger, the very role which he aspired to transcend. But despite his miraculous rise, his doubts about both his capacities and his sins remained, exacerbated by the domestic and foreign-policy troubles that came crowding in on him, troubles to which he responded with increasingly desperate and reckless actions which, rather than consolidating and extending his achievements, ultimately ensured his defeat.

17  N. S. Khrushchev (1894–1971): Materialy nauchnoi konferentsii posviashchennoi 100-letiu so
    dnia rozhdeniia N. S. Khrushcheva (Moscow: Rossiiskii gosudarstvennyi universitet, 1994),
    p. 39.
18  Author's interviews with Ol'ga I. Kosenko, June 1991 and Aug. 1993, Donetsk, Ukraine.

## Succession struggle

The battle to succeed Stalin was largely about power (and the personalities
who competed for it), but it was also about policies which his would-be heirs
wielded as weapons against each other. Stalin's legacy created his successors'
agenda. What was to be done about some 2.5 million prisoners still languishing
in labour camps, and about those who had imprisoned them? How to give the
party elite and the intelligentsia, which had been particularly terrorised, an
increased sense of security? How to allow a cultural thaw without unleashing
a flood? How to revive agriculture, which had virtually been ruined by Stalin,
while boosting the production of housing and consumer goods which the
dictator had so badly neglected? How to breach the isolation in which the USSR
found itself after Stalin managed to alienate almost the whole world – not just
the capitalist West, and influential neutrals like India, but key Communist
allies like Yugoslavia, and even China, whose leader, Mao Zedung, paid Stalin
public obeisance but nursed resentments that would soon boil over? How
to counter American nuclear superiority? How to prevent the strains of the
succession struggle itself from sapping Soviet strength in the Cold War? The
capitalists knew, Khrushchev later recalled, 'that the leadership that Stalin left
behind was no good because it was composed of people who had too many
differences among them'.[19]

Lavrentii Beria, Stalin's former secret police chief, was hardly a closet liberal. Had he prevailed, he would almost certainly have exterminated his colleagues, but in the first months after Stalin's death, he played the reformer
in a vain effort to cleanse his image. He proposed a mass amnesty of non-
political prisoners, and revealed that the Doctors' Plot, which had allegedly
prepared to assassinate the Soviet leaders, was a fabrication. He condemned
the predominance of Russians and Russian language in non-Russian republics.
Confronted with a flood of East Germans fleeing westward, itself a response
to Walter Ulbricht's hyper-Stalinist rule, Beria apparently toyed with the idea
of abandoning East German Communism, allowing reunification of a neutral
Germany in exchange for substantial Western compensation.[20]

It was not deep policy differences that turned his colleagues against Beria;
although they rejected his East German proposal, they later adopted other
reforms of the sort he had proposed. Their main fear was that he would get
them if they did not get him first. Khrushchev led a conspiracy that culminated

19 Nikita S. Khrushchev, *Khrushchev Remembers: The Last Testament*, trans. Strobe Talbott
(Boston: Little, Brown, 1974), p. 194.
20 See Taubman, *Khrushchev*, pp. 245–8.

in Beria's arrest on 26 June 1953. In December, Beria was executed. With him out of the way, Georgii Malenkov, who had succeeded Stalin as head of the Soviet government, and Khrushchev, who had taken the late dictator's other job as party boss, shared the leadership. The two men complemented each other in other ways: Khrushchev was impulsive; Malenkov was steadier. Khrushchev craved the limelight; Malenkov might have settled for a lesser role. The Khrushchev and Malenkov families had socialised frequently since the 1930s. However, Kremlin political culture bred mutual suspicions, and personal resentments sharpened them.

In August 1953, Malenkov proposed a reduction in stifling agricultural taxes, an increase in procurement prices which the state paid for obligatory collective-farm deliveries, and encouragement of individual peasant plots, which produced much of the nation's vegetables and milk. Khrushchev had wanted to announce the new policy, and, according to Presidium colleague Anastas Mikoyan, he was 'indignant' when Malenkov stole the mantle of reformer. Khrushchev tried to grab it back with a speech of his own to the Central Committee in September, but he 'could neither forget nor forgive' Malenkov for 'getting the glory'.[21] The reforms Malenkov proposed involved land already under cultivation, and as such they would take time to boost output. So Khrushchev's next proposal called for a crash programme to develop the so-called Virgin Lands of Kazakhstan and western Siberia. Over the next few years, as Khrushchev precipitously increased the area brought under new cultivation, his gamble raised overall output far above that of Stalin's last years. But it also became a source of dissension between him and Viacheslav Molotov, and by the early 1960s, Virgin Lands output proved to be disappointing.

For both Khrushchev and Malenkov, a prime obstacle to change was the Stalinist image of the outside world. If capitalist states were irredeemably hostile, and new world war was therefore inevitable, then the USSR could hardly afford the luxury of domestic reform. Malenkov challenged these axioms when he insisted there were 'no contested issues in US–Soviet relations that cannot be solved by peaceful means', and warned that a nuclear war could destroy not just capitalism, but 'world civilization'. Khrushchev himself would eventually adopt similar stances, but seeking to attract the arch-Stalinist Molotov into an anti-Malenkov alliance, he attacked the latter's heresies, charging that Malenkov's alarm about nuclear war had 'confused the comrades'.[22]

---

21 Anastas Mikoian, *Tak bylo: Razmyshleniia o minuvshem* (Moscow: Vagrius, 1999), p. 599.
22 Malenkov cited in Vladislav Zubok and Constantine Pleshakov, *Inside the Kremlin's Cold War: From Stalin to Khrushchev* (Cambridge, Mass.: Harvard University Press, 1996),

After a February 1955 Supreme Soviet session demoted Malenkov from prime minister to minister of electrification, Khrushchev's next target was Molotov. The two men collaborated against Beria and Malenkov, and although they disagreed on Virgin Lands development (Molotov favoured investing in previously cultivated areas instead), Khrushchev at first kept clear of Molotov's foreign-affairs bailiwick. In 1954, however, Khrushchev had pushed for rapprochement with Tito's Yugoslavia, partly to correct what he regarded as one of Stalin's most grievous sins, but also as a way to undermine Molotov, who had been a prime architect of the Moscow–Belgrade split in 1948. When Molotov objected to Khrushchev's trip to Belgrade in May 1955, Khrushchev responded with an assault on Molotov at a July 1955 Central Committee plenum. Although he was replaced as foreign minister in mid-1956, Molotov kept his seat on the Presidium. Like Malenkov, who also remained on the Presidium, Molotov would never forgive Khrushchev, would hold every error he made against him and would take the first opportunity to get even. The turmoil of 1956 gave them that chance.

Khrushchev was not the only Soviet leader who favoured addressing the Stalin issue at the Twentieth Congress. Beria's arrest, investigation and trial had widened the circle of those fully aware of Stalin's crimes. After his execution, requests poured in for reconsideration of high-level purges. By the end of 1955 thousands of political prisoners had returned home, bringing stories of what had gone on in the camps, and in the process adding many of their relatives to those who would support de-Stalinisation. Yet the Gulag system was still functioning, the most famous show trials of the 1930s had not been re-examined, and labour camps and colonies still held hundreds of thousands of inmates. Mikoyan recalled that he pressed Khrushchev to denounce Stalin, saying, 'There has to be a report on what happened, if not to the party as a whole, then to delegates to the first congress after his death. If we don't do that at the congress, and someone else does it sometime before the next congress, then everyone would have a legal right to hold us fully responsible for the crimes that occurred.'[23] On 13 February, the day before the congress convened, the Presidium as a whole decided that Khrushchev would address the subject at a closed session.[24] But Molotov, Kaganovich and Voroshilov had grave reservations, and Molotov, in particular, later insisted on the

pp. 155, 166. Khrushchev's remarks in RGANI (Russian State Archive of Recent History), f. 2, op. 1, d. 127.
23 Mikoian, *Tak bylo*, p. 591.   24 RGANI, f. 2, op. 1, d. 181, lines 2, 4–5.

30 June Central Committee statement that in effect revised Khrushchev's secret speech.

Early in 1957, Khrushchev himself began taking back what he had said. At a New Year's Eve reception for the Soviet elite and the diplomatic corps, he declared that he and his colleagues were all 'Stalinists' in the uncompromising struggle against the class enemy. After the invasion of Hungary sparked protests among Soviet students and intellectuals, Khrushchev approved a new round of arrests.[25] Sensing that his authority was eroding, he launched a counter-offensive which ended up further undermining his position. His February move to abolish most national economic ministries and replace them with regional economic councils antagonised central planners and ministers. His May pledge that the USSR would soon overtake the United States in per capita output of meat, butter and milk, made without being cleared with the Presidium, was ill-conceived. His bullying of writers at a gala spring picnic played into the hands of Kremlin colleagues who had no use for literary liberals but used Khrushchev's boorish behaviour to discredit him.

On 18 June 1957, Khrushchev's colleagues (he later labelled them the 'anti-party group') launched their move to remove him as party leader. Molotov, Malenkov and Kaganovich led the assault, supported by Bulganin, Voroshilov, Mikhail Pervukhin, Maksim Saburov and Dmitrii Shepilov. The first seven of these constituted a majority of the Presidium's full members. They lost when Khrushchev and Mikoyan, backed by several Presidium candidate members and Central Committee secretaries, insisted that the Central Committee itself, in which Khrushchev supporters predominated, decide the issue.

The 'anti-party group' (which did not in fact oppose the party and was so racked by internal divisions as hardly to constitute a group) accused Khrushchev of erratic and irrational personal behaviour, but its deeper reason for attacking him was fear that he would use the Stalin issue against them. He did tar them with Stalinist crimes, both at the June 1957 Presidium meeting, which lasted until 22 June, and the Central Committee plenum, which stretched seven more days after that. After the plenum, most of the plotters lost their positions, Molotov, Malenkov, Kaganovich and Shepilov immediately, the others more slowly so as to obscure how many of them had conspired against Khrushchev. It was only in 1961 that Molotov, Malenkov, Kaganovich and

25 Nikolai A. Barsukov, 'Analiticheskaia zapiska: Pozitsiia poslestalinskogo rukovodstva v otnoshenii politicheskikh repressii 30-x–40-x i nachala 50-x godov', unpublished article, pp. 41–6. Barsukov, 'The Reverse Side of the Thaw', paper delivered at conference on 'New Evidence on Cold War History', Moscow, Jan. 1993, pp. 19–20, 32–6.

Shepilov were expelled from the party, but after 1957 Khrushchev faced no more top-level opposition until his own protégés in the Presidium began to conspire against him in 1964. Until then he was free virtually to dictate domestic and foreign policy and to undermine himself as the result.

## Reforming agriculture

Khrushchev's first priority was agriculture. Yet, in addressing this and other areas, he quickly encountered the ideological limits of the Soviet system, social resistance and bureaucratic behaviour that magnified his own errors. At times Khrushchev sounded like a born-again free marketeer: 'Excuse me for talking to you sharply,' he once told state farm workers, 'but if a capitalist farmer used eight kilos of grain to produce one kilo of meat he'd have to go around without trousers. But around here a state farm director who behaves like that – his trousers are just fine. Why? Because he doesn't have to answer for his own mess; no one even holds it against him.'[26] Yet Khrushchev was still wedded to collectivist agriculture. In 1953 he had defended individual material incentives: 'Only people who do not understand the policy of the party . . . see any danger to the socialist system in the presence of personally owned productive livestock.'[27] But he himself saw such a danger, and so preferred to rely on party mobilisation and exhortation, and on quick fixes of technology and organisation.

Corn had long been grown in the USSR, but Khrushchev took the United States as his model. His American guru when it came to corn, Iowa farmer Roswell Garst, stressed necessary preconditions – hybrid seeds, fertilisation, irrigation, mechanisation, plus use of insecticides and herbicide – but Khrushchev pushed on without them, not just in suitable southern regions but in Siberia and the north as well. Collective farmers resisted planting corn because its cultivation was particularly labour intensive. That drove Khrushchev to press his corn campaign all the harder, while zealous bureaucrats who wanted to please him exacerbated the situation by insisting on extending corn acreage without adequately preparing peasants first.

Despite these and other mistakes (such as the virtually overnight abolition of machine tractor stations, which provided collective farms with machinery and the people to run it), agriculture at first boasted big gains. Between 1953

---

26 Nikita S. Khrushchev, *Stroitel'stvo kommunizma v SSSR i razvitie sel'skogo khoziaistva* (Moscow: Gosudarstvennoe izdatel'stvo politicheskoi literatury, 1962–4), vol. I, p. 170.
27 Speech in Thomas F. Whitney (ed.), *Khrushchev Speaks* (Ann Arbor: University of Michigan Press, 1963), p. 101.

and 1959 farm output rose 8.5 per cent annually and 51 per cent overall. But 1960 proved to be the worst year for agriculture since Stalin's death, and despite optimistic forecasts in the summer of 1961, that autumn's harvest was no better. Khrushchev's response was to resort to more institutional tinkering. In 1962 he moved to abolish district party committees, the fabled *raikomy* which had overseen agriculture for decades, and to replace them with 'territorial production administrations', which added another layer of bureaucracy between the countryside and the capital. That same autumn he proposed dividing the Communist Party into two separate branches, one specialising on agriculture, the other on industry. Ever since Lenin, the party had jealously guarded its monopoly of power by centralising its own ranks. Khrushchev was convinced that local party officials shied away from rural problems, and he was determined to force them to concentrate on feeding the people.

These panaceas also failed. The 1963 harvest was disastrous: only 107.5 million tons compared to 134.7 in 1958; the Virgin Lands produced their smallest crop in years, although the sown area was now 10 million hectares larger than in 1955. As a result Moscow had to buy wheat from the West. 'Father didn't understand what was wrong', his son, Sergei, remembered. 'He grew nervous, became angry, quarreled, looked for culprits and didn't find them. Deep inside he began subconsciously to understand that the problem was not in the details. It was the system itself that didn't work, but he couldn't change his beliefs.'[28]

## Industry and housing

Energising industrial management and rendering it more efficient, another post-Stalinist task, also encountered systemic obstacles. The centralised Soviet planning system, which excelled at 'extensive' heavy industrial development, was not suited for 'intensive' development of an increasingly complex and diversified economy. Yet Soviet leaders of the Khrushchev period were not inclined to pursue proposals for fundamental, structural reform. Although the Moscow-based ministries, which Khrushchev abolished in February 1957, had favoured the narrow needs of their own industries at the expense of local areas in which their plants were located, the *sovnarkhozy* which replaced them fostered localism while losing sight of all-Union interests. That soon led to a process of recentralisation in which the number of regional economic councils was reduced, a new agency called the Supreme Economic Council was created

---

28  Sergei Khrushchev, *Nikita Khrushchev and the Creation of a Superpower*, pp. 700–1.

to co-ordinate them and a series of state committees was formed to duplicate the role of the departed ministries. Nor did Khrushchev's division of the party produce positive industrial results. Although Soviet GNP grew at a rate of 7.1 per cent until 1958, after that it dipped down to 5.4 per cent in 1964, not nearly enough to allow the USSR to 'catch up and overtake' the United States which, although it was growing more slowly, had a much larger economic base.

While the economy did not grow fast enough to satisfy Soviet leaders, the lives of ordinary citizens improved. Wages rose, meat consumption increased, consumer goods like televisions, refrigerators and washing machines became widely available. Stalin's legacy included a dreadful housing crisis: massive overcrowding, armies of young workers living in dormitories, multiple families crowded into communal apartments, with each family occupying one room and all sharing a single kitchen and bathroom. In the Khrushchev period, the annual rate of housing construction nearly doubled. Between 1956 and 1965, about 108 million people moved into new apartments, many of them in standardised five-storey apartment houses built out of prefabricated materials in rapid, assembly-line fashion. Millions were grateful, but Khrushchev encouraged ever higher expectations, particularly by promising, in a speech presenting a new party programme to the Central Committee in June 1961, that the communist utopia itself would be 'just about built' by 1980.[29]

## Culture

Members of the scientific and artistic intelligentsia were a natural constituency for reform. Having been singled out for special suffering under Stalin, many of them enthusiastically welcomed de-Stalinisation. 'I like [Khrushchev] ever so much', gushed Andrei Sakharov in 1956. 'After all, he so differs from Stalin.'[30] However, they were also increasingly dismayed – not only by Khrushchev's continual retreats from anti-Stalinism, but by the incredibly boorish behaviour of a man whom artist Ernst Neizvestny described as 'the most uncultured man I've ever met'.[31] Anticipating just such condescension from intellectuals, Khrushchev dreaded encounters with them even as he craved their respect. They did not realise that their resistance to his calls for ideological discipline challenged not just the party line but his self-esteem. That is why clashes

29 Speech in Nikolai Barsukov, 'Mysli vslukh: zamechaniia N. S. Khrushcheva na proekt tret'ei programmy KPSS', unpublished article, p. 75.
30 Andrei Sakharov, 'Vospominaniia', Znamia 11 (1990): 147.
31 Ernst Neizvestnyi, 'Moi dialog s Khrushchevym', Vremia i my 4 (May 1979): 182.

with recalcitrant intellectuals provoked him into swirls of angry rhetoric, simultaneously offensive and defensive, lashing out at his audience in a violent disconnected way.

What has been called the 'Thaw' began after Stalin's death but picked up momentum after the Twentieth Party Congress. After the long night of Stalinism, with its pogrom against writers and artists, critic Maya Turovskaya recalled, 'the coming of Khrushchev and the Twentieth Congress felt like a great holiday of the soul'.[32] Ilya Ehrenburg's novel *The Thaw* (*Otepel'*) included biting criticism of the ruling elite. In Vladimir Dudintsev's *Not By Bread Alone* (*Ne Khlebom edinym*), an idealistic engineer is thwarted by mindless, heartless officialdom. *Literaturnaia Moskva* (*Literary Moscow*), a literary almanac of prose, poetry, plays, criticism and social commentary published in 1956, included works mocking the official image of 'the new Soviet man'. Mikhail Kalatozov's film, *The Cranes are Flying* (*Letiat zhuravli*), Grigorii Chukhrai's *Ballad of a Soldier* (*Ballada o soldate*) and Sergei Bondarchuk's *Destiny of a Man* (*Sud'ba cheloveka*) took a fresh look at the sacred subject of the Russian soldier in the Second World War (see Plate 22). Concern for the individual, rather than the nation or the state, began to appear in the work of a new generation of film-makers such as Andrei Tarkovsky.

During the World Youth Festival in Moscow in 1957, thousands of young people from around the globe flooded the city, singing and dancing late into the night to the beat of African drums, Scottish bagpipes and jazz bands, cheering open-air poetry readings and carousing along gaily decorated streets. Masses of young Muscovites turned out to meet the foreign guests. The jamboree impressed the world with Moscow's new openness, but the Soviet young people who turned out were even more impressed with Western popular culture. After the Twenty-Second Congress in October 1961, at which Khrushchev launched another attack on Stalin, the Thaw gathered more momentum. Prompted by Khrushchev, the Presidium approved publication of Aleksandr Solzhenitsyn's *One Day in the Life of Ivan Denisovich* (*Odin den' Ivana Denisovicha*), and on 21 October 1962, *Pravda* published Evgenii Evtushenko's poem, 'The Heirs of Stalin' (*Nasledniki Stalina*), which had been circulating privately without hope of publication.

However, Khrushchev recoiled at the very process of liberalisation which he encouraged. When Boris Pasternak allowed his novel, *Doctor Zhivago*, to be published in the West, Khrushchev ordered his Komsomol chief to 'work over' Pasternak, telling him to compare the great poet unfavourably to a pig

32 Author's interview with Maya Turovskaya, March 1995, Amherst, Massachusetts.

who 'never makes a mess where it eats and sleeps', and to invite 'this internal emigrant' to become 'a real emigrant and go to his capitalist paradise'.[33] After his overthrow in 1964, Khrushchev finally read *Doctor Zhivago*. 'We shouldn't have banned it', he said. 'I should have read it myself. There's nothing anti-Soviet in it.'[34]

As Khrushchev's troubles mounted, he sought new ways to motivate and inspire the Soviet people while attacking old traditions like religion, which in his view was distracting them from the task of building Communism. 'Within twenty years', he told the Central Committee in presenting the new party programme in June 1961, the USSR would 'steadily win victory after victory' in economic competition with the United States. The Soviet countryside would blossom with 'such an array of appurtenances – apartment houses equipped with all modern conveniences, enterprises providing consumer services, cultural and medical facilities – that in the end the rural population will enjoy conditions of life comparable to those found in cities'.[35] Khrushchev was a true believer, impatient for the day when his fellow citizens, who had sacrificed so much for so long, would at last enjoy the good life.

Although religion had always been anathema to the Bolsheviks, Stalin had eased religious persecution, if only to unite the populace for the war effort, and to impress his wartime Western allies. It was Khrushchev who mounted an all-out assault that reached its peak in 1961: anti-religious agitation was intensified, taxes on religious activity increased, churches and monasteries closed, with the result that the number of Orthodox parishes dropped from more than 15,000 in 1951 to less than 8,000 in 1963. Khrushchev's anti-religion campaign was a price he paid for de-Stalinisation – in the sense that it was popular with Stalinist ideologues like Central Committee secretary Mikhail Suslov – but he may also have seen it as a form of de-Stalinisation, in that it reversed Stalin's compromise with religion and returned to Lenin's more militant approach.

Khrushchev's approach to the 'nationality question' fitted the pattern of trying to remove the Stalinist stain from socialism while at the same time bringing the USSR closer to utopia itself. He allowed small peoples of the North Caucasus, such as Chechens, Ingush and Balkars, to return from their Stalinist exile, although he did not invite the Crimean Tatars to return to Crimea. His

33 Vladimir Semichastnyi, 'Ia by spravilsia s liuboi rabotoi', interview by K. Svetitskii and S. Sokolov, *Ogonek* 24 (1989): 24.
34 Sergei N. Khrushchev, *Khrushchev on Khrushchev: An Inside Account of the Man and his Era*, trans. William Taubman (Boston: Little, Brown, 1990), p. 208.
35 Speech in Barsukov, 'Mysli vslukh', pp. 75–7.

efforts to decentralise political power by transferring some of it to regional leaders strengthened the position of non-Russian nationalities, some of whom were to break away from Russia three decades later. If Khrushchev did not fear that outcome, that was because he could not imagine it. He counted on the various peoples of the USSR to fuse together into a single Soviet nation. He took the borders between Soviet republics so lightly that in 1954 he transferred the Russian-dominated Crimea from the Russian Federation to Ukraine to celebrate the 300th anniversary of a treaty linking Ukraine with Russia.[36]

## The Soviet bloc

Having had little exposure to the outside world (and almost none to the Great Powers) during the first fifty years of his life, Khrushchev was hardly ready to direct Soviet foreign policy, but initially at least, he did not have to. With Beria and Malenkov taking the lead in designing overall strategy, and Molotov conducting diplomacy, Khrushchev did not attend to world affairs until 1954, at which point his focus was on relations with other Communist states. Between 1953 and 1956 Moscow agreed to build, or aid in the construction of, some 205 Chinese factories and plants valued at about $2 billion, with a large proportion of the cost financed with Soviet credits, all when the Russians themselves were suffering shortages. But Khrushchev's failure to consult the Chinese before unmasking Stalin, and his handling of the Polish and Hungarian crises later in 1956, alienated Mao. Khrushchev hoped to play the benevolent tutor to the Chinese leader, so it was personally devastating when Mao began condescending to him, not just denying Khrushchev the satisfaction of outdoing Stalin in Sino-Soviet relations, but returning Khrushchev to his former role of an upstart mortified by a new master.

When Mao came to Moscow to celebrate the fortieth anniversary of the Bolshevik revolution in the autumn of 1957, Khrushchev showered him with attention and hospitality. But Mao practically oozed dissatisfaction and condescension in return.[37] The years 1958 and 1959 brought a sharp downturn in Sino-Soviet relations which two Khrushchev trips to Beijing not only failed to reverse, but actually deepened. The trigger for the dispute was a Soviet request for long-wave radio stations, necessary for communicating with Soviet submarines, on Chinese territory, and a proposal for a joint submarine fleet, both of which, Mao feared, would deepen Chinese dependence on the USSR.

---

36 See Ronald Grigor Suny, *The Soviet Experiment: Russia, the USSR, and the Successor States* (New York: Oxford University Press, 1998), pp. 410–11.

37 See Taubman, *Khrushchev*, pp. 341–2.

Sino-Soviet differences extended to Chinese ideological boasting about the communes they were constructing, the Sino-Indian clash in 1959 and Moscow's pursuit of détente with the United States, all overlaid with growing personal animosity between the two leaders. Alone with Soviet colleagues in a Beijing reception room that must have been bugged, Khrushchev likened Mao in 1959 to old 'galoshes', a term that is colloquial for condoms in Chinese as well as Russian. Mao saw himself as a 'bullfighter', one of his interpreters recalled, and 'Khrushchev as the bull'.[38]

In 1960, Khrushchev suddenly decided to pull all Soviet advisers, of whom there were more than a thousand, out of China, and to tear up hundreds of contracts and scrap hundreds of co-operative projects, a radical step that not only wounded the Chinese but deprived Moscow of the chance to gather invaluable intelligence. Although the two sides adopted an uneasy truce the next year, the dispute flared up again when Zhou En-Lai walked out of the Twenty-Second Party Congress in Moscow, further intensified when Beijing characterised Khrushchev's handling of the Cuban Missile Crisis as 'adventurism' followed by 'capitulationism', and deteriorated beyond repair when the two parties started exchanging propaganda barrages, involving other Communist Parties in their conflict, and even quarrelling about potentially explosive Sino-Soviet border disputes.

Khrushchev's 1955 journey to Belgrade reflected a new, post-Stalinist formula for holding together the Soviet bloc: to tolerate a modicum of diversity and domestic autonomy, to emphasise ideological and political bonds and reinforce economic and political ties, and to weave all this together with Khrushchev's own personal involvement. Yugoslav leader Josip Tito was eager for reconciliation, but on his own terms: his aim was to reform the Communist camp, not buttress it; to preserve Yugoslav independence, including ties with the West, not restrict it. Having broken with Stalin before Khrushchev did, Tito was proud and touchy. Khrushchev needed Yugoslav concessions to prove he was right to conciliate Belgrade, whereas Tito was determined to postpone the closer party-to-party ties that Khrushchev sought until Stalinism was dead and buried in the USSR. As a result, although Soviet–Yugoslav tensions never again plummeted to their post-1948 depths, they did not become as close as Khrushchev wanted either.

The year 1955 also marked the post-Stalin leadership's first major venture into the Third World. For Stalin, who was famous for concentrating on countries of great geopolitical significance, and for cutting his losses in those

38 Recollections of former Soviet and Chinese officials and interpreters at 1997 Symposium on Sino-Soviet Relations and the Cold War, Beijing, 1997.

he could not hope to control, the developing world had been a sideshow. Khrushchev, in contrast, welcomed the prospect of revolutions that might bring the USSR new allies, and courted neutrals whom Stalin had disdained. In October 1955, he and Bulganin undertook a lengthy tour of India, Burma and Afghanistan. In February 1960, he revisited these three while adding Indonesia to his itinerary. Egypt received a visit from him in May 1964. In the meantime, he devoted considerable attention to the Congo, supporting the short-lived, left-leaning presidency of Patrice Lumumba, and of course Cuba, whose fiery new leader seemed intent on turning his island into a Soviet ally only 150 kilometres from Florida (see Plate 17). None of these ventures, however, brought anything like the dividends Khrushchev hoped for.

## East–West relations

While China and Yugoslavia could challenge the USSR, and the Third World tempted it, the United States could destroy it. The centrepiece of Khrushchev's diplomacy was a campaign for what a later era would label détente. As he saw it, reducing Cold War tensions could undermine Western resistance to Communist gains, tempt capitalists to increase East–West trade and project a more appealing image to the world, while at the same time allowing Soviet energies and resources, which had previously been devoted to the military, to be shifted to civilian uses.

Khrushchev's first major achievement was the Austrian State Treaty, signed in May 1955, under which Soviet occupation forces pulled out in return for an Austrian declaration of neutrality. Next came the four-power Geneva summit conference in July 1955. The main issues discussed at Geneva (the German question, European security and disarmament) offered no room for compromise, but Khrushchev's main impression from the meeting, that 'our enemies probably feared us as much as we feared them', would soon encourage him to practise nuclear blackmail so as to play on Western fears.[39] When Israel attacked Egypt, with British and French support, in October 1956, Premier Bulganin ominously asked Prime Minister Anthony Eden, 'What situation would Britain find itself in if she were attacked by stronger states possessing all kinds of modern destructive weapons?' Later, after a Suez ceasefire was agreed to, Khrushchev claimed it was the 'direct result' of this Soviet warning.[40] In fact, it was American rather than Soviet pressure that forced Egypt's attackers

---

39 Nikita S. Khrushchev, *Khrushchev Remembers*, p. 400.
40 Veljko Mićunović, *Moscow Diary*, trans. David Floyd (Garden City, N.Y.: Doubleday, 1980), p. 148.

to cease fire, for Soviet threats had been issued only after that outcome was no longer in doubt.

The Soviet invasion of Hungary, which coincided with the Suez crisis, put Khrushchev's détente campaign on hold. He resumed it in 1957 and 1958, including a series of hints that he would welcome an invitation to come to the United States for informal talks with President Eisenhower, but got little response.[41] In the meantime, the German situation worsened, with East Germany lagging behind West Germany economically, and steadily losing skilled workers and professionals to the West, and with West Germany seeming likely to gain access to nuclear weapons. By the autumn of 1958, recalled Khrushchev's foreign policy adviser, Oleg Troianovskii, West Germany was 'being drawn ever deeper into the Western alliance; the arms race was gathering steam and spreading into outer space; disarmament negotiations were getting nowhere with defence spending weighing more heavily on the economy; East Germany was isolated and under pressure as before; the Soviet Union was being surrounded by American military bases; new military blocs were being set up in Asia and the Middle East'. To make matters worse, Troianovskii remembers 'voices saying ever more distinctly that if the Soviet Union had to choose between the West and China, preference should be given to the latter'.[42]

Khrushchev's answer to practically all these problems was the Berlin ultimatum that he issued in November 1958: If the West did not recognise the German Democratic Republic, Moscow would give it control over access to Berlin, thus abrogating Western rights established in the post-war Potsdam accords. If the West tried forcibly to prevent East Germany from carrying out its new duties, the USSR would fight to defend its ally. This ultimatum was Khrushchev's way of forcing the Western powers into talks, but his 'plan' had several serious flaws. He was not sure exactly where he was going or how to get there. Nor did he realistically assess the obstacles in his way, particularly the shrewdly stubborn German chancellor, Konrad Adenauer, the imperiously disdainful French president, Charles de Gaulle, the well-disposed but insufficiently influential British prime minister, Harold Macmillan and the unexpectedly unreliable President Eisenhower.

The Berlin ultimatum produced a deadlock until Eisenhower suddenly invited Khrushchev to visit the United States in September 1959. While

41 See Taubman, *Khrushchev*, pp. 400–2.
42 Oleg Troianovskii, *Cherez gody i rasstoianiia* (Moscow: Vagrius, 1997), pp. 208–9; Troianovskii, 'The Making of Soviet Foreign Policy', in Taubman, Khrushchev and Gleason (eds.), *Nikita Khrushchev*, p. 216.

Khrushchev's reception was mixed, the very fact of the visit, the first ever by a Soviet leader, was stunning. But the diplomatic results were also mixed: Khrushchev's only concession was to lift the ultimatum, or rather, not to deny that he had done so. All he got in return was Eisenhower's promise to attend Khrushchev's long-sought summit, which neither committed NATO allies to do so, nor ensured that useful accords would ensue if they did.

After a delay of several months (occasioned by French and German resistance), the four-power summit convened in Paris in May 1960, or rather, failed to convene because of a crisis triggered by an American U-2 spy plane's overflight of the USSR on 1 May. Once the summit collapsed, after Eisenhower rejected Khrushchev's demand that he apologise and promise never to do it again, the Soviet leader angrily gave up on Eisenhower and placed his hopes for progress in the next American president, John Kennedy. But their bilateral summit, in June 1961 in Vienna, produced a further stalemate, while convincing Khrushchev that Kennedy was weak. 'What can I tell you?' Khrushchev said to Troianovskii after his first negotiating session with Kennedy. 'This man is very inexperienced, even immature. Compared to him, Eisenhower was a man of intelligence and vision.'[43] So that when the summit was followed by an exchange of threats, which further accelerated the flight of East German refugees, Khrushchev dared to authorise construction of the Berlin wall. The wall was a second-best substitute for the more general German solution he had been seeking since 1958, but Khrushchev was pleasantly surprised when President Kennedy accepted it, an impression that convinced him that he could pressure Kennedy again, thus setting the stage for the most explosive Cold War crisis of all in Cuba.

In the summer and early autumn of 1962, Moscow secretly sent to Cuba missiles capable of reaching the American homeland. The crisis that ensued after Washington discovered the rockets lasted until Khrushchev agreed to remove them in return for an American promise not to invade Cuba, as well as a secret American undertaking to remove US missiles stationed in Turkey. Historians have cited several Soviet motives for the missile deployment: to protect Cuba from an invasion following on from the failed intervention at the Bay of Pigs in April 1961; to rectify what had turned out, despite Khrushchev's atomic boasting, to be a strategic nuclear imbalance in Washington's favour; to prepare a new move to achieve the larger German solution which had eluded Khrushchev since 1958. In fact, all three motives probably played a role, as filtered through the mind of a man who by 1962 was also besieged by

43 Troianovskii, *Cherez gody*, p. 234.

agricultural and other troubles at home and was looking for a Cuban triumph that might solve, or at least overshadow, all these problems.[44]

When the crisis was over, Khrushchev declared a kind of victory: it had proved possible, he told the USSR Supreme Soviet on 12 December, 'to prevent the invasion', and to 'overcome a crisis that threatened thermonuclear war'.[45] 'He made a show of having been brave,' his Presidium colleague Petr Demichev recalled, 'but we could tell by his behaviour, especially by his irritability, that he felt it had been a defeat.'[46]

## Endgame

After the collapse of his Cuban adventure, Khrushchev tried to address foreign and domestic problems whose solutions had so far eluded him, but without the positive momentum which a Cuban triumph would have provided. He did manage to negotiate a treaty with the Americans and the British banning nuclear testing in the air, underwater and in outer space, the most important arms control agreement since the start of the Cold War, as well as one establishing a 'hot line' for communicating during crises. But the assassination of President Kennedy in November 1963 put an end to hopes for another summit which would establish a new Soviet–American relationship, as the Vienna meeting had not.

The division of the Communist Party into agricultural and industrial branches, about which a Soviet journalist heard 'not one good word', but 'only bewilderment and outright rejection' behind the scenes at the November 1962 Central Committee plenum which unanimously adopted the plan, failed to energise agriculture, and neither did a plan for quadrupling Soviet chemical fertiliser production in four years.[47] When drought struck in 1963, the Soviet people found themselves standing in bread queues only two years after having been promised milk and honey without limit in the new party programme. Moscow eventually agreed to purchases of 6.8 million tons of grain from Canada, almost 2 million from the United States, 1.8 million from Australia, even 400,000 from lowly Romania.

As late as November 1962, liberal writers and artists were still pushing the Thaw forward. The publication that month of Solzhenitsyn's *One Day in the Life of Ivan Denisovich* seemed a harbinger of more gains to come. Rather than

44 Taubman, *Khrushchev*, pp. 529–41.      45 *Pravda*, 13 Dec. 1962, p. 2.
46 Author's interview with Petr Demichev, Aug. 1993, Moscow.
47 Nikolai Barsukov, 'The Rise to Power', in Taubman, Khrushchev and Gleason, *Nikita Khrushchev*, p. 62.

sparking a sustained burst of *glasnost'*, however, November marked a retreat as cultural conservatives, who had been waiting for an opportunity to move against their intelligentsia foes, cleverly exploited Khrushchev's sour post-Cuba mood. By moving a small exhibit of avant-garde art from an artist's studio to the huge Manezh exhibition hall, and then inviting Khrushchev to view it, they provoked him into an obscenity-laced tirade against the offending artists. He tried to revert to his more open-minded, benevolent self by inviting some four hundred intellectuals to a lavish reception on 17 December, but instead he erupted again in a vituperative attack on unorthodox art. Yet a third surreal session with artists, writers and others followed in March 1963 at the Kremlin. As in December, Khrushchev's aides had prepared a balanced, moderate text, but once again, one of them recalled, Khrushchev 'did not use a word of it'.[48] Instead he lambasted writers like Andrei Voznesenskii and Vasilii Aksionov so wildly as to raise doubts as to whether Khrushchev himself was in his right mind.

Khrushchev's reformist impulses were not entirely finished. In his last years in office, proposals for radical economic reform developed by Khar'kov economist Evsei Liberman started appearing in *Pravda*. During a visit to Yugoslavia in the late summer of 1963 Khrushchev displayed interest in Yugoslav 'self-management' based on 'workers' councils'. But he was no longer capable of implementing radical new ideas even if he had adopted them. By this time he was also ignoring his Presidium colleagues, having withdrawn instead into an inner circle of aides and advisers. Nor was he listening to high-ranking military men. They had previously been alienated by three rounds of deep cuts in Soviet armed forces which Khrushchev had ordered between 1955 and 1957, in 1958 and again in 1960 (approximately 2 million, 300,000 and another 1.2 million respectively), and by his decision to rely on nuclear missiles rather than conventional forces. Their leader hardly hid his assumption that he knew military affairs better than they did, and they could not conceal their resentment.[49]

## Overthrow

The Soviet Union possessed no established procedure for transferring power. After Lenin and Stalin died, the battle to succeed them had shaken the political system. The trouble with a fixed term for the leader, and a regularised process

48 Author's interview with Georgii Kunitsyn, August 1993, Moscow.
49 See Taubman, *Khrushchev*, pp. 378–81, 618.

for replacing him, was that they would limit the leader himself. Even hand-picking a successor was problematic since an ambitious heir apparent could threaten his sponsor. The way to reduce that danger was to have two rival heirs share power, but that might ensure a destructive contest later on.

In 1962, Frol Kozlov, the former Leningrad party boss who had become Khrushchev's de facto deputy, led the field of future contenders. But Kozlov began to alienate his boss in early 1963 (less because he led a conservative faction as some Western Kremlinologists surmised at the time, and more as a result of what seemed like personal arrogance to Khrushchev), and later that year he suffered a major stroke that removed him from the running. In 1964 Khrushchev in effect elevated Leonid Brezhnev to deputy party leader, but at the same time he made Ukrainian party boss Nikolai Podgornyi a rival heir apparent. Beginning in the spring of that year, the two men put aside their mutual suspicions and combined in a conspiracy against Khrushchev. In March, they began approaching fellow Presidium members about remov-ing Khrushchev. In June Brezhnev went so far as briefly to consider having Khrushchev arrested as he returned from a foreign trip. Instead, he and his fellow plotters spent the summer and early autumn secretly securing the sup-port of Central Committee members so as to avoid the fate of Khrushchev's rivals in 1957.

On the evening of 12 October, Brezhnev telephoned Khrushchev, who was vacationing in Pitsunda on the Black Sea coast, and asked him to return to the Kremlin for a meeting of the Presidium. After initially objecting, Khrushchev agreed to fly back the next day. When he arrived, his Presidium colleagues took turns indicting him for destructive policies both foreign and domestic, ranging from agriculture to Berlin and Cuba. Most of all they emphasised his personal shortcomings: his impulsiveness and explosiveness, his unilateral, arbitrary leadership, his megalomania. After a brief and halting attempt to defend himself, Khrushchev offered no resistance. No one defended him, not even his closest associate on the Presidium Anastas Mikoyan, who was willing to have Khrushchev stay on as prime minister while stepping down as party leader.[50]

The next day the Presidium granted Khrushchev's 'request' to retire 'in connection with his advanced age and deterioration of his health'. Khrushchev lived under what amounted to house arrest for the next seven years. He died on 11 September 1971.

50 See ibid., pp. 10–16.

## Legacy

As a man and a leader, Khrushchev was as two-sided as the Ernst Neizvestny monument, consisting of intersecting slabs of white marble and black granite, which stands at his grave site: Stalinist-turned-de-Staliniser, complicit in great evil yet also the author of much good. The legacy of the Khrushchev period as a whole is more unambiguously positive. Mikhail Gorbachev and his reformist colleagues came to political maturity at the time and remembered its greater openness with optimism and nostalgia. Gorbachev's generation, he once said, considered itself 'children of the Twentieth Congress', and regarded the task of renewing what Khrushchev had begun as 'our obligation'.[51] And in this they had the support of a much wider circle of *shestidesiatniki* (men and women of the 1960s) who had long dreamed of recapturing the hope and idealism of their youth. As Lyudmilla Alexseyeva, who later became a leading dissident, recalled, Khrushchev's speech denouncing Stalin 'put an end to our lonely questioning of the Soviet system. Young men and women began to lose their fear of sharing views, knowledge, beliefs, questions. Every night we gathered in cramped apartments to recite poetry, read "unofficial" prose, and swap stories that, taken together, yielded a realistic picture of what was going on in our country. That was the time of our awakening.'[52]

Beneath the surface, the reforms of the Khrushchev period, awkward and erratic though they were, allowed a nascent civil society to take shape where Stalinism had created a desert. It would take nearly three decades for the seeds that were planted under Khrushchev to bear fruit, but eventually they did.

---

51 *N. S. Khrushchev (1894–1971)*, p. 6.
52 Lyudmilla Alexseyeva and Paul Goldberg, *The Thaw Generation: Coming of Age in the Post-Stalin Era* (Pittsburgh: Pittsburgh University Press, 1993), p. 4.

# II

# The Brezhnev era

STEPHEN E. HANSON

The nature of Soviet politics and society during Leonid Brezhnev's tenure as General Secretary of the CPSU from 1964 to 1982 has until recently remained a comparatively unexplored scholarly topic. Among historians, the turn towards social history 'from below' that has so greatly enriched our understanding of the Soviet regime under Lenin and Stalin has yet to inspire a parallel re-examination of everyday life in the Brezhnev era.[1] Meanwhile, political scientists, with few exceptions, have given up study of the pre-Gorbachev Soviet Union to focus on more contemporary themes.[2] Compounding these gaps within history and political science are continuing problems of documentation. Although the records of Central Committee plenums and many materials from the CPSU General Department archive from the period are now available, and important archival materials are also accessible in many of the former Soviet republics, other key historical archives from the period – in particular, the so-called Presidential Archive containing documentation of meetings of the CPSU Politburo and Secretariat, as well as the KGB, military and foreign intelligence archives – remain largely closed to independent scholars. Post-1991 memoirs by Soviet high officials and their relatives – although many do cover the Brezhnev era – have tended to emphasise developments during the

The author would like to thank Mariana Markova and Toregeldi Tuleubayev for research assistance, and Mark Kramer for invaluable feedback on an earlier draft of this chapter.

1 Useful accounts of everyday life in the Brezhnev era can be found in Caroline Humphrey, *Karl Marx Collective: Economy, Society, and Religion in a Siberian Collective Farm* (Cambridge and New York: Cambridge University Press, 1983); Victor Zaslavsky, *The Neo-Stalinist State: Class, Ethnicity and Consensus in Soviet Society* (Armonk, N.Y.: M. E. Sharpe, 1982); and John Bushnell, *Moscow Graffiti: Language and Subculture* (Boston: Unwin Hyman, 1990).

2 The exceptions include Steven Solnick, *Stealing the State: Control and Collapse in Soviet Institutions* (Cambridge, Mass.: Harvard University Press, 1998); Brian Taylor, *Politics and the Russian Army* (Cambridge and New York: Cambridge University Press, 2003); Matthew Evangelista, *Unarmed Forces: The Transnational Movement to End the Cold War* (Ithaca, N.Y.: Cornell University Press, 2002); and Yitzhak M. Brudny, *Reinventing Russia: Russian Nationalism and the Collapse of the Soviet State, 1953–1991* (Cambridge, Mass.: Harvard University Press, 1998).

Gorbachev period. And despite the presence of millions of eyewitnesses still living in the former Soviet Union today, transcriptions of oral histories of the period are practically non-existent.[3] Finally, scholars also lack a consensual analytical framework for making sense of Brezhnevism as a regime type. Indeed, several contradictory labels for the period continue to coexist in both popular and scholarly accounts.

One influential approach derived from the totalitarian model of Soviet politics saw the Brezhnev era as one of 'oligarchical petrification', in which the essential institutional features of the Stalinist system were left intact with only minor adjustments, leading to a long-term pattern of political immobilism and economic decline.[4] This interpretation later got an unanticipated boost from Mikhail Gorbachev, whose ritual invocation of the phrase 'era of stagnation' (*era zastoia*) to describe the pre-*perestroika* period has greatly influenced the historical accounts of both Russian and Western scholars. Brezhnev and his elite are thus remembered as a group of sick old men, with dozens of meaningless medals pinned to their chests, presiding over an increasingly dysfunctional military-industrial complex.

Of course, this image captures some important part of the reality of the Brezhnev regime, particularly in its later stages. Yet it is instructive to remember that perhaps the most influential school of thought among Soviet specialists during the Brezhnev era itself, the modernisation approach, saw the post-1964 period very differently – as marking the triumph of rationality and development over the 'Utopian' impulses of Lenin, Stalin and Khrushchev.[5] Scholars

3 Memoirs that cover the Brezhnev era in some depth include Luba Brezhneva, *The World I Left Behind: Pieces of a Past* (New York: Random House, 1995); Anatoly Dobrynin, *In Confidence: Moscow's Ambassador to America's Six Cold War Presidents (1962–1986)* (New York: Random House, 1995); Mikhail Gorbachev, *Zhizn' i reformy* (Moscow: Novosti, 1995); Evgenii I. Chazov, *Zdorov'e i vlast': vospominaniia 'kremlevskogo vracha'* (Moscow: Novosti, 1992); Vladimir Medvedev, *Chelovek za spinoi* (Moskva: 'Russlit', 1994); Aleksandr I.Yakovlev, *Omut pamiati* (Moscow: Vagrius, 2000); Viktor V. Grishin, *Ot Khrushcheva do Gorbacheva: politicheskie portrety piati gensekov i A.N. Kosygina: memuary* (Moscow: ASPOL, 1996); A. S. Cherniaev, *Moia zhizn' i moie vremya* (Moscow: Mezhdunarodnye otnosheniia, 1995); and Andrei M. Aleksandrov-Agentov, *Ot Kollontai do Gorbacheva: vospominaniia diplomata, sovetnika A. A. Gromyko, pomoshchnika L. I. Brezhneva, Iu. V. Andropova, K. U. Chernenko i M. S. Gorbacheva* (Moscow: Mezhdunarodnye Otnosheniia, 1994). For a pathbreaking study of the late Soviet era based on eyewitness accounts, see Alexei Yurchak, *Everything was Forever, until it was No More: The Last Soviet Generation* (Princeton; Princeton University Press, 2006).

4 Zbigniew Brzezinski, 'The Soviet Political System: Transformation or Degeneration?', in Brzezinski (ed.), *Dilemmas of Change in Soviet Politics* (New York: Columbia University Press, 1969), pp. 1–34.

5 Richard Lowenthal, 'Development vs. Utopia in Communist Policy', in Chalmers Johnson (ed.), *Change in Communist Systems* (Stanford, Calif: Stanford University Press, 1970), pp. 33–116.

in this camp competed in the 1970s to apply a whole series of models drawn from the comparative politics of developed countries to help interpret the new, seemingly more stable and successful, Soviet reality. Jerry Hough saw the Brezhnev regime as a 'return to normalcy' in which an 'institutional pluralism' similar to that characterising Western democracies had taken shape; Soviet regional party secretaries, in his view, functioned very much like 'prefects' in modern France, using personal initiative to solve local economic problems in an essentially rational manner.[6] Skilling and Griffiths edited a widely read volume of essays applying Western 'interest group theory' to the Soviet case.[7] George Breslauer termed the Brezhnev regime a form of 'welfare-state authoritarianism'; Valerie Bunce and John Nichols, while sharing Breslauer's emphasis on the Soviet regime's social welfare orientation, preferred the term 'corporatism'.[8]

Given that most of these models were designed to explain what was then seen as the relative stability and success of Brezhnevism, it is easy to discount their conceptual utility now. Yet modernisation theory, with its emphasis on understanding how Soviet institutions actually functioned, captured something important about the Brezhnev era that is too often lost in post-1991 analyses. This was, after all, a leadership that endured for nearly two decades, during which time the USSR was universally acknowledged to be second only to the United States in world power and influence. Brezhnev himself initially impressed his subordinates as far more competent and reasonable than his predecessor Khrushchev – at least until his illness in the later 1970s, when as one high-ranking party official put it, 'the Brezhnev we used to know had become completely different'.[9] In the popular mythology of contemporary Russia, too, Brezhnev's reign is often seen as a 'golden era' of stability and consumer abundance, when Soviet achievements in space exploration and sport were the envy of the world. Such nostalgia cannot substitute for objective

6 Jerry F. Hough, *The Soviet Prefects: The Local Party Organs in Industrial Decisionmaking* (Cambridge, Mass.: Harvard University Press, 1969); *The Soviet Union and Social Science Theory* (Cambridge, Mass.: Harvard University Press, 1977); Jerry F. Hough and Merle Fainsod, *How the Soviet Union is Governed* (Cambridge, Mass.: Harvard University Press, 1979).
7 H. Gordon Skilling and Franklyn Griffiths (eds.), *Interest Groups in Soviet Politics* (Princeton: Princeton University Press, 1971).
8 George Breslauer, 'On the Adaptability of Soviet Welfare-State Authoritarianism', in Erik P. Hoffmann and Robin F. Laird (eds.), *The Soviet Polity in the Modern World* (New York: Aldine, 1984); Valerie Bunce and John M. Nichols III, 'Soviet Politics in the Brezhnev Era: "Pluralism" or "Corporatism"?', in Donald R. Kelley (ed.), *Soviet Politics in the Brezhnev Era* (New York: Praeger, 1980), pp. 1–26.
9 Ziia Nuriev, quoted in Evan Mawdsley and Stephen White, *The Soviet Elite from Lenin to Gorbachev: The Central Committee and its Members, 1917–1991* (Oxford and New York: Oxford University Press, 2000), p. 182.

historical understanding of the period, but its persistence and power among many who lived through the period must nonetheless be explained.

In short, the Brezhnev era was somehow both a time of modernisation, stability and accomplishment and a time of decay, stagnation and corruption. How are we to make sense of this paradox? This chapter will argue that the complex nature of Brezhnevism must be understood through a deeper analysis of the underlying ideological project of the Soviet regime from 1917 to 1991. The totalitarian model interpreted the Bolshevik revolution as a power grab by revolutionary extremists whose ultimate goal was total control over society; Brezhnevism from this perspective was simply a degenerate form of one-party rule in the same basic mould as its Stalinist predecessor. The modernisation approach saw the Bolshevik revolution as containing the seeds of a breakthrough towards 'modern' forms of political and economic organisation; Brezhnevism (like Khrushchevism before it and Gorbachevism after it) was thus seen as another stage in the inevitable emergence of a more fully 'rational' Soviet system. Neither school, however, fully grasped the ways in which Lenin, Stalin and their successors interpreted their own historical mission: as the creation of a new, socialist way of life, meant to make modernity itself 'revolutionary'. Lenin's invention of the Bolshevik 'party of professional revolutionaries', and Stalin's imposition of a socio-economic system built upon 'planned heroism', can both be understood as institutional expressions of this attempted synthesis of modern bureaucratic rationality and charismatic transcendence of social constraints.[10]

With Brezhnev's emergence as party leader in 1964, power passed to the first generation to come of age under Soviet rule, whose promotions within the party and state apparatuses were a direct reward for their fidelity to this project and success in implementing it (including their willingness to arrest and kill millions of supposed 'enemies' of socialism).[11] Five decades after the Bolshevik revolution, however, the revolutionary dream of transforming the nature of modernity itself was increasingly giving way to complacency among the older generation – who had already proven their credentials as socialist heroes – and to cynicism on the part of many Soviet young people, for whom ideological rhetoric about perfecting socialism sounded increasingly irrelevant and embarrassing. Given the regime's professed goal of making modernity

---

10  Ken Jowitt, *New World Disorder: The Leninist Extinction* (Berkeley: University of California Press, 1992); Stephen E. Hanson, *Time and Revolution: Marxism and the Design of Soviet Institutions* (Chapel Hill: University of North Carolina Press, 1997).

11  Sheila Fitzpatrick, 'Stalin and the Making of a New Elite, 1928–1939', *Slavic Review* 38, 3 (1979); Mawdsley and White, *The Soviet Elite from Lenin to Gorbachev*.

revolutionary, the Soviet 'way of life' began to lose coherence precisely when it had become successful enough to be ordinary.

The Brezhnev period can be best understood, then, as marking the routinisation of Soviet revolutionary modernity. Such an interpretation helps to explain why those focusing on the Soviet regime's professed revolutionary aspirations (including Gorbachev) have tended to see Brezhnevism as a bankrupt and stagnant compromise, while those focusing on the USSR's efforts at modernisation could see genuine progress in Soviet administration during the 1960s and 1970s. At the same time, such an approach highlights a further paradox: namely, as maintaining 'revolutionary modernity' in a stable society proved to be increasingly oxymoronic in practice, 'neo-traditional' forms of political and economic organisation, based on personal networks and communal identities, emerged as the dominant principle governing everyday Soviet social life – simultaneously subverting the regime's aspirations to generate a new type of communist personality and its efforts to maintain bureaucratic rationality in order to catch up and overtake the capitalist West.[12]

In what follows, I will first trace the emergence of the Brezhnev leadership's 'orthodox Leninist' consensus from 1964 through the Soviet invasion of Czechoslovakia in 1968. I will then examine the 'social contract' that emerged as the basis of social stability in the years of 'high Brezhnevism' from 1969 to 1976, noting the important role of détente in Brezhnev's political economy. Finally, I will discuss the decline of Brezhnevism from 1976 to 1982, both domestically and internationally.

## The rejection of Khrushchevism

Brezhnev's brand of orthodox Leninism was a direct reaction to the perceived failures of his predecessor as General Secretary, Nikita Khrushchev. Khrushchev's strategy for building a socialist culture while rejecting Stalinist methods of coercion involved perpetual heroic campaigns designed to rekindle the revolutionary enthusiasm of ordinary Soviet citizens – the Virgin Lands campaign, the meat and milk campaign, the chemicals campaign and so on. But in each case, the initial promise of such campaigns had given way to declining production, extraordinary economic waste and exhausted human and natural resources. In international affairs, too, Khrushchev's style was impulsive and often reckless, as his nuclear brinkmanship during the Berlin Crisis and the Cuban Missile Crisis demonstrated. Even the 1956 'Secret Speech'

---

12 Ken Jowitt, *New World Disorder*, pp. 121–58.

to the Twentieth Party Congress denouncing Stalin's cult of personality and terror launched a campaign of sorts – one that endeavoured to replace the charisma of Stalin with a new mythology of the 'heroism of the Soviet people'. In sum, Khrushchev appeared to take his famous promise to achieve full communism 'in the main' by 1980 quite literally, even if this meant adopting increasingly unrealistic domestic and foreign policies. By the early 1960s, resistance to Khrushchev's leadership had spread to every major Soviet institution, from the military-industrial complex to the party itself. Khrushchev's last-ditch attempts to maintain his power and programme – introducing the rotation of party cadres to new positions every five years, dividing the party apparatus into parallel hierarchies for agriculture and industry, and encouraging rank-and-file party members to criticise party officials – thus only hastened the bloodless coup against him in October 1964.

To a great extent, a common loathing of Khrushchev's chaotic style of rule was the key factor uniting the 'collective leadership' proclaimed by the inner core of the Brezhnev Politburo after 1964 (consisting of chairman of the USSR Council of Ministers Aleksei Kosygin, chief CPSU ideologist Mikhail Suslov, chairman of the Presidium of the Supreme Soviet Nikolai Podgornyi, deputy chairman of the RSFSR Central Committee Andrei Kirilenko and of course Brezhnev himself). These five men had had remarkably similar life experiences: all were born between 1902 and 1906, all had been promoted rapidly as party and state officials during Stalin's First Five-Year Plan, and all had reached positions of leadership in large part due to Stalin's Great Terror in the mid-1930s, which eliminated the Old Bolsheviks previously making up the Soviet elite. Khrushchev was born in 1894 and was thus old enough to remember life under tsarism; he had still judged revolutionary success in terms of the transformational ethos of the Bolshevik revolution and civil war. The Brezhnev generation, by contrast, were barely teenagers in 1917, and their careers as mature revolutionaries were coterminous with, and essentially due to, the rise of Stalin. Khrushchev's struggles to reach pure communism must have struck them as quite irrelevant to the real issues facing the USSR: above all, the need for domestic and international consolidation of the Soviet system, which in their view had proven almost miraculously successful. For the Brezhnev generation, the post-Stalin USSR already represented a successful 'dictatorship of the proletariat' – after all, all of them had been Leninist proletarians in the 1920s, and now they ruled the second most powerful country in the world!

Thus the first two years of the Brezhnev era witnessed the rapid reversal of just about every institutional and cultural initiative undertaken during the preceding decade. The bifurcation of the party apparatus was repealed, plans for rotation in office were quietly dropped and a new policy of 'trust in cadres' was loudly proclaimed. In September 1965, Khrushchev's experiment with *sovnarkhozy* (regional economic councils), which had been designed to spur local economic initiative, was abandoned in favour of a return to hierarchical control over production by planning officials and state ministries. At the Twenty-Third Party Congress in March 1966, the 'Presidium' was renamed the Politburo, and the 'First Secretary' was renamed the General Secretary, restoring the standard terminology of the Stalin era.

These institutional measures were accompanied by a parallel rejection of Khrushchev's optimistic revolutionary timetable. References to the 'full-scale construction of Communism' and to the 'party' and 'state of the whole people' in the Soviet press became more and more infrequent; the USSR was instead now described as being at the stage of 'developed socialism' – a formulation that focused attention on the successes of the past rather than the promise of the future. Khrushchev was no longer referred to by name, either; Khrushchevian policies were instead ritually dismissed as 'hare-brained scheming' and 'voluntarism', so that the history of the CPSU leadership now oddly appeared to skip directly from Lenin to Brezhnev.

Finally, consistent with the neo-Stalinist ideological tendencies cited above, the Brezhnev Politburo sharply curtailed the tentative moves towards free cultural expression that had been permitted as part of Khrushchev's 'Thaw'. De-Stalinisation came to a halt, although the major party newspapers continued to avoid positive references to Stalin himself; in more conservative publications, however, a return to hagiographic treatments of Stalin's leadership became increasingly common.[13] The works of openly critical writers such as Aleksandr Solzhenitsyn – who had already run afoul of Khrushchev after the publication of his Gulag memoir *One Day in the Life of Ivan Denisovich* – were now entirely suppressed. In August 1965, authors Andrei Siniavskii and Iulii Daniel', whose *samizdat* writings had been smuggled out of the USSR and published in the West, were arrested, and in February 1966 both were sentenced to years of forced labour. A petition signed by prominent cultural figures such as Solzhenitsyn and Soviet physicist Andrei Sakharov on behalf of Siniavskii and Daniel' led only to greater repression of the emerging dissident movement, with new articles inserted into the Soviet Criminal Code in December 1966 to outlaw the dissemination of 'anti-Soviet slander' in any form. Dissent on issues of nationality and ethnicity was also dealt with ruthlessly; activists bold enough to fight publicly for such causes were arrested or committed to mental

13 Viktor Zaslavsky, *The Neo-Stalinist State*, pp. 3–21.

asylums.[14] The power of the KGB, placed under the leadership of hard-liner Iurii Andropov in 1967, grew precipitously.

In sum, the new collective leadership of the CPSU had, within a few years, undone all of the major reforms of the Khrushchev period – except, of course, for his decision to abandon mass terror as an instrument of rule. But there were still significant divisions of opinion within the Politburo concerning precisely how to manage future socialist economic development, both in the USSR and in the Soviet bloc. In particular, Prime Minister Kosygin, who had been a textile factory manager in the 1920s and whose entire career had involved work in light industry, began to articulate a strategy for economic change with striking similarities to that promoted by Prime Minister Georgii Malenkov in the early post-Stalin period. Like Malenkov, Kosygin declared that so-called 'Group B' industries – those producing consumer goods – should receive greater priority relative to 'Group A' heavy industries. Under Kosygin's sponsorship, Soviet economists began to argue for a more decentralised style of management, in which enterprise directors would orient themselves towards attaining profits rather than simply trying to meet and exceed gross output targets set by Gosplan. Innovations such as the 'Shchekino experiment' – in which factories capable of achieving planning targets with fewer personnel were allowed to shed excess labour and split the total wage funds among the remaining workers – were introduced, albeit only on a small scale. At the same time, Kosygin argued for lower levels of investment in unproductive collective farms in order to finance the expansion of light industry.[15]

The greater leeway in the Soviet academic press given to arguments for economic decentralisation inspired similar calls for reform in the East European Soviet bloc states, whose economies had never fully recovered from the ravages of the Stalinist occupation. In Hungary, where the 'goulash communism' of János Kádár had already reversed much of the hypercentralisation of the Stalin period, the 'New Economic Mechanism' formally adopted on 1 January 1968 successfully enacted most of the Kosygin reform programme. In Czechoslovakia, however, similar arguments for reform eventually sparked an escalating rebellion against Leninist rule, especially after the removal of the hard-line Stalinist party leader Antonín Novotný and his replacement by Alexander Dubček in February 1968. The resulting 'Prague Spring' saw censorship

14 Lyudmilla Alexseyeva, *Soviet Dissent: Contemporary Movements for National, Religious, and Human Rights* (Middletown, Conn.: Wesleyan University Press, 1985).

15 Alec Nove, *An Economic History of the USSR, 1917–1991*, 3rd edn (London and New York: Penguin, 1992); George Breslauer, *Khrushchev and Brezhnev as Leaders: Building Authority in Soviet Politics* (London and Boston: Allen and Unwin, 1982).

abolished, restrictions on freedom of assembly lifted and clear moves towards a multi-party system. Ukrainian party leader Petro Shelest' began to warn of the potential spread of secessionist sentiment from Ukrainian populations in Czechoslovakia to the USSR itself. By the summer, the entire Soviet Politburo – including Kosygin himself – became convinced that the Prague Spring represented a grave threat to socialism.[16] On 20 August 1968, the Soviet Union, along with Warsaw Pact allies Poland, Hungary, Bulgaria and East Germany, sent 500,000 troops to crush the Czechoslovak rebellion (see Plate 19). Within the USSR, the 'Kosygin reforms' were largely dropped from public discussion.

The crushing of the Prague Spring marked the full consolidation of Brezhnevian orthodoxy: a reassertion of Leninist principles of hierarchical authority and obedience, Stalinist principles of central planning and a neo-Stalinist cultural policy based upon an insistence on fidelity to ideological dogma and severe repression of all forms of dissent. The Politburo's public announcement that 'socialist internationalism' required Soviet armed intervention wherever a threat of 'capitalist restoration' appeared in the Soviet bloc – the 'Brezhnev Doctrine', as it later became known both in the USSR and in the West – made Brezhnevian orthodoxy mandatory for Eastern Europe as well. By and large, the 'little Brezhnevs' in the Soviet satellite states enforced this 'really existing socialism' for the rest of the Brezhnev era.

## Brezhnev's social contract

By 1969, Brezhnev had clearly emerged as the *primus inter pares* in the Politburo. The tentative experimentation with economic decentralisation sponsored by Kosygin gave way to a renewed emphasis on the authority of the planners and industrial ministries in overseeing production. Although increased consumer goods production remained a formal priority for Soviet planners, the military-industrial complex received the lion's share of investment.[17] In agriculture, tentative efforts to improve productivity through new incentive systems were halted, replaced by Brezhnev's preferred policy of investing massively in new farm equipment and fertiliser while increasing agricultural subsidies. In 1967, Kosygin could still represent the USSR at the Glassboro summit meeting with

---

16 Mark Kramer, 'The Czechoslovak Crisis and the Brezhnev Doctrine', in Carole Fink, Philipp Gassert and Detlef Junker (eds.), *1968: The World Transformed* (Cambridge and New York: Cambridge University Press, 1998), pp. 111–71; Kieran Williams, 'New Sources on Soviet Decision Making during the 1968 Czechoslovak Crisis', *Europe–Asia Studies* 48, 3 (May 1996).

17 Clifford Gaddy, *The Price of the Past: Russia's Struggle with the Legacy of a Militarized Economy* (Washington: Brookings Institution Press, 1996).

United States President Lyndon Johnson; by 1969, Brezhnev had taken full personal control over Soviet foreign policy as well. When the Twenty-Fourth Party Congress of the CPSU in 1971 ratified the expansion of the Central Committee to include forty-six new Brezhnev appointees, and Brezhnev allies Dinmukhamed Kunaev, Viktor Grishin, Fedor Kulakov and Vladimir Shcherbitskii (replacing Shelest') were subsequently added to the Politburo, the General Secretary's dominance over the Soviet political system was complete.

The political and social stability of the Brezhnev regime at its height has led numerous scholars to conclude that it rested on a sort of 'social contract' between the party and the Soviet population.[18] This terminology has its weaknesses, overemphasising the degree of social consensus underlying the Soviet dictatorship; Ken Jowitt, for example, has argued that Brezhnevism operated more like a 'protection racket' than a social contract.[19] Still, as widespread post-Soviet nostalgia for the Brezhnev era suggests, important features of Brezhnevian stability really did appeal to broad strata within Soviet society. Moreover, the unravelling of the Brezhnev social contract under Gorbachev played an important role in delegitimating the Soviet regime altogether.

The Brezhnev social contract consisted of five key elements: job security, low prices for basic goods, the de facto toleration of a thriving 'second economy', a limited form of social mobility and the creation of tightly controlled spheres for the expression of non-Russian national identities.[20] The first of these elements, job security, had been an implicit component of the Stalinist economic system ever since its foundation in the 1930s; the declaration that the capitalist problem of unemployment had been 'solved' by socialism was an important and perennial Soviet propaganda theme. But such 'security' was undercut under Stalin by constant blood purges affecting all ranks of society, and under Khrushchev by general institutional turbulence. After the roll-back of the Kosygin reforms, however, politically loyal Soviet citizens in every occupational category could expect to keep their positions – except in cases of extreme incompetence or insubordination – until retirement or death. The Stalinist system's emphasis on plan target fulfilment as the sole criterion of success meant that enterprise managers had every incentive to hoard labour, and no incentive at all to use it efficiently. Wage funds were set in proportion to an enterprise's workforce, so it made sense for enterprise managers

18 Linda J. Cook, *The Soviet Social Contract and Why it Failed: Welfare Policy and Workers' Politics from Brezhnev to Yeltsin* (Cambridge, Mass.: Harvard University Press, 1993); Peter Hauslohner, 'Gorbachev's Social Contract', *Soviet Economy* 3, 1 (1987): 54–89.
19 Ken Jowitt, *New World Disorder*, p. 227.
20 The analysis in this section closely follows that of Zaslavsky, *Neo-Stalinist State*.

to hire hundreds of otherwise superfluous workers to use in periods of 'storming' to fulfil the plan. Typical industrial enterprises were thus absurdly overstaffed by comparison with their Western competitors. Brezhnev's agricultural subsidies, meanwhile, perpetuated a system of inefficient collective farms supporting millions of unproductive farmers. Meanwhile, due to the 'trust in cadres' policy, party and state bureaucrats themselves no longer had to worry about being replaced either.

The Brezhnev regime's subsidies for basic foodstuffs, housing and welfare provision eliminated another long-standing source of worry for ordinary Soviet citizens. After Khrushchev's 1962 price hikes touched off riots in Novocherkassk that were put down by military force, the prices of such staples as baked goods and dairy products were left unchanged for more than two decades.[21] Health care, public transportation, education and a variety of recreational and vacation facilities were available at nominal cost to most Soviet citizens. Rent and domestic utilities, too, were provided practically free of charge to most Soviet workers. Of course, such artificially low prices inevitably led to massive shortages and queues for a wide range of products. Everyday goods such as underwear or toilet paper sometimes disappeared for months at a time. Meanwhile, luxuries such as automobiles remained far beyond the means of typical Soviet families. Still, for a Soviet population whose parents and grandparents made up an impoverished peasantry just a generation earlier, the cheap consumer and welfare goods of the Brezhnev era were a genuine achievement.

Moreover, Brezhnev's de facto toleration of a vast, informal 'second economy' during the 1970s helped further ameliorate the rigidities of the Soviet planning system.[22] The free market for agricultural products grown on peasants' private plots, officially legalised under Stalin, continued to supply the majority of fresh fruits and vegetables consumed by Soviet citizens. Technically illegal 'free markets', however, existed for almost all other consumer goods as well. Workers in Soviet retail stores sold the choicest items from their inventories after official store hours at inflated prices or bartered them for other hard-to-obtain products. Soviet youth, especially those who had learned some English or German, bargained with Western tourists for otherwise unattainable designer blue jeans, popular cassette tapes and portable appliances. Special stores open only to the Soviet elite sold a wider variety of

21 Samuel H. Baron, *Bloody Sunday in the Soviet Union: Novocherkassk, 1962* (Stanford, Calif.: Stanford University Press, 2001); Cook, *The Soviet Social Contract*, p. 85.
22 Gregory Grossman, 'The "Second Economy" of the USSR', *Problems of Communism*, 26 (Sept.–Oct. 1977): 25–40.

consumer products; these supplies, too, often found their way onto the black market. Although cheap vodka sold by the state alcohol monopoly was one of the mainstays of the official Brezhnev economy, myriad forms of *samogon* (moonshine) were always available in the informal sector as well. The importance of personal connections – or *blat*, in the Soviet slang – for success in the second economy could be exasperating, even humiliating, for less well-positioned consumers. Yet such informal economic networks also played an important role in humanising life under orthodox Leninist dictatorship.

A fourth component of the Brezhnev social contract was a limited form of social mobility – one hardly comparable to the massive promotions of Soviet workers during the Stalinist 1930s, yet still important in channelling the energies of Soviet citizens in officially approved directions.[23] With the routinisation of the Stalinist socio-economic system in the 1970s, a kind of locational hierarchy had emerged in Soviet society, and ambitious young people did their best to climb it. At the bottom of this hierarchy were the *kolkhozy* and *sovkhozy*; Soviet villages often still resembled Russian villages of the nineteenth century, with unpaved roads, few modern conveniences and only rudimentary welfare services. Unsurprisingly, young and energetic individuals did their utmost to escape agricultural employment; as a result, Soviet collective farms were left with an ageing, largely unskilled population.[24] Somewhat better life chances were available in 'open cities', that is, those with few or no residency controls. Here, a wider variety of consumer goods was available, greater educational opportunities existed and everyday life was a little less boring. Higher up the locational hierarchy were the 'closed cities' – those where political, scientific and / or military activities supposedly demanded a higher degree of control over residency and where, not coincidentally, one found the greatest variety of consumer goods and most exciting cultural opportunities. Access to such cities, for those outside the elite, depended upon proven loyalty to the CPSU, high levels of educational attainment, marriage to a city resident and / or good personal connections with, or bribes of, Communist Party officials. At the very apex of the residential hierarchy stood Leningrad and especially Moscow, where the standard of living was famously and dramatically better than anywhere else in the USSR, and where dependable access to foreign tourists meant an even greater range of consumer products on the black market. Desire to live in Moscow was so great, in fact, that a substantial population of workers allowed into the city on temporary work permits – the so-called *limitchiki* – stayed there

---

23 Viktor Zaslavsky, *The Neo-Stalinist State*, pp. 130–64.
24 Alexander Yanov, *The Drama of the Soviet 1960s: A Lost Reform* (Berkeley: Institute of International Studies, University of California, 1984).

as illegal migrants, working in the shadow economy and constantly trying to avoid expulsion. Thus, the Brezhnev economy, though intensely frustrating for skilled workers assigned to jobs that were often poorly compensated and outside their areas of specialisation, still offered opportunities to 'work the system' so as to ascend the residential hierarchy. Those who had managed to attain 'higher' spots in this hierarchy had a substantial incentive not to challenge the system that maintained it.

The final element of the Brezhnev social contract involved the institutionalisation of what Terry Martin has called the 'affirmative action empire' – that is, the creation of opportunities for career advancement and limited cultural expression by non-Russian minorities within the USSR.[25] As scholars such as Ronald Suny, Rogers Brubaker and Yuri Slezkine have shown, Soviet nationalities policy in the Brezhnev era, while officially still committed to the creation of a supranational 'Soviet man', nevertheless inadvertently reinforced national and ethnic identities in the Soviet republics and in other administrative units formally designated for titular ethnic groups.[26] Of course, it would be a mistake to overstate the degree of freedom for national self-expression in a regime that brutally suppressed all forms of independent political organisation. Russian (and to a lesser extent Ukrainian) dominance over the USSR as a whole was ensured through such policies as appointing ethnic Russians as the 'second secretaries' of every Soviet republic, requiring Russian-language education for all elite positions and forcing non-Russians in the Soviet army to serve outside their home republics.[27] Still, Soviet federalism under Brezhnev, however circumscribed, had significant cultural effects. Each of the Soviet republics had the right to provide education in the titular language and – with the important exception of the Russian Soviet Federative Socialist Republic (RSFSR) itself – its own Academy of Sciences and its own republican party and state bureaucracies. National identities were inscribed as well on the obligatory Soviet passport, which essentialised and made hereditary the official

25 Terry Martin, *An Affirmative Action Empire: Nations and Nationalism in the Soviet Union, 1923–1939* (Ithaca, N.Y.: Cornell University Press, 2001).
26 Ronald Grigor Suny, *The Revenge of the Past: Nationalism, Revolution, and the Collapse of the Soviet Union* (Stanford, Calif.: Stanford University Press, 1993); Rogers Brubaker, *Nationalism Reframed: Nationhood and the National Question in the New Europe* (Cambridge and New York: Cambridge University Press, 1996); Yuri Slezkine, 'The USSR as a Communal Apartment, or How a Socialist State Promoted Ethnic Particularism', *Slavic Review* 53, 2 (Summer 1994): 414–52.
27 Seweryn Bialer, *Stalin's Successors: Leadership, Stability, and Change in the Soviet Union* (Cambridge and New York: Cambridge University Press, 1980); Gail Lapidus, 'Ethnonationalism and Political Stability: The Soviet Case', *World Politics* 36, 4 (July 1984): 555–80; Victor Zaslavsky, *Neo-Stalinist State*, pp. 91–129.

ethnic identities established and enforced under Leninist rule. Propaganda endeavouring to show the 'friendship of the peoples' of the USSR highlighted the regime's support for 'indigenous' folk music and art, museums of (regime-approved) republican history and ethnography and official national literatures. At the same time, the 'trust in cadres' strategy allowed powerful ethnic networks to become politically entrenched in such places as Kazakhstan under Kunaev, Ukraine under Shcherbitskii, Uzbekistan under Sharaf Rashidov and Azerbaijan under Heidar Aliev.[28] Taken as a whole, such policies fostered nationalist subcultures that would later, under Gorbachev, generate significant resistance to Soviet rule.

Taken together, these five elements of the Brezhnev social contract – job security, low prices, the second economy, limited social mobility and controlled avenues for ethnic self-expression – allowed ordinary Soviet citizens to eke out something like a 'normal life', even within the confines of CPSU dictatorship. Still, the quiescence of much of the Soviet population in this period did not suffice to generate any deeper allegiance to the regime's numbing official Marxist-Leninist orthodoxy. Instead, the gap between the CPSU leadership's formal proclamations of Soviet revolutionary modernity and the social reality of widespread political apathy and cultural alienation became increasingly glaring. The leadership's attempts to counter such alienation with official propaganda touting continued Soviet achievements in space, sport and science often came across as laughable. Indeed, it is no coincidence that the 1970s were the heyday of the classic Soviet joke (*anekdot*).

## The rise and decline of détente

The immobilism and social alienation of the Brezhnev era has given rise to the mistaken idea that Brezhnev himself did not care about his reputation as a revolutionary. Even concerning domestic policy, this view is not entirely accurate, as Brezhnev's promotion throughout the 1970s of the Baikal–Amur Railway (BAM) project as a 'heroic' and 'Stakhanovite' endeavour demonstrates.[29] But it was largely in the realm of foreign policy that Brezhnev hoped to prove his credentials as a visionary and dynamic Leninist leader in his own right. The policies known in the West as 'détente' – in Russian, *razriadka*, or

28 John P. Willerton, *Patronage and Politics in the USSR* (Cambridge and New York: Cambridge University Press, 1992).
29 Christopher J. Ward, 'Selling the "Project of the Century": Perceptions of the Baikal–Amur Mainline Railway (BAM) in the Soviet Press, 1974–1984', *Canadian Slavonic Papers* 43, 1 (Mar. 2001): 75–95.

'relaxation' of international tension – were, contrary to the perceptions of some contemporary Western analysts and policy makers, a major constitutive element of Brezhnev's orthodox Leninist strategy for consolidating 'developed socialism' in the USSR. Brezhnev's 'Peace Programme', announced in 1969, was predicated above all on the notion that the Soviet Union had now achieved military 'parity' with the United States – and, at least in terms of the number of long-range nuclear missiles each superpower now had pointed at the other side, this was in fact the case. Given this 'shift in the correlation of forces' towards the Soviet Union, Brezhnev argued, the United States and other main 'imperialist' powers could now be expected to make pragmatic concessions to Soviet interests.

Beyond this simple – but symbolically, extremely important – claim to equal superpower status, Brezhnev's vision of détente also represented an alternative, less politically dangerous strategy for addressing the rigidities of the Soviet economy. Grain purchases from world markets could ameliorate the continuing deficiencies of collectivised agriculture, while West European, Asian and US capitalists could be lured to invest in the development of Soviet industry and, especially, Siberian oil and gas reserves. Brezhnev could, and did, justify this approach to the capitalist powers as classically 'Leninist', just as in the early Soviet period, the imperialists would sell the Soviet Union the rope that would eventually be used to hang them. Given the 'inevitability' of new capitalist 'crises' – and indeed, the 1970s saw plenty of these, from the first oil crisis of 1973 to the 'stagflation' of the latter part of the decade – the USSR had no need to fear that increased economic ties with the West would undermine socialism in the long run.

Remarkably, just a year after the Soviet invasion of Czechoslovakia, and in a period when tensions with Maoist China erupted in bloody border clashes in the Russian Far East, Brezhnev found a receptive audience for his Peace Programme in both Western Europe and the United States. In West Germany, the 1969 election of Social Democrat Willy Brandt as chancellor led within a few years to treaties ratifying the borders of the German Democratic Republic and settling the legal status of East Berlin, as well as significant new West German purchases of Soviet natural gas. Better relations with Western Europe led, in turn, to new loans by Western banks and governments to various Eastern European socialist states, temporarily easing the growing economic problems in the Soviet trade bloc, the COMECON. At the same time, in the United States, new President Richard Nixon and his chief foreign policy adviser Henry Kissinger saw improved relations with the Soviet Union as the key to extrication of US forces from Vietnam (and their strategic opening to Communist China was designed in large part to increase American leverage over Soviet decision makers in pursuit of this goal). On both sides, too, a genuine desire to curtail the escalating, expensive US–Soviet arms race provided another significant reason for compromise. Nixon's visit to Moscow in May 1972 led to the signing of several US–Soviet treaties, including the Anti-Ballistic Missile Treaty limiting each side to a single missile defence system, the SALT I treaty setting ceilings on nuclear missile deployments and a three-year agreement authorising American grain sales to the Soviet Union. Follow-up visits by Brezhnev to the United States in 1973, and by Nixon to the USSR in 1974, symbolically furthered the momentum of détente while negotiations on the stricter regulation of nuclear missiles outlined in the SALT II treaty continued.

The early promise of détente, however, soon began to fade amidst a series of international challenges. Domestic opponents of rapprochement with Brezhnev's USSR in both the United States and Western Europe increasingly demanded an end to the denial of basic human liberties by the Soviet regime as the price for further co-operation; the April 1973 promotion to the Polit-buro of hard-liners such as Iurii Andropov of the KGB, Minister of Defence Andrei Grechko, and Foreign Minister Andrei Gromyko hardly inspired con-fidence in this respect. Nixon became embroiled in the Watergate scandal, drastically weakening his control over United States policy. Soviet support for Egypt during the surprise October 1973 attack against Israel nearly brought the two superpowers into direct military conflict. In the US Congress, Senator Henry M. Jackson argued successfully for the Jackson–Vanik amendment to the 1974 bill granting most-favoured nation status to the USSR, tying Soviet MFN status to freedom of emigration for Jews and other persecuted citizens; the Soviet leadership abrogated the US–Soviet Trade Agreement in response. Even the crowning achievement of Soviet diplomacy in these years – the 1975 signing of the Helsinki Accords legally ratifying the new borders of the East-ern European states conquered and reconfigured by Stalin during the Second World War – was attained only with accompanying Soviet pledges to uphold United Nations human rights standards in the socialist bloc. Dissident groups throughout the region quickly organised 'Helsinki watch groups' to monitor Soviet compliance with the Helsinki human rights accords, further exposing the repressive nature of Leninist politics and the hypocrisy of Soviet foreign policy.[30]

A final asymmetry between the Soviet and Western understanding of détente became clear by the mid-1970s, this time connected to foreign policy

---

30 Daniel C. Thomas, *The Helsinki Effect: International Norms, Human Rights, and the Demise of Communism* (Princeton: Princeton University Press, 2001).

towards the Third World. Kissinger had assumed that the 'linkage' between Soviet trade agreements and Soviet foreign policy would induce the Brezhnev Politburo to cut back its growing engagements in post-colonial Africa, Asia, the Middle East and Latin America. Meanwhile, Brezhnev assumed that the shift of the correlation of forces in the USSR's favour would allow enhanced Soviet support for 'national liberation movements' and 'countries of socialist orientation'. A clash between these two interpretations, at some point, was inevitable. The close relations between newly unified Communist Vietnam and the Soviet Union after the US withdrawal were one sign of this. But the issue broke into the open when, in November 1975, the USSR helped to transport 11,800 Cuban troops to support the Marxist-Leninist MPLA faction in recently decolonised Angola against the US-supported UNITA coalition. Later Soviet interventions in Mozambique, Ethiopia and Yemen would lead to a growing disillusionment with détente throughout the West.

## Brezhnevism in decline, 1976–82

As the Twenty-Fifth Party Congress of the CPSU opened in Moscow in February 1976, Brezhnev thus faced serious challenges to his orthodox Leninist domestic and foreign-policy strategy. Despite the initial success of détente, the boom in Western investment and trade anticipated by the Soviet leadership had failed to materialise. Loans to East European states were beginning to generate significant levels of indebtedness, further increasing their economies' dependence on Soviet energy subsidies. Soviet agriculture remained a disaster, despite ever-increasing levels of state support; widespread drought in 1975 had led to a particularly poor harvest. Meanwhile, the absolute job security of the Brezhnev social contract was quickly eroding work incentives in Soviet industrial enterprises. Declining labour productivity and worker alienation became a subject of serious and intense discussion among Soviet social scientists.[31]

Yet Brezhnev introduced no major institutional reforms in response to these growing challenges. His four-hour speech to the Twenty-Fifth Party Congress reiterated many of the General Secretary's favourite themes, including the priority of military and heavy industrial production, the importance of international support for 'countries of socialist orientation' such as Vietnam and Cuba, the need for new investments in agriculture and, above all, the imperative of

31 John Bushnell, 'Urban Leisure Culture in Post-Stalin Russia: Stability as a Social Problem?', in Terry L. Thompson and Richard Sheldon (eds.), *Soviet Society and Culture: Essays in Honor of Vera S. Dunham* (Boulder, Colo.: Westview Press, 1988).

rapid development of Siberian energy reserves.[32] Notwithstanding the banality of Brezhnev's presentation, those assembled greeted it with paroxysms of praise. Rashidov called Brezhnev 'the most outstanding and most influential political figure of contemporary times', and Petras Griškevičius, the first secretary of the Lithuanian Central Committee, rhapsodised that he was 'a man with a great soul in whom is embodied all the best qualities of Man in capital letters'.[33] Shortly after the congress, Brezhnev received the rank of Marshal in the Red Army. In 1977, the politically ambitious Podgornyi was purged as chairman of the USSR Supreme Soviet, and Brezhnev took over this position as well. Formally, Brezhnev's power and authority appeared stronger than ever.

But Brezhnev's growing personality cult and multiple new formal titles masked a rapid, serious decline in his health. As early as 1973, in fact, Brezhnev had begun to experience periods of incapacitation due to arteriosclerosis, and, in part to reduce the stress of his tense relationship with his family, he became dangerously addicted to sedatives.[34] By 1975, the General Secretary's poor health became an increasingly public problem; he frequently had to be given powerful stimulants before official meetings with foreign leaders, his speech became slurred and he appeared increasingly disoriented.[35] As the 1970s wore on, Brezhnev spent more and more time relaxing with a handful of intimate friends at the Zavidovo hunting lodge, and less and less time at work. By the early 1980s, Politburo meetings often lasted only fifteen or twenty minutes, so as not to wear out the General Secretary.[36]

Nor was Brezhnev the only leading figure within the CPSU leadership to be experiencing health problems. The inevitable result of the 'trust in cadres' policy, by the late 1970s, was an ageing and increasingly infirm Central Committee and Politburo. Yet the Brezhnev generation remained largely unwilling to cede real power to younger party members. Minister of Defence Grechko died in 1976 at the age of seventy-three, and was replaced by the sixty-eight–year-old Dmitrii Ustinov. Brezhnev's sidekick from his days in Moldavia, Konstantin Chernenko, was promoted to full Politburo membership in 1978 at the age of sixty-seven. Aleksei Kosygin died in 1980 at the age of seventy-six, and was replaced by the seventy-five-year-old Brezhnev crony Tikhonov.

32 Breslauer, *Khrushchev and Brezhnev as Leaders*; Thane Gustafson, *Crisis amidst Plenty: The Politics of Soviet Energy under Brezhnev and Gorbachev* (Princeton: Princeton University Press, 1989).
33 Quoted in Hough and Fainsod, *How the Soviet Union is Governed*, p. 260.
34 Chazov, *Zdorov'e i vlast'*, pp. 115–17.
35 Dmitri Volkogonov, *Sem' vozhdei: galereia liderov SSSR*, vol. II (Moscow: Novosti, 1995), p. 68.
36 Gorbachev, *Zhizn' i reformy*, p. 202; Aleksandrov-Agentov, *Ot Kollontai do Gorbacheva*, pp. 271–3.

The only major exception to this pattern was the selection of the forty-seven-year-old Mikhail Gorbachev to replace Fedor Kulakov as Central Committee Secretary with responsibilities for agriculture upon the latter's death in 1978.

The senescence of the CPSU leadership only symbolised the larger sclerosis of the Soviet system as a whole during the last years of Brezhnev's reign. By the late 1970s, the combination of continued wasteful state spending on defence and agriculture, the declining productivity of Soviet labour, and the lack of serious investment in emerging new production technologies combined to reduce Soviet GDP growth nearly to zero. The Soviet economy had become increasingly reliant on revenues from oil and gas exports, and thus falling world energy prices in the early 1980s led to an incipient crisis. At the same time, the Brezhnev social contract began to unravel. Job security meant little in a society where, as the famous joke put it, 'we pretend to work and they pretend to pay us'. Officially cheap prices for consumer goods, similarly, were moot when even basic necessities were often unavailable in state stores; the profits made by 'speculators' who sold such goods on the black market now seemed especially unfair and exploitative. The limited social mobility that had allowed at least some ambitious Soviet citizens to rise through the hierarchy of *kolkhozy*, open cities and closed cities was transformed into an increasingly frustrating zero-sum competition for favoured positions – most of them, seemingly, obtained through high-level connections or outright corruption. Finally, with rising popular frustration at Soviet stagnation and decline, expressions of nationality and ethnic identity were harder to contain within approved limits. Within the RSFSR itself, the perception of Soviet affirmative action in favour of non-Russians had given rise to a strong Russian nationalist subculture that paradoxically resented the treatment of the Slavic population by what was ostensibly a Russia-dominated empire. In some of its manifestations, this new Russian nationalism shaded over into anti-Semitic fascism.[37]

In sum, Brezhnevian stability, by the end of the 1970s, had degenerated into a 'neo-traditional' form of rule in which Marxism-Leninism became a set of quasi-religious rituals, party bureaucracy was corrupted by pervasive patron–client networks and covert resistance to formal Soviet priorities spread throughout society.[38] Social pathologies such as alcoholism and worker absenteeism became overwhelming problems; even among Soviet émigrés, who

37 Brudny, *Reinventing Russia.*     38 Jowitt, *New World Disorder*, pp. 121–58.

might have been expected to come predominantly from better-managed enterprises, nearly 40 per cent of those from blue-collar backgrounds surveyed reported that alcoholism and absenteeism had been problems at their place of work 'nearly all the time' or 'often'.[39]

Along with these growing signs of internal crisis, the Brezhnev elite at the turn of the decade faced a whole series of new challenges on the international arena: the turmoil caused by revolution and civil war in Afghanistan, the rise of the Solidarity movement in Poland, and the election of the staunch anti-Communists Margaret Thatcher in Britain and Ronald Reagan in the United States. Taken together, these challenges simultaneously undermined the USSR's international prestige in the Third World, in Europe and in the United States, at a time when the CPSU leadership as a whole was far too old and sick to respond with any vigour or creativity.

The Soviet invasion of Afghanistan in December 1979 was the single most disastrous decision of the Brezhnev leadership. The origins of this intervention lay in Afghanistan's April 1978 Communist revolution by the People's Democratic Party of Afghanistan (PDPA) against the dictator Mohammad Daoud – with whom the USSR had previously had quite good relations. By the summer, the Khalq faction of Nur Mohammad Taraki and Hafizullah Amin had manoeuvred to defeat the rival, more moderate Parcham faction, led by Babrak Karmal, and instituted a radical programme to achieve socialism in Afghanistan in short order. Agricultural collectivisation was initiated, Islamic religious leaders were attacked and women were unveiled and brought into schools and universities. In response, mass resistance broke out in much of the country. With the success of Ayatollah Khomeini's revolution in Iran in February 1979, the civil war in Afghanistan appeared even more threatening to the USSR, with the potential to provoke Islamic uprisings throughout Soviet Central Asia and into the Russian heartland itself. In March, several dozen Soviet advisers and their families were killed during anti-Communist uprisings in Herat; Taraki and Amin began to request direct Soviet military support. Still, at this stage, the Soviet leadership remained opposed to direct military intervention in Afghanistan. Then, in September, immediately after a trip to Moscow to meet with Brezhnev, Taraki was killed in a gunfight with Amin's forces, and was replaced by Amin as PDPA leader. With the unpredictable Amin now in charge of Afghanistan, and reports that Chinese, Pakistani, Iranian and

---

39 Paul Gregory, 'Productivity, Slack, and Time Theft in the Soviet Economy', in James Millar (ed.), *Politics, Work, and Daily Life in the USSR: A Survey of Former Soviet Citizens* (Cambridge: Cambridge University Press, 1987), p. 266.

Saudi Arabian arms were flowing to support the mujahedeen forces, pressure on the Soviet Union to intervene increased. Finally, on 12 December 1979, a group of just four Politburo members – Ustinov, Andropov, Gromyko and Brezhnev himself, who was in such poor health that he was barely able to sign his name to the intervention order – made the decision to send 40,000 Soviet troops into Afghanistan.

The results were catastrophic. The Soviet military presence only further inspired the diverse anti-communist forces in Afghanistan to rally against the foreign invader. The USSR's reputation in the post-colonial world as a supporter of 'national liberation movements' was fatally undermined; the US and the USSR now seemed to be two equally imperialistic superpowers. President Jimmy Carter, who had previously tried to sustain the momentum of détente, despite increasing public criticism of the Soviet human rights record and growing scepticism about Soviet intentions in the Third World – in particular, through efforts to convince the US Senate to sign the unratified SALT II treaty – now broke with Brezhnev completely. Carter announced an embargo on further US grain sales to the USSR, the cancellation of American participation in the Moscow Olympic Games of 1980 and a rapid increase in US defence spending. As the Soviet presence in Afghanistan dragged on, morale in the Red Army plummeted. Soviet soldiers, told that they would be fighting American and Chinese troops to defend socialism in Afghanistan, instead found themselves shooting at ordinary Afghan citizens waging a determined guerrilla struggle. Returning Afghan veterans suffered problems of psychological adjustment and drug addiction, contributing to the general social malaise of the late Brezhnev era.

Meanwhile, an equally serious challenge to Soviet legitimacy emerged in Poland with the rise of the Solidarity trade union movement, led by electrician Lech Wałęsa. Poland had long been one of the most restive countries in the Soviet bloc, and due to Soviet compromises with Gomułka made after the uprisings of 1956, it still maintained a private agricultural sector and an independent Catholic Church. The Workers' Defence Committee (KOR), formed in 1976 in the wake of the signing of the Helsinki Accords and party leader Gierek's announced price rises, marked an important advance in the co-ordination of intellectual and working-class opposition to Polish Communism. The election in 1978 of the Polish Pope John Paul II, and his subsequent 1979 visit to greet millions of supporters in Poland, further galvanised social resistance to the regime. When Gierek announced additional price hikes in 1980 in response to the growing economic crisis brought about by severe

Polish indebtedness, the stage was set for a genuinely revolutionary uprising. Strikes in the Lenin Shipyards of Gdańsk soon led to an anti-Communist
protest movement that quickly spread through every sector of the Polish
population.

The rise of Solidarity confronted the Brezhnev elite with a severe ideological
dilemma. How could one make Marxist-Leninist sense of a true workers'
revolution – directed against the Polish United Workers' Party (PUWP)? Were
the Soviet Union to intervene militarily to crush the Solidarity movement, the
notion that Communism represented the fruits of a workers' revolution would
appear utterly farcical. Moreover, the last chances for détente with the West
would surely disappear, and the resulting burden on the Red Army (already
engaged in bloody battles in Afghanistan) might be overwhelming. While
the Brezhnev Politburo debated, Wałęsa and Solidarity fought courageously
to wrest political and economic power away from the PUWP. The ailing
Gierek was replaced as party leader by Stanisław Kania in September 1980;
Kania, unable to stem the tide of Polish opposition, was in turn replaced
by General Wojciech Jaruzelski, head of the Polish army, in October 1981. On
13 December, with full Soviet support, Jaruzelski declared martial law in Poland
and immediately arrested the Solidarity leadership. Over 10,000 Solidarity
activists and supporters were jailed in the following months.[40] Jaruzelski's
repression of Solidarity in Poland, while temporarily successful in quelling the
direct threat of anti-Communist revolution, was nonetheless another major
international defeat for the USSR. The need to rely on armed force to run the
Polish party-state exposed the naked coercion underlying Soviet rule in Eastern
Europe. Nor did there seem to be any long-term solution to the growing
economic burden of the failing East European economies on the Soviet Union.
Solidarity itself continued its activities underground, and Communist control
over Poland remained tenuous.

Jaruzelski's declaration of martial law also further validated the vehement
anti-Communism of the new Western leaders: Margaret Thatcher in Britain
(elected in 1979) and Ronald Reagan in the United States (elected in 1980).
Indeed, the rise of Reagan and Thatcher constituted a third international challenge to Brezhnev's orthodox Leninism. Their passionate anti-Soviet rhetoric
and consistent focus on the sorry Soviet human rights record placed supporters
of co-operation with the USSR in both countries very much on the defensive.

---

40 Mark Kramer, 'Jaruzelski, the Soviet Union, and the Imposition of Martial Law in Poland:
New Light on the Mystery of December 1981', *Cold War International History Project
Bulletin* 11 (Winter 1998): 5–16.

Given the symbolic importance of 'parity' with the United States to Brezhnev's conception of 'developed socialism', Reagan's triumphant patriotism constituted a particularly difficult ideological challenge. Reagan's straightforward declaration that the Soviet Union was 'evil', his absolute dismissal of the idea of détente and his commitment to accelerate the rapid defence build-up of the late Carter years all came as something of a shock to an ageing Politburo that had interpreted the stagflation of the 1970s as presaging the 'final crisis of capitalism'.

Indeed, the Brezhnev Politburo was by this stage in no position to respond effectively to Reagan and Thatcher – or anything else. The CPSU Twenty-Sixth Party Congress in the winter of 1981 had a farcical air; despite the multiple international crises swirling around the Soviet Union, Brezhnev's keynote speech began by proclaiming the triumphant addition to the socialist camp of such powerful new allies as Ethiopia, Mozambique and North Yemen. Brezhnev's personality cult reached new depths of absurdity with the prolonged public celebration of the General Secretary's seventy-fifth birthday in December 1981. Not long afterward, the news broke that Brezhnev's daughter Galina, along with her lover Boris the Gypsy, a circus performer, was involved in running a huge diamond-smuggling ring in which diamonds were shipped abroad while hidden in circus animals. The leak probably came from Andropov in an effort to position himself as an anti-corruption candidate for the succession to Brezhnev; in any case, it highlighted the truly ludicrous forms of corruption taking place at the top levels of the CPSU. Indeed, as Gorbachev later revealed, Galina's husband Iurii Churbanov had, during the same period, been conspiring with Uzbekistan's party boss Rashidov in a scam to pocket billions of roubles by falsely inflating Uzbek cotton production statistics.[41]

The death of staunch Brezhnev supporter Mikhail Suslov on 25 January, at the age of seventy-nine, marked the beginning of an open struggle for Soviet leadership succession, with the Andropov faction generally outmanoeuvring the status quo-oriented Chernenko circle. With both Andropov and Chernenko themselves now already quite unwell, the problem of generational change in the Soviet leadership was obviously still far from resolution. But change was clearly coming, as Brezhnev was growing weaker by the month. In September 1982, in a particularly embarrassing incident, Brezhnev startled an audience in Baku when he spoke for several minutes about the future prospects of 'Afghanistan' – before distraught advisers handed him the

41 For Churbanov's view of events, see Yurii M. Churbanov, *Ia rasskazhu vse, kak bylo* – (Moscow: Nezavisimaia Gazeta, 1992).

correct speech about Azerbaijan.[42] With the help of his doctors, Brezhnev managed to witness one last military parade in honour of the anniversary of the Bolshevik revolution from the top of Lenin's mausoleum. Three days later, on 10 November 1982 he died of a heart attack. On 12 November, Iurii Andropov was announced as the new General Secretary of the CPSU.

42 Stephen White, *Russia's New Politics* (Cambridge and New York: Cambridge University Press, 2000), p. 5.

# 12

# The Gorbachev era

ARCHIE BROWN

No period in peacetime in twentieth-century Russia saw such dramatic change as the years between 1985 and 1991. During this time Russia achieved a greater political freedom than it had ever enjoyed before. The Soviet system moved from being highly authoritarian to essentially pluralist. This process ended with the disintegration of the Soviet state, although even after the fifteen union republics went their separate ways, Russia remained the largest country in the world. The break-up itself was remarkably peaceful, in sharp contrast to the extensive violence that accompanied the separation of the constituent parts of Yugoslavia. Within what was sometimes called 'the outer empire', the Soviet leadership broke with the past by ruling out military intervention when, one after another, the countries of Eastern Europe became non-Communist and independent. The Cold War, which had begun with the Soviet takeover of East-Central Europe, ended definitively in 1989 when the Central and Eastern European states regained their sovereignty.

Before these remarkable changes are examined in greater detail, the immediate prelude to the Gorbachev era deserves attention, albeit briefly. When Leonid Brezhnev died in November 1982 he was succeeded by Iurii Andropov who had earlier in the same year become the second secretary of the Communist Party of the Soviet Union, following Mikhail Suslov. Andropov had spent the previous fifteen years as chairman of the KGB and that organisation had left its mark on him. Immediately prior to running the security police, he had been an anti-Stalinist secretary of the Central Committee. Appointed by Nikita Khrushchev, Andropov gathered around him in the first half of the 1960s a team of highly capable consultants, who were to acquire a justified reputation as 'progressives' in the Brezhnev years and some of whom (especially Georgii Shakhnazarov) were to be among the most influential contributors to the 'New Political Thinking' of the Gorbachev era.

Andropov, once he had become General Secretary, continued the policy of cracking down on any sign of overt dissidence which he had pursued as KGB chief, but somewhat widened the bounds of permissible discussion by speaking more about economic and social problems than the complacent Brezhnev had done. At the same time he demanded greater discipline in the workplace and made examples of some of the more notoriously corrupt officials who had prospered under his predecessor.[1] Although prepared to contemplate reform within strict limits, Andropov showed no sign during his fifteen months at the helm of being willing to engage in fundamental transformation of the Soviet system. Nevertheless, he made an unwitting contribution to that more ambitious task. Andropov was an admirer of the abilities and energy of Mikhail Gorbachev and he accorded him greater responsibility within the Secretariat of the Central Committee. Gorbachev was already a full member of the Politburo as well as a Central Committee secretary when Andropov reached the top post in 1982. At that time, however, his duties were confined to agriculture. Andropov gave him responsibility for the economy as a whole and also brought into the Secretariat two people who were to work with Gorbachev and who, in turn, were to become significant political actors in the *perestroika* (reconstruction) era, Egor Ligachev and Nikolai Ryzhkov.

Andropov had hoped that Gorbachev would be his direct successor and, as illness prevented him from working normally during the second half of his tenure of the top post, he relied increasingly on the younger man. In December 1983 he sent an addendum to a speech at a plenary session of the Central Committee, which he was too ill to attend in person, proposing that Gorbachev be designated to chair the Politburo and lead the Secretariat during his absence. That was a clear attempt to move Gorbachev from the third to the second position in the party hierarchy and to make him, rather than the more senior Konstantin Chernenko, Andropov's successor as party leader. Such a move was anathema to the old guard within the Politburo who, while they were as yet unaware of just how radical a reformer Gorbachev would be, were conscious that he was likely to wield a new broom that could sweep them aside. Chernenko, in consultation with two members of the top leadership team even older than himself, Chairman of the Council of Ministers Nikolai Tikhonov and Defence Minister Dmitrii Ustinov, took the decision to suppress the extra six paragraphs Andropov had added to his earlier text.[2]

When Andropov died in February 1984 he was succeeded by Chernenko, already aged seventy-two and in poor health. Several Politburo members who

1 Luc Duhamel, 'The Last Campaign against Corruption in Soviet Moscow', *Europe–Asia Studies* 56, 2 (Mar. 2004): 187–212.
2 For further detail on this episode, see Archie Brown, *The Gorbachev Factor* (Oxford: Oxford University Press, 1996), pp. 67–9.

were worried about granting Gorbachev the role of Chernenko's heir apparent tried to prevent him acceding to the vacant slot of second secretary. As a compromise it was agreed that Gorbachev would carry out the duties of the second-in-command without formally being recognised as such. This meant that he led the Secretariat and, when Chernenko was indisposed, chaired the Politburo as well. Later Gorbachev was recognised within the party apparatus as the second secretary, and responsibility for ideology and foreign affairs was added to his overlordship of the economy. However, there were many attempts to undermine him and to prevent him becoming the sole serious candidate to succeed Chernenko, whose health was in visible decline. It was, for example, only at the last minute that Gorbachev would be informed that Chernenko was too unwell to chair Politburo meetings.[3] A Central Committee plenum on scientific and technological progress that Gorbachev had been preparing was postponed, and Chernenko himself telephoned Gorbachev on the very eve of a December 1984 conference devoted to ideology to propose the postponement also of that event.[4] Chernenko's own immediate circle, strongly supported by the editor of the party's theoretical journal, *Kommunist* (Richard Kosolapov), was anxious to put a stop to the rise of Gorbachev. It seized upon the text of Gorbachev's speech prepared for the conference which, on the instigation of Chernenko's aides, had been circulated to members of the Politburo and Secretariat.[5] In it Gorbachev had used some of the new vocabulary of politics which would become commonplace during the period of *perestroika* and he attacked as irrelevant to the problems of real life a number of the tired formulae of Soviet doctrine, complaining about the attempt 'to squeeze new phenomena into the Procrustean bed of moribund conceptions'.[6] In a gesture of defiance that was very unusual in the strictly hierarchical Soviet Communist Party, Gorbachev firmly refused to go along with Chernenko's wishes that he change the formulations in his speech to which the General Secretary objected and that he postpone the conference.[7]

The conference had some reverberations in the highest echelons of the CPSU, but Gorbachev was still not clearly perceived to be a reformer. For his elderly colleagues in the Politburo, he was primarily a young man in a hurry.

3 Yegor Ligachev, *Inside Gorbachev's Kremlin*, trans. Catherine A. Fitzpatrick et al. (New York: Pantheon Books, 1993), pp. 53–4.
4 Ibid., pp. 46–8; Vadim Medvedev, *V kommande Gorbacheva* (Moscow: Bylina, 1994), p. 22; and Aleksandr Iakovlev, *Sumerki* (Moscow: Materik, 2003), pp. 369–70. For the text of the speech, see M. S. Gorbachev, *Zhivoe tvorchestvo naroda* (Moscow: Politizdat, 1984).
5 Iakovlev, *Sumerki*, p. 369.
6 Gorbachev, *Zhivoe tvorchestvo naroda*, p. 41.
7 Iakovlev, *Sumerki*, pp. 368–70; Vadim Medvedev, *V komande Gorbacheva*, p. 22.

When Chernenko died on 10 March 1985, this was just a week after Gorbachev's fifty-fourth birthday. He was still the youngest person in the top leadership team. Making full use of the possibilities offered by his position as second secretary, he lost no time in convening a meeting of the Politburo. It was held on the same evening that Chernenko died and it was agreed that the election of a new General Secretary would take place the next day. Less than twenty-four hours after Chernenko's death Gorbachev had not only been nominated as General Secretary by the Politburo but had also been elected to that office by the Central Committee. Both votes were unanimous, for when it came to the point Gorbachev's enemies within the leadership knew that they could not find a viable alternative leader, although both the Moscow party first secretary, Viktor Grishin, and the former Leningrad first secretary, Grigorii Romanov (whom Andropov had brought to Moscow to join the Secretariat of the Central Committee), had aspired to the top post.[8]

## Launching political reform

While there had been an accumulation of problems over several decades, including a secular decline in the rate of economic growth and rising rates of infant mortality and alcoholism, and though the gulf between Soviet rhetoric and reality had led to an increase in popular cynicism, there was no strong pressure from below for change in 1985. The dissident movement had been crushed and the atmosphere was primarily one of political apathy and fatalism. In Brezhnev's time there had been a lot of talk about the 'scientific and technological revolution', but technologically the Soviet Union was lagging far behind the advanced Western countries and not faring well in comparison with the newly industrialising countries of Asia. Moreover, the war in Afghanistan was proving costly and becoming increasingly unpopular. Yet all the mechanisms of political control were firmly in place and it is highly likely that the system – and, accordingly, the Soviet state – could have survived into the twenty-first century had not radical reform, or 'revolution from above', shaken its foundations. Although Gorbachev, with some justification, spoke

8 Gorbachev's allies, among them two people who were later to find themselves on opposite sides of the political struggle, Egor Ligachev and Aleksandr Yakovlev, who in 1984 was still the director of the Institute of World Economy and International Relations (IMEMO), had also not been idle in preparing for Gorbachev's succession to Chernenko. See Iakovlev, *Sumerki*, pp. 459–63; Anatolii Gromyko, *Andrei Gromyko. V labirintakh kremlia: vospominaniia syna* (Moscow: Avtor, 1997), pp. 92–5; Mikhail Gobachev, *Zhizn' i reformy* (Moscow: Novosti, 1995), vol. 1, pp. 266–7; and Ligachev, *Inside Gorbachev's Kremlin*, pp. 72–9.

of the presence of 'pre-crisis phenomena' in the Soviet Union he inherited, it was not so much a case of crisis forcing radical reform as of radical reform generating crisis.[9]

The General Secretary in the post-Stalin era did not have a completely free hand in making appointments to the Politburo and Secretariat of the Central Committee. Generally, Soviet leaders required time to build up their power base, gradually bringing in known supporters who had worked with them in the past. Gorbachev was unusual in that no one whom he promoted to either of the two highest organs of the CPSU was from his native Stavropol' where he had spent the whole of his career in the Komsomol and party between graduating from the Law Faculty of Moscow University in 1955 and being brought to Moscow as a secretary of the Central Committee in 1978.[10] Nevertheless, he used to the full his authority as General Secretary to make radical personnel changes in his first year. Among those who were ousted from the Politburo were Grishin, Romanov and Tikhonov. Ligachev was given full membership of the Politburo in April 1985 and became the second secretary within the party. Nikolai Ryzhkov was also promoted to the Politburo in April and was appointed chairman of the Council of Ministers in succession to Tikhonov in September 1985. An appointment that turned out to be even more important in retrospect than it appeared at the time was that of Boris Yeltsin as first secretary of the Moscow party organisation, in succession to Grishin, in December 1985.

Much of the focus of the new leadership team was on getting the country moving again and one of the early catchwords of the Gorbachev era was *uskorenie* (acceleration). Gorbachev himself was from the outset, however, interested also in what he called 'democratisation', which included a greater tolerance of, and even encouragement for, a variety of views, although it did not yet signify for him or anyone in a position of authority fully-fledged pluralist democracy. Yet, it was symbolic of the way in which political reform edged ahead of economic change in Gorbachev's priorities that when in 1987 two important Central Committee plenary sessions put radical reform on the political agenda, it was the first of these, the January plenum, that was devoted to political reform and only the second, the June plenum, that focused on

---

9 For interesting elaboration of that point, see Stephen Kotkin, *Armageddon Averted: The Soviet Collapse 1970–2000* (New York and Oxford: Oxford University Press, 2001).

10 The nearest thing to an exception was Vsevolod Murakhovskii, who had been Gorbachev's subordinate and later his successor as first secretary of the Stavropol' regional party organisation. Murakhovskii was brought to Moscow as head of a newly created State Committee for the Agro-Industrial Complex. It was not, however, a particularly powerful post, and Gosagroprom, as it was known, was abolished in early 1989, having failed to live up to Gorbachev's expectations.

the economy. At the January plenary session, Gorbachev introduced some measures of intra-party democratisation and announced that there would be a special all-Union conference in the summer of 1988 'to discuss matters of further democratising the life of the party and society as a whole'.[11] That event, the Nineteenth Party Conference (discussed later in this chapter), was to be the point at which Gorbachev and his allies moved beyond reform and embarked on a path of systemic transformation. Already in January 1987 Gorbachev launched a strong attack on the stagnation in Soviet political thinking which, he claimed, had not advanced much beyond the level of the 1930s and 1940s. The June plenum on economic reform, accompanied by a document outlining the principles of economic reform, inaugurated an attempt to decentralise economic decision-making in the Soviet Union. While the assumption at this stage was that the economy would remain a centrally planned one, the aim was to try to keep the focus of central planners on issues of national importance, 'leaving all operational decisions to lower levels'.[12] The reform also extended the rights of workers to participate in factory decision-making.

While in the summer of 1987 a majority of the members of the Politburo and Secretariat were far from being committed to fundamental reform, four of the five most important politicians in the country by that time had been brought into those positions since Gorbachev succeeded Chernenko. The three most powerful politicians after Gorbachev, following the June 1987 plenum, were Ligachev, Ryzhkov and Aleksandr Yakovlev, followed by Eduard Shevardnadze. Of the top five, three – Gorbachev, Yakovlev and Shevardnadze – were firmly in the radically reformist camp, although Gorbachev often played the role of a 'centrist' in order to carry more conservative colleagues along with him. Ryzhkov had a more limited and technocratic view of reform, while Ligachev was increasingly identifying with those who felt that freedom to criticise the Soviet past and present was getting out of hand.

Yakovlev's promotion had been extraordinarily speedy. He was not one of the 470 people elected to full or candidate membership of the Central Committee in March 1981 at the end of the Twenty-Sixth Party Congress. Thus, Yakovlev could not be promoted to the Secretariat until that deficiency had been rectified at a party congress. He was not only duly elected to the Central Committee at the Twenty-Seventh Congress in February–March 1986 but also simultaneously promoted by Gorbachev to a secretaryship of that body. At

11 M. S. Gorbachev, 'O perestroike i kadrovoi politike partii', in Gorbachev, *Izbrannye rechi i stat'i*, vol. IV (Moscow: Politizdat, 1987), p. 354.
12 Ed A. Hewett, *Reforming the Soviet Economy: Equality versus Efficiency* (Washington: Brookings Institution Press, 1988), p. 349.

the January 1987 plenum he became a candidate member of the Politburo and at the June plenum a full member. The diversity of view which had long existed within the Soviet Communist Party (although carefully concealed from most outside observers) was now increasingly clearly represented in the highest echelons of the CPSU. Yakovlev and Ligachev vied with each other for predominant influence within the Secretariat. Their disagreement and rivalry not only exemplified but also facilitated a growing intra-party as well as societal pluralism. According to their disposition, editors and party functionaries could take their cue from the radically reformist Yakovlev or the conservative Ligachev.

## The new freedoms

One of the most important developments in the Soviet Union following Gorbachev's selection as General Secretary was a change of political language. New concepts were introduced into Soviet political discourse and old ones shed the meanings they had been accorded hitherto by Soviet ideology. A case in point was the idea of freedom. Instead of freedom meaning the recognition of (Marxist-Leninist) necessity, it acquired in the Soviet political lexicon its everyday meaning of freedom from constraints or, simply, 'ordinary freedom, as established and practiced in the liberal democratic countries of the world'.[13] The term 'pluralism' had hitherto been used in Soviet publications and speeches only pejoratively in the context of attacks on East European 'revisionism' and on 'bourgeois democracy'. It was Gorbachev who broke that taboo by speaking positively about a 'socialist pluralism' and a 'pluralism of opinion' in 1987.[14] This gave a green light to social scientists and journalists to advocate pluralism and frequently to leave out the adjective 'socialist'.

From 1987 onwards there was also advocacy of checks and balances, separation of powers, a state based upon the rule of law and a market economy. Some writers qualified these concepts by placing 'socialist' in front of them. Others did not. Since there was also, however, increasingly vigorous argument as to what constituted socialism (with the writer Chingiz Aitmatov using his speech to the First Congress of People's Deputies in 1989 to name, among other countries, Switzerland as a fine example of socialism!),[15] the use of 'socialist' was

---

13 Andrzej Walicki, *Marxism and the Leap to the Kingdom of Freedom: The Rise and Fall of the Communist Utopia* (Stanford, Calif: Stanford University Press, 1995), pp. 554–5. See also Archie Brown, 'Ideology and Political Culture', in Seweryn Bialer (ed.), *Politics, Society, and Nationality inside Gorbachev's Russia* (Boulder, Colo.: Westview Press, 1989), p. 31.

14 *Pravda*, 15 July 1987, p. 2; and *Pravda*, 30 Sept. 1987, p. 1.

15 *Izvestiia*, 4 June 1989, p. 2.

not the constraint upon debate it would have been in the Soviet past. From very early in the Gorbachev era one of the key concepts given emphasis was *glasnost'*, meaning openness or transparency, although *glasnost*, like *perestroika*, was about to enter the English and other languages, such was the international impact of the changes in the Soviet Union. In each year that followed 1985 *glasnost'* became increasingly indistinguishable from freedom of speech. There were, nevertheless, occasions when *glasnost'* was conspicuous by its absence. The most notable was the disaster at the Chernobyl' nuclear power station in Ukraine on 26 April 1986. The news of what turned out to be the world's worst nuclear accident thus far came to Soviet citizens from the West by foreign radio (in a reversion to what was common in the unreformed Soviet system). It was not until 28 April that the accident was noted by Soviet television and much later before any detailed account was provided. Those within the Soviet Union who wished change to progress faster used Chernobyl', however, as an illustration of what was wrong with the system – from shoddy work at the nuclear plant, to the local attempt to cover up the scale of the disaster, to the reluctance of the Soviet leadership and mass media to provide prompt and accurate information about the catastrophe. The more reform-oriented parts of the mass media were soon carrying articles very critical of the absence of *glasnost'* on this occasion, a development that in itself would have been impossible prior to 1985 when even air crashes and some natural disasters in the Soviet Union went unreported in order to convey the impression that all was well on the home front. When, following Chernobyl', every catastrophe, whether natural (such as the Armenian earthquake in 1988) or man-made, was extensively reported and commented on, it appeared to some Soviet citizens that the incidence of misfortune had increased.

The growing freedom of speech was a mixed blessing for the General Secretary who had allowed it to happen. On the one hand, it served Gorbachev's interests that radical reformists were now free to criticise party and state bureaucrats who were opposed to change. On the other hand, almost every social and national group had an accumulation of grievances which had been impossible to air publicly in the unreformed Soviet system. These problems now spilled out into the open and overloaded the political agenda with highly contentious issues. Nowhere was that more true than in the sphere of relations among different nationalities, a topic on which more will be said later in the chapter.

Some of the new freedoms, which were soon to be taken for granted, represented a huge advance for Soviet citizens. Among the most important was the ending of the persecution of religion. A new religious tolerance prevailed and many places of worship were reopened. The year of the major turning point for this, as for much else, was 1988. In June the celebration of the millennium of Russian and Ukrainian Christianity took place with state support. New legislation gave the Church the right to publish literature and to engage in religious education. Other traditional religions of the Soviet Union also benefited from the change of policy. The jamming of Russian-language foreign broadcasts to the Soviet Union was ended and foreign travel for Soviet citizens became easier. By the last years of the Soviet Union financial constraints had become more important than bureaucratic obstacles to freedom of travel.

The Soviet press acquired a spectacular diversity in the Gorbachev era. There were weeklies such as *Ogonek* (Little light) and *Moskovskie novosti* (Moscow news) (with new editors and transformed content from the summer of 1986) that were in the vanguard of reform and *glasnost'* and publications such as the newspaper *Sovetskaia Rossiia* (Soviet Russia) or the Komsomol journal *Molodaiia gvardiia* (Young Guard), which combined political conservatism with Russian nationalism. One periodical which published information that would have been unthinkable in the past, and was at times in a battle of words even with the more tolerant authorities of the *perestroika* era, *Argumenty i fakty* (Arguments and facts), sold, at the peak of its circulation, as many as 33 million copies a week. In general, the circulation of newspapers and journals reached far greater heights during the *perestroika* period than either before or since in Russia. An entirely new and independent newspaper, which incorporated the word 'independent' in its title, *Nezavisimaia gazeta*, began publication in 1990.

Films which had failed to pass the censor in the unreformed Soviet system were now screened and made a great impact – none more so than the anti-Stalinist Georgian film, *Pokoianie* (Repentance), which went on general release in November 1986. The backlog of forbidden literature was even longer. The solid monthly literary journals were able to fill their pages with high-quality creative writing and revealing memoir material that had failed to pass the censor in times past. Many of the works of Aleksandr Solzhenitsyn appeared in official Soviet publications for the first time, including his devastating indictment of the Soviet system, *The Gulag Archipelago*, which was serialised in the large-circulation literary monthly, *Novyi mir* (New world), in 1989. Other works deemed in the past to be especially dangerous, the very possession of which was a criminal offence – among them George Orwell's *Animal Farm* and *Nineteen Eighty-Four*, Arthur Koestler's *Darkness at Noon*, Vasilii Grossman's *Life and Fate*, *Doctor Zhivago* (Boris Pasternak's Nobel prize-winning novel) and Anna Akhmatova's poem, *Requiem*, about the victims of Stalin – were published in large editions.

From early in the Gorbachev era criticism of Stalin and Stalinism – which had been banned in the Brezhnev years – resumed and the critiques became much more fundamental than Khrushchev's attack which had condemned *some* of Stalin's purges but did not question the system that had allowed him to get away with mass murder. It was in 1988 that the much bolder step, in the Soviet context, of criticising in print Marx and Lenin was taken. The first author to achieve this breakthrough was Aleksandr Tsipko in the pages of the popular science monthly, *Nauka i zhizn'* (Science and life). Tsipko, who had been brought into the Central Committee apparatus in 1986, was still working in the CPSU headquarters when he published a series of articles, beginning in November 1988, that were critical of the Bolsheviks and the consequences of their revolution. In his own words, he set the precedent of 'legal anti-Communism' and did so under the protection of Central Committee Secretaries Yakovlev and Vadim Medvedev.[16] It is one of the paradoxes of the dismantling of the Communist system that the most decisive steps in that process were taken by high-ranking members of the Communist Party, including, crucially, the highest. These new freedoms, it is important to note, occurred at a time before Yeltsin was playing any part in national decision-making. Aleksandr Bovin rightly sees as one of Yeltsin's principal merits that he *preserved* the inheritance of freedom that Gorbachev introduced.[17] To see freedom of speech and publication as a product of post-Soviet Russia would be a serious distortion. The many new liberties were, on the contrary, among the most notable achievements of *perestroika*, although they contributed also to its ultimate undoing.

## From political reform to systemic transformation

New concepts and a greatly enhanced freedom were accompanied by insti-tutional change. The point at which the policy pursued by Gorbachev and his supporters moved beyond an attempt to reform the existing system was in the run-up to the Nineteenth Party Conference in the summer of 1988. Encouraged by the removal of Boris Yeltsin in November 1987 from his post as Moscow party chief after he had criticised the party leadership and, in partic-ular, Ligachev at a Central Committee meeting the previous month, conser-vatives within the CPSU Central Committee began to fight back against the

16 Alexander Tsipko, 'The Collapse of Marxism-Leninism', in Michael Ellman and Vladimir Kontorovich (eds.), *The Destruction of the Soviet Economic System: An Insiders' History* (Armonk, N. Y.: M. E. Sharpe, 1998), pp. 169–86, esp. pp. 184–5.
17 Aleksandr Bovin, *XX vek kak zhizn': vospominaniia* (Moscow: Zakharov, 2003), pp. 682–3.

developing radicalism of Gorbachev's reforms.[18] (Yeltsin saw himself as being in the vanguard of *perestroika*, although his emphasis at that time was more on a greater social egalitarianism than on democracy. Gorbachev was the first to call for competitive elections.)

In early 1988 the apparatus backlash against radical reform became more apparent. A letter appeared under the name of Nina Andreeva, a hitherto unknown Leningrad lecturer, in *Sovetskaia Rossiia* on 13 March 1988, which attacked the processes under way in Russia from a neo-Stalinist standpoint. It received immediate support from within the Central Committee apparatus. Its publication date was deliberately chosen for a Sunday just before Gorbachev left for Yugoslavia and Yakovlev for Mongolia. In their absence Ligachev commended the article to journalists as 'a benchmark for what we need in our ideology today'.[19] There was a gap between publication of this document, which appeared to many to portend a dramatic change of official course, and its rebuttal. Most Russian intellectuals, including some who were later to criticise Gorbachev for 'half-measures' and 'indecisiveness', waited to see which way the wind was blowing. On Gorbachev's insistence, the Politburo discussed the Andreeva letter at a session that lasted for two days and it turned out that at least half the membership were basically sympathetic to the anti-reformist line it had expressed.[20] It was not until 5 April that an article appeared in *Pravda* rebutting 'Andreeva' point by point. It was given additional party authority by being unsigned, though it was drafted by Yakovlev, with the participation of Gorbachev, and represented a clear victory for the reformist wing of the leadership.

This, in turn, enabled Gorbachev, with particularly important help both from Yakovlev and from his recently appointed adviser on reform of the political system, Shakhnazarov, to radicalise the political agenda and to oversee the production of documents presaging far-reaching reform that were presented to the Nineteenth Party Conference in June 1988. The conference itself produced more open debate than had occurred at a party forum since the 1920s. Politburo members Mikhail Solomentsev, Gromyko and Ligachev were

18 For the transcript of the Central Committee meeting which led to Yeltsin's removal from his Moscow party post and from candidate membership of the Politburo (although he remained a member of the Central Committee), see *Izvestiia TsK CPSU*, no. 2 (1989): 209–87. On Yeltsin's break with the party leadership in late 1987, see Leon Aron, *Boris Yeltsin: A Revolutionary Life* (London: HarperCollins, 2000), pp. 200–17; and Brown, *The Gorbachev Factor*, 169–72 and 356–7.

19 For a more detailed account of the 'Nina Andreeva affair', see Brown, *The Gorbachev Factor*, pp. 172–5.

20 For the main points of that discussion, see 'O stat'e N. Andreevoi i ne tol'ko o nei', in M. S. Gorbachev, *Gody trudnykh reshenii* (Moscow: Al'fa-Print, 1993), pp. 98–110.

criticised by name and Gorbachev, though not yet explicitly named as some-one guilty of social democratic deviation from Communist orthodoxy, was the clear implicit target of several critical speeches from conservative Communists. Nevertheless, at that time the party remained notably hierarchical and Gorbachev still benefited from the authority traditionally enjoyed by the General Secretary. As a result, he was able to get the conference delegates to approve reforms that were both against the inner judgement of many of them and which constituted a fundamental departure from Soviet practice. The most important decision was to move to contested elections for a new legislature, the Congress of People's Deputies, which would in turn elect an inner body, the Supreme Soviet. The latter was to be in session for some eight months of the year – unlike the existing rubber-stamp Supreme Soviet which met for only a few days each year.

Until these elections were held in March 1989 the political institutional changes constituted what Yakovlev and many others have called a 'revolution from above'.[21] The elections, however, galvanised Soviet society – some republics and nations more than others – and brought entirely new actors on to the political stage. They also provided the opportunity for one demoted politician, Boris Yeltsin, who had remained a nominal member of the Central Committee, to make a spectacular comeback and begin his ascent to power. Yeltsin stood for election in a constituency that comprised the whole of Moscow and he overwhelmingly defeated the favoured candidate of the party apparatus. A third of the seats were reserved for candidates from 'public organisations' (which ranged from the Communist Party itself to the Academy of Sciences and the Writers' Union and Film-Makers' Union). This was both a concession to institutional interests within the Soviet system and also, in the minds of some reformers, a way of getting talented people from outside the political class into the new legislature. Among the deputies chosen from the Academy of Sciences was Andrei Sakharov. In the ballot by the electorate as a whole for the remaining two-thirds of the deputies, there was real contestation between two or more candidates in a majority of seats. About a quarter of the constituencies had only one name on the ballot paper. This, however, did not guarantee election, for the support of more than half of those voting was required. A number of officials, who had contrived to have no competitor, found themselves spurned. Among those thus defeated was a candidate member of the Politburo, Iurii Solov'ev, in Leningrad.[22] These

---

21 See e.g. Aleksandr Iakovlev, *Predislovie, obval, posleslovie* (Moscow: Novosti, 1992), p. 267.
22 Stephen White, Richard Rose and Ian McAllister, *How Russia Votes* (Chatham, N.J.: Chatham House, 1997), pp. 28–9.

first contested national elections marked a breakthrough to real political pluralism in the Soviet Union and kindled great public enthusiasm. The voter turn-out was higher than for any subsequent Russia-wide election up to and including the presidential election of 2004. Only a minority of those elected to the new Soviet legislature were committed to further transformative change, but some of those who were formed the Inter-Regional Group of Deputies which numbered Sakharov, Yeltsin, and the historian Iurii Afanas'ev among its leaders.

Other elections followed – in 1990 for the legislatures of all fifteen republics of the Soviet Union (which saw Yeltsin emerge as chairman of the Supreme Soviet of the Russian Republic) and in 1991 for newly created republican presidencies. The most important of those elections was in June 1991 when Yeltsin got more votes than all his opponents put together to become president of the Russian Republic and the first popularly elected leader in Russian history. In March 1990 the institution of the presidency had been created at the level of the Soviet Union. There was debate among reformers whether this should be a nationwide election or an indirect election by the legislature, the Congress of People's Deputies. Even a number of reformers (including the distinguished scholar, Academician Dmitrii Likhachev) urged Gorbachev to opt for the latter. Some were for prompt indirect election on the grounds that, with tension rising as a result of nationalist discontent and economic problems, the sooner a new executive was formed the better. Other supporters of Gorbachev were worried that he could lose the election, although it was in May 1990 that Yeltsin for the first time moved ahead of Gorbachev in the surveys conducted by the All-Soviet (later All-Russian) Institute for Public Opinon (VTsIOM), the most reliable of the opinion pollsters at the time. Gorbachev's election by the Congress of People's Deputies of the USSR to become the Soviet Union's first executive president in March 1990 was a tactical victory, but probably a strategic error. If he had competed in a general election and won, he would have greatly strengthened his legitimacy in an era – which he himself had inaugurated – when this could no longer be conferred by the practice of seven decades whereby a group of senior Communist Party officials got together behind closed doors and chose the party leader who then automatically became the country's leader.

A systemic transformation occurred in the Soviet Union between 1988 and 1990. By March 1990 at the latest it was no longer meaningful to describe the Soviet state as Communist. The two most fundamental political characteristics of a Communist system were the monopoly of power of the Communist Party and 'democratic centralism' (meaning hierarchical subordination, strict discipline and absence of open debate, with the centralism a reality and 'democratic' a misnomer). Both of these features had disappeared. The process had begun with Gorbachev's abolition of most of the economic departments of the Central Committee and of lower party economic organs in the autumn of 1988. Hitherto, ministerial and other state economic institutions had been under close party supervision. Now they acquired a new autonomy. Competitive elections, even when they were not multi-party elections, meant the end of democratic centralism. There was much intra-party debate, some of it conducted in the mass media, from 1986 onwards, and the elections for the new Soviet legislature in 1989 pitted one CPSU member against another, frequently displaying radically different political outlooks and advocating widely divergent policies. Their fate was decided by the electorate, among whom only 10 per cent of adults were members of the CPSU. Thus the Communist Party's monopoly of power was fast disappearing de facto in 1989 before it was removed de jure from the Soviet Constitution at a session of the Congress of People's Deputies of the USSR in March 1990.[23]

The creation of the Soviet presidency, while it did little to help Gorbachev at a time when his popularity was slipping and Yeltsin was emerging as a serious challenger to his authority, signalled the end of party hegemony. The Politburo had from early in the Soviet period been the ruling body of the country as well as of the party. From March 1990 onwards a state institution, the presidency, was more powerful than the highest party organs, although Gorbachev held on to his office of General Secretary to ensure that it did not fall into the hands of a conservative Communist who might attempt to reverse the process under way. A Presidential Council was created which was more authoritative than the Politburo, although it suffered from the absence of institutional underpinnings, a chain of command analogous to that which had prevailed in the CPSU.

At the same time as the new Soviet presidency and the Presidential Council were created in March 1990, so was a body known as the Federation Council. It was composed of the presidents or the chairmen of the supreme soviets of the union republics. As such, it was created from below – from the republics. Neither Gorbachev, as president of the Soviet Union, nor the Communist Party apparatus was able to determine who sat on the Federation Council. As the Presidential Council was chosen by Gorbachev, listening to advice but with full responsibility for the ultimate choice, it is evident that the loser of the power

---

23 On the emergence of new legislative and executive institutions and the switch from party to state power, see Brown, *The Gorbachev Factor*, pp. 188–205.

of appointment in both cases was the central CPSU apparatus. Moreover, the introduction of competitive elections in the republics as well as at the Centre meant that politicians had to take more account of public opinion than ever before. Whereas previously nothing was more important for a political leader in Estonia or Ukraine than the opinion held of him in the Central Committee building in Moscow, now the views of Estonians and Ukrainians assumed greater significance.

The president himself, Gorbachev, was the chief arbiter of executive decision-making – even more so than in the days when his power rested entirely on the General Secretaryship, for when party organs reigned supreme, he still had to take some account of opinion within the Politburo. However, the constraints from outside the federal executive were far greater in 1990–1 than at any time since the consolidation of the Soviet regime in the 1920s. These came partly from republican institutions and, for Gorbachev, the challenges to his authority from Yeltsin in 1990–1 were of especial significance. There was also, however, a new politics at street level. The second half of the 1980s saw the development of new and independent organised groups. After the Nineteenth Party Conference and the decision to move to contested elections, it was clear that the dangers of engaging in such activity – which hitherto had been very real – were becoming a thing of the past. Two authors who have studied Russian independent groups in contrasting ways agree at least that '1989 stands out as the crucial takeoff phase for autonomous political activity in Russia'.[24] Put another way: 'Elections of the People's Deputies of the USSR in 1989 and to the Russian Federation federal and local soviets in 1990 completely changed the character of Russian independent political groups. Before this, despite various impressive names, the "democratic" movement actually consisted of many small clubs.'[25] Some of the new groups turned into mass movements, most notably Democratic Russia, a loosely organised body which held its founding congress in October 1990 and played a significant part in mobilising support for Boris Yeltsin in the Russian presidential election the following summer.

By the time the Communist Party of the Soviet Union held its Twenty-Eighth (and last) Congress in the summer of 1990 it was no longer playing a decisive role in the political process, at least at the central level. A document adopted by the congress, 'Towards a Humane, Democratic Socialism', which

24 M. Steven Fish, *Democracy from Scratch: Opposition and Regime in the New Russian Revolution* (Princeton: Princeton University Press, 1995), p. 35.
25 Alexander Lukin, *The Political Culture of the Russian 'Democrats'* (Oxford: Oxford University Press, 2000), p. 81.

would have been a sensation at the previous party congress in 1986, no longer made a significant impact. Work began on a new party programme and a draft of it was presented to a Central Committee plenum in the summer of 1991. It fully reflected Gorbachev's own intellectual journey in a little over six years from Communist reformer to democratic socialist of a type familiar in Western Europe (although not in Russia or the United States). However, among those who duly voted for what was essentially a Social Democratic platform, it appears that a majority had no intention of implementing it. Some of those present had already turned their minds to the issue of how to remove Gorbachev from office.

## The failure of economic reform

The most immediate stimulus to change in the Soviet Union at the beginning of the Gorbachev era was the long-term decline in the rate of economic growth and the fact that the Soviet economy was not only lagging behind the most advanced Western countries but also was being overtaken by some of the newly industrialising countries in Asia. There was, however, no agreement on what should be done to remedy matters. The most radical reformers in the mid-1980s thought not in terms of a fully-fledged market economy but simply of making significant concessions to market forces along the lines of the Hungarian economic reform, launched in 1968. Others believed that what was needed was more discipline of the kind which Andropov had begun to impose. An influential group, which included the chairman of the Council of Ministers, Ryzhkov, was from early in the Gorbachev era in favour of raising prices but very cautious about leaving prices entirely to market forces. By the end of the 1980s large numbers of specialists had lost all faith in state planning of the economy and, instead of looking for a combination of plan and market, were ready for a more radical shift to the market. The economist Nikolai Petrakov, soon after he became Gorbachev's aide on economic matters at the beginning of 1990, told Ryzhkov that the State Committee on Prices should be abolished, since it made no sense for the state to be fixing prices. Ryzhkov agreed in principle but said the phasing-out of that State Committee should occur in a few years' time. Petrakov responded: 'Nikolai Ivanovich, you talk about the market as we used to talk about communism – it's always sometime later.'[26]

26 Author's interview with Petrakov, Moscow, June 1991.

An economic error committed as early as May 1985 (and for which Ryzhkov was entirely blameless, since he opposed the policy on the grounds that it would lead to a serious reduction of state revenue) was the adoption of an anti-alcohol programme. The production of alcohol in state distilleries and wineries was drastically reduced, many retail outlets were closed, and illicit alcohol production filled the gap. The state's monopoly of this industry had previously, given the high level of alcohol consumption (especially of vodka in the Slavic parts of the Soviet Union), made a massive contribution to the revenue side of the budget. Since alcoholism and drunkenness were alarmingly widespread in Russia, the measure had some support, especially from women; but, in spite of apparent early success in reducing alcohol consumption, it was ultimately a failure. The prime movers in the Politburo for a major effort to reduce alcohol consumption were Egor Ligachev and Mikhail Solomentsev, but Gorbachev became associated with the campaign in the minds of most of the public, for he supported the principle of a fresh attempt to tackle what he recognised to be a serious social and moral problem.

A combination of the policy's growing unpopularity and Ligachev's loss of his position as second secretary of the CPSU in 1988 meant that from that year on the campaign was quietly abandoned.[27] There had been previous propaganda campaigns against excessive alcohol consumption, but none had been successful in the long term. By making it much harder for alcohol to be obtained legally at convenient locations and times, this new assault on the hard drinking culture did produce a sharp drop in legal sales which was reflected both in the official statistics, suggesting that vodka consumption in 1987 was less than half of what it had been in 1985, and by the hole that was left in the state budget.[28] However, if moderate drinkers drank less because of a reluctance to stand in long queues at the reduced number of shops selling alcohol, those at whom the measure was primarily aimed were less easily deterred. Hardened drinkers were prepared to queue for as long as it took or to fill the gap in legal supplies with 'moonshine', thus depriving the state of the large element of turnover tax on each bottle of liquor.

Bad luck as well as bad decisions complicated economic policy during *perestroika*. Whereas a rise in oil prices had partially disguised Soviet economic inefficiency in the 1970s, a fall in oil prices in the second half of the 1980s did nothing to cushion economic reform. It is arguable, though, that this may have

27 Stephen White, *Russia Goes Dry: Alcohol, State and Society* (Cambridge: Cambridge University Press, 1996), p. 183.
28 Ibid., p. 141.

been a blessing in disguise in that it became increasingly clear that the existing economic system needed to be replaced by one operating on fundamentally different principles. Very few Soviet economists, not to speak of party and government officials, held such a view in 1985. Between then and 1990, however, the economic philosophy of many of the social scientists, in particular, underwent a fast evolution. By 1990 the view was widely held among them that central planning would have to give way to an essentially market economy. There were, though, differences of opinion among reformers between those who favoured a mixed ownership system (state, co-operative and private) and those who wished to go the whole hog to private ownership.

The first move towards recognising a role for non-state economic enterprise was the Law on Individual Economic Activity of November 1986. This legalised individual and family-based work, such as car repairs, taxi services and private tuition. A much more ambitious piece of legislation was introduced the following year. The Law on the State Enterprise, a compromise measure following debate within the leadership, in which Gorbachev played a leading role, devolved more authority than hitherto to the enterprise level – in particular, to factory managers. While the diagnosis that the Soviet economy was too centralised and that economic ministries had too much power was correct, the law did not achieve any of its intended results. The State Planning Committee (Gosplan) and the economic ministries found ways of maintaining many of their powers over the enterprises, even though the number of plan indicators was cut drastically. To the extent that there was some real devolution of authority to the factory level, it did more harm than good. Enterprises were able to charge higher prices for work of no higher quality than before. The law thus had inflationary consequences and also contributed to an increase in inter-enterprise debt. Decentralisation without price liberalisation and competition was doomed to failure, although at the time many Soviet reformers and Western observers saw the Enterprise Law as a step forward. This was so only in the sense that since the attempt to reform the Soviet economy proceeded on the basis of trial and error, and in conditions of *glasnost'*, the failures could soon be brought into the light of day. One of the most important of the unintended consequences of the Enterprise Law became apparent in the last years of the Soviet Union and in early post-Soviet Russia when a process of insider privatisation occurred. Taking advantage of the enhancement of their legal rights provided by the 1987 law, factory managers, often aided and abetted by local party officials, began to convert their control of industrial enterprises into ownership.

A more successful legislative act was the Law on Co-operatives of 1988. Going well beyond the law which had legalised individual economic enterprise, this law prescribed no maximum to the number of people who could be employed in a 'co-operative'. Many of the co-operatives became indistinguishable from private enterprise but it was an advantage in the late 1980s that the former terminology could be supported by quotations from Lenin who in 1989 still topped a serious poll of Soviet citizens who perceived him as being by far the greatest person who had ever lived.[29] An open acceptance of large-scale private economic activity would have been seen as an embrace of capitalism to which a majority of the population, as well as a majority of the political elite, were at the time opposed.

Nevertheless, as political tensions rose in 1990 and the economy showed no signs of the 'acceleration' which one of the earlier slogans of the Gorbachev era had demanded, Gorbachev and Yeltsin came to an agreement in the summer of that year to set up a team of specialists to come up with concrete proposals for transition to a market economy. The group was to be drawn in equal numbers from Gorbachev and Yeltsin nominees. The leader of Gorbachev's team was Stanislav Shatalin, a sophisticated critic of the Soviet command economy of an older generation, while Yeltsin, in his capacity as chairman of the Russian Supreme Soviet, nominated Grigorii Iavlinskii, a much younger enthusiast for the market. In endorsing this project, Gorbachev completely bypassed the Communist Party hierarchy and offended the head of the government, Ryzhkov. The document that the Shatalin–Iavlinskii group produced became known as the '500-Days Plan', an ambitious attempt to make the transition to a market economy within that time period.[30] The 238-page programme did not so much as mention 'socialism' and made no concessions to traditional Soviet ideology. It envisaged the speedy construction of market institutions, large-scale privatisation and extensive devolution of power to the republics of the Soviet Union. Gorbachev, after reading the document more than once, and Yeltsin, without reading it, both gave the programme their initial enthusiastic endorsement. In response to the backlash from within the ministerial network, including the strong objections of Ryzhkov and the first deputy prime minister, Leonid Abalkin (himself a reformist economist), as well as from CPSU, military

29 Even in 1994 and 1999 when the same question was put to Russian respondents by the leading survey research organisation which had conducted the 1989 survey, Lenin came second only to Peter the Great in the list of 'most outstanding people of all times and nations' in the perception of respondents. See Boris Dubin, 'Stalin i drugie: Figury vysshei vlasti v obshchestvennom mnenii sovremennoi Rossii', *Monitoring obshchestvennogo mneniia* (Moscow: VTsIOM), 1 (Jan.–Feb. 2003): 13–25, at p. 20.
30 *Perekhod k rynku: Chast' 1. Kontseptsiia i Programma* (Moscow: Arkhangel'skoe, 1990).

and KGB critics, Gorbachev retreated from his earlier support for the '500-days' document.

The issue was not by this time whether to move to a market economy, but rather when, how and to what kind of market economy. The Shatalin–Iavlinskii proposals were less a plan or programme and more a set of aspirations which were subsequently agreed to have been over-optimistic. Egor Gaidar, a member of the team which produced the document, subsequently saw its desiderata as more of a political than an economic statement and regarded them, on the basis of his own post-Soviet experience, as having been naive.[31] The political salience of the issue was, however, very great. Gorbachev's retreat from support of the Shatalin–Iavlinskii proposals undoubtedly lost him credibility among Russian radical reformists as well as within the republics most desirous of greater sovereignty. The mantle of leader of reform appeared now, in the eyes of many intellectuals, to be passing to Yeltsin. Finding himself deserted by a significant part of the constituency for change, Gorbachev became increasingly reliant on the more conservative elements within the leadership during the winter of 1990–1.

There is no doubt that the attempt to reform the Soviet economy ended in failure. Part of the reason for that was the tension between reforming an existing system to make it work better and replacing that system by one which had a quite different logic. In the early years of *perestroika* the first aim was being pursued – and with only very limited success. By 1990–1, while there was not a consensus, there was at least a broad body of support among specialists for the idea that the command economy had to give way to a market economy. It was clearer to Gorbachev than to Yeltsin that this would mean tens of millions of citizens becoming worse off for some years to come. Freeing prices would improve the supply of goods and services but would also raise those prices to a level the majority could ill afford. That factor, together with the institutional opposition to change of the type proposed by the Shatalin–Iavlinskii group, and concern about the possibly deleterious impact of economic systemic change on the territorial integrity of the USSR, made Gorbachev hesitate about pushing through the move to a market economy in practice that he had already accepted in principle. Much of the economic legislation of the *perestroika* years – not least the Law on Co-operatives – had helped to pave the way for marketisation, but the Soviet economy remained in limbo at the end of the Gorbachev era. It was no longer a functioning command economy but not yet a market system.

---

31 Egor Gaidar, *Dni porazhenii i pobed* (Moscow: Vagrius, 1996), p. 65.

## Ending the Cold War

If the results of economic reform during the *perestroika* period were, to say the least, disappointing, the outcome of the new direction of Soviet foreign policy was a dramatic improvement in Soviet relations with the outside world. Gorbachev came to power intent on making a qualitative change in this respect. He was determined to end the war in Afghanistan and to improve relations with the United States, Western Europe and China. He wished to move away also from Soviet tutelage of Eastern Europe. At a meeting with the East European Communist leaders as early as Chernenko's funeral Gorbachev told this disbelieving group that the Soviet Union would respect their sovereignty and independence and they, in turn, would have to take full responsibility for developments in their countries. In other words – and Gorbachev was to make this more explicit in November 1986 – the ruling parties of Eastern Europe had better earn the trust of their own people, for there would be no more Soviet military interventions if they ran into trouble.[32] Granting more independence to Communist leaders in Eastern Europe and respecting the full autonomy of those states were not, of course, the same thing. It was in 1988–9 that Gorbachev went beyond the former position to embrace the latter.

The issue of how decisive in ending the Cold War was the role played by political leaders – in particular, Gorbachev – is still a subject for debate, as are explanations in terms of material resources, ideas and Soviet domestic politics.[33] Some see these as alternative explanations. For others they are complementary, each having some bearing on the eventual outcome but to greatly varying extent. One argument which would accord primacy to American pressure – stressing, at the same time, the disparity between the material resources of the Soviet Union and the United States – holds that by stepping up military expenditure in a way the USSR would find difficult to match, the Reagan administration was inviting its Soviet adversary either to 'spend itself to death' or to capitulate. Expressed more moderately, this is stated as: 'The end of

---

32 Gorbachev, *Zhizn' i reformy*, p. 311; and Alex Pravda, 'Soviet Policy towards Eastern Europe in Transition: The Means Justify the Ends', in Neil Malcolm (ed.), *Russia and Europe: An End to Confrontation* (London: Pinter, for the Royal Institute of International Affairs, 1994), pp. 123–50, at p. 134. Within the Soviet Politburo Gorbachev sometimes used more traditional language. See Mark Kramer, 'The Collapse of East European Communism and the Repercussions within the Soviet Union (Part I)', *Journal of Cold War Studies* 5, 4 (Fall 2003): 178–256, at p. 183.

33 See esp. Richard K. Herrmann and Richard Ned Lebow (eds.), *Ending the Cold War: Interpretations, Causation, and the Study of International Relations* (New York: Palgrave Macmillan, 2004).

the Cold War was caused by the relative decline of Soviet power and the reassurance this gave the West.'[34]

However, the relative strength of the United States in relation to the Soviet Union was greater in the early post-war years when Stalin's takeover of Eastern Europe *began* the Cold War. Moreover, the Soviet Union, if less militarily strong than the United States in the mid-1980s, had enough nuclear weapons to destroy life on earth. It did not need to match the US, weapon for weapon, in order to maintain the division of Europe. At home, living standards, while low in comparison with Western Europe, were much higher than Soviet citizens had put up with over many decades. Even if there had been more widespread domestic dissatisfaction with Soviet foreign policy and with the domestic political order than, in fact, there was in 1985, the regime had sophisticated means of maintaining control and an apparatus of repression that had very successfully eliminated dissent. It could have continued to do so, using the mass media to present a propagandistic interpretation of Western aggressive intentions and the need for the Soviet Union to strengthen still further its defences, had the leadership opted for continuity rather than change in foreign policy.

Gorbachev was in a minority of one in the Politburo at the time he took over as General Secretary in believing that the Soviet Union as well as the United States had to react to the realities of the nuclear age in a new way. He was concerned that President Reagan's Strategic Defense Initiative (SDI) increased the chance of Cold War turning into hot war by increasing reliance on fallible technology and technocratic rather than political decisions. He wished also to divert excessive military expenditure to civilian purposes, but he was initially alone also within the top leadership in being willing to tackle the power of the Soviet military-industrial complex. And even as leader, aware that he could be replaced as General Secretary at short notice by a CPSU Central Committee plenum, Gorbachev had to proceed cautiously in challenging the most powerful institutional interests within the Soviet system.

A combination of new Soviet leadership and new ideas was more important than the difference in material resources between the USSR and the USA in bringing about change. Domestic Soviet politics were also more important than the international environment between 1985 and 1988. This changed in 1989 when the citizens of East European countries demanded and secured their independence. The speed at which this happened left Gorbachev responding to

---

34 William C. Wohlforth, 'Realism and the End of the Cold War', *International Security* 19, 3 (Winter 1994/5): 91–129, at p. 96.

events, rather than setting the international agenda, as he had done, to a great extent, in his earliest years in office. One of the features that distinguished Gorbachev from his predecessors as Soviet leader was a strong aversion to violence. This is, on the whole, recognised both by those who think well of Gorbachev and by his severe critics in post-Communist Russia. In the words of Vladislav Zubok: 'The principle of non-violence was not only Gorbachev's sincere belief, and the foundation of his domestic and foreign policies, but it also matched his personal "codes" . . . The critics claim that Gorbachev "had no guts for blood", even when it was dictated by *raison d'état*.'[35] There was, moreover, as Anatolii Cherniaev has affirmed, 'a total lack in Gorbachev of undue respect for the military or any kind of special fascination with military parades and demonstrations of military power'.[36]

By bringing in a new foreign-policy team early on, consisting of Eduard Shevardnadze as foreign minister, Cherniaev as main foreign policy adviser, Anatolii Dobrynin as head of the International Department of the Central Committee, and Vadim Medvedev in charge of the Socialist Countries Department of that body, Gorbachev opened the way for both new thinking on foreign policy and new behaviour. From the outset Aleksandr Yakovlev was also an influential adviser and from 1988 he was the overseer of international affairs within the Central Committee. While Gorbachev pursued what George Breslauer has characterised as a 'concessionary foreign policy', the Soviet Union was not forced into this.[37] It was, rather, a price that a minority of the Soviet elite – including, however, the principal power-holder – was prepared to pay for what they (perhaps, in retrospect, naively) believed would be a more peaceful and self-consciously interdependent world. The policy was intimately bound up with the changes that the same people wished to make at home. Liberalisation, followed by democratisation, within the country was linked to abandoning imperial pretensions abroad. Ronald Reagan, contrary to the belief of most of the Soviet experts on American politics, turned out to be a valuable partner for Gorbachev in international negotiations. His anti-Communist credentials were sufficiently strong to offer him protection at home, and although there were important inter-agency tensions within the American administration,

35 Vladislav M. Zubok, 'Gorbachev and the End of the Cold War: Perspectives on History and Personality', *Cold War History* 2, 2 (Jan. (2002): 61–100, at p. 82.
36 Anatolii Cherniaev, 'Forging a New Relationship', in William C. Wohlforth (ed.), *Cold War Endgame: Oral History, Analysis, Debates* (University Park, Pa.: Pennsylvania State University Press, 2003), p. 21.
37 On Gorbachev's way of justifying his change of Soviet foreign policy, see George W. Breslauer, *Gorbachev and Yeltsin as Leaders* (New York and Cambridge: Cambridge University Press, 2002), esp. pp. 70–8.

Reagan believed that change within the Soviet Union (and of Soviet international conduct) was possible, and, in the words of his ambassador to Moscow, 'always came down ultimately in support of dialogue'.[38]

The coming to power of Gorbachev led to the toppling of ideological orthodoxy in Soviet thinking on international affairs even more quickly than on the economy and the political system. The concept of 'reasonable sufficiency' in military expenditure (rather than fully matching the potential adversary), the idea that 'all-human values' had supremacy over class values and that there were universal interests which took precedence over those of any one country led to an emphasis on interdependence that marked a qualitative step forward from the old Soviet doctrine of 'peaceful coexistence'. International relations were no longer seen as a zero-sum game, a deadly struggle between socialism and capitalism, but rather an arena where, through co-operation, all countries could benefit.[39]

The first fruits of the new co-operation were to be seen in arms reduction agreements. There were summit meetings between Gorbachev and Reagan at Geneva (1985), Reykjavik (1986), Washington (1987) and Moscow (1988). The Reykjavik meeting came close to outlawing a wide range of nuclear weapons, but ultimately foundered on disagreement over whether work on SDI should or should not be confined to the laboratory. Although both leaders left that meeting greatly disappointed, it did not sour the Gorbachev–Reagan relationship. The Washington summit in December 1987 ended by eliminating a whole category of nuclear weapons, both Soviet SS-20s and the American cruise and Pershing missiles. This 'zero option' had been Reagan's policy since 1981, and so he could take some pride in the outcome. However, hardline Washington critics, as well as hard-line Moscow ones, were upset, for the former had believed that no Soviet leader would dare admit that installing the SS-20s had been a mistake, and they had counted on the continued presence of American medium-range missiles in Europe.

The improvement in East–West relations was further enhanced by the Soviet Union's decision to withdraw its troops from Afghanistan. Gorbachev had been looking for an exit strategy from the beginning of his General

---

38 Jack F. Matlock, Jr., *Reagan and Gorbachev: How the Cold War Ended* (New York: Random House, 2004), p. 64. See also Archie Brown, 'Gorbachev and the End of the Cold War', pp. 31–57, esp. 50–2, and George W. Breslauer and Richard Ned Lebow, 'Leadership and the End of the Cold War: A Counterfactual Thought Experiment', in Herrmann and Lebow, *Ending the Cold War*, pp. 161–88, esp. 180–4.

39 Robert D. English, *Russia and the Idea of the West: Gorbachev, Intellectuals, and the End of the Cold War* (New York: Columbia University Press, 2000), esp. pp. 193–228; and Brown, *The Gorbachev Factor*, esp. pp. 220–5.

Secretaryship but he had to take account of the reluctance of the Soviet military to depart in a manner which looked like a defeat. He wished, therefore, to encourage reconciliation among the warring parties in Afghanistan and sought American help in doing so. In April 1987 Gorbachev told American Secretary of State George Shultz that the Soviet Union wanted to get out of Afghanistan but the United States was not doing anything to make it easier.[40] In July of the same year Gorbachev stated in a newspaper interview that 'in principle, Soviet troop withdrawal from Afghanistan has been decided upon'.[41] Eduard Shevardnadze repeated the request for American help in September 1987, in order that 'a reactionary fundamentalist Islamic regime' would not take power in Afghanistan. He made it clear, however, that the Soviet Union was committed to withdrawal, in any event.[42] It was April 1988 before an agreement on the Soviet army's withdrawal was actually signed. Soviet troops began leaving in substantial numbers the following month and the process was completed by the agreed date of 15 February 1989. By that time President Reagan had already made his celebrated visit to Moscow. Asked by a reporter inside the grounds of the Kremlin what had happened to the 'evil empire', the term Reagan had applied to the Soviet Union in 1983, the American president responded: 'I was talking about another time, another era.'[43]

Appropriately, since the Cold War had begun with the Soviet takeover of Eastern Europe, it ended with the Central and East European countries achieving independent statehood. The key shift of Soviet policy which facilitated this occurred, along with so much else of immense future significance, in the summer of 1988. In his major speech to the Nineteenth Conference of the CPSU on 28 June, Gorbachev followed a passage in which he had been speaking about the Communist countries of Eastern Europe with these words:

> The concept of freedom of choice holds a key place in the new thinking. We are convinced of the universality of this principle in international relations at a time when the most important general problem has become the very survival of civilisation . . . That is why the policy of force [*politika sily*] in all its forms and manifestations has become historically obsolete.[44]

Gorbachev could scarcely have been more explicit in opposing military intervention as a policy, even though up until then Western governments had taken

40 George P. Shultz, *Turmoil and Triumph: My Years as Secretary of State* (New York: Macmillan, 1993), p. 895.
41 Ibid., p. 910.   42 Ibid., p. 987.
43 Don Oberdorfer, *The Turn: How the Cold War Came to an End – the United States and the Soviet Union, 1983–1990* (London: Jonathan Cape, 1992), p. 299.
44 Gorbachev, *Izbrannye rechi i stat'i*, vol. VI, pp. 347–8.

it for granted that, in the last resort, the Soviet Union would use force of arms to maintain Communist regimes in Eastern Europe. Gorbachev expressed similar sentiments to those in his party conference speech in his address to the United Nations in December 1988, although they were given less publicity than the 'hard news' of substantial Soviet troop withdrawals from Eastern Europe.[45]

In 1989 the Central and East Europeans took Gorbachev at his word. One after another the countries of the region rejected their ruling parties and the Moscow connection and became independent and non-Communist. Except in Romania, where the deposed president, Nicolae Ceauşescu was executed by firing squad, the 'revolutions', if they can be called that, were peaceful. Soviet troops remained in their barracks and not a shot was fired in Eastern Europe by a Russian. The contrast with Hungary 1956 and Czechoslovakia 1968 could not have been more stark.[46] The final piece of the jigsaw fell into place with the tearing down of the Berlin Wall in November 1989. A summit meeting between Gorbachev and the new American President George Bush in December 1989 in Malta was the first time a Soviet and American top leader gave a joint press conference at the end of it and treated each other as partners. The Soviet Foreign Ministry's adroit press spokesman, Gennadii Gerasimov, was able to announce: 'We buried the Cold War at the bottom of the Mediterranean Sea.'[47]

The Cold War was pronounced dead many times, but it is safe to say that the ideological reasons for its continued existence had ceased to exist before the end of 1988 and that it ended in political reality in 1989. The reunification of Germany in 1990 was a natural consequence of Soviet acquiescence in the destruction of the Berlin Wall.[48] The suddenness of the process, nevertheless, took both the Soviet leadership and its Western counterparts by surprise.

45 Pavel Palazchenko (citing George Shultz), *My Years with Gorbachev and Shevardnadze: The Memoir of a Soviet Interpreter* (University Park, Pa.: Pennsylvania University Press, 1997), p. 370.
46 For an excellent study of the events of that year, see Jacques Lévesque, *The Enigma of 1989: The USSR and the Liberation of Eastern Europe* (Berkeley: University of California Press, 1997).
47 Michael R. Beschloss and Strobe Talbott, *At the Highest Levels: The Inside Story of the End of the Cold War* (London: Little, Brown, 1993), p. 165.
48 On the political process of German unification, see Timothy Garton Ash, *In Europe's Name: Germany and the Divided Continent* (London: Jonathan Cape, 1993); Philip Zelikow and Condoleezza Rice, *Germany Unified and Europe Transformed: A Study in Statecraft* (Cambridge, Mass.: Harvard University Press, 1995); Mikhail Gorbachev, *Kak eto bylo* (Moscow: Vagrius, 1999); and Viacheslav Dashichev, 'On the Road to German Unification: The View from Moscow', in Gabriel Gorodetsky (ed.), *Soviet Foreign Policy, 1917–1991: A Retrospective* (London: Cass, 1994), pp. 170–9.

Gorbachev had become the first Soviet leader since the end of the Second World War to recognise in 1987 that Germany might not remain divided for ever, but neither he nor, at that time, Chancellor Helmut Kohl imagined for a moment that within three years unification would have occurred. Given, however, Gorbachev's aversion to the use of force to preserve unpopular Communist regimes in East-Central Europe, the logic of events led to his telling Chancellor Kohl in February 1990 that it was up to the Germans to decide in what kind of state they wished to live and the speed with which they would attain it.[49] Both within the International Department of the Central Committee and in Soviet military circles, there was criticism of Gorbachev and Shevardnadze for not striking a tougher bargain over Germany. Against that, the countries of what had been the 'Soviet bloc' were returned to the citizens of East-Central Europe in a remarkably peaceful process. While events had passed beyond the control of Moscow, the Soviet Union could have greatly complicated them. Had not Soviet troops been kept in their barracks throughout the region, the short-term outcome might have been different and would certainly have been bloodier. In the specific case of German unification, Gorbachev's conduct of negotiations (that were delicate and dangerous for him in the context of Soviet domestic politics) left a legacy of German goodwill both for him personally and for Russia.

## From pseudo-federation to disintegration

From the outset of *perestroika*, its proponents had stressed how crucially inter-related were both domestic and foreign policy. Whereas in the first three and a half years of *perestroika*, this meant that domestic change in the Soviet Union was having a dramatic impact on international relations, from early 1989 the boot was on the other foot. Developments in Eastern Europe began to feed back into Soviet domestic politics in a way which threatened and ultimately destroyed the unity of the Soviet state.

The break-up of the Soviet Union had several proximate causes in addition to the legacy of the past. That legacy, however, was especially important in two respects. First, the suppression of national aspirations and the severe per-secution of even peaceful manifestations of nationalism meant that there was an underlying resentment of the Soviet political order that existed to some degree in all the union republics, but was more widespread in some than oth-ers. It amounted to outright disaffection in the three Baltic states which had

49 Dashichev, 'On the Road to German Unification', p. 176.

been forcibly incorporated into the Soviet Union against the will of the great majority of their populations in 1940. The second legacy was an institutional one. The fact that the union republics had their own 'national' branches of the Communist Party (with the exception of Russia – until 1989), their own Councils of Ministers, Supreme Soviets and Academies of Sciences meant that under conditions of liberalisation and democratisation they had available to them institutions through which they could articulate distinctive national sentiments and demands. The significance of this element of institutional path determinism is indicated by the fact that the only Communist states which disintegrated in the course of transition from Communist rule were the three that had federal forms (the Soviet Union, Czechoslovakia and Yugoslavia) and by the equally significant datum that it was the fifteen union republics of the USSR, which were the best endowed with institutional resources – and not other national territories, such as the so-called 'autonomous republics' or 'autonomous regions' – that achieved independent statehood. Thus, though the power structure of the unreformed Soviet Union could fairly be characterised as 'pseudo-federal', the federal forms which up until 1985 played an extremely circumscribed role in the political life of the country were of great latent importance.[50]

Yet another legacy of the pre-*perestroika* Soviet period that played its part in fomenting national discontent was, paradoxically, one of the success stories – the achievement of near-universal literacy in the USSR and the existence of a substantial stratum of the population in all of the republics who had received a higher education. It is, as a rule, intellectuals rather than peasants who are the bearers of nationalist ideology. In the Central Asian republics, in particular, a native intelligentsia and national consciousness were equally the creations of the Soviet period. New ways of looking at the world were both a result of higher education and broadening intellectual horizons, on the one hand, and the federal forms, on the other, even though it was well into the Gorbachev era before the latter acquired federal substance. Contrary to the predictions of some scholars, however, it was not from the Asian and Islamic parts of the Soviet Union but from its most westerly European republics that the strongest pressure for sovereignty emanated.[51] The majority of citizens of Soviet Central Asia, like a majority of inhabitants of Belarus, had

50 See Rogers Brubaker, *Nationalism Reframed: Nationhood and the National Question in the New Europe* (Cambridge and New York: Cambridge University Press, 1996), esp. chs. 1 and 2; and Valerie Bunce, *Subversive Institutions: The Design and the Destruction of Socialism and the State* (Cambridge: Cambridge University Press, 1999).

51 Cf. Hélène Carrère d'Encausse, *L'Empire Éclaté* (Paris: Flammarion, 1978).

independent statehood thrust upon them in 1991. Only a minority had been striving for it.

*Perestroika* produced its own impetus for centrifugal pressures. *Glasnost'* brought to the surface injustices and discontent that it would have been dangerous to air earlier. These revelations, in turn, had a radicalising effect on opinion within several of the republics. Moreover, the reduction and subsequent removal of the 'leading role' of the Communist Party took away a key institutional pillar not only of the Soviet *system* but of the *Union*. The federal forms had been tolerated by Soviet leaderships prior to *perestroika* because they were outweighed by the 'leading role' of the party. The party remained strictly hierarchical and even republican party first secretaries had to be highly responsive to instructions coming down the line from the Central Committee in Moscow. This meant that the party, at the level of the union republic Central Committee, could, and did, place limits on the extent to which republican ministries or republican institutes of the Academy of Sciences might ignore Moscow's wishes.

As already noted, both democratic centralism and the monopoly of power of the Communist Party had ceased to exist by 1989 when competitive elections for a new legislature, the Congress of People's Deputies of the USSR, took place and were followed a year later by contested elections for legislatures in the republics. While the institutional changes were especially important in permitting national movements to gain a strong foothold within a system in flux, the withering away of Marxism-Leninism also played a part. Although many officials, not to speak of ordinary citizens, had paid only lip-service to the ideology, its thorough debunking by the end of the 1980s left space open for other ideologies, of which nationalism turned out to be especially important for the future (or, more precisely, non-future) of the Union. As Ronald Suny has aptly put it:

> [National] pasts were constructed and reconstructed; traditions were selected, invented, and enshrined; and even those with the greatest antiquity of pedigree became something quite different from past incarnations. While alternative discourses of affiliation, like class and gender, were silenced, the dominance of the national discourse defined its constituents almost exclusively as subjects of the nation, effacing the multiplicity of possible identities.[52]

A series of flashpoints in particular republics exemplified and exacerbated nationality-related problems. The appointment of a Russian, Gennadii Kolbin,

---

52 Ronald G. Suny, *The Revenge of the Past: Nationalism, Revolution, and the Collapse of the Soviet Union* (Stanford, Calif.: Stanford University Press, 1993), p. 160.

Plate 1. The last emperor of Russia, Nicholas II (1894–1917), dressed in seventeenth-century national costume, 1903.

Plate 2. Jean Cocteau. Poster for the 1911 Ballets Russes season showing Nijinsky in costume for *Le Spectre de la Rose*, Paris, 1911.

Plate 3. Portrait of Metropolitan Sergei. Detail from a painting by Pavel Korin, *Bygone Russia*, in P. Korin's house-museum, Moscow.

Plate 4. Demonstration of soldiers' wives demanding an increase in the welfare payments to the families of soldiers, 'the defenders of freedom and the people's peace', 1917.

Plate 5. The three comrades: Trotsky, Lenin, Kamenev, May 1920.

Plate 6. Baroness Ol'ga Wrangel's visit to the Emperor Nicholas Military School in Gallipoli, c.1921.

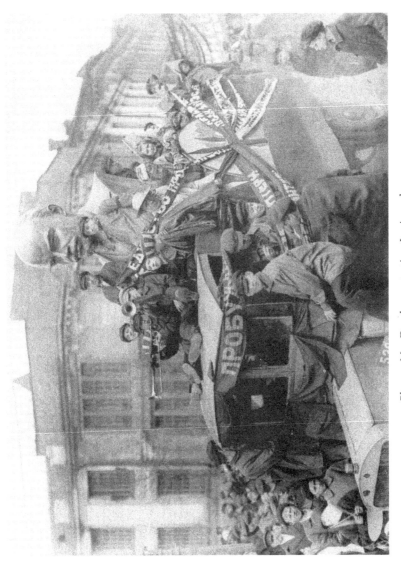

Plate 7. May Day demonstration, Leningrad, 1924.

Plate 8. Soviet poster by I. Nivinskii: 'Women join the co-operatives!'

Plate 9. Anti-religious poster by N. B. Terpsikhorov: 'Religion is poison. Safeguard the children' (1930).

Plate 10. Soviet poster by Konstantin Zotov: 'Every collective farm peasant . . . has the opportunity to live like a human being' (1934).

Plate 11.  P. Filonov, *Portrait of Stalin* (1936).

Plate 12.  Photograph by Evgenii Khaldei of the outstanding miner Aleksei Stakhanov
with the car presented to him as a gift (1936).

Plate 13. Two posters celebrating the multinational character of the Soviet Union:
(a) Stepan Karpov's 'The brotherhood of the peoples' (1923–4)
(b) Dmitrii Piatkin's 'Hail Stalin!' The caption reads: 'In celebration of our free
Fatherland, the trusty bulwark of the friendship of the peoples' (1951).

Plate 14. Muscovites listen as Prime Minister Viacheslav Molotov announces the outbreak of the war, 22 June 1941.

Plate 15. Red Army soldiers fighting in the streets in Stalingrad during the
Second World War, winter 1942–February 1943.

Plate 16. Soviet poster by Viktor Govorkov: 'Who receives the national income? In
capitalist countries the lion's share goes to the exploiters. In the USSR it goes to the
working people' (1950).

Plate 17. Nikita Khrushchev and Fidel Castro.

Plate 18. Soviet space capsule *Vostok* being assembled in 1965 by a group of Soviet technicians; photograph released by an official Soviet source in connection with the USSR Economic Achievement Exhibition in Moscow.

Plate 19. Russian tanks in the streets of Prague, Czechoslovakia, after the Soviet invasion that brought the 'Prague Spring' of 1968 to an end.

Plate 20. Parade float of the factory named 'Comintern' proclaiming 'More, Better', 7 November 1968.

Plate 21.  General Secretary Leonid Il'ich Brezhnev and President Gerald R. Ford sign a joint communique for the limitation of strategic offensive arms, Vladivostok, USSR, 24 November 1974.

Plate 22.  Still from *Ballad of a Soldier* (1959), directed by Grigorii Chukhrai.

МАТЕРИАЛЬНАЯ ОСНОВА МОГУЩЕСТВА СТРАНЫ

Plate 23. Soviet poster from the early years of *perestroika* (1986) showing General Secretary Mikhail Gorbachev meeting with energy workers in Tiumen'. Caption: 'The material base of the power of the country'. The text reads, in part: 'By the labour of generations of Soviet people, a powerful economic, scientific-technical and cultural potential has been created.'

Plate 24. Groznyi, the capital city of the republic of Chechnya, in ruins after battles between the Russian armed forces and nationalist resisters, 1996.

Plate 25. Outgoing president of the Russian Federation, Boris Yeltsin, and his successor at the inauguration of President Vladimir Putin, Moscow, 7 May 2001.

as first secretary of the CPSU in Kazakhstan (on the recommendation of the outgoing first secretary, Dinmukhamed Kunaev) in December 1986 provoked riots in Alma Ata (Almaty). In July 1987 Moscow's Red Square was the scene of a sit-down demonstration by Crimean Tatars demanding to be allowed to return to the homeland from which they had been exiled by Stalin. From February 1988 the temperature of the dispute between Armenia and Azerbaijan over the land of Nagorno-Karabakh was seldom below boiling point. The federal authorities found this an especially intractable problem, since both Armenians and Azeris were utterly convinced of their historic claim to the territory. The fact that this predominantly Armenian enclave was within the Soviet republic of Azerbaijan had long been a sore point for Armenians. It was – for Gorbachev and the federal authorities – just one of the unintended consequences of liberalisation that Armenians in their tens of thousands felt able to raise the issue sharply less than three years into *perestroika*. The dispute led to inter-ethnic violence in 1988 with at least thirty-two people, mainly Armenians, killed in the city of Sumgait in Azerbaijan where many more Armenian homes were wrecked. In turn there were fatal attacks on Azeris in Nagorno-Karabakh and in Armenia itself. A further escalation of violence occurred in 1990 when a pogrom of Armenians in Baku killed at least sixty people. This led Gorbachev's special envoy, Evgenii Primakov, to urge strong action against the Popular Front in Azerbaijan. The indiscriminate nature of the onslaught subsequently ordered by Soviet senior officers on the spot produced an official death toll of eighty-three, though according to Azeri nationalist sources several hundred people may have died. The cycle of violence merely further inflamed national passions and did nothing to resolve the problems.

This was never more evident than in the case of the violent suppression of a peaceful demonstration by young people in Tbilisi in April 1989. Soviet troops, with the support of the first secretary of the CPSU in Georgia (and against the explicit wishes of Gorbachev who had asked Shevardnadze to fly to Georgia to negotiate a peaceful end to the stand-off), brutally attacked the protestors. Nineteen of the demonstrators (mainly young women) were killed and several hundred were injured. From that time on, Georgian nationalism was more than ever a force to be reckoned with. Similarly, violence against protesters in the Lithuanian capital, Vilnius, and the Latvian capital, Riga, in early 1991 merely added fuel to the fires of national discontent. Gorbachev, in the winter of 1990–1, had made a tactical shift in the direction of more conservative forces and at times his rhetoric was a throwback to an earlier period. He desperately wished to preserve the Union, but was not willing to pay the price of bloodily suppressing nationalist movements. Each use of excessive force by

Soviet troops was intended by their chiefs in the power ministries to be but the beginning of a more general crackdown on all fissiparous movements. They also hoped to separate Gorbachev from the most liberal-minded members of his team and from the democratic movement that had developed after 1989 in Russian society. In the latter aim in particular the conservatives had some success. Yet – in contrast with the sustained violence in Chechnya in post-Soviet Russia – each incident in which force was used in the Gorbachev era was a one-day event. The forces favouring violent suppression of national and separatist movements were never given their head to 'finish the job', partly because of Gorbachev's reluctance on moral grounds to shed blood and partly because he realised that such violence as had been applied was entirely counter-productive.

Separatist movements in the Soviet Union were given a huge impetus by developments in Eastern Europe in 1989. It was at this point that the radicalisation of the political agenda came full circle. Developments within the Soviet Union itself had been the key to change in the rest of Communist Europe. The peoples of Central and Eastern Europe had decided to test the sincerity of Gorbachev's professed willingness to let the people of each country decide for themselves the character of their political system. They could not fail to notice that, to their surprise, domestic liberalisation had gone further by the end of 1988 within Russia than it had in most of the Warsaw Pact countries. The outcome of taking Gorbachev at his word was that in the course of one year Eastern European countries became non-Communist and independent. For Estonians, Latvians and Lithuanians, this was especially significant. They were no longer ready to argue simply for greater sovereignty within a renewed Soviet Union but for an independent statehood that would be no less than that enjoyed by Czechs, Hungarians and Poles.[53] Moreover, competitive elections had brought to the fore politicians – including, in the case of Lithuania, even the Communist Party first secretary (Algirdas-Mikolas Brazauskas) – ready to embrace the national cause.

When Gorbachev had declared each people's 'right to choose', he had in mind existing states. He truly believed that there was a 'Soviet people' who had a lot in common which transcended national differences. His doctrine of liberation was not intended to lead to separatism in the USSR. When he came round to recognising the reality of the Soviet Union's own 'nationality problem', his preferred solution was to turn pseudo-federation into genuine

---

53 Archie Brown, 'Transnational Influences in the Transition from Communism', *Post-Soviet Affairs* 16, 2 (Apr.–June 2000): 177–200.

federation – even, as a last resort, in late 1991 into a loose confederation. In April 1991 Gorbachev initiated a new attempt to negotiate a Union Treaty that would preserve a renamed Union on a voluntary basis. Only nine out of the fifteen republics participated in the talks. The fact that they went ahead regardless reflected the fact that Gorbachev and the liberal wing of the leadership (people such as Yakovlev, Shakhnazarov and Cherniaev) had come to accept de facto that the Union would not consist of as many as fifteen republics in the future. They wished, however, that secession, where it had become a political necessity, would be orderly and legally defined.

Events conspired against the preservation of even a smaller union. The election of Yeltsin as Russian president in June 1991 gave him a legitimacy to speak for Russia that was now greater than that of Gorbachev, who had been only indirectly elected by a legislature representing the whole of the USSR more than a year earlier. For some time Yeltsin had been pressing for Russian sovereignty within the Union. In May 1990 he insisted that Russian law had supremacy over Union law. This was a massive blow against a federalist solution to the problems of the Union.[54] The same claim had been made on behalf of Estonia, but Russia contained three-quarters of the territory of the USSR and just over half of its population, so the threat to the future of a federal union was of a different order. Nevertheless, by the summer of 1991, the nine plus one negotiations had produced a draft agreement which Yeltsin and the Ukrainian president, Leonid Kravchuk, were prepared to sign. The president of Kazakhstan, Nursultan Nazarbaev, at that time a strong supporter of preserving a Union, played a constructive role in securing the agreement.[55] Gorbachev had made many concessions. A vast amount of power was to be devolved to the republics, so much so that the conservative majority within the CPSU apparatus, the army and the KGB were convinced that this would be but a stepping-stone to the break-up of the Soviet Union.

Thus, with the draft Union Treaty due to be signed on 20 August 1991, and with Gorbachev preparing to fly back to Moscow from his holiday home in Foros on the Crimean coast, the final blow to the Union was struck by people whose main aim was to preserve it. Gorbachev, his wife and family and one or two close colleagues (including Cherniaev) were put under house arrest on 18 August and a state of emergency was declared in Moscow early in the morning of 19 August. A self-appointed State Committee for the State of Emergency was set up in which the Soviet vice-president, Gennadii Ianaev,

---

54 See Aron, *Boris Yeltsin*, p. 377.
55 Georgii Shakhnazarov, *Tsena svobody: Reformatsiia Gorbacheva glazami ego pomoshchnika* (Moscow: Rossika Zevs, 1993), p. 233.

had been persuaded to play the most public role. In order to provide a fig leaf of legality, the plan had been to persuade Gorbachev to hand over his powers (temporarily, he was told) to the vice-president.

From the moment that Gorbachev denounced the delegation which had been sent to cajole or intimidate him into acquiescing with their action (which had begun with cutting off all his telephones) the putschists were in trouble.[56] The key figures in this attempt to turn the clock back (which, if it had succeeded, would logically have resulted in severe repression in the most disaffected republics and a return to a highly authoritarian regime in the Soviet Union as a whole) were, unsurprisingly, the chairman of the KGB, Vladimir Kriuchkov, the powerful head of the military-industrial complex of the Soviet Union, Oleg Baklanov, and the minister of defence, Dmitrii Iazov. Many senior Communist Party officials sympathised with them and one Politburo member, Oleg Shenin, was intimately involved in the coup attempt. Because, however, the CPSU had by this time lost whatever prestige it once enjoyed, the emphasis of the plotters was on patriotism and preserving the Soviet state. There was no reference to restoring the monopoly of power of the Communist Party or to Marxism-Leninism. Many people demonstrated in Moscow against the coup, but throughout the country as a whole most citizens waited to see who would come out on top. Many republican and most regional party leaders assumed that those who had taken such drastic action would prevail and hastened to acknowledge the 'new leadership'.

It emerged, however, that even the most conservative section of the Soviet party and state establishment had been affected by the changes in Soviet society and the new norms that had come to prevail over the previous six and a half years. Yeltsin, in the Russian White House (the home at that time of the Russian government), became the symbol of resistance to the coup. He received strong support from Western leaders, although a few had initially been prepared to accept the coup as a *fait accompli*, among them President Mitterrand of France. The tens of thousands of Muscovites (several hundred thousand over several days when account is taken of comings and goings) who surrounded the White House raised the political cost of its storming, but would not have prevented the building and its occupants being seized, if the army, Ministry of Interior and KGB troops had acted with the kind of ruthlessness they displayed in

56 On the coup, see Mikhail Gorbachev, *The August Coup: The Truth and the Lessons* (London: HarperCollins, 1991); Anatoly Chernyaev, *My Six Years with Gorbachev*, trans. and ed. Robert English and Elizabeth Tucker (University Park, Pa.: Pennsylvania State University Press, 2000), esp. 'Afterword to the U.S. Edition', pp. 401–23; and V. Stepankov and E. Lisov, *Kremlevskii zagovor: Versiia sledstviia* (Moscow: Ogonek, 1992).

pre-*perestroika* times. Yet, faced with political resistance, the forces of coercion themselves became divided. Since the coup leaders were people who had for several years been denouncing Gorbachev – at first, in private, and of late in public – for 'indecisiveness', it is ironic that their own indecision made certain the failure of the coup. They lacked the resolution to carry it to its logical conclusion and gave up the attempt as early as 21 August.

The putsch was, however, a mortal blow both for the Union and for the leadership of Gorbachev. Having seen how close they had been to being fully reincorporated in a Soviet state which would have been a throwback to the past, the Baltic states instantly declared their independence. This was recognised by the Soviet Union on 6 September. Four days later Armenia followed suit, while Georgia and Moldova already considered themselves to be independent. While Gorbachev had been isolated on the Crimean coast, Yeltsin had been the public face of resistance to the coup, and Gorbachev's position became weaker and Yeltsin's stronger in its aftermath. Taking full advantage of this further shift in the balance of power, Yeltsin was no longer content with the draft Union Treaty that was to have been signed in August. New negotiations saw further concessions from Gorbachev which would have moved what remained of a Union into something akin to a loose confederation. Ultimately, this did not satisfy the leaders of the three Slavic republics – Yeltsin, Leonid Kravchuk of Ukraine, and Stanislav Shushkevich of Belarus. At a meeting on 8 December 1991 they announced that the Soviet Union was ceasing to exist and that they were going to create in its place a Commonwealth of Independent States (see Map 12.1). Not the least of the attractions of this outcome for Yeltsin was that with no Union there would be no Gorbachev in the Kremlin. In the months following the coup he had been sharing that historic headquarters of Russian leaders with Gorbachev, but, given their rivalry, such a 'dual tenancy', like 'dual power' in 1917, could not last.

In a televised 'Address to Soviet Citizens' on 25 December 1991, just as the Soviet state itself was coming to an end, Gorbachev announced that he was ceasing to be president of the USSR. He said that, although he had favoured sovereignty of the republics, he could not accept the complete dismemberment of the Soviet Union and held that decisions of such magnitude should have been accepted only if ratified by popular will. Looking back on his years in power, he observed that all the changes had been carried through in sharp struggle with 'the old, obsolete and reactionary forces' and had come up against 'our intolerance, low level of political culture and fear of change'. Yet, he could justly claim that the society 'had been freed politically and spiritually', with the establishment of free elections, freedom of the press and freedom of

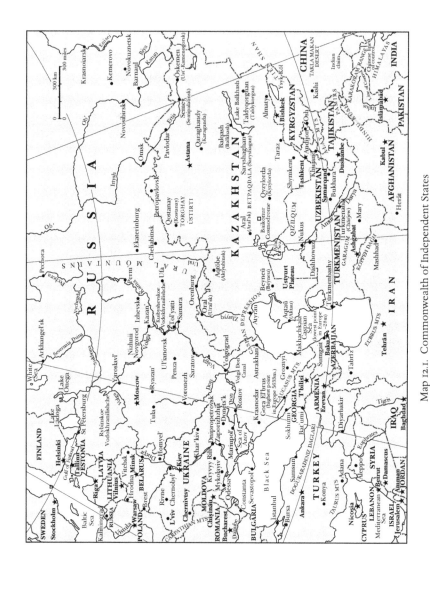

Map 12.1. Commonwealth of Independent States

worship. On foreign policy the gains seemed to Gorbachev to be especially clear:

> An end has been put to the 'Cold War', the arms race and the insane militarisation of our country, which disfigured our economy, social thinking and morals. The threat of world war has been removed.

Moreover:

> We opened ourselves up to the rest of the world, renounced interference in the affairs of others and the use of troops beyond our borders. In response, we have gained trust, solidarity and respect.

Looking ahead, Gorbachev had words of warning:

> I consider it vitally important to preserve the democratic achievements of the last few years. We have earned them through the suffering of our entire history and our tragic experience. We must not abandon them under any circumstances or under any pretext. Otherwise, all our hopes for a better future will be buried.[57]

---

57 The full text of Gorbachev's resignation speech is to be found in Mikhail Gorbachev, *Zhizn' i reformy*, vol. 1, pp. 5–8; and in the abbreviated English translation of that book: Gorbachev, *Memoirs* (London: Transworld, 1996), pp. xxvi–xxix.

13

# The Russian Federation

MICHAEL McFAUL

The immediate afterglow of the failed coup attempt in August 1991 must rank as one of the more optimistic periods in Russian history. In August 1991, like many other times in Russia's past, Kremlin rulers had issued orders to suppress the people. This time around, some of the people resisted. For three days, a military stand-off ensued between those defending elected representatives of the people in the White House – the home to Russia's Congress of People's Deputies – and those carrying out orders issued by non-elected leaders in the Kremlin.[1] Popular resistance to the coup attempt was not widespread. In fact, except for Moscow, St Petersburg and the industrial centres in the Urals, there were no signs of resistance at all.[2] But this concentrated opposition, especially in Moscow, produced major consequences for Russia's history. In this round of conflict between the Russian people and their rulers, the people prevailed. The victory created an atmosphere of unlimited potential. One Western publication declared, 'Serfdom's End: a thousand years of autocracy are reversed'.[3]

The triumph, however, also fuelled inflated expectations about what was to come next. The victors immediately accomplished some symbolic gestures, such as the arrest of the coup plotters and the destruction of Feliks Dzerzhinsky's statue outside the KGB's headquarters. But the bigger tasks of creating a new state, economy and polity soon erased the euphoria of August 1991 for Russia's political leadership. Russian President Boris Yeltsin, the unquestioned hero of the dramatic August events, most certainly seemed overwhelmed. He spent three weeks in September outside Moscow on vacation.

---

[1] The situation represented a classic revolutionary situation of dual sovereignty. See Charles Tilly, *From Mobilization to Revolution* (New York: McGraw-Hill, 1978), ch. 9.

[2] For assessments of national resistance, see John Dunlop, *The Rise of Russia and the Fall of the Soviet Empire* (Princeton: Princeton University Press, 1993), pp. 236–7.

[3] This title is from *Time*, 2 Sept. 1991, p. 3.

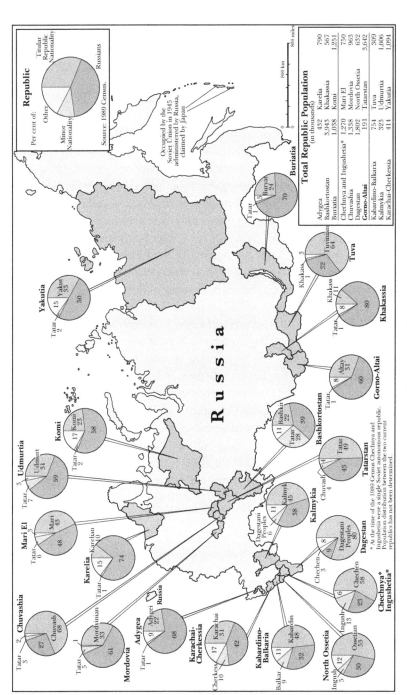

## Republic

Per cent of:
- Titular Republic Nationality
- Other
- Russians
- Minor Nationality

Source: 1989 Census.

Occupied by the Soviet Union in 1945, administered by Russia, claimed by Japan

### Total Republic Population
(in thousands)

| | | | | |
|---|---|---|---|---|
| Adygea | 432 | Karelia | 790 |
| Bashkortostan | 3,943 | Khakassia | 567 |
| Buriatia | 1,038 | Komi | 1,251 |
| Chechnya and Ingushetia* | 1,270 | Mari El | 750 |
| Chuvashia | 1,338 | Mordovia | 963 |
| Dagestan | 1,802 | North Ossetia | 632 |
| Gorno-Altai | 191 | Tatarstan | 3,642 |
| Kabardino-Balkaria | 754 | Tuva | 309 |
| Kalmykia | 323 | Udmurtia | 1,606 |
| Karachai-Cherkessia | 414 | Yakutia | 1,094 |

* At the time of the 1989 Census Chechnya and Ingushetia were a single Soviet autonomous republic. Population distribution between the two current republics has not been determined.

Map 13.1. Ethnic Republics in 1994

August 1991 may have punctuated the end of one regime, but did little to define the contours of what was to follow. As in all revolutions, destruction of the *ancien régime* came easier and more quickly than the construction of a new order.[4] Throughout the autumn of 1991, it remained uncertain what kind of political regime or economic system would fill the void left by the collapsing Soviet state. Some within Russia were convinced that the command economy had to be dismantled and replaced by a market system. Others had a different view. Likewise, many within Russia spoke about the need to destroy the last vestiges of autocracy and erect a democracy. But among these advocates of regime change, there was little agreement about the ultimate endpoint. And with hindsight, we now know that many powerful actors within the Soviet Union had no intention of building democracy, as the majority of regimes in place today in the states of the former Soviet Union are forms of dictatorship, not liberal democracies.[5] Even the borders of the new political units were unclear. And those who had a notion of what the endpoint should be regarding political and economic change did not have a roadmap in hand for how to get there.

Even if Yeltsin and his supporters had known precisely what they wanted and had a blueprint for creating it, they still did not have the political power to implement their agenda. In August 1991, Yeltsin of course was the most popular figure in Russia. Yet, this popularity was ephemeral and perhaps not as widespread as observers stationed in Moscow made it out to be. Yeltsin's authority was not institutionalised in either political organisations or state offices. Even the powers of his presidential office – created just two months earlier – were not clear. Equally ambiguous was the strength of those political forces that favoured preservation of the Soviet political and economic order. The coup had failed, but those sympathetic to the coup's aims were still in

---

4 For elaboration of the frame of revolution as a method for understanding change in post-Communist Russia, see Vladimir Mau and Irina Starodubrovskaya, *The Challenge of Revolution: Contemporary Russia in Historical Perspective* (Oxford: Oxford University Press, 2001).

5 In his classifications of regimes in the former Soviet space at the end of 2001, Larry Diamond ranks only three (Estonia, Latvia and Lithuania) as liberal democracies, one (Moldova) as an electoral democracy, three (Armenia, Georgia, Ukraine) as ambiguous regimes, two (Russia and Belarus) as competitive authoritarian regimes, five (Azerbaijan, Kazakhstan, Kyrgyzstan, Tajikistan and Uzbekistan) as hegemonic electoral authoritarian regimes, and one (Turkmenistan) as a politically closed authoritarian regime. See Larry Diamond, 'Thinking about Hybrid Regimes', *Journal of Democracy* 13, 2 (Apr. 2002): 30. For arguments explaining this variation, see Steven M. Fish, 'Democratization's Requisites', *Post-Soviet Affairs* 14, 3 (1998): 212–47; Steven Levitsky and Lucan Way, 'The Rise of Competitive Authoritarianism, *Journal of Democracy* 13, 2 (Apr. 2002): 51–65; and Michael McFaul, 'The Fourth Wave of Democracy *and* Dictatorship: Noncooperative Transitions in the Postcommunist World', *World Politics* 54, 2 (Jan. 2002): 212–44.

power in the government, the army, the KGB, in local governments and even in the Russian Congress of People's Deputies. Fearing a replay of 1917, Yeltsin and his band of revolutionaries decided not to use force against their enemies. In attempting to advance a peaceful revolution, however, the new leaders in Moscow were constrained by lingering legacies of the Soviet era for the rest of the decade.

Yeltsin and his allies, therefore, did not enjoy a *tabula rasa* in constructing a new state, economy and political system after the 1991 coup. Although Russia's abrupt, revolutionary mode of transition removed guideposts for navigating the transition, the non-violent nature of the transition also allowed many individuals, institutions and social forces endowed with certain rights and powers in the Soviet system to continue to play important political and economic roles in the post-Soviet era. The clash between fading old institutions and groups, emerging new actors, forces and practices, and robust mutations between the old and the new defined the drama in Russian history throughout the 1990s.[6]

## Dissolving the Soviet Union

In tackling the triple agenda of state formation, economic transformation and regime change, Yeltsin made the creation of an independent Russian state his first priority. He had no popular mandate for this momentous task. Only a few months earlier, in March 1991, over 70 per cent of Russian citizens had voted to preserve the Soviet Union. After the August coup attempt, however, Yeltsin saw the dissolution of the Soviet Union as both inevitable and desirable. The Baltic republics took immediate advantage of the power vacuum in Moscow after the coup to push for complete independence from the Soviet Union. Other republics followed the Baltic lead. The week after the coup attempt, the Ukrainian Supreme Soviet voted overwhelmingly (321 in favour, 6 against) to declare Ukraine an independent state, and set 1 December 1991 as the date for a referendum to obtain a popular mandate for their decision. Georgia and Armenia quickly followed by voting in September for full independence. At the time, Gorbachev was still formally the president of the Soviet Union, but in actuality he had little authority or power left to sanction these rebellious

---

6 At the beginning of the 1990s, the losers from change in the post-Communist order were thought to be the greatest enemies of reform. See, most importantly, Adam Przeworski, *Democracy and the Market: Political and Economic Reforms in Eastern Europe and Latin America* (Cambridge: Cambridge University Press, 1991). Later in the decade, those that benefited from partial reform emerged as the real threat. See Joel Hellman, 'Winners Take All: The Politics of Partial Reform in Postcommunist Transitions', *World Politics* 50 (1998): 203–34.

republics, and Yeltsin most certainly was not going to order troops into these places to defend Soviet territorial integrity. After all, he had declared Russia a sovereign country a year earlier. Instead, Yeltsin devoted his energies to guiding the Soviet Union to peaceful disintegration.

Yeltsin first banned the Communist Party of the Soviet Union, dissolving the only organisation potentially capable of making and implementing policy at the all-Union level. Yeltsin also suspended the publication of several Communist newspapers, and purged the leadership at other important media outlets. Though most were senior CPSU officials, leaders in other republics did the same in their territories. Next, Yeltsin and his allies moved quickly to recast most of the ministries and organisations of the Soviet state as Russian entities. The strategy regarding most of these state organs was co-option, not coercion or dissolution.[7] Yeltsin and his government adopted a more cautious strategy regarding the so-called power ministries. With the CPSU in disarray, the Soviet armed forces, the KGB and the Ministry of Internal Affairs were the only organisations that had the capacity (and quite possibly the legitimacy) to construct an alternative all-Union administrative authority. After all, most of the Soviet Union's armed and best-trained troops were stationed beyond the Russian Republic's borders.[8] To begin to neutralise these institutions, therefore, Yeltsin appointed loyal allies to head them. But in contrast to his strategy towards other ministries, Yeltsin allowed the power ministries to remain under Soviet jurisdiction during this transitional period. He eventually incorporated these ministries into the Russian government after Soviet dissolution, but without initiating any serious internal reforms within these ministries.[9] Nor did Yeltsin establish firm civilian control over these bodies. Above all else, Yeltsin, as well as other republican leaders, feared a divided and polarised army.

There were two Soviet state institutions that Yeltsin did not want to seize, but rather destroy – the Soviet Congress of People's Deputies and the Soviet presidency. He and his government first sought to discredit the Soviet parliament by blaming Soviet legislators for tacit acquiescence to the coup. As Yeltsin stated the week after the coup attempt, 'During the days of the putsch, there was no supreme legislative power in the country, there was no parliament. The junta had a free hand. Through its inaction, the Supreme Soviet provided the

7 On the process, see Egor Gaidar, *Dni porazhenii i pobed* (Moscow: Vagrius, 1996).
8 Dale Herspring, 'Putin and the Armed Forces', in Dale R. Herspring (ed.), *Putin's Russia: Past Imperfect, Future Uncertain* (Armonk, N.Y.: M. E. Sharpe, 2003), p. 155.
9 Yeltsin did divide the KGB into three separate bureaucracies. Reforms within the Ministry of Internal Affairs and the Ministry of Defence were minimal.

junta with most-favored status.'[10] In response to Yeltsin's prodding, the Soviet Congress approved on 5 September 1991 a new law on governing the Soviet Union during a transitional period in which the Congress de facto surrendered its governing authority to an executive body called the USSR State Council. The axe fell next on the Soviet presidency. Although enjoying Gorbachev's co-operation during this volatile period, Yeltsin wanted to use the opportunity of the failed August putsch to eliminate his nemesis from politics forever.[11] To eliminate Gorbachev's position and prevent the Soviet leader from attempting to create a new looser union, Yeltsin met with his counterparts from Ukraine and Belarus to sign the Belovezhskaia Accord on 8 December 1991. This short accord effectively dismantled the USSR.[12] Amazingly, it met little resistance in any of the three signatory countries. By the end of the year, the largest country in the world ceased to exist.

## The new political system

Like many other revolutionary leaders in similar situations, Yeltsin could have taken advantage of August 1991 to establish an authoritarian regime.[13] Several of Yeltsin's advisers did urge him to consider an authoritarian strategy, at least as an interim solution to collapsing state power throughout the country and as a means for introducing unpopular economic reforms. On the other hand, Yeltsin could have taken steps to consolidate a democratic polity. He could have disbanded old Soviet government institutions, adopted a new constitution codifying the division of power between executive, legislative and judiciary as well as federal and regional bodies, and called new elections to stimulate the development of a multi-party system. Many leaders in the democratic movement expected him to do so. Yeltsin, however, pursued neither strategy.

10 Yeltsin, speech to Extraordinary Congress of the USSR Congress of People's Deputies, in *Izvestiya*, 4 Sept. 1991, pp. 4–7; reprinted in *The Current Digest of the Soviet Press* 53, 37 (16 Oct. 1991): 3.
11 Yeltsin and Gorbachev despised each other. On their criticisms of each other during the autumn of 1991, see Mikhail Gorbachev, *Memoirs* (New York: Doubleday, 1996), chs. 30 and 31; and Boris Yeltsin, *The Struggle for Russia* (New York: Random House, 1994), ch. 3. For an independent assessment of this complicated relationship, see George Breslauer, *Gorbachev and Yeltsin as Leaders* (Cambridge: Cambridge University Press, 2002), ch. 7.
12 'Agreement of the Creation of the Commonwealth of Independent States', 8 Dec. 1991; reprinted in Alexander Dallin and Gail Lapidus (eds.), *The Soviet System: From Crisis to Collapse*, revised edn (Boulder, Colo.: Westview Press, 1995), p. 638.
13 On this pattern, see Theda Skocpol, 'Social Revolutions and Mass Military Mobilization', *World Politics* 40, 2 (Jan. 1988): 147–68.

Although he did not attempt to erect a dictatorship, he did little to consolidate a new democratic polity. Importantly, he resisted calls for new national elections and actually postponed regional elections scheduled for December 1991. He also did not form a political party. He delayed the adoption of a new constitution, even though his own constitutional commission had completed a first new draft as early as October 1990. Yeltsin also failed to dismantle many Soviet-era governmental institutions, including, most importantly, the Supreme Soviet and the Congress of People's Deputies of the Russian Republic.[14]

## Launching economic transformation

Yeltsin's priority was not the creation or consolidation of a new democratic political system (or a new authoritarian regime). Rather, once the borders of the new Russian state were secure, Yeltsin turned his attention to dismantling the command economy and creating a market economy. He and his new government inherited a bankrupt economy – no hard currency reserves, a ballooning budget deficit, foreign debt of $80 billion, declining industrial production, a monetary overhang and a scarcity of goods that compelled many experts to predict starvation. After some hesitation, Yeltsin came to believe that only radical reforms could redress these desperate economic conditions. He hired a team of young reformers, led by his new deputy prime minister for the economy, Egor Gaidar, to initiate such reforms, which acquired the unfortunate label of 'shock therapy'.[15]

Gaidar's programme for economic reform called for immediate liberalisation of prices and trade while at the same time achieving macroeconomic stabilisation through control of the money supply and government spending.[16] Once stabilisation had been accomplished, massive privatisation was to follow. Gaidar's plan was consistent with his neo-liberal approach to markets and market development; the less the state intervened in the market the better.

14 On the reasons for inaction, see Michael McFaul, *Russia's Unfinished Revolution: Political Change from Gorbachev to Putin* (Ithaca, N.Y.: Cornell University Press, 2001), ch. 4.
15 On the general formula, see Anders Aslund, *Post-Communist Economic Revolutions: How Big a Bang?* (Washington: Center for Strategic and International Studies, 1992); and Jeffrey Sachs, *Poland's Jump to the Market Economy* (Cambridge, Mass.: MIT Press, 1993).
16 On the formation of this team, see Anders Aslund, *How Russia Became a Market Economy* (Washington: Brookings Institution Press, 1995).

## The consequences of Yeltsin's reform
## sequence and strategy

Yeltsin's greatest achievement as president was the peaceful dissolution of the Soviet Union. Initiating economic reform was another important accomplishment. Executing the measures successfully, however, was not.

In January 1992, Yeltsin and Gaidar did succeed in introducing dramatic price liberalisation. Prices on most food items (exceptions were milk, bread and other main staples) as well as almost all consumer durables were freed overnight. Significant price controls, however, remained in the energy sector. At the time, government officials, trade union chiefs and journalists all predicted riots, work stoppages and general social unrest. Gaidar himself predicted his own dismissal by the end of the month. None of these scenarios transpired. This peaceful transition towards free prices represented a monumental step for a country where prices had been controlled for over sixty years. By the end of the decade, few goods were rationed, long queues were rare and Russian shops were filled with goods to sell.

The January 1992 price liberalisation produced a sharp rise in inflation. What is striking in retrospect, however, is how low inflation was in comparison with the rates to follow. Monthly inflation rates steadily declined from 38 per cent in February 1992 to 9 per cent in August 1992. Politics, however, quickly eroded Gaidar's ability to implement macroeconomic stabilisation.[17] Tight government money threatened directors and workers of large state enterprises. These groups used the moment of the Sixth Congress of People's Deputies in the spring of 1992 to launch an assault against Gaidar's reforms. Rather than call for Gaidar's dismissal, leaders of the parliamentary faction, Industrial Union, mobilised other conservative forces in the parliamentary body to strip the president of his extraordinary powers. Ambiguously defined rules of the game, including most importantly the absence of a new Russian constitution, made possible this kind of strategy. Although Yeltsin fought and defeated the original move to dilute his executive powers, he did later compromise with the anti-reform coalition in the parliament by agreeing to appoint three new deputy prime ministers closely associated with the industrial lobby – Vladimir Shumeiko, Georgii Khizha and Viktor Chernomyrdin – into his government. During the painful first year of the transition from the command economy, Yeltsin began to lose confidence in his young team of economic

---

17 For details, see Andrei Shleifer and Daniel Treisman, *Without a Map: Political Tactics and Economic Reform in Russia* (Cambridge, Mass.: MIT Press, 2000), ch. 3.

advisers.[18] By the end of the year, Yeltsin acquiesced to pressure from the Russian Congress and dropped his acting prime minister Gaidar. Yeltsin replaced Gaidar with the more conservative Chernomyrdin, the former head of the gas company, Gazprom. For many, this was the end of economic reform in Russia.

The consequences of these political battles for macroeconomic stabilisation were profound.[19] By the summer of 1992, government transfers to state enterprises began to increase dramatically. Even more importantly, however, Gaidar and his team lost control of monetary policy. As part of this compromise with the industrialists, Viktor Gerashchenko was appointed head of the Russian Central Bank. Soon after his appointment, Gerashchenko approved the clearing of inter-enterprise debt as well as cheap credit lines for state enterprises. As a result of these changes in both fiscal and monetary policies, inflation began to soar again in the autumn of 1992, reaching 25 per cent per month by the end of the year. Central Bank credits amounted to 31 per cent of GDP.[20]

Though sequenced to begin after liberalisation and stabilisation, privatisation has been singled out as the 'driving force behind economic reform in Russia' and 'the heart of the transformation process'.[21] As defined by Yeltsin's first post-Communist government, the policy of privatisation of large state enterprises aims to create privately owned, profit-seeking corporations owned by outside shareholders that do not depend on government subsidies for survival. If enterprises must generate profits to cover expenditures and pay dividends to stockholders, then they will be compelled to rationalise assets, a process that will include downsizing, restructuring and bankruptcy.

On paper, Russian privatisation looked successful. By January 1994, 90,000 state enterprises had been privatised. The record on the actual creation of real private property rights, however, was less rosy. Privatisation of small shops and services created actual owners endowed with clearly delineated property rights. Privatisation of large state enterprises did not. Instead, by the summer of 1993, insiders had acquired majority shares in two-thirds of Russia's privatised and privatising firms, state subsidies accounted for 22 per cent of

18 Yeltsin, *The Struggle for Russia*, p. 165.
19 See Timothy Frye, 'The Perils of Polarization: Economic Performance in the Postcommunist World', *World Politics* 54, 3 (Apr. 2002): 308–37.
20 Bridget Granville, *The Success of Russian Economic Reforms* (London: Royal Institute of International Affairs, 1995), p. 67.
21 Stanley Fisher and Alan Gelb, 'The Process of Socialist Economic Transformation', *Journal of Economic Perspectives* 5, 4 (Fall 1991): 98.

Russia's GDP, while indicators of actual restructuring (bankruptcies, downsizing, unemployment, unbundling) were not positive.[22]

Again, the problem was politics. Well before the collapse of the Soviet regime, the Soviet institutional arrangements governing property rights allowed directors to appropriate many of the rights associated with ownership. When the Yeltsin government's privatisation programme threatened to re-allocate property rights, these directors organised to defend their claims.[23] Their venue of struggle once again was the Congress of People's Deputies. While Gaidar and his privatisation tsar, Anatolii Chubais, had hoped to implement their original privatisation programme through presidential decree, industrialists in the Congress argued that such an important act had to have the force of law. After some hesitation, Yeltsin agreed to submit the privatisation programme for parliamentary approval. Over a hundred amendments were added to Chubais's original privatisation programme, including two new options for privatisation, which allowed managers to acquire control of their firms. Not surprisingly, insiders acquired the majority of enterprises privatised under this new law.

Polarisation over economic issues between the president and his government on the one hand and the Russian Congress on the other eventually provoked conflict over basic political issues. The absence of well-defined political rules of the game fuelled ambiguity, stalemate and conflict both between the federal and sub-national units of the state. Both confrontations ended in armed conflict.

## October 1993

The Russian Congress of People's Deputies was an odd foe for Boris Yeltsin. In 1990, this body had elected Yeltsin as its chairman. After Yeltsin became president, this Congress then elected Yeltsin's deputy chairman, Ruslan Khasbulatov to become speaker. In August 1991, Yeltsin, Khasbulatov and their supporters huddled inside the Congress building – the White House – as their chief defensive strategy for thwarting the coup. In November 1991, the Congress voted overwhelmingly to give Yeltsin extraordinary powers to deal with economic

---

22 Joseph Blasi, Maya Kroumova and Douglas Kruse, *Kremlin Capitalism: Privatizing the Russian Economy* (Ithaca, N.Y.: Cornell University Press, 1997). For an even more critical assessment, see Clifford Gaddy and Barry Ickes, *Russia's Virtual Economy* (Washington: Brookings Institution Press, 2002).
23 Michael McFaul, 'State Power, Institutional Change, and the Politics of Privatization in Russia', *World Politics* 47, 2 (Jan. 1995): 210–43.

reform. In December 1991, the Supreme Soviet of the Russian Congress ratified Yeltsin's agreement to dissolve the Soviet Union. Only six deputies voted against the agreement.

The portrayal, therefore, of the Congress as a hotbed of *Communist* conservatism is misleading. To be sure, Communist deputies controlled roughly 40 per cent of the seats in the Congress and the anti-Yeltsin coalition – which included Communists and non-Communists – grew over time.[24] Yet, the initial balance of power within the Congress did not prevent Yeltsin from being elected chairman. It should not have prevented him from reaching agreement with this Congress about the rules of the game that governed their interaction with each other.

Initially after the putsch attempt, the institutional ambiguity between the president and Congress did not have a direct impact on politics, as most deputies in the Congress at that time supported Yeltsin. After price liberalisation and the beginning of radical economic reform in January 1992, however, the Congress began a campaign to reassert its superiority over the president. The disagreement over economic reform in turn spawned a constitutional crisis between the parliament and president.[25] With no formal institutions to structure relations between the president and the Congress, polarisation crystallised yet again, with both sides claiming to represent Russia's highest sovereign authority. During the summer of 1993, in preparing for the Tenth Congress of People's Deputies, deputies drafted a series of constitutional amendments that would have liquidated Russia's presidential office altogether. Yeltsin pre-empted their plans by dissolving the Congress in September 1993. The Congress, in turn, declared Yeltsin's decree illegal and recognised Vice President Aleksandr Rutskoi as the new interim president. In a replay of the 1991 drama, Russia suddenly had two heads of state and two governments each claiming sovereign authority over the other. The October 1993 'events' – the euphemism coined to describe the armed conflict between the president and the parliament on 3–4 October 1993 – was a national tragedy for Russia. For the second time in as many years, debates about institutional design moved beyond the realm of peaceful politics and into the arena of military confrontation. In 1991, the military stand-off took the lives of three defenders of the White House. In 1993, several hundred people died in the fighting between warring branches of the Russian state. In addition to the loss of life, the October events ended

24 Josephine Andrews, *When Majorities Fail: The Russian Parliament 1990–1993* (Cambridge: Cambridge University Press, 2002).
25 See Thomas Remington, *The Russian Parliament: Institution Evolution in a Transitional Regime, 1989–1999* (New Haven: Yale University Press, 2001), ch. 4.

Russia's romantic embrace of democracy. If the end of the military stand-off in 1991 triggered rapturous support for the new regime and the democratic ideals that it claimed to represent, the end of fighting in 1993 marked a nadir of support for the Russian government and the end of optimism about Russia's democratic prospects.

This tragic moment also created opportunity. After dissolving the parliament in October 1993 through the use of force, Russian President Yeltsin was free to draft the constitution as he and his aides saw fit. This new constitution spelled out a set of basic guarantees for all Russian citizens and codified a new system of government, which included the office of the president, a prime minister and the government, and a bicameral parliament, consisting of a lower house, the State Duma, and an upper house, the Federation Council. In the first election to the Duma, held in December 1993, a presidential decree ruled that half the seats (225) were to be determined by a majoritarian system in newly drawn electoral districts while the other half (225) were to be allocated according to a system of proportional representation (PR). Parties had to win at least 5 per cent to win seats on the PR ballot.[26] Later codified as law, these rules for electing the Duma have remained in place ever since. Two representatives from each region of Russia – that is eighty-nine republics, krais, and oblasts of the Russian Federation – constitute the Federation Council, though the process of selecting these two representatives has changed over time.

The new constitution gave the president extraordinary powers, compelling some to label the new regime a form of authoritarianism.[27] The president appoints the prime minister. The lower house of parliament, the State Duma, must approve the president's choice for prime minister. But if they reject the president's candidate three times, then the Duma is dissolved and new elections are held. Not surprisingly, votes against the prime minister have been few and far between. The president also has the right to issue decrees, which have the power of law until overridden by a law passed by both the upper and lower houses of parliament and signed by the president. The president also controls the nomination process of judges in the Constitutional Court and Supreme Court.[28]

---

26 See Robert Moser, *Unexpected Outcomes: Electoral Systems, Political Parties, and Representation in Russia* (Pittsburgh: University of Pittsburgh Press, 2001).

27 Donald Murray, *A Democracy of Despots* (Boulder, Colo.: Westview Press, 1995); Lilia Shevtsova, *Yeltsin's Russia: Myths and Realities* (Washington: Carnegie Endowment for International Peace, 1999); and Peter Reddaway and Dmitrii Glinski, *The Tragedy of Russia's Reforms: Market Bolshevism against Democracy* (Washington: U.S. Institute of Peace, 2001).

28 For details, see Eugene Huskey, *Presidential Power in Russia* (Armonk, N.Y.: M. E. Sharpe, 1999).

Yeltsin's opponents ridiculed this new basic law, claiming not without merit that the new constitution gave the president extraordinary powers and the process of drafting the constitution was undemocratic. There was no compromise between different parties or regional leaders in the making of this constitution. Rather, Yeltsin imposed his will and then offered voters the choice to reject or accept *his* constitution. Nonetheless, most of Yeltsin's opponents participated in the December 1993 elections, in effect signalling that they were willing to acquiesce to these newly imposed rules. Perhaps most importantly, the leadership of the Communist Party of the Russian Federation decided that it was in the party's best interest to participate in rather than boycott the December 1993 vote.[29] In a referendum in December 1993 marred by claims of fraud, a majority of voters approved the constitution.[30] After the referendum, no major political force in Russia mobilised to challenge the constitution. After years of ambiguity, Russia had a new set of formal rules for organising politics accepted both by the majority of the population and by all strategic political actors.

## Chechnya

The same constitutional ambiguity that fuelled conflict between Yeltsin and the Congress also allowed federal conflicts to fester. Eventually, one of them – Chechnya – exploded into a full-scale war.

Tensions between Moscow and the regions arose well before the 1993 executive–legislative stand-off.[31] Immediately after the August 1991 coup attempt, General Jokhar Dudayev and his government declared Chechnya's independence. In March of the following year, Tatarstan held a successful referendum for full independence. The first of several federal treaties were signed in March 1992, but negotiations over a new federal arrangement embedded within a constitution dragged on without resolution into the summer

29 Joan Barth Urban and Valerii Solovei, *Russia's Communists at the Crossroads* (Boulder, Colo.: Westview Press, 1997), p. 107.
30 Timothy Colton, 'Public Opinion and the Constitutional Referendum', in Timothy Colton and Jerry Hough (eds.), *Growing Pains: Russian Democracy and the Election of 1993* (Washington: Brookings Institution Press, 1998), pp. 291–310; and A. A. Sobianin and V. G. Sukhovolskii, *Demokratiia, ogranichennaia falsifikatsiiami: vybory i referendumy v Rossii v 1991–1993 gg.* (Moscow, 1995).
31 For overviews, see Steven Solnick, 'Is the Center Too Weak or Too Strong in the Russian Federation?', in Valerie Sperling (ed.), *Building the Russian State: Institutional Crisis and the Quest for Democratic Governance* (Boulder, Colo.: Westview Press, 2000), pp. 137–56; and Kathryn Stoner-Weiss, 'The Russian Central State in Crisis', in Zoltan Barany and Robert Moser (eds.), *Russian Politics: Challenges of Democratization* (Cambridge: Cambridge University Press, 2001), pp. 103–34.

of 1993, prompting several other republics as well as oblasts to make their own declarations of independence complete with their own flags, customs agents and threats of minting new currencies. Yeltsin allowed these federal ambiguities to linger. Consumed with starting market reform and then distracted by the power struggle with the Congress, Yeltsin opted not to devote time or resources towards constructing a Russian federal order. Moreover, the Russian state was too weak to exercise sovereignty over a breakaway republic like Chechnya, which enjoyed de facto independence during this period. After the October 1993 stand-off, Yeltsin did put before the people a new constitution, ratified in December 1993, which formally spelled out a solution to Russia's federal ambiguities (see Map 13.1). The new constitution specified that all constituent elements were to enjoy equal rights vis-à-vis the Centre. Absent from the document was any mention of a mechanism for secession.

The formal rules of a new constitution did not resolve the conflicts between the Centre and the regions. Negotiation over the distribution of power between the central and sub-national governments continued. But all sub-national governments except one – Chechnya – acquiesced to a minimalist maintenance of a federal order. Ironically, the clarity of rules generally highlighted the specific problem of Chechnya's status.

After solidifying his power with the defeat of the Russian Congress and the adoption of a new constitution, Yeltsin committed to a military solution following a series of challenges from Dudayev regarding Russian sovereignty during negotiations over the federal treaty in the spring of 1994 and a spate of bus hijackings in the region that summer. A failed coup attempt orchestrated by Russia's Federal Security Service was followed by a ground assault on 1 December 1994 and a full-scale air attack beginning on 11 December 1994.[32] For the second time in as many years, Yeltsin had ordered the deployment of Russian military forces against his own people.[33]

On the eve of attack, Defence Minister Pavel Grachev predicted that the military action would be over within hours. The results of the invasion, however, were disastrous as Russia's armed forces proved ill-prepared to fight such a war (see Plate 24). By the time Russia finally sued for peace in the summer of 1996, an estimated 45,000–50,000 Russian citizens had lost their lives.[34] Moreover, the

32 Shevtsova, *Yeltsin's Russia*, p. 111.
33 For accounts of the war, see John Dunlop, *Russia Confronts Chechnya: Roots of a Separatist Conflict* (Cambridge: Cambridge University Press, 1998); and Anatol Lieven, *Chechnya: Tombstone of Russian Power* (New Haven: Yale University Press, 1998).
34 John Dunlop, 'How Many Soldiers and Civilians Died during the Russo-Chechen War of 1994–1996?' *Central Asian Survey* 19, 3 and 4 (2000): 338.

negotiated settlement that ended the war did not resolve Chechnya's sovereign status, an ambiguity that would later help to spark a second war (discussed below).

## Founding elections: 1993–6

In addition to the constitutional referendum, Yeltsin also decreed that elections for the State Duma and the Federation Council would take place on 12 December 1993. These new parliamentarians were to serve only an interim two-year term, and then face election again in 1995 for a full four-year term. Earlier in the year, Yeltsin had pledged to hold early elections for the presidency. After the October 1993 events, he withdrew that pledge and instead scheduled the next presidential election for 1996. After two years of no elections in post-Communist Russia, this electoral calendar offered voters a chance to choose their national leaders three times in as many years.

Between June 1991 – the timing of the last national election in Soviet Russia – and December 1993 when the first set of competitive elections in the post-Soviet era were held, monumental changes unfolded in Russia, making predictions about electoral outcomes difficult. During this interval, the Russian economy as well as the Russian state had continued to contract, while political polarisation had generated instability and then outright military confrontation. Voter turn-out in December 1993, reported officially at 54.8 per cent, was markedly lower than any previous competitive elections in Russia in 1989, 1990 and 1991.

Some outcomes from 1993 went according to the Yeltsin administration's plan. In the referendum, the official count claimed that 58.4 per cent supported Yeltsin's constitution, while 41.2 per cent opposed it. Elections to the upper house, the Federation Council, and elections in single-mandate districts for the Duma were unremarkable, producing pro-Yeltsin victories in most contexts. The one extraordinary electoral outcome in 1993 occurred on the proportional representation ballot for the Duma. Vladimir Zhirinovsky and his extreme nationalist Liberal Democratic Party of Russia (LDPR) won almost a quarter of the popular vote. At the same time, the pro-Yeltsin Russia's Choice secured a paltry 15 per cent, less than half of what was expected, while the other 'democratic' parties all won less than 10 per cent of the popular vote. The Communist Party of the Russian Federation and their allies, the Agrarian Party of Russia, won less than 20 per cent of the vote, while new 'centrist' groups combined for nearly a quarter of the vote.

Zhirinovsky's splash onto the Russian national stage shocked governmental officials in both Moscow and the West.[35] Because he spouted a venomous brand of racism and chauvinism and criticised in equal proportion the Communists and democrats, Zhirinovsky appeared to represent a new, third force in Russian electoral politics – militant nationalism. Russian fascism seemed ascendant, while both pro-democratic (and pro-Western) forces and pro-Communist forces seemed to be on the decline.[36] At this moment, Russia's political and economic future seemed highly uncertain. Public opinion surveys indicated a rise in the degree of trust in the fairness of the electoral process.[37] At the same time, pro-Yeltsin elites in Moscow hinted that the Kremlin would never allow someone like Zhirinovsky to come to power, no matter what the voters said, suggesting that the elections were not the final determinant of who ruled Russia.

With the advantage of hindsight, it is clear that Zhirinovsky's 1993 victory did not mark the beginning of fascism's ascendance in Russia. Rather it was the unique circumstances of the autumn of 1993 that allowed his star to rise. After two and a half years of falling production, double-digit inflation and general economic uncertainty, everyone expected the opposition or protest vote in 1993 to be substantial. In the immediate aftermath of this mini-civil war in downtown Moscow, the Communists were still regrouping in December. Weeks before the December vote, it was uncertain whether members of the Russian Communist Party would even be allowed to participate. Communist disarray allowed Zhirinovsky to capture the opposition, protest vote. In addition, Zhirinovsky's brilliant television campaign, the first real mass-media campaign in Russian electoral history, established his party as the most aggressive and abrasive enemy of the status quo.[38]

Over the next years leading up to the next parliamentary election in 1995, economic conditions in Russia did not improve, leaving the distribution of

---

35 In the wake of the election, the *Journal of Democracy* commissioned several articles from Russian and American scholars and practitioners. The editors gave the cluster of articles the title, 'Is Russian Democracy Doomed?' See *Journal of Democracy* 5, 2 (Apr. 1994): 3–41.

36 For a flavour of his views at the time, see Vladimir Zhirinovsky, *Poslednii brosok na iug* (Moscow: TOO Pisatel', 1993).

37 Matthew Wyman, Stephen White, Bill Miller and Paul Heywood, 'Public Opinion, Parties, and Voters in the 1993 Russian Elections', *Europe–Asia Studies* 47 (1995): 602.

38 The importance of the PR electoral system cannot be underestimated in accounting for Zhirinovsky's surprising victory. In single-mandate races, LDPR candidates won only five seats in the Duma and no seats in the Federation Council. In a pure majoritarian electoral system, the Liberal Democratic Party would have won less than ten seats in the parliament.

support between pro-government and opposition voters relatively the same. In this two-year interval, however, Zhirinovsky's appeal among opposition voters faded at the same time as the Communist Party reorganised and grew once again as Russia's most important opposition force. Although the Communist Party was challenged by important splinter groups on the Left, including Viktor Anpilov's radical Working Russia, the party entered the 1995 campaign as the most united and best organised political party in Russia. Building upon networks and structures left from several decades of Communist Party rule in Russia, the CPRF used the resources accorded to the party by the Duma to strengthen regional party organisations during the two-year interval between parliamentary votes.

This organisational work paid off as the CPRF made impressive gains over its 1993 showing by winning almost a quarter of the popular vote and thereby reclaiming its role as the leader of the opposition. Buoyed by party identification on the ballot, CPRF candidates also dominated single-mandate races, winning an astonishing fifty-eight seats. Zhirinovsky's LDPR won less than half its 1993 total, but was still placed second with 11 per cent of the popular vote. The total percentage of votes for anti-governmental parties well exceeded 50 per cent, giving hope to the opposition, CPRF leader Ziuganov in particular, that Yeltsin could be defeated in the presidential context in the following year.

Division and poor electoral performances among those considered pro-government or pro-reform helped to fuel optimism in the opposition's camp. The number of electoral blocs that registered for the ballot rose dramatically, from thirteen in 1993 to forty-three in 1995 and most of the new contestants were considered reformist or centrist blocs. Eight of the new electoral blocs in 1995 were direct descendants of Russia's Choice from 1993, while an amazing twenty electoral blocs emerged from the Democratic Russia of 1991. Early in the campaign period, the Yeltsin administration openly promoted the formation of two new electoral blocs led by Prime Minister Viktor Chernomyrdin and Duma speaker Ivan Rybkin that would be loyal to the Yeltsin regime. Chernomyrdin's Our Home Is Russia was supposed to represent the Right of centre, while Rybkin was ordered to form a left-of-centre bloc. The Rybkin project all but collapsed before the vote, but even Chernomyrdin's new 'party of power' did not perform well, just barely breaking into double digits. Grigorii Iavlinskii's *Iabloko* (Apple), the self-proclaimed leader of Russia's democratic opposition, won 7 per cent, well below expectations and almost a full percentage point below *Iabloko's* 1993 showing. Former acting prime minister Egor Gaidar and his Democratic Choice of Russia (DVR) suffered the greatest setback in 1995, winning just 3.9 per cent of the popular vote, less than one-third of their 1993 total.

Most analysts interpreted these results as a firm rebuff of both Yeltsin and Prime Minister Chernomyrdin.[39] Yeltsin subsequently began the 1996 presidential campaign looking as if he would follow other first time post-Communist leaders and be defeated in the second election. To defeat Ziuganov and stay in power a second term, Yeltsin turned the 1996 presidential election into a referendum on the revolution.[40] Yeltsin obviously could not ask voters to judge him by the achievements of his administration over the previous four years – a list of accomplishments that included economic collapse, armed conflict with parliament and war in Chechnya (discussed above and below). Instead Yeltsin's strategy was to convince voters that Russia had to proceed with what he and his allies had started in 1991 – the transformation of Russia into a market economy and democratic polity. In making this case, Yeltsin's campaign also emphasised that the current president was the lesser of two evils. The Yeltsin campaign also scared voters into thinking that revolutionary turmoil would ensue should Ziuganov win. To make it easier for voters to support Yeltsin, his campaign first worked to eliminate or mute the president's negatives. First, Yeltsin's image had to be changed. The president lost twenty pounds, stopped drinking and began to appear frequently in public again. Second, negative policies had to be changed. Public opinion polls demonstrated that two were most salient – unpaid wages and the war in Chechnya. To create a sense of urgency around the issue, Yeltsin created a special government commission tasked with paying all salaries by 1 April. In the process of fulfilling this goal, Yeltsin sacked numerous regional government heads as well as several of his own cabinet officials including his deputy prime minister, Anatolii Chubais. Yeltsin also raised pensions, increased salaries of government employees (including military personnel), and began doling out government transfers on the campaign trail. Yeltsin addressed his other big negative at the end of March when he pledged to end the war in Chechnya. In May, the first Russian troops began to leave.

Parallel to this positive campaign to remake Yeltsin's image, policies and government, Yeltsin's team also unleashed a hard-hitting negative media blitz

---

39 Peter Reddaway, 'Red Alert', *The New Republic*, 29 Jan. 1996, p. 15; Daniel Singer, 'The Burden of Boris', *The Nation*, 1 Apr. 1996, p. 23; and Jerry Hough, Evelyn Davidheiser, Susan Goodrich Lehmann, *The 1996 Russian Presidential Election* (Washington: Brookings Institution Press, 1996).

40 The following two paragraphs are adapted from Michael McFaul, *Russia's 1996 Presidential Election: The End of Polarized Politics* (Stanford, Calif.: Hoover Institution Press, 1997).

against Communism at the end of the campaign. The Yeltsin campaign successfully defined the election as a referendum on seventy years of Soviet Communism, and deftly avoided letting the vote be about Yeltsin's record. Ziuganov tried to bring the focus back to Yeltsin's record, but did not succeed, in part because he enjoyed little access to the national media and in part because he offered no viable alternative to Yeltsin's reforms. Instead of tracking to the centre and becoming a Social Democrat, Ziuganov fused his traditional Communist slogans with nationalist themes. The strategy did not attract new voters. Instead, the campaign became defined by the mass media (virtually monopolised by Yeltsin), as a contest not between two individuals, but between two ways of life.

By 1996 Russia had in place a political system that no longer seemed on the verge of collapse or overthrow. The 1996 vote reaffirmed that elections were the only legitimate means for obtaining political power. At one critical moment in the spring campaign, Yeltsin seemed ready to postpone the vote, ban the Communist Party and rule by decree.[41] But he did not. In surviving this important milestone, Russia's constitution also seemed to be strengthening. Moreover, those elected under the guise of this new law also seemed to be acquiescing to the new political rules. Though the Duma had been dominated by anti-Yeltsin forces between 1994 and 1996, the relationship between the new parliament and president survived new elections for the parliament in 1993 and 1995, votes of no confidence in the government during the summer of 1995, a presidential election in 1996 and the subsequent legislative approval of the prime minister soon thereafter. Co-operation between these two branches was becoming routinised and rules-based.

A return of the Communists also faded as a threat after the 1996 vote. Whether President Ziuganov actually would have tried to resurrect a command economy is a hypothetical question. That he would not have the chance to try ever again seemed certain after the 1996 vote. Instead, prospects for deepening market reforms seemed better than ever. The following year, Russian government officials as well as several Western financial institutions predicted positive growth rates for the first time since the collapse of the Soviet Union. In 1997, Yeltsin also reorganised his government to empower a group of young reformers.[42] He made an even bolder reconfiguration of the government in the

41 Lilia Shevtsova,'El'tsin ostanetsya, dazhe esli proigraet', *Nezavisimaya gazeta*, 26 Apr. 1996, p. 3. Yeltsin admits that he contemplated such a plan, but then rejected it. See Boris Yeltsin, *Midnight Diaries* (New York: Public Affairs, 2000), pp. 24–5.
42 Yeltsin appointed Chubais deputy prime minister in charge of the economy, including the Finance Ministry, and named Boris Nemtsov, a young reformist from Nizhnii Novgorod and a darling of Western aid programmes, as another deputy prime minister.

spring of 1998 when he dismissed Prime Minister Viktor Chernomyrdin and appointed an even younger, and more reformist government headed by Sergei Kirienko. Called a reformer's 'dream team' by many Russian and Western commentators, the new government came into office with an express desire to finally truly reform Russia's ailing economy.

There was some good economic news. Annual inflation dropped to 22 per cent in 1996 and 11 per cent in 1997, while the exchange rate on the rouble remained relatively stable. In 1997, Russia finally did record positive growth – albeit very small growth – for the first time in the decade.[43] That same year, Russia's new stock market boomed, helping in part to fuel upbeat forecasts about Russia's economic future.[44]

Beneath the surface, however, the Russian polity and economy still had many ills. On the political side, it was actual illness – Yeltsin's illness – that crippled the president's second term from the outset. Yeltsin spent the first months of his second term recovering from multiple-bypass heart surgery. After a brief appearance in the Kremlin in December, Yeltsin finally returned to active duty as president in the spring of 1997. Throughout his entire second term, however, Yeltsin never seemed fully engaged. As a result, a small group of Yeltsin confidants – called the Yeltsin 'family' – seemed to rule Russia from inside the Kremlin. This family – which included Yeltsin's daughter – wielded power by working closely with Russia's oligarchs, and one – Boris Berezovsky – in particular.[45]

## The August 1998 financial crisis

In addition to a crisis in leadership, the negative consequences of Russia's partial economic reform were beginning to accumulate in the second half of the 1990s. Shock therapy in Russia failed because it was never attempted. Instead, throughout most of the 1990s, Yeltsin allowed Chernomyrdin and his government to creep along with partial reforms – reforms that included big budget deficits, insider privatisation and partial price and trade liberalisation, which in turn combined to create amazing opportunities for corruption and spawned a decade of oligarchic capitalism. The nadir of this period was loans-for-shares,

---

43 Daniel Treisman, 'Fighting Inflation in a Transitional Regime: Russia's Anomalous Stabilization', *World Politics* 50 (1998): 235–65.
44 See most famously, Richard Layard and John Parker, *The Coming Russian Boom: A Guide to New Markets and Politics* (New York: Free Press, 1996).
45 On this period, see David Hoffman, *The Oligarchs: Wealth and Power in the New Russia* (New York: Public Affairs, 2002); and Chrystia Freeland, *Sale of the Century: Russia's Wild Ride from Communism to Capitalism* (New York: Crown Publishers, 2000).

a scheme under which Yeltsin and his government gave away Russia's most valuable companies to these oligarchs for a song.

After the ratification of the constitution in 1993, the Russian government did acquire control over Russia's Central Bank and thereafter pursued a more stringent monetary policy. But budget deficits persisted throughout the 1990s, as the government continued to fail to pass balanced budgets through the parliament.[46] Last-minute deals needed to pass the budget, particularly with the Agrarian Party, consistently resulted in the proliferation of financial obligations that the government could never meet, which in turn necessitated the constant sequestering of expenditures. Persistently poor tax collection also undermined sound fiscal policy. Russia's oligarchs were particularly notorious for not paying taxes, creating real revenue-raising problems for the government. In 1998, the deficit was still 150 billion roubles ($25 billion) – more than 5 per cent of GDP.

In the early part of the decade, the Central Bank simply printed new money and issued new credits to compensate for the deficit, a policy that fuelled inflation and undermined the stability of the exchange rate. In the latter half of the decade, after the enactment of the constitution gave the executive branch control over the Central Bank, the government deployed a new set of non-inflationary methods to deal with the deficit.

First, the Central Bank stopped printing money. The lack of liquidity in the economy also stimulated the use of barter, a highly inefficient method of transaction.[47] By 1998, experts estimated that over half of all industry transactions took place through barter. In addition, tight monetary policy exacerbated the accumulation of debt between enterprises. According to one estimate, inter-enterprise debts increased from 33.9 per cent of GDP in 1993 to 54.2 per cent of GDP by the end of 1997.[48]

A second method was simply not to pay money owed to state employees. This strategy resulted in an explosion of wage and pension arrears. Because workers and pensioners were not organised collectively to protest against the state's nefarious behaviour, the Russian government could get away with this method of 'macroeconomic stabilisation'.[49]

46 Sergei Aleksashenko, *Bitva za rubl'* (Moscow: AlmaMater, 1999).
47 See David Woodruff, *Money Unmade: Barter and the Fate of Russian Capitalism* (Ithaca, N.Y.: Cornell University Press, 1999); and Vadim Medvedev, *Obshchii krizis ekonomiki: prichini i posledstviia* (Moscow: Mezhdunarodnyi fond sotsial'no-ekonomicheskih isledovanii [Gorbachev-fond], 1999), esp. pp. 94–8.
48 *Rossiiskii statisticheskii ezhegodnik* (Moscow: Goskomstat, 1997), p. 535.
49 See Debra Javeline, *Protest and the Politics of Blame: The Russian Response to Unpaid Wages* (Ann Arbor: University of Michigan Press, 2003).

Third, in addition to their debts with the International Monetary Fund (IMF) and the World Bank, the Russian government began borrowing money from international markets. The Eurobond was the instrument of choice. By the summer of 1998, the Russian government had borrowed $4.3 billion through such medium and long-term instruments.[50]

As a fourth new method for raising revenue, the Russian Finance Ministry introduced new debt instruments in 1995, the short-term bond or *gosudarstvennye kratkosrochnye obligatsii* or GKO and the medium-term bond known by its acronym, OFZ. GKOs matured after three or six months, making them especially attractive to those investors looking for quick turnaround on their money. Many celebrated the GKOs as a particularly useful innovation since it brought money into the Russian state coffers in a non-inflationary way, while at the same time gave investors an incentive for maintaining low inflation rates and a stable currency.

As a package, however, these schemes for maintaining stabilisation were not sustainable in the long run. The GKO market grew exponentially. In 1994, the short-term bond market amounted to only $3 billion. By 1997, GKO debts outstanding totalled $64.7 billion, which ballooned to $70 billion in the summer of 1998.[51] In this same summer, two related external shocks – the Asian financial crisis and falling oil prices – began to reverberate in Russia. The same people who were losing money in South Korea had money tied up in Russia.[52] To provide incentives for these investors to keep their money in Russia, the Finance Ministry responded by continually raising the return rates on GKOs.[53] A month before the crash, yields on these treasury bills had reached 113 per cent.[54] The fall in oil prices decreased Russian export revenues, causing the Russian current account to go from a $3.9 billion surplus in 1997 to an estimated $4.5 billion deficit in 1998.[55] Russian tax receipts fell dramatically, as did Central Bank reserves. In effect, the Russian government was bankrupt.

50 Joseph Kahn and Timothy L. O'Brien, 'Easy Money: A Special Report: For Russia and its U.S. Bankers, Match Wasn't Made in Heaven', *New York Times*, 18 Oct. 1998, p. 1.
51 Hoffman, *The Oligarchs*, p. 469.
52 On the worldwide crisis, see Paul Blustein, *The Chastening: Inside the Crisis that Rocked the Global Financial System and Humbled the IMF* (New York: Public Affairs, 2001).
53 At first, the Russian government resisted IMF advice of raising interest rates, preferring instead to spend foreign currency reserves to defend the rouble. Eventually, however, they were compelled to raise interest rates. See US GAO Report to the House Committee on Banking and Financial Services, 'Foreign Assistance: International Efforts to Aid Russia's Transition Have Had Mixed Results', Nov. 2000, GAO-01-8, p. 46.
54 John Thornhill, 'IMF and Russia in a New Loan Accord', *Financial Times*, 8 July 1998, p. 2.
55 William H. Cooper, 'The Russian Financial Crisis: An Analysis of Trends, Causes, and Implications', Report for Congress, 18 Feb. 1999, pp. 98–578. Available online at: www.cnie.org/nle/inter-16.html

In a drastic, desperate move, the Russian government announced on 17 August 1998 a compulsory conversion of short-term GKOs into longer-term debt instruments. The Russian debt market immediately collapsed as investors refused to believe that the Russian government would ever pay back this borrowed money. On this same day, the Russian government also announced a ninety-day moratorium on payment of all hard-currency loans owed to Western commercial banks. Simultaneously, the government announced a new trading price for the rouble at 30 per cent lower than the day before. In one day, the two alleged economic achievements of the Yeltsin era – control of inflation and a stable, transferable currency – were wiped away.

These emergency measures did little to halt the economic crisis. The stock market all but disappeared, the rouble continued to fall and banks began to close. Responding desperately to a desperate situation, Yeltsin fired Kirienko and his government the next week and nominated Viktor Chernomyrdin as his candidate for prime minister. As the confirmation process for Chernomyrdin dragged on throughout September, the economy continued to collapse. The rouble continued to plummet, banks refused to allow withdrawals, prices soared and stores emptied as people started to stockpile durable goods such as cigarettes, sugar and flour.

## Renewed political polarisation

The August 1998 financial meltdown jolted the regime in Russia like no other event since the October 1993 stand-off. In combination with a subsequent banking scandal, the August 1998 crisis sparked a 'who lost Russia' debate in the West.[56] At the time, Russia looked as if it had failed at making the transition from a command economy to a market system.

Russia's transition from authoritarian rule to democracy also looked less certain. In the immediate aftermath, the financial crisis changed the de facto distribution of power between political actors and institutions in the country in favour of the parliament. This shift in the distribution of power, in turn, threatened to undermine Russia's constitutional stability. The Duma demonstrated its new (if temporary) importance by dominating the selection process of a new prime minister. Unlike previous votes for a new prime minister, Duma deputies did not capitulate to Yeltsin's demands, but made it clear that they would vote down his candidate, Viktor Chernomyrdin, if the president

56 John Lloyd, 'Who Lost Russia? The Devolution of Russia', *New York Times Magazine*, 15 Aug. 1999.

nominated him for a third time. Yeltsin relented and nominated the Duma's preferred candidate, Evgenii Primakov. Though not obligated constitutionally to consult the Duma on ministerial appointments, Primakov (with Yeltsin's acquiescence) nonetheless co-operated with Duma leaders to form a coalition government. Taking advantage of Yeltsin's weakness, Primakov and his Communist allies in the Duma floated the idea of limiting the powers of the presidency through an extra-constitutional pact. Yeltsin worried about even more radical challenges to his authority, warning potential conspirators, 'we have enough forces in order to stop any plans for taking power'.[57] That these ideas were even circulating demonstrated that the political rules of the game established in 1993 were still vulnerable in 1998.

From August 1998 until May 1999, Russia's Communists had their best opportunity to challenge the existing economic and political order after their candidate, Primakov, became prime minister against Yeltsin's wishes in the wake of the August 1998 financial meltdown. Upon assuming office, Primakov invited a Communist Party member, Iurii Masliukov, to serve as his economic tsar. Rhetorically, Primakov and Masliukov promised to reverse radical economic reforms, raise pensions and wages, curtail the activities of Western agents of influence such as the International Monetary Fund and the World Bank, toss 1,000 bankers in jail and hinted at restoring state control over prices and property.[58] In practice, Primakov and his Communist allies in the government pursued none of these policies but instead proved to be as fiscally conservative and monetarily stringent as previous reform governments.[59] Instead of chasing the IMF out of Russia, Primakov continued to negotiate with this 'tool of imperialism' and even agreed to introduce a package of legislation recommended by the IMF. In its negotiations with the World Bank, the Primakov government actually rejected the bank's recommendation for pension payments as too high. When offered the opportunity to roll back capitalism, Russia's Communists instead adhered to the general principles of the system in place.

Another challenge to constitutional stability erupted in the spring of 1999 when the Duma opened impeachment proceedings against the president. In the week leading up to the impeachment vote, held on 15 May 1999, Yeltsin looked certain to be impeached by the Duma on at least one count – his decision to invade Chechnya in 1994. In a bold counter-attack, just days before

57 Yeltsin, quoted in Bill Powell and Evgeniya Albats, 'Summer of Discontent', *Newsweek* (International edition), 19 Jan 1999.
58 John Thornhill, 'Primakov Defies IMF Advice', *Financial Times*, 17 Sept. 1998, p. 2.
59 As to why, see Evgenii Primakov, *Vosem' mesyatsev plyus . . .'* (Moscow: Mysl', 2001).

the impeachment vote, Yeltsin fired Primakov. Yeltsin's dismissal of the popular prime minister inched Russia closer to a constitutional crisis. If the Duma had impeached Yeltsin and also rejected his nominee for prime minister, Sergei Stepashin, the Russian constitution is silent on what should have happened next. Push did not come to shove, however, as the Duma did not muster the necessary two-thirds vote to pass any of the five impeachment articles. Days later, Duma deputies overwhelmingly approved Yeltsin's nominee for prime minister. In August 1999, Yeltsin fired Stepashin and nominated Vladimir Putin as his replacement. The Duma approved Yeltsin's candidate without a fuss.

## Invading Chechnya again

Just as the political crisis in Moscow began to subside in the summer of 1999, a new crisis of even greater proportions ignited again in the Caucasus.[60] In early August, a multi-ethnic force headed by Chechen commander Shamil Basaev invaded the Russian republic of Dagestan, claiming Dagestan's liberation from Russian imperialism as their cause. Russian armed forces responded by launching a major counter-offensive against the Chechen-led 'liberation' movement.[61] On 1 September, the war came to Moscow, when an explosion in downtown Moscow wounded forty-one people.[62] Further terrorist attacks in Moscow and elsewhere killed more than 300 Russian civilians in one month. Russians understood the terrorist attacks to be acts of war committed by Chechnya and its foreign supporters. Society demanded a response, and the Russian government responded.[63] In October Russian troops crossed into Chechen territory for the second time that decade.[64] Chechnya was to be liberated from the bandits and terrorists by any means necessary. Over 100,000 troops were sent to the theatre to accomplish this objective.

---

60  For accounts of the second Chechen war, Matthew Evangelista, *The Chechen Wars: Will Russia Go the Way of the Soviet Union?* (Washington: Brookings Institution Press, 2003); Anne Nivat, *Chienne de Guerre: A Woman Reporter Behind the Lines of the War in Chechnya* (New York: Public Affairs, 2000); and Anna Politkovskaya, *A Dirty War: A Russian Reporter in Chechnya* (London: Harvill Press, 2001).

61  ITAR-TASS, 'Operatsiia nachalas', goriachaia khronika', *Rossiiskaia gazeta*, 14 Aug. 1999, p. 3.

62  Vladimir Zainetdinov, Aleksei Siviv, Maria Beloklova, 'Vchera v shkolakh ot Chukhotki do Kaliningrada prozvenel pervyi zvonok. A v Okhotnom riadu poslednii zvonok', *Rossiiskaia Gazeta*, 2 Sept. 1999, p. 1.

63  David Hoffman, 'Russian Premier Pins Bombing on Chechens', *Washington Post*, 16 Sept. 1999, p. A26.

64  'Goriachaia Khronika: Konechnaia tsel' unichtozhit' banditov', *Rossiiskaia gazeta*, 6 Oct. 1999, p. 1.

Initially, Russian armed forces were more successful in this second war.[65] More methodical and relying to a greater extent on air power, Russian forces eventually recaptured Groznyi and most of Chechnya's cities by the beginning of 2000, while the Chechen fighters remained in the mountains. The nature of human rights violations in this second war increased dramatically (or they were better documented).[66] Western experts estimate that 400,000 people have been displaced.[67] But final victory proved elusive. Resistance continued. In September 2004 Chechens held hundreds of children hostage in a school in Beslan, North Osetia. Russian troops stormed the school, and over 340 people died in the assault.

## The end of Yeltsin's Russia and the beginning of Putin's Russia

The combination of a massive economic crisis, a new war and an ailing and unpopular president created real uncertainty about the 1999–2000 electoral cycle. In the run-up to the 1999 parliamentary elections, a new political coalition called Fatherland–All Russia seemed poised to compete with the Communist Party for the highest vote totals. Led by former Prime Minister Primakov, Fatherland–All Russia looked at the 1999 parliamentary vote as a primary for the 2000 presidential vote – the real prize in Russia's political system. In the summer of 1999, Primakov polled well ahead of all other presidential hopefuls. A changing of the guard – a final test of Russia's democratic institutions – looked imminent.[68]

---

65 Mark Kramer, 'Civil-Military Relations in Russia and the Chechnya Conflict', *Policy Memo Series* 99 (Cambridge, Mass.: Program on New Approaches to Russian Security, December 1999).

66 Human Rights Watch, 'Now Happiness Remains: Civilian Killings, Pillage, and Rape in Alkhan-Yurt', Chechnya, *Russia/Chechnya* 12, 5 (D) (Apr. 2000): 1–33; Human Rights Watch, 'February 5: A Day of Slaughter in Novye Aldi', *Russia/Chechnya* 12, 9 (D) (June 2000): 1–43; Human Rights Watch, 'The "Dirty War" in Chechnya: Forced Disappearances, Torture, and Summary Executions', *Russia* 13, 1 (D) (Mar. 2001): 1–42; and Human Rights Watch, 'Burying the Evidence: The Botched Investigation into a Mass Grave in Chechnya', *Russia/Chechnya* 13, 3 (D) (May 2001): 1–26. The *Chechnya Weekly*, published by the Jamestown Foundation, also has provided comprehensive coverage of events related to the war, including extensive reporting on human rights violations. Amnesty International, Physicians for Human Rights, Doctors of the World, and Doctors without Borders have also contributed to the documentation of human rights abuses. In Russia, Memorial has provided the most comprehensive coverage of human rights abuses inside Chechnya.

67 This figure is cited in Sarah Mendelson, 'Russia, Chechnya, and International Norms: The Power and Paucity of Human Rights? *NCEEER Working Paper*, 17 July 2001, p. 11.

68 See Michael McFaul, Andrei Ryabov and Nikolai Petrov (eds.), *Rossiia v izbiratel'nom tsikle: 1999–2000 godov* (Moscow: Moscow Carnegie Center, 2000).

For Yeltsin, allowing Primakov to replace him would have signalled defeat for reform. So he anointed an alternative, Vladimir Putin. By selecting Putin to become his new prime minister in August 1999, Yeltsin made it clear that he considered this former KGB agent his heir apparent.[69] Few others believed that Putin had a chance. He displayed little charisma, had no political party or other interest groups behind him and had never run for office. In his first month in office, his approval rating hovered in the single digits. By the end of the year, however, his popularity had soared to well above 70 per cent.[70] In the 1999 parliamentary election, a new pro-Kremlin electoral bloc, Unity, rode Putin's coat-tails to a surprising second-place finish, just behind the Communist Party.[71] As the result of a major negative campaign launched by media outlets friendly to the Kremlin, Fatherland–All Russia suffered a devastating defeat in the 1999 vote, winning only 13 per cent of the popular vote. Primakov subsequently decided not to compete against Putin in the presidential election the following year, guaranteeing a Putin landslide in the first round of the 2000 vote.[72]

Putin's popularity exploded in the autumn of 1999 due first and foremost to his handling of the Chechen war. It was an odd formula for gaining popularity. After all, Yeltsin's first war with Chechnya was extremely unpopular and had to be ended before he could win re-election in 1996. In this second intervention, the Russian people believed that the rationale for this war was self-defence. Second, relying more on air power, the Russian military appeared to be more successful in the second war. Consequently, this second Chechen war was initially very popular. During the 2000 presidential campaign, public support remained steady at roughly 60 per cent; it did not waver, as many had predicted, when Russian casualties increased. Opinion polls conducted in the autumn of 1999 demonstrated that people were grateful to Putin for accepting responsibility for the security of the Russian people. He looked like a leader who had taken charge during an uncertain, insecure time and had delivered on his promise to provide stability and security.

In addition to Chechnya, Putin benefited from several other factors. He was young, energetic and new while his competitors were the opposite. Putin

69 Yeltsin, *Midnight Diaries*, p. 337.
70 Agentstvo regional'nykh politcheskikh issledovanii (ARPI), *Regional'nyi Sotsiologicheskii Monitoring* 49 (10–12 Dec. 1999): 39. Sample size: 3,000 respondents in 52 Federation subjects.
71 On how, see Timothy Colton and Michael McFaul, 'Reinventing Russia's Party of Power: Unity and the 1999 Duma Election', *Post-Soviet Affairs* 16, 3 (Summer 2000): 201–24.
72 For details on the campaign, see Timothy Colton and Michael McFaul, *Popular Choice and Managed Democracy: The Russian Elections in 1999 and 2000* (Washington: Brookings Institution Press, 2003).

also positioned himself as a candidate different from Yeltsin. Putin's youth and energy provided a striking contrast to his old and sick predecessor. He was also unknown, allowing people to project into his candidacy all sorts of images and orientations. With the exception of his policy towards Chechnya, he was a *tabula rasa* on which voters could write what they wanted. In addition the economy had begun to turn around as devaluation from the August 1998 crisis and rising oil prices had helped to make 1999 Russia's first year of economic growth in a decade. Finally, Putin benefited from extensive positive coverage in the Russian media, most of which was still owned by the state or was friendly to the Kremlin (see Plate 25).

## Conclusion

In leaving office on 31 December 1999, Yeltsin bequeathed to his successors several serious political and economic conundrums. Russian democratic institutions were weak, the economy was growing but still in need of further reforms and corruption and crime remained rampant. Most tragically, the war in Chechnya continued with little prospect for genuine resolution. Yeltsin already has earned his place in history as one of Russia's most important leaders. What kind of adjectives will modify his legacy, however, will only become clear after the resolution of these lingering issues. He could be remembered as the father of Russian democracy and the initiator of Russia's market economy and sustained economic growth. Or he could be remembered as the first post-Communist leader who squandered Russia's first chance of becoming a liberal democracy and a capitalist economy. Yeltsin's last important decision – his appointment of Vladimir Putin as prime minister and then as acting president – will have a profound effect on how the Yeltsin legacy is finally judged. To date, Putin has pressed forward with furthering economic reforms, but at the same time has undermined Russia's already fragile democratic institutions.[73]

Yet, Yeltsin also created the foundation for his successors to succeed and secure for him the more positive modifiers to his legacy. The revolution is not over, but it also has not reversed. The Soviet Union is gone and will never be resurrected. Communism also will never return to Russia. Russia has not gone to war with Ukraine, Latvia or Kazakhstan to defend Russians living there and is less likely to do so today than when Yeltsin first took office. Though

73 See the articles on political and economic developments under Putin in Herspring, *Putin's Russia: Past Imperfect, Future Uncertain*, as well as the more negative assessment of Putin in Lilia Shevtsova, *Putin's Russia* (Washington: Carnegie Endowment for International Peace, 2003).

they threatened with periodic electoral splashes, neither neo-fascists nor neo-Communists ever succeeded in coming to power in the 1990s and do not seem poised to do so in the near future. Even the Russian Communist Party has lagged behind its counterparts in Eastern Europe in not being able to recapture the Kremlin. Individual freedoms in Russia have never been greater.

Finally, by avoiding the temptation of dictatorship, Yeltsin also established an important precedent of democratic behaviour that will raise the costs for future authoritarian aspirants. In defiance of his critics, he did not cancel elections in 1996, he did not suspend the constitution after the August 1998 financial crisis, and he did not stay in power by any means necessary. On the contrary, he won re-election in 1996, abided by the constitution and even invited Communists into his government in the autumn of 1998, and then stepped down willingly, peacefully and constitutionally. Although Putin has shown little proclivity for deepening democratisation in Russia, his cautious approach to decision-making will make it very difficult for him to break this precedent. If dissolving the Soviet Union was Yeltsin's most important destructive act, his seizure and surrender of power through democratic means may be his most important constructive act.

PART TWO

★

# RUSSIA AND THE SOVIET UNION: THEMES AND TRENDS

14

# Economic and demographic change: Russia's age of economic extremes

PETER GATRELL

The enduring fascination with Russia's twentieth-century economic history has its roots in the politics of revolution. For the Bolshevik leadership, the events of 1917–18 presaged the foundation of a more equitable, humane and modern economic and social order, one that would hold out hope to millions of oppressed and impoverished people within and beyond Russia's borders. For the Bolsheviks' opponents, the revolution was destructive and barbaric, reversing a half-century of prior economic progress under the tsarist regime, for the sake of what seemed to many of them to be dubious social and economic goals. These sharply polarised opinions have, to a greater or lesser extent, coloured the way in which later generations have assessed the aspirations and the performance of the Russian economy during the twentieth century. When Stalin launched an extraordinarily ambitious programme of economic modernisation and social change upon the Soviet Union after 1928, jettisoning traditional forms of agricultural organisation and cementing a system of central economic planning, the controversy between enthusiasts and sceptics only deepened. The enthusiasts pointed to rapid economic growth and dramatic technological change during the 1930s, contrasting this with the prolonged depression in the capitalist West. Victory in the war against Nazism seemed to them to have validated the Stalinist industrial revolution. For their part, the sceptics questioned the magnitude of economic growth, drew attention to systemic deficiencies and highlighted the widespread terror and population losses. After Stalin's death, attempts at economic reform – sometimes hesitant, sometimes more purposeful – did nothing to lessen a divergence of opinion between those who saw reform as a dead end and those who regarded it as a worthwhile attempt to redesign the socialist system, in order to respond to fresh challenges from the Soviet Union's rivals, beneficiaries of the post-war

I am grateful to Nick Baron, Paul Gregory, Mark Harrison and Nat Moser for their comments on an earlier version of this chapter.

economic miracle. Finally, the disintegration of the Soviet system after 1991 enabled the sceptics to claim that the planned economy had been built on shallow foundations all along. The enthusiasts, bruised by the sudden collapse of Soviet socialism, bemoaned the high costs of 'transition'. By the end of the twentieth century, they had become the sceptics, whilst those who hitherto pinpointed the shortcomings of the Soviet economic experiment now enthusiastically endorsed Russia's attempt to create a functioning capitalist economy.

For these reasons, it is not difficult to understand why the eminent American sovietologist and economist, Alexander Gerschenkron, wrote of Russia's twentieth century that 'it always was a political economic history'. It was bound up with a vision of an economic future that could be deliberately engineered by administrative means, in order to fashion a developed yet egalitarian society. That vision was compelling far beyond Russia. Differences of history and culture notwithstanding, the Soviet economic project inspired politicians, economists and engineers in countries as far apart as Romania, China, Cuba and Tanzania, not to mention in those non-socialist societies where the exchange of ideas operated freely. The 'second world' of socialism enjoyed enormous prestige in the 'third world'. It affected no less the course of intellectual debate and political practice in developed parts of the globe.

The political and ideological context of economic decision-making did not remain stable throughout the twentieth century. The tsarist regime was deeply unsettled by the Revolution of 1905, to which it responded by embarking upon a major reform of property rights in the countryside. Nor did the installation of the Soviet regime bring about greater stability: on the contrary, the civil war unleashed a period of political uncertainty and economic collapse. Following the relatively stable era of the New Economic Policy (1921–8), the Stalinist 'revolution from above' ushered in a fresh period of turmoil. For many peasants, collectivisation had echoes of the wartime exactions that they had rejected in 1920 and carried connotations of the serfdom that had been abolished in 1861. For enterprise managers, the dictates of central planning created a climate of uncertainty rather than security; there was little refuge from arbitrary intervention by the party in economic affairs. The post-war era brought about a more prolonged degree of political stability, but the collapse of Soviet authority in the late 1980s engendered fresh turmoil, from which the post-Communist successor states have not been immune.

Notwithstanding this recurrent political turbulence, Russia's twentieth century displays certain continuities in the style of governance. At a macro level, economic policy was governed by a pronounced sense of the imperial, Soviet and post-Soviet mission of economic modernisation. At stake was the need to tame reckless nature, to improve (and transcend) human capabilities, to arrange population 'rationally' and above all to overcome economic backwardness. The economic history of Russia can thus be read as a kind of Nietzschean struggle that rationalised overt political intervention in the affairs of subordinate institutions and their agents. Tsarist officials prescribed in microscopic detail the conduct of corporate bodies, whether joint-stock enterprises or trade unions. The Communist Party established formal political departments in economic commissariats (ministries) and in collective farms. To be sure, both regimes might periodically laud the 'heroic' and decisive individual, whether the entrepreneur (before the revolution) or the Soviet factory director who exceeded plan targets. But the imperatives of modernisation – the subjugation of space and the transcendence of time – ascribed particular significance to the state and limited the formal autonomy of agents, whether managers, workers or farmers. These ambitions introduced a campaign style to Russia's economic history. The tsarist programme of land reform, the war on *nouveaux riches* during the 1920s, the Stakhanovite movement in 1935–6, Khrushchev's Virgin Lands campaign, Gorbachev's project for economic 'acceleration' – all these are characteristic of a belief that the state had a duty to intervene in order to circumvent potential obstacles to the tasks of economic modernisation.

As already implied, these imperatives had profound implications for Russia's demographic history. The emphasis upon the transformation of space imparted particular significance to population migration. At one level this meant the use of political instruments to promote the settlement of regions earmarked for economic development and expansion. At another it meant that some regions were 'cleared' of 'alien elements' and others were set aside for the incarceration and deployment of forced labour. In the tsarist and Soviet eras alike, defence considerations as well as colonising impulses were at work. As recent work has made clear, this population politics was closely bound up with the global pursuit of 'modernity'.[1]

These preliminary remarks serve to suggest a framework for understanding the mixed fortunes of the Soviet economy during the twentieth century. No attempt is made here to survey all aspects of Russian economic history or to provide a full picture of economic growth and development.[2] Instead, this

---

1 David Hoffmann and Yanni Kotsonis (eds.), *Russian Modernity: Politics, Knowledge, Practices* (London: Macmillan, 2000).
2 The most important works are listed in the Bibliography. No detail is provided here on the economy during the two world wars, for which see Peter Gatrell, *Russia's First World War: A Social and Economic History* (Harlow: Longman, 2005); and Mark Harrison, *Accounting*

chapter provides a way of thinking about the economic and demographic consequences of the ambitions expressed by successive political leaders in Russia.

## Great leaps forward (1): late tsarist industrialisation

The long boom in Russian industry began after 1885 and, after a brief interruption in 1899–1907, finally came to an end in 1916. It rested upon a mixture of direct and indirect initiatives on the part of the state. Under Minister of Finances Sergei Witte the tsarist government embarked on a massive programme of railway-building, including the construction of the Trans-Siberian Railway, designed in part to open up markets in the Far East and Central Asia. Railway construction in turn helped kick-start the expansion of heavy industry. By its adoption of the gold standard in 1897 the government created an environment favourable to foreign investment. Russia became increasingly integrated into the international economy, through the medium of capital movements and the export trade in commodities such as grain and oil. International movements of labour were less significant, although Russia suffered a net outflow of migrants to the New World, partly because of discriminatory policies towards the empire's Jewish population.

The results were impressive: a growth rate for total income of around 5 per cent per annum during the 1890s and again after 1907, combined with technological modernisation in key industrial sectors such as iron and steel, oil and engineering. New industrial regions came into existence, including the Donbass coal basin and the oil industry of the Caucasus, although it is worth noting that tsarist industrialisation tended to consolidate pre-existing regional disparities. For example, investment in modern metalworking and textile factories in the Baltic lands took place in an environment that was already relatively highly developed in terms of educational attainment and income per head.

Russia's industrial upsurge sparked controversy at the time, and its welfare consequences have been debated ever since. Conservatives bemoaned the intrusion of a modern financial sector and foreign investment in Russia, and charged Witte with the neglect of agriculture. In an influential assessment Alexander Gerschenkron defended Witte's strategy, on the grounds that it enabled the Russian state to substitute for factors of production that were

for War: Soviet Production, Employment, and the Defence Burden, 1940–1945 (Cambridge: Cambridge University Press, 1996).

missing or in short supply. Chief amongst these were skilled labour and capital. By stabilising the exchange rate, imposing high tariffs and launching a
propaganda offensive, the tsarist state encouraged the inflow of foreign direct
investment. Advanced technology imported from Western Europe enabled
Russian entrepreneurs to substitute capital for labour. Yet underpinning the
strategy was a government willingness to maintain a high level of demand for
the output of heavy industry, and this entailed in the view of some observers
injurious taxation of the peasant population and depressed levels of household
consumption. Gerschenkron believed that this was a small price to pay for
economic development. Elements in this story have been challenged: thus
Gerschenkron neglected regional differences in peasant welfare, understated
autonomous industrial growth and discounted the impact of state-financed
rearmament in asserting that the state's role diminished after 1905. However,
his overall interpretative framework has proved remarkably stimulating and
durable.

Industrialisation had important demographic consequences. The rate of
migration to new centres of industry increased (Witte's critics decried the
squalor of new settlements, and bemoaned the crime that they associated
with urban overcrowding). As a result, on the eve of the First World War
around 16 per cent of the population lived in urban centres. Witte deliberately encouraged population migration, partly because he saw colonisation
as a solution to 'rural overpopulation' in Russia's central agricultural region.
The tempo of economic development greatly increased the settlement of Russians in far-flung corners of the empire, including Central Asia, the Caucasus,
Poland and the Baltic lands. Non-Russian minorities in turn began to settle
in larger numbers in Russia's expanding cities. By 1914, for example, around
15 per cent of the empire's Latvian population lived outside the Baltic region,
the result of a generation of economic development and migration to European Russia. However, few observers attributed any significance to this at the
time.

These developmental imperatives continued to operate during the First
World War. Around 140,000 workers, including prisoners of war, were set to
work building railway lines, such as between Petrozavodsk and Murmansk.
They included Kazakh rebels who were punished for having opposed conscription in 1916. In general, however, the mainsprings of wartime migration
betrayed other, non-developmental impulses. Jews, Germans and other 'alien'
populations were forcibly removed from the borderlands during 1915, and
resettled in European Russia (for Russia's Jews this forced migration marked
the end of the infamous Pale of Settlement).

Historians have been relatively kind in their assessment of the tsarist great leap forward. The growth rates and structural change were remarkable. All the same, on the eve of the First World War the gap between Russia and more developed countries had actually widened in terms of income per capita – a consequence of Russia's rapid population increase and the size of the unreconstructed rural sector. Traditional forms of tsarist governance persisted; in particular, there was a surfeit of arbitrary intervention in economic life that probably had a corrosive effect on entrepreneurship. The post-revolutionary generation would continue to grapple with the issue of Russia's relative economic backwardness and to experiment with forms of economic administration.

## The radical privatisation impulse (1): pre-1917 experiments with land reform

The majority of the population in tsarist Russia continued to support itself from agriculture. Peasant farming gave cause for concern, because it was believed that traditional methods of cultivation condemned successive generations to poverty. Hence attention shifted to the prevailing forms of peasant agriculture. Following widespread peasant unrest in 1905 and 1906 Prime Minister Stolypin targeted the traditional land commune (*obshchina*), in the expectation that it would be replaced by a class of 'sturdy and strong' farmers who enjoyed full title to the land. A growing number of economists and other social scientists bemoaned the restrictions that the commune was believed to impose on peasant farmers and its deleterious consequences for the growth of agricultural productivity. Particular attention focused on the custom of redistributing allotment land, which was believed to act as a disincentive to improvements in cultivation, and on the fragmentation of peasant allotments. The edict of 9 November 1906 enabled peasant heads of household to petition for communal allotment land to be transferred into their personal ownership. Where such a household had more land than would be allotted at the next redistribution, its head was entitled to purchase the excess on very favourable terms, with the help of a Peasant Land Bank. The commune was obliged to comply with any such request within one month. Furthermore, the head of a household was entitled to demand the consolidation of scattered strips. Provision was also made for the entire commune to embark on land consolidation, provided two-thirds of its members agreed. Where a commune appeared to resist, the government was entitled to intervene on behalf of the 'separator'.

The reformers faced an uphill struggle to convert – the word is used advisedly, since so many embarked on their task with missionary zeal – Russian peasants from subsistence farming to a capitalist ethic. Much of their analysis overlooked the fact that the land commune governed all aspects of peasant life, from the allocation of scattered strips of land (itself a kind of insurance against risk) and the use of communal pasture to the maintenance of rural infrastructure and the apportionment of taxation. Thus a householder's request to privatise his plot had far-reaching consequences, which the government sought to minimise by insisting that the household retained other rights of membership of the commune, such as access to meadows and pasture. Many peasants resented the claims of their neighbours who sought to take advantage of the new legislation, and there were stories of intimidation. Besides, subordinate members of the separating household begrudged the new powers vested in the hands of the paterfamilias. Nor did the reformers dissuade the majority from the view that their prospects would be greatly enhanced by a revolutionary redistribution of the land privately held by noble landowners. But the reform impulse amongst a new generation of Russian agronomists swept all before it, and these enthusiasts themselves did not shrink from intimidation. Much publicity attended the creation of independent farms (*khutora*), idealised and actively promoted by government Land Organisation Committees. More than one million households took advantage of consolidation between 1907 and 1915; this implies that around 8 per cent of peasant communal land underwent full reorganisation. Particular enthusiasm for enclosure was demonstrated in the southern provinces of European Russia where cereal production became increasingly commercialised.

The reforms themselves are thus of considerable interest, because they reveal a concerted willingness to impose modern patterns of land organisation as well as new kinds of behaviour upon a sceptical peasantry. These grand ambitions (like the land commune itself) persisted into the Soviet period. Yet, in economic terms, the direct results of the Stolypin land reforms were quite modest. As Esther Kingston-Mann and others have pointed out, the reformers refused to accept that the land commune was quite compatible with improved cultivation on peasant farms. In truth, of much greater consequence for the advance of Russian agriculture before the war was the growth of new markets and the improvement in the terms of trade for food producers, which enabled farmers to diversify into new products and to invest in agricultural equipment. Institutions such as co-operatives helped to sustain this activity.

Equally important in economic terms was the continued process of internal migration. The land reforms gave an added impulse to migration, primarily by cancelling the redemption payments that peasants had incurred as a result of emancipation in 1861 and by enabling poorer peasants to sell land (although they could not sell to non-peasants) and to move from depressed regions such as the lower Volga. Some sought work in the expanding urban economy of European Russia, becoming workers and (as Lenin had suggested) consumers with 'civilised habits and requirements'.[3] Others decided to explore opportunities further east. The government's Siberian Committee and the Colonisation Department for Turkestan provided peasant migrants with maps and itineraries – a noteworthy contrast to the much more chaotic population displacement that occurred in the First World War. Between 1896 and 1915 around 4.5 million peasants settled permanently in western Siberia and Central Asia, where a thriving rural economy began to develop on the eve of war. But the government continued to impose tight restrictions on the mobility of the *inorodtsy* ('foreigners'), including Jews and the indigenous population of Siberia, Central Asia and the Caucasus. Freedom of settlement was not an option available to all.

## The reform impulse in Russian economic history (1): New Economic Policy

The New Economic Policy (NEP) had its roots in the shift away from 'War Communism', a system that heralded imminent utopia so far as some enthusiasts were concerned, demonstrating the kind of economic fundamentalism that would become fashionable in the 1930s and again during the 1990s. Between 1918 and 1920 money virtually lost its function as a medium of exchange, and capitalist institutions evaporated. But the underlying economic reality showed War Communism in a disastrous light. Production collapsed (industrial output in 1921 was a mere 12 per cent of the 1913 level) and established economic links were broken, being replaced by somewhat arbitrary bureaucratic determination of priorities for the supply of inputs. This was an economy of absolute shortage. Deprivation and dictatorship went hand in hand. The collapse of workers' control during the civil war represented defeat for a more libertarian vision of Soviet socialism, and the triumph of one-man management. Workers who held on to their jobs received payment in kind, and bartered goods in order to survive. Others returned to the village. Russia suffered a demographic haemorrhage. Thanks to the 'Red Terror', the

---

3 V. I. Lenin, *The Development of Capitalism in Russia* (Moscow: Progress Publishers, 1977), p. 582. Lenin's work was first published in 1899.

propertied elite (including many former landlords, whose estates were seized by the peasantry in 1917–18) decided to emigrate. Those who remained on Russia's war-ravaged territory were exposed to infectious disease and famine, which domestic and foreign aid organisations (such as the American Relief Administration and the Society of Friends) struggled valiantly to overcome.

In 1921 what came to be seen as the hallmarks of War Communism – compulsory deliveries of produce by peasant farmers (according to assigned quotas, or *prodrazverstka*), the nationalisation of enterprises and the administrative allocation of goods and labour, particularly to support the war effort against the Bolsheviks' enemies – were abandoned. In their stead came greater commercial freedom, although NEP led neither to complete deregulation nor to the abandonment of the ultimate objective of a planned socialist economy. (In a significant indication of the new state's ambitions, Gosplan was established in 1921.) Crucial to the transition to NEP was the decision to introduce a single tax on peasants' output and to permit them to retain the residual product. It is not difficult to see this as a political accommodation that the Bolshevik Party reached with the peasantry, and that brought with it profound economic implications. Other policy decisions logically followed: the creation of a stable currency (finally completed in 1924), the stabilisation of the state budget (a factor contributing indirectly to a rising level of unemployment), the abolition of restrictions on trade, and the introduction of commercial principles in enterprise transactions (*khozraschet*). Private traders (Nepmen) replaced the 'bagmen' who had engaged in illegal trade in grain during the civil war. By 1923 private traders accounted for more than 75 per cent of all retail trade. The Communist Party – which enjoyed a monopoly of political power – did not abandon all forms of economic intervention. In particular, it forced down industrial prices in 1924, in order to offset the consequences of the 'scissors' crisis' (Trotsky's famous expression describing the relative movement of agricultural and industrial prices in 1923–4) and to encourage peasants to bring grain to the market. This was consistent with the social contract between party and peasantry.

How dynamic was NEP? The question is important (and has been much debated), because it raises issues concerning the mainsprings of economic growth beyond 1928. The official Soviet view was that the potential for stimulating further growth within the NEP framework had been exhausted by 1928. However, Paul Gregory argues that the economy had still not recovered pre-war (1913) levels of output by that date, the implication being that part of the subsequent Stalinist economic transformation was a consequence of utilising reserve capacity. Other scholars have taken an intermediate position, arguing that Gregory overstated the prosperity of the Russian economy in 1913 and thus understated the rate of growth in 1913–28. Certainly, the Soviet economy under NEP had important achievements to its credit, for example by greatly extending the tsarist experiment with electrification and introducing new products, such as oil-drilling equipment. Yet some important sectors (iron and steel, food and drink) lagged considerably. Non-Bolshevik economic specialists had to answer criticism from the political leadership that NEP was failing to address issues of technological backwardness in industry, against a backdrop of greater dynamism in the developed capitalist West.

'All economy comes down in the last analysis to an economy of time.' Marx's words were quoted approvingly by Trotsky, for whom socialism meant not only the removal of capitalist exploitation but also a greater economy of time, 'that most precious raw material of culture'. Most commentators, whether tsarist or Soviet, had a more narrow conception of labour productivity, but they all agreed that Russian labour productivity had to be improved if the gap on economically more advanced countries were to be closed. That perception was shared by V. I. Grinevetskii, the pre-revolutionary engineer, and by Aleksei Gastev, the Soviet populariser of 'scientific organisation of labour' (NOT, *nauchnaia organizatsiia truda*), whose manuals continued to find favour as late as the 1960s. By 1925 the main authority for state industry (Vesenkha, the Supreme Council of the National Economy) called for the 'rationalisation' of production, by means of improved working methods and management. The strategy was crucial to NEP, because an improvement in labour productivity made possible a lowering of costs of production, thereby enabling enterprises to realise profits, without simply forcing up prices and jeopardising the relationship with the peasantry, as happened in the scissors' crisis. But the pace of modernisation remained relatively sluggish.

To some of its chief advocates, NEP held out the prospect of greater Soviet exposure to the international economy, which had been severely curtailed between 1914 and 1920 (although in March 1920 Lenin signed a huge order for foreign railway equipment). In fact, foreign intervention during the civil war suggested that European powers had extensive economic ambitions for the Russian borderlands, such as the Caucasus. Could those interests be harnessed to the task of socialist economic construction? To be sure, trade agreements were signed and some foreign capitalists established concessions in sectors such as timber and minerals (manganese, lead and precious metals). Technical assistance was imported – the memoirs of foreign specialists provide valuable insights into the birth pangs of the Soviet economy – but the results were far less impressive than Grinevetskii had envisaged. The diminished grain marketings mentioned below hindered the recovery of foreign trade, and the trade deficit continued to increase. By 1926 the Soviet rouble had ceased to be a convertible currency. This hardly betokened a commitment to internationalisation.

Meanwhile, the early years of NEP coincided with the formation of the Soviet Union. During the period of War Communism large and resource-rich parts of the country such as Siberia, the Caucasus and Ukraine had been controlled by the Bolsheviks' opponents. The challenge now was to recon-figure the internal economic relations of the new country. The creation of national republics and autonomous regions meant, according to one dyspep-tic observer, that the national question was looked at 'through "economic eyes" – Turkestan means cotton, lemons, etc.; Kirgizia wool, cattle; Bashkiria timber, hides, cattle'.[4] That description appeared to confirm rather than to overturn existing regional specialisation. Indeed the Soviet policy of 'nativisa-tion' (korenizatsiia) did not extend to the economic sphere, at least so far as the division of labour was concerned. Programmes for 'national' development might reduce the economic role of non-indigenous groups, who sometimes portrayed themselves as victims of 'bullying' by the indigenes. Yet there were limits to the latter's leverage: in regions of labour shortage, such as Karelia, the nationalist leadership complained about Russian in-migration, but no con-stituent republic was allowed to place restrictions on population resettlement (the new word for colonisation). Capital investment and migration were to be determined by the broad strategic goals of all-Union modernisation and security. Any resulting economic 'equalisation' would be a by-product rather than a guiding principle of economic policy.

Why did NEP come to an end? Opinions have been divided between struc-turalists, for whom the system was inherently unstable, and intentionalists, who point to the consequences of policy mistakes at the end of the decade. It is clear that important issues remained unresolved under NEP. Unemploy-ment persisted to an unacceptably high extent (in industry it reached around 14 per cent in 1927); transport, education, health and defence were deprived of resources; the technological level of Soviet industry left much to be desired; and the pattern of industrial location remained largely pre-Soviet. Yet the system was evidently capable of delivering economic growth and marked improve-ments in the quality of life. The difficulty was that these advantages seemed to count for little when set alongside the manifestations of social division and defence concerns. The system was dealt a fatal blow in 1927–8. In spring 1927 the

---

4 Quoted in E. H. Carr, *A History of Soviet Russia: The Bolshevik Revolution 1917–1923*, vol. I, (Harmondsworth: Penguin, 1973), p. 288.

party committed itself to more rapid industrialisation, increasing investment and credits to state enterprises, and simultaneously reducing the retail price of industrial products. The Russian countryside suffered a goods shortage, exacerbating existing problems (grain marketings had declined as a proportion of agricultural output, and by the mid-1920s were little more than half the pre-war level). In 1928 the authorities resolved to criminalise 'speculation', in a measure designed to put pressure on those, particularly rich 'kulaks' and Nepmen, who were believed to be hoarding grain. In essence Stalin's adoption in January 1928 of the 'Urals–Siberian method', so called because of the regions where the measures were first applied, abrogated the social contract that had been instituted with the peasantry in March 1921. Stalin did not refrain from speaking of 'tribute' in justifying the need to apply force in order to procure grain at low prices.[5]

The New Economic Policy has had a good press from many Western observers (as well as from the advocates of *perestroika* during the 1980s), who associate it with an era of relative political freedom and cultural experimentation before the onset of Stalinism. However, the underlying rationale of NEP was at odds with the cultural intelligentsia's contempt for the profane world of commerce and the profit motive – 'romantic anti-capitalism', in Katerina Clark's words.[6] In less exalted society, too, NEP failed to register except as a framework that promoted the visibility and the prosperity of the 'money-grabbing' merchant (Nepman), the 'kulak', and the 'bourgeois specialist' – all of whom actually provided important services – without apparently doing much to improve job prospects and social welfare. The Stalinist political leadership took advantage of this disaffection, as well as with the misgivings mentioned earlier about housing, health and so forth, to launch a radically different system after 1928.

## Great leaps forward (II): the Five-Year Plans and collectivisation

The adoption of the First Five-Year Plan in 1928 marks the next attempt to engineer rapid economic growth by means of concerted state intervention. With its ambitious targets for capital investment, increased labour productivity and the expansion of output, the Five-Year Plan (FYP) reflected a clear redirection in Soviet life. Cultural revolution affected economics no less than other

5 His use of this term was only made public in 1949.
6 Katerina Clark, *Petersburg: Crucible of Cultural Revolution* (Cambridge, Mass.: Harvard University Press, 1995).

forms of intellectual activity. Enthusiasts such as Strumilin, who espoused a 'teleological' commitment to economic planning, triumphed over economists such as Groman, Varzar and Kafengauz, who preferred an 'organic' approach to growth. In this atmosphere, one hallmark of which was a pronounced militarisation of economic rhetoric, it took considerable courage to proclaim the need for caution. As Strumilin put it in 1929, 'specialists prefer to stand for high rates of growth rather than to sit in jail (*sidet'*) for low ones'.

Why then did the Communist Party commit itself to a new course? Apart from the distasteful encouragement that NEP appeared to give to 'hostile' elements, the existing economic system had not 'solved' the questions of unemployment and the foreign trade deficit. A commitment to rapid industrial growth implied the absorption of unemployed labour, import substitution and the creation of a modern defence industry, something that a war scare in 1927 made yet more imperative. The decision to embark on industrialisation meant a decision, in the words of Maurice Dobb, to forsake 'the slow rhythm of the plough for the more complex rhythm of the machine', with Gosplan conducting from Stalin's score and Stalin tolerating no dissent from the orchestral forces.

Tsarist officials sometimes referred to 'His Excellency, the Harvest' as the factor governing economic affairs in pre-revolutionary Russia. Their counterparts in Stalin's Russia acknowledged the dictatorship of the plan. 'His Excellency, the Plan' lay at the core of the economic system. Unlike the harvest, plans took a monthly, quarterly and annual form, whilst for broad strategic purposes the FYP dominated decision-making. Plans were imposed upon state-owned enterprises by superior authorities, notably Gosplan and the economic ministries or commissariats. Targets normally took the form of physical indicators, that is in terms of tons of steel or yards of cloth, but could also be expressed in money terms, such as of the gross value of output in 'constant prices'. Other elements of planned performance might include targets for product assortment, cost reduction, labour productivity and so forth. Quality considerations were secondary. Accompanying the targets were centrally allocated supplies to industrial enterprises. Preparation for this level of intervention had already taken place under NEP, when 'control figures' were formulated and published from 1925 onwards. In the FYP period this process became much more extensive. A large economic bureaucracy supported this hugely ambitious exercise in co-ordination, and intervened when needed to restore a degree of balance.

The consequences were profound in terms of economic behaviour. A complex interplay of interests between the party, the planning agencies, economic ministries, republican, regional and local authorities, and the enterprises (farms, factories, etc.) determined the formulation and the implementation of plans.[7] In principle, Soviet planners dictated the targets, but at each level subordinate agents within the system entered into complex strategies with their superiors to obtain the best possible set of instructions, in other words to negotiate a plan that was achievable. Since no superior had access to perfect information, subordinates were able to understate and conceal productive capacity. Similarly, plan fulfilment required astute and timely action on the part of enterprises. No manager could afford to be exposed to failure to meet the targets, and in these circumstances horizontal networks and contacts flourished; thus managers engaged 'pushers' (*tolkachi*) to obtain inputs over and above the planned allocation. Ultimately, firms and ministries came to an understanding that the completion of the plan mattered more than the notional budget that underpinned it; hence the phenomenon of the 'soft' budget constraint, whereby struggling enterprises could in the last resort rely upon credits or subsidies in order to survive. Farm managers likewise concealed some of their grain, rather than deliver it to the authorities, in order to boost the seed fund for the next harvest. Thus the formal system of subordination disguised the fact that the principal (the state) did not have perfect information about the behaviour of its agents (enterprises), about which it frequently remained ignorant. In a sense, therefore, the system was sustained less by the hierarchical character of central economic planning than by the interaction of dictators and subordinates. It should also be remembered that from time to time the party-state 'mobilised' resources on an ad hoc basis, disrupting the targets agreed with subordinates and thereby contributing to pervasive uncertainty. Sometimes, too, unforeseen external circumstances, such as war scares, wreaked havoc with the assumptions that planners had made.

The First FYP rested upon a significant planned increase in labour productivity, as a means of financing the increased investment. Attempts were made to improve the productivity of Soviet workers, by means of 'shock work', by widening wage differentials, and by creating differential access to rationed goods. But the mass influx of unskilled peasant migrant labour made it difficult to improve output per person. During the mid-1930s the Soviet leadership acknowledged that the productivity gap between the USSR and its capitalist rivals remained wide. All sectors were demanding increased investment, making it imperative to look for ways of reducing costs. The most famous such initiative, the Stakhanov movement, took place during the Second FYP,

7 For discussion of this 'nested dictatorship' in theory and practice see Paul Gregory and Andrei Markevich, 'Creating Soviet Industry: The House that Stalin Built', *Slavic Review* 61 (2002): 787–814.

at a time when the Soviet leadership had embarked on a fresh surge of capital investment. *Pravda* (1 January 1936) explained this in orthodox Marxist terms: 'every newly emerging social system triumphs over the old outdated mode of production because it brings about a higher productivity of labour'. But most workers responded passively at best, and managers regarded the entire campaign as a pointless distraction. The outcome of Stakhanovism was chaos. By the beginning of 1937 more modest targets for labour productivity were being contemplated. Recent work has pinpointed concerns about financial stability as a major factor; the state budget was already under great strain as a result of increased spending on defence, infrastructure and consumer subsidies. Campaigns, such as the Stalinist drive to boost labour productivity and to over-fulfil output targets, could not but create a climate of uncertainty for Soviet managers and factory directors as well – they suffered a mass purge in 1937 and 1938, at a time when Stalinist ideology celebrated managerial power. In general it proved much more straightforward to draft millions of additional workers to the task of social and economic construction than it was to engineer an improvement in output per person.

What then were results in economic terms? The magnitude of industrial growth in particular has provoked endless debate as well as ingenious attempts to deal with measurement problems. Much of the available statistical record took the form of data on physical output, but apart from issues of concealment and falsification these data raise difficult issues of aggregation. Decisions have to be reached about the appropriate weights to be applied. Next, there is the problem of deciding which prices to apply to the data; according to the 'Gerschenkron effect', the adoption of early year prices overstates growth in an economic system that is undergoing rapid structural transformation. Problems arise from the introduction of new types of product that substitute for old; how quality change is to be measured poses particular difficulties for the measurement of Soviet economic change. For these reasons no final judgement of the growth record is likely to be reached. However, it is now clear that official Soviet estimates greatly overstated total economic growth; Girsh Khanin has revised the official rate of increase of national income from 13.9 per cent to 3.2 per cent for the years 1928–41.

The allocation of additional output reflected the priorities given to investment and to government spending, notably on defence. The total stock of capital more than doubled between 1928 and 1941; this increase was all the more remarkable, given the sharp fall in livestock herds. Defence production increased twenty-eight-fold during the 1930s (far in excess of total industrial production), imposing a heavy burden, particularly after 1936. The Stalin era witnessed Russia's emergence as a modern military power. The hallmarks were the new tank and aviation industries, supported in turn by steel, metalworking, fuel, chemicals and rubber production. Qualitative improvements had also taken place. But difficulties remained: the defence sector was not immune from the inefficiency prevalent in the economic system as a whole, and by 1941 much of the stock of military equipment was already obsolete. Much reliance continued to be placed upon sheer manpower. The Red Army's increased demand for manpower was met largely by peasant conscription.

The world of the Russian peasantry was turned upside down by a concerted attempt to reorganise peasant land tenure, not (as in 1906–11) to create individual enclosed farms but to realise a vision of collectivised agriculture. Those who framed the collectivisation project shared with Stolypin's surveyors and agronomists a firm belief in the need for a more rational organisation of the land and in the inability of peasants to bring about real change on their own initiative. In 1929 the order was given to collectivise peasant farms. After a short interruption following Stalin's famous speech, 'Dizziness from success' (March 1930), the process recommenced. 'Kulaks' (demonised as 'peasant barons') were dispossessed and deprived of the opportunity to enter the new farms. Nomadic groups (such as Roma, and the 'small peoples of the North') were compulsorily settled in collectives, in order to create the basis for a new 'proletariat'. Soviet official propaganda treated collectivisation as a progressive measure (Dovzhenko's film *Earth* (*Zemlia*, 1930), gave it a more subtle and aesthetic treatment). Stalin and his entourage accused peasants of 'sabotage' and of starving workers and soldiers, and expressed concern about the 'counter-revolutionary chauvinism' of Ukrainian peasants. The outcome was uncompromising state violence. Out of a total of 25 million peasant households, around one million were identified as kulaks and deported, many of them to Central Asia, where they were exposed to infectious disease and a shortened life expectancy.

Land reorganisation was accompanied by a far more concerted attempt to extract grain from producers. The government overcame widespread peasant opposition by a combination of repression (theft of 'socialist property', including grain, became a capital offence on 7 August 1932) and reform (the legalisation of trade by peasant households in May 1932 and the creation of a legal framework for the *kolkhoz*). In another echo of the Stolypin reforms, some peasants welcomed the new dispensation as an opportunity to get ahead. In the short term, however, the outlook was entirely bleak. The famine of 1933, following disastrous harvests in 1931 and 1932, devastated large parts of Ukraine, the Volga region and the North Caucasus. Stalin has been accused of preventing shipments of grain from reaching areas of starvation, leading some scholars to argue that collectivisation-induced famine represented a deliberate programme of 'genocide'. Others are unconvinced, citing the overall decline in food production and the limited room for government manoeuvre.[8] In purely economic terms collectivisation resulted in the devastation of livestock herds (nowhere more so than in Kazakhstan) and the decline of animate power. It took a generation for the agricultural sector to recover. Only on the very eve of war did the total stock of power (animate and inanimate) finally exceed pre-collectivisation levels.

Gerschenkron famously pinpointed continuities between the 'Witte system' and Stalinism. According to this interpretation, Stalin exploited the 'advantages of backwardness' to press the claims of heavy industry for investment, which were secured on the basis of a sharp curtailment of overall consumption.[9] Certainly, for ordinary people, this turbulent economic transformation imposed severe strain. Day-to-day survival required the adoption of imaginative strategies: sufficient goods could be secured only by recourse to the legal and illegal markets, in order to supplement organised (planned) distribution. Workers' families traded output from domestic food production and artisanal activity. Peasants relied upon sales of produce from their private plots; their income from the *kolkhoz*, calculated as 'labour-day payment', was neither reliable (it was treated as a residual claim on the farm's product) nor adequate.[10] Other than the prison-camp population, those of pensionable age were hardest hit (peasants counted as self-employed and were not entitled to a pension).

The Stalinist economic transformation promoted upward social mobility. Some peasants escaped the *kolkhoz*, making use of well-established village networks and institutions in order to seek a more secure future than could be obtained in the uncertain world of the collective farm. Many worked as seasonal labourers, as their parents' generation had done in pre-revolutionary times. Between 1926 and 1939 around 23 million people flocked to Soviet cities, including 2 million to the Moscow conurbation. This mass influx owed very little to organised recruitment. Indeed the government sought to restrict the movement of peasants, by denying them an entitlement to the internal passport

8  For a summary of the arguments see R. W. Davies, M. B. Tauger and S. G. Wheatcroft, 'Stalin, Grain Stocks, and the Famine of 1932–33', *Slavic Review* 54 (1995): 642–57. Important remarks on the politics of collectivisation, based on new archival research, are to be found in Terry Martin, *The Affirmative Action Empire: Nations and Nationalism in the Soviet Union, 1923–1939* (Ithaca, N.Y.: Cornell University Press, 2001), pp. 302–7.
9  This is not to say that the investment programme was sacrosanct: in 1933 and 1938 the Politburo ordered cuts in investment, in order to improve the supply of consumer goods.
10  Peasants who were employed on state farms received a money wage.

that was reintroduced in 1932. But this discriminatory measure had little effect on overall geographical mobility, because peasants could enter the urban economy by various means, for example as domestic servants employed by the emerging Soviet elite so bitterly denounced by Trotsky.

Notwithstanding these pressures, or perhaps because of them, Stalinist industrialisation supported a growing ethos of consumption, particularly after the abolition of rationing in 1935–6. Soviet advice literature emphasised the need to maintain standards, at least by members of the new elite, in the preparation of food and the provision of one's apartment with furniture and books. In general, housing left a great deal to be desired – throughout the 1930s the majority of the population had to make do with communal arrangements, in shared apartments, workers' hostels or barracks. Pervasive shortages of consumer goods and accommodation gave rise to a variety of practices, at all levels of Soviet society, to smooth access to goods and services by circumventing the official system of distribution. The Soviet lexicon designated these informal reciprocal practices as *blat*. They long outlived Stalin.

Impressive resources were devoted to education and cultural improvement. The Stalin revolution entailed the construction of schools and universities, public parks and squares, theatres, cinemas and sports arenas and department stores. Campaigns to improve school attendance and to extend adult learning opportunities resulted in significant gains in literacy. Particular importance was attached to vocational training for the new generation of engineers and managers. These projects were accompanied by injunctions to self-improvement, supported by advice literature that related this to the construction of a new, socialist society and a duty to one's fellow citizens. By 1939 the total numbers employed in social and cultural projects, as well as health, housing and economic administration, exceeded 8 million, compared with fewer than 2 million in 1926.

The demographic consequences of Stalinism were related to this profound economic transformation, and to the terror that accompanied it. Collectivisation prompted a mass exodus of peasants in 1931–2, and as a result the government closed the borders of Ukraine and the Kuban' in January 1933. But the state also directly engineered population displacement. Thus 'dekulakisation' resulted in the deportation of peasants (of all nationalities) to 'special settlements'; by 1933 these housed around 1.1 million men, women and children. Other forced labour was concentrated in prisons, in labour camps, and in labour colonies. All of these – a combined population of 2.52 million in 1933, rising to 3.35 million by 1941 – provided an important source of labour for the Stalinist economy. Ostensibly, the Gulag had impressive 'achievements' to its credit. Construction of mines, roads, railways and urban transport systems (such as the Moscow metro), canals and waterways (for example, the White Sea Canal), and new industrial towns, such as Magnitogorsk and Komsomol'sk-na-Amure, depended upon the labour of dispossessed kulaks and other forced labour, celebrated by Maxim Gorky as a demonstration of the potential to rehabilitate the criminal 'element'. The NKVD also used forced labour to produce non-ferrous metals and for the felling of timber. But the Gulag imposed a heavy burden, because productive workers were wrenched from the occupations for which they had been trained and because immense resources were tied up in monitoring the work of prisoners.

Terror also meant the forced migration of entire 'enemy' populations, beginning with Ingrian peasants who were designated as 'kulaks' and deported to Murmansk and to Central Asia in 1930. Further deportations, of Koreans, Germans and Poles took place before the Second World War; during the war Crimean Tatars and Chechen and Ingush civilians suffered the same fate. Deportation disrupted and even destroyed viable economic activity. The Soviet occupation of Central and Eastern Europe after 1945 brought forth fresh deportations, notably in the Baltic lands, but these were related to economic development only in so far as they 'encouraged' the incorporation of hitherto independent states into the socialist economy. Meanwhile, post-war construction in the USSR, such as the creation of the closed city of Krasnoiarsk-26, a major centre of producing weapons-grade plutonium, depended heavily upon forced labour.

The welfare consequences of the Stalinist economic transformation have proved particularly controversial where the interests of nationalities are concerned. During the Second FYP the Soviet leadership sought to reduce the development gap between the more advanced and less-developed parts of the Soviet Union. The main plank in this strategy was to encourage rapid growth by means of investment in production, infrastructure and education. The results were undoubtedly impressive, at least in terms of accelerating the economic development of less-developed regions such as Central Asia, where new factories, power stations and transport links were built, along with hospitals, schools and universities. These policies produced a nationalist backlash. In pre-war Ukraine, for example, the Soviet regime faced accusations of having expanded heavy industry in the eastern region, at the expense of light industry and agriculture in the ethnically more homogeneous western parts of Ukraine. And in Kazakhstan, the construction of the Turksib railway – achieved in part by the recruitment of native labour – was accompanied by the charge that this grand project had destroyed the 'traditional' Kazakh nomad way of life.

## Great leaps forward (III)

The Second World War left an enduring imprint on the Soviet economy. Economic reconstruction was rendered difficult by the magnitude of wartime devastation and by the shock of sudden famine in 1946–7. Recent work has demonstrated that key industrial sectors, notably coal mining, ferrous metallurgy and construction, experienced a desperate labour shortage that was made good by prisoners (by 1953 the forced labour system incarcerated 5.5 million persons) and by semi-free workers recruited from the village.[11] These workers were bound by the draconian labour legislation introduced in 1938 and 1940 that imposed rigorous controls over job mobility. These controls were not lifted until 1951, by which time managers were refusing to enforce them, lest they deprive the enterprise of scarce skilled labour.

The campaign style in Soviet economic policy was reiterated during the 1950s by Nikita Khrushchev, whose regime became synonymous with fresh ideological fervour, such as supporting the ambitious goals of building communism and overtaking the USA. Khrushchev denounced the spread of ownership of dachas and attacked the private plot. None of these campaigns had any pronounced economic impact. Much more consequential was his decision to promote population migration to Siberia and Central Asia, in order to settle new farmland. Constant pressure to maintain sowings on virgin land quickly led to soil erosion. In general, however, the continued de-ruralisation of Russia continued: by 1970 only 44 per cent of households were rural, compared to 66 per cent on the eve of the Second World War. The relatively poor quality of life in villages, particularly in Russia's non-Black Earth region, encouraged rural depopulation, a process that persisted throughout the final quarter of the century notwithstanding formal restrictions on rural out-migration.[12] One other campaign attracted enormous international publicity: in 1957 the Soviet Union launched the world's first satellite into orbit, heralding the onset of a major space programme. These campaigns went hand in hand with continued economic growth. During the 1950s, according to Khanin, Soviet national income grew at an annual average rate of 7.2 per cent, falling to 4.4 per cent in 1960–5. Further campaigns were launched by Khrushchev's successors to secure improved economic performance by means of institutional reform. In 1965

---

11 The definition of forced labour is the same as used earlier, comprising those in prison, in labour camps, in labour colonies and in special settlements. By 1953 the latter housed 2.75 million. Gulag workers began to receive wages after 1950, although they were set at no more than half the wages paid to free workers.

12 L. N. Denisova, *Ischezaiushchaia derevnia Rossii: nechernozem'e v 1960–1980 gody* (Moscow: RAN, 1996).

industrial ministries were empowered to use 'economic levers', such as bonus payments and retained profits, in order to stimulate enterprise performance.

This era was also associated with a renewed emphasis upon consumption. Consumption was in part a purely 'private' matter, but it was also secured by informal social networks (*blat*) and an extensive range of practices (such as petty pilfering and the theft of state property) that have been grouped together in the term 'second economy' and that enabled consumers to reroute goods from the state to other sectors of the economy. Officialdom frequently turned a blind eye, partly because officials themselves participated in these informal transactions.[13] From one point of view, consumption in its official and unofficial variants helped to cement the legitimacy of the regime. But consumers' access to goods imposed constraints, in that Soviet citizens became accustomed to price subsidies. Consumers were prepared to overlook shortages and poor-quality products provided there were no untoward increases in their price. When working-class consumers went on strike in protest against price increases in Novocherkassk in 1962, they met with brutal state repression. This exceptional episode proved the rule (and helped cost Khrushchev his job): Brezhnev's lengthy tenure of office as General Secretary rested in large part upon the use of retail price subsidies, whereby the state absorbed increases in the procurement prices paid to Soviet farmers during the late 1960s and 1970s.[14] At least for a while, the state budget became the opium of the masses.

The post-Stalinist transformation also brought about Soviet exposure to the international economy. In the first instance this meant the creation of closer links with the countries that made up the 'Soviet bloc'. Here the Council for Mutual Economic Assistance (Comecon) promoted socialist economic integration, meaning the transfer of engineering products from Eastern Europe in exchange for cheap energy from Russia. Meanwhile during the 1970s and early 1980s the Soviet Union extended its international profile by importing Western technology (and some consumer goods) and exporting oil during a period of rapidly rising energy prices on the world market. The great oil boom, and its availability at below-market prices, did nothing to discourage wasteful energy consumption. Policies to accelerate technological progress did not improve overall economic performance, partly because Soviet enterprises lacked the ability to assimilate foreign technology. To all intents and purposes the Soviet

---

13 Gregory Grossman, 'The Second Economy of the USSR', *Problems of Communism* 26 (1977): 25–40.

14 As a result, and taking into account farmers' incomes from their private plots, the disparity between rural and urban incomes that was a feature of the Stalinist economy all but disappeared under Brezhnev.

economy under Brezhnev suffered the same shortcomings as in the era of NEP. In both periods the Soviet Union lagged behind more dynamic economies in the capitalist West.

## The reform impulse in Russian economic history (II): *perestroika*

*Perestroika* (literally, 'restructuring') was a bold attempt to address economic deceleration and to revitalise Soviet society. In the first instance, *perestroika* represented the triumph of a generation of reform-minded social scientists, such as Abel Aganbegian and Tat'iana Zaslavskaia, who had been arguing since the 1970s that the socio-economic system was outmoded. Created at a time when factors of production, labour and capital were relatively abundant and when the general level of educational attainment amongst the population was low, they maintained that the 'administrative-command economy' discouraged the kind of energy and enterprise that the modern economy required and whose absence was reflected in the poor level of labour productivity. Long-serving officials, accustomed to interfere in the affairs of firms, were encouraged to devote their time instead to broad strategic issues. Chief amongst these was the need (in the words of Mikhail Gorbachev) for a 'renewal of socialism'.

Publicity campaigns once more accompanied economic reform initiatives. A remarkable burst of 'openness' (*glasnost'*) far exceeded anything witnessed in the Khrushchev era. The Soviet press and intelligentsia rediscovered the New Economic Policy, which was trumpeted (somewhat misleadingly) as a kind of golden age of economic freedom and dynamism.[15] Technocrats deplored widespread wastage (*brak*) in industry. Gorbachev denounced alcohol abuse and absenteeism. In a concerted attempt to boost economic growth, the leadership pinned its hopes on technological change in key sectors such as engineering. This policy of acceleration (*uskorenie*), closely associated with Prime Minister Nikolai Ryzhkov, failed to live up to expectations. Little came of an attempt to establish joint ventures with foreign firms. In 1987–8 more radical measures were introduced to reform property relations, extending from the legalisation of co-operative and private enterprise to the removal of restrictions on state enterprise. Unfortunately, the Law on State Enterprise (May 1987) failed to have the desired impact. The revival of the doctrine of commercial accounting (*khozraschet*), first formulated in the NEP era, implied

---

15 R. W. Davies, *Soviet History in the Gorbachev Revolution* (London: Macmillan, 1989); Alec Nove, *Glasnost' in Action: Cultural Renaissance in Russia* (London: Unwin Hyman, 1989).

that enterprises would no longer receive support from the state but would instead respond to consumer wants. However, firms were still expected to give priority to orders placed by the state authorities. In 1990, Gorbachev appeared to endorse a still bolder but hastily put together initiative for a '500-day' transition programme, which envisaged the privatisation of around three-quarters of all state enterprises and a liberalisation of prices. Responding perhaps to public anxieties about the consequences of radical reform, Gorbachev held back from committing himself to the adoption of the programme in its entirety.[16]

What went wrong? The budget deficit spiralled out of control, a consequence of reduced tax receipts and a decision to maintain huge spending on consumer subsidies, as well as social welfare and defence. In 1984, before *perestroika*, the deficit was approximately 4 per cent of GNP. By 1989 it stood at 10 per cent. Two years later it had ballooned to 20 per cent. No serious attempt was made to institute a significant reform of the price system. Gorbachev negotiated fresh foreign loans, bequeathing a mountain of debt to his successors. The state kept the system afloat by printing roubles, whilst enterprises survived by granting one another vast credits. Inflation was rampant. The basic problem in late Soviet Russia, namely the failure to engineer economic and technological modernisation, continued unabated.

*Perestroika* unleashed a wave of dissatisfaction, from vested interests whose secure position in Soviet society was threatened, from workers who demanded improvements in food supplies and housing and from nationalists who declared that only independence could restore the fortunes of the Soviet republics. The reformers' stance appeared likely to threaten the perquisites of the Soviet elite. Yet not all Soviet bureaucrats opposed radical economic reform. Paul Gregory has distinguished between planners (*apparatchiki*) and entrepreneurs (*khoziaistvenniki*). The former were directly threatened by attempts to erode the supremacy of Gosplan, whereas the latter entertained the possibility of greater leverage within a more mixed economic system. Post-Soviet reform would subsequently demonstrate that they were well placed to take advantage of full-scale economic liberalisation. Workers also took to the streets to demand wage rises and greater enterprise 'autonomy'; to the extent that their demands were satisfied, costs increased and inter-enterprise debt accumulated. Gorbachev refused to sanction significant increases in retail prices.

16 Ed Hewett described it as 'a valiant effort to reconstruct the union virtually out of whole cloth, on the basis of economic interests, rather than fear' (E. A. Hewett and V. H. Winston (eds.), *Milestones in Glasnost and Perestroyka: The Economy* (Washington: Brookings Institution Press, 1991), p. 457).

As a result shortages of goods continued to mount, queues lengthened and popular disquiet intensified.

Did Soviet integration hinder economic progress in the various republics, as national activists claimed? Membership of the Soviet Union entailed subordination to an increasingly sclerotic planned economy, underwritten by the authority of the Communist Party. Arguably, it was the failings of the economic system, not their incorporation in the Soviet Union per se, that disadvantaged the constituent republics. The slowdown in economic growth that became apparent from the 1970s helped to encourage nationalist dissatisfaction. Some nationalists saw opportunities to profit from secession rather than from continued membership of the Soviet state, regarding independence as a means of escape from Soviet (Russian) domination and exploitation. It dawned on them that tight central control and the imposition of uniform solutions to economic problems had disastrous consequences. Dissatisfaction over the deceleration in economic growth went hand in hand with cultural complaint, which *glasnost'* fuelled in uncompromising fashion. The process was not confined to the non-Russian republics; Boris Yeltsin appropriated and Russified the most important all-Union institutions. Given the opportunity to secede, the nationalists took it unhesitatingly.

## The radical privatisation impulse (II): post-1991 experiments and consequences

The collapse of Communism ushered in a period of prolonged political uncertainty and socio-economic turmoil. Output plummeted. Investment remained weak and expectations of an influx of foreign capital went unrealised, thereby compounding the problems posed by an already obsolescent capital stock. Consumption declined. The Russian Federation found it immensely difficult to establish a secure and viable tax base. Economic relations with others in the Commonwealth of Independent States remained fragile. At the same time, this was an era of radical experimentation with capitalist economic forms. The advocates of economic transformation maintained that the costs of transition were exaggerated.

The post-Communist governments set great store by a radical privatisation of enterprise. In echoes of the Stolypin land reforms, the contemporary exponents of economic transition pinned much of their hopes on privatisation and the entrepreneurial flair that it was expected to unleash. However, the results were mixed. To be sure, the private sector expanded; by 1996 around two-fifths of the labour force was employed in the private sector, compared to one-tenth a decade earlier. But there were significant costs. The so-called 'voucher privatisation' scheme in 1992–4 transferred ownership of thousands of enterprises, mostly to existing management and employees. It guaranteed neither good management of those enterprises nor the prospect of attracting outside investment. The loans-for-shares scheme of 1995–7 enabled powerful oligarchs to acquire cheaply from the state through rigged auctions some of Russia's most valuable oil companies including Yukos, Sibneft and Sidanco. In addition, predatory and criminal cliques flourished, hindering the potential viability of new enterprises and limiting the possibility for engaging with new markets and embracing technical change. So far as the agricultural sector is concerned, little land was transferred into private ownership from 1991. As under Soviet socialism, Russian peasants produced fruit and vegetables on household plots. The large collective farms continued in existence, but this probably testified to inertia rather than to their viability as integrated institutions that once supplied a range of services to the rural population. Peasant farmers did not rush to embrace the institutions of a market economy.

Some authors, such as Anders Aslund, offer a more upbeat assessment of the post-Communist economy. They point out that official output data need to be adjusted to take account of unregistered activity. Allowance must also be made for the high degree of waste in Soviet-era GDP. Taking these factors into account, the decline in output was much less marked. More broadly, they emphasise the shortcomings of the old economic system and the magnitude of the crisis that was bequeathed to the new regime. Even privatisation, it is argued, contributed to a strengthening of democratic potential in the former Soviet Union. (One might add that the results of privatisation, like the Stolypin land reform, will take at least a generation to be fully realised.) Finally, if transition was so disastrous, the argument runs, why was there so little resistance to radical reform?

One explanation may be the short-term recourse to mechanisms of self-help and barter. Barter reflects a loss of confidence in the domestic currency and a readiness to conceal transactions from the tax authorities. The partners involved in non-monetary transactions are predisposed to trust one another rather than to put their faith in the market and in financial institutions. The consequences of barter include disincentives to develop new methods of production or new products. The phenomenon represents a diversion of entrepreneurial talent and time, and promotes other inefficiencies, because resources are tied up in storing and offloading stocks. But, as Paul Seabright suggests, barter arrangements are not unlike *krugovaia poruka* ('collective obligation', or 'mutual responsibility') whereby peasants sustained themselves by a system of mutual dependency. Barter became widespread in Russia and Ukraine during the 1990s, even though inflation was brought under control and confidence in money was restored. Enterprises engaged in barter as a means of exchange and as settlement of inter-enterprise debt. Firms lacking sufficient working capital (perhaps because the government failed to settle its obligations) paid wages in the form of their own output. As well as being an inefficient arrangement the increased recourse to barter were a symptom of wider political and economic dislocation. But equally its prevalence suggests the durability of social networks that were established prior to the 'transition'.

The rupture of inter-republican links following the collapse of the USSR posed major problems of adjustment. Enterprises had to renegotiate contracts with suppliers or to find new sources of supply. Products were now traded at world market prices, rather than being subsidised by the Soviet state. Some of the successor states exploited opportunities to engage in international trade, specialising on the basis of natural resource endowments, such as natural gas in Turkmenistan. Political instability and military conflict in Tajikistan and Georgia, for example, helped to depress economic activity. On the other hand, the Baltic states successfully stabilised their budgets, reduced inflation rates and promoted foreign direct investment, as preparation for joining the enlarged European Union in May 2004. Within the resource-rich Russian Federation, non-Russian ethnic groups sought to redress 'wrongs' done during the Soviet period. Thus a vocal Siberian lobby, speaking on behalf of 32 million people, demanded compensation for environmental damage.

Demographically the transition was extremely painful. To be sure, the project of Soviet 'modernity' itself bequeathed a legacy of environmental degradation, declining health conditions and increasing infant mortality. But transition has thus far done little to reverse the decline. Adult male life expectancy plummeted. Many citizens, including some of the former inmates of remote Soviet prison camps, reverted to a subsistence economy. Ordinary citizens often required two or more jobs in order to compensate for meagre and/or uncertain wages. Again, mutual support networks played an important part in maintaining a basic standard of living. A more extreme response was emigration; according to official figures between 1992 and 1998 some 700,000 people left Russia to settle in countries outside the former Soviet Union. Germany was by far the most popular destination.[17]

Account also needs to be taken of the demographic consequences of the sudden disintegration of the USSR in 1991. Around 280 million ex-Soviet citizens

17 Julie DaVanzo and Clifford Grammich, *Dire Demographics: Population Trends in the Russian Federation* (Santa Monica, Calif.: Rand, 2001), ch. 2.

were now scattered amongst fifteen sovereign states. More than 25 million Russians lived beyond the borders of the Russian Federation (this figure is taken from the 1989 census), and it has not been difficult to portray them as vestiges of Soviet 'colonialism'.[18] Throughout the 1990s concerns were expressed about their status, entitlements and prospects. Those who made their way to Russia survived by capitalising where possible upon networks of mutual support. But the lack of housing and of state benefits has rendered their position in Russia precarious.

## Conclusions and assessment

The economic history of Russia's twentieth century is full of absolutist prescriptions for improved economic performance. Before the revolution, the talk was of foreign investment and enterprise (under Witte), and of 'rational' land consolidation (under Stolypin). Under NEP the emphasis shifted to a combination of state control and circumscribed private enterprise, with continued espousal of the doctrine of improvement for the peasant economy, primarily by means of expert intervention from outside the rural sector. Stalin preferred the twin instruments of central economic planning and terror, in order to realise his vision of Soviet socialist modernisation. Khrushchev pinned his hopes on extracting greater efforts from workers and peasants, partly by means of incentives, but also by exhorting them to work harder and to become pioneer settlers on virgin land. The advocates of *perestroika* after 1985 believed in a mixture of state control and market mechanisms, accompanied by the reform of property rights. Post-Soviet prescriptions have favoured the route of privatisation, claiming that the shortcomings of transition are the result of timidity in engaging with the challenge of economic transition. Each successive nostrum has been accompanied by a set of campaigns, to pinpoint the 'problem' (including aberrant personal behaviour) and/or to identify the 'enemy' to be confronted, unmasked and defeated.

What have been the results of these various economic visions? The Soviet economic project came to dominate the twentieth century. It is worth reflecting on what this means. First, for more than seven decades the experience of millions of Soviet citizens was closely bound up with a centralised system of economic administration and a lack of exposure to overseas economic stimuli. But the domination of the Soviet system did not rest wholly or even

---

18 The Russian census originally scheduled for 1999 was delayed by the financial crisis in 1998. It finally took place in October 2002.

largely on the instruments of terror, even under Stalinism. The state also derived a degree of legitimacy from the promise and the reality of economic growth, technological modernisation and social progress. There were genuine and important gains in literacy and life expectancy from one generation to the next. In the words of a broadly hostile critic, Soviet economic policies secured 'some broad acquiescence on the part of the people'.[19] That acquiescence rested upon Soviet-style welfare provision and opportunities for upward social mobility, which generated a sense of civic commitment and left a positive legacy. On the other hand, Soviet economic modernisation also left scars on the landscape, in the form of large, dirty and obsolescent factories, decrepit farms and polluted waterways and lakes.

There is another dimension to the Soviet economic project. The USSR confronted capitalism with a rival economic system. As Eric Hobsbawm has pointed out, capitalism 'won', but it differed greatly from the system that had conquered the world during the nineteenth century. One reason for its transformation was the challenge it faced from Soviet socialism.[20] Nor should an exposure of the failings of the Soviet economic experiment blind us to the shortcomings of capitalism. To be sure, the Soviet Union left a legacy of debt, environmental degradation and struggling enterprises. But those who gloat over flaws in the system and its uneven economic performance would do well to reflect on the evidence of poverty, malnutrition, illiteracy, ill-health, environmental damage, debt burden and inequality that are the hallmarks of large parts of the globe. No amount of triumphalism from the privileged few can disguise the fact that the fortunes of so much of twentieth-century humanity have been mixed. An objective reading of the Soviet 'experiment' might conclude that the laudable ambition to realise the social and economic potential of the majority remains as relevant today as it was nearly a century ago.

19 Alexander Gerschenkron, *Economic Backwardness in Historical Perspective* (Cambridge, Mass.: Harvard University Press, 1962), p. 29.
20 Eric Hobsbawm, *The Age of Extremes: The Short Twentieth Century 1914–1991* (London: Michael Joseph, 1994).

# 15

# Transforming peasants in the twentieth century: Dilemmas of Russian, Soviet and post-Soviet development

ESTHER KINGSTON-MANN

## Contexts for change

By the dawn of the twentieth century, most predominantly peasant societies were already colonised or otherwise subjugated by the world's industrialised modern empires. For nations not yet subjected to the full force of this process, the penalties of backwardness were increasingly manifest. In Imperial Russia and the Soviet Union, the fear that backwardness might invite foreign conquest led a succession of heads of state to target peasants as producers of the grain needed to finance ambitious, government-sponsored projects for industrialisation. However, although peasants were crucial to the success of any development scenario, both reforming and revolutionary elites tended to discount the possibility of peasant agency. Peasants typically viewed as 'raw material' rather than as co-participants in the development process were – in the words of Caroline Humphrey – 'never in possession of the master narrative of which they were the objects, and had no access to the sources from which it was reaching them'.[1] The following discussion is intended to situate the peasant majority of the population as both agents and victims within the history of Imperial Russia and the Soviet Union, and to locate them on the shifting terrain of the post-Soviet era.

In 1900, the peasants of Imperial Russia continued to struggle – like their parents and grandparents before them – against the constraints of a land and climate largely inhospitable to productive farming. In regions where rainfall was reliable, soils were poor; more fertile areas were routinely afflicted by drought.

I am deeply indebted to the work of Moshe Lewin, Teodor Shanin and Caroline Humphrey, and to the insightful readings of this essay by David Hunt, Rochelle Ruthchild and James Mann.

1 Caroline Humphrey, 'Politics of Privatisation in Provincial Russia: Popular Opinions Amid the Dilemmas of the Early 1990s', *Cambridge Anthropology* 18, 1 (1995): 46.

These drawbacks persisted regardless of prevailing political or socio-economic systems, and despite historical efforts either to privatise or collectivise the land. As the most impoverished and least literate of the tsar's subjects, peasants bore the economic and non-economic burdens imposed by a variety of more or less importunate elites. By 1900, they constituted 80 per cent of the population; the majority were women, and a substantial proportion of them were ethnically non-Russian. As in other predominantly peasant societies, the rural populace of the imperial, Soviet and post-Soviet eras opposed some changes – often in collective fashion, with women in the forefront – but selectively appropriated others. In times of crisis, they deployed the symbols and rituals of their secular and religious cultures to reinforce demands for social justice and for vengeance against malign forces within and outside the household and community.

## Labour, communes, households

Like many other peasantries, the rural inhabitants of Imperial Russia viewed labour as an economic necessity, as the source of legitimate rights to land use and as the basis for status claims within the household and community. In the communes to which most peasants belonged, the number of adult labourers per household frequently determined land-allotment size. In times of unrest and rebellion, peasants asserted that the gentry had 'stolen' the land from the tillers of the soil who were its rightful owners. In the Revolutions of 1905 and 1917, they demanded that land be 'returned' to the labouring peasantry. At no time did peasants acknowledge the legitimacy of claims to landownership by persons who did not labour on it. In 1900, labour claims infused the operations of the peasantry's basic institutions: the commune and the peasant household.

The peasant commune (*mir* or *obshchina*) was the dominant institution in the early twentieth-century Russian countryside. The object of centuries of idealisation and demonisation by a variety of radicals, reformers and government officials, its distinguishing feature was the periodic repartition of land among member households according to family size, number of adult labourers per household or some other collective social principle. Within the commune framework, member households possessed exclusive but temporary rights to use scattered strips of land (allotments) and could freely decide how to dispose of the product of their farm labour. Neither wholly collective nor private, communes were mixed economies within which individual, household and communal rights to ownership coexisted in social configurations that varied regionally and changed over time. Individual members owned their personal belongings and could bequeath them to others. Women possessed unconditional ownership rights to a 'woman's box' (the product of weaving and other gendered activities).

Within the commune, households possessed collective and hereditary rights to a house, garden plot and livestock – the latter properties constituted a key source of economic inequality between peasant households. Periodic repartition was relatively rare in the north and west of the empire, where most peasants held land in hereditary (*podvornoe*) tenure. However, it is significant that even in more privatised areas, peasants relied on the use of common lands. More like English commons-users than yeoman farmers, they collectively shared out and collected the obligations owed to landlords and the state, devised and enforced rules for use of common lands and provided a variety of welfare supports to their members.[2]

Although the powers that the patriarch (*bol'shak*) exercised over the daily life of his household were virtually absolute, when he died, household property reverted to the household group under a new head (a son, brother or sometimes a widow). In the case of household divisions, a village assembly (*skhod*) composed of the heads of member households and led by elected village elders generally oversaw the distribution of property. Although communes were plagued by corruption, nepotism and individual profit-seeking, they nevertheless obliged wealthier families to link their fate with poorer neighbours and required ambitious individuals to obtain the consent of their neighbours before introducing significant changes. At best, they provided a framework capable of satisfying both a family's desire for a holding of its own, and the desire for protection against the monopolising of resources by wealthier families / households within the community.

In many parts of the Russian Empire, the social identities of peasants were organised according to a set of hierarchies that subordinated younger people and females to the authority of the household patriarch. In addition to childcare, women were expected to cook the household's food, fetch water, sew, wash clothes, weave cloth, care for poultry and livestock, endure beatings and tend the family's 'private' garden plot (*usad'ba*). Granted a modicum of respect for their labour contributions and a right to the product of 'women's work' (weaving, poultry raising, etc.), women were otherwise

---

2 Esther Kingston-Mann, 'Peasant Communes and Economic Innovation', in Esther Kingston-Mann and Timothy Mixter (eds.), *Peasant Economy, Culture and Politics of European Russia* (Princeton: Princeton University Press, 1991), pp. 23–51; Steven Grant, 'Obshchina and Mir', *Slavic Review* 35, 4 (1976): 636–51.

wholly subordinated to the authority of fathers, husbands and elder sons; they gained a measure of power only after achieving the status of mother-in-law (with authority over daughters-in-law).

In 1900, most peasant households were primarily devoted to agricultural pursuits. But particularly in the northern provinces of St Petersburg, Moscow, Archangel and Nizhnii Novgorod, an increasing number sought to meet escalating tax burdens by leaving their villages to become hired labourers (*otkhodniki*). In workplaces far distant from their homes, peasants absorbed new ideas, customs and practices and took care to establish strategic relationships grounded in networks of kin and neighbours.[3] However, leaving the village rarely signified a repudiation of village ties; *otkhodniki* frequently 'raided the market' by sending money back to their home villages[4] (where opportunities for women expanded in the absence of the usually dominant males).[5] Peasants did not retain their 'old ways' unchanged. Instead, they infused time-honoured traditions with new combinations of indigenous and imported meanings. As Moshe Lewin has suggested, the rural populace was changing, but 'the interplay between new and old formations did not conform to theory and kept complicating the picture and baffling the thinker and the politician'.[6]

Although wealthy peasants exerted a disproportionate influence in village life, scholars continue to debate the extent to which early twentieth-century economic differences were reproduced from generation to generation as class formations or mitigated through periodic repartition. Since commune repartitions usually apportioned allotments according to family size or labour capacity, larger households were often 'richer' in land; newer and smaller households received smaller allotments.[7]

In general, rural innovation was not confined to 'privatised' farming districts. In Tobol'sk and Kazan', contemporary statisticians and economists

3 Timothy Mixter, 'The Hiring Market as Workers' Turf: Migrant Agricultural Labourers and the Mobilisation of Collective Action in the Steppe Grainbelt of European Russia, 1853–1913', in Kingston-Mann and Mixter, *Peasant Economy, Culture*, pp. 294–340.
4 J. Burds, 'The Social Control of Peasant Labor in Russia: The Response of Village Communities in Labor Migration in the Central Industrial Region, 1961–1904', in Kingston-Mann and Mixter, *Peasant Economy, Culture*, pp. 52–100.
5 See B. Engel, *Between Fields and the City: Women, Work and Family in Russia, 1861–1914* (Cambridge: Cambridge University Press, 1996), pp. 34–63.
6 Moshe Lewin, The *Making of the Soviet System* (New York: Pantheon Books, 1985), p. 290.
7 See the early discussion of this process in N. N. Chernenkov, *K kharakteristike krest'ianskogo khoziaistva* (Moscow, 1905), its later elaboration in A. V. Chaianov, *On the Theory of Peasant Economy*, ed. D. Thorner et al. (Homewood, Ill.: R. D. Irwin, 1966), and a valuable more recent discussion in Teodor Shanin, *The Awkward Class: Political Sociology of Peasantry in a Developing Society, Russia 1910–1925* (Oxford: Clarendon Press, 1972).

documented commune strategies specifically crafted to reward individual innovation while limiting the growth of rural differentiation. In Tambov, commune peasants who fertilised their allotments either received special monetary payments at the time of repartition, a similar allotment or the right to retain their original holdings. In 1900, 127 commune villages in a single district of Moscow province introduced many-field crop rotations; by 1903, 245 out of 368 villages had done so.[8] While innovation was not widespread either within or outside the commune, irreversible changes in farming practices were becoming manifest in the early years of the twentieth century.

## Breaking the peasant commune (1): Stolypin's 'wager on the strong'

In 1905, when Russia's first twentieth-century revolution erupted, communes organised the seizure of gentry land, and commune-sponsored petitions demanding land and liberty, abolition of private property rights and 'return' of land to the tillers of the soil poured into the capital from every corner of the empire.[9] In response, the government introduced a programme to eliminate the peasant commune and replace it with a rural constituency of 'strong' and conservative private farmers. Between 1906 and 1911, Prime Minister Stolypin's reforms invited peasant households to separate from the commune and establish themselves on enclosed, self-contained farms (*otruby* and *khutora*); in this process the household property formerly owned by the household was to become the private property of the *bol'shak*.

In the decade that followed, few of the government's hopes for privatisation were realised. Many requests for separation came not from the strong, but from 'weak' families that had suffered misfortune that could cost them land in repartitions determined according to family size or labour capacity.[10] Equally significant was the depth of peasant opposition, and the role of women. Because soldiers were traditionally less likely to fire on women, and because the income and status of women were so intimately linked with the household's garden plot that had been transferred to the *bol'shak*, women were frequently

---

8 For other examples, see Kingston-Mann, 'Peasant Communes', pp. 36–9.
9 See discussion in Teodor Shanin, *Russia, 1905–07: Revolution as a Moment of Truth: The Roots of Otherness: Russia's Turn of Century*, vol. II (New Haven: Yale University Press, 1986), pp. 79–137.
10 P. N. Zyrianov, *Krest'ianskaia obshchina evropeiskoi Rossii 1907–1914* (Moscow: Nauka, 1992), pp. 111–15.

visible at the forefront of anti-enclosure confrontations with the authorities.[11] Although the government offered 'separators' generous legal and extra-legal support, financial subsidies and preferential credit rates, peasants nevertheless returned to the commune in increasing numbers on the eve of the First World War. By 1916, violence against 'separators' had become so intense that the Stolypin reforms were suspended.

In general, privatisation did not lead 'separators' to change their farming practices. Communities that chose to eliminate periodic land repartition took care to retain not only their common lands but also the welfare supports that communes traditionally provided.[12] Overall, the Stolypin reforms failed to demonstrate that newly enclosed private farms were significantly more or less productive or profitable than communes. Ironically, the most dramatic change in the Russian countryside during this period was initiated not by the government but by commune peasants, who engaged in massive purchases of gentry holdings and appreciably levelled the economic playing field between 1906 and 1914.[13]

## War and revolution, 1914–17

In 1914, world war, invasion, military disaster and a state-sponsored scorched-earth policy destabilised and displaced the populace of Russia's western provinces; by 1916, a predominantly peasant army had suffered 2.5 million casualties and internal refugees numbered 2 million. In this brutal and brutalising context, Russia's second twentieth-century revolution erupted in February 1917 and quickly toppled the regime of Tsar Nicholas II. As in 1905, peasant communes took centre stage by organising land seizures and forcibly returning 'separators' to their former communes. From a political standpoint, the Revolution of 1917 was significant because peasants participated in it not only as soldiers but in their own right, as peasants, in the urban-led revolutionary movement to establish soviets nationwide. Inspired by traditional labour principles, the first 'Order' issued by the All-Russian Conference of Soviet Peasant Deputies in May 1917 declared: 'All peasants deserve the right to labour on the land; private ownership is abolished.' Throughout 1917, the language of peasant

11 Judith Pallot, *Land Reform in Russia 1906–1917: Peasant Responses to Stolypin's Project of Rural Transformation* (Oxford: Clarendon Press, 1999), pp. 181–3 and 193–4; see also J. Humphries, 'Enclosures, Common Rights, and Women', *Journal of Economic History* 50, 2 (1990): 17–41.
12 O. Khauke, *Krest'ianskoe zemel'noe pravo* (Moscow, 1914), p. 355.
13 G. Ioffe and T. Nefedova, *Continuity and Change in Rural Russia: A Geographical Perspective* (Boulder, Colo.: Westview Press, 1997), p. 56.

petitions invoked 'God-given' rights to land 'stolen' by wicked landlords and officials.

During the second half of 1917, peasant political allegiances shifted – not towards Marxism, about which they knew little – but towards a Bolshevik Party that consistently demanded the immediate transfer of land to the peasantry and withdrawal from the war. In the face of economic collapse and the devastation produced by German invasion, peasants in Ukraine, Estonia and Latvia as well as Russia began to voice support – or at least neutrality – towards a Bolshevik seizure of power.[14] However, although peasant support was crucial to Bolshevik success, it never convinced the Bolsheviks that they needed to rethink their urban-centred perspectives. While Lenin optimistically declared that in future peasants would test their petty bourgeois illusions 'in the fire of life'[15] (and presumably move towards socialism), such remarks were no substitute for a principled Marxist peasant policy.

## War Communism, 1918–20

They [the Bolsheviks] didn't understand peasants very well.
(Moshe Lewin, *The Making of Soviet Society*)

The policy of War Communism emerged in response to a series of material disasters, each one sufficient to overwhelm and destroy a stable political order, much less a fragile hierarchy of soviets controlled at the top by a few hundred revolutionaries wholly without administrative experience. Between 1918 and 1921, the Soviet Union was invaded and dismembered by Imperial Germany, torn apart by civil war, weakened by Allied military intervention and deprived of its major grain and fuel-producing territories. The destruction of gentry privilege and the relative powerlessness of the central government provided peasants with the opportunity – for perhaps the first time in their history – to construct their lives free of the constraints traditionally imposed by various social and political elites. In what has been described as a post-October 'anti-Stolypin revolution',[16] 96 per cent of the rural population in thirty-nine out of forty-seven provinces had become commune members by 1920.[17] Attempting

---

14 See discussion in R. G. Suny, *The Revenge of the Past: Nationalism, Revolution, and the Collapse of the Soviet Union* (Stanford, Calif.: Stanford University Press, 1993), p. 57.
15 V. I. Lenin, *Polnoe sobranie sochinenii*, vol. xxxv (Moscow, 1958–65), p. 27.
16 See S. Maksudov, *Neuslyshannye golosa: Dokumenty Smolenskogo Arkhiva*, bk. 1: *Kulaki i Partiitsy* (Ann Arbor: Ardis, 1987), p. 23.
17 D. G. Atkinson, *The End of the Russian Land Commune, 1905–1930* (Stanford, Calif.: Stanford University Press), pp. 209 and 254.

to foster traditional labour principles and social equality (*poravnenie*) in the countryside, peasants were on occasion even willing to allot land to former squires as commune members on condition that the squires were themselves willing to labour on it.[18]

Unsurprisingly, peasants placed a low priority on meeting the needs of urban proletarians who provided them with little in exchange for the grain they produced. Terrified at the prospect of urban workers fleeing to the countryside in search of food, the Soviet government organised 'Committees of the Poor' (*kombedy*) to incite a rural class war between proletarians and kulaks, and confiscate the latter's ill-gotten gains. But since peasants were in 1918 more materially and socially equal than ever before in their history, they chose instead to close ranks against the *kombedy* and rejected Soviet efforts to divide them.

While the economist Preobrazhenskii contended that War Communism embodied the highest socialist principle of taking from each according to ability and giving to each according to need, Lenin was more honest: 'we actually took from the peasants all their surpluses, and sometimes even what was not surplus but part of what was necessary to the peasant. We took it to cover the costs of the army and to maintain the workers . . . Otherwise we could not have beaten the landowners and the capitalists.'[19] By the end of 1918, the *kombedy* were dissolved, but the food crisis continued. Alongside the legal channels of distribution, peasants constructed a black market and devised systems of barter that rendered the formal organs of state control irrelevant to the process of exchange.

Although government statistics indicated that most peasants produced no merchandise, sold a fraction of their produce and reserved most of it for internal family consumption,[20] it is significant that they remained – from the Soviet standpoint – an eternally petty bourgeois element, mired in the 'idiocy of rural life'. Urban-educated party enthusiasts confidently assumed that peasants understood nothing about farming, and inundated them with exhortations and prescriptions for what, how much and even where they should sow their crops. Although the Soviet government made use of peasant communes to collect taxes, the Land Statute of 1919 oddly categorised communes as 'individual' holders of land. Trusting only their own institutions, Lenin and his supporters constructed a network of rural soviets, and vainly encouraged peasants to join collective and state farms. To obscure the commune's dominant presence in

18 O. Figes, 'Peasant Farmers and the Minority Groups of Rural Society: Peasant Egalitarianism and Village Social Relations during the Russian Revolution (1917–1921)', in Kingston-Mann and Mixter, *Peasant Economy, Culture*, pp. 382–5.
19 Lenin, *Polnoe sobranie sochinenii*, vol. XLIII, pp. 219–20.     20 Lewin, *Making*, p. 51.

the countryside, official documents referred to it as a rural society (*sel'skoe obshchestvo*); but peasants themselves generally used the word *mir*.

From an economic and political standpoint, the policies of War Communism were disastrous. By 1920, grain production stood at 60 per cent of its pre-war level, and Soviet leaders were powerless either to constrain or to mobilise the peasantry. For their part, the peasantry's 1917 support for the Bolsheviks, subsequent action to minimise economic inequalities and support for labour rights in the countryside did not win them acceptance as a core political constituency for the Soviet Marxist leadership. It was extremely fortunate for the latter that their enemies in the civil war were frequently even more brutal and repressive in their treatment of the peasant population.[21]

## NEP, 1921–8

Peasants are satisfied with their situation ... We consider this more important than any sort of statistical evidence. No one can doubt that the peasantry is the decisive factor with us.                                                    (Lenin, 1922)

By March 1921, the civil war and the US / Allied intervention were over, and forcible repression of the Kronstadt uprising was under way. The Red Army's brutal show of force against dissenters coincided with the abandonment of War Communism. In its place, a New Economic Policy (NEP) attempted to defuse peasant discontent and foster economic recovery by restoring a more freely functioning market and more flexible approaches to economic and non-economic issues. An infinitely cynical Stalin – expertly capturing the party's new and more tolerant stance towards the peasantry – derided the carelessness with which the term 'kulak' was frequently used. 'If a peasant puts on a new roof,' he joked, 'they call him a kulak.'[22]

Described by Lenin as a 'retreat' in the direction of capitalism, NEP revealed in full measure the improvisatory political skills that originally propelled the Bolsheviks to victory in October 1917. Replacing forced grain requisitions with fixed taxes on individual households, the state left peasants free to trade with the remainder, and granted freedom of choice in forms of landholding. The Land Code of 1922 permitted individuals to farm the land with their own labour, and hire labour on condition that employers worked alongside employees. In a 'balancing act' typical of the NEP era, the Soviet state reverted to pre-1905 peasant customary law by abrogating Stolypin's transfer of household

21 P. Kenez, *Civil War in South Russia* (Berkeley and Los Angeles: University of California Press, 1977), pp. 8–9; 316.
22 Stalin, quoted in Atkinson, *End*, p. 281.

property to the *bol'shak*, but challenged peasant tradition by declaring women to be equal members of the household, with equal rights to participate in the commune assembly alongside males.

Hopeful that state-created rural soviets could persuade 'middle' and poorer peasants to join collective and state farms, NEP reformers celebrated the economic achievements of the so-called 'Red *khutors*' of Nizhnii Novgorod. At the same time, the economic successes unexpectedly manifest in commune districts briefly inspired M. I. Kalinin to hope for 'the transformation of the *mir* from an organisation of darkness, illiteracy and traditionalism into, as it were, a productive cooperative organisation'.[23] In the words of K. Ia. Bauman, socialisation of the individual production process of the whole village (cultivation, threshing and so on) was proceeding 'like an avalanche (*sploshnoi lavinoi*)'. In a single district in Moscow province, 5,204 out of 6,458 commune villages introduced new systems of crop rotation during the year 1926 alone.[24]

In the 1920s, the agricultural picture was indeed mixed. Old-fashioned, low-technology farming continued to persist among most small producers; in 1925, one-third of the spring sowing and half of the grain harvest was still being gathered by hand.[25] Nevertheless, a no longer wholly backward Russian countryside restored grain production to its pre-1914 level by 1926. In 1927, the total land area sown in grain increased slightly, but adverse climatic conditions produced a harvest 6 per cent lower than the previous year's bumper crop.[26] Agricultural recovery was fairly steady – but given the Russian Empire's always unpredictable climatic fluctuations – as precarious as ever.

## Breaking the peasant communes (ii): forced collectivisation and the liquidation of the kulaks as a class

Who will direct the development of the economy, the kulaks or the socialist state? (M. I. Kalinin, 1929)

Although the revival of the economy's agricultural sector had been a key Soviet priority ever since the Bolshevik seizure of power, the recovery of the agricultural population was met with some ambivalence. Changes that would have

23 Kalinin, quoted in Hiroshi Okuda, 'The Final Stage of the Russian Peasant Commune: Its Improvement and the Strategy of Collectivisation', in Roger Bartlett (ed.), *Land Commune and Peasant Community in Russia* (New York: St Martins Press; Basingstoke: University of London, 1990), p. 257.
24 Okuda, 'Final Stage', pp. 259–62.    25 Atkinson, *End*, p. 259.
26 Ibid., p. 250. On subsequent revisions of the data, see S. G. Wheatcroft, 'The Reliability of Russian Prewar Grain Statistics', *Soviet Studies* 26, 2 (1974): 157–80.

been joyfully welcomed in other developing societies – increased grain deliveries to urban centres, rising consumer demand and revitalised community institutions – appeared somehow ominous in the Soviet context. The spectre of a resurgent peasantry aroused fears that a primitive, consumption-hungry rural populace might dictate its own terms in the disposal of agricultural output.[27] If peasants possessed a significant measure of autonomy, would they proceed to reject state directives that set price levels far below what the market could provide? By the late 1920s, manifestations of peasant autonomy were becoming intolerable to a party bureaucracy and Soviet that wished to use peasants as a reservoir to supply the needs of more strategically and politically desirable social groups, and to assert the claims to unlimited power and control characteristic of 'high Stalinism'.

In 1927, V. M. Molotov warned against the dangerously rapid growth of kulaks, contending that as many as 5 per cent of the peasantry fell into this category.[28] However, the term 'kulak' was never legally defined, and official data failed to demonstrate that kulak numbers were increasing – the government's own figures indicated instead that the peasant 'upper strata' remained negligible in comparison with the 15 per cent level of the pre-1917 era. During the late 1920s, kulaks were accordingly charged with quite contradictory failings. Evidence of heavy involvement in marketing grain was taken as proof that they were capitalist enemies of socialism, but evidence that they marketed less grain – were guilty of hoarding – inspired identical accusations.[29] Images of a Janus-like peasant enemy – in one guise, a cunning and crafty investor of capital (the kulak) and in another, a hopeless primitive – were deployed to justify abandonment of the New Economic Policy. Reports on commune-based innovation disappeared from press publications after 1929,[30] as Stalinists vanquished critics like Bukharin and Chaianov (as well as alleged 'communophiles' like N. N. Sukhanov and A. Suchkov).[31] A Gosplan recommendation that

27 See Esther Kingston-Mann, *In Search of the True West: Culture, Economics, and Problems of Russian Development* (Princeton: Princeton University Press, 1999), pp. 175–80; and discussion by Akhiaser, cited in Ioffe and Nefedova, *Continuity*, p. 60.
28 V. M. Molotov, *Piatnadtsatyi s"ezd vsesoiuznoi kommunisticheskoi partii (b) Stenograficheskii otchet* (Moscow, 1928), vol. II, p. 1183.
29 Atkinson, *End*, pp. 282–7. One government survey reported that 750,000 rural entrepreneurs employed a grand total of 1 million labourers in 1927; the most prosperous possessed two to three cows and up to 10 hectares of sowing area for an average family of seven. Lewin, *Making*, p. 212.
30 Okuda, 'Final Stage', p. 266.
31 See esp., N. Sukhanov, 'Obshchina v sovetskom agrarnom zakonodatel'stve', *Na agrarnom fronte* 11–12 (1926); and A. Suchkov, 'Kak ne nado rassmatrivat' vopros o formakh zemlepol'zovaniia', *Bolshevik* 2 (1928).

communes be considered one of the institutional variants that could facilitate a transition to collectivisation was ignored.[32]

Claiming that the survival of socialism was at stake, the party demanded a drastic upward revision of the state's grain procurement quotas; grain allocation requirements for the cities and the army were increased by 50 per cent in 1930. When – unsurprisingly – state demands were not met, the shortfall was attributed to a 'kulak grain strike'.[33] However, since the state's own data suggested (and Stalin himself admitted) that current shortages were due to escalating government demands for grain,[34] it seems fair to say that the crisis that triggered the 'Great Turn' was more political than economic. In a series of wildly unrealistic pronouncements, party leaders allotted one and a half years for the wholesale collectivisation of the rural population.[35]

Forced collectivisation was to replace an 'Asiatic' peasant agriculture with modern, scientific, large-scale farming.[36] Peasant land, livestock and tools became the property of collective or state farms. Tasks traditionally the responsibility of peasants – ploughing, sowing, weeding and harvesting – became state activities, planned and regulated according to a variety of 'scientific' quotas and indicators. Peasants were to work a minimum number of labour days (*trudodni*) under the supervision of managers who ensured fulfilment of state directives. To counter peasant resistance, the Soviet state deployed the tactics of all-out war, complete with the murder of suspected kulaks, mass killings and deportations to forced labour camps. The RSFSR Criminal Code was cited to justify the bombardment of peasant villages judged guilty either of 'failure to offer goods for sale on the market' or unwillingness to meet state-assigned grain quotas.

To many peasants, the government-directed onslaught of the 1930s represented the coming of the anti-Christ. Proclamations 'from the Lord God' prohibiting peasants from entering collective farms mysteriously appeared in one part of Siberia; in European Russia, a peasant proclamation declared, 'God has created people to be free on the land, but the brutality of communism has put on all labourers a yoke from which the entire *mir* is groaning'.[37] Yet within this apocalyptic discourse of opposition lay a complex challenge to a

32 Lewin, *Making*, p. 117.
33 Chris Ward, *Stalin's Russia* (London: Arnold, 1993), pp. 556–9.
34 Atkinson, *End*, p. 324 and R. W. Davies, *The Industrialization of Soviet Russia* vol. 1: *The Socialist Offensive: The Collectivisation of Soviet Agriculture 1929–1930* (Cambridge, Mass.: Harvard University Press, 1980), p. 432.
35 Lewin, *Making*, pp. 269–70.
36 A. I. Rykov, *V bor'be za sukhoi i golodom* (Moscow, 1924), p. 1.
37 However, as Viola notes, much of the discourse of peasant opposition was quite secular, and couched in political and economic terms. See Lynne Viola, *Peasant Rebels Under Stalin* (New York: Oxford University Press, 1996), pp. 55–64, 118.

Soviet state that repeatedly forced peasants to choose between compliance or obliteration. For their part, Soviet leaders remained ideologically blind to the wide array of collectivist economic and non-economic practices characteristic of pre-1917 peasant village life, and to the similarities between the labour principles enshrined in the collective farm statutes of the 1930s and the traditions of the pre-revolutionary village.

Peasant resistance thus represented more than the familiar conflict between collectivism and the individual. It reflected as well a refusal to accept (1) the loss of hard-won individual, household and commune-based autonomy, (2) the state's appropriation of the material basis of peasants' livelihood, and (3) the government's savage effort to annihilate everything that peasant families and communities had built up over many generations.[38] Official promises of a brilliant future were cold comfort to peasants whose lives were quite devoid of material security.

In regions distant from Moscow, forced collectivisation was not always imposed with equal brutality. In Tajikistan, new collective farms drew on traditional kinship networks, while in Georgia, collectivisation frequently replicated traditional settlement patterns and distributions of wealth.[39] But in areas where change was most inflexibly imposed, many peasants not only denied to the Soviet state the fruits of their labour but attempted as well to avoid the dread designation of 'kulak' by destroying massive quantities of grain and slaughtering their livestock. In Kazakhstan, where collectivisation entailed the forcible settlement of a nomadic population, the populace responded by destroying 80 per cent of their herds.[40] By the end of the 1930s, acts of 'self-de-kulakisation' erupted from Siberia to European Russia and resulted in a 45 per cent decline in the number of livestock.[41] Although Soviet officials downplayed all evidence of peasant solidarity, collective resistance seems to have been a significant feature of rural opposition.

By all accounts, women played a leading role in the resistance to forced collectivisation; in 1930 alone, 3,712 mass disturbances (total 13,754) were almost exclusively women; in the other cases, women constituted either a majority or a significant proportion of the participants. A contemporary Soviet report noted that 'in all kulak disturbances the *extraordinary activity of women is evident*'.[42] As

38 Caroline Humphrey, 'The Domestic Mode of Production in Post-Soviet Siberia', *Anthropology Today* 14, 3 (1998): 5.
39 Suny, *Revenge*, pp. 113–17.
40 M. B. Olcott, *The Kazakhs* (Stanford, Calif.: Hoover Institution Press, 1987), pp. 179–87.
41 Caroline Humphrey, *Karl Marx Collective: Economy, Society and Religion in a Siberian Collective Farm* (Cambridge: Cambridge University Press, 1977), p. 171.
42 Viola, *Peasant Rebels*, pp. 183–5.

*Pravda* explained it, women's 'petty bourgeois instincts' were regrettable manifestations of the 'individualistic female spirit'.[43] However, it is useful to recall that women were also frequently in the forefront of opposition to Stolypin's privatisation reforms. In 1930 as in 1906, they resisted appropriation of the household garden plot upon which a significant measure of their security and household status depended. Together with the men of their households, women fought to secure the survival of their families.

Peasants were unable to block the government's onslaught. However, rural resistance – above all, by women – won an extraordinary and rare concession from the Stalinist state. In 1935, a Model Collective Farm Code legitimised peasant claims to a measure of personal and household autonomy in the form of 'private' household allotments of land and farm animals. These plots of land were not freehold property in the Western sense of the term. Households did not purchase their plots, and could neither sell nor lease them. Collectives provided seeds, farm implements and hay from the common meadow and granted pre-1917 commune-style household rights to pasture animals on common land. Nevertheless, the 'private' plots introduced – on however minimal a level – a traditional peasant notion of mixed economy into the brutally dichotomised, 'all or nothing' strategies of the Soviet state. As in the days of the commune, women bore primary responsibility for labour on the 'new' private plots, cared for livestock and marketed their produce. Then and later, Soviet officials downplayed both the magnitude of the state's capitulation and the women's agency that triggered it. Stalin himself took care to trivialise the conflict as 'a little misunderstanding with collective farm women. This business was about cows.'[44]

Although the household plots were categorised by the state as 'temporary', subsidiary (*podsobnoe*) property, they acquired immense significance at a time when collective farm wages were paid only after the state appropriated its share – in 1937, 15,000 collective farms paid no salaries at all to their peasant labourers. In addition, the cruel dislocations of collectivisation – exacerbated by the dismal climatic conditions that defeated Russian and Soviet expectations in both more and less repressive times – produced millions of famine dead in Ukraine, the North Caucasus and Kazakhstan.[45] In this precarious context, private plots became a relatively secure source of material support. As peasants

---

43 Atkinson, *End*, p. 367.     44 Lewin, *Making*, pp. 178–9.
45 A particularly useful discussion of this controversial topic is M. Tauger, R. W. Davies and S. G. Wheatcroft, 'Stalin, Grain Stocks and the Famine of 1932–1933', *Slavic Review* 54, 3 (1995): 642–57.

fled their villages at a rate of 3 million per year, the state responded by imposing an internal passport system to prevent unauthorised departures. Additional millions were deported as kulaks, as were peasants arrested for the theft of collective farm property or failure to meet minimum work norms. Sent to forced labour camps in the north and east, peasant deportees built much-needed roads and canals, and were largely responsible for the construction of new cities like Magnitogorsk.

Lacking representatives of their own or legal rights to organise in defence of their interests, peasants assiduously cared for their 'private' plots. The slow agricultural recovery that began in the second half of the 1930s was dispropor-tionately fuelled by these 'subsidiary' holdings. By 1938, 45 per cent of Soviet agriculture's total farm output was being produced on 3.9 per cent of the sown (private) land (approximately 0.49 hectares per household).[46] On this predominantly women's 'turf', women turned out to be the most productive and efficient – but by far the least acclaimed – economic actors in the Soviet countryside.[47]

The 'private' plots prospered within a radically transformed agricultural sector. By 1940, collective and state farms were cogs in the machinery of a vast, Moscow-based bureaucracy (Gosplan SSSR) whose officials decided what each republic, region, province, district and even state and collective farm should produce; farm managers were then obliged to supply agricultural products for sale to the government at Gosplan-determined prices.[48] The 'false' egalitarianism of the peasant commune gave way to the inequalities of socialism, with each person rewarded for personal contributions to the collective effort. Rural Stakhanovites like Pasha Angelina – the first woman tractor driver in the Soviet Union – were rewarded for over-fulfilment of plan quotas.[49] But since quotas were typically set at levels far beyond the capacity of the farms to fulfil, the new system accelerated the growth of a vast informal network of insider negotiations, nepotism and other forms of favouritism, and massive corruption all along the bureaucratic chain of command.

The brutal decade of the 1930s was framed by an official discourse that demonised opponents and evoked public fear that devious internal and external enemies were joined in a conspiracy to weaken the Soviet Union and leave it

---

46 Lewin, *Making*, pp. 180–3.
47 S. Bridger, *Women in the Soviet Countryside: Women's Roles in Rural Development in the Soviet Union* (Cambridge: Cambridge University Press, 1987), p. 14.
48 Caroline Humphrey, 'Introduction', *Cambridge Anthropology* 18, 2 (1995): 2.
49 R. T. Manning, 'Women in the Soviet Countryside on the Eve of World War II, 1935–40', in B. Farnsworth and L. Viola (eds.), *Russian Peasant Women* (New York: Oxford University Press, 1992), pp. 218–20.

vulnerable to foreign attack. Evoking memories of the First World War and its devastating aftermath, Stalin justified the brutalities of the 1930s as a necessary modernising strategy. In his words:

> those who fall behind get beaten. One feature of the history of old Russia was the continual beatings she suffered for falling behind . . . She was beaten because to do so was profitable and could be done with impunity. Either we perish, or we overtake and outstrip the advanced capitalist countries.[50]

Stalin thus invited the public to join in targeting 'enemies of the people' who undermined the Soviet Union's heroic struggle to become so powerful that no outsider would ever again dare to invade 'with impunity'.

Stalin's gift for manipulating popular fears served him well in the years to come, when the Nazi invasion provided a nightmare confirmation of his paranoid vision of the outside world. Between 1941 and 1945, the genocidal invaders of the Soviet Union set themselves the task of exterminating twenty million, and they massively over-fulfilled their quotas.

## The Second World War and its aftermath

In 1941, European Russia was overrun by Nazi forces (aided by enthusiasts from the Baltic states appropriated by the Soviets in the Nazi–Soviet pact of 1939). In areas like Ukraine, hatreds engendered by the brutalities of collectivisation overshadowed – at least initially – the Nazi threat to exterminate all Slavic populations. However, in the course of the war, the brutal Nazi treatment of 'subhuman Slavic races' convinced many opponents of forced collectivisation that genocide was far worse. Also important in engineering a public opinion shift was a Soviet defence strategy framed in surprisingly patriotic, religious and 'peasant-friendly' terms – complete with posters that featured 'Mother Russia' as an attractive middle-aged woman in a red peasant dress, with her arm raised in summoning gesture, and the caption: 'The Motherland is Calling!'[51]

Under the pressures of war, state planning gave way to ad hoc measures intended to meet the requirements of the front. Private plots were expanded, and the war mobilisation of adult males enabled women to enter occupations from which they had previously been excluded. Many became heads of households, and some even became collective farm managers. Although few

---

50 Joseph Stalin, 'The Breakneck Speed of Industrialisation', quoted in M. McCauley (ed.), *Stalin and Stalinism* (London: Longman, 1995), pp. 92–3.
51 Sheila Fitzpatrick, *Stalin's Peasants: Resistance and Survival in the Russian Village after Collectivization* (New York and Oxford: Oxford University Press, 1994), p. 314.

women were able to emulate Pasha Angelina's exemplary achievements in the 1930s, by 1943, they comprised 50 per cent of Soviet tractor drivers.[52] In the absence of men, and despite the long-term German occupation of the best agricultural land and worsening shortages of agricultural machinery, peasant women, children and older people were able – against all odds – to supply the cities and the army with a significant measure of their food requirements.

After the war, the extraordinary public trauma of 27 million dead was targeted by Stalin, who warned an exhausted populace that the Soviet Union was once again threatened by economic collapse, internal enemies and foreign nations intent on obliterating 'the Red menace'. Accordingly, Stalin demanded the forcible relocation of 'suspect' populations, and crackdowns on suspect economic activity. Millions of Volga Germans, Crimean Tatars and Chechens were deported to Central Asia, the Urals and Siberia, where collective and state farms were required to accept them as new members. An accelerated policy of forced collectivisation was imposed in the former Baltic states and other newly acquired territories; in Estonia alone, peasant resistance in 1949 triggered the deportation of several thousand supposed kulaks to Siberia.[53]

In the late 1940s, Stalin also targeted 'suspect' economic activity on the peasantry's private plots, and increased taxes upon their agricultural output. The peasantry's time-honoured niche at the bottom of the Soviet hierarchy left them with wages and benefits far lower than those accorded urban workers. Within the rural population itself, state farmers received a fixed wage, but collective farmers still received only what remained after compulsory deliveries were provided to the state. In 1947, fears of a too-quickly resurgent peasantry triggered a carefully designed currency reform that completely wiped out peasant savings. By the late 1940s, Soviet women – like America's 'Rosie the Riveter' – were displaced from their wartime positions of leadership and higher status. Although males were still in short supply, the number of women managers and policy makers declined after 1945, as did the number employed as tractor drivers. By 1959, only 0.7 per cent of the latter group were women.[54]

## Post-Stalin: the question of reform

From the peasantry's perspective, the most notable feature of the post-Stalin era was the abandonment of mass murder and deportations as core

---

52 Bridger, *Women*, pp. 15–17.
53 R. Abraham, 'The Regeneration of Family Farming in Estonia', *Sociologia Ruralis* 34, 4 (1993): 355.
54 Bridger, *Women*, p. 19.

instruments of state policy. The familiar alternation of abundant harvests and crop failure did not result in massive purge trials, executions or accusations of treason. In the 1950s and 1960s, official exhortations and economic 'campaigns', and a variety of non-lethal pressures and constraints fostered agricultural initiatives that relied on ever-larger economic enterprises managed by ever-larger contingents of supervisors and inspectors. In the reforms of this era, the southern-born Nikita Khrushchev played a central role. Notorious for the failure of his grandiose agricultural projects, Khrushchev was also notably responsible for initiating a fundamental reversal in the relationship between the rural sector and the rest of the economy. Under Khrushchev, the traditional Soviet view of the countryside as 'an internal colony' that supplied funds for industrial development began at last to give way. By the 1960s, the rural sector became – for the first time in Soviet history – the recipient of significant government investment.

It turned out to be far easier for the Soviet 'command system' to foster dramatic, nationwide increases in income, educational levels and life expectancy than to guarantee consistent improvement in rates of agricultural productivity. Between 1953 and 1967, the average income of the collective farm worker increased by 311 per cent in real terms.[55] In 1956, pension benefits for the aged, disabled and sick were significantly expanded, and in the 1960s, the wages for collective farm workers were fixed (and made no longer dependent on the requirements of the latest Five-Year Plan). Peasants began to enjoy higher incomes from labour on collective and state farms than from their private plots. During the Khrushchev years, agricultural workers were at last restored their freedom to move from one job to another. Compulsory grain deliveries to the state were abolished, and some collective farms were permitted to set up small teams of family members and neighbours to cultivate a given number of fields. Allowed to sign contracts with state enterprises and determine their own production objectives,[56] team members also received individual wages and bonuses based upon the success of the team. Although such reforms produced only mixed results, they represented an outbreak of economic flexibility within the Soviet Union's command economy.

By the 1960s, collective and state farms had become a source of important social benefits, particularly in the area of education. While in 1938, only 9.4 per cent of the rural population possessed eight years of schooling, by the 1960s

55 Gertrude Schroeder, 'Rural Living Standards in the Soviet Union', in Robert Stuart (ed.), *The Soviet Rural Economy* (Totowa, N.J.: Rowman and Allanheld, 1983), p. 243.
56 Moshe Lewin, *Stalinism and the Seeds of Soviet Reform: The Debates of the 1960s* (Armonk, N.Y.: M. E. Sharpe, 1991).

the figure stood at over 55 per cent, with women frequently better educated than men. Although literacy levels for Soviet rural women far outpaced those of women in predominantly peasant societies like Turkey or India, women who became teachers, nurses, veterinarians and agronomists did not thereby gain entry into positions of leadership. They continued as well to bear primary responsibility not only for childcare and other traditional 'women's work', but also for labour on the private plots – where even by the 1960s most farming was still done by hand.[57] These tasks, in addition to the collective farm's labour requirement continued to constitute the Soviet peasant woman's 'triple burden'.

In important respects, the Khrushchev era introduced the dichotomies and contradictions that eventually contributed to the downfall of the Soviet system. Between 1953 and 1958, agricultural productivity increased by 50 per cent, with private plots continuing to significantly out-perform the collective and state farms. Exhorting the rural populace to 'double and triple' their agricultural output, Khrushchev launched a massive 'Virgin Lands' campaign in Kazakhstan and Siberia. This venture was fatally undermined not only by the usual climatic reversals, but also by the Soviet state's penchant for bureaucratic national directives that ignored local conditions and local knowledge. In Kazakhstan, for example, collective and state farmers were ordered to expand the land area sown with corn regardless of whether the necessary equipment or seeds were available; tractor drivers were everywhere paid according to the size of the area they ploughed (thus encouraging them to plough as shallowly as possible).[58] In 1963, a disastrous harvest – together with the setbacks of the Cuban Missile Crisis – contributed to Khrushchev's fall from power.

## The Brezhnev era: stagnation, or deepening contradiction?

Although the Brezhnev years are frequently described as an era of stagnation, from the perspective of the rural populace, they were not. Less constrained than in the 1950s, the rural populace began to create a world that differed from the Stalinist model, recalled the values of an older peasant community and incorporated changes that not only widened village perspectives, but inspired many peasants to abandon the countryside for the city.

---

57 Bridger, *Women*, pp. 108–9.
58 Alec Nove, *Soviet Agriculture: The Brezhnev Legacy and Gorbachev's Cure* (Los Angeles: Rand/UCLA Center for the Study of Soviet International Behavior, 1988), p. 15.

By the 1970s, the more horrific memories of the Second World War and the 1930s had started to recede, and a semblance of 'normality' began to re-emerge in the Soviet countryside. Despite the burden of Moscow-devised plans and quotas, observers reported that the pace of rural life in the 1970s reflected the rhythms of the crop-growing cycle – slow in winter and active during the hay-making and harvest times.[59] Like their counterparts elsewhere in the world, Soviet farmers performed a great variety of tasks at different seasons of the year, worked irregular hours and faced unpredictable weather fluctuations. Deliberations by farm assemblies (*skhody*) were frequently skewed by gender and age considerations or by patronage connections that individuals and households established with the authorities – but the latter no longer freely exercised the life and death powers of their predecessors.

Particularly in regions distant from Moscow, both the formal structures of the collective farm and the requirements imposed by central planners were significantly modified by informal relations and negotiations within the collective farm itself. New legislation gave collective farms the right to assign 'private' plots to member households, and village assemblies continued to honour the pre-1917 commune principles that legitimised land claims on the basis of labour and need. As in earlier years, private plots out-performed the collective and state farms, but they were less crucial to peasant survival once farm wage levels began to rise.[60]

By the 1970s and 1980s, most of the rural populace were state employees, but they bore little resemblance to their Western counterparts. Collective and state farm workers expected – and received from their enterprises – guarantees of education, health, shelter, old-age assistance, month-long vacations, 112 days of paid maternity leave and old-age pensions. Income differentials between city and countryside began to narrow, as did the considerable wage disparities between collective and state farms.[61] In the Soviet Union, agricultural 'jobs' conferred far more than a wage; they mediated as well a set of social, economic and cultural relations and obligations between individuals and a wider community.[62]

---

59 Basile Kerblay, *Modern Soviet Society*, trans. Rupert Sawyer (London: Methuen, 1983), pp. 74–5.
60 Ibid., p. 87.
61 V. George and N. Manning, *Socialism, Social Welfare and the Soviet Union* (London: Routledge and Kegan Paul, 1980), pp. 31–128.
62 Susan Bridger and Frances Pine, 'Introduction', *Surviving Post-Socialism: Local Strategies and Regional Responses in Eastern Europe and the Former Soviet Union* (London: Routledge, 1998), pp. 7–8.

The Brezhnev era featured not only an increased reliance on material incentives in the form of bonuses, increased procurement prices, education / welfare benefits and improvements in diet, but also a persistent refusal either to appreciably diminish levels of political constraint, corruption or favouritism, or to increase opportunities for individual freedom of action. Brezhnev's massive grain purchases from abroad provided the Soviet public with a diet based on meat consumption (then considered a global indicator of rising affluence). Between 1960 and 1973, foreign grain purchases increased from 42.6 million to 99.2 million tons, and domestic food consumption rose by 400 per cent.[63] The so-called 'grain deficits' of this era were in fact an indicator neither of food shortages nor of disastrous decline in agricultural production; they were instead attributable to what one post-Soviet study describes as 'excessive' consumption of animal feed and non-food derivatives.[64] According to reform economist Tat'iana Zaslavskaia, Brezhnev's policies were a cynical effort at 'pacification through material incentives'.[65]

During the 1970s, educational advances, greater freedom of movement and a diminishing reliance on the private plot and household as guarantees of security began to transform farming into an occupation rather than an inherited status. However, the exercise of free choice increasingly included decisions to abandon the collective farm. Rural women, eager to escape their 'triple burden', moved into non-agricultural occupations as nurses, clerks and teachers – and above all, as independent wage earners. Like their male counterparts – particularly of the younger generation – they left the security of village life for the equal security but higher pay and greater autonomy available in new 'agrotowns' and in the cities. While many sought greater autonomy and higher social status, the surveys conducted by Zaslavskaia in the 1970s suggested that physically arduous working conditions, inequitable wage rates and corrupt officials who rewarded lackeys rather than hard-working people far outweighed the desire for upward mobility as motives for departure from the countryside.[66] The highest levels of out-migration came from European agricultural regions of the country; the lowest were in Central Asia, Kazakhstan

63 Harry Shaffer, 'Soviet Agriculture: Success or Failure?' in Shaffer (ed.), *Soviet Agriculture: An Assessment of its Contributions to Economic Development* (New York: Praeger, 1977), pp. 79–81.
64 See Ioffe and Nefedova, *Continuity*, p. 76.
65 Zaslavskaia, quoted in Andrew Rosenthal, 'A Soviet Voice of Innovation Comes to Fore', *New York Times*, 28 Aug. 1987.
66 Kerblay, *Soviet Society*, p. 232.

and the Caucasus. In 1959, 51 per cent of the population of the Soviet Union lived on the land; by 1979, the figure stood at 37 per cent.[67]

In the 1970s, living standards, incomes and literacy rates rose dramatically, even as a repressive state bureaucracy fostered the creation of ever-larger collective and state farm enterprises. The Soviet state raised procurement prices for grain and livestock by 50 per cent in 1965, and awarded bonuses for deliveries that exceeded plan requirements. Productivity rates rose between 1966 and 1970 (followed by significant declines due to crop failures in 1972, 1979 and 1980). Yet overall, according to United Nations estimates, Soviet agriculture achieved a faster rate of growth in volume and per capita than any other major region of the world (including North America, Europe, Africa and Asia). Between 1950 and 1975, Soviet agricultural output more than doubled.[68]

During the Brezhnev years, the tension between socio-economic improvements and a command system of economic and political governance continued to mount. A highly literate populace no longer feared starvation, and the lives of its younger generation were not shaped by the war, invasion and attempted genocide that had so traumatised their parents and grandparents. These generational shifts undermined a Stalinist social contract that had repeatedly promised modernisation and national security in exchange for repression and bureaucratic control. Throughout the Stalin era, a constant state of emergency was invoked to justify brutal constraints on rural and urban freedom of action; a 'crisis mentality' was subsequently reinforced by the Cold War between the United States and the USSR.[69] However, by the 1980s, a far healthier and better-educated populace had come to believe – with good reason – that no nation was likely to invade the USSR with what Stalin had called 'impunity'.

It was in this context that Mikhail Gorbachev emerged as the embodiment of the Soviet social contract and its contradictory tensions. Born on a collective farm and raised by grandparents after losing his father in the Second World War, Gorbachev began work at fourteen as an assistant to a combine harvester operator, and received a Red Banner of labour in 1948 for helping to produce a record harvest on his collective farm. Making the leap from a North Caucasus

---

67 While these figures mark a dramatic rise in rural out-migration, it is useful to recall that between 1950 and 1980, the rates of rural exodus from the American countryside were far higher than in the Soviet Union. See G. Clark, 'Soviet Agriculture', in Shaffer, *Soviet Agriculture*, p. 38.

68 H. Shaffer, 'Soviet Agriculture: Success or Failure?' p. 93.

69 B. P. Kurashvili, 'Ob"ektivnye zakony gosudarstvennogo upravleniia', *Sovetskoe gosudarstvo i pravo* 43 (1983).

secondary school to the acquisition of a law degree at Moscow University and eventually to a position at the top of the party hierarchy, he took advantage of the best opportunities offered by the Soviet system. A beneficiary of Soviet guarantees of education and social welfare, Gorbachev made a name for himself as a proponent of incentive-based projects for raising agricultural productivity rates. As the Politburo member responsible for agriculture under Brezhnev during the 1980s, he spoke out in the name of others like himself for economic restructuring (*perestroika*) that would significantly diminish the powerful Soviet constraints upon individual freedom of action.

## *Perestroika* and the further transformation of Russian rural life

As General Secretary of the party, Gorbachev emphasised the production needs of agriculture and the interests of the rural populace. Building on the rural experiments of the 1960s and 1970s, his reforms encouraged single families or co-operative groups to take land and implements out of the large-scale collective farm for a given period, and use their own labour and management skills to maximise production and increase their incomes. In 1990, new legislation legitimised a variety of forms of tenure, ranging from outright ownership, possession for life, leasehold and indefinite, permanent or temporary use. Committed to socialism and to economic growth, Gorbachev's reforms produced a 21 per cent increase in health, education and other welfare benefits, a 48 per cent rise in per capita income and an 8 per cent increase in productivity rates.[70] Explicitly rejecting Soviet and pre-Soviet notions of the rural populace as 'raw material' for industrial development, Gorbachev appealed for public input into economic and non-economic decision-making at every level, but especially within the agricultural and industrial workplace.

Gorbachev's appeal unleashed a storm of criticism that touched every aspect of Soviet life. Farm managers, agricultural specialists, teachers, writers, ordinary farmers and social scientists denounced the incidence of alcoholism, domestic abuse and disparities in health, housing, education and income between the rural populace and their urban counterparts. Playwrights portrayed heroic collective farmers who demanded the right to 'speak the Truth' to collective farm managers,[71] while a resolution of the Twenty-First Congress

70 W. Liefert, 'The Food Problem in the Republics of the Former USSR', in D. Van Atta, *The Farmer Threat: The Political Economy of Agrarian Reform in Post-Soviet Russia* (Boulder, Colo.: Westview Press, 1993), p. 29.
71 *Sovetskaia kul'tura*, 23 Jan. 1986, p. 5.

of the Uzbek Communist Party denounced corrupt officials who overstated the amount of raw cotton produced by hundreds of thousands of tons.[72] Farm managers, workers and intellectuals targeted the 'gigantomania' that repeatedly led policy makers to assume that an unlimited increase in inputs – in the form of supervisors, mechanisation, chemical fertiliser and the creation of ever-larger economic enterprises – automatically produced increased agricultural outputs.

Above all, rural critics rejected the notion – so deeply ingrained in the minds of Soviet (and pre-Soviet) policy makers – that agriculture and the rural inhabitants who made it work constituted 'the bottleneck of the country's development and the main reason for its backwardness'.[73] Calls for the revitalisation of farming communities coexisted with demands for market socialism, greater opportunities to pursue long-term, enlightened self-interest, to acquire land of one's own, to be rewarded according to merit and to win respect and acknowledgement for local knowledge, experience and expertise.

In the 1990s, the fall of Gorbachev, the break-up of the Soviet Union and the accession to power of Boris Yeltsin marked an accelerated turn away from the precarious, socialist/capitalist 'balancing acts' of the previous decade. In its place, 'shock therapists' launched a revolutionary effort at social engineering that was to transform peasants into productive rural entrepreneurs. The first step in this process was to disentangle and sever property rights and economic activity from the reciprocal social obligations within which – from the peasantry's perspective – they had always been historically embedded. Convinced that the 'natural' desire to receive a piece of national wealth for free would serve as a powerful engine for agricultural land reform, Russia's neo-liberal reformers proposed a series of '500' and '1,000-day' schemes for the wholesale privatisation of the national economy. By 1994, the Union of Private Peasant Farmers (AKKOR) reported that there were 280,000 private farms in the Russian Federation alone.[74] However, among the former collective and state farmers (and urban dwellers with no previous farming experience) who became rural entrepreneurs, there was strikingly meagre enthusiasm for Western-style 'rugged individualism'.

In Nizhnii Novgorod, provincial governor Boris Nemtsov (later the first deputy prime minister of the Russian Republic) was hailed for his efforts to

72 *Pravda vostoka*, 31 Jan. 1986, pp. 2–6.
73 T. Shanin, 'Soviet Agriculture and Perestroika: The Most Urgent Task and the Furthest Shore', unpublished paper (1988).
74 L. Perotta, 'Divergent Responses to Land Reform and Agricultural Restructuring in the Russian Federation', in Bridger and Pine, *Surviving*, p. 150.

construct a fair, open and transparent exchange of land for shares,[75] but some observers raised doubts about the efficiency and productivity levels of these private farming ventures.[76] Even more troubling were reports that the successes in Nizhnii were due to extra-legal pressures from local authorities that recalled – in the words of economist Carol Leonard, 'something that is reminiscent of the tragic collectivisation campaigns of the 1930s'.[77] But in any event, few collective farms emulated the Nizhnii model during the 1990s. Frequently, collectives 'privatised' by becoming joint-stock companies led by former collective farm managers who attempted to obtain for their members the welfare benefits previously provided in the Soviet workplace. On occasion, collective farm members voted to become individual peasant farmers in order to guarantee themselves secure individual ownership of lands that they continued to work and manage collectively. Although, legally, they had split up, their intention was to 'stay together'.[78] In the 1990s, insider trading and asset stripping by farm managers, their cronies and friends undermined both the aims and the legitimacy of efforts to establish a rural regime based on independent and private economic activity. The most successful entrepreneurs often turned out to be former farm managers whose networks and 'social capital' gave them decided advantages in the new market economy.[79]

In 1992, the price liberalisation policies introduced by Russia's shock therapists produced a devastating 2,600 per cent rise in consumer goods prices. By December 1996, per capita monthly income in the Russian Republic stood at 47 per cent of its 1992 level.[80] In the cities and in the countryside, a black market and systems of barter began to flourish – and even to eclipse more normal mechanisms of exchange. In this precarious context, many farm workers and pensioners decided to remain on their collective farms and to rely – as in the

---

75 Introduced in the 1990s, this programme divided collective and state farm land into private shares that could be redeemed in exchange for plots of land and other agricultural assets that permitted individuals to farm independently. Shares were to be apportioned by collective and state enterprises; individual claims were to be assessed in traditional, pre-1917 village fashion – in accordance with current and past investments of labour (i.e. with shares granted to both actively employed and retired workers). S. K. Wegren, 'Political Institutions and Agrarian Reform in Russia', in Van Atta, *Farmer Threat*, p. 124.
76 Perotta, 'Divergent', p. 154.
77 C. S. Leonard, 'Rational Resistance to Land Privatisation: The Response of Rural Producers to Agrarian Reforms in Pre- and Post-Soviet Russia', *Post-Soviet Geography and Economics* 41, 8 (2000): 608.
78 Perotta, 'Divergent', p. 165.
79 M. Lampland, 'The Advantages of Being Collectivised: Collective Farm Managers in the Postsocialist Economy', in C. M. Hann (ed.), *Postsocialism: Ideals, Ideologies and Practices in Eurasia* (London: Routledge, 2002), pp. 31–56.
80 P. Caskie, 'Back to Basics: Household Food Production in Russia', *Journal of Agricultural Economics* 51, 2 (2000): 206.

1930s – on their private plots and communal traditions. By the mid-1990s, over 60 per cent of Russian households were producing a significant proportion of their own food needs on private rural and urban garden plots. Some 14 million were sited in the countryside, and depended on former collectives for the material prerequisites for farming – that is, seeds, machinery and fuel.[81]

Under these circumstances, the rage and despair of a rural populace in decline soon overshadowed the 1980s critiques of the Soviet era. As in other societies that experienced 'structural adjustment', rural women (and children) were the most hard hit; women were particularly threatened by 'land for shares' programmes that failed to acknowledge their special claims and – given their childcare responsibilities – their disproportionate need for the social welfare supports of the Soviet era. It is also worth noting that although women had for years borne major responsibility for the productive private plots of the Soviet era, they were not targeted as potential entrepreneurs either by local officials, by aid agencies or by the rural population itself.[82] In the words of a seventy-two-year-old woman farm worker from Voronezh province in 1995:

> 'what do I think about restructuring? We've been restructured about once every five years for as long as I can remember. And every time things get worse instead of better. I don't see why it should be any different this time. Restructuring usually means that things get worse.'[83]

In important respects, farm women may have represented in its most extreme form the challenge that the rural populace posed to would-be reformers and tormentors throughout the twentieth century. Opposed to the single-minded privatisation measures of the Stolypin era and to the incomparably more brutal and single-minded collectivism of the 1930s, they were averse in the 1990s to the 'either/or' choices presented to them by the Russian government. Although they were no longer the illiterates of the pre-Soviet era, many farm women (and men) nevertheless continued to believe that labour legitimised claims to property. Like their forebears, they were suspicious of individuals who bought land but did not use it, or misused it, or purchased land only to sell it at a higher profit, denouncing them as 'speculators' (*spekulanty*) rather than 'true owners'.[84]

For their part, the Union of Private Landed Proprietors, understandably enraged by the destruction of harvests and burning of tractors carried out by collective farmers during the early 1990s, denounced the archaic 'traditions of

81 Ibid., p. 207.     82 Perotta, 'Divergent', p. 164.     83 Ibid., pp. 148–9.
84 Myriam Hivon, 'The Bullied Farmer: Social Pressure as a Survival Strategy', in Bridger and Pine, *Surviving*, pp. 42–3.

egalitarianism' and the survival of the Soviet era's 'culture of envy'.[85] Frustrated enthusiasts like Boris Nemtsov complained that 'the primary hindrance to privatisation of land in Nizhnii Novgorod province is the lack of people who want to become owners'.[86] In the newly independent Baltic state of Estonia, reformers denounced the machinations of Soviet-era 'Red barons' who reclaimed former privileges at the expense of former employees.[87] In general, advocates of privatisation attributed the problems of agriculture to the irreconcilable contradiction between collectivism and private economic initiative.

For their part, collective and state farm workers argued that when private enterprise became the only legitimate and legally protected form of farm ownership, the state subsidised private farmers, granted them preferential credit arrangements and praised them for their achievements. In contrast, the state deprived collective farmers of their former advantages and then vilified them for laziness and incompetence.[88] Former collective and state farm managers were particularly prone to argue that small-scale family farms were incapable of meeting the food needs of the Russian Republic. In general, critics of privatisation attributed the inefficiency of collective enterprises to external causes and in particular to government policies that privileged some groups at the expense of others.[89]

There is plenty of evidence to support arguments on both sides of this issue. Among both defenders and enemies of privatisation, peasants differed with each other and with the government over the acceptable costs of change, the services and benefits to which citizens should legitimately be able to lay claim, and the role of the state as either a promoter of social cohesion or a catalyst for an individualistic, almost Darwinian struggle for survival.

## Post-Soviet rural life: prospects and dilemmas

In the Russian Republic, agricultural production was 36 per cent lower in 1997 than in 1990. Reasserting the economic priorities of the Stalin and pre-1917 years, Yeltsin-era investment in agriculture declined from 16 per cent of the total in 1992 to 2.5 per cent in 1997. By 2000, over 90 per cent of Russian grain still came from former collective and state farms; private farms had made

---

85 Ibid., pp. 34–43.   86 Quoted in Ioffe and Nefedova, *Continuity*, p. 158.
87 Abraham, 'Regeneration', pp. 356–7.
88 Myriam Hivon, 'Local Resistance to Privatization in Rural Russia', *Cambridge Anthropology* 18, 2 (1995): 18.
89 Perotta, 'Divergent', p. 161.

only a very modest impact and did not perform appreciably better than the former public sector.[90] Despite the brevity of the privatisation experiment and the rapid rates at which rural land has been bought and sold since 1991, there are few signs that privatisation has – as yet – positively affected agricultural productivity rates.[91]

Both the enduring and changing dilemmas of the post-Soviet era are evident in the case of Estonia – an outstanding success story of the 1990s. Newly privatised Estonian family farms have produced high agricultural yields (together with the stark economic divisions between the prosperous and the poor that recall the inter-war years of Estonian independence). Particularly troubling, however, are the late 1990s reports that both supporters and opponents of private farms believed that up to a third of the private farms in Estonia would fail due to shortages of machinery and materials, the absence of social services like health care and a scarcity of capital.[92] In the Russian Republic, among the approximately 30 million who still lived on the land and owned shares in former collective and state farms, the limited access to credit, poor infrastructure and high cost of social protections were bankrupting even the more efficient former Soviet farm enterprises. It was estimated in 1998 that only 20 per cent of the former collective farms/joint-stock companies in the Russian Republic were capable of surviving within a competitive and capital-scarce environment.[93]

In 2003, many public opinion polls indicated that most former collective farmers – who still controlled three-quarters of Russia's arable land – were opposed to the private ownership of land. At the same time, new land laws have further undermined traditional links between labour claims and land use by permitting foreign investors to purchase landed property for capitalist agribusinesses. Such moves aroused opposition not only from labourers who still owned shares in former collective farms, but also from new private farmers who had leased collective farm fields and worked hard to improve them. Reflecting on the events of the past decade, the Agrarian Party's Iurii Savinok declared: 'Look what happened in the 90s – all Russia's industries and resources were grabbed by a few rich oligarchs . . . Does anyone doubt that the same will happen when land goes on the block? . . . Ordinary Russians will be dispossessed again.'[94]

From the perspective of the rural populace at the dawn of the twenty-first century, survival and success seem more dependent on the ability of

90 Caskie, 'Back', pp. 200–1.    91 Ioffe and Nefedova, *Continuity*, p. 296.
92 Abraham, 'Regeneration', p. 367.    93 Caskie, 'Back', p. 206.
94 Quoted in F. Weir, 'This Land is My Land', *In These Times*, 11 Nov. 2002.

individuals and households to mobilise a broad range of political and economic resources than on a talent for generating and reinvesting private profits. In the words of new private farmer A. I. Poprov in 2003, 'Ownership is an empty symbol. What's important is who possesses the land and how he uses it.'[95]

It has been suggested that a sustainable and productive Russian agriculture might well be compatible with an economic system that permits diverse farm sizes and ownership structures that range from large-scale to independent peasant farms to semi-subsistence household plots.[96] Such a proposal would be quite consistent with the history of mixed economies that peasants created whenever there were choices available to them. But the adoption of such a strategy would require reformers to abandon their dichotomised 'either/or' approach to development for one that is far more sensitive to the social impact of economic change upon the rural populace. As we have seen, economic pluralism has rarely appealed either to Russian or Soviet governments. As a policy, it remains – at least so far – starkly at odds with those currently being deployed or contemplated in the Russian Republic.

95 Weir, 'This Land', *In These Times*.    96 Caskie, 'Back', p. 208.

# 16

# Workers and industrialisation

LEWIS H. SIEGELBAUM

'What is the contemporary factory worker in Russia', asked Mikhail Tugan-Baranovskii towards the end of the nineteenth-century, 'a peasant living on the land who makes up the deficiencies of his agricultural income by occasional factory work, or a proletarian bound closely to the factory who lives by selling his labour power?'[1] Tugan-Baranovskii, among Russia's foremost political economists, seemed unsure how to answer the question. Citing earlier studies showing a decline in seasonal employment among workers in Moscow province, he nevertheless had to acknowledge that 'the tie of the factory worker to the soil, although waning, is still very strong', that it was 'economically necessary and therefore is tenaciously maintained'. Yet, echoing an article of faith among Russian Marxists, he confidently predicted that 'a complete severance of this tie . . . is inevitable, and the sooner it takes place the better'.[2]

What was thus on one level an empirical question that lent itself to statistical enquiry into patterns of labour mobility, employment and workers' ties to the land, on another implied more complex issues. Central to the Marxist paradigm of historical evolution, the formation of an industrial proletariat in Russia was a question that came to the fore during the 1890s because of the unprecedentedly rapid growth of factory industry, associated social dislocations and the political implications of these developments. Retrospectively, it served as the opening chapter in the revolutionary narrative that the Bolsheviks would tell about themselves and the society they were determined to transform.[3]

Fast-forwarding nearly a hundred years, we find the authors of a book about post-Soviet Russia's transition to capitalism asking: 'What about the

---

1 M. I. Tugan-Baranovskii, *Russkaia fabrika v proshlom i nastoiashchem*, 2nd edn (St Petersburg: O. N. Popova, 1900), p. 441.
2 Ibid., pp. 449, 451.
3 Arthur Mendel, *Dilemmas of Progress in Tsarist Russia: Legal Marxism and Legal Populism* (Cambridge, Mass.: Harvard University Press, 1961); Igal Halfin, *From Darkness to Light: Class, Consciousness, and Salvation in Revolutionary Russia* (Pittsburgh: University of Pittsburgh Press, 2000).

workers?'[4] This question does not so much recapitulate Tugan-Baranovskii's as imply the reversal of the situation that precipitated it. By the mid-1990s, de-industrialisation was well under way, and industrial workers, who comprised some 50 million people, were in imminent danger of becoming redundant. The once heroic *rabochie*, the universal class of Marxist dreams, had become *rabotiagi*, working stiffs, embodiments of the failure of the Soviet experiment.

For much of the twentieth century, labour historians conventionally employed the concept of the working class as an objective description of a distinct social group with measurable characteristics and factory workers as the core element within that class. Thanks to feminist scholarship, the linguistic turn in the social sciences and humanities and the arrival of the post-industrial era, this convention gave way to an understanding that such terms as 'class', 'industrial' and even 'factory' are linguistically constructed and culturally specific, that statistics bearing on these categories are neither self-evidently reflective of the real world nor value-neutral but rather derive from the nexus of knowledge and power, and that the same can be said of determinations of core and marginal elements.

These reconceptualisations provide a fresh opportunity to revisit some of the terrain already 'covered'. Thinking through whether class is to be under-stood as a sociological aggregate, a linguistic construction, an 'imagined com-munity', or the sum total of certain cultural practices is not to bid farewell to the working class, but to enrich our sense of what a good deal of the struggles of (at least) the twentieth century were about.[5]

This is particularly so in the case of Russia where throughout much of the century 'the working class' had extraordinary political salience and workers experienced radical, often wrenching, changes in the nature and validation of the work they performed. In this chapter workers' experiences are related to the social and cultural spaces they occupied. Four chronologically overlapping themes span the twentieth century. The first two comprise key elements of the Bolshevik narrative of the path to communism; the others represent com-ponents of a counter-narrative that emerged out of the party's abandonment of the model of the heroic working class and, ultimately, the dissolution of the Soviet Union. Two dimensions – the discursive and the experiential – were

---

4 Simon Clarke et al., *What About the Workers?: Workers and the Transition to Capitalism in Russia* (London: Verso, 1993).
5 William H. Sewell, Jr., 'Towards a Post-materialist Rhetoric for Labor History', in Lenard Berlanstein (ed.), *Rethinking Labor History: Essays on Discourse and Class Analysis* (Urbana and Chicago: University of Illinois Press, 1993), pp. 15–38. See also Geoff Eley and Keith Nield, 'Farewell to the Working Class?', *International Labor and Working-Class History* (Hereafter *ILWCH*) 57 (2000): 1–30.

always in dynamic tension and often became blurred as workers both collectively and individually appropriated others' ideas about who they were, what they needed and how they should act to fulfil their needs. The 'contemporary factory worker' of Tugan-Baranovskii's enquiry was thus both an object of others' imaginings and a subject with agency.

## Peasants into workers

The factory worker, observed the governor of Khar'kov province in his official report for 1899 (a year after the publication of Tugan-Baranovskii's book) 'is losing many of the worthy and distinctive traits that are characteristic of the villager, especially the latter's positive, undemanding, traditional worldview, so rooted in religious teachings and in the biddings of his ancestors'. This loss of 'spiritual equilibrium', he added, was providing 'a very convenient opening for those who wish to awaken his dissatisfaction with his own situation and with the social system, which is precisely what the enemies of the existing order have recently been attempting, unfortunately with some success'.[6]

The image of the undemanding, tradition-bound peasant, a mainstay among tsarist officials and conservatives more generally, had its analogue among the liberal and socialist intelligentsia of the nineteenth century. It was of the 'grey muzhik' – 'dark', superstitious, in need of being rescued from benightedness, but almost inaccessible.[7] These images persisted even while peasants in the post-emancipation decades regularly tramped off to labour markets to be hired for off-farm work, engaged in extensive commerce with townsfolk, came under and made use of the new court system, attended schools, entered the army, consumed cheaply produced popular literature and otherwise expanded their contacts with the wider world.[8] By the turn of the century there already existed a substantial ethnographic literature, much of which noted the increasing

---

6 Quoted in Iurii I. Kir'ianov, 'The Mentality of the Workers of Russia at the Turn of the Twentieth Century', in Reginald E. Zelnik (ed.), *Workers and Intelligentsia in Late Imperial Russia: Realities, Representations, Reflections* (Berkeley: University of California Press, 1999), p. 96.
7 Cathy A. Frierson, *Peasant Icons: Representations of Rural People in Late Nineteenth-Century Russia* (New York and Oxford: Oxford University Press, 1993).
8 Jeffrey Burds, 'The Social Control of Peasant Labor in Russia: The Response of Village Communities to Labor Migration in the Central Industrial Region, 1861–1905', in Esther Kingston-Mann and Timothy Mixter (eds.), *Peasant Economy, Culture, and Politics of European Russia, 1800–1921* (Princeton: Princeton University Press, 1991), pp. 52–100; Jeffrey Brooks, *When Russia Learned to Read: Literacy and Popular Literature, 1861–1917* (Princeton: Princeton University Press, 1985).

penetration of urban-originated ideas, practices and goods into the village and the dying out of old, village-based customs.[9]

Peasant labour migration assumed huge proportions in the late nineteenth century. During the 1890s, an average of 6.2 million passports were issued every year by peasant communes to departing peasants (*otkhodniki*) in the forty-three provinces of European Russia. The heaviest out-migration was in the eight Central Industrial provinces of Iaroslavl', Moscow, Vladimir, Kostroma, Kaluga, Nizhnii Novgorod, Tula and Riazan', followed by the north and north-west, the Southern Agricultural Region and the Central Black Soil Region.[10] Agricultural workers made up the largest contingent of *otkhodniki*, but substantial numbers sought and found work in the cities and industrial sites of the country. Some 100,000 to 150,000 immigrants arrived in Moscow every year between 1880 and 1900; in St Petersburg the city's working population increased by two-thirds in the 1890s, mostly on account of peasant in-migration.[11] Peasants also travelled to and found work in the burgeoning metallurgical and coal-mining industries of the south.[12]

The contemporary (and later Soviet) fixation on the factory and the rapid growth of its labour force obscured the fact that substantially larger numbers of peasant migrants found employment in smaller-scale artisanal workshops, commercial establishments, domestic service, prostitution, transportation, public utilities and unskilled construction jobs.[13] Workers all, they were more evenly divided between men and women than was the case among factory workers who were overwhelmingly male.[14] But they did take up

---

9 See e.g. Ministerstvo zemledeliia i gosudarstvennogo imushchestva. Otdel sel'skoi ekonomiki i sel'sko-khoziaistvennoi statistiki, *Otchety i issledovaniia po kustarnoi promyshlennosti v Rossii*, 11 vols. (St Petersburg: Kirshbaum, 1892–1915).

10 Burds, 'Social Control of Labor', pp. 56–7.

11 Joseph Bradley, *Muzhik and Muscovite: Urbanization in Late Imperial Russia* (Berkeley and Los Angeles: University of California Press, 1985), p. 104; Gerald D. Surh, *1905 in St. Petersburg: Labor, Society, and Revolution* (Stanford, Calif.: Stanford University Press, 1989), p. 18.

12 Charters Wynn, *Workers, Strikes, and Pogroms: The Donbass-Dnepr Bend in Late Imperial Russia, 1870–1905* (Princeton: Princeton University Press, 1992), pp. 45–7.

13 Victoria E. Bonnell, *Roots of Rebellion: Workers' Politics and Organizations in St. Petersburg and Moscow, 1900–1914* (Berkeley and Los Angeles: University of California Press, 1983); Bonnell (ed.), *The Russian Worker: Life and Labor under the Tsarist Regime* (Berkeley and Los Angeles: University of California Press, 1983), pp. 186–208; Barbara Alpern Engel, *Between Fields and the City: Women, Work and Family in Russia, 1861–1914* (Cambridge: Cambridge University Press, 1995), pp. 126–238.

14 Olga Crisp, 'Labour and Industrialization in Russia', in Peter Mathias and M. M. Postan (eds.), *The Cambridge Economic History of Europe*, 8 vols. (Cambridge: Cambridge University Press, 1978), vol. VII, pt. 2, p. 368; Rose L. Glickman, *Russian Factory Women: Workplace and Society, 1880–1914* (Berkeley and Los Angeles: University of California Press, 1984), pp. 80, 83.

residence in the same districts of cities, partook of many of the same pastimes and, generally speaking, inhabited the same cultural world as recently arrived factory workers.

The image of the authentic proletarian – a factory worker employed year-round and totally dependent on his wage – nevertheless continued to exercise its hold over the Marxist intelligentsia, representing for them the maturity of Russian capitalism and the possibility of recruiting workers into the fledgling social democratic movement. On the basis of such criteria as literacy, sobriety and a secular world-view, workers could be judged as to whether they were merely part of the masses, incomplete proletarians as it were, or had attained the status of (politically) 'conscious workers'.[15] This distinction corresponded to the trajectory of some factory workers who, shedding their peasant appearance and 'outlook', came to understand their place in society in the terms described by the literature they encountered in the revolutionary underground circles. As proud of their skills as they were resentful of the petty tyranny of foremen and the dissolute ways of their fellow workers, they entered the ranks of the Russian Social Democratic Party, agitated among other workers, organised strikes and embraced the cause of proletarian revolution.[16]

They were, however, a tiny minority among workers. More commonly, and especially in the Central Industrial Region, workers effected a 'symbiosis' between the village and the factory. Facilitated by the location of most factories on the outskirts of cities or in relatively autonomous industrial settlements, their retention of kinship ties and landholding gave them a 'tactical mobility' that city-dwellers and 'pure' proletarians lacked.[17] Several labour historians, focusing on the 1905 Revolution and its aftermath, have challenged the Bolshevik master narrative of working-class formation and the development of a corresponding class consciousness by emphasising the overlapping of parochial (e.g. craft, trade union) allegiances among artisanal workers with broader class identities, the volatility of mining and metallurgical workers as evidenced by their participation in both social democratic-organised strikes and anti-Semitic pogroms, and 'vanguard' workers' expression of a

15 Allan Wildman, *The Making of a Workers' Revolution: Russian Social Democracy, 1891–1903* (Chicago: University of Chicago Press, 1967); Tim McDaniel, *Autocracy, Capitalism, and Revolution in Russia* (Berkeley and Los Angeles: University of California Press, 1988), pp. 162–212.
16 See Reginald E. Zelnik (ed.), *A Radical Worker in Tsarist Russia: The Autobiography of Semen Ivanovich Kanatchikov* (Stanford, Calif.: Stanford University Press, 1986).
17 Robert E. Johnson, *Peasant and Proletarian: The Working Class of Moscow in the Late Nineteenth Century* (New Brunswick, N.J.: Rutgers University Press, 1979), pp. 155–62.

sense of self in the eclectic language of universal human rights and religious eschatology.[18]

'At least until the early twentieth century', writes Barbara Alpern Engel, 'the working-class couple who shared a roof was a relative rarity in Russia's major cities.' Although a gradual trend towards an urban-based family life accelerated after the 1905 Revolution and the Stolypin reforms of 1906–7, cohabitation of the working-class family never became the norm in tsarist Russia. This undoubtedly was because the cost of maintaining a family on the wage paid to most male workers was prohibitive, at least in a city like St Petersburg where it amounted to roughly three times the average annual wage for the country during 1905–9.[19] Hence factory owners' provision of (notoriously crowded and insalubrious) barracks or dormitory accommodation, and the absorption by the village of the costs of reproduction, elderly care and other welfare functions. This too suggests the 'tactical mobility' of workers.

The persistence of workers' ties to the village would save many of them when, during the desperate years of civil war, they fled from the starving cities. Statistics on the industrial workforce from 1917 onwards generally tell a story of diminution. From a high-point of 3.5 million, the number of workers in 'census' industry (i.e. industrial enterprises employing more than sixteen workers) dropped to slightly over 2 million in 1918, and remained at between 1.3 and 1.5 for the remainder of the civil war.[20]

Losses were greatest in the most populous industrial centres, that is, Petrograd, Moscow, the Donbass and the Urals. The number of industrial workers in Petrograd dropped from 406,000 in January 1917 to 123,000 by mid-1920. Workers also declined as a proportion of the city's population – from 45.9 per cent of able-bodied adults in 1917, to 34 per cent by the autumn of 1920. Between 1918 and 1920 Moscow experienced a net loss of about 690,000 people, of whom 100,000 were classified as workers. Over the same period, the number of factory and mine workers in the Urals dropped from 340,000 to 155,000. Large enterprises where the Bolsheviks had concentrated their agitational and recruitment efforts suffered disproportionately, partly owing to the shutting

18 Bonnell, *Roots of Rebellion*, pp. 439–55; Wynn, *Workers, Strikes, and Pogroms*; Mark Steinberg, 'Vanguard Workers and the Morality of Class', in Lewis H. Siegelbaum and Ronald G. Suny (eds.), *Making Workers Soviet: Power, Class, and Identity* (Ithaca, N.Y.: Cornell University Press, 1994), pp. 66–84.
19 Engel, *Between the Fields and the City*, pp. 126–29, 201 (quotation on p. 201); Crisp, 'Labour and Industrialization in Russia', pp. 404–13.
20 D. A. Baevskii, *Rabochii klass v pervye gody sovetskoi vlasti (1917–1921 gg.)* (Moscow: Nauka, 1974) p. 238; Iu. A. Poliakov, *Sovetskaia strana posle okonchaniia grazhdanskoi voiny: territoriia i naselenie* (Moscow: Nauka, 1986), pp. 214–19.

down of entire shops and partly due to heavy mobilisation for the Red Army and food procurement detachments.[21]

De-proletarianisation was not only demographic. Lenin could lament the 'petty-proprietor outlook' of the 'newcomers' who sought to escape the military draft or increase their rations, but this was an all too convenient excuse for the demoralisation of those workers who had not fled or been enlisted and the party's loss of support among them.[22] In any case, the party – and at least some workers – weathered this crisis, albeit just barely. The haemorrhaging of the proletarian body was staunched within a few years of the introduction of the New Economic Policy in 1921. Old blood flowed back, but as new blood poured in towards the end of the 1920s, a 'crisis of proletarian identity' could be discerned among skilled workers.[23]

Stalin's 'great turn' towards industrialisation, accompanied by the collectivisation of agriculture, provoked massive out-migration from the villages. Between 1928 and 1932, approximately 12 million people departed, some to swell the ranks of forced labourers in labour camps and special settlements, and others to escape starvation or, at best, unremunerated labour in the *kolkhoz*. Those who left voluntarily were mainly young males. Some were consigned by their collective farms for a given period to industrial enterprises or construction sites, usually located in remote regions, under conditions specified in 'organised labour recruitment' (*orgnabor*) contracts. Others headed on their own or in groups to the cities which swelled in population but not, for the most part, in accommodation, services and infrastructure. Still others were absorbed by state farms (*sovkhozy*) whose employed population increased from 663,000 in August 1929 to nearly 2.7 million three years later.[24]

These migration flows were by no means one-way. Nor did migrants necessarily settle in their first place of residence. The demand for labour was such that migrants frequently shopped around, 'flitting' like 'rolling stones' from one construction site or factory to another, clogging railroad stations and other collection points, and otherwise disrupting the state's attempts to gain control

21 Baevskii, *Rabochii klass*, pp. 246–7, 254; V. B. Zhiromskaia, *Sovetskii gorod v 1921–1925 gg.* (Moscow: Nauka, 1988), pp. 22–3; Diane Koenker, 'Urbanization and Deurbanization in the Russian Revolution and Civil War', in Diane Koenker, William Rosenberg and Ronald Suny (eds.), *Party, State, and Society in the Russian Civil War* (Bloomington: Indiana University Press, 1989), pp. 81–104.
22 V. I. Lenin, *PSS*, 5th edn, 55 vols. (Moscow: Gosizdpolit, 1958–65), vol. XLIII, pp. 24, 42.
23 Hiroaki Kuromiya, 'The Crisis of Proletarian Identity in the Soviet Factory, 1928–1929', *Slavic Review* 44 (1985): 280–97.
24 Sheila Fitzpatrick, *Stalin's Peasants: Resistance and Survival in the Russian Village after Collectivisation* (New York and Oxford: Oxford University Press, 1994), pp. 80–90.

over the labour market. Those attempts culminated in the introduction of compulsory internal passports for every citizen, sixteen years and older, living in towns and at construction sites or employed in transport and on state farms. The law, issued on 27 December 1932, initially targeted 'yesterday's peasants' who were 'undigested by the proletarian cauldron'. Eventually, it was used as a filtering device to remove the itinerant population and all 'people who are not involved in socially useful labour' from designated 'regime cities' (*rezhimnye goroda*).[25]

These measures worked, but only temporarily. During 1933, the number of new migrants who settled in cities declined to three-quarters of a million compared to 2.7 million in the previous year. Industry actually shed jobs, and what new employment opportunities existed were taken up by the other 'reserve army of labour', namely, the wives and daughters of workers already based in the towns.[26] By 1935, however, rural to urban migration was almost back to pre-passportisation levels.

The huge numbers of peasants absorbed by industry in the 1930s utterly transformed the factories where they worked and the cities in which they resided. They too were transformed, although usually not as rapidly as, or in ways that, party agitators would have liked and Soviet historians later contended.[27] The shock worker heroes and especially the outstanding Stakhanovites were represented in the Soviet media as embodying success stories from which the new Soviet workers could take instruction not only about work but about other dimensions of life.[28] But even after they had entered the 'proletarian cauldron', peasant migrants chose selectively from what was on offer by the party and state. Like more experienced workers, they learned when it was necessary to express approval of or affirmation for decisions made elsewhere (to 'speak Bolshevik' in Stephen Kotkin's inimitable phrase), but also how to circumvent the limits of state provisioning.[29] They may even have

25 *Trud*, 29 Dec. 1932, p. 2; Gijs Kessler, 'The Passport System and State Control over Population Flows in the Soviet Union, 1932–1940', *Cahiers du monde russe et soviétique* 42 (2001): 477–504.

26 Wendy Goldman, *Women at the Gates: Gender and Industry in Stalin's Russia* (Cambridge: Cambridge University Press, 2002).

27 cf. David Hoffmann, *Peasant Metropolis: Social Identities in Moscow, 1929–1941* (Ithaca, N.Y.: Cornell University Press, 1994); Kenneth Straus, *Factory and Community in Stalin's Russia: The Making of an Industrial Working Class* (Pittsburgh: University of Pittsburgh Press, 1997).

28 Lewis H. Siegelbaum, *Stakhanovism and the Politics of Productivity in the USSR, 1935–1941* (Cambridge: Cambridge University Press, 1988), pp. 210–46.

29 Stephen Kotkin, *Magnetic Mountain: Stalinism as a Civilization* (Berkeley and Los Angeles: University of California Press, 1995), pp. 198–237.

learned how to 'think Soviet', but this did not preclude them engaging in practices frowned upon or proscribed by Soviet officials.[30]

The story of peasants' transformation into workers during succeeding decades is one of massive recruitment for defence industries, construction and transport during the Great Patriotic War, followed by a renewal of the stream of voluntary departures from the collective farms which continued to deplete rural society of its younger, skilled and ambitious workforce.[31] Peasants left to further their education or learn a trade. They joined construction crews to build the high-rise apartment buildings that replaced the forests and fields on the outskirts of cities and into which they hoped to move. Whatever their intentions were and to whatever extent they were realised, these migrants did not abandon the village entirely. As late as the mid-1980s, one could see them – young and old, recently and not-so-recently arrived migrants – gathering in urban parks on Saturdays to sing, dance, play the accordion or the spoons and otherwise re-create a bit of village culture in the city.[32]

## Labour discipline and productivity

'The Russian is a bad worker compared with the advanced peoples', wrote Lenin in 1918, echoing complaints that factory owners and managers had made for decades before the October Revolution.[33] International comparisons of output per worker in the main factory-based industries were very much to Russia's disadvantage in the pre-revolutionary era. Indeed, even small-scale and artisan industry within Russia often enjoyed a competitive advantage thanks to the relatively high fixed costs and overhead expenditures in metalwork factories and employers' reliance on unskilled, often seasonal forms of labour.[34]

Lenin's sobering observation was followed by an equally categorical injunction: 'The task the Soviet government must set the people in all its scope is – learn to work.' For the next seventy odd years, the Soviet state would pursue this task, one that the bourgeoisie had performed in nineteenth-century Europe and North America. It did so by a combination of vocational

---

30 Jochen Hellbeck, 'Speaking Out: Languages of Affirmation and Dissent', *Kritika: Explorations in Russian and Eurasian History* 1 (2000): 92.

31 John Barber and Mark Harrison, *The Soviet Home Front, 1941–1945* (London: Longman, 1991), pp. 145–49; Sheila Fitzpatrick, 'Postwar Soviet Society: The "Return to Normalcy", 1945–1953', in Susan J. Linz (ed.), *The Impact of World War II on the Soviet Union* (Totawa, N.J.: Rowman and Allanheld, 1985), pp. 129–56.

32 A. Khaniutin, dir., *Piatachok*, documentary film (1987).

33 Lenin, *PSS*, vol. XXXVI, p. 189.

34 Crisp, 'Labour and Industrialization in Russia', pp. 401–4, 414.

training programmes, political campaigns, legal compulsions and financial inducements. Some of the measures to which it resorted were adaptations of techniques pioneered in capitalist countries; others were of its own devising. All held out the promise of advancing the country along the path towards socialism and then communism while improving the lot of its working population.

Lenin repeatedly stressed the importance of 'nationwide accounting and control of production and the distribution of goods', advocated use of Taylorism (see below), piecework and other 'up-to-date achievements of capitalism', and excoriated violators of labour discipline as 'responsible for the sufferings caused by the famine and unemployment'.[35] He invoked labour discipline both as an 'immediate task' for combating anarchy and hunger and as 'the peg of the entire economic construction of socialism'.[36] Based on the notion that workers were now collectively the ruling class and therefore were working for themselves, labour discipline was an emblem of the new class consciousness the Bolsheviks sought to promote.

During the civil war, the state demanded that workers remain at the bench, but assumed responsibility for their 'social maintenance', providing employment and at least a caloric minimum in the form of rations. With little in the way of material incentives to offer, the party appealed to workers' 'revolutionary conscience', and publicised examples of labour heroism such as the unpaid 'voluntary Saturdays' (*subbotniki*). Violators of labour discipline were punished via trade union-based comrades' disciplinary courts and other coercive mechanisms.[37]

These and other initiatives were inflected by ideology, but they also were driven by the emergency situation of civil war and economic collapse. Many were phased out after the introduction of the New Economic Policy only to return in more systematic fashion with the abandonment of NEP towards the end of the decade. In the meantime, paralleling a European-wide trend, the cult of man-the-machine took hold among Bolshevik intellectuals who marvelled at what Henry Ford had accomplished and Frederick Winslow Taylor's 'scientific management' promised. Under the banner of 'the scientific organisation of labour' (*nauchnaia organizatsiia truda* – NOT), they preached time-consciousness, efficiency and rationalisation in not only industrial work but

35 Lenin, *PSS*, vol. xxxvi, pp. 188–90, 197. On the Russian application of Taylorism before 1917, see Heather Hogan, *Forging Revolution: Metalworkers, Managers, and the State in St. Petersburg, 1890–1914* (Bloomington: Indiana University Press, 1993), pp. 187–93.
36 Lenin, *PSS*, vol. xl, pp. 301–2.
37 William Chase, 'Voluntarism, Mobilization and Coercion: *Subbotniki* 1919–1921', *Soviet Studies*, 41 (1989), 111–28.

the army, schools and other institutions.[38] However, the technocratic implications of NOT were not lost on the party, and most of the institutes and
laboratories promoting it did not survive the 1930s.

For workers there were more immediate concerns such as unemployment
which, despite the recovery of industry, grew throughout the 1920s. This was
due to a number of factors: the demobilisation of the army which threw several million men onto the labour market, rural to urban migration, protective
legislation covering the conditions of employment for women and juveniles
and the cost-accounting basis (*khozraschet*) on which industry was compelled
to operate.[39] Between 1925 and 1928, the Commissariat of Labour recorded an
increase from approximately one million to 1.5 million unemployed, figures
that almost certainly understated the actual numbers. White-collar workers
comprised about one-third of the total, and women and youth were dispropor-
tionately represented.[40] The scourge of unemployment was mitigated for at
least some workers by a rudimentary system of unemployment insurance and
the maintenance of ties to the land, but many resorted to selling home brew
(*samogon*), and engaging in prostitution and thievery, petty and otherwise.[41]

Workers with jobs in industry experienced a steady increase in their wages,
at least until 1927. Wage levels, based on collective agreements co-signed by
respective trade unions, were considerably higher in heavy industry where
the workforce was predominantly male than in textiles and other female-
dominated industries. They also were some 80 per cent higher for technical and
office personnel than for blue-collar workers. Overall, wage increases outpaced
productivity gains, notwithstanding campaigns to reduce expenditures and
rationalise production processes.[42] These campaigns and other measures to
raise productivity did bring output levels within striking distance of pre-war
indices. Intensified after the introduction of the seven-hour work-day in early

---

38 Richard Stites, *Revolutionary Dreams: Utopian Vision and Experimental Life in the Russian Revolution* (New York: Oxford University Press, 1989), pp. 145–59.

39 Lewis H. Siegelbaum, *Soviet State and Society between Revolutions, 1918–1929* (Cambridge: Cambridge University Press, 1992), pp. 100–7.

40 L. S. Rogachevskaia, *Likvidatsiia bezrabotitsy v SSSR, 1917–1930 gg.* (Moscow: Nauka, 1973), pp. 92, 147; E. H. Carr and R. W. Davies, *Foundations of a Planned Economy, 1926–1929*, 2 vols. (Harmondsworth: Penguin, 1971–4), vol. 1, pp. 486–90, 502–4.

41 Carr and Davies, *Foundations*, vol. 1, pp. 643–4; Chris Ward, *Russia's Cotton Workers and the New Economic Policy: Shop-floor Culture and State Policy, 1921–1929* (Cambridge: Cambridge University Press, 1990), pp. 35–50; Jean-Paul Depretto, *Les Ouvriers en U.R.S.S., 1928–1941* (Paris: Publications de la Sorbonne, 1997), pp. 59–67; Nataliia Lebina, *Povsednevnaia zhizn' sovetskogo goroda: normy i anomalii, 1920/1930 gody* (St Petersburg: Letnii sad, 1999), pp. 51–67, 86–94.

42 Carr and Davies, *Foundations*, vol. 1, pp. 516–36, 1013–14; William J. Chase, *Workers, Society, and the Soviet State: Labor and Life in Moscow, 1918–1929* (Urbana and Chicago: University of Illinois Press, 1987), pp. 217–43.

1928, they were accompanied by an appallingly high rate of accidents on the job – about twice that of Germany – and a good deal of conflict on the shop floor.[43]

The party, acknowledging that a breach had opened between itself and the working class, made much of its policy of proletarian preference in access to higher education and party membership.[44] But for all its rhetoric about the proletarian dictatorship, the conditions under which Soviet industrial workers laboured and lived in the 1920s did not differ appreciably from elsewhere in Europe. This in itself was something of an achievement, for material conditions had been immeasurably worse at the outset of the decade. Then again, working and living conditions for workers were far from fulfilling hopes engendered by the 1917 Revolution that the world – or at least their world – would be made anew. The 'big bourgeoisie' had been eliminated, but class enmity at the point of production persisted. Fanned by workers' insecurity, the ubiquity of the language of class and the contradictoriness of a policy that involved building socialism via capitalist techniques, it was manifested in strikes, 'specialist baiting' (spetsedstvo) and altercations with foremen and other low-level supervisors over job assignments, rate-setting and fines. Gender was also a fault-line on the shop floor, as the intrusion of women into previously male-dominated trades such as printing provoked some ugly incidents and much taunting by male workers.[45] In Central Asia, Russian workers behaved similarly towards their indigenous counterparts who were the beneficiaries of 'affirmative action' policies.[46]

Some of these tensions dissipated during the 1930s, but the force-paced industrialisation of the First Five-Year Plan years (1928–32) intensified them and fomented others. The utopianism of this 'socialist offensive' and its accompanying rhetoric of class war were matched by the harshness of repression against 'bourgeois specialists' in industry, Rightists within the party, and other

---

43 Ibid., pp. 243–7; Lewis H. Siegelbaum, 'Industrial Accidents and Their Prevention in the Interwar Period', in William O. McCagg and Lewis Siegelbaum (eds.), The Disabled in the Soviet Union: Past and Present, Theory and Practice (Pittsburgh: University of Pittsburgh Press, 1989), pp. 92–5.

44 Sheila Fitzpatrick, Education and Social Mobility in the Soviet Union, 1921–1934 (Cambridge: Cambridge University Press, 1979); John Hatch, 'The "Lenin Levy" and the Social Origins of Stalinism: Workers and the Communist Party in Moscow, 1921–1928', Slavic Review, 48 (1989): 558–77.

45 Chase, Workers, pp. 235–9; Diane Koenker, 'Men against Women on the Shop Floor in Early Soviet Russia', Americal Historical Review, 100 (1995): 1438–64.

46 Terry Martin, The Affirmative Action Empire: Nations and Nationalism in the Soviet Union, 1923–1939 (Ithaca, N.Y.: Cornell University Press, 2001), pp. 146–54; Matthew Payne, Stalin's Railroad: Turksib and the Building of Socialism (Pittsburgh: University of Pittsburgh Press, 2001), pp. 146–52.

'nay-sayers'. The ratcheting up of targets, shortages of all kinds, the depression of living standards and the general coarsening of daily life created tremendous stress, strain and, in some well-documented cases, strikes and other protests.[47]

Through it all, the party ceaselessly beat the drum for raising productivity. From the summer of 1929, factories and offices were put in continuous operation throughout the week with workers rotating days off every four or five days. This 'continuous working week' (*nepreryvka*) promised several advantages: an increase in the number of working days from 300 to 360, a lessening of pressure on workers' clubs and other leisure and service facilities, a blow against religion (Sunday would become a normal working day) and, perhaps above all, a rise in output of up to 20 per cent without infusions of additional working capital. It turned out, however, that the *nepreryvka* put enormous strain on the supply system, on equipment and on workers' conjugal and family lives. It also encouraged a lack of personal responsibility towards the tools of one's trade.[48] Two years after its introduction, the *nepreryvka* was quietly abolished in most industries, and work schedules reverted to the interrupted six-day week.

More long-lasting, indeed what would become a characteristic feature of Soviet socialism, was socialist competition. This was the practice of workers within an enterprise, shop or brigade setting goals for a period of time and challenging their counterparts to better their performance. Those meeting or exceeding the goals earned the title of shock workers (*udarniki*), with shock work (*udarnichestvo*) and socialist competition proceeding in tandem. Assuming mass proportions from 1929 onwards, these 'movements' were hailed (by V. Kuibyshev) as representing 'an historical breakthrough in the psychology of the worker', and (by Stalin) as 'a fundamental revolution in the attitude of people to labour'.[49] The trade unions, purged of their leading cadres and mandated by the party to turn their 'face to production', assumed the main responsibility for popularising, organising and recording the results of this 'revolution'.

Many workers (and managers) were either indifferent to socialist competition or resented it for imposing additional burdens on them. Hence their ironic reference to shock workers as 'gladiators', 'Americans' and 'shock

---

47 Jeffrey Rossman, 'The Teikovo Cotton Workers' Strike of April 1932: Class, Gender, and Identity Politics in Stalin's Russia', *Russian Review* 56 (1997): 44–69.
48 William Chase and Lewis Siegelbaum, 'Worktime and Industrialization in the U.S.S.R., 1917–1941', in Gary Cross (ed.), *Worktime and Industrialization: An International History* (Philadelphia: Temple University Press, 1988), pp. 202–5; R. W. Davies, *Crisis and Progress in the Soviet Economy, 1931–1933* (Basingstoke: Macmillan, 1996), pp. 44–6, 89–90.
49 Quoted in R. W. Davies, *The Soviet Economy in Turmoil, 1929–1930* (Cambridge, Mass.: Harvard University Press; Basingstoke: Macmillan, 1989), pp. 131, 257.

worker-idiots' (*chudaki-udarniki*).[50] Still, notwithstanding its eventual routinisation and the exaggeration of its results, some, particularly younger, workers responded enthusiastically to socialist competition. The opportunity to prove oneself, participate in the grandiose project of socialist construction, and, not incidentally, earn privileges associated with shock-worker status were only some of the reasons.[51] Others were evident in the case of production collectives and communes that pooled wages and divided them either equally or on the basis of skill grades. They included the desire to practise self-management and cushion the effects on output and wages of irregular supply and variations in the quality of raw materials.[52]

Production collectives and communes proliferated during 1929–31, especially in the metalworks and textile industries. But party leaders were ambivalent, even hostile to them, and the party's campaigns against collective piece-rates, 'depersonalisation' of responsibilities (*obezlichka*), and excessive egalitarianism (*uravnilovka*) in wages led to their disbandment. When, in 1935, the Stakhanovite movement ignited a new wave of socialist competition, circumstances were very different. Wage differentials had been widened significantly, nearly 70 per cent of industrial workers were paid on the basis of individual piece-rates, and of them, 30 per cent were eligible for the *progressivka* according to which rates would rise progressively above the level of output norms.

At no time in Soviet history did raising labour productivity assume such importance as during the heyday of the Stakhanovite movement in the mid-1930s.[53] The production records set by outstanding Stakhanovites, the showering of goods and other rewards on them and the results of Stakhanovite ten-day periods (*dekady*) and months received enormous coverage in the media. Prototypes of the New Soviet Man and Woman, Stakhanovites were represented both as living for their work and enjoying the fruits of their 'cultured' lives.[54] Yet, the objective of achieving a general breakthrough in productivity remained as elusive as ever. Resistance on the part of workers was certainly a factor. Fearing that Stakhanovites' records would be used to raise output norms (as they were in the spring of 1936), individuals engaged in acts of intimidation and

---

50 Ibid., pp. 260–1.
51 Hiroaki Kuromiya, *Stalin's Industrial Revolution: Politics and Workers, 1928–1932* (New York and Cambridge: Cambridge University Press, 1988), pp. 115–28.
52 Lewis H. Siegelbaum, 'Production Collectives and Communes and the "Imperatives" of Soviet Industrialization, 1929–1931', *Slavic Review* 45 (1986): 65–84.
53 Francesco Benvenuti, *Fuoco sui sabotari! Stachanovismo e organizzazione industriale in URSS 1934–1938* (Rome: Valerio Levi, 1988); Siegelbaum, *Stakhanovism*; Robert Maier, *Die Stachanov-Bewegung, 1935–1938* (Stuttgart: Franz Steiner Verlag, 1990).
54 Siegelbaum, *Stakhanovism*, pp. 210–46.

assaults against Stakhanovites, simply refused to adjust to a new division of labour, and otherwise sabotaged the movement.[55]

Ironically, the Stakhanovite movement itself militated against sustained increases in productivity. Whatever benefits were derived from improvements in work organisation and technique were counteracted by the intensification of problems in the delivery of supplies, the disproportionality between different phases of the production process and the neglect of maintenance and repair. Indeed, to the extent that it raised expectations of production breakthroughs that were not fulfilled, Stakhanovism indirectly contributed to accusations against enterprise directors and their staffs of sabotage and wrecking that undermined managerial authority during the Great Purges of 1936–8. Although claims that workers were taking advantage of the situation were probably exaggerated, the drawing of millions of men into the armed forces in connection with the military build-up made cracking down on labour turnover and absenteeism imperative. Such was the intent of the series of decrees, typically characterised by historians as 'draconian', that were issued between December 1938 and June 1940. These introduced labour books containing information about workers' past employment, called for the dismissal and eviction from enterprise housing of workers who were repeatedly truant or late to work, criminalised these violations of labour discipline and extended the normal work-day from seven to eight hours.[56]

What on paper amounted to the militarisation of labour in reality fell considerably short of that thanks to massive non-compliance on the part of management. Eager to retain workers almost at any cost, managers, often with the collusion of trade union committees, turned a blind eye towards truancy and lateness, extracted fictitious sick notes from physicians and issued retroactive notes for unpaid leave.[57] With the Great Patriotic War, the stakes rose in this and all other respects. Between 1940 and 1942 the Soviet industrial workforce declined from 11 million to 7.2 million. Women's share in industrial employment rose from 41 per cent to 52 per cent. The work-week was extended from 48 to 54 hours, and key workers (munitions workers from December 1941 and railroad workers from April 1943) were conscripted and subject to military tribunals for the slightest infraction of labour discipline. Elsewhere, workers continued to respond to bad living and working conditions by leaving their

---

55 Ibid., pp. 91–6, 190–204; Donald Filtzer, *Soviet Workers and Stalinist Industrialization: The Formation of Modern Soviet Production Relations, 1928–1941* (Armonk, N.Y.: M. E. Sharpe, 1986), pp. 200–5.
56 Filtzer, *Soviet Workers*, pp. 233–6.     57 Ibid., pp. 236–43.

jobs or not showing up, and an average of one million were taken to court every year of the war for these 'crimes'.[58]

Compulsion, though, only went so far even in wartime, and the diversion of resources to military production and the front made economic incentives even less available than they had been before the war. Political campaigns and moral appeals thus played a larger role. These included the expansion of the 'two-hundreder' movement that had appeared before the war but took on new meaning with the slogan, 'Work not just for yourself but also for your comrade sent to the front'. By February 1942, individual workers were being celebrated for having fulfilled two and three times their shift norms, and in the case of D. F. Bosyi, a milling machine operator at the Nizhnii Tagil armaments plant in the Urals, over fourteen times the norm. Much larger numbers of workers were involved in Komsomol front-line youth brigades, whose slogan, 'Work in the factory as soldiers fight at the front', typified the patriotic appeals of wartime socialist competition.[59]

As for productivity, the picture was mixed. In the munitions industry, output per worker more than doubled between 1940 and 1944. This was primarily due to the replacement of small batch by flow production on assembly lines, as well as deferments for skilled workers. Civilian industry, which comprised only 20.8 per cent of net national product in 1944 compared to 29.1 per cent in 1940, did not fare so well. Net output per worker dropped 11 per cent between 1940 and 1942 and barely recovered by 1944.[60] Given that average work time had increased by six hours per week, output per hour remained well below pre-war levels.

Wartime devastation followed by harvest failure and famine in 1946–7 consigned workers to a penurious existence in the immediate post-war years. Despite the persistence of penalties which made 'wilful' job-changing a criminal offence, labour turnover remained high, threatening production plans. So too did malnutrition, epidemic outbreaks of typhus, dysentery and tuberculosis, and shortages of basic necessities such as clothing, vegetables and soap.[61] Increasing productivity, advertised as the formula for improving workers' standard of living, was thus held hostage by the very conditions it was supposed to overcome.

58 Barber and Harrison, *The Soviet Home Front*, pp. 164, 216; A. V. Mitrofanova, *Rabochii klass SSSR v gody Velikoi Otechestvennoi voiny* (Moscow: Nauka, 1971), pp. 434–6.
59 Barber and Harrison, *The Soviet Home Front*, pp. 174–6.    60 Ibid., pp. 177–8, 220.
61 Donald Filtzer, 'The Standard of Living of Soviet Industrial Workers in the Immediate Postwar Period, 1945–1948', *Europe–Asia Studies* 51 (1999): 1013–38.

This vicious cycle somewhat abated after 1948. Reconstruction, which involved the extensive use of prisoner-of-war labour, was followed by nearly two decades of sustained industrial growth. During the 1950s, electric power generation and oil production increased fourfold, while natural gas production rose by a factor of eight. While the production of consumer goods lagged as usual, certain items such as refrigerators, washing machines, vacuum cleaners, sewing machines and television sets were turned out in exponentially increasing numbers and began to make their appearance in workers' households.[62] Significant efficiencies were achieved in steel-making, machine-building and other branches of heavy industry that received priority in supplies and other resources, upgraded their equipment and were able to recruit skilled workers and engineers. But even these privileged sectors exemplified certain phenomena that limited productivity gains and can be regarded as endemic to the Soviet system of production relations. They included the hoarding of workers and supplies by enterprises; the overconsumption of materials; the dearth of spare parts that resulted from the emphasis on producing heavier, more expensive items; disincentives against technical innovation; and the largely successful manoeuvring of workers to avoid speed-ups, de-skilling and other attempts to reduce their control over the labour process.[63]

Operating within these limits, the Khrushchev administration initiated reforms through which it sought to invigorate workers' commitment to fulfilling production goals. Infractions of labour discipline were de-criminalised in 1956 after having been in abeyance for several years. A major revision of the wage structure was instituted beginning in 1956 with coal mining and some metalworks enterprises and extending to all branches of industry by 1960. It entailed increases in base rates and production quotas, a reduction in the number of wage scales and the simplification of rates within each scale, the elimination of progressive piece-rates and a modest shift of pieceworkers to time-based wages. Finally, the education system was overhauled to combine academic learning with vocational training for all students in their last three years of secondary school.[64]

The reforms should be seen as a partial response to the emergence of a post-war generation that was more urbanised, better educated and more

62 Roger A. Clarke, *Soviet Economic Facts, 1917–1970* (London: Macmillan, 1972), pp. 85–8, 91.
63 Donald Filtzer, *Soviet Workers and De-Stalinization: The Consolidation of the Modern System of Soviet Production Relations, 1953–1964* (Cambridge: Cambridge University Press, 1992), pp. 13–34, 160–76; Paul R. Gregory and Robert C. Stuart, *Soviet Economic Structure and Performance* (New York: Harper and Row, 1974), pp. 113–231.
64 Filtzer, *Soviet Workers and De-Stalinization*, pp. 38–41, 72–5, 92–9.

demanding than its predecessors. That they proved inadequate was spectacularly demonstrated by the tragic events in Novocherkassk in early June 1962. Provoked by a Union-wide increase in the prices of meat and butter as well as the insensitivity of the factory administration, workers at the Novocherkassk Electric Locomotive Works walked off their jobs, marched on the city centre and seized the party headquarters. Fired upon by troops, some twenty-four were killed, eighteen of whom were under the age of thirty. Mass arrests followed, and 114 persons – officially dubbed 'hooligans', 'bandits', 'extremists' and 'anti-Soviet elements', that is, anything but 'workers' – were tried, among whom seven were sentenced to death and executed.[65]

Official concern that the appeals to patriotism and self-sacrifice were no longer adequate to inspire Soviet youth facilitated the establishment of sociology as an academic discipline. Throughout the 1960s Soviet sociologists conducted numerous studies, using questionnaires and other methods of 'concrete' sociological research, to chart young workers' attitudes. Several found alarmingly high levels of occupational dissatisfaction, low prestige of industrial work and individualistic and material considerations as the main reason for job-changing.[66] Other studies addressed the problem of the 'double-shift' for wage-earning women, which also was the subject of Natalia Baranskaia's story, 'A Week Like Any Other', that appeared in Novyi mir in 1969.[67]

Identifying these problems was not the same as solving them. In any case, by the 1970s the Brezhnev administration had effectively curbed industrial reform efforts and the bolder forays of labour sociologists, preferring instead to tout the 'scientific-technological revolution' (NTR – nauchno-tekhnicheskaia revoliutsiia) as a panacea.[68] Clothed in Soviet Marxist ideological garb, the revolution was to promote inter alia 'the formation of a new type of worker who has mastered scientific principles of production and can ensure that the functioning of production and its future development will be based on the achievements

65 Samuel H. Baron, Bloody Saturday in the Soviet Union: Novocherkassk, 1962 (Stanford, Calif.: Stanford University Press, 2001).
66 L. S. Bliakhman, A. G. Zdravomyslov and O. I. Shkaratan, Dvizhenie rabochei sily na promyshlennykh predpriiatiiakh (Moscow: Ekonomika, 1965); and A. G. Zdravomyslov, V. P. Rozhin and V. A. Iadov, Man and His Work, trans. Stephen P. Dunn (White Plains, N.Y.: International Arts and Sciences Press, 1970).
67 E. Z. Danilova, Sotsial'nye problemy truda zhenshchiny-rabotnitsy (Moscow: Mysl', 1968); A. G. Kharchev and S. I. Golod, Professional'naia rabota zhenshchin i sem'ia (Leningrad: Nauka, 1971); Natalia Baranskaya [Baranskaia], A Week Like Any Other and Other Stories (Seattle: Seal Press, 1990).
68 Vladimir Shlapentokh, The Politics of Sociology in the Soviet Union (Boulder, Colo.: Westview Press, 1987), pp. 49–84; Erik P. Hoffmann and Robbin F. Laird, Technocratic Socialism: The Soviet Union in the Advanced Industrial Era (Durham, N.C.: Duke University Press, 1985).

of science and technique'. According to a post-Brezhnev-era assessment, however, 'CPSU leaders [had] yet to devise successful means of nurturing the NTR or of enhancing ample creative rather than duplicative capabilities'.[69] It remained for Gorbachev to try to break through the 'stagnation', first by emphasising the need for the 'acceleration of productive processes', and then when that accomplished little, by adopting more radical measures.

## Enterprise paternalism

Despite the centralised nature of resource appropriation and redistribution imposed under Stalin and perpetuated by his successors, the day-to-day experience of workers was with enterprise administration, local party and trade union officials and fellow workers. Whatever came down from above in the way of plans, slogans, campaigns and resources, implementation ultimately depended on production relations in the workplace. Thus, rather than interpreting workers as having entered into some sort of 'social contract' with the state, it would be more appropriate to conceive of a mutuality of dependencies between managers and workers structured around what has been called enterprise paternalism.

Paternalism frequently crops up in both contemporary descriptions and historians' accounts of factory relations in pre-revolutionary Russia. While some owners are said to have been 'despotic' and others 'enlightened', the notion that their relationship with workers was more than purely contractual, that it involved a moral obligation to provide for workers' educational, cultural, spiritual and medical needs, seems to have been expected of them and, in many cases, was internalised. This was famously true of the textile magnates of the Central Industrial provinces, many of whom traced their ancestry to humble, serf origins and were of Old Believer faith.[70] But Muscovite and St Petersburg printing employers as well as southern mining and metallurgical owners (who were neither Old Believers nor, in many cases, Russian) also exhibited paternalism towards their workers.[71] In this respect, they were not all that far removed from the welfare capitalism practised by American firms during the Progressive Era.

69 Hoffmann and Laird, *Technocratic Socialism*, pp. 9, 31.
70 Thomas Owen, *Capitalism and Politics in Russia: A Social History of the Moscow Merchants, 1855–1905* (Cambridge: Cambridge University Press, 1981); T. P. Morozova and Irina V. Plotkina, *Savva Morozov* (Moscow: Russkaia kniga, 1998).
71 Mark Steinberg, *Moral Communities: The Culture of Class Relations in the Russian Printing Industry, 1867–1907* (Berkeley and Los Angeles: University of California Press, 1992), pp. 12–20; Theodore Friedgut, *Iuzovka and Revolution: Life and Work in Russia's Donbass, 1869–1924*, 2 vols. (Princeton: Princeton University Press, 1989–94), vol. I, pp. 41–2.

Whether inspired by personal piety, civic responsibility or more calculating motives, factory paternalism could raise expectations among workers that, when unfulfilled, provoked strikes. In these as well as less volatile instances, the image of the beneficent father could quickly give way to less flattering ones. In any event, even before the revolutionary thunderstorm of 1905–6, workers were beginning to develop alternative conceptions of themselves which by emphasising the dignity of the individual, fraternal ties and class affiliation (as in 'the proletarian family') excluded owners and management.[72] Subsequent legislation providing for trade unions, sick-benefit funds, and other forms of worker representation further eroded the basis on which factory paternalism rested, and, of course, the October Revolution would sweep away the entire factory-owning class.

During the civil war years, enterprises experimented with a variety of collective or 'collegial' forms of management, usually involving shared responsibility among representatives of factory committees, trade unions and economic associations. Though favoured by many within the party and the trade unions, enterprise democracy could not withstand the economic collapse and the needs of state institutions on the one hand and the dwindling number of employees on the other. Lenin, who likened the harmoniously run factory to a symphony orchestra, emphasised strict accountability and 'one-man management' (*edinonachalie*), and it was this model that eventually prevailed.[73]

Directorships in industry were occupied throughout the 1920s by former trade union or factory committee activists of working-class origin, 'bourgeois specialists' whose social backgrounds and pre-revolutionary experience often dictated their shadowing by party officials, and party trouble-shooters. These Red Directors were cast by the party as 'commanders of production' and charged with reviving output, avoiding cost overruns and maintaining proper relations with the trade union committee, the party cell and their specialist assistants. Judging by a 1922 *Pravda*-sponsored contest for the best and worst directors, workers appreciated personal qualities such as simplicity, accessibility and energy. While some workers characterised a good director in paternal terms (Korshunov 'loves his workers, he takes pride in them, cares about them as if he were their own father'), others employed images of friendship and brotherhood.[74] As Diane Koenker concluded, the contest revealed

72 Steinberg, *Moral Communities*, pp. 110–22, 212–14, 230–49.
73 E. H. Carr, *The Bolshevik Revolution, 1917–1923*, 3 vols. (Harmondsworth: Penguin, 1966), vol. I, pp. 190–4; Lenin, *PSS*, vol. XXXVI, p. 200.
74 Diane Koenker, 'Factory Tales: Narratives of Industrial Relations in the Transition to NEP', *Russian Review* 55 (1996): 384–411.

a 'fundamental ambivalence between the *workers'* director and the *workers' state's* director'.[75]

It would appear that with the launching of the 'socialist offensive' in the late 1920s that ambivalence was resolved in favour of directors' accountability to the state. The party's public campaign for *edinonachalie*, which was intended to eliminate the managerial parallelism of the director, party secretary and the factory trade union committee, and which culminated in new 'Model Regulations of Production Enterprises' of January 1930, certainly pointed in that direction.[76] So too did several resolutions of the party's Central Committee that granted ownership of factories' capital, the authority to plan production and set quotas and organise supplies and sales to superordinate production associations (trusts, *ob"edineniia, glavki*).[77]

However, these rules and resolutions were routinely violated for the simple reason that it was impossible for directors to abide by them and fulfil their production plans. From Stalin's standpoint, they were acting like 'conceited bigwig bureaucrats' who behaved as if 'party decisions and Soviet laws are not written for them, but for fools'. They had to be brought down a peg or two and be 'put in their proper place', as he told the Seventeenth Party Congress in 1934.[78] As for labour policy, the same directors exhibited the opposite tendency, namely, an unwillingness to exercise the punitive powers vested in them. Addressing a meeting of economic executives in 1934, M. M. Kaganovich attacked directors who wanted 'to play the "liberal" . . . The ground must shake when the director goes around the factory,' he asserted. 'A director who has become a liberal isn't worth half a kopeck. Workers do not like such a director. They like a powerful leader.'[79]

Shake the ground though they might, directors were unlikely to obtain and hold onto a sufficient number of workers or extract from them the necessary co-operation without concessions. Successful managers down to the level of foreman thus were those who learned how to combine acting like bigwigs with playing the liberal, covering their sleights of hand and indulgence with professions of loyalty to the party line and claims to have fulfilled their responsibilities. This was both the cause and effect of the system of 'taut' planning and the irregularity of supplies, the effects of which made a mockery of planning and efforts to standardise production. In addition to features already cited as

---

75 Ibid., p. 408.    76 Kuromiya, *Stalin's Industrial Revolution*, pp. 52–77.

77 David Shearer, *Industry, State, and Society in Stalin's Russia, 1926–1934* (Ithaca, N.Y.: Cornell University Press, 1996), pp. 167–83.

78 J. V. Stalin, *Works*, 13 vols. (Moscow: Foreign Languages Publishing House, 1952–5), vol. XIII, p. 378.

79 Cited in Siegelbaum, *Stakhanovism*, p. 34.

endemic to the Soviet system of production relations, mention should be made of paying workers at grades higher than those outlined in wage handbooks, granting bogus 'bonuses' that amounted to permanent additions to their basic pay, paying for fictitious piecework during down time and defective output during the (inevitable) storming sessions at the end of the month or quarterly plan period, and building 'family nests' feathered by the mutual interests of managers and party officials in perpetuating such practices.[80]

Enterprise paternalism thus had little to do with the social backgrounds or 'party-mindedness' of managers. It also was not a vestige of pre-revolutionary times, but rather emerged as a 'neo-traditional' response to an otherwise unworkable set of systemic conditions. The degree to which it was exercised, of course, varied according to the strategic significance of the enterprise, the ingenuity of the enterprise administration in obtaining resources and other factors. Generally, where local or municipal soviet budgets did not permit supporting social infrastructure (and this was more often the case than not) the enterprise assumed the role of community organiser not unlike American company towns of the late nineteenth and early twentieth centuries. It provided accommodation (or the materials with which to build housing), childcare, dining facilities, access to scarce food supplies, clothing and durable household goods, and a host of other services.

In this context the well-known aphorism, 'as long as the bosses pretend they are paying us a decent wage, we will pretend that we are working', becomes fully comprehensible.[81] Wages and the buying power to which they are connected in market-based societies had less significance in the Soviet economy where the verb 'to get' or 'obtain' (*dostat'*) replaced 'buy' in common parlance. Workers who got on the wrong side of management or the trade union committee jeopardised their opportunity to receive goods and services, but management risked losing workers if it pushed them too hard. These unwritten rules of the game extended to promotion, time off for family emergencies, pilferage (notoriously extensive in the Brezhnev era), use of enterprise materials and facilities for production 'on the side' and other informal arrangements based on personal ties.[82]

As for pretending to work, it has been argued on the basis of observation and interviews at a Samara factory in the early 1990s that 'workers love their

80 Filtzer, *Soviet Workers*, pp. 212–22; David Granick, *Management of the Industrial Firm in the USSR: A Study of Soviet Economic Planning* (New York: Columbia University Press, 1954), pp. 74–5, 161–8.
81 Cited in Hedrick Smith, *The Russians* (London: Sphere, 1976), p. 265.
82 Walter D. Connor, *The Accidental Proletariat: Workers, Politics, and Crisis in Gorbachev's Russia* (Princeton: Princeton University Press, 1991), pp. 171–9.

work, dedicate themselves to it completely, although in discussion they often curse it'. This 'particular kind of love' stemmed not only from the workplace having been a refuge from overcrowded housing conditions and the primary site of sociability, but also because the 'non-technological' (i.e. unstandardised) nature of production presented workers with opportunities for exercising their ingenuity and creativity.[83] Or, as Michael Burawoy (drawing on his extensive personal experience) has put it, 'under state socialism uncertainties in materials, machinery, and labor call for flexible autonomy on the shop floor'.[84]

It is important here to distinguish between 'work', which included many self-defined (and self-defining) tasks, and the job for which workers were hired. It is also important to disaggregate workers. One distinction stressed by the party was between the supposedly more reliable, politically 'conscious', core or cadre workers, and the rest of the labour force. The former could be expected to contribute to rationalisation proposals to production conferences, participate in socialist competition and serve on trade union committees. This distinction, however, did not necessarily coincide with the status hierarchy among workers themselves. Having internalised Soviet propaganda's emphasis on the dignifying, self-realising dimensions of material labour, industrial workers tended to have greater respect for production than auxiliary workers regardless of skill level.[85] Finally, gender stereotyping, deeply ingrained in both official and popular cultures, produced and perpetuated the segregation of occupations, and the marginalisation of women as poorly paid, low-status auxiliary workers.[86] Female workers were therefore less likely to experience the 'particular kind of love' than their male counterparts, although the affective relationships formed with other workers in their brigade or *kollektiv* could be no less meaningful or strong.

## The end of the Soviet working class

The Gorbachev years were hardly kind to industrial labour. It is not that the last Soviet leader set out to antagonise workers, although his early campaigns for 'acceleration' and a crackdown on alcoholic consumption and labour truancy

---

83 Sergei Alasheev, 'On a Peculiar Kind of Love and the Specificity of Soviet Production', in Simon Clarke (ed.), *Management and Industry in Russia: Formal and Informal Relations in the Period of Transition* (Aldershot: Edward Elgar, 1995), pp. 69–98.
84 Michael Burawoy, 'From Capitalism to Capitalism via Socialism: The Odyssey of a Marxist Ethnographer, 1975–1995', *ILWCH* 50 (1996): 85.
85 Simon Clarke, 'Formal and Informal Relations in Soviet Industrial Production', in Clarke, *Management and Industry*, pp. 7–13.
86 Filtzer, *Soviet Workers and De-Stalinization*, pp. 182–96.

hardly won him many friends on the shop floor. Rather, the interests of labour often appeared as an afterthought in the elaboration of *glasnost'* and *perestroika*. Even the Law on State Enterprises (1987), whose provisions for managerial elections and expanded powers for councils of labour collectives (STKs) were hailed as a great breakthrough for industrial democracy and self-management, changed little. According to one estimate, over 90 per cent of managers retained their positions in Soviet industry after elections, and, at least until 1989, the STKs were stacked with directors' favourites.[87]

On a broader level, while *perestroika* rapidly eroded the centralised redistributive powers of the ministries, it did not succeed in replacing the integrative functions of the command economy or the disciplinary powers of the party. In the resultant scramble for resources (raw materials, labour, consumer goods, credits), debts piled up, rationing was reintroduced for the first time since the end of the Second World War, inflation rose sharply and workers and their unions became increasingly dependent on handouts from enterprise directors.[88] By 1991 when Gorbachev adopted a watered-down version of the '500-day plan' for the marketisation of the economy, it was too late. A condition of lawlessness accompanied the frenzy of privatisation of industry, two-thirds of whose capital stock was judged to be obsolete.[89] The 'socialist market economy' turned out to be an oxymoron.

What has been termed '*perestroika* from below' was best represented by the coal miners' strike of the summer of 1989.[90] Alarmed but at the same time emboldened by the disintegration of the state, the miners' strike committees advanced two kinds of demands. One was for more from higher authorities – more goods, more money for wages and pensions and more benefits. Another category of demands was for the restructuring of their industry, namely, full autonomy for enterprises to enable them to contract with both domestic and foreign customers at 'world' prices that were considerably higher than what the state paid and the right to retain the proceeds. Such 'bread and butter demands' gave the strike its predominantly economic cast and, despite their internal inconsistency, were not incompatible with the spirit of *perestroika* from above. But other, more political demands soon surfaced, including the repeal

---

87  Paul T. Christensen, *Russia's Workers in Transition: Labor, Management, and the State under Gorbachev and Yeltsin* (DeKalb: Northern Illinois University Press, 1999), pp. 67–72.

88  Michael Burawoy and Kathryn Hendley, 'Between Perestroika and Privatisation: Divided Strategies and Political Crisis in a Soviet Enterprise', *Soviet Studies* 44 (1992): 371–402.

89  Gertrude Schroeder, 'Dimensions of Russia's Industrial Transformation, 1992 to 1998: An Overview', *Post-Soviet Geography and Economics* 39, 5 (1998): 251.

90  Theodore H. Friedgut and Lewis H. Siegelbaum, 'The Soviet Miners' Strike, July 1989: Perestroika from Below', *Carl Beck Papers in Russian and East European Studies*, no. 804 (Pittsburgh: Center for Russian and East European Studies, 1990).

of Article 6 of the Soviet constitution that enshrined the Communist Party's 'leading role', and the election of the Congress of People's Deputies and its president by universal suffrage.[91]

During the remaining two-and-a-half years of the Soviet Union's existence, coal miners exhibited a militancy and degree of organisation unparalleled among Soviet workers. Their strike/workers' committees and Independent Miners' Union (NPG) spearheaded a second all-Union miners' strike in March–April 1991 which called for Gorbachev's resignation. Reflecting miners' bitterness about the centralised allocation of resources (commonly referred to as 'ministerial feudalism'), their organisations also advocated unrestricted freedom of prices and markets.[92] As their hostility to the 'centre' increased, so did their support for alternative political arrangements – the complete sovereignty of the RSFSR under Boris Yeltsin, and independence for Ukraine.

An analysis of the miners' movement suggests at least two ironies. First, as Stephen Crowley has argued, 'Soviet coal miners fought against the Soviet system and for liberal reforms, including the market, but for reasons that were at odds with those of their liberal allies, reasons that at root were quite socialist'.[93] Producers of material wealth, they felt cheated by a system in which those who redistributed the wealth enriched themselves without doing real work. 'We don't earn', Crowley was told by a leader of the Kuzbass miners in May 1991. 'They give out, and they give out not according to labor but by how much they figure you need.' The market, understood as the means by which 'I earn my own, I buy my own, having sold my labor power', represented the antithesis of this system. It was a key ingredient of the 'normal', 'civilised' society for which miners and other Soviet citizens yearned.[94]

Second, although the movement threw its weight behind Democratic Russia in 1991 and continued to back Yeltsin and successive 'parties of power' after the Soviet Union's collapse, neither in the 1991 and 1996 presidential elections nor in the intervening parliamentary elections of 1993 and 1995 did the Kuzbass, Russia's principal mining district, vote in favour of Yeltsin or the parties supporting his administration.[95] As for Ukraine, the movement's support

91 Simon Clarke, Peter Fairbrother and Vadim Borisov, *The Workers' Movement in Russia* (Aldershot: Edward Elgar, 1995), pp. 17–130; Stephen Crowley, *Hot Coal, Cold Steel: Russian and Ukrainian Workers from the End of the Soviet Union to the Post-Communist Transformations* (Ann Arbor: University of Michigan Press, 1997), pp. 25–45, 102–4.
92 Clarke, Fairbrother and Borisov, *Workers' Movement*, pp. 105–12; L. N. Lopatin (ed.), *Rabochee dvizhenie Kuzbassa: Sbornik dokumentov i materialov* (Kemerovo: Sovremennaia otechestvennaia kniga, 1993), pp. 373–468.
93 Crowley, *Hot Coal, Cold Steel*, p. 130.      94 Ibid., p. 136.
95 Rob Ferguson, 'Will Democracy Strike Back? Workers and Politics in the Kuzbass', *Europe–Asia Studies* 50 (1998): 445–68.

for independence, as characterised by one of its leaders, was predicated on the assumption that it would at last fulfil the Bolsheviks' slogan of October 1917: land to the peasants, factories to the workers.[96] What happened instead, according to another miner activist speaking in February 1992, was that 'we have changed from one political machine to another, with practically the same people [in power]'.[97]

Miners' activism, which extended into the post-Soviet period, was neither continuous nor universal. Nor were miners in this and other respects any more typical of Soviet workers than those in other occupations who stolidly tried to keep their heads above water in the rising tide of political and economic disintegration. The articulation of class varied a great deal in the late Soviet period, overlapping with occupation in some cases (e.g. the miners) and being overshadowed by national and regional identities in others. What was common across republic boundaries and branches of industry was that the collapse of the administrative command system and the Communist Party did not weaken but rather strengthened alliances between workers and management. This was because managerial control of enterprises and managers' role as the personification of the labour collective increased and would continue to do so in the post-Soviet era.[98]

Since the collapse of the Soviet Union workers have been major losers. Official statistics show that real wages indexed to 1985 (1985 = 100) declined to 55 by 1995. Thereafter, wages rose slightly, but in the wake of the financial crisis of 1998, fell again, and by the end of the century were approximately 50 per cent of their 1990 level. On top of this, workers in most if not all sectors of the economy experienced delays or non-payment of wages, the shrinking of benefits and a psycho-social disorientation which, though difficult to quantify, was no less real and goes a long way towards explaining an unprecedented rise in rates of alcoholism, suicide and mortality. Whatever else privatisation and other 'reforms' accomplished, they did not reverse the downward spiral in living standards that most workers experienced in the late Soviet period.

The first phase of privatisation (voucherisation and employee buy-outs) was completed by June 1994, by which time only 20 per cent of the total workforce remained within the state sector. Privatisation turned workers into shareholders. As of December 1994, some 53 per cent of the shares in medium

---

96 Lewis H. Siegelbaum and Daniel J. Walkowitz, *Workers of the Donbass Speak: Survival and Identity in the New Ukraine, 1989–1992* (Albany, N.Y.: SUNY Press, 1995), p. 120.
97 Ibid., p. 144.
98 Simon Clarke, 'Privatisation and the Development of Capitalism in Russia', in Clarke, *What About the Workers?*, pp. 216–19.

and large-scale enterprises that had been privatised were held by employees. This proved to be the high-point of worker 'ownership'. By June 1995, as workers sold their shares to make ends meet and the second ('loans for shares') phase of privatisation got under way, the proportion dropped to 43 per cent and continued downward thereafter.[99] All the while, as the state reduced its subsidies to industry and directors siphoned off funds for other purposes, wage arrears mounted. By 1996, they comprised 7.7 billion roubles, or 131 per cent of the monthly wage bill in 'indebted enterprises', and by August 2000 the total wage debt stood at 40.5 billion roubles.[100]

This disguised form of unemployment was accompanied by others: the assignment of part-time work to wage earners interested in full-time employment, and the placement of workers on unpaid administrative leave. According to the standard definition recognised by the ILO, there were 3.6 million people (4.8 per cent of the active workforce) unemployed in 1992 but 8.9 million (10 per cent) by 1998. Nearly three-quarters of unemployed men were listed as workers, as compared to 53 per cent of women. Women were far more likely to leave the workforce 'voluntarily', either because of declining employment opportunities or curtailment of childcare services. Thus, the proportion of women in the workforce diminished from 51 per cent in 1991 to 47 per cent in 1997.[101]

Sectorally, there were 8.2 million fewer wage earners in industry in 1998 than in 1991, a decline of 36.8 per cent. Other sectors showing significant declines over these years included 'science' (which lost more than half of its workforce), transport and construction. Net gainers included finance and insurance (where employment rose by 73 per cent), and wholesale and retail trade.[102] Not included in official statistics but also increasing significantly in numbers were the self-employed, those involved in the sex trade and bodyguards.

Ethnographies expose dimensions of what workers have endured since the collapse of the Soviet Union that official data and journalists' accounts do not reveal. 'No newspaper report or set of statistics', writes Rob Ferguson in relation to the Kuzbass miners, 'can convey the accumulation of privations,

99 Linda J. Cook, *Labor and Liberalization: Trade Unions in the New Russia* (New York: Twentieth Century Fund, 1997), p. 70.
100 Goskomstat Rossii, *Trud i zaniatost' v Rossii, Statisticheskii sbornik* (Moscow: Goskomstat, 1996), p. 104; 'Goskomstat Rossii soobshchaet osnovnye itogi o sotsial'no-ekonomicheskom polozhenii Rossii (v 1 ianvare–iiule 2000 goda)', *www.government.ru:8014/institutions/committees/gks2308.html*
101 Goskomstat Rossii, *Uroven zhizni naseleniia Rossii* (Moscow: Goskomstat, 1996), p. 24; Goskomstat Rossii, *Rossiiskii statisticheskii ezhegodnik, Statisticheskii sbornik* (Moscow: Goskomstat, 1998), p. 182.
102 Goskomstat Rossii, *Rossiiskii statisticheskii ezhegodnik*, p. 179.

nor the mix of bitterness, anger, despondency and loss of self-esteem that wage non-payment brings in its train.' 'The scale of injustice', he adds, 'invokes rebellion and fatalism in the same breath: "Something must be done ... There is nothing one can do".'[103] The contemporary factory (and mine) worker remains an endangered species in Russia and the other former Soviet republics.

103 Ferguson, 'Will Democracy Strike Back?', p. 461.

17

# Women and the state

BARBARA ALPERN ENGEL

By the early twentieth century, far-reaching changes had begun to challenge Russia's traditional gender hierarchies. Industrialisation and the proliferation of market relations, the growth of a consumer culture and the expansion of education, among other processes, touched the lives of Russia's rural as well as urban population. Economic change expanded women's employment opportunities, while new cultural trends encouraged the pursuit of pleasure in a populace long accustomed to subordinating individual needs to family and community. At the same time, patriarchal relations served as both metaphor and model for Russia's political order. The law upheld patriarchal family relations, as did the institutions and economies of the peasantry, still the vast majority of Russia's people. Religious institutions governed marriage and divorce, which the Russian Orthodox Church permitted only for adultery, abandonment, sexual incapacity and penal exile, and then only reluctantly. Marital law required a woman to cohabit with her husband, regardless of his behaviour.

In the second half of the nineteenth century, this system encountered a range of challenges. Liberal reformers sought to revise Russia's laws, those governing the family in particular, as a means to reconfigure the entire social and political order.[1] Among the challengers were women, who also strove to make their voices heard. Yet women were rarely in a position to influence decisively the discourse on women, or to exercise authority decisively on women's behalf. Instead, as a revolutionary wave mounted, broke and receded, women's voices grew muted, and a gendered hierarchy re-emerged that echoed pre-revolutionary patterns while assuming novel forms.

1 William Wagner, *Marriage, Property and Law in Late Imperial Russia* (Oxford: Clarendon Press, 1994), pp. 61–138; Laura Engelstein, *The Keys to Happiness: Sex and the Search for Modernity in Fin-de-Siecle Russia* (Ithaca, N.Y.: Cornell University Press, 1992).

## On the eve

Women had established a significant presence in public life by the early twentieth century. Nearly half a million women, mainly of peasant origin, laboured in Russia's factories, constituting almost 30 per cent of the industrial labour force. Tens of thousands of educated women occupied professional or semi-professional positions. Approximately 750 women physicians practised medicine in 1904, many of them employed in the public sector. Less extensive and costly training as nurses, midwives and medical aides provided employment to thousands of others. The number of women teaching in rural schools grew from 4,878 in 1880 to 64,851 in 1911.[2] Although barred by law from the civil service, ever-increasing numbers of women held clerical positions in private and government offices. Women also took up their pens, becoming novelists, poets, critics, playwrights, journalists and editors or publishers of journals. By enabling women to earn their own living, employment opportunities eroded institutions that conservatives sought to preserve, such as the patriarchal family.

The burgeoning marketplace had much the same effect, encouraging the desire for individual pleasure and gratification, and fostering patterns of consumption that could cut across social divides. The advertising industry enticed women to consume the fashionable clothing and other items displayed in windows of department stores and on the pages of popular magazines. New pastimes such as bicycling enhanced women's mobility and personal independence. In fact, the ideology of domesticity that so dominated the world-view of the middle classes of Europe and the United States had never gained hegemony in Russia, despite support from the throne. To be sure, domestic ideas had circulated since the early nineteenth century, and after 1905, liberal professionals embraced a modernised version of them, according to which mothers, guided by scientific precepts, would exert a disciplinary influence on society by appropriately raising the future generation.[3] Members of the middle class expected respectable women to be good wives and selfless mothers, echoing Victorian

---

2 Rose Glickman, *Russian Factory Women: Workplace and Society, 1880–1914* (Berkeley: University of California Press, 1984), p. 83; 'Alfavitnyi spisok zhenshchin-vrachei', *Meditsinskii departament. Rossiisskii meditsinskii spisok* (St Petersburg: MVD, 1904), pp. 416–31; Ben Eklof, *Russian Peasant Schools: Officialdom, Village Culture and Popular Pedagogy, 1861–1914* (Berkeley: University of California Press, 1986), p. 195.

3 Diana Greene, 'Mid-Nineteenth Century Domestic Ideology in Russia', in Rosalind Marsh (ed.), *Women and Russian Culture* (Oxford: Berghahn Books, 1998), pp. 78–97; Engelstein, *Keys*, pp. 248, 422.

ideals. Physicians campaigned to modernise motherhood in the countryside. Prompted by exceedingly high infant mortality rates – almost half of rural infants perished before the age of five – physicians sought to replace the traditional practices of village midwives with their own professional expertise, much as physicians had already done in the West. Nevertheless, domestic discourses faced considerable competition from others that endorsed women's productive role. Elite wives had long enjoyed the right to own and manage property independently of their husbands. Members of the progressive elite expressed scant sentimentality about the working class or peasant family, and stressed women's role in the workforce over motherhood. Socialists believed that the family confined women, and that women's workforce participation provided the key to their emancipation. Prominent women rarely identified themselves with the home. Marketing their own images, for example, women writers never embraced the 'rigorously domesticated' womanhood still prevalent in Western societies.[4]

The Revolution of 1905 briefly heightened women's public presence, while gaining them very little. Women industrial workers, clerical workers, professionals, even domestic servants, joined unions and walked off their jobs to attend mass meetings and demonstrations that called for an end to autocracy and representative government. Women's movements re-emerged on a substantial scale. Their primary goal was women's suffrage and an expansion of women's legal and political rights, including reform of marital law. The most active organisation, the Union for Women's Equality, also sought in vain to forge cross-class alliances. As one member lamented, to establish circles among labouring women was relatively easy, but when their political consciousness was raised, 'they quickly join the ranks of one of the [socialist] parties and become party workers'.[5] The October Manifesto enfranchised only men.

The Revolution of 1905 demonstrated that no organisation or individual could speak for women as a group. Undermined by political divisions, the women's movement lost membership and momentum in the post-1905 reaction. Educated women activists only rarely succeeded in melding socialism and feminism, and were more prone to join socialist organisations than feminist ones. Women constituted some 15 per cent of the membership of the

---

4 Adele Lindenmeyr, 'Maternalism and Child Welfare in Late Imperial Russia', *Journal of Women's History* 5, 2 (1993): 114, 123; Beth Holmgren, 'Gendering the Icon: Marketing Women Writers in Fin-de-Siecle Russia', in Helena Goscilo and Beth Holmgren (eds.), *Russia. Women. Culture* (Bloomington: Indiana University Press, 1996), p. 341.

5 GIAgM, fond 516, op. 1, ed. kh. 5, l. 73. Report of the Third Congress, 22 May 1906.

Socialist Revolutionary Party and 10 per cent of the Russian Social Democratic Workers' Party on the eve of the First World War.[6]

## War and revolution

The First World War set the stage for the upheavals to follow. It upset gendered hierarchies and drew out to work hundreds of thousands, perhaps millions of women for the first time. Women replaced men on the factory floor, their proportion in industry rising to 43.2 per cent by 1917. Thousands volunteered as nurses. Women broke into new occupations such as the postal service and transport; some even took up arms. Women's vastly expanded roles in the public arena enhanced their claims for civil rights. Even soldiers' wives (*soldatki*) became assertive, gaining an unprecedented sense of entitlement to public resources because of their husbands' service. Mounting female dissatisfaction contributed to the collapse of the autocracy. Although women workers played a relatively minor role in the strike movement, women were prominent in the subsistence riots that rocked Russia's cities and towns, and sometimes spilled over onto the factory floor. This is what happened on International Women's Day, 23 February (8 March) 1917, when angry working-class women staged an enormous demonstration, summoning workers to join them. Their actions sparked the February Revolution.

Immediately, women claimed citizenship rights in the new order. Feminist leaders campaigned, successfully, for long-standing goals. In June 1917 women lawyers gained the right to serve as attorneys and represent clients in court. Women obtained equal rights with men in the civil service. On 20 July, all adults over the age of twenty gained the right to vote for the forthcoming Constituent Assembly. For lower-class women, economic rights appeared the higher priority. *Soldatki* fought to raise their monetary allotment. In May, over 3,000 laundresses struck, demanding an eight-hour day and a minimum daily wage of four roubles. They persisted in the face of employers' resistance and won a modest victory. Another strike of mainly female dye workers, lasting four months, ended in failure.

Nevertheless, as a group, women workers were far less visible than men during 1917. Many proved reluctant to strike, fearful that plants would close, depriving them of the ability to support themselves and their children. Women's fears were surely heightened by the demands of male workers, when threatened

---

6 Beate Fieseler, 'The Making of Russian Female Social Democrats, 1890–1917', *International Review of Social History* 34 (1989): 204–5; Barbara Evans Clements, *Bolshevik Women* (Cambridge: Cambridge University Press, 1997), p. 1.

with lay-offs, that women be let go first. Lower-class women were poorly represented in the trade unions, factory committees and soviets that upheld workers' interests. Women were also marginalised by revolutionary rhetoric, which reflected an intensely masculinised working-class culture. For decades, swearing, telling dirty jokes and boasting about sexual adventures with women had demonstrated the masculinity of ordinary male workers, while politically and socially 'conscious' men forged a community of brothers. Women family members served both as figures against which to define themselves.[7] In 1917, this masculine brotherhood assumed symbolic significance. Images of male workers were ubiquitous, 'either as the brother of the male peasant and/or the soldier . . . or else as the liberator of the world, breaking chains and crowns'.[8] Working-class women might themselves adopt the language of brotherhood and identify themselves with the family. 'Let us, Russian women and mothers, be proud knowing that we were the first to extend our brotherly [sic!] hand to all the mothers the world over', reads one socialist proclamation.[9]

## The Bolsheviks seize power

During 1917, the Bolshevik Party made only half-hearted efforts to attract women. As membership burgeoned, the proportion of women dropped to 2 per cent; few were workers.[10] After October, the Bolsheviks suppressed the autonomous women's movement, condemning it as 'bourgeois'. For the next seventy years, the party's view of women's emancipation would determine its parameters. As Marxists, they regarded working-class men and women's interests as identical and women's full and equal participation in waged labour as the key to their liberation. Thus, they proposed to equalise the relations between the sexes by socialising housework – that is, entrusting child-rearing and other household tasks to paid workers, enabling women to work full time for wages. Once free of the need to exchange domestic and sexual services for men's financial support, women would encounter men as equals. The

7 S. A. Smith, 'Masculinity in Transition: Peasant Migrants to Late-Imperial St. Petersburg', in Barbara Clements et al. (eds.), *Russian Masculinities in History and Culture* (New York: Palgrave, 2002), p. 99.
8 Orlando Figes and Boris Kolonitskii, *Interpreting the Russian Revolution: The Language and Symbols of 1917* (New Haven: Yale University Press, 1999), p. 110.
9 Mark D. Steinberg (ed.), *Voices of Revolution, 1917*, trans. Marian Schwartz (New Haven: Yale University Press, 2001), p. 98.
10 R. C. Elwood, *Inessa Armand: Revolutionary and Feminist* (Cambridge: Cambridge University Press, 1992), pp. 234–5.

family itself would eventually wither away as society assumed its functions; thereafter, women and men would unite their lives solely for love.

Initially, the Bolsheviks attempted to legislate social change. In 1918, the government produced a family code that equalised women's status with men's, allowed a marrying couple to choose either the husband's or the wife's surname and granted illegitimate children the same legal rights as legitimate ones. Marriage was secularised. Divorce became easily obtainable at the request of either spouse. Labouring women gained eight weeks of paid maternity leave before and after childbirth; women engaged in mental labour gained six. In 1920, abortion became legal if performed by a physician. The law promised equal pay to women whose work equalled men's 'in quantity and in quality'. Whenever possible, new decrees used language that was deliberately gender-neutral. 'Spouses' could retain their nationality upon marriage. A 'spouse' unable to work could request support from the other.[11] Co-education became the rule.

Yet gender distinctions persisted, enhanced by the militarised atmosphere of the civil war. When the authorities decided against obligatory military service for women, the Red Army, the crucible of citizenship in the new order, became identified as a masculine domain: 'I, a *son* of the labouring people, citizen of the Soviet Republic, take on the calling of warrior in the Worker and Peasants Army,' pledged all new recruits (my emphasis).[12] Women experienced difficulty acquiring the toughness demanded of party members in brutalising circumstances. In any case, women's toughness evoked an ambivalence that men's did not. Moreover, even as it tried to efface distinctions of gender, the leadership emphasised the uniquely feminine contribution that women could make to the war effort. Women's independent citizenship was undermined by propaganda and entitlements based on a woman's relationship to a man.[13] Slogans that addressed working women as mothers reinforced the notion that women's responsibility was to care for fighting men and men's, to protect women and children: 'Proletarka! The Red Army soldier is defending you and your children. Ease his life. Organize care for him.'[14] Post-revolutionary iconography consistently portrayed the heroic worker as male, at the centre of action, battling the opponents of revolution or refashioning the world.

---

11 Elizabeth Wood, *The Baba and the Comrade: Gender and Politics in Revolutionary Russia* (Bloomington: Indiana University Press, 1997), p. 50.

12 Ibid., p. 53.

13 Joshua Sanborn, 'Family, Fraternity and Nation-Building in Russia, 1905–1925', in Ronald Grigor Suny and Terry Martin (eds.), *A State of Nations: Empire and Nation-Making in the Age of Lenin and Stalin* (New York: Oxford University Press, 2002), pp. 102–6.

14 Ibid., p. 59.

Thus, proletarian domination, connected rhetorically and visually to male domination, confirmed a gendered hierarchy.[15]

Women occupied the margins of the new civic order. They were identified with private life and family, spheres denigrated by a post-revolutionary culture that privileged public life, the collective and the point of production. The leadership viewed lower-class women as inherently more 'backward' than men, more attached to the family, religion and traditional values and, consequently, as a potential threat to the revolution. (Formerly privileged women the leadership dismissed altogether, apart from party loyalists.) Women's historians argue that it was women's alleged backwardness, more than concern for women's emancipation as such, which convinced the leadership to authorise efforts to mobilise them. Thus, concern over women's lack of support during the civil war led the party to approve the first All-Russian Conference of Working Women, which took place in November 1918, and in September 1919 to authorise a Women's Bureau (Zhenotdel) to co-ordinate the party's work among women. Inessa Armand was designated its first director; after her death in 1920, Aleksandra Kollontai, the party's leading advocate of women's emancipation, replaced her. The party conceived of the Zhenotdel as a transmission belt from the top downwards to mobilise women to support party objectives and inform women of their new rights.

Instead, some Zhenotdel activists became advocates on women's behalf. Empowered as well as constrained by the Marxist vision, they regarded the emancipation of women as an end in itself and the Zhenotdel as a means to achieve it. Kollontai, the most radical, tested the limits of the organisation's mandate. Viewing women's freedom to act on their sexual feelings as essential to their emancipation, as head of the Zhenotdel she rhapsodised about the future when everyone would live in communes and 'women would be free to choose whatever sorts of romantic relationships met their needs'.[16] Kollontai's efforts to link personal with political change won no converts among the party's leadership. And her aggressive advocacy on behalf of women's emancipation alienated other party members. Kollontai was removed as head of the Zhenotdel early in 1922, following her association with the Workers' Opposition. Subsequent Zhenotdel leaders proved more politically astute, but also more tractable and willing to remain within the limits of their charge.

15 Victoria Bonnell, *Iconography of Power: Soviet Political Posters under Lenin and Stalin* (Berkeley: University of California Press, 1997), p. 77.
16 Clements, *Bolshevik Women*, p. 227.

How effective was the Zhenotdel as an agent of proletarian women's emancipation? Activists sought to mobilise lower-class women on their own behalf, to keep women's issues on the party agenda, to fight for the rights of labouring women and to ensure the transformation of everyday life.[17] They fought an uphill battle. Zhenotdel-style feminism had little support even among female party members; some of them actively opposed it. Zhenotdel members themselves disagreed over tactics and goals. And in regional and local organisations, prejudice against the Zhenotdel and its work was endemic. Many party cadres resisted women's emancipation and barely concealed their contempt for the Zhenotdel. Trade union leaders, too, often disliked co-operating with the Zhenotdel or providing facilities for its meetings. In the course of the 1920s, Zhenotdel funding decreased: the organisation operated on a shoestring, many of its activists really volunteers. The Zhenotdel found itself in an impossible position, dependent on party largesse and charged with mobilising a group whose negative qualities (backwardness, ignorance) justified their mission.[18]

In any case, efforts to emancipate women were often ill-suited to material realities. During the civil-war years, urban dwellers, now mostly women and children, starved or froze to death. Millions of homeless children wandered the streets. Instead of serving as shining examples of the socialist future, state-sponsored efforts to assume domestic functions, starved of resources, repelled those who used them. The New Economic Policy in some respects made matters worse. Men returning from the civil war took jobs from women. In an effort to protect their superior status in the workplace and monopoly on skilled 'male' trades, male workers routinely sabotaged women's efforts to acquire advanced skills and upgrade their work status.[19] Managers often preferred to hire men, who had higher skill levels and would not require costly maternity leave and day care. Despite decrees that forbade it, managers discriminated against women workers and dismissed pregnant and nursing women on leave. They used laws banning night work for women as an excuse to lay off women workers. To save money, the state cut back on childcare centres. As a result, working mothers had no place to leave their children and the largely female staffs found themselves without employment. Women's share of the labour force dropped from 45 per cent in 1918 to under 30 per cent,

---

17 Wendy Zeva Goldman, 'The Death of the Proletarian Women's Movement', *Slavic Review* 55, 1 (1996): 46–54.
18 Wood, *Baba and Comrade*, p. 212.
19 Diane Koenker, 'Men against Women on the Shop Floor in Early Soviet Russia', *American Historical Review* 100, 5 (Dec. 1995): 1438–64.

where it remained throughout the 1920s, even as the number of workers slowly grew.[20] Zhenotdel complaints about the situation fell on deaf ears.

Family upheaval intensified women's vulnerability. Millions of Russians, mostly urban residents, exercised their new right to divorce. Courts became swamped with alimony suits, many of them initiated by unmarried women who had borne children in unregistered unions, for which the 1918 law made no provision. Unprepared to devote resources to implementing women's equality in the workplace or restructuring the family, the state instead revised the law. A new family code was issued in 1926 after considerable discussion. Designed 'to shield women and children from the negative effects of NEP', but also to promote the withering away of the family, the code granted new rights to women in unregistered unions and further simplified divorce procedures, transferring contested divorces from the courts to registry offices.[21] The code failed to ameliorate the problems it sought to address.

Other policies that targeted women served to replicate women's subordinate status. Reaffirming the connection between women's sexuality and reproduction, the 1920 abortion law referred to abortion as a serious 'evil', necessitated by the 'moral survivals' of the past and by difficult economic conditions. Once those conditions disappeared, the assumption went, so would the need to limit births.[22] Contraception was legalised only in 1923. Physicians gained greater control over reproduction and authorisation to pursue their campaign to modernise motherhood. Only qualified doctors, not midwives, were certified to perform legal abortions, which deprived most village women of access to them. Propaganda vilified village midwives, the primary source of medical care for village women, and portrayed physicians as male. Posters intended for urban women represented healthy female sexuality as linked to reproduction and offered viewers images of mothers surrounded by healthy children. Yet mothering, propaganda emphasised, was a craft that had to be learned from the physicians who best understood it. To oversee the process, the government created an organisation for the Protection of Motherhood and Infancy (OMM).[23] Women's attempts to control their own reproductive lives through the use of abortion encountered increasing criticism. Facing difficult material conditions, perhaps eager to seize new opportunities, women

20 Wendy Zeva Goldman, *Women, the State and Revolution: Soviet Family Policy and Social Life, 1917–1936* (Cambridge: Cambridge University Press, 1993), pp. 101–44.
21 Ibid., pp. 212–13.
22 Rex Wade (ed.), *Documents of Soviet History*, vol. II: *Triumph and Retreat, 1920–1922* (Gulf Breeze, Fla.: Academic International Press, 1991), p. 145.
23 Elizabeth Waters, 'The Modernization of Russian Motherhood, 1917–1936', *Soviet Studies* 44, 1 (1992): 124–9.

ignored pro-natalist propaganda. By the late 1920s, abortions had become so commonplace that in some cities they considerably outnumbered births. Experts expressed profound concern about the extent of abortion, a threat to population growth in their view. Referring to the 'antisocial' nature of abortion and its 'epidemic' dimensions, they emphasised the state's need for children, not women's need to control their fertility.[24]

## Revolution comes to the countryside

By contrast with urbanites, village women remained largely unaffected by post-revolutionary upheavals. To be sure, the land code that the Bolsheviks introduced in 1922 promised much on paper: it equalised women's legal position in the peasant household, and entitled women to an equal right to land and other property and to equal participation in village self-government; it provided protection for pregnant women and introduced maternity leave for agricultural labourers. The Zhenotdel and press campaigned to educate village women and mobilise them on their own behalf – to set up nurseries for their children, to divorce abusive husbands. But most of these initiatives went nowhere. The state lacked the means to pursue them, or back up its promises with the resources necessary to support real change.

Only with the collectivisation drive did the Soviet state decisively intrude on peasant women's lives, and the impact was mostly negative. The collectivisation campaign threatened the sphere of women. Activists seized as collective property the livestock that women customarily tended; they broke up families and dispersed their members. Although by depriving male household heads of control of household property and labour, collectivisation promised to undermine the peasantry's patriarchal order, it failed to attract peasant women. In the regime's view, women's bitter opposition further demonstrated their greater 'backwardness' and susceptibility to 'kulak' manipulation.[25] Taking advantage of the immunity that such perceptions ensured, enormous numbers of women engaged in acts of resistance. Women also demonstrated against the closing of churches and continued to baptise their children despite prohibitions against the practice. Baptism became a 'conspicuous site of resistance' to official values, if largely a hidden one.[26]

24 Goldman, *Women, the State*, pp. 288–9.
25 Lynne Viola, 'Bab'i Bunty and Peasant Women's Protest during Collectivization', *Russian Review* 45 (1986): 28–38.
26 David Ransel, *Village Mothers: Three Generations of Change in Russia and Tataria* (Bloomington: Indiana University Press, 2000), p. 164.

The regime mobilised to overcome women's resistance. In 1929, it instructed the Zhenotdel to work with this 'backward layer', organising peasant women to support collectivisation. Posters and films trumpeted the advantages that collectivisation brought to women and recast the image of the peasant woman to portray her as a collective farm woman (*kolkhoznitsa*), the antithesis of the backward peasant *baba* who opposed collectivisation. Young and slim, the *kolkhoznitsa* had become a 'new woman', the rural counterpart of her liberated urban sisters.[27] Enthusiastic about constructing socialism, earning her own income and prizing her independence, she was fully committed to the goals of the party-state. Those peasant women who embraced their government's values received considerable publicity, which often emphasised their freedom from traditional constraints on women and subordination to men. The regime rewarded its female supporters more concretely, too. In addition to meeting important functionaries and having their pictures displayed, such women became eligible for goods in short supply. Whether in traditionally male occupations such as tractor driver, or, far more commonly, in traditionally female ones such as milkmaid, such women became poster-children of the new era in the countryside, symbols of the success of the Stalinist revolution and its commitment to promoting women.

Most rural women, however, enjoyed none of these benefits. Comprising roughly 58 per cent of collective farm workers by the late 1930s, women supplied two-thirds of the backbreaking labour. A rigid sexual division of labour prevailed, making it hard for women to work in trades labelled 'male'. Access to health and maternity care improved only slowly. By 1939, there were 7,000 hospitals, 7,503 maternity homes, 14,300 clinics and 26,000 medical assistants in the entire USSR, serving a rural population of over 114,400,000.[28] A genuine advance over the previous decade, these facilities nevertheless remained a drop in the bucket. The network of rural day-care centres intended to free women from childcare fell far short of the goals set by the Five-Year Plan. As always, it was women who shouldered the burden of housework, and without basic amenities such as running water, indoor plumbing and electricity. Women also assumed primary responsibility for tending the private plot that fed most families. Consequently, women's work-days lasted far longer than men's. Women earned far less, however, because most of their work was considered 'unskilled' and they devoted a smaller fraction of it to collective production. In any case,

27 Bonnell, *Iconography*, pp. 109–10.
28 Roberta Manning, 'Women in the Soviet Countryside on the Eve of World War II', in Beatrice Farnsworth and Lynn Viola (eds.), *Russian Peasant Women* (New York: Oxford University Press, 1992), pp. 208, 217.

despite celebration of the newly independent collective farm woman with her own individual wage, collective farm payments, such as they were, customarily went to the household and not the individual.

## A great retreat?

During the First Five-Year Plan, the leadership ceased even to pay lip-service to women's emancipation as a goal in itself; emancipation became linked exclusively with women's participation in production and contribution to building socialism. In December 1928, the government eliminated all women's organisers within trade unions, thereby halting efforts to train, promote and defend women workers on the shop floor. On 5 January 1930, the Zhenotdel itself was abolished, ending advocacy within party circles on behalf of women. Some women in other official organs tried but failed to fill the gap. The absence of persistent advocacy on women's behalf left the leadership free to deploy the female labour force as it chose and at the lowest possible cost. Slowly at first, and then at breakneck speed, the industrialisation drive encouraged women to take up new trades and opened the gates of the industrial labour force to them. In 1928, there were 2.8 million women in the labour force; by 1932, there were twice as many and over four times as many by 1940.[29]

However, despite claims to the contrary, industrialisation failed to provide women with equal employment opportunity. During the First Five-Year Plan, women's share of every branch of industry increased, including those branches, such as chemicals, metallurgy and mining, traditionally dominated by men. The introduction of machinery made women's lack of skill and education less of an obstacle to hiring them, enabling the state to replace men with women and to transfer men where needed. Old lines of gender segregation gave way. However, new ones took their place, as industries and sectors of the economy were designated 'best suited' for women's labour. Entire sectors of the economy became 'female', including food processing, textiles and the production of consumer goods, and the lower and middle ranks of white-collar and service professions.[30]

The 1930s brought some women unprecedented social mobility. The proportion of women in institutions of higher education grew from 31 per cent in 1926 to 43 per cent in 1937. Women's progress was particularly marked in fields

29 Gail Warshofsky Lapidus, *Women in Soviet Society: Equality, Development and Social Change* (Berkeley: University of California Press, 1978), p. 166.
30 Wendy Zeva Goldman, *Women at the Gates: Gender and Industry in Stalin's Russia* (Cambridge: Cambridge University Press, 2002), p. 149.

such as economics, law, construction and transport, where the proportion of women students had hitherto been quite low. Most of the women who benefited derived from lower-class backgrounds. Female role models encouraged women to choose new paths. In September 1938, Valentina Griazodubova, Marina Raskova and Polina Osipenko set a world record for non-stop flight by women. Yet despite the highly acclaimed breakthroughs of a few, the majority of women workers continued to fill the lowest-paid and most physically arduous positions. Concentrated in light industries, such women were left behind by investment policies that favoured heavy industry and neglected consumption. Some experienced a worsening of working conditions and living standards so severe that they staged protests, as did about 16,000 mostly female workers in 1932.[31]

Moreover, because the state failed to socialise domestic labour as promised, working women often did two jobs rather than one. Despite ambitious goals in both the First and Second Five-Year Plans, only modest progress was made because heavy industry took priority. Managers even commandeered for other purposes buildings designated for childcare. According to official figures, the number of children in childcare centres in 1936 numbered 1,048,309, a tenfold increase from 1928, but still far short of the goals.[32] The First Five-Year Plan actually made housekeeping more difficult. Collectivisation severely disrupted food production. Having abolished private trade with the onset of the plan, the state experienced substantial difficulties in distributing goods. Women, not men, were encouraged to assume the housekeeping burden. In 1936, employed wives spent on housework a total of 147 of their leisure hours each month, as compared to thirty spent by husbands. Women spent almost as many hours on housework as they spent on the job.

Women's reproduction was likewise harnessed to the needs of the state. Between 1927 and 1935, the birth rate declined from 45 births per 1,000 people to 30.1; the working-class family decreased in size. Officials found the change alarming. As did other European states, the Soviet state sought to increase the size of its population to meet the demands of industry and modern warfare. Bearing and raising children ceased entirely to be a private matter; instead, they became women's responsibility to society and the state. As Joseph Stalin put it, the fact that a Soviet woman enjoyed the same rights as a man did not release her from the 'great and honourable duty' of being a mother.

31 Jeffrey Rossman, 'The Teikovo Cotton Workers' Strike of April 1932: Class, Gender, and Identity Politics in Stalin's Russia', *Russian Review* 56 (1997): 48–9.
32 Goldman, *Women at the Gates*, p. 274.

Not a private matter, motherhood had 'great social significance'.[33] Efforts to
modernise motherhood continued, now entirely directed by the state and
linked to productivist goals. Media portrayed motherhood as a natural part of
women's lives and avoiding motherhood as 'abnormal'.

The state attempted to strengthen the family, employing legislation and
propaganda similar to that of other European nations. In 1934, homosexual
acts between consenting males became a criminal offence; the regime did not
outlaw female homosexuality, less publicly visible.[34] In 1936, the regime circulated for discussion the draft of a new family law, which would recognise only
registered marriages, make divorce more complicated and expensive, and pro-
hibit abortion except when childbearing threatened the mother's life or health.
The draft also included incentives, similar to those offered by Catholic countries and Nazi Germany, designed to encourage childbearing. Women who
bore more than six children would receive a 2,000-rouble annual bonus for
each additional child and a 5,000-rouble bonus for each child over ten children. The law raised both the level of child support and penalties for men
who failed to pay it. Despite letters from women protesting against the pro-
hibition on abortion, it was retained when the draft became law in 1936. In
1936, a secret directive from the Commissariat of Health ordered contraceptive
devices to be withdrawn from sale.[35] Socialism had solved the 'woman question', the regime proudly declared. Soviet women had become the freest in the
world.[36]

The state's pro-natalist efforts enjoyed only short-lived success. The birth
rate increased to 39.7 births in 1937, but thereafter declined. In 1938, as the nation
prepared for war, maternity leave was reduced from sixteen weeks to nine
and became contingent on seven continuous months of prior employment.
The birth rate in 1940 dropped below that of 1936, partly in consequence.
Underground abortion was primarily responsible for the decline. Despite the
'sin' they attached to it, rural women resorted to it frequently, learning to
perform abortions on themselves or turning to local abortionists. Women's

33 Choi Chatterjee, 'Soviet Heroines and Public Identity, 1930–1939', *Carl Beck Papers in
Russian and East European Studies*, no. 1402 (Pittsburgh: Center for Russian and East
European Studies, 1999), p. 13.
34 Dan Healey, *Homosexual Desire in Revolutionary Russia: The Regulation of Sexual and Gender
Dissent* (Chicago: University of Chicago Press, 2001), pp. 184–5.
35 David Hoffman, 'Mothers in the Motherland: Stalinist Pronatalism in its Pan-European
Context', *Journal of Social History* (Fall, 2000): 39.
36 Mary Buckley, *Women and Ideology in the Soviet Union* (Ann Arbor: University of Michigan
Press, 1989), pp. 108–13.

use of illegal abortion constituted a form of resistance to the demand that they produce and reproduce without support from the state. At a terrible physical, and in the case of peasant women, moral price, women took control of their fertility as best they could.[37]

The new emphasis on the family brought a redefinition of wifehood. Devoting oneself to one's man assumed new importance for all but peasant women. Honouring a Soviet hero, the press would also lavish praise on his wife. The celebration of socially conscious wifehood reached its peak in the movement of wife-activists (*obshchestvennitsy*), which lasted from 1936 until 1941. For the first time since 1917, full-time housewives were treated respectfully and invited to contribute their unpaid labour to the creation of a new society. At its height in 1936–7 the movement mobilised tens of thousands of housewives to organise kindergartens and camps for children, furnish workers' dormitories, plant flowers and the like. Dominated by the wives of industrial managers and engineers, the movement extended women's domestic responsibilities into the public sphere and provided social services neglected by economic planners. At the same time, the neatly groomed and fashionably dressed *obshchestvennitsy* served as exemplars of the 'cultured' society of the future. Working-class women often resented *obshchestvennitsy*, whose celebration signified increased acceptance of class distinctions.[38]

Family ties sometimes brought arrest and imprisonment. Women constituted 11 per cent of those formally prosecuted by the legal system during the Terror, and 8 per cent of the prison population in 1940.[39] Many of the women political prisoners were mothers, daughters, sisters and, most commonly, wives of arrested men. So many wives of arrested Old Bolsheviks were themselves arrested in 1937 that special camps were created to hold them. The motherhood that the regime now celebrated intensified the sufferings of women prisoners. Their children were frequently sent away to children's homes, their names changed, their pasts effaced. In the communal prison cells described by Evgenia Ginzberg and others, women who had remained stalwart under brutal interrogation and in punishment cells would succumb to hysterical weeping when they permitted themselves to think of their children.

37 Ransel, *Village Mothers*, p. 115.
38 Rebecca Balmas Neary, 'Mothering Socialist Society: The Wife-Activists' Movement and the Soviet Culture of Daily Life', *Russian Review* 58, 3 (July 1999): 396–412; Sheila Fitzpatrick, *The Cultural Front* (Ithaca, N.Y.: Cornell University Press, 1992), pp. 216–37; Sarah Davies, '"A Mother's Cares": Women Workers and Popular Opinion in Stalin's Russia', in Melanie Ilic (ed.), *Women in the Stalin Era* (New York: Palgrave, 2001), p. 100.
39 Clements, *Bolshevik Women*, p. 280.

## The Second World War and its aftermath

The massive mobilisation during the Second World War both obscured and intensified gender differences. The line separating men's work from women's work dissolved. Tens of thousands of women were compelled to prepare defences when German forces threatened. To replace the labour of men under arms, on 13 February 1942, the Soviet government ordered full labour mobilisation, incorporating into the labour force the 'non-working' population aged sixteen to forty-five, except for pregnant women, nursing mothers and mothers without access to childcare. By the beginning of October 1942, women comprised 52 per cent of the labour force in military-related industry and 81 per cent of the labour in light industry (up from 60 per cent on the eve of invasion). In 1945, 56 per cent of the entire industrial labour force was female. Seventy per cent of the agricultural labour force was female in 1943, 91.7 per cent in 1945. Between 1940 and 1944, the proportion of tractor drivers who were women rose from 4 to 81 per cent.[40] The war created opportunities for women to advance on the job and in party and state institutions.

Millions of women served at the front. The government immediately drafted women medical students and established crash courses to prepare front-line medics and nurses. Forty-one per cent of physicians at the front were female, as were 43 per cent of field surgeons, 43 per cent of medical assistants and 100 per cent of nurses. Other women participated directly in the fighting, rendering the Soviet Union's wartime experience unique. Women constituted 9.3 per cent of partisan forces that appeared behind enemy lines. To shore up resistance against the invaders, Communist Party and Komsomol members were mobilised for combat immediately after war broke out, without regard to gender. Early in 1942 the Central Committee of the Communist Party formally accepted women into the military. By the end of 1943, when female participation reached its peak, over 800,000 served in the armed forces and partisan units; by the end of the war, over a million had performed military service. Women fought on every front and in all branches of the services, constituting about 8 per cent of military personnel overall.[41]

Yet while gender distinctions disappeared in much of early wartime practice, they resurfaced in wartime propaganda and towards the end of the war,

40 John Erickson, 'Soviet Women at War', in John and Carol Garrard (eds.), *World War 2 and the Soviet People: Selected Papers from the Fourth World Congress for Soviet and East European Studies, Harrogate, 1990* (New York: St Martin's Press, 1993), pp. 53–6.
41 K. Jean Cottam, 'Soviet Women in World War II: The Ground Forces and the Navy', *International Journal of Women's Studies* 3 (1980): 345.

in state policy. Media reinforced the gendered imagery that had evolved by the end of the 1930s, representing women first and foremost as mothers but, more generally, as embodiments of the home and family for which men fought. Women's front-line responsibilities received relatively little attention during the war. In the rare cases when the media did depict women soldiers, it almost invariably portrayed them as feminine and girlish, by contrast with brave and manly men.[42] Towards the end of the war, gender distinctions became newly institutionalised. In 1943, co-education, the norm since 1918, was abolished in urban secondary schools in order to give proper attention to the different requirements of boys' and girls' 'vocational training, practical activities, preparation for leadership and military service'.[43] A new family code was issued on 8 July 1944, the 1936 code having failed to reduce the divorce rate. Intended to strengthen the family, the code reinforced marital ties by making divorce still more difficult. The new law deprived people in unregistered unions of legal benefits and access to housing, and restored the distinction between legitimate and illegitimate children. It barred women from bringing paternity suits. At the same time, the code was unabashedly pro-natalist: single people were taxed, as were married couples with fewer than three children, except for those under the age of twenty-five and attending college full time, or who had lost children during the war. The new legislation also augmented the cult of motherhood. Even unmarried mothers, otherwise stigmatised by the new laws, were eligible for additional financial support from the state. In the summer of 1944, the state instituted military-style 'motherhood medals', almost identical to those awarded by the Nazis and graduated according to the number of children a woman had borne and reared. After 1944, when the press began publishing the names of women who won these awards, mothering became women's most publicised work.

In the post-war period, celebration of women's domestic roles intensified. Demobilised men often replaced women in the responsible and well-paid positions the women had gained during the war and thanks to new entry requirements that favoured male veterans, in institutions of higher education, too. The proportion of women enrolled in higher education dropped from the wartime high of 77 per cent to 52 per cent in 1955, then to 42 per cent in 1962. However, the majority of the adult female population continued to work, their

42 Katharine Hodgson, 'The Other Veterans: Soviet Women's Poetry of World War 2', in Garrard and Garrard, *World War 2*, p. 81.
43 Rudolf Schlesinger (ed.), *The Family in the USSR: Documents and Readings* (London: Routledge and Kegan Paul, 1949), p. 363.

labour essential to rebuilding the Soviet Union. To ensure that they did, food distribution was tied to the workplace. Between 1945 and 1950, the number of women in the workforce grew by over three million, although the proportion of women workers dropped from 56 to 47 per cent because of returning soldiers.[44] Yet despite the need for women's labour, fiction treated women's waged work as 'a mere adjunct' to women's domestic responsibilities, which consisted primarily of restoring men's self-esteem and faith in their own manhood. 'Images of wives welcoming mutilated and traumatized husbands and fiancés home functioned as a promise and a hope for men and as a suggestion and instruction to women.'[45]

To an unprecedented extent, the post-war media celebrated personal and family happiness. Love, peripheral at best in 1930s fiction, became central to the fiction of the post-war era, reflecting as well as shaping popular priorities. The media encouraged women to make themselves more attractive. Magazines intended for women featured advice on beautifying the home and housekeeping, skin care, exercise, gardening and cooking. Exhorted to work hard, make a home, comfort their shell-shocked husbands, bear children and be feminine, in the post-war period women were expected to be all things to all people. While the Soviet government continued to proclaim the equality of men and women, women were now asked to accept the 'Orwellian doctrine' that men were the more equal.[46]

Fertility rates once again reflected the pressures on women. True, roughly a quarter of a million unmarried women bore children in 1946 and sizeable numbers of single women continued to bear children into the 1950s, helping to replenish the decimated population. Nevertheless, despite policies penalising small families and encouraging large ones, most women continued to limit their fertility. The means they employed were the usual: abortion. In 1954, abortions numbered 6.84 per thousand women, according to official figures that undoubtedly underestimate them.[47] The result of women's refusal to reproduce was that as of 1954–5, the birth rate per thousand women remained approximately 60 per cent of its pre-war level.

---

44 Lapidus, *Women in Soviet Society*, pp. 150, 166.
45 Anna Krylova, '"Healers of Wounded Souls": The Crisis of Private Life in Soviet Literature, 1944–1946', *Journal of Modern History* 73, 2 (2001): 324–5, 326.
46 Vera S. Dunham, *In Stalin's Time: Middle Class Values in Soviet Fiction* (Durham, N.C.: Duke University Press, 1990), p. 216.
47 Christopher Williams, 'Abortion and Women's Health in Russia and the Soviet Successor States', in Rosalind Marsh (ed.), *Women in Russia and Ukraine* (Cambridge: Cambridge University Press, 1996), p. 137.

## De-Stalinising the 'woman question'

The death of Joseph Stalin and the rise of Nikita Khrushchev brought a shift in the state's relationship to the 'question of women'. For the first time since the 1930s, the leadership toned down propaganda celebrating women's emancipation and took steps to address some of the worst shortcomings. Yet policies were contradictory and results limited. Reproductive politics provide one example. In 1955, the leadership legalised abortion, claiming the need to protect women's health. While continuing to maintain that the duty of women was to reproduce, and to warn of the danger of abortion, the Soviet state explicitly acknowledged women's freedom to choose for the first time. It was up to women to decide 'the question of motherhood', declared the newspaper *Izvestiia*. Women in state enterprises, although not collective farm women, regained sixteen weeks of fully paid maternity leave. Legal abortion remained a painful and humiliating procedure, however, and contraception unavailable.[48]

Family policy reflected similar contradictions. In conformity with increased openness, the leadership permitted a highly critical discussion of the 1944 family law. Many of the proponents of liberalising the law were women, beneficiaries of post-revolutionary educational opportunities. Possessing the expertise to participate in policy debates and drawing upon early Bolshevik discourse, they spoke forcefully for a more egalitarian view of marriage and the family than that embodied in existing legislation. Reformers called for freedom of marriage and divorce and equal rights for all children, regardless of whether the biological parents were legally married. Reformers' stance evoked fierce opposition from conservatives, who upheld the double standard and feared the threat to men and family stability of women bringing unfounded paternity suits. Khrushchev sided with the conservatives; family law remained unchanged. Yet divorce became more accessible. Taking advantage of greater freedom to exercise initiative, judges responded favourably to applications for divorce, resolving a growing proportion of them in favour of the plaintiff. Perhaps in response, the number of divorce applications increased dramatically. Women initiated the majority of divorces, a sign of new assertiveness. Between 1950 and 1965, divorce rates per thousand people quadrupled.[49]

The leadership also drew attention to women's secondary economic status, but did little to ameliorate it. The entire Soviet economy rested upon the unpaid

48 Buckley, *Women and Ideology*, p. 158.
49 Lapidus, *Women and Soviet Society*, pp. 238–9, 251; Deborah Field, ' "Irreconcilable Differences": Divorce and Conceptions of Private Life in the Khrushchev Era', *Russian Review* 57, 4 (Oct. 1998): 599–613.

and underpaid labour of women. Women comprised two-thirds of the agricultural labour force, and virtually all collective farm women engaged in manual labour. The majority of the work was seasonal, unskilled and poorly paid; it remained difficult for women to advance. The most highly paid, year-round work to which rural women could aspire was dairying, which also ranked among the most arduous labour that collective farm workers performed. In the industrial sector, the low wages paid to women in female-dominated trades such as textiles helped to subsidise the entire industrial economy. Almost a quarter of all women workers were employed in the textile or garment industry. Work in these light industries was as intense as industrial work ever became: women were on the job more than 95 per cent of the time, with only 8 to 10 minutes of break per shift. Poorly designed machinery, inadequate ventilation and shifting schedules exacted an enormous physical toll. The stress of the job put workers 'right at the physiological limit of human capabilities'. Yet such workers received less annual leave than all other industrial workers, and earned less than 80 per cent of the average wage of an industrial worker and two-thirds of that of a metalworker. Women's low wages meant that light industry turned a profit, which the state used to subsidise investment in heavy industry. Women's low wages also made it 'unprofitable' to invest in the costly machinery that would have lightened their work. Gendered assumptions also contributed to restricting women to the least desirable positions. Where machinery was introduced, men often took charge of it, leaving women to perform the remaining unskilled, manual labour. This arrangement was simply too advantageous for the state to abandon voluntarily, and women lacked the clout to force a change from the shop floor. The economic position of women workers continued to deteriorate.[50]

A major cause of women's poor bargaining position was their infamous 'double burden', that is, keeping house as well as working full time for wages. The double burden served to maintain Soviet women's subordinate status at work, while saving the government millions of roubles. In the post-war period, urban women spent at least an hour a day on shopping, then another one and a half to two hours preparing food and cleaning up. In the countryside, running water, indoor plumbing and central heating remained almost non-existent. Rural women, facing empty shelves in village shops, had to travel

50 Susan Bridger, *Women in the Soviet Countryside: Women's Roles in Rural Development in the Soviet Union* (Cambridge: Cambridge University Press, 1987), pp. 19, 46–9; Donald Filtzer, *Soviet Workers and De-stalinization: The Consolidation of the Modern System of Soviet Production Relations, 1953–1964* (Cambridge: Cambridge University Press, 1992), pp. 104, 193–4.

periodically to a nearby city to stock up on necessities. Roughly 13 per cent of children aged one to six could be accommodated in children's institutions, whereas over 75 per cent of women of childbearing age worked outside the home.[51]

Under Khrushchev's leadership, the state tried to ease the double burden, which prevented women from joining the labour force in the desired numbers. Besides, consumption and comfort had become an important dimension of the socialist promise, and failure to provide them, a source of humiliation internationally.[52] Khrushchev redirected resources away from defence and heavy industry and towards consumer-related production for the first time since the industrialisation drive of the 1930s. The government undertook vast new housing projects: between 1955 and 1964, the state's housing stock nearly doubled. Many of the new structures, although poorly built, were nevertheless supplied with heat and water. The number of pre-school institutions increased, providing spaces for 22.5 per cent of eligible children by 1965 – about half of urban children, less than 12 per cent of rural ones. The standard of living improved modestly. However, because most women worked outside the home, the need remained greater. Women still had to compensate with their time and energy for the many shortcomings of the Soviet production and distribution system – figuring out where to obtain scarce goods and cultivating the personal relations that provided access to them, standing in queues and performing by hand the work that Westerners performed by machine. Women's 'titanic efforts' kept the Soviet system functioning.[53] Their onerous double burden prevented them from upgrading skills and advancing on the job; prevented most from even seeking more demanding and well-paid employment, because such employment took more energy than most women had. As a result, many women filled positions for which they were over-qualified. Ironically, such decisions confirmed people's prejudices about women's inability to perform skilled or responsible work.

Under Leonid Brezhnev the leadership finally reformed family law. In December 1965, a new divorce law simplified procedures and reduced costs. A new family law of 1968 permitted paternity suits and enabled mothers to eliminate the blank space on the birth certificate of an out-of-wedlock child.

---

51 Michael Sacks, *Women's Work in Soviet Russia: Continuity in the Midst of Change* (New York: Praeger, 1976).
52 Susan Reid, ' "Masters of the Earth": Gender and Destalinization in Soviet Reformist Painting of the Khrushchev Thaw', *Gender and History* 11, 2 (July 1999): 295–9.
53 Alla Sariban, 'The Soviet Woman: Support and Mainstay of the Regime', in Tatyana Mamonova (ed.), *Women and Russia: Feminist Writings from the Soviet Union* (Boston: Beacon Press, 1984), p. 208.

It also contained a definition of rape that included forced sexual intercourse between spouses. Birth control became available on a limited basis, mainly barrier methods, intra-uterine devices, and the condoms that men half-jokingly referred to as 'galoshes' and often refused to use. Without abandoning the priority given to heavy industry and defence, the leadership nevertheless redirected greater resources to consumer goods. By the mid-1970s, about half of Soviet families owned a refrigerator and two-thirds, a washing machine; the places in childcare centres had grown to accommodate about 45 per cent of pre-school children. Still, improvement was relative, shortages remained endemic and women continued to bear a heavy double burden.

Growing numbers of women expressed discontent with their situation. A survey published in 1970 found that 50 per cent of women who declared themselves unhappily married were dissatisfied with the division of labour in their household.[54] Discontent spread to the countryside, where the educational level of rural women had risen substantially in the post-war period. By 1979, almost half of the rural female population over the age of ten had received secondary or higher education. Well-educated rural women became far less inclined than their mothers to tolerate lack of consumer amenities and low-paying jobs that required heavy labour. In the European part of the Soviet Union, the outcome was massive migration of rural women away from the countryside and to the cities in pursuit of higher education and more appealing work. Men, faced with a 'bride problem', abandoned collective farms, leaving behind them dying villages, where only ageing women laboured.[55]

Everywhere in the European sectors of the Soviet Union, although not in Central Asia, urbanisation and women's rising expectations led to a reduction of the birth rate and increase in divorce. The birth rate steadily dropped, from 26.7 births per 1,000 people in 1950, to 24.9 in 1960, to 23.8 in 1970, to 22.53 in 1980. Divorce rates doubled between 1963 and 1974; by 1978 a third of all marriages ended in divorce, half in Moscow and St Petersburg. Divorce also grew more common in the countryside. Women initiated most divorces, often citing men's alcohol abuse as the primary reason. To the leadership, the declining birth rate and family instability appeared a threat to productivity and military strength, and aroused fears that the European population of the Soviet Union would become a minority.

54 Lapidus, *Women and Soviet Society*, p. 283.
55 Susan Allott, 'Soviet Rural Women: Employment and Family Life', in Barbara Holland (ed.), *Soviet Sisterhood* (Bloomington: Indiana University Press, 1985), pp. 197–202.

Debate on the 'woman question' intensified. Women as a 'demographic resource' set the tone, as scholars and experts explored ways to induce women to bear more children. Some methods, such as encouraging women to leave the workforce, they ruled out immediately. The economy still depended on women's labour, and besides, ideology taught that labour provided the key to women's emancipation. Introducing part-time work and flexible schedules, which many women requested, was discussed but never implemented. Instead, the leadership offered more legal protection and financial incentives to mothers. Thus, according to the new family code of 1968, it became illegal for a man to divorce his wife without her consent while she was pregnant or raising a child under the age of one. In addition to the already existing, fully paid maternity leave of fifty-six days before and after birth, in March 1981, the government introduced a partially paid leave for working mothers, to enable them to care for a child up to the age of one. Women (but not men) gained the option of taking an additional six months of unpaid leave, with no loss of position or job status, replacing the previous policy, which offered a year's unpaid leave. Women also received a lump sum payment of 50 roubles for their first child, with double that amount for the second and third. These policy changes failed to affect the birth rate, however. Starting in 1960, abortions outnumbered live births every year, and were the primary cause of the decline.[56]

Concern with family instability permitted critics to attack women's alleged 'emancipation' for the first time. Ever since women began to work outside the home, men had lost 'the title of family breadwinner', 'experts' declared. Without this role, 'the very earth slips from beneath [a man's] feet'. Newly publicised social problems, such as hooliganism and alcoholism, were blamed on women's failure to be yielding and feminine. A truly feminine woman could even cure the problems of men: 'Marriage with a really feminine girl instills in a man two things. On the one hand, he becomes more masculine from the need to protect and defend her, and on the other hand, sharp traits in his character soften; gradually, he becomes more tender and kind.'[57] To preserve marital harmony, articles warned young rural women to avoid jealousy or possessiveness, and most importantly, not to nag.[58] Many women came to believe that the much-vaunted emancipation, rather than incomplete emancipation, was the source of their difficult lives.

56 Williams, 'Abortion and Women's Health', p. 137.
57 Lynne Attwood, 'The New Soviet Man and Woman – Soviet Views on Psychological Sex Differences', in Holland, *Soviet Sisterhood*, p. 73.
58 Allott, 'Soviet Rural Women', p. 194.

## Gorbachev and after

Criticisms of the shortcomings in women's emancipation and complaints that emancipation had gone too far both intensified in the Gorbachev era. At a conference in January 1987, members of the Soviet Women's Committee, an officially sponsored organisation hitherto utterly loyal, launched biting critiques of numerous party policies involving women. The head of the Committee, the former astronaut Valentina Tereshkova, accused the leadership of disregarding women workers' health and implied that men in positions of authority blocked the advance of women. Speakers even referred to infant mortality, a topic so sensitive that for decades no statistical information about it had been published. Noting that the Soviet Union's infant mortality rate exceeded rates in capitalist countries, they blamed the inadequacies of Soviet medical care and environmental pollution.[59] Their statements prepared the way for still more radical critiques. For the first time since 1930, the accusation that the Soviet Union was 'patriarchal' appeared in print. The annual yearbook *Women in the USSR*, having hitherto celebrated Soviet success in emancipating women, in 1990 offered instead a depressing summary of women's working conditions.

At the same time, the 'back to the home movement' erupted into the open. Male candidates in the election campaign of 1989 repeatedly called for the 'emancipation' of women from the double burden by returning them to the home. Increasingly, political leaders, the media and even the general public embraced the idea that women should withdraw from the workforce. The 'back to the home' movement was usually couched in the language of women's choice: women could be *either* workers *or* mothers; it was their choice.[60] But if 'choice' was the language, policy pointed in a different direction. Virtually every policy initiative aimed to encourage women to bear and raise children, rather than help women advance on the job or combat discrimination at the workplace. In 1987, two weeks were added to the period of fully paid maternity leave, extending it from fifty-six to seventy days after the birth, and the period of partially paid maternity leave was extended from one year to eighteen months. Women also gained up to fourteen days' paid leave each year to care for a sick child. Making the pro-natalist intent of such legislation clear, its provisions were introduced gradually, starting in the regions with the lowest birth rates. In the context of Gorbachev's economic reforms, this legislation disadvantaged working women. Generous in principle, the legislation failed

59 Buckley, *Women and Ideology*, pp. 201–3.
60 Sue Bridger, Rebecca Kay and Kathryn Pinnick, *No More Heroines? Russia, Women and the Market* (New York: Routledge, 1996), p. 26.

to obligate the government to pay for the leaves it decreed. Instead, employers bore the cost of funding maternity-related leaves, as they had for years. Now, however, enterprises had to watch their budgets carefully and consequently, when they laid off workers, women with children were often first to go.[61]

With the fall of Gorbachev, the state completely abandoned the responsibility it had assumed in 1917 as an agent of women's emancipation and social welfare. The results were both positive and negative. Negatives included a dramatic decline in women's standard of living. Millions of women lost their jobs. Poverty became feminised. By the late 1990s, at least a quarter and perhaps as much as half of the Russian population qualified as 'poor' or 'very poor', and over two-thirds of those poor were female. In 1990, responsibility for childcare establishments was transferred from the federal to the local level, with no provision made for funding. Between 1990 and 1995, the number of children in nurseries and kindergartens declined from 9 million to 6 million. The cost of existing places escalated.[62] Such changes raised serious obstacles to women's work outside the home, although some studies suggested that on the whole, women coped better than men in the new economy, and that younger women, presumably unburdened by children, adapted to it successfully.

The quality of life deteriorated. Divorce rates rose, as did rates of mortality. Between 1990 and 1997, women's life expectancy at birth dropped from 74.3 to 72.8; men's dropped even more drastically. The birth rate declined as well, from 13.4 per 1,000 in 1990 to 8.6 per 1,000 in 1997. Between 1991 and 2000, the population of Russia decreased by 3 million.[63] Motherhood itself became more dangerous as a result of maternal ill-health and the drastic deterioration of the public health system. Between 1987 and 1993, the number of mothers who died during pregnancy or in childbirth rose from 49.3 to 70 for every 100,000 births; by 1998, the number had dropped to 50, still more than twice the average European level of 22. Women's sexuality became commodified: product advertisements featured semi or fully nude women; job advertisements sometimes openly solicited women's sexual services. The traffic in women from the former Soviet Union to Asia, the Middle East, Europe and the United States became an internationally recognised problem.

On the positive side, the collapse of the Soviet era also ended the state's monopoly on defining women's emancipation and brought new opportunities

61 Judith Shapiro, 'The Industrial Labor Force', in Mary Buckley (ed.), *Perestroika and Soviet Women* (New York: Cambridge University Press, 1992), p. 26.
62 Bertram Silverman and Murray Yanowitch, *New Rich, New Poor, New Russia: Winners and Losers on the Russian Road to Capitalism* (Armonk, N.Y.: M. E. Sharpe, 1997), p. 73.
63 'Russians Vanishing', *New York Times*, 6 Dec. 2000, p. 8

for women to organise and express themselves. By the mid-1990s, hundreds of women's groups had registered with Russia's Ministry of Justice; countless more operated 'unofficially'. Professional women, their thinking stimulated by foreign travel and contact with Western feminists, led many of the feminist-oriented organisations. Groups that sought to improve the lot of women adopted a range of strategies, almost none of them permissible in the Soviet period. They organised conferences; campaigned for women candidates and against the war in Chechnya; ran charity events to assist women and children; established support groups for single mothers or women artists and rape crisis centres and domestic violence hotlines; offered retraining opportunities; published journals and newsletters and much, much more. Gender and women's studies centres generated women-oriented scholarship; young scholars began to explore hitherto neglected realms of women's experience. Women writers, more numerous than ever before, experimented with new forms of expression.

The movement scored one of its greatest victories in 1992, when the Supreme Soviet considered a bill on the 'Protection of the family, motherhood, fatherhood and childhood' that would have seriously eroded women's civil rights. Had the bill been passed, the family rather than the individual would have become the basis of many civil rights, such as owning an apartment or a plot of land. The law would have required women with children under fourteen to work no more than thirty-five hours a week. The women's movement successfully mobilised to defeat the bill.[64] But such clear-cut victories were few. Women experienced difficulty placing woman-oriented concerns on the political agenda. The Soviet regime had appropriated the language of women's emancipation, making it difficult to discuss women-related issues. Once quotas for female representation ended, the number of women elected to governing bodies declined precipitously. From over a third of delegates to Republic-level Supreme Soviets in the 1970s and 1980s, the proportion of women dropped to 5.4 per cent in Russia and 7 per cent in Ukraine.[65] Despite the efforts of feminists and other women activists, politics remained a man's game, even as the arena expanded.

Yet women enjoyed greater success in informal sectors of power and the cultural sphere. For the first time since 1917, autonomous organisations offered women the possibility of actively shaping social change. Everywhere, the end of

---

64 Valerie Sperling, *Organizing Women in Contemporary Russia: Engendering Transition* (New York: Cambridge University Press, 1999), p. 114.
65 Mary Buckley, 'Adaptation of the Soviet Women's Committee: Deputies' Voices from "Women of Russia"', in Mary Buckley (ed.), *Post-Soviet Women: From the Baltic to Central Asia* (New York: Cambridge University Press, 1997), p. 162.

the state's monopoly on media has meant the end of its monopoly on images of women, too. Women artists, film-makers, journalists, television personalities and writers have presented the public with a profusion of images of women: 'in contrast to the unified "ideal mother and worker" of the Soviet period, there are now a myriad of masculine and feminine types'.[66] These have complicated and enriched ideas about womanhood, and offer alternatives to the essentialist notions left over from the late Soviet era, still propounded by conservatives and some experts. Nevertheless, essentialist notions remain powerful. Not least among the ironies of the Soviet legacy is the intensely gendered nature of the backlash against it. Rejecting the 'emancipation' that Stalinism celebrated, many post-Soviet Russians have nevertheless embraced the domesticity that became its counterpart. A blend of Soviet and pre-revolutionary gender discourses, and linked to dreams of national revival, these ideas have assumed new life in the vacuum left by Communism.

66 Hillary Pilkington, *Gender, Generation and Identity in Contemporary Russia* (New York: Routledge, 1996), p. 16.

# 18

# Non-Russians in the Soviet
# Union and after

JEREMY SMITH

The end of the First World War was followed by a total reorganisation of the
political geography of Europe and parts of Asia, not so much as a direct
result of the defeat of Germany and her allies, as through the break-up
of the three great land-based empires of the region – the Russian, Austro-
Hungarian and Ottoman. From the rubble of the latter two, new nation-
states emerged. From the Russian Empire, some nations followed suit –
Finland, Poland, Latvia, Estonia and Lithuania – but for the others the outcome was different. Although Lenin avowedly espoused a doctrine of national
self-determination similar in many ways to US President Woodrow Wilson's
on which the new East European order was based, after a few years all the
remaining territories of the Russian Empire had been incorporated into the
world's first socialist state, renamed in 1923 as the Union of Soviet Socialist
Republics, or Soviet Union. Instead of encouraging outright independence,
Lenin and his successors implemented nation-building policies within a territorially defined federal structure. The constitutional structure of the Soviet
Union and many elements of the early policies remained largely unchanged
until 1991. In other respects, however, treatment of individual nationalities
varied greatly while an increasingly overt elevation of the political and cultural dominance of the Russian nation contradicted earlier policies. The incorporation of Latvia, Estonia, Lithuania and Moldova into the USSR after the
Second World War further upset the balance of a system that collapsed in
1991.

   The nineteenth century was the high-point of nation-building in Western
Europe, and in Eastern Europe minorities also began to articulate national
demands. In only a handful of cases, however, did national movements based
on the intelligentsia manage to obtain anything like broad popular support.
This was especially true of the Russian Empire, where from the 1880s onwards
the tsars' policies of Russification initially succeeded in further radicalising

the nationalist intelligentsia while in most cases limiting the spread of their influence.[1]

The general radicalisation which spread across all three empires as a result of the First World War greatly enhanced popular support for nationalist leaders. With central authority diminishing by the day, and the Western allies keen on promoting the development of nation-states across Europe and the Middle East,[2] national parties across the Russian Empire shifted their demands from support for broad autonomy and rights to insistence on outright independence.

Ukraine led the way, with the formation of the Ukrainian Central Rada under the presidency of the popular historian Mykhailo Hrushevsky on 17 March 1917. The Rada's First Universal of 23 June declared the right of the Ukrainian people to order their own lives without breaking away from Russia. In Baku, Tiflis and elsewhere in Transcaucasia, effective power lay with socialist-dominated soviets, which sought to work with the Provisional Government. A series of all-Russian Muslim Congresses affirmed the right of Muslims to autonomy within Russia. The Provisional Government, however, dragged its feet over both the constitutional structure of the post-tsarist state and the question of land reform, which was crucial to the interests of the vast majority of non-Russians, and the demand for independence was raised with growing frequency. The Bolshevik revolution in October 1917 marked, for many national leaders, the end of any hope of autonomy or federalism within a democratic Russian state. The Rada declared Ukrainian independence on 25 January 1918, and a Transcaucasian Sejm made up of Georgian, Armenian and Azerbaijani representatives followed suit on 22 April, only to split into three fully independent republics a month later. The fourth Muslim Congress held in Kokand in November–December declared autonomy for Turkestan, but soon became a focus for both Russian and non-Russian anti-Bolshevik forces in the region.

By this time, however, most of the non-Russian regions were engulfed by the civil war. As well as the Reds and Whites, the war was fought between independent peasant and nationalist armies fighting for local self-rule. No less than eight separate armies were active on Ukrainian soil at some point between 1918 and 1920.[3] The nationalist forces of Simon Petliura and Denikin's

1 Andreas Kappeler, *The Russian Empire: A Multiethnic History* (London and New York, Longman, 2001).
2 Aviel Roshwald, *Ethnic Nationalism and the Fall of Empires: Central Europe, Russia and the Middle East, 1914–1923* (London: Routledge, 2001).
3 Arthur E. Adams, *Bolsheviks in the Ukraine: The Second Campaign, 1918–1919* (New Haven: Yale University Press, 1963); Jurij Borys, *The Sovietization of Ukraine, 1917–1923* (Edmonton: Canadian Institute of Ukrainian Studies, 1980).

White Army were finally defeated by November 1920, although the Ukrainian peasant bands under the anarchist Nestor Makhno continued to disrupt Soviet power until the following summer. In Central Asia resistance lasted longer in the form of the 'Basmachestvo' – a broad and disparate movement made up of a loose alliance of politically motivated opponents of Bolshevism and pan-Turkists together with local warlords. Although the movement was never united or organised enough to pose any serious threat to Soviet power, it continued to cause disruption until the end of the 1920s.[4] In Transcaucasia, following the withdrawal of Turkish forces in the summer of 1918, the three independent republics survived with little interference until Soviet power was established in Azerbaijan in April 1920, in Armenia in December and in Georgia the following February.

Richard Pipes's account of the formation of the Soviet Union describes the establishment of Bolshevik rule in these areas essentially as a series of military campaigns in which the Red Army eventually overwhelmed weak national armies.[5] Only in Georgia, however, was the picture almost as straightforward as this. Elsewhere a number of complex factors undermined the independent governments. Outside Transcaucasia, workers and administrators in the cities were predominantly Russian, even where the surrounding countryside was populated by non-Russian peasants, providing an urban base for Bolshevism and opposition to separation from Russia. Bolshevik promises of land reform and the guarantee of national rights appealed to many non-Russians, among whom the idea of independence had weak roots in any case. In some areas, the Bolsheviks were able to exploit splits in the national movement and base Sovietisation on one or other sympathetic group or party, as with the Azerbaijani socialist Hummet Party. In Armenia, the Dashnaks reluctantly accepted Soviet power as the lesser evil when faced with the imminent possibility of invasion from Turkey. Finally, even where the national governments enjoyed broad popular support, they were led mostly by intellectuals with little or no experience of either government administration or military affairs and whose political programme was not coherent or developed enough to satisfy the aspirations of even their natural supporters.[6]

By the middle of 1921, then, Soviet power extended across most of the former territory of the Russian Empire. The Bolsheviks then faced the problem of

---

4 Marie Broxup, 'The Basmachis', *Central Asian Survey* 2 (1983): 57–82; Mustafa Chokaev, 'The Basmaji Movement in Turkestan', *Asiatic Review* 24 (1928): 273–88.
5 Richard Pipes, *The Formation of the Soviet Union: Communism and Nationalism, 1917–1923*, Revised edn (Cambridge, Mass.: Harvard University Press, 1997).
6 Orest Subtelny, *Ukraine: A History* (Toronto: University of Toronto Press, 1989), pp. 353–4.

how to administer the non-Russian areas and to build a socialist society there. On the one hand, they needed to ensure at least the passive support of the local population, and Lenin in particular was concerned to avoid any impression that the new Soviet state was a continuation of the old Russian-dominated one, and to hold up Soviet rule as a shining example to anti-colonial movements elsewhere in the world. On the other hand, the non-Russian nationalities were overwhelmingly peasant in composition, had even lower levels of literacy than Russians, and were less receptive to the demands of socialism than were Russian workers, leaving them vulnerable to the propaganda efforts of nationalists and religious leaders. From early 1918 onwards, the numerous smaller nationalities of Soviet Russia itself were granted limited self-rule in the form of autonomous republics and regions, whose purpose was both to satisfy the national aspirations of the population and sections of their elites, and to provide an avenue for the introduction of socialism together with cultural and economic development. In the summer of 1922 Joseph Stalin, as commissar for nationality affairs, drew up a plan which would have extended this system to Ukraine, Belorussia and Transcaucasia, by incorporating them directly into the existing Russian Soviet Federative Socialist Republic (RSFSR). Lenin opposed this on the basis that the overt subordination of the major nationalities to a Russian state would alienate their populations and send out the wrong message internationally. The alternative scheme he proposed was a formal federation of equals into what eventually became the Union of Soviet Socialist Republics at the end of 1923.

The constitutional structure was only one part of early Soviet policies towards the non-Russians. Equally important was the process of *korenizatsiia* – roughly translated as 'indigenisation' – a set of policies aimed at developing and promoting national identity: the recruitment and promotion of members of the local nationality in the Communist Party and Soviet system; positive discrimination in other areas of employment; the creation or standardisation of national languages and scripts, together with national cultures based on earlier writers and folk traditions; the extension of local self-rule for national minorities outside the republics through a system of national soviets; and building up a network of national schools with instruction in the mother tongue for all non-Russians.[7] Some historians have interpreted these measures as a

7 Hélène Carrère d'Encausse, *The Great Challenge: Nationalities and the Bolshevik State 1917–1930* (New York and London: Holmes and Meier, 1992), pp. 157–94; Terry Martin, *The Affirmative Action Empire: Nations and Nationalism in the Soviet Union, 1923–1939* (Ithaca, N.Y., and London: Cornell University Press, 2001), pp. 1–56; Jeremy Smith, 'The Education of National Minorities: The Early Soviet Experience', *Slavonic and East European Review* 75 (1997): 281–307.

product of the weakness of Bolshevik appeal to the non-Russians, as a series of temporary concessions to national feeling.[8] Terry Martin, however, emphasises that the policies of *korenizatsiia* went far beyond what might have been needed to ensure loyalty from the non-Russians. Rather than representing a concession, the policies were aimed at undermining anti-Soviet nationalism through promoting national identity in a Soviet form.[9]

*Korenizatsiia* had a profound impact in the non-Russian republics. By 1927 local nationality representation in Soviet executive committees in the republics ranged from 68.3 per cent (Turkmen SSR) to 80.5 per cent (Armenian SSR).[10] By the end of the 1920s, the Communists were claiming that almost all children were receiving education in their mother tongue.[11] Opportunities in higher education also opened up for non-Russians with the nativisation of universities in Tashkent, Belorussia and Ukraine, and the operation of a quota system across the country.

This strategy was not without problems. From the beginning, it aroused opposition among local Russians who felt not only a loss of their previous privileges, but actual negative discrimination, while Communist leaders in the republics were frequently seen to be pushing the policies to the extent that they were denounced as nationalists. The result was a series of local crises and clashes between different wings of the republican Communist parties, which reached their most acute in Ukraine.[12]

The first signs of a change of direction in policy came in 1928–9 with a series of high-profile show trials of intellectuals and less public purges of leading republican figures in Ukraine, Belorussia, the Tatar Autonomous Soviet Republic, Crimea and Kazakhstan. A more general assault on the nation-building approaches of the 1920s was signalled at the turn of the decade over the question of the interpretation of Russian history. In the 1920s a new school of history (the 'Pokrovsky School'), supported by the regime, interpreted the Russian Empire as an exploitative, brutal colonial regime. But in the 1930s the Russian people, history and culture were advanced as being superior to those of non-Russians, and the Russian Empire was now portrayed as having brought enlightenment and other benefits to the territories it had conquered. This revival of the Russians was symbolised by a law of 1938 which made

---

8 E.g. Stephen Blank, *The Sorcerer as Apprentice – Stalin as Commissar of Nationalities, 1917–1924* (Westport, Conn.: Greenwood Press, 1994).
9 Martin, *An Affirmative Action Empire*, pp. 2–9.
10 *Natsional'naia politika VKP(b) v tsifrakh* (Moscow: Kommunisticheskaia Akademiia, 1930), pp. 209–12.
11 Ibid., pp. 278–9.     12 Martin, *The Affirmative Action Empire*, pp. 75–124; 211–72.

Russian, already the effective lingua franca of the Soviet Union, a compulsory subject of study in all schools.

These changes did not amount to a policy of Russification. Religion and other practises, such as nomadism, did come under attack, threatening the traditional way of life for minorities,[13] as well as for Russians, as a consequence of the ideological assault and the drive to industrialise the country. But throughout the 1930s, a renewed emphasis on non-Russian folk cultures was exemplified by a series of festivals held in Moscow, and language rights and the territorial structure were not threatened. The tone, however, had shifted from one of promoting entirely separate national cultures to emphasising a 'Brotherhood of Peoples' in which different cultures could share a common space within the Soviet framework, and in which the leading place went to the Russians. By the end of the decade, those national leaders who had risen to the most senior positions in the republics in the 1920s had been eliminated, without exception, before or during the Great Terror, opening the way for a new generation of leaders who perhaps did not share their commitment to nation-building.

The shifts in policy and tone of the 1930s are open to a variety of interpretations. For those historians such as Pipes and Blank who viewed the approach of the 1920s as a purely temporary concession, the turn against national leaders and cultures was merely a recognition of the fact that Soviet power was securely established and an 'internationalist' programme of national assimilation could now be implemented without fear. For some, most notably the historian Robert Conquest, the turn against non-Russian nationalities went much further, amounting in some cases to a policy of virtual genocide. In particular, controversy has raged over the devastating famines of 1932–3, which hit the Ukrainian (and Kazakh) countryside to a far greater extent than it did in Russia. Conquest has argued that the famine was deliberately engineered by Stalin in an effort to break the back of the Ukrainian nation through the purposeful starvation of a large part of its population.[14] Others have challenged both his figures and interpretation, concluding that the famine was a natural disaster, albeit one which the leadership did little to alleviate, and which also devastated Russian areas.[15]

---

13 Alexandre Bennigsen and Chantal Lemercier-Quelquejay, *Islam in the Soviet Union* (London: Pall Mall, 1967), pp. 138–52.
14 Robert Conquest, *The Harvest of Sorrow* (London: Hutchinson, 1986).
15 R. W. Davies, M. B. Tauger and S. G. Wheatcroft, 'Stalin, Grain Stocks, and the Famine of 1932–1933', *Slavic Review* 54 (1995): 642–57.

More recently scholars have predominantly accepted the picture of the 1920s as an era of nation-building, and have offered various interpretations of the new direction in the 1930s. The persistence of the federal form and the emphasis on national cultures has led Yuri Slezkine to underplay the extent of changes in the 1930s.[16] Other interpretations invariably see the change in national policies against the background of the dramatic political, social, economic and international developments of the decade. Geoffrey Hosking has noted that the destruction of traditional ways of life associated with collectivisation and industrialisation was an inevitable consequence of economic modernisation which applied to Russians and non-Russians alike.[17] But in itself this is not enough to explain the more positive attitude to Russians vis-à-vis other nationalities in the 1930s. A direct consequence of the combined impact of collectivisation and industrialisation was a massive mobility of population across the Soviet Union as peasants flocked to the cities, and workers and administrators moved from the more industrialised regions to those embarking on the rapid building of industry. In particular, this meant a movement of Russians into the non-Russian republics. The proportion of Russians in the overall population increased between 1926 and 1939 from 21.2 per cent to 40.3 per cent in Kazakhstan and from 52.7 per cent to 72 per cent in the Buriat ASR, for example.[18] Given that a high proportion of these new migrants were engineers and skilled workers, maintaining the earlier anti-Russian stance in the republics was no longer tenable.

A further factor was the growing prospect of the Soviet Union being involved in a major war, the fear of which increased in the late 1920s and early 1930s. The possibility of protracted conflict raised the importance of the loyalty of the disgruntled members of the largest nationality, the Russians.[19] The overt appeal to Russian national feeling contained in the new history books and, increasingly, in the public statements of Stalin and other leaders, underlined the shift from the development of separate national identities towards a Brotherhood of Nations united under the Soviet system and in which Russians had pride of place.[20]

---

16 Yuri Slezkine, 'The Soviet Union as a Communal Apartment, or How a Socialist State Promoted Ethnic Particularism', *Slavic Review* 53, 2 (Summer 1994): 414–52; 436–44.

17 Geoffrey Hosking, *A History of the Soviet Union* (London: Fontana, 1985), p. 249.

18 Robert J. Kaiser, *The Geography of Nationalism in Russia and the USSR* (Princeton: Princeton University Press, 1994), p. 118.

19 Martin, *An Affirmative Action Empire*, pp. 62–7.

20 Ronald Grigor Suny, *The Soviet Experiment: Russia, the USSR, and the Successor States* (Oxford: Oxford University Press, 1998), pp. 287–8.

Connected with this new emphasis was a change in the theoretical underpinning of attitudes towards nationalities in the second half of the 1930s, which now tended to treat national characteristics as something primordial and unchanging.[21] This was no mere theoretical nicety. In the 1930s this thinking was manifested in campaigns of terror against specific groups, the so-called 'national operations' against Cossacks (now regarded as an ethnic group) and, from 1935, Poles, Germans and Finns. The policy reached new levels in the autumn of 1937 with the decision to deport every single ethnic Korean from a large area in the Far East. This set a precedent for even more large-scale deportations during the course of the Second World War. Between September 1941 and November 1944 the following nationalities were deported: 382,000 Germans of the Volga region; 73,737 Karachai; 131,271 Kalmyks; 407,690 Chechens; 92,074 Ingush; 42,666 Balkars; 202,000 Crimean Tatars; 200,000 Meskhetian Turks.[22] The operations were carried out by NKVD squads descending on towns and villages with no notice given to the population – in the Crimea, Tatars were given fifteen minutes to leave their homes[23] – and typically were completed over the course of a few days. Every man, woman and child was loaded into cattle trucks and transported by train across the country to Kazakhstan or Siberia in a journey lasting weeks. Lacking food, water and sanitation, up to half died on the journey. On arrival at their new destinations, the populations were often abandoned on arid land without housing and were left at the mercy of local officials and dependent on charity. Apart from the Meskhetians, each of the deported nationalities had inhabited an autonomous republic, which was subsequently renamed or simply disappeared from the map. The Balkars, Chechens, Ingush, Karachai and Kalmyks had their rights restored by Khrushchev in 1956. The Germans and Meskhetians were never officially allowed to return to their homelands, while many of the Crimean Tatars, after years of protest, eventually returned to the Crimea without official sanction.

Such a large expenditure of NKVD manpower, railway engines and rolling stock at a time when a war was still to be won defies rational explanation. Preventative measures against ethnic Germans can perhaps be explained, and can reasonably be compared to the simultaneous internment of Japanese

21 Terry Martin, 'Modernization or Neo-traditionalism? Ascribed Nationality and Soviet Primordialism', in Sheila Fitzpatrick (ed.), *Stalinism: New Directions* (London: Routledge, 2000), pp. 348–67.
22 Figures from Isabelle Kreindler, 'The Soviet Deportation of Nationalities: A Summary and Update', *Soviet Studies* 38 (1986): 387–405; 387.
23 Ayshe Seytmuratova, 'The Elders of the New National Movement: Recollections', in Edward A. Allworth (ed.), *The Tatars of Crimea: Return to the Homeland* (Durham, N.C., and London: Duke University Press, 1998), pp. 155–179; 155.

Americans in the USA. Similar thinking probably underlay the deportation of the Meskhetian Turks, who inhabited an area of Georgia too close to the Turkish border for comfort. But in the Crimea, which was under German occupation for some time, it seems that anecdotal evidence of collaboration with the occupying forces on the part of a small number of Tatars was enough to convince Stalin and the head of the NKVD, Lavrentii Beria, that the entire national group was worthy of punishment.[24] With the Chechens and Ingush, accusations of collaboration with the Germans were barely credible, and it is more likely that this was a matter of settling scores with peoples who had proved particularly resistant to Soviet rule before and during the war,[25] while the Balkars appear to have been deported on the whim of Beria as an afterthought to the Chechen and Ingush operations.[26] Whatever the exact reasoning, underpinning it was the assumption that all members of a given nationality should be tarred with the same brush.

Although most of the deported nations were eventually allowed to return to their homelands, the long-term consequences were serious. The territories from which they had been removed had been repopulated by others, causing grievances which stoked the ethnic conflicts that erupted in the North Caucasus in the 1980s and 1990s. For the Chechens in particular, the experience of exile produced a hardening of attitudes and an even deeper antipathy to Soviet or Russian rule.[27]

The deported peoples were not the only nationalities to suffer in the course of the Second World War. Ukraine and Belorussia witnessed some of the most destructive battles of the war and were occupied for much of it by a Nazi regime which treated all Slavs as inferior *Untermenschen*, and planned to rid the territories of much of their population in order to make space for Aryan settlers. Greatest suffering was reserved for the substantial Jewish population of the Soviet Union, up to a million of whom were exterminated in the Holocaust. Over 33,000 Jews were shot in the infamous Babii Yar ravine outside of Kiev, where they were joined by similar numbers of Ukrainians and Russians who had dared to put up resistance, while entire villages were wiped out in reprisal for partisan attacks – this in spite of the fact that many

---

24 Aleksander Nekrich, *The Punished Peoples: The Deportation and Fate of Soviet Minorities at the End of the Second World War* (New York: Norton, 1978), pp. 13–35.

25 Abdurahman Avtorkhanov, 'The Chechens and the Ingush during the Soviet Period and its Antecedents', in Marie Bennigsen Broxup (ed.), *The North Caucasus Barrier: The Russian Advance towards the Muslim World* (London: Hurst, 1992), pp. 146–94, 181–4.

26 *Tak eto bylo: natsional'nye repressii v SSSR 1919–1952 gody*, 3 vols. (Moscow: Insan, 1993), p. 265.

27 For the whole of this section, Pavel Polian, *Ne po svoei vole . . . Istoriia i geografiia prinudi-tel'nykh migratsii v SSSR* (Moscow: O.G.I–Memorial, 2001).

Ukrainians had initially welcomed the Germans in 1941 as liberators from the suffering they had endured in the previous decade. The scale of atrocities against the local population inspired many to take up arms behind enemy lines. By mid-1942 up to 100,000 partisans were operational, concentrated in Ukraine. Whatever their initial motivation, many of these partisan groups came to embrace a fully nationalist agenda, leading them to continue to wage their guerrilla war against the Soviets after the German forces were driven out. The Organisation of Ukrainian Nationalists continued to operate in the forests of Ukraine well into the 1950s.

For the rest of the Soviet population, the war meant a number of concessions from a regime desperate to mobilise resistance and enthusiasm for the war effort. While suspect nationalities were subjected to deportation, attempts were made to secure the loyalty of others through organisational and propaganda efforts. National units in the Red Army, abolished as recently as 1938, were restored. Particular attention was paid to publicising the part played by some national units in resisting invasion, such as the Kazakh division's role in the defence of Moscow.[28] The national heroes of the various non-Russian peoples, who had been lauded in the 1920s and vilified in the 1930s, were again restored to favour. National religions, as well as the Russian Orthodox Church, were granted new freedoms to function. The unity and common struggle of the peoples of the Soviet Union were stressed in propaganda, and were symbolised in victory when the Red Army flag was raised over the Reichstag in Berlin in 1945 by an ordinary Russian soldier, M. A. Egorov, together with a Georgian soldier, M. V. Kantaria.

However, following the German occupation of Ukraine it had been Russia which supplied most of the manpower and industry behind the war effort, and it was the Russian people whose role was glorified above all others in official propaganda, especially in the ever more strident glorification of the heroes of Russia's past. The mood of the war led political leaders and academics so far as to declare open support for Russian nationalism. The emphasis was most famously illustrated in Stalin's well-known toast at the end of the war to 'the health of our Soviet people, and in the first place the Russian people . . . the most outstanding nation of all the nations forming the Soviet Union'.[29] In the later years of the war, this apparent contradiction between appeals to non-Russian national sentiment and affirmation of the leading role of the Russians was the cause of serious disputes between leading historians in the USSR, a conflict

28 Shirin Akiner, *The Formation of Kazakh Identity from Tribe to Nation-State* (London: Royal Institute of International Affairs, 1995), p. 49.
29 J. V. Stalin, *Works*, 18 vols. (London: Red Star Press, 1986), vol. XVI, p. 54.

which was ultimately resolved in favour of the pro-Russian line, setting the tone for propaganda and particular interpretations of Russian history for the remainder of the Soviet period.[30] In the post-war period, this line was reinforced by official condemnation of what had previously been considered important parts of national culture – the visual arts and epic poetry especially.[31]

Nevertheless, the net effect of wartime propaganda, the brutality of the Nazi occupation and the eventual victory of the Red Army were to provide the concept of the Brotherhood of Nations under the leadership of the Russians with an effective series of myths that served to promote a deeper sense of Soviet patriotism and affection for the USSR and its leadership than had been possible before the war.

One group of nationalities unable to subscribe to these myths were those that were newly incorporated into the USSR as a direct result of the war. Under the terms of the secret protocols of the Molotov–Ribbentrop pact of August 1939, Nazi Germany recognised the Soviet Union's right to determine the fate of eastern Poland, Bessarabia (eastern Romania), Latvia and Estonia, a sphere of influence that was later extended to include Lithuania. In September–October 1939, the three Baltic republics, which had gained independence in 1918, were forced to accept the stationing of Soviet troops under the pretext of the strategic demands of defence, making it easy for the Soviets to engineer Communist takeovers in the summer of 1940 and formal incorporation into the USSR. In the year before the German invasion, rapid steps were taken towards Sovietisation – nationalisation of industry, confiscation of all bank accounts above a minimal amount, expropriation of large estates, new curricula in the schools and universities. The process was completed following the reoccupation of the republics in 1945, culminating in full collectivisation of agriculture by the end of the decade.

Both the occupations of 1940 and the reoccupations of 1945 were followed by deportations on a massive scale. Unlike the other national deportations, these were targeted against specific groups – members of most political parties, army officers, high-ranking civil servants, clergymen, estate owners, anyone with a dubious past as a White or even an expelled Communist, anyone suspected of collaboration with the Nazis and so on. The numbers of those deported or killed was staggering: in 1940, 61,000 Estonians, 35,000 Latvians and

---

30 David Brandenberger, ' "... It is imperative to advance Russian nationalism as the first priority": Debates within the Stalinist Ideological Establishment, 1941–1945', in Ronald Grigor Suny and Terry Martin (eds.), *A State of Nations: Empire and Nation-Making in the Age of Lenin and Stalin* (Oxford and New York: Oxford University Press, 2001), pp. 275–99.

31 Ben Fowkes, *The Disintegration of the Soviet Union: A Study in the Rise and Triumph of Nationalism* (London: Macmillan, 1997), pp. 74–5.

39,000 Lithuanians; in 1945–6, a further 100,000 Lithuanians, 41,000 Estonians and 60,000 Latvians.[32] Caught between the twin evils of Nazi Germany and Stalin's Soviet Union, large numbers took to the forests and formed partisan units which fought against both sides, many of the 'Forest Brethren' holding out until 1952. Soviet control over the new territories was reinforced by a deliberate long-term policy of migration of Russians and other Slavs into the republics, causing a substantial demographic shift, especially in Estonia and Latvia. Thus, in Estonia the proportion of Estonians in the overall population fell from 88 per cent in 1939 to 76 per cent in 1950 and 61.5 per cent in 1989.

By annexing the Baltic republics and other territories, Stalin had not only secured a strategic advantage on his borders but had gone a long way towards obtaining for the Soviet Union the same borders that had bounded the Russian Empire. But the long-term costs for the USSR were high. Unlike most of the other nationalities who owed much of their sense of mass national identity to the nation-building period of the 1920s, for Lithuanians, Latvians and Estonians, nationhood was linked to the experience of independent statehood between 1918 and 1939. Incorporation into the Soviet Union remained for much of the population an occupation by a foreign power, and the massive influx of Russians after the war, often into top jobs, only served to further antagonise the locals. Lithuanians, Latvians and Estonians never really joined the Brotherhood of Peoples, and it is no coincidence that they played a major part in the events leading to the break-up of the Soviet Union in 1991.

In the last years of Stalin's life, the balance of national rights and republican powers established before the war and reinforced during it continued to consolidate. For one group, however, the situation took a dramatic turn for the worse. Before 1917, Jews had suffered more than any other nationality from official government policies, which in their turn spurred on popular anti-Semitism, culminating in a series of massacres or 'pogroms' of Jews in the late nineteenth and early twentieth centuries. A renewal of pogroms in the civil war, carried out primarily by anti-Bolsheviks, led thousands of Jews to see the Bolsheviks and the Red Army as their surest source of protection, many of them joining the ranks of the Communist Party, which already counted a number of Jews among its leading members. Jews benefited from the policies of *korenizatsiia* on top of the removal of former restrictions, and in the 1920s Jewish organisations, culture and Yiddish schools flourished, with an unusually

32 Aleksandras Shtroma, 'The Baltic States as Soviet Republics: Tensions and Contradictions', in Graham Smith (ed.), *The Baltic States: The National Self-Determination of Estonia, Latvia and Lithuania* (London: Macmillan, 1996), pp. 86–117; 87; Toivo U. Raun, *Estonia and the Estonians* (Stanford, Calif.: Hoover Institution Press, 1991), p. 181.

high proportion of Jews going into higher education. As the Jews did not have their own territory, this made them difficult to fit into the overall pattern of Soviet nationality policies that favoured the construction of distinct national regions and republics, a situation which the Soviet government, enthusiastically spurred on by the USSR President Mikhail Kalinin, sought to remedy by creating a Jewish autonomous region in Birobidzhan in the Far East.[33] Some historians, however, have seen the Birobidzhan project as a continuation of tsarist policies whose main aim was to transform Jews from traditional artisan and entrepreneurial occupations into productive agricultural labourers.[34] In any case, Birobidzhan did not attract enough Jewish migrants to act as an effective homeland or cultural centre for Soviet Jews, although at times it succeeded in attracting positive international attention, funds and even immigrants from the Americas.[35]

There is a good deal of anecdotal testimony to Stalin's personal anti-Semitism,[36] but in many respects Jewish life continued to prosper in the 1930s. Tens of thousands of Jews lost their lives in the Great Terror and Jewish culture, especially religion, was subject to restrictions similar to those imposed on other nationalities, including a marked reduction in university enrolment. After the suffering of the war years, Jews in the Soviet Union were subjected to a further attack. In 1944, leading members of the Jewish Anti-Fascist Committee (JAC), set up in 1942 to co-ordinate Jewish participation in the war effort and to attract international support, began to discuss the idea of an alternative homeland for the Jews in the Crimea or the Volga region. This was later to provide the pretext for accusations of 'bourgeois Jewish nationalism' and Zionism that culminated in the arrest and execution of former JAC leaders in 1952. In January 1948 the prominent Jewish actor Solomon Mikhoels died in mysterious circumstances, almost certainly murdered by the security services. Later that year a campaign against 'cosmopolitanism' provided the pretext for the harassment and arrest of leading Soviet Jews, the closure of theatres and other cultural institutions, and the disbanding of the JAC and other Jewish organisations. From 1948 to 1953, any Jew who had been active in politics or in Jewish culture lived in permanent fear of arrest, a fate

---

33  Chimen Abramsky, 'The Biro-Bidzhan Project, 1927–1959', in Lionel Kochan (ed.), *The Jews in Soviet Russia since 1917* (Oxford: Oxford University Press, 1978), pp. 64–77.

34  Robert Weinberg, 'Jews into Peasants? Solving the Jewish Question in Birobidzhan', in Yaacov Ro'i (ed.), *Jews and Jewish Life in Russia and the Soviet Union* (Ilford: Frank Cass, 1995), pp. 87–102; 88–91.

35  Robert Weinberg, *Stalin's Forgotten Zion: Birobidzhan and the Making of a Soviet Jewish Homeland* (Berkeley: University of California Press, 1998).

36  Edvard Radzinsky, *Stalin* (London: Hodder and Stoughton, 1996), pp. 24–6.

suffered by thousands of them.[37] A series of prominent articles and speeches raised the spectre of an international Jewish conspiracy to overthrow Soviet power. The campaign culminated in the so-called 'Doctors' Plot' early in 1953, when a number of leading Jewish doctors were arrested and charged with having caused the deaths of the former Politburo members Zhdanov and Shcherbakov and of plotting to kill Stalin and other leaders. Goaded on by official propaganda, popular anti-Semitism was turned against Jews from all walks of life. There is now strong evidence that Stalin, Malenkov and others were preparing a plan for the wholesale forced deportation of Jews from the western parts of the Soviet Union to Siberia, with the intention that up to half should die on the way.[38] They were spared this fate only by Stalin's death on 5 March 1953.

The Jews were the only nationality to be persecuted in this way in the post-war years. No clear explanation for the anti-Jewish campaign has yet emerged, but a combination of Stalin's personal anti-Semitism, fear that Jewish organisations would gain undue influence as a result of sympathy for the Holocaust and a foreign policy that supported new-found allies in the Arab world against the new Israeli state all played a role. Although the overt government campaigns died with Stalin, anti-Semitism remained a significant feature of Soviet life and the experience of 1948–53 did much to stimulate the movement for emigration among Soviet Jews in later years.

For other non-Russians, the post-war years were a period of reconstruction, of grief and of the consolidation of a sense of pride in the Soviet system. The overt appeals to Russian nationalism of the war and the subsequent anti-cosmopolitanism campaign encouraged some elements of the leadership to propose a more Russifying line, but by and large these were defeated. Thus proposals to abolish mother-tongue instruction in schools of the autonomous republics of the RSFSR beyond the fourth grade were abandoned in favour of retaining the principle of mother-tongue education for all.[39]

The union republics of the USSR played an important role in the competition for power which followed Stalin's death (1953–57). Of the Politburo contenders to succeed Stalin, Lavrentii Beria, Lazar Kaganovich and Nikita Khrushchev had all spent a significant period of their earlier careers in the

37 Nora Levin, *The Jews of the Soviet Union since 1917*, 2 vols. (London and New York: I. B.Tauris, 1990), vol. I, pp. 488–525; vol. II, pp. 527–50.
38 Iakov Etinger, 'The Doctors' Plot: Stalin's Solution to the Jewish Question', in Ro'i, *Jews and Jewish Life*, pp. 103–26.
39 Peter A. Blitstein, 'Nation-Building or Russification? Obligatory Russian Instruction in the Soviet Non-Russian School, 1938–1953', in Suny and Martin, *A State of Nations*, pp. 253–274; 263–7.

republics. Ultimately the balance of power could be decided by votes in the Central Committee of the CPSU, many of whose members came from the republics, especially Ukraine where both Khrushchev and Kaganovich had served. During the few months of his ascendancy prior to his arrest, Beria had time to launch an attack on Stalin's later nationality policies, accusing him of abandoning Leninist principles, and was able to initiate significant changes in republican leaderships which favoured local nationals over Russians, such as the replacement of Mel'nikov by Kirichenko as party leader in Ukraine. The general principle that the first party secretary in each republic should be a local national was established at this time. Beria also moved quickly to release the accused in the 'Doctors' Plot' from prison and to condemn the anti-Semitism of the late Stalin years.

Although 'activating remnants of bourgeois-nationalist elements in the union republics' was one of the charges laid against Beria at the time of his arrest in June 1953, the republics continued to enjoy advantages relative to their position in the late Stalin years. Khrushchev in particular used his position as General Secretary to promote former colleagues from Ukraine, increasing Ukrainian representation in the Central Committee from sixteen in 1952 to fifty-nine in 1961. Ukraine also benefited from the decision to transfer the Crimean peninsula from the RSFSR to Ukrainian jurisdiction in 1954, while the rehabilitation of most of the deported peoples in 1956–7 also signalled that non-Russians would no longer be subject to the kind of arbitrary treatment they had reason to fear under Stalin. In seeking to impose his authority over economic policy against his rival Malenkov, Khrushchev decentralised a number of economic ministries and the Ministry of Justice, considerably increasing the decision-making powers of the republics. While there was sound economic reasoning behind these moves, Khrushchev also reckoned that such measures might stand him in a more powerful position in any future inner-party conflicts.[40]

The strategy paid off. When his main rivals in the Politburo sought to remove him in June 1957, Khrushchev successfully appealed to the Central Committee, which was by now packed with supporters from Ukraine and other republics. But it would be a mistake to view Khrushchev as a keen supporter of the rights of non-Russians. After all, he owed much of his rise to the top of the Soviet system to the reputation he had earned in crushing all displays of Ukrainian nationalism after 1937. Having consolidated his power in 1957,

---

40 Gerhard Simon, *Nationalism and Policy Toward the Nationalities in the Soviet Union* (Boulder, Colo.: Westview Press, 1991), pp. 231–3.

Khrushchev soon moved to reverse most of the decentralising measures introduced in the preceding years. More significantly, he signalled a far-reaching ideological shift by abandoning talk of the 'Brotherhood of Peoples' in favour of the 'merging of peoples'.

It was inevitable that such a merged identity should be centred on the Slavic languages and cultures. Khrushchev took care to include other Slavs, especially Ukrainians, alongside Russians when it came to defining the leading nations of the state, as evidenced in both his promotions and his cultural policies. No doubt he was mindful of the need to retain his personal base of support among Ukrainians, but some commentators have noted another possible factor: the relatively high birth rate among the Soviet Union's Muslims compared to that of the Russians, which threatened their overall majority in the population.[41] Modernising economic strategies also led to a renewed period of internal migration as Russians and Ukrainians moved into less-developed regions.[42]

Greatest controversy surrounded Khrushchev's proposals for educational reform. The theses on education he presented in November 1958 included a provision, Article 19, which affected the status of non-Russian languages.[43] It gave parents the right to decide in which language their children should receive instruction, and gave schools in the republics the option to drop the teaching of a second language. In practice this meant abandoning Lenin's principle that every child should receive instruction in the mother tongue, while also removing the requirement for Russians in the republics to study the local language. The move was opposed by Communist leaders in almost all the republics, who feared that the move would undermine the position of the titular nationality. In Azerbaijan and Latvia, opposition went as far as refusing to implement the provisions of Article 19 in new republican laws on education, leading to the direct intervention of Moscow and high-level purges in both republics.[44]

The fears of the republic leaders were not immediately realised,[45] but in the longer term there was a substantial decline in the proportion of Ukrainians and Belorussians attending schools in the mother tongue, with Belorussian schools

41 John A. Armstrong, 'The Ethnic Scene in the Soviet Union: The View of the Dictatorship', in Rachel Denber (ed.), *The Soviet Nationality Reader: The Disintegration in Context* (Boulder, Colo.: Westview Press, 1992), pp. 227–56; 239.

42 Kaiser, *The Geography of Nationalism*, pp. 158–90.

43 George S. Counts, *Khrushchev and the Central Committee Speak on Education* (Pittsburgh: University of Pittsburgh Press, 1959), p. 30.

44 Yaroslav Bilinsky, 'The Soviet Education Laws of 1958–59 and Soviet Nationality Policy', *Soviet Studies* 14 (1962): 138–57.

45 Harry Lipset, 'The Status of National Minority Languages', *Soviet Studies* 19 (1967): 181–9; 183–4, 188.

disappearing altogether from the capital Minsk.[46] In the RSFSR itself, mother-tongue education declined dramatically. The number of languages used in schools fell from forty-seven in the early 1960s to seventeen by 1982, twelve of which were taught only as far as the fourth grade. Russian became the standard language of instruction across the North Caucasus.[47] The Russification of schools in Ukraine and Belorussia seems to have been confined mostly to the cities, and so could be explained as a process of natural assimilation rather than a deliberate policy, but for the national minorities of the RSFSR there was a clear policy of linguistic Russification implemented from Khrushchev's time onwards.

Under both Stalin and Khrushchev, republican leaders could consider themselves fortunate to stay in office any longer than a few years. By contrast, one of the central features of Leonid Brezhnev's period of office (1964–82) was the 'stability of cadres'. Nowhere was this policy more apparent than in the union republics. In Estonia, Johannes Käbin was appointed first secretary of the Estonian Communist Party by Stalin in 1950, and came close to out-surviving Brezhnev himself before his replacement in 1978, while in Uzbekistan Sharaf Rashidov stayed in his post from 1959 to 1983. The average length of service for a first secretary in a union republic under Brezhnev was eleven years. Similar levels of stability extended to other posts in the republican leaderships, which also tended to become more dominated by members of the titular nationality.[48] Republican leaders did not have a completely free hand, however. Petro Shelest', first secretary in Ukraine from 1963, pursued a policy of promoting Ukrainian culture and identity to an extent that was not acceptable to the leadership and was consequently dismissed in 1972. Although the Shelest' case established that there were limits to the activities of republican leaders, for the most part they were allowed to run their republics without interference from the Centre. Especially in Transcaucasia and Central Asia, a pattern emerged of long-standing leaders building up a personal power base often centred on members of their own extended families or clans, and riddled with corruption. Ronald Suny has labelled these ruling elites as 'national mafias'.[49] The new

46 Kaiser, The Geography of Nationalism, pp. 255–6; Nigel Grant, 'Linguistic and Ethnic Minorities in the USSR: Educational Policies and Developments', in J. J. Tomiak (ed.), Soviet Education in the 1980s (London: Croom Helm, 1983), pp. 24–49; 28.
47 V. M. Alpatov, 150 iazykov i politika: 1917–1997 (Moscow: IV RAN, 1997), p. 114.
48 Ben Fowkes, 'The National Question in the Soviet Union under Leonid Brezhnev: Policy and Response', in Edwin Bacon and Mark Sandle (eds.), Brezhnev Reconsidered (London: Palgrave, 2002), pp. 68–89; 69.
49 Ronald Grigor Suny, The Revenge of the Past: Nationalism, Revolution, and the Collapse of the Soviet Union (Stanford, Calif.: Stanford University Press, 1993), p. 118.

stability was underpinned by a reversion to the principle of 'Brotherhood of Nations' on Brezhnev's part.

For the most part, members of the titular nationality benefited from the patronage of the party bosses. Higher education flourished in the republics. Most non-Russian citizens shared in the general relative prosperity and stability of the Brezhnev years. But national tensions never disappeared entirely. At the day-to-day level, derogatory references to nationality were commonplace in queues, on crowded public transport, at football or basketball matches or in competition over girls and alcohol.[50] Mass protests erupted over the announcement of results of competitive university entrance exams in the Kazakh capital Alma Ata, and in Tbilisi over an attempt to introduce Russian as a second official language of Georgia, both in 1978. Meanwhile specific national grievances simmered away. From 1956 onwards, a series of protests, mostly by intellectuals, over the status of Abkhazia, Nagorno-Karabakh and the Prigorodnyi district of North Ossetia prefigured the violent upheavals in these areas in the 1980s and 1990s.[51] The Soviet Union's Jews, although spared the extreme official anti-Semitism of the late Stalin years, found that there was little scope for them to practise their religion or culture, leading to a growing movement in favour of emigration to Israel. This right was granted to large numbers between 1971 and 1979, inspired by a thaw in Soviet–US relations, but was denied thereafter, creating a cohort of refuseniks – Jews who had been refused permission to emigrate and faced persecution for applying. By 1968 Crimean Tatars, still denied access to their homeland, had organised an impressive series of petitions with a claimed total of 3,000,000 signatures.

Such examples of popular protest were few and generally small-scale, however. For the most part, national protest was confined to small numbers of intellectuals, who formed an important part of the dissident movement. In the 1960s and 1970s, a flourishing Ukrainian culture circulated in the form of *samizdat* underground publications, and in 1970 a nationalist journal, *Ukrainian Herald*, appeared secretly for the first time. An Estonian National Front was set up in 1971, followed by a Lithuanian National Popular Front in 1974. In a more individual act of protest, in 1972 a Lithuanian student set fire to himself in a

50 Rasma Karklins, *Ethnic Relations in the USSR* (Boston and London: Allen and Unwin, 1986), pp. 68–71.
51 A. A.Tsutsiev, *Osetino-Ingushskii konflikt (1992– . . .) ego predistoriia i faktory razvitiia* (Moscow: Rosspen, 1998), p. 80; Christopher J. Walker, 'The Armenian Presence in Mountainous Karabakh', in John F. R.Wright, Suzanne Goldenberg and Richard Schofield (eds.), *Transcaucasian Boundaries* (London: UCL Press, 1996), pp. 103–4; Stephen F. Jones, 'Georgia: the Trauma of Statehood', in Ian Bremmer and Ray Taras (eds.), *New States, New Politics: Building the Post-Soviet Nations* (Cambridge: Cambridge University Press, 1997), pp. 505–43; 510.

public square in Kaunas under a poster proclaiming 'Freedom for Lithuania'. In Georgia as well, underground journals flourished in the 1970s. These activities were not ignored by the regime, and participants often faced persecution. Waves of arrests of those suspected of Ukrainian nationalist sympathies were conducted in 1965 and 1972, and in 1979 Moscow announced the execution of three Armenian nationalists who had allegedly been involved in a terrorist explosion on the Moscow underground.[52]

Repressions helped to keep protests in check, while the bulk of the population showed little active interest in the national question. The 'years of stagnation', however, produced a dangerous situation. Most non-Russians enjoyed a relatively privileged position in their republics, could use their mother tongue at school and in public and had controlled access to their national cultures. As a consequence, national identity was strong locally. In the Soviet Union as a whole, however, non-Russians were regarded as second rate; significant career progression depended on a sufficient mastery of Russian language; school books and history texts demeaned their national past; and occasional symbolic and arbitrary interferences from the centre could offend national feelings. This did not matter so much as long as relative economic prosperity and an adequate welfare system persisted, and Moscow could rely on the loyalty of a corrupt and affluent national leadership. Any upset to this delicate balance, however, might have drastic results.

Shortly after his appointment as General Secretary of the CPSU in 1985, Mikhail Gorbachev declared that Soviet socialism had definitively resolved the nationalities problem and that the population of the Soviet Union constituted 'a single family – the Soviet people'.[53] This confidence was shattered by mass conflicts between Russians and Yakuts in Yakutia in June 1986, and when in December of that year Gorbachev dismissed the corrupt first secretary of the Communist Party of Kazakhstan, Dinmukhamed Kunaev, and replaced him by a Russian, Gennadii Kolbin, subsequent riots made the capital of Kazakhstan, Alma Ata, ungovernable for days and, according to unofficial estimates, cost the lives of up to 250 protestors and members of the security forces.[54] Subsequently Gorbachev adopted a far more cautious approach to the national question, accusing officials of lack of sensitivity, decentralising economic decision-making, reforming the Council of Nationalities at the apex of the Soviet system and repealing unpopular language laws. In November 1990

52 Hosking, *A History of the Soviet Union*, pp. 432–9.
53 Stephen White, *After Gorbachev* (Cambridge: Cambridge University Press, 1993), p. 172.
54 Martha Brill Olcott, 'Kazakhstan: Pushing for Eurasia', in Bremmer and Taras, *New States, New Politics*, pp. 547–70; 552.

he published the draft of a new Union Treaty, which was to remodel Soviet federalism to the advantage of the republics. Having secured a popular mandate from most of the republics in a referendum held on 17 March 1991 to pursue a new Union Treaty, he was in the final stages of negotiation when a failed coup attempt in Moscow in August 1991 brought the Communist system crashing down around him.

By that time, however, events had proceeded at such a pace that it is unlikely that a new treaty or the continuation of Gorbachev's rule could have preserved the Soviet Union in anything like its old form. For many non-Russians, the introduction of market-style economic reforms led to particular hardship as it meant that relatively underdeveloped regions such as Central Asia and the Caucasus could no longer rely on unconditional central investment. Meanwhile, for more prosperous regions such as the three Baltic republics, economic decline only made clearer the potential benefits of independence from Moscow. Economic decline upset the delicate balance which had underpinned passive acceptance of Soviet central rule in the Brezhnev era. Gorbachev's hamfisted handling of relations with republican elites, typified by the Kunaev case, further undermined the old system and subsequent insecurity led national leaders to begin to mobilise around national demands as a means of securing their own long-term positions.[55]

Gorbachev's policy of *glasnost'* encouraged the articulation of a broad set of demands. Environmentalist movements which sprang up in the republics increasingly couched their complaints in national terms. By the spring of 1988, single-issue campaigns were developing into mass national movements, nowhere more so than in the Baltic republics. Here intellectuals were initially given encouragement by Gorbachev and other reformers who saw the Baltics as an ideal testing ground for building up a market-based economy and developing foreign trade, but found the road to reform blocked by conservative political leaders. For the population, *glasnost'* provided the opportunity to revive memories of independence and the brutality of Sovietisation, to celebrate their resilient national culture and identity and to call for an increased share in the output of their own economies. The first Popular Front was established in Estonia in April 1988, followed in May and October by Latvia and Lithuania respectively. Membership of the popular fronts was open to anyone with a grievance, but was mostly restricted to members of the relevant nationality. The appointment of new reform-minded leaders in all three republics in the autumn led

---

55 Valery Tishkov, *Ethnicity, Nationalism and Conflict in and after the Soviet Union: The Mind Aflame* (London: Sage, 1997), pp. 49–67.

to a period of co-operation between government and popular fronts during which declarations of sovereignty, new language laws and the readoption of separate flags and national anthems emphasised the determination to establish and maintain a separate identity for each nationality. But if the republican leaders, and even Gorbachev, had hoped to co-opt the growing national movements in this way, their actions only served to encourage mass action and an escalation of demands to the point where nothing short of outright independence would satisfy a large section of the population. Huge protest demonstrations became a regular occurrence, culminating on the fiftieth anniversary of the 1939 Molotov–Ribbentrop pact in August 1989 when over a million Estonians, Latvians and Lithuanians joined hands in a human chain stretching across all three republics. By the end of the year the pressure was so great that the Supreme Soviet in each republic had declared their 1940 incorporation into the Soviet Union illegal, providing a strong formal basis for any declaration of independence. This demand was now adopted by all three popular fronts, no doubt encouraged by the ease with which Communism and obedience to Moscow had collapsed across Eastern Europe in 1989. Free elections in 1989 and 1990 resulted in victories for the Popular Fronts, and independence was declared in Lithuania on 11 March 1990, Estonia on 30 March and Latvia on 4 May.[56]

Not far behind the Baltic republics in raising the demand for secession was Georgia, where nineteen demonstrators were killed by the Red Army at an independence rally in April 1989. Elsewhere, economic collapse and the perception that the centre was losing its grip led sections of the population not to demand independence, but to attack other ethnic minorities. Longstanding disputes over territory, living space, access to jobs and resources and the constitutional status of minority territories came to the fore. The most serious and protracted case of ethnic conflict broke out between Armenians and Azeris over the status of the largely Armenian-populated region of Nagorno-Karabakh in late 1987 and spread to large cities like Sumgait and Baku by March 1988. While genuine grievances and irreconcilable claims lay at the root of the conflicts, the population was goaded on by political leaders in both the Armenian and Azerbaijani republics seeking a populist base for their own positions, culminating in all-out war between the two following independence.[57] Serious conflicts also emerged between Georgia and her Abkhaz and Ossetian minorities in 1989, between Ossetians and Ingush in the

56 Graham Smith, 'The Resurgence of Nationalism', in Smith, *The Baltic States*, pp. 121–43.
57 Audrey L. Altsadt, *The Azerbaijani Turks* (Stanford, Calif.: Hoover Institution Press, 1992), pp. 195–219.

North Caucasus in 1992 (a result of the fall-out from the earlier deportations of Ingush) and between Kirgiz and Uzbeks in the Osh region of Kirgizia in 1990.[58]

The final nail in the coffin of the Soviet Union came from the largest republic – the RSFSR (later renamed the Russian Federation). On his election as chairman of the RSFSR Supreme Soviet in March 1990, Boris Yeltsin sought to use the republic as a power base in his personal struggle with Gorbachev. He quickly assured the Baltic republics that he would not stand in the way of their secession, and followed their lead in declaring sovereignty in the summer of 1990. Sensing the power of the national movements in his struggle with Gorbachev, Yeltsin encouraged this process by calling on the autonomous republics to 'take whatever helping of power that you can gobble up by yourselves'.[59] The RSFSR therefore became a major driving force in the break-up of the USSR.

The failed coup of August 1991 served to strengthen Yeltsin's personal standing and to make even more remote the possibility of keeping Estonia, Latvia and Lithuania, which now appealed for international recognition, within the fold. The only remaining question was if any of the other union republics could be retained within some sort of federal system. Fearing the possibility of another coup, encouraged by Yeltsin and seeing how the Baltic bids for independence had been welcomed in the West, the other non-Russians who had voted overwhelmingly for retention of the Union in the March referendum now moved quickly in support of independence. Political elites could no longer be sure of their privileges and power being preserved by either Yeltsin or Gorbachev, and moved to position themselves as leaders of potential new states. As events unfolded at a dizzying pace, popular national movements and Communist politicians engaged in a circular competition of demands, reinforcing the radicalisation of each other in the process. Ukrainian President Leonid Kravchuk was the key player in the Soviet endgame. When he refused to send a representative to sign a Treaty on the Economic Commonwealth on 18 October and the Ukrainian people voted for independence in a separate referendum on 1 December, the fate of the Union was sealed. Estonia, Latvia, Lithuania and Georgia were by now in effect independent states. On 8 December the presidents of Russia, Ukraine and Belarus agreed to the formation of a loose Confederation of Independent States (CIS) (see Map 12.1), and when they were joined at the eleventh hour by Moldova, Armenia, Azerbaijan, Kazakhstan, Kyrgyzstan, Tajikistan and Uzbekistan it was all over. The

58  Tishkov, *Ethnicity, Nationalism and Conflict*, pp. 135–82.
59  Robert Service, *A History of Twentieth-Century Russia* (London: Penguin, 1997), pp. 488–95.

Union of Soviet Socialist Republics was formally dissolved on midnight of 31 December 1991.

For most of the nationalities of the former Russian Empire the process of nation-building was carried out not so much by their own efforts but on their behalf by a multinational state which was, for a time, committed to reinforcing and even creating national identities alongside a radical social and economic agenda. Though the demands of modernisation, centralisation and geographical mobility undermined many of these measures, enough had been achieved to lay the basis for the further development of modern nations. Propaganda and policies that switched clumsily between promoting separate national feelings, developing Soviet patriotism and celebrating the leading role of the Russians, seemed to offer enough to everyone. The rise in urbanisation and education contributed to the growth of personal and group awareness which could be channelled into controllable paths so long as relative prosperity and national elite co-operation was assured. But the crisis in the Soviet economic and political system arrived at a time when three decades of dissident activity and sporadic outbursts of broader national feeling suggested that the non-Russian nations had matured politically to a degree which made separatism a viable and eventually popular option.

For the fourteen new non-Russian states, the period since 1991 was a second, independent, period of nation-building. Lacking alternative sources of experienced political leaders, most of the states remained in the hands of Communists-turned-nationalists who had already been in power locally for many years before the break-up. Across the southern states and in Moldova, a series of border disputes, civil wars and ethnic conflicts in the first part of the 1990s left the impression that independence might have been a mistake and that the region would remain unstable for decades to come. But the resolution of most of the conflicts by force, negotiation or inertia, combined with the return of relative economic stability, made it clear that independence was there to stay, with the possible exception of Belarus, whose overtures for some form of renewed federation with Russia were rebuffed by Moscow.

The biggest controversy for the new states was how to establish a firm basis of united identity and, in particular, how to deal with the substantial Russian populations that remained within their borders. In 1989 over 25 million Russians were living in other republics of the Soviet Union, and in the years after 1990 migration out of some of the republics, most notably in Central Asia, stood at over 5 per cent of the total population each year.[60] Strict language laws were

60 Paul Kolstoe, *Russians in the Former Soviet Republics* (London: Hurst, 1995), pp. 2, 228, 293–300.

introduced in all three Baltic republics which clearly discriminated against Russians, who were further disadvantaged by constitutional moves basing property and citizenship rights on the situation before 1939. Russian protests and threats were backed up by international pressure, leading to revisions of all the language laws by 1996. By the end of the decade, Estonia, Latvia and Lithuania had adapted so successfully to a free-market economy and West European norms of citizenship and human rights that they were preparing for entry into the European Union. The other states did not progress as rapidly in the same direction, partly as a result of different cultural backgrounds and a less sure economic base. In Central Asia, the clan-based patron–client networks, which had become so firmly established in Brezhnev's time, were perpetuated into the post-Soviet period. But in other respects the break with the Communist past was clear-cut, many observers' fears of the potential of Islamic fundamentalism proved unfounded and stable modern nation-states were emerging.[61]

The Russian Federation inherited the Soviet system of autonomous republics and regions, and after the break-up of the USSR over 18 per cent of its population remained non-Russian. Almost all had declared their own sovereignty, with Yeltsin's encouragement, in 1990. In March 1992 Yeltsin, now head of an independent but still multinational state, devised a Federal Treaty that recognised the rights that the republics enjoyed in practice anyway. Even this was not enough for the largest republic, Tatarstan. A popular referendum rejected the treaty and led Russia and Tatarstan to the brink of a secession crisis. The imposition of a new constitution by Yeltsin following the consolidation of his own power in December 1993 restricted the rights granted a year and a half earlier and pushed Tatarstan ever further away. Although a strong Tatar national independence movement, Ittifak, encouraged the brinkmanship of the Tatar leadership, in the end the republic, surrounded by Russian territory and dependent on the Russian economy, could not afford to go it alone, while the Russian Federation could not afford an open conflict with such a large region. The result was a bilateral treaty signed in February 1994 which granted Tatarstan virtual self-rule in return for remaining a loyal part of the federation. In general the nationalities of the autonomous republics, who had seen the status of their national languages seriously eroded from Khrushchev's time on, engaged in an intensive ethno-national revival under *perestroika* and

61 Gregory Gleason, *The Central Asian States: Discovering Independence* (Boulder, Colo.: Westview Press, 1997); for a survey of nation-building in all the post-Soviet republics, see Bremmer and Taras, *New States, New Politics.*

after. While this process fuelled ethnic conflict and disputes with the Centre in some areas, notably the North Caucasus, in most cases it did not lead to secessionist movements or present any serious threat to stability in the Russian Federation (see Map 13.1).

On 11 December 1994, Russian armed forces crossed into the North Caucasian Republic of Chechnya, initiating a conflict which was to cost 40,000 lives in the next eighteen months. The republic's president, former Soviet air force commander Johkar Dudayev, had come to power with Moscow's backing. But on 2 November 1991 the Chechen parliament declared full independence and in June 1992 Dudayev expelled Russian troops from the region. By late 1994, Yeltsin faced a drastic decline in his own popularity which threatened his chances in the next presidential election, due for the summer of 1996. This provided one of the motives for the invasion. In words attributed to the secretary of the Security Council Oleg Lobov, 'We need a small victorious war to raise the President's ratings.'[62] But Dudayev had also done a great deal to antagonise Moscow. Allegations of connections with organised crime groups in the Russian capital, although greatly exaggerated at the time, were not entirely without basis. The hijacking of a bus near the town of Mineral'nye Vody in the North Caucasus by Chechens in July 1994 further reinforced the notion that Chechnya was a threat to Russia's internal security. Moreover, if Chechnya was allowed to get away with a unilateral declaration of independence, what would stop the rest of the North Caucasus and other republics following suit? The presence of a small amount of oil and a major pipeline linking Russia with the major oilfields of Azerbaijan were a further incentive for Russia to re-establish control.

Whatever the motive, it is clear that Russia's leaders and military commanders expected that the overthrow of Dudayev would be an easy task. In November 1994 the defence minister, Pavel Grachev, famously boasted that 'we would need one parachute regiment to decide the whole affair in two hours'.[63] But the invasion was a disaster. The ill-equipped and demoralised Russian army, for all its numerical superiority in manpower and weapons, found the stubbornness and guerrilla tactics of Chechen fighters far more of a handful than they had expected. After fierce fighting, Russian forces captured the Chechen capital, Groznyi, on 26 January 1995, but the Chechen rebels mounted effective resistance in the mountains despite Dudayev's death from

---

62 Carlotta Gall and Thomas de Waal, *Chechnya: A Small Victorious War* (London: Pan, 1997), p. 161.

63 Ibid., p. 157.

a Russian missile in May 1996. On 6 August 1996, the day of Yeltsin's rein-auguration as Russian president, in a move of astonishing daring, Chechen forces attacked and retook Groznyi from a Russian force supposedly three times the size of their own. Yeltsin, faced with military humiliation, and con-demned internationally for human rights abuses, sent his former presiden-tial electoral rival General Aleksandr Lebed' to Khasavyurt in Dagestan to negotiate an effective ceasefire marking the end of the first Chechen war. In January 1997, Aslan Maskhadov was elected president of Chechnya in mostly fair elections.[64]

Under the Khasavyurt agreement, the question of the future status of Chech-nya was deferred for five years. For the next three years Chechnya enjoyed virtual self-rule beyond Moscow's reach, but was divided internally as com-peting 'warlords' squabbled over influence and territory, leaving Maskhadov an often helpless observer. In the summer of 1999, the bombing of apart-ment blocks in Moscow, widely blamed on Chechen terrorists, was followed by an incursion into Dagestan by a Chechen force under Shamil Basaev. These events provided the pretext for a second Russian invasion, although there is ample evidence that preparations had been under way since at least the spring of that year. This time the Russian army was much better pre-pared and benefited from the vigorous political leadership of Vladimir Putin, who was soon to become president of the Russian Federation. Although not without setbacks, the second invasion was more effective than the first, and within a few months the Russian army had established control of Groznyi and most of the Chechen lowlands. Chechen guerrillas continued to hold out in the mountains, however, and a final end to the fighting seemed a long way off.

Having apparently solved the Chechen question, Putin also moved to curtail the powers of the autonomous republics by dividing the Russian Federation into seven 'super-regions', each overseen by a personal appointee. The move was accepted without much protest by the republics, underlining their depen-dence on Moscow and the lack of will for further secession struggles. Putin benefited from a revival in the Russian economy, as well as the weak founda-tion of republican national identity. The policies of Khrushchev and Brezhnev had ensured that the national minorities of the Russian Federation, apart from the Chechens, would not be as vigorous in their pursuit of national demands

64 Anatol Lieven, *Chechnya, Tombstone of Russian Power* (New Haven and London: Yale University Press, 1999).

as the larger nationalities of the union republics. But the failure of the Russian Federation to reach a consensus on a non-ethnic conception of Russian citizenship[65] means the potential remains for the national question to continue to pose problems for Russia's leaders.

65 Tishkov, *Ethnicity, Nationalism and Conflict*, pp. 272–93.

19

# The western republics: Ukraine, Belarus, Moldova and the Baltics

SERHY YEKELCHYK

The Soviet west, an arch of non-Russian republics extending from the Gulf of Finland in the north to the Black Sea in the south and separating Russia proper from other European states, came to the attention of scholars during the late 1960s and early 1970s. While Western sovietologists have long studied each individual country in the region – Estonia, Latvia, Lithuania, Belorussia / Belarus, Ukraine and Moldavia / Moldova – before the 1960s, they did not think of the Soviet west as an entity. But the region's prominence in the dissident movement during the 1960s suggested that the western fringe of the USSR might become a catalyst of nationalist unrest and, possibly, a channel for the spillover of democratic ideas from Eastern Europe. The region was now seen as a place where the Soviet collapse might begin.

Yet, as North American scholars pioneered the use of the term 'Soviet west', they soon discovered the difficulties of defining this region in economic or social terms – which was at the time considered a clue for understanding nationality perseverance there. In his lead article in the 1975 collection *The Soviet West: Interplay between Nationality and Social Organization*, Ralph S. Clem proposed that the area was characterised by 'high to moderate levels of economic development with relation to other areas of the USSR', but had to qualify this generalisation by excluding the republic of Moldavia, as well as some areas of Ukraine, Belorussia and Lithuania. Of the usual social consequences of economic development, except perhaps for low fertility, neither high educational level nor high urbanisation qualified as defining characteristics of the region. In any case, European Russia displayed similar economic and social trends. In the final analysis, history was the only factor unquestionably uniting the western republics and setting them aside from the rest of the Soviet Union. All had historical ties to other European countries. In the recent past, some had experienced independence, while others were divided territorially, with some of their territories forming part of another European country.[1]

Another contemporary collection, *The Influence of East Europe and the Soviet West on the USSR* (1975), takes a more productive approach to the region as defined more by its past and present links to Eastern Europe than by any sociological criteria. Its editor, Roman Szporluk, suggests in his introduction that the USSR's post-1939 extension westward made the Soviet nationality question much more pressing and sensitive.[2] In his subsequent work on Western Ukraine, which was incorporated into the Ukrainian republic during 1939–45, Professor Szporluk shows that, owing to the pre-existing high level of national consciousness, the Soviet authorities never managed to fully absorb this area. Western Ukraine remained the mainstay of popular nationalism, later contributing greatly to the disintegration of the USSR.[3]

Although this argument would not apply to all western republics, it underscores an important factor in their historical development. The vitality of nationalities on the Soviet Union's western fringe was to a considerable degree determined by the successes or difficulties of their pre-Soviet nation-building. The areas that were able to preserve a high level of national consciousness were those where Sovietisation had come late and where during the twentieth century nationalists had had a chance to mobilise the masses for their cause, as was the case especially in the Baltic states and Western Ukraine. In contrast, in countries where an early interruption of nationalist agitation or lack of infrastructure for such work had prevented nationalist mobilisation of the masses, the population's national identities remained frustratingly ambiguous. This was the case in Belorussia, Moldavia and eastern Ukraine.

To be sure, the Soviet state actively interfered in nation-building processes. Scholars have shown that the USSR institutionalised nationality as a form, while attempting to drain it of its content. As a result, it created territorial nations with all the symbols of nationhood but bereft of political sovereignty, although Stalin's successors were to discover the fluid border in modern nationalism between form and content.[4] The Soviet nativisation programmes during

1 Ralph S. Clem, 'Vitality of the Nationalities in the Soviet West: Background and Implications', in Clem (ed.), *The Soviet West: Interplay between Nationality and Social Organization* (New York: Praeger, 1975), pp. 3–5.
2 Roman Szporluk, 'Introduction', in Szporluk (ed.), *The Influence of East Europe and the Soviet West on the USSR* (New York: Praeger, 1975), p. 10.
3 Roman Szporluk, *Russia, Ukraine, and the Breakup of the Soviet Union* (Stanford, Calif.: Hoover Institution Press, 2000).
4 Rogers Brubaker, *Nationalism Reframed: Nationhood and the National Question in the New Europe* (Cambridge: Cambridge University Press, 1996), pp. 25–7; Yuri Slezkine, 'The

the 1920s made nationalities more articulate, and if Stalinist ideologues managed to undo much of what had been achieved at that time, they never questioned the ethnic distinctiveness of non-Russian peoples. During the post-war period, the non-Russians did not make much progress in their nation-building, but managed to preserve many of their previous accomplishments. Thus, especially for the regions that had been incorporated into the USSR during 1939–45, the pre-Soviet experience of nation-building remained a decisive factor in national consolidation.

## Nation-building in the age of revolution

The prominent Czech scholar Miroslav Hroch concluded in his study of Europe's non-dominant ethnic groups that these people usually undergo three stages in their national revival – that of academic interest in the nation's history and culture, creation and propagation of modern high culture and political mobilisation.[5] All the nationalities living on the western borderland of the Russian Empire qualified as Hroch's 'small peoples' because they lacked continuous traditions of statehood, native elites and literature in an indigenous language. However, in the time of total war and global politics, these nations' geopolitical location between Russia and Germany shaped their destinies no less than did the Czech scholar's objective historical criteria.

During the late nineteenth century, Estonians and Latvians were overwhelmingly peasant peoples, albeit with the level of literacy that was one of the highest in Europe – over 90 per cent. (This high level of literacy was due to the spread of the Lutheran faith beginning in the sixteenth century and the Church's adoption of Estonian in its services.) Estonians, whose speech belongs to the Finno-Ugric family of languages and is drastically different from Indo-European languages, in a sense benefited from their cultural isolation. The Russian imperial government encouraged conversion to Orthodoxy but could not enforce serious assimilation of the peasantry. Instead, the centralising efforts of the last two tsars undermined the positions of the Baltic German nobility, the land's traditional ruling caste, while placing no restrictions on the development of Estonian culture, the press and education. The decline of

Soviet Union as a Communal Apartment, or How a Socialist State Promoted Ethnic Particularism', *Slavic Review* 53, 2 (1994): 414–52; Ronald Grigor Suny, *The Revenge of the Past: Nationalism, Revolution, and the Collapse of the Soviet Union* (Stanford, Calif.: Stanford University Press, 1993), pp. 111–12 and 129–31.
5 Miroslav Hroch, *Social Preconditions of National Revival in Europe*, trans. Ben Fowkes (Cambridge: Cambridge University Press, 1985).

the Baltic barons' power, combined with rapid industrialisation and urbanisation at the turn of the century, allowed Estonians to challenge the German domination of their cities, including Tallinn, which had become one of the empire's major ports. In 1897, Estonians constituted 67.8 per cent of urbanites in their ethno-linguistic territory.[6] The Estonian bourgeoisie and Estonian professionals were becoming increasingly prominent in public life and supported national culture, most notably the tradition of all-Estonian song festivals that began in 1869.

The Revolution of 1905 escalated the political and cultural demands of Estonian activists. Moderate loyalists, led by Jaan Tönisson and the Estonian Progressive People's Party, put forward the demand for autonomy, while radical nationalists, headed by Konstantin Päts, combined this aim with that of overthrowing the tsarist regime. But 1905 also marked the entry on the political scene of Estonian socialism. As the peasants were destroying large manors in the countryside, the Russian and Estonian Social Democratic Workers' Parties were recruiting followers among the working class. The suppression of the revolution undermined the growth of the radical Left, but had little effect on the development of Estonian society and culture.

During the First World War, Estonia remained outside the battle zone and did not suffer wartime destruction. The fall of the tsarist regime in February 1917 led to the renewed demands of autonomy. Following an impressive Estonian demonstration in Petrograd (St Petersburg), the Provisional Government indeed agreed to unite the Estonian ethnic lands into a single province and to allow elections to the provincial assembly. The assembly, known in Estonian as *Maapäev*, was elected in May and represented all the major political parties, including the Bolsheviks. When the Bolsheviks seized power in Petrograd in November 1917, their leader in Estonia, Viktor Kingissepp, disbanded the *Maapäev* but was unable to establish an efficient administration. More important, the Bolsheviks alienated many Estonians with their attacks on the Lutheran Church and failure to divide large landed estates.

On 24 February 1918, as the German army was marching into Estonia, the underground representatives of the *Maapäev* proclaimed the country's independence. During the occupation, which lasted until late November 1918, the German military and the local Baltic Germans openly considered Estonia's incorporation into Germany. But as Germany surrendered to the Allies and withdrew its troops from Eastern Europe, Estonia became the scene of a civil

---

6 Toivo U. Raun, *Estonia and the Estonians* (Stanford, Calif.: Hoover Institution Press, 1991), 73.

war among the Bolsheviks, the Baltic Germans and the provisional Estonian government, which was covertly supported by Finland and the Entente. To complicate matters further, the Allies forced the Estonian authorities to accept on their territory White Russian troops, which in 1919 used Estonia as a spring-board in their unsuccessful attacks on Petrograd.[7] In February 1920, the war ended with the Tartu Peace Treaty, by which Soviet Russia recognised Estonia's independence.

Estonia's southern neighbours, the Latvians, although speakers of a distinct Baltic language belonging to the Indo-European family, shared with Estoni-ans many of their twentieth-century historical experiences. Also a Lutheran, mainly peasant people with a high level of literacy, Latvians ended the Ger-man domination of their cities during the industrial spurt of the 1880s–1910s. The formerly German city of Riga emerged not only as a major port and a Baltic metropolis, but also as a Latvian city, with Latvians becoming its largest ethnic group (39.6 per cent in 1913).[8] Still, unlike in Estonia, the Baltic Ger-mans remained firmly in control of municipal government, and their large estates dominated the rural economy. This led to growing frustration among Latvians. While national culture generally developed freely, the plight of the landless peasantry led radical Latvian intellectuals to an exploration of Marx-ism. In 1904, the Latvian Social Democratic Workers' Party came into existence and soon boasted an impressive 10,000 members. In contrast to the Estonian party, Latvian Social Democrats continued to exist after the revolution and subsequently entered into an affiliation with the Bolsheviks. The year 1905 galvanised more moderate nationalists as well, but the greatest literary figure of the Latvian cultural revival, the poet Jānis Rainis, symbolised the intelli-gentsia's embrace of socialism.

The trials of the First World War only increased the sway of political radical-ism in Latvia. Unlike Estonia, the country was devastated by warfare, evacua-tion and the refugee crisis. Aiming to take advantage of the Latvians' traditional hatred of their German masters, the Russian government created separate units of Latvian infantry, known as *strēlnieki* or, in Russian, *Latyshskie strelki* (Latvian sharpshooters). By 1917, the Latvian units were 30,000 strong and, like most of the Russian army, completely demoralised. The Bolsheviks were able to gain mass support among the *strēlnieki*, many of whom would later move to Russia as Lenin's most trusted guards. The collapse of the monarchy briefly

---

7 Rein Taagepera, *Estonia: Return to Independence* (Boulder, Colo.: Westview Press, 1993), p. 46.
8 Andrejs Plakans, *The Latvians: A Short History* (Stanford, Calif.: Hoover Institution Press, 1995), p. 108.

brought to prominence Latvian moderate nationalists, represented politically by Kārlis Ulmanis and the Agrarian Union, but the Left soon regained the initiative. During the November elections to the All-Russian Constituent Assembly, the Bolsheviks, who were led by Pēteris Stučka, won in Latvia an impressive 71.9 per cent.

Nevertheless, following Soviet Russia's diplomatic concessions at Brest-Litovsk, the German forces in February 1918 occupied all of Latvia. After the German capitulation, representatives of most Latvian political parties met secretly in Riga on 18 November 1918 and proclaimed the Republic of Latvia with Ulmanis as prime minister of its provisional government. It soon transpired that the victorious Entente wanted to perpetuate the German occupation as protection against the Bolsheviks, who from December 1918 to May 1919 again controlled a considerable part of Latvian territory. In the ensuing civil war, Latvian nationalists relied on support consecutively from Germany, the Entente and Poland to defeat the Bolsheviks, White Russians and the Baltic German forces. The war ended in early 1920, and in August, Soviet Russia recognised Latvia as an independent state.

Further south, Roman Catholic Lithuanians could not boast the same level of literacy and social organisation. Closely related to Latvians by language, their modern history was, however, shaped by Polish political domination and the Polonisation of native elites. Unlike their two Baltic neighbours, the Lithuanians could claim to be the heirs of a mighty medieval state, the grand duchy of Lithuania, but the tsarist assimilationist drive greatly hindered the development of their modern high culture. Seeking to separate the peasantry from the rebellious Polish nobility in the region, the government outlawed the use of the Roman alphabet and imposed on Lithuanians the Russian educational system. Equally important, in contrast to Estonia and Latvia, at the turn of the century Lithuania remained an agrarian backwater. Landless peasants did not have an option of becoming industrial workers, and Vilnius remained the only big city in the area, a multinational metropolis that Lithuanians, Poles, Belorussians and Jews all claimed as their cultural centre.

After a slow start, the national movement spurted during the Revolution of 1905, when a national congress, the so-called Great Diet of Vilnius, demanded autonomy and political freedom. Although Social Democrats had long been influential in Lithuania, new opportunities for cultural expression channelled the revolutionary events there more in the direction of national liberation. Such a trend suited the Germans, who occupied all of Lithuania early during the First World War and eventually modified plans for annexation towards the creation of a puppet Lithuanian government. However, when the German military allowed the formation of a Lithuanian national assembly or *Taryba*, in September 1917, this body proved less than obedient. It did proclaim independence 'in alliance with the German Reich' (11 December 1917), but immediately pressed for more rights and subsequently issued another declaration of independence without mention of the Germans (16 February 1918).[9] At one point in 1918, the balance of military powers forced the *Taryba* to accept the German Prince Wilhelm of Urach as a Lithuanian king, but the Lithuanian nationalists, led by Antanas Smetona, gradually took over the administration. Following the German capitulation, Lithuanian forces managed to fight off the Bolsheviks and the Whites, yet lost Vilnius to the new Polish state.

Belorussians represented in the extreme the same case of belated national development and German manipulation. Numbering some 5.5 million in 1897, they were an East Slavic nationality close to Russians in language and Orthodox religion. With their cities dominated by Poles, Jews and Russians, the overwhelming majority of Belorussians were illiterate peasants unfamiliar with the modern notion of national identity. Although it distrusted the Polish gentry in the area, the Russian government did not encourage the development of Belorussian culture. On the contrary, it repressed book publishing in Belorussian, and, when it provided the peasants with any education at all, it was in Russian. With less than 3 per cent of them residing in cities and towns, Belorussians were quite possibly the least urbanised people in Europe. Their national awakening began late, the idea of a separate Belorussian nationality emerging only in the 1890s in the work of the poet Francišak Bahuševič. As other nations of the region were entering the mass mobilisation stage, Belorussians during 1906–15 were undergoing a belated literary revival, which was made possible by the temporary softening of restrictions on the Belorussian language. Belorussian cultural life of this period centred around the weekly *Naša niva* (Our Cornfield) edited by the brothers Ivan and Anton Luckievič.[10]

The First World War brought destruction and population dislocation on Belorussian soil. By the time of the February Revolution, half of Belorussian territory was occupied by the Germans, but in the other half, patriotic activists managed in December to convene the All-Belorussian Congress, only to have it disbanded by the Bolsheviks. By the terms of the Brest-Litovsk Treaty, Belorussia was divided between Germany and Soviet Russia. The former allowed the local nationalists to proclaim the Belorussian Democratic Republic (9 March

9 John Hiden and Patrick Salmon, *The Baltic Nations and Europe: Estonia, Latvia and Lithuania in the Twentieth Century*, rev. edn (London: Longman, 1994), pp. 28–9.
10 Jan Zaprudnik, *Belarus: At a Crossroads in History* (Boulder, Colo.: Westview Press, 1993), p. 64.

1918), while the latter created the Belorussian Soviet Republic (1 January 1919). Subsequently, Belorussia became a prize in the Polish–Soviet War, which ended with the final incorporation of western Belorussia into Poland and the re-establishment of the Belorussian SSR.

Belorussia's neighbour to the south, Ukraine, presented a more complex case. Eastern or Dnieper Ukraine, which was part of the Russian Empire, shared many characteristics with Lithuania and Belorussia. A large nation of some 22 million people in 1897, Ukrainians spoke an East Slavic language closely related to Russian and were overwhelmingly Orthodox. The imperial government imposed harsh restrictions on the development of their national culture, but the national revival that had begun in the mid-nineteenth century was unstoppable. By the early twentieth century, the Ukrainian intelligentsia boasted developed literary, theatrical and musical traditions. Still, nationalist agitators did not have free access to the peasant masses, which remained largely illiterate. Cities, including Kiev, changed their Polish cultural character to Russian because the peasants who moved there or joined the industrial workforce adopted Russian identity. The new working class responded better to agitation by Russian socialists, and, indeed, all-Russian socialist parties had an impressive following in eastern Ukraine. Only the Revolution of 1905 enabled Ukrainian activists to publish their first daily newspaper, *Rada* (Council), and to start popular education societies in the countryside – concessions that the government would take back by the beginning of the war. Except for a brief period after 1905, political parties could only operate underground, and only socialist Ukrainian parties could muster any significant support.

Western Ukraine, which was part of the Austro-Hungarian Empire, had a very different historical experience. Numbering 3.5 million in 1910, Ukrainians in East Galicia (with its centre in Lemberg (L'viv)) suffered from Polish dominion in the crown land of Galicia but benefited from education in their native tongue, freedom of cultural development and – however limited – the experience of political participation. Downsides included the lack of industrial development in the region and Polish and Jewish control of the cities. The national movement began in the mid-nineteenth century and, in time, greatly benefited from Ukrainian identification with the Greek Catholic (Uniate) Church that clearly set Ukrainians apart from the Poles. By the turn of the century, a massive network of Ukrainian printed media, co-operatives, reading rooms and cultural societies produced a generation of nationally conscious peasants.[11] Intellectuals, meanwhile, finally established that their people were

---

11 John-Paul Himka, *Galician Villagers and the Ukrainian National Movement in the Nineteenth Century* (Edmonton: Canadian Institute of Ukrainian Studies Press, 1988).

not just 'Ruthenians', but a part of a larger Ukrainian nation. With political parties legally operating, the moderately nationalistic National Democrats dominated Western Ukrainian politics.

In the province of Bukovina, where the ruling class was Romanian, rather than Polish, and most Ukrainians belonged to the Orthodox Church, the growth of the national movement largely followed the Galician model. This was not the case in Transcarpathia, which belonged to the Hungarian part of the dual monarchy. In Transcarpathia, Hungarian upper classes encouraged assimilation and hindered the spread of the Ukrainian national idea.

The First World War initially had the greatest impact on Western Ukraine. As the Russian army occupied Galicia and Bukovina early during the war, it sought to 'reunite' these lands with Russia. In the spring of 1915, Nicholas II paid a triumphant visit to Lemberg, where his civil administration was actively suppressing organised Ukrainian life. Austria-Hungary, in the meantime, authorised the creation of a Ukrainian legion within its army. When the tsarist regime collapsed, Ukrainian activists in Kiev promptly created the Central Rada (council), which was headed by the respected historian Mykhailo Hrushevsky. In December, the nationalists proved unable to organise effective resistance to the Bolshevik army, which had invaded from Soviet Russia. Just before abandoning Kiev, on 22 January 1918, the Central Rada proclaimed the independent Ukrainian People's Republic. However, soon it was back in the capital on the heels of the German advance. Because the German high command disliked the socialist views of the Rada's leaders, such as Volodymyr Vynnychenko, it installed the conservative General Pavlo Skoropadsky as Ukraine's monarch or *hetman* (April–December 1918). Following the German withdrawal, the re-established Ukrainian People's Republic saw its authority collapse in the chaos and violence of the civil war during which the Reds, the Whites, the Ukrainian forces, the anarchists and bands of looters fought each other until, by the end of 1920, the better-organised Reds established their control.

In Western Ukraine, the revolution started later and had a national, rather than social colouring. As the Austro-Hungarian Empire began disintegrating, in November 1918 the Ukrainian activists proclaimed the creation of the Western Ukrainian People's Republic. In January 1919, the republic entered a union with its east Ukrainian counterpart, but the unification was never implemented because Western Ukrainians had to fight their own civil war against the Entente-supported Poles, which they lost in July. Subsequently, the Allies approved Polish control over all Galicia, as well as the inclusion of Bukovina in greater Romania and that of Transcarpathia in the new state of Czechoslovakia.

Bordering Dnieper Ukraine in the south-west was Bessarabia, which we currently know under its historical name of Moldova. (The old Moldavian principality was considerably larger, and the present-day Republic of Moldova is only slightly bigger than Bessarabia proper.) In the early nineteenth century, the tsars wrested this province from the Ottoman Empire, thus depriving Moldavians of a chance to participate in the later unification of Romanian principalities. Although known as Moldavians, the region's population was ethnically Romanian and spoke dialects of the Romanian language. Economically, Bessarabia was the most backward agricultural region on the empire's western fringes, and literacy among ethnic Moldavians stood at a meagre 6 per cent (1897). When the national awakening began after the Revolution of 1905, it manifested itself primarily in the discovery of the common pan-Romanian cultural heritage. Nationalists in Romania proper also sought to establish contacts with Moldavian intellectuals hoping for eventual reunification, but, before the war and revolution, this aim looked more like a pipe dream.

The February Revolution gave Moldavians an unexpected chance to organise. By October 1917, various civic and military groups managed to convene in Chişinău a national assembly, which declared Bessarabia autonomous. The elections to a national council, *Sfatul Ţării*, followed, but before this body could establish its authority, in January 1918 the Romanian army arrived in force – ostensibly by invitation of the Moldavian authorities with the aim of protecting the country from the Bolshevik peril. The *Sfatul Ţării* proclaimed first the independent Moldavian Democratic Republic of Bessarabia (24 January) and then its union with Romania (27 March).[12] However, the USSR never recognised the Romanian annexation of Bessarabia, and Romanians failed to win a complete international recognition of this act.

One productive way to analyse the revolutionary events in the non-Russian borderlands is to look at the complex interaction of 'class' and 'nation' as two principal identity markers, which competed in contemporary political discourse and influenced the nationalities differently.[13] But given that the western borderlands were positioned strategically between Russia and Western Europe, their internal ideological struggles and nation-building projects were time and again overridden by the intervention of the Great Powers, which reshaped states and nations based on their own global interests.[14]

---

12 Charles King, *The Moldovans: Romania, Russia, and the Politics of Culture* (Stanford, Calif.: Hoover Institution Press, 2000), pp. 33–5.
13 Suny, *The Revenge of the Past*, pp. 1–83.
14 Geoff Eley, 'Remapping the Nation: War, Revolutionary Upheaval, and State Formation in Eastern Europe, 1914–1923', in *Ukrainian–Jewish Relations in Historical Perspective* (Edmonton: Canadian Institute of Ukrainian Studies Press, 1988), pp. 205–46.

## States and nations in the era of mass politics

Rogers Brubaker has suggested that the new nation-states that after the First
World War replaced multinational empires were essentially 'nationalising'
states, protecting and promoting the political domination, economic welfare
and culture of their 'core' nations.[15] This is, of course, an ideal model, useful in
comparative analysis but too generalising to be sustained in most case studies.
Nevertheless, the notion of a 'nationalising state' captures a significant feature
of the post-war period, when states, armed with the techniques of mass politics,
interfered aggressively in the nation-building processes.

At the final stages of their wars of independence, the republics of Estonia,
Latvia and Lithuania benefited from the Entente's intention to create a *cordon
sanitaire* around Soviet Russia. But independence brought the need for economic reorientation towards the West, for the region's economy previously
had depended on the Russian market. As hopes of remaining a mediator in
Russia's trade with Western Europe did not materialise, all three countries
moved to create export economies specialising in dairy and meat products.
This task was made easier by the redistribution of large landed estates with
little or no compensation. (Most landlords in any case belonged to another
nationality, Baltic German in Estonia and Latvia, and Polish in Lithuania.) The
new Baltic governments realised that, in order to prevent social discontent,
they needed to turn the landless peasantry into small farmers. Indeed, the
independent farming class eventually came to constitute the backbone of the
Baltic states' social structures. A modest industrial sector survived in Estonia
and Latvia, but failed to develop in Lithuania.

Politically, the 1920s were turbulent. All three states were established as
parliamentary republics, but political parties were numerous and fragmented.
The left and right wings were strong, while the centre weak. Frequent changes
of government indicated the inherent instability of a political system, which
contemporaries perceived as being in permanent danger of a coup from either
the radical Left or the radical Right. Liberal democracy, indeed, did not survive
long in the Baltics, but the authoritarian regimes that emerged in the region
were not established by the extremists – ideological cousins of either Bolsheviks
or Nazis – but by the traditional Right. Lithuania was the first to take flight in
1926, when the army overthrew a coalition government of populists, socialists
and minorities and installed a prominent conservative nationalist, Antanas
Smetona, as an authoritarian president.

15 Brubaker, *Nationalism Reframed*, pp. 83–4 and 103–4.

In Estonia, a coup followed the Great Depression. As disappointment with parliamentary democracy grew, so did the popularity of the fascist-like League of Freedom Fighters, a paramilitary organisation of veterans of the war of independence. Before the veterans' candidate could win the presidential elections of 1934, however, Prime Minister Konstantin Päts organised a pre-emptive coup on 12 March 1934. He declared a state of emergency, dissolved the parliament and all political parties and ruled by decree until the decade's end. Latvia followed the path to authoritarianism later the same month. Faced with the challenge from the extreme right Thunder Cross movement, Prime Minister Kārlis Ulmanis organised a similar coup on 16 March 1934.

Authoritarian regimes in the Baltic region had many features in common. The dictators forbade all political parties (in some cases, except for their own) and censored the press, but did not completely suppress civic rights. Influenced by Italian Fascist corporatism, they actively involved the state in the regulation of the economic and social spheres. In 1938–9, the worsening international situation forced all three leaders to relax their rule somewhat. Although in the 1920s the promotion of the region's national cultures had not infringed the rights of minorities, this changed with the transition to authoritarianism. The regimes of Päts, Ulmanis and Smetona were not racist or xenophobic, but their aggressive support of national languages undermined the system of Polish and German schooling and the cultural autonomy of minorities in the Baltic countries.[16]

In foreign policy, all three states pursued a policy of neutrality. Lithuania was in a more difficult situation as it had long-running territorial conflicts with Poland because of the Polish incorporation of Vilnius in 1920 and with Germany because of the Lithuanian annexation of Memel (Klaipėda) in 1923. (Memel, with a predominantly German population, was then under the control of the League of Nations.) In 1938, Poland forced Lithuania to recognise Vilnius as belonging to Poland, while in March 1939 Germany wrested Klaipėda back by force. During the late 1920s and early 1930s, the Baltic states concluded non-aggression or neutrality agreements with the Soviet Union, followed in 1939 by similar pacts with Nazi Germany. These documents, however, offered little protection when the Great Powers again took it upon themselves to rearrange the map of Europe.

Western Belorussia and the largest part of Western Ukraine found themselves within the new Polish state. In Belorussian lands, where a modern national consciousness was slow in developing, the population's grievances

---

16 Hiden and Salmon, *The Baltic Nations*, pp. 55–7.

found their expression in the popularity of socialism. Following a brief inter-lude in the early 1920s, when minority rights had been well protected, Poland, which became an authoritarian dictatorship after 1926, adopted a policy of assimilating Belorussians by closing their schools and encouraging the spread of Roman Catholicism. In addition, Poland handled the redistribution of large landed estates in such a way that the primary beneficiaries were not the local Belorussian peasants, but Polish colonists. The Polish government repeatedly manipulated census results to play down the domination of Polish colonists in the area that was ethnically Belorussian. As a result of such policies and contin-ued land hunger, the Communist Party of western Belorussia and its legal arm, the Belorussian Peasant and Workers' Union, grew in popularity until they were suppressed in 1927. The 1930s saw further government repressions against Belorussian cultural institutions and the forcible closure of Orthodox churches.

In Galicia, the Polish government attempted similar policies against the local Ukrainian population, but the response was different, namely, the birth of Ukrainian radical nationalism. With civic discipline and a highly developed national consciousness, Ukrainians were frustrated by the defeat of the West-ern Ukrainian People's Republic and the ensuing Polish domination. Assimila-tory pressures only added to their sense of injustice. By the mid-1930s, it became clear that a decade of political participation, including several attempts at com-promise between the leading Ukrainian party, the Ukrainian National Demo-cratic Alliance, and the authorities, had failed to stop the national oppression. A new generation of disaffected young men and women grew disappointed with the fruitless 'collaborationism' of their elders. The moral failure of mod-erate nationalists cleared the way for the radical Right. At a conference in Vienna in 1929, veterans of the Ukrainian–Polish war, students and nationalist intellectuals created the Organisation of Ukrainian Nationalists (OUN). The ideology of the new group emphasised the nation as an absolute value and the willpower of a strong minority as the way to restore a nation to its greatness. The radical Right soon grew into a mass movement.

Ukrainians in inter-war Romania also experienced a policy of assimila-tion, if only formulated more clearly and enforced more strictly. Although the Ukrainian and Romanian languages had little in common, the ideologues of the ruling Romanian National Liberal Party classified the Ukrainian popula-tion in Bukovina as Romanians who had forgotten their ancestral tongue.[17] In contrast, the position of Ukrainians in Transcarpathia improved greatly. The

---

17 Paul Robert Magocsi, *A History of Ukraine* (Toronto: University of Toronto Press, 1996), p. 602.

Czechoslovak Republic, which was the only new state in Eastern Europe that remained a liberal democracy during the entire inter-war period, provided government support for minority education and culture and allowed the use of minority languages in local administration.

When Hitler began his dismemberment of Czechoslovakia in the autumn of 1938, Transcarpathians took advantage of the situation to press for autonomy (October) and even proclaimed the short-lived independent Republic of Carpatho-Ukraine under President Avhustyn Voloshyn (15 March 1939). Nazi Germany, however, assigned Transcarpathia to its Hungarian ally, and in the spring of 1939, Hungarian troops easily overran the Ukrainian defences in what was one of the precursor conflicts of the Second World War.

Finally, Romania spent much of the inter-war period trying to integrate Bessarabia. This effort involved agrarian reform, the construction of roads and railroads and the promotion of literacy. Naturally, the government sought in the process to promote a sense of Romanian patriotism in a backward borderland. Still, the province remained poor. Its only significant export, wine, diminished when the province was separated from the Russian regions. Large minorities such as Russians, Ukrainians and Jews complained about their treatment during the Romanian cultural offensive, and even many Moldavians found it difficult to switch from the Cyrillic alphabet to Latin script. (In addition, the modern Romanian language borrowed most new political, technical and scientific terminology from French, while Moldavians were accustomed to using the Russian words.)[18] All in all, not just minorities, but the Moldavians themselves made it difficult for Romania to 'nationalise' the region.

The Soviet Union, meanwhile, offered its own answer to the challenge of modern nationalism. The Bolshevik state attempted to disarm nationalism by promoting the forms of minority nationhood – national territories, languages, cultures and elites.[19] During the 1920s and early 1930s, the policy of *korenizatsiia* (nativisation) resulted in the creation of national republics or autonomous units, as well as in the state's major investment in the development of non-Russian cultures. The Ukrainian and Belorussian Socialist Soviet (after 1936, Soviet Socialist) Republics were among the beneficiaries of these policies.

Although promulgated in 1923, the policy of Ukrainisation began in earnest in 1925 with the appointment of Lazar Kaganovich as the General Secretary of the Communist Party (Bolshevik) of Ukraine (CP(b)U). Although Kaganovich and his successor Stanislav Kosior were certainly not sympathetic to the

18 King, *The Moldovans*, pp. 43–7.
19 Terry Martin, *An Affirmative Action Empire: Nations and Nationalism in the Soviet Union, 1923–1939* (Ithaca, N.Y.: Cornell University Press, 2001), pp. 1–27.

Ukrainian national cause, they felt it necessary to enforce the 'party line'. The practical guidance of Ukrainisation fell to two remarkable people's commissars of education, Oleksandr Shumsky and Mykola Skrypnyk, both subsequently denounced as nationalist deviationists. Still, the results of state-run Ukrainisation were impressive. Between 1924 and 1933, the Ukrainians' share among CP(b)U members increased from 33 to 60 per cent. Literacy increased markedly, and, by 1929, an impressive 97 per cent of elementary-school students were receiving instruction in Ukrainian. In contrast to 1922, when only one Ukrainian newspaper was in existence, in 1931, 89 per cent of the republic's newspapers were published in Ukrainian.[20] A number of political émigrés returned, including the leading historian and former head of the Central Rada, Mykhailo Hrushevsky.

Like the rest of the USSR, however, in the late 1920s Soviet Ukraine began to experience a violent transition to rapid industrialisation and forced collectivisation of agriculture. Stalinist social transformations went hand in hand with the denunciation of 'national communists' (1928), the trial of the fictitious Union for the Liberation of Ukraine (1930) and the condemnation of Skrypnyk (who shot himself in 1933). The state's murderous grain collection policies in the republic resulted in the catastrophic famine of 1932–3, which took an estimated 4 to 6 million lives. As new archival research demonstrates, Stalin and his associates blamed problems with grain collection on nationalist sabotage within the CP(b)U.[21] This made them even more determined to starve the Ukrainian peasantry into submission. At the same time, active Ukrainisers were condemned as nationalists and many of their reforms reversed, including Skrypnyk's standardisation of the Ukrainian language, which was allegedly designed to distance it from Russian. By the late 1930s, the authorities returned to the promotion in Ukraine of the Russian language and Russian culture.

In the Belorussian SSR, a similar policy of Belorussianisation was implemented during the 1920s. Commissar of Education and later president of the Belarusian Academy of Sciences, Usevalad Ihnatoŭski, initiated the Belorussianisation drive, but he was also among the first victims of the eventual hunt for Belorussian nationalists. (Ihnatoŭski committed suicide in 1930.)[22] Like Ukraine, the Belorussian SSR in the 1930s saw an official effort to bring the national language closer to Russian. The Great Terror of the late 1930s completed the elimination of the generation of radical activists for whom

---

20 Magocsi, *A History of Ukraine*, pp. 538–45.
21 Martin, *An Affirmative Action Empire*, pp. 302–8.
22 Ivan S. Lubachko, *Belorussia under Soviet Rule, 1917–1957* (Lexington: University Press of Kentucky, 1972), pp. 109–11.

socialism and non-Russian nation-building were two potentially compatible projects.

Unlike Ukraine and Belorussia, Soviet Moldavia was not made a union republic, but only an autonomous republic within the Ukrainian SSR (1924). From the very beginning, a Moldavian autonomy on the eastern bank of the Dniester, in Transnistria, was designed as a political magnet for Moldavians across the river, in Bessarabia. Ethnic Moldovans constituted only 30 per cent of the republic's population (Ukrainians had a plurality, at 48.5 per cent), but their existence was important for supporting the Soviet claim on Bessarabia. Following the high-point of Moldavianisation under Commissar for Education Pavel Chior (1928–30), this policy suffered setbacks. In a puzzling turn of events specific to Moldavia, the authorities first ordered the switch from the traditional Cyrillic script to the Latin (1932) to stress the unity of Moldavian and Romanian languages and then, the return to the Cyrillic alphabet (1938) as closer to Russian.

Before the dust settled after the reversal of nativisation policies, the Soviet nationalities policy changed again with the annexation of new territories in the west. Just as mature Stalinism established the Russians' priority status in the Soviet family of nations, Stalinist ideologues came to need an ethnic argument again in their defence of the new conquests. The secret protocol attached to the August 1939 Molotov–Ribbentrop pact assigned Estonia, Latvia, the eastern part of Poland, and Bessarabia to the Soviet sphere of influence (Lithuania was added in September). The Soviet occupation of Western Ukraine and Belorussia in September 1939 was staged as the historic reunification of the Ukrainian and Belorussian nations, respectively.[23] Stalinist ideologues used the same argument to wrest Bukovina from Romania in June 1940 and Transcarpathia from Czechoslovakia in 1945. Ironically, in view of all previous and subsequent efforts at establishing a Soviet Moldovan nationality, the annexation of Bessarabia in June 1940 was likewise justified by this land's allegedly Ukrainian character.[24] Still, Bessarabia became part of the Moldavian autonomous republic. Western Ukraine and western Belorussia joined the existing Ukrainian and Belorussian republics, while Estonia, Latvia and Lithuania became new union republics.

During what post-Communist historians in these countries now refer to as the 'first Soviet occupation', Stalinist authorities did not have time to complete either a collectivisation of agriculture or industrialisation. They did, however,

23 Serhy Yekelchyk, 'Stalinist Patriotism as Imperial Discourse: Reconciling the Ukrainian and Russian "Heroic Pasts", 1938–45', *Kritika: Explorations in Russian and Eurasian History* 3, 1 (2002): 51–80.
24 King, *The Moldovans*, 92.

nationalise existing industry and large farms. While not infringing the rights of local cultures – and in fact, promoting Ukrainian and Belorussian cultures in the former Polish-controlled territories – the bureaucrats carried out mass deportations to Siberia and Soviet Asia of former government officials, bourgeoisie, intellectuals and other 'unreliable elements'. In tiny Estonia, the number of deportees reached 60,000; in Western Ukraine, estimates are in the hundreds of thousands.[25] The Katyn forest in Belorussia became the symbol of another Stalinist crime, the secret execution of thousands of Polish POWs.

The German attack in June 1941 interrupted the Stalinisation of the western republics, but the Nazis had by then abandoned their earlier plans to create a system of puppet states in the Soviet west. In any case, their racial ideology dictated different treatment of the peoples living in the occupied territories. In Estonia, Latvia and Lithuania, local self-government in the form of ministries was set up and universities were allowed to function. In Ukraine and Belorussia, the natives could at best serve in municipal administration, and schooling above Grade Four was abolished. However, all these territories were exploited economically and earmarked for future incorporation into the Reich. Looking for immediate economic benefits, the German administration never really kept its promise to dissolve the collective farms in Ukraine and Belorussia or to allow the restitution of nationalised businesses in the Baltics. In all these regions and usually with the help of local collaborators, the Nazis carried out the extermination of the Jews. Late in the war, in a desperate effort to use the non-Russians' manpower, the Nazis established national SS units composed of Estonians, Latvians and Galician Ukrainians. (This effort failed in Lithuania and was not attempted in Belorussia and eastern Ukraine, but throughout the western republics the locals were actively recruited into auxiliary troops and police.) The Germans suppressed or ignored several attempts by the nationalists to proclaim state independence and, until desperate times came in 1943, were generally wary of working with them. Especially after 1943, Soviet partisans were active in Ukraine, Belorussia and Lithuania. So were the nationalist guerrilla detachments, which originally attacked the Soviet troops but, in view of Nazi mistreatment, soon turned against the Germans as well.

The Soviet army recovered the western regions one by one between the autumn of 1943 (eastern Ukraine) and the spring of 1945 (parts of Latvia). Its advance resulted in the mass westward exodus of the population especially from the regions that had been incorporated before the war. Intellectuals

---

25 Taagepera, *Estonia*, 67; Orest Subtelny, *Ukraine: A History*, 3rd edn (Toronto: University of Toronto Press, 2000), p. 456.

and nationalist activists were over-represented among the so-called 'displaced persons', who, during the late 1940s, resettled primarily in North America, Australia and Britain. Particularly in the Baltics and Western Ukraine, the Soviet army encountered fierce resistance from the nationalist guerrillas, who congregated in the region's forests, but, by the end of the decade, the brutal Soviet counter-measures had succeeded in establishing control over the countryside. This achievement was accompanied by a new wave of mass deportations. Still, the armed resistance in the west profoundly traumatised Soviet ideologues, who subsequently always treated the region as nationalism-prone.

## Between Eastern Europe and the Russian core

Territorial changes at the end of the Second World War favoured the western republics (see Map 8.1). In addition to the 1939 reunion of eastern and Western Ukraine, the Ukrainian SSR acquired Transcarpathia from Czechoslovakia. Lithuania recovered Vilnius from Poland and Klaipėda from Germany. But the population losses and destruction brought by the war made for a long recovery. While Stalinist authorities in the old Soviet regions busied themselves with reconstruction, in the newly acquired western territories their task was Sovietisation. The collectivisation of agriculture was put on hold until the late 1940s, when the authorities established their control over the countryside, but when it finally came, the collectivisation was as violent and disruptive as its all-Union model had been two decades previously.

The post-war international situation also complicated the authorities' choices. New Soviet satellite states in Eastern Europe preserved their independent statehood, and Soviet ideology was at a loss to explain why, for instance, Estonia had to be a part of the USSR, while Poland had not. The very existence of the Soviet republic of Moldavia east of socialist Romania might appear superfluous. As Roman Szporluk has long argued, the emergence of socialist states in Eastern Europe in a fundamental way undermined the legitimacy of Soviet nationality policy.[26] Stalin's new subjects might not feel this theoretical tension. But the Soviet west also became the region most exposed to contacts with East European versions of socialism and served as the USSR's shop window turned to Eastern Europe and Scandinavia.

Either because of this window-dressing function or because of their general ideological vision of the USSR as a highly developed industrial state, the central authorities in Moscow invested heavily in the industrial development of

26 Szporluk, *Russia, Ukraine*, pp. xxv–xxvi.

the western republics. The post-war period saw a quick industrial expansion, particularly in the Baltics and eastern Ukraine. Such previously agricultural areas as Lithuania, Belorussia, Western Ukraine, and Moldavia also, acquired some modern industries. Although not in the short run, industrial growth presented the western nationalities with two problems. First, their specialised production units were included in (and dependent on) the large network of the Soviet command economy. Second, much of the required skilled labour force was – whether intentionally or inevitably – recruited in Russia, thus increasing the share of the Russian population in the western republics. In one extreme case, the Latvian population of the Latvian SSR's capital, Riga, decreased from 63.0 per cent in 1939 to 44.6 per cent in 1959 and to 36.5 per cent in 1989.[27] In Moldavia, Bessarabia remained agrarian, while new industrial development (and new Russian migrants) were concentrated in Transnistria, the former Moldavian autonomy within the Ukrainian republic.

Politically and culturally, life in the western republics stabilised following de-Stalinisation. By the late 1960s and early 1970s, the Baltic republics demonstrated standards of living higher than elsewhere in the USSR, while the rest of the region (except Moldavia) was on a par with the European part of Russia. Especially in urban areas, consumerism set in with the wider availability of cars, furniture, refrigerators, vacuum cleaners and cassette recorders. Except for a brief period during the late 1950s and early 1960s, the central authorities did not openly encourage assimilation to Russian culture, although they were clearly pleased when social processes pushed in this direction. During the 1970s, especially in Belorussia and eastern Ukraine, local party leaders sometimes assisted the Russification of education, the media and urban environment. Needless to say, the Soviet authorities and the KGB remained ever watchful for manifestations of 'bourgeois nationalism' in the western borderlands, suppressing every potential source of resentment.

But the perpetual threat of 'nationalism' was built into the Soviet system, which had itself institutionalised ethnic difference. There were local administrators who, like the deputy premier Eduards Berklāvs in Latvia during the late 1950s or First Secretary Petro Shelest' in Ukraine during the 1960s, developed too strong an identification with their countries and cultures. More important, the functioning of full-fledged national cultures, even Soviet-style, required the existence of national cultural producers, groups of intellectuals who often deviated from the required intricate balance of Sovietness and national pride. There were, too, 'national religions' in some regions of the Soviet west.

27 Plakans, *The Latvians*, pp. 136 and 166.

Persecutions of the Roman Catholic Church in Lithuania, for instance, elicited strong popular protest. Although the Ukrainian Greek Catholic Church had been forcibly dissolved in 1946, it retained a considerable following in Western Ukraine as a 'catacomb Church'.

Publicly, only small groups of intellectuals dared to express their discontent with the Soviet nationalities policy. Although much lionised in post-Soviet nationalist historiographies, the dissident movement did not and could not have brought down the Soviet Empire. Until its rebirth under Gorbachev, the dissident movement remained the cause of hundreds, at most a couple of thousand activists. The dissident movement in fact began with attempts to show that Stalin and his successors had forsaken the 'Leninist' notions of national equality. This was the principal message of *Internationalism or Russification?* by the prominent Ukrainian dissident Ivan Dziuba. Subsequently, the dissenters began openly advocating national rights and self-determination, as well as the advancement of civil rights. In Ukraine, by far the largest western republic, the generation of the 'sixties' first explored the limits of artistic expression but soon established an opposition to the regime on the issues of civil rights and cultural freedoms. The underground *Ukrainian Herald* began appearing in 1970, and a large Ukrainian Helsinki Watch, one of only two such groups in the Soviet west, emerged in Kiev in 1976 under the leadership of the former establishment writer Mykola Rudenko.

Interestingly, in view of its weaker industrial development, Lithuania led Estonia and Latvia in the growth of a nationalist dissident movement. There, workers and peasants were far more prominent than in Russian or Ukrainian dissent, which was dominated by intellectuals. Petitions in defence of the Catholic Church collected tens of thousands of signatures, and the underground *Chronicle of the Lithuanian Catholic Church* appeared steadily from 1972. In 1972, following the self-immolation of a nineteen-year-old non-conformist, mass youth protests took place in the city of Kaunas.[28] In 1976, the Lithuanian Helsinki Watch group came into existence under the leadership of Victoras Petkus. (It was suppressed in two years.) In Latvia, the 1971 letter by '17 Latvian Communists' (who, as was revealed later, included Berklāvs) complained to foreign Communist parties about the advances of assimilation in the republic. In Estonia, the 1972 memorandum to the UN that decried Russification and demanded restoration of independent statehood marked the birth of organised dissent. On the fortieth anniversary of the Molotov–Ribbentrop Pact (1979),

---

28 V. Stanley Vardys and Judith B. Sedaitis, *Lithuania: The Rebel Nation* (Boulder, Colo.: Westview Press, 1997), pp. 84–92.

dissidents of all three Baltic nations issued a declaration demanding its nullifi-cation. Among the signatories were thirty-seven Lithuanians, four Estonians, and four Latvians. In contrast to other nations of the region, the dissident movement in Estonia exploded briefly in 1980–1, under the influence of con-temporary events in Poland, but was immediately weakened by arrests and imprisonments.

In contrast, dissent in Belorussia was unorganised and limited to statements by intellectuals in defence of the national language. In Moldavia, even such sporadic expressions of discontent were rare.

By the early 1980s, the general population in the Soviet west was reasonably informed about living standards in Eastern Europe and the so-called capitalist countries and in its majority was cynical about Soviet ideology. Multiple indi-cations of malfunctions in the Soviet economy and various social problems – from the lowest birth rate Union-wide in Estonia and Latvia to one of the highest child mortality rates Union-wide in rural Moldova – caused citizens to privately question the efficiency of Soviet socialism. Yet, in those years the authorities almost succeeded in rooting out organised dissent. Mass expres-sion of discontent did not emerge until Gorbachev's *glasnost'* began creating a genuine public sphere. Only the reforms originating in Moscow allowed the non-Russian national movements to resume their interrupted (or 'frozen') nation-building projects by returning to what Hroch designates as the stage of mass mobilisation. In all western republics, the national cause acquired a truly mass following only after the long-suppressed economic frustrations and social tensions had flowed into the default channel of nationalistic discourse.

In a recent, fundamental study of the Soviet Union's collapse, Mark R. Beissinger argues that nationalist mobilisation proceeded in 'tides' within which the example of one region could influence developments in others. In the rise of secessionist movements within the USSR, the Balts were in the avant-garde. As Beissinger shows repeatedly in his book, other nationali-ties drew encouragement from their successes and emulated their methods.[29] This, however, applies to the political separatist movement, while the national awakening of the *glasnost'* period was originally a more complex phenomenon, which began as an ecological and cultural movement. Arguably, the movement started after the Chernobyl' disaster in April 1986, which both prompted Gor-bachev to expand the limits of *glasnost'* and gave birth to mass environmentalist movements.

29 Mark R. Beissinger, *Nationalist Mobilization and the Collapse of the Soviet State* (Cambridge: Cambridge University Press, 2002).

Even in the Baltics, the first open protests were against the grand designs of Soviet industry. In Estonia, the first mass meeting opposed Moscow's new phosphorus-mining project, which would damage the country's environment (1987). In 1988, the so-called 'singing revolution' symbolised the breakthrough in cultural revival. The national movement finally reached its organisational stage with the formation of the Estonian Popular Front in April 1988. In Latvia, the first successful effort at open mobilisation of the public was aimed against the construction of a hydroelectric dam on the Daugava River in 1987. Later in the same year, the so-called 'calendar' demonstrations followed, commemorating the 1941 deportations, marking the anniversary of the Molotov–Ribbentrop Pact, and celebrating the proclamation of independence in 1918. In October 1988, a popular front was constituted in the republic. Lithuania, where the Communist Party had been slower in answering the Kremlin's call for reforms, was the last to join the string of demonstrations in the Baltic region, with the first public meeting being organised by a group of Catholic activists on 23 August 1987, to mark the anniversary of the Soviet–German Pact. The popular front known as Sajūdis was established in June 1988.

The transition from the stage of cultural and ecological protests to the stage of political mobilisation took longer in Belorussia. There, national awakening began during 1987–8 with cultural figures petitioning the government for the protection of Belorussian culture against assimilation but escalated into open expressions of discontent in June 1988 with the discovery of mass graves of the victims of Stalinist terror in the Kurapaty forest. As the most powerful symbol of Stalinist crimes – and of what was seen as the Soviet regime's general criminal nature – Kurapaty galvanised public opinion. By October, the Belorussian analogue of Moscow's Memorial Society emerged under the name of the Martyrology of Belorussia Association. Led by the archaeologist Zianon Paźniak, this group immediately began organising the Belorussian Popular Front (BPF) but met fierce resistance from the authorities. At this point, Belorussian activists had already established contacts with Sajūdis. The BPF's founding congress consequently took place in the Lithuanian capital of Vilnius in June 1989.[30] Still, the republic's government effectively prevented the BPF from reaching out to the countryside.

In Ukraine, where the party leadership kept a lid on public opinion until as late as 1989, the development of the national movement combined the traits of the Lithuanian and Belorussian models. In Western Ukraine, a mass

---

30 David Marples, *Belarus: A Denationalized Nation* (Amsterdam: Harwood Academic Publishers, 1999), pp. 47–8.

movement for the restoration of the Greek Catholic Church emerged in 1987. (The authorities finally gave their permission in late 1989.) In the east, the plight of Chernobyl' was the earliest uniting factor as well as the most obvious symbol of the regime's ineffectiveness and criminal secretiveness. The public ecological association, the Green World, was founded in 1987, while the organisation in defence of the national language, the Taras Shevchenko Ukrainian Language Society, was not established until February 1989. But in the same month, a more important political organisation came into existence, namely, the Popular Movement for Restructuring. Better known simply as Rukh (Movement), it was similar in structure and political aims to the Baltic popular fronts at the early stage of their development.

In Moldavia, the party managed to keep the forces of change at bay until mid-1988. But when the breakthrough came in the summer of that year, the republic's intellectuals promptly established both cultural organisations and the more politically oriented Democratic Movement in Support of Restructuring. (These and other pro-reform groups in May 1989 united in the Moldavian Popular Front.) Like the Ukrainian opposition, the Moldavian opposition united around the language issue, which in the Moldavian case entailed not just the status and protection of Moldavian as a state language, but also the recognition of its unity with Romanian and its 'return' to the Latin script. But in all republics of the western belt, the language issue was a political issue.

Although all of them had been created ostensibly to assist Gorbachev in the implementation of his *perestroika* policies, the popular fronts in the Soviet west soon concentrated on the issues specific to their nations. Originally they were limited to language, the environment and Stalinist crimes, but these issues already challenged the Soviet Union's legitimacy. Ultimately, Gorbachev's reforms gave nationalists the opportunity to go public, and the Kremlin proved unable to prevent them from starting mass mobilisations. Initially, popular fronts included reformist Communists and minorities, but the opposition they encountered from the conservative party leadership in most republics, as well as from the emerging minority movements, radicalised their ideology. The seemingly easy collapse of Communist regimes in Eastern Europe was also a contributing factor. By 1990, the popular fronts had evolved from the defence of democratic rights in the republics to the defence of national interests of the titular nations.

During 1989, the national movements went political and succeeded in capturing the protest vote in the Soviet west. Once again, Moscow initiated this turn of events by calling free elections to the All-Union Congress of People's Deputies (March–May 1989). In Lithuania, Sajūdis won all the seats except two that went to national Communists whom the nationalists did not oppose. In Estonia and Latvia, nationalists also won, although on a less impressive scale. On the fiftieth anniversary of the Molotov–Ribbentrop Pact, 23 August 1989, the Baltic popular fronts mounted the most imposing protest action yet when they organised a human chain of some 2 million people from Tallinn to Vilnius. The event drew the world's attention to the growing national unrest in the region.

In 1990, elections to republican parliaments (Supreme Soviets) revealed the emerging political realignment. In Lithuania, where the majority of Communist Party members belonged to the titular nationality, the party proclaimed its independence from the All-Union Party (November 1989). In the months leading to the elections, the reformist Communist leader Algirdas Brazauskas co-operated with the Popular Front, but his party won only a minority of seats. In March 1990, the parliament elected as president the nationalist Vytautas Landsbergis and voted unanimously for the republic's independence, which the Kremlin did not recognise and which was later revoked after a three-month economic blockade.[31] In Estonia and Latvia, the Communist parties captured the votes of primarily ethnic Russians, yet nationalists had a majority and in March 1990 could proclaim – although not as clearly as the Lithuanians had – their republics' intention to re-establish their independence. Perhaps more important, the Baltic governments began asserting their economic independence by stopping financial contributions to the central budget and initiating independent economic reforms.

While Gorbachev was shocked by the mass support for separatism, he remained reluctant to use force in the republics. Although the local press repeatedly warned about an impending crackdown, it never materialised as a large-scale military operation. Rather, in January 1991, a series of smaller incidents took place in the Baltic states, with the Kremlin either denying its involvement or apologising for the 'unintended violence'. In Lithuania, Soviet troops took control of the radio and TV centre, killing fourteen people and injuring 150. In Latvia, five people died and ten were injured when Soviet police special forces captured the building of the Ministry of the Interior. Because these events received extensive media coverage both within and outside the USSR, instead of harassing nationalists as intended, they actually harmed the cause of those in Moscow who had favoured the use of violence in the borderlands.

---

31 Alfred Erich Senn, 'Lithuania: Rights and Responsibilities of Independence', in Ian Bremmer and Ray Taras (eds.), *New States, New Politics: Building the Post-Soviet Nations* (Cambridge: Cambridge University Press, 1997), pp. 356–61.

In contrast, the March 1990 elections to the Supreme Soviet of the Belorussian SSR demonstrated the extent of the authorities' control, with the Communist Party winning 86 per cent of seats. After years of prodding by the intelligentsia, party bureaucrats did agree in January 1990 to pass a law making Belorussian the official language of the state. (Similar laws were by then passed in all other republics of the Soviet west.) Yet, in practice the population of Belorussia remained the most Russified and the least politically active in the region.

In Ukraine, support for Rukh was unevenly distributed geographically. In Western Ukraine, the national movement enjoyed mass support, while in the east it relied primarily on the humanitarian intelligentsia in the cities. Correspondingly, during the 1990 elections, Rukh captured most seats from the western provinces and some in big urban centres, but its total was only 90 out of 450 seats. Hard-line Communists remained policy makers in the republic, although they now had to face opposition in the parliament. Still, following the example of other republics, especially Russia, the majority felt it necessary to pass a declaration of sovereignty (July 1990), which was more an affirmation of the republic's rights than a separatist statement.

In Moldavia, however, the Popular Front, together with the reformist Communists, won the majority of seats during the 1990 elections. The majority pushed through a number of Romanian-oriented cultural reforms, which alienated the minorities. (It is worth noting, nevertheless, that the idea of union with Romania had little support even among Moldavians.) In August 1990, the Turkic-speaking Gagauz population in the south declared a separate Gagauz Republic with its capital in Comrat, and in September, Russians and Russian-speaking Ukrainians in Transnistria created the Dniester Republic with its capital in Tiraspol'. Some 50,000 Moldavian nationalist volunteers immediately marched on the Dniester Republic, where fighting would go on intermittently for several years.

When the abortive coup in August 1991 destroyed the centre's remaining power structures, the Baltic republics were the first to claim their full independence. The Estonian parliament passed a motion to this effect on 20 August, and the first international recognition, from Iceland, followed on 22 August. Yeltsin's Russia was a close second, on 24 August, while both the USA and the USSR hesitated until early September. Although the Soviet military went violent in Riga, Latvia and Lithuania were equally prompt and successful in asserting their independent statehood. At the end of September, all three states already had separate seats at the UN General Assembly.

In Ukraine and Belarus, Communist-dominated parliaments also issued declarations of independence, on 24 and 25 August, respectively. Disoriented by the collapse of the party's centralised controls, local bureaucrats let themselves be persuaded by nationalists and reformers. Moreover, former Communists envisaged their continuing rule after independence. The Ukrainian referendum on independence on 1 December 1991, with over 90 per cent voting in favour of separate statehood, delivered the final blow to the idea of reviving the Soviet Union. The general population, including the minority voters, was swept away by the promises of economic prosperity that state-run media and nationalist agitators issued so easily. Moldova was the last to declare independence, on 27 August 1991, and the question of possible union with Romania that overnight acquired practical significance caused further splits within both the Popular Front and among the reformist Communists.

In the years after the Soviet Union's death, the western republics went their separate roads, albeit the ones determined to a significant degree by Russian politics in the region. But the legacy of twentieth-century nation-building was more important yet. Estonia, Latvia and Lithuania never considered joining the Commonwealth of Independent States, but the treatment of large Russian minorities, especially in Estonia and Latvia, became the major issue between Russia and them. In fact, during the early 1990s, Estonia and Latvia considered all post-1940 immigrants and their children non-citizens requiring naturalisation. The disenfranchisement of minority residents who could not pass a difficult language exam earned Estonia and Latvia reprimands from the European Union and human rights organisations. Although the three states moved quickly to reorient their economies towards the West and introduce market reforms, their continuing connection with Russia was demonstrated as late as 1998, when their economies suffered downturns as a result of the Russian financial collapse. Still, the three Baltic states were extremely successful in what they billed as their 'return to Europe'. In the spring of 2004, all three joined the European Union and NATO.

In contrast, Ukraine still struggles to assert its separateness from Russia, especially in the economic and cultural spheres. Under President Leonid Kravchuk, the state sponsored the Ukrainisation of public life and education, normalised relations with Russia and quelled minority unrest. Yet, the lack of economic reforms caused Kravchuk's downfall. President Leonid Kuchma (1994–2004) came to power on the platform of rebuilding economic ties with Russia and restoring the Russian language to its previously prominent role, but for most of his rule, he tried to maintain a balance between Russia and the West. Still, under Kuchma, Russian financial interests came to control much of Ukraine's industry and mass culture. Late in 2004 Kuchma's attempt to transfer power to a hand-picked successor failed as hundreds of thousands of orange-clad oppositionists occupied Kiev's main square, protesting against the rigged elections. The peaceful 'Orange Revolution' brought to power pro-Western President Viktor Yushchenko (2005– ), who promised to fight corruption and take Ukraine 'back to Europe'.

Finally, Belarus and Moldova experienced a troubled post-Soviet transition. In Belarus, continuous economic decline during the early 1990s eroded already weak support for separate statehood. In 1994, a pro-Russian populist, Aliaksandr Lukashenka, won the presidential elections, putting the country on the path of assimilation, preservation of Soviet-style economy and economic dependence on Russia. Lukashenka's rule eventually deteriorated into an oppressive dictatorship. Formally, Belarus was to enter into union with Russia (1997), a union that was proclaimed but never consummated because of the Russian authorities' reluctance. In Moldova, the early years of independence were marred by political fragmentation over the question of national identity, as well as by ethnic violence, while the second part of the decade saw the reassertion of Russian political and economic influence. The conflict in Transnistria escalated in 1992, and, although Yeltsin's mediation helped to negotiate a ceasefire, the self-proclaimed Dniester Republic remains de facto independent. The faltering economy and huge state salary and pension arrears buoyed the popularity of unreformed Communists, who in 2001 won the parliamentary elections with 50.1 per cent of the votes. The parliament elected as president Vladimir Voronin, who proclaimed a course of closer co-operation with Russia.

At the beginning of the twenty-first century, the former Soviet west no longer exists as a region distinguished by its one-time connection to non-Russian European states or by the brief period of pre-Soviet independence. If the countries of the western belt with their widely disparate economic, political and cultural profiles still have anything in common, it is their Soviet legacy: a considerable Russian minority, economic ties with Russia and Russia's security interest in the area. Only in the cultural sphere, although not without political implications, do local identities continue to be defined in their relation to the Soviet project.

20

# Science, technology and modernity

DAVID HOLLOWAY

## Introduction

Science and technology occupy a central place in the history of all modern states, but their role is particularly significant in twentieth-century Russia. The Soviet Union had at one time a greater number of scientists and engineers than any other country in the world. It made a massive effort to overtake the West in the development of technology. And most important, science and technology were integral to the Soviet claim to offer a vision of modernity that was superior to that of Western capitalism. Not only would science and technology flourish in the Soviet Union, according to this claim; the Soviet system was itself consciously constructed on the basis of a scientific theory and would be guided by that theory in its future development. The Soviet Union presented itself as the true heir to the Enlightenment project of applying reason to human affairs.

## Before the revolution (1901–17)

Science (*nauka*) in Russia was linked with modernisation from the very beginning.[1] Peter the Great imported natural science from Europe in the early eighteenth century as part of his effort to transform Russia into a Great Power. He established the St Petersburg Academy of Sciences in 1724, before there were universities in Russia. For a century and a half, most of the Academy's members were from outside Russia, and many Russians regarded science as alien to Russian culture.[2] In the second half of the nineteenth century a more

---

1 'Nauka' covers both natural and social sciences. 'Nauka' and 'nauchnyi' have a broader meaning than we currently give to 'science' and 'scientific'. This chapter looks primarily at the natural sciences. Where the meaning given to 'science' is broader, I hope it will be clear from the context.
2 Alexander Vucinich, *Science in Russian Culture: A History to 1860* (Stanford, Calif.: Stanford University Press, 1963).

or less cohesive scientific community began to emerge, bound together by learned societies and scientific congresses. A number of Russian scientists, among them N. I. Lobachevskii and D. I. Mendeleev, won international reputations during the nineteenth century, and in the early years of the twentieth century two Russian scientists – I. P. Pavlov and I. I. Mechnikov – were among the first winners of the Nobel Prize for Physiology. Russia had over 4,000 scientists engaged in research at the beginning of the century, and although it lagged behind Britain, Germany and France, it did have areas of real strength – in mathematics and chemistry, for example.[3]

The Academy of Sciences, like academies in other countries, was primarily an honorific society at the beginning of the twentieth century. Most scientific research was done in universities and specialised institutes of higher education. Russia had close scientific ties with Europe, and Russian scientists felt themselves to be part of an international community. They were increasingly conscious of themselves as an important – or at least potentially important – force in Russian society and, like other members of the intelligentsia, they wanted to play a useful role in Russia's development.[4]

In January 1905 a group of 342 St Petersburg university teachers and researchers signed a document criticising the system of higher education for treating university teachers as bureaucrats. They argued that science could flourish only when it was free and protected from external interference. These sentiments were widely shared in the scientific community. In the spring of 1905 a group of leading scientists and scholars founded the Academic Union in order to press for reform of higher education. The Union, which soon included about 70 per cent of all university teachers as members, called on the government to carry through democratic reforms in order to prevent anarchy in the country. Members of the Union helped to found the liberal Constitutional Democratic Party (the Kadets) later in the year. Although there was a significant group of conservative scientists and scholars in Russia, and a small number who supported the revolutionary parties, most scientists were liberal and reformist in their political outlook. With the exception of

3 Alexander Vucinich, *Science in Russian Culture 1861–1917* (Stanford, Calif.: Stanford University Press, 1970); Loren R. Graham, *Science in Russia and the Soviet Union. A Short History* (Cambridge: Cambridge University Press, 1993), pp. 32–75; Robert Lewis, *Science and Industrialisation in the USSR* (London: Macmillan, 1979), p. 5.
4 E. I. Kolchinskii and A. V. Kol'tsov, 'Rossiiskaia nauka i revoliutsionnye krizisy v nachale XX veka', in E. I. Kolchinskii (ed.), *Nauka i krizisy* (St Petersburg: Institut istorii estestvoznaniia i tekhniki, Sankt-Peterburgskii filial, 2003), pp. 291–4.

1905–7, however, they did not play an active role in politics as a corporate group.[5]

Relations with the government remained tense after the Revolution of 1905. When the government sent the police into Moscow University in 1911 to arrest students, 130 professors and instructors – almost one-third of the total number – resigned in protest at the government's infringement of university autonomy. This clash reflected the strains in the relationship: the government wanted the benefits of science and education but was unwilling to grant the scientific community the autonomy it sought.[6]

Russian scientists had little contact with Russian industry, which was largely owned by foreign capital and relied mainly on research done abroad. The absence of a strong industrial research base became painfully apparent with the outbreak of the First World War, when Russia was deprived of the products and raw materials it had been importing from Germany. The government responded by building up research in the War Department and looking favourably on proposals from scientists to put research at the service of the state. In 1915 the Academy of Sciences set up a Commission for the Study of the Natural Productive Resources of Russia under the chairmanship of the mineralogist V. I. Vernadskii. This pointed the way to a new and potentially productive relationship among science, industry and the state.[7]

Science was, for many intellectuals, a force for political change. In the 1860s the Nihilists had advanced the view that science could be used to change the existing social and political order. Science as a mode of enquiry represented, in their view, the highest form of reason; scientific education would eliminate traditional and patriarchal attitudes, thereby destroying the ideological foundation of tsarist rule and opening the way to a new, rational social order. Few intellectuals after the 1860s took quite such an uncompromising view, but reformers and revolutionaries did look on science as a force for progress. The government, for its part, regarded scientific knowledge as indispensable to the modernisation of Russia, but it distrusted the scientific spirit, which it saw as critical of authority.[8]

5 Kolchinskii and Kol'tsov, 'Rossiiskaia nauka', pp. 295–300; Samuel D. Kassow, *Students, Professors and the State in Tsarist Russia* (Berkeley: University of California Press, 1989), pp. 5–8.
6 Kassow, *Students, Professors and the State*, pp. 348–60.
7 Lewis, *Science and Industrialisation*, pp. 1–5; Kendall E. Bailes, *Technology and Society under Lenin and Stalin* (Princeton: Princeton University Press, 1978), pp. 19–43.
8 Vucinich, *Science in Russian Culture 1861–1917*, pp. 14–34, 424–88.

Science was crucial for those who wanted to make Russia a modern state, whatever their vision of modernity might be. Vernadskii, to take one prominent example, believed that the twentieth century would be the 'century of science and knowledge'.[9] To survive and win in international politics, a state had to invest in science and be willing to exploit the knowledge that science produced. Science was inherently democratic, Vernadskii argued, because it was the free thought and free will of individuals that determined the direction of its development. Science needed freedom in order to flourish, and only states that enjoyed freedom would prosper. Vernadskii was one of the founding members of the Kadet Party, and his advocacy of reform was intimately linked to his understanding of science and its place in the development of society.[10]

Marxists claimed that Marxism was both a scientific theory and a guide to revolutionary action. It was based, like the natural sciences, on a materialist conception of reality, and it employed in the analysis of society the same dialectical method that natural scientists used in their study of nature. It enabled them to make a scientific analysis of capitalism and of the revolutionary process that would lead to its replacement by socialism. Precisely how scientific analysis and revolutionary action related to each other was a matter of debate among Marxists, but the claim to scientific status was nevertheless an important source of Marxism's appeal. Both Engels and Lenin took an interest in the philosophy of science and were concerned to show the continuity between Marxist social science and the natural sciences.[11]

## The Bolshevik revolution and its aftermath, 1917–29

Most Russian scientists greeted the February Revolution with enthusiasm because they hoped that a more liberal regime would allow science to flourish, but they regarded the October Revolution with deep suspicion.[12] Like the rest of the population, scientists suffered from the general economic collapse that followed the revolution; many succumbed to illness and died. They lost contact

---

9 V. I. Vernadskii, 'Razgrom', in V. I. Vernadskii, *O nauke* (St Petersburg: Izdatel'stvo Russkogo khristianskogo gumanitarnogo instituta, 2002), vol. II, p. 177.
10 V. I. Vernadskii, 'Mezhdunarodnaia assotsiatsiia akademii', in Vernadskii, *O nauke*, vol. II, p. 19; Vucinich, *Science in Russian Culture 1861–1917*, pp. 414–16, 477–82.
11 David Joravsky, *Soviet Marxism and Natural Science 1917–1932* (London: Routledge and Kegan Paul, 1961), pp. 3–44.
12 Kolchinskii and Kol'tsov, 'Rossiiskaia nauka', p. 329; and E. I. Kolchinskii, 'Nauka i grazhdanskaia voina v Rossii', in Kolchinskii, *Nauka i krizisy*, p. 357.

with colleagues abroad and ceased to receive foreign scientific journals.[13] Yet scientific research did not come to an end, nor was the scientific community destroyed. Scientists taught and did research in buildings that lacked gas and electricity. Scientific publication did not cease entirely. In spite of their mutual hostility, scientists and the Bolsheviks managed to co-operate. The desire to save science was a crucial motive for many scientists, who turned to the Bolsheviks once it became clear that they were consolidating their hold on power. Some scientists took the view that Bolshevik rule would not last long; others believed that science itself would have a civilising effect on the new regime.[14]

Lenin despised the Russian intelligentsia but wanted to harness science to the purposes of the revolution. He was dismissive of calls to create a 'proletarian science'. He wanted to produce a new socialist intelligentsia drawn from the working class and peasantry, and for this he needed the co-operation of those who possessed scientific and technical expertise. He treated scientists differently from other members of the intelligentsia.[15] When he expelled about 200 leading intellectuals from the country in 1922 as ideologically alien to the regime, very few of these were scientists.[16] In the spring of 1919 the Petrograd city government decided to provide a hundred scholars with Red Army rations. By December 1921 the number of scholars receiving 'academic rations' was 7,000.[17]

The Bolsheviks were determined to make science serve the revolution. They quickly rescinded the autonomy for which professors had struggled before 1917. When the People's Commissariat of Education failed to win the co-operation of professors, it proceeded to carry out university reform by decree.[18] By the early 1920s almost all the pre-revolutionary professors of humanities and social sciences had been dismissed, and the last vestiges of university autonomy eradicated. Universities themselves fell out of favour; many were closed and replaced by specialised institutes that offered a narrow

13 Kolchinskii, 'Nauka i grazhdanskaia voina', pp. 357–439. See also S. E. Frish, *Skvoz' prizmu vremeni* (Moscow: Politizdat, 1992), pp. 62–103.
14 E. I. Kolchinskii, 'Sovetizatsiia nauki v gody NEPa (1922–1927)', in Kolchinskii, *Nauka i krizisy*, pp. 440–51.
15 On Lenin's attitude, see Bailes, *Technology and Society*, pp. 45–56.
16 Stuart Finkel, 'Purging the Public Intellectual: The 1922 Expulsions from Soviet Russia', *Russian Review* 62 (2003): 611. See also Kolchinskii, 'Sovetizatsiia nauki', pp. 465–73.
17 Kolchinskii, 'Nauka i grazhdanskaia voina', pp. 409–28.
18 Sh. Kh. Chanbarisov, *Formirovanie sovetskoi universitetskoi sistemy* (Moscow: Vysshaia shkola, 1988), pp. 72–3.

training for the new socialist technical intelligentsia.[19] The Bolsheviks wanted to limit the influence of the old scientific intelligentsia on students, and that was one of the reasons why the Academy of Sciences, which had no students and was besides more pliable than the universities, became the leading scientific research centre in the Soviet Union. The government renamed it the USSR Academy of Sciences in 1925 and acknowledged it formally as the 'highest scholarly institution' in the country.[20]

Scientific research expanded rapidly in the 1920s. By 1925 there were eighty-eight research institutes, seventy-three of which had been established since the revolution. Nineteen of these were devoted to the social sciences, the rest to the natural sciences and applied research. Some of these institutes were in the Academy of Sciences, and some in the universities and higher educational establishments, but most were subordinate to the People's Commissariats.[21] The new institutes were a sign of the emerging collaboration between scientists and the new regime. Both sides believed that science was important for the future of Russia, and although they might have different visions of the future, belief in progress provided a basis for co-operation. This was, moreover, a real, if unequal, partnership. The Bolsheviks did not have plans for the organisation of science in 1917 and they responded favourably to scientists' proposals, many of them formulated in the years before the revolution. Leading scientists quickly adopted the language of the Bolsheviks in arguing that their research would provide the basis for new technology and contribute to the transformation of Russia. It was all the easier for them to do this because, although very few scientists were Communists, many of them shared the belief that science and technology were crucial to Russia's development.[22]

In 1918 the Bolsheviks established the Socialist Academy (renamed the Communist Academy in 1924) to encourage the development of Marxist social science. Independent of the Academy of Sciences, it was one of several Communist institutions designed to revolutionise intellectual life and educate a new intelligentsia. Initially focused on the social sciences, these institutions began to pay attention to the natural sciences in the mid-1920s. The Communist Academy created a Section of the Natural and Exact Sciences, with the task of 'rebuffing attacks on materialism and contributing to the development of materialist science'. The section was to organise a survey of scientific theories

19 Ibid., pp. 189–99; Kolchinskii, 'Sovetizatsiia nauki', pp. 458–65.
20 Ibid., p. 502.  21 For the figures see ibid., pp. 473–80.
22 M. S. Bastrakova, *Stanovlenie sovetskoi sistemy organizatsii nauki (1917–1922)* (Moscow: Nauka, 1973), pp. 34–61.

in order to bring to light the elements of idealism and materialism, and to synthesise the latter into 'purely materialistic general theories'.[23]

There was, however, no agreement among scientists or philosophers about the proper relationship between science and Marxist philosophy. The dominant view in the early 1920s was that of the 'mechanists', who argued that philosophy should confine itself to representing the most general conclusions of science, especially of the natural sciences.[24] There were, on the other hand, those who believed that philosophy could – and should – guide the scientists in their work. That was the position taken by a group of philosophers known as the 'dialecticians' (or the Deborinites, after their leader A. M. Deborin), who saw in the Hegelian dialectic – as reinterpreted by Marx and Engels – the methodological basis of science. 'We are striving for this', Deborin said in 1927, 'that dialectics should lead the natural scientist, that it should indicate the correct path to him.'[25] These philosophical debates did not, however, impinge very much on the conduct of research in the 1920s.[26]

The 1920s were a period of optimism for science in the Soviet Union. A bargain was struck between the Bolsheviks and the scientific community: if the latter would contribute its knowledge to the building of a socialist society, the Bolsheviks would help it to realise its projects for investigating and trans-forming nature. Scientists were relatively well paid, and they were allowed to maintain their foreign contacts.[27] The party's commitment to science was never in question. It was not a divisive issue in the party debates and leadership struggles of the 1920s. Vernadskii, who had gone to Paris in 1921 and thought about staying abroad, was impressed by what was happening in the Soviet Union, to which he returned in 1926.[28]

## The great break and the emergence of Stalinist science, 1929–41

Soviet leaders believed that science had a crucial role to play in helping the Soviet Union to 'catch up and overtake the technology of the advanced

---

23 Kolchinskii, 'Sovetizatsiia nauki', p. 513; Michael David-Fox, *Revolution of the Mind: Higher Learning among the Bolsheviks, 1918–1929* (Ithaca, N.Y.: Cornell University Press, 1997), pp. 201–29.
24 Joravsky, *Soviet Marxism and Natural Science*, pp. 82–3, 93–107; Kolchinskii, 'Sovetizatsiia nauki', pp. 520–1.
25 Quoted by Joravsky, *Soviet Marxism and Natural Science*, p. 176.
26 On these debates see esp. Joravsky, *Soviet Marxism and Natural Science*, pp. 150–214; and Kolchinskii, 'Sovetizatsiia nauki', pp. 508–33.
27 Kolchinskii, 'Sovetizatsiia nauki', pp. 507, 548.
28 I. I. Mochalov, *Vladimir Ivanovich Vernadskii* (Moscow: Nauka, 1982), pp. 246–9.

capitalist countries'.[29] Expenditure on science (in constant terms) grew more than threefold between 1927/8 and 1933. Thereafter the rate of growth slowed down, but it was still impressive, with spending on science almost doubling between 1933 and 1940. The Soviet Union probably spent a greater proportion of its national income than any other country on science in the 1930s.[30] The number of research scientists grew rapidly, from about 18,000 in 1929 to 46,000 in 1935.[31] This expansion took place in the Academy of Sciences, institutions of higher education and the research institutes under the People's Commissariats. The Communist Academy and the other Marxist-Leninist institutions lost much of their influence in the 1930s through closure or merger.

The Soviet Union imported large quantities of foreign machinery and plant during the First Five-Year Plan (1928–32).[32] The Second Five-Year Plan emphasised the development of indigenous technology. This put a heavy responsibility on the scientists and engineers who had predicted in the 1920s that investment in science would produce wonderful results. Such claims had been easy to advance when economic recovery meant little more than the restoration of an economy destroyed by civil war. They were a more serious matter once the party began looking to science to help it achieve the enormously ambitious goals it had set for the economy.

In order to ensure that science did indeed help them to achieve their goals, the authorities imposed rigorous political and administrative controls on the scientific community. In the late 1920s they decided to bring the Academy of Sciences under tighter political control.[33] They changed the procedures for nominating candidates, raised the number of positions in the Academy, and then pressed for the immediate election of eight Communists including N. I. Bukharin. The Academy's leadership acquiesced, but its General Assembly rejected three of the Communist candidates in January 1929. Under government pressure, another ballot was held the following month and the three Communists were elected, though with many abstentions. Administrative control was largely taken over by the newly elected Communist Academicians;

29 I. V. Stalin, 'Ob industrializatsii strany i o pravom uklone v VKP(b)', in I. V. Stalin, *Sochineniia* (Moscow: Gospolitizdat, 1950), vol. XI, p. 248.
30 Robert Lewis, 'Some Aspects of the Research and Development Effort of the Soviet Union, 1924–1935', *Science Studies* 2 (1972): 164.
31 Lewis, *Science and Industrialisation*, pp. 10, 13.
32 Antony C. Sutton, *Western Technology and Soviet Economic Development, 1930–1945* (Stanford, Calif.: Hoover Institution Press, 1971), *passim*.
33 Loren R. Graham, *The Soviet Academy of Sciences and the Communist Party 1927–1932* (Princeton: Princeton University Press, 1967), pp. 80–153; Alexander Vucinich, *Empire of Knowledge* (Berkeley: University of California Press, 1984), pp. 123–49; E. I. Kolchinskii, ' "Kul'turnaia revoliutsiia" i stanovlenie sovetskoi nauki', in Kolchinskii, *Nauka i krizisy*, pp. 586–601.

censorship of Academy publications was introduced for the first time; and tight restrictions were imposed on foreign travel. The Academy's move from Leningrad to Moscow in 1934 signified its absorption into the Soviet state apparatus.

The Academy abandoned the concept of pure science and placed a new emphasis on engineering and applied research. This policy rested on the belief that science did not grow by virtue of an internal logic, but in response to the technological demands that society placed on it.[34] The government introduced planning into science, over the objections of many scientists. In a speech to the first all-Union conference on the planning of scientific research in April 1931, Bukharin stressed that scientists should think beyond their research to the application of scientific knowledge in industrial production.[35]

The relationship between science and Marxist philosophy also underwent a crucial shift. In April 1929, the historian M. N. Pokrovskii, president of the Communist Academy, called on Marxists to end their 'peaceful coexistence' with non-Marxist and anti-Marxist scholars. He urged them 'to begin the decisive offensive on all fronts of scientific work, creating their own Marxist science'.[36] Deborin's claim that dialectical materialism should provide guidance to scientists now appeared too conservative. A group of younger, more radical philosophers called for the 'restructuring of the natural and the mathematical sciences on the basis of the materialist dialectic'.[37] There were sporadic efforts to do just that in the early 1930s, but in the summer of 1932 the Central Committee warned against ill-informed attempts to reconstruct scientific disciplines.[38]

Philosophers were subordinate to the authority of the party Central Committee. They did not constitute an ideological supreme court, passing independent judgement on the acceptability of scientific theories. Stalin made it clear that the primary purpose of theory was to help practice; the correctness of a theory could be judged by its contribution to practice.[39] It was the Central

34 Boris Hessen, 'The Social and Economic Roots of Newton's *Principia*', in J. Needham and P. G. Werksey (eds.), *Science at the Cross Roads*, 2nd edn (London: Frank Cass, 1971), pp. 151–212.
35 N. I. Bukharin, 'Osnovy planirovaniia nauchno-issledovatel'skoi raboty', in Akademik N. I. Bukharin, *Metodologiia i planirovanie nauki i tekhniki: Izbrannye trudy* (Moscow: Nauka, 1989), p. 111.
36 Kolchinskii, ' "Kul'turnaia revoliutsiia" ', p. 610; Joravsky, *Soviet Marxism and Natural Science*, pp. 215–71.
37 Kolchinskii, ' "Kul'turnaia revoliutsiia" ', p. 618.
38 Joravsky, *Soviet Marxism and Natural Science*, p. 269.
39 I. V. Stalin, 'K voprosam agrarnoi politiki v SSSR', in Stalin, *Sochineniia* (Moscow: Gospolitizdat, 1953), vol. xii, p. 142; Joravsky, *Soviet Marxism and Natural Science*, pp. 250ff.

Committee – or, more precisely, its General Secretary – that would decide how useful a theory was and thus whether or not it was correct. Philosophers had little independent authority, but they were responsible for propagating dialectical materialism and they served as ideological watchdogs, on the prowl to see if they could find anything untoward or suspicious in the work of scientists.[40] They were one of the party's instruments for exercising control over the scientific community.

What emerged from the upheavals of 1928–32 was a large, well-funded, party-controlled R&D effort. 'In the USSR, as nowhere else in the world, all the conditions have been created for the flourishing of science,' Karl Bauman, head of the Central Committee's Science Department, claimed in August 1936.[41] But the authorities were not satisfied. The Academy of Sciences, on instruction from the government, organised a conference on physics and industry in March 1936.[42] The main target of criticism was Abram Ioffe, director of the Leningrad Institute of Physics and Technology, the leading Soviet physics institute at the time. He and his institute were attacked for not doing enough to help industry.

In December 1936 the Lenin All-Union Academy of Agricultural Sciences held a conference at which T. D. Lysenko and his followers attacked leading geneticists.[43] Practice was crucial here too. Lysenko was a crop specialist who had won support from those responsible for agricultural policy by proposing various practical measures to improve crop yields. His claims were very appealing in the terrible years following collectivisation. Lysenko, who had no training in genetics, accused some of the geneticists of racism and fascism; he and his followers were in turn charged with being anti-Marx and anti-Darwin.[44] The physicists had resisted the introduction of philosophical issues at their conference. The biology meeting, with its name-calling and political accusations, showed how far scientific debate could become politicised. The Central Committee's assertion of authority in science had opened the way to arguments for and against particular lines of research not merely on the

40 Nikolai Krementsov, *Stalinist Science* (Princeton: Princeton University Press, 1997), pp. 71–80.
41 Quoted in 'Soveshchanie v Narkomtiazhprome o nauchno-issledovatel'skoi rabote', *Sotsialisticheskaia rekonstruktsiia i nauka*, 1936, no. 8: 142.
42 On the conference see V. P. Vizgin, 'Martovskaia (1936 g.) sessiia AN SSSR: Sovetskaia fizika v fokuse', *Voprosy istorii estestvoznaniia i tekhniki*, 1990, no. 1: 63–84; and his 'Martovskaia (1936 g.) sessiia AN SSSR: Sovetskaia fizika v fokuse. II (arkhivnoe priblizhenie)', *Voprosy istorii estestvoznaniia i tekhniki*, 1991, no. 3: 36–55.
43 David Joravsky, *The Lysenko Affair* (Chicago: Chicago University Press, 1970), pp. 97–104.
44 Krementsov, *Stalinist Science*, pp. 59–60; Zhores A. Medvedev, *The Rise and Fall of T. D. Lysenko* (New York: Columbia University Press, 1969), pp. 37–44.

grounds of their scientific validity or practical utility, but also on the basis of their political character. Two types of argument now became available in scientific debates: 'quotation-mongering' (the appeal to the writings of Marx, Engels, Lenin or Stalin in support of one's arguments), and 'label-sticking' (the attempt to defeat an opponent by associating him with a political or philosophical deviation).

Lysenko continued to strengthen his position in the late 1930s. He was made president of the Lenin Academy of Agricultural Sciences in 1938 and a full member of the Academy of Sciences in the following year. The press portrayed him as a scientist of a new type: a man of the people, patriotic and oriented towards practice. This background gave him credibility in party circles. The fact that he understood very little about genetics did not hinder his ascent. He exploited the political context cleverly and destroyed his opponents by accusing them of political and ideological sins. The leading geneticist N. I. Vavilov was arrested in 1940 and died in prison in Saratov in 1943.[45]

Important though the Lysenko affair was, it did not characterise Stalinist science as a whole. While some fields suffered, others thrived. It was in these years, for example, that P. A. Cherenkov, I. M. Frank and I. E. Tamm discovered and explained the Cherenkov effect, for which they received the 1958 Nobel Prize for Physics; L. D. Landau did the work on the theory of liquid helium for which he was awarded the 1962 Nobel Prize; and P. L. Kapitsa did the research in low-temperature physics that won him the 1978 Nobel Prize.[46] The important difference between physics and biology was not that one was compatible with Marxism-Leninism and the other was not. It was the relationship to practice that determined their fate. Geneticists and plant breeders had no ready response to the crisis in agriculture caused by collectivisation. Lysenko, by contrast, found support among agricultural officials. He attacked the geneticists for their failure to provide practical help and explained that failure in terms of the political and ideological defects of the scientists and their theories, converting the crisis in the countryside into a crisis in science. There was no comparable crisis in industry to make physics seriously vulnerable to attacks of that kind.

The scientific community in the 1930s was subject to rigorous political and administrative controls, pressed to contribute to military and economic development and under permanent scrutiny for its political loyalty. Communists were now in key administrative positions; censorship became more stringent;

---

45 Joravsky, *The Lysenko Affair*, pp. 105–30; Krementsov, *Stalinist Science*, pp. 54–83.
46 Graham, *Science in Russia*, pp. 207–13.

and foreign travel came to a virtual stop. Members of the pre-revolutionary scientific intelligentsia still occupied some leading positions, often as institute directors and heads of scientific 'schools', which were networks of patronage and support as well as intellectual communities.[47] Planning, which aimed to eliminate duplication, reinforced these schools and even encouraged the formation of monopolies, with particular fields dominated by individual institutes and their directors. Expansion of the scientific community brought large numbers of young people into science, leading to inter-generational conflicts that sometimes acquired a political character. Careerism and personal rivalries took on a political edge, and the practice of denunciation affected the scientific community as it did society at large.

The growth of science took place against the background of continual investigations and trials. The Shakhty trial of 1928 and the Industrial Party trial of 1930 were only the most prominent instances.[48] Researchers at the Academy were arrested and imprisoned or exiled in the 'Historians' case', the 'Slavists' case', the 'Peasant Labour Party case', the 'Leningrad SR–Narodnik Counter-revolutionary Organisation case', and other cases in the late 1920s and early 1930s. These were widely reported in the press, evidently to frighten scientists and engineers and ensure their loyalty to the regime.[49] Repression became more intense in the late 1930s, with the arrest of tens of thousands of scientists and engineers. Some important institutes were destroyed – the Ukrainian Institute of Physics and Technology in Khar'kov is a notable example.[50] The regime's faith in science was matched by suspicion of scientists; its support of science was counterbalanced by repression of the scientific community. The epitome of this paradox was the *sharashka*, the prison laboratory in which scientists and engineers, who had been arrested for crimes against the state, developed technologies for defending the state.[51]

Leading scientists welcomed the investment in science and the prominence given to science in official propaganda, but they were unhappy with

47 Gennadii Gorelik, *Andrei Sakharov: Nauka i svoboda* (Moscow: R&C Dynamics, 2000), pp. 57–79.
48 Bailes, *Technology and Society*, pp. 69–121.
49 Kolchinskii, ' "Kul'turnaia revoliutsiia" ', pp. 643–50.
50 Alexander Weissberg, *The Accused* (New York: Simon and Schuster, 1951); Iu. V. Pavlenko and Iu. N. Raniuk and Iu. A. Khramov, *'Delo'UFTI 1935–1938* (Kiev: Feniks, 1998); Loren R. Graham, *What Have we Learned about Science and Technology from the Russian Experience?* (Stanford, Calif.: Stanford University Press, 1998), pp. 53–5; M. G. Iaroshevskii (ed.), *Repressirovannaia nauka* (Leningrad: Nauka, 1991); V. A. Kumanev, *Tragicheskie sud'by: repressirovannye uchenye Akademii nauk SSSR* (Moscow: Nauka, 1995).
51 On the *sharashka* of the aircraft designer A. N. Tupolev, see L. L. Kerber, *Tupolev* (St Petersburg: Politekhnika, 1999), pp. 112–86.

the bureaucratic and political controls on the scientific community.[52] Many were of course horrified by the brutality of the regime, and some wrote letters to the authorities to seek the release of colleagues who had been arrested.[53] There were those like Landau who regarded the Stalin regime as no better than fascism, but others thought that the repressive character of Soviet rule would be temporary. Vernadskii, for example, saw in the growth of science a cause for hope in the longer term.[54]

The priority given to science inspired admiration abroad. A Soviet delegation including Bukharin and Ioffe attended a conference on the history of science in London in 1931. The papers they presented, which analysed the development of science in its social context, inspired a group of left-wing British scientists to develop influential ideas about science and its social functions.[55] In the following year, Modest Rubenstein, a member of the delegation to the London conference, described in a pamphlet for foreign readers how science and technology would flourish under socialism. The Soviet Union, he wrote, was the first experiment in which 'a genuinely scientific theory' was being applied to the construction and control of social and economic life, as well as to the management of science and technology.[56]

## The Second World War and the post-war years, 1941–53

Soviet scientists responded to the German invasion by putting themselves and their knowledge at the service of the state. Many volunteered for service in the Moscow and Leningrad militias, which suffered terrible losses in the early months of the war. Research institutes in Moscow and Leningrad were evacuated to the east, where scientists contributed to the war effort by working to

52 Vera Tolz, 'The Formation of the Soviet Academy of Sciences: Bolsheviks and Academicians in the 1920s and 1930s', in Michael David-Fox and Gyorgy Peteri (eds.), *Academia in Upheaval: Origins, Transfers, and Transformations of the Communist Academic Regime in Russia and East Central Europe* (Westport, Com.: Bergin and Garvey, 2000), pp. 39–72.

53 See P. L. Kapitsa's letter in defence of L. D. Landau, P. L. Kapitsa, *Pis'ma o nauke* (Moscow: Moskovskii rabochii, 1989), pp. 174–5.

54 On Landau see Gennady Gorelik, '*Meine antisowjetische Tätigkeit . . .': Russische Physiker unter Stalin* (Wiesbaden: Vieweg, 1993), pp. 184–219; V. I. Vernadskii, 'Nauchnaia mysl' kak planetnoe iavlenie', on which he worked in 1937–8, in V. I. Vernadskii, *Filosofskie mysli naturalista* (Moscow: Nauka, 1988), p. 95.

55 Needham and Werksey, *Science at the Cross Roads*, 2nd edn; for the impact in Britain see P. G. Werksey, *The Visible College* (London: Allen Lane, 1978), pp. 138–49.

56 M. Rubenstein, *Science, Technology and Economics under Capitalism and in the Soviet Union* (Moscow: Co-operative Publishing Society of Foreign Workers in the USSR, 1932), p. 35.

improve arms and equipment as well as production processes.[57] The development of new military technologies did not have high priority until victory was
in sight and it was clear just how much progress other countries had made.

Pre-war research on radar and rocketry had been interrupted by the purges.
Radar development was resumed during the war, and rocket development at
the end of the war.[58] In the spring of 1945 the Soviet Union sent teams of
scientists and engineers to Germany to begin the systematic exploitation of
German science and technology.[59] Soviet physicists had done pioneering work
on nuclear chain reactions, but the German invasion brought that research
to an end. Stalin initiated a small nuclear project in September 1942, but it
was only on 20 August 1945, two weeks after the bombing of Hiroshima, that
he signed a decree converting this project into a crash programme. Special
organisations were set up to manage the atomic project, as well as radar and
rocket development. New institutions of higher education were established to
train the scientists and engineers needed for these programmes.[60]

Stalin more than once expressed the view that another world war was to
be expected in fifteen, twenty, or thirty years. The advanced weapons programmes were intended to prepare the country for what he referred to as
'all contingencies'.[61] He promised to give I. V. Kurchatov, scientific director of
the nuclear project, 'the broadest all-round help'. He told him that he would
improve scientists' living conditions and provide prizes for major achievements.[62] 'I do not doubt', he said in February 1946, 'that if we render the
proper help to our scientists they will be able not only to catch up, but also to
overtake in the near future the achievements of science beyond the borders of
our country.'[63]

On 29 August 1949 the Soviet Union tested an atomic bomb, a copy of
the first American plutonium design, which Klaus Fuchs had given to Soviet

57 B. V. Levshin, *Sovetskaia nauka v gody velikoi otechestvennoi voiny* (Moscow: Nauka, 1983);
   E. I. Grakina, *Uchenye – frontu 1941–1945* (Moscow: Nauka, 1989); E. I. Grakina, *Uchenye
   Rossii v gody velikoi otechestvennoi voiny 1941–1945* (Moscow: Institut rossiiskoi istorii
   Rossiiskoi Akademii nauk, 2000).
58 On radar see M. M. Lobanov, *Razvitie sovetskoi radiolokatsionnoi tekhniki* (Moscow:
   Voenizdat, 1982); on rocketry see B. E. Chertok, *Rakety i liudi* (Moscow: Mashinostroenie, 1994).
59 N. M. Naimark, *The Russians in Germany* (Cambridge, Mass.: Harvard University Press,
   1995), pp. 205–50.
60 David Holloway, *Stalin and the Bomb: The Soviet Union and Atomic Energy, 1939–1956* (New
   Haven: Yale University Press, 1994), pp. 49–133.
61 Ibid., pp. 150–1.    62 Ibid., pp. 147–8.
63 I. V. Stalin, 'Rech' na predvybornom sobranii izbiratelei Stalinskogo izbiratel'nogo
   okruga goroda Moskvy, 9 fevralia 1946g', in *I. V. Stalin, Works*, ed. Robert H. McNeil,
   vol. III: *1946–1953* (Stanford, Calif.: Stanford University Press, 1953), p. 19.

intelligence. In August 1953 it detonated a thermonuclear weapon and two years later, in November 1955, a two-stage thermonuclear design; these were independent Soviet designs.[64] The rocket programme was similarly successful. Building on German technology, Soviet engineers developed generations of rockets with steadily increasing ranges. In August 1957 they carried out the first successful flight test in the world of an intercontinental ballistic missile, and in October they used the same rocket to launch Sputnik.[65] Even with the help of espionage and German technology, these were impressive achievements in science and engineering.

In June 1945 over a hundred foreign scientists took part in a special celebration by the Academy of Sciences to mark its 220th anniversary. At a reception in the Kremlin attended by Stalin, Molotov made a short speech promising the 'most favourable conditions' for the development of science and technology and for 'closer ties of Soviet science with world science'.[66] The latter promise was soon broken. In May 1947 Stalin told the writer Konstantin Simonov: 'the scientific intelligentsia, professors, physicians . . . have an unjustified admiration for foreign culture.'[67] He started a campaign against subservience to the West: foreign contacts were curtailed; science journals stopped reporting on research done abroad and were no longer published in foreign languages. In the summer of 1947 two medical researchers were severely criticised for conveying to American scientists the results of their work on the treatment of cancer.[68]

Lysenko's fortunes had declined during the war, and in the early post-war years the Science Department of the Central Committee supported the geneticists against him. On 10 April 1948, Iurii Zhdanov, newly appointed head of the Science Department and son of Politburo member Andrei Zhdanov, gave a lecture criticising Lysenko's views on evolutionary biology and genetics. Stalin intervened to support Lysenko, telling Zhdanov that the Central Committee could not agree with his position. When Zhdanov replied that the lecture reflected only his personal point of view, Stalin responded: 'the Central Committee can have its own position on questions of science.' 'We in the Party do

64 Holloway, *Stalin and the Bomb*, pp. 138, 213–19.
65 Asif A. Siddiqi, *Challenge to Apollo: The Soviet Union and the Space Race, 1945–1974* (Washington: National Aeronautics and Space Administration, 2000), pp. 160–1, 167.
66 Quoted in Vucinich, *Empire of Knowledge*, p. 206.
67 Konstantin Simonov, *Glazami cheloveka moego pokoleniia* (Moscow: Izdatel'stvo Pravda, 1990), p. 126.
68 V. D. Esakov and E. S. Levina, *Delo KR. Sudy chesti v ideologii i praktike poslevoennogo stalinizma* (Moscow: Institut rossiiskoi istorii i institut istorii estestvoznaniia i tekhniki Rossiiskoi Akademii nauk, 2001), pp. 219–44.

not have personal views and personal points of view,' he said.[69] The Politburo instructed the Lenin Academy of Agricultural Sciences to organise a meeting on biology, and this took place from 31 July to 7 August 1948. Lysenko gave the main report. Some of his opponents were allowed to speak, but the meeting was stacked against them. Stalin had edited Lysenko's report and had made substantial changes to it. On the last day of the meeting Lysenko invoked the highest authority in Soviet science when he told his audience, 'the Central Committee of the Party has examined my report and approved it'.[70] The August session marked his complete triumph, with damaging consequences for teaching and research in biology.[71]

Preparations soon began for a conference on physics, a sequel to the 1936 meeting. The organising committee met forty-two times between 30 December 1948 and 16 March 1949. The discussions were sharp and bitter, with divisions not only between physicists and philosophers but also between different groups of physicists at the Academy of Sciences and at Moscow University.[72] The draft resolution called for a 'struggle against kowtowing and grovelling before the West' and criticised individual physicists such as Ioffe, Kapitsa and Landau. What effect such a resolution would have had on physics is not clear, for it did not attack quantum mechanics and relativity theory directly in the way that Lysenko had condemned genetics. In the event, the physicists were reprieved. The meeting was cancelled in the middle of March, some days before it was due to start.[73]

It appears that leading physicists in the atomic project warned Beria and Stalin that a conference would interfere with the development of nuclear weapons.[74] A similar logic was used by a group of nuclear physicists who wrote to Beria in 1952 to complain about philosophers who 'without taking the trouble to study the elementary bases of physics' try to refute 'the most important achievements of modern physics'.[75] They went on to claim that the

---

69 Krementsov, *Stalinist Science*, pp. 105–57, 161–7; the first remark by Stalin is on p. 166. The second remark by Stalin comes from V. A. Malyshev, 'Dnevnik narkoma', *Istochnik*, 1997, no. 5: 135.

70 Krementsov, *Stalinist Science*, p. 172.

71 T. A. Ginetsinskaia, 'Biofak Leningradskogo universiteta posle sessii VASKhNIL', in Iaroshevskii, *Repressirovannaia nauka*, pp. 114–25; and A. N. Nesmeianov, *Na kacheliakh XX veka* (Moscow: Nauka, 1999), pp. 135–7.

72 G. E. Gorelik, 'Fizika universitetskaia i akademicheskaia', *Voprosy istorii estestvoznaniia i tekhniki*, 1991, no. 2: 31–46.

73 A. S. Sonin, *Fizicheskii idealism: istoriia odnoi ideologicheskoi kampanii* (Moscow: Fizmatlit, 1994); and V. P. Vizgin, 'The Nuclear Shield in the "Thirty-Year War" of Physicists against Ignorant Criticism of Modern Physical Theories', *Physics-Uspekhi* 42, 12 (1999): 1268–70.

74 Vizgin, 'The Nuclear Shield', pp. 1270–4.

75 'Beria i teoriia otnositel'nosti', *Istoricheskii arkhiv*, 1994, no. 3: 217.

philosophers' activities might interfere with the nuclear project.[76] In neither case – 1949 or 1952 – did the party make a definitive ruling in favour of the physicists. The possibility of a conference on physics was held in reserve.

Further discussions took place in the early 1950s, in linguistics, physiology and political economy, and Stalin was deeply involved in each of them.[77] He published his thoughts on linguistics and political economy.[78] He gave Iurii Zhdanov conspiratorial advice on the conference on physiology, telling him to organise the supporters of Pavlov on the quiet, and only then to convene the conference at which 'general battle' could be waged against Pavlov's opponents.[79] But Stalin's interventions raised a fundamental problem: if the Central Committee could have its own position on scientific questions and could adjudicate the truth or falsity of scientific theories, how was it to decide what the correct position was, which theories were true and which false? 'It is generally recognized', Stalin wrote in his commentary on linguistics, 'that no science can develop and flourish without a battle of opinions, without freedom of criticism.'[80] Stalinist discussions, however, were usually initiated in order to destroy, or to reinforce, a particular school or monopoly (Marrist linguistics, Michurinist biology, Pavlovian physiology), and that presupposed that the Central Committee had already decided what it wanted the outcome to be.

In his pamphlet on linguistics, Stalin reasserted Marxism's scientific status. 'Marxism', he wrote, 'is the science of the *laws governing the development of nature and society* ... the science of building communist society' (emphasis added). 'As a science,' he wrote, 'Marxism cannot stand still; it develops and is perfected.' It did not 'recognize invariable conclusions and formulas, obligatory for all epochs and periods. Marxism is the enemy of all dogmatism.'[81] This suggests that he did not regard Marxism as a fixed point on which the Central Committee could base 'its own position on questions of science'. In his comments on Lysenko's 1948 report, he had rejected the idea that socialist natural science was necessarily different from bourgeois natural science.[82] But if Marxism did not provide a key, and scientific monopolies could stifle the truth, how was the Central Committee to make its judgements? It is tempting to see Stalin,

76 Ibid., p. 218.
77 On the post-war sessions see Ethan Pollock, *Stalin and the Soviet Science Wars* (Princeton: Princeton University Press, 2006).
78 I. V. Stalin, *Marxism and the Problems of Linguistics* (Moscow: Foreign Languages Publishing House, 1955); I. V. Stalin, *Ekonomicheskie problemy sotsializma v SSSR* (Moscow: Gosizdat, 1952).
79 I. Stalin to Iu. A. Zhdanov, 6 Oct. 1949, RGASPI f. 558, op. 11, d. 762, pp. 24–5.
80 Stalin, *Marxism and Problems of Linguistics*, p. 41.      81 Ibid., p. 71.
82 Kirill O. Rossianov, 'Editing Nature: Joseph Stalin and the "New" Soviet Biology', *Isis* 84 (1993): 728–45.

in his last writings, struggling with a problem that he himself had created: how could the Central Committee use effectively the authority it claimed on questions of science, without destroying the science on which the power of the state was coming increasingly to depend?

## De-Stalinisation and science 1953–68

Encouraged by success in nuclear weapons development and space flight, the post-Stalin leaders placed great hopes in science and technology. Investment in science grew very rapidly in the fifteen years after Stalin's death, and the number of 'scientific workers' rose from 192,000 in 1953 to 822,000 in 1968.[83] New science cities such as Akademgorodok near Novosibirsk and Zelenograd near Moscow were founded in the expectation that research would flourish there. Boris Slutskii caught the mood of the time in his 1959 poem 'Physicists and Lyric Poets': 'Physicists it seems are honoured, lyric poets are in the shade', the poem begins. There is no point in disputing this, writes Slutskii; greatness is now to be found not in the poet's rhymes, but in logarithms.[84]

The Soviet Union nevertheless lagged behind the West. Kapitsa had written to Stalin in July 1952 to lament the poor condition of Soviet science, and he was not alone in his concern.[85] The tendency towards technological stagnation in the economy was also a source of anxiety.[86] After Stalin's death, the government convened several meetings of engineers, plant directors and scientists to discuss the introduction of new technologies into industrial production. It then established the State Committee for New Technology and created the position of Deputy Minister for New Technology in the industrial ministries.[87] This was the first of a series of administrative reforms designed to stimulate technological progress.

In his letter to Stalin Kapitsa had deplored the way in which science was subordinated to practical needs. It was essential to support fundamental research, he argued, because scientific discoveries could give rise to new technologies; radar, television, jet propulsion and atomic energy were among the examples he mentioned. Kapitsa was challenging the orthodox view that it was the

83 Nauchnye kadry SSSR: dinamika i struktura (Moscow: Mysl', 1991), p. 40.
84 Boris Slutskii, 'Fiziki i liriki', in Boris Slutskii, Sobranie sochinenii (Moscow: Khudozhestvennaia literatura, 1991), vol. 1 Stikhotvoreniia 1939–1961, p. 351.
85 'Nel'zia peredelyvat' zakony prirody (P. L. Kapitsa I. V. Stalinu)', Izvestiia TsK KPSS, 1991, no. 2: 105–9.
86 F. Burlatskii, 'Posle Stalina', Novyi mir, 1988, no. 10: 157.
87 Holloway, Stalin and the Bomb, pp. 356–7; A. B. Bezborodov, Vlast' i nauchno-tekhnicheskaia politika v SSSR serediny 50-kh–serediny 70-kh godov (Moscow: Mosgorarkhiv, 1997), pp. 37–8.

technological needs of society, rather than the internal logic of science, that stimulated scientific progress. Eventually the official position changed, and the 1961 party programme declared that 'science will itself in full measure become a direct productive force'.[88] In the reforms of the Academy of Sciences between 1959 and 1963, a number of technical institutes were moved from the Academy to the appropriate industrial ministries, thus reversing the thrust of the Academy's reform in the late 1920s.[89]

Economic growth was coming to depend more on new technology and higher labour productivity than on the addition of new workers to the labour force. Barriers to technological innovation were, however, deeply embedded in the institutional structure of the economy.[90] First, there was a serious lack of development facilities, because the government had invested heavily in research and production but had neglected engineering development, a crucial phase in the transfer of research into production. Second, factories were reluctant to introduce new products or new processes, because innovation would interfere with their ability to meet plan targets. Third, administrative barriers existed between the R&D system and industrial production, and there were different agencies responsible for R&D, with a resulting lack of policy co-ordination. Khrushchev carried out various administrative reforms, but these did little to improve the situation.[91] Military R&D performed more successfully, not because the defence sector operated according to some ideal of central planning, but because the political leadership devoted considerable resources and effort to overcoming the barriers to innovation that existed elsewhere in the economy.[92]

The scientific community was in a poor state, Kapitsa wrote to Khrushchev in 1955.[93] Scientists had been 'beaten' so often that they were afraid to think for themselves. Excessive secrecy made it impossible for the scientific community at large to form its own judgements about the quality of research. Science was attracting people who were less interested in science than in high salaries and privileges. To remedy this situation, two conditions were needed, in Kapitsa's

88 Vucinich, *Empire of Knowledge*, pp. 298–304; Konstantin Ivanov, 'Science after Stalin: Forging a New Image of Soviet Science', *Science in Context* 15, 2 (2002): 317–38.
89 Graham, *Science in Russia*, pp. 183–5.
90 E. Zaleski et al., *Science Policy in the USSR* (Paris: Organization for Economic Co-operation and Development, 1969), pp. 425–35.
91 Bruce Parrott, *Politics and Technology in the Soviet Union* (Cambridge, Mass.: MIT Press, 1983), pp. 177–9.
92 David Holloway, 'Innovation in the Defence Sector', in R. Amann and J. Cooper (eds.), *Industrial Innovation in the Soviet Union* (New Haven and London: Yale University Press, 1982), pp. 276–367.
93 P. L. Kapitsa to N. S. Khrushchev, 15 Dec. 1955, Kapitsa, *Pis'ma o nauke*, pp. 314–19.

view. The first was that scientists should not be afraid to express their opinions even if those opinions were going to be rejected. It was particularly harmful to decree scientific truths, as the Science Department of the Central Committee had done. The second was that the political leadership should take account of scientific opinion. The situation in biology was a direct result of the leadership's failure to heed the views of the scientific community.

Important changes took place in the mid-1950s. Scientists had had virtually no contact with foreign colleagues since the mid-1930s, apart from a brief period at the end of the Second World War. Now restrictions on foreign travel were eased, though not completely removed.[94] The Soviet Union joined international scientific associations, and some joint research projects were organised with Western countries; information about foreign research became much more accessible. The Soviet Union moved towards closer integration with the international scientific community.[95]

Scientists became less afraid to demand intellectual freedom. In the autumn of 1955 300 biologists signed a letter to the Central Committee calling on it to disavow the August 1948 session. Physicists supported them by writing to draw attention to the harm that the situation in biology was doing to Soviet science as a whole. Khrushchev was unmoved and maintained his support of Lysenko, whose advice on agriculture he valued highly.[96] Scientists also demanded that philosophers stop policing science and looking for ideological deviations in scientific theories; philosophers, they insisted, should understand science before seeking to interpret it.[97] An All-Union Conference on the Philosophical Problems of Contemporary Science in October 1958 enjoined philosophers and scientists to work more closely together, though it also officially, if half-heartedly, endorsed Lysenkoist theories. With the exception of genetics, scientific authority – the right to say what science is – was now clearly vested in the specialist scientific communities, and Lysenko's influence was finally destroyed in October 1964, when Khrushchev fell from power. Philosophers now took their lead from scientists; they no longer claimed, as they had done in the Stalin years, that they should lead the scientists.[98]

94 Zhores A. Medvedev, *The Medvedev Papers: The Plight of Soviet Science Today* (London: Macmillan, 1971) explores the restrictions in detail.
95 Ivanov, 'Science after Stalin', pp. 322–5.
96 D. V. Lebedev, in 'Kruglyi stol. Stranitsy istorii sovetskoi genetiki v literature poslednikh let', *Voprosy istorii estestvoznaniia i tekhniki*, 1987, no. 4: 113–24; 'Genetika – nasha bol'', *Pravda*, 13 Jan. 1989, p. 4; Nesmeianov, *Na kacheliakh XX veka*, pp. 169–70.
97 Nesmeianov, *Na kacheliakh XX veka*, pp. 236–9, 240–3.
98 *Filosofskie problemy sovremennogo estestvoznaniia* (Moscow: Izdatel'stvo AN SSSR, 1959), pp. 602–5.

Lysenkoism was the most striking case of a distinctively 'Soviet' science, and it ended in failure, rejected by Soviet and foreign scientists alike. The rise and fall of Lysenkoism cannot be explained as a clash between genetics and dialectical materialism; it has to be understood in the broader context of the Soviet system and Soviet politics. Soviet leaders supported Lysenko because they believed his ideas were more practical than those of the geneticists and plant breeders. Believing that science would make a huge contribution to socialism, they concluded that there must be something wrong with genetics if it could not offer solutions to the problems they faced in agriculture. The Lysenko affair can provide a misleading picture of Soviet science. It is true that there were efforts to create a distinctively Marxist natural science, but these were largely confined to the early 1930s and were soon reined in by the party. Some scientists found dialectical materialism helpful in thinking about scientific problems. It would be a mistake to believe that the Soviet intellectual climate always hindered science: as Loren Graham has pointed out, there are many cases in which that context helped to shape ideas that proved successful in the sense that the relevant scientific communities, in the Soviet Union and abroad, accepted them.[99]

N. N. Semenov, who won the Nobel Prize for Chemistry in 1956, wrote after Khrushchev's fall that Lysenko and his supporters 'had transferred the struggle against those with different ideas from the level of scientific discussion to the level of demagogy and political accusations'.[100] 'Political' and 'philosophical' became pejorative terms in the scientific community in the 1950s and 1960s. Scientists saw themselves as restoring integrity to science by making it illegitimate to invoke the authority of the Central Committee or of Marxism-Leninism in a scientific argument. This prompted the question: now that science had become less political, why not make politics more scientific? The party claimed, after all, to be guided by a scientific theory in its policy-making: why not strengthen the scientific basis of policy? For at least some elements in the scientific community, this became an important mission in the late 1950s and the 1960s. This was a pivotal moment, because now science provided not only a language of legitimation for the regime, but also a language of criticism with the potential to transform political relationships.[101]

99 Graham, *Science in Russia*, pp. 99–134; Graham, *What Have we Learned*, ch. 1.
100 N. N. Semenov, 'Nauka ne terpit sub"ektivizma', *Nauka i Zhizn'*, 1965, no. 4: 43.
101 David Holloway, 'Physics, the State, and Civil Society in the Soviet Union', *Historical Studies in the Physical and Biological Sciences* 31 (1999), pt. 1: 173–93.

There were two broad approaches to making politics more scientific. The first was technocratic and bound up with cybernetics, which had been condemned in the early 1950s as a 'bourgeois pseudo-science' but rehabilitated in the mid-1950s as an overarching framework for understanding control and communication in machine, animal and society.[102] Cybernetics was linked to the new opportunities that computers opened up for data processing and mathematical modelling, and it provided a framework for thinking about planning and management. Mathematicians and computer specialists helped to revive economics as a discipline, in particular the theory of planning. According to a group of cyberneticians in the mid-1960s, 'the view of society as a complex cybernetic system . . . is increasingly gaining prestige as the main theoretical idea of the "technology" of managing society'.[103]

The second approach was democratic. This drew not on particular concepts and techniques but on a certain conception of science. It is most clearly expressed in Andrei Sakharov's *Reflections on Progress, Peaceful Coexistence, and Intellectual Freedom*, which began to circulate in *samizdat* in 1968 and was published abroad that same year. Sakharov had worked since 1950 at the nuclear weapons institute at Arzamas-16. He opened his essay by writing that his views had been 'formed in the milieu of the scientific and scientific-technical intelligentsia', which was very concerned about the future of the human race. 'This concern', he continued, 'feeds upon consciousness of the fact that *the scientific method of directing politics, economics, art, education, and military affairs, has not yet become a reality. We consider "scientific" that method which is based on a profound study of facts, theories and views, presupposing unprejudiced and open discussion, which is dispassionate in its conclusions.*'[104] For Sakharov intellectual freedom was the key to the scientific method. In March 1970 he, V. A. Turchin and R. A. Medvedev sent a letter to the Soviet leadership in which they wrote: 'a scientific approach demands full information, impartial thinking, and creative freedom.' Talk about scientific management would be meaningless if those conditions were not met.[105]

102 David Holloway, 'Innovation in Science – the Case of Cybernetics in the Soviet Union', *Science Studies*, 1974, no. 4: 299–337. Slava Gerovitch, *From Newspeak to Cyberspeak: A History of Soviet Cybernetics* (Cambridge, Mass.: MIT Press, 2002) provides an excellent full account.
103 B. V. Biriukov et al., 'Filosofskie problemy kibernetiki', in A. I. Berg (ed.), *Kibernetiku – na sluzhbu kommunizmu*, vol. VI (Moscow: Energiia, 1967), p. 303.
104 A. D. Sakharov, *Razmyshleniia o progresse, mirnom sosushchestvovanii i intellektual'noi svobode* (Frankfurt-am-Main: Possev Verlag, 1968), p. 3 (emphasis added).
105 A. D. Sakharov, V. F. Turchin and R. A. Medvedev, 'A Reformist Program for Democratization', in Stephen F. Cohen (ed.), *An End to Silence: Uncensored Opinion in the Soviet Union* (New York: W. W. Norton, 1982), pp. 321–2.

Technocratic ideas appear to have been more widespread in the scientific community than liberal ideas, but the two approaches rested on a set of shared assumptions. They embodied the belief that politics ought to be, in some sense, scientific, and that the scientific-technical revolution presented new challenges that called for new responses. They reflected the conviction that change was necessary and the hope that it might be possible. There were doubtless many scientists – perhaps the great majority – who did not share these assumptions, either because they were not interested in politics or because they did not want change or were sceptical of its possibility. But some scientists believed that, having regained intellectual freedom in the natural sciences, they could seek change in the wider system. This optimism sprang in part from faith in science and technology, in part from the hope that de-Stalinisation would lead to economic and political reform. When signs appeared that Stalin might be rehabilitated at the Twenty-Third Party Congress in 1966, leading scientists wrote to the Central Committee to oppose such a move.[106] Some scientists signed collective letters of protest at the repression of civil rights.[107] Civic engagement of this kind was, for many, a continuation of the struggle for intellectual freedom in the natural sciences.

The post-Stalin years were the period of greatest optimism about science as a force for change, but in 1968 these hopes were dashed.[108] Alarmed by growing political activism among scientists, the party took steps to make it clear that the intellectual freedom that existed in the natural sciences did not extend to politics. M. V. Keldysh, president of the Academy of Sciences, warned dissident scientists not to believe that their status as scientists would protect them. 'These individuals . . . must remember that it is not they who define our science,' he said. 'The development of science will proceed in any event.'[109] This warning foreshadowed the crushing of the Czechoslovak reform movement in August. That was a huge blow to hopes of reform in the Soviet Union itself because it showed how fearful the regime was of democratic change.[110]

In a speech to the Central Committee in December 1969, Brezhnev made it clear that technocratic proposals for reform should not encroach on the party's prerogatives. In an obvious reference to cybernetics, he said that 'systems of

106 Andrei Sakharov, *Vospominaniia* (New York: Izdatel'stvo imeni Chekhova, 1990), pp. 353–4; A. Iu. Semenov, 'Zvezdnoe nebo i nravstvennyi zakon', in *Iulii Borisovich Khariton: put' dlinoiu v vek* (Moscow: Editorial URSS, 1999), pp. 468–9.
107 Raisa Berg, *Sukhovei* (New York: Chalidze Publications, 1983), pp. 262–80, 309–23.
108 Paul R. Josephson, *New Atlantis Revisited: Akademgorodok, the Siberian City of Science* (Princeton: Princeton University Press, 1997), pp. 1–32.
109 M. V. Keldysh, 'Nauka sluzhit kommunizmu', *Pravda*, 1 Apr. 1968, p. 2.
110 Josephson, *New Atlantis Revisited*, pp. 263–304.

information and control created by specialists' were only auxiliary means for solving administrative tasks. Policy-making was the prerogative of the party and the state. 'Problems of management are in the first instance political, not technical, problems,' he said.[111] The party leadership made clear its opposition to the idea that politics could be made more scientific by either democratic or technocratic reform.

## Disenchantment, 1968–91

By the end of the 1960s the Soviet Union had the largest R&D effort in the world, employing about two million people, of whom almost half had higher degrees. The USSR Academy of Sciences had grown into a huge complex, employing 30,000 scientists and researchers. Each union republic, apart from the Russian Federation, had its own Academy of Sciences, most of them established in the 1940s and 1950s, although the Ukrainian and Belorussian academies were older.[112] The universities, which were primarily devoted to teaching, had institutes and laboratories too. The largest element in the R&D effort was the network of institutes and laboratories attached to the industrial ministries and enterprises; most of these worked on military technology. Across the country there were over fifty science cities including ten nuclear cities. Many of these, including all the nuclear cities, were 'closed' and did not appear on Soviet maps.[113]

In some branches of science, most notably in mathematics and physics, Soviet scientists occupied a leading position in the world.[114] But the Soviet Union lagged in technology and, far from closing the technology gap, it was falling further behind in important areas such as computers and electronics.[115] The Brezhnev leadership imported foreign technology and created 'science-production associations' to stimulate technological innovation at home, but these measures did not yield appreciable results.[116] It had been possible in

---

111 'Vystuplenie General'nogo Sekretaria TsK KPSS tov. Brezhneva L. I. na Plenume TsK KPSS, 15 Dec. 1969, RGANI f. 2, op. 3, d. 168, p. 45.

112 E. Zaleski et al., *Science Policy in the USSR*, pp. 207, 216–17, 501–5.

113 Glenn E. Schweitzer, *Swords into Market Shares: Technology, Economics, and Security in the New Russia* (Washington: Joseph Henry Press, 2000), pp. 283–5.

114 Graham, *What have we Learned*, pp. 56–8.

115 This was the general conclusion of the most detailed Western study of Soviet technology. See R. Amann, J. Cooper and R. Davies (eds.), *The Technological Level of Soviet Industry* (New Haven: Yale University Press, 1977), and Amann and Cooper, *Industrial Innovation*.

116 Philip Hanson, 'The Soviet System as a Recipient of Foreign Technology', and Julian Cooper, 'Innovation for Innovation in Soviet Industry', in Amann and Cooper, *Industrial Innovation*, pp. 415–52, 453–512.

the 1930s to explain Soviet technological backwardness by reference to the backwardness of tsarist Russia; and in the 1950s and 1960s the destruction caused by the Second World War offered an explanation for the continuing lag. These explanations became less plausible with the passage of time. It was increasingly clear that technological progress required more than the cautious reforms adopted under Brezhnev.

Military power was the one area in which the Soviet Union achieved its goal of catching up with, and perhaps even overtaking, the advanced capitalist countries. It attained strategic parity with the United States in the late 1960s and early 1970s and continued to develop and deploy new and more advanced strategic weapons systems.[117] The Brezhnev leadership was reluctant to interfere with an economic system that had made it possible to secure what it regarded as an achievement of historic significance. But even in military technology the Soviet Union became concerned about its capacity to compete with the United States. The American strategy of exploiting new electronic technologies for defence worried the General Staff.[118] Ronald Reagan's 1983 Strategic Defense Initiative was also a challenge. Most Soviet specialists understood that, even if the United States deployed a ballistic missile defence system, the Soviet Union would be able to retain its deterrent capability by developing countermeasures. Nevertheless, the American initiatives faced the Soviet Union with the prospect of a new round of intense technological competition.[119]

The party intensified its campaign against dissident scientists after 1968. Regulations were introduced to allow dissertations to be rejected, and higher degrees withdrawn, on grounds of 'anti-patriotic and anti-moral behaviour'.[120] A fierce campaign was launched against Andrei Sakharov, who was nevertheless allowed to live in Moscow until 1980 when he was exiled to Gor'kii.[121] The idea of appealing to science as the inspiration for liberal or technocratic reform now seemed hopeless. Much of the technocratic rhetoric remained, but it was so wrapped up in Marxist-Leninist language that it lost the reformist edge it had had before 1968.[122]

The idea of science as a progressive force was still to be found in dissident writings of the 1970s, but a less optimistic note could be found there too.

117 David Holloway, *The Soviet Union and the Arms Race* (New Haven: Yale University Press, 1983), pp. 43–64.
118 Marshal N. V. Ogarkov, Chief of the General Staff, 'Zashchita sotsializma: opyt istorii i sovremennost', *Krasnaia zvezda*, 9 May 1984.
119 Archie Brown, *The Gorbachev Factor* (Oxford: Oxford University Press, 1996), pp. 226–32.
120 Josephson, *New Atlantis Revisited*, pp. 264–304; Zhores A. Medvedev, *Soviet Science* (New York: W. W. Norton, 1978), pp. 162–96; the quotation is from p. 173.
121 Sakharov, *Vospominaniia*, pp. 528–38.
122 Gerovitch, *From Newspeak to Cyberspeak*, pp. 288–9.

Slanderer (*Klevetnik*), a character in Aleksandr Zinoviev's satirical novel *The Yawning Heights* (*Ziiaiushchie vysoty*), expresses the view that when 'one places one's hopes on the civilising role of science, one commits the gravest error'.[123] That is because science as an activity devoted to the pursuit of truth is subordinate to science as a social system. Slanderer declares that careerism has created a 'moral and psychological atmosphere in science which has nothing in common with those idyllic pictures one can find in the most critical and damning novels and memoirs devoted to the science of the past'.[124] The émigré science journalist Mark Popovsky painted a similar picture.[125] Far from exercising a civilising influence on Soviet society, science had come to embody the worst features of Soviet life: it was dominated by an overpowering bureaucratic apparatus; careerism, patronage and corruption were rife; there was a cynical disregard of ethics and morality; military and security considerations had first priority; the scientific community was riven by national antagonisms, and enmeshed in secrecy. In this disillusioned and perhaps jaundiced view, science could not serve as the model for a free or a moral society.

Early in the 1980s the party leadership decided, after years of putting off the idea, to devote a Central Committee plenary session to the scientific-technical revolution. Preparations began in earnest in the summer of 1984, but the plenum was cancelled.[126] Gorbachev, who had been deeply involved in these preparations, was persuaded of the urgency of the problem. Three months after becoming General Secretary, he told a conference on science and technology: 'an acceleration of scientific-technical progress insistently demands a profound *perestroika* of the system of planning and management, of the entire economic mechanism.'[127] He made it clear that he thought the transition to technology-intensive economic growth should have taken place fifteen years earlier.[128] Subsequent history showed, however, that he himself did not have an effective strategy for making that transition.

The nuclear accident at Chernobyl' on 26 April 1986, dramatised the Soviet Union's technological failings. In the worst nuclear accident ever, explosions

123 Aleksandr Zinov'ev, *Ziiaiushchie vysoty* (Lausanne: L'Age d'Homme, 1976), p. 143.
124 Ibid., p. 143.
125 Mark Popovsky, *Science in Chains: The Crisis of Science and Scientists in the Soviet Union Today* (London: Collins and Harvill Press, 1980). See also Josephson, *New Atlantis Revisited*, p. xix.
126 M. S. Gorbachev, *Zhizn' i reformy*, 2 vols. (Moscow: Novosti, 1995), vol. I, pp. 220, 261; Yegor Ligachev, *Inside Gorbachev's Kremlin* (New York: Pantheon Books, 1993), pp. 45–49; Brown, *The Gorbachev Factor*, pp. 72, 123, 146–7.
127 M. S. Gorbachev, 'Korennoi vopros ekonomicheskoi politiki partii', 11 June 1985, in M. S. Gorbachev, *Izbrannye rechi i stat'i*, vol. II (Moscow: Politizdat, 1987) p. 269.
128 Gorbachev, 'Korennoi vopros', p. 253.

at the nuclear power plant released millions of curies of radioactive particles into the atmosphere.[129] Secrecy and cover-up were the instinctive reaction of the Soviet authorities. It was only after sixty-eight hours – and prodding by the Swedish government – that they issued their first official statement. Once satellite pictures of the burning reactor appeared on television screens around the world, they could not deny that the accident had taken place. *Glasnost'* extended not only to the accident and its consequences, but to its causes as well. It was clear that poor reactor design and human error on the part of the plant operators were part of the picture. But the accident also resulted from the modus operandi of the Soviet bureaucracy, with its insistence on targets, pressure to meet those targets, neglect of safety considerations, secrecy and immunity from public opinion.

Only *glasnost'* would help to remedy the situation.[130] The Soviet press began to publish stories about past accidents. Environmental movements, often linked to nationalist sentiment in the republics, sprang up to oppose the building of new nuclear power plants and to draw attention to environmental damage caused by Soviet policies.[131] It became clear that, in its drive for modernity, the Soviet Union, which ruled one-sixth of the earth's surface, had imposed enormous costs not only on its people, but on its land, air and water too.[132] Chernobyl' – and the *glasnost'* it stimulated – delivered the *coup de grâce* to the regime's claim that, guided by a scientific theory, it was creating a society in which science and technology would flourish for the benefit of the people.

## Science in post-Soviet Russia, 1991–2000

Science in Russia entered what some scientists regard as its most serious crisis in the twentieth century when the Soviet Union collapsed.[133] The depth of the crisis is testimony both to the support that the Soviet Union had given to science and, notwithstanding the failings that critics pointed to in the 1970s and 1980s, to the quality of Soviet science. There was a threefold drop in total expenditure on civilian science in the 1990s, and this was compounded

129 V. G. Bar'iakhtar (ed.), *Chernobyl'skaia katastrofa* (Kiev: Naukova dumka, 1995).
130 Grigorii Medvedev, *Chernobyl'skaia khronika* (Moscow: Sovremennik, 1989); Loren R. Graham, *The Ghost of the Executed Engineer: Technology and the Fall of the Soviet Union* (Cambridge, Mass.: Harvard University Press, 1993).
131 Jane I. Dawson, *Eco-nationalism: Anti-nuclear Activism and National Identity in Russia, Lithuania, and Ukraine* (Durham, N.C.: Duke University Press, 1996).
132 Murray Feshbach and Alfred Friendly, Jr., *Ecocide in the USSR: Health and Nature under Siege* (New York: Basic Books, 1992).
133 V. E. Zakharov, 'Predislovie', in B. M. Bongard-Levin and V. E. Zakharov (eds.), *Rossiiskaia nauchnaia emigratsiia* (Moscow: URSS, 2001), p. 10.

by the removal of price controls, which resulted in sharp increases in the cost of equipment, electricity and other services. The post-Soviet government made a sharp and sudden reduction in defence expenditure in 1992, with a corresponding cut in military R&D.[134]

One indicator of the depth of the crisis was the number of scientists who emigrated or quit science in order to pursue other careers in Russia. According to the Russian Ministry of Science, about 2,000 researchers a year left Russia between 1991 and 1996; after that, the outflow fell to under 1,500 a year. These are conservative figures, however; other estimates suggest that more than 30,000 scientists emigrated in this period. The internal brain drain is even more difficult to estimate, because many researchers remained formally on the staff of research institutes even while devoting themselves to non-scientific activities such as business. It appears that the internal brain drain was far greater than the number of scientists who emigrated.[135]

The international community did not want to see the Russian scientific community destroyed; it especially feared that knowledge of advanced weapons technologies would find its way to states hostile to the West. International organisations and foreign governments took steps to provide assistance to Russian scientists. The financier George Soros set up the International Science Foundation, which over the years 1993–6 granted about $130 million to support basic research in the natural sciences. Learned societies and philanthropic foundations gave significant help. The United States, Japan and the European Union established the International Science and Technology Centre in order to fund civilian projects by scientists who had been engaged in weapons research. By one Russian estimate, about half of Russian basic science was being funded from foreign sources in 1995.[136]

During the twentieth century the scientific community had shown remarkable resilience, and it was called upon to do so again at the century's end. The Academy of Sciences once again displayed considerable powers of survival. No radical reform of scientific institutions took place. Change was evolutionary: co-operation between the Academy of Sciences and the universities began to grow; the government set up a fund to support basic research; collaboration with foreign scientists increased. By the very end of the century there were signs that the situation had stabilised. It was still unclear, however, what shape Russian science would take. Would the universities and the Academy

---

134 Irina Dezhina and Loren Graham, *Russian Basic Science after Ten Years of Transition and Foreign Support* (Washington: Carnegie Endowment for International Peace, 2002), pp. 8, 10.
135 Ibid., pp. 9–10.    136 Ibid., pp. 17–25.

work more closely together? Would the universities become more important centres of research? Was a thoroughgoing reform of science and education needed? Would a capitalist Russia be more successful at commercialising science than the Soviet Union was? Would Russian industry develop advanced civilian technologies? Would the scientific community, which found itself on the sidelines in the 1990s, find a secure position in Russian society?

## Conclusion

Less than six months after the collapse of the Soviet Union, Václav Havel claimed that the end of Communism signified the end not only of the nineteenth and twentieth centuries but also of 'the modern world as a whole'. The modern era, he wrote, had been dominated by the belief that 'the world . . . is a wholly knowable system governed by a finite number of universal laws that man can grasp and rationally direct for his own benefit'.[137] Havel presented the Soviet experience as the perverse extreme of scientific rationalism.

The Soviet Union did indeed appear to many people to offer a vision of modernity that was more attractive than Western capitalism, especially in the 1920s and 1930s when capitalism was in deep crisis, and the commitment to science and the claim to be guided by a scientific theory were important elements in that vision. Optimism about science was high again in the Soviet Union in the late 1950s and early 1960s, when successes in space dramatised the possibilities of scientific-technical progress and de-Stalinisation offered the prospect of political change. These hopes were not realised, however. From the late 1960s on, it became increasingly clear that central planning was not effective at generating technological progress, that the party leadership feared reform and that the state had pursued industrial development with little regard to the consequences for public health or for the environment. The Soviet system began to lose legitimacy at home and abroad. This shook the self-confidence of the political leadership and prompted the attempts at radical reform in the late 1980s.

Andrei Sakharov proposed an alternative approach to politics, derived from his conception of science. The state, in this model, would be guided in its policies by a public opinion formed in the process of reasoned debate and discussion. 'Progress is possible and innocuous only when it is subject to the

137 Václav Havel, 'The End of the Modern Era', *New York Times*, 1 Mar. 1992, section 4, p. 15.

control of reason,' he wrote in his 1975 Nobel Peace Prize lecture.[138] A reasoned approach to the great challenges of the scientific-technical revolution, such as nuclear weapons and environmental change, would be possible only if human rights were guaranteed. Only then would society be able to engage in the process of debate and discussion that would ensure that decisions were grounded in reason. Sakharov's views can be read as a commentary on the Soviet experience of harnessing science to politics: debate and discussion were extremely restricted in the Soviet Union, with harmful consequences for science and for society. Sakharov's views can be taken also as a rejoinder to Havel's equation of modernity with the Soviet experience, by suggesting an alternative vision of the application of reason to human affairs.

138 Andrei Sakharov, 'Peace, Progress, and Human Rights', in Andrei D. Sakharov, *Alarm and Hope* (New York: Vintage Books, 1978), p. 9.

# 21

# Culture, 1900–1945

JAMES VON GELDERN

Russian culture in the first two decades of the twentieth century came under influences that could be found in most European cultures. New audiences transformed taste cultures. The decline of monarchies and ascent of industrial capitalism made art patrons of the bourgeoisie.[1] Modern technology turned the lower classes into a mass audience. Aristocratic arts institutions faced competition from new organisations, many of them private and open to the general public. Cultural life reached social groups once excluded on the basis of class or nationality. The fast-paced, fragmented life of the modern city insinuated itself into all art forms, from the cinema to painting and poetry, and artists struggled to create satisfying art forms from the chaos of modern life.[2]

Russian culture was also influenced by circumstances distinct from other cultures. The first was the intelligentsia, a self-defined class of educated people who sustained social and cultural life under the profoundly undemocratic conditions of tsarism.[3] The second was the October Revolution, which separated Russia from European cultures after 1917, and fundamentally reconfigured the cultural life of the country. The Bolsheviks considered themselves heirs to the great tradition of the intelligentsia when they seized power on 25 October 1917. As an underground party before the revolution, they had organised the working masses by propaganda and education. After the revolution, they used the resources of the state to foster an entirely new consciousness in Soviet citizens, particularly those who came of age after they took power.

---

1 Beverly Whitney Kean, *All the Empty Palaces: The Merchant Patrons of Modern Art in Pre-Revolutionary Russia* (New York: Universe Books, 1983); Edith W. Clowes, Samuel D. Kassow and James L. West (eds.), *Between Tsar and People: Educated Society and the Quest for Public Identity in Late Imperial Russia* (Princeton: Princeton University Press, 1991).
2 Catriona Kelly and David Shepherd (eds.), *Constructing Russian Culture in the Age of Revolution, 1881–1940* (Oxford: Oxford University Press, 1998).
3 Boris Kagarlitsky, *The Thinking Reed: Intellectuals and the Soviet State, 1917 to the Present* (London: Verso, 1988); Christopher Read, *Culture and Power in Revolutionary Russia: The Intelligentsia and the Transition from Tsarism to Communism* (New York: St Martin's Press, 1990).

Few would argue the reach of this cultural programme, though many would dispute the quality of the transformation and the benefits gained by the Soviet people.

If the Bolsheviks felt themselves heirs to the great tradition, others considered them betrayers of the tradition. A deep split had begun to appear within the intelligentsia around the dawn of the twentieth century, as materialists and idealists forwarded alternative versions of the intelligentsia mission. Radical materialists devoted their attention to the sciences or politics as most promising for the betterment of humanity. Some of the most undeviating adherents of materialism could be found in the revolutionary underground, including Vladimir Ul'ianov (Lenin). Other members of the artistic intelligentsia found this unswerving commitment to social change commendable but sterile. They sought a better life in the refined beauty of artistic creation, and their search to recover the unique power of art constitutes the opening chapter of twentieth-century Russian culture.

Modernism had many manifestations and inspirations in Russia and cannot be traced to a single source or moment.[4] A figure who inspired the respect of many, who stood as a symbol of integrity and transcendent talent and whose birth as an artist coincided with the birth of the century was the poet Aleksandr Blok.[5] His first published collection, *Verses on a Beautiful Lady* (*Stikhi o prekrasnoi dame*) (1904), was greeted by older Symbolist poets as an embodiment of their movement, yet Blok stood beyond any specific movement, and spoke to many different readers. His was a poetic world beyond material reality, of ideals that could never be fully expressed and would be destroyed by engagement with everyday life. Though his ethereal early verses were distant from social issues, Blok never turned his back on the world around him. He responded to the social upheavals of his day with poems of urgent foreboding, most remarkably *The Twelve* (*Dvenadtsat'*) (1918), one of the first artistic responses to the October Revolution. Taken by Bolsheviks to be a paean to the revolution, Blok's poem was, much like Andrei Belyi's modernist novel *Petersburg* (1916), an ambivalent recognition of social turmoil, and an attempt to find value in it. The unmatchable lyric power of Blok's verse and his faithfulness to his vision served as inspiration to later generations who suffered under the Soviet

---

4 Boris Gasparov, Robert P. Hughes and Irina Paperno (eds.), *Cultural Mythologies of Russian Modernism: From the Golden Age to the Silver Age* (Berkeley: University of California Press, 1992); Irina Paperno and Joan Delaney Grossman (eds.), *Creating Life: the Aesthetic Utopia of Russian Modernism* (Stanford, Calif.: Stanford University Press, 1994); Stephen C. Hutchings, *Russian Modernism: The Transfiguration of the Everyday* (Cambridge: Cambridge University Press, 1997).

5 Avril Pyman, *The Life of Aleksandr Blok* (Oxford: Oxford University Press, 1979–80).

regime. He insisted that artistic vision gave the clearest view of the future and stayed faithful to his singular genius by avoiding political allegiance.

Organised cultural life in Imperial Russia was dominated by the autocracy until late in the nineteenth century. The Romanov dynasty lavishly supported the performing arts, as with the Bolshoi Theatre in Moscow or the Mariinsky Theatre in St Petersburg, and it sponsored the Academy of Art and schools that discovered and trained Russia's immense artistic talent. The theatre monopoly guaranteed that Russia's finest talents performed on the imperial stages, and produced a performing tradition in drama, opera and ballet that achieved first-rank status in Europe. The imperial grip on the arts world loosened early in the twentieth century. When the theatre monopoly was lifted in 1882, private theatres appeared, such as the Korsh Theatre, Aleksandr Tairov's Chamber Theatre, and the Moscow Art Theatre, home to Konstantin Stanislavsky and his productions of Chekhov's plays.[6] In the visual arts, private art schools, such as the Moscow Art School, introduced young artists to the modernist trends sweeping Europe, and patrons from merchant families, such as the Mamontovs, Morozovs, Shchukins and Tret'iakovs encouraged new directions. These factors and relaxed censorship allowed for a nascent public sphere that freed aesthetic achievement from the narrow tastes of the ruling class. Art could operate according to its own rules, without support from the autocracy or permission from the censor.

The pre-revolutionary capitals of St Petersburg and Moscow offered artists, writers and performers a community in which they mingled intimately and stayed abreast of new developments around the world. They mixed in the same cafés, theatres and private salons, and drew inspiration from each other's work. Poets discovered new techniques in painting; theatre directors looked to poets for new language; painters sought inspiration in the theatre. Informal venues accommodated a greater range of tastes than imperial institutions had. These included nightclubs such as the St Petersburg *Stray Dog*, the *kapustnik* improvisational evenings at the Moscow Art Theatre, or the Wednesday evening literary salons in the 'Tower' apartment of poet Viacheslav Ivanov. The Symbolists organised journals such as *The Golden Fleece, Scales* or *Apollo*.[7]

6 Konstantin Rudnitsky, *Russian and Soviet Theater, 1905–1932* (New York: Abrams, 1988); Robert Russell and Andrew Barratt (eds.), *Russian Theatre in the Age of Modernism* (New York: St Martin's Press, 1990); J. Douglas Clayton, *Pierrot in Petrograd: The Commedia dell'arte/Balagan in Twentieth-Century Russian Theatre and Drama* (Montreal: McGill-Queen's University Press, 1993).
7 Ronald E. Peterson (ed.), *The Russian Symbolists: An Anthology of Critical and Theoretical Writings* (Ann Arbor: Ardis, 1986); Michael Green (ed.), *The Russian Symbolist Theatre: An Anthology of Plays and Critical Texts* (Ann Arbor, Ardis, 1986).

Aleksandr Benois of the World of Art organised yearly art exhibits starting in 1899, which evolved into international exhibitions promoted by Sergei Diagilev. Diagilev's creation of the Ballets Russes in 1909 exported the choreography of Mikhail Fokin, the dancing of Vaslav Nijinsky, and later the music of Igor Stravinsky to Paris and beyond, in such productions as *Firebird* and *Petrushka* (see Plate 2).[8]

The visual arts were perhaps most fractured by competing artistic programmes. Pre-war years saw the Academy and the now influential World of Art challenged by a dizzying array of groups, including Rayonists led by Mikhail Larionov and Suprematists led by Kazimir Malevich. Other artists, including Vasilii Kandinsky, Pavel Filonov, Nataliia Goncharova and Vladimir Tatlin, seemed to defy group definition. The ultimate impact of Russian modernism was not in its organisations, but in the achievements of its brilliant artists, and their legacy to the next generation of artists, whose fate was to encounter the October Revolution at the moment of their maturity.[9]

Many modernists thought of their art as addressing social concerns. Yet it was apparent that the audience for modernist art did not go far beyond the educated classes, and that the lower classes, who did not possess much leisure time or spare income, were largely indifferent to their work. These lower classes were not, as many supposed, lacking in cultural stimulation. The invention of new technologies, such as the gramophone, cinema and mass typography exposed more consumers to cultural expression than ever before. Cheap printing spurred a boom market in paperback detective stories, robber tales, romantic love stories, sometimes even light pornography.[10] The gramophone, which could be purchased for the home or listened to in a public parlour, brought music to listeners who could not afford imperial theatres, music halls or beer gardens. Such luminaries of the imperial stage as opera singer Fedor Chaliapin became popular recording stars, as did *cafés chantants* and variety singers, such as Nadezhda Plevitskaia, Varia Panina, Anastasia Vial'tseva. The Russian film industry, dominated by foreign companies before the First

8 *The World of Art Movement in Early 20th-Century Russia* (Leningrad: Aurora Art Publishers, 1991); Richard Taruskin, *Stravinsky and the Russian Traditions: A Biography of the Works through Mavra* (Berkeley: University of California Press, 1996).

9 John Bowlt (ed.), *Russian Art of the Avant-Garde: Theory and Criticism, 1902–1934* (New York: Viking Press, 1976); *The Russian Avant-Garde in the 1920s–1930s: Paintings, Graphics, Sculpture, Decorative Arts from the Russian Museum in St. Petersburg*, ed. Evgeny Kovtun (St Petersburg: Aurora Art Publishers, 1996).

10 Jeffrey Brooks, *When Russia Learned to Read: Literacy and Popular Literature, 1861–1917* (Princeton: Princeton University Press, 1985); also Louise McReynolds, *The News under Russia's Old Regime: The Development of a Mass-Circulation Press* (Princeton: Princeton University Press, 1991).

World War, boomed when the war isolated the country and created domestic opportunities for Russian studios. By 1917, directors such as Petr Chardynin, Vladimir Gardin, Iakov Protazanov and Evgenii Bauer were presenting viewers with distinctive Russian views of life and history, played by recognisable stars such as Ivan Mozzhukhin and Vera Kholodnaia.[11]

Popular culture was produced by profit-making enterprises, which varied from small family-owned printing presses to the large movie studios. All were subject to the marketplace and responsive to the changing tastes of the popular audience. Disdained by the arbiters of elite culture, popular culture encouraged literacy, exposed audiences to a variety of music, and in the cinema, exposed them to unknown worlds. Lower-class consumers did not seem to share the intelligentsia's assumption that culture need be edifying to be worthwhile. In its sensationalism, popular culture often exposed audiences to social trends ignored by other art forms. Sensational crime stories often revealed the social tensions underlying violence. Sexual innuendo and scandal-mongering encouraged the creation of independent female characters, who in their search for passion transgressed once impenetrable social barriers. Anastasia Verbitskaia, writer of the best-selling novel *Keys to Happiness* (*Kliuchi shchastiia*), and Count Amori (Ippolit Rapgof), wildly successful writer of film scenarios, were two of the many signs that women and non-Russian nationalities were becoming part of Russian culture.[12]

The Bolsheviks showed a great capacity to exploit cultural change when they seized power. The years following the war probably would have seen tremendous cultural innovations even without the Bolsheviks, as was the case in Europe and the United States. Nonetheless, the Bolsheviks made the lower classes the ultimate client of culture. Their long-term policy was to turn cultural institutions to the advantage of the new ruling classes.

Soon after taking power, the Bolsheviks launched an ambitious cultural programme that ran counter to the extremely limited means at their disposal. The

11 Denise Youngblood, *The Magic Mirror: Moviemaking in Russia, 1908–1918* (Madison: University of Wisconsin Press, 1999); Yuri Tsivian, *Early Cinema in Russia and its Cultural Reception* (London: Routledge, 1994).

12 James von Geldern and Louise McReynolds (eds.), *Entertaining Tsarist Russia: Tales, Songs, Plays, Movies, Jokes, Ads, and Images from Russian Urban Life, 1779–1917* (Bloomington: Indiana University Press, 1998); Richard Stites, *Russian Popular Culture: Entertainment and Society since 1900* (Cambridge: Cambridge University Press, 1992); Stephen Frank and Mark Steinberg (eds.), *Cultures in Flux: Lower-Class Values, Practices, and Resistance in Late Imperial Russia* (Princeton: Princeton University Press, 1994); Catriona Kelly, *Petrushka: The Russian Carnival Puppet Theatre* (Cambridge: Cambridge University Press, 1990); Laura Engelstein, *The Keys to Happiness: Sex and the Search for Modernity in Fin-de-Siècle Russia* (Ithaca, N.Y.: Cornell University Press, 1992).

policy, executed by the Commissariat of Enlightenment (Narkompros) and its leader, Anatolii Lunacharskii, relied on the extensive seizure and nationalisation of existing cultural institutions, and on a much smaller and unco-ordinated effort to create new institutions.[13] The first enterprises to fall under Bolshevik power were printing presses.[14] The monopoly on the press, a policy that history has come to associate with the Bolsheviks, came about haphazardly, without a programmatic decision from the party. The two revolutions of 1917 had given birth to a vigorous and diverse press. By early 1918 few non-Bolshevik newspapers were open, and they were subject to strict censorship and closed when their criticisms became too acute. One newspaper to be closed was *New Life (Novaia zhizn')*, edited by Lenin's friend and political sympathiser Maxim Gorky, perhaps the most popular living writer in Russia.[15] Similar actions took place in other institutions inherited from the Old Regime, including imperial theatres, universities, art and music academies. Employees of these institutions had once been members of the privileged elite, and resented their new masters bitterly. It would take several years to bring the institutions under control, a decade in the case of some universities.

Chaos often overwhelmed signs of health and vigour. The economic catastrophes that accompanied the civil war destroyed much of the productive capacity of cultural institutions. Popular education was in disarray, leaving a generation for whom culture, even literacy, was an unattainable luxury. Deep divisions appeared among artists and institutions about the fundamental purpose of art. Before the revolution most artists could, despite their differences, agree that artistic expression had some purposes entirely apart from social progress. The Bolsheviks did not agree. They came to power convinced that culture, politics and society are part of a great whole, infused with the same spirit. It was unimaginable to them that the political and cultural life of a country could function on opposing principles, that the state could pursue a socialist agenda while cultural life was determined by the dictates of the market.[16]

The hope that revolution would liberate the working class to create its own culture had been cherished before the revolution. Some counted on the

13 Sheila Fitzpatrick, *The Commissariat of the Enlightenment: Soviet Organization of Education and the Arts Under Lunacharsky, October 1917–1921* (Cambridge: Cambridge University Press, 1970).
14 Peter Kenez, *The Birth of the Propaganda State: Soviet Methods of Mass Mobilization, 1917–1929* (New York: Cambridge University Press, 1985).
15 Maxim Gorky, *Untimely Thoughts: Essays on Revolution, Culture and the Bolsheviks, 1917–1918* (New Haven: Yale University Press, 1995).
16 Richard Stites, *Revolutionary Dreams: Utopian Vision and Experimental Life in the Russian Revolution* (New York: Oxford University Press, 1989).

so-called 'worker-intellectuals' (*samouchki*, or self-taught intellectuals), uncommon men from the working and lower-middle classes who by force of will found time in their hard lives to read and write. The first worker-intellectuals had become visible in the 1870s, and by the turn of the century, there was a significant body of literature by these men.[17] Aleksandr Bogdanov, a doctor, philosopher, economist and leading Bolshevik thinker, proposed another model of working-class culture. As described in the science fiction classic *Red Star* (*Krasnaia zvezda*) (1908), Bogdanov's vision was one in which work and leisure merged into one, and art reflected the deep-seated principles of freedom and equality. Bogdanov believed that the proletariat could not properly exploit political power before it possessed socialist consciousness, disagreeing with Lenin, who believed that socialist culture could not be created before political power was in proletarian hands. While the Bolsheviks were planning insurrection in the autumn of 1917, Bogdanov and colleagues were creating a cultural network that came to be called Proletkul't.[18] At its peak, the network encompassed over a thousand clubs throughout Russia with a hundred thousand members, most devoted to basic instruction in writing, theatre and the arts. The central leadership of the movement followed an ambitious agenda that claimed to be the sole arm of proletarian cultural management, superseding the state. When the Bolsheviks consolidated their power at the conclusion of the civil war, Proletkul't became an impediment to unified state management. Lenin himself devoted considerable energy to reining in the movement, so that by 1921 its influence was greatly diminished. No fully autonomous proletarian cultural organisation ever again arose in the Soviet Union.

A more immediate need in the years of revolution was to mobilise popular support, by means of agitation, propaganda and education. The classic distinction of agitation and propaganda belongs to Lenin. According to him, agitation was a short-term activity that informed the masses of tasks for the immediate future and enlisted them on the side of progress. Propaganda was instructive and enlightening, aimed at establishing deeper understanding of the goals of the revolution.[19] Agitation was essential during the revolution, for it allowed the Bolsheviks to recruit the worker masses into the Red Guard and Red Army, and to defeat better-situated opponents. Many Bolshevik leaders had been underground journalists and were masterful communicators.

17 Mark D. Steinberg, *Proletarian Imagination: Self, Modernity, and the Sacred in Russia, 1910–1925* (Ithaca, N.Y.: Cornell University Press, 2002).
18 Lynn Mally, *Culture of the Future: The Proletkult Movement in Revolutionary Russia* (Berkeley: University of California Press, 1990).
19 For an earlier distinction, see Allan K. Wildman, *The Making of a Workers' Revolution: Russian Social Democracy, 1891–1903* (Chicago: University of Chicago Press, 1967).

When the newsprint shortage and a transport crisis made communication difficult, they devised ingenious new methods. ROSTA (Russian Telegraph Agency), the first Soviet press agency, hired artists in a number of large cities to produce posters on current events in a popular cartoon style presenting the Bolshevik point of view. The army and Narkompros organised so-called agit-trains. Staffed by journalists, actors, orators and leading members of the government, agit-trains would typically arrive in a town or village, interview local Bolsheviks (if there were any) and residents, write up their findings into a newspaper that was printed aboard the train and then show a movie in the evening. A visible presence could be decisive in bringing locals over to the Bolshevik cause.

Though instrumental in the civil war effort, agitation could not serve the Bolsheviks' long-term needs. Strapped for funds upon conclusion of the war and with an economy in ruins, the government undertook to create a new Soviet consciousness. Schools were rebuilt in villages and towns, and new teachers hired to teach children who, in many cases, had not seen school for five years. The Commissariat of Enlightenment issued new curricula based on the progressive education theories of John Dewey, embodied by the elementary school curriculum borrowed from Dalton, Massachusetts. A reality of under-educated and overworked teachers with poor facilities meant that many reforms were never realised. In higher education, curricular reform was complicated by ambitious programmes to recruit working-class students, who never before had access to higher learning. *Rabfaks* (worker faculties) were created to prepare these students for the rigours of study, laying the ground for years of conflict between students and their professors, most of whom still hailed from the privileged classes. Tensions grew throughout the 1920s until finally a new generation of younger 'Red' professors replaced older faculty members.[20]

The belief that Soviet Russia would breed new forms of culture based on new forms of social life was borne out only partially. The cultural life of most Russians was vastly different by the mid-1920s from what it had been in the final years of the Romanov dynasty. The face of art had changed as well. Artists spoke with a voice unimaginable before the revolution, and in the voices of people – above all the urban working class – silent under the Old Regime. New, revolutionary art forms represented the fragmented consciousness of modern

20 Larry E. Holmes, *The Kremlin and the Schoolhouse: Reforming Education in Soviet Russia, 1917–1931* (Bloomington: Indiana University Press, 1991); Michael David-Fox, *Revolution of the Mind: Higher Learning among the Bolsheviks, 1918–1929* (Ithaca, N.Y.: Cornell University Press, 1997).

urban life and its hostility to traditional ruling norms. The need to respond to new realities, to find new purposes for art, to appeal to a new audience and even to find a new language or mode of expression caused an unrivalled outburst of creative activity.

Writers discovered that the revolution had remade the very stuff of their work, the Russian language. The coherent social structures that had been the foundation of the Russian novel had disappeared, and prose writers retreated to shorter fragmentary forms. Although writers produced very little of lasting value during the revolution, they responded with a burst of innovative prose in the early 1920s. Readers who preferred a traditional narrative found the civil war experience related in *Chapaev* (1923), a novel by Dmitrii Furmanov, who had himself served the real Chapaev as commissar. In *Cement* (1925), Fedor Gladkov gave readers a working-class hero who fought in the civil war and returned to civilian life to reconstruct a local cement factory. These two novels, whose heroes and narratives conformed in many ways to the classic literary canon, were later declared forerunners of the official Soviet literary style, socialist realism.[21] Aleksei Tolstoy published the first two volumes of his trilogy *Road to Calvary* (*Khozhdenie po mukam*), which chronicled the tortured path of a well-born intellectual through the revolution.

The realistic narratives of these and other writers were challenged by a strong element of modernism in Soviet literature. Fragmented narrative styles were well suited for a time when prevailing social structures had broken down. Isaak Babel' 's compact tales of the civil war, published under the title of *Red Cavalry* (*Konarmiia*), provided classic heroes of bravery and natural grace, but disconcerted readers by describing unjustifiable acts of brutality. Boris Pil'niak's *Naked Year* (*Golyi god*) (1921) reflected the era through a town seemingly unaware of the revolution, whose residents slowly succumb to its dislocations. His prose seems plotless and fragmentary, and his language heterogeneous, as if overwhelmed by new words and ideas. A more comic approach to social change was found in the feuilletons of Mikhail Zoshchenko, an enormously popular writer of the NEP era. Set loose in booming urban centres, his narrators and characters absorbed the new language of Soviet Russia without fully understanding it, producing comic malapropisms that cut to the heart of the new Soviet consciousness.

The poetic heirs of Aleksandr Blok and the Symbolists were many and diverse, and they met the revolution with responses ranging from hostility to

21 Edward Brown, *The Proletarian Episode in Russian Literature, 1928–1932* (New York: Columbia University Press, 1953); Robert A. Maguire, *Red Virgin Soil: Soviet Literature in the 1920's* (Princeton: Princeton University Press, 1968).

welcome. Though he had sought to uncover ineffable truths with his verse, Blok's legacy lay equally in changes he brought to Russian poetic language and form. Blok was able to weave ideal beauty and the coarseness of modern urban life into a single poetic form. He perceived and responded to the storm gathering over Russian society in such poems as *The Field of Kulikovo* (*Na pole Kulikovom*) (1908) and *Retribution* (*Vozmezdie*) (1910–21). Poets responded to his challenge either by seeking a new balance for modern verse, as classical verse had once possessed, or by created a fragmented, unbalanced poetic form appropriate to modern life. The poetic ideal once created by Pushkin featured a harmonic expressive control; modern poets no longer had such a world to describe. Futurist poets such as Velimir Khlebnikov and Vladimir Mayakovsky sought inspiration in a non-standard sources, including popular urban ditties called *chastushki*, and introduced new and sometimes vulgar words into the poetic lexicon, to yield a new range of expressive abilities. They grabbed readers' attention with public scandals and manifestos that included *A Slap in the Face of Public Taste* (*Poshchechina obshchestvennomu vkusu*), published by David Burliuk, Aleksandr Kruchenykh, Mayakovsky and Khlebnikov in 1913.[22] The Futurist taste for urban modernism contrasted with the classical balance sought by Acmeists, a group organised by Nikolai Gumilev, whose most elegant voices would be Anna Akhmatova and Osip Mandel'shtam.

The October Revolution saw young poets respond in a number of ways. Mayakovsky declared the revolution to be his own and dedicated his work to its cause. The younger Boris Pasternak was far more ambivalent towards the revolution. Marina Tsvetaeva rejected the revolution and wrote from the Paris emigration. Each found in modernism a fragmentation of metre, rhyme and the poetic line that corresponded to their emotional needs and social experience. Each developed an intensely personal style and lyrical voice. Mayakovsky's claim that poetry was obliged to participate in social change proved fertile in his case, but did not hold true for all. The revolution demanded that literature change with the times. Yet time has proven the value of poetry that cultivated its own values, arranging words in musical patterns and bringing out the distinct and fundamental meaning of language. Poets who gathered under the banner of Acmeism, most prominently Akhmatova and Mandel'shtam, answered to these tasks. Refusing to march with the times, never ignoring

---

22 Vladimir Markov, *Russian Futurism: A History* (Berkeley: University of California Press, 1968); Anna Lawton (ed.), *Russian Futurism through its Manifestoes, 1912–1928* (Ithaca, N.Y.: Cornell University Press, 1988).

the world around them, both Akhmatova and Mandel'shtam wrote verse of tremendous gravity and integrity.[23]

Their fates would be tragic, depriving Russia of one of its greatest poetic generations. Gumilev was executed by the Bolsheviks in 1921 for alleged conspiratorial activities. Lyrical poet Sergei Esenin committed suicide in 1925. Mayakovsky killed himself in 1929. Mandel'shtam would be swallowed by the prison camps in the 1930s, and is believed to have died in 1938. Tsvetaeva eventually returned to an alien Soviet Russia in 1939 and would commit suicide in 1941. Pasternak, whose intense lyricism had little place in Soviet literature after 1934, found refuge in secondary work such as translations. Only after the Second World War did he begin work on his novel *Doctor Zhivago*, which eventually brought him the Nobel Prize. Akhmatova's personal, salon poetry proved the most capable of bearing witness to the times. Akhmatova suffered tragedy when ex-husband Gumilev was shot in 1921, and their son Lev was imprisoned twice in the 1930s. Her *Requiem* and *Poem without a Hero* (*Poema bez geroia*), written in these years and not published till many years later, are in their gravity and control of language the most eloquent testaments to the years of purge and war.

Organisational questions loomed large for other art forms. Music and theatre involve complex issues of financing and distribution; cinema requires a vast investment in technology. Artists cannot work alone in these art forms, and during the revolution they needed to establish a positive relationship with the state to continue work. State-financed theatres found relations with the new rulers problematic from the start. The Bolsheviks and former imperial theatres both entered the relationship with the assumption that ballet, opera and other performing arts were inherently elitist. Opera and ballet, which required a sophisticated audience, years of intense training and the budget for several lavish productions a year, seemed unsustainable in a proletarian state. Only the foresight and tremendous patience of Lunacharskii saved the enterprises, and allowed for the eventual incorporation of the imperial arts into the Soviet pantheon. In the first years of Soviet rule, the imperial theatres seemed bent on defying Soviet power. Beginning with strikes in 1917, and then refusing to adjust the repertory to the tastes of the new audiences, the theatres could find no viable artistic path in Soviet society. Narkompros found itself responsible not only for former imperial theatres, but for theatres that had

23 Clare Cavanagh, *Osip Mandelstam and the Modernist Creation of Tradition* (Princeton: Princeton University Press, 1995); Anatoly Nayman, *Remembering Anna Akhmatova* (New York: Henry Holt, 1991); Alyssa Dinega, *A Russian Psyche: The Poetic Mind of Marina Tsvetaeva* (Madison: University of Wisconsin Press, 2001).

been privately run under the old regime, most prominently the Moscow Art Theatre (MKhAT).[24] The repertory of MKhAT changed little after 1917, featuring the same plays by Chekhov, Gorky, Tolstoy and Dostoevsky, which seemed somewhat irrelevant after 1917. Bewildered by the new realities of the theatre world, Stanislavsky took his troupe into a long period of touring abroad that ended only in 1922. Meanwhile, the banner of change in revolutionary Russia had to be carried by his former student, and later director of the imperial Aleksandrinsky Theatre, Vsevolod Meyerhold, who had the audacity to proclaim an 'October in the Theatre' in 1918.[25]

Independent of the avant-garde, and sometimes independent of the proletarian state, popular culture underwent fundamental change in the years of the New Economic Policy.[26] Members of the working classes who had seen military action or had served in emergency economic conditions during the war now had more leisure time to devote to culture, and possessed a small portion of disposable income. There was a vigorous working press in the capitals and provincial cities. Inexpensive editions of Russian classics were available, and competed for audiences with contemporary literary works. Trade unions, factories and military units gained cheap access to tickets for state-financed theatres, including the once-exclusive imperial theatres. Technologies such as the gramophone, cinema and radio brought culture to the darkest corners of the country.

Despite the wealth of native cultural sources for Soviet Russians, the decade saw a flood of foreign cultural imports, including the same American jazz and movies that were flooding Europe. Jazz music found native adherents such as Leonid Utesov and Aleksandr Tsfasman, whose bands remained popular for decades. Utesov went on to stardom in movie musicals. For all the success of imports, the borrowings were not suited to the ideological purposes of Soviet culture. In fact, jazz would come under heavy restrictions in the 1930s.[27] A more amenable tactic was to graft socialist content onto native cultural tradition. Examples could be found in music, where the so-called 'cruel romance' was recycled, as in Pavel German's 'Brick Factory' (1922), a story of

24 Konstantin Stanislavsky, *My Life in Art* (Boston: Little, Brown, 1924).

25 Edward Braun, *Meyerhold: A Revolution in Theatre* (Iowa City: University of Iowa Press, 1995); Konstantin Rudnitsky, *Meyerhold, the Director* (Ann Arbor: Ardis, 1981).

26 James von Geldern and Richard Stites (eds.), *Mass Culture in Soviet Russia: Tales, Poems, Songs, Movies, Plays, and Folklore, 1917–1953* (Bloomington: Indiana University Press, 1995); Sheila Fitzpatrick, Alexander Rabinowitch and Richard Stites (eds.), *Russia in the Era of NEP: Explorations in Soviet Society and Culture* (Bloomington: Indiana University Press, 1991).

27 S. Frederick Starr, *Red and Hot: The Fate of Jazz in the Soviet Union, 1917–1980* (New York: Oxford University Press, 1983).

working-class woe and redemption.[28] In literature, writers adapted popular genres such as the detective story, known as the 'Pinkerton tale' in Russian. Marietta Shaginian's *Mess-Mend* (*Mess-Mend, ili Ianki v Petrograde*) (1924) featured proletarian detectives who foil a plot by world capitalists to depose the Soviet government. Such work was often successful with audiences, yet critics from the proletarian Left claimed that any work adopted from capitalist cultures could never reflect proletarian consciousness.

No cultural form presented greater competition from the capitalist world, or more opportunity to create distinctly Soviet forms, than the cinema. The movie business requires tremendous investment and organisational support for training, production and distribution. The greater part of the movie industry fled Russia after the October Revolution, taking with it equipment, film stock and a generation of actors, scriptwriters and directors. Faced with rebuilding the movie industry from scratch, and a recognition that cinema would allow the party to spread its message across the country, Lunacharskii established a film school in 1921 that, starting with almost nothing, would soon train a generation of masterful cinematographers and directors. Soviet cinema in the early 1920s faced overwhelming competition from Western imports, particularly American films. Stars such as Douglas Fairbanks and Mary Pickford were proving irresistible to Russian audiences. In response, the young Soviet film industry experimented with the action format. Lev Kuleshov's *The Extraordinary Adventures of Mr West in the Land of the Bolsheviks* (*Neobychainye prikliucheniia Mistera Vesta v strane bol'shevikov*) (1924) told the story of an American visitor to Moscow swindled by a gang of thieves and rescued by honest Soviet police. The message of proletarian virtue and capitalist trickery was relieved by stunts and chases worthy of an American movie.[29]

Soviet film avoided the Hollywood star system by developing a corporate or collective production system. Film studios commissioned work from scriptwriters and directors, and supervised production to ensure ideological responsibility. Actors worked at the behest of the director, who became the focal point of the cinematic creative process. A generation of young directors came of age in the 1920s, producing films of aesthetic daring that they believed embodied the Soviet point of view. The *Kinoglaz* (Film-Eye) series of newsreel

28  Robert A. Rothstein, 'The Quiet Rehabilitation of the Brick Factory: Early Soviet Popular Music and its Critics', *Slavic Review* 39 (1980): 373–88.
29  Jay Leyda, *Kino, a History of the Russian and Soviet Film* (New York: Collier Books, 1973); Denise J. Youngblood, *Movies for the Masses: Popular Cinema and Soviet Society in the 1920s* (Cambridge: Cambridge University Press, 1992); Richard Taylor and Ian Christie (eds.), *The Film Factory: Russian and Soviet Cinema in Documents* (Cambridge, Mass.: Harvard University Press, 1988).

director Dziga Vertov coupled the non-fiction format with aggressive editing techniques to present viewers with a world of socialist values. Directors of the fictional or artistic film followed Kuleshov's lead, coupling action techniques with revolutionary values. Working on state commissions, Sergei Eisenstein created *Strike* (*Stachka*) (1924) and *Battleship Potemkin* (*Bronenosets Potemkin*) (1925), which attracted the attention of critics around the world. Dedicated to events from the tsarist past, the films used action techniques to create vivid images of class struggle. Expressive camera angles and visual metaphors, and editing techniques based on a grammar of conflicting images forced viewers to become active interpreters of events. The films of Vsevolod Pudovkin often concerned the same eras and events, and boasted the same power of persuasion. His *Mother* (*Mat'*) (1926) and *The End of St Petersburg* (*Konets Sankt-Peterburga*) (1927) offered scenes of great violence and revolutionary passion. Pudovkin's editing aimed not at disquieting audiences, as Eisenstein's did, but at providing viewers with a coherent vision of the past.

The moderate policies nurtured by Lunacharskii ensured that Soviet culture under NEP was rich and layered, offering something to many tastes.[30] Adherents could point with pride to advances in the cinema, to the verses of Mayakovsky or plays of Meyerhold, to the vigorous worker club movement. Perhaps their greatest triumph was unprecedented access of the proletariat to culture. Critics who rejected the revolution or felt that art must follow its own path could find solace in the splendid outburst of poetry, in the riches of the art world, in the splendid new theatre productions by directors such as Tairov and Evgenii Vakhtangov, by the reinvigorated opera and ballet companies of the former imperial theatres.[31] They could even read the rich flow of novels and poetry being produced by Russian émigrés in Paris and Berlin.[32] Social ferment ensured a lively and sometime ferocious debate on cultural issues.

Moderate policies ensured that many modes of cultural expression received state support. In practice the Bolsheviks accepted the same cultural hierarchies that radical Leftists would make the primary target of revolution. Despite the obvious disloyalty of their staffs during the revolution, the former imperial theatres received lavish funding. The theatres responded by bringing their work to working-class audiences and creating a new repertory that tried to respond

---

30 Sheila Fitzpatrick, 'The "Soft" Line on Culture and Its Enemies: Soviet Cultural Policy, 1922–1927', *Slavic Review* 33, 2 (June, 1974).

31 Nick Worrall, *Modernism to Realism on the Soviet Stage: Tairov, Vakhtangov, Okhlopkov* (Cambridge: Cambridge University Press, 1989); Spencer Golub, *Evreinov, the Theatre of Paradox and Transformation* (Ann Arbor: UMI Research Press, 1984).

32 Simon Karlinsky and Alfred Appel, Jr. (eds.), *The Bitter Air of Exile: Russian Writers in the West, 1922–1972* (Berkeley: University of California Press, 1977).

to revolutionary thematics. Still, much in the ballet and opera harked back to an aesthetic identified with imperial society.[33] Other innately conservative organisations, such as the musical conservatories and arts academies, continued to receive generous support, undergoing periodic outbursts of internal reform in which the state was as likely as not to support the forces of continuity. Institutions of higher education were still dominated by faculties trained long before the revolution, a situation that grew tense as the worker faculties brought more and more students radicalised by the revolution into universities. Younger people who felt that the revolution had been accomplished in their name found themselves marginalised within many Soviet institutions. Many devoted their energies to building secondary cultural organisations that seemed insignificant within the diversity of the 1920s, but would later mount a powerful assault against prevailing orthodoxies. Institutions that provided refuge for cultural radicals included local branches of the Komsomol, worker clubs and newspapers that gave space to worker correspondents (rabkors), who reported on local working-class affairs and whose exposés of local corruption were so trenchant that several were murdered.

The fate of two independent proletarian organisations that came to dominate cultural life in the late 1920s illustrates the dynamics of the 'Cultural Revolution', the radicalisation and subordination of culture to the party that was initiated in the late 1920s.[34] Artists and critics claiming to speak for the working class created the Russian Association of Proletarian Musicians (RAPM) and Russian Association of Proletarian Writers (RAPP). They insisted on pursuing a narrowly proletarian agenda in the arts, and succeeded for several years during the First Five-Year Plan when the state gave members control of institutions of training, publication and production. The proletarians demanded that art present party agendas and proclaim the slogans of the day. They insisted that only workers could create a proletarian art (this despite the non-proletarian background of many RAPP and RAPM members). Above all they worked to excise certain forms of culture that betrayed bourgeois or aristocratic origins. Noble-born literary classics such as Pushkin and Tolstoy were declared out of

---

33 See Katerina Clark, *Petersburg: Crucible of Cultural Revolution* (Cambridge, Mass.: Harvard University Press, 1995).

34 The term 'cultural revolution' was defined for Russia by Sheila Fitzpatrick in 'Cultural Revolution as Class War', in Sheila Fitzpatrick (ed.), *Cultural Revolution in Russia, 1928–1931* (Bloomington: Indiana University Press, 1978), and her 'Stalin and the Making of a New Elite', in *The Cultural Front: Power and Culture in Revolutionary Russia* (1974; reprinted Ithaca, N.Y.: Cornell University Press, 1992). For discussion, see Michael David-Fox, 'What Is Cultural Revolution?' and 'Mentalité or Cultural System: A Reply to Sheila Fitzpatrick', *Russian Review* 58, 2 (Apr. 1999).

date. Lyric poetry and the realist novel were to be replaced by so-called 'production' novels, which describe the industrial process as experienced by the working class.[35] Folk music, popular urban songs, jazz and most forms of classical music were no longer supported, and some were actively attacked. The tumult that accompanied the rise to power of RAPP and RAPM was replicated in theatres, editorial offices and educational institutions across the country. There was a dismal fall-off of artistic production in all branches of culture, and a wrenching turnover of personnel. Experienced creators and administrators were silenced or removed from office, and classics disappeared from stages and library shelves. Much of this activity took place in the years 1928–33, which coincided with radicalisation of Soviet social life. These were the years of the First Five-Year Plan, and of the collectivisation of agriculture.[36]

Just as it grew wary of policies that alienated common citizens from Soviet power, the party cooled towards proletarian arts organisations. Soviet leaders sought to stabilise cultural life in ways that would allow them to work productively with the 'creative intelligentsia' (as the artistic world came to be known in Soviet parlance) and to win back audiences alienated by radical art forms. Two new policies became the foundation of the state arts administration. The first was the creation of trade unions for creative artists, initially in literature, then in music and the visual arts. The unions allowed party and non-party artists to normalise their professional lives, including the commission and payment for their work. The second was the enunciation of an official Soviet aesthetic, called socialist realism, which rapidly became obligatory for all artistic expression.[37]

Socialist realism was declared the reigning method of Soviet literature at the First All-Union Congress of Soviet Writers in 1934. Defined by Maxim Gorky as a continuation of the Russian realist tradition, the doctrine was infused with the ideology and optimism of socialism. Socialist realism was best characterised by the watchwords accessibility (*dostupnost'*), the spirit of the people (*narodnost'*), and the spirit of the party (*partiinost'*). Joseph Stalin provided an authoritative if vague formulation when he stated that socialist realism was 'socialist in content, national in form'. Writers were wise not to use fancy language, artists and composers not to be too refined in their techniques. The subjects and heroes of these works were usually uncomplicated, reliable and their

---

35 Harriet Borland, *Soviet Literary Theory and Practice during the First Five-Year Plan, 1928–32* (New York: King's Crown Press, 1950).
36 Fitzpatrick, *Cultural Revolution in Russia, 1928–1931*.
37 Boris Groys, *The Total Art of Stalinism: Avant-Garde, Aesthetic Dictatorship, and Beyond* (Princeton: Princeton University Press, 1992).

politics predictable (if not always the core of the tale). Such works could be entertaining, as was Iurii Krymov's *Tanker Derbent* (1938), an adventure tale that hinged on an undisciplined crew brought together by their Communist captain. Socialist realism was unique only in that it was the sole method endorsed by the state. Soviet critics would have denied that this was new. Other ruling classes – the aristocracy, the bourgeoisie – had enforced establishment aesthetics through sponsorship and taste. Of course the proletariat would do the same.

Proclaimed as a unitary method, socialist realism took many different forms depending on the time, the artistic medium and the national culture in which it was created.[38] A form of socialist realism fashionable at the time of its establishment was the so-called production novel. An example of the genre was Valentin Katayev's *Time Forward!* (*Vremia vpered*) (1932), in which young workers attempt to build a gigantic steel plant in record time. Painters produced monumental canvases celebrating the First and Second Five-Year Plans. Music was a more difficult medium, since there is nothing inherently realistic in musical composition. Prescribed methods of socialist realism in all media underwent frequent changes as party factions shifted. At all times the going description was proclaimed to be permanent, rooted in Marxism-Leninism and official. Writers, even loyal and servile writers, found it challenging to follow the line. Soviet culture was riddled with examples of canonic writers being forced to rewrite their work to conform to changing standards. Fedor Gladkov, author of *Cement*, and Aleksandr Fadeev, chairman of the Writers' Union and author of the classic *Rout* (*Razgrom*) (1927) and *Young Guard* (*Molodaia gvardia*) (1945) were forced into rewrites that changed the style of their works entirely.

The Writers' Union regularised the business of literature, providing its members with a dependable living.[39] A writer who submitted to its authority would enjoy a variety of perquisites. The Union distributed assignments to journalists, controlled which house published which books and doled out foreign delicacies, designer clothing and even the highly sought country homes (*dachas*). To be a non-member meant not to be published. By the time of the First Congress, control of printing, distribution, publishing, radio, film and theatre had been firmly centralised, giving the party Central Committee absolute

38 Katerina Clark, *The Soviet Novel: History as Ritual* (Chicago: University of Chicago Press, 1981); Regine Robin, *Socialist Realism: an Impossible Aesthetic* (Stanford, Calif.: Stanford University Press, 1992).
39 A. Kemp-Welch, *Stalin and the Literary Intelligentsia, 1928–39* (Basingstoke: Macmillan, 1991).

power of veto. The Writers' Union served as model for the other creative unions (Cinematographic Workers, Actors, Artists) that were soon established.

While it is apparent in retrospect that these policies were the tools with which the government regimented the arts, it is important to understand why artists in the years 1932–4 might have greeted them with relief. When journals, museums and theatres, arts academies and other cultural institutions fell under the control of the self-proclaimed proletarians, artists found that to sell their work, they must submit to humiliating review by critics with low aesthetic but high political standards. Often these standards were arbitrary and depended on which administrator was in charge. Many artists eventually found it impossible to make a living. The unions and socialist realism regularised commissions and standards of review, and guaranteed payment for artistic work. While the life of a creative artist was very tenuous at the outset of the 1930s, life for a successful artist was extremely profitable by the end of the decade, placing artists among the wealthiest citizens in the land of socialism. Few seemed bothered by the silencing, imprisonment or even death of artists. For the consumers of culture, who had suffered through a long period in which few new movies or books emerged, the policies boded an outburst of culture for popular tastes. Though a good deal of the work labelled socialist realism was mediocre, the decade witnessed a steady stream of literature, movies and popular songs that are read, viewed and sung with great pleasure even today. And since a watchword of the aesthetic was accessibility, all of it was perfectly understandable and enjoyable for the mass consumer.

Socialist realism, first formulated by writers and promulgated by the Writers' Union, was very much a literary principle. It called for clarity of language and narrative, simplicity and steadfastness of character, and a forthright political stance. For a brief few years in the middle of the 1930s, the seeming impracticality of the method gave artists great latitude, particularly in popular music and the cinema. The film industry, restructured into a new organisation called Soiuzkino and headed by Boris Shumiatskii, took as its goal the creation of a popular, self-financing film industry. Shumiatskii felt that the aesthetically ambitious films of Eisenstein, Pudovkin and Kuleshov, as well as the younger Aleksandr Dovzhenko, had alienated the common Soviet spectator. The box office bore him out to a degree. Shumiatskii demanded films that were 'accessible', enjoyable and entertaining. Although political fidelity was still a must, it soon became clear that politics would yield to fun as the primary mission.[40]

---

40 Richard Taylor and Derek Spring (eds.), *Stalinism and Soviet Cinema* (London: Routledge, 1993).

Two films of 1934 carried the banner of the new cinema. The first bore the name of Furmanov's 1923 novel *Chapaev*. The novel depicted Chapaev as a simple soldier, brave and charismatic but politically untutored. Under the guidance of his commissar, he gradually understands the cause he instinctively supports, and teaches his undisciplined troops the primacy of the cause over the individual. On the silver screen, Chapaev's rough-cut personality, full of grand gestures and petty foibles, became the main draw. The second hit of 1934 was *Happy-Go-Lucky Fellows* (*Veselye rebiata*), directed by Grigorii Aleksandrov. Travelling to Hollywood in 1930–2 as Eisenstein's assistant director, Aleksandrov had seen how the musical film could exploit the new talking medium and win a mass audience. He set about creating the Soviet musical, and selected Leonid Utesov as his lead man. Renowned for his performance of the slangy songs of his native Odessa, with a strong admixture of jazz, Utesov played a simple shepherd in the movie. Living in the Crimean village of Abrau, his singing talent is discovered by vacationing Muscovites. He is whisked away to the capital, and soon finds himself leading a jazz band. Anybody, it seemed, could be a star in Soviet Russia.

Music for the film was written by Isaak Dunaevskii, a mainstay of the Soviet song-writing industry. Soviet popular music betrayed the significant influence of jazz, an influence that had not been fully digested when the Cultural Revolution rendered it politically suspect. Soviet audiences loved jazz, both the foreign jazz they heard on records and the native jazz played by Russian bands. From the late 1920s to the early 1930s jazz was rarely heard in officially recognised musical forums, but Utesov's performance in *Fellows* relegitimised jazz in its heavily Russified form. Soviet-Russian jazz was more melodic than rhythmic and it abstained from the improvisation that is problematic in a heavily censored culture. Soviet jazz borrowed its melodic influences from sources ranging from American jazz to Russian folk music. What made it 'jazz' to its Soviet audiences was the use of unfamiliar instruments such as the saxophone and trombone, the unfamiliar rhythms, and the exuberant performance style alien to classical music. Dunaevskii was the composer who most successfully combined these influences; and because of his willingness to write his music for the heavily politicised lyrics of Mikhail Isakovskii and Vasilii Lebedev-Kumach, among other lyricists, he fared well with cultural watchdogs. Other composers, such as the Pokrass Brothers, Matvei Blanter, or A. V. Aleksandrov (founder of the Red Army Chorus) created a more distinctly Soviet style of music in which the march was the favoured genre. The presence of ideological music did not eclipse more traditional musical concerns, and the love song was still the most popular genre of the decade, with the young lyricist Evgenii Dolmatovskii scoring his first successes. As for performers, the Red Army Chorus made its first tours at this time, yet the overwhelming audience favourites remained jazz players like Utesov and Aleksandr Tsfasman, or vocalists such as Izabella Iur'eva, Konstantin Sokol'skii, and Vadim Kozin, who ignored politics and who harkened back to the great torch singers of pre-revolutionary years.

Soviet arts organisations had gained complete control over cultural life by the mid-1930s. In retrospect, these were golden years for average Soviet audiences. Hugely popular songs, novels and movies were easily available, and came out in a fairly steady stream. Audiences had more free time and disposable income than they ever had before. That these resources were paltry in comparison to Western societies seemed to matter little. Yet much of the same witch-hunting that struck the political world during the purge trials of 1936 took place as well in the arts, invisible to the public eye. By the end of the decade, artists as diverse as Mandel'shtam and Kozin were either dead or lost in the prison camps, as were many, many others, including Babel', Meyerhold and Pil'niak. Mikhail Bulgakov's great novel *Master and Margarita*, a decade in the making, was completed and lost deep in a desk drawer, not to emerge until 1966, after which it became perhaps the most beloved Russian novel of the century. Cruel fate struck artists from the most popular to the most elusive, from wholehearted Bolshevik to apolitical elitist, from Russian to Jew.

Emblematic of the unpredictability was the fate of two operas, *Lady Macbeth of Mtsensk*, composed by Dmitrii Shostakovich, and *Ancient Heroes (Bogatyri)*, a libretto written by Demian Bednyi to an old comic opera by Borodin. The young Shostakovich was a rising star in Soviet music, and *Lady Macbeth* one of his first resounding successes. Based on a story by Nikolai Leskov, the opera tells of a strong-willed woman trapped in a loveless marriage in the Russian provinces, ruined finally when her passionate affair leads to the murder of her husband and his father. First performed in 1934, it won instant acclaim for the daring use of instruments such as the trombone and saxophone, and its bold dissonance and discordant rhythms. Yet when Stalin attended a 1936 performance and walked out in evident disgust, Shostakovich was dangerously exposed. Within two days *Pravda* featured an editorial entitled 'Chaos instead of Music', castigating Shostakovich, and performance of the opera ceased.[41] More surprising was the fate of Bednyi. A poet and staunch comrade of Lenin, Bednyi had once defined Soviet political correctness. During the civil war his caustic verse scored points against priests, capitalists and monarchists, and

41 Laurel Fay, *Shostakovich: A Life* (New York: Oxford University Press, 2000).

afterwards he remained an effective political versifier. His libretto for *Heroes* was in the same spirit of mockery, yet much to his shock, *Pravda* denounced its debut performance for disparaging the role of Christianity in Russian history.[42]

Though the final third of the 1930s was a period of profound repression in the arts, to many Soviet citizens it was a time when their tastes were served. Audiences continued to find new movies to suit their tastes, many of them in the musical genre they had come to love. Aleksandrov scored new hits with *Volga-Volga* (1938) and *Radiant Path* (*Svetlyi put'*) (1940), both starring Liubov' Orlova, and he soon found a rival in the young Ivan Pyr'ev, who directed the popular musicals *Rich Bride* (*Bogataia nevesta*) (1938), *Tractor Drivers* (*Traktoristy*) (1939) and *Swineherd and the Shepherd* (*Svinarka i pastukh*) (1940). These films seem today to be clichés of socialist realism, in which *kolkhozniks* and shock workers find true love and happiness, but they resonated deeply with their intended audiences. Music of all kinds continued to be performed, recorded and played on the radio, and if the socialist marches of Aleksandrov and Dunaevskii received the lion's share of official attention, crooners and jazz singers were still commonly available. In fact, one of the most popular entertainments of the era were vast outdoor masquerades and dance parties, such as those arranged in Moscow's Gorky Park, where carefree thousands danced the night away. Here, as well as in dance halls throughout the land, jazz and the cruel romance held sway. The music played on, as long as nobody uttered the word 'jazz'.

Perhaps the most democratic shift in cultural organisation was the state's willingness to sponsor amateur arts to a degree that rivalled the professional. Falling under the broad rubric of *samodeiatel'nost'*, roughly translated as amateur, but meaning 'self-actuating', amateur arts organisations bloomed throughout the Soviet Union. Devoted to all forms of activities and hobbies, clubs provided space, equipment and instruction to the working masses. Although 'Organise Cultured Leisure' was the pervasive if unappealing slogan of cultural authorities, the slogan should not obscure the fact that the movement allowed simple Soviet citizens tremendous opportunity to enjoy themselves, to socialise and to share their accomplishments with friends. Most commonly, amateur arts groups were devoted to singing and dancing, with a repertory that included dollops of officially approved Soviet marches and large shares of the folk music that only a few years before had been the target of proletarian critics. In the Slavic, Transcaucasian and Central Asian ethnic republics,

---

42 Boris Schwarz, *Music and Musical Life in Soviet Russia, 1917–1970* (New York: Norton, 1972).

the revival (often artificial) of folk music and dance was used to demonstrate the deep roots of Soviet nationalities policy. The amateur arts movement allowed common citizens to participate in Soviet cultural life. Oddly the movement, whose folk aesthetics were in utter contradiction to socialist realism, thrived most during the years when the state promoted socialist realism most avidly.[43]

The repressions of the immediate pre-war years undermined the world of culture. Popular song and amateur arts seemed to thrive, but the movie business was producing fewer and fewer films every year, artists were confined to narrow ranges of expression and the literary world lost many of the great writers who had made the first decade of Soviet literature so rich. Arts administrators maintained their jobs by parroting the most recent party line, and in doing so destroyed the careers of talented peers. Artistic unions formed to defend the interests of artists now existed to control them. Soviet culture suffered from a deep split between artists, administrators and audiences.

Similar rifts within Soviet society left the country unprepared for the war that began in June 1941. The army, whose command structure had been destroyed in the purges of 1938, could not resist German attacks; the state found it impossible to organise retreat or resistance in the early months of the war. The party central leadership seemed incapable of response. Yet Soviet artists responded immediately and powerfully to the German invasion, creating songs, posters, newspaper and radio reports and later stories and movies that gave Soviet citizens an outlet for their fury and despair. The ability to adapt to war footing far faster than the army, party or state suggests that Soviet cultural organisations were much stronger than would have seemed possible.[44]

The most difficult years for many Soviet artists were the two between the signing of the Soviet–German Non-aggression Pact in August 1939 and the German invasion. The tremendous pressure on cultural organs to provide ideological support for the never-ending purges, for the growing cult of Stalin and for the forced incorporation of territories into the Soviet Union challenged even loyal minions. Three years of bloody purges left them unsure of whom to praise and wary of paying tribute to any policy line that could, within the space of several days, be declared anathema. The sudden flip-flop into friendship with Hitler's Germany was even more traumatic. Many younger journalists, songwriters and artists had learned their craft by castigating the Nazi scourge.

43 Frank Miller, *Folklore for Stalin: Russian Folklore and Pseudofolklore of the Stalin Era* (Armonk, N.Y.: M. E. Sharpe, 1990).
44 Richard Stites (ed.), *Culture and Entertainment in Wartime Russia* (Bloomington: Indiana University Press, 1995).

Some fell silent, others turned their attention elsewhere. The most popular singers of that era were Kozin (soon to be arrested) and Iur'eva, honey-voiced crooners of love songs. In the cinema the most popular offerings were Pyr'ev's sweet musical comedies. Movies such as Aleksandr Dovzhenko's *Liberation* (*Osvobozhdenie*) (1940), which chronicled the 'reunification' of Western Ukraine (otherwise known as eastern Poland) under the terms of the Soviet–German Treaty, or Vasilii Belaev's *Mannerheim Line* (1940), about the Soviet–Finnish war, quickly passed as embarrassing bows to government campaigns.

Sergei Eisenstein provides an illustration of an artist who continued to identify with the state, yet wished to maintain artistic integrity. When anti-German feeling was at its height, he directed his classic *Aleksandr Nevskii* (1938), which chronicled how in 1242 that Novgorodian prince unified the Russians and repulsed the invasion of the Teutonic Knights. The climactic battle on the ice of Lake Peipus is one of cinema's great action scenes, and the film score composed by Sergei Prokofiev offers one of film's greatest collaborations between composer and director. Unmistakable analogies between the Teutonic Knights and modern Germans, Nevskii's Novgorod and Stalin's Soviet Russia made the film an effective piece of propaganda. The unfortunate shift in foreign policy that followed within a year made the film politically obsolete, and it was removed from circulation. Soon after the signing of the pact, Eisenstein was commissioned to direct Richard Wagner's *Die Walküre*, the apotheosis of the German spirit, at the Bol'shoi Theatre. Meant as a gesture of cultural friendship, the production left German representatives at the 1940 premiere offended by its aesthetic innovations, 'deliberate Jewish tricks' as they called them. The German invasion soon erased the controversy. Wagner was removed from the repertory, and *Nevskii* was once against released to Soviet screens.[45]

Soviet victory in the Great Patriotic War came from an ability of society to rally around the war effort, to tap into deep wells of patriotic faith, to unify itself behind the state and its leader Joseph Stalin. Soviet culture played an integral part in this enterprise. The first rallying cries issued from the pens of the young journalists, artists and songwriters who had made their careers during the purge era. The venom that they so deplorably unleashed against their compatriots seemed entirely appropriate when directed against Fascist invaders. The war seemed to liberate writers and artists who had previously operated inside Soviet cultural rules, to give them a subject matter appropriate

45 *The Eisenstein Reader*, ed. Richard Taylor (London: British Film Institute, 1998); Al LaValley and Barry P. Scherr (eds.), *Eisenstein at 100: A Reconsideration* (New Brunswick, N.J.: Rutgers University Press, 2001).

to their style, allowing them to access once unacceptable cultural idioms. Most remarkable in this regard was the widespread use of Christian symbols as a source of Russian national identity. Only one day after the German attack, Vasilii Lebedev-Kumach, erstwhile lyricist of orthodox Soviet songs ('Life's Getting Better and Happier Too', 1936; 'The Common Soviet Man', 1938), and General Aleksandr Aleksandrov, director of the Red Army Chorus, wrote and recorded 'Holy War', a stirring march that served as anthem for the war. Political cartoonists such as Boris Efimov, who had cut his teeth on anti-Trotskyite caricatures for *Pravda*, and Kukryniksy, a trio of cartoonists who had begun publishing cartoons in 1933, immediately drew anti-German posters that were distributed throughout the country. They continued to do so throughout the war, and remained the most effective graphic propagandists in the country. A similar development took place in journalism, where older political journalists such as Boris Gorbatov, Ilya Ehrenburg and Aleksandr Korneichuk were joined by recent graduates such as Konstantin Simonov in creating an effective brand of wartime journalism. In the earliest months of the war, when the mass media at their worst were pretending that the war effort was going well, these journalists made the perilous journey to the front, addressed the obvious catastrophe and yet offered their readers hope and courage. Ehrenburg proclaimed German barbarity to be the sign of a cultural rot that could not defeat Soviet civilisation. Simonov travelled to western Russia, witnessed the caravans of soldiers and common people streaming east before the German tanks and wrote poems of heartfelt grief. His 'Wait for Me' (Zhdi menia) and 'Smolensk Roads' (Ty, pomnish', Alesha, dorogi Smolenshchiny) were recited as prayers throughout the war and after.

Newspapers, posters and popular songs, which could be generated quickly and distributed throughout the vast country, were the most effective means to rally the people in the first year of the war. Most of the Soviet Union was accessible by radio and print. Radio proved a particularly effective medium. Soviet broadcasting switched from the wire-fed system that had allowed the state to control content and cut off outside broadcasts, to shortwave broadcasts that could reach over enemy lines to the occupied territories. Journalists could report developments on the front immediately, allowing breathless listeners to follow the heroic defences of Stalingrad and Leningrad. Soldiers could hear the latest recordings of their favourite singers singing 1930s classics or new hits. Mark Bernes sang his beloved 'Dark Night' (1942), Klavdiia Shulzhenko her romantic 'Blue Scarf' (1941) and Leonid Utesov recorded his satiric 'Baron von der Pschick' (1942). For all the popularity of Soviet-produced culture, however, listeners on the front and at home most avidly followed readings of Lev Tolstoy's *War and Peace* (*Voina i mir*). The Russian defeat of a foreign invader through persistence and endurance offered a comforting analogy to the present.

The desperation and raw emotion of the first year, which gave birth to short genres with an immediate response to the surrounding world, and a direct route to the emotions of readers and listeners, gave way to more substantial artistic forms later in the war. This was due to the fact partly that artists and writers had more time to work and plan, and partly that cultural institutions that had ceased to function recovered their footing. Censors that had ceded their functions to editors and administrators in the early months of war once again became an effective barrier to unorthodox expression. Arts-funding organisations once again received the political guidance they needed to operate. The Bol'shoi Theatre in Moscow, and the large theatres in Leningrad could again offer the classics of drama, opera and ballet. Productions boosted morale in the big cities where they were performed, and throughout Russia where they were broadcast. They infused Soviet citizens, foremost Soviet Russians, with a pride in their culture at a time when national pride constituted the core of public morale; and they offered proof that civilisation could survive in the face of Fascist barbarity.

The confidence in final victory gained by the summer of 1943 gave Soviet life an unprecedented legitimacy. Soviet culture, commissioned by party and state, accomplished its design. Inspired by Marxism-Leninism, devoted to the cause of the working people, obedient to their representative, the Communist Party; committed to a single message, and receptive to artists of all circumstances of birth: such were the ideals it embodied. Soviet artists and writers had an immediate relationship with their audience that might have been the envy of artists throughout the world. Oddly enough, it was only the German invasion that made the vision of a cultural monolith come true.

## Conclusion

Russian-Soviet culture was fundamentally different after fifty years of social and institutional change. An institutional framework based on the autocracy had given way to private and informal institutions, which were then swept away by the October Revolution. Soviet cultural institutions came into being only slowly, hindered first by financial constraints, then by a shortage of knowledgeable cadres and later by unpredictable ideological shifts. The centrality of social mission to art, an article of faith to the intelligentsia that had been tested by modernism and market-based popular culture, was institutionalised in Soviet times and made obligatory. The modernist impulse so strong in the early years of the century, which had enriched Russian artistic culture and had responded to the revolutionary spirit, was ultimately rejected for the aesthetic of socialist realism. It is important to understand that Soviet popular culture was often genuinely popular, and that the political orthodoxy unpalatable to other cultures and other times did not always bother the intended audience. Many products of Stalinist popular culture were beloved by Soviet audiences long after their political context had faded. Soviet classics enjoy great popular support even today, now that the Soviet Union is a distant memory.

One must not forget, however, that Soviet culture was founded on coercion. The state and party controlled all the institutions of arts education, creation, production and distribution. Artists had no choice but to conform to artistic controls, and audiences knew little but what the state provided them. The audience's apparent enjoyment of Soviet cultural products in pre-war years, and the deep response during the war, took place in the absence of competition. No less a legacy of Soviet culture is the wretched treatment of gifted artists, writers, composers. Those who died, and those who were hounded into silence, were also beloved by Soviet readers, and their legacy lives on.

22

# The politics of culture, 1945–2000

JOSEPHINE WOLL

During the more than half a century covered in this chapter, the Soviet Union experienced a bewildering array of changes, up to and including its own demise. The final years of Stalin's life and rule, when the country had to regenerate itself after the devastation of the Second World War, involved major cultural repressions amid a climate of isolationism and xenophobia. Between Stalin's death in 1953 and the mid-1960s, Soviet officialdom shed its most tyrannical aspects, and despite frequent reimposition of cultural controls, artistic creativity flourished. Brezhnev's reign curtailed much of the dynamism characteristic of the Thaw, whose suppressed energies re-emerged during Gorbachev's five years of *perestroika* and *glasnost'*. Finally, after the upheavals that ended Gorbachev's rule, Russia now vies for attention and profit in a world market. In slightly more than half a century, then, the society has gone from absolute political centralisation to substantial if jagged decentralisation, from state-planned mega-economic structures to market-dependent enterprises, from power- and prestige-based hierarchies to money-based class structures. Its creative artists, once tacit partners with the state in a contract based on mutual support, must fend for themselves in a difficult and competitive environment.

## Paralysis, 1945–53

Although Soviet culture was never entirely monolithic and univocal, it probably came closest to that condition between Victory Day (8 May 1945) and Stalin's death nearly eight years later. Broadly speaking, the arts in those years had nothing whatever to do with an artist's unique and untrammelled creative energies, and little to do with the art prevalent in the 1920s and 1930s, born

My thanks to Caryl Emerson, Julian Graffy, Joan Neuberger, Robert Sharlet and Ron Suny for their extremely helpful comments and corrections on earlier drafts of this essay.

of the marriage between state ideology and individual imagination. Rather, artistic products served 'to *make conscious* that which was *made known* in the language of decrees'.[1]

Within a year of the war's end, the nation's wartime unanimity of patriotic purpose disappeared, replaced by a reshuffled deck of social sectors with new allocations of privileges, rewards and penalties, and a welter of new domestic enemies. A miasma of belligerent isolation and xenophobia stifled wartime exposure to the outside world, and controls over culture tightened with dramatic harshness. Party leaders, often Stalin himself, 'selected the main themes and topics of literature and carefully supervised its ideological content', placing particular emphasis on both Russian and Soviet chauvinism, hatred of everything foreign and glorification of the Communist Party and of the country's ruler,[2] and favouring the epic genres – long novels, marathon narrative poems, historical films, operas – that most readily accommodated themselves to expressing these themes. During the *Zhdanovshchina*, the crudest expression of the regime's general approach to the arts in the post-war years, every newspaper and journal joined the offensive against individual works and artists, excoriating the least suspicion of veracity, artistic independence ('formalism') and apoliticism ('ideological emptiness') and demanding militant, ideologically pure and edifying art. If artists wanted to address the real moral and social dilemmas of their world, they could do so only in the most oblique fashion; *lakirovka*, or make-believe, reigned supreme.

Andrei Zhdanov and his epigones vilified great artists, such as poet Anna Akhmatova, satirist Mikhail Zoshchenko, film director Sergei Eisenstein, composers Dmitrii Shostakovich and Sergei Prokofiev. But they scrutinised with equal vigilance individuals of considerably less talent and reputation: Ukrainian Petro Panch, for the brazen notion that the writer had the 'right' to make mistakes; playwright Aleksandr Gladkov, for his 'complete ignorance of Soviet man and an irresponsible attitude toward his own literature'; scriptwriter Pavel Nilin, whose play provided the basis for Leonid Lukov's film *A Great Life* (*Bol'shaia zhizn'*): 'In the imaginary people portrayed by Nilin there is no power of enthusiasm, no knowledge, no culture, which the Soviet man in the ranks, who matured during the years of the mighty growth of our state, bears

1 Evgeny Dobrenko, 'The Literature of the Zhdanov Era: Mentality, Mythology, Lexicon', in Thomas J. Lahusen with Gene Kuperman (eds.), *Late Soviet Culture: From Perestroika to Novostroika* (Durham, N.C., and London: Duke University Press, 1993), p. 131.
2 Deming Brown, *Soviet Russian Literature since Stalin* (Cambridge and London: Cambridge University Press, 1978), p. 2.

within himself.'[3] The film itself, an attempt to portray with some degree of verisimilitude the life of miners in the Donbass, elicited a Central Committee ban (4 September 1946) as an 'ideologically and politically vicious' film, and artistically weak to boot.[4]

The rhetoric of assault, the shortcomings singled out for attack and the sanctions imposed recurred throughout the years 1945–53, with different segments of the creative intelligentsia targeted at different times. Music, for instance, took its turn on the chopping block in 1948, when the Central Committee made an example of composer Vano Muradeli and his 'vicious and inartistic' opera *The Great Friendship* (*Velikaia druzhba*). The State Museum of Modern Western Art was closed down in 1948, the same year that libraries were instructed to 'process' their holdings of foreign literature captured abroad during the war, and to eliminate once-acceptable domestic works that had slipped into disfavour through political vicissitudes, such as a novel expressing 'friendly feelings' for Communist Yugoslavia, now turned enemy under renegade Tito.

Chauvinist xenophobia rehabilitated the Russian past and hailed all aspects of Soviet life while denigrating everything Western. Seductively attractive foreign art masked a 'putrid, baneful bourgeois culture'. Soviet productions of foreign plays disseminated 'the propaganda of reactionary bourgeois ideology and morals'. Revised editions of books excised favourable references to foreign nations and negative details about Russia. A 1948 edition of *Stepan Razin*, a historical novel set in the seventeenth century, for instance, eliminated obscenities, gory descriptions of torture and details about body odour, bedbugs, flatulence and sex that suggested an 'uncivilized' Russia. New editions of Vsevolod Ivanov's 1922 novel and play, *Armoured Train No. 14–69* (*Bronepoezd No. 14–69*), inserted tributes to the Russian people and interpolations about America's hostile role in the Far East during the civil war, including American plans 'to annex Siberia and China'.[5]

For a few years after the war audiences hungry for entertainment had the chance to see German and American 'trophy' films captured by the Red Army: the regime authorised their distribution partly for revenues, partly to compensate for the absence of new domestic films. Introductory texts and revised titles provided requisite ideological adjustments: *Stagecoach* became

3 George S. Counts and Nucia Lodge, *The Country of the Blind: The Soviet System of Mind Control* (Boston: Houghton Mifflin, 1949), pp. 113, 101, 102.
4 Ibid., p. 125.
5 Herman Ermolaev, *Censorship in Soviet Literature: 1917–1991* (New York and London: Rowman and Littlefields, 1997), pp. 106, 110–11.

*The Journey will be Dangerous*, 'an epic about the struggle of Indians against White imperialists on the frontier', and Frank Capra's *Mr Deeds Goes to Town* became *The Dollar Rules*.[6] Though rarely reviewed, these films were popular enough to annoy the authorities: a central newspaper censured Dom Kino, the film industry's Moscow clubhouse, for screening too many foreign films, including films 'with jazz and fox-trot', to mark the fifth anniversary of the Nazi invasion.[7]

In post-war culture, one blueprint served for all cultural products. Russian chauvinism dictated Russifying the ethnic designations of Greek and Tatar settlements in the Crimea to obliterate their pasts. Eisenstein had repeatedly to answer for the 'lack of Russian spirit' in Part II of *Ivan the Terrible* (*Ivan Groznyi*); composers, a couple of years later, were anathematised for violating the 'system of music and singing native to our people'. Soviet chauvinism dictated rewriting recent history: new editions of Sholokhov's *Quiet Flows the Don* (*Tikhii Don*) (1928), for instance, added quotations from Lenin and Stalin, and cleansed individual Bolsheviks 'of a wide array of personal vices pertaining, among other things, to sex, marriage, foul language, drinking and brutality'. Aleksandr Fadeev cut or altered descriptions of the Red Army's hasty retreat during the war in his novel *The Young Guard* (*Molodaia gvardiia*) (1945) after a critical *Pravda* editorial, and Valentin Katayev increased the 'operational capabilities of [an underground] group' by adding several local Communists to *For the Power of the Soviets* (*Za vlast' Sovetov*) (1949–51) after *Pravda* had a go at him.[8]

The trophy films disappeared from Soviet screens in the late 1940s. Instead audiences could choose from a thin stream of anti-Western films (Aleksandrov's *Meeting on the Elbe* (*Vstrecha na Elbe*), Romm's *Secret Mission* (*Sekretnaia missiia*), Room's *Court of Honour* (*Sud chesti*), historical spectacles explicitly glorifying Stalin (*The Vow* (*Kliatva*), *The Battle of Stalingrad* (*Stalingradskaia bitva*), *The Fall of Berlin* (*Padenie Berlina*)), and biographies of scientists and musicians implicitly doing the same thing.[9] From its outset the anti-cosmopolitan campaign had vilified the intelligentsia, many of whom were Jews, but after 1948 the campaign turned categorically anti-Semitic, first in print – the leading serious film journal, *Iskusstvo kino*, published a list of 'aesthete-cosmopolitans in cinema', nearly all Jews – and then in action, with the NKVD execution of

6 Richard Stites, *Russian Popular Culture: Entertainment and Society Since 1900* (Cambridge: Cambridge University Press, 1992), p. 127.
7 Peter Kenez, *Cinema and Soviet Society: From the Revolution to the Death of Stalin*, 2nd edn (London and New York: I. B. Tauris, 2001), p. 193.
8 Ermolaev, *Censorship*, pp. 120–6 *passim*.
9 See David Caute, *The Dancer Defects: The Struggle for Cultural Supremacy during the Cold War* (Oxford: Oxford University Press, 2003), pp. 112–59.

Solomon Mikhoels, the Soviet Union's leading Yiddish actor, in January 1948 and the execution of thirteen prominent Jews in August 1952, four of them writers.[10]

With very few exceptions, the arts between 1945 and 1953 operated in the realm of fantasy. 'Even the recently ended war,' Dobrenko comments, 'a horrible wound that continued to bleed, was immediately externalized and became yet another thematic.'[11] As Boris Slutskii, a poet who fought in the war, wrote, 'And gradually the cracks were painted over, / The strong wrinkles smoothed out, / And gradually the women grew prettier / And sullen men grew merry.'[12] Painters produced 'meaningless mass scenes', canvases filled with cheerful civilians and clean, well-rested soldiers.[13] Playwrights struggled with the absurd and inherently anti-dramatic theory of 'no conflict drama', premised on 'the alleged impossibility of conflict in a "classless society"',[14] which dominated discourse in the early 1950s. 'Hortatory' writing on rural themes, 'designed to promote discipline and enthusiasm for the painful sacrifices involved in restoring agriculture after the war's devastation', presented the depopulated, devastated countryside as a thriving hive of enthusiasm and productivity.[15] The collision of 'the good and the better' (in one famous formulation), whether on stages or cinema screens, left little space for ambivalence, weakness and death, except for heroic death on the battlefield; it left no room at all for tragedy. As environment – factory, shop, school, field, farm – supplanted human beings and roles replaced character, protagonists became virtually interchangeable, clones identifiable only by their jobs.[16] Thus art shrivelled to function as defined by the Communist Party.

Between 1945 and 1953, nearly every genuine artist fell silent. Authentic popular culture was restricted to the labour camps of the Gulag, and reached a wider public only after Stalin's death. Ersatz, officially sponsored popular culture reflected the regime's conservatism, its determination to preserve the

---

10 See Joshua Rubenstein and Vladimir Naumov (eds.), *Stalin's Secret Pogrom: The Postwar Inquisition of the Jewish Anti-Fascist Committee*, trans. Laura Esther Wolfson (New Haven: Yale University Press, 2002).

11 Dobrenko, 'Literature of the Zhdanov Era', p. 117.

12 Boris Slutskii, '1945 god', in *Segodnia i vchera* (Moscow: 1963), p. 162. Cited by Brown, *Soviet Russian Literature since Stalin*, p. 87.

13 Musya Glants, 'The Images of War in Painting', in John and Carol Garrard (eds.), *World War 2 and the Soviet People* (London: Macmillan and New York: St Martins Press, 1993), p. 110.

14 Melissa T. Smith, 'Waiting in the Wings: Russian Women Playwrights in the Twentieth Century', in Toby W. Clyman and Diana Greene (eds.), *Women Writers in Russian Literature* (Westport, Conn., and London: Praeger, 1994), p. 194.

15 Brown, *Soviet Russian Literature since Stalin*, p. 218.

16 Dobrenko, 'Literature of the Zhdanov Era', p. 123.

status quo, its insistence on stability and normalisation. The rising middle class shared many of those values. At a time when Soviet citizens had little opportunity to amuse themselves in cafés or dance halls and no opportunity to travel, and movie houses recycled hits from a decade before, the bulk of middle-brow reading material – mainly novels – provided diversion, escapist happy endings and 'one of the few ways of meeting the people's need to understand their society's major workaday problems . . . a chance [for the reader] to check his own questions about postwar adjustments against the paradigms of current social issues'.[17] The discrepancy between reality and the 'utterly profane' version[18] advanced in fiction like Babaevskii's *Cavalier of the Golden Star (Kavaler zolotoi zvezdy)* (and Raizman's 1950 screen version) and films like Pyr'ev's *Cossacks of the Kuban' (Kuban'skie kazaki)* troubled the regime not at all. As for the Soviet public, or a large part of it, they suspended belief – willingly or reluctantly – in the pursuit of enjoyment and whatever scraps and tatters of meaning they could relate to their own lives.

## The Thaw, 1953–67(?)

Although the beginning of the Thaw is far easier to date than its terminus, even the death of Stalin did not mark an absolute turning point. After all, individuals and institutions involved in the creation, regulation, dissemination and reception of cultural products did not simply vanish the day Stalin died, nor did their modus operandi. At the same time, signs of renewal pre-dated March 1953, in the arts and in society at large. Valentin Ovechkin's 'District Routine' (*Raionnye budni*), a fictional sketch that began 'the process of returning rural literature to real life',[19] appeared in *Novyi mir* in September 1952. Vsevolod Pudovkin's last film, *The Return of Vasilii Bortnikov (Vozvrashchenie Vasiliia Bortnikova)*, marked by psychological credibility and imaginative camerawork, was shot in 1952. Young people rebelled against grey Soviet monotony by wearing imitations of Western styles, tight trousers and short skirts. Still, Stalin's death unquestionably liberated the psychocultural shifts characteristic of the Thaw years. *Belles-lettres* responded the most quickly. The fine lyric poet Ol'ga Berggol'ts insisted on the poet's right to express personal emotions in her own voice; the established novelist Ilya Ehrenburg and the novice literary critic

17 Vera Dunham, *In Stalin's Time: Middle Class Values in Soviet Fiction*, enlarged edn (Durham, N.C., and London: Duke University Press, 1990), pp. 25–6.
18 Dobrenko, 'Literature of the Zhdanov Era', p. 130.
19 Kathleen Parthé, *Russian Village Prose: The Radiant Path* (Princeton: Princeton University Press, 1992), p. 13.

Vladimir Pomerantsev both demanded more spontaneity and 'sincerity', less official interference in literature.

The termination of the Thaw cannot so readily be pinpointed, in part because it did not skid to a dead halt in one violent action like the 1968 invasion of Czechoslovakia. Indeed, many of the ideas discussed and trends inaugurated during the Thaw years outlasted the political career of the man most clearly associated with it, Nikita Khrushchev, who fell from power in 1964. They endured and evolved over the next two decades, albeit forced into alternative channels as official ones constricted. Most individuals who identified themselves with the goals of the Thaw continued to work within the Soviet cultural sphere, although some emigrated and others confined their audiences to friends or to anonymous purveyors of *samizdat*.

Nonetheless, the term 'Thaw' legitimately denotes a dozen years during which Soviet society moved out from under the worst shadows of the late Stalin years. Artists and audiences alike pressed for greater candour in the arts, an end to mendacious representations of Soviet life, a recognition of the puissance of private concerns, more latitude in subject and style and a 'less paternalistic concern' over what the Soviet reader/film-goer/museum visitor 'should and should not be permitted to know'.[20] Khrushchev's major de-Stalinisation speeches spurred a passion for truth-telling, expressed in a variety of artistic forms that shared a common concern with the moral compromises endemic to Soviet society. And although the party attempted to maintain hegemony over cultural matters, the thawing process persisted despite, beneath and around the ice floes of official reversals, skittish compromises and dogmatic retrenchments.

Already in 1955, before Khrushchev's 1956 'Secret Speech', access to foreign culture increased, with events like the week of French cinema held in October 1955. After Khrushchev's speech the pace accelerated dramatically. Personnel shake-ups replaced bureaucrats with active artists and balanced conservatives with progressives (such as the new, liberal Moscow branch of the national Writers' Union, an organisation Mikhail Sholokhov mordantly dubbed the 'Union of Dead Souls'[21]). The party allocated funds to build or refurbish theatres and movie houses, to buy better equipment, to pay higher authors' fees, to revitalise languishing republican film studios, to rejoin the world's cultural community. (The First Moscow International Film Festival took place in August 1959.) Khrushchev's attempts to decentralise decision-making and encourage

20 Brown, *Soviet Russian Literature since Stalin*, p. 5.
21 John and Carol Garrard, *Inside the Soviet Writers' Union* (New York and London: Free Press, 1990), p. 72.

individual initiative, though formulated to achieve economic goals, had cultural repercussions. The Ministry of Culture, the party's umbrella organisation for all broadcasting, educational and cultural institutions, remained in charge, but official censors relinquished some of their authority to editorial boards of journals and film studio artistic councils; senior literary editors and theatre directors had more access to the ideological watchdogs.

In order to secure the trust of a nation profoundly wary of the repercussions of autonomy, Khrushchev enjoined writers to tell the truth (up to a point) without fear of lethal consequences. As Shimon Markish, a writer and son of one of the Yiddish poets murdered in 1952, wryly – but accurately – observed, while both Stalin and Khrushchev were whimsical and capricious, with Khrushchev 'we knew that whatever happened, it would not be arrest and death'.[22] Artists who felt both anger and guilt at their own acquiescence in falsehood proffered *mea culpas*: in Evgenii Evtushenko's dramatic poem 'Zima Station' (1956), for instance, he reproaches himself for saying 'what I should not have said' and failing to say 'what I should have said'. Censors excised many of the once-obligatory disparaging references to the West and to non-Russian nationalities in new editions of previously published works, and scrapped equally obligatory laudatory references to Stalin: his very name was cropped from phrases like 'Stalin's army' and 'Stalin's generation'. While censors continued to discourage bleak descriptions of the purges, they – emulating Khrushchev – partially rehabilitated the victims of Stalinist repression. 'The censorship did not cease to operate,' Geoffrey Hosking notes, 'but its implementation became less predictable.'[23]

The early years of the Thaw gave artists the chance to scrape the excrescences of Stalinism off what they perceived as the authentic revolutionary idealism of the 1920s. They could retain the possibility of utopian socialism, *sans* Stalin's crippling despotism and Stalinism's lies. Even the relatively orthodox writer Konstantin Simonov, editor of *Novyi mir* in 1956, urged acceptance of any literature imbued with 'socialist spirit', and a large part of Soviet society embraced the opportunity to examine the actual circumstances and dilemmas of Soviet life. For a time, at least, party directives, creative impulses and popular desires galloped along as a troika.

The same desiderata – less embellishment, greater truthfulness, more attention to individuals and their private dramas, the muffling of authorial judgement, multiple perspectives – characterise nearly all fiction and film in the early

22 Ibid., p. 78.
23 Geoffrey Hosking, *Beyond Socialist Realism: Soviet Fiction since Ivan Denisovich* (London: Granada, 1980), p. 20.

Thaw years, whether historical or contemporary. As early as 1954, the novelist Fedor Abramov published a damning survey of post-war rural prose, which centred on the collective farm and frequently came from the pens of urban writers ignorant of country life. He and other *derevenshchiki* – writers of 'village' (rather than *kolkhoz*) prose – began to correct the spurious approach to rural themes characteristic of post-war fiction in favour of sympathetic yet unsentimental portraits of everyday rural reality, including the religious faith that sustained the peasantry. Themselves usually scions of village life, they avoided the (falsely) picturesque, folksy and romantic, and, over the next decade or so, elaborated a set of values virtually opposite to those that dominated *kolkhoz* literature.

Film had less room to manoeuvre, since the party's demand for more and better films 'about agriculture' pointedly implied *kolkhoz* achievements, not retrograde village traditions, and film-makers were understandably reluctant to tackle such a fraught subject. When they did turn to the countryside, however, they starkly contradicted the florid and grotesquely synthetic images of peasant life on display in musicals like *Cossacks of the Kuban'*. Camerawork favoured medium and long shots and pans of the entire environment, as if to offer trustworthy images saturated with reality; the happy ending that reassuringly concluded most *kolkhoz* movies yielded to ambiguity. A wedding opens – rather than closes – Mikhail Shveitser's *Alien Kin* (*Chuzhaia rodnia*, 1955): trouble starts afterwards. Stanislav Rostotskii's *It Happened in Penkovo* (*Delo bylo v Penkove*, 1957) pays lip-service to official rhetoric, encasing a flashback within a narrative framework that shows a poor collective farm becoming prosperous, but for most of the film only drinking, romance and fighting alleviate the tedium of village life.[24] In Vasilii Shukshin's first two films, *A Boy Like That* (*Zhivet takoi paren'*, 1964), and *Your Son and Brother* (*Vash syn i brat*, 1965), exterior shots convey the omnipresence of Siberia's natural environment while interiors are panned matter of factly, their furnishings (wood-burning stoves, vodka decanters, framed photographs) neither quaint, ethnographic objects nor fetishes to be venerated but the stuff of people's lives.

History – the Decembrist uprising of 1825, the populist movement of the 1880s, Bolshevism, the Second World War – served as a template through which to examine the present, both because the past gave writers and film-makers more freedom, and because it had directly engendered the present with which

24 The artistic council sharply criticised the spurious depiction of a neighbouring *kolkhoz*, commenting that peasants would deride its magnificent cowherds and elegant pig-tenders. See Josephine Woll, *Real Images: Soviet Cinema and the Thaw* (London: I. B. Tauris, 2000), p. 67.

they were primarily concerned. With Khrushchev himself calling for a return to Leninist norms, the years during which the Soviet state took shape offered a dramatic framework in which to investigate contemporary hopes and ideals. Thus the Thaw's first historical films – Iurii Egorov's *They Were the First* (*Oni byli pervymi*, 1956), Alov and Naumov's *Pavel Korchagin* (1956), based on Ostrovskii's novel *How the Steel Was Tempered* (*Kak zakalialas' stal'*), Grigorii Chukhrai's *The Forty-first* (*Sorok pervyi*, 1956), Iulii Raizman's *The Communist* (*Kommunist*, 1958) – re-create the civil-war years and the 1920s, not as they had actually been, certainly, but as they were viewed through the lens of the 1950s: as a relatively noble, inspiring and passionate period. Alov and Naumov replaced Ostrovskii's robotic Pavel Korchagin with a hero who renounces personal happiness ('this isn't the time for love') at the cost of horrific, graphically delineated suffering. Chukhrai's protagonists, White Army officer and Red Army sniper, fall so deeply in love, and Chukhrai's cameraman Sergei Urusevskii filmed their idyll with such lyricism and beauty that the lovers' passion and tenderness enjoy parity with – if not primacy over – revolutionary duty.

Throughout the Thaw, and well into the Brezhnev years, the Second World War became a touchstone of Soviet culture, in part because it represented the single unifying experience of a history otherwise bloody with political and ideological divisions. At the Twenty-Second Congress Khrushchev extended his earlier criticism of Stalin to include the army purges of 1937 and the treatment of returning Soviet POWs, unleashing a wave of memoirs, lyrics, autobiographical fiction and movies that reflected the knowledge and experience of the vast majority of Soviet citizens. Finally, civilian dedication to the war effort ranked as no less heroic than combat bravery, and civilian losses as no less painful than death on the battlefield. In fiction by Vasilii Grossman, Boris Balter and Bulat Okudzhava, the private dramas (and melodramas) contingent upon the war took precedence over military strategy, to the point that movies began routinely to avoid battle-scene heroics, instead locating their heroes in the interstices between battles (Tarkovsky's *Ivan's Childhood* (*Ivanovo detstvo*)), in the undramatic hell of the Nazi prison camp, where heroism equalled dogged determination to survive (Bondarchuk's *Fate of a Man* (*Sud'ba cheloveka*, 1959)), or away from the front altogether, as in Chukhrai's *Ballad of a Soldier* (*Ballada o soldate*, 1959) (see Plate 22), where the only 'battle scene' mocks conventional heroics by showing the hero running away from a tank.

The idealism and/or naivety of the early Thaw years disappeared by the end of the decade, its demise hastened by the establishment's loathsome attacks on Boris Pasternak when he won the 1958 Nobel Prize for Literature. As the Thaw lurched into the early 1960s, the 'real, struggling, ascetic' hero morphed into many kinds of hero operating in every sort of context (war, village, *kolkhoz*, factory, scientific institute, rapidly growing city) and genre. Consistently, however, characters were 'no longer apprehended primarily in terms of their attitudes toward the work they perform, their degree of social dedication or the extent to which they have absorbed official dogma and patterns of conduct'.[25] We encounter many vulnerable and/or innocent protagonists: children, whose age protects them from the corruption of adults and whose lack of subterfuge authenticates their vision of the world; teenagers, honest about their fears and tentative about their hopes; young women who fail to live up to their own ideals or who succumb to intolerable pressures. These heroines, not coincidentally, animated the many melodramas that appeared during the Thaw; the genre's 'revival of private life as a legitimate subject for the arts' made it 'an especially apt tool for exploring the individual *within* the collective, the private morality *underneath* the strictures on public performances, the tensions resulting from political manipulations of both public and private morality. [It offered] escape . . . from a social and moral certainty imposed from above.'[26]

So did the poetry recited at open-air readings, a public event revived in the late 1950s that attracted thousands of listeners and turned younger poets – Robert Rozhdestvenskii, Evtushenko and Voznesenskii, Iunna Morits, Bulat Okudzhava, Bella Akhmadulina – into cult figures; so did the concurrent wave of 'youth prose' and its attendant cinematic movement. Although many clichés lurk beneath the colloquialisms, sly humour and taste for rock' n' roll that characterise Vasilii Aksenov and Andrei Bitov's heroes, these authors confronted the painful fissures of Soviet society without proposing easy or dogmatic solutions. Their characters, tired of '*kvass* patriotism, official bombast, and village-style surveillance by the neighbours of their clothing, their morals, and their leisure habits',[27] did not obediently turn to their elders for paradigms. 'Puzzled and concerned about the future, socially disoriented and, in some degree, psychologically bemused',[28] they tried to devise 'ethical standards to replace outworn or suspect ones'.[29]

Khrushchev's speech at the Twenty-Second Party Congress in October 1961 invigorated the liberals and stimulated a year of exciting cultural developments. Stravinsky made his first visit to his homeland in half a century, as did George Balanchine (after forty years away), who brought the New York City

25 Brown, *Soviet Russian Literature since Stalin*, p. 149.
26 Louise McReynolds and Joan Neuberger, 'Introduction', in Louise McReynolds and Joan Neuberger (eds.), *Imitations of Life: Two Centuries of Melodrama in Russia* (Durham, N.C.: Duke University Press, 2002), p. 13.
27 Stites, *Russian Popular Culture*, p. 127.    28 Hosking, *Beyond Socialist Realism*, p. 185.
29 Brown, *Soviet Russian Literature since Stalin*, pp. 142–3.

Ballet. Yehudi and Hepzibah Menuhin toured the Soviet Union; Shostakovich's 'Babii Iar' Symphony, incorporating the text of Evtushenko's poetic memorial to Jewish victims of Nazi slaughter outside Kiev, premiered in December 1962. Moscow museums dusted off and displayed canvases by modernists like Bakst and Larionov. Evtushenko's 'Heirs of Stalin', a passionate and forceful assault on neo-Stalinism, appeared in the autumn, as did the first half of Viktor Nekrasov's account of trips to Italy and the USA, *Both Sides of the Ocean* (*Po obe storony okeana*), in which he criticised isolationist Soviet cultural policies. Most shocking, *One Day in the Life of Ivan Denisovich* appeared in November's *Novyi mir*, principally thanks to editor Aleksandr Tvardovskii and his shrewd campaign for Khrushchev's personal intervention. The top box-office success of 1962, *The Amphibious Man* (*Chelovek-amfibiia*), responded to Khrushchev's revelations by presenting a political allegory about a brilliant scientist's underwater utopia whose only inhabitant – his amphibious son Ikhtiandr – pays for the dreams and desires of his father. 'I wanted to make you the happiest of men,' Dr Salvator apologises to his son, 'and instead I made you unhappy. Forgive me.'

Conservatives fought back, especially after the humiliation of the Cuban Missile Crisis, and Khrushchev retreated: he 'had to give his conservative opponents something', and culture 'was the most disposable part of his reforms'.[30] Throughout 1963, at a series of meetings between party leaders and artists, Khrushchev and his ideological overseer Leonid Ilichev delivered speeches (immediately printed in major newspapers) insisting on party control of the arts, rejecting Western and modernist influences, and shrilly denying anything resembling a generation gap in Soviet society. Khrushchev personally denounced Nekrasov, for *Both Sides of the Ocean* and for the writer's praise of Marlen Khutsiev's *Ilich's Gate* (*Zastava Il'icha*), a particularly provoking film.

The three young heroes of *Ilich's Gate* come of age in the Moscow of 1961–2, and Khutsiev chose as his co-author Gennadii Shpalikov, roughly the age of the film's protagonists, so as to ensure up-to-date language and mood. Characters work on actual construction and demolition sites, enhancing visual/atmospheric veracity; students from the State Institute of Cinematography – future stars of Soviet cinema – play many roles; a poetry reading organised for the film looks as real as the documentary footage of a May Day parade. (In fact, the actors had to elbow their way through the throng crowding in to hear such superstars as Rozhdestvenskii and Akhmadulina.) Much about *Ilich's Gate*'s depiction of the relationship between generations exasperated

30 Robert Sharlet, private letter, 9 Feb. 2003.

Khrushchev, but one scene enraged him. When the twenty-three–year-old hero Sergei asks the ghost of his father, killed during the war, for guidance on how to live, his father replies 'I am twenty-one', and vanishes. 'There's more to this than meets the eye,' fulminated Khrushchev. 'The idea is to impress upon the children that their fathers cannot be their teachers in life, and that there is no point in turning to them for advice. The filmmakers think that young people ought to decide for themselves how to live, without asking their elders for counsel and help.'[31]

Before Khutsiev succeeded in revising and abridging *Ilich's Gate* into a version finally approved for release in 1965, under the title *I Am Twenty (Mne dvadtsat' let)*, well over a year had passed, and Khrushchev himself had been replaced by the team of Brezhnev and Kosygin (in October 1964). The film's sad fate reflects the Soviet Union's general retreat from Thaw liberalism and the onset of a process of calcification that later earned the sobriquet *zastoi*, 'era of stagnation'. Like the Thaw before it, stagnation proceeded unevenly, often imposing itself ruthlessly in the cultural sphere but occasionally permitting new voices to join the cultural chorus. Its crudest and most notoriously repressive manifestations – the trials of Joseph Brodsky, Andrei Siniavskii and Iulii Daniel', the arrest of Ukrainian dissidents, the expulsion of Aleksandr Solzhenitsyn from the Writers' Union and then from the country – conceal a more complex and less uniformly bleak picture. Ideas, instincts and individuals nurtured by the Thaw survived into *zastoi* – indeed, most of them survived into Gorbachev's era of *perestroika* and *glasnost'*, if not beyond. However, in the generally inhospitable cultural atmosphere that prevailed between Khrushchev's fall and Gorbachev's ascension, they faced constricting official possibilities and found themselves compelled to explore alternative channels and outlets.

## Stagnation, 1967–85

Official attempts to suppress debate and to reverse the relative openness of the Thaw dominated cultural life from about 1966 until the early 1970s, with 1967 – the fiftieth anniversary of the revolution – proving particularly stultifying. In 1965 Mikhail Romm's *Ordinary Fascism (Obyknovennyi fashizm)*, a documentary probing the psychology underlying and engendering Nazism, with tacit parallels to Stalinism, attracted 20 million viewers during its first year and won

---

31 Khrushchev's speech appeared in *Pravda*, 10 Mar. 1963. See Priscilla Johnson and Leopold Labedz (eds.), *Khrushchev and the Arts: The Politics of Soviet Culture, 1962–1964* (Cambridge, Mass.: MIT Press, 1965), pp. 152–5.

a prize at the Leipzig festival.[32] By the end of 1965 censors routinely cut 'any parallels, direct or implied, between communism and nazism', any reference to the penal units during the war, to Red Army atrocities, to the official policy that branded as traitors Soviet soldiers imprisoned by the Nazis as prisoners of war (which among other consequences precluded Red Cross assistance), even to venereal disease among combatants.[33] Estonian film-maker Kaljö Kiisk made *Madness (Bezumie)* in 1968, setting its action in Nazi-occupied Estonia and suggesting parallels between Nazism and the Soviet domination of his country: the film was banned until 1986. These proscriptions remained broadly in force until the early 1980s.

The same strictures applied to de-Stalinisation, the purges and the cult of personality. In early 1965, lacking explicit guidelines from the new Central Committee, the script and editorial committee (GSRK) overseeing film production reacted warily to scripts on these subjects. Gradually committee members gained confidence, vetoing one script based on the wartime diary of a girl whose father spent seventeen years in the Gulag, another whose protagonist investigates the rehabilitation cases of those unjustly accused. 'The theme of the cult of personality', they explained, 'is unacceptable at the present time.' By late July, GSRK reacted to a proposal from Armenia's studio with a flat assertion: 'This film should not be about the era of the cult of personality, for there was no such era.'[34]

In May 1967, with domestic publication of *Cancer Ward (Rakovyi korpus)* bogged down indefinitely, Aleksandr Solzhenitsyn mailed 250 signed copies of a thunderous denunciation of censorship and of the literary establishment whose members were about to gather at the Fourth Congress of Soviet Writers. He sent them to 'all the people whom Solzhenitsyn regarded as honest and genuine writers', and to prominent members of the Writers' Union (the two categories rarely overlapped).[35] 'Literature', he wrote, 'cannot develop in between the categories of "permitted" and "not permitted," "about this you may write" and "about this you may not".'[36] Eighty-three members of the Union signed a collective letter to the congress requesting open debate on

32 For attendance figures on Soviet films, see Sergei Zemlianukhin and Miroslava Segida, *Domashniaia sinemateka: otechestvennoe kino 1918–1996* (Moscow: Dubl-D, 1996).
33 Ermolaev, *Censorship*, pp. 206–7.
34 Valerii Fomin, 'Nikakoi epokhi kul'ta lichnosti ne bylo . . .', in Fomin (ed.), *Kino i vlast'* (Moscow: Materik, 1996), pp. 292–9 and *passim*. Originally appeared in *Iskusstvo kino* 1 (1989).
35 Michael Scammell, *Solzhenitsyn: A Biography* (New York and London: Norton, 1984), p. 584.
36 Alexander Solzhenitsyn, 'Letter to the Fourth Congress of Soviet Writers', in John B. Dunlop, Richard Haugh, Alexis Klimoff (eds.), *Alexander Solzhenitsyn: Critical Essays and*

the subject, but the congress resolutely ignored the letter, the author and the issue.

Nevertheless, people like Solzhenitsyn – members of the 'disaffected intelligentsia' – constituted an 'extremely powerful intellectual subculture that challenged the official culture through the power of moral persuasion it exercised . . . through nonofficial channels'.[37] By 1967, official control over culture had substantially shifted from doctrine to praxis, from the once-powerful, now attenuated dogma of socialist realism into the bureaucratic structures that regulated distribution of the arts as a means of regulating what actually reached the consumer. Those structures proved both effective and durable, particularly when manned by orthodox bureaucrats. The unions exercised control over pensions, housing, lecture tours, travel funds: infringement of unwritten rules – whether signing a petition in defence of an arrested human rights activist or writing about a proscribed subject – could entail serious financial hardship. The State Committee for the Press, parallel and complementary to the Writers' Union, expanded its powers, devising a production plan to fulfil economic goals and a thematic plan to fulfil ideological ones.

The system encouraged both conformity and hypertrophy, meeting its goals by producing a certain number of books (movies . . . paintings . . . plays) rather than by satisfying readers or audiences. Production figures, not sales figures, measured success, although studios and publishing houses faced close questioning when ticket sales fell or books gathered dust on shelves. (Since the number of copies printed determined royalties, rather than the number of copies sold, publishers authorised large print runs of 'safe' books – including Brezhnev's ghost-written war memoir *My Little Homeland* (*Malaia rodina*).) Censorship processes – as opposed to self-censorship – began within the intricate hierarchies of journal, publishing house, theatre or film studio, long before a work ever reached official censors.

Vladimir Makanin came of age professionally during the Brezhnev years. He described the unwritten pact:

> As a member of the Writers' Union you got all sorts of advantages: they looked after you if you were ill or disabled . . . they might appeal on your behalf to the Moscow City Council to get you an apartment or a kindergarten place for your child; they guaranteed a good rate of pay for your writing, provided

*Documentary Materials*, 2nd edn (New York and London: Collier, 1975), p. 544; I have modified the translation.

37 Adele Marie Barker, 'The Culture Factory: Theorizing the Popular in the Old and New Russia', in Adele Marie Barker (ed.), *Consuming Russia: Popular Culture, Sex, and Society since Gorbachev* (Durham, N.C.: Duke University Press, 1999), pp. 20–1.

writers' retreats and so forth. . . . But of course the Union of Writers, like any other trade union, had a political edge to it: it guaranteed all these material advantages, but in exchange you had to write as they wanted you to . . . Under such circumstances it's an enormous labour to go your own way and remain an individual.[38]

Nevertheless, even the most repressive years – 1968, 1970, 1972, 1979 – reveal inconsistency and a growing multivocality. Non-conformists willing to remove themselves from the central Moscow–Leningrad axis sometimes found havens in provincial cities. A work proscribed in one city might be published in another. Plays occasionally sneaked onto theatre stages without official permission. Films (like Irakli Kvirikadze's *The Swimmer* (*Plovets*), made and shelved in 1981) might be shown in clubs if not in commercial theatres. Texts by safely dead, once-proscribed writers – Marina Tsvetaeva, Ivan Bunin, Mikhail Bulgakov – reached Soviet readers for the first time, in part to compensate for the disappearance of living writers who, forced into emigration, lost their status as authors along with their citizenship: their books vanished from library shelves, their names from literary history. (Dancers who defected and musicians who transgressed – as Rostropovich did by helping Solzhenitsyn – were similarly erased from officially recorded Russian culture.) When publication was foreclosed, writers often chose to circulate their work unofficially, via *samizdat*, underground distribution of typed or occasionally mimeographed copies of manuscripts, or to send it abroad (*tamizdat*).[39] Liudmila Petrushevskaia, whose unpublished plays were performed in private apartments during the early and mid-1970s, recalled the cachet of illicit art: 'If a play was widely advertised it meant it wasn't worth seeing, no one went. Whereas crowds and crowds would turn up for something that hadn't been advertised at all; everyone would hear about it by word of mouth . . . It would be announced as a "creative evening" or "a meeting with young actors", without mentioning the author or the name of the work.'[40]

Individuals in positions of responsibility often consciously (and occasionally inadvertently) shielded artists. A publishing house held on to Fazil Iskander's story 'Tree of Childhood' (*Derevo detstva*) for years rather than rejecting it outright, simply because the director wanted to avoid controversy, and eventually the story appeared.[41] The editors of *Novyi mir*, although unable to publish

38 Sally Laird, *Voices of Russian Literature: Interviews with Ten Contemporary Writers* (Oxford: Oxford University Press, 1999), p. 65.
39 For a survey of *samizdat* published in the West, see Josephine Woll, 'Introduction', in Josephine Woll and Vladimir G. Treml, *Soviet Dissident Literature: A Critical Guide* (Boston: G. K. Hall, 1983).
40 Laird, *Voices of Russian Literature*, p. 31.     41 Ibid., p. 11.

Petrushevskaia for many years, 'fed me, gave me work, all through the most difficult and hungry times they gave me reviews and book reports to do. They . . . read me and gave me their opinion – always . . . And when the time came [under Gorbachev], they did publish me.' Similarly, her play *Three Girls in Blue* (*Tri devushki v golubom*) appeared in the journal *Contemporary Drama* in 1983 'thanks to the courage of a few people who'd simply taken the responsibility on themselves': specifically, the chief editor of the journal and an apparatchik in the Ministry of Culture who said, 'This play is about me!'[42]

In what amounted to an ongoing tug-of-war between two unequal forces, state and artist, the artist had surprising if insecure resources. The state expelled beyond its borders incorrigible cases, but it did so reluctantly, fully aware of the negative publicity resulting from the departure of some of its most creative individuals. (When authorities bulldozed an outdoor exhibit of paintings by non-conformist artists in 1974, the ensuing negative publicity won a degree of freedom for the artists involved.[43]) Andrei Siniavskii, himself one of those miscreants compelled to emigrate, described the resultant situation:

> With the appearance of ventures which the state interprets as hostile to itself – *samizdat*, the activities of the dissidents and so on – the censorship has tended to be more lenient with certain official writers, who are therefore permitted to deal quite boldly with subjects which, although not the most burning in social and political terms, are nonetheless of considerable peripheral interest, like the subject of the Soviet past and individual destinies . . . The state is obliged to tolerate them, because if they banned them completely they would all go straight into *samizdat* or emigrate to the West.[44]

Artists who chose to remain within the system during *zastoi* adroitly capitalised on their knowledge of its personalities and institutions to evade its constraints. Anatolii Rybakov had never sent his manuscripts abroad for publication, thereby sustaining a reputation for 'loyalty'. Nonetheless, several journals rejected his 1978 novel *Heavy Sand* (*Tiazhelyi pesok*) depicting a Jewish family's life in the Ukraine from about 1900 until 1942, primarily because of its depiction of Belorussian complicity with the Nazis in the destruction of the local Jewish ghetto. He then submitted it to *Oktiabr'*, a journal known for its conservatism, in the hopes that the new editors might want to 'raise the journal's respectability by publishing a daring, sensational work'. Moreover, he knew the censors were less likely to read ahead of time an entire work

42 Ibid., pp. 32–3.
43 Alison Hilton and Norton Dodge, 'Introduction', in *New Art from the Soviet Union* (Washington and Ithaca, N.Y.: Acropolis Books, 1977), p. 10.
44 Andrei Siniavskii, 'Samizdat and the Rebirth of Literature', *Index on Censorship* 9, 4 (Aug. 1980): 9.

scheduled for serial publication in *Oktiabr'* than one scheduled for a known liberal monthly like *Novyi mir.* 'Thus the first, relatively harmless portion of *Heavy Sand* passed through censorship. But the next installment described Soviet repressions of the 1930s and the Nazi's [*sic*] "final solution" . . . The censors were dumbfounded, but deemed it too awkward to interrupt the novel's serialization.'[45] The same tactic enabled Iurii Trifonov to publish *House on the Embankment (Dom na naberezhnoi)* in another 'conservative' journal, *Druzhba narodov.*

Writers frequently relied on Aesopian language, embedding sensitive ideas in a code of allusions, manipulating rigidly defined and instantly recognisable images and topoi in order to suggest parallels to current moral dilemmas and to alert readers to a very different set of values from those officially authorised. 'Since Stalinist socialist realism offered writers a ready-made system of signs with fixed political meanings, it had the potential to be used as . . . a medium for [post-Stalin] writers to express themselves – even if only in a very tentative way – on politically delicate subjects.'[46] Such codes, requiring 'respondents' who share information, point of view or values with the artist,[47] need not be exclusively verbal. In theatre, for instance, an actor's inflected delivery of 'innocent' lines might cue the audience to a coded meaning; in film, juxtaposition of image and sound can signal satiric intent.

The past continued to serve as a template for the present, regardless of the artist's particular politics, but emphasis increasingly shifted to contemporary life. Conservative Iurii Bondarev and liberal Vasil Bykov both chose to link the Second World War with contemporary Soviet life by following 'the behaviour and actions of former soldiers and officers . . . through several decades after the end of the war, and [juxtaposing] the reactions to past events by representatives of different generations'.[48] The revolutionary and Stalinist past 'enters into every facet' of Trifonov's characters and informs – indeed, determines – the moral universe they occupy in the present.[49] In the late 1960s and 1970s, Trifonov, Georgii Baklanov and a handful of others succeeded in publishing fiction about the cynicism and consumerism of the urban intelligentsia, the degraded state of 'that handful of ideals in which scions of the intelligentsia still believed

45 Ermolaev, *Censorship*, pp. 209–10.
46 Katerina Clark, 'Political History and Literary Chronotope: Some Soviet Case Studies', in Gary Saul Morson (ed.), *Literature and History: Theoretical Problems and Russian Case Studies* (Stanford, Calif.: Stanford University Press, 1986), p. 239.
47 Lev Loseff, *The Beneficence of Censorship* (Munich, 1984), p. 110.
48 N. N. Shneidman, *Soviet Literature in the 1970s: Artistic Diversity and Ideological Conformity* (Toronto: University of Toronto Press, 1979), p. 59.
49 Hosking, *Beyond Socialist Realism*, p. 190.

but were unable to act on', and to link the moral expediency of the nation's past with the spiritual degeneration of subsequent generations. Others – Shukshin, Valentin Rasputin – wrote about the 'victims of the transformation of Soviet society, people who had little understanding of and less control over their own lives'. Trifonov wrote from inside the transformation process itself, from 'the point of view of those members of the urban intelligentsia who had "made" the Soviet Union and must live with the results'.[50]

With the present pushing out the past as art's primary focus, village prose diminished in importance, although it remained popular among readers. The phenomenon of *literatura byta*, the literature of everyday reality, expanded, despite consistent official denigration of *bytopisanie* as trivial. (Attacks on *byt* included film: Marlen Khutsiev fielded similar charges against *Two Fyodors* (*Dva Fedora*, 1958), as did Tengiz Abuladze the same year for *Someone Else's Children* (*Chuzhie deti*).) Over time, 'this generally small-scale literature, with its focus on the everyday and the mundane (especially the domestic), carved out a niche for itself within the mainstream of Soviet literature while declining to link the individual with the universal, to resolve personal as well as more general problems, or to comment on ideological or philosophical matters'.[51]

While by no means gender-specific, the literature, drama and cinema of *byt* came to be identified with 'women's themes' and with women artists, especially writers, whose numbers increased dramatically in the Brezhnev years. In films like *A Sweet Woman* (*Sladkaia zhenshchina*, 1976), *A Strange Woman* (*Strannaia zhenshchina*, 1977) and *A Wife Has Left* (*Zhena ushla*, 1979), and in the fiction of many women writers, a throng of lonely women work and raise their children in a feminised world in which men play little part, and that part seldom constructive. The characters live in ugly apartment blocks in neighbourhoods devoid of shops and greenery, miles from the nearest metro stop. They spend inordinate amounts of time acquiring basic foodstuffs and traversing mud- and rubble-filled streets to get to work. 'It is precisely the domestic aspect of life, with its inequitable distribution of labor, its family pressures, the inadequate social and economic services, and above all the necessity of living with alcoholism, that immediately and on a very basic level distinguishes women's lives from those of men.'[52] (That distinction is eroded in later fiction by younger women.) Often enough, these writers treated

---

50 Josephine Woll, *Invented Truth: Soviet Reality and the Critical Imagination of Iurii Trifonov* (Durham, N.C.: Duke University Press, 1991), pp. 13–14.
51 Nicholas Zekulin, 'Soviet Russian Women's Literature in the Early 1980s', in Helena Goscilo (ed.), *Fruits of Her Plume: Essays on Contemporary Russian Women's Culture* (Armonk, N.Y., and London: M. E. Sharpe, 1993), p. 36.
52 Ibid., p. 43.

themes – such as the impact of drunken husbands on family life – that coincided with official concerns (the economic cost of ubiquitous alcoholism). As a result, 'they were able to graft themselves onto a mandate that was actively being promoted' by the authorities.[53]

Given the cost and logistical complexity of film-making, making films required working within the system. Rewards included access to scarce resources like imported film stock, larger shooting budgets, more leisurely schedules, opportunities to shoot co-productions abroad and well-paid managerial positions within the Union of Cinematographers, the studios and the Soviet Union's premier cinema training centre, the State Institute of Cinematography (VGIK). The state stringently controlled distribution: reluctant to ban products that represented substantial financial outlays, the system preferred to limit their impact. With movies, that meant controlling the number of prints made and the venues in which they were shown (in, for instance, central versus outlying locations).

In the 1970s, as cinema attendance sagged in inverse proportion to the rise in TV ownership, the regime tried to encourage the release of entertaining films. (Central TV went over fully to colour programming in 1978.) To that end Filip Ermash, an admirer of Hollywood, replaced the ideological and anti-commercial Aleksei Romanov as head of Goskino, the State Department of Cinema. Ermash ran Goskino from 1972 to 1986, and encouraged a tilt towards 'mass, lightweight film aimed at everyone',[54] like the extraordinarily popular slapstick (and skilful) comedies directed by Leonid Gaidai.

Films became more homogeneous, though generically more diverse, and decidedly less individualistic, especially towards the end of Ermash's tenure. However, not all successful Brezhnev-era film-makers were opportunists, ready to conform to the party's priorities. Eldar Riazanov and Vasilii Shukshin, two significant exceptions, believed no less strongly than Andrei Tarkovsky that film-making should be free of control and dedicated to improvement of society, but they 'rejected formal experimentation in favour of an aesthetic of maximum (or at any rate, widespread) popular accessibility'.[55] Each had occasional difficulties: for years Shukshin fought (unsuccessfully) to make a film on the seventeenth-century Cossack rebel Stenka Razin, and local party chiefs banned Riazanov's bleak 1980 satire *Garage* (*Garazh*), even though it had

53 Ibid., pp. 34, 37.
54 Val S. Golovskoy with John Rimberg, *Behind the Soviet Screen: The Motion-Picture Industry in the USSR 1972–1982* (Ann Arbor: Ardis, 1986), p. 143.
55 George Faraday, *Revolt of the Filmmakers: The Struggle for Artistic Autonomy and the Fall of the Soviet Film Industry* (University Park, Pa.: Pennsylvania State University Press, 2000), p. 98.

been approved for general release. Still, most of their films played in first-run theatres to huge audiences. Fifty million viewers saw Shukshin's *Snowball Berry Red* (*Kalina krasnaia*, 1974) in its first year; seventy million saw Riazanov's *Irony of Fate, or Have a Good Sauna!* (*Ironiia sud'by, ili s legkim parom!*) a year later. Lenfilm's exceptionally gifted Dinara Asanova made eight films in ten years as well as a series on juvenile delinquency for TV. While party leaders censored Asanova's 'portrait of a generation, puzzling in its taste for Western music and punk attire and its search for a new identity',[56] and relegated her films to second-run or run-down theatres, they held none back, and *Kids* (*Patsany*, 1983) won prizes at several Soviet festivals.

After 1967–8 film-makers faced increasing resistance to experimental, folk-loric and stylistically inflected films, with structures based on 'analogical images rather than narrative logic'.[57] Nevertheless, both central and repub-lican studios managed to produce such films until roughly 1975, when local and national pressures combined to promote pedestrian and derivative cin-ema. Ukraine's studio tried to perpetuate the legacy of Dovzhenko and the beleaguered Sergei Paradzhanov, at least until the latter's arrest in 1974 on fabricated charges. Iurii Ilenko's highly stylised *Spring for the Thirsty* (*Rodnik dlia zhazhdushchikh*, 1965) was shelved for twenty years, but two later films, *On St John's Eve* (*Vecher nakanune Ivana Kupala*, 1969) and the award-winning *White Bird with a Black Mark* (*Belaia ptitsa s chernoi otmetinoi*, 1971), ran in theatres, if only briefly. The explosion of cinematic energy that distinguished the studios of Central Asia in the late 1960s continued for several years, with Ishmukhame-dov's *Sweethearts* (*Vliublennye*; Uzbekistan, 1970), Mansurov's *She was a Slave* (*Rabynia*; Kazakhstan, 1970), Narliev's *The Daughter-in-Law* (*Nevestka*; Turk-menia, 1972), Okeev's *The Fierce One* (*Liutyi*; Kirgizia, 1974), and two films by Kirghiz director Shamshiev, *Red Poppies of Issyk-Kul* (*Alye maki Issyk-Kulia*, 1971) and *White Steamship* (*Belyi parokhod*, 1976), both award-winning, though the latter minimally distributed.

Of the republics, only Georgia managed to produce a consistently interest-ing body of work throughout *zastoi*: poetic and visually stunning explorations of Georgia's national past; 'philosophical comedies' that examine 'the incon-gruity between dream and reality, between the desires of the natural man and the structure of a society founded on mechanics and regulations';[58] subtle

56 Anna Lawton, *Kinoglasnost: Soviet Cinema in Our Time* (Cambridge: Cambridge University Press, 1992), p. 24.
57 Ibid., p. 32.
58 Anatoly Vishevsky, *Soviet Literary Culture in the 1970s: The Politics of Irony* (Gainesville, Fla.: University Press of Florida, 1993), p. 34.

psychological dramas exploring the tensions of modern Soviet life. (Distribution was frequently restricted to Georgia.) Otar Ioseliani, who began his career in 1966 with *Leaf fall* (*Listopad*), a feature film of near-documentary verisimilitude, experienced so many problems with later films that he eventually left for France, where he continues to work. Lana Gogoberidze, originally a documentarist, won fame with *Some Interviews on Personal Matters* (*Neskol'ko interv'iu po lichnym voprosam*, 1979), whose forty-something heroine finds she can no longer juggle the complicated balls of her life and whose past – like Gogoberidze's – includes a reunion with a mother released from the Gulag after Stalin's death.

By the last years of *zastoi*, 'the state's intrusion in private life considerably diminished, while the arena for public expression and the possibilities for private pleasure both expanded. Culture and everyday life were, of course, still constricted by political surveillance and economic controls, and censorship still operated . . . But conformity in modes of behavior, public expression, and individual identity became far less coercive, and the politicization of everyday life, the expectation that communal or political goals shaped individual desires, was muted and even ridiculed.'[59] Counter-systems – the cultural equivalents of the black and grey markets that supplemented the stagnant economy – defied, paralleled and in a sense complemented the 'public gloss, monumentalism, desiccated oratory, and relentless ritualism' of state systems.[60] The urban, topical irreverence of *estrada* (*revue*) comedy, acute commentaries on the shortcomings of Soviet life performed most adroitly by Arkadii Raikin and Mikhail Zhvanetskii, appealed to live audiences. And a plethora of voices – from women, from provincial Russia, from non-Russian republics – leaked into and thickened the official chorus.

New technology permitted the spread of culture – primarily, but not exclusively popular culture – with a speed and on a scale previously unimaginable. The advent of cheap audio cassettes allowed everyone from long-distance truckers to high-school students to hear gypsy songs previously banned from the airwaves, the immensely popular songs of Zhanna Bichevskaia, Alla Pugacheva and Valerii Leont'ev, and the far more abrasive ones of bards like Aleksandr Galich and Vladimir Vysotskii. (The Composers' Union fought back, mandating 'that 80% of all songs performed had to be those of Soviet composers' and establishing 'review commissions to vet all rock groups'.[61]) A few

59 Joan Neuberger, 'Between Public and Private: Revolution and Melodrama in Nikita Mikhalkov's Slave of Love', in McReynolds and Neuberger, *Imitations of Life*, pp. 260–1.
60 Stites, *Russian Popular Culture*, p. 149.      61 Ibid., p. 164.

years later video technology, though accessible only to a tiny elite, permitted the beginnings of an underground cinema movement, mainly in Leningrad. What began as 'an underground band of young layabouts and drunken "week-end warriors" who started to film their own debauched and violent free-for-alls in the woods in the early 1980s' went on to make the Soviet Union's first horror movies, where 'crazed "zombies" or necro-denizens wander apoca-lyptic landscapes and commit acts of wanton cruelty, homosexual violence, and murder'.[62] With the increase in the availability of VCRs, pirated foreign films eventually entered Soviet homes without even a token nod to official channels.

Popular fiction during *zastoi* superseded in popularity if not in critical esteem the new generation of 'serious' writers known variously as 'urban', 'the Moscow school', and 'the forty-year-olds'.[63] It satisfied a reading public that had grown substantially thanks to urbanisation, better education and liv-ing conditions and increased leisure time. The *makulatura* scheme, introduced in 1974 to solve the Soviet Union's perpetual paper shortage, enabled read-ers to trade in newspapers and magazines for books. 'Large segments of the population which had previously been uninterested in the printed word out-side newspapers were now introduced to the idea of the book as something valuable to be acquired; they were also encouraged to build a library of ide-ologically neutral and highly readable literature.'[64] Crime fiction burgeoned, both the home-made versions produced by novelists like Arkadii Adamov, Lev Ovalov and Arkadii and Grigorii Vainer, and the imports: fifteen works by Agatha Christie alone appeared in Soviet journals between 1966 and 1970.[65] Iulian Semenov's thrillers fed the hunger for escapist popular fiction, as did Valentin Pikul' 's piquant novels of the diplomatic, aristocratic and dynastic life of eighteenth- and nineteenth-century Russia. The state, eager for its share of the profits, authorised print runs in the millions (that sold out immediately) and screen adaptations. The prestigious Moscow-based journals like *Novyi mir*

62 José Alaniz and Seth Graham, 'Early Necrocinema in Context', in Seth Graham (ed.), *Necrorealism: Contexts, History, Interpretations* (Pittsburgh: Russian Film Symposium, 2001), p. 9.

63 Sally Dalton-Brown, 'Urban Prose of the Eighties', in Arnold McMillin (ed.), *Reconstruct-ing the Canon: Russian Writing in the 1980s* (Amsterdam: Harwood, 2000), pp. 282–3.

64 Stephen Lovell and Rosalind Marsh, 'Culture and Crisis: The Intelligentsia and Literature after 1953', in Catriona Kelly and David Shepherd (eds.), *Russian Cultural Studies: An Introduction* (Oxford: Oxford University Press, 1998), p. 78.

65 Catherine Theimer Nepomnyashchy, 'Markets, Mirrors, and Mayhem: Aleksandra Marinina and the Rise of the New Russian *Detektiv*', in Barker, *Consuming Russia: Popular Culture, Sex, and Society since Gorbachev*, p. 165.

and *Znamia* did not need such material to keep their circulation high, but provincial journals like *Volga*, *Sel'skaia molodezh* (Rural youth) and *Ural'skii sledopyt* (Urals pathfinder) relied on detective novels and/or science fiction to attract subscribers, and the legal journal *Chelovek i zakon* (Man and the law) came out in enormous print runs because it published Georges Simenon's Maigret novels and Semenov's *6 Ogareva Street*.[66]

The Brezhnev regime's final spasm of cultural repression occurred in 1979, with its refusal to publish a 'literary almanac', *Metropolis (Metropol')*. *Metropolis* contained poetry, essays, drama and short fiction by twenty-six writers, famous and obscure. Its editors – Vasilii Aksenov, Viktor Erofeev, Andrei Bitov, Fazil Iskander and Evgenii Popov – justified *Metropolis* as an effort to combat 'the dreary inertia which exists in journals and publishing houses . . . the condition of stagnant, quiet fright'.[67] Deliberately fostering a pluralist approach by including aesthetically diverse material, the editors tried – and failed – to publish via legal channels. The authorities blocked the intended 'book launch' at a downtown café (literally: they sealed off the block and closed the café for 'sanitary' reasons). The Writers' Union expelled five contributors, including Erofeev and Popov, slandered Aksenov and Akhmadulina, intimidated others; several, including Aksenov, emigrated. In the paralysis that ensued, and that persisted until 1986, Soviet culture bifurcated into its official sphere, 'total marasmus, total decay, supercretinism', in Popov's words, and an active, even 'tumultuous' literary underground whose members – mainly born between 1945 and 1955 – had virtually no hope of publication.

> The fact that our generation was immediately confronted with a kind of concrete wall meant that we were forced to go in another direction . . . [We] never identified with Soviet power, absolutely never . . . Whereas that generation, the 'sixtiers', *had* identified with it, they'd gone through the romance of joining the YCL [Komsomol, Young Communists' League] and hearing all these myths and stories about good communists. They'd been seduced by this subtle lie . . . We never felt that. Our only hope was that we might get away with it just a bit, cheat the system a bit, maybe publish a few things. That was our rather minimal ambition . . . None of this was unbearable, unbearable isn't the word . . . but it was simply melancholy, very melancholy, watching what was happening around us, communism and more communism, and wondering when on earth it would end. In fact mostly it seemed it would never come to an end . . . We

66 Viktor Miasnikov, 'The Street Epic', *Popular Fiction*, ed. John Givens, *Russian Studies in Literature* 38, 3 (Summer 2002), (M. K. Sharpe): 14. ('Bul'varnyi epos', *Novyi mir* 11 (2001), trans. Vladimir Talmy.)
67 Cited by Robert Porter, *Russia's Alternative Prose* (Oxford and Providence, R.I.: Berg, 1994), p. 27.

felt that for evermore and eternity there'd be a portrait of Brezhnev hanging there on the wall and someone singing some communist rubbish on the radio. So however much we laughed at Gorbachev, we should all remember very clearly that he played an absolutely enormous role.[68]

## Glasnost' and the post-Soviet decade, 1985–2000

When Gorbachev came to power he hardly intended the end of the Soviet state, with its concomitant dismantling of political, economic and cultural institutions, the resulting need to adapt to altered economic circumstances, cycles of inflation and devaluation that impoverished significant portions of the population, the success of an emergent entrepreneurial class and a myriad of other changes. Initially, glasnost', coupled with perestroika, promised hope, and for some time it delivered on the promise that many men and women, themselves products of Khrushchev's Thaw (the 'sixtiers' to whom Popov refers), felt had been deferred for twenty-five years or more. Throughout 1986, 1987 and 1988, excited, amazed gasps greeted every manifestation of freedom: historical-political rehabilitations, literary and cinematic discoveries and redis-coveries, artistic revelations. Although wary about the durability of those gains without fundamental institutional reform, artists and cultural consumers alike fervently welcomed the recovery of their national pasts, the removal of polit-ical boundaries that had banished into oblivion émigré culture, the exposure of lies that had shaped Soviet life for so long and the opportunity to write and read, produce and watch, compose and listen without supervision. For more than sixty years the Soviet state had controlled the creation and distribution of cultural products; beginning in 1986, that domination disappeared.

Theatre and film unions supported Gorbachev rapidly and energetically, partly because they hoped that the absence of censorship would stimu-late a revamped repertoire with which to lure dwindling audiences. They blamed political and bureaucratic interference for the system's inefficiency, and believed that independence would resolve many of their problems. They swiftly divested themselves of old-style political appointees in favour of those who had accumulated 'moral capital' by suffering from state repression.[69] A new Union of Theatre Workers replaced the All-Russian Theatrical Society, with the aim of 'freeing theatres from the close, pettifogging tutelage of the

---

68 Laird, Voices of Russian Literature, pp. 124–5.
69 Katherine Verdery, What was Socialist, and What Comes Next? (Princeton: Princeton University Press, 1996), pp. 107–8.

Ministry . . . enabling theatre companies themselves to take all the essential decisions and manage their own affairs'.[70] Between January 1986 and 1988, the number of theatres in Moscow increased by 50 per cent, and amateur and semi-professional groups multiplied, including fringe companies offering more experimental productions.

In a parallel process, members of the Cinematographers' Union voted out two-thirds of the board in May 1986, electing in their stead 'uncompromised' directors (most of whom had entered the industry in the 1960s) like Elem Klimov, Eldar Shengelaia and Andrei Smirnov. Cinema studios converted to a financially self-supporting system (*khozraschet*) that permitted virtual autonomy over script selection, budgeting, casting and hiring, though it offered no solutions to the obstructions posed by entrenched interests, the lack of hard currency and the difficulty of gauging popular taste. In 1988 film studios gained the right to distribute their libraries of films directly, bypassing the official government export agency.

Almost immediately the Cinematographers' Union undertook a review of films suppressed during the Brezhnev years, mainly for political transgressions, and authorised their release: Aleksei German's *Roadcheck* (*Proverka na dorogakh*, 1971), its hero a POW suspected of collaboration with the Nazis; Gleb Panfilov's *The Theme* (*Tema*, 1979), with allusions to Jewish emigration; Aleksandr Askoldov's first and last film *The Commissar* (*Komissar*, 1968), with an ambiguous Red Army heroine, montage reminiscent of the 1920s, and a flash forward to the Holocaust. Audiences watched these 'recovered' films with interest, but reserved their passion for the new movies portraying the Soviet Union's painful past and its tumultuous present, just as they devoured investigative journalism in print and on TV. All-Union television, reaching virtually every household in the nation, broadcast a startling number of documentary films.

A few directors (Kira Muratova, Aleksandr Sokurov, Lana Gogoberidze) welcomed *glasnost'* as the chance 'to make films that resist the overpoliticization of culture', rather than as an opportunity to make more openly political films.[71] But the majority of film-makers, freed from the demand to 'construct the future', portrayed the reality that surrounded them, and 'what they saw was a bleak picture: beggars on the streets, impoverished pensioners, economic

---

70 Michael Glenny, 'Soviet Theatre: *Glasnost'* in Action – with Difficulty', in Julian Graffy and Geoffrey A. Hosking (eds.), *Culture and the Media in the USSR Today* (Basingstoke and London: 1989), p. 81.

71 The phrase is Gogoberidze's. Svetlana Boym, 'The Poetics of Banality: Tat'iana Tolstaia, Lana Gogoberidze and Larisa Zvezdochetova', in Goscilo, *Fruits of Her Plume*, p. 75.

chaos, street crime, Mafia shootings, pornographic magazines and videos, decaying houses and ramshackle communal apartments, and the emergence of a new class, the New Russians. . .'.[72] Feature films like Vasilii Pichul's hyper-realistic melodrama *Little Vera* (*Malen'kaia Vera*) and Iurii Mamin's satiric *The Fountain* (*Fontan*), both released in 1988 when ticket prices were still affordable, drew huge audiences (50 million for *Little Vera*) and international prizes.

Within a few years, however, audiences had had enough, preferring to watch Brazilian soap operas and optimistic fortune-tellers on TV in their relatively clean, safe and comfortable living rooms rather than the all-too-familiar grim reality (or Hollywood trash) on offer in decaying dirty theatres. Film production dropped as fast as it had risen: 300 films were released in 1990, 213 in 1991, 68 in 1994, 28 in 1996.[73] More recently annual production has stabilised at about 75, produced by small, privatised companies instead of the unprofitably large studios of yore. Russia's Ministry of Culture currently finances fewer than two dozen films annually, and studios in many of the former Soviet republics struggle to survive, relying on help from organisations like France's Centre National de Cinématographie.

The collapse of the Soviet Union meant the 'wholesale social displacement of the cult of high culture'.[74] Entrenched attitudes compounded enormous practical difficulties. During the Brezhnev years, the polarisation between those artists whom the state favoured and those whom it marginalised strengthened the 'perceived connection between the moral integrity of the film "artist" and the social pessimism and aesthetic difficulty of his or her films'. In other words, inaccessibility denoted honesty, and entertainment meant compromise.[75] That attitude persisted well beyond the system's demise: 'Many people go to movie houses just to relax and enjoy themselves – to stop thinking,' commented a leading film-maker. 'We have to enlighten them and make them want to think.'[76] Yet 'auteur' films, however gratifying the international laurels they may accrue at Cannes, do not fill seats.

72 Birgit Beumers, 'Introduction', in B. Beumers (ed.), *Russia on Reels* (London and New York: I. B. Tauris, 1999), p. 1.
73 Ibid., p. 3.
74 Nancy Condee and Vladimir Padunov, 'The ABC of Russian Consumer Culture', in Nancy Condee (ed.), *Soviet Hieroglyphics: Visual Culture in Late Twentieth-Century Russia* (Bloomington and London: Indiana University Press and British Film Institute, 1995), p. 141.
75 Faraday, *Revolt of the Filmmakers*, p. 87. See also his analysis, pp. 122–3.
76 Elem Klimov, 'Learning Democracy: The Filmmakers' Rebellion', in Stephen F. Cohen and Katrina van den Heuvel (eds.), *Voices of Glasnost: Interviews with Gorbachev's Reformers* (New York: Norton, 1989), p. 240; cited by Faraday, *Revolt of the Filmmakers*, p. 128.

After more than a decade of negotiating between creative autonomy and public taste, Russian film-makers have found no magic formula. Still, a sizeable handful of recent films have succeeded in drawing domestic audiences into theatres. (The construction of modern multiplex cinemas with stadium seating and reliable heating helps as well.) Successful post-Soviet films manipulate generic formulae to probe contemporary concerns. Thrillers like Balabanov's *Brother (Brat*, 1997) offer amoral killer-heroes who may promise safety in a lawless society. Comedies like Dmitrii Astrakhan's *Everything Will Be OK (Vse budet khorosho*, 1995) provide 'escape into another world, imagined or real'. And war films like *Prisoner of the Mountain (Kavkazskii plennik*, 1997) and *The Cuckoo* (*Kukushka*, 2001) feature attractive soldier-heroes who are abandoned by their army and their community.[77] If the film-maker 'with a pragmatic frame of mind and a calculating self-interest has succeeded the figure of the director who was ostentatiously distant from material problems and fully engaged in the problems of art',[78] director Valerii Todorovskii welcomes the shift: 'I think it's a feature of the new generation of Russian filmmakers that they don't try to educate anyone. They understand that cinema should entertain people and give them pleasure, and, if it can, create some original, new world.'[79]

Literature benefited immediately from the steady expansion of opportunity and erosion of prohibitions ushered in by *glasnost'*, despite a tug-of-war between liberals and conservatives that lasted for several years.[80] Censorship was formally abolished on 1 August 1990, but long before that Glavlit had lost most of its teeth. Editors, once the first-line censors, made decisions with little regard for political or ideological criteria, except as they might affect circulation figures. As a result of the 1990 law, formerly underground and unofficial journals gained legal status: more than 400 registered within a few months. Most printing facilities and access to paper supplies remained in the hands of the Communist Party, so the newly independent journals faced an abundance of practical handicaps. For a few years, however, until financial exigencies forced many journals to close down, editors reintegrated into Russian culture an extraordinary range of once-banned material, from poetry and fiction written in the 1920s (Evgenii Zamiatin's 1920 dystopian novel *We (My)*, for one) to novels written thirty or forty years later (Vasilii Grossman's *Forever Flowing*

77 Birgit Beumers, 'To Moscow! To Moscow? The Russian Hero and the Loss of the Centre', in Beumers, *Russia on Reels*, pp. 77, 83.
78 Nina Tsyrkun, 'Tinkling Symbols', in Beumers' *Russia on Reels*, p. 59.
79 Faraday, *Revolt of the Filmmakers*, p. 171.
80 Josephine Woll, 'Glasnost: A Cultural Kaleidoscope', in Harley D. Balzer (ed.), *Five Years that Shook the World: Gorbachev's Unfinished Revolution* (Boulder, Colo., San Francisco and Oxford: Praeger, 1991), pp. 110–15.

(*Vse techet*), Nabokov's novels), from *samizdat* texts by authors living abroad to texts written 'for the drawer' by Soviet authors who had simply waited until circumstances changed. Contemporary authors who had published throughout the years of *zastoi* now took up crusading pens (Rasputin's *Fire* (*Pozhar*, 1985); Astaf'ev's *Sad Detective* (*Pechal'nyi detektiv*, 1986); Aitmatov's *Executioner's Block* (*Plakha*, 1986)), and works appeared by Tatyana Tolstaya, Viktor Erofeev, Mikhail Kuraev – writers whose 'vision of the world evolved prior to glasnost, even if the publication of their works did not'.[81] In addition, readers had access to a bewildering array of pulp fiction – thrillers, romances, pornography – lying cheek by jowl with political pamphlets and 'serious' literature on the stalls outside metro stations.

As the period of Gorbachev's rule drew to an end, writers and critics gradually abandoned the time-honoured civic and social role of literature, its functional utility. Viktor Erofeev, speaking for many, rejected the demand that writers be 'priest, and prosecutor, and sociologist, and expert on questions of love and marriage, and economist, and mystic'.[82] Readers adapted more slowly, rebuffing writers for 'offering no deep thoughts, no beautiful feelings, no attractive characters, not the least ray of hope'.[83] Accustomed to publicistic, polemical and pedagogic prose that sought to expose or ridicule the system, they spurned much of the 'alternative' literature on offer, mainly fiction 'ostensibly divorced from any specific social and historical context . . . sometimes real, sometimes fantastic', and often outrageously explicit in its sexual references and obscenities.[84]

Dubbed by one Russian critic 'post-socialist realist baroque',[85] the fiction of writers like Valeriia Narbikova and Valentin Sorokin is bleak and often shocking, written in response to 'an all-pervasive mass culture [originating] in ideology, deeply permeating the language as well as the visual landscape . . . [Their work] can be read as a passionate response to a society that lived on hypocrisy and shame, combining grandiose pretensions to moral righteousness with an almost unparalleled capacity for violence.' Sorokin, in particular, depicts 'a schizophrenic world in which the stock characters of Soviet literature – solid officials, eager young men, wry old codgers who have seen a thing or two – turn out on inspection to be monsters and perverts, and where everyday

---

81 Helena Goscilo, 'Alternative Prose and Glasnost Literature', in Balzer, *Five Years that Shook the World: Gorbachev's Unfinished Revolution*, p. 120.
82 Viktor Erofeev, 'Pominki po sovetskoi literature', *Literaturnaia gazeta* 17 (1990), reprinted in *Glas* 1 (1991): 221–32.
83 Cited by Porter, *Russia's Alternative Prose*, p. 6.   84 Ibid., pp. 1–2.
85 The phrase is Nadya Azhgikhina's, cited ibid., p. 12.

Soviet language – the language of apparent sense and morality – is seen as no more meaningful than the raving of lunatics'.[86]

Post-Soviet *chernukha* (black fiction), published in serious periodicals, appealed to readers because it 'legitimized their own knowledge that such things [homelessness, prostitution, army hazing, etc.] existed', and its authors spurned any and every kind of ideology in favour of 'corporeal truth'.[87] In time *chernukha* became 'the chief medium for chronicling everyday life', with 'new Russians' (that is, newly and ostentatiously wealthy) replacing the heroes and heroines drawn from the dregs of society, and material abundance – banquets, orgies – replacing suffering and physical humiliation. For the new hero, power alone retains meaning, and 'all other norms that traditionally relate to morality become absolutely arbitrary and are defined by almost insignificant factors'.[88] In Vladimir Tuchkov's 'Master of the Steppes' (*Novyi mir* no. 5, 1998), for example, the protagonist, a successful businessman, values Tolstoy and Dostoevsky for precisely those episodes where evil triumphs. He constructs his own 'hamlet', hires 'serfs' for $2,000/year, abuses them in the manner of Dostoevskian sadists – and his employees eagerly extend their contracts, regarding their master 'not as an eccentric man of means but as their very own father – strict but fair and incessantly concerned for their welfare'.[89] Thus the 'morality' of boundless power prevails over any spiritual value system that condemns such power.

Intriguing, but dispiriting – and hardly enticing to citizens who no longer equate literature with culture, who rarely opt for the self-reflexivity and self-parody of much current 'high' literature, and who much prefer books they enjoy, like the twelve-volume series called 'The Romanovs: A Dynasty in Novels', police procedurals by Aleksandra Marinina, and the escapades of Viktor Dotsenko's hero, an Afghan veteran known as the 'Russian Rambo'.[90] The Russian Centre for Public Opinion Research concluded in 1998 that one-third of Russians do not read at all; 95 per cent of those who do read exclusively choose 'light reading',[91] mostly homegrown products. Various kinds of detective stories – domestic and historical crime novels, female detective

---

86 Laird, *Voices of Russian Literature*, pp. 141–2, 145.

87 Mark Lipovetsky, 'Strategies of Wastefulness, or the Metamorphoses of *Chernukha*' ('Rastratnye strategii, ili metamorfozy "chernukhi"', *Novyi mir* 11 (1999), trans. Liv Bliss), John Givens (ed.), *The Status of Russian Literature, Russian Studies in Literature*, 38, 2 (Armonk, N.Y.: M. E. Sharpe, Spring 2002): 61.

88 Ibid., pp. 70–2 *passim*.      89 Cited by Lipovetsky, 'Strategies of Wastefulness', p. 74.

90 Nepomnyashchy, 'Markets, Mirrors, and Mayhem', pp. 167–8.

91 Published in *Kommersant* 4 (22 Jan. 1999); cited by Mikhail Berg, 'The Status of Literature' ('O statuse literatury', *Druzhba narodov* no. 7, 2000; trans. Liv Bliss), in Givens, *The Status of Russian Literature*, p. 37 n. 2.

novels, 'techno-thrillers' – attract the most readers, principally because they depict 'genuine nobility, people of duty and honor', and because, whatever their time frame, they deal with contemporary concerns: 'how to live in a period of property redistribution, bureaucratic and criminal lawlessness, terrorism, the spread of drug addiction, unsavory public relations campaigns, corruption, loss of social status, and the destruction of public morals'.[92] In Western societies 'high' literature became estranged from popular culture half a century ago. The exigencies of politics and history artificially postponed that rift in the Soviet Union. It is now a reality.

## In lieu of a conclusion

This chapter tells a convoluted story, or rather stories, spanning five decades and a spectrum of leadership ranging from Stalin's absolute dictatorship to Putin's technocracy. It depicts a society where politics and culture have until quite recently been intimately, indeed inextricably, intertwined, and where the imperatives of one frequently conflicted with the essence of the other. Even in today's post-Soviet Russia, where artists grope to find a secure footing in the rubble of the old cultural landscape, the nexus of politics and culture has not entirely disappeared. For better and for worse, each illuminates the other, deepening our understanding of both. The story, then, is as complex as the society – and like the society, with all its metamorphoses and transformations, the story continues, its future unknown.

92 Miasnikov, 'The Street Epic', p. 19, 20.

# 23

# Comintern and Soviet foreign policy, 1919–1941

JONATHAN HASLAM

## The October Revolution

The October Revolution was intended as a prelude to world revolution. Initial disappointment at the failure of other countries to follow suit led to an abrupt change of policy at Brest-Litovsk in March 1918, when Lenin settled for a compromise peace with the Kaiser in order to give time for the creation of a military base for the revolution until Germany was ripe for revolt. The invasion of Russia by the armies of Japan and the Entente Powers, in May and August 1918 respectively, temporarily destroyed the tactic of accommodation with the capitalist world. The option of revolutionary war in the style of Napoleon was thus forced upon the Bolsheviks as a matter of survival. A war of offence against the West therefore became inseparable from the needs for defence. The question hidden behind the ensuing turmoil was the direction of foreign policy once military hostilities ceased. Would Soviet Russia revert to the 'Brest viewpoint' of accommodation? Or, having tasted the excitement, would Moscow once again exercise the option of revolutionary war?

The Bolsheviks had been conducting a fierce campaign to spread the revolution among invading Allied troops since the autumn of 1918 under the Central Executive Committee's Department of Propaganda, which was then moved over into the Communist International (Comintern) on 25 March 1919. The Comintern was thus always conceived and created for more than just furthering the worldwide proletarian revolution: protecting and enhancing the security of Soviet Russia (from 1923 the USSR) was no less a priority. Not everyone immediately understood this ambiguous role. It was reported that at the focal point of its intended activities – Germany – the question of creating the Comintern was viewed 'with great scepticism' because it was not thought that 'anything organisationally could be achieved in the near future'.[1]

In theory no conceptual difference was allowed to exist between these entirely distinct purposes. But the conflict between theory and practice very soon became too blatant to remain unremarked, and as early as 1924 and as late as 1935 even official utterance acknowledged that, at any given moment, these purposes could collide. A further complication also arose from the fact that the Comintern was born out of the October Revolution of 1917, which was Russian in inspiration and implementation. It meant that this global apparatus of power attached to the Soviet Communist Party became embroiled in the struggle for power that divided the party after the death of Lenin. Thus, even as it increasingly became an adjunct to Soviet state power abroad, the Comintern also became an adjunct to one faction within the party that sought to control all Soviet power. Thus the process of Bolshevising the Comintern that took place under Lenin – ostensibly to prepare fraternal parties for revolution – inevitably became a process of Stalinising the Comintern once Stalin crushed all vestiges of formal opposition in 1929.[2]

Therefore, even if we treat the Comintern as the instrument of Soviet foreign policy that it undoubtedly was, the relationship between Soviet state interests and the interests of worldwide revolution was not always entirely clear. Second, even where one can in retrospect see a line dividing the two, the thorny issue remains of a distinction between the interests of the ruling faction in Russia and the interests of the Soviet system as a whole. The Comintern was thus not a marginal and extraneous extension of Soviet power but integral to its very core and purpose, whether original or bastardised by Stalin's autocracy. The legitimacy of the October Revolution in Russia never depended exclusively on what it could do for Russia. Primarily it lay in what Russia could do for the world. Once the German revolution triumphed, Lenin intended to move to Berlin. Thus internal and international purpose could never be separated by a Chinese Wall of indifference without breaching the Leninist legacy in its entirety. Even at the height of his powers and at the peak of his contempt for foreign Communists, Stalin could never fully forswear that legacy, for to do so would have undermined an essential element in the domestic structure of power he was so anxious to dominate completely. Trotsky wrote that Stalin

---

1 Karl Radek, reporting from Berlin, to Lenin, Chicherin and Sverdlov, 24 Jan. 1919: K. Anderson and A. Chubar'ian (eds.), *Komintern i ideia mirovoi revoliutsii: dokumenty* (Moscow: Nauka, 1998), doc. 6.
2 E. H. Carr and R. W. Davies, *Foundations of a Planned Economy, 1926–1929* (London: Macmillan, 1976), vol. III, pts. 1–3.

would not dare desert the Comintern except at risk of appearing 'in the character of a consistent Bonaparte, i.e. break openly with the tradition of October and place some kind of crown on his head'.[3]

## Standing alone

The failure of the Allied war of intervention, signalled by the British decision to pull out by the end of 1919, effectively ensured the survival of Bolshevik rule in Russia and the greater part of its former empire. The Janus faces of Soviet foreign policy thereby emerged: on the one side the face of appeasement and statecraft, the policy of accommodation to the capitalist world (the 'Brest viewpoint'); on the other the contrasting face of violence and revolution to uproot and supplant capitalism in its entirety.

Not least because of the Royal Navy offshore, the Baltic states – Latvia, Lithuania and Estonia – were where Lenin cut his losses. He granted diplomatic recognition to these bourgeois nationalist regimes and sought to make virtue of necessity by dramatically demonstrating Soviet support for the hallowed liberal principle of national self-determination. Similarly in the East, the Bolsheviks projected their solidarity with 'national liberation movements' against Western imperialism even if, in one instance, national liberation was led by a brutal feudal despot (King Amanullah of Afghanistan). This fundamental breach of Marxist principle – to back the bourgeoisie instead of the toiling masses – was dictated by the demands of the Soviet state in a friendless world where revolution was slow to emerge. In the eyes of the Bolsheviks these were merely temporary remedies to a problem for the short term. A breach of principle in the longer term was not expected and would certainly not have been accepted if proposed.

At the same time that Lenin reassured the Baltic that they might stand free of Bolshevik expansionism, other countries were targeted for Sovietisation. The high point of this misplaced euphoria occurred when Poland was seemingly within grasp in late July 1920. Lenin declared 'the situation in the Comintern' to be 'superb'. Zinoviev, Bukharin and Lenin thought it the time to encourage the Italian revolution (this was the time of the factory occupations in Turin). 'My personal opinion', Lenin wrote, 'is that for this we need to Sovietise Hungary, and perhaps also Czechoslovakia and Romania . . .'[4] This bafflingly misplaced optimism was connected to the drive on Warsaw in a desperate

---

3 Published in *Biulleten' Oppozitsii* 44 (July 1935): 13; quoted in E. H. Carr, *Twilight of Comintern, 1930–1935* (London: Macmillan, 1982), p. 427, n. 75.
4 Lenin to Stalin, 23 July 1920: Anderson and Chubar'ian, *Komintern i ideia*, doc. 39.

attempt to create a bridge to the land of revolution, Germany. Even with the dramatic failure of the Polish offensive, Lenin continued to boast. 'The defensive period of the war with global imperialism has ended,' he told the Nineteenth Conference of the Russian Communist Party, 'and we can and must use the military situation for the start of an offensive war.'[5]

The voice of sanity was that of the brilliant Polish Jew, Karl Radek, who was consistently better informed about the state of the world because he moved beyond Soviet borders, and with his eyes wide open. Radek ridiculed the optimism prevalent in the Kremlin. He had no problem with the notion of offensive war; only with the assessment of the international situation. 'Now comrade Lenin is demonstrating a new method of information gathering: not knowing what is going on in a given country, he sends an army there,' he parried. It was, he agreed, entirely possible that a revolution in Italy would transform the scene. 'But in any case we must refrain from the method of sounding out the international situation with the aid of bayonets. The bayonet would be good if it were necessary to aid a particular revolution, but for seeing how the land lies in this or that country we have another weapon – Marxism, and for this we do not need to call upon Red Army soldiers.'[6]

The complete and humiliating collapse of the last all-out attempt at revolution made by German Communists in March 1921 overturned Comintern policy. It underlined the sorry fact that – for all the recrimination heaped upon the KPD leadership for incompetence and lack of conviction – a structural shift was under way outside Russia, reversing the tide accelerated by war from revolution to the 'stabilisation of capitalism' and, though they had yet to recognise it, counter-revolution. And if the Soviet regime was to survive, it had to take careful note and adjust tactics accordingly. Institutionally, the shift was paralleled by the transfer of talent from the Comintern and other party bodies to the diplomatic apparatus, in the form of the People's Commissariat for Foreign Affairs (Narkomindel), whose hitherto precarious existence now became solidified as Soviet Russia established itself as a state in its own right.

It would, however, be wrong to see this shift of emphasis as in any sense final. The two institutions, embodying the Janus faces of the Soviet regime, fought for dominance as an extension of the fact that Comintern sponsorship of revolution inevitably created problems for the Narkomindel. Matters came to a head in mid-August 1921. The issue was to ensure 'that the international position of the RSFSR and the Comintern were not in a condition of antagonism between one another'. The institutional stance of Soviet diplomats was,

5 Ibid., doc. 47.    6 Radek speaking, 22 Sept. 1920: Ibid., doc. 48.

of course, the 'Brest viewpoint': the Peace of Brest-Litovsk of March 1918, where fledgling Soviet Russia traded its principles, indemnities and territory for precious time against the invading Germans. Commissar for Foreign Affairs Georgii Chicherin wrote to party secretary Molotov:

> I do not understand why, thanks to the Comintern, we have to fall out with Afghanistan, Persia and China.
> ...The harm is done in the inadequacy of contacts between the Narkomindel and the Comintern. The line of the Narkomindel consists in enabling the Soviet Republic, the citadel of world revolution, to overcome millions of difficulties. Only from an anti-Brest viewpoint of indifference to the existence of the Soviet Republic can this line be rejected. These difficulties can be counted in the millions; our position is extremely complex. Everyone everywhere mixes up the RSFSR with the Comintern, and an untimely step on its [the Comintern's] part could create a catastrophe for us. We have little in the way of military power. An attack on us from Afghanistan could lead to catastrophe in Turkestan. This is not a game [*etim nel'zia igrat'*]. To consider shameful, vigilance in the face of these dangers – that is truly shameful. [7]

The clash between state interests and revolutionary interests was not so easily resolved in the East, as the revolutionary movement began to swell. In Europe, however, where revolution was effectively in retreat and where the stakes were higher for Soviet security, Comintern tactics had already moved in the direction of the 'united front'. Communist parties formed by splitting Social Democracy were now told to ally with those they believed traitors to the revolution. The parliamentary road to power, anathema months before, was now not just acceptable but also the preferred route to government. The tactical retreat from outright insurrectionism served Soviet state interests because Lenin had by then reached a point of no return in the decision to align Moscow with the pariah of Europe, Weimar Germany. And this alignment rested uneasily upon a common interest between the Right within Germany – extreme nationalists hostile to the Versailles Treaty system, heavy industry in need of markets and the military looking for allies against the Franco-Polish axis – and the Bolsheviks, whose urgent priority was to keep the rest of Europe at loggerheads to forestall any renewed attempt by a common coalition to overturn Soviet power. This alignment was prefigured by secret and unwritten understandings on military co-operation secured before the end of 1921, symbolised in the Treaty of Rapallo in April 1922.[8]

---

7 Chicherin to Molotov, 14 Aug. 1921: Ibid., doc. 86.
8 E. H. Carr, *The Bolshevik Revolution, 1917–1921*, vol. III (London: Macmillan, 1953), and *The Interregnum, 1922–1923* (London: Macmillan, 1954).

Having failed to overthrow the Bolsheviks – though with no idea just how close they had come – the British, led by Lloyd George, decided to rationalise retreat by attempting to prove a fundamental tenet of liberal doctrine: that by trading with Russia, which was now embarking on a market-based New Economic Policy, Britain could undermine its revolutionary essence as individual economic self-interest overwhelmed the spirit of collectivism. The market would thus ultimately triumph. Such a policy might have worked at that time had Lenin – well versed in liberal fundamentals and a keen reader of Maynard Keynes – not immediately blocked off that promising but elusive avenue with institution of a state monopoly of foreign trade. The Anglo-Soviet trade agreement of March 1921 was effectively used by the Bolsheviks to establish Russia as a presence on the international stage, while failing to secure for Britain a ready and peaceful means of ridding the world of Bolshevism. It fast became apparent to all that, with little if any negotiating power at his disposal and with a readiness to make tactical sacrifices as the moment demanded, Lenin had turned the balance of Europe to Russia's advantage, and not through the expected means of revolutionary expansionism but by the time-honoured practices of realpolitik and in a manner worthy of Talleyrand. In this game of deadly chess, under Lenin's skilful direction Moscow always seemed a few steps ahead, leaving the capitalist world insecure, angry and resentful, but with no means yet available of turning that into effective policy to neutralise or destroy the bases of Soviet power.

The real problem for Soviet Russia was, however, that this proved Lenin's last triumph. The assassin's bullet increasingly rendered him senseless, and there existed no one of comparable ability to succeed him. Thus Lenin's tactical moves of the moment – such as Rapallo – were, for want of greater foreign political intuition and ingenuity, fixed in concrete. Where experimentation beyond Lenin's strategy did occur, it not infrequently took place long after it could be truly effective (notably the Popular Front against Fascism) having been blocked by dogma; or it emerged as a desperate scramble to appease a foreign threat, during which every trace of principle was ditched in indecent haste (the Nazi–Soviet pact) and at considerable cost.

## The awakening of the East

The one great asset that emerged after Lenin's demise in January 1924 was what he had predicted two decades before: namely, the 'awakening of the East' – in this instance the Far East. Strategically the prospect of stripping the imperialist powers, above all Britain, of the assets that underwrote empire, was beguiling indeed. India took the greatest share of British export, China stood a close second. The consequences of losing both or even one of these crucial markets, that were also the recipients of billions in capital investment, were both incalculable and uplifting. India, however, trod its own path. The passive resistance movement established by Gandhi differed from the Bolsheviks (and Indian Communists) crucially not only as to ends but also as to means. That left China.

Lenin had been to the fore in establishing Soviet credentials with China's bourgeois nationalist movement under Sun Yat-sen. In 1918 a message had been sent declaring all unequal treaties null and void. Yet nothing was heard in reply. Finally, at the end of 1920, Russian emissaries reported back favourably on Sun as 'violently anglophobe'.[9] But he led no party as such and Moscow saw its job as not merely to found a Chinese Communist Party (CCP) but also build the nationalist movement against the West and Japan. In the summer of 1922 emissary A. A. Ioffe reported to Deputy Commissar of Foreign Affairs (for the East) Lev Karakhan that Beijing was

> for us extremely favourable. The struggle with world capitalism has vast resonance and massive possibilities for success. The spirit of world politics is felt here extremely strongly, much greater than, for instance, in Central Asia, where Lenin attributed it. China is without doubt the focal point of international conflicts and the most vulnerable place in international imperialism, and I think that precisely now, when imperialism is undergoing a crisis in Europe, and when revolution is imminent, it would be very important to deliver imperialism a blow at its weakest point.[10]

Accusations of 'revolutionary opportunism' were met with the rebuttal that 'revolutionary nationalism' was a force to be reckoned with in its own right. 'We have no alternative.'[11]

With Sun's death early in 1925 the Chinese nationalist movement passed into the hands of a less principled successor, Chiang Kai-shek, who formed it into a party: the Guomindang. Even under Sun, however, the interests of the nationalists intersected with those of Russia only at certain key points, not all along the line. Rather like Germany under Stresemann from 1926, the Guomindang saw its close relations with Moscow as a major bargaining

9 Memorandum from A. Potapov to Chicherin, 12 Dec. 1920, M. Titarenko et al. (eds.), *VKP (b), Komintern i natsional'no-revoliutsionnoe dvizhenie v Kitae: Dokumenty*, vol. 1 (Moscow: Russian Akademia nauk, 1994), doc. 7.
10 Telegram from Ioffe to Karakhan, 30 Aug. 1922, in Titarenko et al., *VKP (b)*, doc. 28.
11 Speech by Maring, 6 Jan. 1923, at a session of the Comintern executive committee (IKKI) ibid., doc. 56.

counter to be cashed in when others offered more; an exercise engaged in with the British in the late 1920s and the Japanese from the early 1930s.[12]

By 1925 minimal Soviet investment had paid off handsomely. And when on 30 May the British foolishly fired on unarmed protestors in the Shanghai International Settlement, the entire nationalist movement rose in protest, the fledgling and hitherto insignificant CCP in the vanguard of direct action. The Soviet, and therefore Comintern, commitment to revolutionary nationalism in China was only conditional; yet that very condition – driving the British out – was sufficient to send Anglo-Soviet relations into a tailspin from which it never entirely recovered, and with damaging consequences in the longer term after Hitler came to power in Germany when Moscow needed London as an ally against Berlin.

Thus Comintern aspirations were displaced fortuitously from West to East. Comprehension of the East was, however, not a great deal better than of the West. And the Russians soon got carried away in expectation of cutting the British Empire down to size. They were therefore entirely unprepared when London laid its trap: negotiating a secret compromise with Chiang that not only encouraged but also facilitated the massacre of Communist cadres within his ranks and a breach in diplomatic relations with Moscow that finally foreclosed on the Leninist investment in revolutionary nationalism. London also cut relations with Moscow in the spring of 1927. The Russians therefore had every cause to regret having vested so much in what turned out to be a futile and costly venture. Only the CCP had more reason for regret. Its last outpost of strength was washed away in a tide of blood by Chiang at Canton that December. All that remained were peasants deep in the vast interior, much vaunted by the unknown Mao Zedung but a cause of deep scepticism in Moscow, where decisions were in the making to break the back of recalcitrant peasants resisting the forced collectivisation of agriculture.

## Revolutionary phrase versus cautious pragmatism

Had decisions on Comintern strategy hinged entirely on principles of revolutionary solidarity, the Soviet state would have faced the prospect of extinction, since objective reality did not match up to exaggerated expectations. Rapallo realpolitik would, for instance, never have come about, thus leaving Russia dangerously isolated in a hostile world. Had decisions hinged entirely on reasons

---

12 For the larger picture see E. H. Carr, *Socialism in One Country, 1924–1926* (London: Macmillan, 1964), vol. III, ch. 40.

of state, however, the Comintern would have lost its membership abroad; and although Moscow not infrequently undercut fraternal parties, this was usually only *in extremis*. In the late 1920s, however, neither factor was critical to Comintern strategy. What was critical was the advancement of Stalin within Russia. He had always been deeply sceptical of the Comintern's value – *lavochka* (corner shop) was the dismissive term he used to describe it. None the less the prevailing view was that the Comintern was the sacred repository for the ultimate objective – world revolution – and its membership was inextricably tied into the Soviet party; indeed the Polish party was so difficult to differentiate – it also sprang from the Russian Social Democratic Labour Party – that later Stalin wiped it out.

What made necessary the complete subordination of the Comintern to Stalin was that it was effectively a continuum with the Soviet party – so domination of the latter also necessitated domination of the former. What made possible that subordination were practices begun by Lenin for completely different purposes. Strict discipline was governed by the notorious twenty-first condition of Comintern membership, which originated not from Russian hands but at the enthusiastic suggestion of the founder of the Italian Communist Party, Amadeo Bordiga. This greatly facilitated the process begun by Lenin known as Bolshevisation, which was to ensure that the sections were fine-tuned to (successful) Russian revolutionary standards. The core assumption behind the purge was the fixed and unalterable belief that failure to accomplish revolutionary goals was not the result of the absence of revolutionary conditions but the absence of revolutionary aptitude.

If this were not distortion enough, it rapidly became an instrument to bolster the power and influence of those Russians at the head of the Comintern – initially Zinoviev – to advance their own protégés at the expense of meritocracy. Thus it was that initially the Left (including Bordiga) captured the Comintern, was soon forced to give way to the Right, and both were then obliged to cede to Stalin; precisely parallel to the shift of power within the Soviet Communist Party. Bolshevisation therefore reached its apogee as Stalinisation. And by then whatever virtue there had originally been had long surrendered to bureaucracy. It is no accident that later the indigenous revolutions were accomplished only by those who, one way or another, evaded Moscow discipline (Tito, Hoxha, Mao and Castro).

Stalin notoriously stole the policies of his enemies once he had done with them. Thus it was that, having rid Russia of Trotsky (though not his followers, who were still sulking in their tents), Stalin immediately embarked on policies hitherto heralded by the Left as the domestic solution to Moscow's dilemma:

rapid state industrialisation and the forcible collectivisation of agriculture. This was prefaced by turning the Comintern sharp left against all contacts with Social Democracy and bourgeois nationalism worldwide, proclaimed at the sixth Congress in 1928, ironically under the now helpless leader of the Right, Bukharin. The entire reorientation, domestic and foreign, was effectively harnessed to winning over the Left, even if one allows that events were anyway pressing in this direction. Whether Stalin would have forced the pace without such incentives is open to doubt, for he had hitherto been identified as a Rightist both internationally (by the British Foreign Office no less) and at home (not least by Trotsky). The acute tension within him between innate caution and burgeoning intemperance during moments of gloomy introspection was apt to break dramatically when events allowed, and drive him to lash out in unexpected directions and at unsuspecting victims.

Although the Comintern no longer remained the centre of Soviet foreign policy-making, neither did it become completely irrelevant – not least because the rest of the world saw international revolution as Russia's objective. Thus the shift to the left did have undesirable consequences for the effectiveness of Soviet diplomacy. A near rupture with France at the end of 1927 was followed by a near rupture with Germany early in 1928 and a crisis in China in 1929.[13] That same year ill-considered and overt attempts to recruit the rank and file of the French Communist Party (PCF), the second largest in Europe, for the purpose of spying on military and logistical capabilities resulted in the prompt arrest and imprisonment of the PCF leadership, followed by further tension with Moscow. The atmosphere of fear was such as one might have expected on the eve of war and matched the bellicose rhetoric on the domestic front. The one inevitably spilled easily over into the other.

There was one notable success, however. Patching up relations with the minority Labour administration in Britain provided some compensation, but increasingly France took the lead against international Communism. An unusually enfeebled British Empire – already undermined by the Treasury's short-sighted financial policies – fell easy victim to the Wall Street Crash in October 1929; and by the end of September 1931 Britain was not only forced into devaluation but even the navy had mutinied.

To a Marxist all this should have come as no surprise. The Russians, of course, had long predicted a crash followed by acute social unrest, if not revolution. But as far as Stalin was concerned rhetoric was just rhetoric. Policy was a different matter. With the countryside in revolt, the industrial economy

13 Carr and Davies, *Foundations of a Planned Economy, 1926–1929*, vol. III, pt. I.

overheated and unrest manifest within the ranks of the Red Army, itself backward technologically compared to the Great Powers, the last thing Stalin
wanted was a Communist attempt to seize power and, in so doing, unite the
wrath of the capitalist world in a furious, further and possibly final assault on
the debilitated Soviet Union.[14]

Thus an extraordinary credibility gap emerged by the spring of 1930 between
bellicose Comintern propaganda about the imminence of war and revolution
and the flagrant timidity and conservatism of Stalin's instructions to foreign
Communist parties. In both Germany and China word went out to desist
from grandiose and risky revolutionary adventures.[15] On the diplomatic front
this cautious approach was matched by Commissar Maksim Litvinov, who
had de facto control over the Narkomindel since 1928 before supplanting
his ailing and querulous boss, Georgii Chicherin, in the summer of 1930.
The Litvinov line met Stalin's needs to a tee. It meant following the line
Lenin had chosen in the spring of 1922 for the Soviet delegation to the Genoa
conference, designed to win over the pacifist bourgeoisie of the West with
high-flown talk of increased trade, world peace and general and complete
disarmament; a charade, perhaps, but a proven and effective smokescreen
which required a continued Soviet presence at international conferences –
mostly boring Geneva, where Litvinov indulged himself spinning out the
empty hours in the evenings watching Westerns at the cinema.[16]

## Fear of France eclipses the real danger

France was, of course, the power most set against disarmament, haunted by
fear of a German revival. But it was also an imperial power overseas of some
magnitude, and lines of communication were stretched to the limit. Since
the 1920s, when it led in the losses from nationalisation by the Bolsheviks
of all private property in Russia, France had chafed at irksome but contain-
able Comintern support for troublesome tribes in North Africa. It had been
obliged to follow Britain and Germany in recognising the Soviet regime. Sentiment hardened, however, when, in the spring of 1930, a nationalist revolt of
major proportions took hold in Indochina, in which the young Ho Chi Minh's
Communist group came to play a role disproportionate to its minuscule size.
Paris, on very little evidence but the principle of *cui bono*, immediately blamed

14 Carr, *Twilight*, ch. 1.    15 Ibid., ch. 1.
16 See Jonathan Haslam, *Soviet Foreign Policy 1930–33: The Impact of the Depression* (London: Macmillan, 1983).

Moscow and launched a European-wide campaign to renew the economic blockade of Russia ended by the British in March 1921.[17]

In the bleak circumstances of the Great Depression, with industrialised powers now looking anxiously to capture the few lucrative markets that remained and with the Russians favouring Germany, Sweden, Italy, Britain and the United States with sizeable orders for capital goods, the French stood alone (except for its powerless little allies along the Danube who competed with Moscow on the falling world grain market). Yet, because the Russians still lacked an efficient foreign intelligence service, French hostility came to be magnified out of all proportion to its true effectiveness. And a further factor intervened to compound Soviet anxieties when, on 18 September 1931, Imperial Japan launched its occupation of Manchuria, overran Soviet-owned railroads and raced to the Soviet border with a view to another excursion at Russian expense. Word soon leaked to the press that the French expressed the wish to the Japanese that they now go north (to Russia) rather than south (to Indochina). The Japanese also reinforced existing military and intelligence links with Finland, Poland and Afghanistan, in an attempt at encirclement of the USSR. Soviet efforts to counteract this met stiff resistance in Washington, where the Republican administration under Hoover stubbornly sought recompense for property appropriated by Lenin in 1918 and had no incentive to appease the Russians while they bought US manufactures anyway. And the British, economically holed beneath the waterline and with a navy of doubtful morale, shied away from confrontation with warlike Japan. Worse still, the Red Army in the Far East deterred no one, a fleet had yet to be put together and the single-tracked Trans-Siberian Railway gave little promise of rapid reinforcement in time of war. The need to rearm speedily in the East placed a new burden on a strained economy and the need to stockpile food for war in Siberia further exacerbated the acute shortage of grain that had opened up with famine in the summer of 1932.[18]

Rather than risk allowing the KPD to launch an abortive revolution in Germany, which was sure to fail if merely for the fact that the stooges Stalin had emplaced were better known for unthinking obedience than strategic initiative, Stalin instead chose to encourage German nationalism as the best means of distracting the French. Hitler was seen here, as elsewhere in Europe, to be just another German nationalist. No attempt was therefore made to curb the natural antipathy of the KPD towards long resented 'social Fascists' (the socialists of the SPD), whereas any attempt to open a channel towards

17 Ibid., chs. 4 and 5.     18 Ibid., ch. 8.

them in the name of a still greater threat (the Nazis) was sat upon firmly.[19] The Comintern thus resumed its role as a passive conveyor belt for the furthering of Soviet state interests – as interpreted by Stalin and, in this instance and every other with respect to German matters, by his closest colleague, chairman of the Council of People's Commissars and overseer of the Comintern, the dour and taciturn Viacheslav Molotov.

Throughout, Stalin did receive contrary advice. It was at the time reported that Litvinov, who regarded Molotov as a fool, warned of Hitler as a serious and hostile force to be reckoned with; but he was undermined by his deputy, Nikolai Krestinskii, who had behind him nearly a decade of success as ambassador in Berlin.[20] Krestinskii confirmed Stalin and Molotov in their complacency. From the unthinking Left in the Comintern, the head of the sector dealing with Germany, Knorin, took a position akin to 'the worse the better', since revolution needed to break the fetters of constitutionalism, to which the working class had apparently become wedded. Hitler was in this deluded image a bulldozer with the KPD at the wheel. Were not most Nazi Party members former members of the KPD? The thinking Left, represented by Trotsky in exile, argued very differently and essentially took Litvinov's position. The fact that both Trotsky and Litvinov were Jewish undoubtedly heightened their powers of perception of an anti-Semite like Hitler. But Trotsky's advocacy – which was closely monitored at great distance in the Kremlin – doubtless also confirmed Stalin in his stubborn resistance to such views.

## Salvation too late

From Moscow's vantage point, backing German nationalism was a low-cost policy. Hitler's arrival in power at the end of January 1933 did not occasion an abrupt change of line. Instead the Russians assumed a policy of watchful waiting. At the Comintern the prevailing view was ably expressed by Osip Piatnitskii in a letter to Stalin, Molotov and Kaganovich on 20 March. Piatnitskii carried some weight as head of the international communications section of the Comintern – basically the intelligence section which worked hand in glove with the OGPU – and as a member of the presidium of the Comintern executive committee (IKKI). He reasserted the current myth that in Germany 'the revolutionary crisis is fast developing' and that it would, under Hitler, gather speed and that therefore the resistance of the masses could not but develop. 'The establishment of an open Fascist dictatorship,' he wrote,

19 Carr, *Twilight*, chs. 3–4.    20 Haslam, *Soviet Foreign Policy*, pp. 67–8.

'dispelling all democratic illusions among the masses and freeing the masses from the influence of Social Democracy, will speed up the pace of development of Germany towards a proletarian revolution.'[21] This bizarre misreading was commonplace in Moscow at the time and was sustained even after the successful persecution of the KPD and simultaneous harassment of the mass of Soviet trade and diplomatic employees in Germany took on alarming proportions. By summer the KPD had been suppressed with extraordinary ease and rapidity. Meanwhile in Moscow uneasy inertia began to give way to a more resolute position, though not all illusions – including those of Molotov – were extinguished as late as 1941.[22]

Pressure was building, however, from within Comintern ranks for a change of line. At the head of the British party, Harry Pollitt called for the Comintern presidium to discuss the situation in Germany and the united front strategy (then non-existent). Piatnitskii carefully separated the two, even though they were indissolubly linked in Pollitt's mind and in the minds of others unhappy at the recent course of events.[23] A straw in the wind was the failure of Piatnitskii – then effectively running the Comintern – to prompt what remained of Communist supporters in Germany to have Moscow agree to boycotting the referendum forthcoming in Germany that autumn.[24]

At the level of interstate relations Litvinov fought for a policy based on the assumption that Hitler posed a fundamental threat to the peace of Europe, since, on this view, a war begun anywhere on the subcontinent was destined to spread. Therefore the new Germany had to be contained by a system of alliances – what, in effect, had heretofore been the policy of the French that the Russians had always condemned. France was by now courting the Russians for an alliance premised on the USSR's entry into the League of Nations in order to appease French allies in Eastern Europe, the so-called Little Entente: Poland, Czechoslovakia, Yugoslavia and Romania. Within the Comintern calls for a united riposte to German Fascism had begun to have some impact in Moscow, but dogma as well as the refusal to believe the German revolution was well and truly dead held up progress. And if France had turned to Russia for help, was not reliance on German nationalism paying off? The Leninist policy of

21 N. Komolova et al. (eds.), *Komintern protiv fashizma: dokumenty* (Moscow: Nauka, 1999), doc. 77.

22 Jonathan Haslam, *The Soviet Union and the Struggle for Collective Security in Europe, 1933–39* (London: Macmillan, 1984).

23 Letter from Piatnitskii to Stalin and Molotov, 26 July 1933, in Anderson and Chubar'ian, *Komintern i ideia*, doc. 82.

24 Observe the exchange of letters between Piatnitskii and Soviet leaders in late October: ibid., docs. 83–6.

exploiting contradictions between imperialist powers precluded alliances with them since by definition imperialism meant war. Within the rank and file of the Bolshevik Party opposition to accepting French entreaties was pressed on this basis. The issue came to turn on whether ideological principle or pragmatism should predominate in determining the future course of policy. Domestically ideology had triumphed, duly celebrated at the Seventeenth Party Congress in January 1934, though at a bloody price. Stalin could therefore now afford to accept a degree of ideological heresy abroad as well as at home, provided he could be assured that the Left would not reassert itself and once more accuse him of counter-revolution.

## The Popular Front against Fascism

Whereas the united front of working-class parties against a common enemy was well within Leninist doctrine, what came into being as the Popular Front bore no relationship at all to Leninist doctrine. This was partly as a result of accident. After his trial in Leipzig for setting fire to the Reichstag, which Dimitrov successfully exposed as a charade, the Bulgarian militant was evacuated to Moscow at Soviet behest. Here he used immediate access to Stalin to make the case for dropping the suicidal policy of opposing Social Democracy and for returning to the united front policy dropped in 1928, on the grounds that Fascism was a real danger to one and all. Having agreed to adopt the Litvinov line on collective security, it made little sense for the Kremlin to sustain a Comintern policy so at odds with common sense. Stalin moved cautiously, however, and only gave Dimitrov, now general secretary of the Comintern, freedom to experiment before any policy was finalised by a full Congress. In the teeth of resolute opposition from others within the Comintern apparat – head of the German section Knorin was still prattling on about 'The beginning of the crisis of German Fascism'[25] – and most probably also fundamentalists such as Molotov, who tended to a dogmatic vision on foreign affairs, Dimitrov began to loosen the reins and finally, in the summer of 1934, allowed member parties to open contacts with socialist parties along the lines of an anti-Fascist united front.[26]

25 Speech, 9 July 1934: ibid., doc. 90.
26 See Jonathan Haslam, 'The Comintern and the Origins of the Popular Front, 1934–1935', *Historical Journal* 22, 3 (1979): 673–91. For the core document on this new strategy, see Anderson and Chubar'ian *Komintern i ideia*, doc. 89. This can now also be read in English, with Stalin's comments inserted: A. Dallin and F. Firsov (eds.), *Dimitrov & Stalin 1934–1943: Letters from the Soviet Archives* (New Haven: Yale University Press, 2000), doc. 1.

France was on the front line against Fascism in 1934. The Great Depression hit France late but with as much force as elsewhere. Thus the French political system began to destabilise just as German power was effectively resurrected under Hitler. The initial testing ground for the united front was thus effectively France. Here, however, revolutionary tradition reached back much further than 1917; echoes of 1789, 1830, 1848 and, not least, 1871 still resounded through the capital. Complications lay in the fact that France was also the natural ally of Russia against any German plans for European conquest. How could the governing classes of France be expected to ally with a revolutionary power when they themselves so feared revolution at home from the very people in receipt of continual advice and subsidy from Moscow? The only hope lay in persuading Stalin that it was in Soviet interests not only to ally with France against Germany but also to nullify the effectiveness of the PCF in the domestic arena. The trouble was that Stalin trusted no one, and the PCF was so anti-military, because the French military was so anti-revolutionary, that this circle could not easily be squared.

It was surely because of the potential of France as an ally that Stalin permitted the PCF to go far beyond Comintern orthodoxy in declaring not merely for a united front of workers' parties against Fascism, but also a united front of all parties against Fascism: the so-called *Front Populaire*, declared by Maurice Thorez on 24 October 1934 at Nantes. Acting for the Comintern the Italian party leader Palmiro Togliatti and other comrades had tried to dissuade Thorez from delivering the speech, but to no avail.[27] In Moscow Thorez's call for unity with not only peasant parties but also, implicitly, the Roman Catholic Church and bourgeois parties against the common enemy created uproar within the Comintern. One of the most vigorous of several severe critics of the Comintern's new line was the Hungarian revolutionary, Béla Kun: once subject to Trotsky's caustic wit after a particularly nasty *ad hominem* outburst in the late 1920s – 'la maniera di Bela, non é una bella maniera', quipped the leader of the opposition. On 14 November 1934 Kun wrote a letter to members of the Comintern political secretariat condemning Thorez's position. He objected to the absence from Thorez's statements of any reference to the dictatorship of the proletariat and all power to the soviets in France. 'I once again point out the danger that the PCF is misrepresenting united front tactics. Turning them into a vulgar [coalition] policy, and I propose that such misrepresentation of the tactics of the united front be immediately refuted by a detailed rebuttal.'[28]

27 Haslam, 'The Comintern and the Origins', pp. 688–9.
28 Letter to the political secretariat of the Comintern executive committee, 14 Nov. 1934: Anderson and Chubar'ian *Komintern i ideia*, doc. 211.

The fact that no such rebuttal was issued meant that Thorez read the runes in Moscow better than Kun. And in late July 1935 the Seventh Congress of the Comintern placed a firm seal of approval on the entire venture by generalising it across the world movement.

## The anti-Japanese front

The Popular Front against Fascism, as we have seen, had indigenous roots and did not result merely from instructions issued in Moscow. The Anti-Imperialist Front in the East, however, fits more closely the preconceived pattern of Moscow dictating policy. Yet its implementation, at the hands of Mao Zedung, actually meant that while the letter of policy was observed, the spirit was broken with such consistency that the results Stalin desired – a solid anti-Japanese front – were never forthcoming. This mattered, because although France had reluctantly agreed a mutual assistance pact, it precluded – at French insistence – any undertaking with respect to the Far East. Moscow's concern was quite clearly lest the threat from the East joined the threat from the West. And Stalin well knew that Poland and Finland both had military contacts with Japan. The prospect of creating a firm united front on the ground in China against the Japanese was therefore high priority as compensation for the lack of alliances in the region to secure Siberia from Japanese attack. The most Litvinov had been able to secure from the United States had been diplomatic recognition (1933); any talk of an anti-Japanese alliance was firmly quashed by President Roosevelt. The underlying contradiction in outlook between Moscow and China remained, however: Stalin saw the best hope in a bourgeois anti-imperialist China led by a coalition including a minority of Communists, who had no immediate hope of a workers' revolution in a peasant country; Mao, undeterred by Moscow preferences and prejudices, and too distant for any sustained exertion of Comintern discipline, was looking for a fully-fledged Communist revolution via the peasantry.

The Japanese invasion of Manchuria from 18 September 1931 had long necessitated the unification of resistance in victim China. But the CCP and the Guomindang had long resisted any attempt to draw them back into alliance, not least because of the disastrous experience of the 1920s. Moscow had one major instrument at its disposal – the supply of munitions. The problem was to ensure that these, sent to the Guomindang as the recognised government of China, were used against Japan and not against the CCP. Only an optimist could take a generous view of Chiang Kai-shek. From 1934 to 1935 the Chinese Communists sought escape from encirclement and destruction by the Guomindang through a long march to the north-west of China, an area distant from Chiang's deadly reach and much closer to potential Soviet support from Outer Mongolia. Not surprisingly, therefore, even Stalin's pet Chinese Communist Wang Ming (Chen Shaoyu) had held common cause with Dimitrov's opponents and spoke at the Comintern Congress of Chiang as one of the 'traitors of the nation' – not an encouraging indicator for the prospects of a united front against Japanese imperialism.[29] Mao was still out of reach. Radio contact was not re-established with Moscow until the onset of winter and even then the CCP still lacked reliable codes for transmission. With the party at Wayaobao in northern Shaanxi province, emissaries flew in from Moscow with news of the Comintern Congress and its decisions.[30]

When Chiang came shopping for arms from Moscow, the Russians insisted that agreement must be reached with the Communists for an anti-Japanese front.[31] The Comintern simultaneously now emphasised the need to include Chiang in any united front.[32] But Mao held out against implementing the spirit of the new line and this state of affairs continued even as the Soviet ambassador to the Chiang regime pressed for what amounted to total subjugation of the Chinese Communists to the Guomindang.[33] The signing of the German–Japanese anti-Comintern pact on 25 November 1936, effectively an anti-Soviet alliance, represented precisely the danger Moscow had long feared. Yet CCP policy was to 'force the Guomindang Nanzhing Government and its army to take part in a war of resistance against Japan'.[34] The effective result that December was Chiang's kidnapping in Xian by warlord of Manchuria Zhang Xueliang – then under the influence of pro-Communist advice. 'Some comrades', former CCP Politburo member Zhang Guotao later reported, 'were opposed to a peaceful settlement of the Incident.'[35] The urge on the part of the Communists to do away with their hated enemy had to be restrained. 'When Chou En-lai first came to Sian', Chang's main adviser is quoted as having said, 'he wanted a people's assembly to try Chiang Kai-shek, but a wire came from the Comintern and Chou changed his mind'.[36]

At Moscow's insistence Chiang was permitted to negotiate his freedom, having made some concession to the need for a united front. These concessions remained mere verbiage, however, until 7 July 1937 when the Japanese finally embarked on all-out war across the face of China. Chiang Kai-shek

---

29 Jonathan Haslam, *The Soviet Union and the Threat from the East, 1933–41* (London: Macmillan, 1992), p. 59.
30 Ibid., p. 65.   31 Ibid., pp. 63–4.   32 Ibid., pp. 64–5.
33 Ibid., pp. 68–9.   34 Ibid., p. 78.   35 Ibid., p. 83.
36 This was heard by Nym Wales, wife of intrepid American journalist Edgar Snow.

immediately pressed the Russians to come to his aid. Stalin was not in any haste to oblige. The month before, in an act of supreme folly borne of deep-seated insecurity, Stalin had the cream of his most senior officers shot, though it is interesting that he avoided decapitating the Far Eastern army until later. By the end of August, however, he was persuaded into conceding the Chinese 200 planes and 200 tanks on the basis of $500 million in credit. But getting the equipment into China was no easy task. Planes came in via Xinjiang and Outer Mongolia. Otherwise armaments had to come by sea until the French closed the routes through Indochina, or via a perilous 3,000-mile journey to Lanzhou by road from the end of the Turksib railway.[37] Thus between 1937 and 1941 Chiang received a total of 904 planes, nearly half of which were bombers, but only 82 tanks and a mass of automobiles, heavy and light arms, plus thousands of bombs and some 2 million shells.[38] In May 1938 Deputy Commissar Vladimir Potemkin told the French ambassador that the Soviet government was 'counting on resistance by this country for several years, after which Japan will be too enfeebled to be capable of attacking the USSR'.[39]

In fact more was needed. Collisions between the Red Army and Japanese forces in the summer of that year showed worrying weaknesses in Soviet military capabilities. And not until September 1939 did the Russians, in this case under the command of the ruthless and efficient Georgii Zhukov, overwhelm the Japanese and teach them a lesson they would not soon forget – at the Battle of Khalkhin-Gol on the frontiers of Mongolia. But more important still was the fact that the Russians had retreated from the emerging war in Europe. The Nazi–Soviet pact, to which Hitler had agreed without consulting Japan, came as a grievous blow to Japanese aspirations of forcing the Russians to fight a two-front war. This failure of co-ordination between East and West was vital to Soviet survival, not only between 1939 and 1941, but even more after Hitler decided on war with Russia.

## The Popular Front collapses, 1939

The Popular Front strategy, along with its siamese twin Collective Security, could last only as long as it served Stalin's purpose. The failure to form an effective ring around Nazi Germany highlighted the need to come to terms and drop the distinction hard won by Litvinov between democratic and non-democratic capitalist states. The brutal manner in which the Soviet Union was deliberately kept out of the solution to the crisis over Czechoslovakia by Prime

37 Haslam, *The Soviet Union and the Threat*, pp. 92–3.  38 Ibid., p. 94.  39 Ibid., p. 94.

Minister Neville Chamberlain in September 1938 marked the low point of trust between Moscow and the democracies. Similarly the collapse of Soviet efforts to sustain the Popular Front government in Spain, which received substantial military aid in both men and munitions despite adverse logistical difficulties, spelt the collapse of a policy intended to contain Fascism by other means. No longer would Moscow act to preserve the territorial status quo in Europe created by the Versailles Treaty system. As late as 9 July 1939 Stalin told Chiang Kai-shek that a 'satisfactory result' was not impossible in the negotiations with Britain and France.[40] But Stalin's price was the de facto reabsorption of the Baltic states as protectorates, with a fate not much different for Poland, and that meant the expansion of Soviet power to the West, something Chamberlain feared even more than the Germans. Impatient at the lack of seriousness with which the British approached alliance negotiations with the Soviet Union and ever suspicious that these negotiations were merely there to enhance London's bargaining power vis-à-vis Germany, Stalin cut his losses and signed up with Hitler.

The Nazi–Soviet Non-Aggression Pact signed on 23–4 August 1939 contained within it a secret protocol allowing for the partition of Poland and the Baltic states. This was a tragedy for the victim states. More important for the fate of the world, however, were the assumptions underlying the agreement, which Litvinov, for one – forced into premature retirement in May – considered entirely misconceived. Overestimating British and French power and underestimating that of the Germans, Stalin saw the pact as a means of throwing the entire capitalist world into confusion, from which the Soviet Union would draw unilateral long-term advantage, extending its territory and expanding the reach of socialism at one stroke. 'The extinction of this state [Poland]', Stalin said, 'in current conditions would mean one bourgeois Fascist state less! What would be so bad about extending the socialist system to new territories and populations as a result of the defeat of Poland.'[41] Indeed, Stalin's acts attracted unwanted and backhanded congratulations from Leon Trotsky in his place of exile. He unflatteringly compared the role of Stalin to that of Napoleon: though exterminating the revolution at home, he was obliged to spread it abroad.[42]

---

40 Chiang Kai-shek, *A Summing-up at Seventy: Soviet Russia in China* (London: Harrap, 1957), p. 89.

41 F. Firsov, 'Komintern: opyt, traditsii, uroki – nereshennye zadachi issledovaniia', in *Komintern: opyt, traditsii, uroki. Materialy nauchnoi konferentsii, posviashchennoi 70-letiiu Kommunisticheskogo Internatsionala* (Moscow: Nauka, 1989), pp. 21–2.

42 'SSSR v Voine', *Biulleten' Oppozitsii* (25 Sept. 1939): 79–80.

In an extraordinary outburst that echoed the unreal hopes of 1932–3, which had also led to disaster, Stalin commented thus on Germany and the Allies: 'We would not mind if they got into a good fight and weakened one another,' he said. 'It would be no bad thing if the position of the richest capitalist Powers (particularly England) was shattered at the hands of Germany. Hitler, without understanding or wishing for this, is shattering and blowing up the capitalist system.' The implications for Comintern policy were clear. Before the war, a contradistinction between Fascist and democratic regimes was correct. But, 'At a time of war between the imperialist Powers [it] would no longer be correct. Distinguishing between Fascist and democratic capitalist countries has lost its former significance.'[43] Thus the role now ascribed to the Communist parties in Europe and the United States was to oppose the war.

Nothing could have undermined their strenuous efforts to identify more closely with the nation than this. From the time the instructions went out, fraternal parties conducted a policy of defeatism that undermined the national war effort and made it that much easier for Hitler to conquer the greater part of the subcontinent. Anxious at the speed of the Wehrmacht progress, on 17 September Stalin invaded Poland in haste to meet the incoming German troops. Large numbers of senior Polish officers and other members of the elite were captured; a substantial number were then ordered to be shot by the Politburo on 5 March 1940.[44] Poland out of the way, Stalin moved to force the Baltic states to heel and, with the signature of the Friendship Pact with Berlin at the end of September he included Lithuania in with Latvia and Estonia as new Soviet protectorates. The blunt refusal of Social Democratic Finland to submit then resulted in war on 30 November, a conflict brought to an end after great cost only in March 1940. And by then Hitler was on the way to the total domination of Western Europe.

Stalin believed the Nazi–Soviet agreements had bought the Soviet government time both to expand and to prepare against the eventuality of a German attack. 'A German attack is also possible', he told the Letts. 'For six years German fascists and the communists cursed each other. Now an unexpected turn took place; that happens in the course of history. But one cannot rely upon it. We must be prepared in time. Others who were not ready paid the price'.[45] But Stalin badly miscalculated the speed of the German advance and

43 Firsov, *Komintern: opyt*, p. 21.
44 Excerpt from the minutes of the Politburo, 5 Mar. 1940: S. Stepashin et al. (ed.), *Organy Gosudarstvennoi Bezopasnosti SSSR v Velikoi Otechestvennoi Voine – Sbornik dokumentov*, vol. 1 (Moscow: Kniga i biznes, 1995), doc. 71.
45 Report from Munters, 2 Oct. 1939: A Bilmanis (ed.), *Latvian–Russian Relations: Documents* (Washington, D.C.: Latvian Delegation, 1944), p. 196.

failed to anticipate, as did most others, the rapid collapse of France. The key to sustaining a balance against Germany was French survival. Stalin was caught off guard because his own evaluation of both Britain and France seriously over-estimated their power as against that of Germany. The reigning assessment of the balance of forces suggested stalemate rather than the victory of the Blitzkrieg.

On 9 April 1940 the Germans invaded Denmark and Norway. The Soviet leadership were evidently baffled by this unexpected turn of events. Voroshilov spoke of the international situation being 'extremely muddled' and called for vigilance.[46] Three days later, on 7 May the Soviet government re-established the ranks of General and Admiral. On 10 May the Germans attacked Belgium and the Netherlands. The only good news for the Russians was the resignation of the hated Neville Chamberlain and the reassuring reappearance of Winston Churchill, bent on defeating Hitler. On 14 May Holland surrendered and three days later German troops were taking possession of Brussels. Soon British and French forces evacuated Norway, giving way to German occupation on 10 June. Now the French capital itself lay in imminent danger. Initially, in September 1939, the PCF was strongly instructed to oppose the war for fear that Britain and France would win. Now it was instructed to sustain its opposition for fear of offending the Germans. At the very last minute, on 10 June, Comintern leaders Dimitrov and Manuil'skii sent a text drafted by the leaders of the PCF to Stalin with a request for advice. The draft declaration, though loaded with vituperative denunciation for the leaders of France, the capitalist system, the leaders of the French Socialists and avoiding any mention of Germany (!), ended with what effectively amounted to a call to arms to forestall 'capitulation'.[47] For good measure it was also sent to Molotov. Finally, on 13 June, permission came through for acting upon it and the Comintern secretariat formally approved the dispatch of appropriate instructions.[48] But on the following day German troops entered Paris and on 15 June the secretariat reported that it would not be appropriate to publish the declaration.[49]

Reflecting the abysmal level of defeatism signalled after the surrender was taken on 22 June, the egregious Jacques Duclos, leading the PCF on the ground in Paris, then made moves parallel to the capitulationism of Pétain by attempt-ing to secure Nazi co-operation for party publications and activities. Finally Moscow took fright and issued orders to desist. But it does indicate just how

---

46 *Izvestiia*, 4 May 1940.

47 From the Comintern archives: N. Lebedeva and M. Narinskii (eds.), *Komintern i vtoraia mirovaia voina*, vol. 1 (Moscow: Nauka, 1994), doc. 98.

48 Ibid., doc. 99.    49 Ibid., n. 1. p. 358.

disoriented the entire international Communist movement had become in the face of Moscow's irresolution that the most important party in Western Europe should have descended to such depths.

Stalin's mind was, of course, elsewhere and in some degree of panic. In mid-June he was talked into offering an olive branch to Britain, much against his own inclination. Andrew Rothstein, a leading Stalinist in the British Communist Party, informed the Foreign Office that the Russians wanted Prime Minister Churchill to meet Ambassador Ivan Maiskii for a 'frank discussion'. In passing on this request, Rothstein confessed that the fall of France came as 'something of a surprise, even to the Moscow realists'. He also noted that the takeover of the Baltic and the mobilisation of Soviet troops along the Polish frontier would not please Berlin. The time was ripe, he concluded, for an improvement in relations between London and Moscow.[50] But since Sir Stafford Cripps had already been sent to Moscow to improve relations but had yet to see Stalin, none of this really seemed at all convincing. Clearly something of a vacuum had opened up in Moscow, and Stalin was procrastinating, as he often did when faced with key decisions, allowing others to propose alternatives, until events finally forced a decision upon him.

Meanwhile, as a precautionary measure Russian troops speedily occupied the Baltic states from 17 to 21 June and on 26 June the Supreme Soviet prohibited citizens from leaving their jobs, and imposed a seven-day working week with an eight-hour working day. Then on 28–30 June Stalin took Bessarabia and Northern Bukovina from Romania by force, eventually setting up the bastard republic of Moldavia on 2 August. The Soviet Union now held the Baltic and had a toe-hold in the Balkans, much to Hitler's personal irritation (in reaction on 5 August he issued the first draft plan for the invasion of the Soviet Union).

The key issue, however, was whether Britain would hold out when Operation Sea Lion was launched by Hitler for the invasion of the home islands on 16 July. An article by Eugene Varga, head of the Institute of Global Economics and International Relations (IMEMO) caught the prevalent mood in Moscow:

> We will not be so bold as to give a final prognosis; but it seems to us that from the point of view of purely military possibilities – with aid in only supplies from the USA – England could still continue the war. However, the political side to the question is decisive: is the English ruling class in actual fact determined to conduct the struggle to the end to win or perish?

---

50 G. Gorodetsky, *Stafford Cripps' Mission to Moscow, 1940–42* (Cambridge: Cambridge University Press, 1984), p. 49.

Varga noted there were two camps in London – one for peace; the other for war: 'The scant information available to us now about what is going on in England does not enable us to judge which of these two tendencies is the stronger.'[51] Events answered that question when Churchill rebuffed Hitler's offer of negotiations. A further article that went to press on 24 October argued that the United States would enter the war.[52] The Kremlin was thus deluded, despite a raft of intelligence warnings, that it was safe while Britain remained undefeated. Hitler had in *Mein Kampf* criticised his predecessors for fighting simultaneously on two fronts and gave every indication that he would not repeat that fatal error. Furthermore, on returning from Moscow at the beginning of January 1941 the Soviet military attaché in Paris indicated that 'it was no longer believed in Moscow that the Axis Powers could deliver a definitive victory against Great Britain. There is also scepticism of the possibility of a devastating victory by Great Britain . . . The opinion most widespread in Moscow is that the war must end in a compromise peace acceptable to the British empire and limiting the advantages and the preponderance in Europe that the Reich has conquered.' The notion therefore was that the Soviet Union would not intervene until peace negotiations opened and then it would do so with military power to back up its position.[53] German disinformation conveyed to agents in Berlin trusted by the Russians also played its part. One instance was the dispatch from Berlin on 24 April indicating that the Germans had dropped the idea of going against Russia and were going to focus on pushing the British out of the Middle East.[54]

German troops entered Romania on 12 October 1940 and on 28 October the Italians invaded Greece. The Balkans were now engulfed in war. Molotov's visit to Berlin on 12 November to sort out the state of relations with Hitler personally gave the Russians the impression that the Germans were still committed to the defeat of Britain. Yet little more than a month later, on 18 December, Hitler signed Directive 21, Barbarossa, for the invasion of the Soviet Union. But Moscow continued firmly in the belief that any talk of Germany aiming to attack Russia was merely a smokescreen or an attempt to bluff the Kremlin into conceding some of its territorial gains. And the more the British attempted

51 *Mirovoe khoziaistvo i mirovaia politika* 6 (1940).
52 *Mirovoe khoziaistvo i mirovaia politika* 9 (1940).
53 Report dated 3 June 1941: France, *Ministère des Affaires Etrangères, Archives*. Série Guerre 1939–1945, Vichy Europe. 834. URSS.
54 A. P. Belozerov et al. (eds.), *Sekrety Gitlera na stole u Stalina – Razvedka i kontrrazvedka o podgotovke germanskoi agressii protiv SSSR, mart–iiun 1941g: Dokumenty iz Tsentral'nogo arkhiva FSB Rossii* (Moscow: Mosgorarkhiv, 1995), pp. 35–7.

to persuade the Russians otherwise, the more firmly Stalin and Molotov clung to that conclusion. The signing of a Neutrality Pact with Japan on 13 April also indicated Soviet confidence, because the Russians had turned down a non-aggression pact that the Japanese had been seeking for over a year, evidently believing that no such agreement (which would foreshorten the option of war with Japan) was necessary.[55]

The flight to Britain of Hitler's deputy Rudolf Hess made matters worse. Prior to his arrival and in some desperation, British Ambassador Sir Stafford Cripps recommended a strategy to London that ultimately proved disastrous, because the Russians were reading his mail. His attempts to persuade Stalin that a German invasion was inevitable had come to nothing. The only 'counter-weight', he noted, 'is the fear that we may conclude a separate peace on the basis of a German withdrawal from occupied territories of Western Europe and a free hand for Hitler in the East . . .' 'I realise of course', he continued, 'that this is a most delicate matter to be handled through round about channels. Nevertheless I consider it our most valuable card in a very difficult hand and I trust some means may be found of playing it. Soviet talent for acquiring information through illicit channels might surely for once be turned to our account.'[56]

Hess arrived by plane in Scotland on 10 May. When news of his arrival reached Moscow via Kim Philby, then spying for the Russians within the heart of Whitehall, Stalin demanded to know what peace terms had accompanied him. At the Foreign Office Deputy Secretary Orme Sargent expressed the 'wish we could get out of the Hess incident some material which Sir Stafford Cripps could use on the Soviet Government'.[57] Philby, after some anxious investigation, concluded that 'now the time for peace negotiations has not yet arrived, but in the process of the future development of the war Hess will possibly become the centre of intrigues for the conclusion of a compromise peace and will be useful for the peace party in England and for Hitler'.[58] Sargent did not immediately recommend adoption of the Cripps proposal, but before the end of May he did recommend a variation of it, to be delivered as a 'whisper'. The line was 'to give some assurance to the Soviet Government that they need not buy off Germany with a new and unfavourable agreement because there

55 Haslam, *The Soviet Union and the Threat*, ch. 6.
56 Cripps (Moscow) to London, 23 Apr. 1941: *Foreign Office Archives* (Public Record Office, Kew): FO 371/29480.
57 Comment by Sargent dated 14 May 1941 on Cripps (Moscow) to London, 13 May 1941: ibid., FO 371/29481.
58 From KGB archives: O. Tsarev, 'Iz arkhivov KGB SSSR: Poslednii polet "chernoi berty" ', *Trud*, 13 May 1990.

is clear evidence that Germany does not intend to embark on a war with the Soviet Union in present circumstances'.[59] Cripps's proposal and Sargent's comments were precisely the confirmation that Stalin needed to demonstrate that all talk of a German invasion had been merely a British plot and that, having found out that it no longer served its purpose, London had reversed its line. Thus it was that on 22 June the Soviet government was caught unawares when Hitler attacked. The full consequences of Stalin's misjudgement were to be felt for a long time to come. The tragedy went further than the massive loss of life entailed. The very suspicions that had given rise to the mistake were to multiply as the war proceeded and would lead to the very situation Neville Chamberlain once feared and Churchill hoped would never come to pass: the emergence of Soviet Russia as a mighty power determined to hold the balance of Europe in its own hands. This was not the first time and certainly not the last when Western ignorance of the Soviet Union inadvertently combined with deep-seated Russian suspicions to wreak havoc with a relationship that had never been good.

59 Sargent's comment of 30 May 1941 on Cripps (Moscow) to London, 27 May 1941: Public Record Office, FO 371/29481. The fact that these documents were not declassified under the thirty-year rule but fifty years later indicates that the usual excuse of 'security' is utter nonsense. These materials were retained evidently to save the Foreign Office embarrassment at such monumental incompetence.

# 24

# Moscow's foreign policy, 1945–2000: identities, institutions and interests

## TED HOPF

'A great power has no permanent friends, just permanent interests', an oft-heard aphorism about international politics, assumes these interests are obvious. In Britain's case it was to prevent the domination of continental Europe. For Great Powers in general, it has been to maintain a balance against emerging hegemonic threats, such as Napoleonic France, Hitler's Germany or the post-war Soviet Union.

Advising states to balance against power, the aphorism also warns against treating other states as natural allies, as an enemy today might be a friend tomorrow, as Britain found with the Soviet Union in June 1941. But aphorisms are rarely more than half-truths. States' interests are no more permanent than their allies or enemies. Threats and interests are not obvious or objective. There is nothing about French and British nuclear weapons that make them objectively less threatening to the United States than Chinese warheads.

How, then, does a state become a threat? Realism tells us that power threatens. No Great Power feels threatened by Togo. But power is only necessary, not sufficient, to threaten. Britain, the Soviet Union, the United States and France did not balance against Hitler's Germany before the Second World War. Britain and France did not balance against the United States after the Second World War. Britain, France, China and Russia have not balanced against the United States since the end of the Cold War.

The meaning of power is not given; it is interpreted. Threats are the social constructions of states. States construct threats both by interacting with other states and their own societies.[1] For example, France could have learned that Soviet power was more dangerous than Nazi Germany's through its interactions with Moscow. But France may have felt more threatened by the Soviet Union than Germany because French understanding of itself as a bourgeois

---

[1] For systemic constructivism, see Alexander Wendt, *Social Theory of International Politics* (Cambridge: Cambridge University Press, 1999).

liberal capitalist state made the Communist Soviet Union more dangerous than Fascist Germany.

I explore Moscow's relations with Eastern Europe, China, Western Europe, the decolonising world and the United States (US) since 1945 from the perspective of Soviet and Russian identity relations with these states. Six different identities have predominated in Moscow since the Second World War:

- 1945–7, Soviet Union as part of a Great Power condominium
- 1947–53, Soviet Union within capitalist encirclement
- 1953–6, Soviet Union as natural ally
- 1956–85, Soviet Union as the other superpower
- 1985–91, Soviet Union as normal Great Power in international society
- 1992–2000 Russia as European Great Power

Each of these identities has its roots in the relationship between the state and society.

## Post-war ambiguity, 1945–7

The re-establishment of an orthodox Stalinist identity for the Soviet Union took only eighteen months. From September 1945 to June 1947 uncertainty about Soviet identity was replaced by a strict binary: the New Soviet Man (NSM) and its dangerous deviant Other. The NSM was an ultra-modern, supranational, secular carrier of working-class consciousness. The formal declaration of the triumph of orthodoxy over difference was Andrei Zhdanov's August 1946 speech declaiming authors who offered a 'false, distorted depiction of the Soviet people', that is, who did not write as if the NSM was reality.

*Zhdanovshchina* began with the closure of the literary journals *Zvezda* and *Leningrad* and the expulsion of Anna Akhmatova and Mikhail Zoshchenko from the Writers' Union.[2] A connection was drawn between these deviations and the imperialist threat to the existence of socialism. This was not a wholly imagined danger. Reports from local Ministry of State Security (MGB) and oblast committee (obkom) secretaries to their superiors in Moscow told of widespread rumours among the peasantry that Britain and the United States were threatening to use military force to coerce Stalin to disband collective

---

2 Leonid Mlechin, *MID: Ministerstvo Inostrannykh Del* (Moscow: Tsentrpoligraf, 2001), p. 316. See also Aleksandr A. Danilov and Aleksandr V. Pyzhikov, *Rozhdenie sverkhderzhavy: SSSR v pervye poslevoennye gody* (Moscow: ROSSPEN, 2001).

farms.[3] Meanwhile, the US and Britain were providing military aid to anti-Soviet guerrillas in Poland, Western Ukraine and the Baltic republics, and this was known to Stalin.[4]

The level of danger was tied to parlous economic conditions. As early as September 1945, workers demonstrated at defence plants in the Urals and Siberia. Crime, especially the theft of food, soared. Best estimates are that 100 million Soviets suffered from malnutrition in 1946–7, and 2 million died of starvation from 1946 to 1948. There was no soap or winter clothing. Local party committees cancelled the 7 November 1946 celebration of the Bolshevik revolution, realising people would freeze to death without adequate clothing.[5]

Stalinism itself was the primary institutional carrier of the NSM. All instruments of the party and state both policed Soviet society for deviance and saturated the public space with the dominant discourse. But a peculiar foreign policy institution operated, too. Many post-war East European Communist Party elites had spent the war in the Soviet Union and had formed close ties with Soviet party elites. The latter had their favourites among these allies, and the former curried favour in the Kremlin by energetically fulfilling Soviet wishes in their own countries. Indeed, foreign Communists competed to demonstrate their obedience. This relationship was an institutional route for Moscow's influence in Eastern Europe. East European Communist leaders, identified with Moscow, were often hostage to Soviet elite politics; leadership manoeuvrings in the Kremlin reverberated throughout the alliance in Eastern Europe.[6]

There was a certain 'Frankenstein effect' at work. Eastern European Communists who had remained in Moscow had become more 'orthodox than the Patriarch'. Soviet leaders faced demands from their allies to support more radical Stalinisation than Moscow itself was imagining. In May 1945 Finnish Communists petitioned Moscow to make Finland a Soviet Republic! Zhdanov replied by advising them to become a parliamentary party in coalition with

3 E. Iu. Zubkova, 'Stalin i obshchestvennoe mnenie v SSSR, 1945–1953', in I. V. Gaiduk, N. I. Egorova and A. O. Chubar'ian (eds.), *Stalinskoe desiatiletie kholodnoi voiny: Fakty i gipotezy* (Moscow: Nauka, 1999), pp. 152–62.

4 William Taubman, *Khrushchev: The Man and his Era* (New York: Norton, 2003), p. 197.

5 Elena Zubkova, *Russia after the War* (Armonk, N.Y.: M. E. Sharpe, 1998), pp. 36–49. See also Danilov and Pyzhikov, *Rozhdenie sverkhderzhavy*, pp. 120–32.

6 For Poland, see I. S. Iazhborovskaia, 'Vovlechenie Pol'shi v Stalinskuiu blokovuiu politiku: problemy i metody davleniia na pol'skoe rukovodstvo, 1940-e gody', in A. O. Chubar'ian (ed.), *Stalin i kholodnaia voina* (Moscow: In-t vseobshchei istorii RAN, 1997), pp. 84–101. On Germany, see Norman N. Naimark, *The Russians in Germany* (Cambridge, Mass.: Belknap Press of Harvard University Press, 1995). See also G. P. Murashko and A. F. Noskova, 'Institut Sovetskikh sovetnikov v strankh regiona: tseli, zadachi, rezul'taty', in T. V. Volokitina et al., *Moskva i vostochnaia Evropa. Stanovlenie politicheskikh rezhimov sovetskogo tipa (1949–1953). Ocherki istorii* (Moscow: ROSSPEN, 2002), pp. 645–9.

others in Finland.[7] Soviet leaders reined in their allies. As Stalin told the Czech leader Klement Gottwald in the summer of 1946, 'the Red Army has already paid the price for you. You can avoid establishing a dictatorship of the proletariat of the Soviet type.'[8]

Soviet foreign policy correlates with the evolution of Soviet identity at home. An initial expectation of Great Power condominium rapidly gave way to a binarised conflict with former allies. On 10 January 1944 Maksim Litvinov and Ivan Maiskii gave Molotov a memorandum about the post-war world, in which the world was divided largely between the United States and the Soviet Union, the latter having indirect control over much of Europe.[9] Even as late as November 1946, and from the Soviet leader most closely associated with the division of the world into 'two camps', Zhdanov, there were calls for maintenance of this coalition.

The partially pluralist domestic scene was reflected in Soviet views of the imperialist world as differentiated. In Lenin's contribution to international relations theory, 'Imperialism, the Highest Stage of Capitalism', wars among imperialist powers are inevitable, since they will compete over global resources.[10] The Second World War apparently having validated this theory, Stalin expected differences between Britain and the US after the war, but he was disappointed by British agreement to US policies on Turkey and Iran, and the Truman Doctrine, which assumed British obligations 'east of Suez'. The Marshall Plan, announced only three months after the Truman Doctrine was promulgated, struck Stalin as an effective effort by the US to establish its hegemony over all of Europe, hence muting any differences between Europe and the US, and threatening Stalin's more coercive forms of control. Just as Stalinist society was becoming binarised, so too was international society.

Regimes which had been discouraged from Stalinising were now deemed insufficiently 'friendly' to the Soviet Union. East European publics were turning against their Soviet occupiers and those they perceived as Moscow's local

7 G. P. Murashko and A. F. Noskova, 'Sovetskii faktor v poslevoennoi vostochnoi evrope (1945–1948)', in L. N. Nezhinskii (ed.), *Sovetskaia vneshnaia politika v gody 'Kholodnoi Voiny' (1945–1985)* (Moscow: Mezhdunarodnye otnosheniia, 1995), p. 90. On Hungary, see Volokitina, 'Istochniki formirovaniia partiino-gosudarstvennoi nomenklatury – novogo praviashchego sloia', in Volokitina et al., *Moskva i vostochnaia evropa*, pp. 103–38.
8 Ibid., p. 90. On Poland, see Volokitina, 'Stalin i smena strategicheskogo kursa kremlia v kontse 40-x godov', in Gaiduk, Egorova and Chubar'ian, *Stalinskoe desiatiletie*, p. 14. See also Grant M. Adibekov, *Kominform i poslevoennaia evropa* (Moscow: Rossiia molodaia, 1994), p. 93 and Volokitina, 'Nakanune: novye realii v mezhdunarodnykh otnosheniakh na kontinente v kontse 40-x godov i otvet Moskvy', in Volokitina et al., *Moskva i vostochnaia evropa*, pp. 36–8.
9 Volokitina, 'Nakanune: novye realii', p. 29.
10 Robert Tucker (ed.), *The Lenin Anthology* (New York: Norton, 1975).

agents.[11] The NSM must be replicated in Eastern Europe. The 'peaceful path' to socialism had come to nothing in France, Italy and Finland; and the civil war had been lost in Greece.[12] By the middle of 1947, Molotov and Zhdanov were advising allies in Eastern Europe to 'strengthen the class struggle', that is, stamp out difference that could become dangerous deviation, entailing a turn towards imperialism.[13]

On 5 June 1947 US Secretary of State George Marshall outlined the European Recovery Program. Just two days before the Paris meeting on the plan was to commence, Soviet ambassadors in Eastern Europe delivered the message from Moscow demanding its allies stay away from Paris.[14] If in 1945 and 1946, Soviet embassies in Eastern Europe had active contacts with non-Communist political parties, then by the second half of 1947, these had all but stopped, and completely ended by 1948. Election results in Poland, Romania and Hungary in 1947 were openly falsified. All police forces in Eastern Europe slipped under the control of Moscow's Communist allies. In September 1947, the Cominform was established, an international institution designed to ensure conformity with the Soviet model.[15]

How to explain the self-defeating policies of Stalin in Eastern Europe? Self-defeating in the near term, as they accelerated Western unity before an apparent Soviet threat; in the medium term, as popular support for its allies was very thin; and in the long term, as the Soviet-subsidised alliance stood as evidence of Soviet expansionism. At Yalta in February 1945 Stalin, Churchill and Roosevelt agreed that East European governments should be 'free, and friendly towards the Soviet Union'. This was an oxymoron. Freely elected governments would not choose friendship with Moscow and Moscow's idea of friendship necessitated forms of government that were not free. Some twenty-five years after Yalta, Molotov reminisced that Poland should have been 'independent, but not hostile. But they tried to impose a bourgeois government, which *naturally* would have been an agent of imperialism and hostile towards the Soviet Union'.[16]

---

11 Volokitina, 'Nakanune: novye realii', p. 53; and Volokitina, Murashko and Noskova, 'K chitateliu', in Volokitina et al., *Moskva i vostochnaia evropa*, p. 20.
12 Murashko and Noskova, 'Sovetskii faktor', p. 92.
13 Volokitina, 'Stalin i smena strategicheskogo kursa', p. 17. The authors identify the period from 1945 to 1947 as a time of tolerance of difference. Volokitina et al., *Moskva i vostochnaia evropa*.
14 Danilov and Pyzhikov, *Rozhdenie sverkhderzhavy*, pp. 45–9.
15 Vladislav Zubok and Constantine Pleshakov, *Inside the Kremlin's Cold War* (Cambridge, Mass.: Harvard University Press, 1996), p. 110.
16 Felix Chuev, *Molotov Remembers: Inside Kremlin Politics* (Chicago: I. R. Dee, 1993), p. 54.

Here is captured the connection between the NSM, fear of difference, and Soviet foreign policy. Stalinist identity politics implied that any non-socialist government in Eastern Europe would be naturally hostile to the Soviet Union *and* an ally of the most hostile imperialist Other – the US. Just as the bourgeoisie or landlords at home were dangerous deviants allied with foreign capitalists, so too any deviant governments in Eastern Europe. As Soviet fear of difference becoming bourgeois degeneration increased at home, fears of the threat from the US correspondingly increased, and then so too did the belief that allies must be as similar to the NSM as possible. This helps explain the connection between orthodoxy at home, increased threat abroad and increasing demands on allies in Eastern Europe to become more Stalinist.[17]

The mixed Soviet strategy of formal co-operation with its wartime allies and sympathy for the emergence of new socialist allies abroad was evident in policy towards the Chinese civil war.[18] In August 1945, Moscow signed a treaty of friendship and alliance with Chiang Kai-shek's nationalist Chinese against Japan. This was the legal foundation for the presence of Soviet forces in Port Arthur and Dalian, gave Moscow control over Manchurian railroads and gave Outer Mongolia independence. Soviet military aid to Mao's army in and through Manchuria did not end, however, and when Soviet forces withdrew from China in the spring of 1946, they left this territory to Mao's forces. As late as April 1947 Molotov was assuring Secretary of State Marshall of a continued Soviet commitment to the August 1945 agreement with the Guomindang.[19] But by October 1947, the Soviet Union transferred to the Red Army enough materiel to equip 600,000 soldiers.[20] Stalin later admitted to the Yugoslav Communist Miloslav Djilas that he had mistakenly advised Mao to continue co-operating with Chiang Kai-shek, rather than push for armed victory.[21]

## Stalinism's two camps at home and abroad, 1947–53

The dangerous deviants in these last years of high Stalinism – slavish worshippers of all things Western, rootless cosmopolitans and wreckers and

17 For Germany, see Naimark, *The Russians in Germany*.
18 Niu Jun, 'The Origins of the Sino-Soviet Alliance', in O. A. Westad (ed.), *Brothers in Arms: The Rise and Fall of the Sino-Soviet Alliance, 1945–1963* (Stanford, Calif.: Stanford University Press, 1998), pp. 52–60.
19 Ibid., p. 61.
20 Sergei N. Goncharov, John W. Lewis and Xue Litai, *Uncertain Partners: Stalin, Mao, and the Korean War* (Stanford, Calif.: Stanford University Press, 1993), pp. 14, 74.
21 Ibid., p. 24.

saboteurs – shared one feature. They were all accomplices of the West in overthrowing socialism in the Soviet Union. *Zhdanovshchina* had already condemned as deviant the failure to extol the virtues of the NSM in all cultural products. But kowtowing to the West was associated with disdain for Russian and Soviet achievements, and an unpatriotic preference for life in the West. The official launch of this campaign came a month after the Marshall Plan was announced.[22] It was accompanied by a new official celebration of Russia, punctuated by Moscow's 800th birthday party in September 1947.[23]

After the murder of the director of the Jewish Anti-Fascist Committee in January 1948, a campaign against the Jewish intelligentsia ensued. The Union of Jewish Writers was closed, Jews were purged from political and cultural institutions and works in Yiddish were banned. The accusation was that 'some' Jews had become a fifth column allied with US and British intelligence. Just as the campaign had seemingly lapsed, it was revived in May 1952 with the public trial of those implicated in the 'Anti-Fascist Committee Affair', and then, in the winter of 1952–3, with the announcement of the 'Doctors' Plot', which only ended with Stalin's death. Other campaigns, in Georgia and Estonia, for example, connected local nationalism to an alliance with the West. In the 'Leningrad Affair', in which that party organisation was purged of 'saboteurs and wreckers', from 1949 to 1952, the vulnerability of even the highest ranks of the party to the allure of the West was revealed.[24]

The danger expected from difference was reflected in institutional modifications. In October 1949, the police, or *militsia*, was removed from the Ministry of Internal Affairs (MVD) and shifted to the MGB. In July 1952, the Council of Ministers drafted an order to move all censorship responsibilities from local control to the MGB, as well.[25] The making of foreign-policy decisions remained tightly centralised around Stalin himself, Zhdanov, Molotov, Andrei Vyshinsky, who replaced Molotov in 1949, and Anastas Mikoyan. After 1948, the Presidium rarely met.[26] East European Communist elites continued to have institutionalised channels of communication with their Moscow colleagues.

22  Zubkova, *Russia after the War*, p. 119.
23  Anatolii M. Beda, *Sovetskaia politicheskaia kul'tura cherez prizmu MVD* (Moscow: Mosgorarkhiv, 2002), pp. 32–7.
24  Ibid., pp. 35–6; Murashko and Noskova, 'Repressii kak element vnutripartiinoi bor'by za vlast'', in Volokitina et al., *Moskva i vostochnaia evropa*', p. 547; and Zubkova, *Russia after the War*, pp. 132–6.
25  Beda, *Sovetskaia politicheskaia kul'tura*, p. 38, and Zubkova, *Russia after the War*, p. 129.
26  Taubman, *Khrushchev*, p. 329; Zubok and Pleshakov, *Inside the Kremlin's Cold War*, pp. 76–87; and Zubkova, 'Rivalry with Malenkov', in William Taubman, Sergei Khrushchev and Abbott Gleason (eds.), *Nikita Khrushchev* (New Haven: Yale University Press, 2000), pp. 71–2.

Soviet participation in East European decision-making was as institutionalised as Moscow's participation in obkom decision-making at home.

East Europeans frequently appealed to the Soviet embassy to reverse decisions made by their own governments. Local elites competed to provide Moscow with compromising material (*kompromat*) on each other, hoping to gain Moscow's favour against local rivals. Accusations tracked perfectly with the kinds of dangerous deviance being rooted out in the Soviet Union. The Soviet leadership had its own channels of verification, as well: its embassies, MVD, MGB, the Cominform and members of official Soviet delegations. East European allies adopted institutional forms to look like Soviet ones, right down to the number of members on the Central Committee (CC) Presidium, or number and names of CC departments.[27] MGB advisers would often take over the handling of local interrogations and 'affairs', establishing which charges were appropriate and which confessions should be coerced. All of this was done to ensure that the kinds of deviations revealed in, say, the 'Rajk Affair', would correspond to the particular deviation prevailing in Moscow.[28]

Soviet interests in Eastern Europe did not change from 1945 to 1953: regimes friendly to Moscow. But how Soviets understood what constituted friendly changed dramatically. Replications of the Soviet Union were now necessary. The Soviet need for similarity squandered genuine post-war support for the Soviet Union in Eastern Europe. Soviet practices there pushed the West to unite against it, forgetting about any German threat, and displaced Eastern European memories about Soviet liberation with apprehensions of the Soviets as occupiers. Especially in Poland and Czechoslovakia, the Soviet Union was regarded as protection against Germany into 1947. But by 1948, both the Ministry of Foreign Affairs (MFA) and the CC were reporting less sympathy for Moscow, 'even among progressive parts of the population' in Czechoslovakia and Bulgaria. In January 1949, a poll in Slovakia showed that 36 per cent of those asked would prefer a war between the US and Soviet Union in which the US emerged victorious, versus 20 per cent who favoured a Soviet victory.

27 T. Pokivailova, 'Moskva i ustanovlenie monopolii kompartii na informatsiiu na rubezhe 40–50-x godov', in Volokitina et al., *Moskva i vostochnaia evropa*, pp. 324–41; Volokitina, 'Oformlenie i funktsionirovanie novogo mekhanizma gosudarstvennoi vlasti', in Volokitina et al., *Moskva i vostochnaia evropa*, pp. 232–42, 284; and Volokitina, Murashko and Noskova, 'K chitateliu', p. 11.
28 Murashko and Noskova, 'Institut Sovetskikh sovetnikov', pp. 619–22; and Murashko and Noskova, 'Repressii – instrument podavleniia politicheskoi oppozitsii', in Volokitina et al., *Moskva i vostochnaia evropa*, p. 450.

The poll was broken down by class, and only the working class narrowly supported a Soviet victory (by 35–32 per cent).[29]

Yugoslavia's Tito was doubly deviant, manifesting independence in both foreign and domestic matters. His territorial ambitions alarmed Moscow. It feared other East European allies might mimic Tito's behaviour, and that Tito might use the Cominform as an institutional vehicle to spread his heresy.[30] Tito's popularity in other East European countries was well known to Soviet political elites.[31] Stalin and Molotov deemed Yugoslavia's behaviour adventuristic, as it threatened to unite the US and Britain against Moscow.[32] Moscow withdrew its advisers from Yugoslavia in March 1948, following up with a letter of excommunication distributed to all Cominform members.[33] Tito's codename within the CC was changed from Eagle (*Orel*) to Vulture (*Stervyatnik*).[34] To Moscow's alarm, other East European Communist parties, with the exception of Hungary's, did not immediately support either Moscow's letter or the subsequent June 1948 Cominform resolution repeating Moscow's charges. The Romanian, Czech, Bulgarian and Polish Communist parties had to be prodded to hold meetings to discuss and approve the Soviet position. The problem was not only with Communist elites, but also with average folk on the street, who, it was reported back to Moscow, 'see Tito as a hero worthy of imitation'.[35]

As Volokitina and her co-authors put it, a 'new stage in the history of the region' began in 1948: 'the hot phase of Sovietisation'.[36] The Soviet continuum from difference to danger was evident in East European identity relations. Rudolf Slánský, for example, was initially charged with a 'nationalist deviation', permitting Czechoslovakia to embark upon a 'special path to socialism' which ignored the universality of the Soviet model. This then threatened the 'restoration of capitalism' in the republic, which in turn would have turned

---

29 Murashko and Noskova, 'Sovetskii faktor', pp. 73–7; and Volokitina, 'Stalin i smena strategicheskogo kursa', p. 20.
30 Zubok and Pleshakov, *Inside the Kremlin's Cold War*, pp. 129–35.
31 Murashko and Noskova, 'Sovetskoe rukovodstvo i politicheskie protsessy T. Kostova i L. Raika', in I. V. Gaiduk, N. I. Yegorova and A. O. Chubar'ian (eds.), *Stalinskoe desiatiletie kholodnoi voiny: fakty i gipotezy* (Moscow: Nauka, 1999), p. 24.
32 Volokitina, 'Stalin i smena strategicheskogo kursa', p. 19.
33 Adibekov, *Kominform i poslevoennaia evropa*, 100–2; and Pokivailova, 'Moskva i ustanovlenie monopolii', pp. 349–52.
34 Christopher Andrew and Vasili Mitrokhin, *The Sword and the Shield* (New York: Basic Books, 1999), p. 356.
35 Murashko and Noskova, 'Repressii kak element', pp. 498–50; and Volokitina, 'Nakanune: novye realii', pp. 54–5.
36 Volokitina et al., 'K chitateliu', p. 5.

Czechoslovakia over to 'the English and American imperialists'.[37] A Soviet consulate in Hungary approvingly reported the renaming of hundreds of sites for Lenin, Stalin, Molotov, the Red Army and Gorky, as well as the introduction of Russian language study. The works of Akhmatova, Zoshchenko and other 'disgraced' Soviet authors were removed from Hungarian libraries.[38]

Hungarian party elites told their Soviet counterparts that there was too much Jewish influence in their ranks. But in early 1950, the anti-cosmopolitan campaign had lulled, and so Hungarian reports were ignored. Less than two years later, however, as the Soviet trials in the 'Anti-Fascist Committee Affair' got under way, Hungarian and Czech Communists were instructed to unmask their own cosmopolitan fifth columns.[39] Just as attention to Western art, culture and science was being regarded at home as dangerous, Soviet officials reported that Western culture was exerting too much influence in Eastern Europe. In July 1949, the Soviet Union requested the closure of all Western culture and information centres in Eastern Europe, as well as the reduction of tourism and exchanges to a minimum. The allure of the West was related directly to the vulnerability of socialism in these countries.[40]

Purges also followed Soviet procedures. As Stalin wrote to Hungarian party leader Mátyás Rákosi in September 1949: 'I think that Rajk must be executed, since the people will not understand any other sentence.' And so he was, two weeks later.[41] Moscow measured the effectiveness of campaigns in Eastern Europe as it had in the Soviet Union: by the numbers. Soviets monitored how many people were arrested, purged and executed, recommending more 'vigilance' if too few affairs were being pursued.[42] The 'liberal pacifistic' attitude of Czech comrades was criticised because too many Czech deviants were allowed to emigrate, rather than be incarcerated or executed. Just as political prisoners in the Soviet Union were dragooned into slave labour to build the White Sea canal, Romanian deviants worked on 'socialist projects', such as the Danube–Black Sea canal.[43]

Stalinist fear of difference importing imperialist danger dominated relations with Eastern Europe. But relations with China were not fraught with a fear

---

37 Murashko and Noskova, 'Repressii kak element', p. 561. See also Murashko and Noskova, 'Sovetskii faktor', pp. 93–103.
38 Pokivailova, 'Moskva i ustanovlenie monopolii', pp. 322–3 and 336–8.
39 Murashko and Noskova, 'Repressii kak element', pp. 547–52; and Danilov and Pyzhikov, *Rozhdenie sverkhderzhavy*, pp. 54–5.
40 Pokivailova, 'Moskva i ustanovlenie monopolii', pp. 325–31.
41 Quoted in Murashko and Noskova, 'Repressii kak element', p. 527.
42 Volokitina, 'Istochniki formirovaniia', p. 157; and Murashko and Noskova, 'Institut Sovetskikh sovetnikov', p. 627.
43 Murashko and Noskova, 'Repressii – instrument podavleniia', pp. 440–7.

of difference, but were the external projection of the Stalinist hierarchy of centre and periphery, modernity and pre-modernity. China was the Soviet Union's oldest little brother, a revolutionary comrade-in-arms who aspired to become just like its elder and better. In the summer of 1949 Stalin met six times in Moscow with Liu Shaoqi, one of Mao's closest colleagues. At one meeting, Liu presented a six-hour report on China's political realities in which China was repeatedly described as on the road to becoming the Soviet Union. On Stalin's personal copy are a dozen 'Da!'s written in Stalin's hand after passages that acknowledge China's subordinate position.[44] During these meetings an international division of revolutionary labour emerged. Stalin delegated to China leadership of the anti-colonial movements of Asia, while reserving for Moscow overall leadership of the world Communist movement, including Eastern Europe, and the working-classes of modern North America and Western Europe. China would be the surrogate vanguard for revolutions in places like Vietnam and Indonesia, while the Soviet Union would be China's vanguard. Mao agreed to this hierarchy in his December 1949 meeting with Stalin in Moscow.[45]

This division of labour got its first serious test in Korea. A month after Mao left Moscow, North Korea's leader, Kim Il-Sung, arrived with promises of a quick victory in a short war against South Korea. Stalin agreed to provide the necessary military assistance, but told Kim that no Soviet forces would fight, even if the US did intervene, but that China would. In June 1950, North Korea attacked with initial success. But the US-led counter-attack had, by late September, resulted in US forces approaching the Chinese border. On 1 October, Kim sent a telegram to Stalin warning of a North Korean collapse. Zhou En-lai visited Stalin in Sochi a week later where Stalin suggested that China could demonstrate its identity as vanguard of the Asian national liberation movement (NLM) by saving North Korea. Stalin told Zhou En-lai that it was China's war, but the Soviet Union would provide military equipment and fighter pilots.[46]

During Mao's only meetings with Stalin, the February 1950 treaty of alliance was signed, promising vast quantities of Soviet economic and military aid,

44 In Jun, 'Origins of the Sino-Soviet Alliance', p. 305. The original is in APRF, f. 45, 01, d. 328.
45 Goncharov, Lewis and Litai, *Uncertain Partners*, pp. 46–74; Chen Jian, *Mao's China and the Cold War* (Chapel Hill: University of North Carolina Press, 2001), pp. 50 and 120; Ilya V. Gaiduk, *Confronting Vietnam: Soviet Policy towards the Indochina Conflict* (Stanford, Calif.: Stanford University Press, 2003), p. 2.
46 Goncharov, Lewis and Litai, *Uncertain Partners*, pp. 137–44 and 188–95; Zubok and Pleshakov, *Inside the Kremlin's Cold War*, pp. 62–8; Chen Jian, *Mao's China*, pp. 121–55; and Danilov and Pyzhikov, *Rozhdenie sverkhderzhavy*, pp. 65–6.

along with an alliance against the US and Japan. At the same time, however, Mao had to swallow what he later called 'two bitter pills': continued Soviet control over Port Arthur and the Manchurian railroad, and a secret agreement to keep foreigners and foreign investment, other than Soviet, out of Manchuria and Xinjiang.[47]

Soviet relations with China also revealed relative Soviet indifference towards NLMs. At Chinese behest Ho Chi Minh arrived secretly (a Soviet condition) in Moscow while Mao was there. In his only meeting with Stalin, Ho was advised to work through China, and not through the Soviet Union directly. While China recognised the Democratic Republic of Vietnam (DRV) with great fanfare on 18 January 1950, the Soviet Union did not recognise Hanoi for two weeks, and then most quietly. Moreover, contacts with Ho were handled through the French Communist Party, reflecting the Eurocentrism of Stalin's foreign policy more generally.[48]

The politics of identity between the Soviet Union and its Chinese allies worked differently from the way it did in Eastern Europe. Increasing Soviet intolerance of difference resulted in purges, arrests and executions and the assumption of power in Eastern Europe of Communists with close associations with patrons in the Kremlin. Mao, on the other hand, independently and enthusiastically promoted the adoption of the Soviet model in China. At the March 1949 Chinese Communist Party (CCP) plenum, Mao stated so explicitly.[49] Moscow found itself with a very close ally in its struggle against deviation.

## Difference at home: allies abroad, 1953–6

Stalin's death buried the NSM. The 'us versus them' binarisation of the world was replaced by a continuum of difference, with a broad contested middle ground between the NSM and its dangerous deviant Other, including the possibility of being neither us nor them. The possibility of a 'private' self appeared, an individual personality unconnected to the public performance of being Soviet, socialist or Communist. The recognition of the possibility of irrelevant and innocuous difference entailed as well the acknowledgement of fallibility, of the possibility that errors might be made by even good Soviets. Tolerance for both mistakes and difference spoke of a new level of security and confidence felt by the post-Stalin generation of political elites in Moscow.

---

47  Goncharov, Lewis and Litai, *Uncertain Partners*, pp. 85–126.
48  Chen Jian, *Mao's China*, p. 121; Goncharov, Lewis and Litai, *Uncertain Partners*, pp. 107–8; and Gaiduk, *Confronting Vietnam*, p. 3.
49  Goncharov, Lewis and Litai, *Uncertain Partners*, p. 45.

This said, two important elements of the Stalinist identity of the Soviet Union remained: hierarchy and the Russian nation. The Soviet Union remained the apex and the centre of the world communist community, and the teleological endpoint for all modern humanity. Within the Soviet Union, Russia remained the vanguard for all other republics and peoples, with Central Asians deemed the most peripheral and needful of a vanguard in Russia and Moscow. The Russian nation remained the surrogate nation for a putatively supranational Soviet man.[50]

The political manifestations of these identity shifts in March 1953 were dramatic and almost instantaneous. Within a month, 1.2 million prisoners were amnestied and both the Doctors' Plot and Mingrelian Affair were publicly declared over and mistaken. Within months, Ilya Ehrenburg's novel *The Thaw* was published and Zoshchenko was readmitted to the Writers' Union. All victims of the Leningrad Affair were publicly rehabilitated within a year of Stalin's funeral. In December 1954, the Second Writers' Congress was held, the first since 1938, at which all the issues of Soviet identity were debated publicly for five days. In September 1955, Molotov was forced to write a public recantation in the pages of the single most important theoretical publication of the CPSU, *Kommunist*, in which he admitted socialism had already been built in the Soviet Union, not just had its foundations laid, and so the Soviet system was far more secure than he had hitherto acknowledged. The capstone to the period was the Twentieth Party Congress in February 1956, where Stalin's excesses were revealed and publicly condemned.[51]

The boundaries of permissible difference were revealed in Budapest in November 1956, and were reflected back into Soviet society. But there was no turning back. Molotov persistently struggled against difference, but he, too, was defeated, at the June 1957 CC plenum devoted to the removal of the 'anti-party group'. The next thirty years witnessed a continual contestation of the boundaries of permissible deviation from the Soviet model at home.[52]

50 Ted Hopf, *Social Construction of International Politics* (Ithaca, N.Y.: Cornell University Press, 2002), pp. 39–82; Zubkova, *Russia after the War*, 169–72; Nancy Condee, 'Cultural Codes of the Thaw', in Taubman, Khrushchev and Gleason, *Khrushchev*, pp. 160–76; and Robert English, *Russia and the Idea of the West* (New York: Columbia University Press, 2000), p. 85.

51 Taubman, *Khrushchev*, pp. 246–52; Sergei Khrushchev, *Nikita Khrushchev and the Creation of a Superpower* (University Park, Pa.: Pennsylvania State University Press, 2000), pp. 31–5; Zubkova, *Russia after the War*, pp. 154–66; and James Richter, *Khrushchev's Double Bind: International Pressures and Domestic Coalition Politics* (Baltimore: Johns Hopkins University Press, 1994), pp. 31–73.

52 Zubkova, *Russia after the War*, pp. 189–98; 'SSSR: Narody i sud'by', *Voennye Arkhivy Rossii* 1 (1993): 247–59; Iurii Aksiutin, 'Popular Responses to Khrushchev', in Taubman, Khrushchev and Gleason, *Khrushchev*, p. 193; 'Plenum TsK KPSS Iiun' 1957 goda',

In this initial period after Stalin's death, institutionalisation of a discourse of difference did not occur as much as Stalinism was de-institutionalised. Just one day after Stalin's death, for example, the MVD and MGB were merged, so the police were again being supervised by those responsible for internal law and order, not for finding foreign agents. A year later, the MGB and its intelligence functions were severed from the MVD, so the Stalinist conception of criminality as being connected to a foreign threat was deprived of its institutionalised power.[53] Only two weeks later, the Gulag was transferred from the MVD to the Ministry of Justice.[54] With Georgii Malenkov's demotion in January 1955, Khrushchev packed the CC with his proponents.[55] This strategy paid off in the June 1957 CC meeting that removed Molotov, Malenkov, Lazar Kaganovich and Dmitrii Shepilov.

New institutional carriers for the discourse of difference emerged in society more broadly. The custom of readers writing letters to editors of newspapers and magazines became so widespread that media outlets competed for them. The intelligentsia as a social stratum was revived in strength and confidence, making editorial boards of journals and the meetings and directorates of their official organisations platforms for advancing the boundaries of difference both in everyday discussions and in mass publications.[56]

With regard to foreign policy, the death of Stalin disrupted the institutionalised relationships between East European Communist leaders and their allies in Moscow. And the growing tolerance of difference put them on insecure discursive footing. The abolition of the Cominform in April 1956 was the official end to institutionalised compulsion to adhere to a single Soviet model of socialism.

The new discourse of difference changed Soviet interests in other countries in the world. East Europeans could be good allies without reproducing the Soviet model in detail. NLMs could be good allies just by not being allied with the imperialist West. Russian success at home as vanguard for Central Asia gave Moscow confidence that the Soviet Union could be a surrogate vanguard for dozens of countries trying to become independent of colonial rule. The Soviet Union officially recognised many roads to socialism, including electoral ones.

The recognition of difference was also reflected in relations with the West. The realisation that the US was not the West and that European states, in

*Istoricheskii Arkhiv* 3 (1993): 73; 'Posledniaia "Antipartiinaia" Gruppa. Stenograficheskii', 21; 'Posledniaia "Antipartiinaia Gruppa"', pp. 33–4; Khrushchev, *Nikita Khrushchev*, 203; Taubman, *Khrushchev*, pp. 301–7; and 'Vengriia, Aprel'-Oktiabr' 1956', *Istoricheskii Arkhiv* 4 (1993): 113.

53 Beda, *Sovetskaia politicheskaia kul'tura*, pp. 45–7.    54 Taubman, *Khrushchev*, p. 246.
55 Chuev, *Molotov Remembers*, p. 351.    56 Zubkova, *Russia after the War*, p. 161.

particular, had interests autonomous from Washington, was reflected in a softer foreign policy on Finland, Turkey, Korea and Austria, and unilateral reductions in armed forces, in part, expected to encourage more European independence from the imperialist centre in the US. Recognition of difference dramatically expanded the numbers and kinds of states with which the Soviet Union could develop an interest in allying. Capitalist encirclement was replaced by a zone of peace. And recognition of fallibility, of having made mistakes in the past, made new alliances more probable and rendered existing alliances less problematic.

In Eastern Europe, Soviet confessions that the Doctors' Plot, the anti-cosmopolitan campaign and other purges in the last five years had been misguided put local Communists who had been trying to implement the Soviet model in awkward positions. Those most closely identified with the Stalinist model were discredited; those they had replaced, imprisoned or executed were politically reborn. Władysław Gomułka and Imre Nagy, for example, returned to power in Poland and Hungary, respectively. But, less dramatically in the rest of Eastern Europe, Stalinist leaders were compelled to rehabilitate those they had just purged, many posthumously.[57]

One of the most dramatic changes in Soviet foreign policy came in relations with Yugoslavia. Just three months after Stalin's death, the Soviet Union returned its ambassador to Belgrade. Tito was visited by Khrushchev and a large and apologetic entourage in 1955. New Soviet identity relations helped make this alliance possible. Whereas before, Tito's national brand of socialism was deemed dangerous, by 1955 it was understood as an example of tolerable difference from the Soviet model. In addition, Moscow remained the centre of the world Communist movement, and therefore, Yugoslavia remained subordinate to that centre, at least from Moscow's perspective. Yugoslavia was understood as a younger Slavic brother to the Russian nation. This Slavic fraternity helped mitigate concerns about deviations from the Soviet model. Finally, the Soviet leadership confessed to having erred in its treatment of Yugoslavia in the past.

Each of these understandings was resisted by Molotov. At the July 1955 CC plenum devoted to Yugoslavia, Molotov branded Tito a dangerous deviant, denied the relevance of ethno-national Russian identity to the Soviet model, defended earlier Soviet actions and concluded that the Soviet conferral of a

57 Murashko and Noskova, 'Repressii kak element', pp. 544–73; B. I. Zhelitski, 'Budapesht–Moskva: god 1956', in Nezhinskii, *Sovetskaia vneshniaia politika*, pp. 241–82; Volokitina, 'Oformlenie i funktsionirovanie', pp. 272–302; and Vladislav Zubok, 'The Case of Divided Germany, 1953–1964', in Taubman, Khrushchev and Gleason, *Khrushchev*, p. 289.

socialist identity on Tito would only encourage further deviations from the Soviet model in Eastern Europe.[58]

Molotov's fears were justified. Khrushchev's not-so-secret speech enumerating Stalin's errors at the Twentieth Party Congress was followed by unrest in Poland.[59] In the June 1956 Poznań demonstrations, workers demanded religious freedom and made anti-Soviet and anti-Communist speeches. Seventy were killed and 500 wounded. The Polish party was split between supporters of the orthodox Soviet model and proponents of a Polish path to socialism. In August, Gomułka's party membership was restored, and in October he rejoined the Politburo, becoming first secretary once again on 17 October. Two days later, Molotov, Mikoyan, Kaganovich and Khrushchev arrived in Warsaw. Khrushchev refused to shake hands and called Poles traitors. Gomułka greeted Khrushchev by saying, 'I am Gomułka, the one you kept in prison for three years.' The day after the Soviet delegation left, tens of thousands of Poles participated in pro-Gomułka rallies, culminating in 500,000 demonstrators in Warsaw on 24 October.[60] This mass support for the embodiment of Polish difference was noted in Politburo meetings in Moscow, as was Gomułka's assurance that Poland had no intentions of leaving the Warsaw Pact.[61]

Poland had just missed violating the boundaries of permissible difference; Hungary would not, becoming accused of dangerous deviation for the next thirty years.[62] In June 1953 Mátyás Rákosi was advised by Moscow to abandon Stalinist methods of rule. Rákosi held out, hoping his allies in the Kremlin would overcome this new tolerance of difference. His hopes were realised. In April 1955, Rákosi had his reformist prime minister, Imre Nagy, removed and expelled from the party.[63] But this return to orthodoxy was short-lived, as Khrushchev was welcoming Tito's Yugoslavia into the ranks of socialist allies. As Molotov recalled, 'the turning point was already completed with the Yugoslav question', not the Twentieth Party Congress.[64] Both Poles and Hungarians watched de-Stalinisation carefully, and still more, the rapprochement

58 Hopf, *Social Construction*, pp. 106–23.
59 Unless noted otherwise, my account of the Polish crisis relies on A. M. Orekhov, 'Sobytiia 1956 goda v Pol'she i krizis pol'sko-sovetskikh otnoshenii', in Nezhinskii, *Sovetskaia vneshniaia politika*, pp. 217–40.
60 Mark Kramer, 'New Evidence on Soviet Decision-Making and the 1956 Polish and Hungarian Crises', *Cold War International History Project Bulletin* 8–9 (1996/7): 361.
61 ' "Malin" Notes on the Crises in Hungary and Poland, 1956', *Cold War International History Project Bulletin* 8–9 (1996/7): 389.
62 Unless otherwise noted, my analysis of the Hungarian events relies on Zhelitski, 'Budapesht–Moskva', pp. 241–82; ' "Malin" Notes', pp. 390–9; and Kramer, 'New Evidence', pp. 362–76.
63 'Vengriia, Aprel'–Oktiabr' 1956', pp. 103–5.    64 Chuev, *Molotov Remembers*, p. 351.

with Yugoslavia, the Stalinists with Molotovian dread, the discredited reformers, with hope.[65]

After the Twentieth Party Congress, Hungarian demonstrators demanded de-Stalinisation resume and that Nagy be restored. Iurii Andropov, the Soviet ambassador to Hungary at the time, supported Rákosi, and called his opposition 'dangerous counter-revolutionaries'. The reformist riots in Poznań encouraged Hungarians to push for more reform. In July 1956, Mikoyan went to Budapest to replace Rákosi with a less Stalinist figure. In the following weeks and months, the peculiarly close alliance relationships between Moscow and Eastern Europe were repeatedly demonstrated. Mikoyan participated in Hungarian Politburo meetings in July, János Kádár in Soviet Politburo meetings in November, and Liu Shaoqi in Soviet Politburo meetings about Hungary in the autumn.[66]

By October, student demonstrators had crossed a red line: they demanded not only the restoration of Nagy, but the withdrawal of all Soviet armed forces. Nagy was restored to the Politburo on 23 October, but the Soviet Politburo, save Mikoyan, agreed to deploy Soviet troops against the Hungarian protestors the same day. During Soviet Politburo discussions, Molotov took advantage of the occasion to remind his colleagues how wrong Khrushchev had been about tolerating difference, especially with regard to Yugoslavia. Khrushchev himself was having second thoughts, coming to see Nagy as a dangerous acolyte of Tito. Molotov preferred Ferenc Münnich, who had spent half his life in the Soviet Union, as Nagy's replacement. The rest of the Politburo preferred Kádár, because he had been imprisoned by the Stalinist Rákosi. Molotov opposed him for the very same reason![67]

The pivotal day was 30 October. In a document on relations between the Soviet Union and other socialist countries adopted that day, Moscow admitted it had erred, violated its allies' sovereign equality and was committed to re-examining its troop deployments in Eastern Europe, save Germany. But later the same day, Suslov and Mikoyan reported from Budapest that the Hungarian army could not be trusted and that Nagy had asked that negotiations begin on Hungarian withdrawal from the Warsaw Pact. Difference had already become dangerous disloyalty.

Fear of falling dominoes, loss of credibility and promises of a short war were all evident in Soviet decision-making on Hungary. As Khrushchev told the rest

65 Khrushchev, *Nikita Khrushchev*, p. 148.
66 At the June 1957 plenum, Khrushchev thanked China for its advice on Hungary in October 1956. 'Posledniaia "Antipartiinaia" Gruppa', *Istoricheskii Arkhiv* I (1994): 67.
67 Khrushchev, *Nikita Khrushchev*, pp. 200–1. Quoted in Kramer, 'New Evidence', p. 374.

of the Politburo on 31 October, 'If we leave Hungary . . . the imperialists, the Americans, English, and French, will perceive it as weakness on our part and will go on the offensive.' At the same time, a series of intelligence and foreign ministry reports from embassies, especially in Romania and Czechoslovakia, spoke of the degenerative effect of Hungary on the political situations in these countries. Hungarians along the Romanian border had begun to seek support in Romania; ethnic Hungarians in Romania and Czechoslovakia had begun to manifest sympathy for events in Budapest; and Romanian students demonstrated in support of Nagy. In Moscow and other Soviet cities students were meeting in support of Nagy. By 1 November, Presidium members began invoking the fears of their allies in Eastern Europe, arguing that these friends were losing confidence in Moscow. Finally, Marshal Konev promised Khrushchev and the Politburo that it would take only three to four days to crush the counter-revolution in Hungary. He was right.

The invasion of Hungary stalled the Thaw in the Soviet Union. The limits of tolerable difference had been reached and breached. Hungarian events alerted Soviet elites to the danger of difference at home. Often when Khrushchev would consider reviving the Thaw he was met by references to Hungary, before which 'he would retreat'.[68] And there was reason for such fears. Especially in the Baltic republics, local party leaders reported growing unrest, support for Gomułka and Nagy and anti-Soviet, nationalist and religious demonstrations. On the night of 2 November, for example, in Kaunas, Lithuania, at the Tomb of the Unknown Soldier, 35,000 Lithuanians, mainly students, gathered to demand that Russians end their Communist occupation. In Vilnius, people questioned why the Soviet declaration on relations with other socialist countries did not apply to them, as well![69]

Reformist Communists abroad were so worried about the orthodox reaction that they petitioned the Kremlin not to purge their more tolerant allies in Moscow.[70] Orthodox Soviet allies in the GDR, Romania, Bulgaria and Czechoslovakia, on the other hand, took advantage of Moscow's fear of deviation.[71] Richter shows how Hungary empowered Molotov, Malenkov and Kaganovich in foreign policy, leading to their June 1957 attempt to depose Khrushchev.[72] But Khrushchev, too, had learned the limits of difference. Khrushchev came to regard Tito increasingly as China did, a dangerous deviant

---

68 Sergei Khrushchev, *Nikita Khrushchev and the Creation*, p. 203.
69 'SSSR: Narody i sud'by', pp. 246–70.
70 English, *Russia and the Idea of the West*, pp. 87–8.    71 Kramer, 'New Evidence', p. 377.
72 Richter, *Khrushchev's Double Bind*, pp. 93–6.

within the ranks.[73] The threat from Hungary was reflexively linked to the threat from the US; deviation there was closely associated with US intentions to undermine socialism in Eastern Europe in general. Many future initiatives of Khrushchev in the area of arms control and troop withdrawals from Eastern Europe were opposed by other Politburo members invoking the lessons of Hungary.[74]

One might expect that the discourse of difference would have soured relations with Stalinist China. This prediction is inaccurate, but only in timing. While national roads to socialism violated Chinese adherence to a single Stalinist model, and they did oppose treating Tito's Yugoslavia as a socialist country, Soviet admissions of past mistakes compensated for the toleration of deviance. Moreover, Khrushchev's decision to use force in Hungary, sanctioned and urged by the Chinese leadership at the time, reassured Beijing that there were some limits Khrushchev would thankfully not tolerate.[75]

Soviet aid in the construction of industrial and defence plants accelerated after Stalin's death. In May 1953, the Soviet Union agreed to an additional ninety-one enterprises, and to the replacement of fighter aircraft and tanks with newer models.[76] During Khrushchev's first visit to China in October 1954, Mao asked to acquire nuclear weapons. Khrushchev suggested China concentrate on economic reconstruction, pledging it could rely on the Soviet deterrent, but did offer a civilian nuclear reactor. In March 1955, Moscow agreed to build another 166 industrial enterprises and help China build an atomic reactor and cyclotron. Seventy per cent of China's foreign trade in the 1950s was with the Soviet Union.[77]

Mao cautiously supported Khrushchev's campaign against Stalin, though not the discourse of difference more generally. As Mao told the Soviet ambassador, Iudin, in May 1956, if he 'had always followed Stalin's advice, he would be dead by now'.[78] Mao was dissatisfied with the ambiguity created by the ongoing debates in the Soviet Union between difference and orthodoxy. In April 1956, Mao published his own interpretation of the Twentieth Party Congress, crafting the 70 : 30 rule of thumb about Stalin: he was 70 per cent right (about the economic and political development model) and 30 per cent wrong (on

73 Zubok and Pleshakov, *Inside the Kremlin's Cold War*, p. 187.
74 Sergei Khrushchev, *Nikita Khrushchev and the Creation*, p. 190.
75 Chen Jian, *Mao's China*, pp. 150–6.
76 Boris T. Kulik, *Sovetsko-kitaiskii raskol* (Moscow: Institut Dal'nego Vostoka RAN, 2000), p. 95.
77 Shu Guang Zhang, *Economic Cold War: America's Embargo against China and the Sino-Soviet Alliance, 1949–1963* (Washington: Woodrow Wilson Center Press, 2001), pp. 110–66.
78 Westad, *Brothers in Arms*, p. 15.

treatment of China and murder of colleagues).[79] Mao fashioned his own Thaw, the Hundred Flowers campaign launched in January 1957. But it was aimed not at expanding the boundaries of difference, but at flushing out 'Rightists' who would then be arrested.[80]

In the decolonising world, the discourse of difference greatly expanded potential Soviet allies beyond Communist Parties. The experience of Central Asia provided living proof that a vanguard in Moscow could substitute for the absence of a proletarian vanguard abroad. US support for its allies in the Third World made Soviet support for NLMs that much more natural.

In April 1955, the non-aligned movement was born in Bandung, Indonesia. From the perspective of the new discourse of difference in the Soviet Union, non-aligned meant not aligned with imperialism, permitting closer relations with Moscow. Nehru, Sukarno and Nasser became friends in the struggle against imperialism in the newly christened zone of peace. In August 1955, Moscow approved the sale of Czech arms to Egypt. In November and December 1955, Khrushchev spent four weeks in India, Burma and Afghanistan, during which he compared these three countries to Central Asia. Reading the decolonising world through the Soviet experience in Central Asia, Khrushchev declared that the road to socialism was possible for anybody in the developing world, no matter how meagre their material resources. One need only rely on Soviet experience and help.

Molotov found preposterous the idea of socialism in places like India as he did on difference at home and in Yugoslavia. While not denying the possibility of normal relations with Delhi, he rejected the idea that leaders such as Nehru could ever escape their petit bourgeois nationalist identities, and consequent roles as imperialist lackeys.[81] On 1 June 1956 Molotov was replaced as foreign minister by Dmitrii Shepilov, who had played a key role in the Soviet opening to Egypt in 1955.[82] At the June 1957 CC plenum, Molotov was accused by Mikoyan of not recognising the obvious differences between India, Egypt and Afghanistan, on the one hand, and Pakistan, the Philippines and Iraq, on the other. Instead 'Molotov says the bourgeois camp is united against us . . . He is a bygone conservative . . . This is a left-wing infantile disease in which we cannot indulge . . .We should not be fetishists or dogmatists.' Khrushchev summed matters up: 'Comrade Molotov, if they accept you as one of our leaders, you will ruin your country, take it into isolation . . . Molotov is a hopeless dried-up old man.'[83]

79 Chen Jian, *Mao's China*, p. 65.    80 Ibid., p. 69.
81 Hopf, *Social Construction*, pp. 86–9, 134–42.    82 Richter, *Khrushchev's Double Bind*, p. 85.
83 'Posledniaia "antipartiinaia" gruppa', pp. 33–8.

## Cold peace at home: cold war abroad, 1957–85

At a May 1957 Kremlin meeting with the intelligentsia, Khrushchev warned them that if they ever tried to create a 'Petőfi circle' of reformist intellectuals like they had in Budapest the year before, we 'will grind you into dust'.[84] Khrushchev's fulminations were characteristic of the rest of his rule: support for pushing the boundaries of difference with periodic eruptions of vitriol against what he deemed transgressive. Khrushchev charged Pasternak and others with a lack of patriotism after he was awarded the Nobel Prize for Literature in October 1958. But in May 1960 Khrushchev approved the publication, in *Pravda* no less, of an anti-Stalinist poem by Andrei Tvardovskii. Two years later, Khrushchev was railing at the Manezh exhibit of contemporary Soviet art about 'all this shit' they were producing. But almost simultaneously he was approving, along with the Politburo, which met twice over the manuscript, the publication of Aleksandr Solzhenitsyn's epic anti-Stalinist novel, *One Day in the Life of Ivan Denisovich*.[85]

The removal of Khrushchev from power in October 1964 did not narrow the boundaries of permissible difference. Indeed, Mikhail Suslov, in reading the bill of particulars before the CC, praised 'Khrushchev's positive role in unmasking the cult of personality of Stalin', and agreed with the removal of Molotov in 1957.[86] Under Brezhnev and his two successors, the main targets of official repression were those who engaged in public dissent, especially after August 1968.[87] The Siniavskii/Daniel' trials of February 1966 were an early manifestation of official intolerance. But it grew more comprehensive and more directed against those with manifest political demands to change the Soviet political system.[88] Solzhenitsyn, for example, was finally exiled in February 1974, at Andropov's personal behest.[89] A 1979 KGB report on avant-garde artists could have been written in 1955: 'they produce individualistic works . . . based strictly on personal perceptions'.[90]

This struggle over difference at home was not isolated from identity relations with the outside world: China was a prominent player. The removal of Molotov in 1957 not only marked the triumph of difference over the NSM, but also the

84 'Plenum, TsK KPSS, Iiun' 1957', p. 73.
85 Taubman, *Khrushchev*, pp. 384–8, 527–8, 594–602.
86 'Plenum, TsK KPSS, Oktyabr' 1964 goda. Stenograficheskii otchet', *Istoricheskii Arkhiv* 1 (1993), pp. 7–9. See also Georgi Arbatov, *The System: An Insider's Life in Soviet Politics* (New York: Times Books, 1992), p. 134; and English, *Russia and the Idea of the West*, p. 108.
87 Ibid., p. 135.
88 Condee, 'Cultural Codes of the Thaw', pp. 160–2.
89 Andrew and Mitrokhin, *Sword and the Shield*, pp. 312–18.     90 Ibid., p. 330.

irreversible turn towards alienation from China. China's Stalinist model helped proponents of difference at home point out what restoration of the NSM would mean for socialism in the Soviet Union. This domestic role for Chinese identity continued until the Chinese alliance with the United States after the death of Mao in the late 1970s. By then, however, a new external Other had emerged on the revisionist side of the spectrum: Eurocommunism, or National Social Democracy, personified by Enrico Berlinguer in Italy.[91]

Soviet identity was publicly contested in the discourse of permissible difference in relationship to Chinese dogmatism, Eurocommunist revisionism and competition with the imperialist camp headed by the United States. Meanwhile, identification with Europe was a counter-discourse within the Soviet party elite and intelligentsia. Its public manifestations, whether as Eurocommunism or as Andrei Sakharov's 'Letter to the Soviet Leadership', were officially repressed as anti-Soviet, but identification with European Social Democracy as the desirable Soviet future was already emerging as the alternative beyond the boundaries of permissible difference in the 1950s. Ironically, both the invasion of Czechoslovakia in 1968 and the accession to the Helsinki Treaty in 1975 energised identification with Europe among Soviet elites.[92] By the 1960s, a discourse on ethno-national Russian identity was emerging, especially among the 'village prose writers', led by Valentin Rasputin. While granted more official tolerance to publish its views, it was not as deeply institutionalised as its European alternative.[93]

If the early years of the Thaw were characterised by the de-institutionalisation of Stalinism, then the next thirty years witnessed the institutionalisation of both the dominant discourse and its competitors. There are several related issues here: the institutionalised lack of unbiased information available to decision makers; the position of General Secretary within the decision-making process; the split between the MFA and Central Committee International Department (CCID); the development of research institutes; and the persistence of the intelligentsia as a carrier of the discourse of difference.

Khrushchev, despite making agriculture his primary domestic avocation, continued to receive inflated statistics on harvests, yields and

---

91 Cherniaev, *Moia zhizn' i moe vremia* (Moscow: Mezhdunarodnye otnosheniia, 1995), p. 342; Georgii Shakhnazarov, *S vozhdiami i bez nikh* (Moscow: Vagrius, 2001), p. 271; and Elizabeth Wishnick, *Mending Fences* (London: University of Washington Press, 2001), p. 53.
92 Cherniaev, *Moia zhizn'*, p. 292 and Arbatov, *The System*, p. 132.
93 English, *Russia and the Idea of the West*, pp. 72–91, 122, 136–41, 194; and Ilya Prizel, *National Identity and Foreign Policy* (Cambridge: Cambridge University Press, 1998), pp. 191–211.

technological innovation throughout his tenure as General Secretary.[94] Georgii
Shakhnazarov, an aide to both Andropov in the 1960s and 1970s, and then Gorbachev in the 1980s, relates how party elites, such as CCID secretary Boris
Ponomarev and Defence Minister Dmitrii Ustinov, remained in a state of delusion about the economic conditions of the country, reporting their election
excursions to the countryside, where all had been made ready for them, as if it
were a representative sample of Soviet reality.[95] But this delusion extended to
foreign and security policy as well. It was not until 1990, for example, that Soviets found out that the May 1960 shootdown of Gary Powers's U-2 spy plane had
required thirteen missiles, and had only inadvertently been hit.[96] Soviet ambassadors, especially in the developing world, reported to Moscow just like an
obkom secretary would, exaggerating the industrial, agricultural and political
accomplishments of the piece of territory they considered to be their own.[97]

Oleg Grinevskii, for example, recalls the 'false, at times even absurd, information the KGB and CCID fed the Politburo', representations that reinforced
the Soviet identity of world revolutionary vanguard with regard to countries where a revolutionary situation hardly existed.[98] This discursive bias,
the twin exaggerations of socialism's prospects and imperialism's hostility,
manifested itself with especially baleful consequences in the decision-making
on Afghanistan in 1978–9, but was commonplace.[99] The apocrypha about
Soviet negotiators at arms control talks learning Soviet military secrets from
their Western counterparts are true. Gorbachev himself noted that not even
Politburo members could get basic information about the military-industrial
complex, or even the economy.[100] In response to Andropov's conclusion as
KGB chairman in May 1981 that the US was preparing to launch a nuclear war,
local KGB officers around the world, for the next three years, dutifully collected evidence to support the view held in Moscow.[101] Information contrary
to Soviet policy, such as a memorandum recommending withdrawal from
Afghanistan in early 1980 that went unread until 1986, was ignored, rarely

94  Taubman, *Khrushchev*, p. 261.
95  Shakhnazarov, *S vozhdiami*, pp. 90–1.        96  Taubman, *Khrushchev*, p. 378.
97  Oleg Grinevskii, *Tainy sovetskoi diplomatii* (Moscow: Vagrius, 2000), p. 136.
98  Ibid., p. 9. On the CCID and decision-making on Angola, see Odd Arne Westad, 'Moscow
    and the Angolan Crisis', *Cold War International History Project Bulletin* 8–9 (1996/7): p. 22.
99  English, *Russia and the Idea of the West*, p. 121.
100 Ibid., pp. 73, 323 nn. 32, 33. Vitalii Vorotnikov writes that, as a Politburo member in
    1987, he still could not get a copy of Khrushchev's secret speech at the Twentieth Party
    Congress. V. I. Vorotnikov, *A bylo eto tak . . .* (Moscow: Sovet veteranov knigoizdanii,
    1995), p. 153; and Raymond L. Garthoff, *A Journey through the Cold War* (Washington:
    Brookings Institution Press, 2001), p. 218.
101 Andrew and Mitrokhin, *Sword and the Shield*, pp. 213–14.

contemplated, written up or submitted.[102] As Evgenii Primakov noted in his memoirs, 'we [journalists and scholars who opposed the decision to intervene in Afghanistan] were led mainly by the established custom of unreservedly supporting all decisions taken from above'.[103]

The General Secretary's position was an institution of authority and power. As Shakhnazarov, writing as a political scientist, concluded, the Soviet Union and its socialist allies had one 'basic principle in common, its functioning was one-third defined by institutions and two-thirds by the personality of the leader'. While 'no one would challenge the right of the General Secretary to have the last word in resolving any question, this right did not belong so much to the man as to the position'.[104] Shakhnazarov recounts Andropov receiving a phone call from Khrushchev: 'before my eyes this lively striking interesting man was transformed into a soldier ready to fulfil any order of the commander. Even his voice changed, with tones of obedience and submissiveness.'[105]

The norm of party elite unity reinforced this authority and helps explain how the General Secretary preserved the prevailing discourse. After the post-Stalinist discourse of difference was fixed after 1957, Khrushchev staved off attacks from more orthodox quarters. Only when there was an overwhelming consensus, as in October 1964, did other elites join the attacks.[106] Elite fear of difference helped preserve the norm of unity. The discursive power concentrated in a particular General Secretary also accounts for the possibility of a dramatic shift in discourse once a General Secretary dies, as in the case of Stalin in 1953 and Chernenko in 1985. The institution of the General Secretary, combined with the institutionalised bias for agreeable information, helps explains the staying power of the predominant discourse, as well as the structural disadvantages faced by challengers.[107]

The discourse of difference implied recognition of the decolonising world as a zone of peace, rather than as a zone of imperialist lackeys. This recognition was institutionalised within the CCID, which had responsibility for relations with these revolutionary nationalist movements. The CCID and MFA were competitors for the next thirty years. The MFA, especially after Shepilov's replacement by Gromyko in February 1957, became still more closely associated with the reproduction of a Great Power Soviet identity in competition

102 Carolyn M. Ekedahl and Melvin A. Goodman, *The Wars of Eduard Shevardnadze*, 2nd edn (Washington: Brassey's, 2001), p. 184.
103 Evgenii Primakov, *Gody v bol'shoi politike* (Moscow: Sovershenno sekretno, 1999), p. 51.
104 Shakhnazarov, *S vozhdiami*, pp. 166, 219–21.  105 Ibid., p. 103.
106 Sergei Khrushchev, *Nikita Khrushchev and the Creation*, pp. 148, 463.
107 Andrew Bennett, *Condemned to Repetition? The Rise, Fall and Reprise of Soviet-Russian Military Interventionism, 1973–1996* (Cambridge, Mass.: MIT Press, 1999), pp. 113–15.

with the US and Europe.[108] Within the MFA there emerged a privileged group around Gromyko in Moscow and Ambassador Anatolii Dobrynin in Washington closely associated with Europe and the US.[109] 'Only the US, big European countries and the UN interested Gromyko . . . His heart did not lie in the Third World. He did not consider them to be serious partners. "He considered the Third World only to be a problem," writes Dobrynin. "He himself told me this".'[110]

At one of the meetings in the CC in late 1978 Rostislav Ul'ianovskii (Ponomarev's deputy) said:

'We need to bring things to the point that the NLM of Arabs becomes a socialist revolution. Agreements with American imperialism . . . will only . . . distract the Arab working class from its main political task.'

Ponomarev nodded his head in agreement.

'God!', lamented Robert Turdiev, an MFA expert, on leaving the CC building. 'Do these people understand what is happening on planet Earth? What Arab working class? What socialist revolution in the Middle East? Where do these senile old men live? On the moon, on Mars?'

'In an office on Staraya Ploshchad',' answered Anatolii Filev.

But Gromyko responded completely differently.

'Why have a conversation about a Middle East settlement in the CCID at all? This is not their business. Let them deal with Communist parties and NLMs.'[111]

The CCID preserved the orthodox Soviet identity of vanguard for socialist development in Central Asia. Ponomarev, who had been an aide to Georgii Dimitrov, head of the Comintern in the 1940s, saw himself in that tradition. Shakhnazarov relates details of a meeting of the CC commission on Poland that took place in early 1981 under the chairmanship of Mikhail Suslov. The Soviet ambassador to Poland at the time, Boris Aristov, reported that the Polish peasantry, despite its traditional ideas, had turned out to be a far more reliable support for the regime than the working class, which had fallen under the influence of both Solidarity and the Catholic Church. This is heresy to the orthodox Soviet model of a working-class vanguard, and Ponomarev interrupted, saying that the Polish leadership needed to collectivise its private farms. Aristov demurred, repeating that Polish private farmers mostly supported the government. Ponomarev then reminisced about the 1920s and the great feat

108 Grinevskii, *Tainy sovetskoi diplomatii*, pp. 181–9; and English, *Russia and the Idea of the West*, pp. 103–5 and 278, n. 23.
109 Ibid., pp. 135–50 and 298, n. 181.
110 Mlechin, *MID*, p. 404. See also Grinevskii, *Tainy sovetskoi diplomatii*, p. 12.
111 Grinevskii, *Tainy sovetskoi diplomatii*, pp. 162–3.

of collectivisation. Suslov, 'a reservoir of quotations from Lenin', cited an appropriate one on collectivisation. Suslov and Ponomarev then opined about Lenin and collectivisation. Finally, Ustinov said, 'Mikhail Andreevich, Boris Nikolaevich, why are we talking about communes when with each passing day Solidarity is threatening to remove the party from power!?'[112]

The institutionalisation of information, the authority of the General Secretary and the Great Power and vanguard identities of the MFA and CCID, respectively, help account for the predominance of the orthodox official discourse; the emergence of research institutions, expert advice and the creative associations of the intelligentsia explain the development and deepening of its alternatives.

Shortly after the Twentieth Party Congress the Institute of World Economics and International Relations (IMEMO) was restored from Stalinist oblivion. Over the next ten years, regional institutes associated with the Soviet Academy of Sciences would be established for Latin America (1961), Africa (1962), Asia (1966) and the USA and Canada (ISKAN, 1967).[113] What these, and other research institutions such as the Novosibirsk Institute of Economics and Industrial Organisation and the Public Opinion Research Institute at *Komsomol'skaia Pravda,* had in common was access to information about the outside world unavailable to average party or government officials, let alone the general public.[114] Another important site was in Prague, the editorial headquarters of *Problems of Peace and Socialism,* the journal of the world Communist movement.[115] Not only was there access to foreign publications, but daily discussions with socialists from all over the world, most significantly, Western Europe. The cadre of Soviets who worked in Prague in the 1950s and 1960s became important carriers of a Soviet identification with Europe as a Social Democratic alternative to the Soviet model.[116]

These Soviet scholars and party workers formed a loose network of younger researchers, all informed about the outside world, and all interested in a reformed version of the Soviet model. While they never were a majority in any of the institutions that employed them, they affected and effected both local and national conversations about socialism through years of informal meetings, seminars, conferences and joint work on memos and speeches for political superiors.[117]

112 Shakhnazarov, *S vozhdiami,* pp. 249–51.
113 Jeffrey Checkel, *Ideas and International Political Change: Soviet/Russian Behavior and the End of the Cold War* (New Haven: Yale University Press, 1997), pp. 32–3, 82–105.
114 English, *Russia and the Idea of the West,* pp. 96–113, 131, and 290 n. 78.
115 Primakov, *Gody v bol'shoi politike,* p. 15.      116 Shakhnazarov, *S vozhdiami,* p. 94.
117 English, *Russia and the Idea of the West,* p. 101.

Given how information was organised in these years, this reformist discourse rarely influenced decision-making at the top. But this too began to change slowly over time. Andropov, as CC secretary of the department of relations with socialist countries, recruited heavily from among the reformist cadres who had been in Prague to form his own personal staff of consultants.[118] But this was uncommon. In the late 1970s, for example, it was forbidden to send unsolicited memos directly to the Politburo or CC apparat. They had to be vetted by Chernenko's department, a death sentence for almost all of them. But a revolution of sorts occurred when Andropov became General Secretary in November 1982. He commissioned some 110 reports about Soviet domestic affairs from these reformist experts, and Gorbachev was in charge of this task.

The last institutional carrier of reformist discourse was the intelligentsia. They lived all across the Soviet Union and had their own institutions in creative unions, editorial boards of journals and publishing houses, performance spaces and, of course, their own works. They were the mass base for the reformist cadres who were officially placed in research institutes and party and government positions. The intelligentsia was a vast and authoritative terrain on which the discourse of difference was acted out on a daily basis, keeping contestation alive. I say authoritative because even Brezhnev failed to appoint his own favourites to the Soviet Academy of Sciences. And not even Brezhnev dared ask the academy to expel Sakharov from its ranks.[119]

The Soviet identity of difference, unchallenged after Molotov's removal, contradicted the Chinese identity of Stalinist orthodoxy. The discourse between China and the Soviet Union after 1957 is almost identical to that between Molotov and Khrushchev the previous four years.[120] The Soviet identification of itself as the centre and apex of the world revolutionary movement was in conflict with China's growing understanding of the Soviet Union as a revisionist, degenerate, bourgeois state. 'Each country defined the image of its partner according to whether or not it corresponded to its own ideas about the criteria of socialism.'[121] The identity conflict with China affected Soviet policy all over the world. Challenged by China for leadership of revolutions in the decolonising world, the Soviet Union redoubled its efforts there to counter these charges and establish its credentials as the true socialist vanguard. Criticised for sacrificing the world revolutionary movement on the altar of détente with the US, Khrushchev was increasingly constrained in making concessions

118 Shakhnazarov, S vozhdiami, pp. 133–6; and Wishnick, Mending Fences, p. 75.
119 Primakov, Gody v bol'shoi politike, pp. 22–3.     120 Westad, Brothers in Arms, p. 20.
121 Kulik, Sovetsko-kitaiskii raskol, p. 49, 167–8, 300, 341–4. See also Zubok and Pleshakov, Inside the Kremlin's Cold War, p. 215.

to the West. Moreover, détente with the West increased Soviet interests in supporting NLMs in the developing world, to compensate for the softer line with the imperialists on the issues of Germany and nuclear weapons. The identity conflict with China also had domestic consequences for Soviet identity. If Hungary fixed the limits of difference in 1956, then China in the 1960s empowered Soviet proponents of difference by giving them an example of orthodox Stalinism against which the Soviet Union was officially struggling.[122]

Identity politics helps explain why, as the split reached its climax in the 1960s, it was China, not the Soviet Union, who pushed matters to a complete break. Chinese identity was vulnerable to a reformist understanding of difference, because it had embarked on a neo-Stalinist industrial and cultural revolution. Soviet identity was not threatened, as China's greater orthodoxy was explained away by China's subordinate position on the hierarchy of modernity and revolutionary progress.[123] Soviet deviation could not so easily be explained away by China.

The fact that the Soviet Union never denied China its socialist identity reveals an important discursive bias in Moscow.[124] Difference in the direction of reformism could result in the loss of a socialist identity, as in Hungary and Czechoslovakia; difference in the direction of greater orthodoxy could not. This privileging of orthodoxy helps explain the extraordinary leverage Soviet allies in Eastern Europe and the decolonising world had on the Soviet leadership whenever they invoked more orthodox or revolutionary commitments than prevailed in Soviet discourse at home at the time.

In October 1957, the Soviets agreed to give China a model of an atomic bomb. But in January 1958 Mao announced the 'great leap forward', a neo-Stalinist modernisation programme. In March, Mao told his colleagues that the Soviet model was no longer appropriate.[125] In July 1959, Khrushchev declared the great leap forward to be a Leftist error. In August, the Soviet Union remained neutral on the border clashes between Indian and Chinese forces.[126] The same month, the Soviet Union informed China that nuclear co-operation was over because it was inconsistent with Soviet efforts to get a comprehensive ban on testing nuclear weapons with the United States.[127] A month later, after his trip to the United States, Khrushchev travelled to Beijing where Mao accused him of 'Right opportunism', incidentally, the charge made by Stalin in his purges in

122 Shakhnazarov, S vozhdiami, pp. 105–6; and Arbatov, The System, pp. 97–101.
123 Hopf, Social Construction, pp. 124–34; and Zubok and Pleshakov, Inside the Kremlin's Cold War, p. 230.
124 Kulik, Sovetsko-kitaiskii raskol, p. 466.    125 Chen Jian, Mao's China, pp. 72–3.
126 Taubman, Khrushchev, p. 392, and Chen Jian, Mao's China, p. 79.
127 Khrushchev, Nikita Khrushchev, p. 271; and Chen Jian, Mao's China, p. 78.

the 1930s against Bukharin, Tomskii and Rykov.[128] Suslov, in his report to the December 1959 CC plenum, wrote that Mao had created a cult of personality, parroting Twentieth Party Congress charges against Stalin.[129] In June 1960, at the Romanian party congress, Khrushchev publicly declared Mao to be an 'ultra-leftist, ultra-dogmatist, indeed a Left revisionist', echoing the 1957 charges against Molotov.[130] He announced, upon returning to Moscow, the withdrawal of all Soviet advisers from China. Khrushchev reported to a 1960 CC plenum that 'when he talks to Mao, he gets the impression he is listening to Stalin'.[131]

The change in identity relations with China implied Soviet interests in proving its vanguard identity in the decolonising world.[132] At the December 1960 meeting of Communist and workers' parties in Moscow, the Communist parties from Latin America, south-east Asia, and India all sided with China against the Soviet position of appreciating difference, of collaborating with bourgeois nationalists in decolonising countries. The next month, Khrushchev gave a speech at the Institute of Marxism-Leninism in which he distinguished between just wars of national liberation and local and colonial wars that were both unjust and fraught with the risk of escalation to nuclear war. Soviet reluctance to arm resistance fighters in Algeria and Laos was overcome by the Chinese threat to supplant Moscow as the revolutionary vanguard.[133] In August 1961, Khrushchev approved an unprecedented level of military aid to NLMs in Latin America and Africa.[134] At a 1964 meeting of Latin American Communist parties in Havana, Moscow agreed to more military aid for local rebels on the condition that none of it ended up with factions enjoying Chinese support.[135] An April 1970 KGB memo to the CCID advocating a more aggressive

128 William Taubman, 'Khrushchev vs. Mao', *Cold War International History Project Bulletin* 8–9 (1996/7): 245; Taubman, *Khrushchev*, p. 394; Shu Guang Zhang, *Economic Cold War: America's Embargo against China and the Sino-Soviet Alliance, 1949–1963* (Washington: Woodrow Wilson Center Press, 2001), p. 229; and Head of the Soviet Foreign Ministry's Far Eastern Department, Mikhail 'Zimyanin on Sino-Soviet Relations, September 15, 1959', in Westad, *Brothers in Arms*, pp. 356–9.
129 'More New Evidence', p. 103. For Suslov, see Kulik, *Sovetsko-kitaiskii raskol*, 336.
130 Westad, *Brothers in Arms*, p. 25; and Taubman, *Khrushchev*, p. 470.
131 M. Y. Prozumenshchikov, 'The Sino-Indian Conflict, the Cuban Missile Crisis, and the Sino-Soviet Split' *Cold War International History Project Bulletin* 8–9 (1996/7): 232.
132 Georgii Shakhnazarov, *Tsena svobody: Reformatsiia Gorbacheva glazami ego pomoshchika* (Moscow: Rossika/Zevs, 1993), p. 24; and Arbatov, *The System*, pp. 101, 170; Kulik, *Sovetsko-Kitaiskii Raskol*, pp. 336–47, 375; and 'Records of Meetings of CPSU and CCP Delegations, Moscow, July 5–20, 1963', in Westad, *Brothers in Arms*, p. 386.
133 Richter, *Khrushchev's Double Bind*, pp. 137–8.
134 Zubok and Pleshakov, *Inside the Kremlin's Cold War*, p. 254.
135 Richard D. Anderson, *Public Politics in an Authoritarian State* (Ithaca, N.Y.: Cornell University Press, 1993), p. 164, and Zubok and Pleshakov, *Inside the Kremlin's Cold War*, pp. 268–9.

Soviet policy in Africa justified doing so by citing competition with China for leadership of revolutionary movements on that continent.[136] Together, the CCID and identity relations with China kept Soviet vanguard identity alive throughout the Cold War and pushed Moscow to a series of military interventions there to vindicate that identity.[137]

By 1962, economic activity between the two countries had been reduced to 5 per cent of 1959's level.[138] From September 1963 to July 1964, the CCP published a nine-part open letter in which it developed its case against the Soviet bourgeois deviant.[139] As Kulik put it, relations between the two were now based 'on generally accepted norms, [not] on the principles of socialist internationalism'.[140] From 1965 to 1973, the Soviets engaged in a sustained and massive military build-up in the Far East, punctuated by the armed clashes on the Amur River in 1969. From 1969 to 1973, Soviet manpower tripled to forty divisions, about 370,000 troops, most units of which were equipped with tactical nuclear missiles.[141]

Only in 1978, with the ascension of Deng Xiaoping, and his reformist domestic policy, does the Stalinist Chinese Other disappear from Soviet identity politics. It is replaced within the CCID by a view of China as a revisionist socialist power and within the MFA as a less hostile threat.[142] As Wishnick observes, Suslov, CC secretary in charge of ideology until 1982 and Oleg Rakhmanin, secretary in charge of relations with socialist countries until 1986, were the 'headquarters in opposition to any change in relations with China'. They were uniquely advantaged institutionally by their mandates and by the fact that 'they enjoyed a near monopoly over information and analysis on China'.[143]

The introduction of a 'limited contingent' of Soviet armed forces into Afghanistan in 1979 was the final act of Soviet self-encirclement. Opposed to the coup that toppled Mohammed Daud and brought the People's Democratic Party of Afghanistan (PDPA) to power in April 1978, opposed to the PDPA's radical domestic programme, opposed to deploying Soviet troops to save an unpopular regime, Soviet leaders found themselves in a quagmire

---

136 Westad, 'Moscow and the Angolan Crisis', pp. 22, 30 n. 8.
137 On Cuba, see Aleksandr Fursenko and Timothy Naftali, 'One Hell of a Gamble': Khrushchev, Castro and Kennedy (New York: Norton, 1997), pp. 167–8; on Vietnam, see Chen Jian, Mao's China, pp. 231–5, and Gaiduk, Confronting Vietnam, pp. 132–3; on Angola, see Georgii Kornienko, Kholodnaia voina (Moscow: Mezhdunarodnye otnosheniia, 1994), pp. 166–8, and Westad, 'Moscow and the Angolan Crisis', pp. 21–7; and on Ethiopia, see Ermias Abebe, 'The Horn, the Cold War, and Documents from the Former East-Bloc', Cold War International History Project Bulletin 8–9 (1996/7): 40–2.
138 Kulik, Sovetsko-kitaiskii raskol, p. 357.     139 Ibid., pp. 334–5.
140 Ibid., pp. 298–99.     141 Wishnick, Mending Fences, pp. 29–30.
142 Ibid., pp. 73–86.     143 Ibid., pp. 9–10.

made of their own identity relations, institutional biases, deterrence fears and allied manipulation.

Andropov and Ponomarev told Taraki that a coup would not be welcome in Moscow. On 17 April 1978, the evening of the coup, both the MFA and KGB sent messages to the Soviet embassy in Kabul instructing them to stop it. But Taraki and Amin ignored them. When Ponomarev arrived in Kabul after the coup, Taraki boasted: 'Tell Ul'ianovskii, who always told me that we are a backward country not ready for revolution that I am now sitting in the presidential palace!'[144] While opposing the government's radicalism, the CCID saw a new country of socialist orientation, and Moscow as its vanguard.[145] Meanwhile, Soviet intelligence agencies were, only a bit prematurely, it turns out, reporting about US support for 'reactionary forces', the mujahedin based in Pakistan.[146]

Soviet leaders knew that the Afghan government, despite incessant pleadings from Moscow, was doing little to elicit popular support.[147] At a March 1979 Politburo meeting devoted to Afghanistan, there was unanimity on three things: the People's Republic of Afghanistan (PRA) had little popular support; the Soviet Union would not intervene militarily to support the PRA; the PRA government could not be allowed to fall. Kirilenko made the first point: 'We gave them everything. And what has come of it? Nothing of any value. They have executed innocent people for no reason and then told us that we also executed people under Lenin. What kind of Marxists have we found?'[148] Gromyko declared, 'I completely support Comrade Andropov's proposal to rule out deployment of our troops to Afghanistan.' He went on to point out that 'Afghanistan has not been subjected to any aggression. This is its internal affair', implying no Great Power conflict with the US yet.[149] But Kosygin

144 Grinevskii, *Tainy sovetskoi diplomatii*, pp. 204–6.
145 N. I. Marchuk, 'Voina v Afganistane: "Internatsionalizm" v deistvii ili vooruzhennaia agressiia?', in Nezkinskii, *Sovetskaia vneshniaia politika*, p. 454; Grinevskii, *Tainy sovetskoi diplomatii*, pp. 233–4; Kornienko, *Kholodnaia voina*, pp. 189–90; and 'The Soviet Union and Afghanistan', *Cold War International History Project Bulletin* 8–9 (1996/7): 135.
146 Grinevskii, *Tainy sovetskoi diplomatii*, p. 238. US covert aid to the mujahedin, funnelled through Egypt, Saudi Arabia and Pakistan, began in April 1979, eight months before the Soviet intervention. Zbigniew Brzezinski, *Power and Principle: Memories of a National Security Adviser, 1977–1981* (New York: Farrar, Straus, Giroux, 1983); and Marchuk, 'Voina v Afganistane', p. 460.
147 'The Soviet Union and Afghanistan', pp. 146–51; and Grinevskii, *Tainy sovetskoi diplomatii*, pp. 250–1.
148 Westad, 'Concerning the Situation in "A"', *Cold War International History Project Bulletin* 8–9 (1996–7): 129.
149 'The Soviet Union and Afghanistan', p. 141. For the opposition of Ustinov, Andropov, Kosygin and Kirilenko to Soviet troops, see pp. 141–4.

made a commitment that went unchallenged: 'Naturally, we must preserve Afghanistan as an allied government.'[150]

Kosygin, in a Moscow meeting with Taraki, with Gromyko, Ustinov and Ponomarev present, told him that this was not Vietnam. 'Our mutual enemies are just waiting for Soviet forces to appear on Afghan territory. This would give them an excuse to deploy' their own forces there.[151] Taraki nonetheless begged for Soviet troops to defend Afghanistan against the enemies it was creating, even suggesting Uzbeks dress up like Afghans. In May 1979, the Soviet embassy in Kabul denied an Afghan request for poison gas.[152] From March to December 1979, Kabul requested Soviet military intervention eighteen times.[153] The professional military, represented by then Chief of the General Staff Nikolai Ogarkov and his first deputy, Sergei Akhromeev, both opposed Soviet forces entering Afghanistan.[154]

The mood in Moscow began to turn in October 1979; the Great Power deterrent discourse began to penetrate. After Hafizullah Amin had Taraki murdered after the latter returned from a Moscow meeting with Brezhnev, the KGB began to talk about Amin 'doing a Sadat', turning Afghanistan into a base to replace what the US had lost in Iran.[155] In early December, Andropov sent Brezhnev a memo arguing that Amin might turn to the West to secure his power.[156] Meanwhile, typical of Soviet allied relationships, Moscow had preferred candidates to Amin waiting in the wings, in this case Babrak Karmal, a favourite of the CCID.[157] In this same memo, the consensus on no Soviet troops is preserved, with one exception: the promise of a short successful operation to install Karmal in power, if necessary.[158]

At the 8 December 1979 Politburo meeting, all the discursive pieces added up. Andropov and Ustinov argued that Afghanistan would fall to the US, where they might deploy Pershing II intermediate-range nuclear missiles. A short successful military engagement was the worst-case scenario. Karmal would pursue a more moderate socialist programme where the Soviet vanguard could guarantee success. On 12 December, the decision was taken.[159] Shortly thereafter, Dobrynin asked Gromyko why, as the Americans were now so riled

150 Ibid., p. 144.    151 Ibid., pp. 146–7.
152 Ibid., p. 152.    153 Grinevskii, *Tainy sovetskoi diplomatii*, p. 275.
154 Kornienko, *Kholodnaia voina*, p. 194; Westad, 'Concerning the Situation in "A"', p. 131; and Bennett, *Condemned to Repetition?*, p. 218.
155 Westad, 'Concerning the Situation in "A"', p. 130; and Kornienko, *Kholodnaia voina*, p. 195.
156 Grinevskii, *Tainy sovetskoi diplomatii*, pp. 305–6.    157 Ibid., pp. 307–8.
158 'The Soviet Union and Afghanistan', p. 159.
159 Grinevskii, *Tainy sovetskoi diplomatii*, pp. 311–13.

up. Gromyko answered: It's only for a month; we will do it and then get out quickly.'[160]

A week after the Christmas Eve intervention, Andropov, Gromyko, Ustinov and Ponomarev reported to the Politburo that the new Karmal government intended to correct the revolutionary excesses of the previous regime.[161] But by the first week of February, Ustinov speculated that Soviet troops would remain at least eighteen months. By the first week of March, Gromyko, Andropov and Ustinov reported to the Politburo that Karmal was not achieving the promised reforms.[162] The war continued for nine years.

## Social Democracy at home: normal Great Power abroad, 1985–91

Gorbachev understood the Soviet Union as a failing, yet perfectible, socialist project. If only it were to become more democratic, it could fulfil the Marxist-Leninist promise of being a model of Social Democracy for the world. This understanding had immediate foreign-policy implications. First, by admitting that the Soviet model itself was fraught with problems, the idea of the NSM as infallible was rejected. This rejection entailed the rejection of the Soviet Union as the model for the world revolutionary movement, as the vanguard or centre of Eastern European and Chinese socialism, and NLMs around the world. Difference with the Soviet model was no longer just grudgingly toler-ated, but demanded, as Soviet experience had shown it was grossly inadequate even at home, let alone when emulated abroad in less hospitable contexts.[163] Under Gorbachev, European Social Democracy and Eurocommunism became significant Others to imitate, not oppose.[164] The common roots of Soviet com-munism and European Social Democracy in progressive thought were hailed as promising the integration of the Soviet Union as a normal, civilised, socialist Great Power in a family of Great Powers all committed to common human values of prosperity at home and peaceful resolution of conflict abroad. It was a liberal vision of both the Soviet Union and the world. As Gorbachev himself put it, 'We are merging into the common stream of world civilization.'[165]

160 Quoted in Mlechin, *MID*, p. 420.
161 'The Soviet Union and Afghanistan', pp. 160–3.    162 Ibid., pp. 166–73.
163 Anatoly Chernyaev, *My Six Years with Gorbachev*, trans. and ed. Robert English and Elizabeth Tucker (University Park, Pa.: Pennsylvania State University Press, 2000), p. 61.
164 English, *Russia and the Idea of the West*, pp. 72–91, 140–1, 183–228; Prizel, *National Identity and Foreign Policy*, pp. 191–205; Chernyaev, *My Six Years*, p. 297; and Primakov, *Gody v bol'shoi politike*, p. 33.
165 Quoted in English, *Russia and the Idea of the West*, p. 193.

This new Soviet identity implied a far higher level of security for the Soviet Union. The zone of peace had been discursively expanded beyond Eastern Europe, NLMs and the world proletariat, to include virtually all humankind. What insecurity Soviets experienced was addressable through *perestroika*, *glasnost'*, and democratisation at home, making the country more prosperous and democratic, and new thinking abroad, reassuring the world that the Soviet Union had become a new country with which all could live in liberal harmony.[166] As early as March 1986, Gorbachev told a meeting of foreign ministry officials that domestic Soviet identity was a foreign policy issue, namely, the development of democracy and respect for human rights at home would inspire trust for the Soviet Union abroad.[167]

De-institutionalisation of the NSM began with *glasnost'*, or Gorbachev's demand that the media begin to report about problems confronting the Soviet economy. At first limited to economic issues, ecology and corruption, it was soon extended to political matters and history, and finally to foreign policy and security. The discrediting of the previous Soviet model cleared the way for Gorbachev to begin economic and political reforms. Reformist periodicals, such as *Ogonek* and *Argumenty i fakty* found that revealing shortcomings in the NSM paid: circulation for *Ogonek* went from 260,000 to 4 million, for *Aif* from 10,000 to 32.5 million.[168] In the last years of his rule, Gorbachev was constrained by the discursive changes he authored. Irritated by reporting in *Aif*, he demanded the editor be fired; instead, journalists formed an ad hoc defence committee, and forced Gorbachev to back down from his old thinking.[169]

Gorbachev used the institutions he inherited, empowered ones that were emergent and created new ones. Gorbachev benefited from the inherited institution of General Secretary. Beyond the power it gave him to make all the other institutional and personnel changes noted above, it permitted the consolidation of his vision of Soviet identity as the predominant discourse in the Soviet Union. Within days of becoming General Secretary, he put Ponomarev, with whom he shared virtually no common intellectual ground, in charge of an array of foreign policy issues, in order to undermine Gromyko's MFA monopoly, and create an institutionalised challenge to those positions.[170] But within a year Ponomarev was replaced as CCID secretary by Dobrynin.

166 Chernyaev, *My Six Years*, pp. 104 and 298, 356–7; English, *Russia and the Idea of the West*, p. 219; Primakov, *Gody v bol'shoi politike*, p. 47; and Ted Hopf, *Peripheral Visions* (Ann Arbor: University of Michigan Press, 1994), pp. 90–100.
167 Quoted in English, *Russia and the Idea of the West*, p. 220.
168 Sarah E. Mendelson, *Changing Course: Ideas, Politics, and The Soviet Withdrawal from Afghanistan* (Princeton: Princeton University Press, 1999) p. 108.
169 Shakhnazarov, *Tsena svobody*, p. 310.     170 Chernyaev, *My Six Years*, p. 25.

With this one appointment, the single foreign policy institution most responsible for the maintenance of the Soviet Union's vanguard identity, and for advocating support for NLMs around the world, was cut off at the discursive knees. Moreover, the MFA became *the* single most important foreign-policy institution, no longer competing with the CCID.[171]

In July 1985 Gorbachev replaced Gromyko with Eduard Shevardnadze, who replaced personnel, created a new division on arms control and disarmament, a department of humanitarian and cultural contacts and established a formalised conduit to alternative discourses with the creation of an academic consultative council within the ministry. This council institutionalised the participation of experts, such as Primakov and Arbatov, whose reformist views had been largely ignored until then. Within a year, the MFA had experienced more turnover in personnel than any other Soviet bureaucracy. They brought new thinking and reinforced the MFA's focus on West European and American affairs, at the expense of the developing world and Eastern Europe. Shevardnadze demanded 'unembellished pictures of events', just as Gorbachev was demanding from obkom secretaries and the media at home, and developed an alternative intelligence network of foreign ministry officials and researchers at IMEMO, ISKAN, the new Institute of Europe and the Moscow State Institute of International Affairs (MGIMO).

Shevardnadze's 'very non-professionalism helped him take bolder decisions . . . He would often put his aides off-balance. He would give them a paper, and then ask: "why have we taken this position?" All would shrug their shoulders with surprise, and say: "Well, we have always taken it." Shevardnadze would shake his head, and reply: "That's not an answer. Explain to me the sense of this position."'[172] The new foreign minister compelled his colleagues to think in ways that were literally unimaginable to them before.

The military was one of the MFA's primary targets in the struggle over information. Having created a department of arms control within the MFA, the latter developed expertise and data, independent of the Defence Ministry and General Staff, that undermined arguments about Soviet military inferiority. The military was increasingly on the defensive, faced by a growing group of experts with privileged access to both the General Secretary and sensitive information that, until then, had been its monopoly.[173]

---

171 Ekedahl and Goodman, *Wars of Eduard Shevardnadze*, p. 72; and Bennett, *Condemned to Repetition?*, pp. 117, 254.
172 Mlechin, *MID*, pp. 468–77.
173 Ekedahl and Goodman, *Wars of Eduard Shevardnadze*, pp. 39–41, 70–99 and 137–9; and Bennett, *Condemned to Repetition?*, p. 257.

Aleksandr Yakovlev's CC Ideology Department created a new section on human rights.[174] Gorbachev used the traditional instruments of the General Secretary to purge the apparatus of old cadres. By 1986, there were eight new Politburo members and at the Twenty-Seventh Party Congress in February 1987, 38 per cent of the CC was replaced. Editorial boards of key journals and newspapers were stocked with new thinkers.[175] Gorbachev created 'presidential commissions', ad hoc bodies designed to provide him with advice, while circumventing inherited institutions such as the CC departments.[176]

The Soviet Union's new identity was enacted in Gorbachev's foreign policy of new thinking. Having abandoned the identity of vanguard and centre of the world revolutionary movement, interests in NLMs in the developing world, and in Communist regimes in Eastern Europe and China were transformed.

East European allies lost institutional entrée into the Kremlin and discovered that their own post-Stalinist identities had little in common with the new Soviet understanding of itself as a European Social Democracy in the making. Ponomarev was infuriated by the fact that Gorbachev preferred to meet with Eurocommunists than with East European allies. As Ponomarev put it: 'How can this be? Scores of good communist leaders, and he meets with the bad Italians.'[177] Gorbachev met with the 'bad Italians' because he identified the Soviet future with the revisionist deviant discourse of Eurocommunism. What institutionalised resistance there was in Moscow to Gorbachev's new conceptualisation of relations with Eastern Europe was undercut by the arrival of Dobrynin and Aleksandr Yakovlev to the CCID, and the restoration of the MFA as the centre of Soviet foreign policy.[178] At an October 1985 meeting of the Warsaw Pact Political Consultative Council, Gorbachev told the assembled leaders that it was time for them to act independently of Moscow.[179] In a renunciation of the vanguard discourse of the previous thirty years, Gorbachev said that 'it is time we stopped running fraternal parties like obkoms . . . If we disagree with them, then we have to make our point, not just excommunicate them, scheming and meddling in their internal affairs.'[180]

Gorbachev's expectation that East European states would remain Soviet allies, that they would become Social Democracies, along with the Soviet

174 English, *Russia and the Idea of the West*, pp. 208–14.
175 Mendelson, *Changing Course*, p. 109.
176 Ekedahl and Goodman, *Wars of Eduard Shevardnadze*, p. 68.
177 English, *Russia and the Idea of the West*, pp. 204, 326 n. 64.
178 Chernyaev, *My Six Years*, p. 36; and English, *Russia and the Idea of the West*, p. 204.
179 English, *Russia and the Idea of the West*, p. 43.
180 Ibid., p. 50; Iulii A. Kvitsinskii, *Vremia i sluchai: Zametki professionala* (Moscow, 1999), p. 479; and Ekedahl and Goodman, *Wars of Eduard Shevardnadze*, pp. 157–60.

Union, reflected his confidence in common human values.[181] Deviance was impossible in Eastern Europe since the Soviet vanguard identity was no more. In a meeting with East European Communist leaders in late 1986, Gorbachev told them they could no longer rely on Moscow for support; they would have to generate their own domestic legitimacy.[182] By 1989, Gorbachev had proscribed the use of force in Eastern Europe, and not because the Soviet military was incapable, but because this 'would be the end of perestroika', at home; such actions were incompatible with Soviet identity and its implied interests in a liberal, law-governed, international order.[183] At the December 1989 CC plenum, Yakovlev tied the new democratic Soviet identity to Soviet interests in Eastern Europe: 'If we have proclaimed freedom and democracy for ourselves, then how can we deny it to others?'[184]

The abandonment of the vanguard identity had similar effects on Soviet interests in the 'countries of socialist orientation' inherited from the thirty years of support for NLMs in the decolonising world. The most notable change was the Soviet withdrawal from Afghanistan, a decision made by Gorbachev in principle in March 1985. But its formula of 'national reconciliation', that is, negotiated settlements resulting in coalition governments and subsequent elections, was pursued as well in Angola, Nicaragua and El Salvador.[185] From being a constituent part of the world revolutionary alliance, Gorbachev redefined the developing world as part of a global alliance against nuclear war and for the peaceful resolution of all conflicts. As in other realms of foreign policy, the discourse shifted radically because of the marginalisation of the CCID, and the empowerment of a minority point of view that had been in research institutes all along.[186]

Soviet interests in China were redefined in accordance with the new identity. China was no longer understood along socialist lines within the predominant discourse, though, importantly, within the CCID, they continued to treat China as a revisionist deviation, given Deng Xiaoping's market reforms. Contrariwise,

---

181 Chernyaev, *My Six Years*, p. 54.
182 English, *Russia and the Idea of the West*, p. 224.
183 Quoted in Ekedahl and Goodman, *Wars of Eduard Shevardnadze*, p. 159. See also Vorotnikov, *A bylo eto tak*, pp. 321, 352–3; Susanne Sternthal, *Gorbachev's Reforms: De-Stalinization through Demilitarization* (Westport, Conn.: Praeger, 1997), p. 177; and English, *Russia and the Idea of the West*, p. 203.
184 Vorotnikov, *A bylo eto tak*, p. 353.
185 Ekedahl and Goodman, *Wars of Eduard Shevardnadze*, p. 185; Chernyaev, *My Six Years*, p. 42; Bennett, *Condemned to Repetition?*, pp. 278–87.
186 Hopf, *Peripheral Visions*, pp. 132–9, 166–202, 213–19; Jerry Hough, *The Struggle for the Third World* (Washington: Brookings Institution Press, 1986); and Elizabeth K. Valkenier, *The Soviet Union and the Third World* (New York: Praeger, 1983).

Soviet reformers seized on Chinese reforms as demonstrating the possibilities of the market at home. Control over policy on China shifted from the CCID to the MFA and the General Secretary, and so relations were normalised during the 1980s such that by 1998 trade between the two countries had already reached the level of the 1950s.[187]

Finally, the end of the Cold War with the West was associated with the new identity's acknowledgement of fallibility at home and abroad. Violations of the ideals of Social Democracy by Stalin and his successors had made the Soviet Union into an untrustworthy and threatening state; and its foreign policy actions in Afghanistan, Poland and Czechoslovakia, and its nuclear and conventional military build-up had exacerbated the problem. As a Great Power vanguard, the Soviet Union had encircled itself. By becoming a normal Social Democratic Great Power, the Soviet Union would ally with humanity against common threats, most importantly the danger of nuclear war. The Soviet Union would be more secure because the new discourse recognised the independent sovereignty of each state, thereby dissipating the illusory threat from a monolithic imperialist bloc headed by Washington. Gorbachev told a May 1986 MFA assembly that the most important direction of Soviet foreign policy should be European, and that the ministry was too Americanised.[188]

Gorbachev linked this new Soviet identity with the security dilemma previous Soviet behaviour had created. Reporting to the Politburo after a meeting with the British prime minister, Margaret Thatcher, Gorbachev told his colleagues that what she most wanted to know was 'What is the USSR today? She emphasized trust, and said the USSR had undermined that trust', but that the USSR's domestic reforms were making a deep impression on her, changing her image of the USSR.[189] Gorbachev told his Politburo colleagues that the West European leaders with whom he had met after the summit in Reykjavik with Reagan in November 1986 had said: 'you have no democracy . . . Let's say we trust you personally, but if you are gone tomorrow, then what? . . . Without democracy we will never achieve real trust in Soviet foreign policy abroad.'[190] The new Soviet identity treated public opinion in the West as real, and as partly the product of the Soviet Union's own foreign policy errors.[191]

---

187 Wishnick, *Mending Fences*, pp. 93–116.
188 Kvitsinskii, *Vremia i sluchai*, pp. 483–6. See also Chernyaev, *My Six Years*, pp. 56, 308, 330, 350–1; Ekedahl and Goodman, *Wars of Eduard Shevardnadze*, p. 156; and Vorotnikov, *A bylo eto tak*, p. 137.
189 Quoted in Chernyaev, *My Six Years*, p. 104.
190 English, *Russia and the Idea of the West*, p. 219. See also Mlechin, *MID*, p. 468.
191 Hopf, *Peripheral Visions*, pp. 90–101; Kvitsinskii, *Vremia i sluchai*, p. 483; and Primakov, *Gody v bol'shoi politike*, p. 47.

Among the concessions Gorbachev made to change Soviet identity in the eyes of the West were: a unilateral moratorium on nuclear testing announced in August 1985, repeatedly renewed until February 1987, by which time the US had conducted over twenty tests; acceptance of zero SS-20s, codified in the December 1987 INF Treaty; April 1988 agreement to withdraw from Afghanistan; a unilateral 500,000 cut in conventional forces in Eastern Europe announced in December 1988; delinkage of strategic weapons talks from SDI in September 1989; non-interference in the peaceful liberation of Eastern Europe, culminating in the velvet revolutions of November–December 1989; reunification of Germany accepted in July 1990; and support for the US war against Iraq, autumn 1990. Soviet insecurity was a self-inflicted wound that could be healed through not just changes in Soviet foreign policy, but a transformation of what the USSR was.[192]

Gorbachev spent the last two years of his rule desperately trying to convince the West that the Soviet Union had become something else and that they should invest in his reforms so that world politics could be forever transformed. He was disappointed. In May 1990, he told visiting German bankers that 'An historic turn is occurring in Europe and the world. If this turn is missed . . . then this will be narrow-minded pragmatism . . . *If the Soviet Union does not fundamentally change itself, then nothing will change in the world.* The Soviet people have turned to new forms of life. This is an epochal turn . . . But in the West, and especially in the US, they don't show a sufficiently broad approach.'[193] At the first Group of Eight (G8) meeting in London in July 1991, Gorbachev asked President George Bush explicitly: 'What kind of Soviet Union does the United States want to see?'[194]

## Between Europe and the United States, 1992–2000

There were three main discourses on Russian identity in the 1990s in Moscow: liberal, conservative and centrist. Each understood Russia with respect to internal, external and historical Others.[195] Liberals identified Russia's future,

---

192 Matthew Evangelista, *Unarmed Forces* (Ithaca, N.Y.: Cornell University Press, 1999), and Chernyaev, *My Six Years*, pp. 194–5.
193 Quoted in Kvitsinskii, *Vremia i sluchai*, p. 27. Emphasis added.
194 Chernyaev, *My Six Years*, p. 356.
195 I derive these discourses from popular novels, history textbooks, film reviews and newspaper articles in Hopf, *Social Construction*, pp. 153–210. For taxonomies of Russian foreign policy thought itself in the 1990s, see Richter, *Khrushchev's Double Bind*, pp. 207–10; James Richter, 'Russian Foreign Policy and the Politics of Russian Identity', in C. A. Wallander (ed.), *The Sources of Russian Foreign Policy after the Cold War* (Boulder, Colo.:

at first with the American, and then with the European, present. They identified against the Soviet past and against the internal representation of that Other: the conservative discourse of Communists and far-right national patriots. They recognised the weakness of the Moscow federal Centre vis-à-vis its eighty-nine federal subjects, but felt economic prosperity within a democratic market economy would secure Russia from threats. Russia was understood as part of a universal civilisation of modern liberal market democracy.

Conservatives identified Russia's future with a Soviet past shorn of its Stal-inist brutality and an ethno-national Russian past of Great Power status and strong centralised rule. Its domestic Other were the liberals who were under-stood as a fifth column of the United States and the West. The vulnerability of the Moscow federal Centre to the growing autonomy of the republics was a major source of insecurity, necessitating a more forceful response from Moscow. Russia was understood as a unique, sometimes Eurasian, project to be differentiated from Western conceptions of freedom and economics.

The centrist discourse identified Russia with European Social Democracy, but against American wild west capitalism. It also identified with an idealised Soviet past, but its internal Other was neither liberal nor conservative, but rather the disintegrative processes occurring within the country, most graph-ically, in Chechnya. Centrists explicitly rejected an ethno-national conceptual-isation of Russia, instead adopting a civic national 'Rossian' identity designed to capture the multinational character of the Russian Federation.[196] While Russia was unique, it was situated within a universal civilisation of modern Social Democracy.[197]

In 1992, Russia was polarised between liberal and conservative identities, with liberals implementing their economic and political plans to make Russia

Westview Press, 1996), pp. 69–94; Bennett, *Condemned to Repetition?*, pp. 306–9; Johan Matz, *Constructing a Post-Soviet International Political Reality* (Uppsala: Acta Universitatis Upsaliensis, 2001); English, *Russia and the Idea of the West*; Prizel, *National Identity and foreign policy*, pp. 220–68; Margot Light, 'Post-Soviet Russian Foreign Policy', in Archie Brown (ed.), *Contemporary Russian Politics* (Oxford: Oxford University Press, 2001); Neil Malcolm, 'Russian Foreign-Policy Decision-Making', in Peter Shearman (ed.), *Russian Foreign Policy since 1990* (Boulder, Colo.: Westview Press, 1995), pp. 3–27; and William Zimmerman, *The Russian People and Foreign Policy* (Princeton: Princeton University Press, 2002).

196  Pal Kolsto, *Political Construction Sites: Nation-Building in Russia and the Post-Soviet States* (Boulder, Colo.: Westview Press, 2000), pp. 203–27; and Tadashi Anno, 'Nihonjiron and russkaia ideia: Transformation of Japanese and Russian Nationalism in the Postwar Era and Beyond', in Gilbert Rozman (ed.), *Japan and Russia: The Tortuous Path to Normaliza-tion* (New York: St Martin's Press, 2000), pp. 344–7.

197  Matz, *Constructing Post-Soviet Reality*, p. 169; and English, *Russia and the Idea of the West*, p. 237.

into a liberal market democracy. The collapse of the Russian economy, the failure of the US to provide any significant aid, the rampant and rising crime, corruption and violence associated with privatisation and democratisation and the new issue of 25 million Russians living in the Former Soviet Union, discredited liberal discourse.[198] But conservative discourse did not take its place. Instead, a centrist discourse emerged, which, over the 1990s, became at first the main competitor with conservatives, and finally, by the late 1990s, the predominant representation of Russian identity.

Each of these three discourses had implications for Russian interests and foreign policy. Liberals desired a Russian alliance with the United States and the West. Conservatives desired a Russian alliance with anybody in the world who would balance against the United States and the West. Centrists preferred no alliances with anyone against any particular Other, but rather Russia as one among several Great Powers in a multilateral management of global affairs.

Russia's liberal identity was institutionally privileged in 1992.[199] The MFA under Andrei Kozyrev was initially the only coherent foreign policy institution in Russia, and Kozyrev purged it of Soviet holdovers. But the MFA's monopoly did not go unchallenged. The Russian Ministry of Defence (MOD) and presidential Security Council (SC) were created in the spring. The defence and international relations committees in parliament became sites of conservative and centrist attacks on the liberal MFA. The 'power ministries', the different intelligence and security branches of the federal government, also institutionalised centre-conservative discursive renderings of Russian identity. Moreover, elements of the armed forces, most notably and consequentially, the 14th army in the Trans-Dniestrian area of Moldova and local air force and army personnel in Abkhazia in Georgia, acted independently of the Yeltsin government, creating *faits accomplis* on the ground.[200] It took time for the Russian government to reassert control over armed groups acting in the name of Russia in the FSU.

The conservative Communist Party of the Russian Federation (KPRF) was the only mass national political party. By early 1993, the MFA had become a policy-making arm of the increasingly centrist Yeltsin government, and so liberal identity was to be found mostly in national daily newspapers such as

198 Prizel, *National Identity and Foreign Policy*, pp. 222–47.
199 My discussion of institutions relies on Bennett, *Condemned to Repetition?*, pp. 306–10; Matz, *Constructing Post-Soviet Reality*, pp. 40–143; and Hopf, *Social Construction*, pp. 153–210.
200 Bennett, *Condemned to Repetition?*, pp. 313–23; and Emil A. Pain, 'Contiguous Ethnic Conflicts and Border Disputes along Russia's Southern Flank', in R. Menon, Y. E. Fedorov, and G. Nodia (eds.), *Russia, the Caucasus, and Central Asia* (Armonk, N.Y.: M. E. Sharpe, 1999), p. 185.

*Kommersant* and *Izvestiia*, as well as in the research institutions revived under Gorbachev.[201] In October 1993, Yeltsin crushed a primary institutional carrier of conservative identity, the parliament, replacing it in December 1993 with a no less conservative collection of legislators in the Duma, but in a constitutionally subordinate position to the centrist president. The national TV networks came increasingly under centrist control, although the weekend evening 'analytical news' programmes, such as *Namedni* (Recent events), *Svoboda slova* (Free speech), *Vremena* (Times), *Zerkalo* (Mirror) and others remained national free-for-alls, with all discourses represented. Newspapers also continued to reflect the widest range of Russian identities, and regional TV stations, the instruments of local governors, reflected the political coloration of that particular region. The dominance of the Russian economy by 'oligarchs' also institutionalised that part of the centrist-liberal discourse that identified the recovery of Russian Great Power status in the world, and the strengthening of the federal centre in Moscow, as best achieved through economic growth and development.[202]

We can see the three discourses of Russian identity in relations with Belarus, the FSU or near abroad, NATO, and NATO's war against Yugoslavia in April 1999.[203] Conservative construction of Russian interests in Belarus and the Commonwealth of Independent States (CIS) more generally was the restoration of the Soviet Union in these former Soviet republics. This included the advocacy of the forceful defence of ethnic Russians in these places, and the use of coercion to return these republics, excepting the Baltic, to Moscow's rule. Both the expansion of NATO to the east, and NATO's war against Yugoslavia on the behalf of Kosovo's Albanian majority, were construed as a direct US threat to Russian security, necessitating a Russian military response. Conservatives identified with their Slavic brethren in Belarus and Serbia, generating an ethno-national Russian interest in these countries absent in the other two discourses.

Liberal constructions of Russian interests could not be more different. Understanding the Soviet past as something to be avoided, they were against its restoration in the form of reunification with Belarus or a centralised CIS under Moscow's management. Interests in the FSU should be the product of market economic calculations, not ethno-national fraternity or an atavistic Cold War

201 Prizel, *National Identity and Foreign Policy*, p. 241.
202 Pavel Baev, 'Russian Policies and Non-Policies toward Subregional Projects around its Borders', in R. Dwan and O. Pavliuk (eds.), *Building Security in the New States of Eurasia* (Armonk, N.Y.: M. E. Sharpe, 2000), p. 129.
203 Hopf, *Social Construction*, pp. 211–57.

competition with the US. Liberals did not oppose the expansion of NATO, but for its domestic political empowerment of conservatives.[204] While liberals did not support NATO's war against Yugoslavia, they also saw no security implications for Russia, except for its energising of conservative discourse at home.

Russian foreign policy was neither liberal nor conservative, but centrist, at least after 1992. Integration with Belarus was neither spurned nor accelerated, but rather treated as an issue of economic efficiency.[205] The creation of the CIS was neither treated as trivial nor understood as a way to restore the Soviet Union, but was instead cobbled together to co-ordinate defence and economic policy among its twelve very different members.[206] NATO expansion was neither welcomed nor opposed by arming or allying with other states against it. Instead, it was opposed, with the expectation that Russia's interests would be taken into account as much as was politically feasible as the expansion unfolded. NATO's war in Kosovo was opposed vigorously, but once begun, Russian efforts were aimed at getting Slobodan Milošević to sue for peace as quickly as possible, not at arming him, or encouraging him to resist.[207]

The common centrist thread through the 1990s was to maintain or restore Russia's Great Power status through economic development at home and the empowerment of multilateral international institutions abroad. These main themes were evident in Russian foreign policy towards the diaspora. Despite incessant conservative calls to use military force to rescue Russians from discriminatory citizenship laws in the Baltic states, Moscow consistently worked through multilateral institutions, such as the Council of Europe and the Council for Security and Co-operation in Europe.[208] Meanwhile, Russian multinational companies, such as Yukos, Lukoil and Gazprom, cemented a Russian presence in the FSU through direct investments and debt-for-equity swaps to amortise local energy arrears.[209]

204 Ekedahl and Goodman, *Wars of Eduard Shevardnadze*, pp. 169–76; James M. Goldgeier, *Not Whether but When* (Washington: Brookings Institution Press, 1999), pp. 15–16; Kvitsinskii, *Vremia i sluchai*, pp. 39–43, 67–9; Chernyaev, *My Six Years*, pp. 272–3; Kornienko, *Kholodnaia voina*, pp. 264–7; and Primakov, *Gody v bol'shoi politike*, pp. 232–3.

205 Vyachaslau Paznyak, 'Customs Union of Five and the Russia–Belarus Union', in Dwan and Pavliuk, *Building Security*, pp. 66–79.

206 Martha Brill Olcott, Anders Aslund, and Sherman W. Garnett, *Getting it Wrong* (Washington: Carnegie Endowment for International Peace, 1999); Matz, *Constructing Post-Soviet Reality*; and Lena Jonson, 'Russia and Central Asia', in Roy Allison and Lena Jonson (eds.), *Central Asian Security: The New International Context* (Washington: Brookings Institution Press, 2001).

207 Primakov, *Gody v bol'shoi politike*, pp. 174–6, 305. See also Allen Lynch, 'The Realism of Russia's Foreign Policy', *Europe–Asia Studies* 53, 1 (Jan. 2001): 7–31.

208 Kolsto, *Political Construction Sites*, pp. 208–13.

209 Olcott, Aslund and Garnett, *Getting it Wrong*, pp. 54–66.

## Conclusion

The Stalinist understanding of the Soviet Self squandered pro-Soviet sympathies in Eastern Europe and anti-German feelings throughout Europe so as to reproduce the NSM in the socialist community. The post-Stalinist discourse of difference multiplied allies in the Third World, but entailed the loss of China as an ally and spurred the quest for difference in Eastern Europe. Subsequent suppression of the latter, combined with support for NLMs, led to a Soviet Union encircled by states allied against it. The Gorbachev revolution eliminated that Soviet Great Power vanguard identity that had fixed the Soviet Union and the US in a global competition for international dominance. Soviet interests in the NLMs and control of Eastern Europe disappeared with the old Soviet identity. The Russian Federation understands itself today as a Great Power who can either join European Social Democratic civilisation as a counterweight to US liberal market hegemony, or bandwagon with that hegemony in order to pursue more narrow tactical considerations in defence of its own fissiparous periphery.

What is the Soviet Union? What is Russia? These are questions about a state's identity. The answers are found in how a state understands itself, in relationship to its significant Others, at home and abroad. We have seen that how that question was answered in Moscow from the end of the Second World War to the dawn of the twenty-first century has profoundly affected foreign policy and international order more generally. States interact not only with other states, but also with themselves, with their societies and institutions. Interstate interaction affords an opportunity for other states to help empower or disempower the discourses of identity that are being reproduced at home. But they cannot in and of themselves account for a state's identity. States interact with their own pasts, their own social groups, their own political institutional landscapes. These form the domestic sources of a state's identity, and are fundamental to understanding any state's foreign policy.

25

# The Soviet Union and the road
# to communism

LARS T. LIH

The heart of the governing ideology of the Soviet Union was an image of itself as a traveller on the road to communism. This image was embedded in the narrative of class struggle and class mission created by Karl Marx and first embodied in a mass political movement by European Social Democracy. When Russian Social Democrats took power in October 1917, they founded a regime that was unique in its day because of their profound sense that the country had embarked on a journey of radical self-transformation.

Throughout its history, the Soviet Union's self-definition as a traveller on the road to socialism coloured its political institutions, its economy, its foreign policy and its culture. The inner history of Soviet ideology is thus the story of a metaphor – a history of the changing perceptions of the road to communism. In 1925, Nikolai Bukharin's book *Road to Socialism* exuded the confidence of the first generation of Soviet leaders. Sixty years later, the catch-phrase 'which path leads to the temple?' reflected the doubts and searching of the *perestroika* era. Right to the end, Soviet society assumed that there *was* a path with a temple at the end of it and that society had the duty to travel down that path.

## Marxism and the class narrative

The Soviet Union's vision of the journey's end – socialist society – was in many respects the common property of the European Left as a whole. The distinctive contribution of the Marxist tradition to the new revolutionary regime in Russia was a narrative about how socialist society would come to be. Marxism described the protagonists whose interaction would result in socialism, their motivations, the tasks they set themselves and the dramatic clashes between them that propelled society forward.

Marx shaped the Soviet Union's constitutive narrative in three crucial ways. First, the narrative was about *classes*. The Marxist understanding of 'class' is deeply shaped by seeing classes as characters in a narrative, with motivations, will, purposes and the ability to perceive and overcome obstacles. The role of 'scientific socialism' was to give a strong underpinning to this narrative. The doctrine of surplus value, for example, demonstrated the unavoidable conflict between proletariat and bourgeoisie and this in turn gave the proletariat as a class its essential motivation.

Second, the central episode in Marx's world-historical narrative portrays the process by which the industrial proletariat recognises, accepts and carries out the *historical mission* of taking political power as a class and using it to introduce socialism. This central episode is summed up by the phrase 'dictatorship of the proletariat'. The proletariat needed *political* power in order to carry out its mission for two sets of reasons: the defensive / repressive need to protect socialism from hostile classes and the constructive need for society-wide institutional transformation. Although a class dictatorship was only possible when the class in question was in a position to carry out its class interest fully and without compromise, Marx always assumed that the proletarian class dictatorship would rest securely on the voluntary support of the other non-elite classes.

Third, Marx brought the world-historical narrative home by assigning a mission here and now to dedicated socialist revolutionaries. 'The emancipation of the working classes must be conquered by the working classes themselves.' The famous motto of the First International can be understood in two ways. On one reading, the motto tells revolutionaries from other classes to clear off: the emancipation of the working class is the business of the workers and no one else. The motto was understood in this way by the French Proudhonists who were perhaps the most important constituency within the First International.

On another reading, the motto not only refuses to close the door to non-proletarian revolutionaries but actually invites them in. If only the workers themselves can bring about their liberation, then it is imperative that they come to understand what it is they need to do and that they obtain the requisite organisational tools. This mission of preparing the working class for its mission was incumbent upon *any* socialist who accepted the Marxist class narrative, no matter what his or her social origin.

## Revolutionary Social Democracy: 'The merger of socialism and the worker movement'

The basic self-definition of the Bolsheviks was that they were the Russian embodiment of 'revolutionary Social Democracy'. Their angry rejection of the label 'Social Democracy' in 1918 was meant to be a defiant assertion of continued loyalty to what the label once stood for. When the pioneers of Russian Social Democracy looked West in the 1890s, they saw a powerful, prestigious and yet still revolutionary movement. They saw mass *worker* parties, inspired by the Marxist class narrative, that continued to advance despite the persecutions of such redoubtable enemies as Chancellor Bismarck. They saw a set of innovative institutions – a party of a new type – that set out to bring the message to the workers and instil in them an 'alternative culture'.[1]

The man who gave canonical expression to the elaborated class narrative of Social Democracy was Karl Kautsky. Kautsky is remembered as the most influential theoretician of international Social Democracy, but in certain key respects – particularly in the case of the fledgling Russian Social Democracy – Kautsky's role went beyond influence. In 1892, Kautsky wrote *The Erfurt Programme*, a semi-official commentary on the recently adopted programme of the Social Democratic Party of Germany (SPD). This book *defined* Social Democracy for Russian activists – it was the book one read to find out what it meant to be a Social Democrat. In 1894, a young provincial revolutionary named Vladimir Ul'ianov translated *The Erfurt Programme* into Russian just at the time he was acquiring his lifelong identity as a revolutionary Social Democrat.

In *The Erfurt Programme*, Kautsky defined Social Democracy as 'the merger [*Vereinigung*] of socialism and the worker movement'. This slogan summarised not only the proletarian mission to introduce socialism, but also the Social Democratic mission of filling the proletariat with an awareness of its task. Kautsky's formula also provided Social Democracy with its own origin story. According to the merger formula, Social Democracy was a *synthesis*. As Kautsky put it, each earlier strand of both socialism and the worker movement possessed *'ein Stückchen des Richtigen'*, a little bit of the truth.[2] This little bit of truth could be preserved, but only if its one-sidedness was transcended. In this way, the merger formula implied a two-front polemical war against all who defended the continued isolation of either socialism or the worker movement. The technical term within social democratic discourse for the effort to keep the working-class struggle free from socialism was *Nurgewerkschaftlerei*, 'trade-unions-only-ism'. (Since England was the classical home of this anti-Social Democratic ideology, the English words 'trade union' were used by both German and Russian Social Democrats to make an '-ism' that was equivalent for *Nurgewerkschaftlerei*. To render Lenin's epithet *tred-iunionizm* as

---

1 Vernon Lidtke, *The Alternative Culture: Socialist Labor in Imperial Germany* (New York: Oxford University Press, 1985).
2 Karl Kautsky, *Die historische Leistung von Karl Marx* (Berlin: Vorwärts, 1908), p. 36.

'trade-unionism' is really a mistranslation, since it implies that Lenin was hostile towards trade unions rather than towards a specific ideology that denied the need for a Social Democratic worker party.) A corresponding *'Nur'* term could have been coined for bomb-throwing revolutionaries who continued to think that it was a waste of time to propagandise and educate the working class as a whole prior to the revolution.

By assigning the task of introducing socialism to the working class itself, the merger formula implied an exalted sense of a world historical mission. The most powerful source for this aspect of the Social Democratic narrative was Ferdinand Lassalle, the forgotten founding father of modern socialism. The cult of Lassalle that was an integral part of the culture of the German Social Democratic Party was based on his thrilling insistence during his brief two years of proto-Social Democratic agitation (1862–4) that the workers, the despised fourth estate, accept the noble burden of an exalted mission. 'The high and world-wide honour of this destiny must occupy all your thoughts. Neither the load of the oppressed, nor the idle dissipation of the thoughtless, nor even the harmless frivolity of the insignificant, are henceforth becoming to you. You are the rock on which the Church of the present is to be built.'[3] Anyone who pictures Social Democracy as based on dry and deterministic 'scientific socialism' and overlooks the fervent rhetoric of good news and saving missions has missed the point.

The merger formula also reveals the logic that drove the creation of the party-led alternative culture. The fantastic array of newspapers, the sporting clubs, the socialist hymns, all under the leadership of a highly organised national political party – this entire innovative panoply was meant to merge in the most profound way possible the new socialist outlook with the outlook of each worker.

Social Democracy's self-proclaimed mission of bringing the good news of socialism to the workers meant that it had a profound stake in political democracy and particularly in political liberties such as freedom of speech, press and assembly. Political liberties were only a means – but they were an absolutely essential means. In an image that profoundly influenced Russian Social Democracy, Kautsky asserted that political liberties were 'light and air for the proletariat'.[4] The vital importance of political liberties was a key sector in the two-front polemical war against both isolated trade-union activists and

3 *The Workingman's Programme (Arbeiter-Programm)* (New York: International Publishing Company, 1899), p. 59.
4 *Das Erfurter Programm* (Berlin: Dietz Verlag, 1965), p. 219.

isolated revolutionaries, both of whom tended to ignore or even scorn the need for fighting absolutism and broadening political liberties.

Indeed, Social Democracy pictured itself, accurately enough, as one of the principal forces sustaining political democracy in turn-of-the-century Europe. The reasoning behind this claim is the basis for the political strategy to which the Russian Social Democrats gave the name of 'hegemony in the democratic revolution'. The bourgeoisie does indeed have a class interest in full parliamentary democracy and political liberties, but as time goes by, the bourgeoisie is less and less ready to act on this interest. The same reason that makes Social Democracy eager for democracy (political liberties make the merger of socialism and the worker movement possible and therefore inevitable) douses the enthusiasm of the bourgeoisie. Thus Social Democracy becomes the only consistent fighter for democracy. In fact, some major democratic reforms will probably have to wait until the dictatorship of the proletariat and the era of socialist transformation. In the meantime, bourgeois democracy is much too important to be left to the bourgeoisie.

The defence of democracy was a *national* task in which Social Democracy saw itself as a fighter for the here-and-now interests of *all* the non-elite classes. In the Social Democratic narrative, the proletariat did not look on all the other labouring classes with 'contempt' (as is often stated). The proletariat was rather pictured as the inspiring leader of what might be called follower classes. As Kautsky explained in a section of *The Erfurt Programme* entitled *Die Sozialdemokratie und das Volk*, the leadership role of the proletariat had two aspects. In the long run, peasants and urban petty bourgeoisie would see that their own deepest aspiration – to assert control over their productive activity – could only be attained through the 'proletarian socialism' of centralised social control and not through individual ownership. In the short run, the non-elite classes would realise – sooner rather than later – that nationally organised and militant Social Democracy was the only effective defender of their current perceived interests. In the Marxist texts that most influenced Lenin, the dominant note is not pessimism and fear of, say, the peasants but rather an unrealistic optimism that they would soon accept the leadership of the organised workers.

## Russian Social Democracy

From the point of view of a young Russian revolutionary in the 1890s choosing a political identity, what was the greatest obstacle to choosing to be a revolutionary Social Democrat? A Social Democrat had to reject the pessimistic horror that capitalist industrialisation had inspired in earlier Russian revolutionaries, but this rejection was hardly an obstacle – on the contrary, it was an impetus for optimistic energy in the face of what seemed by the 1890s to be inevitable economic processes. The minuscule dimensions of the new Russian industrial working class also hardly constituted an obstacle, since organising and propagandising even the relatively few Russian workers offered plenty of scope for activity.

The greatest obstacle – the crucial distinction between Russia and the countries where Social Democracy flourished – was the *lack of political liberties*. The tsarist autocracy seemed to make 'Russian Social Democrat' something of an oxymoron. The whole meaning of Social Democracy revolved around propaganda and agitation on a national level. What then was the point of even talking about Social Democracy in a country where even prominent and loyal members of the elite were prohibited from publicly speaking their mind?

Accordingly, many revolutionaries adopted severely modified forms of Social Democratic ideas. Some accepted the importance of achieving political liberty but concluded that a mass movement was a non-starter as a way of overthrowing tsarism. Others accepted the importance of organising the working class but felt that political liberties were not *so* fundamental that overthrowing the autocracy should be a top priority task for the workers.

The central strand of Russian Social Democracy – the strand that ran from the Liberation of Labour group (Georgii Plekhanov, Pavel Aksel'rod and Vera Zasulich) in the early 1880s through the *Iskra* organisation of 1900–3 and then through both the Menshevik and Bolshevik factions that emerged from *Iskra* – tried to be as close to Western-style Social Democracy as circumstances would allow. The guiding principle of Russian Social Democracy can be summed up as: Let us build a party as much like the German SPD as possible under absolutist conditions so we can overthrow the tsar and obtain the political liberties that we need to make the party even more like the SPD!

As worked out by the polemics of the underground newspaper *Iskra* at the turn of the century, this basic principle led to the following assertions. The Russian working class *can* be organised by revolutionaries working in underground conditions. The workers *can* understand the imperative of political liberty both for the sake of immediate economic interests and for the long-run prospects of socialism. Their militant support of a democratic anti-tsarist revolution will instigate other non-elite classes and even the progressive parts of the elite to press home their own revolutionary demands. Thanks primarily to the militancy of the working class, the coming Russian democratic revolution will have a more satisfactory outcome than, say, the half-baked German revolution in the middle of the nineteenth century, since it will attain the greatest possible amount of political liberty. And these political liberties will allow the education and organisation of the Russian working class on an SPD scale, thus creating the fundamental prerequisite of socialist revolution, a class ready and able to take political power.

Compared to the trends they were combating, the *Iskra* team stands out by its *optimism* about the potential of the Russian working class to organise and become an effective and indeed leading national political force under tsarism. *Iskra* believed that this potential could only be realised given the existence of a well-organised and highly motivated Social Democracy – a lesson they learned from the astounding success of German Social Democracy. Many readers of Lenin's *What Is To Be Done?* have concluded that Lenin wanted a nationally organised party of disciplined activists because he had pessimistically given up on the revolutionary inclinations of the workers. In reality, Lenin wanted an SPD-type party – one with a national centre and a full-time corps of activists – because of his optimistic confidence that even the relatively backward Russian proletariat living under tsarist repression would enthusiastically respond to the Social Democratic message. Lenin's opponents were the sceptical ones on this crucial issue.

It is completely anachronistic to see Lenin assuming in 1902 that the party could accomplish its task only if it had control of the state and a monopoly of propaganda. His idea of an effective party in 1902 was an organisation that was efficient enough to publish and distribute a national underground newspaper in regular fashion and that was surrounded by a core of activists who were inspired by and could inspire others with the good news of Social Democracy. Thus the key sentence in *What Is To Be Done?* is: 'You brag about your practicality and you don't see (a fact known to any Russian *praktik*) what miracles for the revolutionary cause can be brought about not only by a circle but by a lone individual.'[5]

Given later events, it is difficult to remember that a central plank in the *Iskra* platform was the crucial importance of political liberties. *Iskra* insisted to other socialists that achieving political liberty had to be an urgent priority. It insisted to other anti-tsarist revolutionaries that only proletarian leadership in the revolution would ensure the maximum achievable amount of political liberty. They drummed home in their propaganda and agitation the vital importance of what might be called the four S's: *svoboda slova, sobraniia, stachek*, freedom of speech, assembly and strikes. The Social Democratic narrative absolutely required these freedoms to operate.

---

5 *What Is To Be Done?*, in Lenin, *PSS*, 5th edn, vol. VI, p. 107.

Overthrowing the autocracy was a *national* task that would advance the interests of almost every group in Russian society. Following the logic of the Social Democracy class narrative, *Iskra* assumed that a socialist party could and should assume the leadership role in achieving democracy. They engaged in a complicated political strategy whereby they supported anti-tsarist liberals, fought with the liberals for the loyalty of the non-elite classes and tried to make the non-elite classes aware of the necessity of winning as much political liberty as possible in the upcoming revolution.

*Iskra* conducted the usual Social Democratic two-front polemical war. The prominence of *What Is To Be Done?* means that we see only one front of the war, namely, the attack against the 'economists' who allegedly wanted to keep the workers aloof from the great merger. In *Iskra*'s activity (and in Lenin's writings) as a whole during this period, the other front in the war was just as prominent or even more so: the attack against the terrorists who allegedly believed that an organised mass worker movement was a pipe dream that would only delay the revolution.

After 1903, the *Iskra* organisation broke up into two Social Democratic factions. The Menshevik/Bolshevik split has achieved mythic status as the place where two roads diverged and taking one rather than the other made all the difference. Counter-intuitive as it may seem, the Menshevik leaders originally dismissed Lenin as someone who put *too high* a priority on achieving political liberties, who would allow Social Democracy to be exploited by bourgeois revolutionaries and who neglected the specifically *socialist* task of instilling hostility between worker and capitalist.

Similarly, Bolshevism prior to the First World War can almost be defined as the Social Democratic faction most fanatically insistent on the importance of political liberties. Lenin's precepts were: *Don't* be satisfied with bourgeois leadership of the bourgeois revolution because the liberals will not push the revolution to achieve its maximum gains. *Don't* be satisfied with the meagre liberties provided by the post-1905 Stolypin regime. *Search* for the most radically democratic allies among the non-elite classes. *Preserve* at all costs a party base in the illegal underground that is the only space in Russia for truly free speech.

## The class narrative in a time of troubles

In 1914 a group of Bolsheviks – the party's representatives in the national legislative Duma – met to compare impressions about the stunning news that the German SPD had voted in favour of war credits for the German government. This news shook them profoundly because 'all Social Democrats had "learned from the Germans" how to be socialists'. The deputies agreed on one thing: the erstwhile model party had betrayed revolutionary socialism.[6]

Six years later, at the Second Congress of the Third International, another party presented itself as an international model: the Bolsheviks themselves. This new Bolshevik model, profoundly marked by the intervening six years of war and civil war, could not have been predicted from knowledge of pre-war Bolshevism. A party that had put the achievement of 'bourgeois democracy' in Russia at the centre of its political strategy now angrily rejected bourgeois democracy and all its works. A party that had propagandised the crucial importance of political liberties had become notorious for dictatorial repression and a state monopoly of mass media.

And yet, despite all these changes, the Bolsheviks claimed to remain loyal to the old class narrative – indeed, they claimed to be the *only* loyal ones. Bolshevism as a factor in world history – as an alternative model for a socialist party and as the constitutive myth of the Soviet Union – was based on the Social Democratic class narrative as it emerged from the severe and distorting impact of an era of world crisis.

Three major developments influenced the new version of the class narrative. The first was the sense of betrayal by Western Social Democracy. The Western European party leaders had announced in solemn convocation that they would make war impossible by using the threat of revolution – and now they not only refused to make good on this threat but turned into cheerleaders for their respective national war machines! The next influence was the apocalyptic world war. The adjective is hardly too strong: the war seemed to the Bolsheviks to present mankind with a choice between socialism and the collapse of civilisation.

The third influence was the Bolshevik experience as a ruling party. The Bolsheviks understood the October Revolution as the onset of the central episode of the class narrative – the long-awaited proletarian conquest of power. All their experiences in power were deeply informed by this narrative framework. In turn, the rigours and emergencies of the civil-war period modified their understanding of the framework. Just as fundamentally, the very concept of a class in power was discovered in practice to contain a host of hitherto unsuspected consequences and implications.

The experience of being a ruling party responsible for all of society meant dealing with other classes. This necessity intensified a fear already latent in the

6 A. G. Shliapnikov, *Kanun semnadtsatogo goda. Semnadtsatyi god*, 3 vols. (Moscow: Izdatel'stvo politicheskoi literatury, 1992–4), vol. I, p. 61.

class narrative – the fear of becoming infected by contact with other classes and losing the proletarian qualities needed to accomplish the great mission. A group often hailed as the conscience of the party, the Worker Opposition of 1920–1, was also the one that most energetically followed out the resulting logic of purge, purification and suspicion.

When the Bolsheviks closed down the bourgeois and even the socialist press, they shocked many socialists into realising their own commitment to 'bourgeois democracy'. The short-term justification was that coercion was needed to complete any revolution, as shown by the record of bourgeois revolutions. This argument was not as fateful as the decision to create an exclusive state monopoly of the mass media. This decision paradoxically had strong roots in the pre-war class narrative. The central reason that Social Democracy required freedom of speech was to be able to raise the consciousness of its worker constituency, and Social Democrats had always envied the tools of indoctrination at the command of the elite classes. If one mark of an SPD-type party was the massive effort to inculcate an alternative culture, then one possible path for an SPD-type party in power was to create what has been called the 'propaganda state'. Grigorii Zinoviev explained why the Bolsheviks chose this path:

> As long as the bourgeoisie holds power, as long as it controls the press, education, parliament and art, a large part of the working class will be corrupted by the propaganda of the bourgeoisie and its agents and driven into the bourgeois camp . . . But as soon as there is freedom of the press for the working class, as soon as we gain control of the schools and the press, the time will come – it is not very far off – when gradually, day by day, large groups of the working class will come into the party until, one day, we have won the majority of the working class to our ranks.[7]

The Bolshevik self-definition as the proletariat in power implied that the new regime had begun the process of socialist transformation. It did not necessarily imply anything definite about the depth of that transformation at any one time nor even about its tempo. Unfortunately, there are two deep-rooted misunderstandings about what the Bolsheviks actually did claim about the road to socialism in the early years of the regime. The first misunderstanding is associated with the phrase 'smash the state'. Many have felt that Lenin's use of this phrase in *State and Revolution* (written in 1917) was a promise (whether sincere or not) to bring about an immediate end to any repressive or centralised state. Some writers have gone further and posited a genuine if temporary

---

7 *Workers of the World and Oppressed Peoples, Unite!: Proceedings and Documents of the Second Congress, 1920*, ed. John Riddell, 2 vols. (New York: Pathfinder, 1991), vol. 1, p. 153.

conversion to anarchism that led to a massive attempt in 1917–18 to create a 'commune-state' that was the polar opposite of the 'dictatorship of the proletariat'.[8] The other misunderstanding is associated with the phrase 'short cut to communism'. Although the Bolsheviks never used this phrase, scholars invariably employ it when describing the policies of 'war communism' in 1917–20. According to the short-cut thesis, the Bolsheviks thought that measures put in place to fight the civil war had accelerated the pace of social transformation to the point of bringing Russia to the brink of a leap into full socialism.

These two myths obscure the real innovation in the Bolshevik version of the class narrative – one which the Bolshevik leaders themselves insisted upon. This innovation was the thesis that a proletarian revolution was *necessarily* accompanied by a massive, society-wide political and economic crisis. As Leon Trotsky summed it up in an epigram from 1922: 'Revolution opens the door to a new political system, but it achieves this by means of a destructive catastrophe.'[9] Far from implying any acceleration of socialist transformation – as suggested by both 'smash the state' and 'short cut to communism' – this quasi-inevitable crisis meant that the new era in world history would be inaugurated by a series of severe challenges to any meaningful transformation.

Lenin's use of 'smash the state' in 1917 was conducted entirely within the framework of the class narrative: the proletariat wrests political power away from the bourgeoisie and uses it to gradually remove the class contradictions that make a repressive state necessary. In his celebrated epigram about the cook running the affairs of the state, Lenin promised only that the new regime would set about *teaching* the cook how to administer society. 'Smash the state' always meant 'smash the bourgeois state *in order* to replace it with a proletarian state'. The new proletarian state might have many of the same institutions and even many of the same personnel – and yet class rule would have changed hands and this made *all* the difference.

Bukharin drew out another implication of the 'smash the state' scenario. If the bourgeois state had to be smashed and the proletarian state had to be built up, a time of breakdown would have to be endured – and therefore social breakdown was no argument against revolution. The paradigmatic instance of this process was the army. Naturally the old bourgeois army *had* to disintegrate, since its use as a weapon against the revolution had to be forestalled, its officers could not be trusted and anyway soldiers in a revolutionary period would simply no longer obey orders. The army thus falls apart, but 'every revolution

---

8 Neil Harding, *Leninism* (Durham, N.C.: Duke University Press, 1996).
9 Lev Trotsky, *Sochineniia*, only 12 vols. published (Moscow: Gosudarstvennoe izdatel'stvo, 1925–7), vol. XII, pp. 327–31.

smashes what is old and rotten: a certain period (a very difficult one) must pass before the new arises, before a beautiful home starts to be built upon the ruins of the old pig-sty'. Eventually a new proletarian army arises. This army would fight according to the standard rules for an effective war machine and it would recruit as many 'bourgeois military specialists' as possible – of course, under the watchful eye of the commissars appointed by the new proletarian state authority.[10]

Much confusion will be avoided once we realise that the Bolsheviks saw the mighty Red Army not as a refutation but as a paradigm of the 'smash the state' scenario. When the Bolsheviks took stock as the civil war wound down in 1920, they were proud that they had successfully defended their right to go down the road to socialism, and they certainly felt they were moving in the right direction – but they also realised that the civil war had set them back in a major way. The Bolshevik economist Iurii Larin told foreign visitors in 1920 that the real economic history of the new regime would begin *after* the civil war. In December 1920 (supposedly the height of the euphoria of 'War Communism'), Trotsky put it this way: 'We attack, retreat and again attack, and we always say that we have not traversed even a small portion of the road. The slowness of the unfolding of the proletarian revolution is explained by the colossal nature of the task and the profound approach of the working class to this task.'[11]

Thus, remarkably, the Bolsheviks had committed themselves to promising the workers a vast social crisis in the event of a successful proletarian revolution. This strand of Bolshevism only makes sense when seen in the context of the all-embracing disaster of the world war. What reasonable worker or peasant would refuse the sacrifices needed to put into practice the only possible escape from a recurrence of this tragedy?

The new themes and emphases that Bolshevism brought to the old class narrative during this time of troubles were not ironed out into a completely consistent whole. Underneath the aggressive defiance, some embarrassment can be detected on issues such as freedom of speech. Still, the heart of this new amalgam was the same as the old class narrative: the proletariat's mission to conquer state power and to use it to construct socialism, and, just as important, the inspired and inspiring leadership that fills the proletariat with a sense of its mission. This underlying faith that the proletariat could and would respond to inspiring leadership informed what outsiders could hardly help seeing as a cynical and manipulative strategy. It was this same faith that

---

10 Nikolai Bukharin, *Programma kommunistov (bol'shevikov)* (Moscow: Izdatel'stvo VTsIK, 1918), pp. 54–8.
11 Trotsky, *Sochineniia*, vol. xv, p. 428 (2 Dec. 1920).

became the real constitution of the new regime and a central influence on its institutions and policies.

## 'Who-whom' and the transformation of the countryside

Nowhere is the influence of the class narrative more evident than in the crucial decisions made in the 1920s about the best way to effect the socialist transformation of the countryside. The link between the class narrative and Bolshevik thinking about the peasantry is the scenario summarised by the phrase *kto-kogo* or 'who-whom'.

*Kto-kogo* – usually glossed as 'who will beat, crush or dominate whom?' – is widely seen as the hard-line heart of Lenin's outlook. Eric Hobsbawm writes: '"Who whom?" was Lenin's basic maxim: the struggle as a zero-sum game in which the winner took, the loser lost all.'[12] This understanding of *kto-kogo* fits in with a standard account of the origins of Stalin's collectivisation drive that goes like this: the Bolsheviks tried to force communism on the peasants during the period of War Communism but found that the task was beyond their strength. Harbouring a deep contempt and resentment of the peasantry, they retreated in 1921 by introducing NEP (New Economic Policy), after which they waited for the day when they would have the strength to renew their assault on the countryside.

Given the almost folkloric status of *kto-kogo* as Lenin's favourite phrase, it is something of a shock to discover that Lenin's first and only use of the words *kto-kogo* is in two of his last public speeches given at the end of his career and that his aim in coining the phrase was to explain the logic of NEP. After the Bolsheviks legalised various forms of capitalist activity at the beginning of NEP, the Bolshevik leaders had to demonstrate – to themselves as well as to their audience – that permitting capitalist activity could actually redound to the ultimate advantage of socialism. In speeches of late 1921 and early 1922, Lenin put it this way: yes, we are giving the capitalists more room to manoeuvre in order to revive the economy – and therefore it is up to us to ensure that this revival strengthens socialist construction rather than capitalist restoration. The question therefore is, who will outpace whom (*kto-kogo operedit*), who will take ultimate advantage of the new economic policies? This question in turn boiled down to a problem in class leadership:

12 Eric Hobsbawm, *The Age of Extremes: A History of the World, 1914–1991* (New York: Vintage Books, 1996), p. 391.

From the point of view of strategy, the essential question is, who will more quickly take advantage of this new situation? The whole question is, whom will the peasantry follow? – the proletariat, striving to build socialist society, or the capitalist who says 'Let's go back, it's safer that way, don't worry about that socialism dreamed up by somebody.'[13]

Lenin pounded this basic point home in a great many formulations and the phrase *kto-kogo* would have pass unnoticed if it had not been picked up by Zinoviev when he gave the principal political speech at the Thirteenth Party Congress in 1924. Zinoviev glossed the phrase as follows: '*Kto-kogo?* In which direction are we growing? Is the revival that we all observe working to the advantage of the capitalist or is it preparing the ground for us? . . . Time is working – for whom?'[14]

Thus the *kto-kogo* scenario was indeed built around the class struggle, but the enemy class was not the peasantry but NEP's 'new bourgeoisie'. Victory would be achieved by using the economic advantages of socialism to win the loyalty of the peasantry. This scenario was not a product of NEP-era rethinking, but rather a variant of the class leadership scenario operative during the civil-war era. Basing themselves on the peasant scenario of Marx, Engels and Kautsky, the Bolsheviks saw the peasants as a wavering class but a crucial one, since the fate of the revolution would be decided by which class the peasants chose to follow. As the Bolsheviks saw it, they had been compelled during the civil war to place heavy burdens on the peasantry. Nevertheless, when push came to shove, the mass of the peasantry realised that the Bolsheviks were defending peasant interests as the peasants themselves defined them and therefore gave the Bolsheviks just that extra margin of support that ensured military victory. This scenario meant that, far from looking back at the civil war as a time of fundamental conflict between worker and peasant, leaders like Bukharin urged Bolsheviks to look back at the successful military collaboration of the civil war as a model for the economic class struggle of the 1920s.

Official Bolshevik scenarios assumed that complete socialist transformation of the countryside – large-scale collective agricultural enterprises operating as units in a planned economy – would not be possible without an extremely high level of industrial technology. The transformative power of technology was symbolised by the slogans of electrification and tractorisation that Lenin coined prior to NEP. This task of economic transformation was so gargantuan that many Bolsheviks assumed it would not occur until a European socialist

13 Lenin, *PSS*, vol. XLIV, p. 160. For uses of *kto-kogo*, see vol. XLIV, pp. 161, 163 (speech of 17 Oct. 1921) and vol. XLV, p. 95 (speech of 27 Mar. 1922).
14 *Trinadtsatyi s"ezd RKP(b)* (Moscow: Izdatel'stvo politicheskoi literatury, 1963), pp. 45, 88.

revolution released resources unavailable to Russia alone. As good Marxists, the Bolsheviks felt that the use of force to create fundamentally new production relations (as opposed to defending the revolution) was not so much wrong as futile. Precisely in 1919, when the Bolsheviks were putting extreme pressure on the peasantry in order to retain power, can be found Lenin's most eloquent denunciations of any use of force in the establishment of communes or collective farms.

The *kto-kogo* scenario is thus an application of an underlying scenario of class leadership of the peasants to the new post-1921 situation of a tolerated market and a tolerated 'new bourgeoisie'. The Bolshevik understanding of the dynamics of this situation was based heavily on pre-war Marxist theories of the evolution of modern capitalism. According to Bolshevik theorists, these evolutionary trends were immanent in *any* modern economy, whether capitalist or socialist – although of course the socialist version would be more democratic and less socially destructive. General European capitalist trends could thus serve the Bolsheviks as rough guides to their own near future. One such trend was the steady movement towards organised and monopolistic forms and the consequent self-annulment of the competitive market. The Bolsheviks also took over Kautsky's assertion that the city was always the economic leader of the countryside. These two factors together implied a steady process of 'squeezing-out' (*Verdrängung, vytesnenie*) of small-scale forms by more efficient and larger ones – petty traders by large-scale trading concerns, small single-owner farms by large-scale collective enterprises (which could be either capitalist or socialist).

These perceived trends informed the Bolshevik scenario of class leadership during the 1920s. The Bolsheviks had no doubt that the countryside would eventually be dominated economically by large-scale, urban-based and society-wide monopolistic institutions. The perceived challenge was not here but in the *kto-kogo* question: what class would be running these institutions? To use another term coined by Lenin at the same time as *kto-kogo*: what kind of *smychka* would be forged between town and country? *Smychka* is usually translated 'link' but this can be misleading if it is taken to imply that the Bolsheviks were unaware prior to NEP of the need for town–country economic links. The *smychka* slogan is specific to NEP because it evokes the economic aspect of the *kto-kogo* struggle against a tolerated bourgeoisie for the loyalty of the peasants. As Bukharin put it in 1924: 'The class struggle of the proletariat for influence over the peasantry takes on the character of a struggle against private capital and for an economic *smychka* with the peasant farm through co-operatives and state trade.'[15] The Bolsheviks assumed that 'the advantages of socialism' – the efficiencies generated by large-scale, society-wide institutions in general and *a fortiori* by the planned and rationalised socialist version of such institutions – would steadily come into play and fund the class leadership struggle by providing economic benefits to the peasants.

Stalin presented the mass collectivisation of 1929–30 as the triumphal outcome of Lenin's *kto-kogo* scenario. *Kto-kogo* acquired its aura of hard-line coercion from Stalin's use of it during this period: 'we live by the formula of Lenin – *kto-kovo*: will we knock them, the capitalists, flat and give them (as Lenin expresses it) the final, decisive battle, or will they knock us flat?'[16] Yet Stalin's claim to embody the original spirit of *kto-kogo* contains some paradoxes. Lenin and the Bolshevik leaders who picked up on his phrase had used *kto-kogo* to justify an *economic* competition with the Nepmen who dominated trade activities – a competition that would result in new forms of agricultural production only *after* an extremely high level of industrial technology was available. Stalin used *kto-kogo* to justify a policy of mass *coercion* against *peasant* kulaks to implant collective farms *long before* industry reached a high level.

These paradoxes make the often-heard claim that Stalin was simply carrying out Lenin's plan a bizarre one. Nevertheless, a close reading of Stalin's speeches in 1928–9 shows that the rationale – and perhaps even the real motivation – for his radical strategy was strongly based on the narrative of class leadership. His key assertion was that 'the socialist town can *lead* the small-peasant village in no other way than by *implanting* collective farms [*kolkhozy*] and state farms [*sovkhozy*] in the village and transforming the village in a new socialist way'. This was because class leadership would be qualitatively different *within* the collective farms from what it would be in a countryside dominated by single-owner farms:

> Of course, individualist and even kulak habits will persist in the collective farms; these habits have not fallen away but they will definitely fall away in the course of time, as the collective farms become stronger and more mechanised. But can it really be denied that the collective farms as a whole, with all their contradictions and inadequacies but existing as an *economic fact*, basically represent a new path for the development of the village – a path of *socialist* development as opposed to a kulak, *capitalist* path of development?[17]

---

15 Nikolai Bukharin, *Izbrannye proizvedeniia* (Moscow: Ekonomika, 1990), p. 256.
16 Stalin, *Sochineniia*, 13 vols. (Moscow: Izdatel'stvo politicheskoi literatury, 1947–52), vol. xii, p. 37, see also vol. xii, p. 144.
17 Stalin, *Sochineniia*, vol. xii, pp. 162–5 (Dec. 1929).

The role of the collective farms as an incubator of the new peasantry helps account for de-kulakisation, the most brutal aspect of Stalin's strategy. If the kulaks were not removed from the village or, even worse, they were allowed into the collective farms, they would simply take over and continue to exercise leadership in the wrong direction. As Stalin lieutenant Mikhail Kalinin put it, excluding the kulaks was a 'prophylactic' measure that 'ensures the healthy development of the *kolkhoz* organism in the future'.[18]

In Kalinin's defence of Stalin's murderous form of class leadership, we still hear a faint echo of the original meaning of *kto-kogo*: 'You must understand that de-kulakization is only the first and easiest stage. The main thing is to be able to get production going properly in the collective farms. Here, in the final analysis, is the solution to the question: *kto-kogo.*' Nevertheless many Bolsheviks were appalled by Stalin's version of *kto-kogo*. In the so-called 'Riutin platform' that was circulated in underground fashion among sections of the Bolshevik elite in 1932 (it is unclear how much of the 100–page document was written by Martemian Riutin himself), it is argued that the Leninist path towards liquidation of the class basis of the kulak meant showing the mass of peasants 'genuine examples of the genuine advantages of collective farms organised in genuinely voluntary fashion'. But Stalin's idea of class leadership of the peasants had the same relation to real leadership as Japan's Manchuria policy did to national self-determination. As a result, 'pluses have been turned into minuses, and the best hopes of the best human minds have been turned into a squalid joke. Instead of a demonstration of the advantages of large-scale socialist agriculture, we see its defects in comparison to the small-scale individual farm.'[19]

We have traced the path of *kto-kogo* starting with Lenin's coinage of the term to express the logic of NEP and ending with Stalin's contested claim that mass collectivisation was the decisive answer to the *kto-kogo* question: who will win the class allegiance of the peasantry? *Kto-kogo* establishes a link between Lenin and Stalin but it also demonstrates the inadvisability of turning that link into an equation. Most importantly, *kto-kogo* refers us back to the narrative of class leadership and the basic assumptions guiding the Bolsheviks as they tackled their most fateful task, the socialist transformation of the countryside.

18 *Pravda*, 21 Jan. 1930.
19 The title of the 'Riutin platform' was 'Stalin and the Crisis of the Proletarian Dictatorship'; it can be found in *Reabilitatsiia: Politicheskie protsessy 30–50-kh godov* (Moscow: Biblioteka zhurnala Izvestiia TsIK, 1991), pp. 334–442.

## From path to treadmill: the next sixty years

Out of the turmoil of the early 1930s emerged the system that remained intact in the Soviet Union until near the very end: collective farms, centralised industrial planning, monopolistic party-state. The construction of this system entailed a fundamental shift in the nature of the authoritative class narrative. Stalin officially declared that no hostile classes still existed in the Soviet Union, nor were there any substantial numbers of still unpersuaded waverers. This new situation meant that although there still existed a long road ahead to full communism, the heroic days of class leadership were over.

In one sense, the new class narrative of the early 1930s remained unchanged for the next six decades. Within its framework, there were various attempts to realise 'the advantages of socialism', either in frighteningly irrational attempts to rid the system of saboteurs or more reasonable attempts to tinker with the parameters of the planning system. This 'treadmill of reform' (as the economist Gertrude Schroeder famously described the process) was bathed in an atmosphere of constant celebration about the achievements and prospects of the united Soviet community as it journeyed towards communism. But underneath this resolutely optimistic framework we can discern a real history of the changes in the way people related to the narrative emotionally and intellectually – a history in which uncertainty and anxiety play a much greater role. By focusing on certain key moments in the presentation of the authoritative class narrative, we can provide an outline of this history.

In March 1938, the big story in *Pravda* was the trial of the Right-Trotskyist bloc – the last of the big Moscow show trials at which Bukharin, Rykov and other luminaries were condemned as traitors and sentenced to death. But alongside transcripts and reports 'from the courtroom' were continuing stories on topics such as Arctic exploration, the party's attempts to apply the plenum resolution of January 1938, campaigns to fulfil economic targets and the crisis-ridden international situation.

The Moscow show trial was intended to dramatise the need for 'vigilance' and for a 'purification' of Soviet institutions from disguised saboteurs and spies. The terror of 1937–8 was paradoxically explained and justified by the premiss that there no longer existed hostile classes and undecided groups in the Soviet Union. Therefore, if the 'advantages of socialism' were not immediately apparent, the problems were not caused by the understandable interests of an identifiable group – and certainly not by structural problems – but only by *individual* saboteurs who were wearing the mask of a loyal Soviet citizen or even party member. Stalin insisted that the danger of isolated saboteurs was potentially immense. Class leadership was therefore no longer described as persuading wavering groups to follow the lead of the party but simply as 'vigilance', as ripping the mask from two-faced *dvurushniki* or 'double-dealers'.

But on the same *Pravda* pages as the trial coverage were other stories that stressed the *damage* done by the vigilance campaign. In January 1938, the Central Committee passed a resolution that tried to cool down the prevailing hysteria – and yet the leadership proved singularly unable to move past the metaphor of the hidden enemy within:

> All these facts show that many of our party organisations and leaders still to this day haven't learned to see through and expose the artfully masked enemy who attempts with cries of vigilance to mask his own enemy status . . . and who uses repressive measures to cut down our Bolshevik cadres and to sow insecurity and excessive suspicion in our ranks.[20]

*Pravda* also printed resolutions from economic officials that say in effect: 'Yes, we know we have problems fulfilling our plan directives, but what can you expect, with all those wreckers running around? But now the wreckers have been caught and we promise to do better.' One can perhaps see in these stories the beginnings of a new approach to improving poor economic performance: tinkering with reforms rather than catching wreckers.

March 1938 was also the month of the Nazi takeover of Austria. *Pravda* stories about international tension were used to underscore the necessity of vigilance. But the shadow of the looming war also strengthened the desire of many to move beyond the internecine paranoia of the purification campaign.

The pages of *Pravda* were not exclusively devoted to the anxiety-provoking evils of two-faced wreckers, super-vigilant party officials, poor economic performance and international tension. Its pages in March 1938 were also filled with a symbolic triumph of Soviet society: the return of Arctic explorers Ivan Papanin and his team from a dangerous and heroic expedition. As Papanin and his men travelled closer and closer to the capital, the stories about them became bigger and bigger. With exquisite timing, they hit Moscow only a few days after the trial closed and several issues of *Pravda* were entirely devoted to the ecstatic welcome they received. A smiling Stalin made an appearance in order to greet the heroes.

This sense of a triumphal progression after overcoming heroic difficulties was for many participants – including the top leaders – as much or more a part of the meaning of the 1930s as the traumas associated with collectivisation or

---

20 Richard Kosolapov, *Slovo tovarishchu Stalinu* (Moscow: Paleia, 1995), pp. 151–2, 148–9.

the purification campaign. This way of remembering the 1930s should be kept in mind when we approach the speech given by Andrei Zhdanov in September 1946 which denounced the alleged pessimistic outlook of the great literary artists Anna Akhmatova and Mikhail Zoshchenko. More than just a clamp-down on literature, this speech served as a signal that the political leadership was going to try to re-create the triumphal mood that it remembered before the war. The complex of hopes and illusions, disappointments and strivings generated in Soviet society by the anti-Nazi war stood in the way of this project and were therefore perceived as an unsettling and dangerous threat. Thus the key passage in the speech – undoubtedly reflecting Stalin's own preoccupations – is: 'And what would have happened if we had brought up young people in a spirit of gloom and lack of belief in our cause? The result would have been that we would not have won the Great Fatherland war.'

Zhdanov presented the Soviet Union as a traveller on a long journey in which the present moment lacked meaning. 'We are not today what we were yesterday and tomorrow we will not be what we are today.' Writers were enlisted as guides and leaders on the journey whose job was 'to help light up with a searchlight the path ahead'.

In this version of the constitutive Soviet narrative, 'class' has almost dropped out while 'leadership' remains. Thankfully, the spotlight is not directed towards searching out hidden enemies. Yet an atmosphere of doubt and anxiety emanates from the speech: can we meet the difficulties ahead if the coming generation does not see itself as participants in a triumphal progression? Thus the core of the attack on Akhmatova was her concern with her own 'utterly insignificant experiences', her 'small, narrow, personal life' – a tirade in which 'personal' (*lichnyi*) is a synonym for 'small' and 'narrow'. The Stalin era is often called the era of the 'cult of personality [*lichnost'*]', but it might just as well be called the era of the *fear* of a personal life.[21]

When the Stalin era came to an end in early 1953, things immediately started to change, and the leadership came face to face with a task which it never really solved: how to account for these changes within the framework of the overarching narrative? The key problem was brought up as early as June 1953 at the Central Committee plenum during which the Politburo (called Presidium during this period) announced and justified to the party elite the arrest of Lavrentii Beria, head of the NKVD. The archival publication of these deliberations in 1991 showed how the leadership had to face up to an embarrassing question (as

---

21 *The Central Commmitte Resolution and Zhdanov's Speech on the Journals* Zvezda *and* Leningrad, bilingual edn (Royal Oak, Mich.: Strathcona Publishing Company, 1978), pp. 19–20, 35–6, 16.

formulated by Lazar Kaganovich): 'It's good that you [leaders] acted decisively and put an end to the adventurist schemes of Beria and to him personally, but where were you earlier and why did you allow such a person into the very heart of the leadership?'[22] The question is here a narrow one about individual leaders, but the same question was bound to expand to the much more difficult issue of why the Soviet system as a whole allowed Stalinism.

The June plenum revealed two different narratives about the downfall of Beria, one mired in the past and the other struggling towards the future. The paradigmatic examples of these contrasting narratives can be found in the speeches by Kaganovich and Anastas Mikoyan. Kaganovich insistently defined the present situation as another 1937. More than once he approvingly referred to Stalin's 1937 speech 'On Inadequacies in Party Work', a speech that served as a signal for the terroristic purification campaign of 1937–8. Using 1937 rhetoric, Kaganovich condemned Beria as a spy in the pay of imperialist powers. Accordingly, Kaganovich called for renewed 'vigilance' and 'purification'. 'Much of what was said in 1937 must be taken into account today as well.'

Mikoyan also employed 1937 rhetoric such as 'double-dealerism' (*dvurush-nichestvo*). But the spirit behind his use of such terms is almost comically opposed to the spirit of 1937. Here is Mikoyan's proof of Beria's double-dealerism: 'I asked him [after Stalin's death]: why do you want to head the NKVD? And he answered: we have to establish legality, we can't tolerate this state of things in the country. We have a lot of arrested people, we have to liberate them and not send people to the camps for no reason.' Mikoyan had no problem with this statement as a policy goal, but he argued that Beria was a *dvurushnik* because – he did not move fast enough during the three months since Stalin's death to introduce legality and release prisoners!

Kaganovich was genuinely angry at Beria, who 'insulted Stalin and used the most unpleasant and insulting words about him'. Beria's insulting attitude towards Stalin did not seem to bother Mikoyan – indeed, in his low-key way, Mikoyan made it clear that Stalin was mainly responsible for Beria's rise to power. Mikoyan rejected the 1937 scenario as simply irrelevant: 'We do not yet have direct proof on whether or not [Beria] was a spy, whether or not he received orders from foreign bosses, but is this really what's important?' He was clearly anxious to get past Beria and talk about issues of economic reform. He described the ludicrous situation in which the government offered unrealistically low prices for potatoes, the *kolkhozniki* had therefore no economic

---

22 The Plenum proceedings were first published in *Izvestiia TsK KPSS*, 1991, nos. 1 and 2. Lazar Kaganovich's remarks are in no. 1: 187–200 (this hypothetical question found on p. 188), Anastas Mikoyan's remarks in no. 2: 148–56.

interest in growing them, and government institutions sent out highly paid white-collar workers every year to plant them while 'the *kolkhozniki* look on and laugh'.

The same only partially successful struggle to shed the old language in order to present new concerns can be seen in many of the literary works of the 'Thaw' that took place in the period 1953–6. A novel such as Vladimir Dudintsev's *Not By Bread Alone* (1956) resembles in many respects the old narrative of unmasking evildoers who carry a party card. The noble inventor Lopatkin is thwarted at every turn by officials such as Drozdov. Drozdov is not a spy who should be shot or sent to the camps, but he *is* an enemy of the people who should be purged.

The historic originality of *Not by Bread Alone* and other literary productions of the 'Thaw' does not come from its muck-raking narrative but rather from its mode of being. The novel is a personal statement by an individual, Vladimir Dudintsev, who wrote it to express *his* views on the country's situation. For the first time in Soviet history, the party-state's monopoly on shaping the authoritative narrative was challenged. This aspect was magnified by the enormous and unprecedented public discussion generated by the book. Again for the first time in Soviet history, an autonomous public opinion used public channels to hear and deliberate, pro and con, on vital issues.

The narrative of *Not by Bread Alone* also affirmed an autonomous space for 'small, narrow, personal life'. Lopatkin has an affair with Drozdov's estranged wife who has left Drozdov partly because of his inability to have any sort of personal life. Indeed, Lopatkin, the counter-Drozdov, has trouble accepting his own need and right to have a personal life. The real climax of the novel is not when Lopatkin's invention is officially introduced but when he decides to ask Nadia to marry him – or rather, when he decides he *can* ask her to marry him.

Some aspects of Dudintsev's novel are more evident today than they could have been to contemporary observers. In a brief episode towards the end of the novel, Dudintsev touches on another great turning-point in Soviet history: the return of Gulag inmates to Soviet society. In hindsight we can also see that Lopatkin is a proto-dissident. Lopatkin survives on the margin of society, outside state service, relying on the support of fellow eccentrics, odd jobs, material aid from sympathisers and finally on occasional patronage from people within the system. Given the new possibility of independent material existence and armed with a ferocious self-righteousness, Lopatkin sets out to reform the system.

The last lines of the novel evoke the path metaphor. 'Although Lopatkin's machine was already made and handed over to the factories, he again suddenly saw before him a path that lost itself in the distance, a path that most likely had no end. This path awaited him, stretched in front of him, luring him on with its mysterious windings and with its stern responsibility.'[23] Lopatkin's personally chosen and mysterious road without an end subverts the narrative of society's triumphal journey to communism.

Yet the triumphal official version of the path metaphor still had some life in it. One of the most exuberant, optimistic and inclusive speeches in Soviet history is Nikita Khrushchev's comments on the new party programme at the Twenty-Second Party Congress in 1961. Here Khrushchev updated the path metaphor in an allusion to the successful exploits in space that appeared to validate Soviet claims to leadership: 'The Programmes of the Party [1903, 1919, 1961] may be compared to a three-stage rocket. The first stage wrested our country away from the capitalist world, the second propelled it to socialism, and the third is to place it in the orbit of communism. It is a wonderful rocket, comrades! (*Stormy applause*).'

The new programme ratified a fundamental shift in the conception of class leadership within the narrative. The official formula that summarised this shift was the replacement of the 'dictatorship of the proletariat' by the 'state of the whole people'. The proletarian dictatorship was defined as not only a time of repression but also of class leadership:

> The workers' and peasants' alliance needed the dictatorship of the proletariat to combat the exploiting classes, to transform peasant farming along socialist lines and to re-educate the peasantry, and to build socialism . . . The working class leads the peasantry and the other labouring sections of society, its allies and brothers-in-arms, and helps them to take the socialist path of their own free will.

In essence, this shift had been announced already in the early 1930s, but Khrushchev now drew the full implications without obsessing about the enemy within. 'The transition to communism [in contrast to the transition from capitalism to socialism] proceeds in the absence of any exploiting classes, when all members of society – workers, peasants, intellectuals – have a vested interest in the victory of communism, and work for it consciously.' The transformative function of class leadership was now transferred to the more or less automatic results of economic growth.[24]

23 V. Dudintsev, *Ne khlebom edinym* (Munich: Izdatel'stvo TsOPE, 1957), p. 296. An English translation by Edith Bone was published by E. P. Dutton (New York) in 1957.
24 *The Road to Communism* (Moscow: Foreign Languages Publishing House, n.d.), pp. 292, 250, 194, 247.

On the basis of this combination of class collaboration and institutional tinkering, Khrushchev promised the realisation of full communism within twenty years. But this less dramatic and more inclusive version of the path metaphor ran into trouble when the expected 'advantages of socialism' failed to materialise. During the post-Khrushchev period, the journey to communism seemed stalled. The Brezhnev period is now known to history as the era of stagnation, but an even more sardonic label can be found in a song by Vladimir Vysotskii. Vysotskii was a figure scarcely conceivable in earlier phases of Soviet society – a hugely popular actor and singer who was also famous for his contribution to the genre of *magnitizdat*, the guitar poetry that circulated unofficially on tape cassettes.

One of his more hilarious songs is entitled 'Morning Gymnastics'. Sung up-tempo with manic cheerfulness, the song urges us to preserve our health by doing push-ups every morning until we drop.[25] The climactic final verse is given special emphasis:

> We don't fear any bad news.
> Our answer is – to run on the spot!
> Even beginners derive benefits.
> Isn't it great! – among the runners, no one is in first place and no one
>    is backward.
> Running on the spot reconciles everybody!

'Morning Gymnastics' was not an underground song – it can be found on a record sold in Soviet stores around 1980. To read the final verse as a satirical comment on Soviet society may be over-interpreting a highly entertaining comic song (although this kind of over-interpretation was also a feature of this complex and ambiguous period). Nevertheless, whether Vysotskii meant it this way or not, his image of 'running on the spot' is a highly appropriate symbol of the class leadership narrative in its last days. A sense of frantic activity without real movement, a loss of the earlier dynamic arising from a vanguard seeking to inspire backward strata, a 'hear-no-evil' refusal to acknowledge problems – many Soviet citizens, even the most loyal, saw their society increasingly in these terms. Khrushchev had called for conflict-free progress towards communism, and what was the result? 'Running on the spot reconciles everybody!'

When the *perestroika* era began in 1985, there was a widespread feeling that running on the spot could now finally be transformed into real movement forward. Instead, the *perestroika* era was marked by an ever-intensifying

---

25 The text to 'Morning Gymnastics' (*Utrenniaia gimnastika*) can be found in Vladimir Vysotsky, *Pesni i stikhi* (New York: Literary Frontiers Publishers, 1981), pp. 230–1.

feeling that no one really knew any more *where* society should go. This de-enchantment of the narrative of the path to socialism took place in two interlocking processes. The first process was the development of reform thinking away from the question 'how do we realise the advantages of socialism?' and towards the question 'how do we avoid the disadvantages of socialism?' The other process was a painful rethinking of Soviet history. How and when did we lose the true way and what must we do to get back on track?

Now that the lid was off, Soviet society had to face up to the full implications of the question that Kaganovich dimly perceived back in 1953. Mikhail Gorbachev tried to give an answer that fully acknowledged the disasters of Soviet history while preserving the sense that Soviet society still had a mission to complete the great journey. 'Neither flagrant mistakes nor the deviations from socialist principles that were allowed could turn our people or our country off the road on which they set out when they made their choice in 1917. The impulse of October was too great!'[26]

The two processes – the rapid evolution of reform thinking and the agonising reappraisal of Soviet history – came together in the use of NEP as a symbol of the path not taken. On the one hand, NEP represented a type of socialism that co-existed with market elements and that could therefore be used to delegitimise the 'administrative command system' associated with the Soviet planned economy. On the other hand, NEP seemed to represent a genuine alternative *within* Soviet history to Stalinist crimes and inefficiency.

But NEP provided only a temporary barrier between the glory of the revolution and the taint of Stalinism. The actual NEP had meant the short-term toleration of the market on the road to socialism. If the reformers of *perestroika* were indeed on the same road, they were travelling in the opposite direction. And the more closely the reformers looked at the political institutions of NEP, the less it looked like a genuine alternative to Stalinism. As the novelist Fazil Iskander wrote sadly in 1988, 'the awful thing is that, remembering the party arguments of the time, I somehow cannot remember one man who put forward a Programme for the democratisation of the country. There were arguments about inter-party democracy but I don't remember any others . . . In such conditions Stalin, naturally, proved to be the best Stalinist, and won.'[27]

The feeling grew stronger that perhaps 'the impulse of October' opened up a fundamentally false path and made it impossible to get off that path – or even

26 Gorbachev, 'Oktiabr' i perestroika', *Kommunist*, 1987, no. 17: 9–15.
27 *Moscow News*, 1988, no. 28: 11.

that the path metaphor is simply not a useful way of thinking about a society's development. When in 1991 the Soviet Union collapsed not with a bang but a whimper, this unexpected outcome was partly the result of the previous de-enchantment of the narrative of class leadership. The Soviet Union had always been based on fervent belief in this narrative in its various permutations. When the binding power of the narrative dissolved, the Soviet Union itself dissolved.

# Bibliography

## THE PRE-REVOLUTIONARY PERIOD

Ascher, Abraham, *Pavel Axelrod and the Development of Menshevism* (Cambridge, Mass.: Harvard University Press, 1972).

    *The Revolution of 1905*, vol. I: *Russia in Disarray*, vol. II: *Authority Restored* (Stanford, Calif.: Stanford University Press, 1988, 1992).

    *P. A. Stolypin: The Search for Stability in Late Imperial Russia* (Stanford, Calif.: Stanford University Press, 2001).

Bernstein, Laurie, *Sonia's Daughters: Prostitutes and their Regulation in Imperial Russia* (Berkeley: University of California Press, 1995).

Black, Cyril E. (ed.), *The Transformation of Russian Society* (Cambridge: Cambridge University Press, 1960).

Bonnell, Victoria, *Roots of Rebellion: Workers' Politics and Organizations in St. Petersburg and Moscow, 1900–1914* (Berkeley: University of California Press, 1983).

    (ed.), *The Russian Worker: Life and Labor under the Tsarist Regime* (Berkeley and Los Angeles: University of California Press, 1983).

Bradley, Joseph, *Muzhik and Muscovite: Urbanization in Late Imperial Russia* (Berkeley: University of California Press, 1985).

    'Subjects into Citizens: Societies, Civil Society, and Autocracy in Tsarist Russia', *American Historical Review* 107, 4 (Oct. 2002): 1094–123.

Brooks, Jeffrey, *When Russia Learned to Read: Literacy and Popular Literature, 1861–1917* (Princeton: Princeton University Press, 1985).

Brower, Daniel, *The Russian City between Tradition and Modernity, 1850–1900* (Berkeley: University of California Press, 1990).

    and Edward Lazzerini (eds.), *Russia's Orient: Imperial Borderlands and Peoples, 1700–1917* (Bloomington: Indiana University Press, 1997).

Burds, Jeffrey, *Peasant Dreams and Market Politics: Labor Migration and the Russian Village, 1861–1905* (Pittsburgh: University of Pittsburgh Press, 1998).

Byrnes, Robert, *Pobedonostev: His Life and Thought* (Bloomington: Indiana University Press, 1968).

Carlson, Maria, *'No Religion Higher Than Truth': A History of the Theosophical Movement in Russia, 1875–1922* (Princeton: Princeton University Press, 1993).

Clark, Katerina, *Petersburg, Crucible of Cultural Revolution* (Cambridge, Mass.: Harvard University Press, 1995).

Clements, Barbara, Engel, Barbara, and Worobec, Christine (eds.), *Russia's Women: Accommodation, Resistance, Transformation* (Berkeley: University of California Press, 1991).

Clowes, Edith, Kassow, Samuel, and West, James (eds.), *Between Tsar and People: Educated Society and the Quest for Public Identity in Late Imperial Russia* (Princeton: Princeton University Press, 1991).

Edmondson, Linda, *Feminism in Russia, 1900–17* (Stanford, Calif.: Stanford University Press; London: Heinemann, 1984).

Eklof, Ben, *Russian Peasant Schools: Officialdom, Village Culture, and Popular Pedagogy, 1861–1914* (Berkeley: University of California Press, 1986).

and Stephen Frank (eds.), *The World of the Russian Peasant: Post-Emancipation Culture and Society* (Boston: Unwin Hyman, 1990).

Elchaninov, Major-General A., *The Tsar and his People* (London: Hodder and Stoughton, 1913).

Engel, Barbara, *Between Fields and the City: Women, Work and Family in Russia, 1861–1914* (Cambridge: Cambridge University Press, 1995).

Engelstein, Laura, *Moscow, 1905* (Stanford, Calif.: Stanford University Press, 1982).

*The Keys to Happiness: Sex and the Search for Modernity in Fin-de-Siècle Russia* (Ithaca, N.Y.: Cornell University Press, 1992).

*Castration and the Heavenly Kingdom* (Ithaca, N.Y.: Cornell University Press, 1999).

'The Dream of Civil Society in Tsarist Russia: Law, State, and Religion', in Nancy Bermeo and Philip Nord (eds.), *Civil Society before Democracy: Lessons from Nineteenth-Century Europe* (Oxford: Rowman and Littlefield, 2000).

and Stephanie Sandler (eds.), *Self and Story in Russian History* (Ithaca, N.Y.: Cornell University Press, 2000).

Evtukhov, Catherine, *The Cross and the Sickle: Sergei Bulgakov and the Fate of Russian Religious Philosophy, 1890–1920* (Ithaca, N.Y.: Cornell University Press, 1997).

Frank, Stephen, *Crime, Cultural Conflict, and Justice in Rural Russia, 1856–1914* (Berkeley, University of California Press, 1999).

and Mark Steinberg (eds.), *Cultures in Flux: Lower-Class Values, Practices, and Resistance in Late Imperial Russia* (Princeton: Princeton University Press, 1994).

Freeze, Gregory, 'Counter-Reformation in Russian Orthodoxy: Popular Response to Religious Innovation, 1922–1925', *Slavic Review* 54, 2 (Summer 1995): 305–39.

'Subversive Piety: Religion and the Political Crisis in Late Imperial Russia', *Journal of Modern History* 68 (June 1996): 308–50.

Frierson, Cathy, *Peasant Icons: Representations of Rural People in Late Nineteenth-Century Russia* (New York and Oxford: Oxford University Press, 1993).

Galai, Shmuel, *The Liberation Movement in Russia, 1900–1905* (Cambridge: Cambridge University Press, 1973).

Garafola, Lynn, *Diaghilev's Ballets russes* (New York: Oxford University Press, 1989).

Gatrell, Peter, *The Tsarist Economy, 1850–1917* (London: Batsford, 1986).

*Government, Industry and Rearmament in Russia 1900–1914: The Last Argument of Tsarism* (Cambridge: Cambridge University Press, 1994).

Geldern, James von, and McReynolds, Louise, *Entertaining Tsarist Russia* (Bloomington: Indiana University Press, 1998).

Geraci, Robert, *Window on the East: National and Imperial Identities in Late Tsarist Russia* (Ithaca, N.Y.: Cornell University Press, 2001).

Getzler, Israel, *Martov: A Political Biography of a Russian Social Democrat* (Cambridge: Cambridge University Press, 1967).

Gitelman, Zvi, *A Century of Ambivalence: The Jews of Russia and the Soviet Union, 1881 to the Present* (Bloomington: Indiana University Press, 2001).

Gray, Camilla, *The Russian Experiment in Art, 1863–1922* (London: Thames and Hudson, 1962).

Haimson, Leopold, *The Russian Marxists and the Origins of Bolshevism* (Cambridge, Mass.: Harvard University Press, 1955).

'The Problem of Social Stability in Urban Russia, 1905–1917', pt. 1, *Slavic Review* 23, 4 (Dec. 1964): 619–42; 24, 1 (Mar. 1965): 1–20.

Halfin, Igal, *From Darkness to Light: Class, Consciousness, and Salvation in Revolutionary Russia* (Pittsburgh: University of Pittsburgh Press, 2000).

Hildermeier, Manfred, *The Russian Socialist Revolutionary Party before the First World War* (New York: St Martin's Press, 2000).

Kelly, Aileen, *Toward Another Shore: Russian Thinkers Between Necessity and Chance* (New Haven: Yale University Press, 1998).

Kelly, Catriona, and Shepherd, David (eds.), *Constructing Culture in the Age of Revolution: 1881–1940* (Oxford: Oxford University Press, 1998).

Khalid, Adeeb, *The Politics of Muslim Cultural Reform: Jadidism in Central Asia* (Berkeley: University of California Press, 1998).

Kir'ianov, Iu. I., and Volin, M. S. (eds.), *Rabochii klass Rossii ot zarozhdeniia do nachala XX v* (Moscow: Nauka, 1989).

Kizenko, Nadieszda, *A Prodigal Saint: Father John of Kronstadt and the Russian People* (University Park, Pa.: Pennsylvania State University Press, 2000).

Kline, George L., *Religious and Anti-Religious Thought in Russia* (Chicago: University of Chicago Press, 1968).

Kotsonis, Yanni, *Making Peasants Backward: Agricultural Co-operatives and the Agrarian Question in Russia, 1861–1914* (New York: St Martin's Press, 1999).

Lawton, Anna (ed.), *Russian Futurism through its Manifestoes, 1912–1928* (Ithaca, N.Y.: Cornell University Press, 1988).

Lieven, Dominic, *Nicholas II: Emperor of All the Russias* (New York: St Martin's Press, 1994).

McDaniel, Tim, *Autocracy, Capitalism, and Revolution in Russia* (Berkeley: University of California Press, 1988).

McKee, W. Arthur, 'Sobering up the Soul of the People: The Politics of Popular Temperance in Late Imperial Russia', *Russian Review* 58, 2 (Apr. 1999): 212–33.

McReynolds, Louise, *The News under Russia's Old Regime* (Princeton: Princeton University Press, 1991).

*Russia at Play: Leisure Activities at the End of the Tsarist Era* (Ithaca, N.Y.: Cornell University Press, 2002).

Markov, Vladimir, *Russian Futurism: A History* (Berkeley: University of California Press, 1968).

Marx, Steven, *Road to Power: The Trans-Siberian Railroad and the Colonization of Asian Russia, 1850–1917* (Ithaca, N.Y.: Cornell University Press, 1991).

Melancon, Michael, *The Socialist Revolutionaries and the Russian Anti-War Movement, 1914–1917* (Columbus: Ohio State University Press, 1990).

and Pate, Alice, *New Labor History: Worker Identity and Experience in Russia, 1840–1918* (Bloomington, Ind.: Slavica, 2002).

Mendel, Arthur, *Dilemmas of Progress in Tsarist Russia: Legal Marxism and Legal Populism* (Cambridge, Mass.: Harvard University Press, 1961).

Mironov, Boris, with Eklof, Ben, *The Social History of Imperial Russia, 1700–1917* (Boulder, Colo.: Westview Press, 2000).

Moon, David, *The Russian Peasantry, 1600–1930: The World the Peasants Made* (London: Longman, 1999).

Nathans, Benjamin, *Beyond the Pale: The Jewish Encounter with Late Imperial Russia* (Berkeley and Los Angeles: University of California Press, 2002).

Neuberger, Joan, *Hooliganism: Crime, Culture, and Power in St. Petersburg, 1900–1914* (Berkeley: University of California Press, 1993).

Owen, Thomas C., *The Corporation Under Russian Law: A Study in Tsarist Economic Policy* (Cambridge: Cambridge University Press, 1991).

Pachmuss, Temira, *Zinaida Gippius: An Intellectual Profile* (Carbondale: Southern Illinois University Press, 1971).

Pallot, Judith, *Land Reform in Russia 1906–1917* (Oxford: Clarendon Press, 1999).

Pipes, Richard, *Struve*, 2 vols. (Cambridge, Mass.: Harvard University Press, 1970–80).

Poggioli, Renato, *The Poets of Russia, 1890–1930* (Cambridge, Mass.: Harvard University Press, 1960).

Radkey, Oliver, *The Agrarian Foes of Bolshevism* (New York: Columbia University Press, 1958).

Rashin, A. G., *Naselenie Rossii za 100 let (1811–1913 gg): statisticheskie ocherki* (Moscow: Gosudarstvennoe statisticheskoe izdatel'stvo, 1956).

Read, Christopher, *Religion, Revolution and the Russian Intelligentsia, 1900–1912* (London, 1979).

Rogger, Hans, *Russia in the Age of Modernisation and Revolution, 1881–1917* (London: Longman, 1983).

Rosenberg, William, *Liberals in the Russian Revolution: The Constitutional Democratic Party, 1917–1921* (Princeton: Princeton University Press, 1974).

Rosenthal, Bernice Glatzer, 'Eschatology and the Appeal of Revolution: Merezhkovsky, Bely, Blok', *California Slavic Studies* 11 (1980): 105–39.

(ed.), *Nietzsche in Russia* (Princeton: Princeton University Press, 1986).

(ed.), *The Occult in Russian and Soviet Culture* (Ithaca, N.Y.: Cornell University Press, 1997).

*New Myth, New World: From Neitzsche to Stalinism* (University Park, Pa.: Pennsylvania State University Press, 2002).

Ruane, Christine, 'Clothes Shopping in Imperial Russia: The Development of a Consumer Culture', *Journal of Social History* 28, 4 (Summer 1995): 765–82.

Scherrer, Jutta, '"Ein gelber und ein blauer Teufel": zur Entstehung der Begriffe "bogostroitel'stvo" und "bogoiskatel'stvo"', *Forschungen zur osteuropäischen Geschichte* 25 (1978): 319–29.

'L'Intelligentsia russe: sa quête da la "vérité religieuse du socialisme"', *Le temps de la réflexion* 2 (1981): 134–51.

Schneiderman, Jeremiah, *Sergei Zubatov and Revolutionary Marxism: The Struggle for the Working Class in Tsarist Russia* (Ithaca, N.Y.: Cornell University Press, 1976).

Service, Robert, *Lenin: A Political Life*, 3 vols. (Bloomington: Indiana University Press, 1985–95).

*Lenin: A Biography* (Cambridge, Mass.: Harvard University Press, 2000).

Shevzov, Vera, 'Chapels and the Ecclesial World of Prerevolutionary Russian Peasants', *Slavic Review* 55, 3 (Fall 1996): 585–613.

'Miracle-Working Icons, Laity, and Authority in the Russian Orthodox Church, 1861–1917', *Russian Review* 58, 1 (Jan. 1999): 26–48.

*Russian Orthodoxy on the Eve of Revolution* (Oxford: Oxford University Press, 2004).

Steinberg, Mark, *Moral Communities: The Culture of Class Relations in the Russian Printing Industry, 1867–1907* (Berkeley: University of California Press, 1992).

*Proletarian Imagination: Self, Modernity, and the Sacred in Russia, 1910–1925* (Ithaca, N.Y.: Cornell University Press, 2002).

Stites, Richard, *The Women's Liberation Movement in Russia* (Princeton: Princeton University Press, 1978).

*Russian Popular Culture* (Cambridge: Cambridge University Press, 1992).

Stockdale, Melissa, *Paul Miliukov and the Quest for a Liberal Russia, 1880–1918* (Ithaca, N.Y.: Cornell University Press, 1996).

Surh, Gerald. 'Petersburg's First Mass Labor Organization: The Assembly of Russian Workers and Father Gapon', *Russian Review* 40, 4 (Oct. 1981): 412–41.

*1905 in St. Petersburg* (Stanford, Calif.: Stanford University Press, 1989).

Terras, Victor (ed.), *Handbook of Russian Literature* (New Haven: Yale University Press, 1985).

Tucker, Robert (ed.), *The Lenin Anthology* (New York: Norton, 1975).

Verner, Andrew, *The Crisis of the Russian Autocracy: Nicholas II and the 1905 Revolution* (Princeton: Princeton University Press, 1990).

Von Laue, T. H., *Sergei Witte and the Industrialization of Russia* (New York: Atheneum, 1969).

Weeks, Theodore, *Nation and State in Late Imperial Russia* (DeKalb: Northern Illinois University Press, 1996).

Williams, Robert, *The Other Bolsheviks* (Bloomington: Indiana University Press, 1986).

Worobec, Christine, *Peasant Russia: Family and Community in the Post-Emancipation Period* (Princeton: Princeton University Press, 1991).

*Possessed: Women, Witches, and Demons in Imperial Russia* (DeKalb: Northern Illinois University Press, 2001).

Wortman, Richard, *Scenarios of Power: Myth and Ceremony in Russian Monarchy*, 2 vols. (Princeton: Princeton University Press, 1995–2000).

Wynn, Charters, *Workers, Strikes, and Pogroms* (Princeton: Princeton University Press, 1992).

Yaney, George, *The Urge to Mobilize: Agrarian Reform in Russia 1861–1930* (Urbana: University of Illinois Press, 1982).

Youngblood, Denise, *The Magic Mirror: Moviemaking in Russia, 1908–1918* (Madison: University of Wisconsin Press, 1999).

Zelnik, Reginald (ed. and trans.), *A Radical Worker in Tsarist Russia: The Autobiography of Semen Ivanovich Kanatchikov* (Stanford, Calif.: Stanford University Press, 1986).

'Russian Bebels', *Russian Review* 35, 3 and 4 (July 1976): 249–89; (Oct. 1976): 417–47.

Zernov, Nicolas, *The Russian Religious Renaissance of the Twentieth Century* (New York: Harper and Row, 1963).

## THE FIRST WORLD WAR, 1914–18

Eley, Geoffrey, 'Remapping the Nation: War, Revolutionary Upheaval, and State Formation in Eastern Europe, 1914–1923', *Ukrainian–Jewish Relations in Historical Perspective* (Edmonton: Canadian Institute of Ukrainian Studies Press, 1988), pp. 205–46.

Engel, Barbara Alpern, 'Not by Bread Alone: Subsistence Riots in Russia during World War One', *Journal of Modern History* 69 (1997): 696–721.

Florinsky, Michael T., *The End of the Russian Empire* (New Haven: Yale University Press, 1931).

Galili y Garcia, Ziva, 'Origins of Revolutionary Defensism: I. G. Tsereteli and the "Siberian Zimmerwaldists"', *Slavic Review* 41 (Sept. 1982): 454–76.

Gatrell, Peter, *A Whole Empire Walking* (Bloomington: Indiana University Press, 1999).
    *Russia's First World War: A Social and Economic History* (Harlow: Longman, 2005).

Gleason, William Ewing, 'The All-Russian Union of Towns and the All-Russian Union of Zemstvos in World War I: 1914–1917', Ph.D. diss., Indiana University, 1972.

Holquist, Peter, *Making War, Forging Revolution: Russia's Continuum of Crisis, 1914–1921* (Cambridge, Mass.: Harvard University Press, 2002).

Lieven, Dominic, *Russia and the Origins of the First World War* (New York, 1983).

Lohr, Eric, *Nationalizing the Russian Empire: The Campaign against Enemy Aliens during World War I* (Cambridge, Mass.: Harvard University Press, 2003).

Pearson, Raymond, *The Russian Moderates and the Crisis of Tsarism, 1914–1917* (New York: Barnes and Noble, 1977).

Sanborn, Joshua A., *Drafting the Russian Nation: Military Conscription, Total War, and Mass Politics, 1905–1925* (DeKalb: Northern Illinois Press, 2003).

Siegelbaum, Lewis, *The Politics of Industrial Mobilization, 1914–1917: A Study of the War-Industries Committees* (New York: St Martin's Press, 1983).

Stone, Norman, *The Eastern Front, 1914–1917* (London: Hodder and Stoughton, 1975; New York: Penguin, 1998).

Wheeler-Bennett, John W., *Brest-Litovsk: The Forgotten Peace, March 1918* (London: Macmillan, 1938).

Zeman, Z. A. B. (ed.), *Germany and the Revolution in Russia, 1915–1918: Documents from the Archives of the German Foreign Ministry* (London: Oxford University Press, 1958).

## REVOLUTION, 1917–18

Acton, Edward, Cherniaev, Vladimir Iu., and Rosenberg, William G. (eds.), *Critical Companion to the Russian Revolution, 1914–1921* (London: Arnold, 1997).

Anweiler, Oskar, *The Soviets: The Russian Workers', Peasants' and Soldiers' Councils, 1905–21* (New York: Pantheon, 1974).

Brovkin, Vladimir N., *The Mensheviks after October: Socialist Opposition and the Rise of Bolshevik Dictatorship* (Ithaca, N.Y.: Cornell University Press, 1987).

Browder, R. P. and Kerensky, A. F., *The Russian Provisional Government*, 3 vols. (Stanford, Calif.: Stanford University Press, 1961).

Brzezinski, Zbigniew, *The Grand Failure: The Birth and Death of Communism in the Twentieth Century* (New York: Scribner, 1989).

Burdzhalov, E. N., *Russia's Second Revolution: The February 1917 Uprising in Petrograd*, trans. Donald J. Raleigh (Bloomington: Indiana University Press, 1987).

Carr, E. H., *A History of Soviet Russia: The Bolshevik Revolution 1917–1923*, 3 vols. (London: Macmillan, 1953; Pelican Books, 1966).

Channon, John, 'The Bolsheviks and the Peasantry: The Land Question during the First Eight Months of Soviet Power', *Slavonic and East European Studies* 66, 4 (1988): 593–624.

Deutscher, Isaac, *Trotsky*, 3 vols. (Oxford: Oxford University Press, 1954–63).

Donald, Moira, 'Bolshevik Activity among Working Women of Petrograd in 1917', *International Review of Social History* 27 (1982): 129–60.

Engerman, David C., *Modernization from the Other Shore: American Intellectuals and the Romance of Russian Development* (Cambridge, Mass.: Harvard University Press, 2003).

Farnsworth, Beatrice, *Aleksandra Kollontai: Socialism, Feminism, and the Bolshevik Revolution* (Stanford, Calif.: Stanford University Press, 1980).

Ferro, Marc, *The Russian Revolution of February 1917* (London: Routledge and Kegan Paul, 1972).

   *October 1917: A Social History of the October Revolution* (London: Routledge and Kegan Paul, 1980).

Figes, Orlando, *Peasant Russia, Civil War: The Volga Countryside in Revolution 1917–21* (Oxford: Clarendon Press, 1989).

   *A People's Tragedy: The Russian Revolution, 1891–1924* (London: Jonathan Cape, 1996; New York: Viking, 1997).

   and Kolonitskii, Boris, *Interpreting the Russian Revolution: The Language and Symbols of 1917* (New Haven: Yale University Press, 1999).

Fitzpatrick, Sheila, *The Russian Revolution*, 2nd edn (Oxford: Oxford University Press, 1994).

Flenley, Paul, 'Industrial Relations and the Economic Crisis of 1917', *Revolutionary Russia* 4, 2 (1991): 184–209.

Frankel, E. R., et al. (eds.), *Revolution in Russia: Reassessments of 1917* (Cambridge: Cambridge University Press, 1992).

Friedgut, T. H., *Iuzovka and Revolution, vol. II: Politics and Revolution in Russia's Donbass, 1869–1924* (Princeton: Princeton University Press, 1994).

Galili, Ziva, *The Menshevik Leaders in the Russian Revolution: Social Realities and Political Strategies* (Princeton: Princeton University Press, 1989).

Getzler, Israel, *Kronstadt, 1917–1921: The Fate of a Soviet Democracy* (Cambridge: Cambridge University Press, 1983).

Gill, Graeme J., *Peasants and Government in the Russian Revolution* (London: Macmillan, 1979).

Gimpel'son, E. G., *Formirovanie sovetskoi politicheskoi sistemy, 1917–1923 gg.* (Moscow: Nauka, 1995).

Hasegawa, Tsuyoshi, *The February Revolution: Petrograd, 1917* (Seattle: University of Washington Press, 1981).

Hickey, Michael C., 'Urban *Zemliachestva* and Rural Revolution: Petrograd and the Smolensk Countryside in 1917', *Soviet and Post-Soviet Review* 23, 2 (1996): 143–60.

Hobsbawm, Eric, *The Age of Extremes: The Short Twentieth Century, 1914–1991* (London: Michael Joseph, 1994).

Kaiser, D. H. (ed.), *The Workers' Revolution in Russia, 1917* (Cambridge: Cambridge University Press, 1987).

Katkov, George, *Russia 1917: The February Revolution* (London: Longman; New York: Harper and Row, 1967).

    *Russia 1917: The Kornilov Affair* (London: Longman, 1980).

Keep, J. L. H., *The Russian Revolution: A Study in Mass Mobilization* (New York: Norton, 1976).

    (ed.), *The Debate on Soviet Power: Minutes of the All-Russian Central Executive Committee of Soviets, October 1917–January 1918* (Oxford: Clarendon Press, 1979).

Kerensky, A. F., *The Prelude to Bolshevism: the Kornilov Rebellion* (New York: Haskell, 1972).

Koenker, D. P., 'The Evolution of Party Consciousness in 1917: The Case of Moscow Workers', *Soviet Studies* 30, 1 (1978): 38–62.

    *Moscow Workers and the 1917 Revolution* (Princeton: Princeton University Press, 1981).

    and William G. Rosenberg, *Strikes and Revolution in Russia, 1917* (Princeton: Princeton University Press, 1989).

Kolonitskii, B. I., 'Antibourgeois Propaganda and Anti-*Burzhui* Consciousness in 1917', *Russian Review* 53, 2 (1994): 183–96.

    *Simvoly vlasti i bor'ba za vlast'* (St Petersburg: Dmitrii Bulanin, 2001).

Kowalski, Ronald I., *The Bolshevik Party in Conflict: The Left Communist Opposition of 1918* (London: Macmillan, 1991).

Laqueur, Walter, *The Dream that Failed: Reflections on the Soviet Union* (New York: Oxford University Press, 1994).

Lenin, V. I., *Polnoe sobranie sochinenii*, 55 vols. (Moscow: Gosizdpolit, 1958–65).

Longley, David A., 'Divisions in the Bolshevik Party in March 1917', *Soviet Studies* 24, 1 (1972–3): 61–76.

McDaniel, Tim, *Autocracy, Capitalism, and Revolution in Russia* (Berkeley: University of California Press, 1988).

Malia, Martin, *The Soviet Tragedy: A History of Socialism in Russia, 1917–1991* (New York: Free Press, 1994).

Mandel, David, *The Petrograd Workers and the Soviet Seizure of Power: From the July Days 1917 to July 1918* (London: Macmillan, 1984).

Mawdsley, Evan, *The Russian Baltic Fleet: War and Politics, February 1917–April 1918* (London: Macmillan, 1978).

Medvedev, Roy, *The October Revolution*, trans. George Saunders (New York: Columbia Press, 1979).

Melancon, Michael, *The Socialist Revolutionaries and the Russian Anti-War Movement, 1914–1917* (Columbus: Ohio State University Press, 1990).

Munck, J. L., *The Kornilov Revolt: A Critical Examination of Sources* (Aarhus: Aarhus University Press, 1987).

Pipes, Richard, *Communism, the Vanished Specter* (New York: Oxford University Press, 1994).

Protasov, L. G., *Vserossiiskoe uchreditel'noe sobranie: istoriia rozhdeniia i gibeli* (Moscow: Rosspen, 1997).

Rabinowitch, Alexander, *Prelude to Revolution: The Petrograd Bolsheviks and the July 1917 Uprising* (Bloomington: Indiana University Press, 1968).

    *The Bolsheviks Come to Power: The Revolution of 1917 in Petrograd* (New York: Norton, 1976).

Radkey, O. H., *The Agrarian Foes of Bolshevism* (New York: Columbia University Press, 1958).

Raleigh, Donald J. (ed.), *Provincial Landscapes: Local Dimensions of Soviet Power, 1917–53* (Pittsburgh: University of Pittsburgh Press, 2001).

Read, Christopher, *From Tsar to Soviets* (London: UCL Press, 1996).

Reed, John, *Ten Days that Shook the World* (New York: Boni and Liveright, 1919; Harmondsworth: Penguin, 1970).

Rosenberg, W. G., *Liberals in the Russian Revolution: The Constitutional Democratic Party, 1917–21* (Princeton: Princeton University Press, 1974).

'Social Mediations and State Construction in Revolutionary Russia', *Social History* 19, 2 (1994): 169–88.

Service, Robert, *The Bolshevik Party in Revolution: A Study in Organisational Change, 1917–1923* (London: Macmillan; New York: Barnes and Noble, 1979).

(ed.), *Society and Politics in the Russian Revolution* (London: Macmillan, 1992).

Shliapnikov, A. G., *Kanun semnadtsatogo goda. Semnadtsatyi god*, 3 vols. (Moscow: Izdatel'stvo politicheskoi literatury, 1992–4).

Smele, Jonathan D., *Civil War in Siberia: The Anti-Bolshevik Government of Admiral Kolchak, 1918–1920* (Cambridge: Cambridge University Press, 1996).

Smith, S. A., *Red Petrograd: Revolution in the Factories, 1917–18* (Cambridge: Cambridge University Press, 1983).

*The Russian Revolution: A Very Short Introduction* (Oxford: Oxford University Press, 2002).

Stalin, I. V., *Sochineniia*, 13 vols (Moscow: Gosudarstvennoe izdatel'stvo politicheskoi literatury, 1946–53).

*Works*, 13 vols. (Moscow: Foreign Languages Publishing House, 1952–5).

Steinberg, Mark D., *Voices of Revolution, 1917. Documents*, trans. Marian Schwartz (New Haven: Yale University Press, 2001).

and Khrustalëv, Vladimir M., *The Fall of the Romanovs: Political Dreams and Personal Struggles in a Time of Revolution* (New Haven: Yale University Press, 1995).

Suny, Ronald Grigor, *The Baku Commune, 1917–1918: Class and Nationality in the Russian Revolution* (Princeton: Princeton University Press, 1972).

'Revision and Retreat in the Historiography of 1917: Social History and its Critics', *Russian Review* 53, 2 (1994): 165–82.

'Toward a Social History of the October Revolution', *American Historical Review* 88, 1 (1983): 31–52.

Tsereteli, I., *Vospominaniia o fevral'skoi revoliutsii*, 2 vols. (Paris: Mouton, 1958).

von Hagen, Mark, 'The Great War and the Mobilization of Ethnicity in the Russian Empire', in Barnett R. Rubin and Jack Snyder (eds.), *Post-Soviet Political Order: Conflict and State-Building* (New York: Routledge, 1998), pp. 34–57.

Wade, R. A., *Red Guards and Workers' Militias in the Russian Revolution* (Stanford, Calif.: Stanford University Press, 1984).

*The Russian Revolution, 1917* (Cambridge: Cambridge University Press, 2000).

White, Howard, '1917 in the Rear Garrison', in Linda Edmondson and Peter Waldron (eds.), *Economy and Society in Russia and the Soviet Union, 1860–1930* (London: Macmillan, 1992), pp. 152–68.

White, James D., 'The Kornilov Affair – A Study in Counter-Revolution', *Soviet Studies* 20, 2 (1968–9): 187–205.

'The February Revolution and the Bolshevik District Committee', *Soviet Studies* 4, 41 (1989): 603–24.

*The Russian Revolution, 1917–21: A Short History* (London: Arnold, 1994).

*Lenin: The Practice and Theory of Revolution* (London: Palgrave, 2001).

Wildman, A. K., *The End of the Russian Imperial Army: The Old Army and the Soldiers' Revolt (March–April 1917); The End of the Russian Imperial Army: The Road to Soviet Power and Peace* (Princeton: Princeton University Press, 1980, 1987).

Williams, Beryl, *Lenin* (Harlow: Longman, 2000).

Zhukov, A. F., *Ideino-politicheskii krakh eserovskogo maksimalizma* (Leningrad: LGU, 1979).

Znamenskii, O. N., *Iul'skii krisis 1917 goda.* (Leningrad: Nauka, 1964).

*Intelligentsiia nakanune velikogo oktiabria fevral'–oktiabr' 1917g.* (Leningrad: Nauka, 1988).

CIVIL WAR, 1918–21

Adelman, Jonathan R., 'The Development of the Soviet Party Apparat in the Civil War: Center, Localities, and Nationality Areas', *Russian History* 9, pt. 1 (1982): 86–110.

Argenbright, Robert, 'Bolsheviks, Baggers and Railroaders: Political Power and Social Space, 1917–1921', *Russian Review* 52, 4 (1993): 506–27.

Aves, Jonathan, *Workers against Lenin: Labour Protest and the Bolshevik Dictatorship* (London: Tauris Academic Studies, 1996).

Azovtsev, N. N. (ed.), *Grazhdanskaia voina v SSSR* (Moscow: Voennoe izdatel'stvo Ministerstva oborony SSSR, 1980, 1986).

Bordiugov, Gennadii A., 'Chrezvychainye mery i "Chrezvychaishchina" v Sovetskoi respublike i drugikh gosudarstvennykh obrazovaniiakh na territorii Rossii v 1918–1920 gg.', *Cahiers du Monde russe et soviétique* 38, 1–2 (1997): 29–44.

Brovkin, Vladimir N., *The Mensheviks after October: Socialist Opposition and the Rise of the Bolshevik Dictatorship* (Ithaca, N.Y.: Cornell University Press, 1987).

*Behind the Front Lines of the Civil War: Political Parties and Social Movements in Russia, 1918–1922* (Princeton: Princeton University Press, 1994).

Buldakov, V. P., *Krasnaia smuta: Priroda i posledstviia revoliutsionnogo nasiliia* (Moscow: Rosspen, 1997).

Clark, Katerina, *Petersburg: Crucible of Cultural Revolution* (Cambridge, Mass.: Harvard University Press, 1995).

David-Fox, Michael, *Revolution of the Mind: Higher Learning among the Bolsheviks, 1918–1929* (Ithaca, N.Y.: Cornell University Press, 1997).

Davydov, M. I., 'Gosudarstvennyi tovaroobmen mezhdu gorodom i derevnei v 1918–1921 gg.', *Istoricheskie zapiski* 108 (1982): 33–59.

Figes, Orlando, *Peasant Russia, Civil War: The Volga Countryside in Revolution (1917–1921)* (Oxford: Oxford University Press, 1989).

Fitzpatrick, Sheila, *The Commissariat of the Enlightenment: Soviet Organization of Education and the Arts under Lunacharsky, October 1917–1921* (Cambridge: Cambridge University Press, 1970).

'The Civil War as a Formative Experience', in Abbott Gleason, Peter Kenez and Richard Stites (eds.), *Bolshevik Culture: Experiment and Order in the Russian Revolution* (Bloomington: Indiana University Press, 1985), pp. 57–76.

Rabinowitch, Alexander, and Stites, Richard (eds.), *Russia in the Era of NEP: Explorations in Soviet Society and Culture* (Bloomington: Indiana University Press, 1991).

Getzler, Israel, *Kronstadt, 1917–1921: The Fall of a Soviet Democracy* (Cambridge: Cambridge University Press, 1983).

Gimpel'son, E. G., *Formirovanie Sovetskoi politicheskoi sistemy, 1917–1923 gg.* (Moscow: Nauka, 1995).

Gor'kii, M., et al., *Istoriia grazhdanskoi voiny v SSSR* (Moscow: 'Istoriia grazhdanskoi voiny', 1935, 1942, 1957, 1959, 1960).

Hafner, Lutz, *Die Partei der linken. Sozialrevolutionäre in der russischen Revolution von 1917/18* (Cologne: Beiträge zur Geschichte Osteuropas, 1994).

Helgesen, Malvin M., 'The Origins of the Party-State Monolith in Soviet Russia: Relations Between the Soviets and Party Committees in the Central Provinces, October 1917–March 1921.', Ph.D. diss., SUNY Stony Brook, 1980.

Holmes, Larry E., 'For the Revolution Redeemed: The Workers Opposition in the Bolshevik Party 1919–1921', *Carl Beck Papers in Russian and East European Studies*, no. 802 (Pittsburgh: Center for Russian and East European Studies, 1990): 1–46.

Holquist, Peter, *Making War, Forging Revolution: Russia's Continuum of Crisis, 1914–1921* (Cambridge, Mass.: Harvard University Press, 2002).

Kenez, Peter, *Civil War in South Russia, 1919–1920: The Defeat of the Whites* (Berkeley and Los Angeles: University of California Press, 1977).

Koenker, Diane P., Rosenberg, William G., and Suny, Ronald G. (eds.), *Party, State, and Society in the Russian Civil War: Explorations in Social History* (Bloomington: Indiana University Press, 1989).

Leonov, S. V., *Rozhdenie sovetskoi imperii: Gosudarstvo i ideologiia, 1917–1922 gg.* (Moscow: Dialog MGU, 1997).

Lih, Lars T., *Bread and Authority in Russia, 1914–1921* (Berkeley and Los Angeles: University of California Press, 1990).

Lincoln, Bruce W., *Red Victory* (New York: Simon and Schuster, 1989).

Long, James W., 'The Volga Germans and the Famine of 1921', *Russian Review* 51, 4 (1992): 510–25.

McAuley, Mary, *Bread and Justice: State and Society in Petrograd, 1917–1922* (Oxford: Oxford University Press, 1991).

Malle, Silvana, *The Economic Organisation of War Communism, 1918–1921* (Cambridge: Cambridge University Press, 1985).

Mally, Lynn, *Culture of the Future: The Proletkult Movement in Revolutionary Russia* (Berkeley and Los Angeles: University of California Press, 1990).

Mawdsley, Evan, *The Russian Civil War* (Boston: Allen and Unwin, 1987).

Narskii, Igor', *Zhizn' v katastrofe: Budni naseleniia Urala v 1917–1922 gg.* (Moscow: Rosspen, 2001).

Patenaude, Bertrand M., *The Big Show in Bololand: The American Relief Expedition to Soviet Russia in the Famine of 1921* (Stanford, Calif.: Stanford University Press, 2002).

Pavliuchenkov, S. A., *Voennyi kommunizm v Rossii: Vlast' i massy* (Moscow: RKT–Istoriia, 1997).

Pereira, Norman G. O., *White Siberia: The Politics of Civil War* (Montreal and Kingston: McGill-Queen's University Press, 1996).

Pipes, Richard (ed.), *The Unknown Lenin: From the Secret Archive* (New Haven: Yale University Press, 1996).

Radkey, Oliver, *The Unknown Civil War in Soviet Russia: A Study of the Green Movement in the Tambov Region, 1920–1921* (Stanford, Calif.: Hoover Institution Press, 1976).

Radus-Zen'kovich, V. A., *Stranitsy geroicheskogo proshlogo. Vospominaniia i stat'i* (Moscow: Gosudarstvennoe izdatel'stvo politicheskoi literatury, 1960).

Raleigh, Donald J., 'Co-optation amid Repression: The Revolutionary Communists in Saratov Province, 1918–1920', *Cahiers du Monde russe et soviétique* 40, 4 (1999): 625–56.

   *Experiencing Russia's Civil War: Politics, Society, and Revolutionary Culture in Saratov, 1917–1922* (Princeton: Princeton University Press, 2002).

Rigby, T. H., 'The Soviet Political Elite', *British Journal of Political Science* 1 (1971): 415–36.

   *Lenin's Government: Sovnarkom, 1917–22* (Cambridge: Cambridge University Press, 1979).

Roslof, Edward E., *Red Priests: Renovationism, Russian Orthodoxy, and Revolution, 1905–1946* (Bloomington: Indiana University Press, 2002).

Rupp, Susan Z., 'Conflict and Crippled Compromise: Civil-War Politics in the East and the Ufa State Conference', *Russian Review* 56 (1997): 249–64.

Sakwa, Richard, *Soviet Communists in Power: A Study of Moscow during the Civil War, 1918–21* (Basingstoke: Macmillan, 1988).

Sapir, Jacques, 'La Guerre civile et l'économie de guerre: Origines du système soviétique', *Cahiers du Monde russe et soviétique* 38, 1–2 (1997): 9–28.

Schapiro, Leonard, *The Origin of the Communist Autocracy: Political Opposition in the Soviet State. First Phase, 1917–1922*, 2nd edn (Cambridge, Mass.: Harvard University Press, 1977).

Scheibert, Peter, *Lenin an der Macht: das russische Volk in der Revolution, 1918–1922* (Weinheim: Acta Humaniora, 1984).

Singleton, Seth, 'The Tambov Revolt (1920–1921)', *Slavic Review* 25, 3 (1966): 497–512.

Smele, Jonathan, *Civil War in Siberia: The Anti-Bolshevik Government of Admiral Kolchak, 1918–1920* (New York: Cambridge University Press, 1996).

Stites, Richard, *Revolutionary Dreams: Utopian Vision and Experimental Life in the Russian Revolution* (New York: Oxford University Press, 1989).

Swain, Geoffrey, *The Origins of the Russian Civil War* (London and New York: Longman, 1996).

Volkogonov, Dmitrii, *Lenin: Life and Legacy*, trans. Harold Shukman (London: Harper-Collins, 1994).

Von Geldern, James R., *Bolshevik Festivals, 1917–1920* (Berkeley and Los Angeles: University of California Press, 1993).

Von Hagen, Mark, *Soldiers in the Proletarian Dictatorship: The Red Army and the Soviet Socialist State, 1917–1930* (Ithaca, N.Y.: Cornell University Press, 1990).

Wehner, Markus, 'Golod 1921–1922 gg. v Samarskoi gubernii i reaktsiia sovetskogo pravitel'stva', *Cahiers du Monde russe et soviétique* 38, 1–2 (1997): 223–42.

White, Stephen, 'The USSR: Patterns of Autocracy and Industrialization', in *Political Culture and Political Change in Communist States*, 2nd edn, ed. Archie Brown and Jack Gray (New York: Holmes and Meier, 1979), pp. 25–65.

NEW ECONOMIC POLICY, 1921–8

Atkinson, Dorothy, *The End of the Russian Land Commune, 1905–1930* (Stanford, Calif.: Stanford University Press, 1983).

Ball, Alan M., *Russia's Last Capitalists: The Nepmen, 1921–1929* (Berkeley: University of California Press, 1987).

*And Now My Soul is Hardened: Abandoned Children in Soviet Russia, 1918–1930* (Berkeley: University of California Press, 1994).

Carr, E. H., *The Interregnum, 1923–1924* (London: Macmillan, 1954).

*Socialism in One Country 1924–1926*, 3 vols. (London: Macmillan, 1958–64).

and Davies, R. W., *Foundations of a Planned Economy 1926–1929*, 3 vols. (London: Macmillan, 1969–78).

Carrère d'Encausse, Hélène, *The Great Challenge: Nationalities and the Bolshevik State, 1917–1930*, (New York: Holmes and Meier, 1992).

Chase, William, *Workers, Society, and the Soviet State: Labor and Life in Moscow, 1918–1929* (Urbana: University of Illinois Press, 1987).

Cohen, Stephen, *Bukharin and the Bolshevik Revolution: A Political Biography, 1888–1938* (Oxford: Oxford University Press, 1980).

Dan, F. I., *Dva goda skitanii* (Berlin: Sklad izd. Russische Bucherzentrale Obrazowanje, 1922).

Daniels, Robert Vincent, *The Conscience of the Revolution: Communist Opposition in Soviet Russia* (Cambridge, Mass.: Harvard University Press, 1960).

Danilov, V. P., *Rural Russia under the New Regime*, trans. Orlando Figes (London: Hutchinson, 1988).

Erlich, Alexander, *The Soviet Industrialization Debate, 1924–1928* (Cambridge, Mass.: Harvard University Press, 1960).

Fitzpatrick, Sheila, *Education and Social Mobility in the Soviet Union, 1921–1934* (Cambridge: Cambridge University Press, 1979).

Goldman, Wendy Z., *Women, the State and Revolution: Soviet Family Policy and Social Life, 1917–1936* (Cambridge: Cambridge University Press, 1993).

Heinzen, James W., *Inventing a Soviet Countryside: State Power and the Transformation of Rural Russia, 1917–1929* (Pittsburgh: University of Pittsburgh Press, 2004).

Heywood, Anthony, *Modernising Lenin's Russia: Economic Reconstruction, Foreign Trade and the Railways 1917–1924* (Cambridge: Cambridge University Press, 1999).

Husband, William, *'Godless Communists': Atheism and Society in Soviet Russia, 1917–1932* (DeKalb: Northern Illinois University Press, 2000).

Kenez, Peter, *The Birth of the Propaganda State: Soviet Methods of Mass Mobilization, 1917–1929* (Cambridge: Cambridge University Press, 1985).

Lewin, Moshe, *Russian Peasants and Soviet Power: A Study of Collectivization* (Evanston, Ill.: Northwestern University Press, 1968).

*The Making of the Soviet System: Essays in the Social History of Interwar Russia* (New York: Pantheon Books, 1985).

Liber, George, *Soviet Nationality Policy, Urban Growth, and Identity Change in the Ukrainian SSR, 1923–1934* (Cambridge: Cambridge University Press, 1992).

Malle, Silvana, *The Economic Organization of War Communism 1918–1921* (Cambridge: Cambridge University Press, 1985).

Pethybridge, Roger, *One Step Backwards, Two Steps Forward: Soviet Society and Politics in the New Economic Policy* (Oxford: Oxford University Press, 1990).

Rabinowitch, Alexander, and Stites, Richard (eds.), *Russia in the Era of NEP: Explorations in Soviet Society and Culture* (Bloomington: Indiana University Press, 1991).

Reiman, Michel, *The Birth of Stalinism: The USSR on the Eve of the 'Second Revolution'*, trans. George Saunders (Bloomington: Indiana University Press, 1987).

Shearer, David R., *Industry, State, and Society in Stalin's Russia, 1926–1934* (Ithaca, N.Y.: Cornell University Press, 1996).

Siegelbaum, Lewis H., *Soviet State and Society Between Revolutions, 1918–1929* (Cambridge: Cambridge University Press, 1992).

Smith, Jeremy, *The Bolsheviks and the National Question, 1917–23* (New York: St Martin's Press, 1999).

Stites, Richard, *Revolutionary Dreams: Utopian Vision and Experimental Life in the Russian Revolution* (Oxford: Oxford University Press, 1989).

Stone, David R., *Hammer and Rifle: The Militarization of the Soviet Union 1926–1933* (Lawrence: University Press of Kansas, 2000).

Trotsky, Lev, *Sochineniia*, 12 vols. (Moscow: Gosudarstvennoe izdatel'stvo, 1925–7).

Tucker, Robert, *Stalin as Revolutionary, 1879–1929: A Study in History and Personality* (New York: Norton, 1973).

Tumarkin, Nina, *Lenin Lives! The Lenin Cult in Soviet Russia* (Cambridge, Mass.: Harvard University Press, 1983).

Youngblood, Denise, *Movies for the Masses: Popular Cinema and Soviet Society in the 1920s* (Cambridge: Cambridge University Press, 1992).

## STALINISM, 1928–53

Alexopoulos, Golfo, *Stalin's Outcasts: Aliens, Citizens, and the Soviet State, 1926–1936* (Ithaca, N.Y., and London: Cornell University Press, 2003).

Applebaum, Anne, *Gulag, A History* (New York: Doubleday, 2003).

Conquest, Robert, *Power and Policy in the USSR: The Struggle for Stalin's Succession 1945–1960* (London: Macmillan, 1961).

 *The Harvest of Sorrow: Soviet Collectivization and the Terror-Famine* (London: Hutchinson, 1986).

Crowfoot, John, and Harrison, Mark, 'The USSR Council of Ministers under Late Stalinism, 1945–54: Its Production Branch Composition and the Requirements of National Economy and Policy', *Soviet Studies* 42, 1 (1990): 41–60.

Danilov, V. P., et al. (eds.), *Tragediia sovetskoi derevni. Kollektivizatsiia i raskulachivanie. Dokumenty i materialy v 5 tomakh, 1927–1939* (Moscow, 2000–3).

Davies, R. W., *The Socialist Offensive: The Collectivization of Soviet Agriculture, 1929–1930* (Cambridge, Mass.: Harvard University Press, 1980).

 *The Soviet Economy in Turmoil, 1929–1930* (Cambridge, Mass.: Harvard University Press, 1989).

et al. (eds.), *The Stalin–Kaganovich Correspondence, 1931–1936* (New Haven: Yale University Press, 2003).

Davies, Sarah, *Popular Opinion in Stalin's Russia: Terror, Propaganda and Dissent, 1934–1941* (Cambridge: Cambridge University Press, 1997).

Deutscher, Isaac, *Stalin, A Political Biography* (Oxford: Oxford University Press, 1949).

Djilas, Milovan, *Conversations with Stalin*, trans. Michael Petrovich (New York: Harcourt, Brace and World, 1962).

Dunham, Vera S., *In Stalin's Time: Middle Class Values in Soviet Fiction* (Durham, N.C.: Duke University Press, 1990).

Filtzer, Donald, *Soviet Workers and Stalinist Industrialization: The Formation of Modern Soviet Production Relations, 1928–1941* (Armonk, N.Y.: M. E. Sharpe, 1986).

*Soviet Workers and Late Stalinism: Labour and the Restoration of the Stalinist System after World War II* (Cambridge: Cambridge University Press, 2002).

'The Standard of Living of Soviet Industrial Workers in the Immediate Postwar Period, 1945–1948', *Europe–Asia Studies* 51 (1999): 1013–38.

Fitzpatrick, Sheila (ed.), *Cultural Revolution in Russia, 1928–1931* (Bloomington: Indiana University Press, 1978).

'Stalin and the Making of a New Elite, 1928–1939', *Slavic Review* 38, 3 (1979): 377–402.

'Ordzhonikidze's Takeover of Vesenkha: A Case Study in Soviet Bureaucratic Politics', *Soviet Studies* 37, 2 (1985): 153–72.

*Stalin's Peasants: Resistance and Survival in the Russian Village after Collectivization* (New York and Oxford: Oxford University Press, 1994).

*Everyday Stalinism: Ordinary Life in Extraordinary Times: Soviet Russia in the 1930s* (New York and Oxford: Oxford University Press, 1999).

(ed.), *Stalinism: New Directions* (London and New York: Routledge, 2000).

and Gellately, Robert (eds.), *Accusatory Practices: Denunciations in Modern European History, 1789–1989* (Chicago and London: University of Chicago Press, 1997).

Getty, J. Arch, *Origins of the Great Purges: The Soviet Communist Party Reconsidered, 1933–1938* (Cambridge: Cambridge University Press, 1985).

and Manning, Roberta T. (eds.), *Stalinist Terror: New Perspectives* (Cambridge: Cambridge University Press, 1993).

and Naumov, Oleg V. (eds.), *The Road to Terror: Stalin and the Self-Destruction of the Bolsheviks, 1932–1939* (New Haven: Yale University Press, 1999).

Ginzburg, Evgeniya, *Journey into the Whirlwind*, trans. Paul Stevenson and Max Hayward (New York: Harcourt, Brace and World, 1967).

*Within the Whirlwind*, trans. Ian Boland (New York: Harcourt, Brace Jovanovich, 1981).

Goldman, Wendy Z., *Women at the Gates: Gender and Industry in Stalin's Russia* (Cambridge: Cambridge University Press, 2002).

Gor'kov, Iurii, *Gosudarstvennyi Komitet Oborony postanovliaet. 1941–1945. Tsifry i dokumenty* (Moscow: Olma Press, 2002).

Gorlizki, Yoram, 'Ordinary Stalinism: The Council of Ministers and the Soviet Neo-patrimonial State, 1945–1953', *Journal of Modern History* 74, 4 (Dec. 2002): 699–736.

and Khlevniuk, Oleg, *Cold Peace: Stalin and the Soviet Ruling Circle, 1945–1953* (New York: Oxford University Press, 2004).

Gouldner, Alvin W., 'Stalinism: A Study of Internal Colonialism', *Political Power and Social Theory: A Research Annual* (Greenwich, Conn.: 1978): 209–59.

Graziosi, Andrea, 'Collectivization, Peasant Revolts, and Government Policies through the Reports of the Ukrainian GPU', *Cahiers du Monde russe et soviétique* 35, 3 (1994): 437–631.

*GULAG (Glavnoe Upravlenie Lagerei) 1918–1960* (Moscow, 2000).

Hagenloh, Paul, '"Socially Harmful Elements" and the Great Terror', in Sheila Fitzpatrick (ed.), *Stalinism: New Directions* (London: Routledge, 2000), pp. 286–308.

Hahn, Werner G., *Postwar Soviet Politics: The Fall of Zhdanov and the Defeat of Moderation, 1946–1953* (Ithaca, N.Y.: Cornell University Press, 1982).

Harris, James, *The Great Urals: Regionalism and the Evolution of the Soviet System* (Ithaca, N.Y.: Cornell University Press, 1999).

Hoffmann, David, *Peasant Metropolis: Social Identities in Moscow, 1929–1941* (Ithaca, N.Y.: Cornell University Press, 1994).

Hunter, Holland, and Szyrmer, Janusz, *Faulty Foundations: Soviet Economic Policies 1928–1942* (Princeton: Princeton University Press, 1992).

Jasny, Naum, *Soviet Industrialization, 1928–1952* (Chicago: Chicago University Press, 1961).

Khlevniuk, Oleg, *In Stalin's Shadow. The Career of 'Sergo' Ordzhonikidze* (Armonk, N.Y.: M. E. Sharpe, 1995).

*Politbiuro. Mekhanizmy politicheskoi vlasti v 1930-e gody* (Moscow: Rosspen, 1996).

'The Objectives of the Great Terror, 1937–1938', in Julian Cooper, Maureen Perrie and E.A. Rees (eds.), *Soviet History, 1917–53: Essays in Honour of R.W. Davies* (London and Basingstoke: St Martin's Press, 1995), pp. 158–76.

et al. (eds.), *Stalinskoe Politburo v 30-e gody* (Moscow: AIRO-XX, 1995).

et al. (eds.), *Politburo TsK VKPb i Sovet Ministrov SSSR 1945–1953* (Moscow: Rosspen, 2002).

Knight, Amy, *Beria: Stalin's First Lieutenant* (Princeton: Princeton University Press, 1993).

Kostyrchenko, G. V., *Tainaia politika Stalina: Vlast' i Antisemitizm* (Moscow: Mezhdunarodnye otnosheniia, 2001).

Kotkin, Stephen, *Magnetic Mountain: Stalinism as a Civilization* (Berkeley: University of California Press, 1995).

Kozlov, V. A., and Zav'ialov, S. M. (eds.), *Neizvestnaia Rossiia. XX vek*, vols. I–III (Moscow: Istoricheskoe nasledie, 1992, 1993).

Kuromiya, Hiroaki, *Stalin's Industrial Revolution 1928–1932* (Cambridge: Cambridge University Press, 1988).

Kvashonkin, A.V. et al. (eds.), *Sovetskoe rukovodstvo. Perepiska. 1928–1941* (Moscow: Rosspen, 1999).

Larina, Anna, *This I Cannot Forget: The Memoirs of Nikolai Bukharin's Widow* (New York: Norton, 1993).

Lih, Lars T., Naumov, Oleg V., and Khlevniuk, Oleg V., *Stalin's Letters to Molotov* (New Haven: Yale University Press, 1995).

McCagg, William O., *Stalin Embattled, 1943–1948* (Detroit: Wayne State University Press, 1978).

McCauley, Martin (ed.), *Stalin and Stalinism* (London: Longman Press, 1995).

Madieveski, Samson, '1953: La Déportation des Juifs Soviétiques était-elle programmée', *Cahiers du Monde russe et soviétique* 41, 4 (2000): 561–8.

Malyshev, V. A., 'Dnevnik narkoma', *Istochnik*, 1997, no. 5: 103–47.

Martin, Terry, 'The Origins of Soviet Ethnic Cleansing', *Journal of Modern History* 70 (1998): 813–61.

Medvedev, Roy, *Let History Judge: The Origins and Consequences of Stalinism*, revised edn (New York: Oxford University Press, 1989).

Merl, Stephan, *Bauern unter Stalin: die Formierung des sowjetischen Kolchossystems, 1930–1941* (Berlin: Duncker and Humblot, 1990).

Mikoyan, Anastas, *Tak bylo: Razmyshleniia o minuvshem* (Moscow: Vagrius, 1999).

Montefiore, Simon Sebag, *Stalin: The Court of the Red Tsar* (London: Weidenfeld and Nicolson, 2003).

Naumov, Vladimir, and Rubinstein, Joshua (eds.), *Stalin's Secret Pogrom* (New Haven and London: Yale University Press, 2001).

Nove, Alec, *Was Stalin Really Necessary? Some Problems of Soviet Political Economy* (London: George Allen and Unwin, 1964).

Osokina, Elena, *Our Daily Bread: Socialist Distribution and the Art of Survival in Stalin's Russia 1927–1941* (Armonk, N.Y.: M. E. Sharpe, 2001).

Pechenkin, A. A., 'Gosudarstvennyi komitet oborony v 1941 godu', *Otechestvennaia istoriia* 4–5 (1994): 126–41.

Poliakov, Iu. A., et al., *Naselenie Rossii v XX veke. Istoricheskie ocherki*, vol. I: 1900–1939 (Moscow, 2000).

Radzinsky, Edvard, *Stalin* (London: Hodder and Stoughton, 1996).

Randall, Amy, 'The Campaign for Soviet Trade: Creating Socialist Retail Trade in the 1930s', Ph. D. diss., Princeton University, 2000.

Rigby, T. H., 'The Soviet Leadership: Towards a Self-Stabilizing Oligarchy?' *Soviet Studies* 22, 2 (1970): 167–8.

  'Stalinism and the Mono-organizational Society', in Robert C. Tucker (ed.), *Stalinism: Essays in Historical Interpretation* (New York: Norton, 1977), pp. 53–76.

  'Was Stalin a Disloyal Patron?' *Soviet Studies* 38, 3 (1986): 311–24.

Rogovin, Vadim Z., *1937: Stalin's Year of Terror*, trans. Frederick S. Choate (Oak Park, Mich.: Mehring Books, 1998).

Rousso, Henry (ed.), *Stalinism and Nazism: History and Memory Compared* (Lincoln and London: University of Nebraska Press, 1999).

Rubenstein, Joshua, and Naumov, Vladimir (eds.), *Stalin's Secret Pogrom: The Postwar Inquisition of the Jewish Anti-Fascist Committee*, trans. Laura Esther Wolfson (New Haven: Yale University Press, 2002).

Shearer, David, 'Modernity and Backwardness on the Soviet Frontier: Western Siberia during the 1930s', in Donald Raleigh (ed.), *Provincial Landscapes: Local Dimensions of Soviet Power, 1917–1953* (Pittsburgh: University of Pittsburgh Press, 2001), pp. 194–216.

  'Social Disorder, Mass Repression, and the NKVD during the 1930s', *Cahiers du Monde russe et soviétique* 42, 2, 3, 4 (Apr.–Dec. 2001): 505–34.

Siegelbaum, Lewis H., *Stakhanovism and the Politics of Productivity in the USSR 1935–1941* (Cambridge: Cambridge University Press, 1988).

  and Sokolov, Andrei (eds.), *Stalinism as a Way of Life: A Narrative in Documents* (New Haven and London: Yale University Press, 2000).

Solomon, Peter H., Jr., *Soviet Criminal Justice under Stalin* (Cambridge: Cambridge University Press, 1996).

Thurston, Robert W., *Life and Terror in Stalin's Russia, 1934–1941* (New Haven and London: Yale University Press, 1996).

Timasheff, Nicholas S., *The Great Retreat: The Growth and Decline of Communism in Russia* (New York: E. P. Dutton and Co., 1946).

Torkunov, A.V., *Zagadochnaia voina: koreiskii konflikt 1950–1953 godov* (Moscow: Rosspen, 2000).

Trotsky, L. D., *The Revolution Betrayed*, trans. Max Eastman (London: Faber and Faber, 1937; New York: Pathfinder Press, 1972).

Tucker, Robert C., *The Soviet Political Mind* (New York: Norton, 1971).

  *Stalin in Power. The Revolution From Above, 1928–1941* (New York: Norton, 1990).

  (ed.), *Stalinism: Essays in Historical Interpretation* (New York: Norton, 1977).

Ulam, Adam, *Stalin: The Man and his Era* (New York: Viking, 1974).

Viola, Lynne, *The Best Sons of the Fatherland: Workers in the Vanguard of Soviet Collectivization* (New York: Oxford University Press, 1987).

  *Peasant Rebels under Stalin: Collectivization and the Culture of Peasant Resistance* (New York: Oxford University Press, 1996).

  *Contending with Stalinism: Soviet Power and Popular Resistance in the 1930s* (Ithaca, N.Y., and London: Cornell University Press, 2002).

Ward, Chris, *Stalin's Russia* (London: Arnold, 1993).

Wehner, Markus, *Bauernpolitik im proletarischen Staat: Die Bauernfrage als zentrales Problem der sowjetischen Innenpolitik 1921–1928* (Cologne: Boehlau Verlag, 1998).

Zhiromskaia, V. B., *Demograficheskaia istoriia Rossii v 1930-e gody. Vzglad v neizvestnoe* (Moscow, 2001).

Zubkova, Elena, *Russia after the War: Hopes, Illusions, and Disappointments, 1945–1957* (Armonk, N.Y.: M. E. Sharpe, 1998).

## THE SECOND WORLD WAR, 1939–45

Andreyev, Catherine, *Vlasov and the Russian Liberation Movement: Soviet Reality and Émigré Theories* (Cambridge: Cambridge University Press, 1987).

Barber, John (ed.), *Zhizn' i smert' v blokadnom Leningrade. Istoriko-meditsinskii aspekt* (St Petersburg: Dmitrii Bulanin, 2001).

  and Harrison, Mark, *The Soviet Home Front 1941–1945: A Social and Economic History of the USSR in World War II* (London: Longman, 1991).

Beevor, Antony, *Stalingrad* (London: Viking, 1998).

  *Berlin: The Downfall, 1945* (London: Viking, 2002).

Bialer, Seweryn, *Stalin and his Generals: Soviet Military Memoirs of World War II* (New York: Pegasus, 1969; London: Souvenir Press, 1970).

Chuev, Felix, *Molotov Remembers: Inside Kremlin Politics* (Chicago: I. R. Dee, 1993).

Dallin, Alexander, *German Rule in Russia, 1941–1945: A Study of Occupation Policies* (London: Macmillan; New York: St Martin's Press, 1957; revised edn Boulder, Colo.: Westview Press, 1981).

Davies, R. W., and Harrison, Mark, 'The Soviet Military-Economic Effort under the Second Five-Year Plan (1933–1937)', *Europe–Asia Studies* 49, 3 (1997): 369–406.

Dear, I. C. B. (ed.), *The Oxford Companion to the Second World War* (Oxford: Oxford University Press, 1994).

Ellman, Michael, and Maksudov, Sergei, 'Soviet Deaths in the Great Patriotic War', *Europe–Asia Studies* 46, 4 (1994): 671–80.

Erickson, John, *The Soviet High Command: A Military-Political History, 1918–1941* (London: Macmillan, 1962).

  *Stalin's War with Germany*, 2 vols. (London: Weidenfeld and Nicolson, 1975–83).

  and Dilks, David (eds.), *Barbarossa: The Axis and the Allies* (Edinburgh: Edinburgh University Press, 1994).

  'Red Army Battlefield Performance, 1941–1945: The System and the Soldier', in Paul Addison and Angus Calder (eds.), *Time to Kill: The Soldier's Experience of War in the West, 1939–1945* (London: Pimlico, 1997), pp. 233–48.

Glantz, David M., *From the Don to the Dnepr: Soviet Offensive Operations, December 1942–August 1943* (London: Cass, 1991).

  *Stumbling Colossus: The Red Army on the Eve of World War* (Lawrence: University Press of Kansas, 1998).

  and House, Jonathan, *When Titans Clashed: How the Red Army Stopped Hitler* (Lawrence: University Press of Kansas, 1995).

Gorodetsky, Gabriel, *Grand Delusion: Stalin and the German Invasion of Russia* (New Haven: Yale University Press, 1999).

Gutman, Israel, and Rozett, Robert, 'Estimated Jewish Losses in the Holocaust', in Israel Gutman (ed.), *Encyclopedia of the Holocaust*, vol. iv: (New York: Macmillan, 1990).

Harrison, Mark, *Soviet Planning in Peace and War, 1938–1945* (Cambridge: Cambridge University Press, 1985).

  *Accounting for War: Soviet Production, Employment, and the Defence Burden, 1940–1945* (Cambridge: Cambridge University Press, 1996).

  'The Economics of World War II: An Overview', in Mark Harrison (ed.), *The Economics of World War II: Six Great Powers in International Comparison* (Cambridge: Cambridge University Press, 1998), pp. 1–42.

  'Trends in Soviet Labour Productivity, 1928–1985: War, Postwar Recovery, and Slowdown', *European Review of Economic History* 2, 2 (1998): 171–200.

  'Wartime Mobilisation: A German Comparison', in John Barber and Mark Harrison (eds.), *The Soviet Defence Industry Complex from Stalin to Khrushchev* (London: Macmillan, 2000), pp. 99–117.

  'Counting Soviet Deaths in the Great Patriotic War: Comment', *Europe–Asia Studies* 55, 6 (2003): 939–44.

Jolluck, Katherine R., *Exile and Identity: Polish Women in the Soviet Union During World War II* (Pittsburgh: University of Pittsburgh Press, 2002).

Keegan, John, *The Face of Battle* (Harmondsworth: Penguin, 1978).

Kokurin, A.I., and Petrov, N.V. (eds.), *GULAG (Glavnoe Upravlenie Lagerei). 1918–1960* (Moscow: Materik, 2002).

Krivosheev, G. F., Andronikov, V. M., Burikov, P. D., Gurkin, V. V., Kruglov, A. I., Rodionov, E. I., and Filimoshin, M. V., *Rossiia i SSSR v voinakh XX veka. Statisticheskoe issledovanie* (Moscow: OLMA-PRESS, 2003).

Kumanev, G.A., *Ryadom so Stalinym. Otkrovennye svidetel'stva. Vstrechi, besedy, interv'iu, doku-menty* (Moscow: Bylina, 1999).

Lieberman, Sanford R., 'Crisis Management in the USSR: Wartime System of Administration and Control', in Susan Linz (ed.), *The Impact of World War II on the Soviet Union* (Totowa, N.J.: Rowman and Allanheld, 1985).

Linz, Susan J. (ed.), *The Impact of World War II on the Soviet Union* (Totowa, N.J.: Rowman and Allanheld, 1985).

Mawdsley, Evan, 'Crossing the Rubicon: Soviet Plans for Offensive War in 1940–1941', *International History Review* 25, 4 (2003).

Mertsalov, A. N., and Mertsalov, L. A., *Stalinizm i voina* (Moscow: Terra-Knizhnyi klub, 1998).

Moskoff, William, *The Bread of Affliction: The Food Supply in the USSR during World War II* (Cambridge: Cambridge University Press, 1990).

Overy, Richard, *Russia's War* (London: Allen Lane, 1997).

Raack, Richard C., *Stalin's Drive to the West, 1938–1941: The Origins of the Cold War* (Stanford, Calif.: Stanford University Press, 1995).

Reese, Roger R., *The Soviet Military Experience* (London: Routledge, 2000).

Roberts, Geoffrey, *The Soviet Union and the Origins of the Second World War: Russo-German Relations and the Road to War, 1933–1941* (Basingstoke: Macmillan, 1995).

*Victory at Stalingrad: The Battle that Changed History* (London: Longman, 2000).

Rubenstein, Joshua, and Naumov, Vladimir (eds.), *Stalin's Secret Pogrom: The Postwar Inquisition of the Jewish Anti-Fascist Committee*, trans. Laura Esther Wolfson (New Haven: Yale University Press, 2002).

Salisbury, Harrison, *The 900 Days: the Siege of Leningrad* (London: Pan, 1969).

Samuelson, Lennart, *Plans for Stalin's War Machine: Tukhachevskii and Military-Economic Planning, 1925–41* (London and Basingstoke: Macmillan, 2000).

Sapir, Jacques, 'The Economics of War in the Soviet Union during World War II', in Ian Kershaw and Moshe Lewin (eds.), *Stalinism and Nazism: Dictatorships in Comparison* (Cambridge: Cambridge University Press, 1997), pp. 208–36.

Simonov, Konstantin, *Glazami cheloveka moego pokoleniia. Razmyshleniia o I.V. Staline* (Moscow: Novosti, 1989).

Simonov, N. S., '"Strengthen the Defence of the Land of the Soviets": The 1927 "War Alarm" and its Consequences', *Europe–Asia Studies* 48, 8 (1996): 1355–64.

Suny, Ronald Grigor, *The Structure of Soviet History: Essays and Documents* (New York and Oxford: Oxford University Press, 2003).

Suvorov (Rezun), Viktor, *Ice-Breaker: Who Started the Second World War?* (London: Hamish Hamilton, 1990).

Torchinov, V. A., and Leontiuk, A. M., *Vokrug Stalina. Istoriko-biograficheskii spravochnik* (St Petersburg: Filologicheskii fakul'tet Sankt-Peterburgskogo gosudarstvennogo universiteta, 2000).

Ulricks, Teddy J., 'The Icebreaker Controversy: Did Stalin Plan to Attack Hitler?' *Slavic Review* 58, 3 (1999): 626–43.

Volkogonov, Dmitrii, *Triumf i tragediia: politicheskii portret I.V. Stalina*, 2 vols. (Moscow: Novosti, 1989).

Watson, Derek, 'Molotov, the Making of the Grand Alliance and the Second Front, 1939–1942', *Europe–Asia Studies* 54, 1 (2002): 51–85.

Weeks, Albert L., *Stalin's Other War: Soviet Grand Strategy, 1939–1941* (Lanham, Md.: Rowman and Littlefield, 2002).

Wegner, Bernd (ed.), *From Peace to War: Germany, Soviet Russia, and the World, 1939–1941* (Providence, R.I.: Berghahn, 1997).

Weinberg, Gerhard L., *A World at Arms: A Global History of World War II* (Cambridge: Cambridge University Press, 1995).

Weiner, Amir, *Making Sense of War: The Second World War and the Fate of the Bolshevik Revolution* (Princeton: Princeton University Press, 2001).

Werth, Alexander, *Russia at War, 1941–1945* (London: Barrie and Rockcliffe, 1964).

Zhukov, Georgii, *Vospominaniia i razmyshlenniia*, 10th edn (Moscow: APN, 1990).


YEARS OF REFORM AND STAGNATION, 1953–82

Adzhubei, Aleksei, *Te desiat' let* (Moscow: Sovetskaia Rossiia, 1989).

*Krushenie illiuzii* (Moscow: Interbuk, 1991).

Aleksandrov-Agentov, Andrei M., *Ot Kollontai do Gorbacheva: vospominaniia diplomata, sovetnika A.A. Gromyko, pomoshchnika L.I. Brezhneva, Iu. V. Andropova, K.U. Chernenko i M.S. Gorbacheva* (Moscow: Mezhdunarodnye Otnosheniia, 1994).

Alexseyeva, Lyudmilla, *Soviet Dissent: Contemporary Movements for National, Religious, and Human Rights* (Middletown, Conn.: Wesleyan University Press, 1985).

and Paul Goldberg, *The Thaw Generation: Coming of Age in the Post-Stalin Era* (Pittsburgh: Pittsburgh University Press, 1993).

Arbatov, Georgi, *The System: An Insider's Life in Soviet Politics* (New York: Times Books, 1992).

Bacon, Edwin, and Sandle, Mark (eds.), *Brezhnev Reconsidered* (London: Palgrave, 2002).

Baron, Samuel H., *Bloody Sunday in the Soviet Union: Novocherkassk, 1962* (Stanford, Calif.: Stanford University Press, 2001).

Bialer, Seweryn, *Stalin's Successors: Leadership, Stability, and Change in the Soviet Union* (Cambridge and New York: Cambridge University Press, 1980).

Breslauer, George, *Khrushchev and Brezhnev as Leaders: Building Authority in Soviet Politics* (London and Boston: Allen and Unwin, 1982).

'On the Adaptability of Soviet Welfare-State Authoritarianism', in Erik P. Hoffmann and Robbin F. Laird (eds.), *The Soviet Polity in the Modern World* (New York: Aldine, 1984).

Brezhnev, Luba, *The World I Left Behind: Pieces of a Past* (New York: Random House, 1995).

Brudny, Yitzhak M., *Reinventing Russia: Russian Nationalism and the Collapse of the Soviet State, 1953–1991* (Cambridge, Mass.: Harvard University Press, 1998).

Brzezinski, Zbigniew (ed.), *Dilemmas of Change in Soviet Politics* (New York: Columbia University Press, 1969).

Bushnell, John, 'Urban Leisure Culture in Post-Stalin Russia: Stability as a Social Problem?', in Terry L. Thompson and Richard Sheldon (eds.), *Soviet Society and Culture: Essays in Honor of Vera S. Dunham* (Boulder, Colo.: Westview Press, 1988).

*Moscow Graffiti: Language and Subculture* (Boston: Unwin Hyman, 1990).

Chazov, Evgenii I., *Zdorov'e i vlast': vospominaniia 'kremlevskogo vracha'* (Moscow: Novosti, 1992).

Chernaiev, A. S., *Moia zhizn' i moe vremia* (Moscow: Mezhdunarodnye otnosheniia, 1995).

Churbanov, Yurii M., *Ia rasskazhu vse, kak bylo . . .* (Moscow: Nezavisimaia Gazeta, 1992).

Cook, Linda J., *The Soviet Social Contract and Why it Failed: Welfare Policy and Workers' Politics from Brezhnev to Yeltsin* (Cambridge, Mass.: Harvard University Press, 1993).

Counts, George S., *Khrushchev and the Central Committee Speak on Education* (Pittsburgh: University of Pittsburgh Press, 1959).

Dobrynin, Anatoly, *In Confidence: Moscow's Ambassador to America's Six Cold War Presidents (1962–1986)* (New York: Random House, 1995).

Evangelista, Matthew, *Unarmed Forces: The Transnational Movement to End the Cold War* (Ithaca, N.Y.: Cornell University Press, 2002).

Filtzer, Donald, *Soviet Workers and De-Stalinization: The Consolidation of the Modern System of Soviet Production Relations* (Cambridge: Cambridge University Press, 1992).

  *The Khrushchev Era: De-Stalinization and the Limits of Reform in the USSR, 1953–1964* (London: Macmillan, 1993).

Fink, Carole, Gassert, Philipp, and Junker, Detlef (eds.), *1968: The World Transformed* (Cambridge and New York: Cambridge University Press, 1998).

Fleron, Frederick J., Jr. (ed.), *Communist Studies and the Social Sciences: Essays on Methodology and Empirical Theory* (Chicago: Rand McNally, 1969).

Fursenko, Aleksandr, and Naftali, Timothy, *'One Hell of a Gamble': Khrushchev, Castro and Kennedy, 1958–1964* (New York: Norton, 1997).

Gaddy, Clifford, *The Price of the Past: Russia's Struggle with the Legacy of a Militarized Economy* (Washington: Brookings Institute Press, 1996).

Gregory, Paul, 'Productivity, Slack, and Time Theft in the Soviet Economy', in James Millar (ed.), *Politics, Work, and Daily Life in the USSR: A Survey of Former Soviet Citizens* (Cambridge: Cambridge University Press, 1987), pp. 241–75.

Grinevskii, Oleg, *Tysiacha i odin den' Nikity Sergeevicha* (Moscow: Vagrius, 1998).

Grishin, Viktor V., *Ot Khrushcheva do Gorbacheva: politicheskie portrety piati gensekov i A.N. Kosygina: memuary* (Moscow: ASPOL, 1996).

Gromyko, Anatolii, *Andrei Gromyko. V labirintakh kremlia: vospominaniia syna* (Moscow: Avtor, 1997).

Grossman, Gregory, 'The "Second Economy" of the USSR', *Problems of Communism* 26 (Sept.–Oct. 1977): 25–40.

Gustafson, Thane, *Crisis amidst Plenty: The Politics of Soviet Energy under Brezhnev and Gorbachev* (Princeton: Princeton University Press, 1989).

Hanson, Stephen E., *Time and Revolution: Marxism and the Design of Soviet Institutions* (Chapel Hill: University of North Carolina Press, 1997).

Hauslohner, Peter, 'Gorbachev's Social Contract', *Soviet Economy* 3, 1 (1987): 54–89.

Heikal, Mohamed, *The Sphinx and the Commissar: The Rise and Fall of Soviet Influence in the Middle East* (New York: Harper and Row, 1978).

Hough, Jerry F., *The Soviet Prefects: The Local Party Organs in Industrial Decisionmaking* (Cambridge, Mass.: Harvard University Press, 1969).

  *The Soviet Union and Social Science Theory* (Cambridge, Mass.: Harvard University Press, 1977).

and Fainsod, Merle, *How the Soviet Union is Governed* (Cambridge, Mass.: Harvard University Press, 1979).

Jowitt, Ken, *New World Disorder: The Leninist Extinction* (Berkeley: University of California Press, 1992).

Kanet, Roger E. (ed.), *The Behavioral Revolution and Communist Studies: Applications of Behaviorally Oriented Political Research on the Soviet Union and Eastern Europe* (New York: Free Press, 1971).

Kelley, Donald R. (ed.), *Soviet Politics in the Brezhnev Era* (New York: Praeger, 1980).

Khrushchev, Nikita S., *Khrushchev Remembers*, trans. and ed. Strobe Talbott (Boston: Little, Brown, 1970).

*Khrushchev Remembers: The Last Testament*, trans. and ed. Strobe Talbott (Boston: Little, Brown, 1974).

*Khrushchev Remembers: The Glasnost Tapes*, trans. and ed. Jerrold L. Schecter with Vyacheslav Luchkov (Boston: Little, Brown, 1990).

*N. S. Khrushchev: vospominaniia–vremia, liudi, vlast'*, 4 vols. (Moscow: Moskovskie novosti, 1999).

*N. S. Khrushchev (1894–1971): materialy nauchnoi konferentsii posviashchennoi 100-letiu so dnia rozhdeniia N. S. Khrushcheva* (Moscow: Rossiiskii gosudarstvennyi universitet, 1994).

Khrushchev, Sergei N., *Khrushchev on Khrushchev: An Inside Account of the Man and his Era*, trans. and ed. William Taubman (Boston: Little, Brown, 1990).

*Nikita Khrushchev: krizisy i rakety*, 2 vols. (Moscow: Novosti, 1994).

*Nikita Khrushchev and the Creation of a Superpower* (University Park, Pa.: Pennsylvania State University Press, 2000).

Kozlov, V. A., *Massovye besporiadki v SSSR pri Khrushcheve i Brezhneve (1953–nachalo 1980)* (Novosibirsk: Sibirskii khronograf, 1999).

Kramer, Mark, 'Jaruzelski, the Soviet Union, and the Imposition of Martial Law in Poland: New Light on the Mystery of December 1981', *Cold War International History Project Bulletin* 11 (Winter 1998): 5–16.

'The Early Post-Stalin Succession Struggle and Upheavals in East-Central Europe: Internal-External Linkages in Soviet Policy-Making', p. 1–3, *Journal of Cold War Studies* 1 (Winter 1999): 3–55; 2 (Spring 1999): 3–38; 3 (Fall 1999): 3–66.

Lapidus, Gail, 'Ethnonationalism and Political Stability: The Soviet Case', *World Politics* 36, 4 (July 1984): 555–80.

Lewin, Moshe, *Stalinism and the Seeds of Soviet Reform: The Debates of the 1960s* (Armonk N.Y.: M. E. Sharpe, 1991).

Linden, Carl, *Khrushchev and the Soviet Leadership, 1957–1964* (Baltimore: Johns Hopkins University Press, 1966).

McCauley, Martin (ed.), *Khrushchev and Khrushchevism* (Bloomington: Indiana University Press, 1987).

McMillan, Priscilla Johnson, *Khrushchev and the Arts* (Cambridge, Mass.: MIT Press, 1965).

Mawdsley, Evan, and White, Stephen, *The Soviet Elite from Lenin to Gorbachev: The Central Committee and its Members, 1917–1991* (Oxford and New York: Oxford University Press, 2000).

Medvedev, Roi, et al., Iu. Vi. Aksiutin, sostavitel', *L. I. Brezhnev: materialy k biiografii* (Moscow: Izdatel'stvo Politicheskoi Literatury, 1991).

Medvedev, Vladimir, *Chelovek za spinoi* (Moscow: 'Russlit', 1994).

Mićunović, Veljko, *Moscow Diary*, trans. David Floyd (Garden City, N.Y.: Doubleday, 1980).

Miller, R. F., and Feher, F. (eds.), *Khrushchev and the Communist World* (London and Canberra: Croom Helm, 1984).

Naumov, Vladimir P., 'Bor'ba N. S. Khrushcheva za edinolichnuiu vlast', *Novaia i noveishaia istoriia* 5–6 (2000).

Ploss, Sidney, *Conflict and Decision-Making in Soviet Russia* (Princeton: Princeton University Press, 1965).

Rigby, T. H., *Communist Party Membership in the USSR, 1917–1968* (Princeton: Princeton University Press, 1970).

Roeder, Philip, *Red Sunset: The Failure of Soviet Politics* (Princeton: Princeton University Press, 1993).

Rush, Myron, *Political Succession in the USSR* (New York: Columbia University Press, 1968).

Sakharov, Andrei, *Memoirs*, trans. Richard Lourie (New York: Alfred A. Knopf, 1990).

Semichastnyi, Vladimir, 'Ia by spravilsia s liuboi rabotoi', interview by K. Svetitskii and S. Sokolov, *Ogonek* 24 (1989).

Skilling, H. Gordon, and Griffiths, Franklyn (eds.), *Interest Groups in Soviet Politics* (Princeton, N.J.: Princeton University Press, 1971).

Solnick, Steven, *Stealing the State: Control and Collapse in Soviet Institutions* (Cambridge, Mass.: Harvard University Press, 1998).

Solomon, Susan Gross (ed.), *Pluralism in the Soviet Union* (London and New York: Macmillan, 1983).

Tatu, Michel, *Power in the Kremlin: From Khrushchev to Kosygin*, trans. Helen Katel (New York: Viking, 1969).

Taubman, William, *Khrushchev: The Man and his Era* (New York, Norton, 2003).

    Khrushchev, Sergei N., and Gleason, Abbott (eds.), *Nikita Khrushchev* (New Haven: Yale University Press, 2000).

Taylor, Brian, *Politics and the Russian Army* (Cambridge and New York: Cambridge University Press, 2003).

Thomas, Daniel C., *The Helsinki Effect: International Norms, Human Rights, and the Demise of Communism* (Princeton, N.J.: Princeton University Press, 2001).

Tomiak, J. J. (ed.), *Soviet Education in the 1980s* (London: Croom Helm, 1983).

Tompson, William J., *Khrushchev: A Political Life* (New York: St Martin's Press, 1995).

Troianovskii, Oleg, *Cherez gody i rasstoianiia* (Moscow: Vagrius, 1997).

Ulam, Adam B., *Expansion and Coexistence: Soviet Foreign Policy, 1917–1973* (New York: Holt, Rinehart and Winston, 1974).

Volkogonov, Dmitrii, *Sem' vozhdei: galereia liderov SSSR*, vol. II (Moscow: Novosti, 1995).

Ward, Christopher J., 'Selling the "Project of the Century": Perceptions of the Baikal–Amur Mainline Railway (BAM) in the Soviet Press, 1974–1984', *Canadian Slavonic Papers* 43, 1 (Mar. 2001): 75–95.

Willerton, John P. *Patronage and Politics in the USSR* (Cambridge and New York: Cambridge University Press, 1992).

Williams, Kieran. 'New Sources on Soviet Decision Making During the 1968 Czechoslovak Crisis'. *Europe–Asia Studies* 48, 3 (May 1996):

Yakovlev, Aleksandr I., *Omut pamiati* (Moscow: Vagrius, 2000).

Yanov, Alexander, *The Drama of the Soviet 1960s: A Lost Reform* (Berkeley: Institute of International Studies, University of California, 1984).

Zaslavsky, Victor, *The Neo-Stalinist State: Class, Ethnicity and Consensus in Soviet Society* (Armonk, N.Y.: M. E. Sharpe, 1982).

Zubkova, Elena, *Obshchestvo i reformy: 1945–1964* (Moscow: Rossiia molodaia, 1993).

Zubok, Vladislav, and Pleshakov, Constantine, *Inside the Kremlin's Cold War: From Stalin to Khrushchev* (Cambridge, Mass: Harvard University Press, 1996).


### THE GORBACHEV REVOLUTION

Afanas'ev, Iu.N. (ed.), *Inogo ne dano* (Moscow: Progress, 1988).

Aganbegyan, Abel, *Moving the Mountain: Inside the Perestroika Revolution*, trans. Helen Szamuely (London: Bantam Press, 1989).

Bakatin, Vadim, *Doroga v proshedshem vremeni* (Moscow: Dom, 1999).

Balzer, Harley D., *Five Years that Shook the World: Gorbachev's Unfinished Revolution* (Boulder, Colo., San Francisco and Oxford: Praeger, 1991).

Beschloss, Michael R. and Talbott, Strobe, *At the Highest Levels: The Inside Story of the End of the Cold War* (London: Little, Brown, 1993).

Bialer, Seweryn (ed.), *Politics, Society and Nationality inside Gorbachev's Russia* (Boulder, Colo.: Westview Press, 1989).

Boldin, V. I., *Krushenie p'edestala. Shtrikhi k portretu M.S. Gorbacheva* (Moscow: Respublika, 1995).

Bovin, Aleksandr, *XX vek kak zhizn': vospominaniia* (Moscow: Zakharov, 2003).

Braithwaite, Rodric, *Across the Moscow River: The World Turned Upside Down* (New Haven and London: Yale University Press, 2002).

Breslauer, George W., *Gorbachev and Yeltsin as Leaders* (New York and Cambridge: Cambridge University Press, 2002).

Brown, Archie, *The Gorbachev Factor* (Oxford and New York: Oxford University Press, 1996).
   'Mikhail Gorbachev: Systemic Transformer', in Martin Westlake (ed.), *Leaders of Transition* (London: Macmillan, 2000), pp. 3–26.
   (ed.), *The Demise of Marxism-Leninism in Russia* (London and New York: Palgrave Macmillan, 2004).
   and Shevtsova, Lilia (eds.), *Gorbachev, Yeltsin, and Putin: Political Leadership in Russia's Transition* (Washington: Carnegie Endowment for International Peace, 2001).

Brumberg, Abraham (ed.), *Chronicle of a Revolution: A Western-Soviet Inquiry into Perestroika* (New York: Pantheon, 1990).

Brutents, K. N., *Tridsat' let na staroi ploshchadi* (Moscow: Mezhdunarodnye otnosheniia, 1998).

Bunce, Valerie, *Subversive Institutions: The Design and the Destruction of Socialism and the State* (Cambridge: Cambridge University Press, 1999).

Chernyaev, Anatoly, *My Six Years with Gorbachev*, trans. and ed. Robert English and Elizabeth Tucker, Foreword by Jack F. Matlock, Jr. (University Park, Pa.: Pennsylvania State University Press, 2000).
   *Byl li u Rossii shans? On – poslednii* (Moscow: Sobranie, 2003).

Cohen, Stephen F., and van den Heuvel, Katrina, *Voices of Glasnost: Interviews with Gorbachev's Reformers* (New York: Norton, 1989).

D'Agostino, Anthony, *Gorbachev's Revolution, 1985–1991* (London: Macmillan, 1998).

Dallin, Alexander, and Lapidus, Gail W. (eds.), *The Soviet System: From Crisis to Collapse*, revised edn (Boulder, Colo.: Westview Press, 1995).

Davies, R. W., *Soviet History in the Gorbachev Revolution* (London: Macmillan, 1989).

Dobrynin, Anatoly, *In Confidence: Moscow's Ambassador to America's Six Cold War Presidents (1962–1986)* (New York: Random House, 1995).

Duhamel, Luc, 'The Last Campaign against Corruption in Soviet Moscow', *Europe–Asia Studies* 56, 2 (Mar. 2004): 187–212.

Dunlop, John D., *The Rise of Russia and the Fall of the Soviet Union* (Princeton: Princeton University Press, 1993).

Ellman, Michael, and Kontorovich, Vladimir (eds.), *The Destruction of the Soviet Economic System: An Insiders' History* (Armonk, N.Y.: M. E. Sharpe, 1998).

English, Robert D., *Russia and the Idea of the West: Gorbachev, Intellectuals, and the End of the Cold War* (New York: Columbia University Press, 2000).

Falin, V. M., *Bez skidok na obstoiatel'stva: Politicheskie vospominania* (Moscow: Respublika Sovremennik, 1999).

Fish, M. Steven, *Democracy from Scratch: Opposition and Regime in the New Russian Revolution* (Princeton: Princeton University Press, 1995).

Garton Ash, Timothy, *In Europe's Name: Germany and the Divided Continent* (London: Jonathan Cape, 1993).

Goldman, Marshall, *Lost Opportunity: What has Made Economic Reform in Russia so Difficult?* (New York: W. W. Norton, 1996).

Gorbachev, Mikhail, *Zhivoe tvorchestvo naroda* (Moscow: Politizdat, 1984).

    *Perestroika: New Thinking for Our Country and the World* (London: Collins, 1987).

    *Izbrannye rechi i stat'i*, 7 vols. (Moscow: Politizdat, 1987–90).

    *The August Coup: The Truth and the Lessons* (London: HarperCollins, 1991).

    *Gody trudnykh reshenii, 1985–1992 gg.* (Moscow: Al'fa-Print, 1993).

    *Zhizn' i reformy*, 2 vols. (Moscow: Novosti, 1995).

    *Memoirs* (New York: Doubleday, 1996; London: Transworld, 1996).

    *Kak eto bylo* (Moscow: Vagrius, 1999).

    and Mlynář, Zdeněk, *Conversations with Gorbachev: On Perestroika, the Prague Spring, and the Crossroads of Socialism*, trans. George Shriver with Introduction by Archie Brown (New York: Columbia University Press, 2002).

Gorbachev, Raisa, *I Hope: Reminiscences and Reflections* (London: HarperCollins, 1991).

Grachev, Andrei, *Final Days: The Inside Story of the Collapse of the Soviet Union*, trans. Margo Milne with Foreword by Archie Brown (Boulder, Colo.: Westview Press, 1995).

    *Gorbachev* (Moscow: Vagrius, 2001).

Hahn, Gordon A., *Russia's Revolution from Above, 1985–2000: Reform, Transition, and Revolution* (New Brunswick, N. J.: Transaction, 2002).

Hermann, Richard K., and Lebow, Richard Ned (eds.), *Ending the Cold War: Interpretations, Causation, and the Study of International Relations* (New York: Palgrave Macmillan, 2004).

Hewett, Ed A., *Reforming the Soviet Economy* (Washington: Brookings Institution Press, 1988).

Hough, Jerry F., *Democratization and Revolution in Russia, 1985–1991* (Washington: Brookings Institution Press, 1997).

Iakovlev, Aleksandr, *Predislovie, obval, posleslovie* (Moscow: Novosti, 1992).
*Sumerki* (Moscow: Materik, 2003).

Kahn, Jeffrey, *Federalism, Democratization, and the Rule of Law in Russia* (Oxford: Oxford University Press, 2002).

Kotkin, Stephen, *Armageddon Averted: The Soviet Collapse 1970–2000* (Oxford and New York: Oxford University Press, 2001).

Kramer, Mark, 'The Collapse of East European Communism and the Repercussions within the Soviet Union (Part 1)', *Journal of Cold War Studies* 5, 4 (Fall 2003): 178–256.

Kriuchkov, Vladimir, *Lichnoe delo*, 2 vols. (Moscow: Olimp, 1996).

Lévesque, Jacques, *The Enigma of 1989: The USSR and the Liberation of Eastern Europe* (Berkeley: University of California Press, 1997).

Lewin, Moshe, *Russia–USSR–Russia: The Drive and Drift of a Superstate* (New York: Norton, 1995).

Ligachev, Yegor, *Inside Gorbachev's Kremlin*, trans. Catherine A. Fitzpatrick, Michele A. Berdy and Dobrochna Dyrcz-Freeman, with Introduction by Stephen F. Cohen (New York: Pantheon, 1993).

Lukin, Alexander, *The Political Culture of the Russian 'Democrats'* (Oxford: Oxford University Press, 2000).

McFaul, Michael, *Russia's Unfinished Revolution: Political Change from Gorbachev to Putin* (Ithaca, N.Y.: Cornell University Press, 2001).

Matlock, Jack F., Jr., *Autopsy for an Empire: The American Ambassador's Account of the Collapse of the Soviet Union* (New York: Random House, 1995).
*Reagan and Gorbachev: How the Cold War Ended* (New York: Random House, 2004).

Mau, Vladimir, 'Perestroika: Theoretical and Political Problems of Economic Reform in the USSR', *Europe–Asia Studies* 47, 3 (1995): 387–411.

Medvedev, Vadim, *V komande Gorbacheva: Vzglyad iznutri* (Moscow: Bylina, 1994).
*Prozrenie, mif ili predatel'stvo? K voprosu ob ideologii perestroika* (Moscow: Evraziia, 1998).

Miller, John, *Mikhail Gorbachev and the End of Soviet Power* (London: Macmillan; and New York: St Martin's Press, 1993).

Nove, Alec, *Glasnost' in Action: Cultural Renaissance in Russia* (London: Unwin Hyman, 1989).

Oberdofer, Don, *The Turn: How the Cold War Came to an End – the United States and the Soviet Union, 1983–1990* (London: Jonathan Cape, 1992).

Palazchenko, Pavel, *My Years with Gorbachev and Shevardnadze: The Memoir of a Soviet Interpreter* (University Park, Pa.: Pennsylvania University Press, 1997).

Primakov, Evgenii, *Gody v bol'shoi politike* (Moscow: Sovershenno sekretno, 1999).

Ryzhkov, Nikolai, *Perestroika: Istoriia predatel'stva* (Moscow: Novosti, 1992).

Sakharov, Andrei, *Moscow and Beyond 1986 to 1989*, trans. Antonina Bouis (New York: Knopf, 1991).

Sakwa, Richard, *Gorbachev and his Reforms, 1985–1990* (Hemel Hempstead: Philip Allan, 1990).

Shakhnazarov, Georgii, *Tsena svobody: Reformatsiia Gorbacheva glazami ego pomoshchnika* (Moscow: Rossika/Zevs, 1993).

*S vozhdiami i bez nikh* (Moscow: Vagrius, 2001).

Shevardnadze, Eduard, *The Future Belongs to Freedom*, trans. Catherine A. Fitzpatrick (London: Sinclair-Stevenson, 1991).

Shultz, George P., *Turmoil and Triumph: My Years as Secretary of State* (New York: Macmillan, 1993).

Sobchak, Anatolii, *Khozhdenie vo vlast': Rasskaz o rozhdenii parlamenta* (Moscow: Novosti, 1991).

Stepankov, V., and Lisov, E., *Kremlevskii zagovor: Versiia sledstviia* (Moscow: Ogonek, 1992).

Vorotnikov, V. I., *A bylo eto tak ... Iz dnevnika chlena Politbiuro KPSS* (Moscow: Sovet veteranov knigoizdaniia, 1995).

Walicki, Andrzej, *Marxism and the Leap to the Kingdom of Freedom: The Rise and Fall of the Communist Utopia* (Stanford, Calif.: Stanford University Press, 1995).

White, Stephen, *Russia Goes Dry: Alcohol, State and Society* (Cambridge and New York: Cambridge University Press, 1996).

Rose, Richard, and McAllister, Ian, *How Russia Votes* (Chatham, N.J.: Chatham House, 1997).

Whitefield, Stephen, *Industrial Power and the Soviet State* (Oxford: Clarendon Press, 1993).

Wohlforth, William C., 'Realism and the End of the Cold War', *International Security* 19, 3 (Winter 1994/5): 91–129.

*Cold War Endgame: Oral History, Analysis, Debates* (University Park, Pa.: Pennsylvania State University Press, 2003).

*XIX Vsesoiuznaia konferentsiia Kommunisticheskoi partii Sovetskogo Soiuza, 28 iiunia – 1 iiulia 1988 g.: Stenograficheskii otchet*, 2 vols. (Moscow: Politizdat,1988).

Zelikow, Philip, and Rice, Condoleezza, *Germany Unified and Europe Transformed: A Study in Statecraft* (Cambridge, Mass.: Harvard University Press, 1995).

Zubok, Vladislav M., 'Gorbachev and the End of the Cold War: Perspectives on History and Personality', *Cold War History* 2, 2 (Jan. 2002): 61–100.

POST-SOVIET RUSSIA AND THE SUCCESSOR STATES

Andrews, Josephine, *When Majorities Fail: The Russian Parliament 1990–1993* (Cambridge: Cambridge University Press, 2002).

Aron, Leon, *Boris Yeltsin: A Revolutionary Life* (London: HarperCollins, 2000).

Aslund, Anders, *Post-Communist Economic Revolutions: How Big a Bang?* (Washington: Center for Strategic and International Studies, 1992).

Barker, Adele Marie (ed.), *Consuming Russia: Popular Culture, Sex, and Society Since Gorbachev* (Durham, N.C.: Duke University Press, 1999).

Blasi, Joseph, Kroumova, Maya, and Kruse, Douglas, *Kremlin Capitalism: Privatizing the Russian Economy* (Ithaca, N.Y.: Cornell University Press, 1997).

Blustein, Paul, *The Chastening: Inside the Crisis that Rocked the Global Financial System and Humbled the IMF* (New York: Public Affairs, 2001).

Breslauer, George, *Gorbachev and Yeltsin as Leaders* (Cambridge: Cambridge University Press, 2002).

Brown, Archie (ed.), *Contemporary Russian Politics: A Reader* (Oxford: Oxford University Press, 2001).

Colton, Timothy, *Transitional Citizens: Voters and What Influences Them in the New Russia* (Cambridge, Mass.: Harvard University Press, 2000).

and Hough, Jerry, *Growing Pains: Russian Democracy and the Election of 1993* (Washington: Brookings Institution Press, 1998).

and McFaul, Michael, *Popular Choice and Managed Democracy: The Russian Elections in 1999 and 2000* (Washington: Brookings Institution Press, 2003).

Diamond, Larry. 'Thinking about Hybrid Regimes', *Journal of Democracy* 13, 2 (Apr. 2002): 21–35.

Dunlop, John, *The Rise of Russia and the Fall of the Soviet Empire* (Princeton: Princeton University Press, 1993).

*Russia Confronts Chechnya: Roots of a Separatist Conflict* (Cambridge: Cambridge University Press, 1998).

'How many Soldiers and Civilians Died during the Russo-Chechen War of 1994–1996?', *Central Asian Survey* 19, 3–4 (2000): 328–38.

Evangelista, Matthew, *The Chechen Wars: Will Russia Go the Way of the Soviet Union?* (Washington: Brookings Institution Press, 2003).

Fish, Steven M., 'Democratization's Requisites', *Post-Soviet Affairs* 14, 3 (1998): 212–47.

Fisher, Stanley and Gelb, Alan, 'The Process of Socialist Economic Transformation', *Journal of Economic Perspectives* 5, 4 (Fall 1991): 91–105.

Freeland, Chrystia, *Sale of the Century: Russia's Wild Ride from Communism to Capitalism* (New York: Crown Publishers, 2000).

Frye, Timothy, 'The Perils of Polarization: Economic Performance in the Postcommunist World', *World Politics* 54, 3 (Apr. 2002): 308–37.

Gaidar, Egor, *Dni porazhenii i pobed* (Moscow: Vagrius, 1996).

Granville, Bridget, *The Success of Russian Economic Reforms* (London: Royal Institute of International Affairs, 1995).

Hann, C. N. (ed.), *Postsocialism: Ideals, Ideologies and Practices in Eurasia* (London: Routledge, 2002).

Hellman, Joel, 'Winners Take All: The Politics of Partial Reform in Postcommunist Transitions', *World Politics* 50 (1998): 203–34.

Herspring, Dale R. (ed.), *Putin's Russia: Past Imperfect, Future Uncertain* (Armonk, N.Y.: M. E. Sharpe, 2003).

Hoffman, David, *The Oligarchs: Wealth and Power in the New Russia* (New York: Public Affairs, 2002).

Hough, Jerry, Davidheiser, Evelyn, Lehmann, Susan Goodrich, *The 1996 Russian Presidential Election* (Washington: Brookings Institution Press, 1996).

Human Rights Watch, 'Now Happiness Remains: Civilian Killings, Pillage, and Rape in Alkhan-Yurt, Chechnya', *Russia/Chechnya* 12, 5 (D) (Apr. 2000): 1–33.

'February 5: A Day of Slaughter in Novye Aldi', *Russia/Chechnya* 12, 9 (D) (June 2000): 1–43.

'The "Dirty War" in Chechnya: Forced Disappearances, Torture, and Summary Executions', *Russia* 13, 1 (D) (Mar. 2001): 1–42.

'Burying the Evidence: The Botched Investigation into a Mass Grave in Chechnya', *Russia/Chechnya* 13, 3 (D) (May 2001): 1–26.

Humphrey, Caroline, *The Unmaking of Soviet Life: Everyday Economies after Socialism* (Ithaca, N.Y.: Cornell University Press, 2002).

Huskey, Eugene, *Presidential Power in Russia* (Armonk, N.Y.: M. E. Sharpe, 1999).

'Is Russian Democracy Doomed?' *Journal of Democracy* 5, 2 (Apr. 1994): 3–41.

Javeline, Debra, *Protest and the Politics of Blame: The Russian Response to Unpaid Wages* (Ann Arbor: University of Michigan Press, 2003).

Kahn, Joseph, and O'Brien, Timothy L., 'Easy Money: A Special Report: For Russia and its U.S. Bankers, Match wasn't Made in Heaven', *New York Times*, 18 Oct. 1998, p. 1.

Kolsto, Pal, *Political Construction Sites: Nation-Building in Russia and the Post-Soviet States* (Boulder, Colo.: Westview Press, 2000).

Layard, Richard, and Parker, John, *The Coming Russian Boom: A Guide to New Markets and Politics* (New York: Free Press, 1996).

Levitsky, Steven, and Way, Lucan, 'The Rise of Competitive Authoritarianism', *Journal of Democracy* 13, 2 (Apr. 2002): 51–65.

Lieven, Anatol, *Chechnya: Tombstone of Russian Power* (New Haven: Yale University Press, 1998).

McFaul, Michael, 'State Power, Institutional Change, and the Politics of Privatization in Russia', *World Politics* 47, 2 (Jan. 1995): 210–43.

  *Russia's 1996 Presidential Election: The End of Polarized Politics* (Stanford, Calif.: Hoover Institution Press, 1997).

  'The Fourth Wave of Democracy and Dictatorship: Noncooperative Transitions in the Postcommunist World', *World Politics* 54, 2 (Jan. 2002): 212–44.

  *Between Dictatorship and Democracy: Russian Postcommunist Political Reform* (Washington: Carnegie Endowment for International Peace, 2004).

  Ryabov, Andrei, and Petrov, Nikolai (eds.), *Rossiia v izbiratel'nom tsikle: 1999–2000 godov* (Moscow: Moscow Carnegie Center, 2000).

Mau, Vladimir, and Staradubrovskaya, Irina, *The Challenge of Revolution: Contemporary Russia in Historical Perspective* (Oxford: Oxford University Press, 2001).

Moser, Robert, *Unexpected Outcomes: Electoral Systems, Political Parties, and Representation in Russia* (Pittsburgh: University of Pittsburgh Press, 2001).

Murray, Donald, *A Democracy of Despots* (Boulder, Colo.: Westview Press, 1995).

Nivat, Anne, *Chienne de Guerre: A Woman Reporter Behind the Lines of the War in Chechnya* (New York: Public Affairs, 2000).

Politkovskaya, Anna, *A Dirty War: A Russian Reporter in Chechnya* (London: Harvill Press, 2001).

Pravda, Alex (ed.), *Leading Russia: Putin in Perspective* (Oxford: Oxford University Press, 2005).

Primakov, Evgenii, *Vosem' mesyatsev plyus . . .* (Moscow: Mysl, 2001).

Przeworski, Adam, *Democracy and the Market: Political and Economic Reforms in Eastern Europe and Latin America* (Cambridge: Cambridge University Press, 1991).

Reddaway, Peter, and Glinski, Dmitrii, *The Tragedy of Russia's Reforms: Market Bolshevism against Democracy* (Washington: U.S. Institute of Peace, 2001).

Remington, Thomas, *The Russian Parliament: Institution Evolution in a Transitional Regime, 1989–1999* (New Haven: Yale University Press, 2001).

*Rossiiskii statisticheskii ezhegodnik* (Moscow: Goskomstat, 1997).

Sachs, Jeffrey, *Poland's Jump to the Market Economy* (Cambridge, Mass.: MIT Press, 1993).

Service, Robert, *Russia: Experiment with a People: From 1991 to the Present* (London: Macmillan, 2002).

Shevtsova, Lilia, *Yeltsin's Russia: Myths and Realities* (Washington: Carnegie Endowment for International Peace, 1999).

    *Putin's Russia* (Washington: Carnegie Endowment for International Peace, 2003).

Shleifer, Andrei, and Treisman, Daniel, *Without a Map: Political Tactics and Economic Reform in Russia* (Cambridge, Mass.: MIT Press, 2000).

Sobianin, A. A., and Sukhovolskii, V. G., *Demokratiia, ogranichennaia falsifikatsiiami: vybory i referendumy v Rossii v 1991–1993 gg* (Moscow, 1995).

Solnick, Steven, 'Is the Center too Weak or too Strong in the Russian Federation?', in Valerie Sperling (ed.), *Building the Russian State: Institutional Crisis and the Quest for Democratic Governance* (Boulder, Colo.: Westview Press, 2000), pp. 137–56.

Stoner-Weiss, Kathryn, 'The Russian Central State in Crisis', in Zoltan Barany and Robert Moser (eds.), *Russian Politics: Challenges of Democratization* (Cambridge: Cambridge University Press, 2001), pp. 103–34.

Urban, Joan Barth, and Solovei, Valerii, *Russia's Communists at the Crossroads* (Boulder, Colo.: Westview Press, 1997).

White, Stephen, *After Gorbachev* (Cambridge: Cambridge University Press, 1993).

    *Russia's New Politics* (Cambridge and New York: Cambridge University Press, 2000).

Whitefield, Stephen (ed.). *Political Culture and Post-Communism* (London: Palgrave Macmillan, St. Antony's College Series, 2005).

Woodruff, David, *Money Unmade: Barter and the Fate of Russian Capitalism* (Ithaca, N.Y.: Cornell University Press, 1999).

Wyman, Matthew, White, Stephen, Miller, Bill, and Heywood, Paul, 'Public Opinion, Parties, and Voters in the 1993 Russian Elections', *Europe–Asia Studies* 47 (1995): 602.

Yeltsin, Boris, *Against the Grain: An Autobiography*, trans. Michael Glenny (London: Jonathan Cape, 1990).

    *The Struggle for Russia* (New York: Random House, 1994).

    *Midnight Diaries* (New: York: Public Affairs, 2000).

Zhirinovsky, Vladimir, *Poslednii brosok na iug* (Moscow: TOO Pisatel', 1993).

## ECONOMY

Amann, Ronald, and Cooper, J. M. (eds.), *Industrial Innovation in the Soviet Union* (London: Yale University Press, 1982).

Aslund, Anders, *Gorbachev's Struggle for Economic Reform* (London: Pinter, 1991).

    *Building Capitalism: The Transformation of the Former Soviet Bloc* (Cambridge: Cambridge University Press, 2002).

Bailes, Kendall, *Technology and Society under Lenin and Stalin* (Princeton: Princeton University Press, 1978).

Bergson, Abram, *The Real National Income of Soviet Russia since 1928* (Cambridge, Mass.: Harvard University Press, 1961).

Berliner, Joseph, *Factory and Manager in the USSR* (Cambridge, Mass.: Harvard University Press, 1957).

Bukharin, N., and Preobrazhensky, E. A., *The ABC of Communism* (London: CPGB, 1922).

Carr, E. H., and Davies, R. W., *Foundations of a Planned Economy, 1926–1929*, vol. 1 (Harmondsworth: Penguin, 1969; London: Macmillan, 1976).

Coale, Ansley J., *Human Fertility in Russia since the Nineteenth Century* (Princeton: Princeton University Press, 1979).

Coopersmith, Jonathan, *The Electrification of Russia 1800–1926* (Ithaca, N.Y.: Cornell University Press, 1992).

Crisp, Olga, *Studies in the Russian Economy before 1914* (London: Macmillan, 1976).

Danilov, V. P., *Rural Russia Under the New Regime* (London: Macmillan, 1988).

Davies, R. W., *The Formation of the Soviet Budgetary System* (Cambridge: Cambridge University Press, 1960).

  *The Industrialisation of Soviet Russia*, 3 vols. (Basingstoke: Macmillan, 1980–9).

  (ed.), *From Tsarism to the New Economic Policy: Continuity and Change in the Economy of the USSR* (Basingstoke: Macmillan, 1990).

  *Crisis and Progress in the Soviet Economy 1931–1933* (Basingstoke: Macmillan, 1996).

  *Soviet Economic Development from Lenin to Khrushchev* (Cambridge: Cambridge University Press, 1998).

  Harrison, Mark, and Wheatcroft, S. G. (eds.), *The Economic Transformation of the Soviet Union, 1913–1945* (Cambridge: Cambridge University Press, 1994).

Davis, Christopher M., 'Russia: A Comparative Economic Systems Interpretation', in James Foreman-Peck and Giovanni Federico (eds.), *European Industrial Policy: The Twentieth-Century Experience* (Oxford: Oxford University Press, 1999), pp. 319–97.

Dobb, Maurice, *Russian Economic Development since the Revolution*, 2nd edn (London: Routledge, 1929); new edn pub. as *Soviet Economic Development since 1917* (London: Routledge, 1948).

Dubrovskii, S. M., *Stolypinskaia zemel'naia reforma* (Moscow: Nauka, 1963).

Dunmore, Timothy, *The Stalinist Command Economy: The Soviet State Apparatus and Economic Policy 1945–1953* (London: Macmillan, 1980).

Ellman, Michael, and Kontorovich V. P. (eds.), *The Disintegration of the Soviet Economic System* (London: Routledge, 1992).

Gaddy, Clifford, and Ickes, Barry, *Russia's Virtual Economy* (Washington: Brookings Institution Press, 2002).

Gerschenkron, Alexander, *Economic Backwardness in Historical Perspective* (Cambridge, Mass.: Harvard University Press, 1962).

Gregory, Paul, *Russian National Income 1885–1913* (Cambridge: Cambridge University Press, 1982).

  *Restructuring the Soviet Economic Bureaucracy* (Cambridge: Cambridge University Press, 1985).

  (ed.), *Behind the Façade of Stalin's Command Economy: Evidence from the Soviet State and Party Archives* (Stanford, Calif.: Hoover Institution Press, 2001).

  and Stuart, R. C., *Russian and Soviet Economic Performance and Structure*, 7th edn (Boston: Addison Wesley, 2001).

Grossman, Gregory, 'The Second Economy of the USSR', *Problems of Communism* 26 (1977): 25–40.

Guroff, Gregory, and Carstensen, Fred V. (eds.), *Entrepreneurship in Imperial Russia and the Soviet Union* (Princeton: Princeton University Press, 1983).

Harrison, Mark, 'Soviet Economic Growth Since 1928: The Alternative Statistics of G. I. Khanin', *Europe–Asia Studies* 45 (1993): 141–67.

'Trends in Soviet Labour Productivity 1928–1985: War, Postwar Recovery and Slowdown', *European Review of Economic History* 2 (1998): 171–200.

'Coercion, Compliance, and the Collapse of the Soviet Command Economy', *Economic History Review* 55 (2002): 397–433.

and Barber, John (eds.), *The Soviet Defence Industry Complex from Stalin to Khrushchev* (Basingstoke: Macmillan, 2000).

Hewett, E. A., *Reforming the Soviet Economy: Equality versus Efficiency* (Washington: Brookings Institution Press, 1988).

and Winston, V. H. (eds.), *Milestones in Glasnost and Perestroyka: The Economy* (Washington: Brookings Institution Press, 1991).

Hoffmann, David, and Kotsonis, Yanni (eds.), *Russian Modernity: Politics, Knowledge, Practices* (London: Macmillan, 2000).

Humphrey, Caroline, *The Unmaking of Soviet Life* (Cambridge: Cambridge University Press, 2002).

Jasny, Naum, *The Socialized Agriculture of the USSR: Plans and Performance* (Stanford, Calif.: Stanford University Press, 1949).

Kafengauz, Lev B., *Evoliutsiia promyshlennogo proizvodstva Rossii* (Moscow: Epifaniia, 1994).

Khanin, G. I., *Dinamika ekonomicheskogo rosta SSSR* (Novosibirsk: Nauka, 1991).

Kingston-Mann, Esther, *In Search of the True West: Culture, Economics, and Problems of Russian Development* (Princeton: Princeton University Press, 1999).

Ledeneva, Alla, *Russia's Economy of Favours* (Cambridge: Cambridge University Press, 1998).

Lewis, R. A., and Rowland, R., *Population Redistribution in the USSR 1897–1977* (New York: Praeger, 1979).

Lorimer, Frank, *The Population of the Soviet Union: History and Prospects* (Geneva: League of Nations, 1946).

McKay, John P., *Pioneers for Profit: Foreign Entrepreneurship and Russian Industrialization 1885–1913* (Chicago: University of Chicago Press, 1970).

Malafeev, A. A., *Istoriia tsenoobrazovaniia v SSSR* (Moscow, 1964).

Millar, James (ed.), *Politics, Work, and Daily Life in the USSR: A Survey of Former Soviet Citizens* (Cambridge: Cambridge University Press, 1987).

Moorsteen, Richard, and Powell, Raymond P., *The Soviet Capital Stock 1928–1962* (Homewood, Ill.: Irwin, 1966).

Moskoff, William, *Hard Times: Impoverishment and Protest in the Perestroika Years* (Armonk, N.Y.: M. E. Sharpe, 1993).

Nove, Alec, *An Economic History of the USSR*, 3rd edn (London: Penguin Books, 1992).

Pavlovsky, George, *Agricultural Russia on the Eve of the Revolution* (London: Routledge, 1930).

Pilkington, Hilary, *Migration, Displacement and Identity in Post-Soviet Russia* (London: Routledge, 1998).

Poliakov, Iu. A., and Zhiromskaia, V. B. (eds.), *Naselenie Rossii v XX veke*, 2 vols. (Moscow: Rosspen, 2000).

Prokopovich, Sergei N., *Histoire économique de l'U.R.S.S.* (Paris: Le Portulan, 1952).

Raffalovich, A., *Russia: Industries and Trade* (London: P. S. King, 1918).

Schroeder, Gertrude, 'Nationalities and the Soviet Economy', in Lubomyr Hajda and Mark Beissinger (eds.), *The Nationalities Factor in Soviet Politics and Society* (Boulder, Colo.: Westview Press, 1990), pp. 43–71

Schwarz, Solomon M., *Labor in the Soviet Union* (New York: Praeger, 1951).

Seabright, Paul (ed.), *The Vanishing Rouble: Barter Networks and Non-Monetary Transactions in Post-Soviet Societies* (Cambridge, Cambridge University Press, 2000).

Shanin, Teodor, *The Awkward Class: Political Sociology of Peasantry in a Developing Society, Russia 1910–1925* (Oxford: Clarendon Press, 1972).

Spulber, Nicholas, *Russia's Economic Transitions: From Late Tsarism to the New Millennium* (Cambridge: Cambridge University Press, 2003).

Strumilin, S. G., *Statistiko-ekonomicheskie ocherki* (Moscow, 1958).

Timoshenko, V. P., *Agricultural Russia and the Wheat Problem* (Stanford, Calif.: Stanford University Press, 1932).

Urlanis, B.Ts., *Istoriia odnogo pokoleniia: sotsial'no-demograficheskii ocherk* (Moscow: Mysl', 1968).

Vainshtein, A. L., *Narodnoe bogatstvo i narodnokhoziaistvennoe nakoplenie predrevoliutsionnoi Rossii* (Moscow: Gosstatizdat, 1960).

Volkov, E. Z., *Dinamika narodonaseleniia SSSR za vosem'desiat let* (Moscow: Gosudarstvennoe izdatel'stvo, 1930).

Wiles, P. J. D., *The Political Economy of Communism* (Oxford: Blackwell, 1964).

Zaleski, Eugene, *Stalinist Planning for Economic Growth, 1933–1952* (Chapel Hill: University of North Carolina Press, 1980).

Zaslavskaia, Tatiana 'The Novosibirsk Report', *Survey* 28 (1984): 88–108.

*A Voice of Reform: Essays*, trans. Murray Yanovitch (Armonk, N.Y.: M. E. Sharpe, 1989).

Zhiromskaia, V. B., *Demograficheskaia istoriia Rossii v 1930-e gg: vzgliad v neizvestnoe* (Moscow: Rosspen, 2001).

## INDUSTRIALISATION AND WORKERS

Baevskii, D. A., *Rabochii klass v pervye gody sovetskoi vlasti (1917–1921 gg.)* (Moscow: Nauka, 1974).

Baranskaya, Natalia, *A Week Like Any Other and Other Stories* (Seattle: Seal Press, 1990).

Benvenuti, Francesco, *Fuoco sui sabotari! Stachanovismo e organizzazione industriale in URSS 1934–1938* (Rome: Valerio Levi, 1988).

Bliakhman, L. S., Zdravomyslov, A. G., and Shkaratan, O. I., *Dvizhenie rabochei sily na promyshlennykh predpriiatiiakh* (Moscow: Ekonomika, 1965).

Burawoy, Michael, 'From Capitalism to Capitalism via Socialism: The Odyssey of a Marxist Ethnographer, 1975–1995', *International Labor and Working-Class History* 50 (1996): 77–99.

and Hendley, Kathryn, 'Between Perestroika and Privatization: Divided Strategies and Political Crisis in a Soviet Enterprise', *Soviet Studies* 44 (1992): 371–402.

and Krotov, Pavel, 'The Soviet Transition from Socialism to Capitalism: Worker Control and Economic Bargaining in the Wood Industry', in Simon Clarke et al. (eds.), *What about the Workers?: Workers and the Transition to Capitalism in Russia* (London: Verso, 1993), pp. 56–90.

Chase, William, *Workers, Society, and the Soviet State: Labor and Life in Moscow, 1918–1929* (Urbana and Chicago: University of Illinois Press, 1987).

‘Voluntarism, Mobilization and Coercion: *Subbotniki* 1919–1921’, *Soviet Studies* 41 (1989): 111–28.

and Siegelbaum, Lewis, ‘Worktime and Industrialization in the U.S.S.R., 1917–1941’, in Gary Cross (ed.), *Worktime and Industrialization: An International History* (Philadelphia: Temple University Press, 1988), pp. 183–216.

Christensen, Paul T., *Russia's Workers in Transition: Labor, Management, and the State under Gorbachev and Yeltsin* (DeKalb: Northern Illinois University Press, 1999).

Clarke, Roger A., *Soviet Economic Facts, 1917–1970* (London: Macmillan, 1972).

Clarke, Simon (ed.), *Management and Industry in Russia: Formal and Informal Relations in the Period of Transition* (Aldershot: Edward Elgar, 1995).

et al. (eds.), *What About the Workers?: Workers and the Transition to Capitalism in Russia* (London: Verso, 1993).

Fairbrother, Peter, and Borisov, Vadim, *The Workers' Movement in Russia* (Aldershot: Edward Elgar, 1995).

Connor, Walter D., *The Accidental Proletariat: Workers, Politics, and Crisis in Gorbachev's Russia* (Princeton: Princeton University Press, 1991).

Cook, Linda J., *Labor and Liberalization: Trade Unions in the New Russia* (New York: Twentieth Century Fund, 1997).

Crisp, Olga, ‘Labour and Industrialisation in Russia’, in Peter Mathias and M. M. Postan (eds.), *The Cambridge Economic History of Europe*, vol. VII (Cambridge: Cambridge University Press, 1978), pt. 2, pp. 308–415.

Crowley, Stephen, *Hot Coal, Cold Steel: Russian and Ukrainian Workers from the End of the Soviet Union to the Post-Communist Transformations* (Ann Arbor: University of Michigan Press, 1997).

Danilova, E. Z., *Sotsial'nye problemy truda zhenshchiny-rabotnitsy* (Moscow: Mysl', 1968).

Depretto, Jean-Paul, *Les Ouvriers en U.R.S.S., 1928–1941* (Paris: Publications de la Sorbonne, 1997).

Eley, Geoff, and Nield, Keith, ‘Farewell to the Working Class?’, *International Labor and Working-Class History* 57 (2000): 1–30.

Fenin, Aleksandr I., *Coal and Politics in Late Imperial Russia: Memoirs of a Russian Mining Engineer*, trans. Alexandre Fediaevsky (DeKalb: Northern Illinois University Press, 1989).

Ferguson, Rob, ‘Will Democracy Strike Back? Workers and Politics in the Kuzbass’, *Europe–Asia Studies* 50 (1998): 445–68.

Friedgut, Theodore, *Iuzovka and Revolution: Life and Work in Russia's Donbass, 1869–1924*, 2 vols. (Princeton: Princeton University Press, 1989–94).

and Siegelbaum, Lewis H., ‘The Soviet Miners' Strike, July 1989: Perestroika from Below’, *The Carl Beck Papers in Russian and East European Studies*, no. 804 (Pittsburgh: Center for Russian and East European Studies, 1990).

Gimpel'son, E. G., *Rabochii klass v upravlenii sovetskim gosudarstvom: noiabr' 1917–1920 gg.* (Moscow: Nauka, 1982).

Goskomstat Rossii, *Trud i zaniatost' v Rossii, Statisticheskii sbornik* (Moscow: Goskomstat, 1996).

*Uroven' zhizni naseleniia Rossii* (Moscow: Goskomstat, 1996).

*Rossiiskii statisticheskii ezhegodnik, Statisticheskii sbornik* (Moscow: Goskomstat, 1998).

Granick, David, *Management of the Industrial Firm in the USSR: A Study of Soviet Economic Planning* (New York: Columbia University Press, 1954).

Gregory, Paul, and Markevich, Andrei, 'Creating Soviet Industry: The House that Stalin Built', *Slavic Review* 61 (2002): 787–814.

Hatch, John, 'The "Lenin Levy" and the Social Origins of Stalinism: Workers and the Communist Party in Moscow, 1921–1928', *Slavic Review* 48 (1989): 558–77.

Hellbeck, Jochen, 'Speaking Out: Languages of Affirmation and Dissent', *Kritika: Explorations in Russian and Eurasian History* 1 (2000): 71–96.

Hoffmann, Erik P., and Laird, Robbin F., *Technocratic Socialism: The Soviet Union in the Advanced Industrial Era* (Durham, N.C.: Duke University Press, 1985).

Hogan, Heather, *Forging Revolution: Metalworkers, Managers, and the State in St. Petersburg, 1890–1914* (Bloomington: Indiana University Press, 1993).

Johnson, Robert E., *Peasant and Proletarian: The Working Class of Moscow in the Late Nineteenth Century* (New Brunswick, N.J.: Rutgers University Press, 1979).

Kharchev, A. G. and Golod, S. I., *Professional'naia rabota zhenshchin i sem'ia* (Leningrad: Nauka, 1971).

Koenker, Diane, 'Men against Women on the Shop Floor in Early Soviet Russia', *American Historical Review* 100 (1995): 1438–64.

'Factory Tales: Narratives of Industrial Relations in the Transition to NEP', *Russian Review* 55 (1996): 384–411.

Kuromiya, Hiroaki, 'The Crisis of Proletarian Identity in the Soviet Factory, 1928–1929', *Slavic Review* 44 (1985): 280–97.

Lebina, Natalia, *Povsednevnaia zhizn' sovetskogo goroda: normy i anomalii, 1920/1930 gody* (St Petersburg: Letnii sad, 1999).

Lopatin, L. N. (ed.), *Rabochee dvizhenie Kuzbassa: Sbornik dokumentov i materialov* (Kemerovo: Sovremennaia otechestvennaia kniga, 1993).

Maier, Robert, *Die Stachanov-Bewegung, 1935–1938* (Stuttgart: Franz Steiner Verlag, 1990).

Ministerstvo zemledeliia i gosudarstvennogo imushchestva. Otdel sel'skoi ekonomiki i sel'sko-khoziaistvennoi statistiki, *Otchety i issledovaniia po kustarnoi promyshlennosti v Rossii*, 11 vols. (St Petersburg: Kirshbaum, 1892–1915).

Mitrofanova, A. V., *Rabochii klass SSSR v gody velikoi otechestvennoi voiny* (Moscow: Nauka, 1971).

Morozova, T. P., and Plotkina, Irina V., *Savva Morozov* (Moscow: Russkaia kniga, 1998).

Payne, Matthew, *Stalin's Railroad: Turksib and the Building of Socialism* (Pittsburgh: University of Pittsburgh Press, 2001).

Poliakov, Iu. A., *Sovetskaia strana posle okonchaniia grazhdanskoi voiny: territoriia i naselenie* (Moscow: Nauka, 1986).

Rogachevskaia, L. S., *Likvidatsiia bezrabotitsy v SSSR, 1917–1930 gg* (Moscow: Nauka, 1973).

Rosenberg, William G., and Siegelbaum, Lewis H., (eds.), *Social Dimensions of Soviet Industrialization* (Bloomington: Indiana University Press, 1993).

Rossman, Jeffrey, 'The Teikovo Cotton Workers' Strike of April 1932: Class, Gender, and Identity Politics in Stalin's Russia', *Russian Review* 56 (1997): 44–69.

Ruckman, Jo Ann, *The Moscow Business Elite: A Social and Cultural Portrait of Two Generations, 1840–1905* (DeKalb: Northern Illinois University Press, 1984).

Siegelbaum, Lewis H., 'Production Collectives and Communes and the "Imperatives" of Soviet Industrialization, 1929–1931', *Slavic Review* 45 (1986): 65–84.

'Industrial Accidents and Their Prevention in the Interwar Period', in William O. McCagg and Lewis Siegelbaum (eds.), *The Disabled in the Soviet Union: Past and Present, Theory and Practice* (Pittsburgh: University of Pittsburgh Press, 1989), pp. 85–117.

'Masters of the Shop Floor: Foremen and Soviet Industrialisation', in Nick Lampert and Gabor T. Rittersporn (eds.), *Stalinism: Its Nature and Aftermath* (Houndmills: Macmillan, 1992), pp. 127–56.

'Freedom of Prices and the Price of Freedom: The Miners' Dilemmas in the Soviet Union and Its Successor States', *Journal of Communist Studies and Transition Politics* 13 (1997): 1–27.

'Narratives of Appeal and the Appeal of Narratives: Labor Discipline and its Contestation in the Early Soviet Period', *Russian History* 24 (1997): 65–87.

and Suny, Ronald Grigor (eds.), *Making Workers Soviet: Power, Class, and Identity* (Ithaca, N.Y.: Cornell University Press, 1994).

and Walkowitz, Daniel J., *Workers of the Donbass Speak: Survival and Identity in the New Ukraine, 1989–1992* (Albany, N.Y.: SUNY Press, 1995).

Straus, Kenneth, *Factory and Community in Stalin's Russia: The Making of an Industrial Working Class* (Pittsburgh: University of Pittsburgh Press, 1997).

Tugan-Baranovskii, M. I., *Russkaia fabrika v proshlom i nastoiashchem*, 2nd edn (St Petersburg: O. N. Popova, 1900).

Ward, Chris, *Russia's Cotton Workers and the New Economic Policy: Shop-floor Culture and State Policy, 1921–1929* (Cambridge: Cambridge University Press, 1990).

Wegren, Stephen K., Ioffe, Gregory, and Nefedova, Tatyana, 'Demographic and Migratory Responses to Agrarian Reform in Russia', *Journal of Communist Studies and Transition Politics* 13 (1997): 54–78.

Wildman, Allan, *The Making of a Workers' Revolution: Russian Social Democracy, 1891–1903* (Chicago: University of Chicago Press, 1967).

Wynn, Charters, *Workers, Strikes, and Pogroms: The Donbass-Dnepr Bend in Late Imperial Russia, 1870–1905* (Princeton: Princeton University Press, 1992).

Zdravomyslov, A. G., and Iadov, V. A. 'Opyt konkretnogo issledovaniia otnosheniia k trudu', *Voprosy filosofii* 4 (1964): 72–84.

Rozhin, V. P., and Iadov, V. A., *Man and His Work*, trans. Stephen P. Dunn (White Plains, N.Y.: International Arts and Sciences Press, 1970).

Zelnik, Reginald E. (ed.), *Workers and Intelligentsia in Late Imperial Russia: Realities, Representations, Reflections* (Berkeley: University of California Press, 1999).

Zhiromskaia, V. B., *Sovetskii gorod v 1921–1925 gg.* (Moscow: Nauka, 1988).

AGRICULTURE AND PEASANTS

Abraham, Ray, 'The Regeneration of Family Farming in Estonia', *Sociologia Ruralis* 34, 4 (1993): 354–68.

Ananich, B. V., Ganelin, R. S., Dubentsov, B. B., Diakin, V. S., and Potolov, S. I., *Krizis Samoderzhaviia v Rossii, 1895–1917* (Leningrad, 1984).

Atkinson, D. G., *The End of the Russian Land Commune 1905–1930* (Stanford, Calif.: Stanford University Press, 1983).

Barnes, Andrew, 'What's the Difference? Industrialization, Privatization and Agricultural Land Reform in Russia, 1990–6', *Europe–Asia Studies* 50, 5 (1998): 843–57.

Bartlett, Roger, *Land Commune and Peasant Community in Russia: Communal Forms in Imperial and Early Soviet Society* (Basingstoke: University of London, 1990).

Bazhaev, V. G., *Travopol'noe khoziaistvo v nechernozemnoi polose Evropeiskoi Rossii* (St Petersburg, 1902).

Belov, Fedor, *The History of a Collective Farm* (New York: Praeger, 1955).

Bridger, Susan, and Pine, Frances, *Surviving Post-Socialism: Local Strategies and Regional Responses in Eastern Europe and the Former Soviet Union* (London: Routledge, 1998).

Caskie, Paul, 'Back to Basics: Household Food Production in Russia', *Journal of Agricultural Economics* 51, 2 (May 2000): 196–209.

Chaianov, A. V., *On the Theory of Peasant Economy*, ed. D. Thorner et al. (Homewood, Ill.: R. D. Irwin, 1966).

Chernenkov, N. N., *K kharakteristike krest'ianskogo khoziaistva* (Moscow, 1905).

Danilov, V. P., *Rural Russia Under the New Regime*, ed. and trans. O. Figes (Bloomington: Indiana University Press, 1988).

and Danilova, L.V., 'Commune', *Great Soviet Enyclopedia*, trans. of 3rd edn (New York: Macmillan, 1978), vol. XVIII, p. 47.

Davies, R. W., Tauger, M. B., and Wheatcroft, S. G., 'Stalin, Grain Stocks, and the Famine of 1932–33', *Slavic Review* 54 (1995): 642–57.

Denisova, L. N., *Ischezaiushchaia derevnia Rossii: nechernozem'e v 1960–1980e gody* (Moscow: RAN, 1996).

Diamond, Douglas, and Krueger, Constance, 'Recent Developments in Output and Productivity in Soviet Agriculture', in *Soviet Economic Prospects for the Seventies: A Compendium of Papers Submitted to the Joint Economic Committee* (Congress of the United States, Washington, D.C.: Government Printing Office, 1973).

Dubrovskii, S. M., *Stolypinskaia zemel'naia reforma: iz istorii sel'skogo khoziaistva Rossii v nachale XX veka* (Moscow, 1963).

Efimenko, A. I., *Issledovaniia narodnoi zhizni* (Moscow: Kasperov, 1884).

George, Vic, and Manning, Nick, *Socialism, Social Welfare and the Soviet Union* (London: Routledge and Kegan Paul, 1980).

Gibbon, Peter, Havnevik, Kjell, and Hermele, Kenneth, *A Blighted Harvest: The World Bank and African Agriculture in the 1980s* (Trenton: Africa World Press, 1993).

Grant, Steven, 'Obshchina and Mir', *Slavic Review* 35, 4 (1976): 636–51.

Hann, Chris, 'Forward', in Susan Bridger and Frances Pine (eds.), *Surviving Postsocialism* (London: Routledge, 1998), pp. x–xiv.

Hivon, Myriam, 'Local Resistance to Privatisation in Rural Russia', *Cambridge Anthropology* 18, 2 (1995): 13–22.

Humphrey, Caroline, *Karl Marx Collective: Economy, Society and Religion in a Siberian Collective Farm* (Cambridge: Cambridge University Press, 1977).

'Introduction', *Cambridge Anthropology* 18, 2 (1995): 1–11.

'Politics of Privatisation in Provincial Russia: Popular Opinions Amid the Dilemmas of the Early 1990s', *Cambridge Anthropology* 18, 1 (1995): 40–62.

'Myth-Making, Narratives and the Dispossessed in Russia', *Cambridge Anthropology* 19, 2 (1997): 70–92.

'The Domestic Mode of Production in Post-Soviet Siberia', *Anthropology Today* 14, 3 (June 1998): 2–7.

Humphries, Jane, 'Enclosures, Common Rights, and Women: The Proletarianization of Families in the Late Eighteenth and Early Nineteenth Centuries', *Journal of Economic History* 50, 2 (Mar. 1990): 17–41.

Ioffe, Grigory, and Nefedova, Tatyana, *Continuity and Change in Rural Russia: A Geographical Perspective* (Boulder, Colo.: Westview Press, 1997).

'Areas of Crisis in Russian Agriculture: A Geographic Perspective', *Post-Soviet Geography and Economics* 41, 4 (2000): 288–305.

Karcz, Jerzy (ed.), *Soviet and East European Agriculture* (Berkeley: University of California Press, 1967).

Kerblay, Basile, *Modern Soviet Society*, trans. Rupert Sawyer, foreword by M. Lewin (London: Methuen, 1983).

Khauke, O., *Krest'ianskoe zemel'noe pravo* (Moscow, 1914).

Kingston-Mann, Esther, 'The Danger of Universal Principles: Understanding the Soviet Union's Demise', *Challenge: A Magazine of Economic Affairs* (1999): 34–42.

'Deconstructing the Romance of the Bourgeoisie', *Review of International Political Economy* 10, 1 (Feb. 2003): 93–117.

and Mixter, Timothy (eds.), *Peasant Economy, Culture and Politics of European Russia* (Princeton: Princeton University Press, 1991).

Kotz, David, with Weir, Fred, *Revolution from Above: The Demise of the Soviet System* (London: Routledge, 1997).

Leonard, Carol Scott, 'Rational Resistance to Land Privatisation: The Response of Rural Producers to Agrarian Reforms in Pre- and Post-Soviet Russia', *Post-Soviet Geography and Economics* 41, 8 (2000): 605–20.

Maksudov, S., *Neuslyshannye golosa: Dokumenty smolenskogo arkhiva*, bk. 1: *Kulaki i partiitsy* (Ann Arbor: Ardis, 1987).

Moon, David, *The Russian Peasantry 1600–1930: The World the Peasants Made* (London: Longman, 1999).

Nove, Alec, *Soviet Agriculture: The Brezhnev Legacy and Gorbachev's Cure* (Los Angeles: Rand, 1988).

Ofer, Gur, *Soviet Economic Growth: 1928–1985* (Los Angeles: Rand, UCLA Center for the Study of Soviet International Behavior, 1988).

Pallot, Judith, *Land Reform in Russia, 1906–1917: Peasant Responses to Stolypin's Project of Rural Transformation* (Oxford: Clarendon Press, 1999).

Prosterman, Roy, et al., 'Prospects for Family Farming in Russia', *Europe–Asia Studies* 49 (1997): 1383–407.

Pryor, Frederick, 'When is Collectivization Reversible?' *Studies in Comparative Communism* 24, 1 (Mar. 1991): 3–24.

Rykov, A. I., *V bor'be za sukhoi i golodom* (Moscow, 1924).

Shaffer, Harry (ed.), *Soviet Agriculture: An Assessment of its Contributions to Economic Development* (New York: Praeger, 1977).

Shanin, Teodor, *The Rules of the Game: Cross-disciplinary Essays on Models in Scholarly Thought* (London: Tavistock Publications, 1972).

   *The Awkward Class: Political Sociology of Peasantry in a Developing Society, Russia 1910–1925* (Oxford: Clarendon Press, 1974).

   (ed.), *Late Marx and the Russian Road: Marx and the Peripheries of Capitalism* (New York: Monthly Review Press, 1984).

   *Russia as a 'Developing Society'*, 2 vols. (New Haven: Yale University Press, 1985).

   *Russia, 1905–07: Revolution as a Moment of Truth* (New Haven: Yale University Press, 1986).

   'Soviet Agriculture and Perestroika: Four Models', *Sociologia Ruralis* 29, 1 (1989): 7–22.

   *Neformal'naia ekonomika: Rossiia i mir* (Moscow: Logos, 1999).

   (ed.), *Refleksivnoe krest'ianovedenie* (Moscow: Rosspen, 2002).

Shmelev, Gelii Ivanovich, *Lichnoe posobnoe khoziaistvo i ego sviazi s obshchestvennym proizvodstvom* (Moscow, 1971).

Solomon, Susan, *The Soviet Agrarian Debate: A Controversy in Social Science, 1923–1929* (Boulder, Colo.: Westview Press, 1977).

Stepanov, I. P., *Neskol'ko dannykh o sostoianii sel'skogo khoziaistva v Moskovskoi gubernii* (Moscow, 1922).

Stuart, Robert C. (ed.), *The Soviet Rural Economy* (Totowa, N.J.: Rowman and Allanheld, 1983).

Suchkov, A., 'Kak ne nado rassmatrivat' vopros o formakh zemlepol'zovaniia', *Bolshevik* 2 (1928).

Sukhanov, N. N., 'Obshchina v sovetskom agrarnom zakonodatel'stve', *Na agrarnom fronte* 11–12 (1926).

Tauger, Mark, Davies, R. W., and Wheatcroft, S. G., 'Stalin, Grain Stocks and the Famine of 1932–1933', *Slavic Review* 54, 3 (1995): 642–57.

Van Atta, D., *The Farmer Threat: The Political Economy of Agrarian Reform in Post-Soviet Russia* (Boulder, Colo.: Westview Press, 1993).

Wadekin, Karl-Eugen, *The Private Sector in Soviet Agriculture*, ed. J. Karcz; trans. K. Bush (Berkeley: University of California Press, 1973).

Wegren, Stephen K., 'Rural Reform and Political Culture in Russia', *Europe–Asia Studies* 46, 2 (1994): 215–41.

   *Agriculture and the State in Soviet and Post-Soviet Russia* (Pittsburgh: University of Pittsburgh Press, 1998).

   (ed.), *Land Reform in the Former Soviet Union and Eastern Europe* (London: Routledge, 1998).

Wheatcroft, S. G., 'The Reliability of Russian Prewar Grain Statistics', *Soviet Studies* 26, 2 (Apr. 1974): 157–80.

Wilbur, Elvira, 'Was Russian Peasant Agriculture Really that Impoverished? Evidence from Case Study of the "Impoverished Center" at the end of the Nineteenth Century', *Journal of Economic History* 127, 44 (Mar. 1983): 137–44.

Yanov, A., *The Drama of Soviet Reform in the 1960s: A Lost Reform*, trans. Stephen Dunn (Berkeley: Institute of International Studies, 1984).

Zyrianov, P. N., 'Stolypin i sud'ba russkoi derevni', *Obshchestvennye nauki i sovremennost'* 4 (1991): 117–25.

   *Krest'ianskaia obshchina evropeiskoi Rossii 1907–1914* (Moscow: Nauka, 1992).

WOMEN AND GENDER

Bridger, Susan, *Women in the Soviet Countryside: Women's Roles in Rural Development in the Soviet Union* (Cambridge: Cambridge University Press, 1987).

   Kay, Rebecca, and Pinnick, Kathryn, *No More Heroines? Russia, Women and the Market* (New York: Routledge, 1996).

Buckley, Mary, *Women and Ideology in the Soviet Union* (Ann Arbor: University of Michigan Press, 1989).

   (ed.), *Perestroika and Soviet Women* (New York: Cambridge University Press, 1992).

   (ed.), *Post-Soviet Women: From the Baltic to Central Asia* (New York: Cambridge University Press, 1997).

Chatterjee, Choi, 'Soviet Heroines and Public Identity, 1930–1939', *The Carl Beck Papers in Russian and East European Studies*, no. 1402 (Pittsburgh: Center for Russian and East European Studies, 1999).

Clements, Barbara Evans, *Bolshevik Women* (Cambridge: Cambridge University Press, 1997).

   Friedman, Rebecca, and Healey, Dan (eds.), *Russian Masculinities in History and Culture* (New York: Palgrave, 2002).

Cottam, K. Jean, 'Soviet Women in World War II: The Ground Forces and the Navy', *International Journal of Women's Studies* 3 (1980): 345–55.

Edmondson, Linda (ed.), *Women and Society in Russia and the Soviet Union* (Cambridge: Cambridge University Press, 1992).

Eklof, Ben, *Russian Peasant Schools: Officialdom, Village Culture and Popular Pedagogy, 1861–1914* (Berkeley: University of California Press, 1986).

Elwood, R. C., *Inessa Armand: Revolutionary and Feminist* (Cambridge: Cambridge University Press, 1992).

Engel, Barbara Alpern, *A History of Russia's Women: 1700–2000* (New York: Cambridge University Press, 2003).

   and Posadskaya-Vanderbeck, Anastasia (eds.), *A Revolution of their Own: Voices of Women in Soviet History* (Boulder, Colo.: Westview Press, 1998).

Engelstein, Laura, *The Keys to Happiness: Sex and the Search for Modernity in Fin-de-Siècle Russia* (Ithaca, N.Y.: Cornell University Press, 1992).

Erickson, John, 'Soviet Women at War', in John and Carol Garrard (eds.), *World War 2 and the Soviet People: Selected Papers from the Fourth World Congress for Soviet and East European Studies, Harrogate 1990* (New York: St Martin's Press, 1993), pp. 50–76.

Farnsworth, Beatrice, and Viola, Lynne (eds.), *Russian Peasant Women* (New York: Oxford University Press, 1992).

Field, Deborah, ' "Irreconcilable Differences": Divorce and Conceptions of Private Life in the Khrushchev Era', *Russian Review* 57, 4 (Oct. 1998): 599–613.

Fieseler, Beate, 'The Making of Russian Female Social Democrats, 1890–1917', *International Review of Social History* 34 (1989): 193–226.

Fitzpatrick, Sheila, and Slezkine, Yuri (eds.), *In the Shadow of Revolution: Life Stories of Russian Women from 1917 to the Second World War* (Princeton: Princeton University Press, 2000).

Glickman, Rose, *Russian Factory Women: Workplace and Society, 1880–1914* (Berkeley: University of California Press, 1984).

Goldman, Wendy Zeva, *Women, the State and Revolution: Soviet Family Policy and Social Life, 1917–1936* (Cambridge and New York: Cambridge University Press, 1993).

'The Death of the Proletarian Women's Movement', *Slavic Review* 55, 1 (1996): 46–77.

*Women at the Gates: Gender and Industry in Stalin's Russia* (New York and Cambridge: Cambridge University Press, 2002).

Goscilo, Helena, and Holmgren, Beth (eds.), *Russia. Women. Culture* (Bloomington: Indiana University Press, 1996).

Healey, Dan, *Homosexual Desire in Revolutionary Russia: The Regulation of Sexual and Gender Dissent* (Chicago: University of Chicago Press, 2001).

Hodgson, Katharine, 'The Other Veterans: Soviet Women's Poetry of World War 2', in John and Carol Garrard (eds.), *World War 2 and the Soviet People: Selected Papers from the Fourth World Congress for Soviet and East European Studies, Harrogate 1990* (New York: St Martin's Press, 1993), pp. 77–97.

Hoffman, David, 'Mothers in the Motherland: Stalinist Pronatalism in its Pan-European Context', *Journal of Social History* (Fall 2000): 35–53.

Holland, Barbara (ed.), *Soviet Sisterhood* (Bloomington: Indiana University Press, 1985).

Ilic, Melanie (ed.), *Women in the Stalin Era* (New York: Palgrave, 2001).

Koenker, Diane, 'Men Against Women on the Shop Floor in Early Soviet Russia', *American Historical Review* 100, 5 (Dec. 1995): 1438–64.

Krylova, Anna, ' "Healers of Wounded Souls": The Crisis of Private Life in Soviet Literature, 1944–1946', *Journal of Modern History* 73, 2 (June 2001): 301–31.

Lapidus, Gail Warshofsky, *Women in Soviet Society: Equality, Development and Social Change* (Berkeley: University of California Press, 1978).

Lindenmeyr, Adele, 'Maternalism and Child Welfare in Late Imperial Russia', *Journal of Women's History* 5, 2 (1993): 114–25.

Mamonova, Tatyana (ed.), *Women and Russia: Feminist Writings from the Soviet Union* (Boston: Beacon Press, 1984).

Marsh, Rosalind (ed.), *Women in Russia and Ukraine* (Cambridge: Cambridge University Press, 1996).

(ed.), *Women and Russian Culture* (Oxford: Berghahn Books, 1998).

Neary, Rebecca Balmas, 'Mothering Socialist Society: The Wife-Activists' Movement and the Soviet Culture of Daily Life', *Russian Review* 58, 3 (July 1999): 396–412.

Pilkington, Hillary, *Gender, Generation and Identity in Contemporary Russia* (New York: Routledge, 1996).

Ransel, David, *Village Mothers: Three Generations of Change in Russia and Tataria* (Bloomington: Indiana University Press, 2000).

Reid, Susan, ' "Masters of the Earth": Gender and Destalinization in Soviet Reformist Painting of the Khrushchev Thaw', *Gender History* 11, 2 (July 1999): 276–312.

'Russians Vanishing', *New York Times*, 6 Dec. 2000, p. 8.

Sacks, Michael, *Women's Work in Soviet Russia: Continuity in the Midst of Change* (New York: Praeger, 1976).

Sanborn, Joshua, 'Family, Fraternity and Nation-Building in Russia, 1905–1925', in Ronald Grigor Suny and Terry Martin (eds.), *A State of Nations: Empire and Nation-Making in the Age of Lenin and Stalin* (New York: Oxford University Press, 2002), pp. 93–110.

Schlesinger, Rudolf (ed.), *The Family in the USSR: Documents and Readings* (London: Routledge and Kegan Paul, 1949).

Silverman, Bertram, and Murray, Yanowitch, *New Rich, New Poor, New Russia: Winners and Losers on the Russian Road to Capitalism* (Armonk, N.Y.: M. E. Sharpe, 1997).

Sperling, Valerie, *Organizing Women in Contemporary Russia: Engendering Transition* (New York: Cambridge University Press, 1999).

Stites, Richard, *The Women's Liberation Movement in Russia: Feminism, Nihilism, and Bolshevism* (Princeton: Princeton University Press, 1978).

Viola, Lynne, 'Bab'i Bunty and Peasant Women's Protest during Collectivization', *Russian Review* 45 (1986): 23–42.

Wade, Rex (ed.), *Documents of Soviet History*, vol II: *Triumph and Retreat, 1920–1922* (Gulf Breeze, Fla: Academic International Press, 1991).

Wagner, William, *Marriage, Property and Law in Late Imperial Russia* (Oxford: Clarendon Press, 1994).

Waters, Elizabeth, 'The Modernization of Russian Motherhood, 1917–1936', *Soviet Studies* 44, I (1992): 123–35.

Wood, Elizabeth, *The Baba and the Comrade: Gender and Politics in Revolutionary Russia* (Bloomington: Indiana University Press, 1997).

FOREIGN POLICY

Abebe, Ermias, 'The Horn, the Cold War, and Documents from the Former East-Bloc: An Ethiopian View', *Cold War International History Project Bulletin* 8–9 (1996/7): 40–5.

Adibekov, Grant M., *Kominform i poslevoennaia Evropa, 1947–1956* (Moscow: Rossiia molodaia, 1994).

Allison, Roy, and Jonson, Lena (eds.), *Central Asian Security: The New International Context* (Washington: Brookings Institution Press, 2001).

Anderson, K., and Chubar'ian, A. (eds.), *Komintern i ideia mirovoi revoliutsii: dokumenty* (Moscow: Nauka, 1998).

Anderson, Richard D., Jr., *Public Politics in an Authoritarian State: Making Foreign Policy During the Brezhnev Years* (Ithaca, N.Y.: Cornell University Press, 1993).

Andrew, Christopher and Mitrokhin, Vasili, *The Sword and the Shield: The Mitrokhin Archive and the Secret History of the KGB* (New York: Basic Books, 1999).

Beda, Anatolii M., *Sovetskaia politicheskaia kul'tura cherez prismu MVD: Ot 'Moskovskogo patriotizma' k idee 'bol'shogo otechestva', 1946–1958* (Moscow: Mosgorarkhiv, 2002).

Belozerov. A.P., et al. (eds.), *Sekrety Gitlera na stole u Stalina – Razvedka i kontrrazvedka o podgotovke germanskoi agressii protiv SSSR, mart–iiun, 1941g: Dokumenty iz tsentral'nogo arkhiva FSB Rossii* (Moscow: Mosgorarkhiv, 1995).

Bennett, Andrew, *Condemned to Repetition? The Rise, Fall, and Reprise of Soviet-Russian Military Interventionism, 1973–1996* (Cambridge, Mass.: MIT Press, 1999).

Bilmanis, A. (ed.), *Latvian–Russian Relations: Documents* (Washington: Latvian Delegation, 1944).

Blum, Douglas W., 'Domestic Politics and Russia's Caspian Policy', *Post-Soviet Affairs* 14, 2 (1998): 137–64.

Borkenau, F., *World Communism: A History of the Communist International* (Ann Arbor: University of Michigan Press, 1962).

Carr, E. H., *Twilight of Comintern, 1930–1935* (London: Macmillan, 1982).

Checkel, Jeffrey T., *Ideas and International Political Change: Soviet/Russian Behavior and the End of the Cold War* (New Haven: Yale University Press, 1997).

Chen, Jian, *Mao's China and the Cold War* (Chapel: Hill: University of North Carolina Press, 2001).

Chiang, Kai-shek, *A Summing up at Seventy: Soviet Russia in China* (London: Harrap, 1957).

Chubar'ian, A. O. (ed.), *Stalin i kholodnaia voina* (Moscow: In-t vseobshchei istorii RAN, 1997).

Dallin, A., and Firsov, F. (eds.), *Dimitrov & Stalin 1934–1943: Letters from the Soviet Archives* (New Haven: Yale University Press, 2000).

Danilov, Aleksandr A., and Pyzhikov, Aleksandr V., *Rozhdenie sverkhderzhavy: SSSR v pervye poslevoennye gody* (Moscow: ROSSPEN, 2001).

Dwan, Renata, and Pavliuk, Oleksandr (eds.), *Building Security in the New States of Eurasia: Subregional Cooperation in the Former Soviet Space* (Armonk, N.Y.: M. E. Sharpe, 2000).

Ekedahl, Carolyn McGiffert, and Goodman, Melvin A., *The Wars of Eduard Shevardnadze*, 2nd edn (Washington: Brassey's, 2001).

English, Robert D., *Russia and the Idea of the West: Gorbachev, Intellectuals, and the End of the Cold War* (New York: Columbia University Press, 2000).

Evangelista, Matthew, *Unarmed Forces. The Transnational Movement to End the Cold War* (Ithaca, N.Y.: Cornell University Press, 1999).

Firsov, F, 'Komintern: opyt, traditsii, uroki – nereshennye zadachi issledovaniia', in *Komintern: opyt, traditsii, uroki. Materialy nauchnoi konferentsii, posviashchennoi 70-letiiu Kommunisticheskogo Internatsionala* (Moscow: Nauka, 1989).

Fursenko, Aleksandr, and Naftali, Timothy, *'One Hell of a Gamble': Khrushchev, Castro, and Kennedy, 1958–1964* (New York: W. W. Norton, 1997).

Gaiduk, Ilya V., *Confronting Vietnam: Soviet Policy toward the Indochina Conflict, 1954–1963* (Stanford, Calif.: Stanford University Press, 2003).

Egorova, N. I., and Chubar'ian, A. O. (eds.), *Stalinskoe desiatiletie kholodnoi voiny: fakty i gipotezy* (Moscow: Nauka, 1999).

Garthoff, Raymond L., 'Some Observations on Using Soviet Archives', *Diplomatic History* 21, 2 (1997): 243–57.

*A Journey through the Cold War: A Memoir of Containment and Coexistence* (Washington: Brookings Institution Press, 2001).

Goldgeier, James M., *Leadership Style and Soviet Foreign Policy* (Baltimore: Johns Hopkins University Press, 1994).

*Not Whether but When: The U.S. Decision to Enlarge NATO* (Washington: Brookings Institution Press, 1999).

Goncharov, Sergei N., Lewis, John W., and Litai, Xue, *Uncertain Partners: Stalin, Mao, and the Korean War* (Stanford, Calif.: Stanford University Press, 1993).

Gorodetsky, Gabriel, *Stafford Cripps' Mission to Moscow, 1940–42* (Cambridge: Cambridge University Press, 1984).

(ed.), *Soviet Foreign Policy, 1917–1991: A Retrospective* (London: Cass, 1994).

Grinevskii, Oleg, *Tainy sovetskoi diplomatii* (Moscow: Vagrius, 2000).

Haslam, Jonathan, 'The Comintern and the Origins of the Popular Front, 1934–1935', *Historical Journal* 22, 3 (1979): 673–91.

*Soviet Foreign Policy 1930–33: The Impact of the Depression* (London: Macmillan, 1983).

*The Soviet Union and the Struggle for Collective Security in Europe, 1933–39* (London: Macmillan, 1984).

'Political Opposition to Stalin and the Origins of the Terror in Russia, 1932–1936', *Historical Journal* 29, 2 (1986): 395–418.

*The Soviet Union and the Threat from the East, 1933–41: Moscow, Tokyo and the Prelude to the Pacific War* (London: Macmillan, 1992).

'Russian Archival Revelations and Our Understanding of the Cold War', *Diplomatic History* 21, 2 (1997): 217–28.

Hopf, Ted, *Peripheral Visions: Deterrence Theory and American Foreign Policy in the Third World, 1965–1990* (Ann Arbor: University of Michigan Press, 1994).

*Social Construction of International Politics: Identities and Foreign Policies, Moscow, 1955 and 1999* (Ithaca, N.Y.: Cornell University Press, 2002).

Hough, Jerry, *The Struggle for the Third World* (Washington: Brookings Institution Press, 1986).

Komolova, N., et al. (eds.), *Komintern protiv fashizma: dokumenty* (Moscow: Nauka, 1999).

Kornienko, Georgii M., *Kholodnaia Voina: svidetelstvo ee uchastnika* (Moscow: Mezhdunarodnye otnosheniia, 1994).

Kramer, Mark, 'New Evidence on Soviet Decision-Making and the 1956 Polish and Hungarian Crises', *Cold War International History Project Bulletin* 8–9 (1996/7): 358–84.

Kulik, Boris T., *Sovetsko-Kitaiskii raskol: prichiny i posledstviia* (Moscow: Institut Dal'nego Vostoka RAN, 2000).

Kumanev, Georgii A., *Ryadom so Stalinym: otkrovennye svidetel'stva* (Moscow, 1999).

Kvitsinskii, Iulii A., *Vremia i sluchai: zametki profesionala* (Moscow, 1999).

Lebedeva, N., and Narinskii, M. (eds.), *Komintern i vtoraia mirovaia voina*, vol. 1 (Moscow: Nauka, 1994).

Light, Margot, 'Post-Soviet Russian Foreign Policy: The First Decade', in Archie Brown (ed.), *Contemporary Russian Politics: A Reader* (New York: Oxford University Press, 2001), pp. 419–28.

' "Malin" Notes on the Crises in Hungary and Poland, 1956', *Cold War International History Project Bulletin* 8–9 (1996/7): 385–410.

Mastny, Vojtech, *Russia's Road to the Cold War: Diplomacy, Warfare, and the Politics of Communism, 1941–1945* (New York: Columbia University Press, 1979).

Matz, Johan, *Constructing a Post-Soviet International Political Reality: Russian Foreign Policy towards the Newly Independent States, 1990–95* (Uppsala: Acta Universitatis Upsaliensis, 2001).

'Memorandum of Conversation, East German official with Soviet Ambassador to Ethiopia Ratanov, Addis Ababa, 6 December 1977', *Cold War International History Project Bulletin* 8–9 (1996/7): 82–3.

Mendelson, Sarah E., *Changing Course: Ideas, Politics, and the Soviet Withdrawal from Afghanistan* (Princeton: Princeton University Press, 1999).

Menon, Rajan, Fedorov, Yuri E., and Nodia, Ghia (eds.), *Russia, the Caucasus, and Central Asia: The 21ˢᵗ Century Security Environment* (Armonk, N.Y.: M. E. Sharpe, 1999).

Mlechin, Leonid, *MID: Ministerstvo Inostrannykh Del, romantiki i tsiniki* (Moscow: Tsentrpoligraf, 2001).

'More New Evidence on the Cold War in Asia', *Cold War International History Project Bulletin* 8–9 (1996/7): 220–69.

Morgenthau, Hans, *Politics Among Nations* (New York: Knopf, 1967).

Naimark, Norman M., *The Russians in Germany: A History of the Soviet Zone of Occupation, 1945–1949* (Cambridge, Mass.: Belknap Press of Harvard University Press, 1995).

' "Nasha liniia takaia . . .". Dokumenty o vstreche I.V. Stalina s rukovoditeliami SEPG. Ian.–fev. 1947g.', *Istoricheskii Arkhiv* 4 (1994): 22–44.

Nezhinskii, L. N. (ed.), *Sovetskaia vneshniaia politika v gody 'Kholodnoi Voiny' (1945–1985)* (Moscow: Mezhdunarodnye otnosheniia, 1995).

Olcott, Martha Brill, Aslund, Anders, and Garnett, Sherman W., *Getting It Wrong: Regional Cooperation and the Commonwealth of Independent States* (Washington: Carnegie Endowment for International Peace, 1999).

'Plenum TsK KPSS. Iiun' 1957 goda. Stenograficheskii otchet', *Istoricheskii Arkhiv* 3 (1993): 5–94.

'Plenum TsK KPSS. Oktyabr' 1964 goda. Stenograficheskii otchet', *Istoricheskii Arkhiv* 1 (1993): 6–19.

'Posledniaia "Antipartiinaia" Gruppa', *Istoricheskii Arkhiv* 1 (1994): 4–77; 2 (1994): 4–88.

'Posledniaia "Antipartiinaia" Gruppa. Stenograficheskii otchet iiun'skogo (1957 g.) plenuma TsK KPSS', *Istoricheskii Arkhiv* 3 (1993): 5–94; 4 (1993): 4–82.

Prizel, Ilya, *National Identity and Foreign Policy: Nationalism and Leadership in Poland, Russia, and Ukraine* (Cambridge: Cambridge University Press, 1998).

Prozumenshchikov, M. Y., 'The Sino-Indian Conflict, the Cuban Missile Crisis, and the Sino-Soviet Split, October 1962: New Evidence from the Russian Archives', *Cold War International History Project Bulletin* 8–9 (1996/7): 251–7.

Richter, James, *Khrushchev's Double Bind: International Pressures and Domestic Coalition Politics* (Baltimore: Johns Hopkins University Press, 1994).

Rozman, Gilbert (ed.), *Japan and Russia: The Tortuous Path to Normalization, 1949–1999* (New York: St Martin's Press, 2000).

Shearman, Peter (ed.), *Russian Foreign Policy since 1990* (Boulder, Colo.: Westview Press, 1995).

Shu Guang, Zhang, *Economic Cold War: America's Embargo against China and the Sino-Soviet Alliance, 1949–1963* (Washington: Woodrow Wilson Center Press, 2001).

Shulman, Marshall D., *Stalin's Foreign Policy Reappraised* (Cambridge, Mass.: Harvard University Press, 1963).

Snyder, Jack, 'The Gorbachev Revolution: A Waning of Soviet Expansionism?', *International Security* 12, 3 (1987/8): 93–131.

'SSSR: Narody i sud'by', *Voennye Arkhivy Rossii* 1 (1993): 246–70.

Stepashin, S., et al., *Organy Gosudarstvennoi Bezopasnosti SSSR v Velikoi Otechestvennoi Voine – sbornik dokumentov*, vol. 1 (Moscow: Kniga i biznes, 1995).

Sternthal, Susanne, *Gorbachev's Reforms: De-Stalinization through Demilitarization* (Westport, Conn.: Praeger, 1997).

Taubman, William, 'Khrushchev vs. Mao: A Preliminary Sketch of the Role of Personality in the Sino-Soviet Split', *Cold War International History Project Bulletin* 8–9 (1996/7): 243–8.

'The Soviet Union and Afghanistan, 1978–1989: Documents from the Russian and East German Archives', *Cold War International History Project Bulletin* 8–9 (1996/7): 133–84.

Titarenko, M., et al. *VKP (b), Komintern i natsional'no-revoliutsionnoe dvizhenie v Kitae: Dokumenty*, vol. 1 (Moscow: Russian Academy of Sciences, 1994).

'Transcript, Meeting of East German leader Erich Honecker and Soviet leader Leonid Brezhnev, Crimea, USSR, 25 July 1978', *Cold War International History Project Bulletin* 8–9 (1996/7): 122–3.

'Vengriia, Aprel'–Oktiabr' 1956 goda. Informatsiia Iu. V. Andropova, A. I. Mikoiana, i M. A. Suslova iz Budapeshta', *Istoricheskii Arkhiv* 4 (1993): 103–42.

Volokitina, Tatiana V., Murashko, Galina P., Noskova, Albina F., and Pokivailova, Tat'iana A., *Moskva i vostochnaia Evropa. Stanovlenie politicheskikh rezhimov sovetskogo tipa (1949–1953). Ocherki istorii* (Moscow: Rosspen, 2002).

Wallander, Celeste A. (ed.), *The Sources of Russian Foreign Policy after the Cold War* (Boulder, Colo.: Westview Press, 1996).

Westad, Odd Arne, 'Concerning the Situation in "A": New Russian Evidence on the Soviet Intervention in Afghanistan', *Cold War International History Project Bulletin* 8–9 (1996/7): 128–32.

  'Moscow and the Angolan Crisis, 1974–1976: A New Pattern of Intervention', *Cold War International History Project Bulletin* 8–9 (1996/7): 21–32.

  *The Global Cold War: Third World Interventions and the Making of Our Times* (Cambridge: Cambridge University Press, 2005).

  (ed.), *Brothers in Arms: The Rise and Fall of the Sino-Soviet Alliance, 1945–1963* (Stanford, Calif.: Stanford University Press, 1998).

Wishnick, Elizabeth, *Mending Fences: The Evolution of Moscow's China Policy from Brezhnev to Yeltsin* (London: University of Washington Press, 2001).

Zimmerman, William, *The Russian People and Foreign Policy: Russian Elite and Mass Perspectives, 1993–2000* (Princeton: Princeton University Press, 2002).

Zubok, Vladislav, and Pleshakov, Constantine, *Inside the Kremlin's Cold War* (Cambridge, Mass.: Harvard University Press, 1996).

## CULTURE, SCIENCE, IDEAS AND THE INTELLIGENTSIA

Alaniz, José, and Graham, Seth, 'Early Necrocinema in Context', in Seth Graham (ed.), *Necrorealism: Contexts, History, Interpretations* (Pittsburgh: Russian Film Symposium, 2001).

Amann, R., and Cooper, J. (eds.), *Industrial Innovation in the Soviet Union* (New Haven: Yale University Press, 1982).

and Davies, R. (eds.), *The Technological Level of Soviet Industry* (New Haven: Yale University Press, 1977).

Anninskii, Lev, *Shestidesiatniki i my* (Moscow: Kinotsentr, 1991).

Bailes, Kendall E. *Technology and Society under Lenin and Stalin: Origins of the Soviet Technical Intelligentsia, 1917–1941* (Princeton: Princeton University Press, 1978).

*Science and Russian Culture in an Age of Revolutions: V. I. Vernadsky and his Scientific School, 1863–1945* (Bloomington: Indiana University Press, 1990).

Balzer, Harley D., *Soviet Science on the Edge of Reform* (Boulder, Colo.: Westview Press, 1989).

Bar'iakhtar, V. G. (ed.), *Chernobyl'skaia katastrofa* (Kiev: Naukova dumka, 1995).

Barker, Adele Marie (ed.), *Consuming Russia: Popular Culture, Sex, and Society since Gorbachev* (Durham, N.C.: Duke University Press, 1999).

Bastrakova, M. S., *Stanovlenie sovetskoi sistemy organizatsii nauki (1917–1922)* (Moscow: Nauka, 1973).

Berg, Raisa, *Sukhovei* (New York: Chalidze Publications, 1983).

'Beria i teoriia otnositel'nosti', *Istoricheskii arkhiv* 3 (1994): 215–23.

Beumers, Birgit (ed.), *Russia on Reels* (London and New York: I. B. Tauris, 1999).

Bezborodov, A. B., *Vlast' i nauchno-tekhnicheskaia politika v SSSR serediny 50-kh–serediny 70-kh godov* (Moscow: Mosgorarkhiv, 1997).

Biriukov, B. V., et al., 'Filosofskie problemy kibernetiki', in A. I. Berg (ed.), *Kibernetika – na sluzhbu kommunizmu*, vol. VI (Moscow: Energiia, 1967).

Bongard-Levin, G. M., and Zakharov, V. E. (eds.), *Rossiiskaia nauchnaia emigratsiia: dvadtsat' portretov* (Moscow: URSS, 2001).

Bonnell, Victoria E., *Iconography of Power: Soviet Political Posters under Lenin and Stalin* (Berkeley: University of California Press, 1997).

Bowlt, John (ed.), *Russian Art of the Avant-Garde: Theory and Criticism, 1902–1934* (New York: Viking Press, 1976).

Brooks, Jeffrey, *When Russia Learned to Read: Literacy and Popular Literature, 1861–1917* (Princeton: Princeton University Press, 1985).

*Thank You, Comrade Stalin!: Soviet Public Culture from Revolution to Cold War* (Princeton: Princeton University Press, 2000).

Brown, Deming, *Soviet Russian Literature since Stalin* (Cambridge and London: Cambridge University Press, 1978).

Brown, Edward, *The Proletarian Episode in Russian Literature, 1928–1932* (New York: Columbia University Press, 1953).

Bukharin, Nikolai, *Programma kommunistov (bol'shevikov)* (Moscow: Izdatel'stvo VTsIK, 1918).

*Metodologiia i planirovanie nauki i tekhniki: Izbrannye trudy* (Moscow: Nauka, 1989).

*Izbrannye proizvedeniia* (Moscow: Ekonomika, 1990).

and Preobrazhensky, Evgenii, *The ABC of Communism: A Popular Explanation of the Program of the Communist Party of Russia* (Ann Arbor: University of Michigan Press, 1966; originally published 1919).

Bulganin, N., *Doklad na plenume tsentral'nogo komiteta KPSS, 4 iiulia 1955 goda* (Moscow: Politizdat, 1955).

Burlatskii, F., 'Posle Stalina', *Novyi mir* 10 (1988).

*Central Committee Resolution and Zhdanov's Speech on the Journals Zvezda and Leningrad, The* bilingual edn (Royal Oak, Mich.: Strathcona Publishing Company, 1978).

Chanbarisov, Sh. Kh., *Formirovanie sovetskoi universitetskoi sistemy* (Moscow: Vysshaia shkola, 1988).

Chatterjee, Choi, *Celebrating Women: Gender, Festival Culture, and Bolshevik Ideology, 1910–1939* (Pittsburgh: University of Pittsburgh Press, 2002).

Chertok, B. E., *Rakety i liudi* (Moscow: Mashinostroenie, 1994).

Clark, Katerina, *The Soviet Novel: History as Ritual* (Chicago: University of Chicago Press, 1981).

Clyman, Toby, and Greene, Diana (eds.), *Women Writers in Russian Literature* (Westport, Conn. and London: Praeger, 1994).

Cohen, Stephen F. (ed.), *An End to Silence: Uncensored Opinion in the Soviet Union* (New York: W. W. Norton, 1982).

Condee, Nancy (ed.), *Soviet Hieroglyphics: Visual Culture in Late Twentieth-Century Russia* (Bloomington and London: Indiana University Press and British Film Institute, 1995).

Corney, Frederick C., *Telling October: Memory and the Making of the Bolshevik Revolution* (Ithaca, N.Y., and London: Cornell University Press, 2004).

Counts, George S., and Lodge, Nucia, *The Country of the Blind: The Soviet System of Mind Control* (Boston: Houghton Mifflin, 1949).

and Peteri, Gyorgy (eds.), *Academia in Upheaval: Origins, Transfers, and Transformations of the Communist Academic Regime in Russia and East Central Europe* (Westport, Conn.: Bergin and Garvey, 2000).

Dawson, Jane I., *Eco-nationalism: Anti-Nuclear Activism and National Identity in Russia, Lithuania, and Ukraine* (Durham, N.C.: Duke University Press, 1996).

Dezhina, Irina, and Graham, Loren, *Russian Basic Science After Ten Years of Transition and Foreign Support* (Washington: Carnegie Endowment for International Peace, 2002).

Donald, Moira, *Marxism and Revolution: Karl Kautsky and the Russian Marxists, 1900–1924* (London: Yale University Press, 1993).

Draper, Hal, *Karl Marx's Theory of Revolution*, 4 vols. (New York: Monthly Review Press, 1977–90).

Dudintsev, Vladimir, *Ne khlebom edinym* (Munich: Izdatel'stvo TsOPE, 1957).

*Not by Bread Alone*, trans. Edith Bone (New York: E. P. Dutton, 1957).

Dunlop, John B., Haugh, Richard, and Klimoff, Alexis (eds.), *Alexander Solzhenitsyn: Critical Essays and Documentary Materials*, 2nd edn (New York and London: Collier, 1975).

Edelman, Robert, *Serious Fun: A History of Spectator Sport in the USSR* (New York: Oxford University Press, 1993).

Engels, Frederick, *The Dialectics of Nature* (New York: International Publishers, 1940).

*Anti-Duehring: Herr Eugen Duehring's Revolution in Science* (Moscow: Foreign Languages Publishing House, 1962).

Ermolaev, Herman, *Censorship in Soviet Literature: 1917–1991* (New York and London: Rowman and Littlefields, 1997).

Esakov, V. D., and Levina, E. S., *Delo KR. Sudy chesti v ideologii i praktike poslevoennogo stalinizma* (Moscow: Institut rossiskoi istorii i institut istorii estestvoznaniia i tekhniki Rossiiskoi Akademii nauk, 2001).

Faraday, George, *Revolt of the Filmmakers: The Struggle for Artistic Autonomy and the Fall of the Soviet Film Industry* (University Park, Pa.: Pennsylvania State University Press, 2000).

Feshbach, Murray, and Friendly, Alfred, Jr., *Ecocide in the USSR: Health and Nature under Siege* (New York: Basic Books, 1992).

*Filosofskie problemy sovremennogo estestvoznaniia* (Moscow: Izdatel'stvo AN SSSR, 1959).

Finkel, Stuart, 'Purging the Public Intellectual: The 1922 Expulsions from Soviet Russia', *Russian Review* 62 (2003): 589–613.

Fomin, Valerii, *Kino i vlast'* (Moscow: Materik, 1996).

Frish, S. E., *Skvoz' prizmu vremeni* (Moscow: Politizdat, 1992).

Garrard, John and Carol, *Inside the Soviet Writers' Union* (New York and London: Free Press, 1990).

  (eds.), *World War 2 and the Soviet People* (London: Macmillan and New York: St Martin's Press, 1993).

Garros, Véronique, Koenevskaya, Natalia, and Lahusen, Thomas (eds.), *Intimacy and Terror: Soviet Diaries of the 1930s* (New York: New Press, 1995).

Gasparov, Boris, Hughes, Robert P., and Paperno, Irina (eds.), *Cultural Mythologies of Russian Modernism: From the Golden Age to the Silver Age* (Berkeley: University of California Press, 1992).

'Genetika – nasha bol'', *Pravda*, 13 Jan. 1989, p. 4.

Gerovitch, Slava, *From Newspeak to Cyberspeak: A History of Soviet Cybernetics* (Cambridge, Mass.: MIT Press, 2002).

Gibian, George, *Interval of Freedom: Soviet Literature during the Thaw, 1954–1957* (Minneapolis: University of Minnesota Press, 1960).

Golovskoy, Val S., with John Rimberg, *Behind the Soviet Screen: The Motion-Picture Industry in the USSR 1972–1982* (Ann Arbor: Ardis, 1986).

Gorelik, Gennadii, 'Fizika universitetskaia i akademicheskaia', *Voprosy istorii estestvoznaniia i tekhniki* 2 (1991): 31–46.

  *'Meine antisowjetische Tätigkeit . . .': Russische Physiker unter Stalin* (Wiesbaden: Vieweg, 1993).

  *Andrei Sakharov: Nauka i svoboda* (Moscow: R&C Dynamics, 2000).

Goscilo, Helena (ed.), *Fruits of Her Plume: Essays on Contemporary Russian Women's Culture* (Armonk, N.Y., and London: M. E. Sharpe, 1993).

Graham, Loren R., *The Soviet Academy of Sciences and the Communist Party 1927–1932* (Princeton: Princeton University Press, 1967).

  *Science, Philosophy, and Human Behavior* (New York: Columbia University Press, 1987).

  *Science in Russia and the Soviet Union. A Short History* (Cambridge: Cambridge University Press, 1993).

  *The Ghost of the Executed Engineer: Technology and the Fall of the Soviet Union* (Cambridge, Mass.: Harvard University Press, 1993).

  *What Have we Learned about Science and Technology from the Russian Experience?* (Stanford, Calif.: Stanford University Press, 1998).

Grakina, E. I., *Uchenye – frontu 1941–1945* (Moscow: Nauka, 1989).

  *Uchenye Rossii v gody velikoi otechestvennoi voiny 1941–1945* (Moscow: Institut rossiiskoi istorii Rossiiskoi Akademii nauk, 2000).

Groys, Boris, *The Total Art of Stalinism: Avant-Garde, Aesthetic Dictatorship, and Beyond*, trans. Charles Rougle (Princeton: Princeton University Press, 1992).

Halfin, Igal, and Hellbeck, Jochen, 'Rethinking the Stalinist Subject: Stephen Kotkin's "Magnetic Mountain" and the State of Soviet Historical Studies', *Jahrbücher für Geschichte Osteuropas* 44 (1996): 456–63.

Harding, Neil, *Leninism* (Durham, N.C.: Duke University Press, 1996).

Hellbeck, Jochen, 'Fashioning the Stalinist Soul: The Diary of Stepan Podlubyni', *Jahrbücher für Geschichte Osteuropas* 44, H. 3 (1996): 344–73.

    *Revolution on My Mind: Writing a Diary Under Stalin* (Cambridge, Mass.: Harvard University Press, 2006).

Hessen, Boris, 'The Social and Economic Roots of Newton's *Principia*', in *Science at the Cross Roads*, 2nd edn (London: Frank Cass, 1971).

Hilton, Alison, and Dodge, Norton (eds.), *New Art from the Soviet Union* (Washington and Ithaca, N.Y.: Acropolis Books, 1977).

Hingley, Ronald, *Russian Writers and Soviet Society 1917–1978* (New York: Knopf, 1979).

Holloway, David, 'Innovation in Science – the Case of Cybernetics in the Soviet Union', *Science Studies* 4 (1974): 229–337.

    'The Political Uses of Scientific Models: The Cybernetic Model of Government in Soviet Social Science', in Lyndhurst Collins (ed.), *The Use of Models in the Social Sciences* (London: Tavistock Publications, 1976).

    *The Soviet Union and the Arms Race* (New Haven: Yale University Press, 1983).

    *Stalin and the Bomb: The Soviet Union and Atomic Energy, 1939–1956* (New Haven: Yale University Press, 1994).

Holmes, Larry E., *The Kremlin and the Schoolhouse: Reforming Education in Soviet Russia, 1917–1931* (Bloomington: Indiana University Press, 1991).

Horton, Andrew, and Brashinsky, Michael, *Glasnost and Soviet Cinema in Transition* (Princeton: Princeton University Press, 1992).

Hosking, Geoffrey, *Beyond Socialist Realism: Soviet Fiction since Ivan Denisovich* (London: Granada, 1980).

Hutchings, Stephen C., *Russian Modernism: The Transfiguration of the Everyday* (Cambridge: Cambridge University Press, 1997).

Iaroshevskii, M. G. (ed.), *Repressirovannaia nauka* (Leningrad: Nauka, 1991).

*Iulii Borisovich Khariton: put' dlinoiu v vek* (Moscow: Editorial URSS, 1999).

Ivanov, Konstantin, 'Science after Stalin: Forging a New Image of Soviet Science', *Science in Context* 15, 2 (2002).

Johnson, Priscilla, and Labedz, Leopold (eds.), *Khrushchev and the Arts: The Politics of Soviet Culture, 1962–1964* (Cambridge, Mass.: MIT Press, 1965).

Joravsky, David, *Soviet Marxism and Natural Science 1917–1932* (London: Routledge and Kegan Paul, 1961).

    *The Lysenko Affair* (Chicago: Chicago University Press, 1970).

Josephson, Paul R., *Physics and Politics in Revolutionary Russia* (Berkeley: University of California Press, 1991).

    *New Atlantis Revisited: Akademgorodok, the Siberian City of Science* (Princeton: Princeton University Press, 1997).

*Red Atom: Russia's Nuclear Power Program from Stalin to Today* (New York: W. H. Freeman, 2000).

Kagarlitsky, Boris, *The Thinking Reed: Intellectuals and the Soviet State, 1917 to the Present* (London: Verso, 1988).

Kapitsa, P. L., *Pis'ma o nauke* (Moscow: Moskovskii rabochii, 1989).

Karlinsky, Simon, and Appel, Alfred, Jr. (eds.), *The Bitter Air of Exile: Russian Writers in the West, 1922–1972* (Berkeley: University of California Press, 1977).

Kassow, Samuel D., *Students, Professors and the State in Tsarist Russia* (Berkeley: University of California Press, 1989).

Keldysh, M. V., 'Nauka sluzhit kommunizmu', *Pravda,* 1 Apr. 1968, p. 2.

Kelly, Catriona, and Shepherd, David (eds.), *Constructing Russian Culture in the Age of Revolution, 1881–1940* (Oxford: Oxford University Press, 1998).

(eds.), *Russian Cultural Studies: An Introduction* (Oxford: Oxford University Press: 1998).

Kenez, Peter, *The Birth of the Propaganda State: Soviet Methods of Mass Mobilization, 1917–1929* (New York: Cambridge University Press, 1985).

*Cinema and Soviet Society: From the Revolution to the Death of Stalin,* 2nd edn (London and New York: I. B. Tauris, 2001).

Kerber, L. L. *Tupolev* (St Petersburg: Politekhnika, 1999).

Kharkhordin, Oleg, *The Collective and the Individual in Russia: A Study of Practices* (Berkeley and Los Angeles: University of California Press, 1999).

Kneen, Peter, *Soviet Scientists and the State* (Albany, N.Y.: State University of New York Press, 1984).

Kojevnikov, A., 'President of Stalin's Academy', *Isis* 87 (1996): 18–50.

'Rituals of Stalinist Culture at Work: Science and the Games of Intraparty Democracy ca. 1948', *Russian Review* 57 (1998): 25–52.

Kolchinskii, E. I. (ed.), *Nauka i krizisy* (St Petersburg: Institut istorii estestvoznaniia i tekhniki, Sankt-Peterburgskii filial, 2003).

Kosolapov, Richard, *Slovo tovarishchu Stalinu* (Moscow: Paleia, 1995).

Kovtun, Evgeny, *The Russian Avant-Garde in the 1920s–1930s: Paintings, Graphics, Sculpture, Decorative Arts from the Russian Museum in St. Petersburg* (St Petersburg: Aurora Art Publishers, 1996).

Krementsov, Nikolai, *Stalinist Science* (Princeton: Princeton University Press, 1997).

'Kruglyi stol. Stranitsy istorii sovetskoi genetiki v literature poslednykh let', *Voprosy istorii estestvoznaniia i tekhniki* 4 (1987): 113–24.

Kumanev, V. A. (ed.), *Tragicheskie sud'by: repressirovannye uchenye Akademii nauk SSSR* (Moscow: Nauka, 1995).

Lahusen, Thomas J., with Kuperman, Gene (eds.), *Late Soviet Culture: From Perestroika to Novostroika* (Durham, N.C., and London: Duke University Press, 1993).

Laird, Sally, *Voices of Russian Literature: Interviews with Ten Contemporary Writers* (Oxford: Oxford University Press, 1999).

Lawton, Anna, *Russian Futurism through its Manifestoes, 1912–1928* (Ithaca, N.Y.: Cornell University Press, 1988).

*Kinoglasnost: Soviet Cinema in Our Time* (Cambridge: Cambridge University Press, 1992).

Legasov, V., 'Moi dolg rasskazat' ob etom . . .', *Pravda,* 20 May 1988, p. 8.

Lenin, V. I., *Materialism and Empiriocriticism* (New York: International Publishers, 1972).

Levshin, B. V., *Sovetskaia nauka v gody velikoi otechestvennoi voiny* (Moscow: Nauka, 1983).

(ed.), *Dokumenty po istorii Akademii nauk SSSR* (Leningrad: Nauka, 1986).

Lewis, Robert, 'Some Aspects of the Research and Development Effort of the Soviet Union, 1924–1935', *Science Studies* 2 (1972).

*Science and Industrialisation in the USSR* (London: Macmillan, 1979).

Leyda, Jay, *Kino, A History of the Russian and Soviet Film* (New York: Collier Books, 1973).

Lih, Lars T., 'Bukharin's "Illusion": War Communism and the Meaning of NEP', *Russian History/Histoire russe* 27, 4 (Winter 2000): 417–60.

*Lenin Rediscovered: What Is To Be Done? In Context: A Commentary and New Translation* (Leiden: Brill, 2006).

Lobanov, M. M., *Razvitie sovetskoi radiolokatsionnoi tekhniki* (Moscow: Voenizdat, 1982).

Loseff, Lev, *The Beneficence of Censorship* (Munich: 1984).

Lubrano, Linda, and Solomon, Susan Gross (eds.), *The Social Context of Soviet Science* (Boulder, Colo.: Westview Press, 1980).

McMillin, Arnold, *Reconstructing the Canon: Russian Writing in the 1980s* (Amsterdam: Harwood, 2000).

McReynolds, Louise, and Neuberger, Joan (eds.), *Imitations of Life: Two Centuries of Melodrama in Russia* (Durham, N.C.: Duke University Press, 2002).

Maguire, Robert A., *Red Virgin Soil: Soviet Literature in the 1920's* (Princeton: Princeton University Press, 1968).

Mally, Lynn, *Culture of the Future: the Proletkult Movement in Revolutionary Russia* (Berkeley: University of California Press, 1990).

Markov, Vladimir, *Russian Futurism: A History* (Berkeley: University of California Press, 1968).

Morson, Gary Saul, *Literature and History: Theoretical Problems and Russian Case Studies* (Stanford, Calif.: Stanford University Press, 1986).

Medvedev, Grigorii, *Chernobyl'skaia khronika* (Moscow: Sovremennik, 1989).

*No Breathing Room: The Aftermath of Chernobyl* (New York: Basic Books, 1993).

Medvedev, Zhores A., *The Rise and Fall of T. D. Lysenko* (New York: Columbia University Press, 1969).

*The Medvedev Papers: The Plight of Soviet Science Today* (London: Macmillan, 1971).

*Soviet Science* (New York: W. W. Norton, 1978).

Mochalov, I. I., *Vladimir Ivanovich Vernadskii* (Moscow: Nauka, 1982).

Naiman, Eric, *Sex in Public: The Incarnation of Early Soviet Ideology* (Princeton: Princeton University Press, 1997).

Naimark, Norman M., *The Russians in Germany* (Cambridge, Mass.: Harvard University Press, 1995).

*Nauchnye kadry SSSR: dinamika i struktura* (Moscow: Mysl', 1991).

Nazarov, A. G., *Nauka i bezopasnost' Rossii* (Moscow: Nauka, 2000).

'Nel'zia peredelyvat' zakony prirody (P. L. Kapitsa I. V. Stalinu)', *Izvestiia TsK KPSS* 2 (1991): 104–10.

Nesmeianov, A. N., *Na kacheliakh XX veka* (Moscow: Nauka, 1999).

Paperno, Irina, and Grossman, Joan Delaney (eds.), *Creating Life: The Aesthetic Utopia of Russian Modernism* (Stanford, Calif.: Stanford University Press, 1994).

Parrott, Bruce, *Politics and Technology in the Soviet Union* (Cambridge, Mass.: MIT Press, 1983).

Parthé, Kathleen, *Russian Village Prose: The Radiant Path* (Princeton: Princeton University Press, 1992).

Pavlenko, Iu. V., Raniuk, Iu. N., and Khramov, Iu. A., *'Delo' UFTI 1935–1938* (Kiev: Feniks, 1998).

Peterson, Ronald E., *The Russian Symbolists: An Anthology of Critical and Theoretical Writings* (Ann Arbor: Ardis, 1986).

Petrone, Karen, *Life Has Become More Joyous, Comrades: Celebrations in the Time of Stalin* (Bloomington and Indianapolis: Indiana University Press, 2000).

Pollock, Ethan, *Stalin and the Soviet Science Wars* (Princeton: Princeton University Press, 2006).

Popovsky, Mark, *Science in Chains: The Crisis of Science and Scientists in the Soviet Union Today* (London: Collins and Harvill Press, 1980).

Porter, Robert, *Russia's Alternative Prose* (Oxford and Providence, R. I.: Berg, 1994).

Read, Christopher, *Culture and Power in Revolutionary Russia: The Intelligentsia and the Transition from Tsarism to Communism* (New York: St Martin's Press, 1990).

Riabev, L. D. (ed.), *Atomnyi proekt SSSR: Dokumenty i materialy*, 2 vols. (Moscow-Sarov: Nauka; Fizmatlit, VNII Vniief, 1998–9).

*Road to Communism, The* (Moscow: Foreign Languages Publishing House, n.d.).

Rossianov, Kirill O., 'Editing Nature: Joseph Stalin and the "New" Soviet Biology', *Isis* 84 (1993): 728–45.

Rubenstein, M., *Science, Technology and Economics under Capitalism and in the Soviet Union* (Moscow: Co-operative Publishing Society of Foreign Workers in the USSR, 1932).

Rudnitsky, Konstantin, *Russian and Soviet Theater, 1905–1932* (New York: Abrams, 1988).

Russell, Robert, and Barratt, Andrew (eds.), *Russian Theatre in the Age of Modernism* (New York: St Martin's Press, 1990).

Sakharov, Andrei D., *Razmyshleniia o progresse, mirnom sosushchestvovanii i intellektual'noi svobode* (Frankfurt-am-Main: Possev Verlag, 1968).

   *Alarm and Hope* (New York: Vintage Books, 1978).

   *Vospominaniia* (New York: Izdatel'stvo imeni Chekhova, 1990).

Scammell, Michael, *Solzhenitsyn: A Biography* (New York and London: Norton, 1984).

Schweitzer, Glenn E., *Swords into Market Shares: Technology, Economics, and Security in the New Russia* (Washington: Joseph Henry Press, 2000).

Semenov, N. N., 'Nauka ne terpit sub" ektivizma', *Nauka i zhizn'* 4 (1965).

Shlapentokh, Vladimir, *The Politics of Sociology in the Soviet Union* (Boulder, Colo.: Westview Press, 1987).

Shneidman, N. N., *Soviet Literature in the 1970s: Artistic Diversity and Ideological Conformity* (Toronto: University of Toronto Press, 1979).

Siddiqi, Asif A., *Challenge to Apollo: The Soviet Union and the Space Race, 1945–1974* (Washington: National Aeronautics and Space Administration, 2000).

Siniavskii, Andrei, 'Samizdat and the Rebirth of Literature', *Index on Censorship* 9, 4 (Aug. 1980):

Sonin, A. S., *Fizicheskii idealizm: istoriia odnoi ideologicheskoi kampanii* (Moscow: Fizmatlit, 1994).

'Soveshchanie v Narkomtiazhprome o nauchno-issledovatel'skoi rabote', *Sotsialisticheskaia rekonstruktsiia i nauka* 8 (1936).

'Stalin and the Crisis of the Proletarian Dictatorship' (known as the 'Riutin platform'), in *Reabilitatsiia: Politicheskie protsessy 30-50-kh godov* (Moscow: Biblioteka zhurnala Izvestiia TsIK, 1991), pp. 334–442.

Stalin, I. V., *Ekonomicheskie problemy sotsializma v SSSR* (Moscow: Gosizdat, 1952).

    *Marxism and the Problems of Linguistics* (Moscow: Foreign Languages Publishing House, 1955).

Starr, S. Frederick, *Red and Hot: The Fate of Jazz in the Soviet Union, 1917–1980* (New York: Oxford University Press, 1983).

Stuart, Robert, *Marxism at Work: Ideology, Class and French Socialism during the Third Republic* (Cambridge: Cambridge University Press, 1992).

Sutton, Antony C., *Western Technology and Soviet Economic Development, 1930–1945* (Stanford, Calif.: Hoover Institution Press, 1971).

Taylor, Richard, and Christie, Ian (eds.), *The Film Factory: Russian and Soviet Cinema in Documents* (Cambridge, Mass.: Harvard University Press, 1988).

Todes, Daniel, 'Pavlov and the Bolsheviks', *History and Philosophy of the Life Sciences* 17 (1995): 379–418.

Tsivian, Yuri, *Early Cinema in Russia and its Cultural Reception* (London: Routledge, 1994).

Tucker, Robert C., *Political Culture and Leadership in Soviet Russia: From Lenin to Gorbachev* (New York: Norton, 1987).

Vernadskii, V. I., *Filosofskie mysli naturalista* (Moscow: Nauka, 1988).

    *O nauke*, 2 vols. (St Petersburg: Izdatel'stvo Russkogo khristianskogo gumanitarnogo instituta, 2002).

Vishevsky, Anatoly, *Soviet Literary Culture in the 1970s: The Politics of Irony* (Gainesville, Fla.: University Press of Florida, 1993).

Vizgin, V. P., 'Martovskaia (1936 g.) sessiia AN SSSR: Sovetskaia fizika v fokuse', *Voprosy istorii estestvoznaniia i tekhniki* 1 (1990): 63–84; 3 (1991): 36–55.

    'The Nuclear Shield in the "Thirty-Year War" of Physicists against Ignorant Criticism of Modern Physical Theories', *Physics-Uspekhi* 42, 12 (1999): 1268–70.

    *Vlast' i nauka, uchenye i vlast' 1880-e–nachalo 1920-kh godov* (St Petersburg: Izdatel'stvo 'Dmitrii Bulanin', 2003).

von Geldern, James, and Stites, Richard (eds.), *Mass Culture in Soviet Russia: Tales, Poems, Songs, Movies, Plays, and Folklore, 1917–1953* (Bloomington: Indiana University Press, 1995).

Vucinich, Alexander, *Science in Russian Culture: A History to 1860* (Stanford, Calif.: Stanford University Press, 1963).

    *Science in Russian Culture 1861–1917* (Stanford, Calif.: Stanford University Press, 1970).

    *Empire of Knowledge* (Berkeley: University of California Press, 1984).

Vysotsky, Vladimir, *Pesni i stikhi* (New York: Literary Frontiers Publishers, 1981).

Weissberg, Alexander, *The Accused* (New York: Simon and Schuster, 1951).

Werskey, P. G., *The Visible College* (London: Allen Lane, 1978).

Woll, Josephine, *Invented Truth: Soviet Reality and the Literary Imagination of Iurii Trifonov* (Durham, N.C.: Duke University Press, 1991).

*Real Images: Soviet Cinema and the Thaw* (London: I.B. Tauris, 2000).

and Treml, Vladimir G., *Soviet Dissident Literature: A Critical Guide* (Boston: G. K. Hall, 1983).

*Workers of the World and Oppressed Peoples, Unite!: Proceedings and Documents of the Second Congress, 1920*, 2 vols., ed. John Riddell (New York: Pathfinder, 1991).

*World of Art Movement in Early 20th-Century Russia* (Leningrad: Aurora Art Publishers, 1991).

Zaleski, E., Kozlowski, J. P., Wienert, H., Davies, R. W., Berry, M. J., and Amann, R., *Science Policy in the USSR* (Paris: Organization for Economic Co-operation and Development, 1969).

Zemlianukhin, Sergei, and Segida, Miroslava, *Domashniaia sinemateka: otechestvennoe kino 1918–1996* (Moscow: Dubl-D, 1996).

Zinov'ev, Aleksandr, *Ziiaiushchie vysoty* (Lausanne: L'Age d'Homme, 1976).

### NATIONALITIES

Adams, Arthur E., *Bolsheviks in the Ukraine: The Second Campaign, 1918–1919* (New Haven: Yale University Press, 1963).

Akiner, Shirin, *The Formation of Kazakh Identity from Tribe to Nation-State* (London: Royal Institute of International Affairs, 1995).

Allworth, Edward A. (ed.), *The Tatars of Crimea: Return to the Homeland* (Durham, N.C., and London: Duke University Press, 1998).

Alpatov, V. M., *150 iazykov i politika: 1917–1997* (Moscow: IV RAN, 1997).

Altstadt, Audrey L., *The Azerbaijani Turks* (Stanford, Calif.: Hoover Institution Press, 1992).

Anderson, Barbara A., and Silver, Brian D., 'Estimating Russification of Ethnic Identity among Non-Russians in the USSR', *Demography* 20, 4 (Nov. 1983): 461–89.

'Equality, Efficiency, and Politics in Soviet Bilingual Education Policy, 1934–1980', *American Political Science Review* 78 (1984): 1019–39.

Armstrong, John A., *Ukrainian Nationalism, 1939–45* (New York: Columbia University Press, 1963).

*Nations Before Nationalism* (Chapel Hill: University of North Carolina Press, 1982).

Arutiunov, Iurii, *Sotsial'noe i natsional'noe: Opyt etnosotsiologicheskikh issledovanii po materialam Tatarskoi ASSR* (Moscow: Nauka, 1973).

Aster, Howard, and Potichnyj, Peter J. (eds.), *Ukrainian–Jewish Relations in Historical Perspective* (Edmonton: Canadian Institute of Ukrainian Studies Press, 1988).

Balmaceda, Margarita M., Clem, James I., and Tarlow, Lisbeth L. (eds.), *Independent Belarus: Domestic Determinants, Regional Dynamics, and Implications for the West* (Cambridge, Mass.: Ukrainian Research Institute and Davis Center for Russian Studies, Harvard University, 2002).

Beissinger, Mark R., *Nationalist Mobilization and the Collapse of the Soviet State* (Cambridge: Cambridge University Press, 2002).

Bennigsen, Alexandre, and Lemercier-Quelquejay, Chantal, *Islam in the Soviet Union* (London: Pall Mall, 1967).

Bilinsky, Yaroslav, 'The Soviet Education Laws of 1958–59 and Soviet Nationality Policy', *Soviet Studies* 14 (1962): 138–57.

Blank, Stephen, *The Sorcerer as Apprentice – Stalin as Commissar of Nationalities, 1917–1924* (Westport, Conn.: Greenwood Press, 1994).

Blitstein, Peter, 'Stalin's Nations: Soviet Nationality Policy between Planning and Primordialism, 1936–1953'. Ph. D. diss., University of California, Berkeley, 1999.

Borys, Jurij, *The Sovietization of Ukraine, 1917–1923* (Edmonton: Canadian Institute of Ukrainian Studies, 1980).

Brandenberger, David, *National Bolshevism: Stalinist Mass Culture and the Formation of Modern Russian National Identity, 1931–1956* (Cambridge, Mass.: Harvard University Press, 2002).

Bremmer, Ian, and Taras, Ray (eds.), *New States, New Politics: Building the Post-Soviet Nations* (Cambridge: Cambridge University Press, 1997).

Bromlei, Iulii V., *Sovremennye etnicheskie protsessy v SSSR* (Moscow: Nauka, 1975).

Broxup, Marie, 'The Basmachis', *Central Asian Survey* 2 (1983): 57–82.

(ed.), *The North Caucasus Barrier: The Russian Advance towards the Muslim World* (London: Hurst, 1992).

Brubaker, Rogers, *Nationalism Reframed: Nationhood and the National Question in the New Europe* (Cambridge and New York: Cambridge University Press, 1996).

Burds, Jeffrey, 'The Early Cold War in Soviet West Ukraine, 1944–1948', *Carl Beck Papers in Russian and East European Studies*, no. 1505 (Pittsburgh: Center for Russian and East European Studies, University of Pittsburgh, 2001).

Carrère d'Encausse, Hélène, *L'Empire Éclaté* (Paris: Flammarion, 1978).

*Decline of an Empire: The Soviet Socialist Republics in Revolt* (New York: Newsweek Books, 1979).

*The Great Challenge: Nationalities and the Bolshevik State 1917–1930*, trans. Nancy Festinger (New York and London: Holmes and Meier, 1992).

Chokaev, Mustafa, 'The Basmaji Movement in Turkestan', *Asiatic Review* 24 (1928): 273–88.

Clem, Ralph S., *The Soviet West: Interplay between Nationality and Social Organization* (New York: Praeger, 1975).

Dawisha, Karen, and Parrott, Bruce (eds.), *Democratic Changes and Authoritarian Reactions in Russia, Ukraine, Belarus, and Moldova* (Cambridge: Cambridge University Press, 1997).

Denber, Rachel (ed.), *The Soviet Nationality Reader: The Disintegration in Context* (Boulder, Colo.: Westview Press, 1992).

Dreifelds, Juris, *Latvia in Transition* (Cambridge: Cambridge University Press, 1996).

Dyczok, Marta, *Ukraine: Movement without Change, Change without Movement* (Amsterdam: Harwood Academic Publishers, 2000).

Edgar, Adrienne Lynn, *Tribal Nation: The Making of Soviet Turkmenistan* (Princeton: Princeton University Press, 2004).

Eley, Geoff, and Suny, Ronald Grigor, *Becoming National: A Reader* (New York: Oxford University Press, 1996).

Fedor, Helen (ed.), *Belarus and Moldova: Country Studies* (Washington: Federal Research Division, Library of Congress, 1995).

Feshbach, Murray, 'The Soviet Union: Population Trends and Dilemmas', *Population Bulletin* 37, 3 (Aug. 1982): 1–44.

Fowkes, Ben, *The Disintegration of the Soviet Union: A Study in the Rise and Triumph of Nationalism* (London: Macmillan, 1997).

Gall, Carlotta, and de Waal, Thomas, *Chechnya: A Small Victorious War* (London: Pan, 1997).

Gitelman, Zvi Y., *Jewish Nationality and Soviet Politics: The Jewish Sections of the CPSU, 1917–1930* (Princeton: Princeton University Press, 1972).

Gleason, Gregory, *The Central Asian States: Discovering Independence* (Boulder, Colo.: Westview Press, 1997).

Hajda, Lubomyr, and Beissinger, Mark (eds.), *The Nationalities Factor in Soviet Politics and Society* (Boulder, Colo.: Westview Press, 1990).

Hiden, John, and Salmon, Patrick, *The Baltic Nations and Europe: Estonia, Latvia and Lithuania in the Twentieth Century*, revised edn (London: Longman, 1994).

Himka, John-Paul, *Galician Villagers and the Ukrainian National Movement in the Nineteenth Century* (Edmonton: Canadian Institute of Ukrainian Studies Press, 1988).

'Western Ukraine between the Wars', *Canadian Slavonic Papers* 34, 4 (Dec. 1992): 391–412.

Hroch, Miroslav, *Social Preconditions of National Revival in Europe: A Comparative Analysis of the Social Composition of Patriotic Groups among the Smaller European Nations*, trans. Ben Fowkes (Cambridge: Cambridge University Press, 1985).

Huttenbach, Henry R. (ed.), *Soviet Nationality Policies: Ruling Ethnic Groups in the USSR* (London: Mansell, 1990).

Iwaskiw, Walter R. (ed.), *Estonia, Latvia, and Lithuania: Country Studies* (Washington: Federal Research Division, Library of Congress, 1996).

Kaiser, Robert J., *The Geography of Nationalism in Russia and the USSR* (Princeton: Princeton University Press, 1994).

Kappeler, Andreas, *The Russian Empire: A Multiethnic History* (London and New York: Longman, 2001).

Karklins, Rasma, *Ethnic Relations in the USSR* (Boston and London: Allen and Unwin, 1986).

*Ethnopolitics and Transition to Democracy: The Collapse of the USSR and Latvia* (Washington: Woodrow Wilson Center Press, 1994).

King, Charles, *The Moldovans: Romania, Russia, and the Politics of Culture* (Stanford, Calif.: Hoover Institution Press, 2000).

Kochan, Lionel (ed.), *The Jews in Soviet Russia since 1917* (Oxford: Oxford University Press, 1978).

Kolstoe, Paul, *Russians in the Former Soviet Republics* (London: Hurst, 1995).

Krawchenko, Bohdan, *Social Change and National Consciousness in Twentieth-century Ukraine* (London: Macmillan, 1985).

Kreindler, Isabelle, 'The Soviet Deportation of Nationalities: A Summary and Update', *Soviet Studies* 38 (1986): 387–405.

Kuzio, Taras, *Ukraine under Kuchma: Political Reform, Economic Transformation and Security Policy in Independent Ukraine* (London: Macmillan, 1997).

*Ukraine: State and Nation Building* (London: Routledge, 1998).

and Wilson, Andrew, *Ukraine: Perestroika to Independence* (London: Macmillan, 1994).

Lapidus, Gail W., 'The Nationality Question and the Soviet System', in Erik P. Hoffmann (ed.), *The Soviet Union in the 1980s, Proceedings of the Academy of Political Science* 35, 3 (1984): 98–112.

Levin, Nora, *The Jews of the Soviet Union since 1917*, 2 vols. (London and New York: I. B. Tauris, 1990).

Lieven, Anatol, *The Baltic Revolution: Estonia, Latvia, Lithuania and the Path to Independence* (New Haven: Yale University Press, 1993).

Lipset, Harry, 'The Status of National Minority Languages', *Soviet Studies* 19 (1967): 181–9.

Lubachko, Ivan S., *Belorusia under Soviet Rule, 1917–1957* (Lexington: University Press of Kentucky, 1972).

Magocsi, Paul Robert, *A History of Ukraine* (Toronto: University of Toronto Press, 1996).

Marples, David R., *Belarus: From Soviet Rule to Nuclear Catastrophe* (London: Macmillan, 1996).

*Belarus: A Denationalized Nation* (Amsterdam: Harwood Academic Publishers, 1999).

Martin, Terry, *The Affirmative Action Empire: Nations and Nationalism in the Soviet Union, 1923–1939* (Ithaca, N.Y., and London: Cornell University Press, 2001).

Massell, Gregory J., *The Surrogate Proletariat: Moslem Women and Revolutionary Strategies in Soviet Central Asia, 1919–1929* (Princeton: Princeton University Press, 1974).

Misiunas, Romuald J., and Taagepera, Rein, *The Baltic States: Years of Dependence, 1940–1990*, revised edn (London: Hurst and Co., 1993).

Motyl, Alexander J., *Will the Non-Russians Rebel? State, Ethnicity, and Stability in the USSR* (Ithaca, N.Y.: Cornell University Press, 1987).

*Sovietology, Rationality, Nationality: Coming to Grips with Nationalism in the USSR* (New York: Columbia University Press, 1990).

Nahaylo, Bohdan, and Swoboda, Victor, *Soviet Disunion: A History of the Nationalities Problem in the USSR* (London: Hamish Hamilton, 1990).

Naimark, Norman M., *Fires of Hatred: Ethnic Cleansing in Twentieth-Century Europe* (Cambridge, Mass.: Harvard University Press, 2001).

*Natsional'naia politika VKP(b) v tsifrakh* (Moscow: Kommunisticheskaia Akademiia, 1930).

Nekrich, Aleksander Moiseevich, *The Punished Peoples: The Deportation and Fate of Soviet Minorities at the End of the Second World War* (New York: Norton, 1978).

Northrop, Douglas, *Veiled Empire: Gender and Power in Stalinist Central Asia* (Ithaca, N.Y.: Cornell University Press, 2004).

Olcott, M. B., *The Kazakhs* (Stanford, Calif.: Hoover Institution Press, 1987).

Pipes, Richard, *The Formation of the Soviet Union: Communism and Nationalism, 1917–1923* (Cambridge, Mass.: Harvard University Press, 1954; revised edn 1997).

Plakans, Andrejs, *The Latvians: A Short History* (Stanford, Calif.: Hoover Institution Press, 1995).

Polian, Pavel, *Ne po svoei vole . . . Istoriia i geografiia prinuditel'nykh migratsii v SSSR* (Moscow: O.G.I –Memorial, 2001).

Rauch, Georg von, *The Baltic States: Estonia, Latvia, Lithuania: The Years of Independence, 1917–1940*, trans. Gerald Onn (London: Hurst, 1974).

Raun, Toivo U., *Estonia and the Estonians* (Stanford, Calif.: Hoover Institution Press, 1991).

Ro'i, Yaacov (ed.), *Jews and Jewish Life in Russia and the Soviet Union* (Ilford: Frank Cass, 1995).

Roshwald, Aviel, *Ethnic Nationalism and the Fall of Empires: Central Europe, Russia and the Middle East, 1914–1923* (London: Routledge, 2001).

Senn, Alfred Erich, *Lithuania Awakening* (Berkeley: University of California Press, 1990).

Simon, Gerhard, *Nationalismus und Nationalitatenpolitik in der Sowjetunion: Von der totalitaren Diktatur zur nachstalinschen Gesellschaft* (Baden-Baden: Nomos Verlagsgesellschaft, 1986).

    *Nationalism and Policy Toward the Nationalities in the Soviet Union* (Boulder, Colo.: Westview Press, 1991).

Slezkine, Yuri, *Arctic Mirrors: Russia and the Small Peoples of the North* (Ithaca, N.Y., and London: Cornell University Press, 1994).

    'The Soviet Union as a Communal Apartment, or How a Socialist State Promoted Ethnic Particularism', *Slavic Review* 53, 2 (Summer 1994): 414–52.

    *The Jewish Century* (Princeton and Oxford: Princeton University Press, 2004).

Smith, Graham (ed.), *The Baltic States: The National Self-Determination of Estonia, Latvia and Lithuania* (London: Macmillan, 1996).

    *The Post-Soviet States: Mapping the Politics of Transition* (London: Arnold, 1999).

Smith, Jeremy, *The Bolsheviks and the National Question, 1917–1923* (London: Macmillan, 1997).

    'The Education of National Minorities: The Early Soviet Experience', *Slavonic and East European Review* 75 (1997): 281–307.

    'The Origins of Soviet National Autonomy', *Revolutionary Russia* 10 (1997): 62–4.

Subtelny, Orest, *Ukraine: A History* (Toronto: University of Toronto Press, 1989; 3rd edn 2000).

Suny, Ronald Grigor, *Looking Toward Ararat: Armenia in Modern History* (Bloomington: Indiana University Press, 1993).

    *The Revenge of the Past: Nationalism, Revolution and the Collapse of the Soviet Union* (Stanford, Calif.: Stanford University Press, 1993).

    *The Making of the Georgian Nation* (Bloomington: Indiana University Press, 1988; 2nd edn, 1994).

    (ed.), *Transcaucasia: Nationalism and Social Change: Essays in the History of Armenia, Azerbaijan, and Georgia* (Ann Arbor: Michigan Slavic Publications, 1983; revised edn, Ann Arbor: University of Michigan Press, 1996).

    and Kennedy, Michael D. (eds.), *Intellectuals and the Articulation of the Nation* (Ann Arbor: University of Michigan Press, 1999).

    and Martin, Terry (eds.), *A State of Nations: Empire and Nation-Making in the Age of Lenin and Stalin* (Oxford and New York: Oxford University Press, 2001).

Szporluk, Roman (ed.), *The Influence of East Europe and the Soviet West on the USSR* (New York: Praeger, 1975).

    *Russia, Ukraine, and the Breakup of the Soviet Union* (Stanford, Calif.: Hoover Institution Press, 2000).

Taagepera, Rein, *Estonia: Return to Independence* (Boulder, Colo.: Westview Press, 1993).

*Tak eto bylo: natsional'nye repressii v SSSR 1919–1952 gody*, 3 vols. (Moscow: Insan, 1993).

Tishkov, Valery, *Ethnicity, Nationalism and Conflict in and after the Soviet Union: The Mind Aflame* (London: Sage, 1997).

Tsutsiev, A. A., *Osetino-Ingushskii konflikt (1992 . . .) ego predistoriia i faktory razvitiia* (Moscow: Rosspen, 1998).

Vakar, Nicholas P., *Belorussia: The Making of a Nation* (Cambridge, Mass.: Harvard University Press, 1956).

Vardys, V. Stanley, and Sedaitis, Judith B., *Lithuania: The Rebel Nation* (Boulder, Colo.: Westview Press, 1997).

Weinberg, Robert, *Stalin's Forgotten Zion: Birobidzhan and the Making of a Soviet Jewish Homeland* (Berkeley: University of California Press, 1998).

Wilson, Andrew, *Ukrainian Nationalism in the 1990s: A Minority Faith* (Cambridge: Cambridge University Press, 1997).

Wright, John F. R., Goldenberg, Suzanne, and Schofield, Richard (eds.), *Transcaucasian Boundaries* (London: UCL Press, 1996).

Yekelchyk, Serhy, 'Stalinist Patriotism as Imperial Discourse: Reconciling the Ukrainian and Russian "Heroic Pasts", 1938–1945', *Kritika: Explorations in Russian and Eurasian History* 3, 1 (2002): 51–80.

   *Stalin's Empire of Memory: Russian-Ukrainian Relations in the Soviet Historical Imagination* (Toronto, Buffalo, London: University of Toronto Press, 2004).

Zaprudnik, Jan, *Belarus: At a Crossroads in History* (Boulder, Colo.: Westview Press, 1993).

Zaslavsky, Victor, *The Neo-Stalinist State: Class, Ethnicity and Consensus in Soviet Society* (Armonk, N.Y.: M. E. Sharpe, 1982).

# Index

Abalkin, Leonid 334
Abkhazia 512, 515, 702
abortion
    illegal 481, 485
    legalised 473, 476
    re-criminalised 209, 481
    re-legalised (1955) 486, 490
Abramov, Fedor 613
Abuladze, Tengiz 623
Academic Union (1905) 550
Academy of Art 581
Academy of Sciences 550, 572
    1936 conference 558
    Commission for the Study of Natural
        Productive Resources (1915) 551
    political control over 556–7
    reforms 567
    research
        applied 556
        post-Soviet 576
        and research institutes (ISKAN) 687,
            696
    reserved seats in Congress (1989) 327
    status under Bolshevik government 554
    in Union republics 572
Acmeists 588
Adamov, Arkadii, novelist 627
Adenauer, Konrad, West German chancellor
    286
aestheticism 79
Afanas'ev, Iurii 328
Afghanistan
    decision-making on 684, 691–4
    Khrushchev's visit 285, 681
    national liberation movement (1920) 638
    Soviet invasion of (1979) 54, 311–12, 319
    withdrawal of troops (1989) 339–40, 698
Africa 690
Aganbegyan, Abel, economist 404

agit-trains 586
agitation, Bolshevik 585–6
    see also propaganda
Agrarian Party of Russia 366, 372, 438
agriculture
    backwardness of 177, 308, 420
    corn (maize) 278
    importance of private plots 424–5, 429, 436,
        478
    inflated statistics on 683
    innovation in communes 414, 421
    livestock 423, 477
    loss of cultivated land (civil war) 167
    and Lysenkoism 558–9, 569
    and market privatisations 434
    and markets 389
    migration from 88, 303, 399, 402, 431
    post-Soviet 407, 437
    and privatisation of collectives 435, 436–7
    productivity
        criticism of central planning (1990s) 433
        effect of collectivisation 196–7, 422, 424
        failure of policies (1962–3) 288
        post-war 429, 432
        under War Communism 419
    prospects for 438–9
    reforms
        Gorbachev's 433–4
        Khrushchev's 278–9, 428
        tsarist experiments 388–90
    relaxation of controls 205
    subsidies 300, 302
    Virgin Lands campaign (Khrushchev) 275,
        279, 296, 402, 429
    see also collective farms; collectivisation;
        grain
Aitmatov, Chingiz 322
    Executioner's Block 633
Akademgorodok, science city 566

Akhmadulina, Bella 615
Akhmatova, Anna 588, 589, 606, 663,
725
*Requiem* (poem) 324, 589
Akhromeev, Sergei 693
Aksel'rod, Pavel 711
Aksenov, Vasilii 289, 615, 628
alcohol, state monopoly and 'moonshine' 303,
332
alcoholism 83, 85, 310, 404
and anti-alcohol policy (1985) 332,
462
*Aleksandr Nevsky* (film) 208
Aleksandrinsky Theatre 590
Aleksandrov, A.V., composer 597
Aleksandrov, General Aleksandr, 'Holy War'
anthem 602
Aleksandrov, Grigorii
*Happy-Go-Lucky Fellows* (film) 597
*Meeting on the Elbe* 608
*Radiant Path* 599
*Volga-Volga* (film) 599
Alekseev, General Mikhail, Chief of Staff
(1915) 97
and democratisation of army command
120
Alekseeva, Ludmilla 291
Alexandra, Empress 100
Aliev, Heidar, president of Azerbaijan 305
All-Russian Conference of Working Women
(1918) 474
All-Russian Congress of Students (May 1917)
131
All-Russian Muslim Congress 151, 496
All-Russian Peasant Union 87
All-Russian Soviet of Peasant Deputies 416
and Central Committee of the Soviets
(VTsIK) 137
All-Russian Theatrical Society 629
All-Russian Union for the Relief of Sick and
Wounded Soldiers 105
All-Soviet (All-Russian) Institute for Public
Opinion (VTsIOM) 328
All-Union Congress of Soviet Writers (1934)
594
All-Union Congress of Soviets (1924) 176
Alma Ata (Almaty), Kazakhstan, riots (1986)
345, 513
Almond, Gabriel 29
*The Civic Culture* (with Verba) 29
Alov, Aleksandr and Naumov, Vladimir, *Pavel
Korchagin* 614
Amanullah, King of Afghanistan 638

American Committee for the Defense of
Leon Trotsky 17
American Relief Association (ARA) 11, 172, 391
Amin, Hafizullah, Afghan Khalq faction 311,
692, 693
Amori, Count (Ippolit Rapgof) 583
Andreev, Andrei, and membership of
Politburo 249
Andreeva, Nina, letter in *Sovetskaia Rossiia* 326
Andropov, Iurii 314, 685
and Afghanistan 692, 693–4
as ambassador to Hungary 678
and KGB 299, 307, 684
promotion of Gorbachev 317, 688
and researchers 688
as successor to Brezhnev 314, 316–17
Angola 308, 698
*Annales* school, Paris 37
Anpilov, Viktor, Working Russia party 368
Anti-Ballistic Missile Treaty (1972) 307
Anti-Fascist Committee Affair (1952) 668,
671
anti-Semitism 92, 101
and 1952–3 Doctors' Plot 264, 507–8
in films 608
and 'pogroms' 90
under Brezhnev 310
and Western view of Bolshevism 9
*see also* Jews
Arctic expedition (1938) 724
Arendt, Hannah (1906–75) 23
*Argumenty i Fakty*, reformist periodical 695
Aristov, Boris, ambassador to Poland 686
armaments *see* defence industry; nuclear
weapons
Armand, Inessa, Zhenotdel director 474
Armenia 95, 102
ambiguous (democratic) regime 354
and Commonwealth of Independent States
516
Dashnak regime 150, 497
dispute with Azerbaijan 345, 515
independence 349, 355
and Nagorno-Karabakh 515
nationalism in 91, 102, 513
relationship to RSFSR 174
and Transcaucasian Republic (1922) 175
Armenians, refugees from Turkish massacres
(1915) 103
Armstrong, John 31
army, imperial
and abdication of Nicholas II 115
desertions 97, 125

execution of officers by Provisional
  Government 109
and February uprising 114, 120
and formation of volunteer army 143
and imposition of martial law 97–100
Jewish conscripts 101
and Kerensky's offensive (1917) 125
loss of influence (1917) 109–10
national units (First World War) 102, 109
officers recruited into Red Army 144
at outbreak of First World War 95, 96
role of parastatals in military supply
  administration 106
shortage of rifles 96
Volynskii regiment 114
women's 'death battalions' (1917) 122
*see also* Red Army
art
  avant-garde exhibition (1962) 289, 682
  modern 79, 586–7
  socialist realism in 207
art schools 581
artisan culture, revival of 206
artists 581, 582
  and Bolshevik policies 584
  defections 620
  and purges 598–9, 600
  and socialist realism 595
  trade unions for 594, 596, 600
Asanova, Dinara 625
Asia, financial crisis (1998) 373
Askoldov, Aleksandr, *The Commissar* 630
Astaf'ev, Viktor, *Sad Detective* 633
Astrakhan, Dmitrii, *Everything will be OK*
  632
Austria 285, 676
  Nazi control over (1938) 724
Austria-Hungary
  capitulation and fall of monarchy (1918) 111,
    495
  First World War 95, 97
  Western Ukraine and 529, 530
Austrian State Treaty (1955) 285
autocracy
  legacy of 153
  political ideology of 70–2
  and political liberties 711
  Western view of 8
autonomous regions 343, 498
  *see also* republics
Azerbaijan 95, 103, 305, 510
  and Commonwealth of Independent States
    516

dispute with Armenia 345, 515
hegemonic electoral authoritarian regime
  354
Hummet party 497
Musavat regime 150
and Nagorno-Karabakh 515
relationship to RSFSR 174
and Transcaucasian Republic (1922) 175
Azeri Turks 103

Babaevskii, Semen, *Cavalier of the Golden Star*
  610
Babel', Isaak 598
  *Red Cavalry* 587
Bahuševič, Francišak, Belorussian poet 528
Baikal–Amur Railway (BAM) project 305
Bailes, Kendall E. 53
Bakhtin, Mikhail 57
Baklanov, Georgii 622
Baklanov, Oleg 348
Bakst, Leon, artist 616
Baku, Azerbaijan, Armenian refugees in 103
Balabanov, Aleksei, *Brother* 632
Balanchine, George 615
Balkan Wars (1912–13) 70
Balkar people
  allowed to return 282
  deportation of 502, 503
Balter, Boris 614
Baltic States 130, 342, 532, 545
  and anniversary of Molotov–Ribbentrop
    Pact 541, 543, 545
  authoritarian regimes 532–3
  economies 408, 540, 545
  and European Union 518, 547
  German nobility 524, 526, 532
  German occupation 538
  and Hungarian uprising 679
  inter-war independence 515, 516, 638
  neutrality 533
  Popular Fronts 514–15
  post-Soviet independence 349, 355
  Russian minorities in 506, 547
  Soviet annexation and occupation 222, 537,
    658
  Stalin's ambitions for 655, 656
  *see also* Estonia; Latvia; Lithuania
Balts, nationalism among 91
bandits, in rural areas 205
banks
  and August 1998 crisis 372, 374
  scandal 374
baptism 477

Baptist churches 81
Baranskaia, Natalia, 'A Week Like Any Other'
     (story) 457
Barber, Benjamin R. 26
Barghoorn, Frederick 42
Barnaul, Siberia
    lack of facilities 204
    population growth 201
barter
    in post-Soviet economy 372, 407–8, 435
    to compensate for shortages 198, 390
    *see also blat*
Basaev, Shamil, Chechen commander,
     invasion of Dagestan 376, 520
Bashkiria 393
Basmachestvo movement 497
Bauer, Evgenii 55, 583
Bauman, Karl 558
Bauman, K.Ia. 420
Bauman, Zygmunt 59
Beatty, Bessie, *San Francisco Bulletin* 8
Bednyi, Demian, libretto to *Ancient Heroes* 598
Belaev, Vasilii, *Mannerheim Line* 601
Belarus (from 1991) 528–9
    and Commonwealth of Independent States
     516
    as competitive authoritarian regime 354
    independence (1991) 547
    post-Soviet transition 548
    relations with Russian Federation 703–4
    *see also* Belorussia
Belarusian Peasant and Workers' Union 534
Belarusian Popular Front (1988–9) 543
Belarusian Socialist Soviet 535
Belgium, German invasion 657
Belorussia
    and 1990 elections 546
    Belarusianisation policy of Soviet Union
     536
    ceded by treaty of Brest-Litovsk 136,
     528
    cultural revival (from 1890s) 528
    dissent 542
    First World War 95, 528
    German occupation 528, 538
    independence 517
    national education 499, 510
    nationalism in 102, 150, 528, 543
    relationship to RSFSR 174
    reunification (1939) 537
    western (within Poland) 533–4
    *see also* Belarus (from 1991)
Belovezhskaya Accord (1991) 357

Belyi, Andrei 82
    *Petersburg* (novel) 580
Benua (Benois), Aleksandr 581
    World of Art movement 81
Berezovsky, Boris 371
Berggolts, Ol'ga 610
Beria, Lavrentii 242, 261, 263
    and deportations 503
    fall and execution (1953) 274–5, 276, 509,
     725–7
    and foreign policy 283
    and formation of GKO 255, 257
    head of NKVD 215, 240, 252
    membership of Politburo 252
    and Molotov 259
    and scientists 564
    and succession to Stalin 508
Berklāvs, Eduards, Latvia 540, 541
Berlin, Red Army entry into (1945) 504
Berlin, Isaiah (1909–97) 36
Berlin Ultimatum, by Khrushchev (1958)
     286–7, 296
Berlin wall
    construction of 287
    demolition 341
Berliner, Joseph (1921–2001) 31
Berlinguer, Enrico 683
Bernes, Mark, singer 602
Bessarabia (Eastern Romania) 505, 531
    Soviet occupation (1940) 222, 658
    *see also* Moldavia (Moldova from 1991)
Bichevskaia, Zhanna, singer 626
Birmingham, University of, Centre for
     Russian and East European Studies 36
Birobidzhan, Jewish Autonomous Region
     507
Bitov, Andrei 615, 628
*Black Book of Communism* 63
black markets 198, 399
    and 1990s inflation 435
    exploitative 310
    peasants' 418
    tolerated under Brezhnev 302–3
    *see also* commodities
Blanter, Matvei, composer 597
*blat* (informal distribution practices) 400, 403
    *see also* barter
Blok, Aleksandr, modernist 580, 587
    *The Field of Kulikovo* 588
    *Retribution* 588
    *The Twelve* (poem) 580
Bobrinskii, Georgii, military governor of
     L'viv 99

Bogdanov, Aleksandr
  and 'God-Building' 82
  and Proletkul't 585
Bohlen, Charles 'Chip', American diplomat 13
Bolshevik government (dictatorship)
    (1917–22) 135–9, 166–7
  alienation of peasants 159–60
  attempts to establish 'peaceful
    reconstruction' 165
  authoritarianism of 139
  Central Control Commission 245, 248
  collegial nature of 245
  and corruption 154–5
  Council of People's Commissars (October
    1917) (Sovnarkom) 137
  cultural policies 155–7, 583–5
  economic policy *see* War Communism
  effect of power on concept of class 714–16
  Land decree 136–7
  and Orthodox Church 148
  and Party-State 151–5, 166
  peace decree 135–6
  policies towards women 472–7
  political control over Academy of Sciences
    556–7
  popular revolts against 147–8
  relations with borderlands and
    nationalities 148–51, 497–8
  relations with workers 163–6
  and scientific education 553–4
  socialist opposition to 147
  suppression of women's movement 472
  Zhenotdel (Women's Bureau) 474–5
  *see also* Communist party; War
    Communism
Bolsheviks 68, 125
  appeal of Stalin's group to rank and file 247
  attempts to inspire revolution among allies
    636–43
  and class narrative 713–18
  concerns about NEP 180–1
  economic ambitions 383
  as embodiment of revolutionary Social
    Democracy 707, 713, 714
  and February Revolution 114, 123, 125
  as heirs of intelligentsia tradition 579
  Kerensky's suppression of (July 1917) 126
  and notion of 'capitalist encirclement' 113
  opposition to war 104, 138
  peasants' support for 417
  renamed Communists (1918) 143
  seizure of power 133–5
  support for self-determination 149

urban base of 497
use of terror in civil war 145–6
view of peasants 160–1, 417, 718, 719
war administration (1917–18) 110–11
workers' support for 84, 121, 129
*see also* Bolshevik government
  (dictatorship); Bolshevism
Bolshevisation 644
Bolshevism
  aspirations and failures of 44–5
  marginalisation of women 472
  Western views of 8–9, 33–7
Bol'shoi theatre, Moscow 581, 603
Bondarchuk, Sergei, *Fate of a Man* 281,
  614
Bondarev, Iurii 622
border guard forces 215
Bordiga, Amadeo, Italian communist 644
Bosyi, D. F., machine operator 455
Bourdieu, Pierre 57
'bourgeois specialists' 459
  Stalin's attack on 189, 451, 460
bourgeoisie
  fear of 714
  and Social Democracy 710
  tolerated under NEP 719–20
  *see also* middle classes
'brain-washing' 24
Brandt, Willy, West German chancellor 306
Brazauskas, Algirdas-Mikolas, Lithuania 346
Brest-Litovsk, fall of 97
Brest-Litovsk, Peace of 9, 110, 111, 636
  as compromise of principles 640
  Russian territorial losses 136, 144, 527
'Brethren' (*brattsy*) movement 81
'Brezhnev Doctrine' (orthodoxy) 300
Brezhnev, Galina (daughter), corruption
  scandals 314
Brezhnev, Leonid 290, 305–6
  control over Politburo 300–1
  and cultural stagnation (*zastoi*) 298–9,
    617–29
  death 314, 316
  decline of administration 308–15
  economy 302–3, 310, 403–4
  and family law reforms 488–90
  foreign policy and détente 305–8
  historiography 292–5
  ill health 309, 312, 314
  and invasion of Afghanistan 311–12
  *My Little Homeland* memoir 619
  and path to communism 729
  Peace Programme (1969) 306

Brezhnev, Leonid (*cont.*)
  personality cult 309, 314
  and rejection of Khrushchevism 296–300
  repression under 618, 682
  and response to Polish Solidarity
    movement 312–13
  and science 571
  social contract 300–5, 310
  stability under 294
  'trust in cadres' policy 297, 298, 302, 305,
    309, 511
  visit to USA 307
Brodsky, Joseph, trial 617
Brotherhood of Nations, concept of 500, 501,
    505, 510, 512
  Baltic states' exclusion from 506
Broun, Heywood 18
Brown, Archie 42
Brumberg, Abraham 21, 374
Brusilov, General Aleksei, 1916 offensive 97
Bryant, Louise, radical 8
Brzezinski, Zbigniew
  definition of totalitarianism 22, 27, 31, 52, 55
  as US national security adviser 54
Budennyi, Simeon 257
*Buford*, USS (the 'Red Ark') 9
Bukhara, captured by Bolsheviks 151
Bukharin, Nikolai 144, 191, 246, 719
  and Academy of Sciences 556
  and Comintern 645
  and London science conference 561
  and prospect of Italian revolution 638
  *Road to Socialism* 706
  and Stalin 185, 186
  support for NEP 185–7, 194, 247, 421
  trial (1938) 723
  view of class revolution 716, 720
Bukovina, Northern, Soviet invasion 658
Bukovina province, Ukraine 530
  to Romania 530, 534
Bulgakov, Mikhail 620
  *Master and Margarita* 598
Bulganin, Nikolai 242, 263
  as deputy to Stalin 265
  and Khrushchev 277, 285
  and Politburo 260
  and Suez 285
Bullitt, William, US ambassador to USSR 13
Bunin, Ivan 620
'Bureau for Sociopolitical Enlightenment'
    (Provisional Government) 111
bureaucracy
  as basis of Stalinist state 17, 51

in Communist systems 41
  for Five-Year Plan 395
Burliuk, David (and others), *A Slap in the Face
    of Public Taste* 588
Burma, Khrushchev's visit 285, 681
Bush, George, US President 341
  and Gorbachev 700
Bykov, Vasilii 622

capitalism
  critique of 12, 14
  and modernity 29, 58
  optimism about 6
  *see also* socialism; West, the
Carnegie Corporation 22
Carpatho-Ukraine, Republic of (1939) 535
Carr, E.H. (1892–1982), historian 22, 33–4, 36
Carter, Jimmy, US President 54, 312
cartoons, anti-German 602
Castro, Fidel 271, 285
casualties
  1921–3 famine 148, 166
  1932–3 famine 196
  civil war 166, 475
  during deportations 502
  First World War 416
  German in Second World War 224
  Soviet civilian deaths under German
    occupation 226
  Soviet deaths in Second World War 225–7
  *see also* death rate
Catholic Church
  in Lithuania 541
  in Poland 312, 686
Caucasus *see* Armenia; Azerbaijan; Georgia;
    Transcaucasia
Caucasus, North
  ethnic conflict in 503
  *see also* Chechnya; Dagestan
Ceauşescu, Nicolae 341
censorship 208–9
  abolished (1990) 632
  inconsistencies 620
  relaxation of (pre-revolution) 581
  relaxation under Khrushchev 612
  Second World War 603
  State Security (MGB) control over 668
  under Brezhnev 618
  under martial law (First World War) 99
censuses
  1926–37 200
  1937 203
  Russia (2002) 409

Central Asia
  anti-European uprisings (1916) 151
  and civil war 497
  film-making 625
  industrialisation 401
  labour camps 202
  nationalisms in 343
  policies towards women 56, 174
  post-independence states 518
  Soviet Union as vanguard in 675, 681
Central Committee
  and 1928 'emergency measures' 247
  ageing (1970s) 309
  economic departments abolished (1988) 329
  expansion under Brezhnev 301, 618
  Gorbachev and 697
Central Committee International
      Department (CCID) 683, 695
  relations with MFA 685–7
Central Control Commission 245, 248
  *see also* State Control Commission
Central Executive Committee of the Soviets
    (VTsIK) 126, 246
  and All-Russian Soviet of Peasant Deputies
    137
  Lenin and 134
Central Industrial region
  peasant out-migration 443
  workers' 'symbiosis' with village life 444
Chadaev, Iakov 254
Chaianov, Aleksandr Vasilevich (1888–*c*.1938)
  421
Chaliapin, Fedor 582
Chamberlain, Neville, British prime minister
  655, 657
Chamberlin, William Henry (1897–1969),
  *Christian Science Monitor*
  correspondent 15
Chambers, Whittaker 35
Chancellery for Civilian Administration 98
*Chapaev* (film) 208, 587, 597
Chardynin, Piotr 583
charivari (*vozhdenie*) rituals 86
Chase, Stuart, economist 14
Chechens
  allowed to return 282
  deportations of 502, 503
    to Central Asia 202, 226, 401
Chechnya 346, 519
  declaration of secession (1992–4) 364–6
  invasion (1999) 376–7, 378, 520
  Putin's policy on 378
  Russian invasion (1994–6) 365, 519–20

Cheka, terror commission 146, 214
Cheliabinsk, Siberia, population growth 201
Cheremukhin, N. A., armed repression in
  Saratov province (1919) 161
Cherenkov, P. A., physicist 559
Chernenko, Konstantin 309, 688
  as General Secretary 317–19
  and succession to Brezhnev 314
Cherniaev, Anatolii, foreign policy adviser to
  Gorbachev 338, 347
Chernobyl' nuclear disaster (1986) 323, 542,
  574–5
Chernomyrdin, Viktor 359, 368
  as prime minister 371, 374
Chernov, Viktor
  centrist SR leader 124
  as chair of Constituent Assembly 138
Chiang Kai-shek, Chinese nationalist 642, 643,
  652, 655
  captured 653–4
  USSR support for 667
Chicago, University of 22
Chicherin, Georgii, commissar for foreign
  affairs 640, 646
child support laws 209
childcare
  centres 480, 488, 489, 492
  collective 172, 180
  mothers' role in 209
children, destitute and orphaned 475
  from mass deportations 203
  police control over 214
  street 172
  from Volga famine 172
China 641–3
  arms supplies to 654
  border clashes (1969) 306, 691
  civil war (1945–7) 667
  Communist party (CCP) 652
  destruction of communist movement
    (1927) 199, 246, 643
  and end of Cold War 698
  Hundred Flowers campaign 681
  identity relations with 688–90, 691
  Khrushchev and 284, 680–1
  market reforms 698
  and Stalin 274, 667, 671–2
  Stalinist model 682, 689
  as surrogate vanguard 672, 690
  treaty of alliance (1950) 672
  and Vietnam 673
  war with Japan 653
Chior, Pavel, Moldova 537

*chrezvychaishchina* (government based on mass terror) 153
Chubais, Anatolii 361, 369, 370
Chubar, Vlas 249, 251
Chukhrai, Grigorii
   *Ballad of a Soldier* 281, 614
   *The Forty-first* 614
Churbanov, Yuri 314
church
   separation from state 156
   *see also* Orthodox Church
Churchill, Winston 9, 657
CIA (Central Intelligence Agency) 21
   funding for CENIS 30
cinema *see* film industry; films
Cinematographers' Union 630
cities
   'closed' 241, 303, 401
   nuclear 572
   'open' 303
   science 572
   *see also* towns and urban areas
civic education 11, 24
civil rights, as goal of liberals 73
civil society
   changes in pre-revolutionary Russia 77–80
   emergence under Khrushchev 291
   and parastatal organisation in First World War 105–7
   repression of 167
civil war (1918–22) 143–51, 497
   de-urbanisation 163, 167, 170
   devastation of 166–7
   effect on development of Bolshevik party-state 153, 167
   historiography 140–2
   labour discipline 449
   loss of industrial workers 445–6
   and nationalities 496
   origins of 143
   role of international intervention 112, 145, 638
   *see also* War Communism
class
   as basis of privileges and repression 211
   Bolshevik application to transformation of countryside 159, 160, 418, 718–22
   in Bolshevik ideology 157, 164, 713–18
   and fear of bourgeoisie 714
   and food rationing 158
   and identity 129

Marxist narrative of 706–7
   and nationalism 131
   and revolutionary consciousness 48, 49
   and victory of socialism 205, 211, 214, 723
   women and 482
   *see also* class leadership; proletariat; workers
class conflict 159, 160, 418
   exacerbated (1917) 128–30
   and Stalin's attack on kulaks and Nepmen 189, 195, 721–2
class consciousness
   development of 444
   of industrial workers (1917) 121, 451
class leadership
   Bolshevik concept of 720
   Khrushchev's redefinition of 728
   and 'Who-Whom?' (*kto-kogo*) scenario 718–19, 720, 721–2
Clem, Ralph S., *The Soviet West* 522
coal production 194, 386
coalminers
   militancy (1990s) 464–5
   strike (1989) 463
coercion
   Bolshevik justification of 158, 159, 720
   Gorbachev's refusal to use 349
   Stalin's use of 243
   to force peasants to sell grain (1928) 188
   *see also* repression; violence, state
Cohen, Stephen F. 50
Cold War 682–91
   and collapse of USSR 61–2
   and concept of totalitarianism 23
   end of 336–42, 697
   factors in end of 336–7
   Khrushchev's attempts to reduce tensions 285
   professional Sovietology 20–2
   and revisionist historiography 43–4
   and US policy 43
   and Western assumption of Soviet expansionist ambitions 20–1, 25
   *see also* détente; foreign policy
collective farms (*kolkhozy*) 195, 303, 398, 420
   less formal structure 430
   low productivity of 302
   model 179, 186
   and privatisations 435
collectivisation 192, 194–8, 398–400, 420–6, 721
   concession on private plots 424

costs of 197
extent of 196
and nationalities 501, 539
relaxation of rules 196
social effects of 197, 446
women's resistance to 423–4, 477–9
*see also* agriculture
Columbia University, Russian Institute 21, 22
COMECON (Council for Mutual Economic
    Assistance) trade bloc 306, 403
comedy
    cartoons 602
    *estrada* (revue) 626
Cominform (1947) 666, 669
    abolition (1956) 675
    and Tito 670
Comintern (Communist International)
    and China 653
    and communism in China 643
    move to Left 644–5
    relations with Narkomindel 639–40
    relationship to Communist Party 644
    role and purpose of 636–7
    Sixth Congress (1928) 645
Commissariat of Enlightenment
    (Narkompros) 584, 589
    and education under Bolsheviks 586
Commissariat of Food Supply (Narkomprod)
    158
Commissariat for Foreign Affairs
    (Narkomindel), relations with
    Comintern 639–40
Commissariat of Local Affairs 152
Commissariat of Nationalities (Narkomnats)
    149, 151
Committee to Save the Constituent Assembly
    (*Komuch*), in Samara 144
commodities
    consumer goods 456, 488, 489
    shortages 198, 249, 302, 310, 400, 455
    stores for Soviet elite 302–4
    subsidised 302
    *see also* black markets
Commonwealth of Independent States 349,
    406, 516, 703–4
commune (*obshchina*) organisation (in
    villages) 86, 389, 412–13
    reforms (1906) 88, 388, 415–16
    return to 416, 417
'commune state', Lenin's vision of 134
communications 192
    *see also* information; media
communism

criticism of (under Gorbachev) 325
decline of 379
and social democracy 694
Western interpretations of Soviet 33–7
Communist Academy 554, 556
Communist International *see* Comintern
communist parties
    and change of Comintern strategy 640, 645
    in decolonising countries 690
    emergence from Western Social
        Democracy 8, 706
    and world research movement 687
Communist Party
    banned (1991) 356
    and Comintern 637, 644
    control over NKVD and police 215
    'Cultural Revolution' 593–4
    declining support for 199
    economic intervention 391
    fear of peasant autonomy 420
    hierarchical control within 297, 327
    intolerance of rival socialists 144, 165
    Khrushchev's division into agriculture and
        industry branches 279, 280, 288
    loss of monopoly power 328, 344
    membership of 153–4
    merger with RCs (1920) 144
    Nineteenth Party Conference (1988) 321,
        325, 326, 340–1
    patronage in 310
    perception of threats 213–14, 258
    and problem of accounting for Stalinism
        725–7
    proportion of nationalities in 176
    purges (1920–1) 154
    and resistance to break-up of Union 347–8
    Russian national domination of 211
    *see also* Central Committee; Communist
        Party Congresses; Communist Party
        of the Russian Federation; Politburo;
        Stalinism
Communist Party (Bolshevik) of Ukraine
    (CP(b)U) 535
Communist Party Congresses
    Eighth (1919) 152
    Tenth (1921) 168
    Eleventh (1922) 181
    Twelfth (1923) 182
    Seventeenth (1934) 205, 650
    Eighteenth (1939) 252, 266
    Nineteenth (1951) 263
    Twentieth (1956) 268–9
    Twenty-Second (1961) 281, 284, 728

Communist Party Congresses (*cont.*)
Twenty-Third (1966) 298
Twenty-Fourth (1971) 301
Twenty-Fifth (1976) 308
Twenty-Sixth (1981) 314, 321
Twenty-Seventh (1986) 321
Twenty-Eighth (last) (1990) 330
Communist Party of the Russian Federation
366, 367, 702
and premiership of Primakov 375, 377
revival of 368
Communist Youth League (Komsomol) 455,
593
women's section 174
computers, technological lag in 572
'comrade', as form of address 129
Congo, Khrushchev and 285
Congress of People's Deputies 327, 344
communists within 362
elections (1989) 327–8, 544
and opposition to economic reforms 359,
360, 361, 362
Yeltsin and 356, 361–3
Conquest, Robert 39–40, 52, 500
conscription
First World War 95
Second World War 238
Constituent Assembly 109, 137
closure of 139, 144
elections 122, 146
Constitutional Democratic Party *see* Kadets
consumer culture
among peasants 88
development of 79, 400, 403, 468
in early years of NEP 171
women and 469
contraception 476, 481, 489
'convergence thesis' 20, 32
Coolidge, Archibald Cary (1866–1928),
historian 10
co-operative farms (*kolhozy*) 195, 303
co-operatives
co-optation of (1919) 158
Law on (1988) 333
rural 178, 186, 389
corporal punishment, abolished (1904)
88
corruption 153
Bolshevik government and 154–5
in state economy 199
under Brezhnev 310, 314
in Yeltsin's economic reforms 371
Cossacks, in White Army 143

Council of Defence (Bolsheviks') 111
Council of Europe 704
Council of Ministers (Sovmin) 260–1
Buro of the Presidium 263
Council of People's Commissars (October
1917) (Sovnarkom) 137
armed opposition to 143
Stalin as head of 240
Council for Security and Cooperation in
Europe (CSCE) 704
Counts, George (1889–1974) 14
*The Country of the Blind* (with Lodge) 24
Crimea, transferred to Ukraine 283, 509
Crimean Tatars
allowed to return 282, 502
demonstration in Moscow (1987) 345
deported to Central Asia 202, 401, 502
Jadidist 151
petition (1968) 512
Cripps, Sir Stafford 658, 660–1
Crossman, Richard, (ed.) *The God that Failed*
35
Cuba
Bay of Pigs (1961) 287
Khrushchev and 285
military support for Angola 308
missile crisis (1962) 287–8, 296
'cultural turn' 57
culture
adaptations 590
amateur arts 599–600
American influence (1920s) 171, 590
artists' trade unions 594, 596, 600
Bolshevik policies on 155–7, 583–5
and capitalist 'decadence' 187
counter-culture 626–7
dominance of Russian 211, 304, 495
European influence on 281, 579, 590
*glasnost'* and 629–34
historical themes 613–14, 622
individualism and private morality 615
intelligentsia and 579–80
Khrushchev's policies on 280–2, 675
*kolkhoz* prose, rural sentimental 609, 613
mass entertainment 79
and morality 206–10, 607
national 210
political critics 596
popular 582–3, 596, 603–4, 609
post-war repression 605–10, 682
proletarian 592–4
Proletkul't 155, 585
reversal of thaw (under Brezhnev) 298–9

science as alien to 549
and Second World War 600–3
socialist realism 207–8, 594–600
stagnation (1967–85) (*zastoi*) 617–29
Stalinist xenophobia 211, 605–10
state control over 207, 208–9, 604, 612
state support for 592–3
thaw (1953–67) 281, 288–9, 610–17, 675, 682
*see also* art; films; literature; music; propaganda; theatre
currency
reforms 170, 427
ruble no longer convertible (1926) 393
stabilisation 391
Custine, Marquis de 7
cybernetics 570
Czechoslovak legionnaires 144
Czechoslovakia
crisis (1938) 219, 654
federal form of 343
and Hungarian uprising 679
relations with USSR 669
'special path to socialism' 670, 671
suppression of 1968 'Prague Spring' 41, 299–300, 306
Transcarpathian Ukrainians in 530, 534–5

dachas, spread of ownership of 402
Dagestan 520
Chechen invasion (1999) 376, 520
Dalian 667
Dallin, Alexander (1924–2000) 33
Dan, Fedor 171
dance halls 599
Daniel', Iulii 298
trial 617, 682
Daniels, Robert Vincent 30, 38
Daud, Mohammed, Afghanistan 311, 691
Davies, Joseph E., US ambassador to USSR 18
*Mission to Moscow* 19
Davies, R.W. 34, 36
Davies, Sarah 54
Davis, Jerome, sociologist 12
de-Stalinisation 276–7, 614, 725–7
and Eastern Europe 677
end of 298
of 'woman question' 485–90
de-urbanisation, civil war 163, 167, 170
Dean, Vera Micheles 13
death penalty
executions under Stolypin 69
Kerensky's restoration of 132

death rate 170
among urban industrial workers 83
Deborin, A. M., dialectician 555, 557
'decadence', in pre-revolutionary culture 79
defeatism, punishment of 231
defence industry 193
concentration of scientific research on 572–3, 576
Five-Year Plan 397
post-war 241–2, 300, 308, 337
wartime production 234, 238
*see also* nuclear weapons
defencism
ideology of 105
revolutionary 108, 110
Demichev, Petr 288
democracy
and aims of February Revolution 119–20
and Bolshevik coup 138, 139
in former Soviet states 354
Gorbachev's interest in 320–1
in industry 163
as norm of modernisation 29
prospects for 19, 354, 379–80
Putin and 379, 380
democratic centralism, end of 328
Democratic Centralists (DC) 152
Democratic Choice of Russia party 368
Democratic Conference (14–19 September 1917) 133
Democratic Russia movement 330
demography
effect of collectivisation on 400–1
effect of economic policies on 385–6
effect of post-Soviet economy on 408–9
*see also* population
Deng Xiaoping 691
market reforms 698
Denikin, General Anton, commander of Whites 112, 146, 496
Denmark, German invasion 657
Department of Propaganda 636
deportations
during Second World War 502–3
of kulaks and peasants 195, 201, 203, 400–1
of nationalities and 'socially dangerous' elements 202, 212, 401, 427, 502–3
and returns under Khrushchev 282, 502
social disruption and disorder resulting from 203–5
of suspected collaborators 239
war deaths as result of 226
from western republics 538

desertions
  on Eastern Front 231
  imperial army 97, 125
  Red Army 160
détente 54, 305–8
  Brezhnev's vision of 305–7
  decline of 307
  and Third World 307–8
  *see also* Cold War
Deutscher, Isaac (1907–67) 33, 35–6
Deutscher, Tamara 34
development
  and democracy 29
  and post-colonialism 29
  Stalinism as stage in 50
Dewey, John 14, 15, 19
  American Committee for the Defense of
    Leon Trotsky 17
Diagilev, Sergei 582
dictatorship of the proletariat 52
difference
  and identity relations with China 688–90
  limits of (Hungary) 678
  Stalinist fear of 666, 667
  toleration of (1953–6) 673–5
  *see also* Soviet identity
Dimitrov, Georgii, Comintern 650, 657,
    686
disease 455
  among urban industrial workers 83
dissidents
  as accomplices in Western plots against
    socialism 667–8
  Eastern Europe 307
  repression of 298, 319, 682
  and science 573–4
  western republics of USSR 522, 540–2
district (*uezd*) committees, formed after
    February Revolution 117
divorce
  Bolshevik laws on 173, 473, 476
  rates 489, 492
  re-liberalisation (1950s) 486
  reversal of liberalisation 209, 481, 484
Djilas, Miloslav 667
Dniprostroi, hydroelectric dam at 193
Dniester Republic 546, 548
Dobb, Maurice (1900–76) 33
Dobrynin, Anatolii 338, 693
  as ambassador in Washington 686
  as CCID secretary 695, 697
Doctors' Plot (1952–3) 264, 267, 274, 508, 668
  public declaration of error 674

Dolmatovskii, Evgenii 598
Donbass coalfields 386
Dostoevsky, Fedor 634
Dotsenko, Viktor 634
Douglas, Paul, labour economist 13
Dovzhenko, Aleksandr 596, 625
  *Earth* 398
  *Liberation* 601
Dreiser, Theodore, novelist 12, 18
*Druzhba narodov* (journal) 622
'dual power' 115, 116
Dubček, Alexander, Czechoslovakia 299
Duclos, Jacques, French communist 657
Dudayev, General Johkar 519–20
  declaration of Chechnya's independence
    364, 365
Dudintsev, Vladimir, *Not by Bread Alone* 281,
    727–8
Dunaevskii, Isaak, composer 597
Durant, Will, historian 14
Duranty, Walter, *New York Times*
    correspondent 12
Durkheim, Emile 29
Dzerzhinsky, Feliks
  head of Cheka 146
  statue destroyed (1991) 352
Dziuba, Ivan, Ukrainian dissident 541

Eastern Europe (Soviet bloc)
  calls for economic reform 299–300
  COMECON trade bloc 306, 403
  demands for independence 337, 342
  economic weakness 308
  Gorbachev's view of 336, 340, 697–8
  and Helsinki Accords (1975) 307
  independence (1989) 341
  institutions 668
  purges 671
  relations with Moscow 664–5, 669, 675,
    676
  Soviet control over 665–6
  state autonomy in 26, 41, 539
Eastman, Max, journalist 16, 19
*L'Echo de Paris*, on Bolsheviks 9
economic reform (from 1987)
  500-day Plan (1990) 334–5, 405
  attempts at macroeconomic stabilisation
    359–61
  effect on republics 514
  failure of 331–5, 702
  Gorbachev's policies 321, 333–4, 404–5
  insider privatisations 333, 360
  Law on Co-operatives (1988) 333, 335

Law on Individual Economic Activity
(1986) 333
Law on the State Enterprise (1987) 333, 404,
463
monetary reforms 360
moves away from central planning (late
1980s) 333–4, 384
perestroika 404–6, 463–4
privatisation of large state enterprises 360–1
prospects for (1991) 354
prospects for (1996) 370
threat by Primakov to reverse 375
*uskorenie* (acceleration) under Gorbachev
320, 334, 404, 462
Yeltsin's move to market economy 358
*see also* economy, post-Soviet
economics, and mathematics 570
economy 383–6
assessment of Soviet experiments 409–10
and barriers to technological innovation
567
central planning 169–70, 198, 279, 300, 383
commodity shortages 198, 249
crisis of 1917 128
decentralisation experiment (under
Kosygin) 299
delusional information about 395–6, 684
economic councils (*sovnarkhozy*) 158, 279
effect of Second World War on 227, 233–4,
241, 402
failure to revive (1970s) 308, 405
inter-war (self-contained) 219–21
Khrushchev's policies 277–83, 289, 402–3
long-term instability 384
political intervention in 157, 385
post-Stalinist 402–4
post-war concentration on defence 241–2
prescriptive visions of 409
private trading 169, 180, 187, 198
and pursuit of modernisation 384–5
stagnation (1970s–1980s) 308, 310, 319, 383
state markets 198
tsarist 157, 386
under Brezhnev 302–3, 403–4
War Communism 147, 157–63, 164, 390–1
*see also* collectivisation; economic reform
(from 1987); economy, post-Soviet;
Five-Year Plans; industry; New
Economic Policy (NEP)
economy, post-Soviet 406–9
assessment of transition 406–7
attempts at stabilisation 372–4
August 1998 crisis 371–4

bankruptcy of (1991) 358, 366
budget deficits 372
effect of break-up of Soviet Union on
supplies 408
inflation 372
international debt 372, 374
loans-for-shares schemes 371, 407
recovery (1999) 379
short-term bonds (GKOs) 373–4
Eden, Anthony, UK prime minister 285
*edinolichniki* (private peasant farms), survival
of 196, 206
*edinonachalie* (one-man management) 459,
460
education
Bolshevik 586
co-education 473, 484
curriculum reform 586
expansion of 468
higher, for women 479, 484
Khrushchev's reforms 510–11
in national languages 499, 536
rural schooling 88, 428, 431
rural women 489
Stalinist expansion of 206–7, 400
vocational training 400, 456
*see also* literacy; universities
Efimov, Boris, cartoonist 602
Egorov, Iurii, *They Were the First* 614
Egorov, M.A. 504
Egypt 681
Khrushchev's visit 285
Soviet support for (1973) 307
Ehrenburg, Ilya
novelist 602, 610
*The Thaw* 281, 674
Eikhe, Robert Indrikovich 251
Eisenhower, Dwight D., US president 286–7
Eisenstein, Sergei, film-maker 208, 606
*Aleksandr Nevsky* 601
*Battleship Potemkin* 592
*Ivan Groznyi* 608
and Richard Wagner's *Die Walküre* 601
*Strike* 592
Ekaterinburg *see* Sverdlovsk
El Salvador 698
elections
parliamentary (1999) 377
and popular politics 330
referendum on Federation constitution
364, 366
regional (postponed 1991) 358
Russian Federation (1993–6) 366–71

elections (*cont.*)
 Russian presidential (1996) 369–70
 to Communist Party, manipulation of 152
 to Congress of People's Deputies (1989)
  327–8
 to Duma (1993) 363
 to legislatures of republics (1990) 328
 to Presidency (indirect) 328
 to Soviet legislature (1989) 329
 *see also* political parties
electoral law
 reforms (1907) 69
 Russian Federation 363, 367
electronics 572
elites
 and communes 418
 identification with Europe 683
 initial reaction to outbreak of First World
  War 95
 nationalist 109
 women 470
emigration
 during civil war 166, 390
 Jews 307, 508, 512
 from post-Soviet Russia 408, 576
 from tsarist Russia 386, 387
 from western regions (Second World War)
  538
émigrés
 radicalisation of 99
 return of (1917) 109
empires
 and international trade 219
 Stalinist view of imperialism 665
employers' organisations 84
employment
 job security (under Brezhnev) 301–2
 post-Soviet unemployment 466
 unemployment under NEP 391, 393,
  450
energy production 194
 *see also* coal; natural gas; oil
Engels, Friedrich 552
enterprise paternalism 458–62
entrepreneurs 405
environment, degradation of 408, 410
environmentalist movements 542
Ermash, Filip 624
Erofeev, Viktor 628, 633
Esenin, Sergei 589
Estonia 495, 524–6
 deportations (1940s) 505–6, 538
 dissidents 542

economy 532
 First World War 95, 525
 incorporated in USSR 505
 inter-war independence 150, 525, 533
 land privatisation 437, 438
 liberal democracy 354, 518
 National Front 512
 nationalism 131, 543, 545
 post-Soviet independence 346, 546
 Revolution of 1905 525
 Russians in 506, 547
Estonian Popular Front (1988) 543
Estonian Progressive People's Party 525
Estonian Social Democratic Workers' Party
  525
Ethiopia 308, 314
ethnic minorities *see* nationalities
ethnography, in Stalinist USSR 210
Eurobonds 373
Eurocommunism 683, 694
 Gorbachev and 697
Europe
 balance of power 95
 and Brezhnev's Peace Programme
  306
 cultural influence on Russia 579, 590
 fear of 'contagion' of revolution 111
 Little Entente (1934) 649
 political geography 495
 relations with USA 675
 *see also* West, the
European Union
 and Baltic States 518, 547
 enlargement 408
Evlogii, Archbishop 99
Evtushenko, Evgenii 615, 616
 'Heirs of Stalin' 616
 'Zima Station' 612
executions
 of imperial army officers 109
 of Jews 609
 under Stolypin 69
 *see also* Great Purges; show trials
Extraordinary Commission to Combat
  Counter-revolution and Sabotage
  (Cheka) 146
Ezhov, N. I., head of political police 212, 214,
  215
*Ezhovshchina see* Great Purges

Fadeev, Aleksandr
 *Rout* 595
 *Young Guard* 595, 608

Fainsod, Merle 27
*How Russia is Ruled* 25
*Smolensk Under Soviet Rule* 25
families
Bolshevik legislation on 173–4, 472–3
collective child-rearing ideal 180
collective rights in communes 413
hierarchies within 413
household organisation 86, 412, 445
patriarchy within 413, 468
return to traditional model 209–10, 476–7
family law codes
1926 Family Code 173, 476
1936 209, 481–2
1944 484, 486
1968 488, 490
1992 bill defeated 493
famine
1921–3 11, 148, 162, 166, 171–2, 178
1931–3 Ukraine 16, 40, 196, 398, 424, 500, 536
1946–7 455, 664
death tolls 148, 166, 196, 201
Farrell, James T., novelist 17, 19
fascism
comparison with Marxism 24–5
effect of rise of on Western ideological
loyalties 17, 649
Popular Front against 650–2
Fatherland-All Russia political coalition 377
Federation Council (1990) 329
Federation Council, Russian Federation (1993)
363
elections to 366
Filev, Anatolii 686
film industry 582, 591–2, 600, 624
in decline 631–2
and *glasnost'* 630
Soiuzkino organisation 596
films 208, 582
'about agriculture' 613
anti-Semitic 608
anti-Western 608
French cinema week (1955) 611
historical 613–14
Hollywood 171, 591
Moscow International Film Festival (1959)
611
musical 599
pirated foreign videos 627
portrayal of women 623
republican studios 625–6
Russian nationalist rewriting 608–9
screening of previously forbidden 324, 630

socialist realism in 596–7
*The Amphibious Man* 616
'trophy' German and American 607
under *zastoi* 624–6
*see also* Eisenstein
Filonov, Pavel 582
Finland 676
communism in 664
independence 150, 495
and Japan 652
nationalism in 130, 149
Soviet war in 18, 222, 228, 236, 656
Finns
deportations 202, 502
nationalism among 91, 102
First All-Russian Congress of Soviets (June
1917) 123
First Congress of Peasant Soviets (May 1917)
123
First International 707
First World War 94, 219
Bolshevik demand for peace 135–6
and Bolshevik view of socialism 714
Eastern Front 95
and effect of revolution in Russia 107–11
German occupation of borderlands (1918)
111–13
Great Retreat (1915) 100, 104
June offensive (1917) 109
and labour migration 387
military campaigns (1914–16) 96–7
munitions crisis 96, 104
outbreak of 94–6
and peasants 416–17
politics of war 104–7
Provisional Government's policy (1917)
122–6
women in industry 471
Fischer, Louis (1890–1977), *The Nation*
correspondent 12, 18
*Assignment in Utopia* 16
*The Soviets in World Affairs* 16
Fischer, Ruth 35
Fitzgerald, F. Scott 15
Fitzpatrick, Sheila 51–2, 53, 57, 58
Five-Year Plan, First (1928–32)
assessment of 397–8
bureaucracy for 395
Gerschenkron effect (on data) 397
intention of rapid economic growth 394
investment in heavy industry 193
and labour productivity 396–7
Stakhanovism 396

Five-Year Plan, First (1928–32) (*cont.*)
  targets and budgets 395–6
  Western enthusiasm for 14
  workers' enthusiasm for 54
Five-Year Plans 394–8
Fokin, Mikhail 582
folk traditions 500
  music 599
  and rural religion 87
Food Army (*Prodarmiia*) 159
food supplies
  after February Revolution 117
  food crimes (1941) 229
  forced requisitioning of (1919) 161–2
  problems under Bolshevik government
    158–63
  rationing 158
  Second World War 233
  subsidised 302
  *see also* grain
Footman, David 36
forced labour 203, 402
  under Stalinism 193, 400, 401
  *see also* Gulag labour camps
Foreign Office (British), Information and
    Research Department (IRD) 39
foreign policy
  Afghanistan 311–12, 691–4
  alignment with Weimar Germany 640
  and alliance with Britain (1940) 658–61
  anti-Japanese front 652–4
  arms reduction talks (1985–8) 339
  China 641–3, 688–90, 691
  conflict between revolutionary rhetoric
    and pragmatism 643–6
  détente 54, 305–8
  as European great power (1992–2001) 699,
    700–4
  and expectation of world revolution (1917)
    636–7
  fear of France 646–7
  institutions of 668–9
  natural allies of (1953–6) 675–81
  as normal great power (1985–91) 694–700
  as part of great power condominium 663–7
  perception of capitalist encirclement 113,
    667–73
  Popular Front against Fascism 650–2, 654
  purpose of Comintern 636–7
  relations between Comintern and
    Narkomindel 639–40
  shift away from revolution in Europe 638–9
  and Soviet identity 705

as superpower 682–91
and threat of Nazi Germany 648–50
*see also* Cold War; international relations;
    Soviet identity
Foucault, Michel 57, 59
France 219
  academic study of Russia 7
  anti-fascism 651–2
  and Far East 646, 652
  *Front Populaire* 651
  and perception of threat 662
  policy against international communism
    645, 646
  relations with 645, 646–7, 649–50, 651–2
  surrender (1940) 657
Francis, David, US ambassador to Russia 9
Francis Ferdinand, Archduke, assassination of
    95
Frank, I.M., physicist 559
Frankfurt School 28
freedom
  cultural 629–34
  Gorbachev's use of word 322
  intellectual 550, 570–1
freedom of speech 323, 715
  *see also* censorship; liberties; press freedom
French Communist Party (PCF) 645, 651
French Revolution, symbols of liberty 119
Friedrich, Carl (1901–84), political scientist 22,
    55
Frunze, Mikhail Vasilevich, and Red Army
    235
Fülöp-Miller, René 42
Fundamental Laws (1906) 68
  and definition of autocratic power 70
Furmanov, Dmitrii, *Chapaev* 208, 587, 597
Futurists 79, 588

Gaidai, Leonid, film-maker 624
Gaidar, Egor 335, 368
  market liberalisation plans (1991–2) 358, 360
Galich, Aleksandr 626
Galicia 95, 99
  expulsion of enemy aliens 99
  nationalism in 529, 534
  Russian occupation (1914) 96, 99
  scorched earth policy (1915) 99
  to Poland 530
Gardin, Vladimir 583
Garst, Roswell, American farmer 278
gas *see* natural gas
Gaugauz Republic (Moldova) 546
Gaulle, Charles de, French president 286

*Gazeta-Kopeika* (St Petersburg daily
    newspaper) 78
Gdansk, Poland, Lenin Shipyards strike 313
Geertz, Clifford 57
gender studies 55
General Secretary
    powers of (late 1980s) 320, 327, 695
    role in central decision-making 685
genetics, and Lysenko affair 558–9
Geneva
    four-power conference (1955) 285
    US–USSR summit (1985) 339
Genoa Conference (1922) 175
Georgia 95, 354
    collectivisation in 423
    effect of conflict on economy 408
    film-making 625
    independence 349, 355, 515
    Mensheviks in 94, 124, 150, 497
    and minorities 92, 515
    nationalism in 91, 131, 345, 512, 513
    relationship to RSFSR 174, 702
    subsumed into Transcaucasian Republic
        (1922) 175
Gerashchenko, Viktor, head of Russian
    Central Bank 360
Gerasimov, Gennadii, Gorbachev's press
    spokesman 341
German, Aleksei, *Roadcheck* 630
German, Pavel, 'Brick Factory' 590
German Social Democratic Party (SPD) 709,
    711, 713
Germans in Russia
    deportations 202, 226, 401, 502
    popular aggression towards (First World
        War) 100
Germany
    anti-Comintern pact with Japan (1936) 653
    and Belorussia 528, 538
    and Bolsheviks 135–6, 145, 200
    economy 107, 233
    First World War 102
        capitulation and fall of monarchy (1918)
            111
        invasion of Russia (1917–18) 110
        offensive on Eastern Front (1914) 96
        Schlieffen Plan 96
    and Georgia 150
    invasion of Soviet Union (1941) 18, 222, 223,
        225, 230
    retreat (1942–5) 223
    KPD (Communist party) 647, 648, 649
    Lenin's hopes for revolution in 636, 637, 639

    and Non-Aggression Pact with USSR (1939)
        18, 221, 659
    reunification (1990) 341
    rise of Nazism 647–8
    rise of 95, 219
    science in 562
    Second World War 225, 228
Germany, East 286
    and Berlin Ultimatum (1958) 286–7
Germany, West 286
    and Brezhnev 306
Gerschenkron, Alexander (1904–78) 38, 384
    'Gerschenkron effect' (on data) 397
Getty, J. Arch 53
Gierek, Edward, Polish communist 312, 313
Ginzberg, Evgenia 482
Gitelman, Zvi 56
GKO (*Gosudarstvennyi Komitet Oborony*) (State
    Defence Committee) 229, 240, 242,
        255
    autonomy of members 257
    compared with Politburo 256
    dissolution (1945) 259
Gladkov, Aleksandr, playwright 606
Gladkov, Fedor, *Cement* 587, 595
Glasgow University, Institute of Soviet and
    East European Studies 36
*glasnost'*
    and Chernobyl' disaster 574–5
    concept of 323, 404, 695
    cultural freedom under 629–34
    and nationalism 344, 514, 542–4
    and visibility of economic failures 333
Glassboro, summit meeting (1967) 300
'God-Seeking', spiritual searching 80
Gogoberidze, Lana, film-maker 626, 630
Gold Standard, adoption (1897) 386
Golder, Frank (1877–1927), historian 11
Goldman, Emma, anarchist 10
Gomułka, Władysław, Poland 312, 676
    relations with Khrushchev 677
Goncharova, Nataliia 582
Gorbachev, Mikhail 46, 61, 684
    agricultural incentive schemes 432–3
    Andropov's support for 317, 688
    attempt to preserve Union (1991) 346–8,
        514
    attempted coup (August 1991) 347–9
    aversion to violence 338, 340, 349, 545
    on Brezhnev era 293
    as Central Committee secretary (1978) 310
    and democratisation 320–1
    and economic reform 321, 333–4, 404–5

Gorbachev, Mikhail (*cont.*)
  election as president (1990) 328
  and ending of the Cold War 336–42
  foreign policy 695–700
  introduction of contested elections 327
  meeting with Bush (1989) 341
  move from reform to systemic change
    (*perestroika*) 325–31
  and need for scientific-technical progress
    574
  and new freedoms 322–5
  and normalisation of relations with West
    699–700
  overview of changes 316
  plans to remove 331, 357
  policy on nationalities 513–14, 544
  relations with Politburo 317–19
  resignation address (25 December 1991)
    349–51
  retreat from economic reform plan 335
  security concessions 700
  and Social Democracy 694
  speech to Central Committee conference
    (1984) 318
  view of Eastern Europe 336, 340, 697–8
  view of Khrushchev 291
  view of 'path to socialism' 697, 730
Gorbatov, Boris, journalist 602
Gorer, Geoffrey 23
Gorky, Maxim 401
  and 'God-Building' 82
  and *New Life* newspaper 584
  and socialist realism 207, 594
Goskino (State Department of Cinema) 624
Gosplan (state planning agency) 169, 198, 391
  and agricultural output quotas 425
  and Five-Year Plan 395
  and *perestroika* 405
Gottwald, Klement, President of
    Czechoslovakia 665
government
  relations with parastatals (First World
    War) 105, 106
  *see also* Provisional Government
Grachev, Pavel, defence minister 365, 519
grain
  crises (1927–8) 188–9, 194, 199
  exports to fund industrialisation 188–9, 190,
    194
  imports from West (1960s and 1970s) 279,
    288, 306, 431
  procurements in 1930s 194, 197, 394, 398, 422
  quota assessment (Bolshevik) 158

state monopoly 127
taxes (to replace requisitioning) 169, 178,
    419
  *see also* food supplies
gramophone 582, 590
Gramsci, Antonio 57
Granick, David 31
Great Britain 225, 647
  alliance negotiations 655, 658–61
  and Armenia 150
  and China 643
  Communist Party in 649
  foreign policy interests 219, 662
  and Georgia 150
  and India 641
  mutual assistance pact (1941) 223
  post-war relations with USA 665
  relations with Labour administration 645
  relations severed (1927) 200, 246, 643
  as threat to USSR and socialism 663
  trade agreement (1921) 641
  withdrawal from Russia (1919) 638
Great Depression (from 1929) 219
Great Purges (*Ezhovshchina*) 40, 52–3, 212, 213,
    251, 266
  and arts 598–9, 600
  and industry 454
  labour camps 202
  mechanisms of 213
  operational order no. 447 212
  and perception of threat 213–14
  Red Army command staff (1937–38) 221,
    228, 236
  statistics on 40
  xenophobia in 213
  *see also* deportations; purges; repression
Grechko, Andrei, minister of defence 307,
    309
Greece, Italian invasion (1940) 659
Green movement (peasants) 147
  rebellions (1918–21) 161–2
Griazodubova, Valentina 480
Grinevetskii, V. I. 392
Grinevskii, Oleg 684
Grishin, Viktor 301, 319, 320
Griškevičius, Petras 309
Groman, Vladimir, economist 395
Gromyko, Andrei, foreign minister 307, 326,
    685, 695
  and Afghanistan 692
Grossman, Vasilii 614
  *Forever Flowing* 632
  *Life and Fate* 324

Groznyi, Chechnya 377, 519
Guchkov, Aleksander, War Minister in
    Provisional Government 107
Gulag labour camp colonies 203, 215, 400
    deaths 226
    institutional responsibility for 675
    popular culture in 609
    release of political prisoners (1955) 276
Gumbinnen, Battle of 96
Gumilev, Nikolai 588, 589
Guomindang, Chinese nationalist party 642,
    652, 653, 667
Gurian, Waldemar 23

Habermas, Jürgen 57
hammer-and-sickle emblem 178
*Happy-Go-Lucky Fellows* (film) 597
Harper, Samuel Northrop (1882–1943) 11, 12,
    42
    *The Government of the Soviet Union* 12
Harvard Interview Project 21
Harvard Project on the Soviet Social System
    (Ukraine) 55
Harvard University, Russian Research Center
    21, 22
harvests 171, 178, 180
    drought (1963) 288
    drought (1975) 308
    poor (1960s) 279
Havel, Václav, president of Czech Republic 577
Haxthausen, Baron August de 7
Hazard, John N. 22
health
    infant mortality 470, 491, 542
    post-Soviet 408, 492
    *see also* disease
health care, under Stalinism 206
Hellman, Lillian 18
Helsinki Accords (1975) 307, 312
Helsinki Watch human rights groups
    in Lithuania 541
    in Ukraine 541
Henderson, Loy, American diplomat 13
Herberstein, Sigismund von, *Notes upon
    Russia* (1517–49) 7
Hess, Rudolf, flight to Britain 660
Hindus, Maurice (1891–1969), journalist 12, 15
historiography
    archives 292
    of Brezhnev era 292–5
    of the civil war 140–2
    exceptionalism of Sovietology 41
    methodologies

modernisation theory 293
move from political science to social
    history 37–43
oral histories 293
Pokrovsky School of history (1920s) 499
post-Soviet 57–64
problems of 5–6, 63–4
revisionist 43–54
shifts in
social history of Soviet west 522–3
Hitler, Adolf
    and invasion of Soviet Union 658, 659
    Non-Aggression Pact with Stalin (1939)
        221
    perception of 647, 648
    plans for invasion of Britain 658–9
    war aims on eastern front 219, 232
Ho Chi Minh 646, 673
Hobsbawm, Eric J., historian 22
homosexuality, outlawed 481
Hook, Sidney 19
Hoover, Herbert, US president 11, 172, 647
Horney, Karen, *Neurosis and Human Growth* 43
housing
    communal 280, 400, 445
    Khrushchev's policies 280, 488
    subsidised 302
    urban 83
*How the Steel was Tempered* (film) 209
Hrushevsky, Mykhailo, Ukrainian president
    496, 530, 536
Hughes, H. Stuart 22
Hughes, Langston (1902–67) 14
human rights (liberties)
    CC Ideology Department and 696
    in Chechnya 377
    Helsinki Watch groups 541
    Western demands for 307, 312
Hungarian Soviet Republic 145
Hungary
    conformity with Moscow 671, 677
    economic model 299, 331
    elections (1947) 666
    suppression of 1956 uprising 41, 277, 286,
        677–9
    and Transcarpathia 535
Huntington, Samuel P. 29, 32

Iabloko party 368
Ianaev, Gennadii 347
Ianushkevich, Nikolai, chief of staff (1915) 98,
    101
Iaroslavl' province, peasant out-migration 443

Iavlinskii, Grigorii 368
  economic reform plans 334
Iazov, Dmitrii, minister of defence 348
ideology 13
  centrality of 20, 57
  Communist party 156–7
  power of 44
  withering of Marxism-Leninism 344
Ilenko, Iurii, film-maker 625
Ilichev, Leonid, ideological adviser to
    Khrushchev 616
Imperial Navy, Baltic Fleet at Kronstadt 120
imperialism
  Stalinist view of 665
  and trade 219
Independent Miners' Union 464
India 641
  Khrushchev's visit 285, 681
individualism 62
  in cultural thaw 727–8
  as liberal goal 73
  socialist view of 73
Indochina 646
Indonesia, Khrushchev's visit 285
Industrial Party, trial (1930) 560
industrialisation 48, 67
  deindustrialisation in 1990s 441
  Five-Year Plans 394–8, 451
  and formation of urban proletariat 440
  and growth of urban working population
    83, 387
  and rearmament 220–1, 238
  tsarist 386–8
  under NEP 187, 190, 394
  under Stalin 192, 200
  western republics 539
industrialists
  and February Revolution 121
  reaction to 1917 strikes 129
industry
  collapse of (1918–19) 164, 167, 390
  consumer goods 488
  cost-accounting (*khozraschet*) system for
    factories 169, 404, 450
  councils of labour collectives (STKs) 463
  efficiencies 456
  enterprise paternalism 458–62
  factory committees of workers (1917) 121,
    129, 163
  factory provision of housing and food 199,
    461
  falling productivity 308
  foreign investment 306

investment (first Five-Year Plan) 193
  iron and steel production 194
  large-scale state 169, 258
  and Law on the State Enterprise (1987) 333
  liberalism among managers 460–1
  management 459–61
  nationalisation 158
  opposition to economic transformation
    (1991–2) 359–60
  post-war growth 456
  and research institutes 572
  scientists and 551, 558
  secret 'company towns' 241
  technological levels 386, 387, 392, 393, 551
  trust groupings 169
  under Khrushchev 279–80
  under NEP 190
  under War Communism 157
  use of forced labour 401
  war mobilisation 106, 230
  work force 83, 454
    reductions 445–6, 466
  workers' control of 157, 158
  *see also* defence industry; economy; labour
infant mortality 470, 491, 542
inflation
  1990s 372, 405, 463
  after 1992 price liberalisation 359, 435
  crisis of 1917 128
  and currency reform 170
  hidden 198
information
  institutionalised lack of 683–5
  on military inferiority 696
Ingrian peasants, deported to Murmansk
    401
Ingush people
  allowed to return 282
  deportations 401, 502, 503
  and Ossetians 515
Inkeles, Alex 55
Institute of Europe 696
Institute of Global Economics and
    International Relations (IMEMO) 658,
    687, 696
institutions
  effect on Russian character 7
  of foreign policy 668–9
  under Stalin 215
  *see also* State Duma
insurance, unemployment 450
intellectuals (intelligentsia)
  and Bolshevik cultural policy 155, 579

and February Revolution 131
identification with Europe 683
materialist-idealist split 580
and nationalist protests 512, 540–1
and political ideologies of dissent 72–6
and reformist discourse 688
and Russian culture 579–80
and spiritual revivalism 82
'worker-intellectuals' 585
Inter-Regional Group of Deputies, within
 Congress 328
International Monetary Fund 373
international relations
 arms reduction talks (1985–8) 339
 détente 54, 305–8
 doctrine of 'reasonable sufficiency' of
  weapons (Gorbachev) 339
 interpretation of threat 662
 nature of power in 662–3
International Science Foundation
 576
International Science and Technology Centre
 576
internationalism 123
 among radical opposition 105
Ioffe, A. A., emissary to China 642
Ioffe, Abram, physicist 558, 564
 and London science conference 561
Ioseliani, Otar 626
Iran, Khomeini revolution (1979) 311
Irkutsk, revolutionary committee (March
 1917) 117
iron and steel production 194
Isakovsky, Mikhail, lyricist 597
Ishmukhamedov, Elier, film-maker 625
Iskander, Fazil
 editor 628, 730
 'Tree of Childhood' 620
*Iskra* organisation (1900–3) 711–12
 and political liberties 712–13
 split 713
*Iskusstvo kino* film journal 608
Islam
 Bolshevik government and 150–1
 fears of post-Soviet fundamentalism 518
Israel, war with Egypt (1973) 307
Italy, imperial ambitions 219
Ittifak, Tatarstan independence movement
 518
Iudin, Pavel, ambassador to China 680
Iur'eva, Izabella, singer 598
*Ivan Groznyi* (film) 208
Ivanov, Viacheslav 581

Ivanov, Vsevolod, *Armoured Train No.14–69*
 607
*Izvestiia* newspaper 703

Jackson, Senator Henry M., and
 Jackson–Vanik amendment (1974)
 307
Jadid Muslims 150
James, C.L.R. 19
Japan 68
 anti-Comintern pact with Germany (1936)
  653
 conflict with 652–4
 invasion (1918) 636
 invasion of Manchuria 647, 652
 and Nazi–Soviet pact 654
 Neutrality Pact (1940) 660
 Second World War 219, 222,
  223
 troops in Siberia 145
 war with China 653
Jaruzelski, General Wojciech, Poland 313
jazz 208, 590, 597
Jewish Anti-Fascist Committee (JAC) 507,
 668
Jews 56, 90
 Autonomous Region in Birobidzhan for
  507
 Babii Yar massacre (Ukraine) 503
 blamed for 1905 unrest 90
 deaths within Soviet Union 226
 and Doctors' Plot (1952–3) 264, 508,
  668
 emigration movement 307, 508, 512
 executions 609
 in First World War 99, 100–2, 387
 Holocaust deaths 225, 226
 and *korenizatsiia* 506
 massacred by Whites 146
 nationalism among 91–2
 'pogroms' against 90, 506
 Stalinist policies against 506–8, 668
 *see also* anti-Semitism
John of Kronstadt, Father (d.1908) 80
John Paul II, Pope 312
Johnson, Lyndon, US president 300
journalists
 accounts of Bolshevik revolution 8
 accounts of Soviet Russia 10, 15–16
 ideological interpretations by 15–16
 investigative 630
 Second World War 602
 Western, disillusionment of 15

journals 627, 632
    closed 663
    Symbolist 581
Jowitt, Kenneth 60

Kádár, János 299, 678
Kadets (Constitutional Democratic Party) 73,
    550, 552
    defence of imperial-national state 116, 130
    Provisional Siberian Government 145
    resignation from Provisional Government
        126
    and second coalition of Provisional
        Government 126
Kafengauz, Lev, economist 395
Kaganovich, Lazar 242, 263, 508, 675
    and downfall of Beria 726
    and Khrushchev 276, 277, 677
    membership of Politburo 249, 260
    as party General Secretary in Ukraine 535
    and Stalin 186
Kaganovich, M. M. 460
Kaiser, Robert 15
Kalatozov, Mikhail, *Cranes are Flying* (film) 281
Kaledin, General 149
Kalinin, Mikhail 251, 420
    and de-kulakisation 722
    and Jewish Autonomous Region 507
    president of USSR 246, 248
Kalmyks, deportation of 502
Kaluga province, peasant out-migration 443
Kamenev, L. B. (1883–1936) 125
    and Lenin's plan to overthrow Provisional
        Government 134
    and Stalin 184
    and Trotsky 185, 245
Kandinskii, Vasilii 582
Kania, Stanisław, Polish communist 313
Kantaria, M.V. 504
Kapitsa, P. L. 559, 564
    letter to Khrushchev 567
    letter to Stalin 566
Karachai people, deportation of 502
Karakhan, Lev, and China 642
Karelia
    deportation of Finns from 202
    Russian settlement 393
Karmal, Babrak, Afghan Parcham faction 311,
        693
Karpovich, Michael (1888–1959) 38, 39
Katayev, Valentin
    *For the Power of the Soviets* 608
    *Time Forward!* 208, 595

Katyn forest, massacre 538
Kautsky, Karl
    *The Erfurt Programme* 708, 710
    and theory of Social Democracy 708–9
Kazakhstan 305, 354
    and Commonwealth of Independent States
        516
    famine (1932–3) 500
    industrialisation 401
    nationalism 344, 512
    resistance to collectivisation 423
    Russians in 501
    Virgin Lands programme 275, 429
Kazakhs, in First World War 103
Kazan' 151, 414
Keenan, Edward 42
Keldysh, M.V. 571
Kemerovo, Siberia, urban growth 201
Kennan, George 13, 20–1
    *Siberia and the Exile System* 7
Kennedy, John F., US president 287, 288
Kent, Rockwell 18
Kerblay, Basile 37
Kerensky, Aleksandr 131, 135
    and Kornilov rebellion 132–3
    preparations for military offensive 125–6
    Provisional Government 109, 111, 116
Kerner, Robert, historian 13
KGB
    power of under Andropov 299
    resistance to dissolution of USSR 347
    and transition under Yeltsin 356
Khabarovsk, population growth 201
Khalkhin-Gol, battle of (1939) 654
Khasbulatov, Ruslan 361
Khiva, captured by Bolsheviks 151
Khizha, Georgii 359
Khlebnikov, Velimir 588
Kholodnaia, Vera 583
Khomeini, Ayatollah, Iran 311
*khozraschet* (cost-accounting system) 169, 404,
        450
Khrulev, General 256
Khrushchev, Nikita 26, 242, 683
    and 22nd Congress (1961) 614, 615, 728–9
    agricultural policies 278–9
        Virgin Lands scheme 275, 279, 296, 402,
            429
    attempt by 'anti-party group' to depose
        (1957) 277–8
    biography 272–3
    and China 284, 680–1, 689–90
    and Cuban Missile Crisis 287–8

and cultural thaw 281, 288–9, 610–17, 675, 682
and de-Stalinisation 276–7, 614
death (1971) 290
deposition 289–90, 682
and economy 402, 683
and Kennedy 286, 287
as leader 270–1, 296, 685
legacy 41, 291
and Malenkov 275–6, 277, 675, 679
membership of Politburo 252, 265
and Molotov 275, 276
and nationalities 282, 509–11
and nuclear test-ban treaty 288
personality and rise of 263, 270–2
policies towards women 486–8
and relations with West 272, 285–8
relations with writers and artists 277, 280–2, 288–9, 616
retreat from cultural thaw (1963) 616
role in Stalinism 273
and science 567–8
'Secret Speech' (1956) 268–9, 276, 296, 611, 674
and succession struggle 274–8
suppression of religion 282
and Third World 284, 681, 690
and toleration of difference 673–9
and Ukraine 509
visits to Beijing 283
and Yugoslavia 276, 284
Khrushchev, Sergei (son) 269, 279
Khutsiev, Marlen 623
  *Ilich's Gate* 616
Kiev 529
  taken by Germany (1941) 222
Kiisk, Kaljö, Estonian film-maker, *Madness* 618
Kim Il-Sung, Korea 672
Kingissepp, Viktor, Estonian Bolshevik 525
*Kinoglaz* newsreel series 591
Kirgizia republic 393
  *see also* Kyrgyzstan
Kirichenko, Aleksei Illarionovich, Ukraine 509
Kirienko, Sergei, prime minister 371, 374
Kirilenko, Andrei 297
  and Afghanistan 692
Kirov, Sergei 186, 249
  murder of (1934) 250
Kissinger, Henry, US foreign policy adviser 306, 308
Klimov, Elem, film director 630
Knorin, Vil'gel'm Georgievich, Comintern 648, 650

Koestler, Arthur (1905–83), *Darkness at Noon* 18, 62, 324
Kohl, Helmut, German chancellor 342
Kolbin, Gennadii, Kazakhstan 344, 513
Kolchak, Admiral, leader of Whites 112, 145
*kolkhozy see* collective farms
Kollontai, Aleksandra, director of Zhenotdel 122, 474
*kombedy* (committees of village poor) 159, 160, 418
*Kommersant* newspaper 703
Komsomol (Communist Youth League) 174, 455, 593
Komsomol'sk-na-Amure industrial town 401
Konev, Marshal Ivan Stepanovich 679
Korea 676
Korean War 241, 672
Koreans in eastern Russia, deportations of 202, 401, 502
*korenizatsiia* (indigenisation) 176, 180, 210, 498–9
  and Jews 506
  Ukraine 535
Korneichuk, Aleksandr, journalist 602
Kornilov, General Lavr 110
  rebellion 132–3
Korsh theatre 581
Kosior, Stanislav 249, 251, 535
Kosolapov, Richard, editor of *Kommunist* 318
Kosovo, NATO war in 703, 704
Kostroma province, peasant out-migration 443
Kosygin, Aleksei 297, 309
  and Afghanistan 692
  economic decentralisation 299
Kotkin, Stephen 58
Kozin, Vadim, singer 598, 601
Kozlov, Frol, deputy to Khrushchev 290
Kozyrev, Andrei, Russian foreign minister 702
Krasin, L. B., Communist party leader 154
Krasnoiarsk-26 closed city 401
Kraval', I. A., statistical agency 203
Kravchuk, Leonid, president of Ukraine 347, 349, 516, 547
Krestinskii, Nikolai 648
Kriachkov, A. D., architect of Novosibirsk 204
*Kritika* (journal) 59
Kritsman, L., on War Communism 157
Kriuchkov, Vladimir, KGB 348
Kronstadt, naval uprising (1921) 148, 166, 168
Kronstadt soviet, in 1917 118
Kruchenykh, Aleksander 588
Krymov, Iurii, *Tanker Derbent* 595

*kto-kogo* (Who-Whom?) scenario of class
    leadership 718–19, 720
    Stalin's interpretation of 721–2
Kuchma, Leonid, president of Ukraine 547
Kuibyshev, Valerian, chair of Central Control
    Commission 245, 452
Kukryniksy, cartoonists 602
Kulakov, Fedor 301, 310
kulaks (peasant elite) 179, 394, 421
    collectivisation as campaign against 195–6,
        201, 203
    de-kulakisation 213, 398, 400, 721–2
    demonisation of 421–2
    Stalin's view of 189, 194, 419
Kuleshov, Lev, *Adventures of Mr West...* (film)
    591
Kulik, Grigorii Ivanovich 257
Kun, Béla, Hungarian revolutionary 145,
    651
Kunaev, Dinmukhamed, Kazakhstan 301, 305,
    344
    dismissed 513
Kuraev, Mikhail 633
Kurapaty forest, Belarus, graves of Stalinist
    victims 543
Kurchatov, I.V., nuclear project 562
Kursk, German offensive (1943) 223
Kuzbass mining district 464
Kuznetsov, A. A., and Leningrad Affair 261,
    262
Kuznetsstroi 193
Kvirikadze, Irakli, *The Swimmer* 620
Kyrgyz (Kirgiz) peoples
    ethnic conflict in First World War 103
    and Uzbeks 516
Kyrgyzstan 354
    and Commonwealth of Independent States
        516

labour
    and employment security 301–2, 308
    forced 193, 203, 400, 401, 402
    gendered division 443, 451, 478, 479
    militarisation of 158, 454
    peasant view of 412, 436
    prisoner-of-war 456
    shortages (Second World War) 402, 454
    slave 671
    work force reductions 445–6, 466
    *see also* workers
labour camps 202, 274, 400
    Second World War deaths in 226
    *see also* Gulag penal colonies

labour discipline 448–50, 451
    reforms under Khrushchev 456–7
labour history 45, 47–9
labour legislation
    labour books (workers' records) 454
    restrictions on job mobility 402
    on working conditions 83
labour migration
    under Stalinism 446–7
    women and 122
labour productivity 392, 404
    absenteeism 310
    and management 454
    pre-Revolution 448
    production collectives 453
    Second World War 455
    socialist competition strategy 452–3
    Stakhanovism 396, 453–4
    under Brezhnev 457–8
    under Five-Year Plan 396–7
    under Khrushchev 456–7
    under NEP 450
Land Code (1922) 419
Land decree (October 1917) 136–7
land ownership
    among peasants 87
    confiscations (1917–18) 136–7
    labour and rights to 412, 436
    noble, decline in 87
    peasant purchases of gentry lands 416
    and privatisation of collectives 435, 436–7,
        438–9
land reform
    demand for (1917) 127
    illegal seizures by peasants (1917) 127–8
    post-Soviet experiments 434
    tsarist experiments 388–90
Land Statute (1919) 418, 477
Landau, L. D. 559, 561, 564
Landsbergis, Vytautas, president of Lithuania
    545
language, Communist ideological 156,
    164
languages
    Estonian 524
    and formalisation of minority cultures 210
    Hebrew and Yiddish 91
    and Khrushchev's reforms 510–11
    Latvian 526
    minority 89, 177, 508, 510
    and nationalism 544
    Russian made compulsory in schools 499
    Ukrainian 529

Lansing, Robert, US secretary of state 8
Lapidus, Gail 55
Larin, Iurii 717
Larionov, Mikhail 582, 616
Lasch, Christopher 6
Lassalle, Ferdinand, and modern socialism
    709
Latin America 690
Latvia 495, 526–7
    authoritarian regime (1934) 533
    Bolshevism in 526–7
    deportations (1940s) 505–6
    dissidents 541
    economy 532
    emigration (pre-First World War) 387
    First World War 95, 526
    incorporated in USSR 505
    inter-war independence 150, 527
    liberal democracy 354, 518
    nationalism 131, 345, 510, 543, 545
    post-Soviet independence 346
    Russians in 506, 547
    *strēlnieki* infantry 526
Latvian Social Democratic Workers' Party
    526
Laue, Theodore von (1916–2000) 33
law *see* Fundamental Laws
Law on Co-operatives (1988) 333, 335
Law on Individual Economic Activity (1986)
    333
law, rule of 73
Law on the State Enterprise (1987) 333,
    404
League of Foreign Peoples of Russia 102
League of Nations 649
Lebed', General Aleksandr 520
Lebedev-Kumach, Vasilii, lyricist 597, 602
Lee, Andrea 15
legitimacy, laws on 473, 484
Leites, Nathan 23
Lemberg *see* L'viv (L'vov)
Lena goldfields (Siberia), strikes 70
Lenin, V. I. 135, 182, 708
    and ambition of revolution in Germany
        636, 637, 639
    *April Theses* 125
    and assassination of royal family 145
    attempted assassination of 145
    and Baltic states 638
    and China 642
    and Comintern 637
    criticism of (under Gorbachev) 325
    illness and death (1924) 182, 183

and industry 446, 459
and interpretation of 'smash the state'
    phrase 715, 716
Marxism of 75
materialism of 580
misgivings about Transcaucasian Republic
    175, 498
and nationalities 498
and New Economic Policy (NEP) 168,
    181–2, 718
opposition to liberalism and
    parliamentarism 124, 137
and party 712
on peasant Green rebellions 161
and prospect of world revolution 112,
    638–9
and prospects for socialism 149, 181
realpolitik of 641
return from exile 110, 124
and Stalin 175–6, 184
*State and Revolution* 134, 152, 715
*Testament* 183, 184
view of science 552, 553
view of worker–peasant co-operation 178,
    418, 720
view of workers 448
*What is to be Done?* (1902) 75, 712, 713
Lenin All-Union Academy of Agricultural
    Sciences 558, 564
Leningrad
    German siege of (1941–5) 222, 226, 229
    living standards 303
    population growth 201
    underground cinema movement 627
    war deaths 226
Leningrad Affair (1949) 261–3, 266, 674
Leningrad Institute of Physics and
    Technology 558
*Leningrad* (journal) 663
Leninism, relationship to Stalinism 16, 38, 46,
    50–1
Leont'ev, Valerii 626
Leroy-Beaulieu, Anatole 7
Lewin, Moshe 33, 36–7, 58
    on Stalinism 50, 52
Lewis, Sinclair 12
Liberal Democratic Party of Russia (LDPR)
liberals
    'banquet campaign' (1904) 68
    political parties 72–3
    and traditions of *intelligentsia* 72
Liberation of Labour movement 711
Liberman, Evsei, economist 289

liberties
  political 709, 711, 712
  under Gorbachev 322–5
  *see also* human rights
liberty, symbols of (1917) 119
libraries, removal of foreign books
  607
life expectancy 408
Ligachev, Egor 317, 318, 320, 321, 326
  and anti-alcohol campaign 332
  criticism of reforms 326
Likhachev, Dmitrii, Academician 328
linguistics 565
Lippmann, Walter 9, 20
Lipset, Seymour Martin, *The Political Man* 29
literacy 192, 206
  among peasants 88, 180
  among urban workers 83
  in Estonia and Latvia 524
  and nationalism 343
  and popular culture 77, 583
  rural women 429
  spread of 78, 400
  Ukraine 536
literary salons 581
literature
  bleakness of modern 633–4
  bowdlerised 607
  *chernukha* 634
  and *glasnost'* 632–3
  Jewish 91
  *kolkhoz* prose 613
  Muslim 92
  'no conflict drama' 609
  no longer equated with culture 634–5
  popular 77, 79, 88, 582, 590
  popular crime stories 583, 627, 634
  popular fiction 627, 633, 634–5
  production novel (socialist realist) 595
  proletarianisation of 593
  publication of previously forbidden
    324
  publishing quotas 619
  and small-scale reality in 623–4
  socialist realism in 595, 596
  under Bolsheviks 587–9
  *see also* poetry; writers
*Literaturnaia Moskva* 281
Lithuania 495, 527–8
  authoritarian regime (1926) 532
  declaration of independence 545
  deportations (1940s) 505–6
  dissident movement 541

  economy 532
  First World War 95, 527
  foreign relations 533
  Great Diet of Vilnius 527
  and Hungarian uprising 679
  incorporated in USSR 505
  inter-war independence 150
  liberal democracy 354, 518
  National Popular Front 512
  nationalism 345, 543
  and Poland 527
  post-Soviet independence 346
  relations with Germany 533
  relations with Poland 533
  Revolution of 1905 527
  Russians in 506
  Sajudis popular front 543
  *Taryba* national assembly 528
Litvinov, Maksim
  foreign affairs commissar 646, 655
  and post-war world 665
  view of Hitler 648, 649
Liu Shaoqi 672, 678
Lobachevskii, N. I., mathematician 550
Lobov, Oleg 519
local government
  councils of people's commissars
    (*sovnarkomy*) 152
  liberal goals for 73
  organisation after February Revolution
    117–19
  political power during civil war 152
  problems of rural areas 204–5
Lodge, Nucia, *The Country of the Blind* (with
  Counts) 24
Lominadze, Vissarion 249
London, history of science conference (1931)
  561
London, University of, School of Slavonic
  Studies 10
Luckievič, Ivan and Anton, Belorussian
  editors 528
Lukashenka, Aliaksandr, president of Belarus
  548
Lukov, Leonid, *A Great Life* 606
Lumumba, Patrice, president of Congo 285
Lunacharskii, Anatolii 584, 589, 592
  and 'God-Building' 82
Lutheranism, and literacy 524
L'viv
  L'vov (Lemberg), occupation of 96
  as capital of Galicia 529
  fall of 97

L'vov, Prince G.E.
chairman of Union of *Zemstvos* 107
as prime minister of Provisional
Government 107, 116, 123
Lyons, Eugene (1898–1985), journalist 15
Lysenko, T. D. 558–9, 563–4
influence of 563–4, 568
Lysenkoism 569

*Maapäev* assembly 525
McCarthy, Senator Joseph 15
McCarthyism 21
MacDonald, Dwight 19
McFaul, Michael 62
Macmillan, Harold, British prime minister
286
Magnitogorsk, creation of 193, 401
Maiskii, Ivan, Soviet ambassador in London
658, 665
Makanin, Vladimir 619
Makhno, Nestor, Ukrainian anarchist 149, 497
Maklakov, Nikolai, interior minister (1914) 98
Malenkov, Georgii 242, 252, 261, 263
demotion 675
as deputy to Stalin 265
economic strategy 299
and foreign policy 283
and formation of GKO 255
and Molotov 259
rivalry with Khrushchev 275–6, 277, 679
Malevich, Kazimir 582
Malia, Martin (1924–2004) 39, 46, 271
*The Soviet Tragedy* 57
Malinovka, Saratov province 161
malnutrition 455
Malraux, André 35
Mamin, Iurii, *The Fountain* 631
Mamontov family, as arts patrons 581
Manchuria, Japanese invasion 647, 652
Mandel'shtam, Osip 588, 598
Mansurov, Bolat, film-maker 625
Manuilov, Andrei Appolonovich, minister in
Provisional Government 107
Manuil'skii, Dmitrii Zakharevich, Comintern
657
Mao Zedung 643, 652, 653
'great leap forward' 689
relations with Khrushchev 283–4, 680
and Stalin 274
visit to Moscow (1949) 672
visit to Moscow (1957) 283
Marinina, Aleksandra 634
market economy, move towards 358, 360

markets
and agriculture 389
liberalisation 434, 436
private trading under NEP 169, 180, 187
small-scale exchange permitted 205
state 198
*see also* black markets
Markish, Shimon 612
marriage, laws on 468
Marriage, the Family and Guardianship Code
(1918) 173
Marshall, George, US secretary of state 666
Marshall Plan (European Recovery
Programme) 665, 666
martial law (1914) 97–100
expulsion of enemy aliens 99
occupation policy 99
and political control over civilian
population 99
in provinces (1917) 128
Martov, Iulii (Tsederbaum) L., Marxism of 74
internationalist Menshevik 123
Martyrology of Belarus Association 543
Marx, Karl
criticism of (under Gorbachev) 325
and narrative of class 706
Marxism
and class narrative 706–7
comparison with fascism 24–5
and dialectical materialism 555, 557, 569
and formation of urban proletariat 440
and science 552, 554–5, 557–8, 565–6, 569
as theory of modernisation 29
US view of 20
Marxist Russian Social Democratic Workers'
Party 68, 74
*see also* Bolsheviks; Mensheviks
Marxists
as political opposition (to 1914) 74–6
and spiritual revivalism 82
view of proletariat 82
Maskhadov, Aslan, president of Chechnya 520
Masliukov, Yurii, economic minister 375
mass politics, replacement of class politics by
23
Massell, Gregory J. 56
Masurian Lakes, First Battle of 96
Masurian Lakes, Second Battle of 97
materialism
dialectical (Marxism) 555, 557, 569
discontent with and spiritual revivalism
81–2
and political radicalism 580

maternity leave 473, 475, 486
  additional 490, 491
  for agricultural workers 477
  reduced 481
mathematics, and economics 570
Mayakovsky, Vladimir 588
Mead, Margaret 23
Mechnikov, I. I., Nobel prizewinner
      550
media *see* press; television
Medvedev, R. A. 570
Medvedev, Vadim 325, 338
Mehnert, Klaus, German sociologist 13
Mekhlis, Lev Zakharevich 257
Mel'nikov, Leonid, Ukraine 509
Memel (Klaipėda), annexed by Lithuania 533,
      539
Mendeleev, D. I. 550
Mensheviks 68
  and Bolshevik Sovnarkom 137
  condemnation of Petrograd insurrection
      (October 1917) 135
  and February uprising 115
  opposition to war 104
  and political liberties 713
  and Provisional Government 116, 123–4
  relations with Bolshevik government 144,
      147
  as trade union leaders 84
  Western Social Democrat support for 17
Menuhin, Yehudi and Hepzibah 616
merchants, as arts patrons 581
Merriam, Charles E. (1874–1953) 11
  *The Making of Citizens* 11
Merz, Charles 9
Meshketian Turks, deportation of 502
messianism 82
*Metropolis*, literary almanac 628
Meyer, Alfred G. (1920–98) 31
Meyerhold, Vsevolod 590, 598
MFA *see* Ministry of Foreign Affairs
MGB *see* Ministry of State Security (MGB)
middle classes
  as art patrons 579
  and February Revolution 122, 131
  women 469–70
  *see also* bourgeoisie
midwives 476
migration, internal 389–90
  labour 446–7
  of peasants to towns (post-emancipation)
      443
  to urban areas 88, 170, 303, 387

women 431, 489
  *see also* emigration; urbanisation
Mikhail, Grand Duke, refusal to take throne
      115
Mikhailov, P., popular singer 208
Mikhoels, Solomon, actor 507
  execution (1948) 609
Mikoyan, Anastas 242, 249, 263
  and deposition of Khrushchev 290
  and fall of Beria 726–7
  and foreign policy-making 668
  and Hungary 678
  and Khrushchev 275, 276
  and Molotov 259
  and Poland 677
  and Stalin 186, 259, 264, 265
military-revolutionary committees 135, 137
Miliukov, Pavel, foreign minister in
      Provisional Government 10, 123
Millikan, Max, at MIT 30
Milošević, Slobodan 704
ministers, tsarist, influence of 70–1
Ministry of Culture 612
Ministry of Defence (1992) 702
Ministry of Foreign Affairs (MFA)
  relations with CCID 685–7
  under Gorbachev 696
  under Yeltsin 702
Ministry of Internal Affairs (MVD) 668
  responsibility for Gulag administration
      675
  and transition under Yeltsin 356
Ministry of State Security (MGB) 663
  control over police (*militsiia*) 668
  and East European states 669
  merged with MVD 675
  *see also* KGB
Mirbach, Count, German ambassador,
      assassination of 145
*Mission to Moscow* (film) 19
MIT (Massachusetts Institute of Technology),
      Center of International Studies
      (CENIS) 30
Mitterrand, François, president of France 348
mobility
  geographical 78, 400
  *see also* migration; social mobility
Model Collective Farm Code (1935) 424
Model Regulations of Production Enterprises
      460
modernisation
  admiration for First Five-Year Plan 14
  in Brezhnev era 295–6

liberal goals for 73
material economic progress 77
negative aspects of (pre-revolutionary)
78–9, 85
and science 549, 577–8
modernisation paradigm 28–32
*see also* development
modernism
cultural 580–1, 582
in literature 587
modernity, 'totalitarian' effects of 28
Moldavia (Moldova from 1991) 495, 531
and Commonwealth of Independent States
516
Democratic Movement in Support of
Restructuring 544
dissent 542
independence 349, 517, 531
independence (1991) 547
Moldovanisation policy in Transnistria
537
Muslim population in 546
nationalist movements 544
post-Soviet transition 354, 548
republic (1940) 658
separatism 546, 702
under Romanian rule 531, 535, 546
*see also* Bessarabia
Moldovan Popular Front 544
Molotov, Viacheslav 242, 246, 263,
657
and Comintern 648, 649, 650
deposed 681, 682
and Eastern Europe 666
and foreign policy 283, 668, 681
and formation of GKO 255
and Hungary 677, 678
and Khrushchev 275, 276, 277
on kulaks 421
and Non-Aggression Pact with Germany
221, 659
and Poland 677
recantation in *Kommunist* 674
and science programme 563
and Stalin 186, 246
Stalin's attacks on 253–4, 259, 264, 265
view of Tito 670, 676
Molotov–Ribbentrop Pact (1939) 18, 221, 505,
537, 655–7
denounced (1979) 541, 543
human chain protest (Tallinn to Vilnius)
545
Japan and 654

money, loss of function (1918–20) 390
Montesquieu, Baron Charles de 7
Moore, Barrington, Jr. 25
Morits, Iunna 615
*Morning Post*, London newspaper 9
Morozov family, as arts patrons 581
Moscow
Bol'shoi theatre 581, 603
Chechen terrorist attacks 376
as cultural centre 581–2
German advance on (1941) 222, 229
living standards 303
martial law in 97
peasant immigration 443
population growth 83, 201
population losses (civil war) 170
US–USSR summit (1985) 339
*zemstvo* relief committee 105
Moscow Art School 581
Moscow Arts Theatre 581, 590
Moscow International Film Festival (1959)
611
Moscow Machine Building Trust 169
Moscow province, peasant out-migration
443
Moscow State Institute of International
Affairs (MGIMO) 696
Mosely, Philip 30
Mozambique 308, 314
Mozzhukhin, Ivan 583
Muggeridge, Malcolm, *Manchester Guardian*
correspondent 16
*Mulla Nasreddin* (Muslim magazine) 92
Munich (Germany), Institute for the Study of
the USSR 21
Münnich, Ferenc, Hungary 678
Muradeli, Vano, composer 607
Murakhovskii, Vsevolod 320
Muratova, Kira, film director 630
Muscovy, foreign perceptions of 6
music
audio cassettes 626
classical 209
folk 599
jazz 208, 590, 597
love songs 598
marches 597, 602
opera 598–9
popular 582, 599
post-war repression 607
Red Army Chorus 597
and socialist realism 595
wartime popular songs 602

Muslims
    Bolshevik policies to emancipate women
        174
    cultural reform 92
    in First World War 103
    nationalism among 91, 92
    *see also* Islam
mutinies, Volynskii regiment (February
        uprising) 114
mysticism 80

Nabokov, Vladimir 633
Nagorno-Karabakh 345, 512, 515
Nagy, Imre, Hungarian prime minister 676,
        678
    dismissed 677
Narbikova, Valeriia 633
Narkomindel *see* People's Commissariat for
        Foreign Affairs
Narliev, Khojakuli, film-maker 625
nation-building
    Europe 495
    in pre-revolution western states 524–31
    stages in 524
national character 11, 42, 55
    as 'Asiatics' 20
    formed by climate 7, 10
    formed by swaddling of infants 23
    role of institutions 7
    Western assumptions about 6–7
national identity
    Russian 90
    in USSR 211, 498
national liberation movements (NLMs) 26
    Afghanistan (1920s) 638
    and First World War 102, 496
    Gorbachev and 698
    Gromyko's view of 685–6
    rivalry with China over 690
    Stalin's policy towards 673
    support for 308, 312, 689
    USSR as natural ally for 675
    *see also* Third World
nationalism 56, 91
    among non-Russians (1917) 130–1, 148,
        149
    and class 131
    and dissent 540–2
    and *glasnost'* 344, 514, 542–4
    and *perestroika* 406, 544
    reconstruction of 344
    and revolution 130
    and separatism 544–7

under Brezhnev 304, 310, 512–13
    *see also* Russian nationalism
nationalities
    Bolshevik government and 148–51,
        497–8
    and break-up of USSR 355–7, 516–17
    and collectivisation 501
    contradictory policies in pre-revolutionary
        Russia 89–93
    deportations 202, 502–3
    in First World War 100–4, 109
    formalisation of 210
    historiography of 55–6
    Khrushchev's policies 282
    and *korenizatsiia* (indigenisation) 176, 180,
        210, 498–9
    local policies on 89
    and migration to urban areas 387
    Muslim 150–1
    NEP policy towards 174–7, 393
    and post-Soviet nation-building 517–18
    in the Soviet West 522–3
    Stalinist reconstruction of 210–12
    under Brezhnev 304–5
    in USSR 176–7, 192, 220, 342, 498
    view of socialism among 498
    and White movement 112
nationality, as basis of privileges and
        repression 241, 513
NATO
    Russian Federation view of expansion
        (1990s) 703–4
    and war in Kosovo 703, 704
natural gas 194, 306
    exports from Turkmenistan 408
    production 456
*nauchnaia organizatsiia truda* (NOT), scientific
        organisation of labour 449
Nazarbaev, Nursultan, president of
        Kazakhstan 347
Nearing, Scott 12
Neizvestny, Ernst 280, 291
Nekrasov, Viktor, *Both Sides of the Ocean* 616
Nemtsov, Boris, provincial governor of
        Nizhnii Novgorod 370, 434, 437
neo-traditionalism 60–1
NEP *see* New Economic Policy (NEP) (1921–8)
Nepmen (private traders) 179, 181, 182, 187,
        391, 394
    Stalin's view of 189, 721
Netherlands
    colonies 219
    German invasion 657

New Economic Policy (NEP) (1921–8) 51, 159, 166, 384, 390–4
assessment of 391–3
Bolshevik concerns over 180
central planning 169–70
effect of death of Lenin on 182
end of 190–1, 393–4
and nationalities 174–7, 393
as new approach 168, 169
and popular culture 590–1
recovery 170–1, 392
retrospective view of 404, 730
as stage in progress towards socialism 180, 187, 718
state capitalism of 199
under Stalin 185–91
and women's status 475–6
and work force 446
*New Life* newspaper 584
*New Republic*, and Russian invasion of Finland 18
New Soviet Man (NSM), concept of 663, 666, 673
*New York Times*
misreadings of Bolshevik revolution 9
publication of Khrushchev's speech (1956) 269
newspapers *see* press
Nicaragua 698
Nicholas II, Tsar 71
abdication 107, 115
assassination at Ekaterinburg with family 145
and concept of nation 71, 90
October Manifesto (1905) 68, 70
order to crush February uprising 115
personal command of army 97
prorogation of Duma 104
relations with government 104, 107
and Ukraine 530
nightclubs, St Petersburg 581
Nijinsky, Vaslav 582
Nikolai Nikolaevich, Grand Prince, as supreme army commander 96
Nilin, Pavel, scriptwriter 606
Nixon, Richard, US president 306, 307
Nizhnii Novgorod
land reform proposals (1990s) 434, 435
peasant out-migration 443
NKVD (Commissariat of the Interior)
control over police 214

methods of deportation 502
powers of 239, 240
use of forced labour 401
Nobel prizes 550, 559
nomads and nomadism
collectivisation of 398
suppression of 500
Non-Aligned Movement 681
North Africa 646
Norway, Second World War 657
Nove, Alec (1915–94) 32, 33
Novocherkassk, 1962 price riots 302, 403, 457
Novosibirsk 201
opera house 204, 206
urban planning 204
Novotný, Antonín 299
*Novyi mir* (journal) 610, 616, 627
protection of writers 620
NSM *see* New Soviet Man (NSM)
nuclear research 562
nuclear test-ban treaty 288
nuclear weapons 289, 566
assumption of US–Soviet parity 306, 573
Chinese request for 680, 689–90
first atomic test 562
intercontinental ballistic missile 563
limitation treaties (1972) 307
reduction agreement (Washington 1987) 339
thermonuclear test 563
unilateral moratorium on testing (1985) 700

*obshchestvennitsy* (wife-activists) 482
October Manifesto (1905) 68, 70, 84
Octobrists (Union of 17 October) 73
Ogarkov, Nikolai, chief of the general staff 693
*Ogonek*, reformist periodical 695
oil
Caucasus 386, 519
consumption 403
price falls 332, 373
Russian multinational companies 407, 704
Siberian reserves 306
Okeev, Tolomush, film-maker 625
*Oktiabr'* (journal) 621
Okudzhava, Bulat 614, 615
Old Believers 458
Olearius, Adam, on Muscovy 7
oligarchs, rise of (1990s) 371, 703
oligarchy, defined 244
Olympic Games, Moscow (1980) 312

Omsk
  Kadets' anti-Bolshevik government in 145
  soviet (1917) 118
opera 598–9
opinion polls 328, 687
  *see also* public opinion
Ordzhonikidze, Sergo 175, 249
  and 1928 'emergency measures' 247
  and Stalin 246, 250–1
  suicide (1937) 251
Orel province, martial law (1917) 128
Organisation of Ukrainian Nationalists
      (OUN) 504, 534
Orlova, Liubov' 599
Orthodox Church
  attempts to revitalise 80
  Bolshevik government and 148
  and family law 468
  Khrushchev's restrictions on 282
  millennium of Christianity celebration 324
  missionary work in borderlands 90
  and sectarian movements 81
  wartime freedom for 504
Orwell, George (1903–50) 18
  *1984* 23, 62, 324
  *Animal Farm* 23, 324
Osipenko, Polina 480
Ossetia 515
Ostrovskii, Nikolai Alekseevich (1904–37),
      *How the Steel was Tempered* 614
*otkhodniki* (hired labourers) 414
Ottoman Empire, and First World War 95,
      103, 495
Our Home is Russia party 368
Outer Mongolia 667
Ovalov, Lev, novelist 627
Ovechkin, Valentin, 'District Routine' 610

paganism, and folk religion 87
Pale of Settlement, Jewish 91
  formal end of (1915) 101
Pan-Islamism 92
Pan-Turkism 92, 497
Panch, Petro, Ukrainian writer 606
Panfilov, Gleb, *The Theme* 630
Panina, Varia 582
Papanin, Ivan, Arctic explorer 724
Paradzhanov, Sergei 625
parastatal complex
  emergence of during First World War 105–7
  and Provisional Government 107, 108
Pares, Bernard (1867–1949), historian 10
Paris, four-power summit (1960) 287

parliament, democratic, as goal of liberals 73
Pasha Angelina, first woman tractor driver
      425
passports, internal (1932) 211, 425, 447
Pasternak, Boris 209, 588
  *Doctor Zhivago* 207, 281, 324, 589
  Nobel prize 614, 682
Pasvolsky, Leo 13
paternalism
  enterprise 458–62
  in pre-revolutionary Russia 458
paternity suits 484, 486, 488
patriarchalism 76, 413, 468
Patriotic War *see* Second World War
patriotism 230
  and defence campaign 426
  oppositionist 104
  study of indoctrination methods 11
Päts, Konstantin, Estonian nationalist 525, 533
Pavlov, I.P., Nobel prizewinner 550, 565
Paźniak, Zianon, Belarusian archaeologist 543
peasants 412, 442–3
  and 1906 commune reforms 389, 415–16
  alienated by Bolshevik food procurement
      policies 147, 159–60, 419
  Bolshevik categorisation of 179
  and Bolshevik class narrative 718–22
  in Brezhnev era 429–32
  and collectivisation 420–6
      resistance to 195–6, 422–4
      social effects of 197
  and election of township committees 117
  and elections to Constituent Assembly
      139
  and First World War 416–17
  Green rebellions (1918–21) 161–2, 168
  growth of political discontent among 87–8
  as hired labourers 414
  Khrushchev's view of 427
  and land settlement 127–8, 136–7, 160, 177
  migration to towns 88, 443
  and NEP 177–80, 188–9, 419–20
  and parastatals under Provisional
      government 108
  and *perestroika* 433–7
  in pre-revolutionary Russia 86–9, 411–12
  prospects for in post-Soviet Russia 437–9
  rejection of communal land tenure 163
  and religious and spiritual revival 81
  restrictions on mobility of 197, 399
  Revolution (autumn 1917) 126–8
  right to cultivate plots and own livestock
      196, 206, 407, 424–5

sale of surplus on free market 169, 186, 194, 391

and Second World War 231–2, 426–7

as targets of mass repression 213, 427

transformation into proletarian workers 442–8

view of labour 412

and War Communism 417–19

*see also* agriculture; kulaks

penal colonies

deportation of kulaks to 195

deported populations in 202

*see also* labour camps

Penza province, martial law (1917) 128

People's Democratic Party of Afghanistan 311, 691

*perestroika* 325–31, 344

backlash 326, 405–6

economic reforms 404–6, 463–4

effect on rural life 433–7

'from below' 463–4

and nationalism 406, 544

and rethinking of path to socialism 729

Pervukhin, Mikhail, and Khrushchev 277

Pétain, Marshal Henri 657

Peter the Great, Tsar, and science 549

*Peterburgskii listok* (daily newspaper) 78

Petkus, Victoras, Helsinki Watch in Lithuania 541

Petliura, Simon, Ukrainian nationalist 496

Petrakov, Nikolai, economist 331

Petrograd

demonstrations at Tauride Palace (July 1917) 126

February 1917 revolution in 114–16

industrialists 121

population losses (civil war) 170, 445

renaming of St Petersburg 97

storming of Winter Palace (1917) 135

*see also* Leningrad; St Petersburg

Petrograd Soviet 108, 115

agitational literature for rural areas 126

insurrection in support of garrison 135

invitation to join Provisional Government 116

Military Revolutionary Committee (MRC) 135

Order No.1 (destruction of army command) 120

Petrovskii, Grigorii 249

Petrushevskaia, Liudmila, playwright 620

Philby, Kim 660

philosophy, and science 557, 568

physics 559, 564

Piatnitskii, Osip 648, 649

Pichul, Vasilii, *Little Vera* 631

Pikul', Valentin 627

Pil'niak, Boris 598

*Naked Year* 587

Pipes, Richard 39, 45, 46, 497

on US National Security Council 54

Plehve, Viacheslav, assassination of (1904) 68

Plekhanov, Georgii 711

Plevitskaia, Nadezhda 582

pluralism, socialist (Gorbachev's use of term) 322

Pobedonostsev, Konstantin, chief procurator of Orthodox Church 70

Podgornyi, Nikolai 290, 297

dismissed (1977) 309

poetry

open-air readings 615

under Bolsheviks 587–9

poets 581

fate of 589

pogroms

First World War 99, 103

of Jews 90, 506

*Pokoianie* (Repentance) (film) 324

Pokrass Brothers, composers 597

Pokrovskii, M.N., and Marxist science 557

Pokrovsky School of history 499

Poland 95, 495

assimilated by USSR 222, 505

conflict with Bolsheviks 146, 638

elections (1947) 666

German invasion 219

German offensive against (1914) 96

German–Russian agreement on (1939) 221

and Japan 652

murder of Soviet ambassador (1927) 246

nationalism in 130, 149

relations with USSR 669, 677, 686

and repression of Belorussia 533–4

rise of Solidarity movement 312–13, 542, 686

scorched earth policy (1915) 99

Stalin's ambitions for 655, 656

Ukrainian nationalism in 534

Poles in Russia

deportations of 99, 202, 401, 502

during First World War 99, 102

nationalism among 91

in Ukraine 529

police, civil (*militsiia*) 215
    State Security (MGB) control over 668
    subordinated to political police 215
police, political, and mass repressions 212,
        214–15
police, secret 264
    *see also* NKVD
Polish United Workers' Party 313
Politburo (Political Bureau)
    ageing (1970s) 309
    appointments to 260, 320
    attempt to block Gorbachev 317–19
    collective leadership under Brezhnev 297
    conflicts within 249
    and creation of Presidency (1990) 329
    and 'emergency measures' (1928) 247
    and expulsion of Trotsky 245
    manipulation of decision-making 252
    personal rights and networks 250, 320
    promotion of younger cohort to (1938–9)
        252
    purges within 251
    relationship to Sovmin 260–1
    relative autonomy of members 246, 248,
        249–50
    resistance to Gorbachev's reforms 321
    ruling group ('quintet') 253
    Stalin's domination of 195, 240, 248, 260
    working methods of 'septet' in Stalin's
        absences 263
    *see also* Presidium
Political Directorate of the War Ministry 111
Political Directorate of the Workers' and
        Peasants' Red Army (1918) 111
political parties, in Russian Federation
        366–9
    new coalitions (1999) 377–8
political prisoners
    amnestied (1953) 674
    released from Gulags 276
political science
    'behaviouralist revolution' (1960s) 41
    move towards social history 37–43
    political culture approach 42
    and 'totalitarian model' 22–8
politics
    opposition in First World War 104–5
    radicalisation of (1917) 109
    re-emergence of popular (1980s) 330
    and science 550–2, 569–70, 571, 577
    *see also* Marxism
*politruk* system of dual command (Red Army)
        235, 236

Pollitt, Harry, British communist 649
Pomerantsev, Vladimir 611
Ponomarev, Boris, CCID secretary 684, 686,
        695
    and Afghanistan 692
    on Gorbachev 697
Popkov, P.S., and Leningrad Affair 261,
        262
Popov, Evgenii 628
    on 'sixtiers' 628
Popovsky, Mark, émigré scientist 574
Poprov, A.I., farmer 439
population
    birthrate 481, 489, 490
    fall (1990s) 492
    in labour camps 202
    life expectancy 492
    recovery in early 1920s 170
    under Stalinism 200–1
Populist socialists, compared with Marxists 74
Port Arthur 667, 673
Portal, Roger 37
Poskrebyshev, Aleksandr 265
Possony, Stefan 23
post-colonialism
    and development 29
    *see also* national liberation movements
Postyshev, Pavel Petrovich, purged 251
Potemkin, Vladimir 654
Potsdam accords 286
poverty
    as precondition for communism 30
    women 492
Powers, Gary, U-2 spy plane pilot 287, 684,
        686
Poznan, Poland, demonstrations 677
Praeger, Frederick A., publisher 40
Prague, *Problems of Peace and Socialism*
        headquarters 687
*Pravda*
    1938 stories 723–4
    publication of Yevtushenko's poem 'The
        Heirs of Stalin' 281
Preobrazhenskii, Evgenii, economist 418
Presidency, office of (1990) 328, 329
    and constitutional crisis (1993) 362
    constraints on 330
    and transition under Yeltsin 356
Presidency, Russian Federation (1993), powers
        of 363–4
Presidential Council 329
Presidium (of the Central Committee of the
        Communist Party) 264, 277–8

and attempt to depose Khrushchev (1957)
277–8
reverted to name of Politburo 298
press
Bolshevik control over 584
diversification under Gorbachev 324
foreign broadcasts to Russia 324
and liberal Russian identity 703
mass circulation daily newspapers 77, 78,
79, 88
reporting of disasters 323
state monopoly 715
underground nationalist 512
wartime 602
*see also* censorship; journalists; television
press agency, use of posters 586
press freedom
in 1905 reforms 69, 77
Stolypin's restrictions on 69
under Gorbachev 324
prices
liberalisation (1992) 359, 435
rises (1990s) 435
subsidised 302, 403
Prigorodnyi, North Ossetia 512
Primakov, Evgenii 345, 685
and 1999 presidential elections
377–8
prime minister 375–6
prime minister, office of 363
printing presses
Bolshevik control over 584
family-owned 583
*see also* publishing
privatisations (of state enterprises) 360–1, 406,
463, 465–6
and agriculture 434
insider 333, 360
loans-for-shares schemes 371, 407
'voucher' 407
*Problems of Communism* (journal) 21
professionals
and February Revolution 132
women as 469
Progressive Bloc, in First World War 104
Prokofiev, Igor 606
Prokofiev, Sergei 208
proletariat (urban workers)
and Bolshevik class ideology 121, 164,
444
and culture 592–4
dictatorship of 52
historical mission of 707, 710

Marxist image of 82, 444
'moral' demands of 84
in pre-revolutionary Russia 82–6
relations with Bolshevik government
163–6
transformation of peasants into 442–8
Proletkul't 155, 585
propaganda
Bolshevik use of 585–6, 715
collectivisation campaign 195, 398, 478
military use of in First World War 100
of motherhood 473, 476–7, 480, 484
and nationalities 504
and popular alienation (under Brezhnev)
305
wartime 601–2, 636
property
Bolshevik abolition of private 156
creation of new rights (1990s) 360
Protazanov, Iakov 583
Protection of Motherhood and Infancy
organisation 476
Proudhonists, French 707
provincial committees, formed after
February Revolution 117
Provisional Government 112, 123
and 'dual power' 115–16
failure of 138
and local authority 117
origins in parastatal complex 107
planned overthrow of 134
relations with army 108
relations with nationalities 109, 496
Przemysl, fall of (1915) 97
psycho-history 43
public opinion
All-Soviet (All-Russian) Institute for Public
Opinion (VTsIOM) 328
and expansion of civic life 77
and failed coup (1991) 349, 352
Public Opinion Research Institute 687
publishing
and protection of writers 620
state control of 595
*see also* press; printing presses
Pudovkin, Vsevolod 592
*The Return of Vasilii Bortnikov* 610
Pugacheva, Alla 626
purges
Communist Party (1920–1) 154
Eastern Europe 671
within Politburo 251
*see also* Great Purges

Putilov works, Petrograd 114
Putin, Vladimir 62, 376, 377
  and Chechen war 378, 520
  and nationalities 520–1
  rising popularity of 378–9
Pyr'ev, Ivan 599, 601

radar, development of 562
Radek, Karl 639
radio, wartime 602
Radus-Zen'kovich, V.A. 161
Raeff, Marc 38
Raikin, Arkadii 626
railways
  inadequate for troop movement 96
  labour for 387
  Trans-Siberian 67, 386, 647
  Turksib railway 401, 654
  under NEP 171
Rainis, Jānis, Latvian poet 526
Raizman, Iulii, *The Communist* 614
Rajk, Laszlo, Hungarian foreign minister 671
Rakhmanin, Oleg 691
Rákosi, Mátyás, Hungarian communist 671,
  677
Rambaud, Alfred 7
ranks and titles, abolition of 156
Ransome, Arthur, journalist 8
Rapallo, Treaty of (1921) 640
Rashidov, Sharaf, Uzbekistan 305, 309, 314
Raskova, Marina 480
Rasputin, Valentin 623, 683
  *Fire* 633
rationing 158, 198
  under *perestroika* 463
Rayonist movement 582
Reagan, Ronald, US president 54, 313
  relations with Gorbachev 338, 339, 340,
    699
  Strategic Defense Initiative (SDI) 337,
    573
red, symbolism of (February uprising) 114, 119
Red Army 144, 150, 473
  demobilisation 170
  desertions (1918–20) 160
  doctrine of the offensive 235, 237
  and doctrine of pre-emptive strike 221
  dual command with political commissars
    235, 236, 238
  encirclement (1941) 222
  frontier defence 237
  Khrushchev's cuts 289
  low morale 228, 238

morale in Afghanistan 312
political and military compromise in
  organisation 235
reliance on nuclear weapons 289
role in revolution 717, 719
Second World War 234–9
  conscription 238
  military deaths 225, 233
  national units 504
  obsolete equipment 398
  women in 483
size of 235
Stalin's purge of command staff (1937–8)
  221, 228, 236, 654
Stalin's *Stavka* command structure 237
*strēlnieki* Latvian infantry 526
  and transition under Yeltsin 356
  war against Finland 228
Red Cross, and war relief (First World War)
  105
Red Guards (Petrograd October 1917) 135
  allowed to challenge orders 234
Reed, John, American journalist 8, 119
reformist discourse
  intelligentsia and 688
  and new thinking under Gorbachev
    696
  and research institutes 687–8
reforms, (after 1905 revolution)
  contradictory nature of 68–9
  *see also perestroika*
refugees, First World War 99, 101, 416
relief organisations, First World War
  refugee 101
  war relief (parastatals) 105–7
religion
  national variations 504
  revivals 80–2, 205
  in rural areas 87, 205
  suppression of 282, 500
  in western republics 540
  *see also* Orthodox Church
religious societies 80
religious tolerance
  in 1905 reforms 91
  under Gorbachev 323
Remnik, David 15
repression
  of civil society 167
  class basis of 211
  of dissidents 298, 319, 682
  as instrument of policy 214
  mass 212–16, 425

peasants 213, 427
post-war cultural 605–10, 682
role of police in 212, 215
of scientists 560–1
of women 482
*see also* collectivisation; deportations; Great
      Purges; terror
republics (of USSR)
Academies of Science 572
and autonomous regions 343, 498
elections to legislatures (1990) 328, 330
film studios 625–6
institutional autonomy 343
movement of Russians into 501
relations with USSR 342–3
role in leadership struggle (1953) 508–9
republics, post-independence
conflicts within 517
and Russian populations 517–18
research institutes
and liberal identity 703
and reformist discourse 687–8, 698
revolution
and Bolshevik view of class narrative 716–18
Deutscher's law of 35
as illegitimate 46
modernism as 295
as tradition 156
Revolution of 1905 68, 77, 459
Estonia 525
and land reform 388
Lithuania 527
and movement for women's emancipation
      76, 470
scientists and 551
Revolution of 1917
and autonomy for nationalities 496
effect on Russian culture 579
effect on Russia's war 107–11
and expectation of world revolution 636–7
February Revolution 8, 114–17, 122, 131
    local government organisation 117–19
    politics of war (March-July) 122–6
    'July Days' 125–6
October Revolution
    and failure of democracy 44
    revisionist historiography of 43–9
    Western liberal view of 8
poets and 588
political polarization (summer 1917) 128–33
role of peasants in 416
scientists and 552–4
*see also* Provisional Government

Revolutionary Communists (RC) 144
'revolutionary defencism' 108, 110
    Tsereteli's 123
Reykjavik, US–USSR summit (1985) 339
Rhys Williams, Albert 8
Riazan' province, peasant out-migration
      443
Riazanov, Eldar 624
    *The Irony of Fate* 625
Ribbentrop, Joachim von, and
      Non-Aggression Pact with USSR 221
Rieber, Alfred 37
Riga, Latvia 526, 540
Riga, Treaty of (1921) 146, 150
Rittersporn, Gabor T. 53
Riutin, Martemian 722
Robinson, Geroid Tanquary, *Rural Russia
      Under the Old Regime* 13
Rodionov, M. I., and Leningrad Affair 261,
      262
Romania
    elections (1947) 666
    German invasion (1940) 659
    and Hungarian uprising 679
    independence 341
    and Moldova 546
    Ukrainian nationalists in 534
    *see also* Bessarabia; Moldavia
Romanian National Liberal Party 534
Romanov, Aleksei 624
Romanov dynasty
    end of 115
    patronage of arts 581
Romanov, Grigorii 319, 320
Romm, Mikhail
    *Ordinary Fascism* 617
    *Secret Mission* 608
Room, Abram, *Court of Honour* 608
Roosevelt, F.D., US president 652
*Rossiia*, concept of 90, 701
Rossman, Jeffrey 54
ROSTA (Russian Telegraph Agency) 586
Rostotskii, Stanislas, *It Happened in Penkovo*
      613
Rostov-on-Don, Soviet army at 231
Rostow, Walt Whitman (1916–2003)
    *The Dynamics of Soviet Society* 30–1
    *The Stages of Economic Growth* 30
Rostropovich, Mstislav 620
Rothstein, Andrew, British communist 658
Rozhdestvenskii, Robert 615
Rubenstein, Modest, scientist 561
Rudenko, Mykola, Helsinki Watch 541

Rudzutak, Ian 246, 248, 251
rural areas
    effect of February Revolution 117
    and German advance (1941) 228
    unrest in 87, 204–5
    *see also* agriculture; collectivisation;
        commune; villages
*Rus'*, concept of 90
Russell, Bertrand 10
Russia, pre-revolutionary 7, 354
    attempts to understand 13–14, 15–16
    imperial foreign policy 95
    legacy of autocracy 153
    martial law regime in First World War
        97–100
    optimist–pessimist debate (1900–14) 67, 93
    politics of First World War 104–7
    science in 549–52
    and transition from tsarism to
        Communism
    western borderlands in First World War 95,
        97, 110, 111–13
    *see also* Russian empire; Russian
        Federation; USSR
Russian Association of Proletarian Musicians
    (RAPM) 593
Russian Association of Proletarian Writers
    (RAPP) 593
Russian Central Bank, and 1998 economic
    crisis 372
Russian empire
    and eastern Ukraine 529
    and ethnic minorities 89–93
    nationalisation of during First World War
        100–4
    Russification policies 495
Russian Federation 518
    centrist discourse 701, 702
    conservative discourse in 701
    declaration of independence (1990) 347, 356,
        516, 546
    and demand by Chechnya for secession
        364–6
    liberal discourse in 700, 702–3
    new constitution (1993) 363–4
    and Tatarstan 518
Russian nationalism
    radical 366–8
    Stalin's promotion of 504
    tsarist promotion of 90
    use of Christian symbols of 602
Russian Social Democratic Workers' Party
    124, 144, 525

Russian Soviet Federative Socialist Republic
    (RSFSR) 174, 498
    *see also* Russian Federation
Russians
    in Baltic states 506, 547
    movement into non-Russian republics 501,
        540
    *see also* national character
Russia's Choice party (pro-Yeltsin) 366, 368
'Russification', policy of 90–1, 495
Russo-Japanese War (1904–5) 68
Rutskoi, Aleksandr, declared president by
    Congress 362
Ryazan' province, martial law (1917) 128
Rybakov, Anatolii, *Heavy Sand* 621
Rybkin, Ivan 368
Rykov, Aleksei 246, 249
    and 1928 'emergency measures' 247, 248
    and Stalin 185, 186
    trial (1938) 723
Ryzhkov, Nikolai 317, 320, 321
    and economic reform 331, 334, 404

Saburov, Maksim 277
St Petersburg
    'Bloody Sunday' (Jan. 1905) 68
    as cultural centre 581–2
    daily newspapers 78
    Mariinsky Theatre 581
    population 83, 443
    Religious-Philosophical Meetings (1901–3)
        80
    *see also* Petrograd
St Petersburg Academy of Sciences 549
Sakharov, Andrei 280, 298, 577
    campaign against 573
    election to Congress (1989) 327
    'Letter to the Soviet Leadership' 683
    *Reflections on Progress . . .* 570
salaried workers (*sluzhashchie*), and February
    Revolution 132
SALT II Treaty (1972) 307
    negotiations 307, 312
Samara, Committee to Save the Constituent
    Assembly (*Komuch*) 144
*samizdat* (underground distribution of
    proscribed literature) 620, 621
Saratov province
    forcible requisitioning of food (1919) 161
    martial law (1917) 128
    strike (1921) 166
    township committees (1917) 117
Sargent, Orme, British Foreign Office 660

Savinok, Iurii 438
Schapiro, Leonard, *Origins of the Communist Autocracy* 36
Scheffer, Paul, *Berliner Tageblatt* correspondent 16
Schlesinger, Rudolf (1901–69) 36
Schlieffen Plan 96
Schulenberg, Count Friedrich Werner von der, German ambassador to USSR 255
Schuyler, Eugene 7
Schwarz, Solomon, Menshevik historian 48
science
  applied to war effort (Second World War) 561–3
  and dissidence 573–4
  effect of Chernobyl' disaster on 574–5
  expenditure on 556, 566
  Hegelian dialectic and 555
  and intellectual freedom 570–1
  international investment in (from 1991) 576
  and modernisation 549, 577–8
  and politics 550–2, 569–70, 571, 577
  in post-Soviet Russia 575–7
  restrictions on foreign contacts 563–4, 568
  Soviet inferiority to West 566
  Stalinist use of 558–60
  *see also* technology
scientific research 550
  concentration on military technology 572–3, 576
  effect of 1917 Revolution on 553
  under Bolshevik government 554
scientific socialism 707, 709
'scientific-technological revolution' (*nauchno-tekhnicheskaia revoliutsiia* NTO) 457
scientists
  'academic rations' 553
  emigration (after 1991) 576
  numbers of 566
  political activism 571
  and Revolution of 1917 552–4
  and Stalinist repression 560–1
scorched earth policy
  First World War 99
  Second World War 223
Scott, James 59
Scott, Joan Wallach 49
Second Congress of Soviets 143
Second World War
  international origins of 217–19
  war in Europe (to 1941) 654–61

Second World War (Great Patriotic War in Soviet Union, 1941–5) 192, 217
  and arts 600–3, 622
  deportations 502
  the Eastern Front 222–7
  effect on economy 227, 241, 402
  effect on Stalinist state 227, 239–42
  in film and fiction 614
  German invasion of Soviet Union (1941) 18, 222, 223, 225, 228–9, 230
  patriotic defence campaign 426
  peasants and 426–7
  science in 561–3
  Soviet resistance 229–34
  treatment of civilians under German occupation 226, 231–2
  turning point for Allies 224
  victory 239
  *see also* Red Army
sectarianism 81
secularism, among Jews 92
sedition, trials for (1906–7) 69
Semenov, Iulian, novelist 627
Semenov, N. N., chemist 569
Semichastnyi, Vladimir 269
Serbia, Austrian ultimatum to 95
serfdom, abolition of (1861) 86, 87
Seton Watson, Hugh (1916–84) 36
Sewell, William H., Jr. 49
sex, civic discussion of 78
Shaginian, Marietta, *Mess-Mend* 591
Shakhnazarov, Georgii 316, 326, 347, 684, 686
  on role of General Secretary 685
Shakhty trial (mining engineers) 189, 560
Shamshiev, Bolotbek, Kyrgyz film-maker 625
Shanghai International Settlement 643
Shatalin, Stanislav 334
Shaw, George Bernard 15
'Shchekino experiment' 299
Shcherbakov, Aleksandr Sergeevich 252, 508
Shcherbitskii, Vladimir, Ukraine 301, 305
Shchukin family, as arts patrons 581
Shelest', Petro, Ukraine 300, 511, 540
Shengelaia, Eldar, film director 630
Shenin, Oleg 348
Shepilov, Dmitrii 681, 685
  and Khrushchev 277, 675
Shevardnadze, Eduard 321
  as foreign minister 338, 340, 696
  and Georgian nationalism 345
Shipler, David 15
Shliapnikov, A.G., Workers' Opposition 164

Sholokhov, Mikhail 611
  *Quiet Don* 608
shops and shopping 77, 79
  stores for Soviet elite 302–4
  *see also* black markets; commodities
Shostakovich, Dmitrii 208, 209, 606
  'Babii Yar' Symphony 616
  *Lady Macbeth of Mstensk* 598
show trials 617, 682
  1936–8 723–4
  and loss of support for USSR 17
  republican nationalists (1928–9) 499
  scientists 189, 560
Shpalikov, Gennadii 616
Shtiurmer, B.V., chairman of Council of
    Ministers 107
Shukshin, Vasilii 613, 623, 624
  *Snowball Berry Red* 625
Shultz, George, US secretary of state 340
Shulzhenko, Klavdiia, singer 602
Shumeiko, Vladimir 359
Shumiatskii, Boris 596
Shumsky, Oleksandr, and Ukrainisation
  536
Shushkevich, Stanislav, president of Belarus
  349
Shveitser, Mikhail, *Alien Kin* 613
Siberia
  demand for compensation for
    environmental damage 408
  labour camps 202
  peasant uprising 161
  urban growth 201
  Virgin Lands programme 203, 275, 390, 402,
    429
  Whites in 146
Sibneft, oil company 407
Sidanco oil company 407
Simmons, Ernest J. 22
Simonov, Konstantin, journalist 563, 602, 612
Siniavskii, Andrei 298, 621
  trial 617, 682
Skoropadsky, General Pavlo, Ukrainian
  *hetman* 530
Skrypnyk, Mykola, and Ukrainisation 536
Slánský, Rudolf 670
*Slavonic Review, The* 10
Slutskii, Boris 609
  'Physicists and Lyric Poets' (poem) 566
Smetona, Antanas, Lithuanian nationalist 528,
  532
Smirnov, Andrei 630
Smith, Hedrick 15

*smychka* (worker–peasant co-operation) 178,
  720
Social Democracy, Russian 710–13
  revolutionary modification of 711
Social Democracy, Western 8, 706
  Kautsky and 708–9
  perception of betrayal by 714
  and worker movement 707–10
Social Democrats
  and February Revolution 114, 706
  *see also* Bolsheviks, Mensheviks
social disorder, resulting from collectivisation
    and deportations 203–5
social history
  and concept of working class 441–2
  and labour politics 47
  and totalitarian model of USSR 27–8
social mobility 78, 399
  in early Soviet state 51
  limited form of (under Brezhnev) 303
social reforms
  liberal goals for 73
  Stolypin's commitment to 69
Social Revolutionary Party (SR) 74, 104
  alliance of Left SRs with Bolsheviks 143
  attempt to form anti-Bolshevik
    government 144
  and Bolshevik Sovnarkom 137
  and elections to Constituent Assembly 138
  expelled from soviets 144
  and February Revolution 114, 124
  and October Revolution 135
  and peasant revolt (1918–21) 162
  and Provisional Government 116
  relations with Bolshevik government 147
social sciences, changes in terminology 21
socialism
  failure of in Soviet Russia 35–6, 58
  influence as economic model 384
  interpretations of 322
  Lenin's belief in 125, 149, 181
  'path to' 697, 730
  scientific 707, 709
  Stalin's proclamation of victory of 205, 211,
    214, 723
  *see also* Bolshevism; capitalism;
    communism; Marxism
Socialist Academy *see* Communist Academy
socialist realism 207–8, 594–600
socialists
  and nationalist movements 91
  political ideologies of 73–4
  relations with Bolsheviks 143

societies
  and voluntary associations 77
  *see also* parastatal complex
Society of Friends (Quakers), relief efforts
  (1918–20) 391
Soiuzkino (film industry organisation) 596
Sokol'skii, Konstantin 598
Sokurov, Aleksandr 630
soldiers
  appeal of Provisional Government to 108
  First World War 95, 97, 101
  role in February Revolution 120
  and rural agitation (1917) 126
  Second World War 238
Solidarity movement, Poland 312–13
Solomentsev, Mikhail 326, 332
Solov'ev, Iurii 327
Solzhenitsyn, Aleksandr 298
  *Cancer Ward* 618
  expulsion 617, 682
  *Gulag Archipelago* 40, 52, 324
  *One Day in the Life of Ivan Denisovich* (1962)
    281, 288, 616, 682
Sorokin, Pitirim 19
Sorokin, Valentin 633
Soros, George, International Science
  Foundation 576
*Sotsialisticheskii vestnik (Socialist Herald)* 17
Soviet identity
  and democratisation under Gorbachev
    695–700
  and foreign policy 705
  NSM 663, 666, 673
  and 'private' self 673
  reinforced by false information 684
  and toleration of difference 673–5
  as vanguard 674, 675, 681, 684, 688, 697
  *see also* difference
*Soviet Studies* (journal) 36
Soviet Union *see* USSR (Union of Soviet
  Socialist Republics)
Soviet West, the 522–3
  German occupation 226, 231–2, 503–4, 538
  and Molotov-Ribbentrop Pact 537
  *see also* Baltic States; Belarus; Moldova;
    Ukraine
Soviet Women's Committee 491
Soviet Writers, Fourth Congress (1967) 618
soviets
  Council of People's Commissars (October
    1917) 137
  and party centralisation 152–3
  popular support for 137–8

rise of (1917) 117, 118–19, 134
rural 418, 420
view of war 123
*see also* Central Committee of the Soviets
  (VTsIK)
*sovkhozy see* cooperative farms
*sovnarkhozy* (economic councils) 158, 279
Sovnarkom *see* Council of Ministers (Sovmin);
  Council of People's Commissars
space progamme 402, 563
Spain 655
Special Council for Defence (1915) 106
spiritual revival 80–2
  and discontent with materialism 81–2
  'God-Seeking' 80
Spiro, Herbert J. 26
*Sputnik* (satellite), launched (1957) 40, 402, 563
Stakhanovism 396, 453–4
  rural 425
Stalin, Joseph (1878–1953) 125, 253, 261
  anti-Semitism 507
    and fabrication of Doctors' Plot (1951)
      264, 267, 508
  attacks on Molotov 253–4, 259, 264
  character 244, 262
    personality 216, 243–4
  and China 274, 667, 671–2
  and Comintern 637–8, 644–5
  as commander-in-chief of army 237, 256
  control of secret police 264
  cult of 43, 244, 258, 600, 601
  and de-Stalinisation 269, 276–7, 725–7
  death (1953) 265–6, 508
  as dictator 254, 258–63, 266
    anti-oligarchic strategy (1952) 263–5
    consolidation of personal dominance
      239–40, 253
    lack of challenges to 265
    move from oligarchy to dictatorship
      249–54
    nature of control over state 243–5
    subjugation of close advisers 258–60
  and Five-Year Plan 395
  foreign relations
    and alliance with Britain 658
    Non-Aggression Pact with Hitler (1939)
      18, 221, 655–7
    relations with foreign communist
      parties 645
  and formation of Transcaucasian Republic
    175, 498
  grain requisitions (1928–9) 188–9, 194, 394
  and Hitler 221, 647–8

Stalin, Joseph (1878–1953) (*cont.*)
interventions in science 563, 565–6
Khrushchev's condemnation (1956) 268–9
'Left Opposition' to 185–6
legacy of 274
and Lenin 175–6
and Leningrad Affair 261–3
and nationalities 210, 498
head of Commissariat of Nationalities (Narkomnats) 149
and NEP 185–6
change of policy on 186, 188–9
and nuclear weapons project 562
Order no.227 231
Order no.270 231
perception of threats
post-war external 258, 264, 427, 667–73
to revolution 199, 211, 216
and Politburo
control of 248, 260
manipulation of decision-making in 252
promotion of younger cohort (1938–9) 252
status in (1922) 183
politics
interpretation of *kto-kogo* scenario of class leadership 721–2
'socialism in one country' 185, 193, 200
and post-war cultural ideology 594, 606
relations with deputies 244–5
rise to power 184–5, 189–90, 191, 245–8
rivalry with Trotsky 183–5
Second World War
delegation of powers during 256–8
invasion of Poland 656
punishment of defeatism 231, 237
reaction to German invasion 223, 229, 237, 254–6
and threat from enemies of socialism 205, 425, 723
use of repression 212–16, 425
Great Purges 52–3, 266
as instrument of policy 214
purge of Red Army officers (1937–8) 221, 228, 236
view of Tito 670
*see also* Stalinism
Stalingrad, siege of 223
Stalinism 216, 394–401
consolidation of 205–6
contradictions within 192, 664
criticism of (under Gorbachev) 324
and cultural xenophobia 605–10

culture and morality 206–10, 607
demographics and population movements 200–5
as epitome of totalitarianism 23, 27, 40
and family law 481–2
forced collectivisation 192, 194–8, 398–400, 721
industrialisation 192, 200, 394–8
international context of 199–200
labour migration 446–7
mass repressions 212–16
nationalities under 210–12, 500–3
new hierarchies in 19
and official optimism 724–5
relationship to Bolshevism of civil war 140
and relationship to Leninism 16, 38, 46, 50–1, 142
revisionist historiography of 49–54
and science 555–61
Western Communist support for 17
*see also* Five-Year Plans
Stanford University, Hoover Institute of War, Peace and Revolution 11
Stanislavsky, Konstantin 581, 590
state
civil institutions under Stalin 215
limitations on Stalinist 243
mechanisms of political control 319
*see also* autocracy; totalitarianism
State Association of Metal Factories 169
state capitalism *see* New Economic Policy
State Committee for New Technology 566
State Committee for the Press 619
State Control Commission, and corruption (1919) 155
State Council, and martial law regime 98
State Department of Cinema (Goskino) 624
State Duma (1906–17) 68
authority of 68, 98
formation of committee (February 1917) 115
Fourth 98
prorogued 104
representation of minorities in 90
State Duma, Russian Federation 363
elections to 366
political crisis (1998–9) 374–6
proportional representation vote (1993) 366
threat to impeach Yeltsin 375
State Institute of Cinematography 616, 624
State Museum of Modern Western Art 607
state, tsarist
and industrialisation 67
popular protests against 69

*Stavka* (General Headquarters), established (1941) 237, 256
Stedman Jones, Gareth 49
Steffens, Lincoln, writer 8
Stepashin, Sergei, prime minister 376
Stolypin, Petr, prime minister 69, 71
  assassination 69
  commitment to social reforms 69
  and Duma 98
  reform of peasant communes (1906) 88, 103, 388, 415–16
Stravinsky, Igor 582, 615
strikes 83
  1910–14 70, 84
  against food shortages (1920–1) 168
  coalminers (1989) 463
  February 1917 Petrograd 114–15
  legalised 69, 84
  Lena goldfields (Siberia) 70
  Moscow 166
  Petrograd 166
  summer 1917 128, 471
Strumilin, Stanislav Gustavovich (1877–1974) 395
Struve, P. V. 130
Stučka, Pēteris, Latvian Bolshevik 527
students
  and February Revolution 131
  radical 593
Suchkov, A. 421
Suez Crisis (1956) 285
Sukhanov, N. N. 421
Sukhomlinov, General, minister of war (1914) 96
Sun Yat-sen, and Chinese nationalists 642
Suprematists 582
Supreme Council of the National Economy (Sovnarkhoz) 158, 169, 279
Supreme Soviet, Gorbachev's new 327
Suslov, Mikhail 297, 316, 678, 682
  Central Committee secretary 282, 686, 691
  death 314
  on Mao 690
Sverdlovsk (Ekaterinburg)
  assassination of royal family at 145
  population growth 201
Sviatopolk-Mirskii, Prince Dmitrii 68
symbolism
  February Revolution 119
  Second World War use of Christian 602
Symbolists 82, 580, 581
Syrtsov, Sergei 249

Szporluk, Roman, *The Influence of East Europe and the Soviet West on the USSR* 523

Tairov, Aleksandr, Chamber Theatre 581, 592
Tajikistan 354, 408
  collectivisation in 423
  and Commonwealth of Independent States 516
Tallinn, Estonia 525
Tambov province
  communes 415
  martial law (1917) 128
  peasant uprising 161, 168
Tamm, I. E., physicist 559
Tannenberg, Battle of 96
Taraki, Nur Mohammed, Afghan Khalq faction 311, 692, 693
Tarkovsky, Andrei 281, 624
  *Ivan's Childhood* 614
Tartu Peace Treaty (1920) 526
Tashkent 151
  university 499
Tatarstan 518
  referendum on independence (1992) 364
Tatlin, Vladimir 582
Tatyana Society, refugee relief organisation 101
taxes
  collective responsibility for, abolished (1904) 88
  inefficient collection (1990s) 372
  under NEP 391
Taylor, Frederick Winslow, 'Taylorism' 449
technology
  attempt to stimulate (1950s–60s) 566–7
  barriers to innovation 567
  Bolshevik faith in 719
  imported from West 403
  lag in computing and electronics 572
  levels of 386, 387, 392, 393
  Soviet investment in 556
  and spread of culture 626–7
  *see also* science
television
  documentary films 630
  and film industry 624
  imported soap operas 631
  political centrism in 703
'Temporary Statute of Military Censorship' (by martial law regime) 99
Tereshchenko, Mikhail Ivanovich (1886–1956), minister in Provisional Government 107

Tereshkova, Valentina 491
terror
  and *Black Book of Communism* 63
  Stalin's use of 243
  use of in civil war 145–6
  use of by totalitarian regimes 22, 25, 27
terrorism, Chechen, in Moscow 376
textile industry 121, 458
Thatcher, Margaret, UK prime minister 313
  and Gorbachev 699
theatre
  freedoms under Gorbachev 629
  pre-revolutionary 581
  under Bolsheviks 589–90
Third Communist International 145
Third World
  and détente 307–8
  Khrushchev and 284
  and Western development model 30
  *see also* national liberation movements
    (NLMs)
Thomas, Dorothy 12
Thomas, Norman 19
Thompson, E.P. 49
Thorez, Maurice 651
Tikhonov, Nikolai 309, 317, 320
Timasheff, Nicholas S., *The Great Retreat* 19
Timoshenko, General, head of Stavka 256
Tito, Josip 284
  and Khrushchev 676–7
  Soviet view of 670
Tobol'sk, communes 414
Todorovskii, Valerii, film director 632
Togliatti, Palmiro, Italian communist 651
Tolstaya, Tatiana 633
Tolstoy, Aleksei, *Road to Calvary* 587
Tolstoy, Lev [Leo]
  adulation of 69, 81
  death (1910) 69
  popularity of *War and Peace* (Second World
    War) 603
Tomskii, Mikhail 194
  and 1928 'emergency measures' 247, 248
  and Stalin 185, 186
Tõnisson, Jaan, Estonian nationalist 525
'totalitarian model', in study of Soviet Russia
    22–8
totalitarianism
  applied to both communism and fascism
    18, 22, 24–5
  critiques of 26–8
  and modernisation 31–2
  'spontaneous' 31

*tovaroobmen* system of food procurement
    159
towns and urban areas 105, 137
  'cleansing' and deportations 202
  de-urbanisation 163, 167, 170
  and German advance (1941) 229
  growth in size and population 77, 83, 387,
    447
  influx of dispossessed and fugitives into
    203–4
  migration to 88, 170, 303, 387
  religious revival among workers
    81
  secret defence industry 241
  strained public services 204
  *see also* cities; urbanisation
township (*volost'*) committees, formed after
    February Revolution 117
trade, international
  with Britain 641
  and Comecon 403
  and imperial ambitions 219
  nineteenth-century 219, 386
  Soviet need for control over 220
  by successor states 408
  under NEP 392
trade unions 13, 128, 459
  legalised 69, 84
  role for under Bolsheviks 163
traditional society, in development
    (modernisation) model 30
Transcarpathia province
  in Czechoslovakia 530, 534–5
  Ukraine 530, 539
Transcaucasia
  as front in First World War 95
  mass deportations from 212
  nationalism in 130, 150
  oil in 386, 519
  soviet governments 496
  *see also* Armenia; Azerbaijan; Chechnya;
    Dagestan; Georgia; Transcaucasia
Transcaucasian Republic (1922) 175,
    497
transition (transitology) 61–62
Transnistria 537, 40
  and Dniester Republic 546
travel, foreign 324
Tret'iakov family, as arts patrons 581
Trifonov, Iurii 622
  *House on the Embankment* 622
Triple Entente (Russia, France and Great
    Britain) 95

Troianovskii, Oleg, Khrushchev's foreign
    policy adviser 286
Trotsky, Leon 125, 182
    expulsion of 185–6, 245, 246
    *History of the Russian Revolution* 16
    and Lenin's plan to overthrow Provisional
        Government 135
    *The Lessons of October* 184
    and Red Army 144, 235
    rivalry with Stalin 183–5, 655
    trial and Western support for 17
    use of term Stalinism 49
    view of class revolution 716, 717
    view of Hitler 648
    view of Stalinist USSR 17
Trotskyists, Western 17
Trudovik (Labourist) faction (in State Duma)
    74
Truman Doctrine 665
tsar
    personal power of 71
    *see also* autocracy
Tsederbaum, Iulii *see* Martov
Tsereteli, Iraklii (I.G.) 45
    and 'revolutionary defencism' 123
Tsfasman, Aleksandr 590, 598
Tsipko, Aleksandr 325
Tsvetaeva, Marina 588, 620
tuberculosis 83
Tuchkov, Vladimir, 'Master of the Steppes' 634
Tucker, Robert C. 23, 26, 33, 42–3
    on Stalinism 50, 52
Tugan-Baranovskii, Mikhail 440
Tukhachevskii, Mikhail, and concept of 'deep
    battle' 235, 237
Tula province
    martial law (1917) 128
    peasant out-migration 443
Turchin, V.A. 570
Turdiev, Robert 686
Turkestan 103, 390, 393, 496
Turkey 676
    and Azerbaijan 150
Turkic peoples, ethnic conflict in First World
    War 103
Turkmenistan 354
    natural gas exports 408
Turovskaya, Maya 281
Tvardovskii, Aleksandr 616, 682

U-2 spy plane incident (1960) 287, 684, 686
Ufa Conference (1918) 145
Ukraine 529–30

as autonomous Socialist Soviet 535
Babii Yar massacre of Jews 146, 503
Bukovina province 530, 534, 537
and civil war 496
and collectivisation 398, 536
deportations 538
dissident movement 541, 617
Eastern 529
    Ukrainisation policy in 535–6
ethnic networks in 305
famine (1931–33) 16, 40, 196, 398, 424, 500,
    536
film studios 625
First World War 95, 530
German occupation 225, 426, 503–4, 538
Greek Catholic (Uniate) Church 529, 541,
    544
Green World ecological movement 544
Harvard study project 55
industrialisation 401
Khrushchev and 508–9
land seizures 128
mass deportations from 212
nationalism 91, 102, 149–50, 496, 512
    cultural 529
    nationalist movement (1987–9) 529, 543–4
    native university 499
    nature of 130, 523
    partisans 503
    western 529
peasant uprising 161
post-Soviet 354, 547–8
    and break-up of USSR 516
    independence (1991) 355, 547
    'Orange Revolution' 548
    workers' demand for independence 464
Rada (Central Council) 530
*Rada* newspaper 529
relationship to RSFSR 174, 529
reunification (1939) 537, 539
Rukh movement (Popular Movement for
    Restructuring) 544, 546
Taras Shevchenko Ukrainian Language
    Society 544
Transcarpathia province 530, 539
*Ukrainian Herald* 541
Western 529–30
    ceded by treaty of Brest-Litovsk 136
    nationalism in 529
    *see also* Galicia
Ukrainian Institute of Physics and
    Technology, Khar'kov 560
Ukrainian People's Republic 530

Ukrainians
  deportation (First World War) 99
  radical nationalism in European states
    534–5
Ulam, Adam B. 27
Ulbricht, Walter, East German president 274
Ul'ianov, Vladimir *see* Lenin, V. I.
Ul'ianovskii, Rostislav 686, 692
Ulmanis, Karlis, Latvia 527, 533
Unger, A. L. 53
Uniate (Greek Catholic) Church, in Ukraine
    529, 541, 544
Union of 17 October (Octobrists) 73
Union of Cinematographers 624
Union of Landowners and Farmers 128
Union of Private Landed Proprietors 436
Union of Private Peasant Farmers 434
Union of Theatre Workers 629
Union for Women's Equality 470
United Nations 224
  human rights standards 307
  recognition of former Soviet states 546
United States of America 21, 26, 219
  and Afghanistan 312, 692
  and America as 'good society . . . in
    operation' 28
  assumption of USSR as threat 20–1, 22–8,
    241, 306
  and Brezhnev 306
  cultural influence (early 1920s) 171, 590, 591
  and early Soviet Russia 10, 13–14
  economic aid to USSR 223, 233
  influence over Europe 665, 675, 680
  and Japan 652
  Khrushchev and 286
  and Korean War 672
  and nuclear threat 241, 306
  and nuclear weapons parity 306, 573
  relations with 20, 54, 307, 647
  relative strength 241, 306, 336
  and Second World War 225, 659
  Soviet studies in 10, 37–9, 40
  as threat to USSR and socialism 663
  view of Bolshevism 9
  view of show trials (1936–8) 17
  *see also* Reagan, Ronald
Unity political coalition 378
universities 572
  and academic freedom (1905) 550
  national (native) 499
  women at 479, 484
uprisings and demonstrations, 1905
    Revolution 68

Urals
  labour camps 202
  peasant uprising 161
  urban growth 201
urban workers *see* proletariat (urban workers)
urbanisation 192, 387, 402
  under Stalin 200–1
  *see also* towns and urban areas
Urusevskii, Sergei 614
USSR State Council, transitional executive
    body (1991) 357
USSR (Union of Soviet Socialist Republics)
  in 1985 319–20
  in 1991 352–5
  constitution 176, 215
  contribution to Second World War 224–5
  dissolution of (1991) 61–2, 349, 352–7, 516–17,
    731
    attempt to preserve union (1991) 346–8
    resistance to Union Treaty (1991) 347
  end of Communist Party power in 328
  federal structure of 304, 495–6
  foundation (1922) 151, 175–7, 495
  as global power 239, 685–700
  Gorbachev revolution 322–5
  as imperialist 39
  international isolation 199, 274
  legacy of Stalinism 271, 274
  nationality in 176–7, 498, 523–4
    and fear of nationalism 540–2
  perceived threat of invasion (from 1920s)
    220–1
  as perverse model of modernisation 30–1,
    58
  popular discontent and resistance in 53
  Russian cultural dominance in 211, 304, 495,
    499
  as scientific system 549
  separatist movements 346
  social histories of 58–61
  and Soviet Bloc under Khrushchev 283–5,
    674
  and threat of war (1927) 199, 220
  and transfer of power between leaders
    289
  transformation under Stalin (from 1928)
    192–3
  war preparations from mid-1930s 221
  Western European view of (late 1930s) 221
  Western views of communist experiment
    12–20
  *see also* economy; foreign policy; Russian
    Federation; Soviet identity; Stalinism

Ustinov, Dmitrii, minister of defence 309, 317, 684
and Afghanistan 693
Utesov, Leonid 590, 597, 598
'Baron von der Pschick' 602
Uzbekistan 305, 354
and Commonwealth of Independent States 516
Uzbeks, in Osh region 516

Vainer, Arkadii and Grigorii, novelists 627
Vakhtangov, Evgenii 592
Varga, Eugene, Institute of Global Economics and International Relations 658
Varzar, Vasilii Egorovich, economist 395
Vavilov, N. I., geneticist 559
Veblen, Thorstein, critique of capitalism 14
Verba, Sidney, *The Civic Culture* (with Almond) 29
Verbitskaia, Anastasia, novelist 583
Vernadskii, V. I. 551, 555, 561
and political reform 552
Vernadsky, George (1887–1973) 38
Vertov, Dziga 591
Vialtseva, Anastasia 582
video technology 627
Vietnam, USSR and 308, 673
Vietnam War 306
and effect on US policy 26, 43
villages 86, 126, 414
effect of February Revolution on 117
and NEP co-operatives 179
Soviet 303
workers' links with 444, 445, 448
*see also* commune
Vilnius 527
ceded to Poland 528, 533
returned to Lithuania 539
Viola, Lynne 53
violence, state 153
between president and parliament (1993) 362
in collectivisation campaign 195, 398, 422
*see also* coercion; terror
Vladimir province, peasant out-migration 443
Vladivostok, population growth 201
Vlasov, General, capture by Germans 228, 239
*voennizatsiia* (militarisation of state institutions) 215
Volga provinces 128, 161
civil war conflicts 144
deportation of Germans from 226

famine (1921–2) 171–2
urban growth 201
Voloshyn, Avhustyn, president of Carpatho-Ukraine 535
volunteer army, formation of 143
Volunteer Army of South Russia *see* Whites
Volynia, German population in 100
Voronin, Vladimir, president of Moldova 548
Vorontsov-Dashkov, viceroy in Georgia 103
Voroshilov, Kliment 242, 657
and formation of GKO 255
and Khrushchev 276, 277
and Stalin 186, 246, 257
Voznesenskii, Andrei 289
Voznesenskii, Nikolai 242, 252, 615
and Leningrad Affair 261–2
in Politburo 260
and Stalin 253
trial and execution of 262
VTsIK *see* Central Executive Committee of the Soviets
Vynnychenko, Volodymyr 530
Vyshinsky, Andrei 668
Vysotskii, Vladimir 626
'Morning Gymnastics' 729

wage funds 301
wages
agricultural 428, 430
arrears (to 2000) 466
and bonus pay 164, 461
differentials 453
increase under NEP 450
and informal strategies 461
post-Soviet 465
unpaid 198, 372, 465
women's 487
Wagner, Richard, *Die Walküre* 601
Walder, Andrew 60
Wałęsa, Lech 312
Walker, Martin 15
Wall Street Crash (1929) 645
Wallace, Donald Mackenzie 7
Wallace, Henry A., US vice president 20
Wang Ming (Chen Shaoyu), Chinese communist 653
War Communism 147, 157–63, 164, 167, 390–1
peasants and 417–19
as short-cut to communism 716, 718
war industries committees 105, 106, 115
Warsaw, German campaign against (1914) 97
Washington, US–USSR summit (1985) 339
*A Wealthy Bride* (film) 208

Webb, Sidney and Beatrice 33
Weber, Max 29, 60
welfare
  provision in rural areas 430
  sick-benefit funds 459
  supplied by workplace 458, 461
Werth, Alexander 15
West, Nathaniel 18
West, the
  academic study of post-war USSR 20–2
  anti-communist leaders (in 1980s) 313
  assumption of Western master narrative 28
  and détente (*c.*1965–75) 54, 305–8
  economic crises (1970s) 306
  and Gorbachev's reforms 699–700
  influence of popular culture 281
  left-wing enthusiasm for Bolshevism 8
  left-wing ideological support for Soviet
    Russia 17–18
  optimism about capitalist democracy 6
  and perception of international revolution
    645
  right-wing views of Bolshevism 8
  views of communist experiment 12–20
  views of visiting writers on Soviet
    experiment 10, 12–13, 15–16
  and Yeltsin 348
  *see also* Europe; United States of America
White Sea Canal 193, 401, 671
White, Stephen 42
Whites (White Army) 143
  Allies' support for 112, 145
  defeat of 146–7
  and Muslim populations 151
  use of terror 146
Wilhelm II, Emperor of Germany 95
Wilhelm of Urach, German prince 528
Wilson, Edmund 19
  *An Appeal to Progressives* 14
  *To the Finland Station* 18
Wilson, Woodrow, US president 112, 495
  view of February 1917 Revolution 8
Witte, Sergei, prime minister 71
  and completion of Trans-Siberian railway
    67, 386
  industrialisation 386
'woman question'
  de-Stalinisation of 485–90
  in pre-revolutionary politics 76
women
  and 1905 Revolution 76, 470
  and 1917 Revolution 471–2
    February Revolution 114, 122, 471

  attempted emancipation of Muslim 174
  Bolshevik emancipation of 156, 173–4
  and class 85, 482
    social mobility (1930s) 479–80
  commodification of sexuality 492
  discontent (1970s) 489
  domestic responsibilities ('double burden')
    480, 484, 487–8
  education
    co-education 473
    literacy rates 207, 429
    of rural women 489
  and effect of market liberalisation 436
  elite 470
  and end of state regulation 492–3
  gendered roles
    in employment 172, 427
    post-war 483–5
    traditional hierarchies 468, 473, 494
  and labour movement 122
  life expectancy 492
  middle-class 122, 469–70
  migration to towns 431, 489
  *obshchestvennitsy* (wife-activists) 482
  political organisation (1990s) 492–3
  portrayal in films and literature 623–4
  poverty 492
  pre-revolution
    and 1905 Revolution 76, 470
    in public life 469–70
    resistance to Stolypin's commune
      reforms 415
  as prisoners 482
  in professions 469
    as physicians 469, 483
  and reforms under Brezhnev 488–90
  resistance to collectivisation 423–4,
    477–9
  return to traditional model 209–10
    'back to home' movement 491–2
    and ideology of domesticity 469–70
    and propaganda of motherhood 473,
      476–7, 480, 484
    and redefinition of wifehood 482
  rights within communes 413, 420, 477
  rural
    and cultivation of private plots 425, 429,
      478
    in peasant households 86, 413
    workers on collectives 478–9
  and rural religion 87, 477
  Second World War
    in armed forces 483

employment 483
and wartime food production 426
single mothers 173
social and cultural success 493–4
socialist activists 470
soldiers' wives 471
under NEP 172–4, 475–6
unemployment 466, 475, 492
voting in Constituent Assembly elections
122, 471
workers 462, 468, 485
industrial 469, 479, 487
working-class 85
*see also* women's emancipation
*Women in the USSR* yearbook (1990) 491
women's emancipation
abandoned 479, 490
Bolshevik reforms 156, 173–4, 471, 472
debate under *perestroika* 491–2
movement for 76, 122, 470
work and 490
and Zhenotdel (Women's Bureau) 474–5
work permits, temporary, for Moscow
303
worker club movement 592
'worker-intellectuals' 585
Worker Opposition group (1920–1) 715
workers 45, 462
adaptation to the system 447–8
artisanal 443, 444
continuing links with villages 440, 444, 445,
448
enthusiasm for rapid industrialisation 48
increasing discontent 456
informal strategies for acquiring goods and
services 461
labour discipline 448–50
and *perestroika* 405, 465
relations with Bolshevik government 163–6
relationship with workplace management
458–62
reliance on workplace provision 198
resistance to Stakhanovism 397, 453, 455
role in revolution 120–21, 129
'shock' 452
socialist competition strategy 452–3
and trade unionism 708
*see also* labour history; proletariat (urban
workers); working class
workers' consciousness (*soznatel'nost'*),
Marxist concept of 83
Workers' Defence Committee (KOR), Poland
312

Workers' Group of War Industries
Committee, and February uprising 115
Workers' Opposition 164
workers' organisations
relations with Provisional Government 108
role of Marxists in 75
Workers'–Peasants' Inspectorate (1920) 155
working class 441–2
end of (under Gorbachev) 462–7
and establishment of soviet power 137–8
and mass culture 579, 582, 590
participation in war industries committees
106
political consciousness among 84–5, 444
rarity of family households 445
reduction in size (during civil war) 163
resistance to Bolshevik practices 163, 165
and Social Democracy 707–10, 711
*see also* proletariat (urban workers);
workers
working conditions 83, 450
continuous working week (*nepreryvka*)
452
working hours 83
World of Art movement 81, 582
World Bank 373
World Youth Festival, Moscow (1957) 281
Wrangel, Baron N. 9
Wrangel, Petr, commander of Whites 112, 146
writers
expelled 620, 621
Khrushchev's relations with 277
tactics to avoid censorship 621–2
women 469, 470, 493
Writers' Union 595, 596, 618
powers of control 619, 628
revival of 611

xenophobia
cultural 605–10
in Great Purges 213

Yakovlev, Aleksandr 269, 318, 696, 697
and foreign policy 338
rebuttal of Andreeva letter 326
as reformist 321–2, 325, 347
Yakut peoples, relations with Russians 513
Yalta Agreement (1945) 666
Yeltsin, Boris 61, 369, 702
and 1998 economic crisis 371–4
banning of Communist Party 356
as challenger to Gorbachev 328, 348–9, 352,
357, 516

Yeltsin, Boris (*cont.*)
  and Chechnya's declaration of
    independence 365
  conflict with Congress of People's
    Deputies 361–3
  and creation of market economy (1991) 358
  and dissolution of USSR (1991) 348–9, 355–7,
    516
  Duma threat to impeach 375
  election to Congress (1989) 327, 328
  and events of October 1993 361–4
  'family' network 371
  as First Secretary of Moscow Party 320,
    325
  illness 371, 378
  indecision on political system 357–8
  legacy 379–80
  and new constitution (1993) 363–4
  and new freedoms 325
  and *perestroika* 326
  and political crisis (1998–9) 374–6
  popular support for 330, 335, 354, 377
  as president of Russian Republic 328
  and presidential elections 366, 369–70
  and proposals for economic reform (1990)
    334
  and Russian Republic independence 347,
    516
  and Tatarstan 518
Yemen 308, 314
Yevtushenko, *see* Evtushenko
Yudenich, General 112
Yugoslavia 289, 343
  Khrushchev's relations with 276, 284,
    676–7
  NATO intervention in Kosovo 703, 704
Yukos oil company 704
Yushchenko, Viktor, president of Ukraine 548

Zamiatin, Evgenii, *We* (novel) 632
Zaslavskaia, Tat'iana, economist 404, 431
Zasulich, Vera 711

Zelenograd, science city 566
*zemstvos*
  democratisation of (1917) 117
  union of (parastatal) 105
Zhang Guo-tao, Chinese communist 653
Zhang Xueliang, Manchurian warlord 653
Zhdanov, Andrei 242, 252, 261, 508, 606
  and concept of Soviet identity (NSM) 663,
    725
  and Eastern Europe 666
  and Finland 664
  and foreign policy-making 668
  as Stalin's deputy 253
Zhdanov, Iurii, scientist 563, 565
Zhdanovshchina (cultural repression) 606,
  663, 668
Zhelezniakov, A. G., sailors' leader 138
Zhemchuzhina, Polina, wife of Molotov 251
Zhenotdel (Women's Bureau) 474–5, 477, 478
  abolition 479
Zhirinovsky, Vladimir, radical nationalist
  366–8
Zhou En-lai 672
  at Twenty-Second Congress 284
Zhukov, General Georgii 255, 654
Zhvanetskii, Mikhail 626
Zinoviev, Aleksandr, *The Yawning Heights* 574
Zinoviev, Grigorii (1883–1936) 125, 134, 638
  and Comintern 644
  expulsion from Party 186, 190, 246, 250
  and *kto-kogo* phrase 719
  and prospect of Italian revolution 638
  and Stalin 184
  and Trotsky 185, 245
  and use of propaganda 715
Zionism 91
Ziuganov, Gennadii Andreevich, presidential
  candidate (1996) 369
*Znamia* (journal) 627
Zoshchenko, Mikhail, satirist 587, 606, 663,
  674, 725
*Zvezda* (journal) 663